Money, Banking, and Financial Markets

Sixth Edition

Stephen G. Cecchetti
Brandeis International Business School

Kermit L. Schoenholtz
New York University
Leonard N. Stern School of Business

MONEY, BANKING, AND FINANCIAL MARKETS

Published by McGraw-Hill Education, 2 Penn Plaza, New York, NY 10121.

This book is printed on acid-free paper.

1 2 3 4 5 6 7 8 9 LWI 25 24 23 22 21 20

ISBN 978-1-260-57136-3
MHID 1-260-57136-X

Cover Image: ©NASA images/Shutterstock

mheducation.com/highered

Dedication

To my father, Giovanni Cecchetti, who argued tirelessly that financial markets are not efficient; and to my grandfather, Albert Schwabacher, who patiently explained why inflation is destructive.

Stephen G. Cecchetti

To my wife, Elvira Pratsch, who continues to teach me what is true, good, and beautiful.

Kermit L. Schoenholtz

About the Authors

Stephen G. Cecchetti is Rosen Family Chair in International Finance at the Brandeis International Business School (http://people.brandeis.edu/~cecchett/). He previously taught at Brandeis from 2003 to 2008. Before rejoining Brandeis in 2014, Cecchetti completed a five-year term as Economic Adviser and Head of the Monetary and Economic Department at the Bank for International Settlements in Basel, Switzerland. During his time at the Bank for International Settlements, Cecchetti was involved in numerous postcrisis global regulatory reform initiatives, including the work of the Basel Committee on Banking Supervision and the Financial Stability Board.

He has also taught at the New York University Leonard N. Stern School of Business and at The Ohio State University. In addition to his other appointments, Cecchetti served as Executive Vice President and Director of Research, Federal Reserve Bank of New York (1997–1999); Editor, *Journal of Money, Credit, and Banking* (1992–2001); Research Associate, National Bureau of Economic Research (1989–2011); and Research Fellow, Centre for Economic Policy Research (2008–present), among others.

Cecchetti's research interests include inflation and price measurement, monetary policy, macroeconomic theory, economics of the Great Depression, and the economics of financial regulation.

Cecchetti received an SB in Economics from the Massachusetts Institute of Technology in 1977 and a PhD in Economics from the University of California at Berkeley in 1982. In 2016, he received an Honorary Doctorate in Economics from the University of Basel.

Kermit L. Schoenholtz is the Henry Kaufman Professor of the History of Financial Institutions and Markets in the Department of Economics of New York University's Leonard N. Stern School of Business, where he teaches courses on money and banking (http://pages.stern.nyu.edu/~kschoenh). He also directs NYU Stern's Center for Global Economy and Business (www.stern.nyu.edu/cgeb). Schoenholtz was Citigroup's global chief economist from 1997 until 2005.

Schoenholtz joined Salomon Brothers in 1986, working in its New York, Tokyo, and London offices. In 1997, he became chief economist at Salomon, after which he became chief economist at Salomon Smith Barney and later at Citigroup.

Schoenholtz has published extensively for the professional investment community about financial, economic, and policy developments; more recently, he has contributed to policy-focused scholarly research in economics. He is a member of the Financial Research Advisory Committee of the U.S. Treasury's Office of Financial Research, a panel member of the U.S. Monetary Policy Forum, and a member of the Council on Foreign Relations. He also has served as a member of the Executive Committee of the London-based Centre for Economic Policy Research.

From 1983 to 1985, Schoenholtz was a Visiting Scholar at the Bank of Japan's Institute for Monetary and Economic Studies. He received an MPhil in economics from Yale University in 1982 and an AB from Brown University in 1977.

Preface

The world of money, banking, and financial markets is constantly evolving. Every year, people explore new ways to pay for purchases, save for the future, and borrow to meet current needs.

New technology is an ongoing source of change. Internet banking makes it easier than ever for individuals to take control of their finances. And smartphones not only allow American college students to pay for their morning coffee but also are giving hundreds of millions of people in poor countries their first access to the financial system.

In some instances, crises provided the impetus for change. For example, new regulations aimed at making the financial system safer have pushed many banks to take fewer risks than they did just a few years ago. Financial markets also have become more resilient and less likely to need public support. And monetary policymakers, especially in places where economic growth has slowed and deflation is a risk, have adopted a slew of policies never seen before. In much of Europe and Japan, interest rates have fallen below zero—breaking through what had long been seen as a permanent barrier—while new policies are in place to boost bank lending and restore inflation and growth to precrisis levels.

The same things that are reshaping the global financial system also are transforming the study of money and banking. Some old questions are surfacing with new intensity: How can individuals use the changing financial system to improve their lives? How can governments ensure that the financial system remains stable? How should we balance the need for financial resilience with the goals of competition, efficiency, and innovation? And how can monetary policymakers keep inflation low, employment high, and both of them stable?

Against this background, students who memorize the operational details of today's financial system are investing in a short-lived asset. Our purpose in writing this book is to focus on the basic functions served by the financial system while deemphasizing its current structure and rules. Learning the economic rationale behind current financial tools, rules, and structures is much more valuable than concentrating on the tools, rules, and structures themselves. It is an approach designed to give students the lifelong ability to understand and evaluate whatever financial innovations and developments they may one day confront.

The Core Principles Approach

Toward that end, the entire content of this book is based on five *core principles.* Knowledge of these principles is the basis for understanding what the financial system does, how it is organized, how it is linked to the real economy, and how it is changing. If you understand these five principles, you will understand the future:

1. Time has value.
2. Risk requires compensation.
3. Information is the basis for decisions.
4. Markets determine prices and allocate resources.
5. Stability improves welfare.

These five core principles serve as a framework through which to view the history, current status, and future development of money and banking. They are discussed in detail in Chapter 1; throughout the rest of the text, marginal icons remind students of the principles that underlie particular discussions.

Focusing on core principles has created a book that is both concise and logically organized. This approach does require some adjustments to the traditional methodology used to teach money and banking, but for the most part they are changes in emphasis only. That said, some of these changes have greatly improved both the ease of teaching and the value students draw from the course. Among them are the emphasis on risk and on the lessons from the financial crisis; use of the term *financial instrument;* parallel presentation of the Federal Reserve and the

European Central Bank; a streamlined, updated section on monetary economics; and the adoption of an integrated global perspective.

Innovations in This Text

In addition to the focus on core principles, this book introduces a series of innovations designed to foster coherence, relevance, and timeliness in the study of money and banking.

The Money and Banking Blog

The global economy and financial system of the 21st century is evolving quickly. Changes in technology, in the structure of financial institutions and markets, and in monetary and regulatory policy are occurring at a pace that far outstrips the normal three- or four-year cycle at which textbooks are revised. We designed the *Money and Banking* blog to keep examples and applications current. Available at www.moneyandbanking.com, the blog provides timely commentary on events in the news and on questions of more lasting interest.

The blog is closely linked to this book. Like the book, it aims to enhance students' understanding of the world around them. Based on the five core principles of money and banking, each blog entry is associated with a specific chapter. Students following the blog will learn how current events affect the various parts of the financial system—money, financial instruments, financial markets, financial institutions, financial regulators, and central banks.

The material from the blog also is integrated into the book in two ways. First, each chapter includes a "Money and Banking Blog" boxed reading. These are short versions of postings that have appeared on www.moneyandbanking.com since the publication of the previous edition of this text. These excerpts describe current issues that highlight the lessons in the body of the chapter. Second, the website includes a listing of the posts by chapter. This listing allows students and instructors alike to find new, up-to-date material that illustrates the lessons and core principles emphasized in each chapter.

To receive the latest commentary as it is posted every week or so, subscribe to the blog at www.moneyandbanking.com. You can also follow the authors on Twitter (@MoneyBanking1).

Federal Reserve Economic Data (FRED)

Money, Banking, and Financial Markets systematically integrates the use of economic and financial data from FRED, the online database provided free of charge to the public by the Federal Reserve Bank of St. Louis. As of this writing, FRED offers nearly 600,000 data series from more than 85 sources, including indicators for about 200 countries. Information on using FRED appears in Appendix B to Chapter 1.

Through frequent use of FRED, students will gain up-to-date knowledge of the U.S. and other economies and an understanding of the real-world challenges of economic measurement; they will also gain skills in analysis and data manipulation that will serve them well for years to come. Many of the graphs in this book were produced (and can be easily updated) using FRED. In addition, end-of-chapter Data Exploration problems call on students to use FRED to analyze key economic and financial indicators highlighted in that chapter. (For detailed instructions for using FRED online to answer the Data Exploration problems in Chapters 1 to 10, visit www.mhhe.com/moneyandbanking6e and click on Data Exploration Hints.) Students can even do some assignments using the FRED app for their mobile devices.

Impact of the Crises

The effects of the global financial crisis of 2007–2009 and the euro-area crisis that began in 2010 transformed money, banking, and financial markets. Accordingly, from beginning to end, the book integrates the issues raised by these crises and by the responses of policymakers.

The concept of a liquidity crisis surfaces in Chapter 2, and the risks associated with leverage and the rise of shadow banking are introduced in Chapter 3. Issues specific to the 2007–2009 crisis—including securitization, rating agencies, subprime mortgages, over-the-counter trading, and complex financial instruments like credit-default swaps—are included in the appropriate intermediate chapters of the text. Chapter 16 explores the role of the European Central Bank in managing the euro-area crisis. More broadly, the sources of threats to the financial system as a whole are identified throughout the book, and there is a focused discussion on regulatory initiatives to limit such systemic threats. Finally, we present—in a logical and organized manner—the unconventional monetary policy tools, including the use of negative interest rates and the concept of the effective lower bound, that have become so prominent in postcrisis policy debates and remain relevant today.

Early Introduction of Risk

It is impossible to appreciate how the financial system works without understanding risk. In the modern financial world, virtually all transactions transfer some degree of risk between two or more parties. These risk trades can be extremely beneficial, as they are in the case of insurance markets. But there is still potential for disaster. In 2008, risk-trading activity at some of the world's largest financial firms threatened the stability of the international financial system.

Even though risk is absolutely central to an understanding of the financial system, most money and banking books give very little space to the topic. In contrast, this book devotes an entire chapter to defining and measuring risk. Chapter 5 introduces the concept of a risk premium as compensation for risk and shows how diversification can reduce risk. Because risk is central to explaining the valuation of financial instruments, the role of financial intermediaries, and the job of central bankers, the book returns to this concept throughout the chapters.

Emphasis on Financial Instruments

Financial instruments are introduced early in the book, where they are defined based on their economic function. This perspective leads naturally to a discussion of the uses of various instruments and the determinants of their value. Bonds, stocks, and derivatives all fit neatly into this framework, so they are all discussed together.

This approach solves one of the problems with existing texts, use of the term *financial market* to refer to bonds, interest rates, and foreign exchange. In its conventional microeconomic sense, the term *market* signifies a place where trade occurs, not the instruments that are traded. This book follows standard usage of the term *market* to mean a place for trade. It uses the term *financial instruments* to describe virtually all financial arrangements, including loans, bonds, stocks, futures, options, and insurance contracts. Doing so clears up the confusion that can arise when students arrive in a money and banking class fresh from a course in the principles of economics.

Parallel Presentation of the Federal Reserve and the European Central Bank

To foster a deeper understanding of central banking and monetary policy, the presentation of this material begins with a discussion of the central bank's role and objectives. Descriptions of the Federal Reserve and the European Central Bank follow. By starting on a theoretical plane, students gain the tools they need to understand how all central banks work. This avoids focusing on institutional details that may quickly become obsolete. Armed with a basic understanding of what central banks do and how they do it, students will be prepared to grasp the meaning of future changes in institutional structure.

Another important innovation is the parallel discussion of the two most important central banks in the world, the Federal Reserve and the European Central Bank (ECB). Students of the 21st century are ill-served by books that focus entirely on the U.S. financial system. They need a global perspective on central banking, the starting point for which is a detailed knowledge of the ECB.

Modern Treatment of Monetary Economics

The discussion of central banking is followed by a simple framework for understanding the impact of monetary policy on the real economy. Modern central bankers think and talk about changing the interest rate when inflation deviates from its target and output deviates from its normal level. Yet traditional treatments of monetary economics employ aggregate demand and aggregate supply diagrams, which relate output to the *price level*. Our approach is consistent with that in the most recent editions of the leading macroeconomics textbooks and directly links output to *inflation,* simplifying the exposition and highlighting the role of monetary policy. Because this book also skips the IS-LM framework, its presentation of monetary economics is several chapters shorter. Only those topics that are most important in a monetary economics course are covered: long-run money growth and inflation and short-run monetary policy and business cycles. This streamlined treatment of monetary theory is not only concise but more modern and more relevant than the traditional approach. It helps students to see monetary policy changes as part of a strategy rather than as one-off events, and it gives them a complete understanding of business cycle fluctuations.

Integrated Global Perspective

Technological advances have dramatically reduced the importance of a bank's physical location, producing a truly global financial system. Twenty-five years ago money and banking books could afford to focus primarily on the U.S. financial system, relegating international topics to a separate chapter that could be considered optional. But in today's financial world, even a large country like the United States cannot be treated in isolation. The global financial system is truly an integrated one, rendering separate discussion of a single country's institutions, markets, or policies impossible. This book incorporates the discussion of international issues throughout the text, emphasizing when national borders are important to bankers and when they are not.

Organization

This book is organized to help students understand both the financial system and its economic effects on their lives. That means surveying a broad series of topics, including what money is and how it is used; what a financial instrument is and how it is valued; what a financial market is and how it works; what a financial institution is and why we need it; and what a central bank is and how it operates. More important, it means showing students how to apply the five core principles of money and banking to the evolving financial and economic arrangements that they inevitably will confront during their lifetimes.

Part I: Money and the Financial System. Chapter 1 introduces the core principles of money and banking, which serve as touchstones throughout the book. It also presents FRED, the free online database of the Federal Reserve Bank of St. Louis. The book often uses FRED data for figures and tables, and every chapter calls on students to use FRED to solve end-of-chapter problems. Chapter 2 examines money both in theory and in practice. Chapter 3 follows with a bird's-eye view of financial instruments, financial markets, and financial institutions. (Instructors who prefer to discuss the financial system first can cover Chapters 2 and 3 in reverse order.)

Part II: Interest Rates, Financial Instruments, and Financial Markets. Part II contains a detailed description of financial instruments and the financial theory required to understand them. It begins with an explanation of present value and risk, followed by specific discussions of bonds, stocks, derivatives, and foreign exchange. Students benefit from concrete examples of these concepts. In Chapter 7 (The Risk and Term Structure of Interest Rates), for example, students learn how the information contained in the risk and term structure of interest rates can be useful in forecasting. In Chapter 8 (Stocks, Stock Markets, and Market Efficiency), they learn about stock bubbles and how those anomalies influence the economy. And in Chapter 10 (Foreign Exchange), they study the Big Mac index and learn to understand the concepts of purchasing power parity and interest rate parity. Throughout this section, two ideas are emphasized: that financial instruments transfer resources from savers to investors, and that in doing so, they transfer risk to those best equipped to bear it.

Part III: Financial Institutions. In Part III, the focus shifts to financial institutions. Chapter 11 introduces the economic theory that is the basis for our understanding of the role of financial intermediaries. Through a series of examples, students see the problems created by asymmetric information as well as how financial intermediaries can mitigate those problems. The remaining chapters in Part III put theory into practice. Chapter 12 presents a detailed discussion of banking, the bank balance sheet, and the risks that banks must manage. Chapter 13 provides a brief overview of the financial industry's structure, and Chapter 14 explains financial regulation, including a discussion of regulation to limit threats to the financial system as a whole and of efforts to limit the increased regulatory burden.

Part IV: Central Banks, Monetary Policy, and Financial Stability. Chapters 15 through 19 survey what central banks do and how they do it. This part of the book begins with a discussion of the role and objectives of central banks, which leads naturally to the principles that guide central bank design. Chapter 16 applies those principles to the Federal Reserve and the European Central Bank, highlighting the strategic importance of their numerical inflation objectives and their communications. Chapter 17 presents the central bank balance sheet, the process of multiple deposit creation, and the money supply. Chapters 18 and 19 cover operational policy, based on control of both the interest rate and the exchange rate. Chapter 18 also introduces the monetary transmission mechanism and presents a variety of unconventional monetary policy tools, including negative interest rates and the concept of the effective lower bound, that have become so prominent in recent years. The goal of Part IV is to give students the knowledge they will need to cope with the inevitable changes that will occur in central bank structure.

Part V: Modern Monetary Economics. The last part of the book covers modern monetary economics. While most books cover this topic in six or more chapters, this one does it in four. This streamlined approach concentrates on what is important, presenting only the essential lessons that students truly need. Chapter 20 sets the stage by exploring the relationship between inflation and money growth. Starting with inflation keeps the presentation simple and powerful, and emphasizes the way monetary policymakers think about what they do. A discussion of aggregate demand, aggregate supply, and the determinants of inflation and output follows. Consistent with the presentation in recent editions of leading macroeconomic textbooks, Chapter 21 presents a complete macroeconomic model with a dynamic aggregate demand curve that integrates monetary policy directly into the presentation, along with short- and long-run aggregate supply curves. In Chapter 22 the model is used to help understand the sources of business cycles, as well as a number of important applications that face monetary policymakers in the world today. Each application stands on its own, and the applications are ordered in increasing difficulty to allow maximum flexibility in their use. Finally, Chapter 23 explores the monetary transmission mechanism in some detail and addresses key challenges facing central banks, such as asset price bubbles, the effective lower bound for nominal rates, and the evolving structure of the financial system.

For those instructors who have the time, we recommend closing the course with a rereading of the first chapter and a review of the core principles. What is the future likely to hold for the six parts of the financial system: money, financial instruments, financial markets, financial institutions, regulatory agencies, and central banks? How do students envision each of these parts of the system 20 or even 50 years from now?

What's New in the Sixth Edition?

Many things have happened since the last edition. For that reason, all of the figures and data have been updated to reflect the most recent available information. In addition, the authors have made many changes to enhance the sixth edition of *Money, Banking, and Financial Markets*. What follows is only a sample of these changes.

New Topics in the Integrated Global Perspective

The sixth edition reflects the wide range of monetary and regulatory developments that have taken place since 2018. New topics introduced or discussed in much greater detail include:

- The role of paper money and virtual currencies
- Mobile banking and financial inclusion
- Modernizing the payments system
- Bond market liquidity
- The distribution of wealth
- Replacing LIBOR
- Private versus public equity
- Intangible capital
- Fiscal sustainability
- Stress testing banks to ensure resilience
- Cyber risk
- Negative interest rates
- Chinese exchange rate policy
- The threat to Fed independence

- Measuring tail risk
- Big data and the macroeconomy
- Secular stagnation
- Balance of payments crises

The most extensive changes are in Chapter 12, which includes a new section on cyber risk; in Chapter 14, which includes a discussion of continued reforms to financial regulation in the aftermath of the financial crisis; and in Chapter 18, which includes a full treatment of the Federal Reserve's evolving operational policy regime.

Changes at the Federal Reserve and the ECB

The discussion of the Federal Reserve and the ECB now considers their evolving communications strategy (Chapter 16); the use of unconventional policy tools, including negative interest rates and the dramatic growth in central bank balance sheets, aimed at addressing first the financial crisis and then the weak economic recoveries that followed (Chapter 18); the interactions between monetary policy and financial stability (Chapter 18); and the impairment of the monetary transmission process during the crisis (Chapter 23). It also reflects the sharply increased threat to Fed independence under President Trump (Chapter 15).

Updated Coverage of Current Events

Overall, nearly 30 of the 140 inserts in the previous edition have been replaced or altered substantially. These changes capture new developments in the key areas of technological change, the financial crisis, inequality, regulatory reform, and monetary policy.

Here is a partial list of the new or revised features:

Money and Banking Blog
Virtual Frenzies: Bitcoin and Blockchain (Chapter 2)
Banking the Masses: 2018 Edition (Chapter 3)
Investing in College (Chapter 4)
On the Distribution of Wealth (Chapter 5)
Bond Market Liquidity: Should We Be Worried? (Chapter 6)
The Cloudy Future of Peer-to-Peer Lending (Chapter 12)
Fiscal Sustainability (Chapter 15)
Is 2 Percent Still the Right Inflation Target? (Chapter 18)
Sudden Stops: Understanding Balance-of-Payments Crises (Chapter 19)
The Phillips Curve (Chapter 21)
Secular Stagnation (Chapter 22)
GDP at Risk (Chapter 23)

Applying the Concept
Modernizing U.S. Payments: Faster, Cheaper and More Secure (Chapter 2)
Raising Equity: Public versus Private (Chapter 8)
Financing Intangible Capital (Chapter 11)
Eclipsing LIBOR (Chapter 13)
Better Capitalized Banks Lend *More* and Lend *Better* (Chapter 14)
The Threat to Fed Independence (Chapter 15)
Time Consistency (Chapter 15)
Central Bank Digital Currency (Chapter 16)
What Should the Fed Own? (Chapter 17)
GDP: One Size No Longer Fits All (Chapter 18)
China's Changing Exchange Rate Regime (Chapter 19)
GDP-Linked Bonds (Chapter 22)

Lessons from the Crisis
Central Counterparties and Systemic Risk (Chapter 9)
The Three Phases of the Financial Crisis of 2007–2009 (Chapter 14)

Supplements for Instructors

The following ancillaries are available for quick download and convenient access via the Instructor Resource material available through McGraw-Hill Connect®.

Solutions Manual

Prepared by James Fackler (University of Kentucky) and Roisin O'Sullivan (Smith College), this manual contains detailed solutions to the end-of-chapter questions—Conceptual and Analytical problems and Data Exploration questions.

Test Bank

The revised test bank includes more than 2,500 multiple-choice and 600 short-answer and essay questions. The test bank can be used both as a study guide and as a source for exam questions. It has been computerized to allow for both selective and random generation of test questions.

Test Builder

Available within Connect, Test Builder is a cloud-based tool that enables instructors to format tests that can be printed or administered within an LMS. Test Builder offers a modern, streamlined interface for easy content configuration that matches course needs, without requiring a download.

Test Builder allows you to:

- access all test bank content from a particular title.
- easily pinpoint the most relevant content through robust filtering options.
- manipulate the order of questions or scramble questions and/or answers.
- pin questions to a specific location within a test.
- determine your preferred treatment of algorithmic questions.
- choose the layout and spacing.
- add instructions and configure default settings.

Test Builder provides a secure interface for better protection of content and allows for just-in-time updates to flow directly into assessments.

PowerPoint Slides

Updated presentation slides outline the main points in each chapter and reproduce major graphs and charts. This handy, colorful supplement can be edited, printed, or rearranged to fit the needs of your course.

Assurance of Learning Ready

Many educational institutions today are focused on the notion of *assurance of learning,* an important element of some accreditation standards. *Money, Banking, and Financial Markets* is designed specifically to support your assurance of learning initiatives with a simple, yet powerful solution.

Instructors can use Connect to easily query for learning outcomes/objectives that directly relate to the learning objectives of your course. You can then use the reporting features of Connect to aggregate student results in similar fashion, making the collection and presentation of assurance of learning data simple and easy.

AACSB Statement

McGraw-Hill Global Education is a proud corporate member of AACSB International. Understanding the importance and value of AACSB accreditation, *Money, Banking, and Financial Markets* has sought to recognize the curricula guidelines detailed in the AACSB standards for business accreditation by connecting questions in the text and test bank to the general knowledge and skill guidelines found in the AACSB standards.

The statements contained in *Money, Banking, and Financial Markets* are provided only as a guide for the users of this text. The AACSB leaves content coverage and assessment within the purview of individual schools, the mission of the school, and the faculty. While *Money, Banking, and Financial Markets* and the teaching package make no claim of any specific AACSB qualification or evaluation, we have within *Money, Banking, and Financial Markets* labeled questions according to the general knowledge and skills areas.

McGraw-Hill Customer Care Contact Information

At McGraw-Hill, we understand that getting the most from new technology can be challenging. That's why our services don't stop after you purchase our products. You can reach our Product Specialists 24 hours a day to get product-training online. Or you can search our knowledge bank of Frequently Asked Questions on our support website. For Customer Support, call **800-331-5094**, or visit **www.mheducation.com/highered/contact.html**. One of our Technical Support Analysts will be able to assist you in a timely fashion.

Learning Tools Walkthrough

Learning Objectives

The learning objectives (LOs) introduced at the start of each chapter highlight the material and concepts to be mastered. Every end-of-chapter problem is denoted by the LO to which it relates for reinforcement.

Learning Objectives

After reading this chapter, you should be able to:

- **LO1** Define money and describe its functions.
- **LO2** Discuss the different methods of payment and the future of money.
- **LO3** Explain how the money supply is measured and how it is linked to economic growth and inflation.

Core Principle Icons

The entire text discussion is organized around the following five core principles: *Time* has value; *risk* requires compensation; *information* is the basis for decisions; *markets* set prices and allocate resources; and *stability* improves welfare. Exploring these principles is the basis for learning what the financial system does, how it is organized, and how it is linked to the real economy. They are discussed in detail in Chapter 1; throughout the rest of the text, marginal icons remind students of the principles that underlie particular discussions.

you agree to make a $225 loan, and the borrower offers to repay you either $100 a year for three years or $125 a year for two years. Which offer should you take? Answering this question means figuring out the current value of the promised payments on the dates when they will be made. To do that, we'll use the concept of present value, sometimes referred to as *present discounted value.*

The Definition In our discussion of future value, we used the term *present value* to mean the initial amount invested or deposited. The way we used the term suggests its technical definition: Present value *is the value today (in the present) of a payment that is promised to be made in the future.* Put another way, present value is the amount that must be invested today in order to realize a specific amount on a given future date. Financial instruments promise future cash payments, so we need to know how to value

Debit Cards versus Credit Cards
YOUR FINANCIAL WORLD

When you go shopping, should you pay with a credit card or a debit card? To decide, you need to understand the difference between the two. First make sure you know which one of your cards is which. Usually an ATM card (the one that you got from the bank when you opened your checking account) is a debit card. But check to make sure.

What's the real difference, from the shopper's point of view? A debit card works just like a check, only faster. When you write a paper check, it usually takes a day or two to go through the system. A debit card transaction goes through right away. The electronic message gets to your bank on the same day, and your account is debited immediately. So, if you want to use your debit card, your account balance has to be higher than the payment you want to make. During and after the financial crisis that began in 2007, debit card use sharply outpaced credit card activity, as lenders and borrowers sought to slow the expansion (or even reduce the outstanding level) of household debt.

A credit card creates a deferred payment. The issuer agrees to make the payment for you, and you repay the debt later. That sounds good, but there's a catch. If you're late paying, there's a late fee. And if you don't pay the entire debt every month, you pay interest on the balance—at what is usually a very high interest rate. If you do pay your entire credit card debt every month, however, there is no late fee and no interest charge. Hence, you get an interest-free loan from the time you make the purchase to the time you pay the balance. If you can pay off your credit cards in full and on time, it's to your advantage to use them.

Credit cards have another advantage over debit cards. They help you build a credit history, which you'll need when the time comes to buy a car or a house. Because debit cards are just extensions of your bank account, they don't show potential lenders that you are creditworthy. In fact, some businesses, like car rental companies, require their customers to use credit cards for this reason.

Your Financial World

These boxes show students that the concepts taught in the text are relevant to their everyday lives. Among the topics covered are the importance of saving for retirement, the risk in taking on a variable-rate mortgage, the desirability of owning a diversified portfolio, and techniques for getting the most out of the financial news.

Lessons from the Crisis

These boxes explain concepts or issues that are both integral to the chapter and central to understanding how the financial crisis of 2007–2009 and the subsequent crisis in the euro area transformed the world of money, banking, and financial markets. The topics range from specific aspects of the crisis such as shadow banks and central bank policy responses to broad concepts like liquidity, leverage, sovereign default, and systemic risk.

Leverage
LESSONS FROM THE CRISIS

Households and firms often borrow to make investments. Obtaining a mortgage for a new home or selling a corporate bond to build a new plant are common examples. The use of borrowing to finance part of an investment is called *leverage.** Leverage played a key role in the financial crisis of 2007–2009, so it is worth understanding how leverage relates to risk and how it can make the financial system vulnerable.

Modern economies rely heavily on borrowing to make investments. They are all leveraged. Yet, the more leverage, the greater the risk that an adverse surprise will lead to bankruptcy. If two households own houses of the same value, the one that has borrowed more—the one that is more highly leveraged and has less net worth—is the more likely to default during a temporary slump in income. This example could apply equally well to firms, financial institutions, or even countries.

Financial institutions are much more highly leveraged than households or firms, typically owning assets of about 10 times their net worth. During the crisis, some important financial firms leveraged more than 30 times their net worth.†

When highly leveraged financial institutions experience a loss, they usually try to reduce their leverage—that is, to *deleverage*—by selling assets and issuing securities that raise their net worth (see accompanying figure). However, everyone in the financial system cannot deleverage at once. When too many institutions try to sell assets simultaneously, their efforts will almost surely prove counterproductive: falling prices will mean more losses, diminishing their net worth further, raising leverage, and making the assets they hold seem riskier, thereby compelling further sales.

This "paradox of leverage" reinforces the destabilizing liquidity spiral discussed in Chapter 2 (see Lessons from the Crisis: Market Liquidity, Funding Liquidity, and Making Markets). Both spirals feed a vicious cycle of falling prices and widespread deleveraging that was a hallmark of the financial crisis of 2007–2009. The financial system steadied only after massive government interventions in response to the plunge of many asset prices.

*For a technical definition of leverage, see the Tools of the Trade

Virtual Frenzies: Bitcoin and Blockchain
MONEY AND BANKING BLOG

Bitcoin is the oldest and most prominent of more than 2,500 cryptocurrencies—sometimes called "virtual currencies"—that have come into existence since 2008. Devotees hope these "tokens" will revolutionize many aspects of finance, including everyday payments. Cryptocurrencies like Bitcoin are a type of digital currency based on a peer-to-peer network designed to allow for the verification of transfers without the need for a government authority or any trusted third party. The technology used to record ownership—blockchain—is an ever-growing, encrypted public ledger of transactions spread over a network of

Let's have a closer look at Bitcoin itself. Some countries classify Bitcoin as a commodity, subjecting it to capital gains taxation, or severely restricting its use. In no country can Bitcoin be widely exchanged for goods and services. As a result, in early 2019 Bitcoin accounted for less than 200 *thousand* daily transactions globally, compared with more than 500 *million* dollar transactions in the United States alone.

Bitcoin's value is extremely unstable: The dollar value of a single Bitcoin surged from just pennies in 2010 to nearly $20,000 at the peak in December 2017, before plunging

Money and Banking Blog

One article per chapter is featured from the authors' blog at www.moneyandbanking.com. These readings show how concepts introduced in the chapter are applied to contemporary issues in money and banking, including changes in technology, regulation, and the mechanisms of monetary policy.

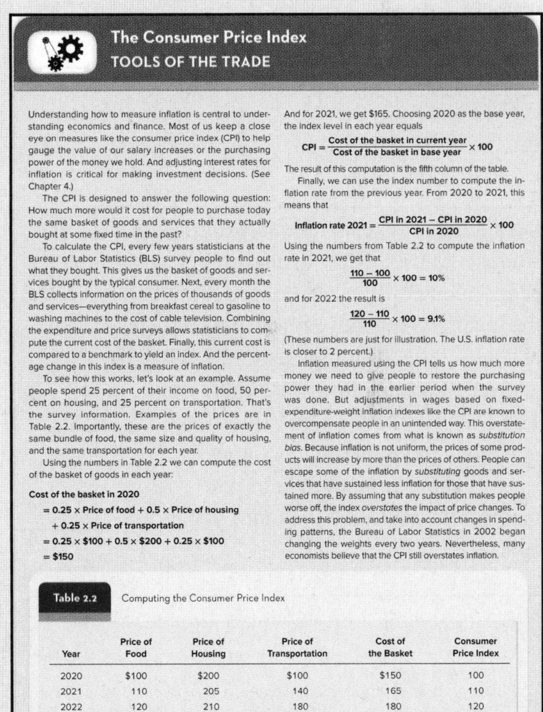

The Consumer Price Index
TOOLS OF THE TRADE

Understanding how to measure inflation is central to understanding economics and finance. Most of us keep a close eye on measures like the consumer price index (CPI) to help gauge the value of our salary increases or the purchasing power of the money we hold. And adjusting interest rates for inflation is critical for making investment decisions. (See Chapter 4.)

The CPI is designed to answer the following question: How much more would it cost for people to purchase today the same basket of goods and services that they actually bought at some fixed time in the past?

To calculate the CPI, every few years statisticians at the Bureau of Labor Statistics (BLS) survey people to find out what they bought. This gives us the basket of goods and services bought by the typical consumer. Next, every month the BLS collects information on the prices of thousands of goods and services—everything from breakfast cereal to gasoline to washing machines to the cost of cable television. Combining the expenditure and price surveys allows statisticians to compute the current cost of the basket. Finally, this current cost is compared to a benchmark to yield an index. And the percentage change in this index is a measure of inflation.

To see how this works, let's look at an example. Assume people spend 25 percent of their income on food, 50 percent on housing, and 25 percent on transportation. That's the survey information. Examples of the prices are in Table 2.2. Importantly, these are the prices of exactly the same bundle of food, the same size and quality of housing, and the same transportation for each year.

Using the numbers in Table 2.2 we can compute the cost of the basket of goods in each year:

Cost of the basket in 2020

$$= 0.25 \times \text{Price of food} + 0.5 \times \text{Price of housing} + 0.25 \times \text{Price of transportation}$$
$$= 0.25 \times \$100 + 0.5 \times \$200 + 0.25 \times \$100$$
$$= \$150$$

And for 2021, we get $165. Choosing 2020 as the base year, the index level in each year equals

$$\text{CPI} = \frac{\text{Cost of the basket in current year}}{\text{Cost of the basket in base year}} \times 100$$

The result of this computation is the fifth column of the table.

Finally, we can use the index number to compute the inflation rate from the previous year. From 2020 to 2021, this means that

$$\text{Inflation rate 2021} = \frac{\text{CPI in 2021} - \text{CPI in 2020}}{\text{CPI in 2020}} \times 100$$

Using the numbers from Table 2.2 to compute the inflation rate in 2021, we get that

$$\frac{110 - 100}{100} \times 100 = 10\%$$

and for 2022 the result is

$$\frac{120 - 110}{110} \times 100 = 9.1\%$$

(These numbers are just for illustration. The U.S. inflation rate is closer to 2 percent.)

Inflation measured using the CPI tells us how much more money we need to give people to restore the purchasing power they had in the earlier period when the survey was done. But adjustments in wages based on fixed-expenditure-weight inflation indexes like the CPI are known to overcompensate people in an unintended way. This overstatement of inflation comes from what is known as *substitution bias*. Because inflation is not uniform, the prices of some products will increase by more than the prices of others. People can escape some of the inflation by *substituting* goods and services that have sustained less inflation for those that have sustained more. By assuming that any substitution makes people worse off, the index *overstates* the impact of price changes. To address this problem, and take into account changes in spending patterns, the Bureau of Labor Statistics in 2002 began changing the weights every two years. Nevertheless, many economists believe that the CPI still overstates inflation.

Table 2.2 Computing the Consumer Price Index

Year	Price of Food	Price of Housing	Price of Transportation	Cost of the Basket	Consumer Price Index
2020	$100	$200	$100	$150	100
2021	110	205	140	165	110
2022	120	210	180	180	120

How Much Is Our Distant Future Worth?
APPLYING THE CONCEPT

Many people worry about the challenges their descendants will face. There are plenty of things to fret about, ranging from the threat of rising sea levels in this century to the long-range challenge of managing radioactive waste, which can be toxic for many thousands of years. Physicist Stephen Hawking has argued that human beings "won't survive another 1,000 years without escaping our fragile planet."

How much ought we be willing to spend now to avoid damage 100 years from now that will cost $1 at that time? The answer depends on many factors, including the relative affluence of our descendants, the degree of uncertainty about the future, and the possibility of existential threats.

To simplify the question, suppose that the only thing we care about is the present value of the expected losses associated with a preventable future disaster. In that case, the discount rate we use is critical for determining what we should do today. For example, for a disaster that is 100 years away, the value today of a $1 future loss at an annual discount rate of 1 percent is $0.37. But at a discount rate of

What discount rate should we use to value things in the distant future? For questions like this, economists usually look at market prices.

Various measures suggest that the appropriate rate is in the range of 1 to 2½ percent. For example, in recent years the long-term U.S. Treasury inflation-indexed bond yield has averaged around 1 percent. At the upper end of the range, research examining land leases with several hundred years of maturity points to a rate close to 2½ percent.

Policy disagreements among serious analysts of climate change are closely related to their views on the appropriate discount rate. One well-known report applied a relatively low discount rate of 1.4 percent and called for a large tax on carbon emissions to limit future losses from climate change. A different analysis used a relatively high 4.3 percent discount rate and called for a carbon tax only about *one-tenth* the level implied by the 1.4 percent rate analysis. Why? The low discount rate puts a great deal more weight on losses that are predicted to occur hundreds of years in the future.

Of course, it's not just about discount rates. It's about the scale of future losses, too. If policy actions today can prevent a

Applying the Concept

These sections showcase history and examine issues relevant to the public policy debate to illustrate how ideas introduced in the chapter can be applied to the world around us. Subjects include central bank digital currency, the replacement of LIBOR, and the heightened threat to Fed independence.

Tools of the Trade

These boxes teach useful skills, including how to read bond and stock tables, how to read charts, and how to do some simple algebraic calculations. Some provide brief reviews of material from the principles of economics course, such as the relationship between the current account and the capital account in the balance of payments.

End-of-Chapter Features

Using FRED: Codes for Data in This Chapter

Data Series	FRED Data Code
1-year Treasury bill rate	TB1YR
3-month Treasury bill rate	TB3MS
Consumer price index	CPIAUCSL
1-year inflation expectations (Michigan survey)	MICH
Brazil Treasury bill rate	INTGSTBRM193N
Brazil consumer price index	BRACPIALLMINMEI
China discount rate	INTDSRCNM193N
China consumer price index	CHNCPIALLMINMEI
10-year Treasury constant maturity rate	GS10
10-year Treasury inflation-indexed yield	FII10
5-year Treasury constant maturity rate	GS5
5-year Treasury inflation-indexed yield	FII5

FRED Data Codes

The FRED table lists key economic and financial indicators relevant to the chapter and the codes by which they are accessed in FRED, the free online database provided by the Federal Reserve Bank of St. Louis. With the data codes, students can use FRED to analyze key economic patterns and illuminate the ideas in the chapter. See Appendix B to Chapter 1 for help using FRED and refer to www.mhhe.com/moneyandbanking6e.

Data Exploration

Detailed end-of-chapter questions ask students to use FRED to analyze economic and financial data relevant to the chapter. Appendix B to Chapter 1 provides information on using FRED and sets the stage for its use thereafter. The Data Exploration questions have now been integrated into Connect as assignable content to help you incorporate real-time data into your course!

Data Exploration connect

For detailed instructions on using Federal Reserve Economic Data (FRED) online to answer each of the following problems, visit www.mhhe.com/moneyandbanking6e *and refer to the FRED Resources and Data Exploration Hints.*

1. Find the most recent level of M2 (FRED code: M2SL) and of the U.S. population (FRED code: POP). Compute the quantity of money divided by the population. (Note that M2 is measured in billions of dollars and population is in thousands of individuals.) Do you think your answer is large? Why? *(LO1)*
2. Reproduce Figure 2.3 from 1960 to the present, showing the percent change from a year ago of M1 (FRED code: M1SL) and M2 (FRED code: M2SL). Comment on the pattern over the last five years. Would it matter which of the two monetary aggregates you looked at? *(LO3)*
3. Which usually grows faster: M1 or M2? Produce a graph showing M2 divided by M1. When this ratio rises, M2 outpaces M1 and vice versa. What is the long-run pattern? Is the pattern stable? *(LO3)*
4. To complete payments, do you think people need more or less currency per dollar of transactions than they did 30 years ago? After stating your hypothesis, plot currency in

Conceptual and Analytical Problems connect

1. Describe four ways you could pay for your morning cup of coffee. What are the advantages and disadvantages of each? *(LO2)*
2. You are the owner of a small sandwich shop. A buyer may offer one of several payment methods: cash, a check drawn on a bank, a credit card, or a debit card. Which of these is the least costly for you? Explain why the others are more expensive. *(LO2)*
3. Explain how money encourages specialization, and how specialization improves everyone's standard of living. (LO3)

4.* Could the dollar still function as the unit of account in a totally cashless society? *(LO2)*

5. Give four examples of ACH transactions you might make. *(LO2)*
6. A subset of European Union countries have adopted the euro, while the remaining member countries have retained their own currencies. What are the advantages of a common currency for someone who is traveling through Europe? *(LO1)*
7. Why might each of the following commodities not serve well as money? *(LO2)*
   a. Tomatoes
   b. Bricks
   c. Cattle

Conceptual and Analytical Problems

Each chapter contains at least 18 conceptual and analytical problems at varying levels of difficulty, which reinforce the lessons in the chapter. All of the problems are available as assignable content within Connect, McGraw-Hill's homework management platform, organized around learning objectives to make it easier to plan, track, and analyze student performance across different learning outcomes.

Acknowledgments

I owe thanks to many more people than I can possibly list, including a large number of academics, central bankers, and financial market participants around the world. A few of these deserve special mention. I would like to thank Robert M. Solow, who set me on the path doing economics as a 20-year-old undergraduate; George A. Akerlof, whose inspiration still guides me, even more than 35 years after he signed my dissertation; William J. McDonough, who gave me the opportunity to watch and ask questions from inside the Federal Reserve; Peter R. Fisher, who was my day-to-day guide to what I was seeing during my time at the Fed; and Jaime Caruana and Hervé Hannoun, whose patience and understanding helped me appreciate the global central bank community.

Of my numerous collaborators and colleagues over the years, Nelson Mark (now at the University of Notre Dame) is the most important. In addition, Michael Bryan has been a constant source of help and encouragement, as have numerous friends throughout the central banking world.

Among all of the professional colleagues who took the time to read early versions of the manuscript, I would like to single out Jim Fackler for his insight and patience. This book is much better for the time he generously devoted to correcting my logical mistakes and helping ensure that the exercises would reinforce the lessons in each chapter.

Without all the people at McGraw-Hill this book would never have been written. Gary Burke and Paul Shensa first convinced me that I could write this book, and then taught me how. Erin Strathmann worked tirelessly (and daily) to improve the book. Betty Morgan made my sentences and paragraphs readable. And all of the people in production and design turned the words and charts into a beautiful, readable book. Starting with the third edition, Gregg Forte has made notable contributions through his skilled editing of the manuscript. And, for the last three editions, Christina Kouvelis has done the hard work of ensuring everyone maintained the high standard.

Without students, universities would not exist. And without a class in money and banking to teach, I would not have written this book. I owe a debt to every student who has sat in a classroom with me. Several deserve special mention for the time and effort they put into helping with the manuscript: Margaret Mary McConnell of the Federal Reserve Bank of New York, Roisin O'Sullivan of Smith College, Stefan Krause formerly of the Banque de France, Lianfa Li of Peking University, Craig Evers of Brevan Howard, and Georgios Karras of the University of Illinois at Chicago.

And finally, there is my family; my wife, Ruth, and our sons, Daniel and Ethan. For years they put up with my daily routine of writing, rewriting, and rewriting again and again. To them I owe the biggest thanks.

Stephen G. Cecchetti

Brandeis International Business School

There is not enough space here to thank the many people who taught me about financial markets and institutions during my more than two decades of work as a market economist, but a few deserve special mention. Hugh Patrick was an inspiration in graduate school and remains a friend and guide. In the financial markets, I benefited especially from the wisdom of Henry Kaufman and the economists he gathered at Salomon Brothers in the 1980s—Richard Berner, Robert DiClemente, John Lipsky, and Nicholas Sargen. The members of the economics team that I was privileged to lead at Salomon (and later at Citi) continued my education, including (among many others) Lewis Alexander, Robert DiClemente, Don Hanna, Michael Saunders, Christopher Wiegand, and Jeffrey Young.

I also owe an extraordinary debt to my colleagues at the New York University Leonard N. Stern School of Business, who welcomed me, gave me the privilege of teaching excellent students, and entrusted me with the honor of directing Stern's Center for Global Economy and Business (www.stern.nyu.edu/cgeb). For their sustained support and guidance, I thank former Deans Thomas Cooley and Peter Henry, current Dean Rangarajan Sundaram, former Vice Dean Ingo Walter, and the distinguished current and former chairs of the Department of Economics—the late David Backus, Luis Cabral, Paul Wachtel, Lawrence White, and Stanley Zin. David Backus, Kim Ruhl, and Michael Waugh gave me the tools to teach MBA students. Jennifer Carpenter has been my partner as Associate Director of the Center for Global Economy and Business, while John Asker, Michael Dickstein, Thomas Philippon, Kim Ruhl, Laura Veldkamp, Paul Wachtel, and Michael Waugh have all served as Center research group coordinators and my advisors. Jonathan Robidoux keeps the Center operating efficiently and with a smile each day. Many others deserve thanks for making Stern the thriving research and teaching environment that it is today, but I am especially grateful for the support of Viral Acharya, Gian Luca Clementi, Christopher Conlon, Robert Engle, Mervyn King, Matthew Richardson, Maher Said, Bruce Tuckman, Vaidyanathan Venkateswaran, and Robert Whitelaw. Finally, many thanks to Corey Feldman for his research assistance in the preparation of this sixth edition.

Of course, my greatest debt is to my wife, Elvira Pratsch. I also thank my sister and brother, Sharon and Andy.

Kermit L. Schoenholtz
New York University Leonard N. Stern School of Business

Reviewers

Thank you to the following contributing reviewers for this and previous editions.

Burton Abrams
University of Delaware

Douglas Agbetsiafa
Indiana University at South Bend

Pedro Albuquerque
University of Minnesota at Duluth

Abdiweli Ali
Niagara University

Thomas Martin Allen
Texas A&M University

Brad Altmeyer
South Texas College

Harjit Arora
Lemoyne College

Foued Ayari
Bernard M. Baruch College

Raymond Batina
Washington State University

Clare Battista
California Polytechnic State University

Larry Belcher
Stetson University

Robert Boatler
Texas Christian University

Christa Bouwman
Case Western Reserve University

Latanya Brown
Bowie State University

James Butkiewicz
University of Delaware

Anne Bynoe
Pace University

Douglas Campbell
University of Memphis

Giorgio Canarella
California State University at Los Angeles

Bolong Cao
Ohio University, Athens

Tina Carter
Florida State University at Tallahassee

Matthew S. Chambers
Towson University

Dong Cho
Wichita State University

Nan-Ting Chou
University of Louisville

Isabelle Delalex
Pace University

Mamit Deme
Middle Tennessee State University

Seija Doolittle
Delaware Technical Community College at Wilmington

David Doorn
University of Minnesota at Duluth

Demissew Ejara
William Patterson University

Paul Emberton
Texas State University
Robert Eyler
Sonoma State University
Gregory Fallon
College of Saint Joseph
Richard Froyen
University of North Carolina at Chapel Hill
Craig Furfine
University of Chicago
William Gavin
Washington University
Ronald Gilbert
Texas Tech University
Gregory Gilpin
Montana State University
Lance Girton
University of Utah
Stuart Glosser
University of Wisconsin at Whitewater
William L. Goffe
Oswego State University of New York
Stephan F. Gohmann
University of Louisville
Elias Grivoyannis
Yeshiva University
Joanne Guo
Pace University
David Hammes
University of Hawaii at Hilo
Scott Hein
Texas Tech University
Ying Huang
Manhattan College
Julio Huato
Saint Francis College
Owen Irvine
Michigan State University at East Lansing
Aaron Jackson
Bentley College
Yongbok Jeon
University of Utah at Salt Lake City
George Jouganatos
California State University at Sacramento
Chulhee Jun
Texas Technical University
Chris Kauffman
University of Tennessee at Knoxville
Andrew Kayanga
Dillard University
Kathy Kelly
University of Texas, Arlington
Kent Kimbrough
Duke University
Paul Kubik
DePaul University
Pamela Labadie
George Washington University
Larry Landrum
Virginia Western Community College
Tom Lee
California State University at Northridge
Serpil Leveen
Montclair State University
Melissa Lind
University of Texas, Arlington
Mark Longbrake
Ohio State University at Columbus
Fiona Maclachlan
Manhattan College
Michael Madaris
William Carey University
Ellie Mafi-Kreft
Indiana University
Vincent Marra
University of Delaware
Ralph May
Southwestern Oklahoma State University
Robert McAuliffe
Babson College
Chris McHugh
Tufts University
Alice Melkumian
Western Illinois University
Alla Melkumian
Western Illinois University
Jianjun Miao
Boston University
Peter Mikek
Wabash College
Ossama Mikhail
University of Central Florida

Kyoko Mona
Bernard M. Baruch College
Ray Nelson
Brigham Young University
James Nguyen
Southeastern Louisiana University
David O'Dell
McPherson College
Roisin O'Sullivan
Smith College
Dennis O'Toole
Virginia Commonwealth University
Daniel Owens
University of North Dakota
Hilde Patron-Boenheim
University of West Georgia
Robert Pennington
University of Central Florida
Dennis Placone
Clemson University
Hamideh Ramjerdi
William Patterson University
Ronald Ratti
University of Western Sydney, Australia
Rupert Rhodd
Florida Atlantic University at Davie
Kevin Salyer
University of California, Davis
Julia Sampson
Malone College
Drew Saunders
Purdue University
Timothy J. Schibik
University of Southern Indiana
Sherrill Shaffer
University of Wyoming
Eugene Sherman
Baruch College
Anna Shostya
Bernard M. Baruch College
Harindar Singh
Grand Valley State University
Robert Sonora
Fort Lewis College
Souren Soumbatiants
Franklin University
Richard Stahl
Louisiana State University at Baton Rouge
Herman Stekler
George Washington University
Mark Strazicich
Appalachian State University
William Stronge
Florida Atlantic University
Scott Sumner
Bentley College
Philip Tew
University of Mississippi
Sven N. Thommesen
Auburn University
Mark Toma
University of Kentucky at Lexington
Kudret Topyan
Manhattan College
Brian Trinque
University of Texas at Austin
Rubina Vohra
New Jersey City University
William Walsh
University of St. Thomas
Dale Warmingham
Rutgers University at New Brunswick
Chao Wei
George Washington University
Mark Weinstock
Pace University
Niklas Westelius
Hunter College
Eugene White
Rutgers University at New Brunswick
Ruhai Wu
Florida Atlantic University
King-Yuen Yik
University of Michigan at Ann Arbor
Derek Yonai
Campbell University

Brief Contents

FOR INSTRUCTORS

You're in the driver's seat.

Want to build your own course? No problem. Prefer to use our turnkey, prebuilt course? Easy. Want to make changes throughout the semester? Sure. And you'll save time with Connect's auto-grading too.

65%
Less Time Grading

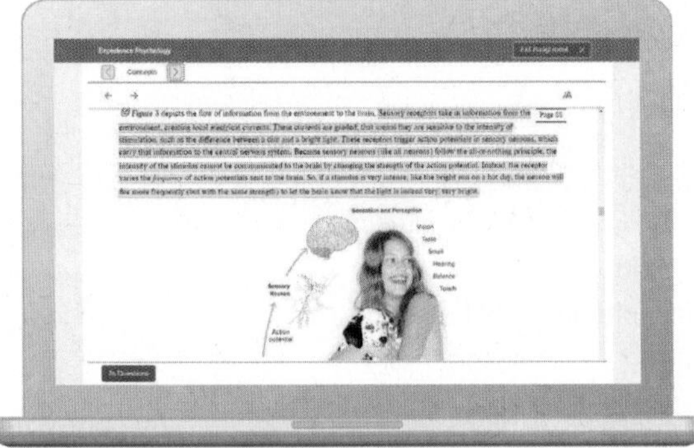

Laptop: McGraw-Hill; Woman/dog: George Doyle/Getty Images

They'll thank you for it.

Adaptive study resources like SmartBook® 2.0 help your students be better prepared in less time. You can transform your class time from dull definitions to dynamic debates. Find out more about the powerful personalized learning experience available in SmartBook 2.0 at **www.mheducation.com/highered/connect/smartbook**

Make it simple, make it affordable.

Connect makes it easy with seamless integration using any of the major Learning Management Systems—Blackboard®, Canvas, and D2L, among others—to let you organize your course in one convenient location. Give your students access to digital materials at a discount with our inclusive access program. Ask your McGraw-Hill representative for more information.

Padlock: Jobalou/Getty Images

Solutions for your challenges.

A product isn't a solution. Real solutions are affordable, reliable, and come with training and ongoing support when you need it and how you want it. Our Customer Experience Group can also help you troubleshoot tech problems—although Connect's 99% uptime means you might not need to call them. See for yourself at **status.mheducation.com**

Checkmark: Jobalou/Getty Images

FOR STUDENTS

Effective, efficient studying.

Connect helps you be more productive with your study time and get better grades using tools like SmartBook 2.0, which highlights key concepts and creates a personalized study plan. Connect sets you up for success, so you walk into class with confidence and walk out with better grades.

Study anytime, anywhere.

Download the free ReadAnywhere app and access your online eBook or SmartBook 2.0 assignments when it's convenient, even if you're offline. And since the app automatically syncs with your eBook and SmartBook 2.0 assignments in Connect, all of your work is available every time you open it. Find out more at **www.mheducation.com/readanywhere**

"I really liked this app—it made it easy to study when you don't have your text-book in front of you."

- Jordan Cunningham, Eastern Washington University

Calendar: owattaphotos/Getty Images

No surprises.

The Connect Calendar and Reports tools keep you on track with the work you need to get done and your assignment scores. Life gets busy; Connect tools help you keep learning through it all.

Learning for everyone.

McGraw-Hill works directly with Accessibility Services Departments and faculty to meet the learning needs of all students. Please contact your Accessibility Services office and ask them to email accessibility@mheducation.com, or visit **www.mheducation.com/about/accessibility** for more information.

Top: Jenner Images/Getty Images, Left: Hero Images/Getty Images, Right: Hero Images/Getty Images

Contents

Part V Modern Monetary Economics

Learning Tools

Chapter

1 An Introduction to Money and the Financial System

Learning Objectives

After reading this chapter, you should be able to:

LO1* List and explain the six parts of the financial system.

LO2 Identify the five core principles of money and banking.

LO3 Describe the special features and organization of the book.

This morning, a typical American college student bought coffee at the local café, paying for it with a debit card. Then she jumped into her insured car and drove to the university, which she attends thanks to her student loan. She may have left her parents' home, which is mortgaged, a few minutes early to avoid construction work on a new dormitory, financed by bonds issued by the university. Or perhaps she needed to purchase this book online, using her credit card, before her first money and banking class began.

Beneath the surface, the financial transactions embedded in this story—even the seemingly simple ones—are quite complicated. If the café owner and the student use different banks, paying for the coffee will require an interbank funds transfer. The company that insures the student's car has to invest the premiums she pays until they are needed to pay off claims. The student's parents almost surely obtained their home mortgage through a mortgage broker, whose job was to find the cheapest mortgage available. And the bonds the university issued to finance construction of the new dormitory were created with the aid of an investment bank.

This brief example hints at the complex web of interdependent institutions and markets that is the foundation for our daily financial transactions. The system is so efficient that most of us rarely take note of it. But a financial system is like air to an economy: If it disappeared suddenly, everything would grind to a halt.

In the autumn of 2008, we came closer to such a financial meltdown than at any time since the 1930s. In the earlier episode, the collapse of the banking system led to the Great Depression. In the recent crisis, some of the world's largest financial institutions failed. Key markets stopped functioning. Credit dried up, even for sound borrowers. As a result, vibrant companies that relied on short-term loans to pay their employees and buy materials faced potential ruin. Even some fundamental ways that we make payments for goods and services were threatened.

*LO, Learning Objective.

Gasping for air in this financial crisis, the global economy during 2008 and 2009 sank into the deepest, broadest, and longest downturn since the 1930s. Around the world, tens of millions of people lost their jobs. In the United States, millions lost their homes and their life's savings. Others became unable to borrow to buy a home or go to college. And the weakness added to financial fragility elsewhere, especially in Europe, where the viability of the euro, the world's leading currency after the U.S. dollar, was threatened. The chances are good that you know someone—in your neighborhood, your school, or your family—whose life was changed for the worse by the crisis.

So, what happens in the financial system, whether for good or for bad, matters greatly for all of us. To understand the system—both its strengths and its vulnerabilities—let's take a closer look.

The Six Parts of the Financial System

The **financial system**[1] has six parts, each of which plays a fundamental role in our economy. Those parts are money, financial instruments, financial markets, financial institutions, government regulatory agencies, and central banks.

We use the first part of the system, **money**, to pay for our purchases and to store our wealth. We use the second part, **financial instruments**, to transfer resources from savers to investors and to transfer risk to those who are best equipped to bear it. Stocks, mortgages, and insurance policies are examples of financial instruments. The third part of our financial system, **financial markets**, allows us to buy and sell financial instruments quickly and cheaply. The New York Stock Exchange is an example of a financial market. **Financial institutions**, the fourth part of the financial system, provide a myriad of services, including access to the financial markets and collection of information about prospective borrowers to ensure they are creditworthy. Banks, securities firms, and insurance companies are examples of financial institutions. Government **regulatory agencies** form the fifth part of the financial system. They are responsible for making sure that the elements of the financial system—including its instruments, markets, and institutions—operate in a safe and reliable manner. Finally, **central banks**, the sixth part of the system, monitor and stabilize the economy. The **Federal Reserve System** is the central bank of the United States.

While the essential functions that define these six categories endure, their form is constantly evolving. *Money* once consisted of gold and silver coins. These were eventually replaced by paper currency, which today is being eclipsed by electronic funds transfers. Methods of accessing means of payment have changed dramatically as well. As recently as 1970, people customarily obtained currency from bank tellers when they cashed their paychecks or withdrew their savings from the local bank. Today, they can get cash from practically any ATM anywhere in the world. To pay their bills, people once wrote checks and put them in the mail, and then waited for their monthly bank statements to make sure the transactions had been processed correctly. Today, payments can be made automatically, and account holders can check the transactions at any time on their bank's website or on their smartphone.

Financial instruments (or securities, as they are often called) have evolved just as much as currency. In the last few centuries, investors could buy individual stocks through stockbrokers, but the transactions were costly. Furthermore, putting together a portfolio of even a small number of stocks and bonds was extremely

[1]Throughout the book, terms in bold red are "key terms" listed at the end of each chapter and defined in the glossary.

time-consuming; just collecting the information necessary to evaluate a potential investment was a daunting task. As a result, investing was an activity reserved for the wealthy. Today, financial institutions offer people with as little as $1,000 to invest the ability to purchase shares in *mutual funds,* which pool the savings of a large number of investors. Because of their size, mutual funds can construct portfolios of hundreds or even thousands of different stocks and/or bonds.

The markets where stocks and bonds are sold have undergone a similar transformation. Originally, *financial markets* were located in coffeehouses and taverns where individuals met to exchange financial instruments. The next step was to create organized markets, like the New York Stock Exchange—trading places specifically dedicated to the buying and selling of stocks and bonds. Today, most of the activity that once occurred at these big-city financial exchanges is handled by electronic networks. Buyers and sellers obtain price information and initiate transactions from their desktop computers or from handheld devices. Because electronic networks have reduced the cost of processing financial transactions, even small investors can afford to participate in them. Just as important, today's financial markets offer a much broader array of financial instruments than those available even 50 years ago.

Financial institutions have changed, as well. Banks began as vaults where people could store their valuables. Gradually, they developed into institutions that accepted deposits and made loans. For hundreds of years, in fact, that was what bankers did. Today, a bank is more like a financial supermarket. Walk in and you will discover a huge assortment of financial products and services for sale, from access to the financial markets to insurance policies, mortgages, consumer credit, and even investment advice.

The activities of government regulatory agencies and the design of **regulation** have been evolving and have entered a period of more rapid change, too. In the aftermath of the financial crisis of 1929–1933, when the failure of thousands of banks led to the Great Depression, the U.S. government introduced regulatory agencies to provide wide-ranging financial regulation—rules for the operation of financial institutions and markets—and **supervision**—oversight through examination and enforcement. The U.S. agencies established in the 1930s to issue and enforce these financial rules still operate.

Yet, the evolution of financial instruments, institutions, and markets has led to many changes in the ways that regulatory agencies work. A bank examiner used to count the money in the cash drawers and call borrowers to see if the loans on a bank's books were real. The examiner might even visit workplaces to see if the loans were used as designed to buy equipment or build a factory. Today, banks engage in millions of transactions, many of which are far more complex and difficult to understand than a loan or a mortgage. So, a government examiner also looks at the systems that a bank uses to manage its various risks. In doing so, regulators try to encourage best practices throughout the financial industry.

However, the failure of regulators in the United States and elsewhere around the world to anticipate or prevent the financial crisis of 2007–2009 has led many governments to undertake far-reaching changes to financial regulation and the regulatory agencies. The Dodd-Frank Wall Street Reform and Consumer Protection Act, adopted in 2010 and known as the **Dodd-Frank Act**, is the largest U.S. regulatory change since the 1930s. Also in 2010, regulators of many nations agreed on a third, major update of standards for internationally active banks—known as **Basel III** after the Swiss city where the policymakers meet. Both reforms took years to implement, and have prompted further changes to tailor the rules and limit the resulting regulatory burden. Their influence will continue to shape the financial system for decades.

Finally, *central banks* have changed a great deal. They began as large private banks founded by monarchs to finance wars. For instance, King William of Orange created the Bank of England in 1694 for the express purpose of raising taxes and borrowing to finance a war between Austria, England, and the Netherlands on one side and Louis XIV's France on the other. Eventually, these government treasuries grew into the modern central banks we know today. While only a few central banks existed in 1900, now nearly every country in the world has one, and they have become one of the most important institutions in government. Central banks control the availability of money and credit to promote low inflation, high growth, and the stability of the financial system. Because their current mission is to serve the public at large rather than land-hungry monarchs, their operating methods have changed as well. A central bank's decisions used to be shrouded in mystery, but today's policy-makers strive for transparency in their operations. Officials at the **European Central Bank (ECB)** and the U.S. Federal Reserve—two of the most important central banks in the world—go out of their way to explain the rationale for their decisions.

Though the changing nature of our financial system is a fascinating topic, it poses challenges for both students and instructors. How can we teach and learn about money and banking in a way that will stand the test of time, so that the knowledge we gain won't become outmoded? The answer is that we must develop a way to understand and adapt to the evolutionary structure of the financial system. That means discussing money and banking within a framework of core principles that do not change over time. The next section introduces the five core principles that will guide our studies throughout this book.

The Five Core Principles of Money and Banking

Five core principles will inform our analysis of the financial system and its interaction with the real economy. Once you have grasped these principles, you will have a better understanding not only of what is happening in the financial world today but of changes that will undoubtedly occur in the future. The five principles are based on **time, risk, information, markets,** and **stability.**

Core Principle 1: Time Has Value

TIME

The first principle of money and banking is that *time has value.* At some very basic level, everyone knows this. If you take a job at the local supermarket, you will almost surely be paid by the hour. An hour's worth of work equals a certain number of dollars. Literally, your time has a price.

On a more sophisticated level, **time** affects the value of financial transactions. Most loan contracts allow the borrower to spread out the payments over time. If you take out an auto loan, for example, the lender will allow you to make a series of monthly payments over three, four, or even five years. If you add up the payments, you'll discover that the total exceeds the amount of the loan. At an interest rate of 4 percent, a four-year, $10,000 car loan will require 48 monthly payments of $226 each. That means you will repay a total of $10,848 (48 times $226). The reason your repayments total more than the loan amount is that you are paying interest to compensate the lender for the time during which you use the funds. That is, the resources you borrowed have an opportunity cost to the lender so you have to pay rent on them.

Interest payments are fundamental to a market economy. In Chapter 4, we will develop an understanding of interest rates and how to use them. Then, throughout the remainder of Part II (Chapters 4–10), we will apply the principle that time has value in our discussion of the valuation of bonds, stocks, and other financial instruments involving future payments. How much should you be willing to pay for a particular stock or bond? Figuring out what alternative investments are worth, and comparing them, means valuing payments made on different future dates. The same principle applies to the question of how much you must invest today to achieve a particular financial objective in the future. How much of your salary, for example, do you need to save each month to meet your goal of buying a house? The length of time your savings will be earning interest is a key to answering this question.

Core Principle 2: Risk Requires Compensation

The world is filled with uncertainty. More events, both good and bad, *can* happen than *will* happen. Some of the possibilities, such as the likelihood of your home doubling in value after you buy it, are welcome. Other possibilities, such as the chance that you might lose your job and not be able to make your car payments, are distinctly unwelcome. Dealing effectively with **risk** requires that you consider the full range of possibilities in order to eliminate some risks, reduce others, pay someone to assume particularly onerous risks, and just live with what's left. Needless to say, no one will assume your risks for free, which brings us to the second core principle of money and banking: *Risk requires compensation.* In the financial world, compensation is made in the form of explicit payments. That is, investors must be paid to assume risk; the higher the risk, the bigger the required payment.

Car insurance is a common example of paying someone else to shoulder a risk you don't want to take. If your car is wrecked in an accident, you will want to be able to repair it. But beyond that, auto insurance shelters drivers from the possibility of losing all their wealth in the event that they cause an accident in which someone is seriously injured. Although the chances of causing such an accident are quite small, the results can be so serious that, even if the government didn't require it, most of us would voluntarily purchase auto insurance. Driving without it just isn't worth the risk. The insurance company pools the premiums that policyholders pay and invests them. Even though some of the premiums will be spent to settle claims when cars are stolen or damaged by collisions, the chance to make a profit is good. So both the insurance company and the drivers who buy policies are ultimately better off.

Bearing in mind that time has value and risk requires compensation, we can begin to see the rationale behind the valuation of a broad set of financial instruments. For example, a lender will charge a higher interest rate on a loan if there is a chance that the borrower will not repay. In Chapters 6 and 7, we will use this principle when we examine the interest rates on bonds. As we will see, a company or a government that is on the verge of being unable to pay its bills may still be able to issue bonds (called *junk bonds*), but it will have to pay an extremely high interest rate to do so. The reason is that the lender must be compensated for the substantial risk that the company will not repay the loan. Risk requires compensation.

Core Principle 3: Information Is the Basis for Decisions

Most of us collect **information** before making decisions. The more important the decision, the more information we gather. Think of the difference between buying a $5

sandwich and a $10,000 used car. You will surely spend more time comparing cars than comparing sandwiches.

What's true for sandwiches and cars is true for finance as well. That is, *information is the basis for decisions.* In fact, the collection and processing of information is the foundation of the financial system. In Chapter 11, we will learn how financial institutions like banks funnel resources from savers to investors. Before a bank makes a loan, a loan officer will investigate the financial condition of the individual or firm seeking it. Banks want to provide loans only to the highest-quality borrowers. Thus, they spend a great deal of time gathering the information needed to evaluate the creditworthiness of loan applicants.

To understand the problem faced by the two parties to any financial transaction, think about a home mortgage. Before making the loan, the mortgage broker examines the applicant's finances and researches the home's value to make sure the applicant can afford the monthly payments and the property is more valuable than the loan.

And before the broker transfers the funds to the seller, the new homeowner must purchase fire insurance. All these requirements arise from the fact that the lender doesn't know much about the borrower and wants to make sure the loan will be repaid. When lenders fail to assess creditworthiness properly, they end up with more borrowers who are unable to repay their loans in the future. Large mistakes like these were a key factor in the wave of U.S. mortgage delinquencies and defaults that preceded the financial crisis of 2007–2009. Even as recently as 2018, mortgages on more than two million U.S. homes still exceeded the underlying property value.

Information plays a key role in other parts of the financial system as well. In Chapters 2 and 3, we'll see that many types of transactions are arranged so that the buyer doesn't need to know anything about the seller. When merchants accept cash, they don't need to worry about the customer's identity. When stocks change hands, the buyer doesn't need to know anything about the seller, or vice versa. Stock exchanges are organized to eliminate the need for costly information gathering, facilitating the exchange of securities. In one way or another, information is the key to the financial system.

Core Principle 4: Markets Determine Prices and Allocate Resources

Markets are the core of the economic system. They are the place, physical or virtual, where buyers and sellers meet, where firms go to issue stocks and bonds, and where individuals go to trade assets. Financial markets are essential to the economy, channeling its resources and minimizing the cost of gathering information and making transactions. In fact, well-developed financial markets are a necessary precondition for healthy economic growth. For the most part, the better developed a country's financial markets, the faster the country will grow.

The reason for this connection between markets and growth is that *markets determine prices and allocate resources.* Financial markets gather information from a large number of individual participants and aggregate it into a set of prices that signals what is valuable and what is not. Thus, markets are sources of information. By attaching prices to different stocks or bonds, they provide a basis for the allocation of capital.

To see how prices in the financial markets allocate capital, think about a large firm wishing to finance the construction of a new factory costing several hundred million dollars. To raise the funds, the firm can go directly into the financial markets and issue stocks or bonds. The higher the price investors are willing to pay in the market, the more appealing the idea will be, and the more likely it is that the firm will issue securities to raise the capital for the investment.

We will refer to the financial markets throughout much of this book. While our primary focus in Part II (Chapters 4–10) will be the nature of financial instruments, we will also study the markets in which those instruments are traded. Chapters 6 through 10 describe the markets for bonds, stocks, derivatives, and foreign currencies.

Importantly, financial markets do not arise by themselves—at least, not the large, well-oiled ones we see operating today. Markets like the New York Stock Exchange, where billions of shares of stock change hands every day, require rules in order to work properly, as well as authorities to police them. Otherwise, they will not function. For people to be willing to participate in a market, they must perceive it as fair. As we will see, this creates an important role for the government. Regulators and supervisors of the financial system make and enforce the rules, punishing people who violate them. When the government protects investors, financial markets work well and help promote economic growth; otherwise they don't.

Finally, even well-developed markets can break down. When they do—as some did during the financial crisis of 2007–2009—the financial system as a whole can be at risk. So today, governments must also play a role in promoting the healthy operation of markets.

Core Principle 5: Stability Improves Welfare

Most of us prefer stable to variable incomes. We like getting raises, but the prospect of a salary cut is not a pleasant one. This brings us to the fifth core principle of money and banking: *Stability improves welfare*. **Stability** is a desirable quality, not just in our personal lives but in the financial system as a whole. As we saw at the start of this chapter, financial instability in the autumn of 2008 brought us closer to a collapse of the system than at any time since the 1930s, triggering the worst global downturn since the Great Depression. And the banking and government debt crisis in the euro area partly reversed Europe's financial integration, a cornerstone of its successful economic and political framework in recent decades.

If you are wondering whether this principle is related to Core Principle 2 (risk requires compensation), you are right. Because volatility creates risk, reducing volatility reduces risk. But while individuals can eliminate many risks on their own (we'll see how when we study financial instruments in Part II—Chapters 4–10), some risks can be reduced only by government policymakers. Business cycle fluctuations are an example of the sort of instability individuals can't eliminate on their own. And though "automatic stabilizers" like unemployment insurance and the income tax system reduce the burden of recessions on individuals, they cannot eliminate an economic slowdown. Monetary policymakers can moderate these downswings by carefully adjusting interest rates. Central banks also have powerful tools to steady fragile financial systems and to repair or support dysfunctional markets. In stabilizing the economy as a whole, they eliminate risks that individuals can't, improving everyone's welfare in the process.

As we will learn in Part IV (Chapters 15–19) of this book, stabilizing the economy is a primary function of central banks like the Federal Reserve and the European Central Bank. Officials of these institutions are charged with controlling inflation and reducing business cycle fluctuations. That is, they work to keep inflation low and stable and to keep growth high and stable. They also have key roles in securing financial stability. When they are successful, they reduce both the risk that individuals will lose their jobs and the uncertainty that firms face in making investment decisions. Not surprisingly, a stable economy grows faster than an unstable economy. Stability improves welfare.

Throughout the book you will notice icons like this TIME in the margin in various places. These will guide you to the core principle that provides the foundation for what is being discussed at that point in the text.

Special Features of This Book

The very first special feature of every chapter in this book is its introduction—each one presents a real-world example that leads to the big questions the chapter is designed to answer, such as: What is money? What do banks do? How does the bond market work? What does the Federal Reserve do to prevent or limit financial crises?

After that real-world setup, the text of each chapter presents the economic and financial theory you need to understand the topics covered. Learning objectives listed at the beginning of the chapter outline the core concepts that are discussed and should be mastered. Each chapter also contains a series of inserts that apply the theory. There are five types of inserts: Your Financial World, Applying the Concept, Lessons from the Crisis, Money and Banking Blog, and Tools of the Trade. Finally, the end of each chapter is divided into four sections: Key Terms, Using FRED, Chapter Lessons, and Problems. Here are some guidelines for using the inserts and end-of-chapter materials.

Your Financial World

When most people decide to make a major purchase, they begin by collecting information. If they are considering buying a car, they will first try to decide which model is best for them and then work hard to pay the lowest price possible. Even for smaller purchases, like clothes or groceries, people first gather information and then buy.

Financial transactions should be no different from consumer purchases. Become informed first, and then buy. If you're thinking, "That's easier said than done," you're right. The problem is that most people have very little knowledge of the financial system, so they don't know how to start or what kind of information to collect.

That's where Your Financial World comes in. These inserts provide basic guidelines for applying economic theory to the bread-and-butter financial decisions you make nearly every day. Your Financial World answers questions about:

- Banking and Payments
    - What's the difference between credit and debit cards?
    - Are your bank deposits insured?
- Investments
    - Should you own stocks or bonds or gold?
    - Should you invest in the company you work for?
- Credit, Loans, and Mortgages
    - What do you need to know about your mortgage?
    - What is your credit score and why is it important?

Guard Your Identity
YOUR FINANCIAL WORLD

There is an old video advertisement in which a middle-aged man is sitting in his living room drinking a beer. Out of the man's mouth comes the voice of a woman describing some very expensive clothing she just bought. She didn't care how much the clothes cost because she wasn't paying—she used a credit card that was in the man's name. The ad catches viewers' attention because it is funny. But its primary purpose is to serve as a warning about *identity theft*, in which one person takes on the identity of another to do things like make credit card purchases.

Someone who has a few pieces of key information about you can get a credit card in your name. To prevent this, you need to protect personal information. Do your best never to tell anyone your birth date and birthplace, your address, or your mother's maiden name. Most importantly, guard your Social Security number. Because it is unique, it is the key to identity theft. Give out your Social Security number only when absolutely necessary—on tax forms, for employment records, and to open bank accounts. If a business requests it, ask if there is an alternative number they can use. Importantly, beware of *phishing*–fraudulent e-mails purporting to be from reputable companies trying to get you to reveal passwords, credit card information, or other personal information. Give that information only to people you know to be legitimate.

Beyond protecting your personal information, you need to monitor your financial statements closely, looking for things that shouldn't be there. Be on the lookout for unauthorized charges. This means maintaining careful records so that you know what should be on your bank and credit card statements.

The risks of identity theft have grown substantially in recent years. In 2017, hackers gained unauthorized access to more than 140 million records at Equifax, one of the three large U.S. consumer credit reporting agencies. The personal information obtained through the security breach included names, addresses, birth dates, Social Security numbers, and driver's license numbers.

Unfortunately, even though it is a serious crime, Identity theft occurs frequently. For more information about identity theft, and how to avoid being a victim, see the U.S. Department of Justice's website: www.justice.gov/criminal-fraud/identity-theft/identity-theft-and-identity-fraud.

- Insurance
  - How much life insurance do you need?
  - Why do we all need disability income insurance?

Applying the Concept

Applying the Concept inserts show how to put theory into practice. They provide real-world examples of the ideas introduced in the chapter, drawn primarily from history or from relevant public policy debates. Here are some of the questions examined in Applying the Concept:

- Why do interest rates rise when inflation goes up?
- Under what conditions is a fixed exchange rate vulnerable?
- Why do large-scale frauds that damage investors occur repeatedly?
- Why is it important for central banks to be free of political influence?
- Can monetary policy be used to stabilize the economy?
- What determines inflation?
- How is China's exchange rate policy evolving?

Lessons from the Crisis

These inserts cover episodes from the financial crisis of 2007–2009 and from the European banking and government debt crisis that began shortly thereafter. One goal is to give you a framework for understanding these crises and how they are transforming the world of finance. Another goal is to highlight the relevance and power of the ideas in the book more generally. Along the way, the various Lessons from the Crisis offer you insight into the sources and effects of financial instability. They also address the means that governments—including regulators and central bankers—use to counter financial instability. Most chapters contain one such insert.

The topics range from specific aspects of the crises to key issues that have wide application. Here are some of the questions examined in Lessons from the Crisis:

- What factors led to the financial crisis of 2007–2009?
- What made financial institutions especially vulnerable in this period?
- Why do financial markets sometimes stop functioning?
- How do threats to the financial system differ from threats to specific financial institutions?
- When a crisis erupts, what can central banks do to prevent another Great Depression?
- What factors link banks and governments in the euro-area crisis?

Money and Banking Blog

One of the primary purposes of this textbook is to help you understand the business and financial news. Critically evaluating what you read, hear, and see means developing a clear understanding of how the financial system works, as well as reading the news regularly. Like many other skills, critical reading of contemporary economic and financial analysis takes practice. You can't just turn to an economics blog, newspaper, or magazine and skim through it quickly and efficiently; you need to learn how. Your instructor will make suggestions about what you should read. See Table 1.1 for a list of reliable sources of information on the economy and the financial system.

Given your need to become a skilled consumer of financial information, each chapter in this book closes with an article drawn from our blog www.moneyandbanking.com under the heading Money and Banking Blog. Each provides an example of how the concepts introduced in the chapter are discussed in the real world.

Tools of the Trade

Many chapters in this book include an insert called Tools of the Trade that concentrates on practical knowledge relevant to the chapter. Some of these inserts cover basic skills, including how to read bond and stock tables, how to read charts, and how to do some simple algebraic calculations. Others provide brief reviews of material from principles of economics classes, such as the relationship between the current account and the capital account in the balance of payments. Still other Tools of the Trade inserts address questions such as:

- What is leverage, and how does it affect risk?
- What are hedge funds?
- What tools did the Fed use to address the financial crisis?
- How is a recession defined?

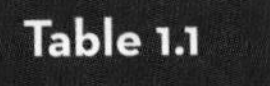

Table 1.1 Sources of Economic and Financial News and Data

Sources of Daily News

The Wall Street Journal* and *www.wsj.com

Published six days a week, and available both in print and on the Internet, *The Wall Street Journal* provides news, as well as comprehensive coverage of business and finance. Some content on the website is free.

Financial Times* and *www.ft.com

The *Financial Times* offers reporting, analysis, and commentary on major business, political, financial, and economic events. The *FT* is written from a distinctly European perspective and includes detailed coverage of non-U.S. business and financial news. Free registration gives access to some of the *FT* web content.

Bloomberg *(www.bloomberg.com)*

Bloomberg offers a wide range of financial market services, including news. A wide variety of news and data can be found on the free portion of its website.

Yahoo! Finance *(http://finance.yahoo.com)*

Yahoo! Finance provides free quotes on stocks, bonds, currencies, and commodities. It also presents news from various sources about business finance and portfolio management.

Sources of Weekly News

The Economist* and *www.economist.com

The Economist covers global politics, economics, business, finance, and science. It not only reports the facts but also analyzes them and draws policy conclusions. The Finance and Economics section, located roughly three-quarters of the way into each print issue, is of particular interest.

Bloomberg Businessweek* and *www.bloomberg.com/businessweek

Bloomberg Businessweek is a U.S.-based publication that offers balanced reporting and analysis of top economic, financial, business, and technological issues.

Economic and Financial Data

The Federal Reserve Bank of St. Louis maintains a comprehensive database called FRED (**F**ederal **R**eserve **E**conomic **D**ata) that you can access by going to https://fred.stlouisfed.org. This website includes tutorials for using FRED that will help you answer the end-of-chapter problems.

The Bureau of Labor Statistics supplies data on prices, employment, and unemployment at www.bls.gov.

The Bureau of Economic Analysis provides information on gross domestic product, consumption, investment, and other macroeconomic data at www.bea.gov.

The Federal Reserve Board website, www.federalreserve.gov, provides a variety of banking, monetary, interest rate, and exchange rate data.

Personal Finance Information

Many financial websites offer a variety of personal finance resources, including financial calculators to help you with mortgages, auto loans, and insurance. These include:

- www.choosetosave.org
- www.dinkytown.net
- www.consumerfinance.gov/consumer-tools

End-of-Chapter Sections

Key Terms A listing of all the technical terms introduced (in bold red) and defined in the chapter. The key terms are defined in full in the glossary at the end of the book.

Using FRED: Codes for Data in This Chapter A table identifying economic and financial data highlighted in the chapter together with the data code (identifier) that is used to retrieve the data from the Federal Reserve's online database, FRED.

Chapter Lessons A list of the key lessons in the chapter summarized in the form of an outline that matches the chapter headings—a format designed to aid comprehension and retention.

Problems Each chapter contains two types of problems at varying levels of difficulty: (1) conceptual and analytical problems and (2) data exploration problems using FRED. The problems are designed to reinforce the lessons in the chapter. The data exploration problems ask you to manipulate economic and financial data from FRED (Federal Reserve Economic Data, https://fred.stlouisfed.org), the extensive online resource maintained and provided free of charge by the Federal Reserve Bank of St. Louis. Many of the graphs in this book are based on data in FRED. See Appendix B of this chapter for further information on FRED and how to use it.

The Organization of This Book

This book is organized into five sections (Parts). Each one employs core principles to illuminate a particular part of the financial system and applies economic theory to the world around us. The next two chapters will continue our overview of the financial system. First, we'll study money—what it is and how it is used. We'll see that currency allows transactions to be made anonymously, which reduces the need to gather information. This advantage of currency is related to Core Principle 3: Information is the basis for decisions. In Chapter 3, we'll take a bird's-eye view of financial instruments, financial markets, and financial institutions. At various points in that chapter, we'll refer to the first four core principles.

Part II (Chapters 4-10) includes detailed descriptions of financial instruments. We'll study bonds, stocks, and derivatives, as well as exchange rates for foreign currency. The valuation of financial instruments requires a comparison of payments made on different dates as well as an estimate of the risk involved in each instrument. Thus, these chapters focus on Core Principles 1 and 2: Time has value and Risk requires compensation.

Throughout Part II and continuing in Part III, we'll discuss financial markets, whose purpose is to facilitate the buying and selling of financial instruments. No one would buy stocks or bonds if they could not be easily resold at little cost. Financial markets also provide the information necessary to understand the value and risk that are associated with particular financial instruments. Core Principles 3 and 4 (Information is the basis for decisions and Markets determine prices and allocate resources) are both relevant to our discussion of markets.

Part III (Chapters 11-14) covers financial institutions, especially banks and their regulation. Earlier in this chapter, we emphasized that financial institutions spend a great deal of time collecting and processing information. Without that information, many financial transactions could not take place. This dependence of banks on information is an example of Core Principle 3: Information is the basis for decisions. Financial regulation is driven by Core Principle 5: Stability improves welfare.

Part IV (Chapters 15-19) describes central banks, especially the Federal Reserve and the European Central Bank. These institutions exist to stabilize the real economy as well as the financial system. Thus, like financial regulators in Part III of the book, they embody Core Principle 5: Stability improves welfare. We'll see how central banks manipulate interest rates and other less conventional policy tools to stabilize the economy.

Finally, Part V (Chapters 20-23) brings together material covered in the first four sections to explain how the financial system influences the real economy. We'll use a macroeconomic model to analyze the mechanism through which central banks influence the economy, paying particular attention to the role of the financial system in determining inflation and growth.

Learning money and banking is going to be hard work. Reading and working through the remaining 22 chapters of this book will take lots of time and energy. But when you are done, you will be armed with the tools you need to understand how the financial system works and why it changes as it does. You will be an informed reader of the financial and economic news and know how to put the financial system to use for you. You will understand the various ways that you can pay for your morning coffee and how each one of them works. You will understand the usefulness of bonds and stocks as well as what financial institutions do and how central banks work. You will know how to make sound financial decisions for the rest of your life. You will understand how financial crises arise, how they threaten economic stability, and what can be done to prevent and contain them. Regardless of the career you choose to follow, a solid background in money, banking, and financial markets will help you make sound financial decisions for the rest of your life.

Key Terms

Using FRED: Codes for Data in This Chapter

Data Series	FRED Data Code
Nominal GDP	GDP
Real GDP	GDPC1
GDP deflator	GDPDEF
Consumer price index	CPIAUCSL

To learn more about the changing financial system, visit www.moneyandbanking.com.

Chapter Lessons

1. A healthy and constantly evolving financial system is the foundation for economic efficiency and economic growth. It has six parts:
   a. Money is used to pay for purchases and to store wealth.
   b. Financial instruments are used to transfer resources and risk.
   c. Financial markets allow people to buy and sell financial instruments.
   d. Financial institutions provide access to the financial markets, collect information, and provide a variety of other services.
   e. Government regulatory agencies aim to make the financial system operate safely and reliably.
   f. Central banks stabilize the economy.
2. The core principles of money and banking are useful in understanding all six parts of the financial system.
   a. Core Principle 1: Time has value.
   b. Core Principle 2: Risk requires compensation.
   c. Core Principle 3: Information is the basis for decisions.
   d. Core Principle 4: Markets determine prices and allocate resources.
   e. Core Principle 5: Stability improves welfare.

Conceptual and Analytical Problems

1. List the financial transactions you have engaged in over the past week. How might each one have been carried out 50 years ago? *(LO1)*
2. How were you, or your family or friends, affected by the failure of the financial system to function normally during the financial crisis of 2007–2009? *(LO1)*
3. List three items you formerly bought with cash but now purchase with a debit card. *(LO1)*
4. Various financial instruments usually serve one of two distinct purposes: to store value or to transfer risk. Name a financial instrument used for each purpose. *(LO1)*
5. Financial innovation has reduced individuals' need to carry cash. Explain how. *(LO1)*
6.* Many people believe that, despite ongoing financial innovations, cash will always be with us to some degree as a form of money. What core principle could justify this view? *(LO2)*
7. When you apply for a loan, you are required to answer lots of questions. Why? Why is the set of questions you must answer standardized? *(LO2)*
8. Name two distinct financial markets and describe the kind of asset traded in each. *(LO1)*
9.* Why do you think the global financial system has become more globally integrated over time? Can you think of any downside to this increased integration? *(LO1)*
10. The government is heavily involved in the financial system. Explain why. *(LO1)*

*Indicates more difficult problems.

11. If offered the choice of receiving \$1,000 today or \$1,000 in one year's time, which option would you choose, and why? *(LO2)*
12. If time has value, why are financial institutions often willing to extend you a 30-year mortgage at a lower annual interest rate than they would charge for a one-year loan? *(LO2)*
13. Using Core Principle 2, under what circumstances would you expect a job applicant to accept an offer of a low base salary and an opportunity to earn commission over one with a higher base salary and no commission potential? *(LO2)*
14. Suppose medical research confirms earlier speculation that red wine is good for you. Why would banks be willing to lend to vineyards that produce red wine at a lower interest rate than before? *(LO2)*
15.* If the U.S. Securities and Exchange Commission eliminated its requirement for public companies to disclose information about their finances, what would you expect to happen to the stock prices for these companies? *(LO2)*
16. If 2 percent growth is your break-even point for an investment project, under which outlook for the economy would you be more inclined to go ahead with the investment: (1) a forecast for economic growth that ranges from 0 to 4 percent, or (2) a forecast of 2 percent growth for sure, assuming the forecasts are equally reliable? What core principle does this illustrate? *(LO2)*
17.* Why are large, publicly listed companies much more likely than small businesses to sell financial instruments such as bonds directly to the market, while small businesses get their financing from financial institutions such as banks? *(LO2)*
18.* During the financial crisis of 2007–2009, some financial instruments that received high ratings in terms of their safety turned out to be much riskier than those ratings indicated. Explain why markets for other financial instruments might have been adversely affected by that development. *(LO2)*
19. Suppose financial institutions didn't exist but you urgently needed a loan. Where would you most likely get this loan? Using core principles, identify an advantage and a disadvantage this arrangement might have over borrowing from a financial institution. *(LO2)*
20. In broad terms, explain how a central bank tries to maintain economic and financial stability and encourage economic growth. *(LO1)*
21. The Dodd-Frank Act, enacted in the United States in the aftermath of the 2007–2009 financial crisis, includes provisions aimed at enhancing the coordination of various regulatory agencies. Which two core principles might best explain these reforms? *(LO2)*
22. In a sequence of nine steps between December 2015 and December 2018, the Federal Reserve increased its policy interest rate target range by 2.25 percentage points from a historically low level of close to zero. If central banks use interest rates to moderate business cycle swings in the economy, what might you infer about the Fed's view of the strength of the economy over this time period? *(LO2)*
23. What steps should you take to protect yourself from identity theft and why is it so important to do so in the context of the financial system? *(LO3)*

*Indicates more difficult problems.

Data Exploration connect

For detailed instructions on using Federal Reserve Economic Data (FRED) online to answer each of the following problems, visit www.mhhe.com/moneyandbanking6e *and refer to the FRED Resources and Data Exploration Hints.*

1. Go to the FRED website (https://fred.stlouisfed.org). Register to set up your own account. Doing so will allow you to save and update graphs, alter them for submitting assignments and making presentations, and receive a notice whenever the data are updated.
2. To begin using FRED, plot the consumer price index (FRED code: CPIAUCSL) and find the date and level of the latest monthly observation. Then, plot the inflation rate as measured by the percent change from a year ago of this index.
3. Plot the level of real GDP (FRED code: GDPC1). Then, plot the rate of economic growth as the percent change from a year ago of this index. Describe how real GDP behaves in recessions, which are denoted in the FRED graph by vertical shaded bars. If you registered on FRED (as in Data Exploration Problem 1), save the graph so that you can recall and update it easily when new observations become available.
4. Examine nominal GDP (FRED code: GDP) based on a figure showing percent change from a year ago. What was special about the behavior of nominal GDP during the financial crisis of 2007–2009 compared to previous decades?
5. Plot on one figure the percent change from a year ago of both the GDP deflator (FRED code: GDPDEF) and real GDP (FRED code: GDPC1). How does the GDP deflator link nominal and real GDP? Since the mid-1980s, does it fluctuate more or less than real GDP?

Appendix A to Chapter 1

Measuring Economic Activity, Prices, and the Inflation Rate

Measuring Economic Activity

Gross domestic product (GDP) is the most commonly used measure of economic activity. In order to see if the economy is improving, you can look at whether GDP is growing (or shrinking) and the rate of that growth. And to compare well-being in two countries, you can look at the GDP per person in each country—*per capita GDP.*

The definition of GDP is *the market value of final goods and services produced in a country during a year.* Let's look at the pieces of this definition:

- **Market value:** In order to add together production of cars, corn flakes, and computers, we take the market price of each and multiply it times the quantity of each that is produced, and sum the products together. That is, add up (Market price of cars × Quantity of cars produced) plus (Market price of corn flakes × Quantity of corn flakes produced), and so on.
- **Final goods and services:** We take only the price of the final product purchased by the person who uses it. For example, when a consumer buys a car, the car is considered a final good so it's included. But when the automobile manufacturer buys steel from a steel company in order to build the car, the steel is an intermediate product so it is not included.
- **In a country:** Only production within the country counts. This means that if a U.S. company owns a factory in China, the production of the factory is included in China's GDP.
- **During a year:** To measure production we need to specify a time period, and the time period is usually one year.

So, to compute U.S. GDP in 2020, for example, we sum the quantity of goods and services produced in the United States in 2020 times their 2020 prices. In an economy with only cars and corn flakes, the calculation would look like this:

GDP in 2020 = (2020 Price of cars × Quantity of cars produced in 2020)
+ (2020 Price of corn flakes × Quantity of corn flakes produced in 2020)

Note that we could always measure incomes rather than production. That is, instead of measuring total production, we can measure the total payments made to factors used to produce the output—the payments to labor, capital, and land. Because the revenue from selling all of the goods and services produced must always go to the people responsible for making them—the workers and the owners—total income equals GDP as well.

Real versus Nominal GDP

It is essential when measuring the level of economic activity to distinguish changes in prices from changes in quantities. As defined so far, GDP confuses the two changes. For example, U.S. GDP rose from \$19.485 trillion in 2017 to \$20.501 trillion in 2018. Computing the annual growth rate, the percentage change from one year to the next, means that the U.S. economy grew by 5.21 percent.

$$\text{GDP growth rate from 2017 to 2018} = \frac{\$20.501\ trillion - \$19.485\ trillion}{\$19.485\ trillion} \times 100$$
$$= 5.21\%$$

This number alone only tells us the sum of the growth in the quantity of output produced (something that is beneficial) and the change in prices (which is not so good). To see the point, look back at the computation for the car and corn flakes economy and note that GDP can rise either because quantities rise or because prices go up.

Separating changes in the quantities from changes in the prices requires computing *real* GDP. To do this, government statisticians fix the prices at a base-year level and then calculate the sum of the quantities times these base-year prices. Currently, real GDP in the United States is reported in year-2012 dollars. That is, statisticians sum up the value of all production in the United States during a year measured at the prices at which the goods and services were sold in the year 2012. This procedure isolates the part of change in GDP that is due to growth in the quantity produced from the part that came from changes in prices.

For the car and corn flakes economy, the formula looks like this:

$$\text{Real GDP in 2020} = (\text{2012 Price of cars} \times \text{Quantity of cars produced in 2020}) + (\text{2012 Price of corn flakes} \times \text{Quantity of corn flakes produced in 2020})$$

To see what this means for the United States as a whole, we can look at the government's website www.bea.gov and find that, in 2017, real GDP (in year-2012 dollars) was \$18.051 trillion. In 2018, real GDP (again in year-2012 dollars) had increased to \$18.571 trillion. That's an increase of 2.89 percent.

$$\text{Real GDP growth rate from 2017 to 2018} = \frac{\$18.571\ trillion - \$18.051\ trillion}{\$18.051\ trillion} \times 100$$
$$= 2.89\%$$

The GDP Deflator and the Inflation Rate

It should come as no surprise that from nominal and real GDP we get a measure of prices on average in the economy as a whole. We can start by thinking about nominal GDP as the product of real GDP times a measure of prices in the economy as a whole. That is:

$$Nominal\ GDP = Prices \times Real\ GDP$$

Looking at this expression, you can see that by taking the ratio of nominal GDP to real GDP we get a measure of prices. This is what's called the GDP *deflator,* and using the data from 2017 and 2018, we get

$$\text{GDP deflator in 2017} = \frac{\text{Nominal GDP in 2017}}{\text{Real GDP in 2017}} = \frac{\$19.485\text{ trillion}}{\$18.051\text{ trillion}} = 1.079$$

$$\text{GDP deflator in 2018} = \frac{\text{Nominal GDP in 2018}}{\text{Real GDP in 2018}} = \frac{\$20.501\text{ trillion}}{\$18.571\text{ trillion}} = 1.104$$

No one spends much time worrying about the level of the GDP deflator. Instead, we are concerned with the rate at which the index is changing. The inflation rate is defined as the rate of growth in the price level. Using the GDP deflator from 2017 to 2018, we get an inflation rate of 2.31 percent.

$$\text{Inflation rate} = \frac{(1.104 - 1.079)}{1.079} \times 100 = 2.31\%$$

This result makes sense. Because real GDP is designed to strip out the effect of price changes, the inflation rate (2.31 percent) should equal the growth rate of nominal GDP minus the growth rate of real GDP (5.21% – 2.89% = 2.32%). Approximation error accounts for the small difference between these two rates (2.31 percent versus 2.32 percent).

While it is the easiest to explain and compute, the GDP deflator is unfortunately not the most commonly used price index. The consumer price index, or CPI, designed to measure the changes in the cost of living, lays claim to that title. We will learn more about the CPI throughout this book, starting with the Tools of the Trade in Chapter 2.

Appendix B to Chapter 1

Using FRED

A key feature of this book is its extensive use of the Federal Reserve Economic Database (FRED), an online resource provided free of charge to the public by the Federal Reserve Bank of St. Louis.

Using FRED, you can easily display and examine economic data in graphic form on your computer, tablet, or smartphone. From the online FRED interface, you can download data into an Excel spreadsheet for further analysis; or, if you prefer, you can install an Excel "add-in" from the FRED website that allows you to more quickly access and manipulate FRED data.

As of October 2019, FRED contains nearly 600,000 economic time series from more than 85 sources covering more than 200 countries! The database is updated daily. If you register for a free FRED account, you can save your datasets and your graphs for automatic updating whenever you need them.

The purpose of studying economics, especially money and banking, is to better understand the world around you. That means addressing *quantitative* questions. How much does a change in central bank policy alter prospects for growth and inflation? How does the stock market affect the economy? What do bond yields tell us about inflation expectations? Answering these questions, and a myriad of others, requires a blending of theoretical knowledge and core principles with the up-to-date statistics that FRED delivers quickly and easily.

FRED is a great laboratory for exploring ideas. The use of FRED challenges you to convert economic concepts into the quantitative measures needed to understand everyday economic and financial developments. Looking carefully at data will help you grasp the nature and cause of business cycles, the tools of monetary policy, and much more. When reading about money and finance, you can also use FRED to dig deeper, furthering your understanding of what is in the news and elsewhere.

This book uses FRED in many ways. When figures are based on data from FRED, the caption at the bottom will include the FRED codes (identifiers) that let you find and update the data. For those figures that can be created directly in FRED, the electronic version of this book includes a link that brings you online to an updated version of the figure. The problems at the end of each chapter include a Data Exploration section that requires you to use FRED. And at the end of each chapter, you will find a table of the data series used in the chapter along with their FRED data codes.

To learn how to use FRED, you can start with the FRED Lessons page (www.moneyandbanking.com/fred-lessons/) on our Money and Banking website (www.moneyandbanking.com). You can also go directly to the FRED website (https://fred.stlouisfed.org) and click on the "Need Help?" link to find a set of training tools.

These online aids show you how to make and alter graphs using the FRED interface. They teach you how to change the chart type (line, area, bar, scatter, or pie), add data series to a chart, change the observation period or frequency of a data series, transform the data (e.g., percent change, percent change from a year ago, percent change at an annual rate), and use a variety of other useful tools. After looking at these, and with a bit of practice, you will be able to make a variety of complex, up-to-date charts using a wide range of economic and financial data.

Getting acquainted with FRED as you start reading this book will prepare you to answer the FRED-linked end-of-chapter problems. When you have finished using the book, you will have a thorough theoretical knowledge of money and banking. You will also have the tools to find and analyze the data needed to deepen your understanding as the world around you continues to change.

Chapter

2 Money and the Payments System

Learning Objectives ///

After reading this chapter, you should be able to:

LO1 Define money and describe its functions.

LO2 Discuss the different methods of payment and the future of money.

LO3 Explain how the money supply is measured and how it is linked to economic growth and inflation.

Parker Brothers's bestselling board game.

Dave Donaldson/Alamy Stock Photo

The makers of the board game Monopoly print on average about $50 billion of Monopoly money every year. Every new game has bills totaling 20,580 Monopoly dollars. At a cost of less than 20 U.S. dollars per set, this "money" would be a good deal if you could buy things other than Boardwalk and Park Place with it. Unfortunately, attempts to pay for groceries, books, or rent with this particular form of money have been unsuccessful. And that's probably a good thing. Since the mid-1930s, Parker Brothers has sold more than 250 million Monopoly games, containing more than 4 trillion Monopoly dollars, or more than twice U.S. official currency in circulation as of 2019.

When we pay for our purchases in the real world, we have lots of choices: crisp new $20 bills, credit cards, debit cards, checks, or more complicated electronic methods. Regardless of the choice we make, we are using *money* to buy our food and clothes and pay our bills. To make sure we can do it, thousands of people work through every night, for the payments system really never sleeps. And the volume of payments is astounding. The Federal Reserve reports that in 2016 there were nearly 150 billion noncash payments made in the United States, less than 12 percent of which were paper checks. That means something like 69 million paper checks and over 500 million electronic payments were processed on an average business day. And, regardless of how you choose to pay, the path that the payment follows is pretty complicated.

To understand why money is so important to the smooth functioning of the economy and how it improves everyone's well-being, we need to understand exactly what money is. Just why is a $20 bill issued by the U.S. government much more useful than $20 in Monopoly money? Furthermore, to quantify the impact of money on the economy, we need to be able to measure it. Those are the goals of this chapter: to understand what money is, how we use it, and how we measure it.

Money and How We Use It

When people use the word *money* in conversation, they mean many different things. Someone who "makes lots of money" has a high income; a person who "has lots of money" is wealthy. We will use the word *money* in a narrower, specialized sense to mean anything that can readily be used to make economic transactions. Formally defined, **money** *is an asset that is generally accepted as payment for goods and services or repayment of debt.* Income, in contrast, is a flow of earnings over time. **Wealth** is the value of assets minus liabilities. Money is one of those assets, albeit a very minor one.

Money, in the sense we are talking about, has three characteristics. It is (1) a means of payment, (2) a unit of account, and (3) a store of value. The first of these characteristics is the most important. Anything that is used as a means of payment must be a store of value and thus is very likely to become a unit of account. Let's see why this is so.

Means of Payment

INFORMATION

The primary use of money is as a **means of payment**. Most people insist on payment in money at the time a good or service is supplied because the alternatives just don't work very well. Barter, in which a good or service is exchanged directly for another good or service, requires that a plumber who needs food find a grocer who needs a plumbing repair. Relying on this "double coincidence of wants" surely causes the economy to run less smoothly. The plumber could pay for his breakfast cereal with a "promise" of plumbing services, which the grocer could then transfer to someone else. But while it would be possible to certify the plumber's trustworthiness, taking payment in money is easier. Money finalizes payments so that buyers and sellers have no further claim on each other. That is money's special role. In fact, so long as a buyer has money, there is nothing more the seller needs to know.

As economies have become more complex and physically dispersed, reducing the likelihood that a seller will have good information about a buyer, the need for money has grown. The increase in both the number of transactions and the number of potential buyers and sellers (the vast majority of whom may never see one another) argues for something that makes payment final and whose value is easily verified. That something is money.

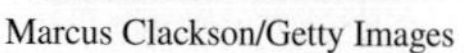
Marcus Clackson/Getty Images

Unit of Account

Just as we measure length using feet and inches, we measure value using dollars and cents. Money is the **unit of account** that we use to quote prices and record debts. We could also refer to it as a standard of value.

Having a unit of account is an incredible convenience. Remember from microeconomics that prices provide the information consumers and producers use to

Debit Cards versus Credit Cards
YOUR FINANCIAL WORLD

When you go shopping, should you pay with a credit card or a debit card? To decide, you need to understand the difference between the two. First make sure you know which one of your cards is which. Usually an ATM card (the one that you got from the bank when you opened your checking account) is a debit card. But check to make sure.

What's the real difference, from the shopper's point of view? A debit card works just like a check, only faster. When you write a paper check, it usually takes a day or two to go through the system. A debit card transaction goes through right away. The electronic message gets to your bank on the same day, and your account is debited immediately. So, if you want to use your debit card, your account balance has to be higher than the payment you want to make. During and after the financial crisis that began in 2007, debit card use sharply outpaced credit card activity, as lenders and borrowers sought to slow the expansion (or even reduce the outstanding level) of household debt.

A credit card creates a deferred payment. The issuer agrees to make the payment for you, and you repay the debt later. That sounds good, but there's a catch. If you're late paying, there's a late fee. And if you don't pay the entire debt every month, you pay interest on the balance—at what is usually a very high interest rate. If you do pay your entire credit card debt every month, however, there is no late fee and no interest charge. Hence, you get an interest-free loan from the time you make the purchase to the time you pay the balance. If you can pay off your credit cards in full and on time, it's to your advantage to use them.

Credit cards have another advantage over debit cards. They help you build a credit history, which you'll need when the time comes to buy a car or a house. Because debit cards are just extensions of your bank account, they don't show potential lenders that you are creditworthy. In fact, some businesses, like car rental companies, require their customers to use credit cards for this reason.

ensure that resources are allocated to their best uses. What matters are the *relative* prices of goods and services. When the price of one product is higher than the price of another, that product is worth more to both producers and consumers. Using dollars makes these comparisons easy. Imagine what would happen if we needed to compute relative prices for each pair of goods. With two goods, we would need only one price. With three goods, we would need three prices. But with 100 goods, we would need 4,950 prices, and with 10,000 goods (substantially less than the 42,000 products in a typical supermarket), we would need nearly 50 million prices.[1] Using money as a yardstick and quoting all prices in dollars certainly is easier.

Store of Value

For money to function as a means of payment, it has to be a **store of value**, too. That is, if we are going to use money to pay for goods and services, then it must retain its worth from day to day. Sellers are much less likely to accept things that are perishable, like milk or lettuce. So the means of payment has to be durable and capable of transferring purchasing power from one day to the next. Paper **currency** does degrade with use ($1 bills have an estimated life span of 70 months in circulation), but regardless of its physical condition, it is usually accepted at face value in transactions.

Of course, money is not the only store of value. We hold our wealth in lots of other forms—stocks, bonds, houses, even cars. Many of these are actually preferable to money as stores of value. Some, like bonds, pay higher interest rates than money. Others, like stocks, offer the potential for appreciation in nominal value, which money

[1]The general formula is that for n goods we need $n(n-1)/2$ prices, so for 10,000 goods, the number would be $10{,}000(9{,}999)/2 = 49{,}995{,}000$.

does not. Still others, like houses, deliver other services over time. Yet we all hold money because money is liquid. **Liquidity** *is a measure of the ease with which an asset can be turned into a means of payment,* namely money. For example, a bond is much more liquid than a house because it is so much easier and cheaper to sell. The more costly it is to convert an asset into money, the less liquid it is. Because constantly transforming assets into money every time we wished to make a purchase would be extremely costly, we keep some money around.

Financial institutions often use a more specific term—**market liquidity**—for their ability to sell assets for money. A second, related concept—**funding liquidity**—refers to their ability to borrow money to buy securities or make loans. For financial institutions, liquidity in both those senses is critical to their daily operations: A shortfall of either type can lead to their outright failure (see Lessons from the Crisis: Market Liquidity, Funding Liquidity, and Making Markets on page 31).

The Functions of Money

1. ***Means of payment:*** Used in exchange for goods and services.
2. ***Unit of account:*** Used to quote prices.
3. ***Store of value:*** Used to transfer purchasing power into the future.

The Payments System

The **payments system** is the web of arrangements that allow for the exchange of goods and services, as well as assets, among different people. Because the efficient operation of our economy depends on the payments system, a critical public policy concern is that it function well. As we will see in Part IV (Chapters 15–19), that is why central banks are directly involved.

Money is at the heart of the payments system. Whether we realize it or not, virtually every transaction we engage in involves the use of money at some point. Let's go through all the possible methods of payment to see how the system works.

Commodity and Fiat Monies

The first means of payment were things with intrinsic value. These **commodity monies** included everything from silk in China to butter in Norway, whale teeth in Fiji, and salt in Venice. All these things had value even if they were not used as money. The worth of a block of salt, for instance, came from its value as a preservative. But successful commodity monies had other characteristics: They were usable in some form by most people; they could be made into standardized quantities; they were durable; they had high value relative to their weight and size so that they were easily transportable; and they were divisible into small units so that they were easy to trade. For most of human history, gold has been the most common commodity money. It is widely accepted as payment; can be purified and made into standard weight units like coins; and is extremely durable because it does not corrode or tarnish. Moreover, gold is rare (there is only enough in existence to fill about one-third of the Washington Monument with solid gold), so it has high value relative to weight. And it can be cut into smaller pieces without losing its value.

A Revolutionary War "continental" issued by the Continental Congress in 1775. The new government of the United States eventually printed $200 million worth, and by 1781 they no longer had any value.

Courtesy of Stephen Cecchetti

An assignat issued by the French revolutionary government in 1793. Faced with the need to finance wars and food shortages, the government eventually printed 40 billion of them and by the late 1790s they were worthless.

Courtesy of Stephen Cecchetti

In 1656, a Swede named Johan Palmstruck founded the Stockholm Banco. Five years later he issued Europe's first paper money.[2] At the time, the Swedish currency was copper ingots, which work poorly as money because of their low value per unit of weight. (Today, copper is worth only about 17 cents per ounce, or roughly 1/85 the value of silver and 1/8800 the value of gold.) Thus, easy-to-handle paper was welcomed, at least at first.

After a few years of printing paper currency, Palmstruck and his sponsor, the king of Sweden, became overly enamored of the new money. The king needed to finance some wars he was fighting, so he convinced Palmstruck to print more and more notes. Because the bills were redeemable on demand for metal, the system worked only as long as people believed there was enough metal sitting in Palmstruck's vaults. As the number of notes increased, Swedes lost confidence in them and started to redeem them for the metal they supposedly stood for. But Palmstruck had issued too many notes, and his bank failed.

Other people tried issuing paper money during the early 1700s. Eventually governments got into the act. In 1775, the newly formed Continental Congress of the United States of America issued "continentals" to finance the Revolutionary War. Twenty years later, revolutionary France issued the "assignat." Lacking any other source of funding for their wars, both governments issued huge quantities of the currencies, and both currencies eventually became worthless.

The reaction was predictable: People became suspicious of government-issued paper money. But governments need funds and will use all available means to get them. In the United States, the Civil War put pressure on government finances and the two warring parties had little choice but to issue paper money to pay for salaries and supplies. Beginning in 1862, both the Confederate and the Union governments printed and used paper money with no explicit backing. The North's "greenbacks" are still legal tender in the United States, but collectors are the only people who value the Confederate currency.

[2]The Chinese were the real monetary pioneers, issuing their first paper currency in the 7th century, 1,000 years before the Europeans.

After the Civil War, the United States reverted to the use of gold as money. Both gold coins and notes backed by gold circulated well into the 20th century. Today, though, we use paper money—high-quality paper, nicely engraved, with lots of special security features. This type of currency is called **fiat money**, because its value comes from government decree, or *fiat*. Some countries print notes that are durable and attractive, bearing famous works of art in multiple colors. The Australians pioneered making notes out of plastic. But in all cases the money has very little intrinsic worth, and the cost of production is only a small fraction of the face value. The U.S. Treasury's Bureau of Engraving and Printing pays 5½ cents to print a $1 bill, 10½ cents to print a $20 bill, and a bit over 13 cents to print a $100 bill.

Why are we willing to accept these bills as payment for goods or in settlement of debts? There are two reasons. First, we take them because we believe we can use them in the future; someone else will take them from us. Second, the law says we must accept them. That is, the U.S. government stands behind its paper money. Since the first greenbacks were issued in 1862, all U.S. currency has borne the short and simple phrase "This note is legal tender for all debts, public and private." In practice, this means that private businesses accept dollar bills as payment. More important, the U.S. government is committed to accepting the currency it has issued in settlement of debts. We will always be able to pay our taxes in dollars.

Today, some critics of fiat money advocate a return to the gold standard.[3] Their fear is that governments will issue too much paper money, threatening its value and use. Even if a government promises today to limit fiat money, it can renege on that commitment in the future, casting doubt today on the money's value. This credibility problem exemplifies the challenge of making policy **time consistent**.[4] Policy lacks time consistency whenever policymakers have a strong incentive to give up in the future on their current promises or plans.

Supporters of a gold standard argue that removing future policy discretion will ensure a reliable store of value, resulting in greater economic and price stability (Core Principle 5). They view the government's ability to tinker with the volume of fiat money as an unnecessary source of risk. Yet, a gold standard also may not be time consistent. For example, in a crisis, governments can renege on their commitment to use gold as a unit of account. Indeed, many countries, including the United States, exited the gold standard during the Great Depression to restore economic stability (see Chapter 19, Applying the Concept: The Gold Standard: An Exchange Rate Regime Whose Time Has Passed).[5]

Ultimately, if a fiat currency is to outperform a commodity currency, policymakers must be credibly committed—by law or custom—to limiting the volume in circulation. As long as the government stands behind its paper money and doesn't issue too much of it, we will use it. In the end, money is about trust.

Checks

Checks are another way of paying for things. Unlike currency, the checks you use to pay your rent and electric bill are not legal tender. In fact, they aren't money at all. A **check** is just an instruction to the bank to take funds from your account and transfer

[3]See, for example, Ron Paul, *End the Fed* (New York: Grand Central Publishing, 2009).

[4]Acting in a time-consistent fashion is a big challenge in many settings, from parenting to military strategy. In the world of finance, where expectations about the future (including future policy) are critical, time consistency plays a major role in government oversight of the financial system (Chapter 14) and in monetary policy (Part IV—Chapters 15–19).

[5]For a policymaker's assessment of the gold standard, see the first in the series of online lectures by former Federal Reserve Board Chairman Ben Bernanke at www.federalreserve.gov/newsevents/lectures/origins-and-mission.htm.

them to the person or firm whose name you have written on the "Pay to the order of" line. Thus, when you give someone a check in exchange for a good or service, it is not a final payment—at least, not in the same sense as currency. Instead, your check sets in motion a series of transactions that eventually lead to the final payment.

Here are the usual steps. You hand over the check to a merchant, who then takes it to the bank or sends an electronic image. Depending on the arrangement, the bank will credit the amount of the check to the merchant's account either immediately or with a short lag. At the end of the day, the bank sends an electronic image of the check through the check-clearing system along with the other millions of images of checks to be processed that night by a check-processing center run by the Federal Reserve or a private check clearinghouse. (The first check clearinghouses were pubs where bank employees met to have a drink and exchange checks.) At the center, the check is transferred from the bank that sent it to the bank on which it is written—your bank. The account of the bank presenting the check is credited, and the account of the bank on which the check is written is debited (see Figure 2.1). This is the step that uses *money*.

Figure 2.1 The Path of a Paper Check

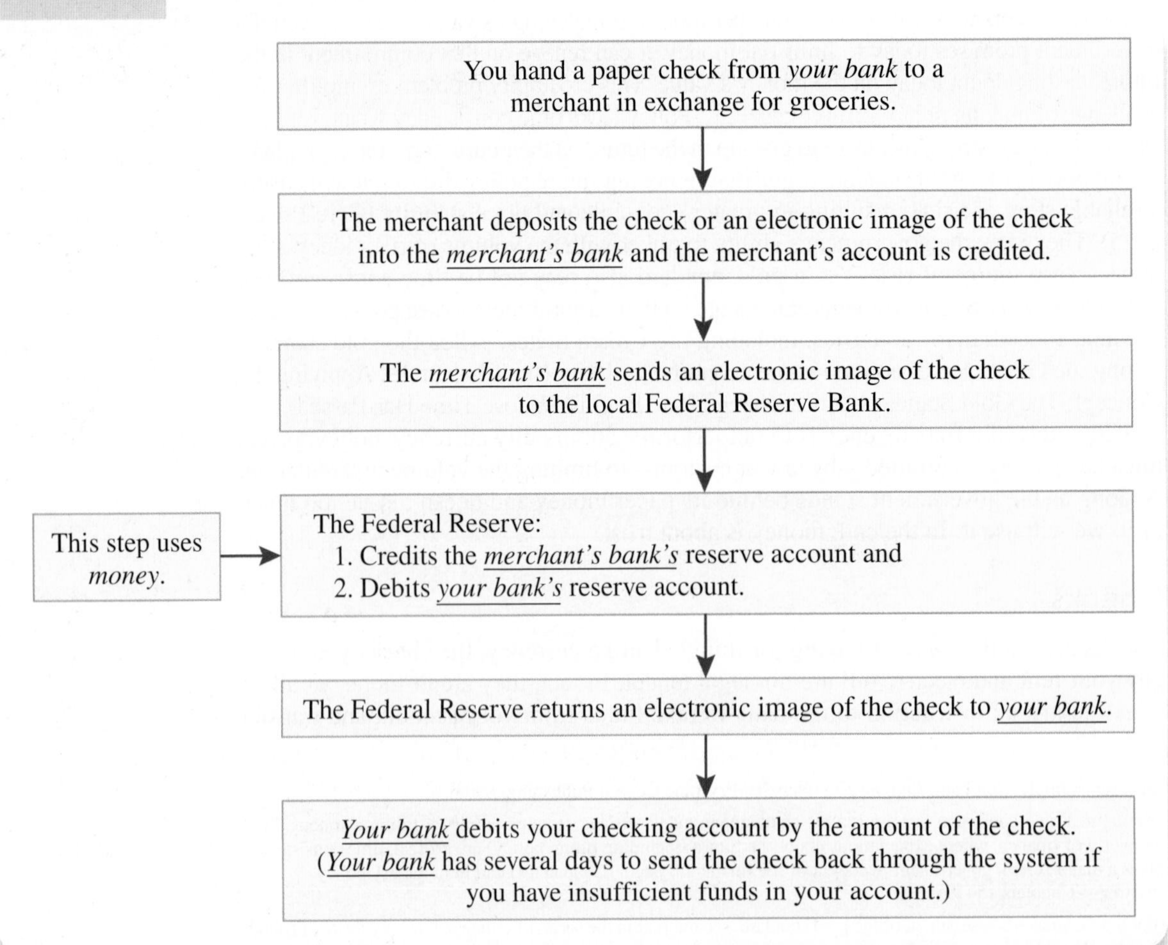
You hand a paper check from your bank to a merchant in exchange for groceries.
The merchant deposits the check or an electronic image of the check into the merchant's bank and the merchant's account is credited.
The merchant's bank sends an electronic image of the check to the local Federal Reserve Bank.
This step uses money.
The Federal Reserve:
1. Credits the merchant's bank's reserve account and
2. Debits your bank's reserve account.
The Federal Reserve returns an electronic image of the check to your bank.
Your bank debits your checking account by the amount of the check. (Your bank has several days to send the check back through the system if you have insufficient funds in your account.)

Modernizing U.S. Payments: Faster, Cheaper, and More Secure

YOUR FINANCIAL WORLD

When it comes to domestic payments, the U.S. financial system lags the efficiency in many advanced economies. In 2016, paper checks—a 14th-century innovation—still accounted for 11½ percent of U.S. noncash payments in value. Europeans typically use very few checks. Not only that, but many countries have something that the United States does not: a real-time electronic payments system where everyone can make and receive payments of all sizes almost instantly.

Why is the home to Amazon, Apple, Facebook, Google, and Microsoft behind in an information- and technology-intensive area like payments?

The reasons are easy to find. First, other countries have leapfrogged outdated technologies. Much as some parts of the world bypassed landline telephones, some advanced economies have replaced paper checks as they rebuilt their financial infrastructure following World War II. Second, in the United States, checks remained dominant partly because they benefit from government support. At its founding in 1914, the Fed created a unified check-based payments system and has continued to maintain the system ever since. Third, the U.S. legal framework supported this system: Canceled paper checks were legal proof of payment. Fourth, payment systems exhibit what economists call a *network externality*–the more people adopt one form of payment, the more valuable that method is to the people who are already using it. Fifth, there are large and powerful firms that profit from the current system. For example, Visa charges between 1 and 3 percent of the value on the roughly 150 million transactions it processes every day.

Adding to these institutional and network obstacles to innovation is the fact that a noncash payment (such as a payment with a debit card, a credit card, a check, or a wire transfer) is a complex operation involving a series of steps. Someone has to start the process, the identity of the participants has to be verified, accounts have to be identified and the payer must have the funds, confirmation has to be received, obligations need to be discharged, and the transaction must be verified. If even one of these steps fails, the payment will not go through.

So, how can we develop a new U.S. payments system that is universal, cheap, fast, and secure? The solution involves a combination of *technology* and *coordination*. With this in mind, in 2015 the Federal Reserve convened the Faster Payments Task Force to help overcome barriers to the introduction of technology into the U.S. payments system in a manner that is similar to what they did for checks 100 years ago. And, in August 2019, the Federal Reserve announced that it will develop an around-the-clock system ("FedNow Service") for real-time settlement of retail payments that provides immediate access to funds.

Finally, on receipt of the check, your bank debits your account. (If the balance in your account is insufficient to cover the check, your bank has a few days to return it to the sending bank, so the transaction isn't actually final until that period has passed.) In the past all paper checks were returned to the people who originally wrote them. Today, they are scanned and customers can view electronic images on their bank's websites.

Electronic Payments

The third and final method of payment is electronic. We are all familiar with credit cards and debit cards. A less well-known form of payment is electronic funds transfers. While there are a large number of credit and debit card transactions, electronic funds transfers account for the bulk of the $151 trillion worth of noncash, noncheck payments made each year in the United States.

What is the difference between debit cards and credit cards? A **debit card** works the same way as a check in that it provides the bank with instructions to transfer funds from the cardholder's account directly to a merchant's account. There is usually a charge for this; the processor of the payment takes a fee based on the size of the transaction.

A **credit card** is a promise by a bank to lend the cardholder money with which to make purchases. When a shopper buys a pair of shoes with a credit card, the shoe store's bank account receives payment immediately, but the money that is used for payment does not belong to the buyer. Instead, the bank that issued the credit card makes the payment, creating a loan the cardholder must repay. For this reason, credit cards do not represent money; rather, they represent access to someone else's money.

With relatively rapid growth in the use of debit cards since 2007, the number of debit card transactions is now about double the number of credit card payments. But in terms of dollar amount, the typical credit card transaction is more than twice as large as that of the typical debit card; as a result, the total value of credit card payments is still larger, by about 23 percent. And while checks are used only one-fourth as often as credit and debit cards, the average check size is far larger, so the total value of payments by check is still six times greater than that for the two card types combined.

Electronic funds transfers (EFTs) are movements of funds directly from one account to another. These transactions are used extensively by banks and are becoming increasingly popular for individuals as well. For individuals, the most common form is the **automated clearinghouse (ACH) transaction**, which is generally used for recurring payments such as paychecks and utility bills. Some merchants use them for one-time transactions as well. ACH transactions are just like checks except that they are entirely electronic. Your bank account is debited or credited automatically, and you receive periodic notifications of the activity in your account. Having surpassed the value of checks in recent years, the value of ACH payments now accounts for more than one-half of the value of all noncash payments.

Banks use electronic transfers to handle transactions among themselves. The most common method is to send money through a system maintained by the Federal Reserve, called Fedwire. The volume and value of payments made through this system are substantial. On a typical day in 2018, the system completed 631,000 transactions with a total value of about $2.9 trillion.

Rapid innovation is reducing the cost and increasing the speed of payments and transfers, both domestically and internationally. We see this in the proliferation of smartphone apps and infrastructure created by Alipay, Amazon Pay, Apple Pay, Google Pay, PayPal, TransferWise, Venmo, WeChat, Zelle, and the like. These systems allow individuals to make payments to merchants (online and at brick-and-mortar shops), to make transfers to one another, or both.

In some cases, these digital wallets are simply links to a person's bank or credit card account. In others, the service provider requires the transfer of funds *prior* to any purchase. Since these technologies build on the existing financial system, conventional forms of money play a role at some point in the process. Ultimately, the goal of these digital systems is to minimize transaction costs and ensure security, reliability, and speed while preventing use for criminal purposes.

Payment systems are improving rapidly in the emerging world. The most prominent example over the past decade is the M-Pesa in Kenya. *Pesa* means "money" in Swahili. In 2007, a mobile phone company began allowing Kenyans to deposit, withdraw, and transfer funds using their phones. As of 2017, mobile money transfer subscriptions surpassed 27 million, an extraordinarily rapid adoption that highlights the value of the service. There are more than 110,000 M-Pesa agents,

Market Liquidity, Funding Liquidity, and Making Markets
LESSONS FROM THE CRISIS

A "market maker" in stocks, bonds, or other securities is usually a financial institution that buys and sells securities on behalf of clients. If buy orders exceed sell orders for a particular security, the market maker must be able to act as the seller to clear the market. Therefore, market makers usually hold inventories of the specific financial instruments in which they trade, and they borrow to maintain inventories at adequate levels.

Market liquidity—the ability to sell assets—and *funding liquidity*—the ability to borrow money—are both needed to make financial markets function smoothly. If a loss of funding liquidity prevents market makers from holding adequate inventories, trading and market liquidity suffer. Conversely, if market liquidity for some financial instruments declines, the prices of those instruments will fall as they become less attractive to investors; resulting concerns about the safety of the market makers that hold the assets with falling prices may reduce their ability to borrow.

A sudden loss of liquidity was central to the 2007–2009 financial crisis. Before the crisis, many financial institutions relied on short-term borrowing to hold long-term financial instruments because their managers believed that funding liquidity would remain readily available. They also believed that markets would always be liquid—that is, they would always be able to sell the securities and loans that they held. They were wrong on both counts.

In the summer of 2007, investors began to doubt the value of a wide class of securities. As a result, market liquidity for those instruments disappeared, and financial institutions that held them faced large potential losses. In turn, funding liquidity for these institutions evaporated as the potential losses caused their lenders to worry about their safety.

This double "liquidity shock" led many financial institutions to increase cash holdings that they might otherwise have lent to others. Reduced loan supply intensified the vicious spiral of dwindling liquidity and falling securities prices. The private financial system as a whole could not provide sufficient market liquidity or funding liquidity to satisfy heightened demands.

One lesson from the financial crisis is clear: Liquidity is a highly valuable resource that can disappear when it is most needed, so it should not be taken for granted. Even large and seemingly wealthy financial firms can fail if liquidity evaporates.

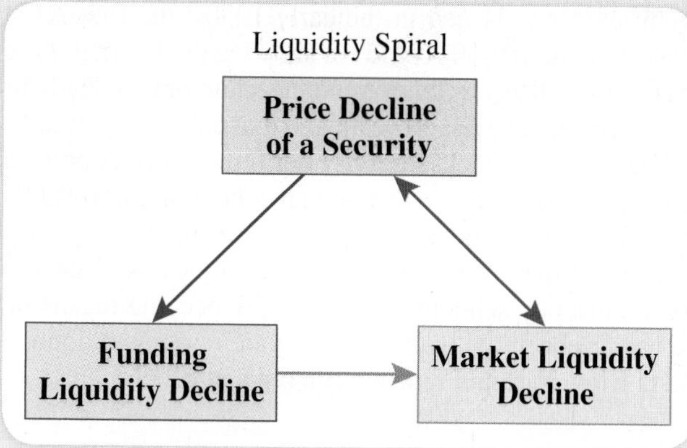

In the accompanying figure, a decline of the price of a security makes it more costly for a financial institution to make a market in that security, resulting in a decline of market liquidity. That decline makes the security less attractive to investors, further reducing its price. If the price falls sufficiently, concern about the well-being of market makers diminishes their funding liquidity, advancing a vicious cycle.

40 times the number of bank ATMs, while 96 percent of households outside the capital have an M-Pesa account.

The M-Pesa has greatly improved access to the financial system, allowing Kenya to technologically leapfrog the more traditional payments mechanisms of far wealthier countries. For many Kenyans, their cell phone substitutes for a conventional bank account. That may be a sign of the future: According to the World Bank, as of 2017, one-third of the world's adults—more than 1.7 billion people—do not have an account at a bank or a mobile money operator. Yet, according to the mobile money industry, as of 2018 more than 860 million customers have mobile money accounts, and both the account totals and usage are rising rapidly in the developing world.[6]

The Future of Money

Let's speculate about what might happen to money and each of its three functions in the future. As a *means of payment,* it has already undergone big changes. The time is rapidly approaching when safe and secure systems for payment will use virtually no money at all.

We will always need money as a *unit of account* in which to quote values and prices; the efficiency of quoting prices in commonly understood terms isn't going to change. But the question is, how many units of account will we need? Today, many countries have their own currencies, which give rise to their own units of account. In the future, though, there will be little reason to maintain different units of account across different countries. Price systems will be more like systems of weights and measures. Today, there are two commonly used systems of weights and measures: English (ounces and yards) and metric (grams and meters). We will likely see a similar sort of standardization of money and a dramatic reduction in the number of units of account.

Finally, money as a *store of value* is clearly on the way out. With the advances in financial markets, many financial instruments have become highly liquid. They are easily bought and sold and can be converted into a means of payment quickly and cheaply, while providing a better store of value than money. These instruments and the financial markets in which they trade are the subject of the next chapter. For now, though, we can conclude that in the future, there will almost surely be less and less money.

One caution is in order. As we look into the future and try to discern what will happen to money, we should remember that 150 years ago there was virtually no paper currency in circulation. The first credit card was issued in the early 1950s; the first ATM was installed around 1970. Not until the mid-1990s could we shop via the Internet. Forecasting most of these developments, as well as any other trend in technology, is nearly impossible. After all, who could have predicted even 20 years ago that today we would be able to check our bank balances, buy and sell stocks, and pay our utility bills 24 hours a day, seven days a week using our smartphones from virtually anywhere in the world? So, as many firms now experiment with new payment technologies, we shouldn't be surprised if one or more of them again transform the payments process over the next decade. Some observers thought that virtual currency schemes might rapidly become means of payment. But so far, that hope has not been realized, and there are reasons to doubt that it will. (see Money and Banking Blog: Virtual Frenzies: Bitcoin and Blockchain).

Measuring Money

Changes in the amount of money in the economy are related to changes in interest rates, economic growth, and, most important, **inflation**. Inflation is the pace at which prices in general are increasing over time—and the **inflation rate** is a measure of that process.[7] With inflation, you need more units of money to buy the same basket of goods you bought a month or a year ago. Put another way, inflation makes money less valuable. And the primary cause of inflation is the issuance of too much money. When the Continental Congress issued too much currency to finance the Revolutionary War, the

[6]For details on worldwide financial access, see the World Bank's *The Little Data Book on Financial Inclusion 2018*.

[7]The terms *inflation* and *inflation rate* are often used interchangeably. We will refer to inflation as the process of prices rising, and inflation rate as the measurement of the process. The relationship between these terms is analogous to that between *heat* and *temperature*. The second is the measure of the first.

number of continentals people needed to purchase food and shelter rose dramatically. Continentals became less valuable. So the value of the means of payment depends on how much of it is circulating.

To use the insight that money growth is somehow related to inflation, we must be able to measure how much money is circulating. This is no easy task. Let's start with money's primary function, as a means of payment. If that were the definition of money, we would measure the quantity of money as the quantity of —currency in circulation—an unrealistically limited measure, because there are many ways to complete transactions (effect final payment) without using currency.

A reasonable alternative would be to consider a broad category of financial assets and sort them by their degree of liquidity. That is, we could rank them by the ease with which they can be converted into a means of payment, arranging them along a spectrum from the most liquid (currency) to the least liquid (art, antique cars, and the like). Figure 2.2 shows what our liquidity spectrum would look like.

Figure 2.2 The Liquidity Spectrum

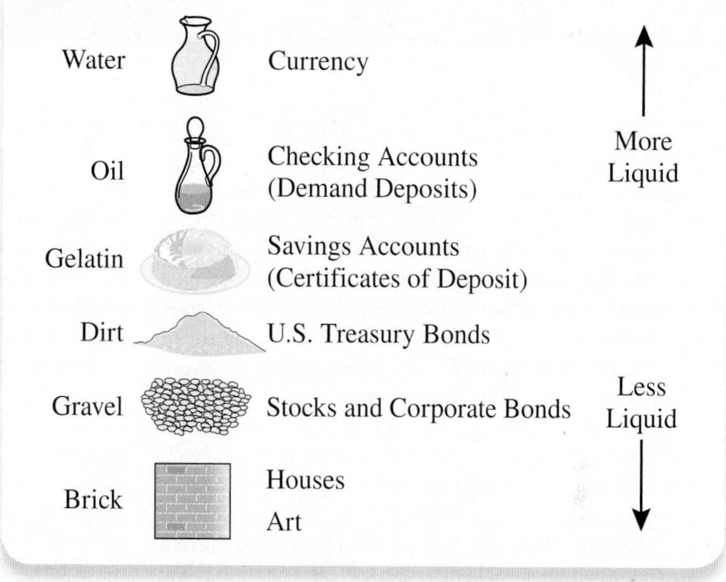

Water	Currency	More Liquid ↑
Oil	Checking Accounts (Demand Deposits)	
Gelatin	Savings Accounts (Certificates of Deposit)	
Dirt	U.S. Treasury Bonds	
Gravel	Stocks and Corporate Bonds	Less Liquid ↓
Brick	Houses Art	

Liquidity is the ease with which you can turn an asset into a means of payment without loss of value.

Once we have our list, we could draw a line and include everything on one side of the line in our measure of money. Over the years, figuring out just where to draw the line has proven very difficult, especially since the introduction of new types of checking accounts. There really is no perfect solution. Instead, we have drawn the line in a number of different places and computed several measures of money, called the **monetary aggregates**: M1 and M2.

Table 2.1 shows the components of the two monetary aggregates as defined by the Federal Reserve, along with the size of each as of February 2019. Let's go through each one to understand how it is constructed. **M1**, the narrowest definition of money, includes only currency and various deposit accounts on which people can write checks. These are the most liquid assets in the financial system. The components of M1 include *currency in the hands of the public,* which is the quantity of dollar bills outstanding excluding the ones in the vaults of banks; *traveler's checks* issued by travel companies, banks, and credit card companies, which are guaranteed by the issuer and usually work just like cash; **demand deposits** at commercial banks, which are standard checking accounts that pay no interest; and other checkable deposits, which are deposits in checking accounts that pay interest.

M2 equals all of M1 plus assets that cannot be used directly as a means of payment and are difficult to turn into currency quickly. These assets in M2 include small-denomination **time deposits** (less than $100,000) that cannot be withdrawn without advance notice; *savings deposits,* including *money-market deposit accounts,* which pay interest and offer limited check-writing privileges; *retail money-market mutual fund shares,* or shares in funds that collect relatively small sums from individuals, pool

Virtual Frenzies: Bitcoin and Blockchain

MONEY AND BANKING BLOG

Bitcoin is the oldest and most prominent of more than 2,500 cryptocurrencies—sometimes called "virtual currencies"—that have come into existence since 2008. Devotees hope these "tokens" will revolutionize many aspects of finance, including everyday payments. Cryptocurrencies like Bitcoin are a type of digital currency based on a peer-to-peer network designed to allow for the verification of transfers without the need for a government authority or any trusted third party. The technology used to record ownership—blockchain—is an ever-growing, encrypted public ledger of transactions spread over a network of computers. Promoters of this "distributed ledger technology" believe that it will have broad applications in supporting payments in any currency.

Advocates claim that Bitcoin and other cryptocurrencies have two important advantages: (1) their value cannot be undermined by government fiat (because its value is created and controlled by the network of users and a set of unchanging rules, not by government), and (2) users can remain anonymous while making payments electronically and efficiently.

However, cryptocurrencies lack the three key characteristics of money: They are not a commonly accepted means of exchange, do not provide a reliable unit of account, and do not offer a stable store of value. As for blockchain, extensive experimentation is underway to determine whether it can beat out existing payments mechanisms.

Let's have a closer look at Bitcoin itself. Some countries classify Bitcoin as a commodity, subjecting it to capital gains taxation, or severely restricting its use. In no country can Bitcoin be widely exchanged for goods and services. As a result, in early 2019 Bitcoin accounted for less than 200 *thousand* daily transactions globally, compared with more than 500 *million* dollar transactions in the United States alone.

Bitcoin's value is extremely unstable: The dollar value of a single Bitcoin surged from just pennies in 2010 to nearly \$20,000 at the peak in December 2017, before plunging back below \$3,200 a year later. Since 2014, the *daily* percentage change in Bitcoin's U.S. dollar value has ranged from –22 percent to +32 percent. Had Bitcoin been employed as a unit of account over this period, all other prices would have been subject to enormous day-to-day swings.

Initially, Bitcoin's anonymity made it popular with money launderers, tax evaders, and drug traffickers. Perhaps the most notorious users of Bitcoin were participants in the online black market known as Silk Road, which the U.S. government shut down in 2013. In 2016, most Bitcoin currency transactions were executed on exchanges in China, probably to get around government controls on moving capital out of the country. A year later, the Chinese government virtually banned these transactions.

Other governments also have paid greater attention to activity in digital currencies in recent years. And, despite

them together, and invest them in short-term marketable debt issued by large corporations. Money-market mutual fund shares can be issued by nonbank financial intermediaries, such as brokerage firms. They do carry check-writing privileges. M2 is the most commonly quoted monetary aggregate in the United States, because its movements are most closely related to interest rates and economic growth.

To clarify what the monetary aggregates mean, let's compare their size to the size of the economy. In the fourth quarter of 2018, nominal U.S. **gross domestic product (GDP)** was \$20.501 trillion. Putting that number into the same units as those in Table 2.1, that's \$20,501 billion. So GDP is nearly five and one-half times larger than M1 and more than 40 percent larger than M2.

Which one of the M's should we use to understand inflation? That's a difficult question whose answer has changed over time. Until the early 1980s, economists and policymakers looked at M1. But with the introduction of substitutes for standard checking accounts, especially money-market mutual fund shares, M1 became less

Bitcoin's complex infrastructure, privacy experts question its security: According to one analysis, about 40 percent of Bitcoin users can be identified by tracking their activity in a blockchain ledger.

Can a private currency—digital or otherwise—do the job better as *money* than what we currently have? So far, the answer is no. Government-issued fiat monies like the dollar, euro, yen, and renminbi are far more reliable than Bitcoin as a means of payment, unit of account, and store of value. And if there's a profit to be made from issuing a currency, it seems reasonable for the public at large to be the beneficiary.

How about blockchain technology? Can it outperform existing payments and record-keeping mechanisms? Advances in payments technology that cut costs and broadened access punctuate the history of modern finance. The rapid spread of credit and debit cards and the rise of Internet banking have generated large cost savings; and over the past decade, mobile telephony has helped millions of the world's poorest people make payments efficiently (think of the mobile money, M-Pesa, launched in Kenya).

The press is full of stories about financial intermediaries experimenting with blockchain, but progress has been slow.

Where is the greatest opportunity? It is surely possible to improve the speed of retail financial transactions and the safety of the payments system (including from cyberattack). Perhaps blockchain technology can help with some of these goals. But, doing so will require a dramatic improvement in the speed at which the system operates. Current technology is not close to the tens of thousands of transactions per second that centralized systems like Visa routinely process.

Making *wholesale* electronic trading platforms and clearinghouses significantly cheaper will be even more difficult. First, some wholesale operations (like those for domestic interbank transfers) are run by public entities based on cost recovery. Second, in derivatives, foreign exchange, securities settlement, and other sectors, clearing utilities have achieved enormous economies of scale, letting them slash costs.

Even where the opportunities for cost cutting are larger—as with retail wire transfers across borders—blockchain technology may not be suitable. The problem is that someone needs to screen and monitor transactions to prevent money laundering, terrorist finance, and other illicit transfers. The anonymity of blockchain collides with the public's legitimate right to thwart criminal transactions.

The bottom line: Blockchain offers potential gains where the current payments system is the least developed. But the innovators must be able to show that, if the technology cuts costs and makes transactions safer, it also will allow for effective oversight where needed. So far, the hopes exceed the reality.

useful than M2. These innovations enabled people to shift their balances out of the noninterest-bearing accounts in M1 and into accounts that paid interest. As Table 2.1 shows, demand deposits and other checkable deposits in M1 total about $2.1 trillion, which represents about one-tenth of GDP. By comparison, the savings deposits, money-market deposit accounts, and retail money-market mutual fund shares in M2 total $10.1 trillion or nearly one-half of GDP. M1 is no longer a useful measure of money.

Looking at Figure 2.3 you can see that from 1960 to 1980 the growth rates of the two measures of money moved together. After 1980, however, M1 behaved very differently from M2. Here's what happened. In the late 1970s and early 1980s, inflation climbed to over 10 percent for a few years. Needless to say, people who had money in zero-interest checking accounts were upset. Their money was losing value at a rapid rate. They went looking for ways to get checking services along with interest. Soon financial firms began to offer "money market" accounts that compensated

Table 2.1 The Monetary Aggregates

Monetary Aggregates			Value as of February 2019 (US$ billions)
M1	=	Currency in the hands of the public	1,633.7
	+	Demand deposits	1,499.8
	+	Other checkable deposits	626.0
		Total M1	**3,759.4**
M2	=	M1	
	+	Small-denomination time deposits	580.6
	+	Savings deposits and money-market deposit accounts	9,276.4
	+	Retail money-market mutual fund shares	861.4
		Total M2	**14,477.8**

NOTE: Sums may differ due to rounding.

SOURCE: Board of Governors of the Federal Reserve System.

depositors at least in part for inflation. These accounts are part of M2. The movement of funds into the non-M1 portion of M2 meant that the two measures no longer moved together. At the same time, the new money-market accounts made M2 accounts more liquid. Analysts interested in the economy's prospects stopped looking at M1 and began to look at M2.

How useful is M2 in tracking inflation? We already know that when the quantity of money grows quickly, it produces very high inflation. A cross-country analysis of

Figure 2.3 Growth Rates of Monetary Aggregates, 1960–2019

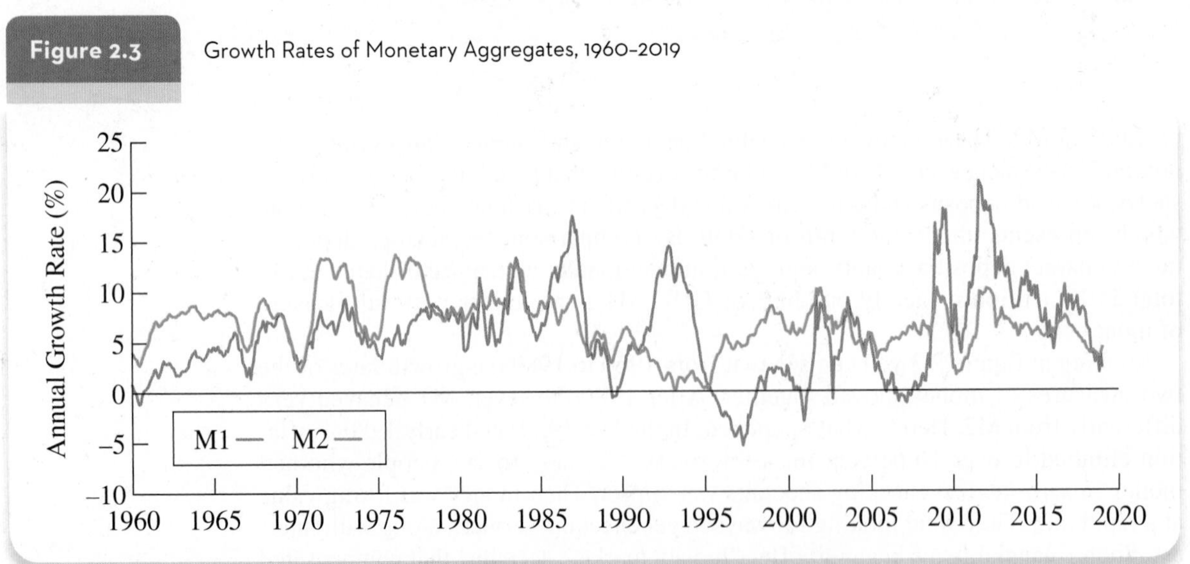

SOURCE: Board of Governors of the Federal Reserve System, Release H.6. (FRED data codes: M1SL and M2SL).

The Consumer Price Index
TOOLS OF THE TRADE

Understanding how to measure inflation is central to understanding economics and finance. Most of us keep a close eye on measures like the consumer price index (CPI) to help gauge the value of our salary increases or the purchasing power of the money we hold. And adjusting interest rates for inflation is critical for making investment decisions. (See Chapter 4.)

The CPI is designed to answer the following question: How much more would it cost for people to purchase today the same basket of goods and services that they actually bought at some fixed time in the past?

To calculate the CPI, every few years statisticians at the Bureau of Labor Statistics (BLS) survey people to find out what they bought. This gives us the basket of goods and services bought by the typical consumer. Next, every month the BLS collects information on the prices of thousands of goods and services—everything from breakfast cereal to gasoline to washing machines to the cost of cable television. Combining the expenditure and price surveys allows statisticians to compute the current cost of the basket. Finally, this current cost is compared to a benchmark to yield an index. And the percentage change in this index is a measure of inflation.

To see how this works, let's look at an example. Assume people spend 25 percent of their income on food, 50 percent on housing, and 25 percent on transportation. That's the survey information. Examples of the prices are in Table 2.2. Importantly, these are the prices of exactly the same bundle of food, the same size and quality of housing, and the same transportation for each year.

Using the numbers in Table 2.2 we can compute the cost of the basket of goods in each year:

Cost of the basket in 2020

$$\begin{aligned}&= 0.25 \times \text{Price of food} + 0.5 \times \text{Price of housing}\\ &\quad + 0.25 \times \text{Price of transportation}\\ &= 0.25 \times \$100 + 0.5 \times \$200 + 0.25 \times \$100\\ &= \$150\end{aligned}$$

And for 2021, we get $165. Choosing 2020 as the base year, the index level in each year equals

$$\text{CPI} = \frac{\text{Cost of the basket in current year}}{\text{Cost of the basket in base year}} \times 100$$

The result of this computation is the fifth column of the table.

Finally, we can use the index number to compute the inflation rate from the previous year. From 2020 to 2021, this means that

$$\text{Inflation rate 2021} = \frac{\text{CPI in 2021} - \text{CPI in 2020}}{\text{CPI in 2020}} \times 100$$

Using the numbers from Table 2.2 to compute the inflation rate in 2021, we get that

$$\frac{110 - 100}{100} \times 100 = 10\%$$

and for 2022 the result is

$$\frac{120 - 110}{110} \times 100 = 9.1\%$$

(These numbers are just for illustration. The U.S. inflation rate is closer to 2 percent.)

Inflation measured using the CPI tells us how much more money we need to give people to restore the purchasing power they had in the earlier period when the survey was done. But adjustments in wages based on fixed-expenditure-weight inflation indexes like the CPI are known to overcompensate people in an unintended way. This overstatement of inflation comes from what is known as *substitution bias*. Because inflation is not uniform, the prices of some products will increase by more than the prices of others. People can escape some of the inflation by *substituting* goods and services that have sustained less inflation for those that have sustained more. By assuming that any substitution makes people worse off, the index *overstates* the impact of price changes. To address this problem, and take into account changes in spending patterns, the Bureau of Labor Statistics in 2002 began changing the weights every two years. Nevertheless, many economists believe that the CPI still overstates inflation.

Table 2.2 Computing the Consumer Price Index

Year	Price of Food	Price of Housing	Price of Transportation	Cost of the Basket	Consumer Price Index
2020	$100	$200	$100	$150	100
2021	110	205	140	165	110
2022	120	210	180	180	120

Cash Is King, but $100 Bills Are for Crooks

APPLYING THE CONCEPT

For years, people have been saying that cash will disappear. They have been spectacularly wrong. Today, there is nearly $1.6 trillion in paper U.S. dollar currency in circulation, double the amount a decade ago. Furthermore, 80 percent of this is in $100 bills—that is, *thirty-eight* $100 bills for each of the 327 million residents of the United States.

Why is this? The most compelling explanation is that large-denomination paper currency facilitates illicit activity. A host of criminal activities, including money laundering, tax evasion, drug dealing, and human trafficking, run on cash. Big banknotes are a convenient way to transfer funds anonymously. A $100 bill weighs less than a gram, so $1 million weighs just over 20 pounds and is small enough to fit in a medium-size briefcase. In other words, criminals are probably the ones using most of the U.S. currency in circulation.

Now, since it costs only about 13 cents to produce one, the U.S. Treasury makes quite a profit from printing all of these $100 bills. This *seignorage* amounts to about $70 billion per year, financing nearly 2 percent of federal government expenditure. Should the U.S. government be financed in part by an activity that facilitates criminal behavior? Or, should we get rid of $100 bills?

Making cash transactions more costly for criminals has great appeal. But, to do it, governments would have to agree jointly to stop issuing large-denomination paper money. Otherwise, crooks will just substitute one country's fiat currency for another. And, even in the extremely unlikely event that all governments cooperate, crooks could turn to one of the many cryptocurrencies available.

Do we really need paper currency? The most compelling argument for cash focuses on the preservation of freedom, not of payment efficiency. Because of its anonymity, paper money limits the reach of dictators and ideological censors. As a result, there is a tradeoff between people abusing the privacy afforded by cash payments and tyrannical societies exploiting the intimate knowledge of people's payments for malevolent control. If someone is going to issue cash to protect freedom, it might as well be the government that collects the revenue, rather than a private agent.

That leaves open the question of whether we have hit the right balance in the tradeoff between protecting privacy and battling criminality. Are governments providing notes in denominations that are too large—making illegal transactions too easy? In May 2015, the ECB halted the production of €500 notes, something the United States did half a century ago. Would it really be so bad if governments eliminated everything that was bigger than a $20, €20, CHF20, or ¥2,000 note? Aside from the legislators who will need to replace the lost seignorage, and from the crooks whose costs will rise, we suspect that few would complain.

money growth supports this conclusion. In Turkey, Venezuela, and Ukraine, where in the last half of the 1990s the inflation rate ranged from 30 to 75 percent per year, the money supply grew at comparable rates.[8] By contrast, in the United States, Canada, and Europe, the inflation rate averaged only about 2 percent, and the money growth rate stayed in the range of 6 to 7 percent. Because high money growth means high inflation, controlling inflation means controlling the money supply. Imagine how much inflation there would be if people could spend the $4 trillion in Monopoly dollars Parker Brothers has printed since 1935!

How useful is money growth in helping us control moderate inflation? We will address this question in detail in Chapter 20 of this book. For now, though, let's look at whether money growth helps forecast inflation.

Figure 2.4 shows M2 growth on the horizontal axis and the inflation rate *two years later* on the vertical axis, both for the United States. The solid red diamonds

[8]From 1995 to 2000, inflation averaged 74 percent in Turkey, 42 percent in Venezuela, and 30 percent in Ukraine. At the same time, a measure of money that is close to U.S. M2 grew in those three countries at 86, 33, and 36 percent per year respectively. Data for these comparisons come from the International Monetary Fund's *International Financial Statistics*.

Figure 2.4 Money Growth and Inflation, Monthly 1960–2019

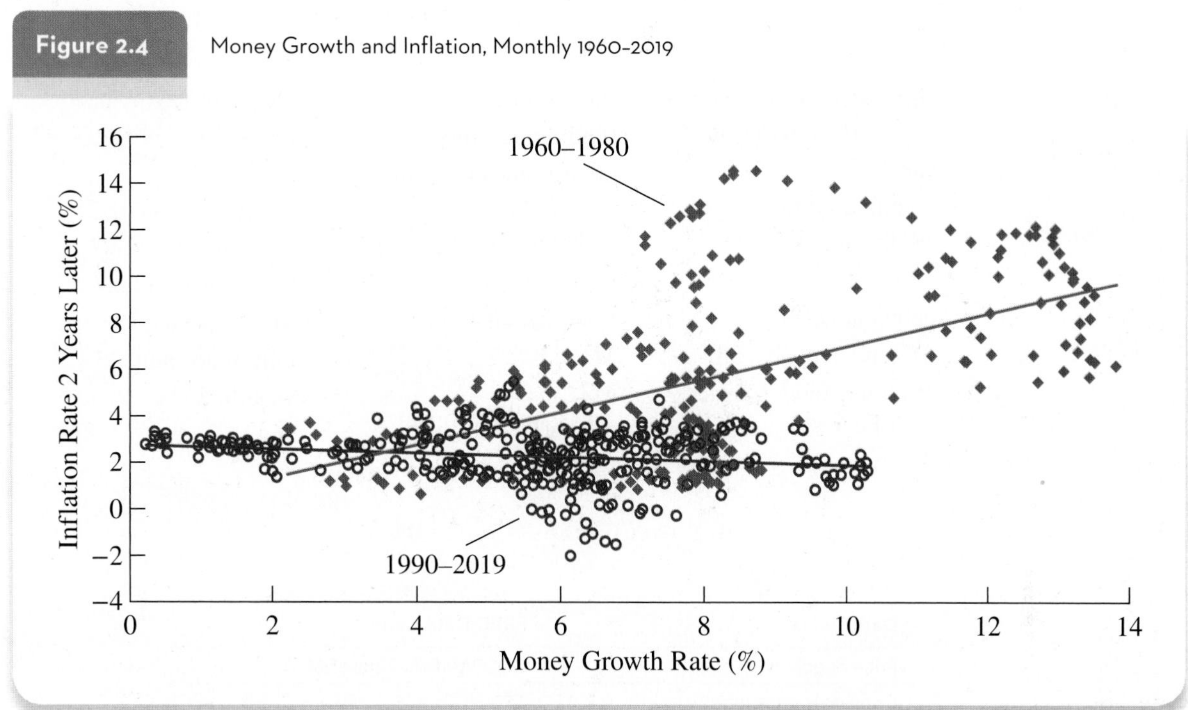

Money growth measured as the 12-month change in M2, and inflation measured as the 12-month change in the consumer price index (FRED data codes: M2SL and CPIAUCSL).

SOURCE: Board of Governors of the Federal Reserve System and Bureau of Labor Statistics.

represent data from 1960 to 1980. Note that, while the relationship is far from perfect in those years, higher money growth was clearly associated with higher inflation two years later. In fact, the correlation was over 0.5.[9] But look at what has happened to the relationship more recently. The hollow blue circles represent data from 1990 to 2019, when there was virtually no relationship between the two measures. (The correlation was slightly negative.) Growth in M2 stopped being a useful tool for forecasting inflation.

There are two possible explanations for the fact that M2 no longer predicts inflation. One is that the relationship between the two applies only at high levels of inflation. Figure 2.4 shows that during the period 1960–1980, the inflation rate often rose higher than 5 percent, but from 1990 to 2019, it rarely did. Maybe the relationship between money growth and inflation doesn't exist at low levels of inflation, or it shows up only over longer periods of time. All we really know is that at low levels of money growth, inflation is likely to stay low.

An alternative explanation is that we need a new measure of money that takes into account recent changes in the way we make payments and use money. Once economists have identified the right measure, perhaps we'll be able to predict inflation again.

[9]Correlation is a measure of how closely two quantities are related, or change together. The numerical value ranges from +1 to −1. A positive correlation signifies that the two variables move up and down together, while a negative correlation means that they move in opposite directions.

Key Terms

Using FRED: Codes for Data in This Chapter

Data Series	FRED Data Code
Price of gold (U.S. dollars)	GOLDAMGBD228NLBM
Consumer price index	CPIAUCSL
M1	M1SL
M2	M2SL
Currency in circulation	CURRSL
Traveler's checks	TVCKSSL
Demand deposits	DEMDEPSL
Other checkable deposits	OCDSL
Small-denomination time deposits	STDCBSL
Savings deposits and MMDAs*	SAVINGSL
Retail MMMFs†	RMFSL
Nominal GDP	GDP
U.S. population	POP

*Money-market deposit accounts.

†Money-market mutual funds.

To learn more about the changing financial system, visit www.moneyandbanking.com.

Chapter Lessons

1. Money is an asset that is generally accepted in payment for goods and services or repayment of debts.
   a. Money has three basic uses:
      i. Means of payment
      ii. Unit of account
      iii. Store of value
   b. Money is liquid. Liquidity is the ease with which an asset can be turned into a means of payment.

c. For financial institutions, market liquidity is the ease with which they can sell a security or loan for money. Funding liquidity is the ease with which they can borrow to acquire a security or loan.

2. Money makes the payments system work. The payments system is the web of arrangements that allows people to exchange goods and services. There are three broad categories of payments, all of which use money at some stage.
   a. Cash
   b. Checks
   c. Electronic payments
3. In the future, money will be used less and less as a means of payment.
4. To understand the links between money and inflation, we need to measure the quantity of money in the economy. There are two basic measures of money: M1 and M2. M1, the narrowest measure, includes only the most liquid assets. M2, a broader measure, includes assets not usable as a means of payment.
   a. Countries with high money growth have high inflation.
   b. In countries with low inflation, money growth is a poor forecaster of inflation.

Conceptual and Analytical Problems

1. Describe four ways you could pay for your morning cup of coffee. What are the advantages and disadvantages of each? *(LO2)*
2. You are the owner of a small sandwich shop. A buyer may offer one of several payment methods: cash, a check drawn on a bank, a credit card, or a debit card. Which of these is the least costly for you? Explain why the others are more expensive. *(LO2)*
3. Explain how money encourages specialization, and how specialization improves everyone's standard of living. (LO3)
4.* Could the dollar still function as the unit of account in a totally cashless society? *(LO2)*
5. Give four examples of ACH transactions you might make. *(LO2)*
6. A subset of European Union countries have adopted the euro, while the remaining member countries have retained their own currencies. What are the advantages of a common currency for someone who is traveling through Europe? *(LO1)*
7. Why might each of the following commodities not serve well as money? *(LO2)*
   a. Tomatoes
   b. Bricks
   c. Cattle
8. Despite the efforts of the U.S. Treasury and the Secret Service, someone discovers a cheap way to counterfeit $100 bills. What will be the impact of this discovery on the economy? *(LO3)*
9. What do you think accounts for the widespread adoption of mobile-based payment services in emerging economies? *(LO2)*
10. Over a nine-year period in the 16th century, King Henry VIII reduced the silver content of the British pound to one-sixth its initial value. Why do you think he did

*Indicates more difficult problems.

www.moneyandbanking.com

so? What do you think happened to the use of pounds as a means of payment? If you held both the old and new pounds, which would you use first, and why? *(LO1)*

11. Under what circumstances might you expect barter to reemerge in an economy that has fiat money as a means of payment? *(LO3)*
12. You visit a tropical island that has only four goods in its economy—oranges, pineapples, coconuts, and bananas. There is no money in this economy. *(LO1)*
    a. Draw a grid showing all the prices for this economy. (You should check your answer using the $n(n - 1)/2$ formula where n is the number of goods.)
    b. An islander suggests designating oranges as the means of payment and unit of account for the economy. How many prices would there be if her suggestion was followed?
    c. Do you think the change suggested in part *b* is worth implementing? Why or why not?
13. Consider a fruit-growing tropical island economy without money. Under what circumstances would you recommend the issue of a paper currency by the government of the island? What advantages might this strategy have over the use of oranges as money? *(LO1)*
14. What factors should you take into account when considering using the following assets as stores of value? *(LO1)*
    a. Gold
    b. Real estate
    c. Stocks
    d. Government bonds
    e. Cryptocurrencies
15.* Under what circumstances might money in the form of currency be the best option as a store of value? *(LO3)*
16. Suppose a significant fall in the price of certain stocks caused the market makers in those stocks to experience difficulties with their funding liquidity. Under what circumstances might that development lead to liquidity problems in markets for other assets? *(LO3)*
17.* Consider an economy that produces and consumes only two goods—food and apparel. Suppose the inflation rate based on the consumer price index is higher during the year than that based on the GDP deflator. Assuming underlying tastes and preferences in the economy stay the same, what can you say about food and apparel price movements during the year? *(LO3)*
18. Assuming no interest is paid on checking accounts, what would you expect to see happen to the relative growth rates of M1 and M2 if interest rates rose significantly? *(LO3)*
19. If money growth is related to inflation, what would you expect to happen to the inflation rates of countries that join a monetary union and adopt a common currency such as the euro? *(LO3)*
20. Why might one doubt that current new forms of digital money, such as Bitcoin, will replace more traditional fiat currencies? *(LO2)*
21. Is the challenge of making "time consistent" policy unique to fiat-based paper money? *(LO3)*

*Indicates more difficult problems.

22. What are some of the main obstacles to a faster, more efficient U.S. payments system and how might they be overcome? *(LO2)*
23. What are some advantages and disadvantages of a government continuing to issue paper currency in the face of widespread financial innovation? *(LO3)*

Data Exploration connect

For detailed instructions on using Federal Reserve Economic Data (FRED) online to answer each of the following problems, visit www.mhhe.com/moneyandbanking6e *and refer to the FRED Resources and Data Exploration Hints.*

1. Find the most recent level of M2 (FRED code: M2SL) and of the U.S. population (FRED code: POP). Compute the quantity of money divided by the population. (Note that M2 is measured in billions of dollars and population is in thousands of individuals.) Do you think your answer is large? Why? *(LO1)*
2. Reproduce Figure 2.3 from 1960 to the present, showing the percent change from a year ago of M1 (FRED code: M1SL) and M2 (FRED code: M2SL). Comment on the pattern over the last five years. Would it matter which of the two monetary aggregates you looked at? *(LO3)*
3. Which usually grows faster: M1 or M2? Produce a graph showing M2 divided by M1. When this ratio rises, M2 outpaces M1 and vice versa. What is the long-run pattern? Is the pattern stable? *(LO3)*
4. To complete payments, do you think people need more or less currency per dollar of transactions than they did 30 years ago? After stating your hypothesis, plot currency in circulation as a percent of GDP from 1990 (FRED Codes: CURRENCY and GDP). Was your intuition consistent with the data? What might account for the trend you observe? *(LO1)*
5. Plot the annual inflation rate based on the percent change from a year ago of the consumer price index (FRED code: CPIAUCSL). Comment on the average and variability of inflation in the 1960s, the 1970s, and the most recent decade. *(LO3)*

Chapter

3 Financial Instruments, Financial Markets, and Financial Institutions

Learning Objectives

After reading this chapter, you should be able to:

LO1 Explain what financial instruments are, how they are used, and how they are valued.

LO2 Discuss the role and structure of financial markets and identify the characteristics of a well-run financial market.

LO3 Describe the role of financial institutions and structure of the financial industry.

Long before formal financial institutions and instruments became common, there were times when people lacked the resources to meet their immediate needs. In the terminology of introductory economics, people's incomes were exceeded by their necessary consumption. When a harvest was poor, they would dip into the reserves stored from previous years or exchange assets like land and livestock for food. But often those measures were insufficient, so communities developed informal financial arrangements that allowed people to borrow or lend among themselves. After a poor harvest, those people with relatively good yields would help those with relatively poor ones. When the tables were turned, help would flow the other way. In some societies, families spread out geographically to facilitate these arrangements. For example, in rural Indian communities, households deliberately married off their daughters to families in different regions to increase the chance that their in-laws would be able to respond in a time of crisis.[1] These informal insurance arrangements ensured that everyone had enough to eat.

While family members and friends still make loans among themselves, the informal arrangements that were the mainstay of the financial system centuries ago have given way to the formal financial instruments of the modern world. Today, the international financial system exists to facilitate the design, sale, and exchange of a broad set of contracts with a very specific set of characteristics.

In recent decades, finance has evolved at an unprecedented pace, and our understanding of it has changed, too. Formerly, economists distinguished sharply between **direct finance** (in which a borrower sells a security directly to a lender) and

[1]See M. R. Rosenzweig, "Risk, Implicit Contracts, and the Family in Rural Areas of Low-Income Countries," *Economic Journal* 98 (December 1988).

indirect finance (in which an institution like a bank stands between the lender and the borrower). If we need a loan to buy a car, we usually get it from a bank or finance company—that's a classic example of indirect finance. Once we get the loan, the car becomes one of our **assets**, and the loan becomes our **liability**. We all have assets and liabilities. Your assets probably include things of value like a bank account and a computer. If you have a student loan or credit card debt, those are among your liabilities. In contrast, if you borrowed directly from your parents or a friend, that would be an instance of direct finance: They own the asset (the loan), and you are obliged to pay them (rather than a bank) directly.

As finance grows increasingly sophisticated and complex, virtually all transactions take on some indirect flavor. Today, even direct finance usually involves a **financial institution** or **intermediary** in some fashion. When a lender purchases a security issued by a specific firm or government, the transaction typically takes place through a securities broker or an investment bank that helps the issuer distribute new stock or bonds. These securities become assets for the lenders who buy them and liabilities to the government or corporation that created them to obtain funds. Frequently, the lenders are themselves intermediaries, such as mutual funds, that gather and hold such securities for their investors.

Reflecting this trend toward *institutionalization,* the only lingering distinction between direct and indirect finance is who owns the underlying asset. Under direct finance, the asset holder has a direct claim on the borrower. In the case of indirect finance, the asset holder owns a claim on a financial institution (like a bank or mutual fund) that, in turn, owns a claim on the borrower.

Put differently, the historical gap between the two forms of finance has narrowed sharply over decades: Whether a modern financial transaction is direct or indirect, intermediaries are usually heavily involved (see Figure 3.1). As we will see later in

Figure 3.1 Funds Flowing through the Financial System

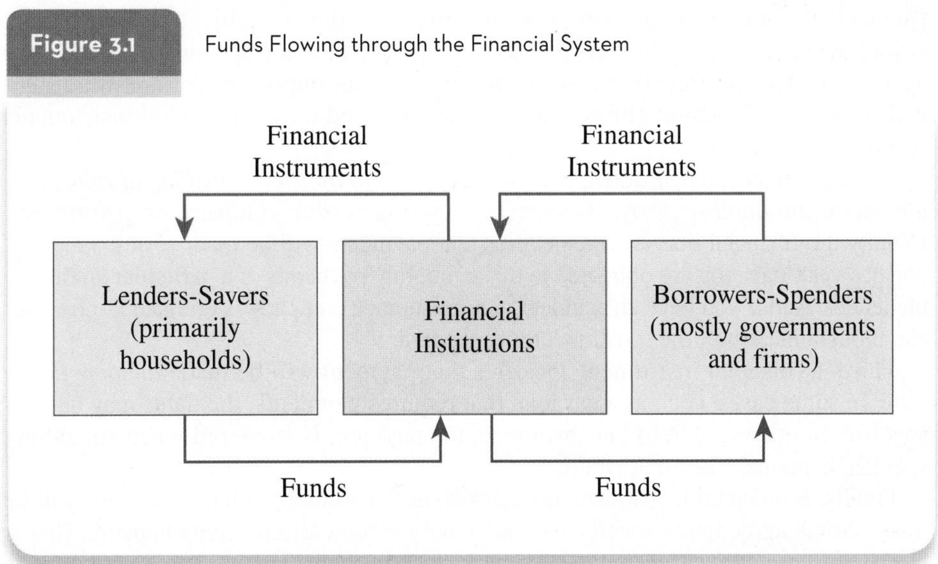

The financial system channels funds from lenders to borrowers through intermediaries. In **indirect finance,** a financial institution like a bank takes the resources from the lender in the form of a deposit (or something like it) and then provides them to the borrower in the form of a loan (or the equivalent). Even in the case of **direct finance,** where the saver acquires a direct claim on the user of the funds, a financial institution like a stockbroker or an investment bank is usually involved in the transaction.

this chapter (and especially in Chapters 11 through 14), the job of intermediaries is to produce and use the information that makes modern finance effective. As a result, users and providers of funds can better satisfy their needs, and economies can expand.

Indeed, such financial development is inextricably linked to economic growth. A country's financial system has to expand as its level of economic activity rises, or the country will stagnate. The role of the financial system is to facilitate production, employment, and consumption. In a prosperous economy, people have the means to pay for things, and resources flow to their most efficient uses. Savings are funneled through the system so that they can finance investment and allow the economy to grow. The decisions made by the people who do the saving direct the investment.

In this chapter, we will survey the financial system in three steps. First, we'll study *financial instruments,* or *securities,* as they are often called. Stocks, bonds, and loans of all types are financial instruments, as are more exotic agreements like options and insurance. Exactly what are these financial instruments, and what is their role in our economy? Second, we'll look at *financial markets,* such as the New York Stock Exchange and the Nasdaq (National Association of Securities Dealers Automatic Quotations), where investors can buy and sell stocks, bonds, and various other instruments. And finally, we'll look at *financial institutions*—what they are and what they do.

Financial Instruments

A **financial instrument** *is the written legal obligation of one party to transfer something of value, usually money, to another party at some future date, under specified conditions.* Let's dissect this definition to understand it better. First, a financial instrument is a *written legal obligation* that is subject to government enforcement. That is, a person can be compelled to take the action specified in the agreement. The enforceability of the obligation is an important feature of a financial instrument. Without enforcement of the specified terms, financial instruments would not exist.[2]

Second, a financial instrument obligates *one party to transfer something of value, usually money, to another party*. By *party,* we mean a person, company, or government. Usually the financial instrument specifies that payments will be made. For example, if you get a car loan, you are obligated to make monthly payments of a particular amount to the lender. And if you have an accident, your insurance company is obligated to fix your car, though the cost of the repair is left unspecified.

Third, a financial instrument specifies that payment will be made *at some future date.* In some cases, such as a car loan that requires payments, the dates may be very specific. In others, such as car insurance, the payment is triggered when something specific happens, like an accident.

Finally, a financial instrument *specifies conditions* under which a payment will be made. Some agreements specify payments only when certain events happen. That is clearly the case with car insurance and with stocks as well. The holder of a stock owns

[2] Myriad financial arrangements that exist outside the legal system, like loan sharking, are also enforced. But those sorts of obligations are not part of the formal financial system.

a small part of a firm and so can expect to receive occasional cash payments, called *dividends,* when the company is profitable. There is no way to know in advance, however, exactly when such payments will be made. In general, financial instruments specify a number of possible contingencies under which one party is required to make a payment to another.

Table 3.1 Uses of Financial Instruments

Means of payment:	Purchase of goods or services.
Store of value:	Transfer of purchasing power into the future.
Transfer of risk:	Transfer of risk from one person or company to another.

Uses of Financial Instruments

Stocks, loans, and insurance are all examples of financial instruments. Taking them as a group, we can see that they have three functions (see Table 3.1). Financial instruments can act as a means of payment, and they can also be stores of value. Thus, they offer two of the three uses of money. (Remember from Chapter 2 that money is a means of payment, a unit of account, and a store of value.) But financial instruments have a third function that can make them very different from money: They allow for the transfer of risk.

Recall that a means of payment is something that is generally accepted as payment for goods and services or repayment of a debt. It is possible to pay for purchases with financial instruments, even if they don't look much like money. An example is the willingness of employees to accept a company's stock as payment for working. (This means of payment was very popular in the late 1990s, when the stock market was booming.) While we cannot yet pay for groceries with shares of stock, the time may come when we can. For now, although some financial instruments may function as means of payment, they aren't terribly good ones.

Having a store of value means that your consumption doesn't need to exactly match your income. For days, months, and years, if necessary, you can spend more than you make, repaying the difference later. Even though most of us are paid weekly or monthly, we eat every day. As stores of value, financial instruments like stocks and bonds are thought to be better than money. Over time, they generate increases in wealth that on average exceed those we can obtain from holding money in most of its forms. These higher payoffs are compensation for higher levels of risk, because the payoffs from holding most financial instruments are generally more uncertain than those that arise from holding money. Nevertheless, many financial instruments can be used to transfer purchasing power into the future.

The third use of a financial instrument lies in its ability to *transfer risk* between the buyer and the seller. Most financial instruments involve some sort of risk transfer. For example, think of wheat farmers. If only one farm has a huge harvest, that farmer does very well. But if everyone's harvest is huge, then prices can plummet and individual farms can lose money. The risk that the harvest will be too good, resulting in low grain prices, is a risk that most individual farmers do not want to take. A *wheat futures contract* allows the farmer to transfer that risk to someone else. A wheat futures contract is a financial instrument in which two parties agree to exchange a fixed quantity of wheat on a prearranged future date at a specified price. By fixing the price at which the crop will be sold well in advance of the harvest, the farmer can forget about what happens in the wheat market because the risk has been transferred to someone else.

Insurance contracts are another example of a financial instrument that transfers risk—in this case, from individuals to an insurance company. Because a car accident can be financially catastrophic, we buy car insurance and transfer the risk to an insurance company. Because insurance companies make similar guarantees to a large group of people, they have the capacity to shoulder the risk. While the timing of an individual automobile accident is impossible to forecast, a predictable percentage of a large group of drivers will experience accidents over a given period.

Characteristics of Financial Instruments: Standardization and Information

As is obvious from the definition of a financial instrument, these sorts of contracts can be very complex. If you don't believe it, take a look at the fine print in a car insurance policy, a student loan, or even a credit card agreement. Complexity is costly. The more complicated something is, the more it costs to create and the more difficult it is to understand. As a rule, people do not want to bear these costs. Yes, the owner of an oil tanker may be willing to go to the expense of negotiating a specific insurance contract for each voyage a ship makes. The same owner may agree to make premium payments based on the load carried, the distance traveled, the route taken, and the weather expected. But for most of us, the cost of such custom contracts is simply too high.

In fact, people on both sides of financial contracts shy away from specialized agreements. Instead, they use standardized financial instruments to overcome the potential costs of complexity. Because of *standardization,* most of the financial instruments that we encounter on a day-to-day basis are very homogeneous. For example, most mortgages feature a standard application process and offer standardized terms. Automobile insurance contracts generally offer only certain standard options.

Standardization of terms makes sense. If all financial instruments differed in critical ways, most of us would not be able to understand them. Their usefulness would be severely limited. If the shares of Microsoft stock sold to one person differed in a crucial way from the shares sold to someone else, for instance, potential investors might not understand what they were buying. Even more important, the resale and trading of the shares would become virtually impossible, which would certainly discourage anyone from purchasing them in the first place. From this, we conclude that arrangements that obligate people to make payments to one another cannot all be one-of-a-kind arrangements.

INFORMATION

Another characteristic of financial instruments is that they communicate *information,* summarizing certain essential details about the issuer. How much do you really want to learn about the original issuer of a financial instrument? Or if you are purchasing an existing instrument, how much do you have to know about the person who is selling it to you? Surely, the less you feel you need to know to feel secure about the transaction, the better. Regardless of whether the instrument is a stock, a bond, a futures contract, or an insurance contract, the holder does not want to have to watch the issuer too closely; continuous monitoring is costly and difficult. Thus, financial instruments are designed to eliminate the expensive and time-consuming process of collecting such information.

A number of mechanisms exist to reduce the cost of monitoring the behavior of the counterparties to a financial arrangement. A **counterparty** is the person or institution on the other side of a contract. If you obtain a car loan from your local bank, then you are the bank's counterparty and the bank is yours. In the case of a stock or bond, the issuing firm and the investors who hold the instrument are counterparties.

Leverage
LESSONS FROM THE CRISIS

Households and firms often borrow to make investments. Obtaining a mortgage for a new home or selling a corporate bond to build a new plant are common examples. The use of borrowing to finance part of an investment is called *leverage*.* Leverage played a key role in the financial crisis of 2007–2009, so it is worth understanding how leverage relates to risk and how it can make the financial system vulnerable.

Modern economies rely heavily on borrowing to make investments. They are all leveraged. Yet, the more leverage, the greater the risk that an adverse surprise will lead to bankruptcy. If two households own houses of the same value, the one that has borrowed more—the one that is more highly leveraged and has less net worth—is the more likely to default during a temporary slump in income. This example could apply equally well to firms, financial institutions, or even countries.

Financial institutions are much more highly leveraged than households or firms, typically owning assets of about 10 times their net worth. During the crisis, some important financial firms leveraged more than 30 times their net worth.† Such high leverage meant that these firms would be vulnerable even to a minor decline in the value of their assets. For example, when a borrower is leveraged more than 30 times, a drop as small as 3 percent in asset prices could eliminate the cushion created by the net worth and lead to bankruptcy.

When highly leveraged financial institutions experience a loss, they usually try to reduce their leverage—that is, to *deleverage*—by selling assets and issuing securities that raise their net worth (see accompanying figure). However, everyone in the financial system cannot deleverage at once. When too many institutions try to sell assets simultaneously, their efforts will almost surely prove counterproductive: falling prices will mean more losses, diminishing their net worth further, raising leverage, and making the assets they hold seem riskier, thereby compelling further sales.

This "paradox of leverage" reinforces the destabilizing liquidity spiral discussed in Chapter 2 (see Lessons from the Crisis: Market Liquidity, Funding Liquidity, and Making Markets). Both spirals feed a vicious cycle of falling prices and widespread deleveraging that was a hallmark of the financial crisis of 2007–2009. The financial system steadied only after massive government interventions in response to the plunge of many asset prices.

*For a technical definition of leverage, see the Tools of the Trade box in Chapter 5. For the evolution of U.S. commercial bank leverage, look at the FRED data series "EQTA."

†A bank's net worth—its assets minus liabilities—is commonly known as *bank capital*. We will discuss this in more detail in Chapter 12.

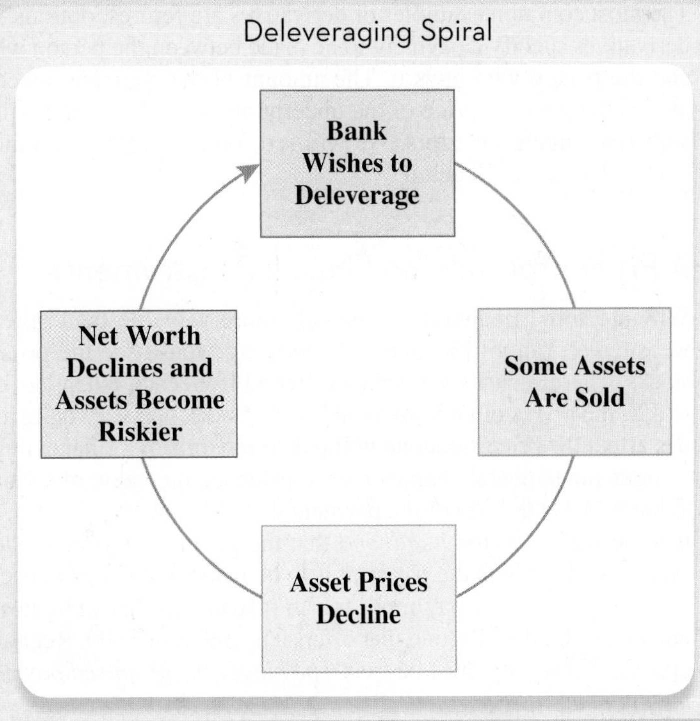

The solution to the high cost of obtaining information on the parties to a financial instrument is to standardize both the instrument and the information provided about the issuer. We can also hire a specialist whom we all trust to do the monitoring. The institutions that have arisen over the years to support the existence of financial instruments provide an environment in which everyone can feel secure about the behavior of the counterparties to an agreement.

In addition to simply summarizing information, financial instruments are designed to handle the problem of *asymmetric information,* which comes from the fact that borrowers have some information they don't disclose to lenders. Instead of buying new ovens, will a bread baker use a $50,000 loan to take an extended vacation in Tahiti? The lender wants to make sure the borrower is not misrepresenting what he or she will do with borrowed funds. Thus, the financial system is set up to gather information on borrowers before giving them resources and to monitor their use of the resources afterward. These specialized mechanisms were developed to handle the problem of asymmetric information.

Underlying versus Derivative Instruments

There are two fundamental classes of financial instruments. The first, **underlying instruments** (sometimes called *primitive securities*), are used by savers/lenders to transfer resources directly to investors/borrowers. Through these instruments, the financial system improves the efficient allocation of resources in the real economy.

The primary examples of underlying securities or instruments are stocks and bonds that offer payments based solely on the issuer's status. Bonds, for example, make payments depending on the solvency of the firm that issued them. Stocks sometimes pay dividends when the issuing corporation's profits are sufficient.

The second class of financial instruments is known as **derivative instruments**. Their value and payoffs are "derived" from the behavior of the underlying instruments. The most common examples of derivatives are futures, options, and swaps. In general, derivatives specify a payment to be made between the person who sells the instrument and the person who buys it. The amount of the payment depends on various factors associated with the price of the underlying asset. The primary use of derivatives is to shift risk among investors. We will see some examples in a moment; Chapter 9 discusses derivatives in detail.

A Primer for Valuing Financial Instruments

Why are some financial instruments more valuable than others? If you look at the websites of Yahoo! Finance or Bloomberg, you'll see the prices of many bonds and stocks. These securities are quite different from each other. Not only that, but from day to day, the prices of an individual bond or stock can vary quite a bit. What characteristics affect the price someone will pay to buy or sell a financial instrument?

Four fundamental characteristics influence the value of a financial instrument (see Table 3.2): (1) the *size* of the payment that is promised, (2) *when* the promised payment is to be made, (3) the *likelihood* that the payment will be made, and (4) the *circumstances* under which the payment is to be made. Let's look at each one of these traits.

First, people will pay more for an instrument that obligates the issuer to pay the holder $1,000 than for one that offers a payment of $100. Regardless of any other conditions, this simply must be true: *The bigger the promised payment, the more valuable the financial instrument.*

Table 3.2 What Makes a Financial Instrument Valuable?

Size: Payments that are larger are more valuable.
Timing: Payments that are made sooner are more valuable.
Likelihood: Payments that are more likely to be made are more valuable.
Circumstances: Payments that are made when we need them most are more valuable.

Second, if you are promised a payment of $100 sometime in the future, you will want to know when you will receive it. Receiving $100 tomorrow is different from receiving $100 next year. This simple example illustrates a very general proposition: *The sooner the payment is made, the more valuable is the promise to make it.* Time has value because of opportunity cost. If you receive a payment immediately, you have an opportunity to invest or consume it right away. If you don't receive the payment until later, you lose that opportunity.

The third factor that affects the value of a financial instrument is the odds that the issuer will meet the obligation to make the payment. Regardless of how conscientious and diligent the party who made the promise is, there remains some possibility that the payment will not be made. Because risk requires compensation, the impact of this uncertainty on the value of a financial instrument is clear: *The more likely it is that the payment will be made, the more valuable the financial instrument.*

Finally, the value of a financial instrument is affected by the conditions under which a promised payment is to be made. Insurance is the best example. We buy car insurance to receive a payment if we have an accident, so we can repair the car. No one buys insurance that pays off when good things happen. *Payments that are made when we need them most are more valuable than other payments.*[3]

Examples of Financial Instruments

We'll have quite a bit to say about financial instruments in Part II (Chapters 4–10) of the book. For now, let's take a look at some of the most common varieties. The best way to organize them is by whether they are used primarily as stores of value or for trading risk.

Financial Instruments Used Primarily as Stores of Value

1. ***Bank loans.*** A borrower obtains resources from a lender immediately in exchange for a promised set of payments in the future. The borrower, who can be either an individual or a firm, needs funds to make an investment or purchase, while the lender is looking for a way to store value into the future.
2. ***Bonds.*** Bonds are a form of loan. In exchange for obtaining funds today, a corporation or government promises to make payments in the future. While bond

[3]This conclusion is related to the principle of declining marginal utility, which you may recall from your study of microeconomics. The idea is that the satisfaction obtained from consumption declines as the level of consumption increases. Each succeeding candy bar brings less pleasure than the last one. Thus, a financial instrument that pays off when marginal utility is high is worth more than one that pays off when marginal utility is low. This means that payoffs that are made when income and wealth are low are more valuable than payoffs that are made when income and wealth are high.

Disability Income Insurance

YOUR FINANCIAL WORLD

People insure their houses so they can rebuild them if they burn down. They insure their cars so they can repair them if they have an accident. And they insure their lives so their families will be financially secure if they die prematurely. But few people insure their most important asset: their ability to produce an income. The biggest risk all of us face is that we will become disabled and lose our earning capacity. Insuring it should be one of our highest priorities.

If you think this advice is alarmist, just look at a few numbers. About one in four 20-year-olds will become disabled for 90 days or longer during their working lives. In fact, the chance you'll become disabled is far higher than the chance of your house suffering a serious fire—which over 40 years is less than 1 in 35.*

Fortunately, you may already have some disability insurance. The government provides some through Social Security; your employer may insure you; and if you're injured on the job and can't work, there is always workers' compensation insurance. But is that enough? You should evaluate what your needs are likely to be. If the disability insurance you already have is not enough, you should buy more. While it isn't very pleasant to think about what would happen if you became disabled, you need to do it. Surely this is one risk you should transfer to someone else.

*Official statistics indicate that a serious fire occurs in roughly 1 of 1,450 houses each year. So there is a 1,449 chance in 1,450 of a house *not* suffering a big fire in any given year. Over a 40-year period, the probability that a serious fire will *not* occur is $(1{,}449/1{,}450)^{40} = 0.973$. That means the chance of a serious fire is 2.7 percent, or fewer than 1 in 35 houses.

payments are often stated in fixed dollars, they need not be. Unlike most bank loans, most bonds can be bought and sold in financial markets. Like bank loans, bonds are used by the borrower to finance current operations and by the lender to store value.

3. ***Home mortgages.*** Most people who wish to purchase a home need to borrow some portion of the funds. A mortgage is a loan that is used to purchase real estate. In exchange for the funds, the borrower promises to make a series of payments. The house is collateral for the loan. **Collateral** is the term used to describe specific assets a borrower pledges to protect the lender's interests in the event of nonpayment. If the payments aren't made, the lender can take the house, a process called *foreclosure.*
4. ***Stocks.*** The holder of a share of a company's stock owns a small piece of the firm and is entitled to part of its profits. The owner of a firm sells stock as a way of raising funds to enlarge operations as well as a way of transferring the risk of ownership to someone else. Buyers of stocks use them primarily as stores of wealth.
5. ***Asset-backed securities.*** **Asset-backed securities (ABS)** are shares in the returns or payments arising from specific assets, such as home mortgages, student loans, credit card debt, or even movie box-office receipts. Investors purchase shares in the revenue that comes from these underlying assets. The most prominent of these instruments are **mortgage-backed securities (MBS)**, which bundle a large number of mortgages together into a pool in which shares are then sold. Securities backed by *subprime* mortgages—loans to borrowers who are less likely to repay than borrowers of conventional mortgages—played an important role in the financial crisis of 2007–2009 (see Chapter 7, Lessons from the Crisis: Subprime Mortgages). The owners of these securities receive a share of the

payments made by the homeowners who borrowed the funds. Asset-backed securities are an innovation that allows funds in one part of the country to find productive uses elsewhere. Thus, the availability of some sorts of financing no longer depends on local credit conditions.[4]

Financial Instruments Used Primarily to Transfer Risk

1. ***Insurance contracts.*** The primary purpose of insurance policies is to ensure that payments will be made under particular, and often rare, circumstances. These instruments exist expressly to transfer risk from one party to another.
2. ***Futures contracts.*** A futures contract is an agreement between two parties to exchange a fixed quantity of a commodity (such as wheat or corn) or an asset (such as a bond) at a fixed price on a set future date. A futures contract always specifies the *price* at which the transaction will take place. A futures contract is a type of derivative instrument, since its value is based on the price of some other asset. It is used to transfer the risk of price fluctuations from one party to another.
3. ***Options.*** Like futures contracts, options are derivative instruments whose prices are based on the value of some underlying asset. Options give the holder the right, but not the obligation, to buy or sell a fixed quantity of the underlying asset at a predetermined price either on a specified date or at any time during a specified period.
4. ***Swaps.*** Swap contracts are agreements to exchange two specific cash flows at certain times in the future (as discussed in Chapter 9). For example, an interest rate swap might involve the exchange of payments based on a fixed rate of interest for payments based on a rate of interest that fluctuates (or "floats") with the market. Swaps come in many varieties, reflecting differences in maturity, payment frequency, and underlying cash flows. The cash flows and other contractual arrangements usually are designed so that there is no upfront fee for the swap.

These are just a few examples of the most prominent financial instruments. Together, they allow people to buy and sell almost any sort of payment on any date under any circumstances. Thus, they offer the opportunity to store value and trade risk in almost any way that one might want.[5] When you encounter a financial instrument for the first time, try to figure out whether it is used primarily for storing value or for transferring risk. Then try to identify which characteristics determine its value.

Financial Markets

Financial markets are the places where financial instruments are bought and sold. They are the economy's central nervous system, relaying and reacting to information quickly, allocating resources, and determining prices. In doing so, financial markets

[4]For an introduction to how asset-backed securities work, see Andreas Jobst, "What Is Securitization?" *Finance and Development*, International Monetary Fund, September 2008.

[5]An important exception is the common desire to borrow using future income as collateral. While young people with good career prospects might wish to spend their future earnings now, lenders worry that such loans will diminish the borrower's incentive to work and repay.

Table 3.3 The Role of Financial Markets

Market liquidity: Ensure that owners of financial instruments can buy and sell them cheaply and easily.

Information: Pool and communicate information about the issuer of a financial instrument.

Risk sharing: Provide individuals with a place to buy and sell risks, sharing them with others.

enable both firms and individuals to find financing for their activities. When they are working well, new firms can start up and existing firms can grow; individuals who don't have sufficient savings can borrow to purchase cars and houses. By ensuring that resources are available to those who can put them to the best use, and by keeping the costs of transactions as low as possible, these markets promote economic efficiency. When financial markets cease to function properly, resources are no longer channeled to their best possible use, and we all suffer.[6]

In this section, we will look at the role of financial markets and the economic justification for their existence. Next, we will examine the structure of the markets and how they are organized. Finally, we will look at the characteristics that are essential for the markets to work smoothly.

The Role of Financial Markets

Financial markets serve three roles in our economic system (see Table 3.3). They offer savers and borrowers *liquidity;* they pool and communicate *information;* and they allow *risk sharing.* We encountered the concept of market liquidity in our discussion of money, where we defined it as the ease with which an asset can be turned into money without loss of value. Without financial markets and the institutional structure that supports them, selling the assets we own would be extremely difficult. Thus, we cannot overstate the importance of liquidity for the smooth operation of an economy. Just think what would happen if the stock market were open only one day a month. Stocks would surely become less attractive investments. If you had an emergency and needed money immediately, you probably would not be able to sell your stocks in time. Liquidity is a crucial characteristic of financial markets.

Related to liquidity is the fact that financial markets need to be designed in a way that keeps transactions costs—the cost of buying and selling—low. If you want to buy or sell a stock, you must pay a licensed professional to complete the purchase or sale on your behalf: A **broker** can find you a counterparty, a **dealer** can act as the counterparty, and a broker-dealer can do either or both. While this service can't be free, it is important to keep its cost relatively low. The very high trading volumes that we see in the stock market—several billion shares per day in the United States—is evidence that U.S. stock markets have low transactions costs and are usually very liquid. (One U.S. market in which transactions costs are high is the market for housing. Once you add together everything you pay agents, bankers, and lawyers, you have spent almost 10 percent of the sale price of the house to complete the transaction. The housing market is not very liquid.)

Financial markets pool and communicate information about the issuers of financial instruments, summarizing it in the form of a price. Does a company have good prospects for future growth and profits? If so, its stock price will be high; if not, its stock price will be low. Is a borrower likely to repay a bond? The more likely repayment is, the

[6]An example demonstrates the point. Following the September 11, 2001, terrorist attacks, the New York Stock Exchange became inaccessible, and other markets were not functioning properly. Alarmed government officials took measures to ensure that markets would open as soon as possible so that trading could proceed. Without these efforts to get the financial markets up and running, the financial system might quickly have come to a standstill.

higher the price of the bond. Obtaining the answers to these questions is time consuming and costly. Most of us just don't have the resources or know-how to do it. Instead, we turn to the financial markets to summarize the information for us so that we can look it up on a website.

Finally, while financial instruments are the means for transferring risk, financial markets are the place where we can do it. The markets allow us to buy and sell risks, holding the ones we want and getting rid of the ones we don't want. As we will see in Chapter 5, a prudent investor holds a collection of assets called a **portfolio**, which includes a number of stocks and bonds as well as various forms of money. A well-designed portfolio has a lower overall risk than any individual stock or bond. An investor constructs it by buying and selling financial instruments in the marketplace. Without the market, we wouldn't be able to share risk.

The Structure of Financial Markets

There are lots of financial markets and many ways to categorize them. Just take a look at any source of business news. You will see charts and tables for domestic stocks, global stocks, bonds and interest rates, the dollar exchange rate, commodities, and more. Keep going and you will find references to stock markets, bond markets, credit markets, currency trading, options, futures, new securities, and on and on. Grasping the overall structure of all these financial markets requires grouping them in some sort of meaningful way—but how?

There are three possibilities (see Table 3.4). First, we can distinguish between markets where new financial instruments are sold and those where they are resold, or traded. Second, we can categorize the markets by the way they trade financial instruments—whether on a centralized exchange or not. And third, we can group them based on the type of instrument they trade—those that are used primarily as a store of

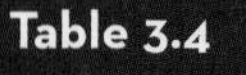

Table 3.4 The Structure of Financial Markets

Primary versus Secondary Markets	
Primary markets:	Markets where newly issued securities are sold.
Secondary markets:	Markets where existing securities are traded.
Centralized Exchanges versus Over-the-Counter Markets	
Centralized exchanges:	Secondary markets where dealers meet in a central, physical location.
Over-the-counter markets:	Decentralized secondary markets where dealers stand ready to buy and sell securities electronically.
Electronic communication networks (ECNs):	An electronic system that brings buyers and sellers together for electronic execution of trades without the use of a broker or dealer.
Debt and Equity versus Derivatives Markets	
Debt and equity markets:	Markets where financial claims are bought and sold for immediate cash payment.
Derivatives markets:	Markets where claims based on an underlying asset are traded for payment at a later date.

Trading in Financial Markets

TOOLS OF THE TRADE

Trading is what makes financial markets work. No one would ever buy a stock or bond if he or she couldn't sell it. Let's take a brief look at how trading works. For this example, we will focus on the stock market.

Placing an order in a stock market is a bit like going to a fast-food restaurant or a coffee shop. You have to enter your order and wait to be served. Not only that, but the order can be very complicated, and how long you wait depends on both what you ordered and how many other people are waiting to be served.

If you place an order, it will have a number of important characteristics:

- The stock you wish to trade.
- Whether you wish to buy or sell.
- The size of the order—how many shares you wish to trade.
- The price at which you would like to trade.

You can place either a *market order*, in which case your order is executed at the most favorable price currently available on the other side, or a *limit order*, which places a maximum on the price you wish to pay to buy or a minimum on the price you will accept to sell. Placing a market order means you value speed over price; you want the trade to occur as soon as possible and are willing to pay for the privilege. By contrast, you can specify a time at which the limit order is canceled if it hasn't been filled.

Executing the trade requires finding someone to take the other side. To do this, you can seek the help of a broker, who might place your order on an exchange, or find a counterparty through a trading system known as an automated electronic communication network (ECN).

ECNs operate in a very simple way. If you want to buy, you enter a bid. If your bid is better than everyone else's, and there is someone willing to sell at or below the price you bid, then you trade immediately. Otherwise, your bid goes into an order book to wait for a seller. Customer orders interact automatically following a set of priority rules established by the network, but with no one acting as an intermediary in the transaction. The liquidity in the market is provided by the customers.

For a stock like IBM or GE, the New York Stock Exchange is an alternative place to send the order. On the NYSE, liquidity provided by customer orders may be supplemented by designated market makers* (DMMs). A DMM is the person on the floor of the stock exchange charged with making a market, ensuring that it is liquid so that people can both buy and sell and that prices aren't overly volatile. For the most part, electronic mechanisms simply match the orders as they come in, keeping track of orders that are outstanding.

On the next page is a portion of the screen from the trading book of the BZX Exchange, which is one of four U.S. equities exchanges operated by the Chicago Board Options Exchange (CBOE). The screen shows outstanding bids and offers for the **exchange-traded fund (ETF)** called SPY just after 4 p.m. on March 19, 2019. An ETF is a marketable security that tracks an index, a commodity, bonds, or a basket of assets like an index fund. The SPY is the most actively traded ETF. It tracks the Standard & Poor's 500 Index of the largest companies in the United States (see Chapter 8).

The system shows more than 15,000 limit orders (bids in green; asks in blue) within a few cents of the most recent

*For a description of designated market makers, see www.nyse.com/publicdocs/nyse/markets/nyse/designated_market_makers.pdf.

value or those that are used to transfer risk. We'll use the vocabulary that is common as of this writing. Bear in mind that there are no hard-and-fast rules for the terminology used to describe these markets, so it may change.

Primary versus Secondary Markets A **primary financial market** is one in which a borrower obtains funds from a lender by selling newly issued securities. Businesses use primary markets to raise the resources they need to grow. Governments use them to finance ongoing operations. Most of the action in primary markets occurs out of public view. While a few companies that want to raise funds go directly to the financial markets themselves, most use an investment bank. The bank examines the company's financial health to determine whether the proposed issue is sound. Assuming that it is, the bank will determine a price and then purchase the securities execution price ($282.04). The system combines the sell (buy) orders of different customers at each price, so we see the aggregate supply (demand) for the security at that price. If a market sell order for 100 shares were to arrive, the system would match that order with the highest bid ($282.03). If a market buy order for 100 shares were to arrive, the system would match that order with the lowest ask ($282.04). Nearly 8 million SPY shares had already traded that day on this exchange, or roughly 40 percent of the SPY ETF trades executed on the four CBOE exchanges.

Book Viewer » **BZX Equities** BYX Equities EDGX Equities EDGA Equities — Market Quality Statistics

Shows the top bids and asks for any symbol.

SPY			Orders Accepted	Total Volume
SPDR S&P 500 ETF TR TR UNIT			2,001,483	7,744,560

	TOP OF BOOK		LAST 10 TRADES		
	Shares	Price	Time	Price	Shares
ASKS	3,100	282.2900	16:02:50	282.2300	100
ASKS	600	282.2800	16:02:50	282.2300	30
ASKS	600	282.2700	16:02:46	282.2300	300
ASKS	2,800	282.2600	16:02:40	282.2600	100
ASKS	100	282.2400	16:02:40	282.2600	88
BIDS	1,300	282.2300	16:02:40	282.2600	12
BIDS	2,900	282.2200	16:02:40	282.2500	30
BIDS	700	282.2100	16:02:39	282.2500	100
BIDS	600	282.2000	16:02:38	282.2600	300
BIDS	2,900	282.1900	16:02:38	282.2550	100

Last updated 16:02:52

SOURCE: CBOE Book Viewer of BZX trading, March 19, 2019, http://markets.cboe.com/us/equities/market_statistics/book/SPY.

in preparation for resale to clients. This activity, called *underwriting,* is usually very profitable, both for the underwriters and the share purchasers. In a few notable instances, however, such as the 2012 offering of Facebook (FB) shares, many investors lost heavily as the value of the new shares quickly plunged. Because small investors are not customers of large investment banks, most of us do not have direct access to these new securities.

Everyone knows about **secondary financial markets**. Those are the markets where people can buy and sell existing securities. If you want to buy a share of stock in ExxonMobil or Microsoft, you won't get it from the company itself. Instead, you'll buy it in a secondary market from another investor. The prices in the secondary markets are the ones we hear about in the news.

Secondary-Market Trading in Stocks Buying a stock is not like buying a pair of shoes. You can't just go into a store, ask for the stock you want, pay for it with your credit card, and walk out with it in a bag. Instead, you typically ask a broker-dealer to buy the stock for you. Whether the broker-dealer obtains it by purchasing it from others or sells it to you from the broker-dealer's own account, your acquisition of the stock is a secondary-market transaction.

The organization of secondary markets for stocks and other securities is changing rapidly. Historically, there have been two types of financial market: **centralized exchanges** and **over-the-counter (OTC) markets**. Some organizations, like the New York Stock Exchange (NYSE) and the large exchanges in London and Tokyo, originated as centralized exchanges, where dealers gathered in person to trade stocks, usually through a system of "open outcry"—shouting bids and offers or using hand signals to make agreements. Others, like the Nasdaq, developed as OTC markets, which are collections of dealers who trade with one another via computer (or, formerly, via phone) from wherever they sit. More recently, **electronic communication networks (ECNs)** have enabled traders (or their brokers) to find counterparties who wish to trade in specific stocks, including those listed on an exchange.

The pace of structural change has accelerated dramatically in the past few years, driven by (1) ongoing technological advances in computing and communications and (2) increasing globalization. The former dramatically lowered the importance of a physical location of an exchange—as new technology allowed the rapid low-cost transmission of orders across long distances—while the latter encouraged unprecedented cross-border mergers of exchanges, integrating larger pools of providers and users of funds.

As part of this process, electronic OTC markets like the Nasdaq and some ECNs have gained the official status of regulated exchanges without establishing a central place of operation. Shifting in the opposite direction, the NYSE has been acquired by Intercontinental Exchange (ICE). And, today a large share of equity trading takes place away from the NYSE floor. Even there, the old system of open outcry has been replaced (as on most exchanges) by computers that record orders, execute transactions, and report trades.[7]

Table 3.5 highlights the multiplicity of trading venues and the fragmentation of U.S. stock trading. For three groups of listed stocks—NYSE, Nasdaq, and NYSE Arca (an all-electronic exchange that includes many exchange-traded funds)—it displays the volume of trading at key venues, as well as the total volume (composite) on one day in March 2019. Most important, the top row—Finra/Nasdaq TRF—is not an exchange, but rather a "trade-reporting facility" that allows broker-dealers to report trades executed off exchange. For example, these trades may occur in "dark pools" that are accessible primarily to institutional investors for the execution of large "block trades." After that, the largest single portion of trading in each group of stocks typically occurs on its listing exchange, but as the table highlights, this may be significantly less than one-half of the daily volume. The right-hand column shows the total trading on each venue, including other shares in addition to the three groups highlighted.

Trading on decentralized electronic exchanges—rather than a physically central one—has advantages and disadvantages. On the plus side, customers can see the orders (look at Tools of the Trade: Trading in Financial Markets on page 56), the orders are executed quickly, trading occurs 24 hours a day, and costs are low. In addition, decentralization reduces a menacing operational risk that became evident on

[7]NYSE still assigns "designated market makers" to provide liquidity in selected stocks, but their importance is declining amid the high volume of rapid electronic trade executions.

Table 3.5 Volume by Market (Millions of Shares), March 15, 2019

Platform	NYSE	Nasdaq	NYSE Arca	Total
Finra/Nasdaq TRF	1,507	1,096	379	3,035
New York	2,720	44	47	2,813
Nasdaq	434	1,464	143	2,051
BZX/BYX Equities	355	199	153	718
NYSE Arca	190	177	271	649
EDGA/EDGX Equities	240	160	95	648
Composite	5,766	3,315	1,198	10,437

NOTE: The table shows only those platforms where volume exceeded 400 million shares that day. The volumes for the BZX and BYX exchanges are summed, as are the volumes for the EDGA and EDGX exchanges. The composite, which shows the reported total volume in each class of shares, includes trading on smaller venues. Similarly, the right-hand column ("Total") includes trading in other shares as well.

SOURCE: Author calculations based on Market Data Center. New York: *The Wall Street Journal*, 2019.

September 11, 2001, a time before computers dominated the floor of the NYSE and people still depended on gathering there to trade. The NYSE building stood only a few blocks from the World Trade Center. Although the NYSE building was not damaged when the Twin Towers fell, the floor of the exchange became inaccessible. Because trading on the NYSE depended on people meeting there, trading stopped; it did not resume until Monday, September 17. Yet, while New York dealers were shut down, dealers elsewhere in the country could trade via the Nasdaq.

But no system of trading is free of problems. On the minus side, electronic operations have proven prone to errors that threaten the existence of brokers. In addition, amid the complex system of multiple, imperfectly linked exchanges, new trading patterns have arisen that render the entire system fragile, raising serious worries among investors about the liquidity and value of their stocks. For example, consider the following events:

- On December 8, 2005, a "fat-finger incident" cost a Japanese broker more than $300 million when an employee mistyped a sell order.
- On May 6, 2010, a rush of electronic sell orders from one mutual fund's **trading algorithm** (a rule-based program for automatically executing hundreds or thousands of trades) immediately preceded the "flash crash," in which the stock prices of leading U.S. corporations plunged to as low as a penny only to recover all or most of their losses within minutes. The willingness of market makers to provide liquidity (by temporarily purchasing the equities offered for sale) may have been overwhelmed by additional sales from risk-sensitive, **high-frequency traders (HFTs),** who can purchase and sell thousands of stocks in a matter of seconds.[8]

[8]For more information on the 2010 flash crash, see the staff report of the Commodity Futures Trading Commission (CFTC) and Securities and Exchange Commission (SEC), *Findings Regarding the Market Events of May 6, 2010*, www.sec.gov/news/studies/2010/marketevents-report.pdf. For details of the 2015 flash crash, see the SEC research note "Equity Market Volatility on August 24, 2015," www.sec.gov./marketstructure/research/equity_market_volatility.pdf.

- On August 1, 2012, a problem with one U.S. broker's trading algorithm triggered large price swings in many stocks, cost the firm an estimated $440 million, and wiped out about three-fourths of its market value in a day.
- On August 24, 2015, in another "flash crash," the Dow experienced its largest intraday point drop (1,089 points) before bouncing back, while the price of several active exchange-traded funds (each of which represents a portfolio of stocks) temporarily plunged well below the net asset value of their constituent stocks (see Applying the Concept: Basics of High-Frequency Trading).
- On February 5, 2018, a day of high price volatility when the S&P 500 Index dropped by 4.1 percent, numerous brokerages and asset managers experienced website outages that prevented their customers from tracking their portfolios and executing orders.

In addition to concerns about fragility of the trading system as a whole, efforts to speed up electronic trading drain resources from more efficient uses. To see this point, imagine that an HFT firm relocates its computing facilities closer to an exchange so that it can cut the transmission time for orders by a few microseconds (millionths of a second). The goal of the move is to profit by trading an instant faster than competitors when new information becomes available, such as a stock issuer's quarterly profit statement or the nation's monthly employment report. Yet microsecond gains in trading speed likely diminish the willingness of market makers to provide liquidity because they don't wish to be "picked off" by well-equipped HFTs.[9]

Finally, the advent of multiple electronic exchanges and ECNs has not resulted in a single, integrated, and transparent U.S. stock market. In such an ideal market, the best

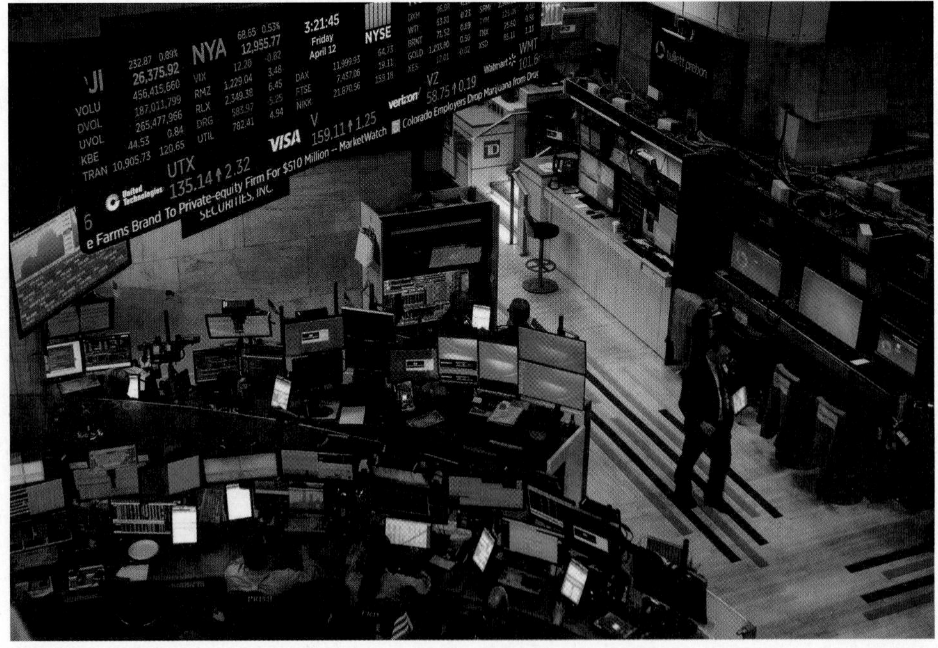

An exchange trading floor now is mostly filled by computers, rather than brokers.

JOHANNES EISELE/AFP/Getty Images

[9] Imagine that the TV quiz show *Jeopardy!* allowed a contestant to install her own faster buzzer. Other contestants might hesitate to play or be compelled to invest in similar (or better) equipment.

Basics of High-Frequency Trading
APPLYING THE CONCEPT

High-frequency trading (HFT) refers to the rapid-fire bids, offers, and executions that now dominate secondary-market trading in stocks, bonds, foreign exchange, and futures. And the frequency is indeed very high—time intervals are measured in nanoseconds (billionths of a second). HFT is based on, but not identical to, electronic trading.

The advantages of electronic trading systems are well known. Customers can see orders and watch as they are executed at low cost. And decentralization of electronic networks increases competition and reduces the likelihood of widespread operational failures, like the shutdown of the New York Stock Exchange that followed the terrorist attack of September 11, 2001.

HFT, however, poses at least five problems. First, it amplifies the risks of electronic operations. HFT depends on computer algorithms—rule-based programs for automatic order submission. When a program goes awry, it can threaten a trading firm's existence, injure its counterparties, and even put an entire market at risk.

A second problem is that the complex real-time interaction of HFT algorithms can overwhelm trading platforms and disrupt the markets. That may be what happened during the flash crash in the equity market on May 6, 2010—when equity prices plunged by nearly 10 percent in minutes only to recover during the following half hour—and in the Treasury flash rally on October 15, 2014, when the 10-year Treasury bond yield plunged by 16 basis points and rebounded—all within 12 minutes.

Third, the prevalence of HFT weakens the position of market makers, who provide liquidity to traditional investors. Market makers must charge a premium on all trades to cover their losses when a speedy algorithm accepts their outdated (by nanoseconds) bids and offers before they can be altered in response to market-moving news. Over time, this situation could undermine market making altogether.

Fourth, HFT creates a temptation for "front-running" (trading ahead of) customer orders, which damages investor confidence in the market and may be the worst impact of HFT. A result is that some investors look for safer places to trade, with the unintended consequence of fragmenting markets. In the U.S. equity market, for example, trading has shifted to electronic networks that need not report their off-market bids and offers to public exchanges. As a result, bids and offers brought to a public exchange may not receive the best possible price execution.

Fifth, HFT can trigger a socially unproductive arms race in which traders spend billions of dollars on equipment to shave a few nanoseconds off the market response to economic news. This behavior diverts resources from more fruitful activities, reducing the productive capacity of the economy as a whole.

Economists have proposed remedies for the problems of HFT. One example is the proposal to use frequent batch auctions (say, at one-second intervals), which would, in the words of one advocate, "transform competition on speed into competition on price." More generally, mechanisms that place a grain of sand in the HFT gears may preserve the liquidity benefits of improved technology while reducing its costly side effects.

bid from any customer would instantly and costlessly be matched against the best offer, and all parties could see the entire schedule of bids and offers prior to trading. Currently, a government rule known as the National Best Bid and Offer (NBBO) mechanism requires brokers to provide the best prevailing prices to customers. Other government rules make all trades visible *after* they occur.

However, not all bids and offers are visible *prior* to a trade. For example, if an ECN is carrying a bid or offer that differs from the latest trade price, it need not be reported to the broader market.[10] In effect, the limit-order books of ECNs are not fully integrated with the limit-order books on regulated exchanges or with each other. The existence of multiple, disconnected order books means that a customer's order may not be executed at the best possible price. So despite all the costly and sophisticated electronic technology, better integration of the U.S. equity market remains an important subject for investors and regulators alike.

[10]The lack of transparency results in a segmentation of market liquidity between an ECN on the one hand and exchanges and other ECNs on the other. Referring to this opacity, observers sometimes use the term *dark pool* to describe the market liquidity in ECNs.

Debt and Equity versus Derivative Markets A useful way to think of the structure of financial markets is to distinguish between markets where *debt and equity* are traded and those where *derivative instruments* are traded. **Debt markets** are the markets for loans, mortgages, and bonds—the instruments that allow for the transfer of resources from lenders to borrowers and at the same time give investors a store of value for their wealth. **Equity markets** are the markets for stocks. For the most part, stocks are traded in the countries where the companies are based. U.S. companies' stocks are traded in the United States, Japanese stocks in Japan, Chinese stocks in China, and so on. In the United States, at the end of 2018, the market value of corporate equities was $42.9 trillion, while debt securities (including government debt) outstanding totaled $45.0 trillion. Derivative markets are the markets where investors trade instruments like futures, options, and swaps, which are designed primarily to transfer risk. To put it another way, in debt and equity markets, actual claims are bought and sold for immediate cash payment; in derivative markets, investors make agreements that are settled later.

Looking at debt instruments in more detail, we can place them in one of two categories, depending on the length of time until the final payment, called the loan's maturity. Debt instruments that are completely repaid in less than a year (from their original issue date) are traded in **money markets**, while those with a maturity of more than a year are traded in **bond markets**. *Money-market instruments* have different names and are treated somewhat differently from *bond market instruments.* For example, the United States Treasury issues Treasury bills, which have a maturity of less than one year when they are issued and are traded in the money market. U.S. Treasury notes, which are repaid at the end of 2 to 10 years, trade in the bond markets, as do U.S. Treasury bonds, which are repaid at the end of 20 to 30 years. The same distinction can be made for large private corporations, which issue commercial paper when borrowing for short periods and corporate bonds when borrowing for long periods.

Characteristics of a Well-Run Financial Market

Well-run financial markets exhibit a few essential characteristics that are related to the role we ask them to play in our economies. First, these markets must be designed to keep transaction costs low. Second, the information the market pools and communicates must be both accurate and widely available. If analysts do not communicate accurate assessments of the firms they follow, the markets will not generate the correct prices for the firms' stocks. The prices of financial instruments reflect all the information that is available to market participants. Those prices are the link between the financial markets and the real economy, ensuring that resources are allocated to their most efficient uses. If the information that goes into the market is wrong, then the prices will be wrong, and the economy will not operate as effectively as it could.

INFORMATION

Finally, investors need protection. For the financial system to work at all, borrowers' promises to pay lenders must be credible. Individuals must be assured that their investments will not simply be stolen. Lenders must be able to enforce their right to receive repayment (or to seize the collateral) quickly and at low cost. In countries that have weak investor protections, firms can behave deceptively, borrowing when they have no intention of repaying the funds and going unpunished. The lack of proper safeguards dampens people's willingness to invest. Thus, governments are an essential part of financial markets, because they set and enforce the rules of the game. While informal lending networks do develop and flourish spontaneously, they can accommodate only simple, small-scale transactions. Because modern financial

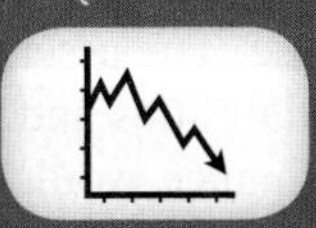

Shadow Banks
LESSONS FROM THE CRISIS

Over the past few decades, financial intermediation and leverage in the United States has shifted away from traditional banks* and toward other financial institutions that are less subject to government rules. These other intermediaries include brokerages, consumer and mortgage finance firms, insurers, investment organizations (such as hedge funds and private equity firms†), money-market mutual funds (MMMFs), and even bank-created asset management firms, such as special investment vehicles (SIVs).

These other intermediaries have come to be known as *shadow banks* because they provide services that compete with or substitute for those supplied by traditional banks. Unlike banks, however, shadow banks do not accept deposits. In addition, the leverage and risk taking of shadow banks can be greater than that of traditional banks while being less transparent.

Beginning in the 1970s, financial innovation sped the shift of intermediation to the shadow banks and was, in turn, stimulated by it. Broader markets, plunging information costs, new profit opportunities, and government practices all encouraged the development of new financial instruments and institutions to meet customer needs at lower cost.

Over time, the rise of highly leveraged shadow banks—combined with government relaxation of rules for traditional banks—permitted a rise of leverage in the financial system as a whole, making it more vulnerable to shocks (see Lessons from the Crisis: Leverage earlier in this chapter).

Rapid growth in some new financial instruments made it easier to conceal leverage and risk taking. Derivatives—options, futures, and the like—allow investors to transfer risks at low cost (see Chapter 9). After 2000, the use of customized derivatives that do not trade in open markets (so-called over-the-counter, or OTC, derivatives) rose dramatically. Those derivatives permitted some large financial institutions to take risks that were unknown to their investors and trading partners and to the public officials who were supposed to monitor them. The spillover from the failure of these firms during the financial crisis nearly sank the entire system.

The financial crisis of 2007–2009 transformed shadow banking. During the fateful week that began with the failure of Lehman Brothers on Monday, September 15, 2008, the largest U.S. brokerages failed, merged, or converted themselves into traditional banks in order to secure access to funding. In the same month, the loss of confidence in MMMFs required a U.S. government guarantee to halt withdrawals. During the crisis, many SIVs failed or were reabsorbed by the banks that created them. Many hedge funds chose to shrink or close as investors fled.

The future of shadow banking remains highly uncertain. The crisis has encouraged governments to scrutinize any financial institution that could, by its risk taking, pose a threat to the financial system. Partly as a result, the scope for leverage and risk taking is lower for now, but incentives to take risk—at others' expense—still can fuel future disruptions.

*One traditional form of bank is a commercial bank, which is defined in Chapter 12 as accepting deposits from and making loans to businesses and individuals.

†Hedge funds (defined in Chapter 13) are private, largely unregulated investment partnerships that bring together small groups of wealthy people who meet certain financial requirements. Private equity funds are investment pools that typically invest directly in private companies to gain management control.

markets require a legal structure that is designed and enforced by the government, countries with better investor protections have bigger and deeper financial markets than other countries.

Financial Institutions

Financial institutions are the firms that provide access to the financial markets, both to savers who wish to purchase financial instruments directly and to borrowers who want to issue them. Because financial institutions sit between savers and borrowers, they are also known as *financial intermediaries,* and what they do is known as intermediation. Banks, insurance companies, securities firms, and pension funds are all financial intermediaries. These institutions are essential; any disturbance to the services they provide will have severe adverse effects on the economy.

To understand the importance of financial institutions, think what the world would be like if they didn't exist. Without an intermediary, individuals and households wishing to save would either have to hold their wealth in cash or figure out some way to funnel it directly to companies or households that could put it to use. The assets of these household savers would be some combination of government liabilities and the equity and debt issued by corporations and other households. All finance would be direct, with borrowers obtaining funds straight from the lenders.

Such a system would be unlikely to work very well, for a number of reasons. First, individual transactions between saver-lenders and spender-borrowers would likely be extremely expensive. Not only would the two sides have difficulty finding each other, but even if they did, writing the contract to effect the transaction would be very costly. Second, lenders need to evaluate the creditworthiness of borrowers and then monitor them to ensure that they don't abscond with the funds. Individuals are not specialists in monitoring. Third, most borrowers want to borrow for the long term, while lenders favor more liquid short-term loans. Lenders would surely require compensation for the illiquidity of long-term loans, driving up the price of borrowing.

A financial market could be created in which the loans and other securities could be resold, but that would create the risk of price fluctuations. All these problems would restrict the flow of resources through the economy. Healthy financial institutions open up the flow, directing it to the most productive investments and increasing the system's efficiency.

The Role of Financial Institutions

Financial institutions reduce transactions costs by specializing in the issuance of standardized securities. They reduce the information costs of screening and monitoring borrowers to make sure they are creditworthy and they use the proceeds of a loan or security issue properly. In other words, financial institutions curb information asymmetries and the problems that go along with them, helping resources flow to their most productive uses.

At the same time that they make long-term loans, financial institutions also give savers ready access to their funds. That is, they issue short-term liabilities to lenders while making long-term loans to borrowers. By making loans to many different borrowers at once, financial institutions can provide savers with financial instruments that are both more liquid and less risky than the individual stocks and bonds they would purchase directly in financial markets.

Figure 3.2 is a schematic overview of the financial system. It shows that there are two types of financial institutions: those that provide brokerage services (top) and those that transform assets (bottom). Broker institutions give households and corporations access to financial markets and direct finance. Institutions that transform assets take deposits or investments or issue insurance contracts to households. They use the proceeds to make loans and purchase stocks, bonds, and real estate. That is their transformation function. Figure 3.3 shows what the balance sheet for such an institution would include.

The Structure of the Financial Industry

In analyzing the structure of the financial industry, we can start by dividing intermediaries into two broad categories called depository and nondepository institutions. *Depository institutions* take deposits and make loans; they are what most people think of as banks, whether they are commercial banks, savings banks, or credit unions. *Nondepository institutions* include insurance companies, securities firms, asset management firms that operate mutual funds and exchange-traded funds, hedge funds, private equity or venture

Figure 3.2 Flow of Funds through Financial Institutions

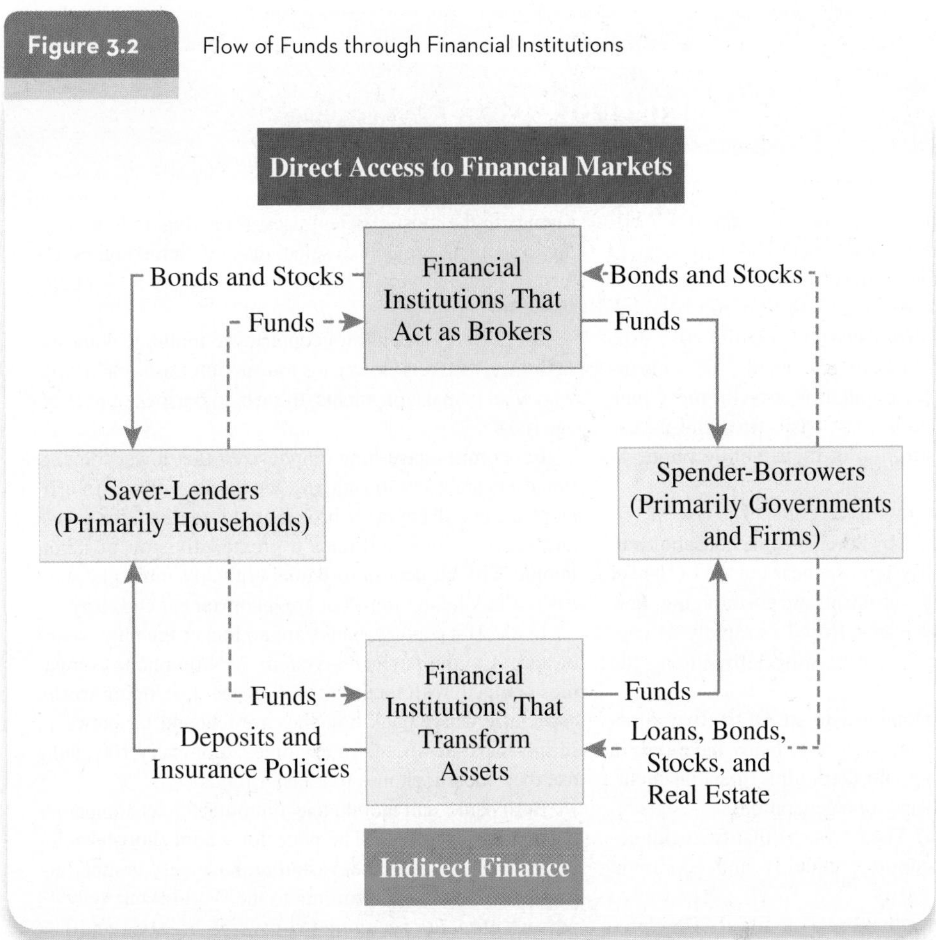

Financial institutions perform both brokerage and asset transformation services. As brokers, they provide access to financial markets, allowing households and firms to buy and sell direct claims on other firms and on governments. Institutions transform assets by taking deposits or investments or issuing insurance contracts to households at the same time that they make loans and purchase stocks, bonds, and real estate.

capital firms, finance companies, and pension funds. Each of these serves a very different function from a bank. Some screen and monitor borrowers; others transfer and reduce risk. Still others are primarily brokers. Here is a list of the major groups of financial institutions, together with a brief description of what they do.

1. ***Depository institutions*** (commercial banks, savings banks, and credit unions) take deposits and make loans.
2. ***Insurance companies*** accept premiums, which they invest in securities and real estate (their assets) in return for promising compensation to policyholders should certain events occur (their liabilities). Life insurers protect against the risk of untimely death. Property and casualty insurers protect against personal injury loss and losses from theft, accidents, and fire.

Figure 3.3 The Simplified Balance Sheet of a Financial Institution

Assets	Liabilities
Bonds	Deposits
Stocks	Shares
Loans	Insurance policies
Real estate	

MON€¥ $ BAN£ING

Banking the Masses

MONEY AND BANKING BLOG

The World Bank estimates that, in 2017, about 1.7 billion adults (aged 15 years and older) had no access to modern finance: no bank deposit, no formal credit, and no means of payment other than cash or barter. As high as that figure is, it was down sharply from the 2011 estimate of more than 2½ billion "unbanked." This means that when we account for population growth, more than 1.2 billion adults gained at least basic financial access through a financial institution or their mobile phone in just six years.

This spectacular progress is welcome. The rise of "financial inclusion"—access by lower-income households to banks and the payments system—is near the top of the list of social advances that governments are encouraging. Few consumer products have ever diffused as rapidly as payments access has in recent years, especially among the world's poor.

Still, we have a very long way to go. Of the two-thirds of adults with some financial access, many have only a tenuous link. Broadening and deepening financial inclusion will remain a challenge for a generation.

Why should we care? The answer is that financial access promotes both economic equality and economic growth.

Think about the things that banks do for us: They provide low-cost access to a sophisticated payments system, they safeguard funds and provide convenient accounting, they reward savers with interest, and they help diversify risks. When the system functions well, banks also allocate savings to the most efficient uses, screening and monitoring investment projects to select those with the highest return to both individual investors and society as a whole. (See Chapter 11.)

In short, finance allows countries to mobilize domestic savings effectively, lowering transaction costs for people who wish to make payments, to save, to borrow, or to manage risks.

Economists have long emphasized that lower transaction costs are a key to spurring economic growth. An efficient means of payment broadens the markets for goods and services and facilitates a greater division of labor. People without access to banks typically must pay with cash or in kind, options that are inconvenient and risky.

In the 21st century, banks are no longer the only means of access to the payments system. Mobile phone companies compete with them in much of the developing world, especially where bank branches are few and far between. In sub-Saharan Africa, for example, 21 of every 100 adults use their mobile phones to transfer funds.

Both banks and mobile telecommunications companies make it easier to save. The poor, for whom short-term income volatility can be devastating, have very compelling reasons to save. Yet, according to the World Bank, only 48 percent of adults accumulated savings in 2017, and just over half (55 percent) of those did so through a financial institution. In some poverty-stricken parts of the world, families may hoard cash or acquire livestock, but they face calamity if their cash is lost or their cattle perish. No

3. ***Pension funds*** invest individual and company contributions in stocks, bonds, and real estate (their assets) in order to provide payments to retired workers (their liabilities).
4. ***Securities firms*** include brokers, investment banks, underwriters, asset management firms, private equity firms, and venture capital firms. Brokers and investment banks issue stocks and bonds for corporate customers, trade them, and advise customers. All these activities give customers access to the financial markets. Asset management firms pool the resources of individuals and companies and invest them in portfolios of bonds, stocks, and real estate. Hedge funds do the same for small groups of wealthy investors. Customers own shares of the portfolios, so they face the risk that the assets will change in value. But portfolios are less risky than individual securities, and individual savers can purchase smaller units than they could if they went directly to the financial markets. Private equity and venture capital firms also serve wealthy investors: They acquire controlling stakes in a few firms and manage them actively to boost the return on investment before reselling them. In contrast, most mutual funds consist of passive investors, who do not seek to influence management.

wonder people welcome bank deposits when low-cost accounts are available.

For those without savings but with good income prospects, borrowing can be a means to finance a new business or to smooth consumption when income fluctuates. According to the World Bank, 48 percent of adults borrowed in 2017. But outside the high-income world, most borrowers obtained funds from their family and friends, partly because banks find it difficult to judge the creditworthiness of the unbanked. As bank access grows, more people will be able to provide the kind of information that banks need—such as saving and spending patterns—to undertake responsible lending; and hence, responsible borrowing should grow.

The correlation across countries between income and financial access is very high: Financial deepening boosts economic growth, while high incomes and wealth naturally create demand for financial services. Unsurprisingly, inhabitants of high-income countries are the most likely to have financial access. But, even some of those countries have made further progress recently. In the United States, for example, 93 of every 100 adults had a financial account as of 2017—up from 88 in 2011.

Within the developing world, financial access varies sharply, ranging from nearly 71 percent in East Asia and the Pacific to less than 43 percent in sub-Saharan Africa. Yet, in seven sub-Saharan economies, more than 50 percent of adults made or received digital payments, some of which are linked to banks (like Kenya's M-Shwari, which builds on the M-Pesa money transfer service).

Both technology and policy point to further sharp gains in financial inclusion. Mobile service providers are spreading out both geographically and across business lines: The GSM Association's Mobile Money for the Unbanked (MMU) tracker reports that the number of deployments more than doubled from 114 in 2011 to 270 in 2017.

Governments are also expanding financial access to promote saving and economic growth. The best example is India's groundbreaking biometric identification project, which has registered more than 1 billion people and offers a free, no-frills bank account to those who want one. According to the World Bank, nearly 450 million Indian adults gained access to basic financial services since 2011, by far the largest increase in any nation. The second-largest gain—of more than 200 million adults—occurred in China.

Rapid gains in financial access are not without risk. One concern is consumer protection because the lack of financial literacy among the newly included makes them targets for fraudsters. And, the technology itself poses a risk of criminal use, such as for money laundering or trading in illegal drugs and other contraband.

But, these are relatively "good" problems. Such challenges exist whenever a financial system is working as it should—helping people make payments, save, and manage risks. Ultimately, the benefits of greater financial inclusion should surface in higher incomes, especially for the poorest of the poor.

5. ***Finance companies*** raise funds directly in the financial markets in order to make loans to individuals and firms. Finance companies tend to specialize in particular types of loans, such as mortgage, automobile, or certain types of business equipment. While their assets are similar to a bank's, their liabilities are debt instruments that are traded in financial markets, not deposits.
6. ***Government-sponsored enterprises (GSEs)*** are federal credit agencies that provide loans directly for farmers and home mortgagors. They also guarantee programs that insure loans made by private lenders. Aside from GSEs, the government also provides retirement income and medical care to older adults through Social Security and Medicare. Pension funds and insurance companies perform these functions privately.

As we continue our study of the relationship between the financial system and the real economy, we will return to the importance of financial institutions, the conduits that channel resources from savers to investors. These intermediaries are absolutely essential to the operation of any economy. When they cease to function, so does everything else. Recall from Chapter 2 that the measures of money (M1 and M2) include checking deposits, savings deposits, and certificates of deposit, among other things. These are all important liabilities of banks. Because they are very liquid, they are accepted as a means of payment. Clearly, the financial structure is tied to the availability of money and credit. But we are getting ahead of ourselves. Before we study financial institutions, we need to look more closely at financial instruments and financial markets, the subjects of Part II (Chapters 4–10) of this book.

Key Terms

assets, 45
asset-backed securities (ABS), 52
bond markets, 62
broker, 54
centralized exchanges, 58
collateral, 52
counterparty, 48
dealer, 54
debt markets, 62
derivative instruments, 50
direct finance, 44
electronic communication networks (ECNs), 58
equity markets, 62
exchange-traded fund (ETF), 56
financial institution, 45
financial instrument, 46
financial markets, 53
high-frequency trader (HFT), 59
indirect finance, 45
intermediary, 45
liability, 45
money markets, 62
mortgage-backed securities (MBS), 52
over-the-counter (OTC) markets, 58
portfolio, 55
primary financial market, 56
secondary financial markets, 57
trading algorithm, 59
underlying instruments, 50

Using FRED: Codes for Data in This Chapter

Data Series	FRED Data Code
U.S. household net worth	TNWBSHNO
Household financial assets	TFAABSHNO
Household deposits	DABSHNO
Market value of equities of nonfarm nonfinancial corporations	MVEONWMVBSNNCB
Financial business assets: debt securities and loans	TCMAHDFS
Credit from U.S. commercial banks	LOANINV
Residential mortgages	HMLBSHNO
3-month U.S. dollar LIBOR	USD3MTD156N
Number of commercial banks	USNUM
Dow Jones Industrial Average	DJIA
Commercial bank equity/assets ratio (inverse of leverage)	EQTA
Wilshire 5000	WILL5000PR
U.S. stock market capitalization (percent of GDP)	DDDM01USA156NWDB
China stock market capitalization (percent of GDP)	DDDM01CNA156NWDB

Chapter Lessons

To learn more about the changing financial system, visit www.moneyandbanking.com.

1. Financial instruments are crucial to the operation of the economy.
   a. Financial arrangements can be either formal or informal. Industrial economies are dominated by formal arrangements.
   b. A financial instrument is the written legal obligation of one party to transfer something of value, usually money, to another party at some future date, under certain conditions.
   c. Financial instruments are used primarily as stores of value and means of trading risk. They are less likely to be used as means of payment, although many of them can be.
   d. Financial instruments are most useful when they are simple and standardized.
   e. There are two basic classes of financial instruments: underlying and derivative.
      i. Underlying instruments are used to transfer resources directly from one party to another.
      ii. Derivative instruments derive their value from the behavior of an underlying instrument.
   f. The payments promised by a financial instrument are more valuable
      i. The larger they are.
      ii. The sooner they are made.
      iii. The more likely they are to be made.
      iv. If they are made when they are needed most.
   g. Common examples of financial instruments include
      i. Those that serve primarily as stores of value, including bank loans, bonds, mortgages, stocks, and asset-backed securities.
      ii. Those that are used primarily to transfer risk, including futures and options.
2. Financial markets are essential to the operation of our economic system.
   a. Financial markets
      i. Offer savers and borrowers liquidity so that they can buy and sell financial instruments easily.
      ii. Pool and communicate information through prices.
      iii. Allow for the sharing of risk.
   b. There are several ways to categorize financial markets.
      i. Primary markets that issue new securities versus secondary markets, where existing securities are bought and sold.
      ii. Physically centralized exchanges, dealer-based electronic systems (over-the-counter markets), or electronic networks.
      iii. Debt and equity markets (where instruments that are used primarily for financing are traded) versus derivative markets (where instruments that are used to transfer risk are traded).
   c. A well-functioning financial market is characterized by
      i. Low transaction costs and sufficient liquidity.
      ii. Accurate and widely available information.
      iii. Legal protection of investors against the arbitrary seizure of their property.
      iv. Ability to enforce contracts quickly at low cost.
3. Financial institutions perform brokerage and asset transformation functions.
   a. In their role as brokers or dealers, they provide access to financial markets.
   b. In transforming assets, they provide loans and other forms of indirect finance.
   c. Intermediation reduces transaction and information costs.
   d. Financial institutions, also known as financial intermediaries, help individuals and firms transfer and reduce risk.

Conceptual and Analytical Problems

1. As the end of the month approaches, you realize that you probably will not be able to pay the next month's rent. Describe both an informal and a formal financial instrument that you might use to solve your dilemma. *(LO1)*

2.* While we often associate informal financial arrangements with poorer countries where financial systems are less developed, informal arrangements often coexist with even the most developed financial systems. What advantages might there be to engaging in informal arrangements rather than utilizing the formal financial sector? *(LO1)*

3. If higher leverage is associated with greater risk, explain why the process of deleveraging (reducing leverage) can be destabilizing. *(LO2)*

4. The Chicago Mercantile Exchange offers a financial instrument that is based on rainfall in the state of Illinois. The standard agreement states that for each inch of rain over and above the average rainfall for a particular month, the seller will pay the buyer $1,000. Who could benefit from buying such a contract? Who could benefit from selling it? *(LO1)*

5. You wish to buy an annuity that makes monthly payments for as long as you live. Describe what happens to the purchase price of the annuity if (1) your age at the time of purchase goes up, (2) the size of the monthly payment rises, and (3) your health improves. *(LO1)*

6. Which of the following would be more valuable to you: a portfolio of stocks that rises in value when your income rises or a portfolio of stocks that rises in value when your income falls? Why? *(LO1)*

7. Has the distinction between direct and indirect forms of finance become more or less important in recent times? Why? *(LO3)*

8. Designated market makers, who historically have provided liquidity (that is, have stood by ready to buy and sell) in markets for specific stocks, have declined in importance. Explain this decline in terms of technology and global economic integration. *(LO2)*

9. The design and function of financial instruments, markets, and institutions are tied to the importance of information. Describe the role played by information in each of these three pieces of the financial system. *(LO2)*

10. Suppose you need to take out a personal loan with a bank. Explain how you could be affected by problems in the interbank lending market such as those seen during the 2007–2009 financial crisis. *(LO2)*

11.* Advances in technology have facilitated the widespread use of credit scoring by financial institutions in making their lending decisions. Credit scoring can be defined broadly as the use of historical data and statistical techniques to rank the attractiveness of potential borrowers and guide lending decisions. In what ways might this practice enhance the efficiency of the financial system? *(LO3)*

12. Commercial banks, insurance companies, investment banks, and pension funds are all examples of financial intermediaries. For each, give an example of a source of their funds and an example of their use of funds. *(LO3)*

*Indicates more difficult problems.

13. Life insurance companies tend to invest in *long-term* assets such as loans to manufacturing firms to build factories or to real estate developers to build shopping malls and skyscrapers. Automobile insurers tend to invest in *short-term* assets such as Treasury bills. What accounts for these differences? *(LO3)*
14. For each pair of instruments below, use the criteria for valuing a financial instrument to choose the one with the highest value. *(LO1)*
    a. A U.S. Treasury bill that pays $1,000 in six months or a U.S. Treasury bill that pays $1,000 in three months.
    b. A U.S. Treasury bill that pays $1,000 in three months or commercial paper issued by a private corporation that pays $1,000 in three months.
    c. An insurance policy that pays out in the event of serious illness or one that pays out when you are healthy, assuming you are equally likely to be ill or healthy.

    Explain each of your choices briefly.
15. Jane and Mike purchase identical houses for $400,000. Jane makes a down payment of $80,000, while Mike puts down only $20,000; for each individual, the down payment is the total of his or her net worth and each finances the remainder of the house price with a mortgage. Assuming everything else is equal, who is more highly leveraged? If house prices in the neighborhood immediately fall by 10 percent (before any mortgage payments are made), what would happen to Jane's and Mike's net worth? *(LO2)*
16.* Everything else being equal, which would be more valuable to you—a derivative instrument whose value is derived from an underlying instrument with a very volatile price history or one derived from an underlying instrument with a very stable price history? Explain your choice. *(LO2)*
17. You decide to start a business selling covers for smartphones in a mall kiosk. To buy inventory, you need to borrow some funds. Why are you more likely to take out a bank loan than to issue bonds? *(LO3)*
18. Splitland is a developing economy with two distinct regions. The northern region has great investment opportunities, but the people who live there need to consume all of their income to survive. Those living in the south are better off than their northern counterparts and save a significant portion of their income. The southern region, however, has few profitable investment opportunities and so most of the savings remain in shoeboxes and under mattresses. Explain how the development of the financial sector could benefit both regions and promote economic growth in Splitland. *(LO2)*
19. What would you expect to happen to investment and growth in the economy if the U.S. government decided to abolish the Securities and Exchange Commission? *(LO2)*
20. Use Core Principle 3 (information is the basis for decisions) to suggest some ways in which the problems associated with the shadow-banking sector during the 2007–2009 financial crisis could be mitigated in the future. *(LO3)*
21. What risks might financial institutions face by funding long-run loans such as mortgages to borrowers (often at fixed interest rates) with short-term deposits from savers? As the manager of a financial institution, what steps could you take to reduce these risks? *(LO3)*
22. Give two examples of how greater financial inclusion might benefit a small farmer who previously did not have access to modern finance. *(LO3)*

*Indicates more difficult problems.

23. How might broader access to finance benefit a country where access was previously very limited? *(LO3)*

24. Secondary-market trading in stocks has become increasingly decentralized. Identify some reasons why you might expect this trend to continue. *(LO2)*

Data Exploration connect

For detailed instructions on using Federal Reserve Economic Data (FRED) online to answer each of the following problems, visit www.mhhe.com/moneyandbanking6e *and refer to the FRED Resources and Data Exploration Hints.*

1. The broadest stock index in the United States is the Wilshire 5000. Plot this index (FRED code: WILL5000PR) over the period from 1971 to the present. *(LO2)*
2. Plot the percent change from a year ago of the Wilshire 5000 (FRED code: WILL5000PR). Discuss the behavior of changes in the index before, during, and after recession periods, which are indicated by the vertical, shaded bars in the graph. *(LO2)*
3. Do changes in stock values affect the wealth of households? Beginning in 1971, plot on a quarterly basis the percent change from a year ago of the Wilshire 5000 (FRED code: WILL5000PR) and the percent change from a year ago of household net worth (FRED code: TNWBSHNO). Compare the two lines. *(LO2)*
4. The Dow Jones Industrial Average is a well-known index of equity prices, but includes only 30 stocks. Consider a much broader measure of the stock market—the market value of corporate equities in nonfinancial corporations (FRED code: MVEONWMVBSNNCB)—which sums the price of each stock times the number of outstanding shares. After plotting it, comment on its pattern since the mid-1990s. *(LO2)*
5. In Data Exploration Problem 3, you looked at changes in household net worth. In Data Exploration Problem 4 you examined stock market wealth. Aside from stock market wealth, what other assets contribute to household net worth? *(LO1)*
6. The role and scale of the stock market differs across countries and over time. Plot stock market capitalization as a percent of GDP for the United States (FRED Code: DDDM01USA156NWDB) and for China (FRED Code: DDDM01CNA156NWDB). Comment on the relative trend since 1995. *(LO2)*

Chapter

4 Future Value, Present Value, and Interest Rates

Learning Objectives

After reading this chapter, you should be able to:

LO1 Compare the value of monetary payments using present value and future value.

LO2 Apply present value to a stream of payments using internal rate of return and bond valuation.

LO3 Explain the difference between real and nominal interest rates and how each is calculated.

Lenders have been despised for most of history. The borrowers must pay for their loans, while the lenders just sit around doing nothing. No wonder people have been vilified for charging interest. No wonder that, for centuries, clerics pointed to biblical passages damning interest. Even philosophers weighed in against the practice, including Aristotle, who called the "breeding of money from money" unnatural.

After scorning lenders for millennia, we now recognize their service as a fundamental building block of civilization. Credit is one of the critical mechanisms we have for allocating resources. Without it, our market-based economy would grind to a halt. Even the simplest financial transaction, like saving some of your paycheck each month to buy a car, would be difficult, if not impossible. And corporations, most of which survive from day to day by borrowing to finance their activities, would not be able to function. Credit is so basic that we can find records of people lending grain and metal from 5,000 years ago. Credit probably existed before common measures of value, and it predates coinage by 2,000 years.

Despite its early existence and its central role in economic transactions, credit was hard to come by until the Protestant Reformation. By the 16th century, views had changed, and interest payments were tolerated if not encouraged, so long as the rate charged was thought to be reasonable. Some historians even point to this shift as a key to the development of capitalism and its institutions. Protestant European countries did develop faster than Catholic ones, at least at first.[1] Since then, credit has exploded, facilitating extraordinary increases in general economic well-being. Yet even so, most people still take a dim view of the fact that lenders charge interest. Why?

The main reason for the enduring unpopularity of interest comes from the failure to appreciate the fact that lending has an opportunity cost. Think of it from the point of

[1]Max Weber makes this argument in his classic work *The Protestant Ethic and the Spirit of Capitalism,* first published in 1905.

view of the lender. People who offer credit don't need to make loans. They have alternatives, and extending a loan means giving them up. While lenders can eventually recoup the sum they lend, neither the time that the loan was outstanding nor the opportunities missed during that time can be gotten back. So interest isn't really "the breeding of money from money," as Aristotle put it; it's more like a rental fee that borrowers must pay lenders to compensate them for lost opportunities.

It's no surprise that in today's world, interest rates are of enormous importance to virtually everyone—individuals, businesses, and governments. Quoted as a percentage of the amount borrowed, interest rates link the present to the future, allowing us to compare payments made on different dates. Interest rates also tell us the future reward for lending today, as well as the cost of borrowing now and repaying later. To make sound financial decisions, we must learn how to calculate and compare different rates on various financial instruments. In this chapter, we'll explore interest rates using the concepts of future value and present value and then apply those concepts to the valuation of bonds. Finally, we'll look at the relationship between interest rates and inflation.

Valuing Monetary Payments Now and in the Future

To compare the value of payments made on different dates, we need a set of tools called *future value* and *present value.* We'll use them to see how and why the promise to make a payment on one date is more or less valuable than the promise to make a payment on a different date. For example, we already know that if you want to borrow $100 today, your repayment needs to be bigger if you promise to make it in a year than if you promise to make it in a month. But how much more will you have to pay? The answer depends on both the date of payment and the interest rate. For the time being, we're going to assume that we know for sure that you will repay the loan. We'll get to the possibility of default when we study risk in the next chapter.

Future Value and Compound Interest

What is the future value of one dollar deposited in an interest-bearing account today? To answer this question, let's start with a definition: **Future value** *is the value on some future date of an investment made today.* Say that today you invest $100 in a savings account that guarantees 5 percent interest per year. After one year, you'll have $105 (the investment at its present value of $100 plus $5 in interest). So the future value of $100 one year from now at an interest rate of 5 percent is $105. We could also say that the $100 investment yields $5, which explains why an interest rate is sometimes called a **yield**. Notice that the same calculation works for a simple loan in which you borrow $100 for one year at 5 percent interest. The amount you will need to repay is $105. Remember Core Principle 1: Time has value.

TIME

To generalize this concept so that we can handle different interest rates and initial investments of any size, we can express it mathematically. First we need to convert the percentage interest rate into a decimal, so that 5 percent becomes 0.05. *Note that in this expression, as in all mathematical manipulations in this chapter, the interest rate is expressed in decimal terms.* Now we can express future value as an equation. If the present value of your initial investment is \$100 and the interest rate is 5 percent, then the *future value* one year from now is

$$\$100 + \$100(0.05) = \$105$$

Present value of the investment + Interest = Future value in one year

It is essential to convert all interest rates to decimals before doing any computation. This is consistent with the fact that we quote interest rates as "parts per 100," so 5 percent means 5 parts per 100, or 0.05.

This expression shows us immediately that the higher the interest rate, the higher the future value. If the interest rate were to rise to 6 percent, then the future value of \$100 would be

$$\$100 + \$100(0.06) = \$106$$

In general, the future value, *FV*, of an investment with a present value, *PV*, invested at an interest rate *i* is

$$\begin{aligned} FV &= PV + PV \times i \\ &= PV \times (1 + i) \qquad (1) \end{aligned}$$

Future value in one year

= Present value of the investment today × (One plus the interest rate)

We can see right away that the higher the interest rate or the amount invested, the higher the future value.

But this example is too simple. Most financial instruments don't make single payments in exactly one year, so we need to figure out what happens when the time to repayment varies. Computing the future value of an investment to be repaid two years from now is straightforward, so let's do that first. But because we quote interest rates on a yearly basis, we need to be careful. Using one-year interest rates to compute the value of an investment that will be repaid more than one year from now requires applying the concept of **compound interest**, *which is interest on the interest.* If you leave an investment in an interest-bearing account for two years, during the second year you will receive interest not only on your initial investment but also on the interest you earned for the first year (because they both have an opportunity cost).

Getting back to our example, let's say that you leave your \$100 deposit in the bank for two years at 5 percent interest per year. The future value of this investment has four parts. The first three are straightforward. They are the initial investment of \$100, the interest on that investment in the first year, and the interest on it in the second year. But because you left the interest from the first year in the bank during the second year, it is as if you made a new deposit at the beginning of the second year, and that earns interest too. So the fourth part of the future value is the interest you receive during the second year on the interest you received in the first year. That's compounding. With an initial deposit of \$100 and an interest rate of 5 percent, we can add up these four parts to compute your investment's future value in two years.

$$\$100 + \$100(0.05) + \$100(0.05) + \$5(0.05) = \$110.25$$

Present value of the initial investment

+ Interest on the initial investment in first year

+ Interest on the initial investment in second year

+ Interest on the interest from first year in second year

= Future value in two years

Table 4.1 Computing the Future Value of $ 100 at 5 Percent Annual Interest

Years into Future	Computation	Future Value
1	$\$100(1.05)$	$105.00
2	$\$100(1.05)^2$	$110.25
3	$\$100(1.05)^3$	$115.76
4	$\$100(1.05)^4$	$121.55
5	$\$100(1.05)^5$	$127.63
10	$\$100(1.05)^{10}$	$162.89

We can use a small amount of algebra[2] to show that this equals

$$\$100(1.05)(1.05) = \$100(1.05)^2$$

Extending it to three years, four years, or more just means multiplying by (1.05) over and over again. The multiplication takes care of the compounding. Table 4.1 shows the calculations. The final line shows that after 10 years, a deposit with a present value of $100 becomes $162.89. That is, it earns $62.89 in interest. If we had ignored compounding and just multiplied 5 percent by 10 years to get 50 percent, the answer would have been $150. Compounding produced an additional $12.89 in interest over 10 years. To put it as clearly as possible, multiplying the number of years times the annual interest rate gives the *wrong* answer!

Using the computations in Table 4.1, we can derive a general formula for future value.

$$FV_n = PV \times (1 + i)^n \tag{2}$$

Future value in n years = Present value of the investment × (One plus the interest rate) raised to n

So to compute future value, all we need to do is calculate one plus the interest rate (measured as a decimal) raised to the nth *power and multiply it by the present value.*

Before we go any further, we should stop to consider an important problem. What if you want to put your $100 into a bank for six months, or 2½ years, or any amount of time that is not a round number of years? The answer is that the formula still works. You can compute the future value using equation (2) regardless of whether n is a whole number. There is one pitfall, however. *In computing future value, both the interest rate and* n *must be measured in the same time units.* We have been measuring interest rates as the percentage per year, so we were careful to measure n in years as well. So, if we want the future value in half of one year, n would be ½; if we wanted it in one month, n would be 1/12; and if we wanted the future value in one day, n would be 1/365.

As you can see, taking advantage of the future-value formula requires an understanding of the transformations needed to convert time from years to months or vice versa. Converting n from years to months is easy—everyone knows there are 12 months

[2]The algebra is as follows: $\$100 + \$100(0.05) + \$100(0.05) + \$5(0.05) = \$100(1 + 0.05 + 0.05 + 0.05^2) = \$100(1 + 0.05)(1 + 0.05) = \$100(1 + 0.05)^2 = \$100(1.05)^2$. This result relies on algebraic factoring: namely, $(1 + i + i + i^2) = (1 + 2i + i^2) = (1 + i)^2$.

How Long Does Your Investment Take to Double?

YOUR FINANCIAL WORLD

You invest \$100 at 5 percent interest. How long will you need to wait until you have \$200? That may seem like a simple question, but compounding makes it difficult. The straightforward (some people would call it "brute force") way to find the answer is to take out your calculator and multiply \$100 times 1.05 over and over again counting how many times it takes to get to an answer that is close to \$200. If you did that, you would find that after the 14th time, you reached \$197.99. And multiplying once more, you would have \$207.89. You would conclude that, at 5 percent interest, your investment takes between 14 and 15 years to double.

While the brute force technique works—you can multiply over and over again—it's clumsy. Fortunately, there is a simpler way called the **rule of 72**. If you want to compute the number of years it takes an investment to double, divide the annual interest rate measured as an integer into 72.* So at an interest rate of 5 percent, we would expect an investment to double in 72/5 = 14.4 years (we can check and see that $1.05^{14.4} = 2.02$). If the interest rate were 8 percent, we would estimate 9 years ($1.08^9 = 2.00$).

The rule of 72 shows the power of compounding. It shows that when the interest rate doubles, the time a \$100 investment takes to become \$200 is cut in half. That is, while it takes 14.4 years to double at 5 percent interest, it takes only 7.2 years at 10 percent (72/10 = 7.2 and $1.10^{7.2} = 1.99$). This rule works for anything that is growing at a constant rate. So, if you want to estimate how long it will take a country's population or company's sales to double, just divide the annual growth rate measured as a percentage per year into 72.

*The rule of 72 is an approximation of the solution to an algebraic problem that requires the use of logarithms. Consider the formula for compound interest, in which the future value after n years is equal to $FV = PV(1 + i)^n$. Setting the present value PV *equal to 1* and the future value FV *equal to 2* and taking logarithms, we get $n = ln(2)/ln(1 + i)$. This formula is exact. Next, we use the approximation that $ln(1 + i) \approx i$ for small i. Substituting this into the equation gives us $n = ln(2)/i$. The $ln(2) = 0.693$, so it might seem that we should be using the rule of 69.3. For very low interest rates, such as we observed after the 2007–2009 financial crisis in Japan, the United States, and parts of Europe, indeed we should. But in the range of interest rates that we often see (4 to 12 percent), 72 works better.

in a year—but converting the interest rate is harder. If the annual interest rate is 5 percent, what is the interest rate for one month? To figure out the answer, we'll start with the future-value formula, but in months. Remember that compounding means you *cannot* just multiply the monthly interest rate by 12 to get the annual interest rate. Instead, if i^m is the one-month interest rate and n is the number of months, then a deposit made for one year will have a future value of $\$100(1 + i^m)^{12}$. We know that this amount equals \$100(1.05), so figuring out the answer means equating the two amounts,

$$(1 + i^m)^{12} = (1.05)$$

and raising each side to the one-twelfth power:

$$(1 + i^m) = (1.05)^{1/12} = 1.0041$$

Converting from decimals to a percentage, the one-month interest rate is 0.41 percent. We can handle any mismatch between the time units of i and n in a similar way (see Tools of the Trade: Computing Compound Annual Rates on page 82).

These fractions of percentage points, like 0.41 percent, are so important in discussing interest rates that they have their own name, basis points. A **basis point** *is one one hundredth of a percentage point*. That is, one basis point equals 0.01 percent.

You're probably wondering how useful all this discussion of future value really is. To see, consider the following question: If you put \$1,000 per year into the bank at 4 percent interest, how much would you have saved after 40 years? The answer is \$98,826—more than twice the \$40,000 you deposited. Figuring out the exact answer is complicated because we need to add up the future values of forty \$1,000 deposits, each made in a different year, but doing so uses the concept of future value. The first \$1,000 is deposited for 40 years, so its future value is

$$\$1{,}000(1.04)^{40} = \$4{,}801.02$$

The second \$1,000 is deposited for 39 years, so its future value is

$$\$1{,}000(1.04)^{39} = \$4{,}616.37$$

and so on. The practical implication of this calculation is that buying one less soda or candy bar per day isn't just good for your physical health; it's good for your financial health, too.

Present Value

It's easy to see why future value is important. We often want to know what savings and investments will be worth in the future. But that isn't the only thing we need to know. There is another, somewhat different task that we face with some regularity. We need to be able to figure out how much a payment promised in the future is worth today. Say you agree to make a \$225 loan, and the borrower offers to repay you either \$100 a year for three years or \$125 a year for two years. Which offer should you take? Answering this question means figuring out the current value of the promised payments on the dates when they will be made. To do that, we'll use the concept of present value, sometimes referred to as *present discounted value.*

TIME

The Definition In our discussion of future value, we used the term *present value* to mean the initial amount invested or deposited. The way we used the term suggests its technical definition: **Present value** *is the value today (in the present) of a payment that is promised to be made in the future.* Put another way, present value is the amount that must be invested today in order to realize a specific amount on a given future date. Financial instruments promise future cash payments, so we need to know how to value those payments. Present value is an integral component of the computation of the price of all financial instruments.

To understand the calculation of present value, go back to future value. Remember that at a 5 percent interest rate, the future value one year from now of a \$100 investment today is \$105. It follows that at this same 5 percent interest rate, the present value of \$105 one year from now is \$100. *All we did was invert the future value calculation.*

Reversing the calculation in general terms is just as easy. Start with the fact that the future value of a payment equals the current investment times one plus the interest rate: $FV = PV \times (1 + i)$ [equation (1)]. Divide both sides of this expression by $(1 + i)$ to get an expression for how much we need to invest today to realize the future value one year from today. The result is

$$PV = \frac{FV}{(1 + i)} \tag{3}$$

Present value = Future value of the payment divided by (One plus the interest rate)

In our example, we see that

$$\frac{FV}{(1 + i)} = \frac{\$105}{(1.05)} = \$100$$

so the present value of \$105 one year from now, at a 5 percent interest rate, is indeed \$100.

Risk Taking and the Search for Yield
LESSONS FROM THE CRISIS

Core Principle 2 teaches us that risk requires compensation. But to secure proper compensation, investors must understand the risks of what they buy.

The present-value analysis of this chapter helps us understand the risk of bonds with different maturities. If interest rates rise, the losses on a long-term bond will exceed the losses on a short-term bond. The reason is that the further in the future the promised payment, the more the present value falls when interest rates rise. As a result, long-term bonds are more sensitive to the risk that interest rates will change. Unsurprisingly, buyers of long-term bonds usually insist on an extra reward as compensation for such *interest rate risk* (see discussion of the yield curve in Chapter 7).

In some circumstances, many investors underestimate the risks of particular assets. For example, investors lacking sufficient regard for risk typically seek higher-yield bonds even if those bonds are riskier (due to longer maturities or higher default probabilities).

What can prompt the underestimation of risk? Experience suggests that some investors extrapolate from recent patterns and pay less attention to the more distant past. If interest rates have been low and stable for some time, investors may expect this pattern to persist even if rates tended to be higher and more volatile in earlier periods.

Extrapolation of recent experience also can lead investors to misjudge default risk. For example, business defaults are relatively infrequent during economic expansions. Because such booms are long and recessions are short, investors can become accustomed to unsustainably low levels of corporate default. Again, naively projecting recent experience underestimates the default risks for which investors should be compensated when buying corporate securities.

Investors also may underestimate risk if their professional investment managers take risks that are not evident or are purposely concealed. As a result, when market interest rates are low, some investment managers may try to generate high interest payments to clients by taking greater risks—a so-called search for yield. Until events compel the manager to reduce payments, the investor may think that the manager is unusually skillful rather than lucky or simply prone to taking risks.

The search for yield can bid up the prices of risky securities and depress the market compensation for risk below a sustainable level. Eventually, when the risk comes to fruition (say, defaults increase), the prices of riskier securities fall disproportionately, potentially triggering large financial losses. During the financial crisis of 2007–2009, the plunge of corporate and mortgage security prices highlighted how forcefully markets can reprice risk when the search for yield has gone too far. In the euro-area crisis that began in 2009, something similar occurred in the markets for bank and government debt.

While future value tells us what today's investment will be worth in the future, present value tells us what promised future payments are worth today. This means that the properties of present value mirror those of future value. In the same way that future value *rises* as the interest rate rises, present value *falls* as the interest rate rises. To see this, first look at the calculation of the present value of \$105 in one year at an interest rate of 6 percent. The answer is

$$\frac{\$105}{1.06} = \$99.06$$

which is less than the \$100 needed when the interest rate is only 5 percent. *Present value falls as the interest rate rises.*

What happens if the payment is going to be made in two years instead of one? What is the present value of \$105 in two years at an interest rate of 5 percent? Again, we can compute the answer using the future-value formula by asking what present value has a future value of \$105 in two years at an interest rate of 5 percent. This is the solution to

$$\$105 = PV(1.05)^2$$

The answer is

$$PV = \frac{\$105}{1.05^2} = \$95.24$$

We can generalize this process by looking at the future value in n years of an investment today: $FV_n = PV(1 + i)^n$. Dividing both sides of this expression by $(1 + i)^n$, we get the general formula for present value:

$$PV = \frac{FV_n}{(1 + i)^n} \tag{4}$$

Present value = Future value of a payment made in n years divided by (One plus the interest rate) raised to n

From this simple expression, we can deduce three important properties of present value. Present value is higher:

1. The higher the future value of the payment, FV_n.
2. The shorter the time until the payment, n.
3. The lower the interest rate, i.

We're going to use equation (4) over and over again. *It is the single most important relationship in our study of financial instruments*, so we have highlighted it in a red rectangle. Once we can figure out the present value of any future payment, then we understand the fundamentals of mortgages, credit cards, car loans, and even stocks.

We will spend the rest of this chapter looking at how present value changes when we change the various components of the formula, and how to use it more generally. But before we do, it is important to note one final similarity between present value and future value. Recall that to calculate future value, n need not be measured in years. We can do the computation even when n is the number of months, so long as the interest rate is measured in months as well. The same is true of present value. So long as we measure n and i in the same time unit, and the interest rate is expressed as a decimal, the formula works.

How Present Value Changes It is useful to go through each of the three properties of present value, looking at the impact of changing each one: the size of the future payment (FV_n), the time until the payment is made (n), and the interest rate (i). Starting with FV_n, we see that *doubling the future value of the payment, without changing the time of the payment or the interest rate, doubles the present value.* For example, at a 5 percent interest rate, a \$100 payment made in two years has a present value of \$90.70. Doubling the payment to \$200 doubles the present value to \$181.40. In fact, increasing or decreasing FV_n by any percentage will change PV by the same percentage, in the same direction.

We have already seen that *the sooner a payment is to be made, the more it is worth.* How much more? To see, let's return to the example of a \$100 payment at 5 percent interest. How sensitive is the present value of this payment to the time until it is made? Plugging some numbers into the general present-value formula [equation (4)], and allowing the time to go from 0 to 30 years, we can construct Figure 4.1, which shows that the present value of the payment is worth \$100 if it is made immediately but declines gradually to \$23 for a payment made in 30 years.

The rate of decline in the present value is related to the same phenomenon that gives us the rule of 72 (described in Your Financial World: How Long Does Your Investment Take to Double? on page 77). Consider this question: At a 5 percent interest rate, how long into the future must a payment of \$100 be made for it to be worth the same as \$50 received today? The answer is 14.4 years. That is, at 5 percent interest, the present value of \$100 paid in 14.4 years is \$50. Note that 14.4 equals 72 divided by 5, so it is also the number of years an investment takes to double in value when the return is 5 percent per year. We can repeat the computation to see that the investment takes 28.8 years to double twice, which tells us that the present value of $100 paid 28.8 years from now is $25. These two points are highlighted in Figure 4.1.

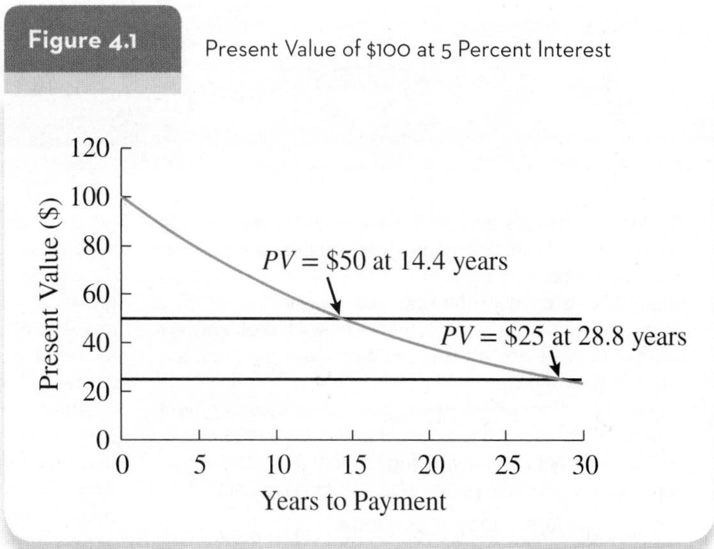

Figure 4.1 Present Value of $100 at 5 Percent Interest

The interest rate is the third important determinant of the present value of a future payment. To see how important it is, let's look at the present value of a $100 payment made 1, 5, 10, and 20 years from now at various interest rates. The general formula [equation (4)] allows us to do this series of computations. Table 4.2 shows the numerical results. Note what happens as the interest rate increases—that is, as you read down a column in the table or move to the right in the figure. You can see immediately that *higher interest rates are associated with lower present values, no matter what the size or timing of the payment.* Conversely, lower interest rates are associated with higher present values.

Table 4.2 Present Value of a $100 Payment

Interest Rate	Payment due in 1 Year	5 Years	10 Years	20 Years
1%	$99.01	$95.15	$90.53	$81.95
2%	$98.04	$90.57	$82.03	$67.30
3%	$97.09	$86.26	$74.41	$55.37
4%	$96.15	$82.19	$67.56	$45.64
5%	$95.24	$78.35	$61.39	$37.69
6%	$94.34	$74.73	$55.84	$31.18
7%	$93.46	$71.30	$50.83	$25.84
8%	$92.59	$68.06	$46.32	$21.45
9%	$91.74	$64.99	$42.24	$17.84
10%	$90.91	$62.09	$38.55	$14.86
11%	$90.09	$59.35	$35.22	$12.40
12%	$89.29	$56.74	$32.20	$10.37
13%	$88.50	$54.28	$29.46	$ 8.68
14%	$87.72	$51.94	$26.97	$ 7.28
15%	$86.96	$49.72	$24.72	$ 6.11

Note, too, that *at any fixed interest rate, an increase in the time until a payment is made reduces its present value.* Read across any row of the table and you will see that as the time increases from 1 to 5 to 10 to 20 years, the present value goes down.

The final lesson to take away from these calculations has to do with how present value changes with both time and the interest rate. Table 4.2 shows what happens to the present value of a payment as the interest rate increases. You can see that if the payment is to be made in one year (column two), as the interest rate increases from 1 percent to 5 percent, the present value falls from $99.01 to $95.24. This is a drop of $3.77, or just under 4 percent. In fact, for the single payment made in one year, the percentage change in the present value is approximately equal to the percentage-point change in the interest rate: A rise of 4 percentage points in the interest rate has caused a decline in present value of 4 percent.

Computing Compound Annual Rates
TOOLS OF THE TRADE

Comparing changes over days, months, years, and decades can be very difficult. If someone tells you that an investment grew at a rate of ½ percent last month, what should you think? You're used to thinking about growth in terms of years, not months. The way to deal with such problems is to turn the monthly growth rate into a *compound annual rate*. Here's how you do it.

An investment whose value grows ½ percent per month goes from 100 at the beginning of the month to 100.5 at the end of the month. Remembering to multiply by 100 to convert the decimal into a percentage, we can verify this:

$$100\left(\frac{100.5-100}{100}\right)=100\left[\left(\frac{100.5}{100}\right)-1\right]=0.5\%$$

To convert this monthly rate to an annual rate, we need to figure out what would happen if the investment's value continued to grow at a rate of ½ percent per month for the next 12 months. We can't just multiply 0.5 times 12. Instead, we need to compute a 12-month compound rate by raising the one-month rate to the 12th power. Assuming that our index starts at 100 and increases by ½ percent per month, we can use the expression for a compound future value to compute the index level 12 months later. Remembering to convert percentages to their decimal form, so that 0.5 percent is 0.005, we find the result is

$$FV_n = PV(1+i)^n = 100\,(1.005)^{12} = 106.17$$

an increase of 6.17 percent. That's the compound annual rate, and it's obviously bigger than the 6 percent result we get from just multiplying 0.5 by 12. The difference between the two answers—the one you get by multiplying by 12 and the one you get by compounding—grows as the interest rate grows. At a 1 percent monthly rate, the compounded annual rate is 12.68 percent.

Another use for compounding is to compute the percentage change per year when we know how much an investment has grown over a number of years. This rate is sometimes referred to as the *average annual rate*. Say that over five years an investment has increased 20 percent, from 100 to 120. What annual increase will give us a 20 percent increase over five years? Dividing by 5 gives the wrong answer because it ignores compounding; the increase in the second year must be calculated as a percentage of the index level at the end of the first year. What is the growth rate that after five years will give us an increase of 20 percent? Using the future-value formula,

$$FV_n = PV(1+i)^n$$
$$120 = 100(1+i)^5$$

Solving this equation means computing the following:

$$i=\left[\left(\frac{120}{100}\right)^{1/5}-1\right]=0.0371$$

This tells us that five consecutive annual increases of 3.71 percent will result in an overall increase of 20 percent. [Just to check, we can compute $(1.0371)^5 = 1.20 = 120/100$.]

Now look at the present value of a payment that will be made in 10 years (column four of Table 4.2). As the interest rate goes from 1 to 5 percent, the present value of a $100 payment 10 years from now falls from $90.53 to $61.39. This is a decline of $29.14, or more than 30 percent. *Not only does the present value of a future payment fall with the interest rate; the further in the future the promised payment is to be made, the more the present value falls.* As a result, a change in interest rates has a much greater impact on the present value of a payment made far in the future than it has on one to be made soon. Remember this principle because it will be extremely important when we discuss bonds in the next section.

Applying Present Value

All of our examples thus far have focused on computing the present value of a single payment on a given future date. Thinking of present value in this way gives us enormous flexibility. It means that we can compute the present value not just of a single payment but also of any group of payments made on any number of dates. As we saw earlier, to use present value in practice, we need to look at sequences, or streams of payments. And valuing a stream of payments means summing their present values. That is, the value of the whole is the sum of the value of its parts. *Present value is additive.* To see how present value is applied to a stream of payments, we will look at two applications: internal rate of return and the valuation of bonds.

Internal Rate of Return

Imagine that you run a sports equipment factory. As part of your strategic planning, you are considering buying a new machine that makes tennis rackets. The machine costs $1 million and can produce 3,000 rackets a year. If you can sell the rackets for $50 apiece (wholesale), the machine will generate $150,000 in revenue each year. To simplify the analysis, we will assume that the machine is the only necessary input in the production of tennis rackets; that we know the exact amount of revenue it will produce (in reality, that has to be estimated); and that the machine will last for exactly 10 years, during which time it will work perfectly, without requiring any maintenance. At the end of the 10 years, the machine will abruptly cease to operate and will have no resale value. Should you buy the machine?

The answer is: It depends. If you borrow the $1 million to pay for the machine, will the revenue from the machine, $150,000 per year, be enough to cover the payments on the loan? If so and you have something left over, then buying the machine may be a good idea. But if you can't make the payments, then buying the machine is a losing proposition. So you need to figure out whether the machine's revenue will be high enough to cover the payments on the loan you would need to buy it. We'll do this in two steps: First, we'll compute the internal rate of return on your investment in the machine, and second, we'll compare that return to the cost of buying the machine. If the cost is less than the return, then you should buy the machine.

The **internal rate of return** *is the interest rate that equates the present value of an investment with its cost.* For the tennis racket machine, it is the interest rate at which the present value of the revenue from the tennis rackets, $150,000 per year for 10 years, equals the $1 million cost of the machine. To find the internal rate of return, we take the sum of the present value of each of the yearly revenues (we can't take the present value of the total revenue) and equate it with the machine's cost. Then we solve for the interest rate, *i:*

$$\$1{,}000{,}000 = \frac{\$150{,}000}{(1+i)^1} + \frac{\$150{,}000}{(1+i)^2} + \cdots + \frac{\$150{,}000}{(1+i)^{10}} \qquad (5)$$

You can solve this equation using a financial calculator or spreadsheet. The answer, 8.14 percent, is the internal rate of return on your investment. That is, the annual rate of return for investing $1 million in the machine is 8.14 percent. But is that rate of return high enough to justify your investment? That depends on the cost of the $1 million you need to buy the machine.

There are two ways you can come up with the $1 million. You can use your company's retained earnings—the funds you've saved from your past profits. Or you can borrow. In the first case, you need to figure out if the machine is more profitable than other ways you might use the funds, just as you might compare interest-bearing investments. The other main use for the retained earnings is to lend them to someone at the

Table 4.3 Fixed Annual Payments on a 10-Year, $1 Million Loan

Interest Rate	Payment
5%	$129,505
6%	$135,868
7%	$142,378
8%	$149,030
9%	$155,820
10%	$162,745

same rate at which you could borrow. That is the opportunity cost of your investment. If you borrow the money to buy the machine, you need to know whether you will have a profit left after paying off the loan. Let's assume you're considering borrowing.

Table 4.3 shows the payments you will have to make if you borrow $1 million at various interest rates. To keep the example fairly simple, we'll assume that the loan requires 10 equal payments, one for each year. This type of loan is called a **fixed-payment loan**, and it is exactly the same as a car loan or a mortgage. Using the present-value formula [equation (4)], we know that the amount of the loan must equal the present value of the 10 payments. If the interest rate is i, then

$$\$1{,}000{,}000 = \frac{\textit{Fixed payment}}{(1+i)} + \frac{\textit{Fixed payment}}{(1+i)^2} + \cdots + \frac{\textit{Fixed payment}}{(1+i)^{10}} \tag{6}$$

$1,000,000 = Present value of 10 equal annual payments at interest rate i.

Using this relationship (and the methods described in the appendix to this chapter), we can compute your loan payment at various interest rates, as shown in Table 4.3. As we would expect, when the interest rate rises, the payments rise too.

At what interest rate can you afford a loan to buy the tennis racket machine? Recall that you have $150,000 a year in revenue, and your internal rate of return is 8.14 percent. So as long as the interest rate is 8 percent or less, you know you can cover the payments. But we can answer this question with more precision. To see why, notice that the internal rate of return equation (5) is virtually identical to the loan equation (6). In fact, the internal rate of return is the interest rate at which $150,000 a year for 10 years will exactly cover the loan. So we really needed to do this computation only once to answer the question. You should buy the tennis racket machine if its internal rate of return exceeds the interest rate on the loan you would need to finance it. In general, *an investment will be profitable if its internal rate of return exceeds the cost of borrowing.*

Before we go on, we can use the concept of internal rate of return to answer the question at the beginning of the present-value section on page 78: If you agree to make a $225 loan, and the borrower offers to repay either $100 a year for three years or $125 a year for two years, which should you take? The first step in figuring out what to do is to compute the internal rate of return of the two payment streams. For the series of three $100 payments, we need to find the interest rate i that solves

$$\$225 = \frac{\$100}{(1+i)} + \frac{\$100}{(1+i)^2} + \frac{\$100}{(1+i)^3}$$

The answer is $i = 0.159$, or 15.9 percent.

Turning to the alternative, we need to calculate the interest rate that solves

$$\$225 = \frac{\$125}{(1+i)} + \frac{\$125}{(1+i)^2}$$

The answer here is $i = 0.073$, or 7.3 percent.

This means that if you choose the three $100 payments, you will earn 15.9 percent interest on the loan, while if you accept the two $125 payments, the interest rate will

How Much Is Our Distant Future Worth?
APPLYING THE CONCEPT

Many people worry about the challenges their descendants will face. There are plenty of things to fret about, ranging from the threat of rising sea levels in this century to the long-range challenge of managing radioactive waste, which can be toxic for many thousands of years. Physicist Stephen Hawking has argued that human beings "won't survive another 1,000 years without escaping our fragile planet."

How much ought we be willing to spend now to avoid damage 100 years from now that will cost $1 at that time? The answer depends on many factors, including the relative affluence of our descendants, the degree of uncertainty about the future, and the possibility of existential threats.

To simplify the question, suppose that the only thing we care about is the present value of the expected losses associated with a preventable future disaster. In that case, the discount rate we use is critical for determining what we should do today. For example, for a disaster that is 100 years away, the value today of a $1 future loss at an annual discount rate of 1 percent is $0.37. But at a discount rate of 2 percent, the present value drops to $0.14. And at 4 percent, it is less than $0.02. Spending more than these amounts today would not make economic sense.

What discount rate should we use to value things in the distant future? For questions like this, economists usually look at market prices.

Various measures suggest that the appropriate rate is in the range of 1 to 2½ percent. For example, in recent years the long-term U.S. Treasury inflation-indexed bond yield has averaged around 1 percent. At the upper end of the range, research examining land leases with several hundred years of maturity points to a rate close to 2½ percent.

Policy disagreements among serious analysts of climate change are closely related to their views on the appropriate discount rate. One well-known report applied a relatively low discount rate of 1.4 percent and called for a large tax on carbon emissions to limit future losses from climate change. A different analysis used a relatively high 4.3 percent discount rate and called for a carbon tax only about *one-tenth* the level implied by the 1.4 percent rate analysis. Why? The low discount rate puts a great deal more weight on losses that are predicted to occur hundreds of years in the future.

Of course, it's not just about discount rates. It's about the scale of future losses, too. If policy actions today can prevent a calamity that threatens life on earth, then people might judge the appropriate discount rate to be quite low because they would not weight the value of future lives any lower than their own.

be 7.3 percent. Clearly, the three payments are better for you as the lender, but we had to do quite a bit of work to figure it out.

Bonds: The Basics

One of the most common uses of the concept of present value is in the valuation of bonds. A **bond** is a promise to make a series of payments on specific future dates. It is issued as part of an arrangement to borrow. In essence, the borrower, or seller, gives an IOU to the lender, or buyer, in return for some amount of money. Both governments and corporations need to borrow, so both issue bonds. Because bonds create obligations, they are best thought of as legal contracts that (1) require the borrower to make payments to the lender and (2) specify what happens if the borrower fails to do so.

Because there are many different kinds of bonds, to focus our discussion, we'll look at the most common type, a **coupon bond**. Say a borrower who needs $100 "issues" or sells a $100 coupon bond to a lender. The bond issuer is required to make annual payments, called **coupon payments**. The annual amount of those payments (expressed as a percentage of the amount borrowed) is called the **coupon rate**. If the coupon rate is 5 percent, then the borrower/issuer pays the lender/bondholder $5 per year per $100 borrowed. The yearly coupon payment equals the coupon rate times the amount

MONEY$ BANKING

Investing in College

MONEY AND BANKING BLOG

Most Americans want a college education, but it is expensive. On average—as of 2019—a four-year school costs about $26,500 per year, or $106,000 for a degree. That's more than one-third the median 2019 house price—a substantial investment. Is it worth it?

The answer for most people is yes. But the outcome is not free of risk, especially for those students who borrow heavily relative to their future income prospects.

To see the benefit and the risk, we need to compute the difference between expected income with and without going to college. As it turns out, the payoff usually remains quite attractive, but it depends on where and what you study and whether you complete your degree.

On average, the returns are high for those who stay the course: One study estimated the present discounted value in 2010 of a college degree net of tuition at more than $500,000 for men and $300,000 for women. For students who get a degree from a highly rated school, and for those who gain skills that are in demand, the present value is especially high.

For example, a group called PayScale estimates that, over the first 20 years of their working lives, people who get an undergraduate degree from Ohio State can expect to make $374,000 in *additional wages* beyond the earnings based on a high school education. If they foot the entire $103,000 bill themselves, the result implies an average annual real return of 8 percent. So long as the real interest rate on any student loan is below 8 percent, an education at Ohio State likely will be worth it.

But Ohio State ranks in the top quarter of the nearly 2,000 four-year colleges that PayScale rates. What about the rest? Well, it turns out that the median real return is 4.6 percent, still above the real interest rates on typical student loans, which are usually in the range of 2 to 4 percent.

Okay, so getting a college degree *usually* pays off. But there are pitfalls.

Most people don't have the luxury of simply writing checks for tens of thousands of dollars each year for four years. As a result, they borrow. And in recent years, they have borrowed an enormous amount. Since 2006, the total value of student loans has increased from $500 billion to nearly $1.5 trillion. According to the Federal Reserve's *Report on the Economic Well-Being of U.S. Households*, as of 2017, 22 percent of adults have education loans outstanding, with the typical amount in the range of $20,000 to $25,000. (For comparison, roughly 40 percent of American households have mortgages, and the median mortgage debt is nearly $114,000.)

Should we encourage people to borrow to go to college? The expected return to a completed college education says yes, but be careful. First, some students do not complete their studies. Second, loans to study at for-profit institutions appear to be very risky. According to the federal Department of Education (DoE), in 2014, for-profit colleges accounted for 13 percent of students and 31 percent of student loans. The DoE estimates that, of all student loans that entered repayment in 2010, nearly one-half of those at for-profit institutions will default, far above the weighted-average default rate of 18 percent.

As a result, in 2014, the federal government tightened eligibility requirements for loans at schools where default rates or loan-to-earnings burdens are high. That basic lending principle—using past default experience to guide future lending practice—also will be a helpful guide to students, who have limited knowledge about their future earning capacity at the start of their higher education.

No one should burden students with loans throughout their lives that they are unlikely to repay. Redirecting federal student loans to those schools (and, eventually, to specific programs within schools) that have the best payback records and the highest returns would benefit students and taxpayers alike.

borrowed. The bond also specifies when the issuer is going to repay the initial $100 and the payments will stop, called the **maturity date** or *term to maturity*. The final payment, a repayment of the initial $100 loan, is often referred to as the **principal**, **face value**, or **par value** of the bond.

Before the advent of computers, an investor buying a bond would receive a certificate with a number of dated coupons attached. To claim the coupon payments, the investor would cut off the coupons and mail them to the bond issuer. At maturity, the investor would redeem the certificate for the final payment. The Reading Railroad Company bond pictured on page 88 still has some coupons attached.[3]

You can see that the borrower who issues a bond is promising to make a series of regular interest payments over the life of the bond, plus a final payment on the maturity date. How much should someone be willing to pay for such a contract? The answer comes directly from present value: *The price of a bond is the present value of its payments.* To see how to value a bond, we'll start with repayment of the principal; then we'll add the coupon payments.

Valuing the Principal Payment Valuing the bond's principal, or final payment, is a straightforward application of present value. Let's look at a bond that promises a principal payment of \$100 on its maturity date n years in the future. The present value of this payment is

$$P_{BP} = \frac{F}{(1+i)^n} = \frac{\$100}{(1+i)^n} \qquad (7)$$

Present value of bond principal (P_{BP}) =

Principal payment (F) divided by (One plus the interest rate) raised to n.

We can see immediately that the value of the principal payment varies with both the time to maturity and the interest rate. The longer the time until the payment is made—the higher the n—the lower the value of the payment. And the higher the interest rate, i, the lower the value of the payment.

To see how this works, let's start with an interest rate of 6 percent and a final payment of \$1,000 to be made in 30 years. If the interest rate is 6 percent, the present value of the final payment is

$$P_{BP} = \frac{\$1000}{(1.06)^{30}} = \$174.11$$

Not surprisingly, this promise to make a payment that far in the future is worth only a fraction of the \$1,000 principal. Lowering the interest rate, say to 4 percent, would increase the present value of the principal payment to \$308.32, but it would still be much less than half of the payment itself.

Valuing the Coupon Payments What about the coupon payments? This series of equal payments resembles the loan payments we examined in our discussion of internal rate of return. There we computed the sum of a series of equal payments by adding up the present value of each payment. Let's look at this process in more detail, starting with two \$10 payments made in consecutive years. Assuming an interest rate of 6 percent, the value of these two payments is

$$\frac{\$10}{1.06} + \frac{\$10}{1.06^2} = \$9.43 + \$8.90 = \$18.33$$

Adding additional payments simply means adding more terms. So for five \$10 payments made over five consecutive years, the present value is

$$\frac{\$10}{1.06} + \frac{\$10}{1.06^2} + \frac{\$10}{1.06^3} + \frac{\$10}{1.06^4} + \frac{\$10}{1.06^5} = \$9.43 + \$8.90 + \$8.40 + \$7.92 + \$7.47 = \$42.12$$

[3]The bond in the picture is a \$1,000 face value 50-year 3½ percent coupon bond issued on May 1, 1945. It promised 100 payments of \$17.35, to be made every six months beginning on November 1, 1945, plus a \$1,000 final payment on May 1, 1995. The vast majority of bonds pay interest biannually.

A coupon bond issued by the Reading Railroad Company on May 1, 1945. Some of the coupons are still attached to the bond.

Courtesy of Stephen Cecchetti

This example highlights two important properties of periodic fixed payments. First, the longer the payments go on—the more of them there are—the higher their total value. Even though the additional payments fall farther into the future, the overall present value still grows. Because a long-term bond (one that lasts for 30 years, for instance) has more payments than a short-term maturity bond (one whose final payment is made, say, in 5 years), the coupon payments on the long-term bond will be worth more than the coupon payments on the short-term bond.

Second, as is always the case in present-value calculations, the higher the interest rate, the lower the present value. Raising the interest rate from 6 to 7 percent, for example, lowers the total value of the five future payments on our short-term bond from \$42.12 to \$41.00.

We can use the present-value expression to write a general formula for a string of yearly coupon payments made over n years. It is simply the sum of the present value of the payments for each year from one to n years:

$$P_{CP} = \frac{C}{(1+i)^1} + \frac{C}{(1+i)^2} + \frac{C}{(1+i)^3} + \cdots + \frac{C}{(1+i)^n} \qquad (8)$$

Present value of a series of bond coupon payments (P_{CP}) = Sum of yearly coupon payments (C) divided by (one plus the interest rate) raised to the power equal to the number of years from now. This formula is messy, but that's why we have calculators and spreadsheets. (For a derivation of a simpler version of this formula, see the appendix to this chapter.)

Valuing the Coupon Payments Plus Principal To value the yearly coupon payments plus the principal, we can combine equations (7) and (8) as follows:

$$P_{CB} = P_{CP} + P_{BP} = \left[\frac{C}{(1+i)^1} + \frac{C}{(1+i)^2} + \frac{C}{(1+i)^3} + \cdots + \frac{C}{(1+i)^n}\right] + \frac{F}{(1+i)^n} \quad (9)$$

Present value of coupon bond (P_{CB})

= Present value of yearly coupon payments (P_{CP})

+ Present value of principal payment (P_{BP})

This formula looks complicated because it is. But we can learn two simple facts just by looking at its parts. The value of the coupon bond, P_{CB}, rises when (1) the yearly coupon payments, C, rise and (2) the interest rate, i, falls. The first of these conclusions follows from the fact that a higher coupon rate means larger payments, and the present value of a larger payment is larger. The second follows directly from the present-value relationship: The lower the interest rate, the higher the present value of any and all future payments.

The fact that lower interest rates mean higher bond prices—and higher interest rates mean lower bond prices—is extremely important. Because bonds promise fixed payments on future dates, the higher the interest rate, the lower their present value. It follows that the *value of a bond varies inversely with the interest rate used to calculate the present value of the promised payment.*

Real and Nominal Interest Rates

In calculating present value, our goal has been to assess the number of dollars you would pay today for fixed dollar payments in the future. To do this, we used the **nominal interest rate**, which is the interest rate expressed in current-dollar terms. We did not worry about the possibility that inflation might change the purchasing power of the dollars. Because borrowers and lenders care about the purchasing power of the money they pay out and receive, they care about inflation. So we need to adjust the return on a loan, looking not just at the nominal interest rate but at the inflation-adjusted interest rate, called the **real interest rate**.

Think about a \$100 loan made at a 5 percent interest rate for one year. The borrower receives \$100 at the beginning of the year and repays \$105 at the end of the year. If prices go up 5 percent during the year—that is, if the inflation rate is 5 percent—then the \$105 returned to the lender at the end of the year will buy exactly what \$100 did at the beginning of the year. The lender's inflation-adjusted return is zero. No lender would be happy with a zero return, so no lender is likely to make a loan at a 5 percent nominal interest rate if expected inflation is 5 percent. (Because the inflation rate can exceed the nominal interest rate, the real interest rate can be negative.)

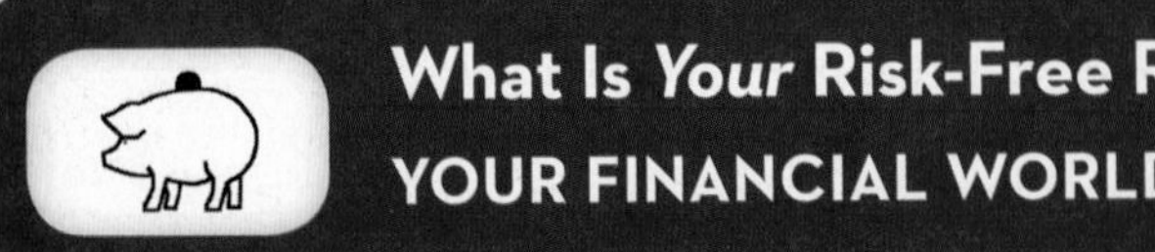

What Is *Your* Risk-Free Rate?

YOUR FINANCIAL WORLD

You received an unexpected bonus at work and wonder what to do with it. A financially savvy friend suggests investing in a balanced portfolio of stocks and bonds. It's never too early to start saving for your retirement, she assures you, so why not put your bonus into one of those target retirement funds?

It sounds reasonable, but you have some questions. A few years ago, you and your partner purchased a house. You made the 20 percent down payment and financed the balance with a 30-year mortgage at 5 percent interest. That raises a new question: Should you use your bonus to invest in stocks and bonds, as your friend suggests, or should you use it to pay down your mortgage?

Assuming that you are not the gambling type, the answer is *pay down your debt*. The reason is pretty simple: The opportunity cost of investing in the retirement fund is the interest rate you are paying on your mortgage. That is, investing the bonus in a mutual fund is equivalent to taking out a loan at your mortgage rate for the purpose of buying stocks and bonds with the proceeds.

From your perspective, your risk-free rate is the mortgage rate. So, to justify investing your bonus rather than using it to pay down your mortgage, your friend would have to convince you that there was a riskless investment with a return in excess of 5 percent out there. There usually is not!

But what about the risk that the value of the house will fall? You bear this risk regardless of what you do with the bonus.

So, if you are fortunate enough to have some extra cash lying around, the best strategy is nearly always to pay down any of your loans—credit card, auto loan, student loan, or mortgage—before you start investing. The reason is that no riskless investment is likely to match the rate you receive when you reduce the size of your debt.

The point of this example is that borrowers look at the inflation-adjusted cost of borrowing, while lenders focus on the inflation-adjusted return. *No one cares only about the number of dollars. People also care about what those dollars can buy. In other words, everyone cares about real interest rates.* This is why economists think of the nominal interest rate as having two parts, the real interest rate and expected inflation.

Say that you want to borrow $100 for one year. You find a lender who is willing to give you a loan, but the two of you need to agree on the interest rate. Both of you care about the inflation rate over the coming year, which will affect the purchasing power of the dollars you will use to repay the loan. But neither of you knows what that rate is going to be, so you need to forecast it to conclude your agreement. That is, the nominal interest rate you agree on must be based on *expected inflation* over the term of the loan, plus the real interest rate you agree on.

Writing down this statement in the form of an equation is helpful. The nominal interest rate, i, equals the real interest rate, r, plus expected inflation, π^e:[4]

$$i = r + \pi^e \tag{10}$$

[4]This equation is an approximation that works well only when expected inflation and the real interest rate are low. The exact relationship among the nominal interest rate, the real interest rate, and the expected inflation rate is $(1 + i) = (1 + r)(1 + \pi^e)$, which translates to $(1 + i) = 1 + r + \pi^e + r\pi^e$; after subtracting 1 from each side, the nominal rate, i, equals $r + \pi^e + r\pi^e$. The approximation, $i = r + \pi^e$, ignores the cross-term $r\pi^e$, the product of the real interest rate and expected inflation, which will not be important when its value is very low (say, $0.05 \times 0.02 = 0.001$). But if, for example, expected inflation is very high, the cross-term can become very important. To illustrate, if the real interest rate is 0.05, or 5 percent, and the expected rate of inflation is 1.00, or 100 percent, the *abbreviated equation* yields a nominal interest rate of $0.05 + 1.00 = 1.05$, or 105 percent. The result implies that, at an inflation rate of 100 percent, an investor would have earned 5 percent after inflation (the real rate) at the end of one year if the nominal interest rate on an investment had been set to 105 percent. But the *full equation* includes the cross-term, $r\pi^e$, which in this case is $(0.05)(1.00) = 0.05$, or 5 percent, meaning that the nominal interest rate would have to be set to 110 percent, not 105 percent, for an investment to earn a real return of 5 percent after one year. In dollar terms, the abbreviated equation produces a one-year real (after-inflation) return on an investment of $100 that is $5 below the true real return calculated with the full equation.

Figure 4.2 The Nominal Interest Rate, the Inflation Rate, and the Real Interest Rate

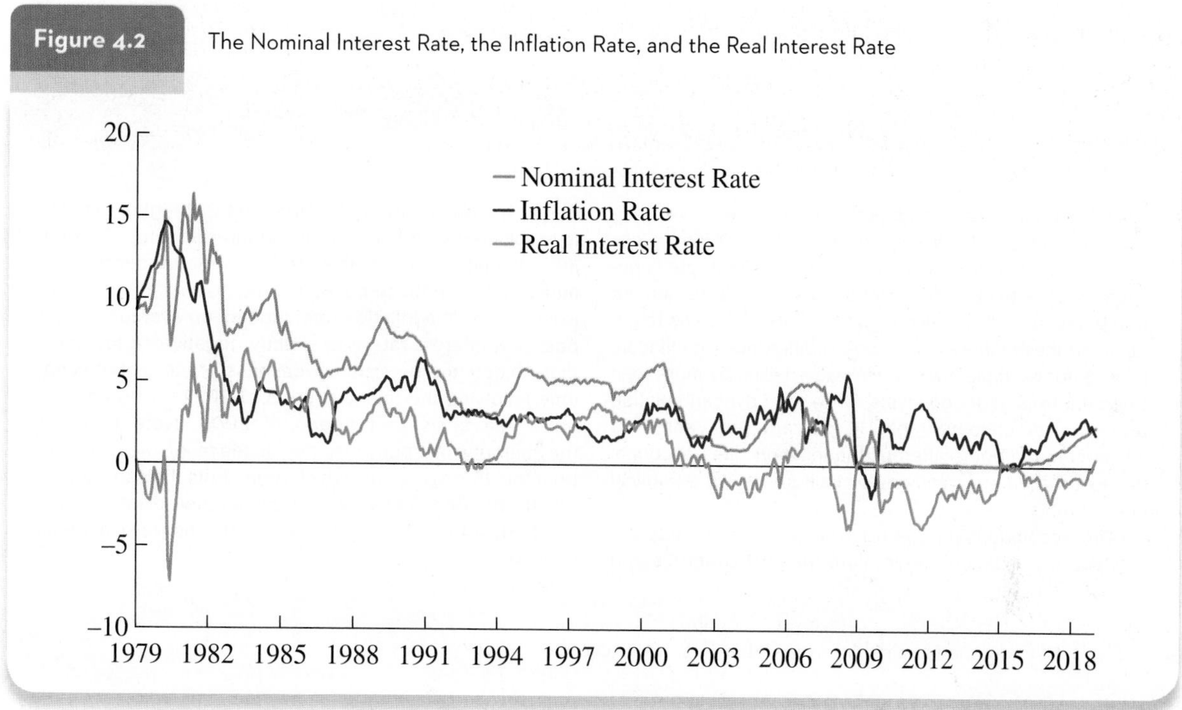

SOURCE: Three-month Treasury bill rates from the Federal Reserve Board and 12-month inflation rates computed from the Bureau of Labor Statistics Consumer Price Index Research Series. The real interest rate is calculated as the nominal rate minus the annual inflation rate. This computation assumes that the expected inflation rate over the next 3 months is equal to the actual inflation rate over the previous 12 months. (FRED data codes: TB3MS and CPIAUCSL)

This is called the *Fisher equation* after the early 20th-century economist Irving Fisher. It shows that in general, the nominal interest rate is positively related to expected inflation. The higher expected inflation, the higher the nominal interest rate. As we can see in Figure 4.2, the data bear this out. While the relationship is not a tight one, higher nominal interest rates are usually associated with higher inflation rates. In 1980 and 1981, for example, U.S. interest rates were sky-high; the U.S. Treasury had to pay more than 15 percent for its short-term borrowing. By 1986, interest rates had dropped to more reasonable levels, close to 5 percent. That's a 10-percentage-point move in just five years! The figure shows that as inflation fell, nominal interest rates also fell. In fact, the declines were almost identical. Real interest rates didn't change much during this period.

The term *real interest rate* can cause confusion. For the most part, the financial markets quote nominal interest rates.[5] When people use the term *interest rate* without qualification, they are referring to the *nominal* interest rate, the one they see every day. We will follow this convention, using the term *interest rate* to mean the nominal rate and the term *real interest rate* to refer to the nominal rate less expected inflation.

Until the advent of *inflation-indexed* bonds (see Your Financial World: Bonds Indexed to Inflation in Chapter 6), we could not directly observe the real interest rate; we had to estimate it. The easiest way to do that was (and still is) to turn the Fisher equation around, rewriting it as

$$r = i - \pi^e \qquad (11)$$

[5]One exception is inflation-indexed bonds, whose interest rates are quoted in real, inflation-adjusted terms.

High Interest Rates, Low Interest Rates
APPLYING THE CONCEPT

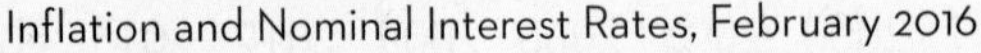

Once we realize that the nominal interest rate moves with expected inflation, big swings in interest rates become less of a mystery. And the fact that the Swiss interest rate is below zero while the Egyptian interest rate exceeds 10 percent also becomes easier to understand. All we need to do to understand these differences is look at differences in inflation. In 2016, for example, Swiss prices were falling by more than 1 percent from year-ago levels, while the Egyptian inflation rate was an uncomfortable 10 percent per year. This 11-percentage-point difference in inflation rates accounts for most of the 12-percentage-point difference in the nominal interest rates.

The accompanying figure shows the nominal interest rate and the inflation rate in more than 50 countries and the euro area in early 2016. Note first that higher inflation is associated with higher nominal interest rates. Second, more than half of the points are below the 45-degree line, meaning that in these countries, the nominal interest rate is lower than the inflation rate. Indeed, on average, the ex post real interest rate was slightly negative—a low level that reflects the persistent weakness of the global economy following the financial crisis of 2007–2009 and the euro-area crisis that began in 2009. Note that, for the majority of countries, the distance of these points from the 45-degree line, which represents the zero real interest rate, does not vary as much as their distance from the horizontal axis, which represents the zero nominal interest rate.

Inflation and Nominal Interest Rates, February 2016

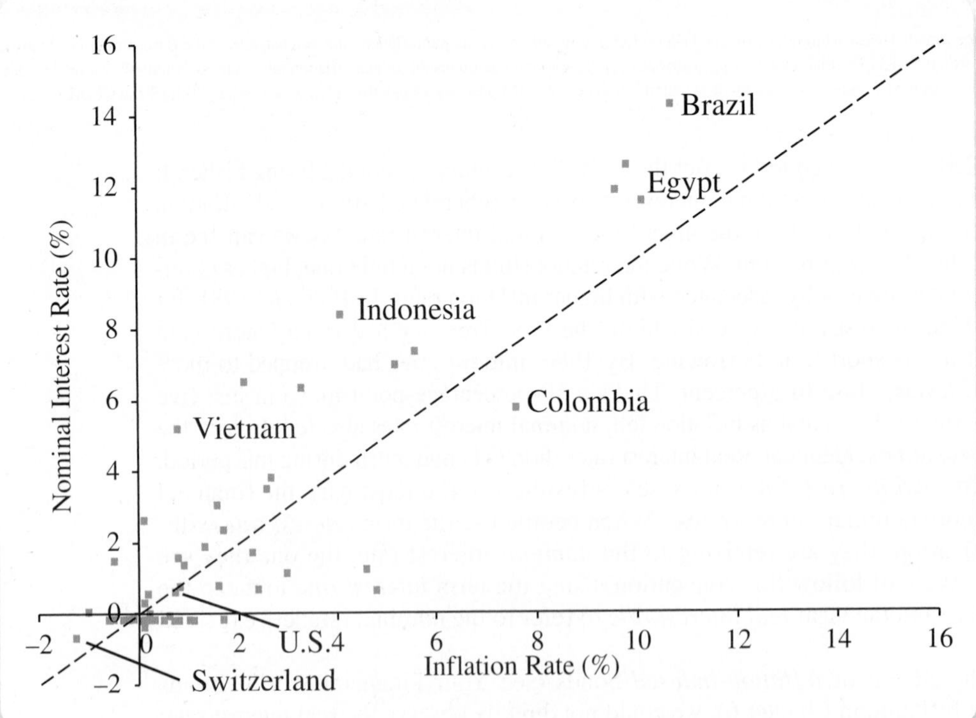

SOURCE: The data come from economic and financial indicators published weekly in *The Economist* magazine.

Because we know the nominal interest rate, *i,* measuring the real interest rate means subtracting forecasted inflation. There are a number of sources for these forecasts. Twice a year the Federal Reserve Bank of Philadelphia publishes professional forecasts. Once a month, the Survey Research Center of the University of Michigan computes consumer inflation expectations.

But because forecasts are often wrong, our estimate will usually differ from the real interest rate that occurs. Someone who is making an economically important decision will do so based on the expected real interest rate. Some time later, that person will look back and compute the real interest rate actually paid or received. The first of these is known as the *ex ante* real interest rate, meaning "before the fact." The second, or realized rate, is the *ex post* real interest rate, meaning "after the fact." We can always compute the ex post real interest rate, because we know the nominal interest rate and the inflation rate there actually was. But it is the ex ante real interest rate that we really want to know.

Key Terms

basis point, 77
bond, 85
compound interest, 75
coupon bond, 85
coupon payment, 85
coupon rate, 85
face value, 86
fixed-payment loan, 84
future value, 74
internal rate of return, 83
maturity date, 86
nominal interest rate, 89
par value, 86
present value, 78
principal, 86
real interest rate, 89
rule of 72, 77
yield, 74

Using FRED: Codes for Data in This Chapter

Data Series	FRED Data Code
1-year Treasury bill rate	TB1YR
3-month Treasury bill rate	TB3MS
Consumer price index	CPIAUCSL
1-year inflation expectations (Michigan survey)	MICH
Brazil Treasury bill rate	INTGSTBRM193N
Brazil consumer price index	BRACPIALLMINMEI
China discount rate	INTDSRCNM193N
China consumer price index	CHNCPIALLMINMEI
10-year Treasury constant maturity rate	GS10
10-year Treasury inflation-indexed yield	FII10
5-year Treasury constant maturity rate	GS5
5-year Treasury inflation-indexed yield	FII5

To learn more about the changing financial system, visit www.moneyandbanking.com.

Chapter Lessons

1. The value of a payment depends on when it is made.
   a. Future value is the present value of an initial investment times one plus the interest rate for each year you hold it. The higher the interest rate, the higher the future value.
   b. Present value is equal to the value today of a payment made on a future date.
      i. The higher the payment, the higher the present value at a given interest rate.
      ii. The higher the interest rate, the lower the present value of a given payment.
      iii. The longer the time until the payment is made, the lower the present value of a given payment at a given interest rate.
      iv. For a given increase in the interest rate, the present value of a promised payment falls more the further into the future the payment is to be made.
      v. When computing present value, the interest rate and the time until the payment is to be made must be measured in the same time units.
2. Present value can be used to value any stream of future payments.
   a. The internal rate of return is the interest rate that equates the present value of the future payments or profits from an investment with its current cost.
   b. A coupon bond is a promise to make periodic interest payments and a final principal payment on specific future dates.
      i. The present value of a bond depends on its coupon rate, date of maturity, and the current interest rate.
      ii. The higher the coupon rate, given the maturity and the interest rate, the higher the present value of the bond.
      iii. The price of a bond is inversely related to the interest rate. The higher the price, the lower the interest rate that equates the price with the present value of the promised payments.
3. The real interest rate is the nominal interest rate minus expected inflation. It expresses the interest rate in terms of purchasing power rather than current dollars.

Conceptual and Analytical Problems Mc Graw Hill connect

1. Compute the future value of $100 at an 8 percent interest rate 5, 10, and 15 years into the future. What would the future value be over these time horizons if the interest rate were 5 percent? Explain the patterns you see in your answers over different time horizons and at different interest rates. *(LO1)*
2. Compute the present value of a $100 investment to be made 6 months, 5 years, and 10 years from now at 4 percent interest. Explain why the present value is lower the further into the future the investment is to be made. *(LO1)*
3. Assuming that the current interest rate is 3 percent, compute the present value of a five-year, 5 percent coupon bond with a face value of $1,000. What happens when the interest rate goes to 4 percent? What happens when the interest rate goes to 2 percent? *(LO2)*
4.* Given a choice of two investments, would you choose one that pays a total return of 30 percent over five years or one that pays 0.5 percent per month for five years? *(LO1)*

*Indicates more difficult problems.

5. A financial institution offers you a one-year certificate of deposit with an interest rate of 5 percent. You expect the inflation rate to be 3 percent. What is the real return on your deposit? *(LO3)*

6. Consider two scenarios. In the first, the nominal interest rate is 6 percent, and the expected rate of inflation is 4 percent. In the second, the nominal interest rate is 5 percent, and the expected rate of inflation is 2 percent. In which scenario would you rather be a lender? In which would you rather be a borrower? *(LO3)*

7. A friend has received an unexpected windfall of $10,000 and is considering whether to use the money to pay down their existing debt, on which they pay 6 percent interest, or invest it in a mutual fund. What advice would you give to your friend? *(LO3)*

8. Most businesses replace their computers every two to three years. Assume that a computer costs $2,000 and that it fully depreciates in 3 years, at which point it has no resale value whatsoever and is thrown away. *(LO1)*
   a. If the interest rate for financing the equipment is equal to *i*, show how to compute the minimum annual cash flow that a computer must generate to be worth the purchase. Your answer will depend on *i*.
   b. Suppose the computer did not fully depreciate, but still had a $250 value at the time it was replaced. Show how you would adjust the calculation given in your answer to part *a*.
   c. What if financing can only be had at a 10 percent interest rate? Calculate the minimum cash flow the computer must generate to be worth the purchase using your answer to part *a*.

9. Some friends of yours have just had a child. Thinking ahead, and realizing the power of compound interest, they are considering investing for their child's college education, which will begin in 18 years. Assume that the cost of a college education today is $125,000. Also assume that there is no inflation and there are no taxes on interest income that is used to pay college tuition and expenses. *(LO1)*
   a. If the interest rate is 5 percent, how much money will your friends need to put into their savings account today to have $125,000 in 18 years?
   b. What if the interest rate were 10 percent?
   c. The chance that the price of a college education will be the same 18 years from now as it is today seems remote. Assuming that the price will rise 3 percent per year, and that today's interest rate is 8 percent, what will your friends' investment need to be?
   d. Return to part *a*, the case with a 5 percent interest rate and no inflation. Assume that your friends don't have enough financial resources to make the entire investment at the beginning. Instead, they think they will be able to split their investment into two equal parts, one invested immediately and the second invested in 5 years. Describe how you would compute the required size of the two equal investments, made 5 years apart.

10. You are considering buying a new house, and have found that a $100,000, 30-year fixed-rate mortgage is available with an interest rate of 7 percent. This mortgage requires 360 monthly payments of approximately $651 each. If the interest rate rises to 8 percent, what will happen to your monthly payment? Compare the percentage change in the monthly payment with the percentage change in the interest rate. *(LO1)*

11.* Use the Fisher equation to explain in detail what a borrower is compensating a lender for when he pays her a nominal rate of interest. *(LO3)*

12. If the current interest rate increases, what would you expect to happen to bond prices? Explain. *(LO2)*

13. Which would be most affected in the event of an interest rate increase—the price of a five-year coupon bond that paid coupons only in years 3, 4, and 5 or the price of a five-year coupon bond that paid coupons only in years 1, 2, and 3, everything else being equal? Explain. *(LO2)*

14. Under what circumstances might you be willing to pay more than $1,000 for a coupon bond that matures in three years, has a coupon rate of 10 percent, and has a face value of $1,000? *(LO2)*

15.* Approximately how long would it take for an investment of $100 to reach $800 if you earned 5 percent? What if the interest rate were 10 percent? How long would it take an investment of $200 to reach $800 at an interest rate of 5 percent? Why is there a difference between doubling the interest rate and doubling the initial investment? *(LO1)*

16. Rather than spending $100 on paint today, you decide to save the money until next year, at which point you will use it to paint your room. If a can of paint costs $10 today, how many cans will you be able to buy next year if the nominal interest rate is 21 percent and the expected inflation rate is 10 percent? *(LO3)*

17. Recently, some lucky person won the lottery. The lottery winnings were reported to be $85.5 million. In reality, the winner got a choice of $2.85 million per year for 30 years or $46 million today. *(LO1)*
    a. Explain briefly why winning $2.85 million per year for 30 years is not equivalent to winning $85.5 million.
    b. The evening news interviewed a group of people the day after the winner was announced. When asked, most of them responded that, if they were the lucky winner, they would take the $46 million up-front payment. Suppose (just for a moment) that you were that lucky winner. How would you decide between the annual installments or the up-front payment?

18. You are considering going to graduate school for a 1-year master's program. You have done some research and believe that the master's degree will add $5,000 per year to your salary for the next 10 years of your working life, starting at the end of this year. From then on, after the next 10 years, it makes no difference. Completing the master's program will cost you $35,000, which you would have to borrow at an interest rate of 6 percent. How would you decide if this investment in your education were profitable? *(LO1)*

19. Assuming the chances of being paid back are the same, would a nominal interest rate of 10 percent always be more attractive to a lender than a nominal rate of 5 percent? Explain. *(LO3)*

20.* Your firm has the opportunity to buy a perpetual motion machine to use in your business. The machine costs $1,000,000 and will increase your profits by $75,000 per year. What is the internal rate of return? *(LO2)*

*Indicates more difficult problems.

21.* Suppose two parties agree that the expected inflation rate for the next year is 3 percent. Based on this, they enter into a loan agreement where the nominal interest rate to be charged is 7 percent. If the inflation rate for the year turns out to be 2 percent, who gains and who loses? *(LO3)*

22. An unusual development in the wake of the 2007–2009 financial crisis was that nominal interest rates on some financial instruments turned negative. In which of the following examples would the nominal interest rate be negative?
    a. The real interest rate is 2 percent and the expected inflation rate is 1 percent.
    b. The real interest rate is zero and the expected inflation rate is 2 percent.
    c. The real interest rate is 1 percent and the expected inflation rate is minus 2 percent.
    d. The real interest rate is minus 2 percent and the expected inflation rate is 3 percent.

    Explain your choice. *(LO3)*

23. Suppose analysts agree that the losses resulting from climate change will reach x dollars 100 years from now. Use the concept of present value to explain why estimates of what needs to be spent today to combat those losses may vary widely. Would you expect this variation to narrow or get wider if the relevant losses were 200, rather than 100, years into the future? *(LO1)*

24. If a climate change analyst applies a discount rate of 2 percent to losses expected in 300 years' time, how much, per $1 of expected loss, might she be willing to spend today to avoid those losses? Would your answer be higher or lower if the losses were expected sooner? Explain your answer. *(LO1)*

Data Exploration connect

For detailed instructions on using Federal Reserve Economic Data (FRED) online to answer each of the following problems, visit www.mhhe.com/moneyandbanking6e *and refer to the FRED Resources and Data Exploration Hints.*

1. How does inflation affect nominal interest rates? *(LO3)*
    a. Plot the three-month U.S. Treasury bill rate (FRED code: TB3MS) from 1960 to the present. What long-run pattern do you observe? What may have caused this pattern?
    b. Plot the inflation rate based on the percent change from a year ago of the U.S. consumer price index (FRED code: CPIAUCSL) from 1960 to the present. How does U.S. inflation history reflect your explanation in part *a*?

2. In Data Exploration Problem 1, you saw the impact of U.S. inflation on short-term U.S. Treasury bill rates. Now examine similar data for Brazil. *(LO3)*
    a. Plot the Brazilian Treasury bill rate (FRED code: INTGSTBRM193N). Notice the range of values and compare them with the range in the U.S. Treasury bill plot from Data Exploration Problem 1.
    b. Plot the inflation rate based on the percent change from a year ago of the Brazilian consumer price index (FRED code: BRACPIALLMINMEI). Comment on the inflation rate in Brazil. Download the data at a quarterly frequency to a spreadsheet. (You may need to widen the spreadsheet column to see the data.) What happens to the index in the 1990–1994 period?

*Indicates more difficult problems.

3. The *expected* real interest rate is the rate that people use in making decisions about the future. It is the difference between the nominal interest rate and the *expected* inflation rate, not the *actual* inflation rate. How does expected inflation over the coming year compare with actual inflation over the past year? Plot the inflation rate since 1978 based on the percent change from a year ago of the U.S. consumer price index (FRED code: CPIAUCSL). Add to this figure as a second line the expected inflation rate from the University of Michigan survey (FRED code: MICH). Is expected inflation always in line with actual inflation? Which is more stable? *(LO3)*
4. Plot the ex ante or *expected* real interest rate since 1978 by subtracting the Michigan survey inflation measure (FRED code: MICH) from the three-month Treasury bill rate (FRED code: TB3MS). Plot as a second line the ex post or *realized* real interest rate by subtracting from the three-month Treasury bill rate (FRED code: TB3MS) the actual inflation rate based on the percent change from a year ago of the consumer price index (FRED code: CPIAUCSL). What does it mean when these two measures are different? *(LO3)*

Appendix to Chapter 4

The Algebra of Present-Value Formulas

In this short appendix, we will derive a formula for computing present value. To do so we need to use some algebra, but the result is worth the trouble. The formula is useful in computing the present value of any series of payments, such as a car loan, a mortgage, or a coupon bond, and the internal rate of return on an investment.

Imagine that you are going to buy a house. You would like to borrow *PV* dollars at interest rate i and agree to make n equal mortgage payments. How large will your payment be? It will be just big enough so that the present value of all your payments, discounted at interest rate i, equals the amount of the loan.

To compute the payment, we will use the present-value formula. If we call the size of the monthly payments C, then we need to solve the following formula:

$$PV = \frac{C}{(1+i)^1} + \frac{C}{(1+i)^2} + \frac{C}{(1+i)^3} + \cdots + \frac{C}{(1+i)^n} \tag{A1}$$

Each term in expression (A1) is the present value of a payment C made on a future date. To simplify (A1), we multiply it by $[1/(1+i)]$ to get

$$\begin{aligned} \frac{1}{(1+i)} PV &= \frac{1}{(1+i)}\left[\frac{C}{(1+i)^1} + \frac{C}{(1+i)^2} + \frac{C}{(1+i)^3} + \cdots + \frac{C}{(1+i)^n}\right] \\ &= \frac{C}{(1+i)^2} + \frac{C}{(1+i)^3} + \frac{C}{(1+i)^4} + \cdots + \frac{C}{(1+i)^n} + \frac{C}{(1+i)^{n+1}} \end{aligned} \tag{A2}$$

Now subtract (A2) from (A1):

$$\begin{aligned} PV - \frac{1}{(1+i)} PV = &\frac{C}{(1+i)^1} + \frac{C}{(1+i)^2} + \frac{C}{(1+i)^3} + \cdots + \frac{C}{(1+i)^n} \\ &- \frac{C}{(1+i)^2} - \frac{C}{(1+i)^3} - \cdots - \frac{C}{(1+i)^n} - \frac{C}{(1+i)^{n+1}} \end{aligned} \tag{A3}$$

to get

$$\frac{i}{(1+i)} PV = \frac{C}{(1+i)^1} - \frac{C}{(1+i)^{n+1}} \tag{A4}$$

Simplifying this result yields the following formula:

$$PV = \left(\frac{C}{i}\right)\left[1 - \frac{1}{(1+i)^n}\right] \tag{A5}$$

To see how to use this formula, suppose you're taking out a $100,000 mortgage that you agree to repay over 30 years at an interest rate of 8 percent. Remember that the interest rate must be quoted in decimal form and at the same frequency as the payments. For example, if you are going to make monthly payments, then i must be a monthly interest rate. To figure out your annual payment (in reality you would make 360 *monthly* payments), just solve the following formula for C:

$$\$100{,}000 = \left(\frac{C}{0.08}\right)\left[1 - \frac{1}{(1.08)^{30}}\right] \tag{A6}$$

Simplifying the right-hand side gives us

$$\$100{,}000 = 11.258C \tag{A7}$$

So your annual payment will be $8,882.57. We can do the same calculation for 360 monthly payments using a monthly interest rate of 0.6434 percent, which annualizes to 8 percent.

Formula (A5) is very useful in computing the fixed payments due on a loan, the coupon payments on a bond, or the internal rate of return on an investment. Notice that as the number of payments increases (as n gets bigger), the term $[1/(1 + i)^n]$ grows smaller. If the payments never end, so that n represents infinity, then $[1/(1 + i)^n]$ shrinks to zero. Thus, the present value of a stream of fixed payments that never ends is $[C/i]$.

Chapter

5 Understanding Risk

Learning Objectives ///

After reading this chapter, you should be able to:

LO1 Interpret risk as a measure of uncertainty about payoffs.

LO2 Explain how to quantify risk.

LO3 Define risk aversion and explain the role the risk premium plays in the risk-return tradeoff.

LO4 Explain the difference between idiosyncratic and systematic risks.

LO5 Demonstrate how to reduce risk through hedging and diversification.

Risk may be a four-letter word, but it's one we can't avoid. Every day we make decisions that involve financial and economic risk. How much car insurance should we buy? Should we refinance the mortgage now or a year from now? Should we save more for retirement, or spend the extra money on a new car? Making any decision that has more than one possible outcome is similar to gambling: We put the money on the roulette table and take our chances.

Interestingly enough, the tools we use today to measure and analyze risk were first developed to help players analyze games of chance like roulette and blackjack. For thousands of years, people have played games based on a throw of the dice, but they had little understanding of how those games actually worked. In ancient times, dice of various sorts were used to consult the gods, so any effort to analyze the odds was thought improper. But even those who ignored religious concerns could not correctly analyze a single throw of a die because they did not understand the concept of zero. That meant that the complex computations necessary to develop a theory of probability were impossible.[1]

Kamira/Shutterstock

By the mid-17th century, the power of religion had waned and mathematical tools had developed to the point that people could begin to make sense out of cards, dice, and other games. Since the invention of probability theory, we have come to realize that many everyday events, including those in economics, finance, and even weather forecasting, are best thought of as analogous to the flip of a coin or the throw of a die. For better or worse, we no longer treat these random events as if they were divinely ordained.

[1]For further details of this history, see Peter L. Bernstein, *Against the Gods: The Remarkable Story of Risk* (Hoboken, NJ: Wiley, 1998).

Still, while experts can make educated guesses about the future path of interest rates, inflation, or the stock market, their predictions are really only that—guesses. And while meteorologists are fairly good at forecasting the weather a day or two ahead, economists, financial advisors, and business gurus have dismal records. So understanding the possibility of various occurrences should allow everyone to make better choices. While risk cannot be eliminated, it can often be managed effectively.

Finally, while most people view risk as a curse to be avoided whenever possible, risk also creates opportunities. The payoff from a winning bet on one hand of cards can often erase the losses on a losing hand. Thus, the importance of probability theory to the development of modern financial markets is hard to overemphasize. People require compensation for taking risks. Without the capacity to measure risk, we could not calculate a fair price for transferring risk from one person to another, nor could we price stocks and bonds, much less sell insurance. The market for options didn't exist until economists learned how to compute the price of an option using probability theory.

In this chapter, we will learn how to measure risk and assess whether it will increase or decrease. We will also come to understand why changes in risk lead to changes in the demand for particular financial instruments and to corresponding changes in the price of those instruments.

Defining Risk

The dictionary definition of *risk,* the "possibility of loss or injury," highlights the perils of putting oneself in a situation in which the outcome is unknown. But this common use of the word doesn't quite fit our purposes because we care about gains as well as losses. We need a definition of *risk* that focuses on the fact that the outcomes of financial and economic decisions are almost always unknown at the time the decisions are made. Here is the definition we will use:

Risk *is a measure of uncertainty about the future payoff to an investment,* assessed over some *time horizon* and *relative to a benchmark.*

This definition has several important elements. First, risk is a *measure* that can be quantified. In comparing two potential investments, we want to know which one is riskier and by how much. All other things held equal, we expect a riskier investment to be less desirable than others and to command a lower price. Uncertainties that are not quantifiable cannot be priced.

Second, risk arises from *uncertainty about the future.* We know that the future will follow one and only one of many possible courses, but we don't know which one. This statement is true of even the simplest random event—more things can happen than will happen. If you flip a coin, it can come up either heads or tails. It cannot come up both heads and tails or neither heads nor tails; only one of two possibilities will occur.

Third, risk has to do with the *future payoff* of an investment, which is unknown. Though we do not know for certain what is going to happen to our investment, we must be able to list all the possibilities. Imagining all the possible payoffs and the likelihood of each one is a difficult but indispensable part of computing risk.

Fourth, our definition of risk refers to an *investment* or group of investments. We can use the term *investment* very broadly here to include everything from the balance in a bank account to shares of a mutual fund to lottery tickets and real estate.

Fifth, risk must be assessed over some *time horizon.* Every investment has a time horizon. We hold some investments for a day or two and others for many years. In most cases, the risk of holding an investment over a short period is smaller than the risk of holding it over a long one, but there are important exceptions to the rule that we will discuss later.[2]

Finally, risk must be assessed *relative to a benchmark* rather than in isolation. If someone tells you that an investment is risky, you should immediately ask: "Relative to what?" The simplest answer is "Relative to an investment with no risk at all," called a *risk-free investment.* But there are other possibilities, often more appropriate. For example, in considering the performance of a particular investment advisor or money manager, a good **benchmark** is the performance of a group of experienced investment advisors or money managers. If you want to know the risk associated with a specific investment strategy, the most appropriate benchmark would be the risk associated with other strategies.

Now that we know what risk is, how do we measure it? We use some rudimentary tools of probability theory, as we will see in the next section.

Measuring Risk

Armed with our definition of *risk*, we are now ready to quantify and measure it. In this section we will become familiar with the mathematical concepts useful in thinking about random events. We have already used some of these concepts. Recall from the last chapter that the *real* interest rate equals the *nominal* interest rate minus *expected* inflation. Without the proper tools, we weren't able to be explicit about what the term *expected inflation* means. The same is true of the term *expected return.* We see now that the best way to think about expected inflation and expected return is as the average or best guess—the *expected value*—of inflation, or the investment's return out of all the possible values.

Possibilities, Probabilities, and Expected Value

Probability theory tells us that in considering any uncertainty, the first thing we must do is *list all the possible outcomes* and then *figure out the chance of each one occurring.* When you toss a coin, what are all the *possible* outcomes? There are two and only two. The coin can come down either heads or tails. What is the *chance* of each one of these two outcomes occurring? If the coin is fair, it will come down heads half the time and tails the other half; that's what we mean by *fair.* If we tossed a fair coin over and over again, thousands of times, it would come down heads half the time and tails the other half. But for any individual toss, the coin has an equal chance of coming down heads or tails. To quantify this statement, we can say that the *probability* that the coin will come up heads is one-half.

Probability is a measure of the likelihood that an event will occur. It is always expressed as a number between zero and one. The closer the probability is to zero, the *less* likely it is that an event will occur. If the probability is exactly zero, we are sure that the event will *not* happen. The closer the probability is to one, the *more* likely it is that an event will occur. If the probability is exactly one, the event *will* definitely occur.

Some people prefer to think of random outcomes in terms of frequencies rather than probabilities. Instead of saying that the probability of a coin coming down heads is one-half, we could say that the coin will come down heads once every two tosses on average. Probabilities can always be converted into frequencies in this way.

To grasp these concepts, it is helpful to construct a table. The table lists everything that can happen (all the possibilities) together with their chances of occurring

[2]In Chapter 8, we will consider evidence that holding stock for 1 year is riskier than holding it for 20 years.

It's Not Just Expected Return That Matters

APPLYING THE CONCEPT

Your life seems to be going well. You enjoy your job, and it pays enough that you can put a little aside each month. You can't resist the dollar-for-dollar match your employer is offering on contributions to your retirement account, so you're slowly building up some long-term savings. But every so often, you wonder if you're saving enough. One day you go home and fire up the financial planning program on your computer, just to check.

Going through the retirement planner, you enter all the standard information: your age now and when you hope to retire; your salary and the value of all your assets; the monthly contribution to your retirement account and the monthly income you want at retirement. When you finish, the program asks what rate of return to assume. That is, how fast do you expect your savings to grow from now until your retirement? Following the suggestion on the screen and adjusting for inflation, you enter 6 percent, which is modestly below the average *real* return on the stock market over the past 75 years.* The light flashes green, signaling that you're on track to meet your financial goals. But are you?

Maybe. The program did a series of future- and present-value calculations like the ones described in Chapter 4. The green light means that if the assumptions you entered are valid, your saving rate is sufficient. That is, *if* your savings grow at 6 percent (adjusted for inflation), you'll be okay. So you need to decide whether you think 6 percent is a reasonable number. While it might be your best guess for the return (that's the *expected return*) over the next few decades, it is surely not the only possibility. You have very little sense of what the average return will be between now and the time that you retire.

To get a 6 percent expected return, you will have to take risk. And risk means that you could end up with less. What if your investment return is only 3 percent per year? Over 40 years that's an enormous difference. At 6 percent annual growth, $1 today is worth more than $10 in 40 years, and if you can save $1,000 per year you'll have more than $160,000 saved up. Reducing the growth rate to 3 percent means that the future value of $1 today 40 years from now falls to about $3.25. The lower return means that with the same $1,000-per-year savings, you're left with less than $80,000 after 40 years.† You'll have to save more than twice as much to meet the same goal. Now that's risk!

You need to know what the possibilities are and how likely each one is. Only then can you assess whether or not your retirement savings plan is risky.

*Inflation complicates computations over very long time periods. Price increases of 2 or 3 percent per year may not seem like much, but over 40 years they add up. At 2 percent inflation, prices double every 36 years. The simplest approach is to ignore inflation and measure income, wealth, and savings in current dollars. Then use a real rate of interest to compute future and present value.

†These numbers are based on future-value calculations. If you save $1,000 per year, after 40 years you will have $\$1{,}000 \times (1.06)^{40} + \$1{,}000 \times (1.06)^{39} + \cdots + \$1{,}000 \times (1.06)^2 + \$1{,}000 \times (1.06) = \$164{,}048$.

Table 5.1 A Simple Example: All Possible Outcomes of a Single Coin Toss

Possibilities	Probability	Outcome
#1	$\frac{1}{2}$	Heads
#2	$\frac{1}{2}$	Tails

(their probabilities). Let's start with a single coin toss. Table 5.1 lists the possibilities—heads or tails—and the probabilities, both equal to one-half.

In constructing a table like this one, we must be careful to list *all* possible outcomes. In the case of a coin toss, we know that the coin can come down only two ways, heads or tails. We know that one of these outcomes *must* occur. We just don't know which one.

One important property of probabilities is that we can compute the chance that one *or* the other event will happen by adding the probabilities together. In the case of the coin flip there are only two possibilities; the probability that the coin will come up either heads or tails must be one. If the table is constructed correctly, then, *the values in the probabilities column will sum to one.*

Let's move from a coin toss to something a bit more complicated: an investment that can rise or fall in value. Assume that for $1,000 you can purchase a stock whose value is equally likely to fall to $700 or rise to $1,400. We'll refer to the amount you could get back as the investment's **payoff**. Following the procedure we used to analyze

Table 5.2 Investing $1,000: Case 1

Possibilities	Probability	Payoff	Probability × Payoff
#1	$\frac{1}{2}$	$ 700	$350
#2	$\frac{1}{2}$	$1,400	$700

Expected value = Sum of (Probability × Payoff) = $1,050

the coin toss, we can construct Table 5.2. Again we list the possibilities and the probability that each will occur, but we add their payoffs (column 3).[3]

We can now go a step further and compute what is called the **expected value** of the investment. We are familiar with the idea of expected value as the **average** or most likely outcome. The expected value is also known as the **mean**. After listing all of the possible outcomes and the probabilities that they will occur, we compute the expected value as the sum of their probabilities times their payoffs. (Another way to say this is that the expected value is the probability-weighted sum of the possible outcomes.)

Computing the expected value of the investment is straightforward. In Table 5.2, the first step is to take the probabilities in the second column and multiply them by their associated payoffs in the third column. The results are in the fourth column. Summing them, we get

$$\text{Expected value} = \tfrac{1}{2}(\$700) + \tfrac{1}{2}(\$1{,}400) = \$1{,}050$$

which appears at the bottom of the table.

The expected value of an investment is a very useful concept, but it can be difficult at first. The problem is that if we make this investment only once, we will obtain either $700 or $1,400, not $1,050. In fact, regardless of the number of times we make this particular investment, the payoff will *never* be $1,050. But what would happen if we were to make this investment 1 million times? About 500,000 of those times the investment would pay off $1,400 and the other 500,000 times it would pay off $700. (Notice that we just converted the probabilities into frequencies.) So the *average* payoff from the 1 million investments would be

$$\frac{500{,}000}{1{,}000{,}000}(\$700) + \frac{500{,}000}{1{,}000{,}000}(\$1{,}400) = \$1{,}050 \text{ (the expected value)}$$

While the world of casino gambling may offer simple bets with just two outcomes, the financial world rarely does. To make the example more realistic, let's double the number of possibilities and look at a case in which the $1,000 investment might pay off $100 or $2,000 in addition to $700 or $1,400. Table 5.3 shows the possibilities, probabilities, and payoffs. We'll assume that the two original possibilities are the most likely; the two new possibilities are much less likely to occur. Note that the probabilities sum to one: 0.1 + 0.4 + 0.4 + 0.1 = 1. Again, we could convert the probabilities to frequencies, so that 0.4

[3]As you go through the examples in the chapter, be aware that it is often very difficult to estimate the probabilities needed to do the risk computations. The best way to do it is often to look at history. Investment analysts usually estimate the possibilities and probabilities from what happened in the past.

Table 5.3 Investing $1,000: Case 2

Possibilities	Probability	Payoff	Probability × Payoff
#1	0.1	$ 100	$ 10
#2	0.4	$ 700	$280
#3	0.4	$1,400	$560
#4	0.1	$2,000	$200

Expected value = Sum of (Probability × Payoff) = $1,050

means 4 out of 10. And again, we can compute the expected value by multiplying each probability times its associated payoff and then summing them. So $100 would be the payoff 1 out of every 10 times, $700 the payoff 4 out of every 10 times, and so on. To compute the expected value, we would find the average of these 10 investments:

$$\$100 + \$700 + \$700 + \$700 + \$700 + \$1{,}400 + \$1{,}400 + \$1{,}400 + \$1{,}400 + \$2{,}000 = \$10{,}500$$

and

$$\frac{\$10{,}500}{10} = \$1{,}050$$

Once again the expected value is $1,050.

Because the expected value of this $1,000 investment is $1,050, the expected gain is $50. But most people don't discuss investment payoffs in terms of dollars; instead, they talk about the percentage return. Expressing the return as a percentage allows investors to compute the gain or loss on the investment regardless of the size of the initial investment. In this case, the **expected return** is $50 on a $1,000 investment, or 5 percent. Note that the two $1,000 investments we just discussed are not distinguishable by their expected return, which is 5 percent in both cases. Does that mean an investor would be indifferent between them? Even a casual glance suggests that the answer is no because the second investment has a wider range of payoffs than the first. The highest payoff is higher and the lowest payoff lower than for the first investment. So the two investments carry different levels of risk. The next section discusses measures of risk.

One last word on expected values. Recall from the last chapter that to compute the real interest rate, we need a measure of *expected inflation*. One way to calculate expected inflation is to use the technique we just learned. That is, list all the possibilities for inflation, assign each one a probability, and then calculate the expected value of inflation.

Measures of Risk

Most of us have an intuitive sense of risk and its measurement. For example, we know that walking on a sidewalk is usually a safe activity. But imagine that one day as you are strolling along, you come upon a 3-foot hole in the sidewalk. The only way across is to jump over it. If the hole is just a few inches deep, it won't stop you. But the deeper it is, the greater the risk of jumping across because the greater the range of injuries you could sustain. We all have an intuitive sense that the wider the range of outcomes, the greater the risk. That's why the investment that has four possible payoffs (Table 5.3) seems riskier than the one with two possible payoffs (Table 5.2).

Thinking about risk in terms of the range of possible outcomes is straightforward. The best way to do it is to start with something that has no risk at all—a sidewalk without a hole in it or an investment with only one possible payoff. We will refer to a financial instrument with no risk at all as a risk-free investment or risk-free asset. A **risk-free asset** *is an investment whose future value is known with certainty and whose return is the* **risk-free rate of return.**[4] The payoff that you will receive from such an investment is guaranteed and cannot vary. For instance, if the risk-free return is 5 percent, a $1,000 risk-free investment will pay $1,050, its expected value, with certainty. If there is a chance that the payoff will be either more or less than $1,050, the investment is risky.

"Come on, Louis. No risk, no reward."

SOURCE: 1992 © Charles Barsotti/The New YorkerCollection/ www.Cartoonstock.com.

Let's compare this risk-free investment with the first investment we looked at, the one in which $1,000 had an equal chance of turning into $1,400 or $700 (see Table 5.2). That investment had the same expected return as the risk-free investment, 5 percent. The difference is that the payoff wasn't certain, so risk was involved. What caused the risk was the increase in the spread of the potential payoffs. The larger the spread, the higher the risk.

These examples suggest that we can measure risk by quantifying the spread among an investment's possible outcomes. We will look at two such measures. The first is based on a statistical concept called the *standard deviation* and is strictly a measure of spread. The second, called *value at risk,* is a measure of the riskiness of the worst case. When the hole in the sidewalk gets deep enough, you risk being killed if you fall in.

Variance and Standard Deviation

The **variance** is defined as the average of the squared deviations of the possible outcomes from their expected value, weighted by their probabilities. We square the differences from the expected value so that high and low payoffs don't cancel each other out and we get a measure of how spread out they are.

It takes several steps to compute the variance of an investment. First, compute the expected value and then subtract it from each of the possible payoffs. Then square each one of the results, multiply it by its probability, and, finally, add up the results. In the example of the $1,000 investment that pays either $700 or $1,400, the steps are:

1. Compute the expected value: $\frac{1}{2}(\$1{,}400) + \frac{1}{2}(\$700) = \$1{,}050$
2. Subtract the expected value from each of the possible payoffs:

   $\$1{,}400 - \$1{,}050 = +\$350$

   $\$700 - \$1{,}050 = -\$350$

[4]In most financial markets, no truly risk-free asset exists, so the risk-free rate of return is not directly observable. Regardless of our inability to measure it exactly, the risk-free rate of return remains a useful concept.

3. Square each of the results: $\$350^2 = 122{,}500(\text{dollars}^2)$ and $(-\$350)^2 = 122{,}500(\text{dollars}^2)$
4. Multiply each result times its probability and add up the results: $\frac{1}{2}[122{,}500(\text{dollars}^2)] + \frac{1}{2}[122{,}500(\text{dollars}^2)] = 122{,}500(\text{dollars}^2)$

Writing this procedure more compactly, we get

$$\text{Variance} = \tfrac{1}{2}(\$1{,}400 - \$1{,}050)^2 + \tfrac{1}{2}(\$700 - \$1{,}050)^2 = 122{,}500(\text{dollars}^2)$$

The **standard deviation** is the (positive) square root of the variance, or

$$\text{Standard deviation} = \sqrt{\textit{Variance}} = \sqrt{122{,}500(\text{dollars}^2)} = \$350$$

The standard deviation is more useful than the variance because it is measured in the same unit as the payoffs: dollars. (Variance is measured in dollars squared.) That means that we can convert the standard deviation into a percentage of the initial investment of $1,000, or 35 percent. This calculation provides a baseline against which we can measure the risk of alternative investments. Given a choice between two investments with the same expected payoff, most people would choose the one with the lower standard deviation. A higher-risk investment would be less desirable.

Let's compare this two-payoff investment with the one that has four possible payoffs. We already concluded that the second investment is riskier, because the payoffs are more spread out. But how much riskier is it? To answer this question, we can compute the standard deviation. That means following the four steps to calculate the variance, and then taking the square root. From the detailed computation in Table 5.4 you can see the standard deviation is $528. This is 1½ times the $350 standard deviation of the first investment, with only two possible payoffs. Because the two investments have the same expected value, the vast majority of people would prefer the first. The greater the standard deviation, the higher the risk.

To see this conclusion graphically, start with Case 1 from Table 5.2 where a $1,000 investment is equally likely to rise in value to $1,400 or fall in value to $700. That is, there are two possibilities, each with probability ½: $700 and $1,400. We can plot this on a bar graph, where the horizontal axis has the payoffs $700 or $1,400 and the height of each bar is the probability (in this case 0.5 for both). The result is in the left panel of Figure 5.1. Recall from Table 5.2 that the expected value of this investment is $1,050, the vertical line in the figure.

Compare this to Case 2 from Table 5.3. Recall that in this case the $1,000 investment has four possible payoffs, $100, $700, $1,400 and $2,000, and these occur with probability 0.1, 0.4, 0.4, and 0.1. As in Case 1, the expected value continues to be $1,050. Using the same method as before, where the height of each bar represents the probability of each outcome, we can plot the right-hand panel of Figure 5.1. Comparing the two figures, we can see that in Case 2, where the investment has four possible payoffs, the distribution is more spread out. This matches the result from computing the standard deviation. *The more spread out the distribution of possible payoffs from an investment, the higher the standard deviation and the bigger the risk.*

Value at Risk Standard deviation is the most common measure of financial risk, and for most purposes it is adequate. But in some circumstances we need to take a different approach to the measurement of risk. Sometimes we are less concerned with the spread of possible outcomes than with the value of the worst outcome. For example, no one wants the local bank to close its doors. Nor is anyone interested in a discount price for a life insurance policy from an insurance company that is in poor

Table 5.4 Expected Value, Variance, and Standard Deviation

To compute the expected value, variance, and standard deviation of the four-payoff investment in Table 5.3, follow the steps described in the text nearby:

1. Compute the expected value.
   - List the possible payoffs and their probabilities.
   - Compute the expected value as the sum of the payoff times the probabilities.
2. Compute the variance.
   - From each payoff subtract the expected value.
   - Square the deviation of the payoff from the expected value.
   - Sum the squared deviations times the probabilities.
3. Compute the standard deviation as the positive square root of the variance.

Here's the information we need:

(1) Probability	(2) Payoff	(3) Payoff − Expected Value	(4) (Payoff − Expected Value)^2
0.1	\$ 100	(\$ 100 − \$1,050) = −\$950	902,500(dollars^2)
0.4	\$ 700	(\$ 700 − \$1,050) = −\$350	122,500(dollars^2)
0.4	\$1,400	(\$1,400 − \$1,050) = +\$350	122,500(dollars^2)
0.1	\$2,000	(\$2,000 − \$1,050) = +\$950	902,500(dollars^2)

1. Using columns (1) and (2), we can compute the expected value:

   Expected value = Sum of (Probability × Payoff)
   = 0.1 × \$100 + 0.4 × \$700 + 0.4 × \$1,400 + 0.1 × \$2,000
   = \$10 + \$280 + \$560 + \$200
   = \$1,050

2. Using column (4), we can compute the variance:

   Variance = Sum of (Probability × Squared deviation of payoff from expected value)
   = 0.1 × 902,500 + 0.4 × 122,500 + 0.4 × 122,500 + 0.1 × 902,500
   = 278,500(dollars^2)

3. Finally, using this result, we can compute the standard deviation:

   Standard deviation = $\sqrt{\text{Variance}}$
   = $\sqrt{278{,}500(\text{dollars}^2)}$
   = \$528

financial condition. Neither the customers nor the government regulators care how well or how badly a financial institution's shareholders fare, so long as they do well enough to keep the doors open. The concept used to assess this sort of catastrophic risk is called **value at risk (VaR)**.

To understand how value at risk works, let's look at an example. Assume you are considering buying a house. In going through your finances, you conclude that you can afford a monthly mortgage payment of \$650 and no more. You find a nice house and a mortgage lender who will lend you \$100,000 to buy it. But you need to decide on the type of mortgage to get. Should it have a fixed or adjustable rate? The answer is different for different people. But let's see if we can organize our thinking.

Figure 5.1 Investing $1,000

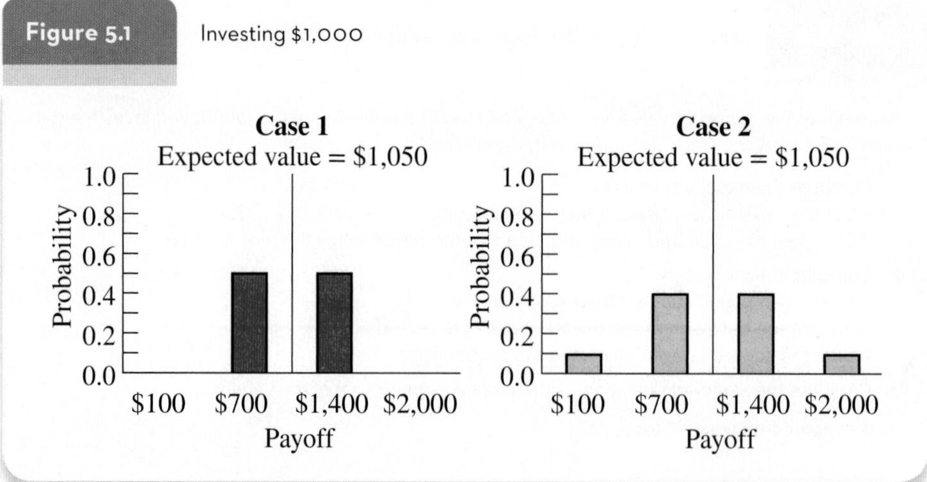

The figure plots the distribution of possible outcomes from a $1,000 investment from Tables 5.2 and 5.3 on pages 105 and 106. In each case, the payoff is on the horizontal axis and the height of each bar equals the probability that outcome will occur.

The Impact of Leverage on Risk

TOOLS OF THE TRADE

In Chapter 3, we saw that leverage added to risks in the financial system (see Lessons from the Crisis: Leverage). Recall that **leverage** is the practice of borrowing to finance part of an investment. Common examples of leverage are borrowing to buy stock (through what is called *margin loans*), corporate borrowing (using bonds), and borrowing to acquire a house (by obtaining a mortgage). In the case of a margin loan, an investor borrows from a brokerage firm to increase the quantity of stock purchased.

How does leverage affect risk and return? To understand the effects of leverage, let's look at an investment of $1,000 with an expected return of 5 percent (a gain of $50) and a standard deviation of 35 percent ($350). That's the example in Table 5.2. What if in addition to investing $1,000 of your own, you borrow $1,000 and invest a total of $2,000? This investment strategy changes the risk involved. The reason is that the lender wants to be repaid the $1,000 loan regardless of how much your investment returns. If the investment's payoff is high, your $2,000 investment will increase in value to $2,800. After repaying the $1,000 loan, you will be left with $1,800—an increase of $800 over your initial investment of $1,000. If your investment falls in value, the $2,000 will become $1,400. After repaying the $1,000 loan, you will be left with $400—a loss of $600.

Because these two results are equally likely, the expected value of your leveraged investment is $\frac{1}{2}$($1,800) + $\frac{1}{2}$($400) = $1,100. Your expected gain—the difference between your investment of $1,000 and its expected value of $1,100—is now $100 and your expected return is 10 percent. That's double the expected return from your investment of $1,000 without any borrowing—double what it would be without leverage. So we have part of the answer to our question: *Leverage increases the expected return.*

But what about risk? To figure it out, let's calculate the standard deviation of your leveraged investment.

$$\textbf{St. Dev.} = \sqrt{\tfrac{1}{2}(1{,}800 - 1{,}100)^2 + \tfrac{1}{2}(400 - 1{,}100)^2} = \$700$$

The standard deviation has doubled: *twice the expected return at twice the risk!*

We can repeat these calculations for any amount of leverage we want. For example, homebuyers commonly pay 20 percent of the price of a house with their savings and borrow the remaining 80 percent. Because mortgage lenders expect to be repaid, changes in the price of the house become gains or losses to the owner. Say you buy a $100,000 house by borrowing $80,000 and paying $20,000 from your savings, often called your *equity*. A 10 percent increase in your home's value would raise the price to $110,000. Subtracting the $80,000 you borrowed, your $20,000 down payment would become $30,000, a

50 percent increase. On the other hand, if your home's value fell by 10 percent, you would *lose* half your $20,000 down payment. *Leverage magnifies the effect of price changes* (see figure below).

The Effect of Leverage on Risk and Return

To understand leverage, picture a set of two gears, one large and one small. The movement in the price of the leveraged investment is measured by the number of revolutions in the big gear. This explains why some people refer to leverage as "gearing." The investor's risk and return are measured by the number of revolutions in the small gear. The bigger the big gear, the more times the small gear goes around with each revolution of the big gear. That's leverage.

We can use these examples to develop a formula for the impact of leverage on the expected return and standard deviation of an investment. If you borrow to purchase an asset, you increase both the expected return and the standard deviation by a leverage ratio of

$$\textbf{Leverage ratio} = \frac{\textbf{Cost of investment}}{\textbf{Owner's contribution to the purchase}}$$

where the "Owner's contribution to the purchase" in the denominator is just the cost of investment minus the amount borrowed. If the expected return and standard deviation of the unleveraged investment are 5 percent and 35 percent (as in our first example), then borrowing half and contributing half means that for each dollar invested, the buyer is contributing 50 cents. The formula tells us that the leverage ratio is 1/0.5, which equals 2. Thus the investment's expected return is 2 × 5 percent = 10 percent, and its standard deviation is 2 × 35 percent = 70 percent. (See the accompanying table.) And if the homeowner borrows 80 percent of the purchase price of the house, his or her contribution is 20 percent, so the leverage ratio is 1/(1 – 80/100) = 1/0.2 = 5 times what it would be for someone who could buy the house outright, with no mortgage.

We have focused on the impact of leverage on risk, but leverage has at least as big an impact on value at risk. Note that for the $1,000 investment without leverage in Table 5.2, the worst case was a loss of $300, or 30 percent, half the time. If an investor borrowed 90 percent of the funds needed to make the investment, half the time the investor would lose not only the entire $100 invested but an additional $200 of borrowed funds as well. *Leverage compounds the worst possible outcome.*

The Impact of Leverage

	No Leverage	Leverage Ratio = 2
Your investment	$1,000	$1,000
+ Amount borrowed	0	$1,000
= Total invested	$1,000	$2,000
Possible payoffs	$1,400 or $700	$2,800 or $1,400
Net of repayment	$1,400 or $700	$1,800 or $400
Expected value (net of repayment)	$1,050 (5%)	$1,100 (10%)
Standard deviation	$350 (35%)	$700 (70%)

The example uses the information from Table 5.2, where a $1,000 investment has an equal probability of a $1,400 or a $700 payoff. In the example with leverage on the right, the investor borrows $1,000, invests a total of $2,000, obtains a payoff of either $2,800 or $1,400, and must repay the $1,000 loan for a net payoff of $1,800 or $400.

Systemic Risk*
LESSONS FROM THE CRISIS

The financial system consists of all the institutions and markets that perform intermediation—matching savers with users of funds. Threats to the system as a whole—known as *systemic risks*—differ from the threats to specific households, firms, or markets. Naturally, governments are more concerned about systemic threats because they can be catastrophic for an economy. Their policy goal is a resilient financial system that cannot be brought down by the failure of specific parts.

Cell biology provides a useful analogy for understanding a financial system. Complex organisms are composed of many cells with specialized purposes. Every day, a large number of these cells die (and new ones are created) without threatening the organism as a whole. In financial systems, too, many intermediaries fail and new ones emerge without posing a systemic threat. Yet, in both biology and finance, some disturbances can undermine both the parts and the whole.

This biological analogy can be taken a step further. Think of financial institutions as the cells of the financial system, and think of markets as the central nervous system that coordinates their actions. Cells operating alone cannot make a complex organism function. Their actions are coordinated by the messages that travel along diverse electrical and chemical pathways. In the same way, an effective financial system requires markets that collect and transmit information necessary to coordinate the behavior of financial institutions and others.

How does the biological analogy help us understand systemic risk? It provides hints about what might threaten the system as a whole, not just its parts.

In the world of finance, systemic risk arises when a set of vulnerabilities in markets and financial institutions threatens to disrupt the general function of intermediation. *Common exposure* to a risk can threaten many intermediaries at the same time. Connections among financial institutions and markets, even when unseen, may transmit and amplify a shock across the system. Obstacles to the flow of information make a system more vulnerable, because information is needed to coordinate the system's parts.

A financial system also may contain critical parts (comparable to a heart or a brain) without which it cannot function. Key markets and exchanges may play such a role. Similarly, the largest, most interconnected financial firms are sometimes called *too big to fail* if their failure threatens a cascade of bankruptcies among other firms.

As one possible source of systemic risk, consider the role of liquidity, which is often called the lifeblood of a financial system (see Chapter 2, Lessons from the Crisis: Market Liquidity, Funding Liquidity, and Making Markets). Usually, the smooth circulation of liquid assets around the financial system makes it possible for financial institutions to convert their holdings easily into cash and to trade in markets. But what happens if that circulation is interrupted or if the overall supply of liquidity is inadequate?

Like a heart attack, obstacles to the flow of liquidity pose a catastrophic threat to the financial system. Some financial institutions may become unable to trade or make payments, while markets for a range of assets may dry up. If these shocks weaken other firms, the result can be a wave of bankruptcies.

*Note that *systemic* risk—which refers to the financial system—differs from *systematic* risk, which is defined in this chapter as an economywide risk that alters the size of the economic pie.

Assume that the current interest rate on a 30-year fixed-rate mortgage (the most popular kind) is 4 percent, so it has monthly payments around $475, which is within your budget.[5] One alternative is a mortgage with the same 30-year term that adjusts once a year, starting at 3 percent. The adjustable-rate mortgage has payments that start at about $420 per month.

This looks great. But remember Core Principle 2: Risk requires compensation. By taking the adjustable-rate mortgage you can save more than $50 per month. But adjustable rates can adjust, meaning they can go up and down. That's a risk. Looking closer, you realize that the mortgage contract specifies that the adjustments can be as much as 2 percentage points per year, and can go as high as 11 percent. Which mortgage should you sign up for?

[5]All of the numbers in this example are approximate. To compare payments on fixed- and adjustable-rate mortgages, you can use the calculators at www.wsj.com or www.choosetosave.org.

The lower initial monthly payments do seem to come with higher risk. Without doing any computations, we know that the standard deviation of monthly payments for a 4 percent fixed-rate mortgage is zero, and that the standard deviation of the payment for the adjustable-rate mortgage is greater than zero. Let's just say that interest rates are not expected to change, so the expected value of the monthly payments in the second circumstance is just $420. But what does that tell us?

The computation of the expected value and standard deviation does not seem to get at the heart of the problem. The reason is that it doesn't take proper account of the worst case. The interest rate could rise 2 percent per year for the next four years. That means that your monthly payments could rise to around $535 in the second year after one adjustment, about $665 in the third year, and go up over $800 in the fourth year. While you can readily make the $535 payments, more than $650 per month is out of the question. If interest rates were to rise by 4 percentage points over the next two years, you would no longer be able to afford the mortgage payments. That's the risk.

This mortgage example highlights the fact that sometimes risk should be measured by the value of the worst case rather than be measured by expected value and standard deviation. Value at risk, which measures risk as the maximum potential loss, is more appropriate in the example we just studied. VaR is the answer to the question: How much will I lose if the worst possible scenario occurs? In the example of the $1,000 investment, summarized in Table 5.2, the worst case was a loss of $300. In the more complex $1,000 investment, summarized in Table 5.3, the value at risk was $900—the most you could possibly lose. In the mortgage example the value at risk is the house: If the payment increases beyond $650 a month, you can't make the payments on your loan and you will be forced to sell the house. There are surely cases where the lower payments of an adjustable-rate mortgage are worth the risk, but this may not be one of them.

A more sophisticated value-at-risk analysis would include a time horizon and probabilities. In fact, the formal definition of *Value at Risk* is *the worst possible loss over a specific time horizon, at a given probability.* VaR is a measure of risk that we will find very useful in discussing the management and regulation of financial institutions. By restricting the sorts of financial instruments banks can hold, bank managers and financial regulators try to limit the chances of a financial collapse. Such a collapse is an example of infrequent but potentially catastrophic events sometimes called *tail risks* or *black swans* (like the enormous 2011 earthquake that produced a tsunami and nuclear disaster in Japan). To address the dangers associated with financial tail risks, banks and regulators employ the concept of value at risk.

Risk Aversion, the Risk Premium, and the Risk-Return Tradeoff

The implication of our discussion so far is that most people don't like risk and will pay to avoid it. While some people enjoy risky activities like skydiving and car racing, most of us are more careful. And while some people gamble large sums, most of us don't because we can't sustain large losses comfortably. In fact, the reason we buy insurance is that we want someone else to take the risk. Insurance is an interesting case; remember, for an insurance company to make a profit, it must charge more than it expects to pay out. Thus, insurance premiums are higher than the expected value of the policyholder's losses. We pay to avoid risks because most of us are *risk averse.*

RISK

Pepgooner/Shutterstock

To understand risk aversion, imagine that you are offered a single chance to play a game in which a fair coin will be tossed. If it comes up heads you will win $1,000; if it comes up tails, you will get nothing. How much would you be willing to pay to play the game just once? The expected value of the game is $500—that is, on average, the game yields $500—but you may play only one time. Would you pay $500 to play the game? If so, you are *risk neutral.* Most people would not play the game at $500, though they would at less than that amount. These people are *risk averse.*

Because the coin toss is similar to an investment, we can apply the same logic to investor behavior and conclude that *a risk-averse investor will always prefer an investment with a certain return to one with the same expected return but any amount of uncertainty.* (A risk-neutral person wouldn't care as long as the expected return is the same.) A risk-free investment with a guaranteed return is clearly preferable to a risky investment with the same expected return but an uncertain outcome. In the case of the coin toss, most people would take $500 with certainty rather than risk tossing the coin and getting double or nothing.

One result of this desire to avoid risk is that investors require compensation for taking risk. That's the flip side of buying insurance. When we buy insurance, we pay someone else to take our risks, so it makes sense that if someone wants us to take on a risk, we need to be paid to do it. A risky investment, then, must have an expected return that is higher than the return on a risk-free asset. In economic terms, it must offer a **risk premium**. In general, *the riskier an investment, the higher the risk premium (the higher the compensation investors require for holding it)* (see Figure 5.2).

By extension, if riskier investments have higher risk premiums, they must have higher expected returns. Thus, there is a tradeoff between risk and expected return; you can't get a high return without taking considerable risk. So if someone tells you he or she made a big return on an investment, you should suspect that it was a very risky investment. No risk, no reward!

To see how the idea of a risk premium works, take the case of a bond. We will study this in much more detail in Chapters 6 and 7, but for now let's compare bonds issued by Johnson & Johnson (JNJ) with those of JCPenney (JCP). As of the first quarter of 2019, JNJ was in top-notch financial condition, while JCP was not. That leads us to expect that the return for holding JCP's bonds would contain a higher risk premium than would the return for holding JNJ bonds. And it did. In early 2019, the two companies had bonds with a maturity range of about five years. Those from JCP paid 25.09 percent, while those from JNJ paid 2.59 percent. Meanwhile, a five-year U.S. Treasury note paid a meager 2.42 percent. Because the U.S. Treasury is highly likely to pay, we'll use 2.42 percent as our estimate of the risk-free rate. So, to get an estimate of the risk premium for the JNJ and JCP bonds, we subtract 2.42 from the rate for each: For JCP, the result is 25.09 − 2.42 = 22.67 percent; for JNJ, we get 2.59 − 2.42 = 0.17 percent. Not surprisingly, the risk premium on the relatively risky company is much bigger—in this case, more than 100 times bigger!

Figure 5.2 The Tradeoff between Risk and Expected Return

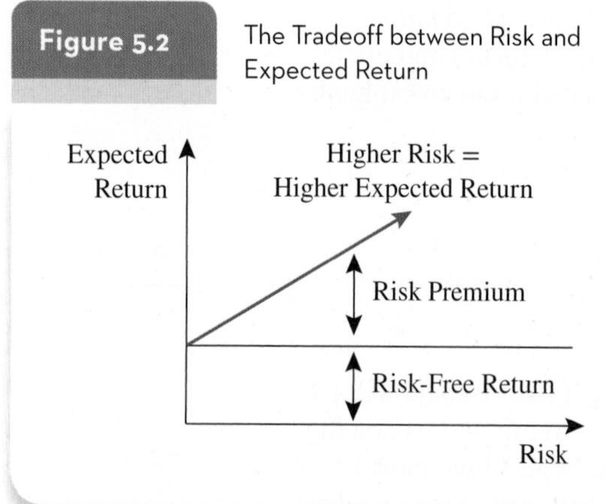

The higher the risk, the higher the expected return. The risk premium equals the expected return on the risky investment minus the risk-free return.

Sources of Risk: Idiosyncratic and Systematic Risk

Risk is everywhere. It comes in many forms and from almost every imaginable place. In most circumstances the sources of risk are obvious. For drivers, it's the risk of an accident; for farmers, the risk of bad weather; for investors, the risk of fluctuating stock prices. Regardless of the source, however, we can classify all risks into one of two groups: (1) those affecting a small number of people but no one else and (2) those affecting everyone. We'll call the first of these **idiosyncratic risks**, or *unique* risks, and the second **systematic risks**, or *economywide* risks.[6]

To understand the difference between idiosyncratic and systematic risk, think about the risks facing Ford Motor Company stockholders. Why should the value of Ford's stock go up or down? There are two main reasons. First, there is the risk that Ford will lose sales to other carmakers. If Ford fares poorly compared with its competition, its market share (and thus its share of all economic activity) may shrink (see Figure 5.3). This risk is unique to Ford, because if Ford does relatively poorly, someone else must be doing relatively better. Idiosyncratic risk affects specific firms, not everyone.

The second risk Ford's stockholders face is that the U.S. industry as a whole will do poorly (see Figure 5.3). This is systematic, economywide risk. If we think of *idiosyncratic risk* as a change in the *share* of the *auto-market* pie, *systematic risk* is a change in the *size* of the pie of the *entire economy*, of which the auto market is a part. In other words, systematic risk is the risk that everyone will do poorly at the same time. The entire economy could slow for reasons that are completely unrelated to any individual company's performance. Macroeconomic factors, such as swings in consumer and business confidence brought on by global economic conditions or changes in the political climate, are the source of systematic risks that affect *all* firms and individuals in the entire economy.

Idiosyncratic risks come in two types. In the first, one set of firms is affected in one way and other firms in another way. An example would be a change in the price of oil. History tells us that when oil prices rise, auto sales fall, and the automobile industry suffers. But higher oil prices improve the profits of firms that supply energy, such as ExxonMobil, Shell, and Texaco. An oil price change that is bad for Ford is good for the oil companies. Looking at the economy as a whole, this is an idiosyncratic risk.

Not all idiosyncratic risks are balanced by opposing risks to other firms or industries. Some unique risks are specific to one person or company and no one else. The risk that two people have an automobile accident is unrelated to whether anyone else has one. We will include these completely independent risks in the category of idiosyncratic risks.

Figure 5.3 Idiosyncratic and Systematic Risk

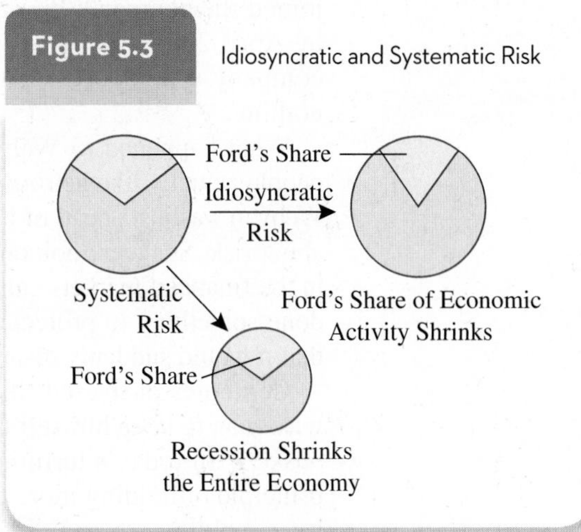

[6]These are also sometimes referred to as *specific* and *common risks*.

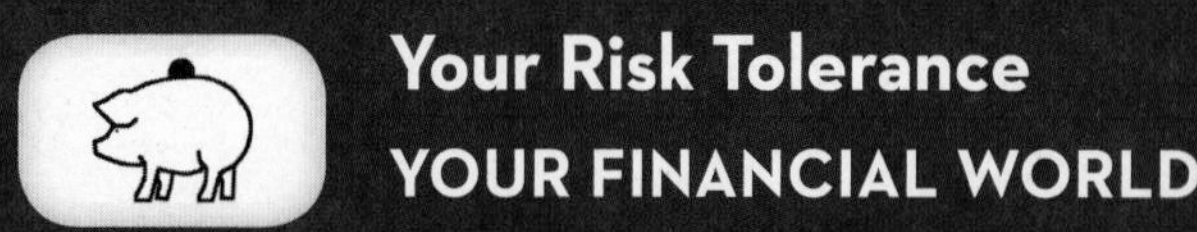

Your Risk Tolerance
YOUR FINANCIAL WORLD

How much risk should you tolerate? Figuring that out isn't easy, but there are a few ways to get some sense of the right level of risk for you. First, there are risk quizzes, short sets of questions financial advisors give their clients to determine the level of risk they can live with. For instance, "What would you do if a month after you invest in the stock market, the value of your stocks suddenly falls by 20 percent?" Answers might include "Sell right away," "Nothing," and "Buy more." Many financial institutions offer one on their websites, so you might want to try one.

But don't stop there. Even if you are willing to take risks, that doesn't mean you should. You may not have time to make back the losses you might suffer. Think about the difference between a 25-year-old and a 60-year-old both saving for their retirement. Which one of these people can afford to suddenly lose a quarter of her savings? Obviously, it is the 25-year-old. If a 60-year-old loses a quarter of her retirement savings, it's a disaster! Likewise, if you're saving to buy a car or a home, the sooner you are planning to make the purchase, the less you can afford to lose what you have. Always ask yourself: How much can I stand to lose? The longer your time horizon (and the wealthier you are), the more risk you can tolerate.

Reducing Risk through Diversification

When George T. Shaheen left his $4 million-a-year job overseeing 65,000 employees of a large management consulting firm to become chief executive of the Webvan Group, he may not have realized how much of a risk he was taking. He thought Webvan would change the way people bought their groceries. Consumers would order their cereal, milk, apples, and ice cream over the Internet, and Webvan would deliver to their door. In November 1999, just a few months after Shaheen joined the company, his stock in Webvan was worth more than $280 million. But by April 2001, his shares were worth a paltry $150,000 and Shaheen had left the company. On July 10, 2001, Webvan collapsed and stockholders were left with nothing.

What happened to Webvan and its plan to change the way people shop? Maybe people actually like getting out of the house and going to the grocery store. Or maybe Webvan was just ahead of its time. But this story is about more than shopping; it's also about risk. Shaheen took on so much risk that a single big loss wiped him out. Traders in the financial markets call this experience "blowing up." Surely Shaheen could have done something to protect at least a portion of his phenomenal wealth from the risk that it would suddenly disappear. But what?

Cervantes answered this question in *Don Quixote* in 1605: "It is the part of a wise man to keep himself today for tomorrow, and *not to venture all his eggs in one basket.*" In today's terminology, risk can be reduced through **diversification**, the principle of holding more than one risk at a time. Though it may seem counterintuitive, holding several different investments can reduce the idiosyncratic risk an investor bears. A combination of risky investments is often less risky than any one individual investment. There are two ways to diversify your investments. You can *hedge* risks or you can *spread* them among the many investments. Let's discuss hedging first.

Hedging Risk

Hedging is the strategy of reducing idiosyncratic risk by making two investments with opposing risks. When one does poorly, the other does well, and vice versa. So while the payoff from each investment is volatile, together their payoffs are stable.

Consider the risk an investor faces from a potential change in the price of oil. Increases in the price of oil are bad for most of the economy, but they are good for oil companies. So an investor might buy stock in both 3M, maker of a wide range of products for consumer, medical and industrial uses; and Texaco, a large oil company. For the sake of our example, let's assume that oil prices have an equal chance of rising or falling. When they rise, owners of Texaco stock receive a payoff of $120 for each $100 they invested. When oil prices fall, Texaco's shareholders just get their $100 investment back. The reverse is true for 3M. When oil prices fall, owners of 3M stock get $120 for each $100 they invested; when oil prices rise, they get $100.

Table 5.5 Payoffs on Two Separate Investments of $100

	Payoff from Owning Only		
Possibility	**3M**	**Texaco**	**Probability**
Oil prices rise	$100	$120	$\frac{1}{2}$
Oil prices fall	$120	$100	$\frac{1}{2}$

Table 5.5 summarizes these relationships.

Let's compare three strategies for investing $100, given the relationships shown in the table:

1. Invest $100 in 3M.
2. Invest $100 in Texaco.
3. Invest half in each company: $50 in 3M and $50 in Texaco.

Regardless of whether you invest $100 in 3M or Texaco, the expected payoff is ½($120) + ½($100) = $110; and the

$$\text{Standard deviation of the payoff} = \sqrt{\tfrac{1}{2}(\$120 - \$110)^2 + \tfrac{1}{2}(\$100 - \$110)^2} = \$10$$

But what about the third option? What if you split your $100 and put half in 3M and half in Texaco? Because $50 is half the size of your initial investment, the payoff is half as big as well—a $50 investment in either stock pays off either $60 or $50. But the important point about this strategy is that it reduces your risk (see Table 5.6). When oil prices go up, Texaco does well but 3M does badly. When oil prices fall, the reverse happens. Regardless of whether oil prices go up or down, you will get back $110 on your $100 investment. Investing $50 in each stock ensures your payoff. Hedging—splitting your investment between two stocks with different payoff patterns—has eliminated your risk entirely.

Table 5.6 Results of Possible Investment Strategies: Hedging Risk
Initial Investment = $100

Investment Strategy	Expected Payoff	Standard Deviation
3M only	$110	$10
Texaco only	$110	$10
$\frac{1}{2}$ and $\frac{1}{2}$	$110	$ 0

Could George Shaheen have hedged the risk of owning so much Webvan stock? To do it, he would have had to find a company whose stock price would rise when Webvan's fell. That would have been difficult, because Webvan's business concept was new and untested. But Shaheen did have another option.

Do U.S. Households Benefit When Growth Is Stable?
APPLYING THE CONCEPT

Something odd has happened to the U.S. economy over the past three decades. Economists call this period the Great Moderation because aggregate income, measured by real GDP, became more stable. But at the household level, the volatility of income *rose* during the Great Moderation. Put differently, families face greater *idiosyncratic* income risk than in the past even though economywide *systematic risk* has receded.

What are the implications? Consider a slowdown of 2½ percent in economic growth—the typical pattern of a U.S. recession in the past half century. If it meant everyone went home an hour earlier on Friday afternoon until growth picked up again, we wouldn't worry much—the burden would be spread evenly across the entire population. But that's not how it works. Instead, in that typical recession, one in every 30 or 40 people becomes unemployed, so the pain is highly concentrated. Business cycle downturns come with lots of idiosyncratic risk.

Disturbingly, even as recessions have become milder, individual income volatility has been rising.* This volatility could reflect more frequent, short-term job changes. If so, the fall in income while between jobs would be quickly reversed. Alternatively, it could be that people who lose their jobs are less likely to find a new one at the same level of pay, in which case the income decline will persist. It's probably a bit of both.

Regardless of why individual income risk has gone up even as aggregate risk has gone down, a key question is whether households can insure themselves against the risk of an interruption or decline in income.

At first glance, you might think that a large group of people facing uncorrelated hazards are perfect candidates for an insurance pool. However, a combination of incentives, complexity, and cost conspire to make private insurance of this kind generally unavailable. For example, someone who is hedged against income risk may be less inclined to seek retraining (or a new job if they lose one). And, while insurers know how to overcome such incentive problems, doing so requires complex and costly contracts. The same is true of creating and operating financial markets needed to hedge risks.

So, U.S. households today face greater idiosyncratic income risk than a generation ago. Can finance specialists and economic policymakers find a way to use financial institutions and markets to help people diversify these income risks? Not yet, but they have good reason to work at it.†

*Karen Dynan, Douglas Elmendorf, and Daniel Sichel, "The Evolution of Household Income Volatility," *The B.E. Journal of Economic Analysis and Policy* 12, no. 2 (2012).

†Robert Shiller, *The New Financial Order: Risk in the 21st Century* (Princeton, NJ: Princeton University Press, 2004).

Spreading Risk

Because investments don't always move predictably in opposite directions, you can't always reduce risk through hedging. Fortunately, there is another way. You can simply **spread risk** around—and that's what George Shaheen should have done. To spread your risk, all you need to do is find investments whose payoffs are unrelated. Let's replace Texaco with Microsoft and assume that 3M and Microsoft's payoffs are independent of each other.[7] So we toss a coin once to see if 3M does well or badly, and then we toss it a second time to see how Microsoft does. As before, a \$100 investment in either company pays off either \$120 or \$100 with equal probability.

Again, we'll consider three investment strategies: (1) 3M only, (2) Microsoft only, and (3) half in 3M and half in Microsoft. The expected payoff on each of these strategies is the same: \$110. For the first two strategies, \$100 in either company, the standard deviation is still \$10, just as it was before. But for the third strategy, \$50 in 3M and \$50 in Microsoft, the analysis is more complicated. There are four possible outcomes, two for each stock.

[7]The assumption of independence makes the calculations easier but is not essential. All that we need to know is that the two payoffs, 3M and Microsoft, are not perfectly correlated so they do not move in lockstep.

Table 5.7 Payoffs from Investing $50 in Each of Two Stocks
Initial Investment = $100

Possibilities	3M	Microsoft	Total Payoff	Probability
#1	$60	$60	$120	$\frac{1}{4}$
#2	$60	$50	$110	$\frac{1}{4}$
#3	$50	$60	$110	$\frac{1}{4}$
#4	$50	$50	$100	$\frac{1}{4}$

To solve the problem, we need to create a table showing all the possibilities, their probabilities, and the associated payoffs (see Table 5.7). We're familiar with possibilities 2 and 3, in which one stock pays off but the other one doesn't, just as in the 3M/Texaco example.

Remember that the standard deviation is the square root of the average of the squared deviations from the expected value, weighted by the probabilities. In this case, that turns out to be the square root of the sum of $\frac{1}{4}(\$120 - \$110)^2$ plus $\frac{1}{4}(\$100 - \$110)^2$, which is $\sqrt{50(\text{dollars}^2)} = \$7.1$.[8]

Figure 5.4 shows the distribution of outcomes from the possible investment strategies. The left-hand panel plots the payoffs from investing the entire $100 in one stock, either 3M or Microsoft. The right-hand panel has the distribution of the payoffs from investing $50 in each of two stocks (from Table 5.7). The figure makes clear that by

Figure 5.4 Spreading Risk Payoffs from Two Investment Strategies

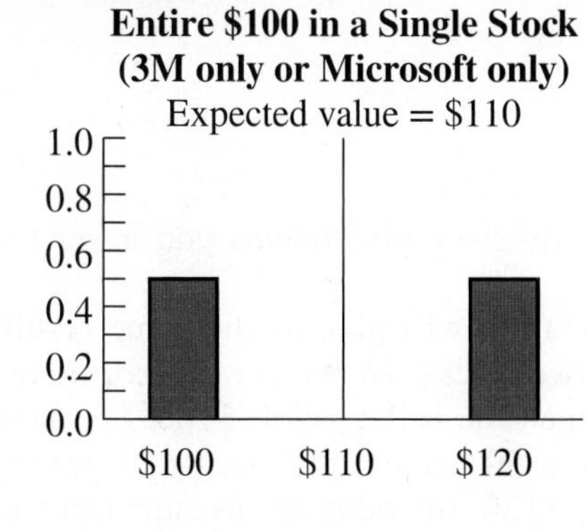

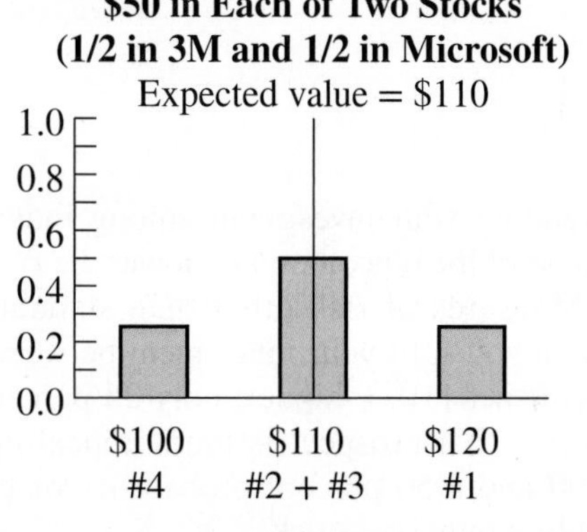

Left panel is the bar plot of the distribution of payoffs from investing all $100 in either 3M or Microsoft, where each pays off either $100 or $110 with probability ½. Right panel is the bar plot of the distribution of payoffs from investing $50 each in 3M and Microsoft, where each pays off either $50 or $60 with probability ½ and both are independent (see Table 5.7).

[8]Following the steps in Table 5.4, we can compute the standard deviation of investing $50 each in 3M and Microsoft as $\sqrt{\frac{1}{4}(\$120 - \$110)^2 + \frac{1}{4}(\$110 - \$110)^2 + \frac{1}{4}(\$110 - \$110)^2 + \frac{1}{4}(\$100 - \$110)^2}$ $= \sqrt{\frac{1}{4}(\$10)^2 + \frac{1}{4}(\$0)^2 + \frac{1}{4}(\$0)^2 + \frac{1}{4}(\$10)^2} = \sqrt{50(\text{dollars}^2)} = \$7.1$.

On the Distribution of Wealth

MONEY AND BANKING BLOG

Over the past half century or so, while the distribution of per capita income around the world has become more equal, *within* many advanced countries income has become distinctly less equal. What is true of income also applies to wealth.

Wealth inequality affects welfare in at least two key respects. First, savings allow households to smooth consumption in the face of temporary bouts of illness or unemployment, but those with little or no wealth have nothing to buffer fluctuations in income. Second, wealth provides resources in retirement, but those with little or no savings face potential hardship in old age.

It turns out that the distribution of wealth is far less equal than that of income. Moreover, in the United States, the wealth distribution has become decidedly more unequal in recent years. As a result, a large portion of U.S. households appear to have little scope for meeting retirement needs out of their current net worth, making federal insurance programs key to their future well-being.

While wealth inequality prevails in virtually every modern economy, the differences across countries are large. Among the advanced economies, wealth inequality appears particularly pronounced in the United States. According to OECD country comparisons, the United States ranks at the top for the wealth shares of the top 10 percent (79.5 percent) and the top 1 percent (42.5 percent). It is also the third lowest for the bottom 60 percent (2.4 percent). At the opposite end of the spectrum is Japan, where the wealth ratio of the top 10 percent to the bottom 60 percent is 2.3, just a fraction of the U.S. ratio of 33.

What factors influence the evolution of the wealth distribution in the United States? One element is the path of incomes. Other things equal, slower income growth means less saving and less wealth accumulation. Moreover, the lower the mobility of people between income groups over generations, the wider the gap between the savings and wealth paths of the wealthy and those of the others. A second factor is that the less well-off hold a different mix of assets and are more reliant on borrowing. A third reason for increased wealth inequality is the evolution of asset prices.

What are the key portfolio differences across the population? The wealthiest Americans invest the largest portion of their wealth in business equity and related instruments, while people in the middle of the distribution concentrate their holdings in a highly undiversified asset—their home. Information from the Federal Reserve's Survey of

spreading your investment among independently risky investments you lower the spread of the outcomes, and lower the risk.

Measures of risk other than standard deviation will give us the same result. When you split your investment between the two stocks, 75 percent of the time the payoff is $110 or higher; only 25 percent of the time is the payoff $100. For most people, that prospect is more appealing than a 50 percent probability of getting $100 and a 50 percent probability of getting $120, the odds an investor faces in holding only one stock.

In the real world, there is no reason for an investor to stop diversifying at two stocks. The more independent sources of risk you hold in your portfolio, the lower your overall risk. Using the same numbers in this example—a payoff of either $100 or $120 per $100 investment, with equal probability—we can increase the number of stocks from two to three to four, and the standard deviation of a $100 investment will fall from $7.1 to $5.8 to $5.0. As we add more and more independent sources of risk, the standard deviation becomes negligible. (The appendix to this chapter explains the algebra behind this statement.)

In summary, spreading the risk is a fundamental investment strategy. As Cervantes put it (and George Shaheen learned), never put all your eggs in one basket. If Shaheen

Consumer Finance tells us that 80.4 percent of the assets held by the top 1 percent are composed of corporate stock, unincorporated business equity, financial securities, mutual funds shares, personal trusts, and real estate *other than their primary residence*. In sharp contrast, for those in the middle three quintiles of the distribution (that is, from the 20th to the 80th percentiles), their principal residence accounts for 61.9 percent of their assets. The two groups also have sharply different levels of borrowing: relative to net worth, debt is an almost imperceptible 2.4 percent for the top 1 percent, but comes in at a whopping 58.9 percent for the middle 60 percent. Most of the latter is mortgage debt.

Despite relatively sluggish income gains at the bottom of the distribution, the general rise of asset prices in the decades prior to 2007 boosted wealth across the board. However, the collapse of housing prices during the 2007–2009 financial crisis triggered a large setback for those below the top 10 percent. In contrast, the post-crisis recovery of stock prices sharply boosted the wealth of those at the top.

Putting all this together leads to the following conclusions. While U.S. aggregate net worth rose by 20 percent from 2007 to 2016, the wealth of the top 10 percent rose by nearly 30 percent. Over the same period, the wealth of the bottom 50 percent plunged by more than 40 percent. Per household, the drop is even larger, more than 50 percent. Over a longer interval, the results also are startling: Per-household wealth in the bottom half of the distribution is not only lower today than it was in 2007, but it is substantially *below* the level in either 1971 or 1989.

Returning to welfare, the recent dramatic increase in wealth inequality has two important implications. First, all but the wealthiest have less capacity to smooth their consumption when faced with transitory income shocks. As a result, there is a risk that recessions will be both deeper and more harmful to the most vulnerable in society.

Second, with the retirement of the baby boom generation now in full swing, tens of millions of U.S. households may have little or no net worth on which to fall back. Absent a sharp and sudden climb in housing prices, it will be difficult for those in the bottom half of the wealth distribution who are currently approaching retirement age to maintain a decent standard of living after leaving the workforce. Many of those who can delay retirement probably will feel compelled to do so, even if their wages stagnate or slide. Those who cannot delay will be even more reliant on government-provided pension and health care in the form of Social Security, Medicare, and Medicaid.

had sold his Webvan stock and invested the proceeds in a portfolio composed of many stocks representative of the stock market as a whole, he would probably still have most of his $280 million. Diversification really works.

Diversification through the spreading of risk is the basis for the insurance business. A large automobile insurer writes millions of policies. It counts on the fact that not everyone will have accidents at the same time, for the risk of any one policyholder crashing is independent of the risk of another policyholder crashing. If it writes enough policies, the company can expect a predictable number of accident claims each year. When you toss a coin a million times, it will turn up heads around 500,000 times; likewise, assembling a large enough pool of independent risks isn't risky.

Now that we understand both what risk is and how to measure it, we can move on to study the impact of risk on the value of bonds, stocks, and other financial instruments. Using the tools from this chapter we will see how risk affects decisions by individual investors, managers of financial institutions, and officials who make public policy decisions. As we do, always remember Core Principle 2: Risk requires compensation.

www.moneyandbanking.com

Key Terms

average, 105
benchmark, 103
diversification, 116
expected return, 106
expected value, 105
hedging, 117
idiosyncratic risk, 115
leverage, 110
mean, 105
payoff, 104
probability, 103
risk, 102
risk-free asset, 107
risk-free rate of return, 107
risk premium, 114
spreading risk, 118
standard deviation, 108
systematic risk, 115
value at risk (VaR), 109
variance, 107

Using FRED: Codes for Data in This Chapter

Data Series	FRED Data Code
Wilshire 5000 stock price index	WILL5000PR
S&P 500 stock price index	SP500
30-year conventional mortgage rate	MORTG
5/1-year adjustable mortgage rate	MORTGAGE5US
Moody's Aaa corporate bond yield	AAA
Moody's Baa corporate bond yield	BAA
BofA Merrill US CCC or below effective yield	BAMLH0A3HYCEY
CBOE Volatility Index: VIX	VIXCLS
CBOE Volatility Index: DJIA	VXDCLS
10-year Treasury constant maturity rate	GS10

To learn more about the changing financial system, visit www.moneyandbanking.com.

Chapter Lessons

1. Risk is a measure of uncertainty about the possible future payoffs of an investment. It is measured over some time horizon, relative to a benchmark.
2. Measuring risk is crucial to understanding the financial system.
   a. To study random future events, start by listing all the possibilities and assign a probability to each. Be sure the probabilities add to one.
   b. The expected value is the probability-weighted sum of all possible future outcomes.
   c. A risk-free asset is an investment whose future value, or payoff, is known with certainty.
   d. Risk increases when the spread (or range) of possible outcomes widens but the expected value stays the same.
   e. One measure of risk is the standard deviation of the possible payoffs.
   f. A second measure of risk is value at risk, the worst possible loss over a specific time horizon, at a given probability.

3. A risk-averse investor:
   a. Always prefers a certain return to an uncertain one with the same expected return.
   b. Requires compensation in the form of a risk premium in order to take risk.
   c. Trades off between risk and expected return: the higher the risk, the higher the expected return risk-averse investors will require for holding an investment.
4. Risk can be divided into idiosyncratic risk, which is specific to a particular business or circumstance, and systematic risk, which is common to everyone.
5. There are two types of diversification:
   a. Hedging, in which investors reduce idiosyncratic risk by making investments with offsetting payoff patterns.
   b. Spreading, in which investors reduce idiosyncratic risk by making investments with payoff patterns that are not perfectly correlated.

Conceptual and Analytical Problems

1. Consider a game in which a coin will be flipped three times. For each heads you will be paid $100. Assume that the coin comes up heads with probability ⅔. *(LO1)*
   a. Construct a table of the possibilities and probabilities in this game.
   b. Compute the expected value of the game.
   c. How much would you be willing to pay to play this game?
   d. Consider the effect of a change in the game so that if tails comes up two times in a row, you get nothing. How would your answers to parts *a–c* change?

2.* Why is it important to be able to quantify risk? *(LO2)*

3. You are the founder of IGRO, an Internet firm that delivers groceries. *(LO4, LO5)*
   a. Give an example of an idiosyncratic risk and a systematic risk your company faces.
   b. As founder of the company, you own a significant portion of the firm, and your personal wealth is highly concentrated in IGRO shares. What are the risks that you face, and how should you try to reduce them?

4. Assume that the economy can experience high growth, normal growth, or recession. Under these conditions you expect the following stock market returns for the coming year: *(LO1, LO3)*

State of the Economy	Probability	Return
High Growth	0.2	+30%
Normal Growth	0.7	+12%
Recession	0.1	−15%

   a. Compute the expected value of a $1,000 investment over the coming year. If you invest $1,000 today, how much money do you expect to have next year? What is the percentage expected rate of return?
   b. Compute the standard deviation of the percentage return over the coming year.
   c. If the risk-free return is 7 percent, what is the risk premium for a stock market investment?

*Indicates more difficult problems.

5. Assume that the economy can experience four possible states: high growth, normal growth, recession, or depression. For each of those states, you expect the following stock market returns for the coming year:

State of the Economy	Probability	Return
High Growth	0.20	+20%
Normal Growth	0.60	+8%
Recession	0.15	−10%
Depression	0.05	−30%

   In dollar terms, what is the value at risk (over a one-year horizon at a 5 percent probability) associated with a $1,000 investment? *(LO2)*

6. Car insurance companies sell a large number of policies. Explain how this practice minimizes their risk. *(LO5)*
7. Mortgages increase the risk faced by homeowners. *(LO2)*
   a. Explain how.
   b. What happens to the homeowner's risk as the down payment on the house rises from 10 percent to 50 percent?
8. Banks pay substantial amounts to monitor the risks that they take. One of the primary concerns of a bank's "risk managers" is to compute the value at risk. Why is value at risk so important for a bank (or any financial institution)? *(LO2)*
9. Explain how liquidity problems can be an important source of systemic risk in the financial system. *(LO4)*
10.* Give an example of systematic risk for the U.S. economy and how you might reduce your exposure to such a risk. *(LO4, LO5)*
11. For each of the following events, explain whether it represents systematic risk or idiosyncratic risk and why. *(LO4)*
    a. Your favorite restaurant is closed by the county health department.
    b. The government of Spain defaults on its bonds, causing the breakup of the euro area.
    c. Freezing weather in Florida destroys the orange crop.
    d. Solar flares destroy earth-orbiting communications satellites, knocking out cell phone service worldwide.
12. You are planning for retirement and must decide whether to purchase only your employer's stock for your 401(k) or, instead, to buy a mutual fund that holds shares in the 500 largest companies in the world. From the perspective of both idiosyncratic and systematic risk, explain how you would make your decision. *(LO4, LO5)*
13. For each of the following actions, identify whether the method of risk assessment motivating your action is due to the value at risk or the standard deviation of an underlying probability distribution. *(LO2)*
    a. You buy life insurance.

*Indicates more difficult problems.

b. You hire an investment advisor who specializes in international diversification in stock portfolios.
c. In your role as a central banker, you provide emergency loans to illiquid intermediaries.
d. You open a kiosk at the mall selling ice cream and hot chocolate.

14. Which of the investments in the following table would be most attractive to a risk-averse investor? How would your answer differ if the investor was described as risk neutral? *(LO1)*

15. Consider an investment that pays off $800 or $1,400 per $1,000 invested with equal probability. Suppose you have $1,000 but are willing to borrow to increase your expected return. What would happen to the expected value and standard deviation of the investment if you borrowed an additional $1,000 and invested a total of $2,000? What if you borrowed $2,000 to invest a total of $3,000? *(LO1)*

Investment	Expected Value	Standard Deviation
A	75	10
B	100	10
C	100	20

16. Suppose an investment pays off $800 or $1,600 with equal probability per $1,000 invested. What is the maximum leverage ratio you could have and still have enough to repay the loan in the event the bad outcome occurred? *(LO1)*

17. Consider two possible investments whose payoffs are completely independent of one another. Both investments have the same expected value and standard deviation. If you have $1,000 to invest, explain why you would benefit from dividing your funds between these investments. *(LO5)*

18.* Suppose you identify 10 possible investments whose payoffs are completely independent of one another. All the investments have the same expected value and standard deviation. You have $1,000 to invest. In terms of risk, would the benefit of spreading your $1,000 across all 10 investments be the same, greater, or smaller compared with dividing your funds between just 2 investments? *(LO5)*

19. You are considering three investments, each with the same expected value and each with two possible payoffs. The investments are sold only in increments of $500. You have $1,000 to invest so you have the option of either splitting your money equally between two of the investments or placing all $1,000 in one of the investments. If the payoffs from Investment A are independent of the payoffs from Investments B and C and the payoffs from B and C are perfectly negatively correlated with each other (meaning when B pays off, C doesn't, and vice versa), which investment strategy will minimize your risk? *(LO5)*

*Indicates more difficult problems.

20. In which of the following cases would you be more likely to decide whether to take on the risk involved by looking at a measure of the value at risk? *(LO2)*
    a. You are unemployed and are considering investing your life savings of $10,000 to start up a new business.
    b. You have a full-time job paying $100,000 a year and are considering making a $1,000 investment in the stock of a well-established, stable company.

    Explain your reasoning.
21. You have the option to invest in either Country A or Country B but not both. You carry out some research and conclude that the two countries are similar in every way except that the returns on assets of different classes tend to move together much more in Country A—that is, they are more highly correlated in Country A than in Country B. Which country would you choose to invest in and why? *(LO5)*
22. The imposition of new trade tariffs has resulted in tensions between the United States and some of its major trading partners. Suppose you are a small business owner in the United States. *(LO3, LO4)*
    a. How would you classify the risk of a U.S. economic downturn that results from such trade conflict?
    b. Do you think a strategy to reduce this risk through hedging or spreading risk within the U.S. economy would be successful? Explain your answer.
23. The rise in wealth inequality in the United States has reduced the capacity of much of the population to cope with transitory income shocks. How might you expect that to impact workers' preferences between fixed-salary jobs versus jobs with a low base salary and the potential for high-commission-based earnings? *(LO2, LO3)*

Data Exploration connect

For detailed instructions on using Federal Reserve Economic Data (FRED) online to answer each of the following problems, visit www.mhhe.com/moneyandbanking6e *and refer to FRED Resources and Data Exploration Hints.*

1. Plot the percent change from a year ago of the Wilshire 5000 stock index at a monthly frequency (FRED code: WILL5000PR). Visually, has the risk of the Wilshire 5000 index changed over time? *(LO2)*
2. Another way to understand stock market risk is to examine how investors *expect* risk to evolve in the near future. The DJIA volatility index (FRED code: VXDCLS) is one such measure. Plot the level of this volatility index at a monthly frequency since October 1997 and, as a second line, the percent change from a year ago of the Wilshire 5000 index, also at a monthly frequency (FRED code: WILL5000PR). Compare their patterns. *(LO2)*
3. For the period since 2005, plot on one graph the 30-year conventional mortgage rate (FRED code: MORTGAGE30US) and a measure of an adjustable mortgage rate (FRED code: MORTGAGE5US). Explain their systematic relationship using Core Principle 2: Risk requires compensation. *(LO2)*
4. Plot the difference since 1979 between the Moody's Baa bond index (FRED code: BAA) and the U.S. Treasury 10-year bond yield (FRED code: GS10). Comment on the trend and variability of this "credit risk premium" (see Chapter 7) before and after the 2007–2009 financial crisis. *(LO1)*

Appendix to Chapter 5

The Mathematics of Diversification

With a small amount of mathematics, we can show how diversification reduces risk. Let's begin with two investments in 3M and Texaco. We'll label the payoffs to these investments *x* and *y*. If *x* is the payoff to buying 3M stock, then it must equal either \$120 or \$100, each with a probability of one-half (see Table 5.5). Then *y* is the payoff to buying Texaco stock.

Hedging Risk

In the chapter, we considered splitting our investment between 3M and Texaco. If *x* and *y* are the payoffs from holding 3M and Texaco, respectively, then the payoff on the investment is

$$\text{Investment payoff} = \tfrac{1}{2}x + \tfrac{1}{2}y \qquad \text{(A1)}$$

What is the variance of this payoff? (Because the standard deviation is the square root of the variance, the two must move together—a lower variance means a lower standard deviation—so we can skip the standard deviations.) In general, the variance of any weighted sum $ax + by$ is

$$\text{Var}(ax + by) = a^2\text{Var}(x) + b^2\text{Var}(y) + 2ab\,\text{Cov}(x,y) \qquad \text{(A2)}$$

where *Var* is the variance and *Cov* is the covariance. While the variance measures the extent to which each payoff moves on its own, the covariance measures the extent to which two risky assets move together. If the two payoffs rise and fall together, then the covariance will be positive. If one payoff rises while the other falls, then the covariance will be negative.

It is useful to express these quantities symbolically. Assume that p_i is the probability associated with a particular outcome x_i. Then the expected value of *x* is the probability-weighted sum of the possible outcomes.

$$\text{Expected value of } x = E(x) = \bar{x} = \sum_i p_i x_i \qquad \text{(A3)}$$

As described in the chapter (page 107), the variance of *x* is the probability-weighted sum of the squared deviations of *x* from the expected value.

$$\text{Variance of } x = \text{Var}(x) = \sigma_x^2 = \sum_i p_i(x_i - \bar{x})^2 \qquad \text{(A4)}$$

The covariance of *x* and *y* is defined analogously as

$$\text{Covariance of } x \text{ and } y = \text{Cov}(x,y) = \sigma_{x,y} = \sum_i p_i(x_i - \bar{x})(y_i - \bar{y}) \qquad \text{(A5)}$$

In our 3M/Texaco examples, $a = b = \tfrac{1}{2}$, so

$$\text{Var(Investment payoff)} = \tfrac{1}{4}\text{Var}(x) + \tfrac{1}{4}\text{Var}(y) + \tfrac{1}{2}\text{Cov}(x,y) \qquad \text{(A6)}$$

We know from Table 5.6 that the expected payoff to 3M and Texaco is \$110 each and the standard deviation is \$10 as well. The variance is the standard deviation squared, so it is 100. What about the covariance? We can compute it easily from Table 5.5:

$$\begin{aligned}&\text{Cov(Payoff on 3M and Texaco)}\\&=\tfrac{1}{2}(100-110)(120-110)+\tfrac{1}{2}(120-110)(100-110)=-100 \qquad \text{(A7)}\end{aligned}$$

Substituting this value into the formula for the variance of the investment payoff, we get

$$\text{Var(Investment payoff)}=\tfrac{1}{4}(100)+\tfrac{1}{4}(100)-\tfrac{1}{2}(100)=0 \qquad \text{(A8)}$$

The fact that the covariance is negative means that the variance, or risk, in a portfolio containing both 3M and Texaco stock is lower than the risk in a portfolio containing one or the other. The stocks act as hedges for each other.

Spreading Risk

Showing how spreading reduces risk is a bit more complex. Let's consider spreading our investment between 3M and Microsoft. Again, the variance of the investment payoff depends on the variances of the individual stock payoffs and on their covariance. But here we must assume that the covariance between the 3M and Microsoft payoffs is zero. That is, they are independent of each other. As before, each stock has a variance of 100, so the variance of a portfolio that is split half and half is

$$\text{Var(Investment payoff)}=\tfrac{1}{4}(100)+\tfrac{1}{4}(100)=50 \qquad \text{(A9)}$$

and the standard deviation is 7.1 (see footnote 8 on page 119).

This result suggests that individual stocks or groups of stocks with independent payoffs are potentially valuable, as they will reduce risk. Let's consider an arbitrary number of independent investments, each with the same individual variance. What is the variance of an equally weighted portfolio of these investments? Assume that the number of investments is n, each with the same expected payoff, $\bar{x}$, and the same variance, σ_x^2. We hold $1/n$ of our portfolio in each stock, so the expected payoff is

$$\text{Expected payoff}=\frac{1}{n}\sum_{i=1}^{n}x_i=\bar{x} \qquad \text{(A10)}$$

Because the payoff on each stock is independent of all the rest, the covariances are all zero. So the variance is

$$\text{Variance of payoff}=\left(\frac{1}{n}\right)^2\sum_{i=1}^{n}\sigma_x^2=\frac{\sigma_x^2}{n} \qquad \text{(A11)}$$

That is, the variance of the payoff on a portfolio of n independent stocks is the variance divided by n. Most important, as n increases, the variance declines, so when the value of n is very large, the variance is essentially zero.

In summary, spreading exposure to risk among a wide range of independent risks reduces the overall risk of a portfolio. As we saw in this chapter, this is the strategy that insurance companies use. While the payoff to an individual policyholder is highly uncertain, the payoffs to a large group of policyholders are almost unrelated. By selling millions of insurance policies, the company simply pays the expected value, and the variance will be nearly zero if the payoffs are truly independent.

Chapter 6

Bonds, Bond Prices, and the Determination of Interest Rates

Learning Objectives

After reading this chapter, you should be able to:

LO1 Explain the relationship between bond pricing and present value.

LO2 Define the relationship among a bond's price and its coupon rate, current yield, yield to maturity, and holding period return.

LO3 Explain how bond prices are determined and why they change.

LO4 Identify the three major types of bond risk: default, inflation, and interest rate changes.

Virtually any financial arrangement involving the current transfer of resources from a lender to a borrower, with a transfer back at some time in the future, is a form of bond. Car loans, home mortgages, even credit card balances all create a loan from a financial intermediary to an individual making a purchase—just like the bonds governments and large corporations sell when they need to borrow.

When companies like Ford, General Electric, or Walmart need to finance their operations, they sell bonds. When the U.S. Treasury or a state government needs to borrow, it sells bonds. And they do it billions of dollars at a time. Following the financial crisis of 2007–2009, U.S. corporations tried to reduce their debt, but their bonds outstanding climbed above the precrisis peak of more than $10 trillion in 2012 and continued to rise. As of 2018, federal, state, and local American governments have more than $28 trillion in outstanding debt as well.[1] The ease with which individuals, corporations, and governments borrow is essential to the functioning of our economic system. Without this free flow of resources through the bond markets, the economy would freeze up.

Historically, we can trace the concept of using bonds to borrow to monarchs' almost insatiable appetite for resources. To maintain lavish lifestyles, fight wars, and explore the globe, kings, princes, and other rulers drew on every available source of financing. Even with these incentives, after thousands of years of civilization only a few possibilities had been developed: outright confiscation; taxation, which is a mild form of confiscation; debasement of currency, in which people are required to exchange their coins for ones that weigh less—in effect, a tax on currency; and borrowing. Monarchs

[1]These numbers come from the *Financial Accounts of the United States,* published quarterly by the Federal Reserve Board.

who borrowed directly from international bankers frequently defaulted or failed to make the loan payments they had promised.[2]

Between 1557 and 1696, the various kings of Spain defaulted 14 times. With that track record, it's no wonder they had to pay interest rates close to 40 percent.

The Dutch invented modern bonds to finance their lengthy war of independence against those same Spanish kings who defaulted on loans in the 16th and 17th centuries. Over the next two centuries, the British refined the use of bonds to finance government activities. The practice then spread to other countries. Alexander Hamilton, the first Secretary of the U.S. Treasury and the man whose face appears on the $10 bill, brought bonds to the United States. One of Hamilton's first acts after the formation of the U.S. Treasury in 1789 was to consolidate all the debt remaining from the Revolutionary War. This resulted in the first U.S. government bonds. While the depth and complexity of bond markets have increased in modern times, many of their original features remain.

If we want to understand the financial system, particularly the bond market, we must understand three things. The first is the relationship between bond prices and interest rates (yet another application of present value). The second is that supply and demand in the bond market determine bond prices. The third is why bonds are risky. Let's get started.

Bond Prices

A standard bond specifies the fixed amounts to be paid and the exact dates of the payments. *How much should you be willing to pay for a bond?* The answer depends on the bond's characteristics. We will look at four basic types:

1. *Zero-coupon bonds,* which promise a single future payment, such as a U.S. Treasury bill.
2. *Fixed-payment loans,* such as conventional mortgages.
3. *Coupon bonds,* which make periodic interest payments and repay the principal at maturity. U.S. Treasury bonds and most corporate bonds are coupon bonds.
4. *Consols,* which make periodic interest payments forever, never repaying the principal that was borrowed. (There aren't many examples of these.)

Let's see how each of these bonds is priced. To keep the analysis simple, we'll ignore risk for now.

Zero-Coupon Bonds

U.S. Treasury bills (commonly known as **T-bills**) are the most straightforward type of bond. Each T-bill represents a promise by the U.S. government to pay $100 on a fixed future date. There are no coupon payments, which is why T-bills are known as **zero-coupon bonds**. They are also called *pure discount bonds* (or just discount bonds), because the price is less than their face value—they sell at a discount. This isn't a discount in the sense of a markdown at a clothing store, however. If a $100 face value

[2]For a detailed analysis of such sovereign defaults, see Carmen M. Reinhart and Kenneth S. Rogoff, *This Time Is Different: Eight Centuries of Financial Folly* (Princeton, NJ: Princeton University Press, 2011).

T-bill sells for \$96, the \$4 difference is the interest, the payment to the lender for making the loan.

Because a Treasury bill makes a single payment on a future date, its price is just the present value of that payment:

$$\text{Price of \$100 face value zero-coupon bond} = \frac{\$100}{(1+i)^n} \quad (1)$$

where i is the interest rate expressed in decimal form and n is the time until the payment is made, measured in the same time units as the interest rate. Suppose the annual interest rate is 5 percent. What is the price of a one-year T-bill? To figure out the answer, take the present value formula, set i at 0.05 and n at 1, and then compute the price:

$$\text{Price of one-year Treasury bill} = \frac{\$100}{(1+0.05)} = \$95.24$$

TIME

The U.S. Treasury doesn't issue T-bills with a maturity of more than one year; six-month T-bills are much more common. At an annual interest rate of 5 percent, what is the price of such a zero-coupon bond? We can use the present-value formula, again, but this time we have to be careful. Recall that we need to measure i and n in the same time units. Because i is the interest rate for one year, we need to measure n in years, and because six months is half a year:

$$\text{Price of a six-month Treasury bill} = \frac{\$100}{(1+0.05)^{1/2}} = \$97.59$$

As you can see, the price of a six-month Treasury bill is higher than that of a one-year T-bill. The shorter the time until the payment is made, the more we are willing to pay for it now. If we go on to compute the price of a three-month T-bill, setting n at 0.25 (one-fourth of a year), we find the answer is \$99.02.

Equation (1) shows that for a zero-coupon bond, the relationship between the price and the interest rate is the same as the one we saw in our discussion of present value. When the price moves, the interest rate moves in the *opposite* direction. Thus, we can compute the interest rate from the price using the present-value formula. For example, if the price of a one-year T-bill is \$95, then the interest rate is $i = (\$100/\$95) - 1 = 0.0526$, or 5.26 percent.

Fixed-Payment Loans

Conventional home mortgages and car loans are called *fixed-payment loans* because they promise a fixed number of equal payments at regular intervals. These loans are *amortized,* meaning that the borrower pays off the principal along with the interest over the life of the loan. Each payment includes both interest and a portion of the principal. Pricing these sorts of loans is straightforward using the present-value formula: The value of the loan today is the present value of all the payments. If we assume that the annual interest rate is i (measured as a decimal) and that the loan specifies n payments, then

$$\text{Value of a fixed-payment loan} = \frac{\text{Fixed payment}}{(1+i)} + \frac{\text{Fixed payment}}{(1+i)^2} + \cdots + \frac{\text{Fixed payment}}{(1+i)^n} \quad (2)$$

Using this formula is complicated, so we won't go any further. But when lenders figure out your monthly payment for a car loan or home mortgage, this is how they do it.

Know Your Mortgage
YOUR FINANCIAL WORLD

Survey evidence tells us that a large number of people with adjustable-rate mortgages underestimate how much their monthly payments can change.* Don't be one of these people! When you buy a home and get a mortgage, know what can happen.

There are two basic types of mortgages: conventional fixed-rate and adjustable-rate, also known as ARMs. Fixed-rate mortgages are the easiest to understand because the payments, like the interest rate, are fixed. That means you make the same monthly payment for the entire term of the mortgage. For most people, that term is 30 years. (You can also get 10-, 15-, and 20-year fixed-rate mortgages.) Because the payments don't change, fixed-rate borrowers are not exposed to the risks of interest rate increases.

ARMs are more complicated, because the interest rate changes. This means that the payments change, too. Getting an adjustable-rate mortgage means knowing about things like interest rate indexes, margins, discounts, caps, negative amortization, and convertibility:†

- On what interest rate index is the mortgage rate based? How much does that index move around?
- How big is the mortgage rate margin above the interest rate index on which it is based?
- How frequently is the rate adjusted?
- Does the ARM have an initial "teaser" interest rate that will almost surely rise? If so, when and by how much?
- What is the maximum change in the interest rate for a single adjustment and what is the highest the interest rate can ever go (the mortgage rate cap)?
- Does the ARM include a payment cap? If you hit the payment cap, will the principal of the loan start to increase? (That's negative amortization.)
- Can you convert the ARM into a fixed-rate mortgage?

This list may seem long, but it is really only the beginning. Getting the right mortgage may be the most important financial decision you ever make, so it is worth spending some time figuring it out. And once you have it, don't forget how your mortgage works.

*In "Do Homeowners Know Their House Values and Mortgage Terms?," Federal Reserve Board Finance and Economics Discussion Paper 2006–3, January 2006, Brian Bucks and Karen Pence estimate that nearly half of people with adjustable-rate mortgages don't know how much the interest rate can move at one time, the maximum rate, or the index to which the mortgage rate is tied.

†The Consumer Financial Protection Bureau's *Consumer Handbook on Adjustable Rate Mortgages*, http://files.consumerfinance.gov/f/201401_cfpb_booklet_charm.pdf, is a great place to start learning about mortgages.

Coupon Bonds

Recall from Chapter 4 that the issuer of a coupon bond promises to make a series of periodic interest payments called coupon payments, plus a principal payment at maturity. So we can value a coupon bond using (you guessed it) the present value formula. The price of the coupon bond is

$$P_{CB} = \left[\frac{\text{Coupon payment}}{(1+i)^1} + \frac{\text{Coupon payment}}{(1+i)^2} + \cdots + \frac{\text{Coupon payment}}{(1+i)^n}\right] + \frac{\text{Face value}}{(1+i)^n} \qquad (3)$$

The right side of this equation has two parts. The first part, in brackets, looks just like the fixed-payment loan—and it is, with the important exception that it represents only the interest. The second part, on the far right, looks just like a zero-coupon bond, and it is. It represents the value of the promise to repay the principal at maturity.

Consols

Another type of bond offers only periodic payments. That is, the borrower pays only interest, never repaying the principal. These loans, called **consols** or **perpetuities**, are like coupon bonds whose payments last forever. Because governments are really the only borrowers that can credibly promise to make payments forever, there are no privately issued consols (although a few corporations have issued 100-year coupon bonds).

The British government retired the last of its consols, originally issued in the 18th century, in 2015. The U.S. government sold consols once in 1900. The bonds had a special provision allowing the Treasury to buy them back starting in 1930. The Treasury bought back all the consols, so you would not be able to find one today.

You won't be surprised to learn that the price of a consol is the present value of all the future interest payments. The fact that the number of payments is infinite complicates things. But we can derive a formula for the price of a consol that makes a coupon payment every year forever.[3] At interest rate *i*,

$$P_{Consol} = \frac{\text{Yearly coupon payment}}{i} \tag{4}$$

The price of a consol equals the annual coupon payment divided by the interest rate. So at an interest rate of 5 percent, a consol that promises $1 per year forever would sell for $20. If the interest rate changes to 4 percent, the price rises to $25. Again, the interest rate and the price move in opposite directions.

Bond Yields

Now that we know how to calculate a bond price given the interest rate, we need to move in the other direction and calculate the interest rate, or the return to an investor, implicit in the bond's price. Doing so means combining information about the promised payments with the price to obtain what is called the *yield*—a measure of the cost of borrowing and the reward for lending. When people talk about bonds they use the terms *yield* and *interest rate* interchangeably, so we will too.

Yield to Maturity

The most useful measure of the return on holding a bond is called the **yield to maturity**, or the yield bondholders receive if they hold the bond to its maturity when the final principal payment is made. Take a $100 face value 5 percent coupon bond with one year to maturity. At maturity, the owner of this bond receives a coupon payment of $5 plus a principal payment of $100.[4] Using the formula from equation (3), we know that the price of the bond is

$$\text{Price of one-year 5 percent coupon bond} = \frac{\$5}{(1+i)} + \frac{\$100}{(1+i)} \tag{5}$$

The value of *i* that solves this equation is the *yield to maturity.* Remembering that present value and interest rates move in opposite directions, we can conclude the following:

1. If the price of the bond is $100, then the yield to maturity equals the coupon rate. (Recall from Chapter 4 that the coupon rate is the ratio of the annual coupon payments to the face value of the bond.)

[3]You may find it troubling that you can add up an infinite number of payments and get a finite number. To see why this works, notice that as the number of years at which the terminal payment occurs increases, $1/(1+i)^n$ grows very small. After 100 years, at an interest rate of 5 percent, it is 0.008. So the present value of $1 promised in 100 years is less than one cent. We could just ignore the payments that come after this and get virtually the same answer. To derive the expression for the price of a consol, use the techniques from the appendix to Chapter 4. Start by calling *C* the coupon payment and writing the price as the sum of the present value of the (infinite) number of payments, $P_{Consol} = \frac{C}{(1+i)} + \frac{C}{(1+i)^2} + \frac{C}{(1+i)^3} + \ldots$. Next, multiply this expression by $[1/(1+i)]$ to get $\frac{1}{(1+i)}P_{Consol} = \frac{C}{(1+i)^2} + \frac{C}{(1+i)^3} + \frac{C}{(1+i)^4} + \ldots$. Then subtract this expression from the original, which gives $P_{Consol} - \frac{1}{(1+i)}P_{Consol} = \frac{C}{(1+i)}$. Solving for the price yields equation (4).

[4]Most bonds offer two semiannual payments, each equal to half the annual coupon. We will ignore this complication.

2. Because the price rises as the yield falls, when the price is *above* \$100, the yield to maturity must be *below* the coupon rate.
3. Because the price falls as the yield rises, when the price is *below* \$100, the yield to maturity must be *above* the coupon rate.

Looking at the one-year 5 percent coupon bond, we can see right away that if the yield to maturity is 5 percent, then

$$\frac{\$5}{(1+0.05)}+\frac{\$100}{(1+0.05)}=\frac{\$105}{1.05}=\$100$$

That's the first point. Now look at what happens when yield to maturity falls to 4 percent. The price becomes

$$\frac{\$5}{(1+0.04)}+\frac{\$100}{(1+0.04)}=\frac{\$105}{1.04}=\$100.96$$

That's the second point. If the yield to maturity rises to 6 percent, then the price falls to

$$\frac{\$5}{(1+0.06)}+\frac{\$100}{(1+0.06)}=\$99.06$$

That's the third point. You can try this process with a more complicated bond—say, one with 10 years to maturity that makes more than just one coupon payment—and get exactly the same results.

The fact that the return on a bond depends on the price you pay for it really isn't that mysterious. If you pay \$95 for a \$100 face value bond, for example, you will receive both the interest payments and the increase in value from \$95 to \$100. This rise in value, referred to as a **capital gain**, is part of the return on your investment. So when the price of the bond is below the face value, the return is above the coupon rate. When the price is above the face value, the bondholder incurs a **capital loss** and the bond's yield to maturity falls below its coupon rate.

Current Yield

Current yield is a commonly used, easy-to-compute measure of the proceeds the bondholder receives for making a loan. It is the yearly coupon payment divided by the price:

$$\text{Current yield}=\frac{\text{Yearly coupon payment}}{\text{Price paid}} \qquad (6)$$

Looking at this expression, we can see that the current yield measures that part of the return from buying the bond that arises solely from the coupon payments. It ignores the capital gain or loss that arises when the price at which the bond is purchased differs from its face value. So if the price is below par, the current yield will be below the yield to maturity.

Let's return to the one-year 5 percent coupon bond and assume that it is selling for \$99. The current yield is easy to calculate as

$$\frac{5}{99}=0.0505$$

or 5.05 percent. The yield to maturity for this bond is the solution to

$$\frac{\$5}{(1+i)} + \frac{\$100}{(1+i)} = \$99$$

which is 6.06 percent. The yield to maturity is higher because, if you buy the bond for \$99, one year later you get not only the \$5 coupon payment but also a guaranteed \$1 capital gain for a total of \$6.

We can repeat these calculations for a case in which the bond is selling for \$101. Then the current yield is

$$\frac{5}{101} = 0.0495$$

or 4.95 percent, and the yield to maturity is

$$\frac{\$5}{(1+i)} + \frac{\$100}{(1+i)} = \$101$$

or 3.96 percent.

Putting all this together, we see the relationship between the current yield and the coupon rate. Again, it comes from the fact that current yield moves in the opposite direction from the price: it falls when the bond's price goes up and rises when the price goes down. So when the price equals the face value of the bond, the current yield and coupon rate are equal. When the price rises above the face value, the current yield falls below the coupon rate. And when the price falls below the face value, the current yield rises above the coupon rate.

Table 6.1 summarizes the relationships among the price, coupon rate, current yield, and yield to maturity. We know that when the bond price is less than face value, the current yield and the yield to maturity are both higher than the coupon rate. But because the yield to maturity takes account of the capital gain the bondholder receives, while the current yield does not, the yield to maturity must be even higher than the current yield. When the price is above the face value, the yield to maturity is lower than the current yield, which is lower than the coupon rate.

Holding Period Returns

We have emphasized that if you buy a bond whose yield to maturity deviates from the coupon rate, the price will not be the face value. Similarly, the return from holding a bond need not be the coupon rate. For example, if you pay \$95 for a one-year 6 percent coupon bond, one year later you will get both the \$6 coupon payment and the \$5 difference between the purchase price and the \$100 face value at maturity. But this example is really too simple, because it assumes that the investor

Table 6.1 Relationship among a Bond's Price and Its Coupon Rate, Current Yield, and Yield to Maturity

Bond price < *Face value:* Coupon rate < Current yield < Yield to maturity
Bond price = *Face value:* Coupon rate = Current yield = Yield to maturity
Bond price > *Face value:* Coupon rate > Current yield > Yield to maturity

holds the bond to maturity. Most holders of long-term bonds plan to sell them well before they mature. And because the price of the bond may change between the time of the purchase and the time of the sale, the return to buying a bond and selling it before it matures—the **holding period return**—can differ from the yield to maturity.

Take an example in which you pay \$100 for a 10-year, 6 percent coupon bond with a face value of \$100. You intend to hold the bond for one year. That is, you are going to buy a 10-year bond and then a year later, you'll sell a nine-year bond. What is your return from holding this bond? If the interest rate doesn't change (that is, it stays at 6 percent) your return will be \$6/\$100 = 0.06, or 6 percent. But if the interest rate changes, calculating your return becomes more complicated. Say that over the year you hold the bond, the interest rate falls from 6 to 5 percent. That is, the yield to maturity falls to 5 percent. Using equation (3), we can figure out that you have bought a 10-year bond for \$100 and sold a 9-year bond for \$107.11. What is your one-year holding period return on the initial \$100 investment? It has two parts: the \$6 coupon payment and the \$7.11 capital gain (the difference between the price at which you bought the bond and the price at which you sold it). So the holding period return is

$$\begin{aligned}\text{One-year holding period return} &= \frac{\$6}{\$100} + \frac{\$107.11 - \$100}{\$100} = \frac{\$13.11}{\$100} = 0.1311 \\ &= 13.11 \text{ percent}\end{aligned}$$

Obviously, bond prices can go down as well as up. Consider what happens if the yield to maturity rises to 7 percent so that the price falls to \$93.48. Now the one-year holding period return is

$$\begin{aligned}\text{One-year holding period return} &= \frac{\$6}{100} + \frac{\$93.48 - \$100}{\$100} = \frac{-\$.52}{\$100} = -0.0052 \\ &= -0.52 \text{ percent}\end{aligned}$$

The coupon payment still represents a 6 percent return, but the capital loss from the price movement is 6.52 percent. The one-year holding period return is negative, as overall there is a small loss.[5]

To generalize these examples, notice that the one-year holding period return is the sum of the yearly coupon payment divided by the price paid for the bond, and the change in the price (price sold minus price paid) divided by the price paid:

$$\text{Holding period return} = \frac{\text{Yearly coupon payment}}{\text{Price paid}} + \frac{\text{Change in price of bond}}{\text{Price paid}} \qquad (7)$$

[5]The multiyear case is somewhat more complex. Say that an investor purchased the same 10-year 6 percent coupon bond at par, and then held it for *two* years. If the interest rate were to rise from 7 percent, the price of the now 8-year bond would fall to \$94.03 per \$100 of face value. This means that the investor would receive \$12 in coupon payments plus a capital loss of \$5.97, for a total payoff of \$106.03. To simplify, let us assume that the first-year coupon cannot be reinvested. Then, using the methods described in the Tools of the Trade on page 82 of Chapter 4, we can compute the annual-rate return as $\left[\left(\frac{106.03}{100}\right)^{1/2} - 1\right] = 0.0297$, or 2.97%. If instead the interest rate were to fall to 4 percent, the price of the bond would rise to \$106.46, the total payoff would be \$118.46, and the annual-rate return would be 8.84 percent.

The first part on the right-hand side of this equation is the current yield (equation 6). The second part is the capital gain. So the holding period return is

$$\text{Holding period return} = \text{Current yield} + \text{Capital gain} \qquad (8)$$

Whenever the price of a bond changes, there is a capital gain or loss. The greater the price change, the more important a part of the holding period return the capital gain or loss becomes. The potential for interest rate movements and changes in bond prices creates risk. The longer the term of the bond, the greater those price movements and the associated risk can be, as we'll see in more detail in the last section of this chapter.

The Bond Market and the Determination of Interest Rates

Now that we understand the relationship between bond prices and various measures of interest rates, we need to figure out how bond prices are determined and why they change. The best way to do that is to look at bond supply, bond demand, and equilibrium prices in the bond market. Once we understand how the bond market determines bond prices, we can figure out why the prices change.

To keep the analysis simple, we need to make a few choices about how to proceed. First, we'll restrict the discussion to the quantity of bonds outstanding, called the *stock of bonds.* (We could look at what causes the changes in the quantity of bonds outstanding—the *flow*—but that would complicate matters.) Second, we are going to talk about *bond prices* rather than interest rates. Because a bond's price, together with its various characteristics, determines its yield, it really doesn't matter whether we talk about yields (interest rates) or bond prices. Once we know the price, we know the yield. Finally, we're going to consider the *market for a one-year zero-coupon bond* (one that makes no coupon payments) with a face value of $100.

If we assume the investor is planning to purchase a one-year bond and hold it to maturity—the investor has a one-year **investment horizon**—then the holding period return equals the bond's yield to maturity, and both are determined directly from the price. The present-value formula shows that the relationship between the price and the yield on such a bond is simply $P = \$100/(1 + i)$, so $i = [(\$100 - P)/P]$.

For example, if a bond sells for $95, then the yield is $i = \$5/\$95 = 0.0526$, or 5.26 percent.

Bond Supply, Bond Demand, and Equilibrium in the Bond Market

How are bond prices (and bond yields) determined? Not surprisingly, by supply and demand. Some investors are supplying bonds, while others are demanding them. The *bond supply curve* is the relationship between the price and the quantity of bonds people are willing to sell, all other things being equal. The higher the price of a bond, the larger the quantity supplied will be for two reasons.

Reading the Bond Page
TOOLS OF THE TRADE

Every day *The Wall Street Journal* lists the previous day's closing yields for a wide variety of bonds that serve as standards—or benchmarks—for comparison with other financial instruments. Table 6.2 shows some representative data on global government bonds published on March 18, 2019, while Table 6.3 presents some data on corporate bonds. Let's see what we can learn from reading these tables.

Global Government Bonds

Governments issue hundreds of bonds. As of early 2019, the U.S. Treasury alone had more than 300 different coupon-bearing instruments outstanding. But investors often focus on the most liquid bonds at key maturities to summarize the evolution of the entire bond market. Table 6.2 uses a two-year bond yield to represent relatively short-term issues and a 10-year bond yield to represent the longer term. In Chapter 7, we'll see how the *term structure of interest rates* relates the level of bond yields to the maturity of the bonds.

The table highlights several points. First, the yields on government bonds vary over time. For example, on March 18, 2019, the "latest" 10-year German government bond yield was 0.087 percent. The table also shows that the latest yield exceeded the day-earlier ("previous") level of 0.086 percent and was lower than the "year-ago" level of 0.572 percent. Assuming that the representative bond had exactly 10 years to maturity on each date, then, as the yield fell, its price in euros rose from €96.88 on March 18, 2018, to €101.62 on March 18, 2019. Similarly, the 10-year U.S. Treasury yield edged lower over the year, from 2.847 percent to 2.602 percent, raising the U.S. dollar price of the bond by $2.11, to $100.20.

Table 6.2 Government Bonds

Yields and spreads over or under U.S. Treasurys on benchmark two-year and 10-year government bonds in selected other countries; arrows indicate whether the yield rose (Δ) or fell (▼) in the latest session.

Coupon (%)	Country/Maturity, in years		YIELD (%) Latest (·)	Previous	Month ago	Year ago	SPREAD UNDER/OVER U.S. TREASURYS, in basis points Latest	Year ago
2.500	**U.S.**	2	2.458 Δ	2.438	2.504	2.291	...	...
2.625		10	2.602 Δ	2.592	2.666	2.847	...	...
0.000	**France**	2	−0.458 Δ	−0.460	−0.451	−0.486	−291.6	−277.7
0.500		10	0.453 ▼	0.464	0.547	0.816	−214.9	−203.1
0.000	**Germany**	2	−0.527 Δ	−0.539	−0.560	−0.590	−298.6	−288.1
0.250		10	0.087 Δ	0.086	0.116	0.572	−251.5	−227.4
3.750	**Italy**	2	0.328 ▼	0.368	0.579	−0.256	−213.0	−254.6
2.800		10	2.425 ▼	2.504	2.768	1.979	−17.7	−86.7
0.100	**Japan**	2	−0.162 ▼	−0.161	−0.176	−0.148	−262.1	−243.8
0.100		10	−0.036 ▼	−0.035	−0.020	0.035	−263.9	−281.2
0.050	**Spain**	2	−0.255 ▼	−0.220	−0.171	−0.271	−271.3	−256.2
1.450		10	1.151 ▼	1.188	1.227	1.368	−145.2	−147.9
2.000	**U.K.**	2	0.754 ▼	0.767	0.724	0.813	−170.4	−147.8
1.625		10	1.198 ▼	1.214	1.068	1.432	−140.4	−141.5

SOURCE: *The Wall Street Journal*, March 18, 2019.

The second point illustrated by the table is that the yields on government bonds differ substantially across countries. The "latest" yield on the 10-year U.S. Treasury bond was much higher than the yield on Germany's bond, but only a bit higher than the yield on Italy's. The difference across countries is also portrayed by the bars in the third column from the right, which show the latest yield spread versus 10-year Treasuries. The spread for Italy's bond—that is, the yield on Italy's bond minus the yield on the U.S. bond—was –17.7 basis points (a basis point is one hundredth of a percentage point); for Germany's bond, the spread was −251.5 basis points—that is, the yield on Germany's bond was lower than the U.S. or Italian bond yield. Recall from the figure on page 92 that the difference between interest rates partly reflects differences in expected inflation. However, in the case of Italy, the difference also reflected risks associated with high government debt and unsettled conditions in the euro area (which will be discussed in Chapter 16).

Third, the latest 10-year yield exceeded the latest two-year yield in every country shown in the table. When we study the term structure of interest rates in Chapter 7, we'll learn why this pattern of higher long-term yields is common but does not always hold.

Finally, the yield on each bond differs from its coupon rate (shown in the first column). As noted elsewhere in this chapter, when the yield is higher (lower) than the coupon, the price of the bond is below (above) the par value of 100.

Corporate Debt

Thousands of corporations in the United States issue bonds, and the bonds vary significantly in default risk (see the discussion of default risk on pages 147–151). In line with Core Principle 2: investors expect to be compensated for those risks. Table 6.3 captures a measure of that compensation—the yield spread over Treasury securities.

The table shows the levels and one-day changes of yield spreads on actively traded corporate bond yields compared to a similar-maturity U.S. Treasury yield. For the bond issued by Deutsche Bank AG (the large German bank), the "current" spread of 550 basis points is the amount by which its previous-day yield exceeded that on the most recent 30-year Treasury issue.

Narrower corporate bond spreads over U.S. Treasuries are associated with lower default risk. Hence, spreads are as diverse as corporate default risks. The narrowest spread shown in the table is 11 basis points, for Cisco Systems, a major technology firm; the widest is 550 for Deutsche Bank AG. Spreads can change significantly day to day: The table shows that the largest swings in spreads on March 18 were the 44-basis-point tightening for Deutsche Bank AG and the 19-basis-point widening for General Motors Financial. These day-to-day changes reflect changing perceptions of each company's default risk over different time horizons.

The last two columns of the table show the stock price level and change for those bond issuers that also issue shares. Note that a gain (loss) in the price of a company's stock, which normally indicates greater (lesser) confidence in the prospects for a company, is not always accompanied by similar change in the yield spread of that company's bond.

Table 6.3 Corporate Bonds

Investment-grade spreads that tightened the most . . .

Issuer	Symbol	Coupon (%)	Maturity	SPREAD*, IN BASIS POINTS Current	Change	Last week	STOCK PERFORMANCE Close	% Chg
Deutsche Bank AG	**DB**	7.500	April 30, '49	550	−44	632	$9.26	4.28
Cisco Systems	**CSCO**	3.000	June 15, '22	11	−14	23	53.51	0.58
Discover Financial Services	**DFS**	4.100	Feb. 9, '27	161	−14	177	...	...
General Electric	**GE**	5.000	Jan. 21, '49	236	−13	241	10.20	2.41

. . . And spreads that widened the most

Issuer	Symbol	Coupon (%)	Maturity	Current	Change	Last week	Close	% Chg
General Motors Financial	**GM**	3.700	May 9, '23	148	19	160	...	...
Apollo Management Holdings	**APO**	4.872	Feb. 15, '29	209	16	212	29.78	2.30
Boeing	**BA**	2.800	March 1, '24	55	13	48	372.28	−1.77
Hexcel	**HXL**	3.950	Feb. 15, '27	152	6	n.a.	69.87	1.01

*Estimated spread over 2-year, 3-year, 5-year, 10-year or 30-year hot-run Treasury; 100 basis points = one percentage point; change in spread shown is for Z-spread.

Note: Data are for the most active issue of bonds with maturities of 2 years or more.

SOURCE: *The Wall Street Journal*, March 18, 2019.

From investors' point of view, the higher the price, the more tempting it is to sell a bond they currently hold. From the point of view of companies seeking finance for new projects, the higher the price at which they can sell bonds, the better. Taking our example of a $100 one-year zero-coupon bond, the quantity supplied will be higher at $95 per bond than it will be at $90 per bond, all other things being equal. This means that *the bond supply curve slopes upward.*

The *bond demand curve* is the relationship between the price and quantity of bonds that investors demand, all other things being equal. As the price falls, the reward for holding the bond rises, so the demand goes up. That is, the lower the price potential bondholders must pay for a fixed-dollar payment on a future date, the more likely they are to buy a bond. Again, think of the zero-coupon bond promising to pay $100 in one year. That bond will attract more demand at $90 than it will at $95 per bond, all other things being equal. Thus, *the bond demand curve slopes downward.* Because the price of bonds is inversely related to the yield, the demand curve implies that the higher the demand for bonds, the higher the yield.

Equilibrium in the bond market is the point at which supply equals demand—point *E* in Figure 6.1. As is always the case with supply and demand analysis, we need to explain how the market adjusts when the price deviates from the price that equates supply and demand—point P_0 in Figure 6.1. Let's look briefly at the two possibilities: Either the price is too high or the price is too low. If bond prices start out above the equilibrium point, somewhere greater than P_0, quantity supplied will exceed quantity demanded. That is, excess supply means that suppliers cannot sell the bonds they want to at the current price. To make the sale, they will start cutting the price. The excess supply will put downward pressure on the price until supply equals demand.

When the price is below the equilibrium point, quantity demanded will exceed quantity supplied. Those people who wish to buy bonds cannot get all they want at the prevailing price. Their reaction is to start bidding up the price. Excess demand continues to put upward pressure on the price until the market reaches equilibrium.

Figure 6.1 Supply, Demand, and Equilibrium in the Bond Market

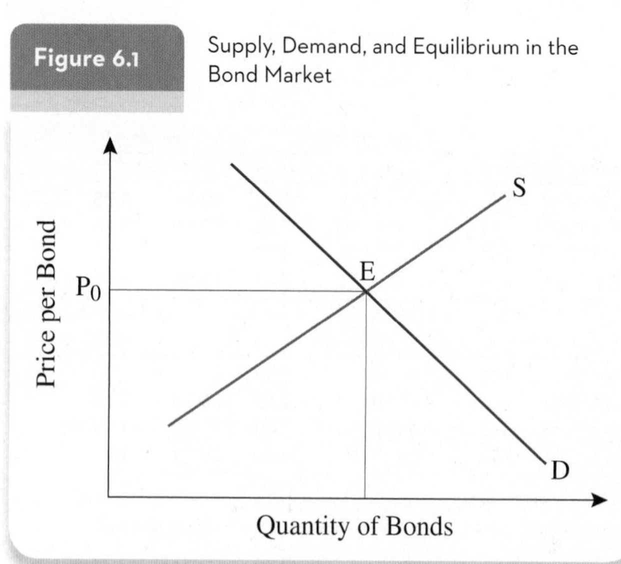

The supply of bonds from borrowers slopes up and the demand for bonds from lenders slopes down. Equilibrium in the bond market is determined by the intersection of supply and demand.

So far, so good. But to really understand how bond prices (and bond yields) change over time, we need to learn what determines the location of the supply and demand curves. Over time they shift around, leading to changes in the equilibrium prices. As we discuss the causes of such shifts in the following section, make sure you remember the distinction between moving *along* a supply or demand curve and *shifting* a curve. When the quantity demanded or quantity supplied changes because of a change in the price, it produces a movement along the curve. But when the quantity demanded or supplied at a given price changes, it shifts the entire curve. More important, in the bond market, a shift in either the supply or the demand curve changes the price of bonds, so it changes the yield as well.

Factors That Shift Bond Supply

What changes the quantity of bonds *supplied* at a given price, shifting the supply curve? We can identify three factors: changes in government borrowing, in general business conditions, and in expected inflation. Let's look at these one at a time.

Changes in Government Borrowing The government's need to issue bonds affects the supply of bonds out there. Both changes in tax policy and adjustments in spending can affect a government's need to borrow. Regardless of the reason, *any increase in the government's borrowing needs increases the quantity of bonds outstanding, shifting the bond supply curve to the right.* The result is an increase in quantity of the bonds supplied at every price (see Figure 6.2). Because the demand curve stays where it is (remember, we're holding everything else constant), the increase in supply drives the price down. The added supply of U.S. government bonds has reduced prices, raising interest rates.

Figure 6.2 A Shift in the Supply of Bonds

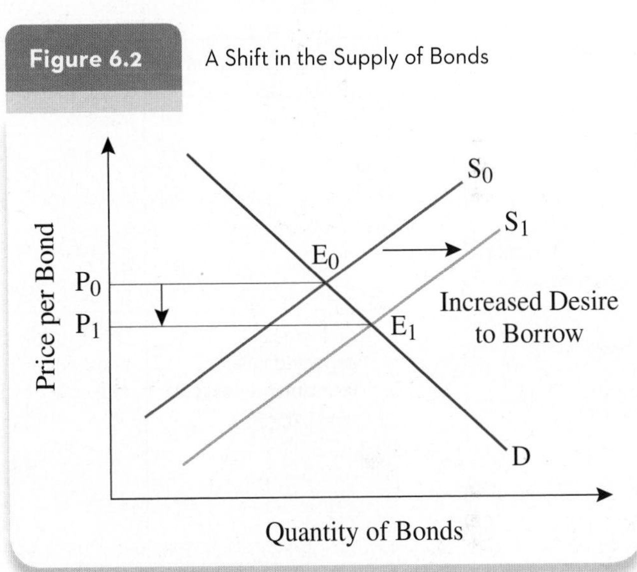

When borrowers' desire for funds increases, the bond supply curve shifts to the right, lowering bond prices and raising interest rates.

Changes in General Business Conditions During business cycle expansions, when general business conditions are good, investment opportunities abound, prompting firms to increase their borrowing. As the amount of debt in the economy rises, the quantity of bonds outstanding with a given risk goes up. So *as business conditions improve, the bond supply curve shifts to the right,* forcing bond prices down and interest rates up. Again, Figure 6.2 shows what happens. This connection between general business conditions and the supply of bonds also helps explain how weak economic growth can lead to rising bond prices and lower interest rates for bonds with unchanged risk.

Changes in Expected Inflation Bond issuers care about the *real* cost of borrowing—the cost of the loan taking inflation into account. At a given *nominal* interest rate, higher expected inflation means a lower *real* interest rate. And at a lower real interest rate, fewer real resources are required to make the payments promised by a bond. So when expected inflation rises, the cost of borrowing falls and the desire to borrow at every nominal interest rate rises. Figure 6.2 shows that *an increase in expected inflation shifts the bond supply curve to the right.* Higher expected inflation increases the bond supply, reducing bond prices and raising the nominal interest rate.

Table 6.4 summarizes the factors that increase the quantity of bonds supplied at every price, shifting the bond supply curve to the right. Before moving on to shifts in the demand for bonds, we should mention that there is one other factor that shifts the bond supply: changes in corporate taxation. Because such changes in the tax code require government legislation, they don't occur very often. But when they do, they can affect the economywide supply of bonds. Corporations pay taxes on their profits,

Table 6.4 Factors That Shift Bond Supply to the Right, Lower Bond Prices, and Raise Interest Rates

Change	Effect on Bond Supply, Bond Prices, and Interest Rates	Shift in Bond Supply
An increase in the government's desired expenditure relative to its revenue	Bond supply shifts to the right, bond prices ↓, and interest rates ↑	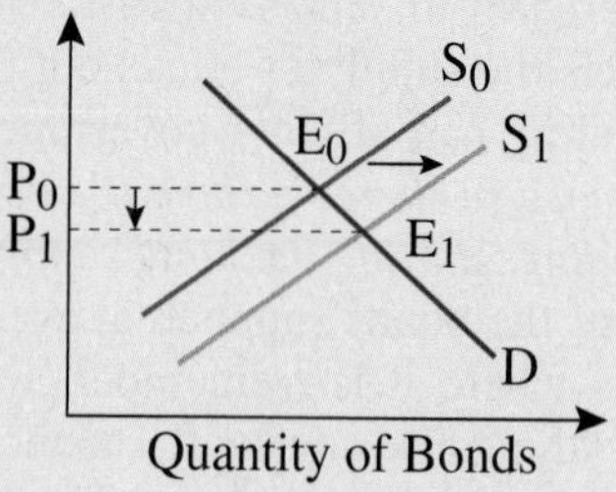 S_0, S_1, E_0, E_1, P_0, P_1, D; Quantity of Bonds
An improvement in general business conditions	Bond supply shifts to the right, bond prices ↓, and interest rates ↑	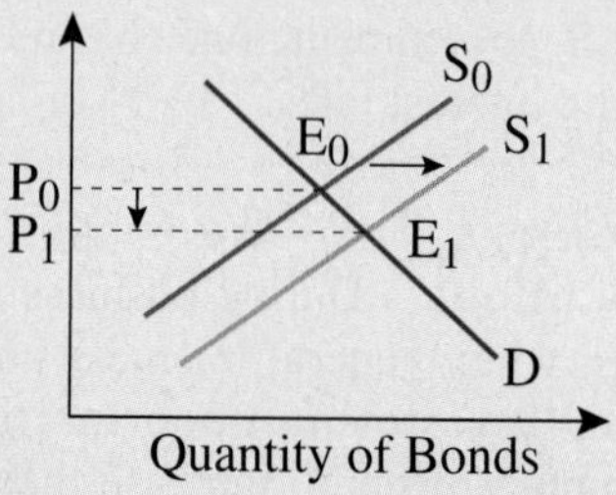 S_0, S_1, E_0, E_1, P_0, P_1, D; Quantity of Bonds
An increase in expected inflation, reducing the real cost of repayment	Bond supply shifts to the right, bond prices ↓, and interest rates ↑	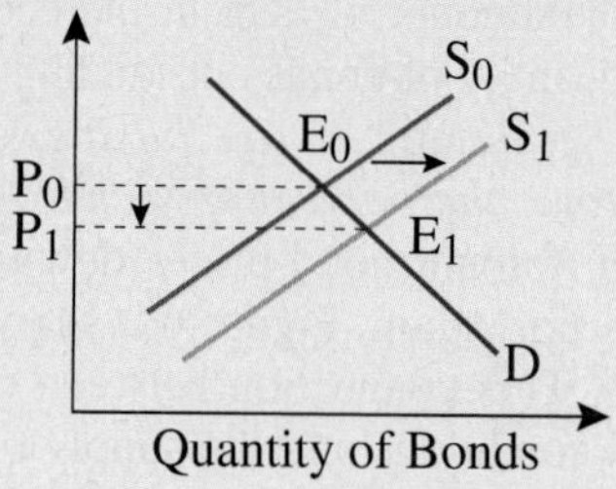 S_0, S_1, E_0, E_1, P_0, P_1, D; Quantity of Bonds

just as individuals pay taxes on their income, so they are concerned with after-tax profits. Governments often create special tax subsidies that make corporate investments less costly. These tax incentives increase the supply of bonds because they raise the after-tax profitability of investing in new equipment purchased with funds raised from selling bonds. Like the other three factors we have considered, government tax incentives increase bond supply, shift the supply curve to the right, and lower the price of bonds.

Factors That Shift Bond Demand

Now we move on to bond demand. Six factors shift the *demand* for bonds at a given price: wealth, expected inflation, the expected return on stocks and other assets, expected interest rates, risk, and the liquidity of bonds (see Table 6.5).

Wealth The more rapidly the economy grows, the wealthier individuals become. As their wealth increases, they increase their investment in stocks, bonds, real estate,

Table 6.5 Factors That Shift Bond Demand to the Right, Raise Bond Prices, and Lower Interest Rates

Change	Effect on Bond Demand	Shift in Bond Demand
An increase in wealth increases demand for all assets including bonds.	Bond demand shifts to the right, bond prices ↑, and interest rates ↓	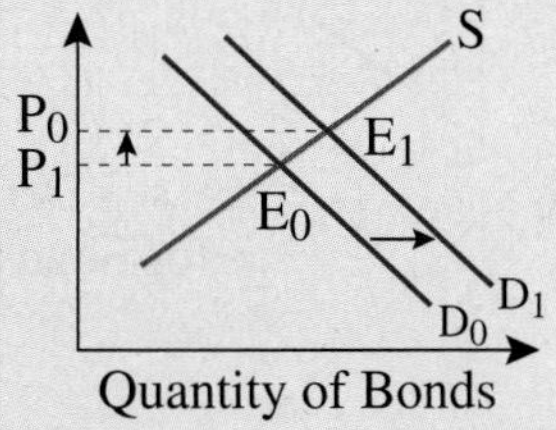 S, P_0, P_1, E_1, E_0, D_1, D_0, Quantity of Bonds
A reduction in expected inflation makes bonds with fixed nominal payments more desirable.	Bond demand shifts to the right, bond prices ↑, and interest rates ↓	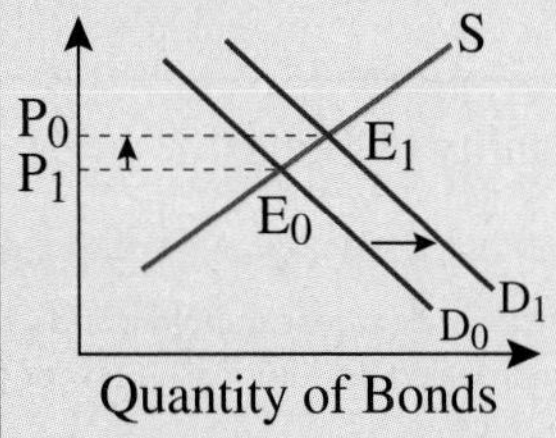 S, P_0, P_1, E_1, E_0, D_1, D_0, Quantity of Bonds
A decrease in the expected future interest rate makes bonds more attractive.	Bond demand shifts to the right, bond prices ↑, and interest rates ↓	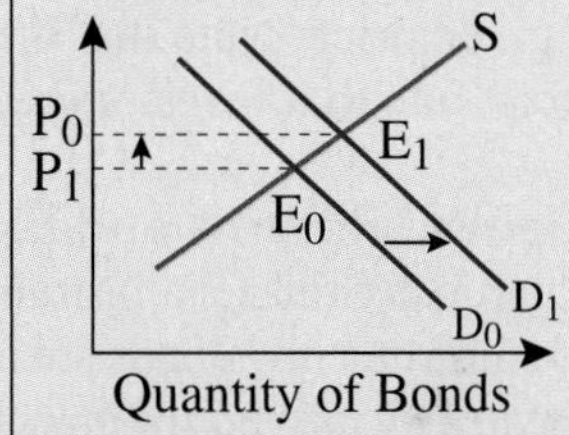 S, P_0, P_1, E_1, E_0, D_1, D_0, Quantity of Bonds
An increase in the expected return on the bond relative to the expected return on alternatives makes bonds more attractive.	Bond demand shifts to the right, bond prices ↑, and interest rates ↓	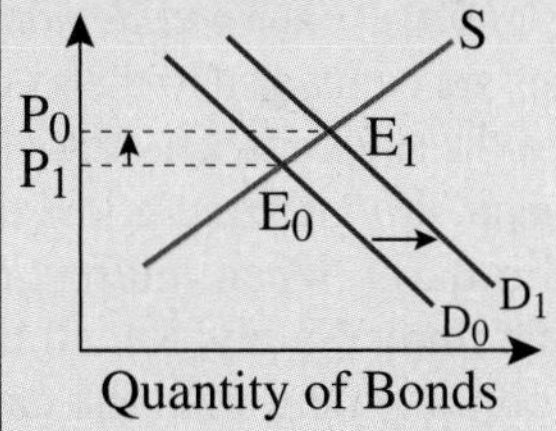 S, P_0, P_1, E_1, E_0, D_1, D_0, Quantity of Bonds
A fall in the riskiness of the bond relative to the riskiness of alternatives makes bonds more attractive.	Bond demand shifts to the right, bond prices ↑, and interest rates ↓	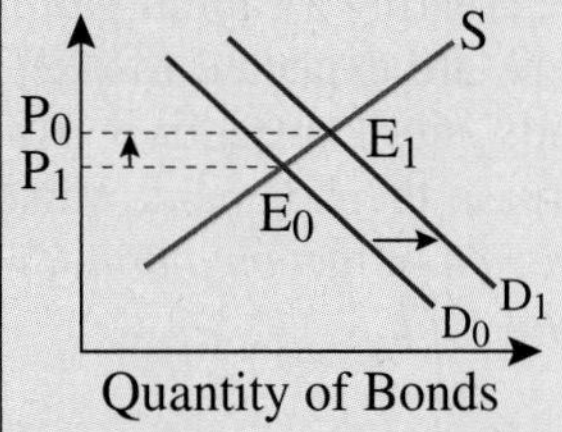 S, P_0, P_1, E_1, E_0, D_1, D_0, Quantity of Bonds
An increase in the liquidity of the bond relative to the liquidity of alternatives makes bonds more attractive.	Bond demand shifts to the right, bond prices ↑, and interest rates ↓	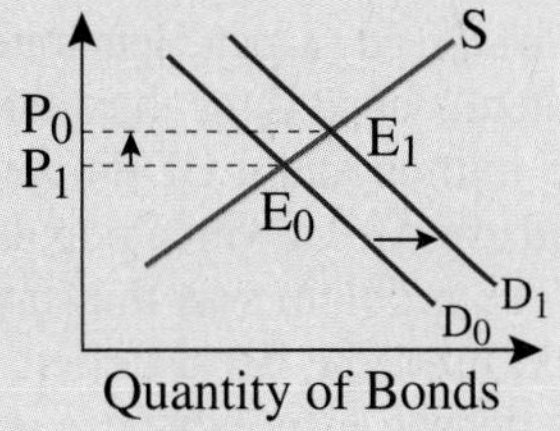 S, P_0, P_1, E_1, E_0, D_1, D_0, Quantity of Bonds

Figure 6.3 A Shift in the Demand for Bonds

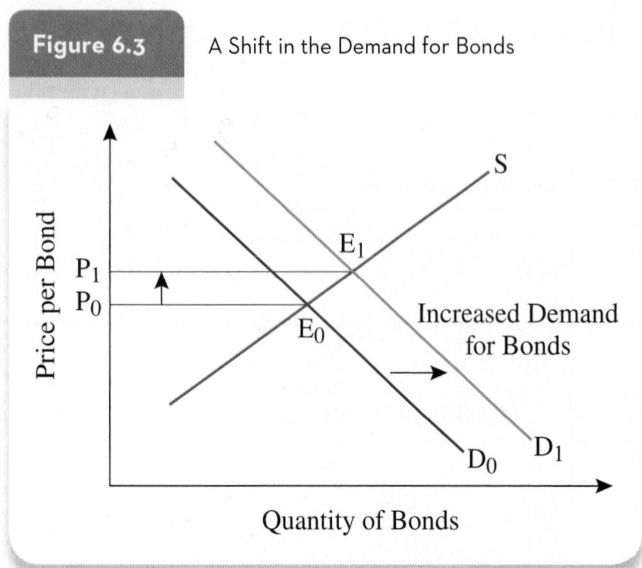

When there is an increase in investors' willingness to hold bonds, the bond demand curve shifts to the right, increasing bond prices and reducing interest rates.

and art. Thus, *increases in wealth shift the demand for bonds to the right,* raising bond prices and lowering yields (see Figure 6.3). This is what happens in a business cycle expansion. In a recession, as wealth falls, the demand for bonds falls with it, lowering bond prices and raising interest rates.

Expected Inflation Changes in expected inflation alter investors' willingness to purchase bonds promising fixed-dollar payments. A decline in expected inflation means that the payments promised by the bond's issuer have a higher value than borrowers originally thought, so the bond will become more attractive. *This fall in expected inflation shifts the bond demand curve to the right,* increasing demand at each price and lowering the yield, as shown in Figure 6.3. In short, the higher real return on the bond increases the willingness of would-be lenders to buy it at any given price. Note that the decline in expected inflation has reduced the nominal interest rate that investors require in order to make a loan.

Expected Returns and Expected Interest Rates An investor's desire to hold any particular financial instrument depends on how its return compares to those of alternative instruments. Bonds are no different. *If the expected return on bonds rises relative to the return on alternative investments, the quantity of bonds demanded at every price will rise, shifting the bond demand curve to the right.* This leads us to conclude that bond prices are connected to the stock market. Investors see bonds as an alternative to stocks, so when the stock market outlook worsens, they shift their portfolios into bonds, increasing demand, driving bond prices up and interest rates down.

Similarly, when interest rates are expected to change in the future, bond prices adjust immediately. Recall that the holding period return on a bond depends on the coupon payment plus the capital gain or loss. When interest rates fall, bond prices rise, creating a capital gain. Whenever interest rates are expected to fall, then bond prices are expected to rise, creating an expectation of a capital gain. This makes bonds more attractive. Knowing that bonds are a good investment, investors increase their demand immediately, driving bond prices up. So *an increase in the expected return on a bond, relative to the return on alternatives, shifts bond demand to the right.*

Risk Relative to Alternatives On May 13, 2002, a headline in *The Wall Street Journal* read "Japan Gets Irate at Having Its Risk Compared to Botswana." What's going on here? Japan is the third-largest economy in the world, with a population of more than 125 million and a GDP approaching $5 trillion. Botswana is a landlocked country in southern Africa with a population of 2 million people and a GDP of about $17 billion.

The problem was that investors had two reasons to question Japan's budget outlook. First, the fiscal deficit was a very high 7 percent of GDP. Second, over the next few decades, the Japanese government would have to find a way to meet its promises

When Russia Defaulted
APPLYING THE CONCEPT

The idea that risk matters to bond investors is not just a textbook theory. On numerous occasions, investors' concerns about increased risk in certain areas of the globe have led to a significant shift in demand for U.S. Treasury bonds. A noteworthy example occurred in August 1998, when the Russian government failed to make the payments on some bonds held by foreign investors. That is, the Russian government defaulted. Suddenly, no one wanted to hold Russian debt. More important, people lost confidence in the debt issued by all emerging market countries, including Brazil, Argentina, Turkey, and Thailand. After dumping anything that they thought at all risky, investors went looking for a safe place to put the proceeds.

Because the safest assets around are U.S. Treasury bonds, that is what they bought. The perception during this episode was that the riskiness of U.S. Treasury bonds had fallen relative to the riskiness of virtually everything else. The result was an increase in the price of U.S. Treasury bonds and a decline in their yield. At the same time, the prices of the more risky alternatives fell and their yields rose.

The data in the following figure show what happened. After the default (at the vertical line in the figure), the price of U.S. Treasury bonds rose by roughly 10 percent while the price of Brazilian bonds fell by more than one-third. Even though it was half a world away from Russia, investors' demand for Brazilian bonds plummeted. Meanwhile, demand for the safe U.S. Treasury debt went up.

Prices of Brazilian Government Debt and U.S. Treasury Bonds, July 1998 to October 1998

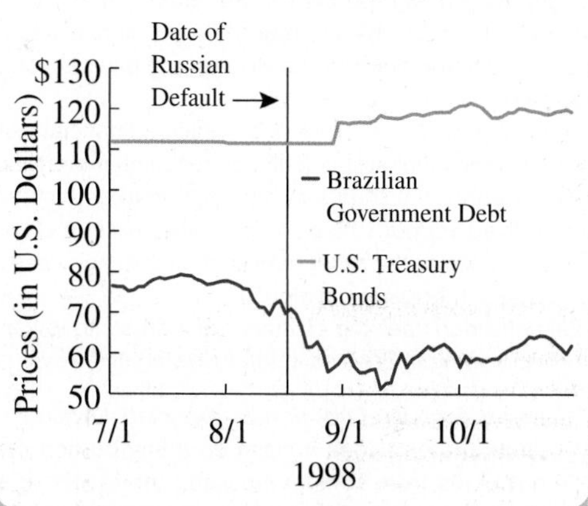

One bond index is for five- to seven-year U.S. Treasury bonds and the other is for Brazilian government bonds. The indexes, which show the movement in the prices of the bonds, were constructed by Lehman Brothers and supplied by Datastream.

SOURCE: Data compiled from Thomson Datastream.

on the bond's return relative to the risk-free rate. That is, we will try to figure out how certain risks affect the premium investors require over the risk-free return. Once again, *risk requires compensation.*

Default Risk

There is no guarantee that a bond issuer will make the promised payments. While we usually ignore default risk in thinking about U.S. Treasury bonds, we cannot do so when discussing bonds issued by many other governments or by private corporations. When corporations or governments fail to meet their payments, what happens to the price of their bonds?

To figure out the answer, let's list all the possibilities and payoffs that might occur, along with their probabilities. We can then calculate the expected value of the promised payments, from which we can compute the bond's price and yield. Suppose, for example, that the one-year risk-free interest rate is 5 percent. Flim.com, an Internet

Securitization
APPLYING THE CONCEPT

In 1997, musician David Bowie issued $55 million worth of bonds backed by royalties from 287 songs he had written and recorded before 1990. The bonds had a 10-year maturity and a 7.9 percent interest rate (somewhat above the 10-year Treasury yield of 6.5 percent at the time). "Bowie bonds" were no accident: By the late 1990s, the U.S. financial system had evolved to the point where virtually any payment stream could be *securitized.*

Securitization is the process by which a financial institution pools individual assets (such as residential mortgages) to back a bond that trades in the open market. Instead of paying a fixed coupon, the bond gives the owner a claim on the payments from the asset pool (in the mortgage case, the homeowners' mortgage payments).

Securitization uses the efficiency of markets to lower the cost of borrowing. It does so in the following five ways:

1. *Diversification of risk* or *risk spreading.* Owning a security that provides a claim on a tiny portion of the payments from several thousand mortgages is less risky than owning a few mortgages in their entirety.
2. *Creating liquidity.* Securitization makes the underlying assets liquid by creating a market for them in the form of a bond.
3. *Fostering specialization.* Some financial institutions are effective in *originating* (creating) the underlying assets (such as a residential mortgage), while others are more proficient at collecting these assets and issuing and *distributing* the securities.
4. *Broadening markets.* Instead of having to rely on a local bank to hold the mortgage, a homebuyer gains access through securitization to investors across the globe.
5. *Promoting innovation.* Financial firms seeking to lower the cost of funds to borrowers can broaden the range of assets that are transformed into securities.

Securitization has grown sharply over the past 35 years, rising from only $0.3 trillion in 1980 to $8.0 trillion in 2018—including $7.3 trillion in home mortgages (see Table 6.7). Thus, mortgage-backed securities (MBS) account for the largest share of securitized debt, by far, although many other forms of debt have also been pooled into bonds, including student loans, auto loans, and credit card debt.

Securitization has clear benefits, but its huge scale also reflects enormous government support. Initially, all securitizations were federally guaranteed, and as of 2018, the fraction guaranteed still stood at 85 percent. Here again, mortgages stood out. In 2018—primarily because of the government-sponsored enterprises (GSEs) Fannie Mae and Freddie Mac—fully 94 percent of all MBS (or nearly two-thirds of all U.S. residential mortgages) were guaranteed.

Table 6.7 U.S. Securitizations and Mortgages Outstanding, 1980 to 2018 (trillions of dollars)

	1980	1990	2000	2018
Total securitizations	0.3	1.6	5.5	8.0
Fraction guaranteed	100%	85%	75%	85%
Total home mortgages	0.9	2.4	4.7	10.9
Home mortgages securitized	0.2	1.1	2.9	7.3
Fraction guaranteed	100%	96%	87%	94%

SOURCE: Federal Reserve Board, "Financial Accounts of the United States," Statistical Release Z.1.

firm hoping to market its own brand of e-cash called "Flam,"[7] has issued one-year, 5 percent coupon bonds with a face value of $100. This represents a promise to pay $105 in one year. What is the price of this bond?

If Flim.com were risk free, and lenders were certain they would be paid back, the price of the bond would be computed as the present value of the $105 payment, calculated using the 5 percent risk-free interest rate.

$$\text{Price of Flim.com bond if it is risk free} = \frac{\$100 + \$5}{1.05} = \$100$$

[7]This example is not farfetched. In the 1990s a company called flooz.com tried to issue e-money called "flooz."

Bonds Indexed to Inflation
YOUR FINANCIAL WORLD

Inflation creates risk that the nominal return you receive on a bond won't be worth as much as you expected. If a bond pays a 6 percent yield but the inflation rate is also 6 percent, then the real return is zero! What can you do? You could accept the inflation risk, buy a regular bond, and hope for the best. But that's not always appealing.

Fortunately, there are alternatives. One is to buy a type of U.S. Treasury bond that compensates you for inflation. This **inflation-indexed bond** is structured so that the government promises to pay you a fixed interest rate plus the change in the consumer price index (the CPI). For instance, if you buy a $1,000 bond with an interest rate of 3 percent plus inflation, and the CPI rises 2 percent, you will get 3 + 2 = 5 percent. If the inflation rate jumps to 5 percent, then you'll get 3 + 5 = 8 percent. Regardless of what inflation turns out to be, you get 3 percent more, so there is no inflation risk. And because the U.S. Treasury issues these bonds, there is little default risk.

The U.S. Treasury sells two types of bonds that are adjusted for inflation, Series I savings bonds and Treasury Inflation-Protected Securities (TIPS). Series I savings bonds have a long list of rules about how many can be purchased and how long they need to be held. You can learn about these bonds on the website of TreasuryDirect at www.treasurydirect.gov. You can buy and sell TIPS in financial markets, or you can buy them directly from the U.S. Treasury through TreasuryDirect.

TIPS, which have been issued regularly since 2003, usually guarantee investors a way to beat inflation. Beginning in late 2011, however, anxieties about future inflation boosted the price of 10-year TIPS so high that the yield fell *below* the annual inflation rate. As of August 2019, the yield was less than 25 basis points, well below its long-term average.

But unlike the U.S. Treasury, Flim.com may not make the payments. People might be unwilling to use Flam, so Flim.com could default. Suppose there is a 0.10 probability (1 chance in 10) that Flim.com will go bankrupt before paying bondholders their $105. To simplify the example, we will assume that in the case of default, the bondholders get nothing. This means that there are two possible payoffs, $105 and $0 (see Table 6.8).

Table 6.8 shows that the expected value of the payment on this bond is $94.50. But even if the payment is made, it will be made one year from now, which means that the price we would be willing to pay for the bond today must be the present value of the future payment. Using the risk-free interest rate for this computation, we find that

$$\text{Expected present value of Flim.com bond payment} = \frac{\$94.50}{1.05} = \$90$$

So the bond will sell for $90. What yield to maturity does this price imply? If the promised payment is $105, the promised yield to maturity is

$$\text{Promised yield on Flim.com bond} = \frac{\$105}{\$90} - 1 = 0.1667$$

Table 6.8 Expected Value of Flim.com Bond Payment

Possibilities	Payoff	Probability	Payoff × Probabilities
Full payment	$105	0.90	$94.50
Default	$ 0	0.10	$ 0

Expected value = Sum of payoffs × Probabilities = $94.50

Bond Market Liquidity: Should We Be Worried?

MONEY AND BANKING BLOG

In recent years, some experts have expressed concern that changes in regulations since the Great Financial Crisis have diminished the functionality of U.S. bond markets.

The loudest complaints are about market liquidity. Participants say that it has become increasingly difficult to execute large trades without affecting prices. The claim is that the heightened cost of complying with regulations has driven banks out of the business of market making in bonds. As a result, not enough intermediaries are holding the inventories required to readily and continuously buy and sell bonds.

We can separate the claims about bond market liquidity into those about U.S. corporate bonds and those regarding Treasury bonds.

Corporate bonds were highly illiquid *before* the crisis as well as after it. To be sure, their turnover—average daily trading as a share of the dollar quantity outstanding—has slipped, from 0.37 percent in 2005 to 0.35 percent in 2018. But corporate bond turnover has always been extremely low—a small fraction of that in Treasury debt (3½ percent in 2018) and mortgage-backed securities (2 percent).

Corporate bonds consist of a large number of small issues, which is one reason that they are so rarely traded—it is very costly to do so. Table 6.9 illustrates the point for a set of U.S. investment-grade corporate bond issuers. For example, JPMorgan has a total of 1,685 separate bond issues, of which only 58 are included in the index. Yet, those 58 issues account for 65 percent of JPMorgan's outstanding corporate bond debt.

If issuing a small number of bonds in large volume would enhance their liquidity, why would a firm choose to issue so many different bonds of small size? One possibility is that doing so allows a single investor, like a pension fund or insurance company, to purchase the entire issue with the intention of holding it until maturity. If so, then the benefit to the issuer of making its bonds more liquid may fall short of the costs of doing so.

Arguably, the chief concern about corporate bond liquidity is its *variation* around the low norm: It declines even further at times of heightened financial volatility. This pattern is a reminder that market liquidity tends to disappear in times of stress.

Concerns about a loss of liquidity in U.S. Treasury debt markets have greater merit. Turnover in Treasury debt fell from 13.3 percent of \$4.25 trillion outstanding in 2005 to 3.6 percent of \$15.3 trillion in 2018. While other common measures of liquidity show only limited deterioration on average, worries surged following the "Treasury flash rally" that occurred on the morning of October 15, 2014, between 9:33 and 9:45 eastern U.S. time. Within those 12 minutes, the yield on the 10-year Treasury issue first spiked downward by 16 basis points for no apparent reason and then recovered.

After the event, government authorities issued a comprehensive report focusing on the rapid technological changes in the Treasury market as a possible source of the problem. The bulk of trading in Treasury securities today is done by institutions called *principal trading firms* (*PTFs*) that use proprietary automated trading strategies, or "bots." PTFs are distinct from hedge funds and bank dealers. And unlike traditional market makers, they often place buy and sell orders that they cancel within fractions of a second, making them high-frequency traders.

Does it matter that the market has shifted from being largely populated by brokers to one inhabited by bots? It may. Bots are driven by the very short-run objectives in their algorithms. They are typically programmed to pull back during times of stress, rather than assist customers who wish to trade. And they trade so rapidly that their interactions dominate market developments over short intervals.

Converting the decimal to a percentage, we get an interest rate of 16.67 percent.[8] Because the default-risk premium is the promised yield to maturity minus the risk-free rate, it is 16.67 percent − 5 percent = 11.67 percent.

In calculating the default-risk premium on Flim.com's bond, we computed the expected value of holding the bond—the yield at which the bond is a fair bet. But we know that risk-averse investors require some compensation for bearing risk. The more risk, the greater the compensation they demand. Only a risk-neutral investor would be

[8]This set of calculations could have been done in reverse. Given the yield of 16.67 percent and the characteristics of the bond, it is straightforward to compute the probability of default as 10 percent.

Table 6.9 Top U.S. Investment-Grade Bond Issuers

Issuer	Number of Bond Issues in Barclays U.S. Corporate Index	Share of Dollar Amount Outstanding (%)*	Total Number of Bond Issues Outstanding
JPMorgan Chase & Co	58	65	1,685
Bank of America	51	68	830
Goldman Sachs	41	62	2,560
Wells Fargo	42	67	489
Citigroup	53	58	2,061
AT&T	48	59	213
Morgan Stanley	33	61	1,171
Comcast	55	77	99
Verizon	35	83	199
Apple	39	82	76

NOTE: Table shows issuers with the largest notional amount outstanding in the Barclays U.S. Corporate Index.
*Share of dollar-denominated bonds that are eligible for inclusion in bond indexes.

SOURCE: Update as of December 12, 2018 of Exhibit 4 in BlackRock Viewpoint, "*Addressing Market Liquidity*," July 10, 2015.

What we don't know is whether a temporary loss of market making poses greater risk to the financial system. So long as the disturbances are brief and do not infect other markets, trading is a zero-sum game that matters solely to the participants. And so long as the intermediaries remain healthy, it's hard to see why a sudden loss of liquidity in a single market would not remain temporary and contained.

Put differently, the resilience of intermediaries and the resilience of markets are mutually reinforcing. With more resilient institutions, someone is more likely to stand ready to make a market in bonds—both Treasury and corporate—so long as the rewards are adequate. So it is natural for policymakers to focus on making intermediaries strong and able to withstand unpleasant market surprises. That helps market liquidity, too.

willing to pay \$90 for this bond. Any risk premium will drive the price down below \$90 and push the yield to maturity above 16.67 percent.

This example shows that the higher the default risk, the higher the probability that the bondholders will not receive the promised payments. Risk reduces the expected value of a given promise, lowering the price an investor is willing to pay and raising the yield. The higher the default risk, the higher the yield.

Inflation Risk

With few exceptions, bonds promise to make fixed-dollar payments. That is, a \$100 face value, one-year bond at 5 percent is a promise to make a \$105 payment in one

Table 6.10 Inflation Risk

	Probabilities		
Inflation Rate	**Case I**	**Case II**	**Case III**
1 percent	0.50	0.25	0.10
2 percent	—	0.50	0.80
3 percent	0.50	0.25	0.10
Expected inflation	2 percent	2 percent	2 percent
Standard deviation	1.0 percent	0.71 percent	0.45 percent

year. If this promise is free of default risk, the bondholder can be sure of receiving the $105 payment. Still, there is a risk of inflation. Remember that what you care about is the purchasing power of the money, not the number of dollars. In other words, bondholders are interested in the *real interest rate,* not just the nominal interest rate. And they don't know what the inflation rate will be.

Let's look at an example that shows how inflation risk affects the interest rate. To begin with, think about the interest rate as having three components: the real interest rate, expected inflation, and a compensation for inflation risk. Suppose the real interest rate is 3 percent but we are unsure what the inflation rate will be. It could be either 1 percent or 3 percent with equal probability (see Case I in Table 6.10). Expected inflation is 2 percent, with a standard deviation of 1.0 percent. This means the nominal interest rate should equal the 3 percent real interest rate plus the 2 percent expected inflation plus the compensation for inflation risk. The greater the inflation risk, the larger the compensation for it will be.

In Cases II and III, expected inflation is the same (2 percent) but the standard deviation is lower because we are more certain that the inflation rate will be close to its expected value. That is, Case III is less risky than Case II, which is less risky than Case I. Because risk requires compensation, we would expect the interest rate to be highest in Case I and lowest in Case III. While we may not see this distinction much in the United States or Europe, where inflation is stable, emerging market countries can go through periods when increases in inflation risk substantially drive up nominal interest rates.

Interest Rate Risk

To explain interest rate risk, we'll focus on a U.S. Treasury bond and assume that it is free of default risk and that we know how much inflation there will be, so there also is no inflation risk. Interest rate risk arises from the fact that investors don't know the holding period return of a long-term bond. Remember that when interest rates change, bond prices move; the longer the term of the bond, the larger the price change for a given change in the interest rate. Now think about what happens if you have a short investment horizon. If you buy a long-term bond, you will need to sell the bond before it matures, so you have to worry about what will happen if the interest rate changes.

Whenever there is a mismatch between your investment horizon and a bond's maturity, there is interest rate risk. Because the prices of long-term bonds can change dramatically, this can be an important source of risk. For example, on March 18, 2019, the 8.75 percent coupon Treasury bond that matures on August 15, 2020, traded at a price of $108.58 (per $100 face value). When it was originally issued as a 30-year bond in August 1990, its price was $98.747.[9] An investor who bought the bond when it was originally issued and sold it nearly 29 years later on March 18, 2019, earned a capital gain of nearly 10 percent. By comparison, an investor who purchased the 2.75 percent coupon 30-year Treasury bond when it was issued on November 15, 2012, at $100.69 and sold it less than 7 years later at its market price of $95.91 on March 18, 2019, suffered a capital loss of nearly 5 percent.

The lesson is that any move in interest rates changes the price of a bond. For investors with holding periods shorter than the maturity of the bond, the potential for a change in interest rates creates risk. The more likely interest rates are to change during the bondholder's investment horizon, the larger the risk of holding a bond.

[9]The U.S. Treasury auctions its bonds, so the original selling price is not the exact par value of the bond.

Key Terms

capital gain, 134
capital loss, 134
consol or perpetuity, 132
current yield, 134
default risk, 146
holding period return, 136
inflation-indexed bond, 149
inflation risk, 146
interest rate risk, 146
investment horizon, 137
U.S. Treasury bill (T-bill), 130
yield to maturity, 133
zero-coupon bond, 130

Using FRED: Codes for Data in This Chapter

Data Series	FRED Data Code
3-month Treasury bill rate	TB3MS
1-year Treasury bill rate	TB1YR
2-year Treasury constant maturity rate	GS2
10-year Treasury constant maturity rate	GS10
30-year Treasury constant maturity rate	GS30
5-year Treasury inflation-indexed yield	FII5
10-year Treasury inflation-indexed yield	FII10
30-year Treasury inflation-indexed yield	FII30
Consumer price index	CPIAUCSL
1-year inflation expectations (Michigan survey)	MICH
Japan Treasury bill rate	INTGSTJPM193N
Brazil Treasury bill rate	INTGSTBRM193N
U.S. Consumer Price Index (less food and energy)	CPILFESL

MON€¥ $ BAN£ING

To learn more about the changing financial system, visit www.moneyandbanking.com.

Chapter Lessons

1. Valuing bonds is an application of present value.
   a. Pure discount or zero-coupon bonds promise to make a single payment on a predetermined future date.
   b. Fixed-payment loans promise to make a fixed number of equal payments at regular intervals.
   c. Coupon bonds promise to make periodic interest payments and repay the principal at maturity.
   d. Consols (perpetuities) promise to make periodic coupon payments forever.
2. Yields are measures of the return on holding a bond.
   a. The yield to maturity is a measure of the interest rate on a bond. To compute it, set the price of the bond equal to the present value of the payments.
   b. The current yield on a bond is equal to the coupon rate divided by the price.
   c. When the price of a bond is above its face value, the coupon rate is greater than the current yield, which is higher than the yield to maturity.
   d. One-year holding period returns are equal to the sum of the current yield and any capital gain or loss arising from a change in a bond's price.
3. Bond prices (and bond yields) are determined by supply and demand in the bond market.
   a. The higher the price, the larger the quantity of bonds supplied.
   b. The higher the price, the smaller the quantity of bonds demanded.
   c. The supply of bonds rises when:
      i. Governments need to borrow more.
      ii. General business conditions improve.
      iii. Expected inflation rises.
   d. The demand for bonds rises when:
      i. Wealth increases.
      ii. Expected inflation falls.
      iii. The expected return, relative to other investments, rises.
      iv. The expected future interest rate falls.
      v. Bonds become less risky relative to other investments.
      vi. Bonds become more liquid relative to other investments.
4. Bonds are risky because of:
   a. Default risk: the risk that the issuer may fail to pay.
   b. Inflation risk: the risk that the inflation rate may be more or less than expected, affecting the real value of the promised nominal payments.
   c. Interest rate risk: the risk that the interest rate may change, causing the bond's price to change.

Conceptual and Analytical Problems

Mc Graw Hill connect

1. Consider a U.S. Treasury bill with 270 days to maturity. If the annual yield is 3.8 percent, what is the price? *(LO1)*

2.* You are an officer of a commercial bank and wish to sell one of the bank's assets—a car loan—to another bank. Using equation (A5) in the appendix to Chapter 4,

*Indicates more difficult problems.

compute the price you expect to receive for the loan if the annual interest rate is 6 percent, the car payment is $430 per month, and the loan term is five years. *(LO1)*

3.* Your financial advisor recommends buying a 10-year bond with a face value of $1,000 and an annual coupon of $80. The current interest rate is 7 percent. What might you expect to pay for the bond (aside from brokerage fees)? *(LO1)*

4.* Consider a coupon bond with a $1,000 face value and a coupon payment equal to 5 percent of the face value per year. *(LO1)*

a. If there is one year to maturity, find the yield to maturity if the price of the bond is $990.

b. Explain why finding the yield to maturity is difficult if there are two years to maturity and you do not have a financial calculator.

5. Which of these $100 face value one-year bonds will have the highest yield to maturity and why? *(LO2)*

a. A 6 percent coupon bond selling for $85.

b. A 7 percent coupon bond selling for $100.

c. An 8 percent coupon bond selling for $115.

6. You are considering purchasing a consol that promises annual payments of $4. *(LO2)*

a. If the current interest rate is 5 percent, what is the price of the consol?

b. You are concerned that the interest rate may rise to 6 percent. Compute the percentage change in the price of the consol and the percentage change in the interest rate. Compare them.

c. Your investment horizon is one year. You purchase the consol when the interest rate is 5 percent and sell it a year later, following a rise in the interest rate to 6 percent. What is your holding period return?

7.* Suppose you purchase a three-year, 5 percent coupon bond at par and hold it for two years. During that time, the interest rate falls to 4 percent. Calculate your annual holding period return. *(LO2)*

8. In a recent issue of *The Wall Street Journal* (or on www.wsj.com or an equivalent financial website), locate the prices and yields on U.S. Treasury issues. For one bond selling above par and one selling below par (assuming they both exist), compute the current yield and compare it to the coupon rate and the ask yield listed. *(LO2)*

9. In a recent issue of *The Wall Street Journal* (or on www.wsj.com), locate the yields on government bonds for various countries. Find a country whose 10-year government bond yield was above that on the U.S. 10-year Treasury bond and one whose 10-year yield was below the Treasury yield. What might account for these differences in yields? *(LO4)*

10. A 10-year zero-coupon bond has a yield of 6 percent. Through a series of unfortunate circumstances, expected inflation rises from 2 percent to 3 percent. *(LO4)*

a. Assuming the nominal yield rises by an amount equal to the rise in expected inflation, compute the change in the price of the bond.

b. Suppose that expected inflation is still 2 percent, but the probability that it will move to 3 percent has risen. Describe the consequences for the price of the bond.

*Indicates more difficult problems.

11. You are sitting at the dinner table and your father is extolling the benefits of investing in bonds. He insists that as a conservative investor he will only make investments that are safe, and what could be safer than a bond, especially a U.S. Treasury bond? What accounts for his view of bonds? Explain why you think it is right or wrong. *(LO4)*

12.* Consider a one-year, 10 percent coupon bond with a face value of $1,000 issued by a private corporation. The one-year risk-free rate is 10 percent. The corporation has hit on hard times, and the consensus is that there is a 20 percent probability that it will default on its bonds. If an investor were willing to pay at most $775 for the bond, is that investor risk neutral or risk averse? *(LO4)*

13. If, after one year, the yield to maturity on a multiyear coupon bond that was issued at par is higher than the coupon rate, what happened to the price of the bond during that first year? *(LO2)*

14. Use your knowledge of bond pricing to explain under what circumstances you would be willing to pay the same price for a consol that pays $5 a year forever and a 5 percent, 10-year coupon bond with a face value of $100 that only makes annual coupon payments for 10 years. *(LO1)*

15.* You are about to purchase your first home and receive an advertisement regarding adjustable-rate mortgages (ARMs). The interest rate on the ARM is lower than that on a fixed-rate mortgage. The advertisement mentions that there would be a payment cap on your monthly payments and you would have the option to convert to a fixed-rate mortgage. You are tempted. Interest rates are currently low by historical standards and you are eager to buy a house and stay in it for the long term. Why might an ARM not be the right mortgage for you? *(LO4)*

16. Use the model of supply and demand for bonds to illustrate and explain the impact of each of the following on the equilibrium quantity of bonds outstanding and on equilibrium bond prices and yields: *(LO3)*
    a. A new website is launched facilitating the trading of corporate bonds with much more ease than before.
    b. Inflationary expectations in the economy fall, evoking a much stronger response from issuers of bonds than investors in bonds.
    c. The government removes tax incentives for investment and spends additional funds on a new education program. Overall, the changes have no effect on the government's financing requirements.
    d. All leading indicators point to stronger economic growth in the near future. The response of bond issuers dominates that of bond purchasers.

17. Suppose that a sustainable peace is reached around the world, reducing military spending by the U.S. government. How would you expect this development to affect the U.S. bond market? *(LO3)*

18. Use the model of supply and demand for bonds to determine the impact on bond prices and yields of expectations that the real estate market is going to weaken. *(LO3)*

19.* Suppose there is an increase in investors' willingness to hold bonds at a given price. Use the model of the demand for and supply of bonds to show that the impact on the equilibrium bond price depends on how sensitive the quantity supplied of bonds is to the bond price. *(LO3)*

20. Under what circumstances would the purchase of a Treasury Inflation-Protected Security (TIPS) from the U.S. government be virtually risk free? *(LO4)*

*Indicates more difficult problems.

21. In the wake of the financial crisis of 2007–2009, negative connotations often surrounded the term *mortgage-backed security*. What arguments could you make to convince someone that she may have benefited from the growth in securitization over the past 50 years? *(LO3)*
22. During the euro-area sovereign debt crisis, the spread between the yields on bonds issued by the governments of peripheral European countries (such as Greece, Ireland, Italy, Portugal, and Spain) and those on bonds issued by Germany widened considerably. Use the model of supply and demand for bonds to illustrate how this could be explained by a change in investors' perceptions of the relative riskiness of peripheral sovereign versus German bonds. *(LO3, LO4)*
23. Not long after the United Kingdom's vote to leave the European Union in 2016, the yields on some British Government bonds (called gilts) turned negative. Assuming that these bonds were issued with a positive coupon rate, would you expect their market prices to be above, below, or equal to their face value when the yields were negative? Explain your choice. *(LO2)*

Data Exploration Mc Graw Hill connect

For detailed instructions on using Federal Reserve Economic Data (FRED) online to answer each of the following problems, visit www.mhhe.com/moneyandbanking6e *and refer to the FRED Resources and Data Exploration Hints.*

1. Graph investors' long-term expected inflation rate since 2003 by subtracting from the 10-year U.S. Treasury bond yield (FRED code: GS10) the yield on 10-year Treasury Inflation-Protected Securities (FRED code: FII10). Do these market-based inflation expectations appear stable? Did the financial crisis of 2007–2009 affect these expectations? *(LO4)*
2. Compare long-run market expectations of inflation with a consumer survey measure of one-year-ahead inflation expectations. Starting with the graph from Data Exploration Problem 1, add as a second line the University of Michigan survey measure of inflation expectations (FRED code: MICH). Why might these measures differ systematically? *(LO4)*
3. How does the variability of annual inflation—an indicator of inflation risk—change over time? Graph the percent change from a year ago of the consumer price index (FRED code: CPIAUCSL) since 1990 and visually compare the decades of the 1990s, the 2000s, and the period that began in 2010. *(LO4)*
4. Download the data from the graph that you produced in Data Exploration Problem 3. Calculate the standard deviation of the annual inflation rate for the three time periods and compare these results against your visual assessment from Data Exploration Problem 3. *(LO4)*
5. Economists sometimes exclude food and energy prices from the "headline" consumer price index and use the resulting "core" price measure to assess inflation prospects. For the period since 1990, plot on one graph the percent change from a year ago of the consumer price index (FRED code: CPIAUCSL) and the percent change from a year ago of the consumer price index excluding food and energy (FRED code: CPILFESL). Visually compare the variability of these two measures of inflation. Why might inflation excluding food and energy be a better predictor of future inflation than headline inflation? *(LO4)*

Chapter

7 The Risk and Term Structure of Interest Rates

Learning Objectives

After reading this chapter, you should be able to:

LO1 Explain the links between credit risk, bond ratings, and bond yields.

LO2 Distinguish taxable and tax-free bonds.

LO3 Define the yield curve and interpret it using the expectations hypothesis and liquidity premium theory.

LO4 Discuss how yields anticipate future economic activity.

On October 5, 1998, William McDonough, president of the Federal Reserve Bank of New York, declared "I believe that we are in the most serious financial crisis since World War II."[1] Since August 17, when the Russian government had defaulted on some of its bonds, deteriorating investor confidence had increased volatility in the financial markets. Bond markets were the hardest hit; as lenders re-evaluated the relative risk of holding different bonds, some prices plummeted while others soared. This simultaneous increase in some interest rates and decline in others—a rise in what are called **interest rate spreads**—was a clear sign to McDonough that the substantial stress the financial markets were experiencing could easily spread to the wider economy, affecting everyone.

Changes in bond prices, and the associated changes in interest rates, can have a pronounced effect on borrowing costs corporations face. The experience of Ford and General Motors (GM), the American automobile manufacturers, provides an instructive example. Like virtually every large company, the two carmakers borrow to maintain and expand their businesses. And the amounts are very large. By 2005, Ford's borrowing exceeded $150 billion while GM's was nearly twice that. The two companies produce almost one-third of the cars and trucks Americans buy. And they buy quite a few—just over 17¼ million in 2018. But for years before the financial crisis that began in 2007, the fortunes of U.S. automakers were declining. Plummeting sales in the recession of 2007–2009 triggered massive losses that eventually led to the bankruptcy of GM. Even before GM's failure, the perceived riskiness of Ford and GM's bonds led to a decline in the price investors were willing to pay for them. A fall in bond prices means an increase in interest rates and a corresponding rise in the cost the auto companies have to pay to borrow.

[1]McDonough's job was to monitor financial market developments for the Federal Reserve System, to devise government reaction to such financial crises, and to formulate policies that prevented crises. As we will see in our discussion of the structure of the Federal Reserve System in Chapter 16, the Federal Reserve Bank of New York is the largest of the 12 district banks in the Federal Reserve System. The president of that bank plays a special role as the eyes and ears of the government in world financial markets.

These examples highlight the need to understand the differences among the many types of bonds that are sold and traded in financial markets. What was it about the movement in the prices of different bonds that McDonough found so informative? How did information about profitability affect investors' willingness to lend to GM and Ford? To answer these questions, we will study the differences among the multitude of bonds issued by governments and private corporations. As we will see, these bonds differ in two crucial respects: the identity of the issuer and the time to maturity. The purpose of this chapter is to examine how each of these affects the price of a bond, and then to use our knowledge to interpret fluctuations in a broad variety of bond prices.

Ratings and the Risk Structure of Interest Rates

Default is one of the most important risks a bondholder faces. Not surprisingly, the risk that an issuer will fail to make a bond's promised payments varies substantially from one borrower to another. The risk of default is so important to potential investors that independent companies have come into existence to evaluate the creditworthiness of potential borrowers. These firms, sometimes called rating agencies, estimate the likelihood that a corporate or government borrower will make a bond's promised payments. The first such ratings began in the United States more than 100 years ago. Since 1975, the U.S. government has acknowledged a few firms as "nationally recognized statistical rating organizations" (NRSROs), a designation that has encouraged investors and governments worldwide to rely on their ratings. In 2010, sweeping financial reform legislation (called the Dodd-Frank Wall Street Reform and Consumer Protection Act) included provisions to reduce reliance on ratings agencies. Let's look at these companies and the information that they produce.

Bond Ratings

The best-known bond rating services are Moody's and Standard & Poor's.[2] These companies monitor the status of individual bond issuers and assess the likelihood that a lender/bondholder will be repaid by a borrower/bond issuer. Companies with good credit—those with low levels of debt, high profitability, and sizable amounts of cash assets—earn high bond **ratings**. A high rating suggests that a bond issuer will have little problem meeting a bond's payment obligations.

SOURCE: grzegorz knec/Alamy Stock Photo

Table 7.1 reports the rating systems of Moody's and Standard & Poor's. As you can see, they are very similar. Both systems are based on letters and bear a broad similarity to the rankings in minor-league baseball. Firms or governments with an exceptionally strong financial position carry the highest ratings and are able to issue the highest-rated bonds, Triple A. Johnson & Johnson, Microsoft, and the government of Canada are all examples of entities with Aaa bond ratings.[3]

[2]Fitch is a third, less well-known bond rating company. In addition to the big three, seven small agencies also now enjoy the U.S. government's NRSRO designation.

[3]U.S. government debt is a standard of comparison for other dollar-denominated debt because it is widely perceived as among the world's safest financial instruments. In August 2011, however, reacting to the rising debt burden and what it called "political risks," Standard & Poor's downgraded long-term U.S. Treasury debt to AA+. In September 2012, Moody's warned that it may downgrade U.S. debt from Aaa to Aa1 (the highest Aa category) if U.S. budget negotiations in 2013 failed to put the ratio of federal debt to GDP on a declining path in the medium term. Nevertheless, as of early 2019, the Moody's rating of U.S. debt remained stable at Aaa.

Table 7.1 A Guide to Bond Ratings

	Moody's	Standard & Poor's	Description	Examples of Issuers with Bonds Outstanding in 2016
Investment Grade	Aaa	AAA	Bonds of the best quality with the smallest risk of default. Issuers are exceptionally stable and dependable.	Johnson & Johnson Microsoft Canada
	Aa	AA	Highest quality with slightly higher degree of long-term risk.	Google/Alphabet Procter & Gamble South Korea
	A	A	High-medium quality, with many strong attributes but somewhat vulnerable to changing economic conditions.	JPMorgan Chase Wells Fargo China
	Baa	BBB	Medium quality, currently adequate but perhaps unreliable over the long term.	Hewlett Packard Italy Portugal
Noninvestment, Speculative Grade	Ba	BB	Some speculative element, with moderate security but not well safeguarded.	Goodyear Tire Nokia Brazil
	B	B	Able to pay now but at risk of default in the future.	Hertz Greece Kenya
Highly Speculative	Caa	CCC	Poor quality, clear danger of default.	Ferrellgas Partners Sable Permian Resources
	Ca	CC	Highly speculative quality, often in default.	
	C	C	Lowest-rated, poor prospects of repayment though may still be paying.	Venezuela*
	D	D	In default.	

*While the Moodys rating for Venezuela is C, the Standard and Poor's rating is SD for "selective default."

For a more detailed definition of ratings see Moody's website, www.moodys.com, or Standard and Poor's website, www.standardandpoors.com.

The top four categories, Aaa down to Baa in the Moody's scheme, are considered **investment-grade bonds**, meaning they have a very low risk of default. These ratings are reserved for most government issuers as well as corporations that are among the most financially sound.[4] Famously, these top ratings also were awarded to many risky mortgage-backed securities (see Lessons from the Crisis: Subprime Mortgages on page 161) that later plunged in value, triggering the financial crisis of 2007–2009 (see Money and Banking Blog: In Search of Better Credit Assessments on page 162). Table 7.1 gives examples of governments and firms in selected rating levels above default in early 2019.

The distinction between investment-grade and speculative, noninvestment-grade bonds is an important one. A number of regulated institutional investors, among them some insurance companies, pension funds, and commercial banks, are not allowed to invest in bonds that are rated below investment grade, that is, below Baa on Moody's scale or BBB on Standard & Poor's scale.[5]

[4]Government debt ratings are important, as they generally create a ceiling on the ratings for private companies in that country.

[5]Restrictions on the investments of financial intermediaries, such as insurance companies, are a matter for government regulators. There is no comprehensive reference for all of the legal restrictions that force financial firms to sell bonds whose ratings fall below Baa. In many cases, such as those of bond mutual funds, the restrictions are self-imposed.

Subprime Mortgages
LESSONS FROM THE CRISIS

The financial crisis of 2007–2009 initially was known as the *subprime crisis* because of the mortgage-backed securities (MBS, see page 52) that helped trigger the crisis in the United States. What is a subprime mortgage? What role does it play in the mortgage market? And how did it contribute to the financial crisis?

A residential mortgage is called *subprime* when it does not meet key standards of creditworthiness that apply to a conventional *prime* mortgage.* Conventional prime mortgages are those that satisfy the rules for inclusion in a collection or *pool of mortgages* to be guaranteed by a U.S. government agency. For this reason, conventional prime mortgages also are called *qualifying* or *conforming* mortgages.† Prime mortgages in which the loan amount exceeds a government-specified limit are called jumbo prime and do not qualify for the government guarantee.

The purpose of the creditworthiness standards is to increase the likelihood that the borrower will be able to repay the loan. Reducing borrower defaults lowers the cost to the government agency of its guarantee for the mortgage pools that back the MBS. The lending standards for qualifying mortgages typically include rules about the borrower's income, wealth, and credit score (see Your Financial World: Your Credit Rating on page 166). The standards also cover the size of mortgage, the price of the home, and the ratio between those two amounts—known as the *loan-to-value ratio,* or LTV ratio.

Subprime loans may fail to meet some or all of these standards for a qualifying mortgage. Typically, a loan is subprime if it is made to someone with a low credit score or whose income may be low relative to the price of the home; or if the LTV is high; or if the borrower does not provide sufficient documentation of his or her ability to pay. All of these factors make the loan more risky. Put differently, a subprime loan has a higher probability of default than qualifying loans.

Like conventional mortgages, the subprime type comes in two forms: fixed-rate and adjustable-rate mortgages (the latter are called ARMs—Chapter 6). And like conventional ARMs, subprime ARMs typically provide a low interest rate—known as a *teaser* rate—for the first two or three years. But once this initial period ends, the interest rate *resets* to a higher level—often, a much higher level—for the remaining term of the loan. This structure gives borrowers an incentive to replace their mortgage after the early years to obtain a new, low teaser rate or a fixed-rate loan. This process is called *refinancing*. Rising house prices make it possible to refinance even when a borrower's ability to pay is low because the lender can sell the house to recover the loan if the borrower fails to make timely payments.

During the housing bubble, starting in 2002, the volume of subprime loans surged as mortgage lenders relaxed their lending standards. Borrowers could obtain loans with lower down payments (high LTVs) and ever-poorer documentation. A complacent belief that the rise in nationwide house prices that had continued since the 1930s would persist indefinitely encouraged lending to borrowers with progressively lower ability to pay. When house prices started to fall in 2006, home values began to sink "below water"—that is, the home price fell to less than the amount of the mortgage—and lenders became unwilling to refinance many subprime loans. A wave of defaults followed. And further house price declines meant that lenders would not be able to recover the loan amounts in the increasingly likely event that borrowers would not be able to pay.

Even at their peak, outstanding subprime mortgages probably accounted for less than 15 percent of overall residential mortgages (which were $11 trillion in 2007)—and only a fraction of these were of really terrible quality. So why did subprime mortgage defaults trigger the financial disruptions of 2007–2009? The key reason is that some large, highly leveraged financial institutions held a sizable volume of MBS backed by subprime mortgages. Buying the MBS had allowed the institutions to increase their leverage and risk taking (see Chapter 5) at the same time that they earned fees for new MBS issuance. In effect, some financial institutions "bet the house" on subprime mortgage securities, and the price collapse of those securities threatened their existence.

*There is another category of nonprime mortgages called alt-A that fall between prime and subprime in their default probability.

†The guarantee on a conforming mortgage pool lowers the default risk on a security backed by the pool. As a result, investors will pay more for the security and borrowers can obtain a cheaper mortgage.

Bonds issued by Goodyear, Hertz, and the governments of Brazil and Kenya are in the noninvestment, speculative grade. These companies and countries may have difficulty meeting their bond payments but are not at risk of immediate default. The final category in Table 7.1, highly speculative bonds, consists of debts that are in serious risk of default. Bonds issued by Venezuela are in this category.

Bonds with ratings below investment grade are often referred to as **junk bonds** or sometimes more politely as *high-yield bonds* (a reminder that to obtain a high yield,

In Search of Better Credit Assessments

MONEY AND BANKING BLOG

Credit rating agencies (CRAs) are businesses that played a central role in the financial crisis of 2007–2009. Almost immediately after the crisis hit, the CRAs' sky-high ratings of mortgage-backed securities (MBS) were seen as one of the villains in the drama. Without the complicity of CRAs, it is hard to see how the lending that fed the housing boom could have been sustained.

In 2014, the Securities and Exchange Commission (SEC) issued two guidelines to reform the operations of CRAs. As one of the regulatory reforms mandated by the Dodd-Frank Act of 2010, the CRA rules were a long time coming, but they are not likely to achieve their intended goals.

During the years before the crisis, financial institutions assembled vast numbers of MBS pools, each composed of several thousand subprime (low-quality) mortgages, yet the vast majority of MBS supported by such pools received the highest-quality credit rating. How could that happen? The basic approach was to cut up each pool into pieces (tranches). All of the cash from the underlying mortgages flowed initially to the highest-grade tranche, which had first claim, and any remaining cash flowed to each successively lower-grade tranche. This "waterfall" pattern of filling the top vessel first was supposed to make the top-quality tranche backed by each pool virtually risk free.

The CRAs were central to this alchemy. They blessed the tranche structure, rewarding MBS pools with extravagant ratings, including (typically) a "super-senior AAA rating" for the top tranche. A key element was that the CRAs used statistical models that did not account for the increased threat of a large nationwide decline of housing prices. These models effectively ignored the vulnerability created by the unprecedented house price boom that began around 2000. Believing that the securities were safe, MBS investors did little to monitor the quality of the underlying mortgages.

But once housing prices across the country tipped lower in 2007 and mortgages started to default in unison, CRAs slashed their ratings, fueling the MBS bust in a mirror image of the process in which their high ratings had propelled the boom. Of all the asset-backed securities (and collateralized debt obligations) rated AAA between 2005 and 2007, *more than 80 percent* had fallen by at least four rating notches by mid-2009 and were no longer investment grade!

CRAs had strong incentives to pump up ratings. Given that the issuer of the securities pays for the rating, the most obvious incentive was the concentration of their paying clients: in the half-dozen years before 2007, the top five MBS issuers accounted for 40 percent of the MBS market, resulting in a large volume of repeat business. The resulting conflict of interest led to a documented bias toward high ratings.

This brings us to the two SEC rules intended to address the problems with bond ratings. The first one

investors must take a large risk).[6] There are two types of junk bonds. The first type, called **fallen angels**, were once investment-grade bonds, but their issuers fell on hard times. The second are cases in which little is known about the risk of the issuer.

MCI WorldCom, the telecommunications giant purchased by Verizon in early 2006, was one company whose bond rating fluctuated between investment grade and junk. When it began issuing bonds in 1997, the firm was below investment grade (Moody's Ba). MCI WorldCom saw its rating rise for several years, until it peaked as a Moody's A from mid-1999 to the end of 2001. Taking advantage of this investment-grade rating, MCI WorldCom issued $11.8 billion worth of bonds in May 2001. Just one year later, MCI WorldCom's rating dropped back to where it started, Ba, and its 10-year bonds were trading for 44 cents on the dollar, less than half of their initial prices. By mid-2002, as the company filed for bankruptcy, its bonds had fallen one more notch to B.

Sovereigns can be "fallen angels," too. For example, bonds issued by Greece were rated A (investment grade) as recently as the spring of 2010. As the financial crisis in the euro area intensified, the rating agencies repeatedly lowered Greece's credit rating

[6] *Junk bond* is an informal term used to mean a highly speculative security that has a low rating; it has no exact or formal definition.

requires CRAs to establish controls to limit the conflict of interest arising from the "issuer pays" arrangement. To improve transparency, the second rule compels the CRAs to publish reams of information about the pools they are rating.

Will this help? Probably not much. Take the transparency rule first. It is addressed to the market for U.S. MBS that are *not* government insured—known as "private-label" MBS. In 2018, however, private-label MBS issuance was less than 5 percent of its peak levels in 2005–2006! The lack of new issues has deprived investors of the long data history necessary to assess the risk of private-label MBS. The additional information required by the transparency rule probably won't improve investors' ability to assess the changing correlations that determine the risks of private-label MBS.

What about CRA conflicts of interest? Here, at least two problems remain. First, however much the new guidelines try to separate a CRA's ratings activity from its business of gathering revenues, the connection is still there. Analysts know that customers shop for ratings, awarding the lucrative job of rating a new bond to the firm that is most optimistic about their prospects.

Second, and more troubling, the desire for inflated ratings is not limited to issuers; many investors, including asset managers and bankers, want inflated ratings, too! That is, the incentive problems are the same on *both sides* of this transaction.

For example, the performance of an asset manager whose portfolio includes bonds is measured relative to a benchmark with bonds in specific rating categories. A manager who buys bonds with an inflated rating will boost the expected return on the portfolio relative to the benchmark while concealing the increased risk—at least until there are actual losses. Because funds that perform poorly are often shut down, the survival of the outperformers makes it look like their managers have superior skills, even if they merely choose riskier portfolios.

For a banker, the riskier the assets, the bigger the regulatory capital buffer required. For small banks, the measurement of risk uses a standardized approach based on credit ratings. Again, a bank that holds bonds that are riskier than their ratings suggest can expect a higher return for a given level of capital.

Addressing all of the issues associated with CRAs—problems including faulty models, insufficient data, and poor incentives—may exceed anyone's current capacity. But regulators can do better than the SEC has done. One example suffices: The SEC rules for CRAs do not address the problem of ratings shopping even though reform proposals to address this deficiency existed well before passage of the Dodd-Frank Act.

(eventually to the lowest grade, C) in the run-up to its March 2012 default. Frequent, sharp downgrades during such periods of market stress raise doubts about the usefulness of the ratings in anticipating default (see also Money and Banking Blog: In Search of Better Credit Assessments). Indeed, for investment-grade sovereign debt, Moody's puts the five-year default rate, as a share of issuers, at nearly 3¼ percent. The one-year-ahead record is better: 12 months before their default, no sovereign issuer was still rated as investment grade, but more than 1 percent of corporate defaults were.[7]

Material changes in a firm's or government's financial conditions precipitate changes in its debt ratings. The rating services are constantly monitoring events and announcing modifications to their views on the creditworthiness of borrowers. If a particular business or country encounters problems (as occurs with some frequency), Moody's and Standard & Poor's will lower that issuer's bond rating in what is called a **ratings downgrade**. Typically, an average of 2 to 3 percent of bonds that begin a year in an investment-grade category—Aaa to Baa—have their ratings downgraded to one of the

[7]For an in-depth assessment of sovereign credit ratings, see International Monetary Fund, *Global Financial Stability Report*, "The Uses and Abuses of Sovereign Credit Ratings," October 2010, Chapter 3. Moody's issuer-weighted cumulative default-rate estimates appear in Exhibit 19 of its report *Sovereign Default and Recovery Rates, 1983–2018*, April 8, 2019.

noninvestment grades. The MCI WorldCom downgrade in May 2002 reflected the agencies' view that the company had too much debt and (given the dismal state of the telecommunications industry at the time) little opportunity to reduce it. **Ratings upgrades** occur as well. Roughly 3 percent of Aa-rated bonds are upgraded to Aaa each year.[8]

Commercial Paper Ratings

Commercial paper is a short-term version of a bond. Both corporations and governments issue commercial paper. Because the borrower offers no collateral, this form of debt is *unsecured.* So only the most creditworthy companies can issue it.[9] Moreover, the amount of commercial paper outstanding plunged during the financial crisis of 2007–2009: After peaking in mid-2007 at $2.1 trillion, it fell to about $1 trillion by 2011 and has remained there ever since. Nevertheless, financial companies, such as JPMorgan and TD Bank, still issued the majority of it.

Like a U.S. Treasury bill, commercial paper is issued on a discount basis, as a zero-coupon bond that specifies a single future payment with no associated coupon payments. For legal reasons, commercial paper usually has a maturity of less than 270 days.[10] Roughly one-third of all commercial paper is held by money-market mutual funds (MMMFs), which require very short-term assets with immediate liquidity. A majority of commercial paper is issued with a maturity of 5 to 45 days and is used exclusively for short-term financing.

The rating agencies rate the creditworthiness of commercial paper issuers in the same way as bond issuers. Again, Moody's and Standard & Poor's have parallel rating schemes that differ solely in their labeling (see Table 7.2). The vast majority of issuance is in the highest category, Moody's P-1, with the remainder rated P-2—the *P* stands for **prime-grade commercial paper**. Speculative-grade commercial paper does exist, but not because it was originally issued as such.

The Impact of Ratings on Yields

RISK

Bond ratings are designed to reflect default risk: The lower the rating, the higher the risk of default. We know investors require compensation for risk, so everything else held equal, the lower a bond's rating, the lower its price and the higher its yield. From Chapter 6 we know that we can think about changes in risk as shifts in the demand for bonds. Increases in risk will reduce investor demand for bonds at every price, shifting the demand curve to the left, decreasing the equilibrium price and increasing the yield (see Figure 7.1 on page 165).

The easiest way to understand the quantitative impact of ratings on bond yields is to compare different bonds that are identical in every way except for the issuer's credit rating. U.S. Treasury issues have long served as a standard for comparison because they are viewed as having little default risk. This is why they are commonly referred to as **benchmark bonds**, and the yields on other bonds are measured in terms of the

[8]Based on authors' estimates for the period 1983–2017 using Moody's *Annual Default Study: Corporate Default and Recovery Rates, 1920–2017,* February 15, 2018, Exhibits 29 and 41.

[9]Recall that collateral is something of value pledged by the borrower that the lender could sell if the loan is not repaid. See also Lessons from the Crisis: Asset-Backed Commercial Paper on page 168.

[10]As described in detail by Thomas K. Hahn, "Commercial Paper," *Instruments of the Money Market* (Federal Reserve Bank of Richmond, 1998, Chapter 9), the Securities Act of 1933 generally requires registration of securities, a time-consuming and expensive process. But Section 3(a) (3) of the act exempts securities with less than 270 days to maturity as long as they meet certain requirements.

Table 7.2 Commercial Paper Ratings

	Moody's	Standard & Poor's	Description	Examples of Issuers with Commercial Paper Outstanding in 2016
Investment or Prime Grade	P-1	A-1+, A-1	Strong likelihood of timely repayment.	Coca-Cola ExxonMobil Yale University
	P-2	A-2	Satisfactory degree of safety for timely repayment.	General Electric General Mills Harley-Davidson
	P-3	A-3	Adequate degree of safety for timely repayment.	
Speculative, below Prime Grade		B, C	Capacity for repayment is small relative to higher-rated issuers.	
Defaulted		D		

SOURCE: Thomas K. Hahn, "Commercial Paper," *Instruments of the Money Market*, Chapter 9, Federal Reserve Bank of Richmond, 1998; www.moodys.com; and www.standardandpoors.com.

spread over Treasuries. (Remember from the definition in Chapter 5: Risk is measured relative to a benchmark. For bonds, the most common benchmark is U.S. Treasury bonds.)

We can think of any bond yield as the sum of two parts: the yield on the benchmark U.S. Treasury bond plus a default-risk premium, sometimes called a **risk spread**.

$$\text{Bond yield} = \text{U.S. Treasury yield} + \text{Default-risk premium} \qquad (1)$$

If bond ratings properly reflect the probability of default, then the lower the rating of the issuer, the higher the default-risk premium in equation (1). This way of thinking about bond yields provides us with a second insight: When Treasury yields move, all other yields move with them.

These two predictions—that interest rates on a variety of bonds will move together and that lower-rated bonds will have higher yields—are both borne out by the data. To see this, let's look at a plot of the **risk structure of interest rates**. Panel A of Figure 7.2 on page 167 shows the yield to maturity for long-term bonds with three different ratings: 10-year U.S. Treasury, Moody's Aaa-rated, and Moody's Baa long-term bonds. As you can see from the figure, all of these yields move together. When the U.S. Treasury yield goes up or down, the Aaa and Baa yields do too. While the default-risk premiums do fluctuate—rising particularly in periods of financial stress—changes in the U.S. Treasury yield account for most of the movement in the Aaa and Baa bond yields. Furthermore, the yield on the higher-rated U.S. Treasury bond is consistently the lowest. In fact, over the years from 1971 to 2019,

Figure 7.1 The Effect of an Increase in Risk on Equilibrium in the Bond Market

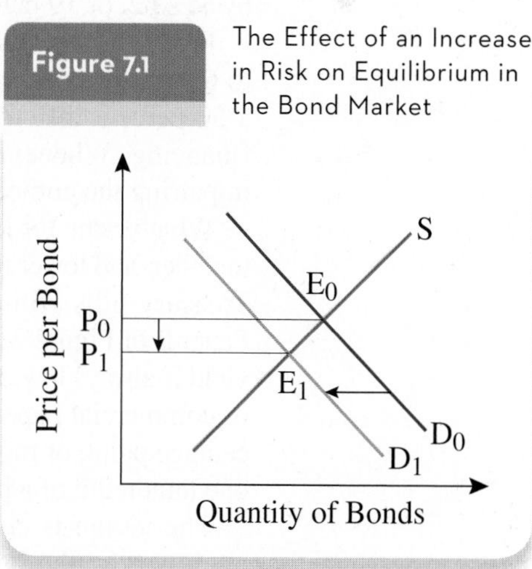

Increased risk reduces the demand for the bond at every price, shifting the demand curve to the left from D_0 to D_1. The result is a decline in the equilibrium price and quantity in the market. Importantly, the price falls from P_0 to P_1, so the yield on the bond must rise.

Your Credit Rating
YOUR FINANCIAL WORLD

Companies aren't the only ones with credit ratings; you have one, too. Have you ever wondered how someone decides whether to give you a loan or a credit card? The answer is that there are companies keeping track of your financial information. They rate your creditworthiness, and they know more about you than you might think. Credit rating companies know all about your credit cards, your car loan or mortgage (if you have one), and whether you pay your bills on time. All of this information is combined in something called a *credit score*. If you have low levels of debt and pay your bills on time, you have a high credit score.

You care about your credit score; here's why. Lenders use *credit scores* to calculate the interest rate they charge on a loan. With a top credit score, a four-year, $10,000 car loan might have an interest rate of 4 percent and monthly payments of $221. But if your credit score was low, because you missed a payment on a credit card or paid your utility bill late, then the interest rate could be as high as 15 percent, which would mean monthly payments as much as $50 higher. The same principle applies to home mortgages; the better your credit score, the lower the interest rate. It pays to pay all your bills on time.*

*Ironically, someone who has never had a credit card and never owed anyone any money has no credit history at all and so will have a low credit score. You cannot start too soon in creating a record as a good credit risk. And you are entitled to a free annual credit report from each of the credit rating companies. To find out how to get it, go to www.annualcreditreport.com.

the 10-year U.S. Treasury bond yield averaged more than a full percentage point below the yield on Aaa bonds and two percentage points below the yield on Baa bonds.

How important is one or two percentage points in yield? To see, we can do a simple computation. At an interest rate of 4 percent, the present value of a $100 payment made 10 years from now is $66.48. If the interest rate rose to 6 percent, the value of this same promise would decline to $53.86. So a two-percentage point increase in the yield, from 4 percent to 6 percent, lowers the value of the promise of $100 in 10 years by $12.62, or 19 percent!

From the viewpoint of the borrower, an increase in the interest rate from 4 percent to 6 percent means paying $6 rather than $4 per year for each $100 borrowed. That is a 50 percent difference. Clearly, ratings are crucial to corporations' ability to raise financing. Whenever a company's bond rating declines, the cost of funds goes up, impairing the company's ability to finance new ventures.[11]

What is true for long-term bond yields is true for short-term bond yields; they move together, and lower ratings imply higher yields. Compare the yields on three-month U.S. Treasury bills with those on A-1/P-1 commercial paper of the same maturity (see Panel B of Figure 7.2). The two yields clearly move together, and the U.S. Treasury bill yield is always lower than the yield on commercial paper. From 1971 to 2019, the spread of commercial paper over U.S. Treasury bills averaged more than one-half of one percentage point, or more than 50 *basis points*. (Recall from Chapter 6 that a basis point is one hundredth of a percentage point, or 0.01 percent.)

The lesson is clear; investors must be compensated for assuming risk. The less creditworthy the borrower, the higher the risk of default, the lower the borrower's

[11]The same is true for individuals. Consider the impact on the monthly payments required to service a 30-year, $100,000 mortgage. At an interest rate of 4 percent, payments would be approximately $477 per month. If the interest rate were to increase to 6 percent, the required monthly payments would rise to more than $600. You can compute these amounts using the formulas in the appendix to Chapter 4.

Figure 7.2 The Risk Structure of Interest Rates

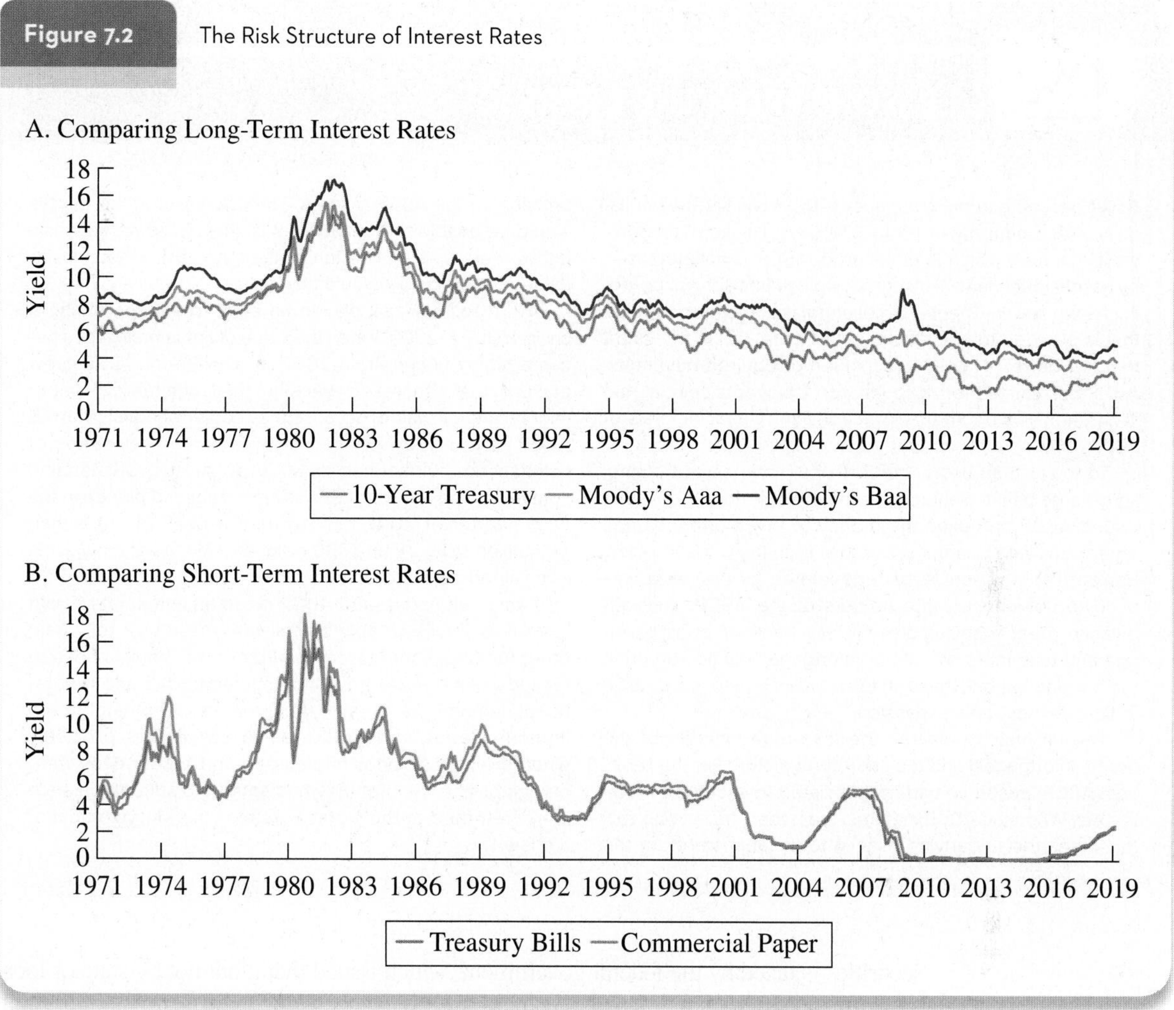

SOURCE: Board of Governors of the Federal Reserve System, [FRED data codes: GS10, AAA, BAA, CPN3M (since 1997), and TB3MS].

rating, and the higher the cost of borrowing. And the lower the rating of the bond or commercial paper, the higher the yield.

Differences in Tax Status and Municipal Bonds

Default risk is not the only factor that affects the return on a bond. The second important factor is taxes. Bondholders must pay income tax on the interest income they receive from owning privately issued bonds. These are **taxable bonds**. In contrast, the coupon payments on bonds issued by state and local governments, called **municipal** or **tax-exempt bonds**, are specifically exempt from taxation.[12]

The general rule in the United States is that the interest income from bonds issued by one government is not taxed by another government, although the issuing government may tax it. The interest income from U.S. Treasury

[12]Municipal bonds come in two varieties. Some are general-obligation bonds backed by the taxing power of the governmental issuer. Others are revenue bonds issued to fund specific projects; these are backed by revenues from the project or operator.

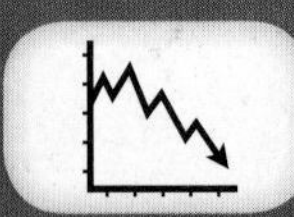

Asset-Backed Commercial Paper
LESSONS FROM THE CRISIS

Asset-backed commercial paper (ABCP) is a short-term liability with a maturity of up to 270 days. Unlike most commercial paper, which is unsecured, ABCP is collateralized by assets that financial institutions place in a special portfolio. As we saw in Chapter 3, collateral is something of value that is pledged to pay a loan (in this case, CP) in the event that the borrower does not make the required payments. ABCP has existed for decades, but it played a special role in the housing boom that preceded the financial crisis of 2007–2009.

To lower their costs and limit their own asset holding, some large banks created firms (a form of *shadow bank*) that issued ABCP and used the money to buy mortgages and other loans (see Chapter 3, Lessons from the Crisis: Shadow Banks). The payment stream generated by the loans was used to compensate the holders of the ABCP. This off-balance-sheet financing also allowed banks to boost leverage and take more risk. When mortgage volume surged in the housing bubble, these shadow banks issued more ABCP to finance their rapid expansion.

The mismatch between the long-term maturity of the assets (mortgages) and the short-term maturity of the liabilities (ABCP) posed an underappreciated threat to the ABCP issuers. When the ABCP matures, the issuers have to borrow (or to sell the underlying assets) to be able to return the principal to the ABCP holders. The risk was that the issuers would be unable to borrow—that is, they faced *rollover* risk. If they were also unable to sell the long-term assets easily, these shadow banks would face failure.

ABCP rollover risk played an early role in the financial crisis of 2007–2009. When the value of some mortgages became highly uncertain in 2007, purchasers of ABCP grew anxious that the assets backing their commercial paper might plunge in value. Because they had erroneously viewed ABCP as a very low-risk security, the sudden awareness of risk caused a virtual halt to ABCP purchases. Outstanding commercial paper from ABCP issuers began to plunge in the third quarter of 2007, sinking from a peak of more than $1.2 trillion to less than $300 billion in 2013. As of early 2019, it remained below that mark.

Firms that had issued ABCP faced an immediate threat to their survival. Unable to sell their assets or to obtain other funding, some failed. In other cases, banks chose to rescue their shadow banks to limit legal risks and reputational damage. As a result, those banks faced heightened liquidity needs and pressures to sell assets precisely when the cost of funds had surged and asset prices were plunging. The risk that they had sought to shift off balance sheet returned at the worst possible time—in the midst of a crisis.

securities is taxed by the federal government, which issued them, but not by state or local governments. In the same way, the federal government is precluded from taxing interest on municipal bonds. In an effort to make their bonds even more attractive to investors, however, state and local governments usually choose not to tax the interest on their own bonds, exempting it from all income taxes.

How does a tax exemption affect a bond's yield? Bondholders care about the return they actually receive, after tax authorities have taken their cut. If investors expect to receive a payment of \$6 for holding a bond but know they will lose \$1.80 of it in taxes, they will act as if the return on the investment is only \$4.20. That is, investors base their decisions on the *after-tax yield.*

Calculating the tax implications for bond yields is straightforward. Consider a one-year \$100 face value taxable bond with a coupon rate of 6 percent. This is a promise to pay \$106 in one year. If the bond is selling at par, at a price of \$100, then the yield to maturity is 6 percent. From the point of view of the government issuers, the bondholder receives \$6 in taxable income at maturity. If the tax rate is 30 percent, the tax on that income is \$1.80, so the \$100 bond yields \$104.20 after taxes. In other words, at a 30 percent tax rate, a 6 percent taxable bond yields the equivalent of 4.2 percent.

This same calculation works for any interest rate and any bond, which allows us to derive a relationship between the yields on taxable and tax-exempt bonds. The rule is that the yield on a tax-exempt bond equals the taxable bond yield times one minus the tax rate:

$$\text{Tax-exempt bond yield} = (\text{Taxable bond yield}) \times (1 - \text{Tax rate}) \qquad (2)$$

For an investor with a 30 percent tax rate, then, we can compute the tax-exempt yield on a 10 percent bond by multiplying 10 percent times (1 – 0.3), or 7 percent. Overall, the higher the tax rate, the wider the gap between the yields on taxable and tax-exempt bonds.

The Term Structure of Interest Rates

TIME

A bond's tax status and rating aren't the only factors that affect its yield. In fact, bonds with the same default rate and tax status but different maturity dates usually have different yields. Why? The answer is that long-term bonds are like a composite of a series of short-term bonds, so their yield depends on what people expect to happen in years to come. In this section, we will develop a framework for thinking about *future interest rates.*

The relationship among bonds with the same risk characteristics but different maturities is called the **term structure of interest rates**.

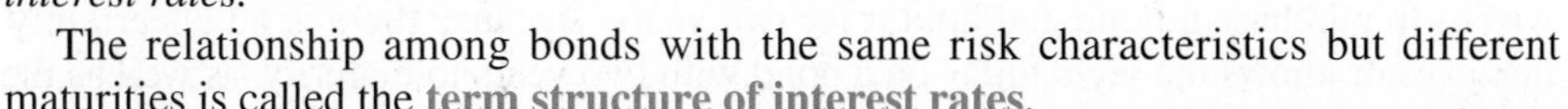

In studying the term structure of interest rates, we will focus our attention on Treasury yields; see Figure 7.3. Comparing information on 3-month (the blue line) and 10-year (the green line) Treasury issues, we can draw three conclusions:

1. *Interest rates of different maturities tend to move together.* The bulk of the variation in short- and long-term interest rates is in the same direction. That is, the blue and green lines clearly move together.
2. *Yields on short-term bonds are more volatile than yields on long-term bonds.* The blue line moves over a broader range than the green line.
3. *Long-term yields tend to be higher than short-term yields.* The green line usually, *but not always,* lies above the blue line.

Figure 7.3 The Term Structure of Treasury Interest Rates

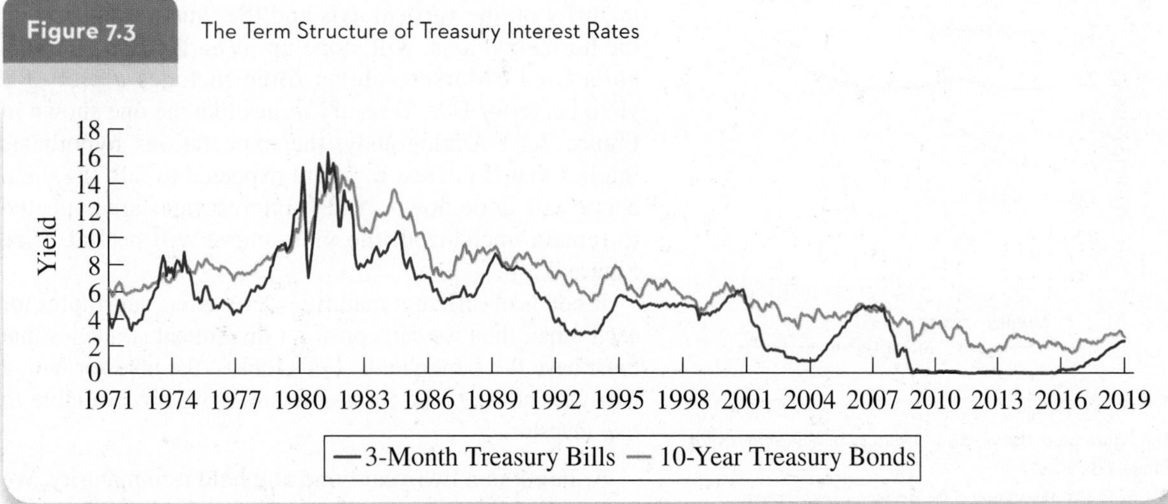

SOURCE: Board of Governors of the Federal Reserve System. [FRED data codes: TB3MS and GS10]

Default risk and tax differences cannot explain these relationships. What can? We will examine two explanations, the expectations hypothesis and the liquidity premium theory.

The Expectations Hypothesis

Over the years, economists have proposed and discarded numerous theories to explain the term structure of interest rates. We can benefit from their hard work and ignore all the ones they found wanting. The first one we will focus on, called the **expectations hypothesis of the term structure**, is straightforward and intuitive. If we think about yields as the sum of a risk-free interest rate and a risk premium, the expectations hypothesis focuses on the first of those elements. It begins with the observation that the risk-free interest rate can be computed, assuming there is no uncertainty about the future. That is, we know not just the yield on bonds available today but the yields that will be available on bonds next year, the year after that, and so on.

To understand the implications of this statement, think about an investor who wishes to purchase a bond and hold it for two years. Because there is no uncertainty, the investor knows the yield today on a bond with two years to maturity, as well as the yields on a one-year bond purchased today and on a second one-year bond purchased one year from now. Being sure about all of these, the investor will be indifferent between holding the two-year bond and holding a series of two one-year bonds. *Certainty means that bonds of different maturities are perfect substitutes for each other.* This is the essence of the expectations hypothesis.

To see how this works, assume that the current one-year interest rate is 5 percent. The expectations hypothesis implies that the current two-year interest rate should equal the average of 5 percent and the one-year interest rate one year in the future. If that future interest rate is 7 percent, then the current two-year interest rate will be (5 + 7)/2 = 6%.

Figure 7.4 The U.S. Treasury Yield Curve

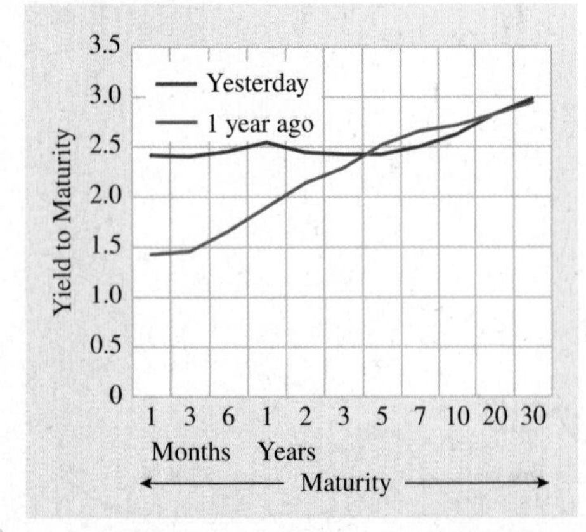

The figure plots the yields on Treasury bills and bonds for January 31, 2019.

SOURCE: U.S. Department of the Treasury, www.treasury.gov/resource-center/data-chart-center/interest-rates/Pages/TextView.aspx?data=yield; or FRED.

According to the expectations hypothesis, then, when interest rates are expected to rise in the future, long-term interest rates will be higher than short-term interest rates. This means that the **yield curve**, which plots the yield to maturity on the vertical axis and the time to maturity on the horizontal axis, will slope up. (*The Wall Street Journal*'s Credit Market column often includes a plot of a yield curve for U.S. Treasury issues like the one shown in Figure 7.4.) Analogously, the expectations hypothesis implies that if interest rates are expected to fall, the yield curve will slope down. And if interest rates are expected to remain unchanged, the yield curve will be flat. (See Figure 7.5.)

If bonds of different maturities are perfect substitutes for each other, then we can construct investment strategies that must have the same yields. Let's look at the investor with a two-year horizon. Two possible strategies are available to this investor:

A. Invest in a two-year bond and hold it to maturity. We will call the interest rate associated with this investment i_{2t} ("i" stands for the interest rate, "2" for two

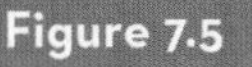
The Expectations Hypothesis and Expectations of Future Short-Term Interest Rates

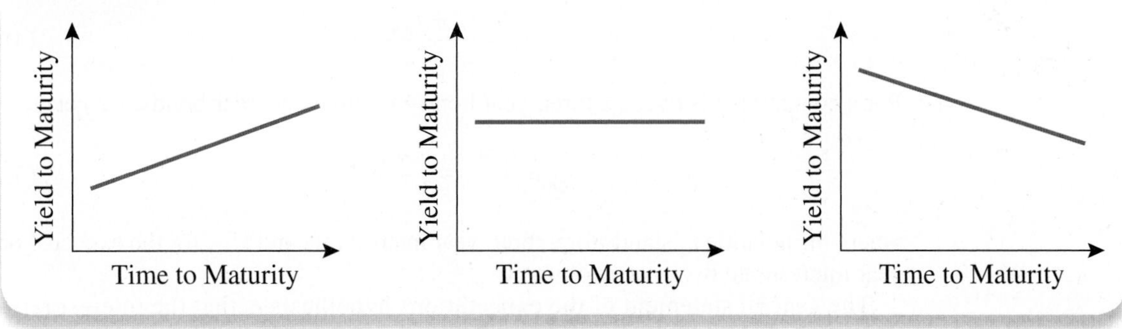

Interest rates are expected to **rise.** Interest rates are expected to **remain unchanged.** Interest rates are expected to **fall.**

years, and "t" for the time period, which is today). Investing one dollar in this bond will yield $(1 + i_{2t})(1 + i_{2t})$ two years later.

B. Invest in two one-year bonds, one today and a second when the first one matures. The one-year bond purchased today has an interest rate of i_{1t} ("1" stands for one year). The one-year bond purchased one year from now has an interest rate of i^e_{1t+1} where "$t + 1$" stands for one time period past period t, or next year. The "e," which stands for *expected,* indicates that this is the one-year interest rate investors *expect* to obtain one year ahead. Because we are assuming that the future is known, this expectation is certain to be correct. A dollar invested using this strategy will return $(1 + i_{1t})(1 + i^e_{1t+1})$ in two years.

The expectations hypothesis tells us that investors will be indifferent between these two strategies. (Remember, the bonds are perfect substitutes for each other.) Indifference between strategies A and B means that they must have the same return, so

$$(1 + i_{2t})(1 + i_{2t}) = (1 + i_{1t})(1 + i^e_{1t+1}) \qquad (3)$$

The Expectations Hypothesis of the Term Structure:

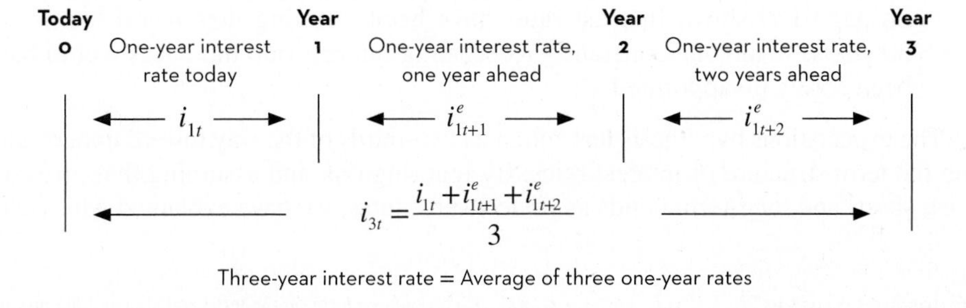

If the one-year interest rate today is $i_{1t} = 5\%$, the one-year interest rate one year ahead is $i^e_{1t+1} = 6\%$, and the one-year interest rate two years ahead, is $i^e_{1t+2} = 7\%$, then the expectations hypothesis tells us that the three-year interest rate will be $i_{3t} = (5\% + 6\% + 7\%)/3 = 6\%$.

Expanding equation (3) and taking an approximation that is very accurate, we can write the two-year interest rate as the average of the current and future expected one-year interest rates:[13]

$$i_{2t} = \frac{i_{1t} + i^e_{1t+1}}{2} \tag{4}$$

For a comparison between a three-year bond and three one-year bonds, we get

$$i_{3t} = \frac{i_{1t} + i^e_{1t+1} + i^e_{1t+2}}{3} \tag{5}$$

where the notation i_{3t} stands for a three-year interest rate and i^e_{1t+2} for the expected one-year interest rate two years from now.

The general statement of the expectations hypothesis is that the interest rate on a bond with n years to maturity is the average of n expected future one-year interest rates:

$$i_{nt} = \frac{i_{1t} + i^e_{1t+1} + i^e_{1t+2} + \cdots + i^e_{1t+n-1}}{n} \tag{6}$$

What are the implications of this mathematical expression? Does the *expectations hypothesis of the term structure of interest rates* explain the three observations we started with? Let's look at each one.

1. The expectations hypothesis tells us that long-term bond yields are all averages of expected future short-term yields—the same set of short-term interest rates—so *interest rates of different maturities will move together.* From equation (6) we see that if the current one-year interest rate, i_{1t}, changes, all the yields at higher maturities will change with it.
2. The expectations hypothesis implies that *yields on short-term bonds will be more volatile than yields on long-term bonds.* Because long-term interest rates are averages of a sequence of expected future short-term rates, if the current 3-month interest rate moves, it will have only a small impact on the 10-year interest rate. Again, look at equation (6).[14]
3. The expectations hypothesis *cannot* explain why *long-term yields are normally higher than short-term yields* because it implies that the yield curve slopes upward only when interest rates are expected to rise. To explain why the yield curve normally slopes upward, the expectations hypothesis would suggest that interest rates are normally expected to rise. But as the data in Figure 7.3 on page 169 show, interest rates have been trending downward for nearly 30 years, so anyone constantly forecasting interest rate increases would have been sorely disappointed.

The expectations hypothesis has gotten us two-thirds of the way toward understanding the term structure of interest rates. By ignoring risk and assuming that investors view short- and long-term bonds as perfect substitutes, we have explained why yields

[13]Expanding (3) gives us $2i_{2t} + i^2_{2t} = i_{1t} + i^e_{1t+1} + (i_{1t})(i^e_{1t+1})$. The squared term on the left-hand side and the product term on the right-hand side of this equation are small, and their difference is even smaller. Using the example of 5 percent and 7 percent for the one-year interest rates, we can see that ignoring the two product terms means ignoring $[(0.06)^2 - (0.05 \times 0.07)]/2 = (0.0036 - 0.0035)/2 = 0.00005$, an error of 0.005 percentage points.

[14]Take a simple example in which the one-year and two-year interest rates, i_{1t} and i_{2t}, are both 5 percent. If the one-year interest rate increases to 7 percent, then the two-year interest rate will rise to 6 percent. The two move together, and the short-term rate is more volatile than the long-term rate.

at different maturities move together and why short-term interest rates are more volatile than long-term rates. But we have failed to explain why the yield curve normally slopes upward. To understand this, we need to extend the expectations hypothesis to include risk. After all, we all know that long-term bonds are riskier than short-term bonds. Integrating this observation into our analysis will give us the *liquidity premium theory* of the term structure of interest rates.

The Liquidity Premium Theory

Throughout our discussion of bonds, we emphasized that even default-free bonds are risky because of uncertainty about inflation and future interest rates. What are the implications of these risks for our understanding of the term structure of interest rates? The answer is that risk is the key to understanding the usual upward *slope* of the yield curve. Long-term interest rates are typically higher than short-term interest rates because long-term bonds are riskier than short-term bonds. Bondholders face both inflation and interest rate risk. The longer the term of the bond, the greater both types of risk.

The reason for the increase in inflation risk over time is clear-cut. Remember that bondholders care about the purchasing power of the return—the *real* return—they receive from a bond, not just the nominal dollar value of the coupon payments. Computing the real return from the nominal return requires a forecast of future inflation, or *expected* future inflation. For a three-month bond, an investor need only be concerned with inflation over the next three months. For a 10-year bond, however, computation of the real return requires a forecast of inflation over the next decade.

In summary, uncertainty about inflation creates uncertainty about a bond's real return, making the bond a risky investment. The further we look into the future, the greater the uncertainty about inflation. We are more uncertain about the level of inflation several years from now than about the level of inflation a few months from now, which implies that *a bond's inflation risk increases with its time to maturity.*

What about interest rate risk? Interest rate risk arises from a mismatch between the investor's investment horizon and a bond's time to maturity. Remember that if a bondholder plans to sell a bond prior to maturity, changes in the interest rate (which cause bond prices to move) generate capital gains or losses. The longer the term of the bond, the greater the price changes for a given change in interest rates and the larger the potential for capital losses.

Because some holders of long-term bonds will want to sell their bonds before they mature, interest rate risk concerns them. These investors require compensation for the risk they take in buying long-term bonds. As in the case of inflation, the risk increases with the term to maturity, so the compensation must increase with it.

What are the implications of including risk in our model of the term structure of interest rates? To answer this question, we can think about a bond yield as having two parts, one that is risk free and another that is a risk premium. The expectations hypothesis explains the risk-free part, and inflation and interest rate risk explain the risk premium. Together they form the **liquidity premium theory of the term structure** of interest rates. Adding the risk premium to equation (6), we can express this theory mathematically as

$$i_{nt} = rp_n + \frac{i_{1t} + i^e_{1t+1} + i^e_{1t+2} + \cdots + i^e_{1t+n-1}}{n} \tag{7}$$

where rp_n is the risk premium associated with an n-year bond. The larger the risk, the higher the risk premium, rp_n, is. Because risk rises with maturity, rp_n increases with n, and the yield on a long-term bond includes a larger risk premium than the yield on a short-term bond.

To get some idea of the size of the risk premium rp_n, we can look at the average slope of the term structure over a long period. From 1985 to early 2016, the difference between the interest rate on a 10-year Treasury bond and that on a 3-month Treasury bill averaged nearly two percentage points. It is important to keep in mind that this risk premium will vary over time. For example, if inflation is very stable or the variability of the real interest rate were to fall, then the 10-year bond risk premium could easily fall below one percentage point.

Can the liquidity premium theory explain all three of our conclusions about the term structure of interest rates? The answer is yes. Like the expectations hypothesis, the liquidity premium theory predicts that *interest rates of different maturities will move together* and that *yields on short-term bonds will be more volatile than yields on long-term bonds.* And by adding a risk premium that grows with time to maturity, it explains why *long-term yields are higher than short-term yields.* Because the risk premium increases with time to maturity, the liquidity premium theory tells us that the yield curve will normally slope upward; only rarely will it lie flat or slope downward. (A flat yield curve means that interest rates are expected to fall; a downward-sloping yield curve suggests that the financial markets are expecting a significant decline in interest rates.)

The Information Content of Interest Rates

The risk and term structure of interest rates contain useful information about overall economic conditions. These indicators are helpful in evaluating both the present health of the economy and its likely future course. Risk spreads provide one type of information, the term structure another. In the following sections we will apply what we have just learned about interest rates to recent U.S. economic history and show how forecasters use these tools.

Information in the Risk Structure of Interest Rates

When the overall growth rate of the economy slows or turns negative, it strains private businesses, increasing the risk that corporations will be unable to meet their financial obligations. The immediate impact of an impending recession, then, is to raise the risk premium on privately issued bonds. Importantly, though, an economic slowdown or recession does not affect the risk of holding government bonds.

The increased risk of default is not the same for all firms. The impact of a recession on companies with high bond ratings is usually small, so the spread between U.S. Treasuries and Aaa-rated bonds of the same maturity is not likely to move by much. But for issuers whose finances were precarious prior to the downturn, the effect is quite different. Those borrowers who were least likely to meet their payment obligations when times were good are even less likely to meet them when times turn bad. There is a real chance that they will fail to make interest payments. Of course, firms for which even the slightest negative development might mean disaster are the ones that issue low-grade bonds. The lower the initial grade of the bond, the more the default-risk premium rises as general economic conditions deteriorate. The spread between U.S. Treasury bonds and junk bonds widens the most.

Panel A of Figure 7.6 shows annual GDP growth over four decades superimposed on shading that shows the dates of recessions. (We'll learn more about recession dating in Chapter 22.) Notice that during the shaded periods, growth is

The Flight to Quality
APPLYING THE CONCEPT

Standing in the middle of an open field during a thunderstorm is a good way to get hurt, so few people do it. Instead, they take shelter. Investors do exactly the same thing during financial storms; they look for a safe place to put their investments until the storm blows over. In practical terms, that means selling risky investments and buying the safest instruments they can: U.S. Treasury bills, notes, and bonds. An increase in the demand for government bonds coupled with a decrease in the demand for virtually everything else is called a **flight to quality**. When it happens, there is a dramatic increase in the difference between the yields on safe and risky bonds—the *risk spread* rises.

When the government of Russia defaulted on its bonds in August 1998, the shock set off an almost unprecedented flight to quality. Yields on U.S. Treasuries plummeted, while those on corporate bonds rose. Risk spreads widened quickly; the difference between U.S. Treasury bills and commercial paper rates more than doubled, from its normal level of half a percentage point to over one percentage point. The debt of countries with emerging markets was particularly hard hit.

This flight to quality was what William McDonough called "the most serious financial crisis since World War II" (see the opening of this chapter). Because people wanted to hold only U.S. Treasury securities, the financial markets had ceased to function properly. McDonough worried that the problems in the financial markets would spread to the economy as a whole. They didn't in the 1998 episode, but they did in the much larger financial crisis of 2007–2009.

usually negative. In Panel B of Figure 7.6, GDP growth is drawn as the red line and the green line is the spread between yields on Baa-rated bonds and U.S. Treasury bonds. Note that the two lines move in opposite directions. (The correlation between the two series is −0.57.) That is, when the risk spread rises, output falls. The risk spread provides a useful indicator of general economic activity, and because financial markets operate every day, this information is available well before GDP data, which is published only once every three months. During the financial crisis of 2007–2009, the spread reached its widest level (5.6 percentage points) since the Great Depression of the 1930s.

Information in the Term Structure of Interest Rates

Like information on the risk structure of interest rates, information on the term structure—particularly the slope of the yield curve—helps us to forecast general economic conditions. Recall that according to the expectations hypothesis, long-term interest rates contain information about expected future short-term interest rates. And according to the liquidity premium theory, the yield curve usually slopes upward. The key term in this statement is *usually*. On rare occasions, short-term interest rates exceed long-term yields. When they do, the term structure is said to be *inverted,* and the yield curve slopes downward.

An **inverted yield curve** is a valuable forecasting tool because it predicts a general economic slowdown. Because the yield curve slopes upward even when short-term yields are expected to remain constant—it's the average of expected future short-term interest rates plus a risk premium—an inverted yield curve signals an expected fall in short-term interest rates. If interest rates are comparatively high, they serve as a brake on real economic activity. As we will see in Part IV, monetary policymakers adjust short-term interest rates in order to influence real economic growth and inflation. When the yield curve slopes downward, it indicates that policy is *tight* because policymakers are attempting to slow economic growth and inflation.

The Risk Spread and GDP Growth

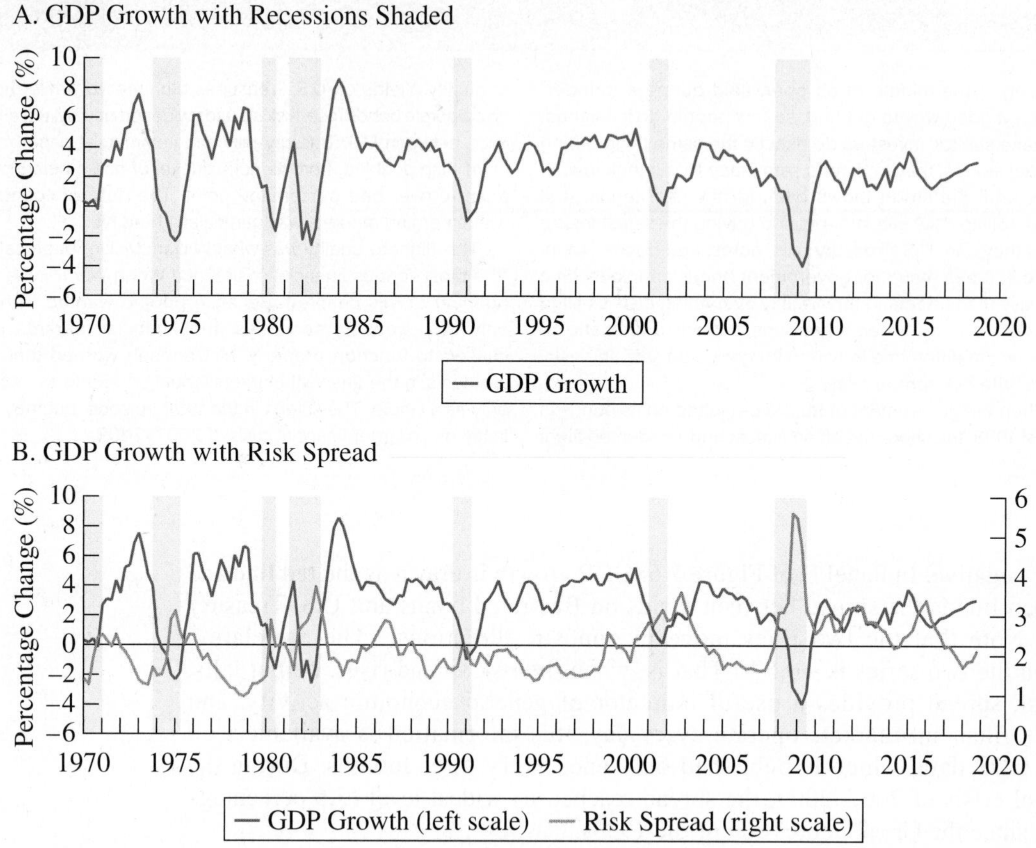

A. GDP Growth with Recessions Shaded

Percentage Change (%)

— GDP Growth

B. GDP Growth with Risk Spread

Percentage Change (%)

Spread (%)

— GDP Growth (left scale) — Risk Spread (right scale)

SOURCE: Bureau of Economic Analysis and Board of Governors of the Federal Reserve System. GDP growth is the percentage change from the same quarter of the previous year, while the yield spread is the difference between the average yield on Baa and 10-year U.S. Treasury bonds during the quarter. Shaded periods denote recessions. (FRED data codes: GDPC1, BAA, GS10, and USREC.)

Careful statistical analysis confirms the value of the yield curve as a forecasting tool.[15] Figure 7.7 shows GDP growth and the slope of the yield curve, measured as the difference between the 10-year and 3-month yields—what is called a **term spread**. Panel A of Figure 7.7 shows GDP growth (as in Figure 7.6) together with the contemporaneous term spread (the growth and the term spread at the same time). Notice that when the term spread falls, GDP growth tends to fall somewhat later. In fact, when the yield curve becomes inverted, the economy tends to go into a recession roughly a year later. Panel B of Figure 7.7 makes this clear. At each point, GDP growth in the current year (e.g., 1990) is plotted against the slope of the yield curve *one year earlier* (e.g., 1989). The two lines clearly move together; their correlation is +0.43. What the

[15]See Arturo Estrella and Frederic S. Mishkin, "The Yield Curve as a Predictor of U.S. Recessions," Federal Reserve Bank of New York, *Current Issues in Economics and Finance* 2, no. 7 (June 1996). To learn what the current yield curve tells about the U.S. economic outlook, see the latest monthly analysis of economists at the Federal Reserve Bank of Cleveland: www.cleveland.fed.org/research/data/yield_curve.

Figure 7.7 The Term Spread and GDP Growth

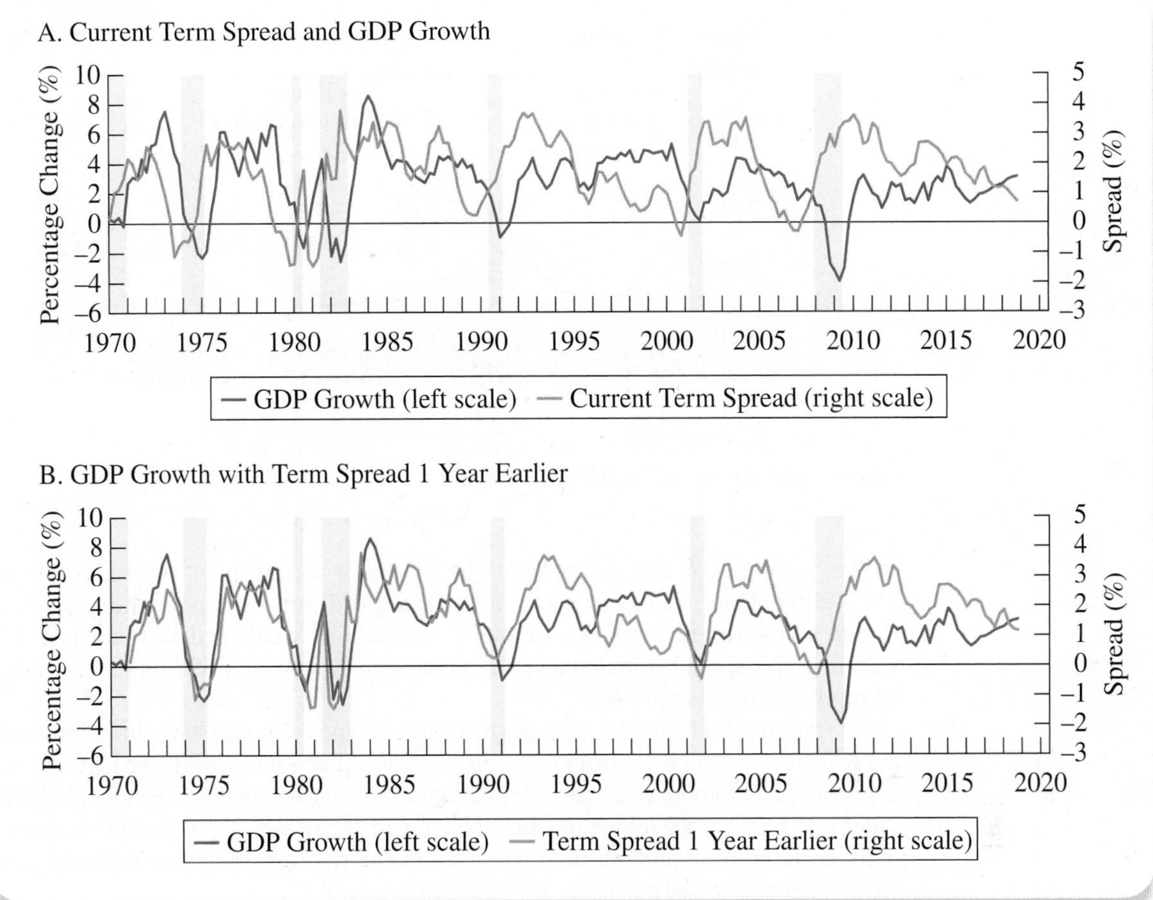

SOURCE: Bureau of Economic Analysis and Board of Governors of the Federal Reserve System. GDP growth is the percentage change from the same quarter of the previous year, while the term spread is the difference between the average yield on a 10-year U.S. Treasury bond and a 3-month U.S. Treasury bill during the quarter. In Panel B, the spread is lagged 1 year. Shaded periods denote recessions (FRED data codes: GDPC1, GS10, TB3MS, and USREC).

data show is that when the term spread falls, GDP growth tends to fall one year later. The yield curve is a valuable forecasting tool.

An example illustrates the usefulness of this information. In the left-hand panel of Figure 7.8, we can see that on January 23, 2001, the yield curve sloped downward from 3 months to 5 years, then upward for maturities to 30 years. This pattern indicated that interest rates were expected to fall over the next few years. Eight months later, after monetary policy had eased and the U.S. economy had slowed substantially, the Treasury yield curve sloped upward again (see the right-hand panel of Figure 7.8). At that point, growth was at a virtual standstill, and policymakers were doing everything they could to get the economy moving again. They had reduced interest rates by more than three percentage points over a period of less than nine months. Thus, investors expected little in the way of short-term interest rate reductions. This prediction turned out to be wrong, however; interest rates kept falling after the terrorist attacks of September 11, 2001. They continued to fall through the remainder of 2001 as the economy went into a mild recession.

Figure 7.8 The U.S. Treasury Yield Curve in 2001

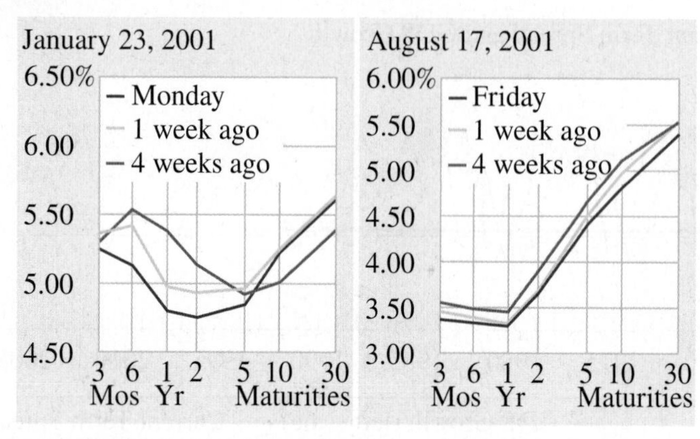

SOURCE: Board of Governors of the Federal Reserve System.

The yield curve did *not* predict the depth or duration of the recession of 2007–2009. One- and two-year market rates did not anticipate the persistent plunge of overnight rates. As financial institutions weakened in the crisis, the widening risk spread signaled a severe economic downturn, providing a more useful predictor in this episode.

We started this chapter by asking why different types of bonds have different yields and what it is we can learn from those differences. After a bit of work, we can now see that differences in both risk and time to maturity affect bond yields. The less likely the issuer is to repay or the longer the time to maturity, the riskier a bond and the higher its yield. Even more important, both increases in the risk spread and an inverted yield curve suggest troubled economic times ahead.

Key Terms

benchmark bond, 164
commercial paper, 164
expectations hypothesis of the term structure, 170
fallen angel, 162
flight to quality, 175
interest rate spread, 158
inverted yield curve, 175
investment-grade bond, 160
junk bond, 161
liquidity premium theory of the term structure, 173
municipal bonds, 167
prime-grade commercial paper, 164
rating, 159
ratings downgrade, 163
ratings upgrade, 164
risk spread, 165
risk structure of interest rates, 165
spread over Treasuries, 165
taxable bond, 167
tax-exempt bond, 167
term spread, 176
term structure of interest rates, 169
yield curve, 170

Using FRED: Codes for Data in This Chapter

Data Series	FRED Data Code
Moody's Aaa corporate bond yield	AAA
Moody's Baa corporate bond yield (monthly)	BAA
BofA Merrill Lynch US corporate BBB effective yield	BAMLC0A4CBBBEY
BofA Merrill Lynch US high-yield BB effective yield	BAMLH0A1HYBBEY
BofA Merrill Lynch US high-yield B effective yield	BAMLH0A2HYBEY
BofA Merrill Lynch US high-yield CCC or below effective yield	BAMLH0A3HYCEY
10-year Treasury constant maturity rate (monthly)	GS10
3-month Treasury bill rate	TB3MS
3-month AA nonfinancial commercial paper rate	CPN3M
Consumer price index	CPIAUCSL
Real GDP	GDPC1
Brazil Treasury bill rate	INTGSTBRM193N
3-month AA financial commercial paper rate	CPF3M
Moody's seasoned Baa corporate bond yield (weekly)	WBAA
10-year Treasury constant maturity rate (weekly)	WGS10YR
St. Louis Fed Financial Stress Index	STLFSI
Long-term U.S. government bond yield	LTGOVTBD

Chapter Lessons

To learn more about the changing financial system, visit www.moneyandbanking.com.

1. Bond ratings summarize the likelihood that a bond issuer will meet its payment obligations.
   a. Highly rated investment-grade bonds are those with the lowest risk of default.
   b. If a firm encounters financial difficulties, its bond rating may be downgraded.
   c. Commercial paper is the short-term version of a privately issued bond.
   d. Junk bonds are high-risk bonds with very low ratings. Firms that have a high probability of default issue these bonds.
   e. Investors demand compensation for default risk in the form of a risk premium. The higher the risk of default, the lower a bond's rating, the higher its risk premium, and the higher its yield.
2. Municipal bonds are usually exempt from income taxes. Because investors care about the after-tax returns on their investments, these bonds have lower yields than bonds whose interest payments are taxable.
3. The term structure of interest rates is the relationship between yield to maturity and time to maturity. A graph with the yield to maturity on the vertical axis and the time to maturity on the horizontal axis is called the yield curve.
   a. Any theory of the term structure of interest rates must explain three facts:
      i. Interest rates of different maturities move together.
      ii. The yields on short-term bonds are more volatile than the yields on long-term bonds.
      iii. Long-term yields are usually higher than short-term yields.

b. The expectations hypothesis of the term structure of interest rates states that long-term interest rates are the average of expected future short-term interest rates. This hypothesis explains only the first two facts about the term structure of interest rates.
c. The liquidity premium theory of the term structure of interest rates, which is based on the fact that long-term bonds are riskier than short-term bonds, explains all three facts in part *a*.

4. The risk structure and the term structure of interest rates both signal financial markets' expectations of future economic activity. Specifically, the likelihood of a recession will be higher when:
   a. The risk spread, or the range between low- and high-grade bond yields, is wide.
   b. The yield curve slopes downward, or is inverted, so that short-term interest rates are higher than long-term interest rates.

Conceptual and Analytical Problems Mc Graw Hill connect

1. Consider a firm that issued a large quantity of commercial paper in the period leading to a financial crisis. *(LO1)*
   a. How would you expect the credit rating of the commercial paper to evolve as the crisis unfolds?
   b. Would you alter your prediction if, rather than commercial paper, the firm was instead issuing asset-backed commercial paper?
2. Suppose that a major foreign government defaults on its debt. What, if anything, will happen to the position and slope of the U.S. Treasury yield curve? *(LO1)*
3. What was the connection between house price movements, the growth in subprime mortgages, and securities backed by these mortgages—on the one hand—and—on the other hand—the difficulties encountered by some financial institutions during the 2007–2009 financial crisis? *(LO1)*
4. Suppose that the interest rate on one-year bonds is 4 percent and is expected to be 5 percent in one year and 6 percent in two years. Using the expectations hypothesis, compute the yields in two- and three-year bonds and plot the yield curve. *(LO3)*
5.* According to the liquidity premium theory, if the yields on both one- and two-year bonds are the same, would you expect the one-year yield in one year's time to be higher, lower, or the same? Explain your answer. *(LO3)*
6. You have $1,000 to invest over an investment horizon of three years. The bond market offers various options. You can buy (i) a sequence of three one-year bonds; (ii) a three-year bond; or (iii) a two-year bond followed by a one-year bond. The current yield curve tells you that the one-year, two-year, and three-year yields to maturity are 3.5 percent, 4.0 percent, and 4.5 percent, respectively. You expect that one-year interest rates will be 4 percent next year and 5 percent the year after that. Assuming annual compounding, compute the return on each of the three investments, and discuss which one you would choose. *(LO3)*
7.* Suppose that the yield curve shows that the one-year bond yield is 3 percent, the two-year yield is 4 percent, and the three-year yield is 5 percent. Assume that the risk premium on the one-year bond is zero, the risk premium on the

*Indicates more difficult problems.

two-year bond is 1 percent, and the risk premium on the three-year bond is 2 percent. *(LO3)*

a. What are the expected one-year interest rates next year and the following year?
b. If the risk premiums were all zero, as in the expectations hypothesis, what would the slope of the yield curve be?

8.* If inflation and interest rates become more volatile, what would you expect to see happen to the slope of the yield curve? *(LO3)*

9. Suppose your local government, threatened with bankruptcy, decided to tax the interest income on its own bonds as part of an effort to rectify serious budgetary woes. What would you expect to see happen to the yields on these bonds? *(LO2)*

10.* Suppose the yields on tax-exempt local government bonds in Problem 9 initially were below the Treasury yields of the same maturity. If the tax-exempt status were then removed from the local government bonds, would you expect their yields spreads versus treasuries to narrow, to disappear, or change sign? Explain your answer. *(LO1, LO2)*

11. Suppose the risk premium on U.S. corporate bonds increases. How would the change affect your forecast of future economic activity, and why? *(LO4)*

12. If regulations restricting institutional investors to investment-grade bonds were lifted, what do you think would happen to the spreads between yields on investment-grade and speculative-grade bonds? *(LO1)*

13. Consider a struggling emerging market economy where, in contrast to developed economies, the perceived risk associated with holding sovereign bonds is affected by the state of the economy. Suppose vast quantities of valuable minerals were unexpectedly discovered on government-owned land. How might the government's bond rating be affected? Using the model of demand and supply for bonds, what would you expect to happen to the yields on that country's government bonds? *(LO1, LO4)*

14. Select the circumstance in which the impact on government bond yields of a new source of revenue (such as a natural resource discovery) would be largest. Explain your choice.

a. Before the discovery, the government was heavily indebted with a crippling debt-service burden *or*

b. Before the discovery, the government had a very low debt burden. *(LO1, LO4)*

15. The misrating of mortgage-backed securities by rating agencies contributed to the financial crisis of 2007–2009. List some recommendations you would make to avoid such mistakes in the future. *(LO1)*

16. How do you think the abolition of investor protection laws would affect the risk spread between corporate and government bonds? *(LO1)*

17. You and a friend are reading *The Wall Street Journal* and notice that the Treasury yield curve is slightly upward sloping. Your friend comments that all looks well for the economy but you are concerned that the economy is heading for trouble. Assuming you are both believers in the liquidity premium theory, what might account for your difference of opinion? *(LO3, LO4)*

*Indicates more difficult problems.

18. Do you think the term spread was an effective predictor of the recession that started in December 2007? Why or why not? *(LO4)*

19.* Given the data in the accompanying table, would you say that this economy is heading for a boom or for a recession? Explain your choice. *(LO4)*

	3-Month Treasury Bill	10-Year Treasury Bond	Baa Corporate 10-Year Bond
January	1.00%	3.0%	7.0%
February	1.05	3.5	7.2
March	1.10	4.0	7.5
April	1.20	4.3	7.7
May	1.25	4.5	7.8

20. Suppose recent regulatory reforms relating to credit rating agencies are perceived to improve the reliability and accuracy of credit ratings of corporate bonds. Imagine further that you manage a corporation interested in issuing new bonds, in addition to past issues by the firm that already trade in the market. Identify one way in which your firm might lose and one way in which it might gain from these reforms. Explain your answer. *(LO1)*

Data Exploration

For detailed instructions on using Federal Reserve Economic Data (FRED) online to answer each of the following problems, visit www.mhhe.com/moneyandbanking6e *and refer to the FRED Resources and Data Exploration Hints.*

1. Did the financial crisis of 2007–2009 affect financial and nonfinancial firms to the same extent? For the period beginning in 2006, plot the spread between the interest rates on three-month nonfinancial commercial paper (FRED code: CPN3M) and three-month Treasury bills (FRED code: TB3MS). Plot a similar spread using the interest rates on three-month financial commercial paper (FRED code: CPF3M) and Treasury bills (FRED code: TB3MS). Compare the evolution of these two spreads. *(LO1)*
2. The Federal Reserve Bank of St. Louis publishes a weekly index of financial stress (FRED code: STLFSI) that summarizes strains in financial markets, including liquidity problems. For the period beginning in 1994 plot this index and, as a second line, the difference between the weekly Baa corporate bond yield (FRED code: WBAA) and the weekly 10-year U.S. Treasury bond yield (FRED code: WGS10YR). Does the index STLFSI provide an early warning of stress? *(LO4)*
3. How did the Great Depression (1929–1933) and the Great Recession of 2007–2009 affect expectations of corporate default? To investigate, construct for each of those periods a separate plot of the corporate bond yield spread. For the Depression period, plot from 1930 to 1933 the difference between the Baa corporate bond yield

*Indicates more difficult problems.

(FRED code: BAA) and the long-term government bond yield (FRED code: LTGOVTBD). For the Great Recession, plot from 2007 to 2009 the difference between the Baa yield (FRED code: BAA) and the 10-year Treasury bond yield (FRED code: GS10). Compare the plots. *(LO1)*

4. How reliably does an inverted yield curve anticipate a recession? How far in advance? Plot from 1970 (as in Figure 7.7A) the difference between the 10-year Treasury yield (FRED code: GS10) and the 3-month Treasury bill rate (FRED code: TB3MS). Discuss the variability of the time between an inversion of the yield curve and the subsequent recession. *(LO3, LO4)*
5. Download the data used from the graph produced in Data Exploration Problem 4 and (a) find the most recent period for which the yield curve was (approximately) flat and (b) the longest time period for which the yield curve was inverted. *(LO3, LO4)*

Chapter 8

Stocks, Stock Markets, and Market Efficiency

Learning Objectives

After reading this chapter, you should be able to:

LO1 Identify the characteristics of common stock.

LO2 Distinguish leading stock market indices and their types.

LO3 Explain how stocks are valued.

LO4 Assess the risk in holding stocks for the long run.

LO5 Describe the stock market's role in the economy.

Stocks play a prominent role in our financial and economic lives. For individuals, they provide a key instrument for holding personal wealth as well as a way to diversify, spreading and reducing the risks that we face. Importantly, diversifiable risks are risks that are more likely to be taken. By giving individuals a way to transfer risk, stocks supply a type of insurance enhancing our ability to take risk.[1]

For companies, they are one of several ways to obtain financing. Beyond that, though, stocks and **stock markets** are a central link between the financial world and the real economy. Stock prices are fundamental to the functioning of a market-based economy. They tell us the value of the companies that issued the stocks and, like all other prices, they allocate scarce investment resources. The firms deemed most valuable in the marketplace for stocks are the ones that will be able to obtain financing for growth. When resources flow to their most valued uses, the economy operates more efficiently.

Mention of the stock market provokes an emotional reaction in many people. They see it as a place where fortunes are easily made or lost, and they recoil at its unfathomable booms and busts. During one infamous week in October 1929, the New York Stock Exchange lost more than 25 percent of its value—an event that marked the beginning of the Great Depression. In October 1987, prices fell nearly 30 percent in one week, including a record decline of 20 percent in a single day. Crashes of this magnitude have become part of the stock market's folklore, creating the popular impression that stocks are very risky.

In the 1990s, stock prices increased nearly fivefold and Americans forgot about the "black Octobers." By the end of the decade, many people had come to see stocks as

[1]This point was central to our discussions of risk in Chapter 5. Our ability to diversify risk either through the explicit purchase of insurance or through investment strategies means that we are able to do risky things that we otherwise would not do.

almost a sure thing; you could not afford not to own them. In 1998, nearly half of all U.S. households owned some stock, either directly or indirectly through mutual funds and managed retirement accounts.

When the market's inexorable rise finally ended, the ensuing decline seemed more like a slowly deflating balloon than a crash. From early 2000 to the week following the terrorist attacks of September 11, 2001, the stock prices of the United States' biggest companies, as measured by the Dow Jones Industrial Average, fell more than 30 percent. While many stocks recovered much of their loss fairly quickly, a large number did not. During the same period, the Nasdaq Composite Index fell 70 percent, from 5,000 to 1,500; it remained below the peak until 2015. Because the Nasdaq tracks smaller, newer, more technologically oriented companies, many observers dubbed this episode the "Internet bubble."

The plunge of the U.S. stock market in the recent financial crisis was much broader and greater, roughly halving the market value by early 2009 from its 2007 peak of about $26 trillion. After accounting for inflation, it recaptured this peak only in 2014.

Yet, contrary to popular mythology, stock prices do tend to rise—even after adjusting for inflation—over the long term, collapsing only on those infrequent occasions when investors broadly reassess risk and return, or when normal market mechanisms are out of alignment. For most people, the experience of losing or gaining wealth suddenly is more memorable than the experience of making it gradually. By being preoccupied with the potential short-term losses associated with crashes, we lose sight of the gains we could realize if we took a longer-term view. The goal of this chapter is to try to make sense of the stock market—to show what fluctuations in stock value mean for individuals and for the economy as a whole and look at a critical connection between the financial system and the real economy. We will also explain how it is that things sometimes go awry, resulting in bubbles and crashes. First, however, we need to define the basics: what stocks are, how they originated, and how they are valued.

The Essential Characteristics of Common Stock

Stocks, also known as **common stock** or **equity**, are shares in a firm's ownership. A firm that issues stock sells part of itself, so that the buyer becomes a part owner. Stocks as we know them first appeared in the 16th century. They were created to raise funds for global exploration. Means had to be found to finance the dangerous voyages of explorers such as Sir Francis Drake, Henry Hudson, and Vasco de Gama. Aside from kings and queens, no one was wealthy enough to finance these risky ventures alone. The solution was to spread the risk through *joint-stock companies,* organizations that issued stock and used the proceeds to finance several expeditions at once. In exchange for investing, stockholders received a share of the company's profits.

These early stocks had two important characteristics that we take for granted today. First, the shares were issued in *small denominations,* allowing investors to buy as little or as much of the company as they wanted; and second, the shares were *transferable,* meaning that an owner could sell them to someone else. Today, the vast majority of large companies issue stock that investors buy and sell regularly. The shares normally are quite numerous, each one representing only a small fraction of a company's total value. The large number and small size of individual shares—prices are usually below $100 per share—make the purchase and sale of stocks relatively easy.

Figure 8.1 Examples of Stock Certificates

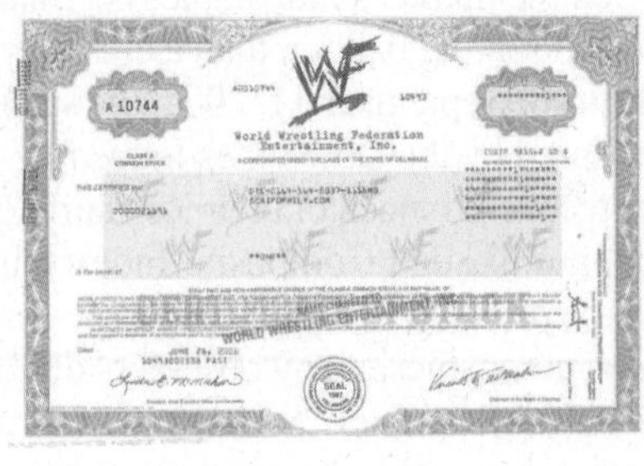

Courtesy of Stephen Cecchetti

Until recently, all stockowners received a certificate from the issuing company. Figure 8.1, on the left, shows the first stock certificate issued by the Ford Motor Company in 1903, to Henry Ford. The right-hand side of the figure shows a more recent stock certificate issued by the World Wrestling Federation (WWF), renamed World Wrestling Enterprises (WWE). The WWE is the media and entertainment company that produces the wrestling events involving characters like The Rock and Hulk Hogan. The former governor of Minnesota, Jesse Ventura, worked for the WWF before entering politics.

Today, most stockholders no longer receive certificates; the odds are that you will never see one. Instead, the information they bear is computerized, and the shares are registered in the names of brokerage firms that hold them on investors' behalf. This procedure is safer because computerized certificates can't be stolen. It also makes the process of selling the shares much easier.

The ownership of common stock conveys a number of rights. First and most importantly, a stockholder is entitled to participate in the profits of the enterprise. Importantly, however, the stockholder is merely a **residual claimant**. If the company runs into financial trouble, only after all other creditors have been paid what they are owed will the stockholders receive what is left, if anything. Stockholders get the leftovers!

To understand what being the residual claimant means, let's look at the case of a software manufacturer. The company needs a number of things to make it run. The list might include rented office space, computers, programmers, and some cash balances for day-to-day operations. These are the *inputs* into the production of the company's software *output*. If we took a snapshot of the company's finances on any given day, we would see that the firm owes payments to a large number of people, including the owner of the office space it rents, the programmers who work for it, the supplier of its computers, and the bondholders and bankers who have lent the firm resources. The company uses the revenue from selling its software to pay these people. After everyone has been paid, the stockholders get the rest of the revenue. In some years, the company does well and there are funds left over, so the stockholders do well. But when the firm does poorly, the stockholders may get nothing. If the firm performs really poorly, failing to sell enough software to cover its obligations, it can go bankrupt and cease operating entirely. In that case, the stockholders lose their entire investment.

The possibility of bankruptcy brings up an interesting question. What happens if a company's revenue is insufficient to cover its obligations to nonstockholders? What if

A Home Is a Place to Live
YOUR FINANCIAL WORLD

A home is a place to live; it is very different from a stock or a bond. When you own a stock, the issuing firm either pays you dividends or reinvests its profits to make the business grow. Bonds pay interest, that's how you are compensated for lending. In either case, you receive an explicit financial return on your investment.

When you buy a house and move in, what you get is a roof over your head. And you do it without paying rent to someone else. That means that you are consuming the dividend or interest payments in the form of what economists call *housing services.* So, if you buy a house, live in it for a while, and then sell it, you should expect to get back the original purchase price, adjusted for inflation. It is as if you bought an inflation-indexed bond and used the coupon payments to live on. What's left at the end is the principal amount, no more.

Data on the long-run real (inflation-adjusted) change in the price of housing are consistent with this. Over the 128 years from 1890 to 2018, the average annual real increase in the value of housing in the United States was only 0.43 percent. That means that if you were to purchase a house for $100,000 and live in it for 30 years (the time it takes to completely pay off a conventional fixed-rate mortgage), you could expect to sell it for around $114,000 plus any adjustment for inflation.

An observer in 2006 might be forgiven for thinking that the long-run rules for housing prices had changed with the millennium. In the first six years of the decade, real house prices surged by 60 percent. By 2009, however, these gains had vanished with the financial crisis, leaving the former long-run pattern intact.

To see the contrast with a financial investment, compare the purchase of the home to the purchase of $100,000 worth of stock. If stocks have an annual average real return of 6 percent, then after 30 years you will have accumulated nearly $575,000. But, unlike the house, this financial investment does not provide you with a place to live. So, when you think about the return to owning a house, remember that you get a place to live—that's the return on your investment.

its revenue is too small to pay the landlord, the programmers, the supplier of the computers, and the bondholders and other lenders? It would appear that the stockholders' promised participation in the firm's profits would yield a liability rather than a payment. If the company does very poorly, will the stockholders have to pay the firm's creditors?

An arrangement in which the stockholders are held liable for the firm's losses is very unappealing and would surely discourage people from buying stock. Stockholders bore that risk until the early 19th century. It ended with the introduction of the legal concept of limited liability.[2] **Limited liability** means that, even if a company fails completely, the maximum amount that shareholders can lose is their initial investment. *Liability* for the company's losses is *limited* at zero, meaning that investors can never lose more than they have invested. Clearly, buying stock is much more attractive if you know that your maximum potential loss is the price you pay for the stock in the first place.

Beyond participating in the firm's profits, owners of common stock are entitled to vote at the firm's annual meeting. Though managers supervise a firm's day-to-day activities, the shareholders elect the board of directors, which meets several times per year to oversee management. Ultimately, the shareholders' ability to dislodge directors and managers who are performing poorly is crucial to their willingness to purchase shares.[3] This ability to elect and remove directors and managers varies with a country's legal structure. In places where shareholders' legal rights are weak, stock ownership is less appealing, and equities are a less important form of corporate financing.

[2]The United States passed the first general law granting limited liability to manufacturing companies in 1811.

[3]Managers and directors may have different priorities and objectives from shareholders. While the firm's owners would like to see the value of their investment increase, managers may be more interested in ensuring that they retain their jobs.

Today, stock ownership is immensely popular. Investors want to own stocks and companies want to issue them. Over the past century, markets have developed in which people buy and sell billions of shares every day. This thriving financial trade is possible because:

- An individual share represents only a small fraction of the value of the company that issued it.
- A large number of shares are outstanding.
- Prices of individual shares are low, allowing individuals to make relatively small investments.
- As residual claimants, stockholders receive the proceeds of a firm's activities only after all other creditors have been paid.
- Because of limited liability, investors' losses cannot exceed the price they paid for the stock.
- Shareholders can replace managers who are doing a bad job.

Measuring the Level of the Stock Market

Stocks are one way in which we choose to hold our wealth. When stock values rise, we get richer; when they fall, we get poorer. These changes affect our consumption and saving patterns, causing general economic activity to fluctuate. We need to understand the dynamics of the stock market, both to manage our personal finances and to see the connections between stock values and economic conditions. From a macroeconomic point of view, we need to be able to measure the level of fluctuation in all stock values. We will refer to this concept as the *value* of the stock market and to its measures as **stock market indexes**.

You are probably familiar with price indexes, like the consumer price index, and output indexes, like industrial production and real gross domestic product. The purpose of an index number is to give a measure of scale so that we can compute percentage changes. The consumer price index, for example, is not measured in dollars. Instead, it is a pure number. In February 2019, the value of the Consumer Price Index for All Urban Consumers was 253.11, which isn't very interesting on its own. If, however, you know that 12 months earlier, in February 2018, the same index was 249.37, then you can figure out that prices rose by 1.50 percent over a 12-month period—that's the percentage change in the index.

Stock market indexes are the same. They are designed to give us a sense of the extent to which things are going up or down. Saying that the Dow Jones Industrial Average is at 10,000 doesn't mean anything on its own. But if you know that the Dow index rose from 10,000 to 11,000, that tells you that stock prices (by this measure) went up 10 percent. As we will see, stock indexes can tell us both how much the value of an average stock has changed and how much total wealth has gone up or down. Beyond that, stock indexes provide benchmarks for performance of money managers, allowing us to measure whether a particular manager has done better or worse than "the market" as a whole.

A quick look at the financial news reveals a number of stock market indexes, covering both domestic stocks and stocks issued by firms in foreign countries. Our goal in this section is to learn what these are and, more important, what question each is designed to answer. We will start with a detailed discussion of the two most well-known U.S. indexes, the *Dow Jones Industrial Average* and the *Standard & Poor's 500 Index*. A brief description of other indexes and a short history of the performance of the U.S. stock market will follow.

The Dow Jones Industrial Average

The first, and still the best-known, stock market index is the **Dow Jones Industrial Average (DJIA)**. Created by Charles Dow in 1884, the DJIA began as an average of the prices of 11 stocks. Today, the index is based on the stock prices of 30 of the largest companies in the United States. The DJIA measures the value of purchasing a single share of each of the stocks in the index. That is, adding up the per-share prices of all 30 stocks and dividing by 30 yields the index. The percentage change in the DJIA over time is the percentage change in the sum of the 30 prices. Thus, the DJIA measures the return to holding a portfolio of a single share of each stock included in the average.

The Dow Jones Industrial Average is a **price-weighted average**. Price-weighted averages give greater weight to shares with higher prices. To see how this works, take the example of an index composed of just two companies, one with an initial price of $50 and the other with an initial price of $100. The purchase of two shares of stock, one from each company, would cost $150. Now consider the effect of a 15 percent increase in the price of the first stock. It raises the value of the two-stock portfolio by $7.50, or 5 percent, to $157.50. Yet a 15 percent increase in the value of the second stock raises the value of the portfolio by $15, or 10 percent, to $165. The behavior of higher-priced stocks, then, dominates the movement of a price-weighted index like the DJIA.[4]

Since Charles Dow first created his index of 11 stocks, nine of which were railroad stocks, the structure of the U.S. economy has changed markedly. At various times, steel, chemical, and automobile stocks have dominated the DJIA. The index now includes the stocks of information technology firms, such as Microsoft and Intel, as well as of retailing firms, such as Walmart and Home Depot. In 2018, General Electric, the last of the original 11 stocks, was removed from the index.[5] The DJIA is a large-company index, but as of the start of 2019, it did not include 4 of the top 10 firms in terms of market value: Alphabet Inc. (parent of Google), Berkshire Hathaway, Amazon, and Facebook.

The Standard & Poor's 500 Index

The **Standard & Poor's 500 Index** differs from the Dow Jones Industrial Average in two major respects. First, it is constructed from the prices of many more stocks. Second, it uses a different weighting scheme. As the name suggests, the S&P 500 Index is based on the value of 500 firms, the largest firms in the U.S. economy. And unlike the DJIA, the S&P 500 tracks the total value of owning the entirety of those firms. In the index's calculation, each firm's stock price receives a weight equal to its total market value. Thus, the S&P 500 is a **value-weighted index**. Unlike the DJIA, in which higher-priced stocks carry more weight, larger firms are more important in the S&P 500.

To see this, we can return to the two companies in our last example. If the firm whose stock is priced at $100 has 10 million shares outstanding, all its shares together—its total market value, or **market capitalization**—are worth $1 billion.

[4]You may wonder how the DJIA has climbed to over 18,000 if it is the average of 30 stock prices, all less than $200 per share. The answer is that the averaging process takes stock splits into account and that the companies included in the index change periodically. There is a simple way to compute the change in the index level: (1) Take the list of 30 stocks in the DJIA and add up the changes from the previous day's close, so if each stock rose by $1, that's $30. (2) Using an online search engine, locate something called the DJIA "divisor." It's a number like 0.14748071991788 (that's the value for January 4, 2019). (3) Divide the sum of changes in the prices of the DJIA stocks by the divisor and add that to the previous day's close. The result is the current level of the DJIA.

[5]For a description of the DJIA, visit its website, www.djindexes.com.

Reading Stock Indexes in the Business News

TOOLS OF THE TRADE

Each morning, the business news brings reports of the prior day's changes in all the major stock market indexes. Table 8.1, reproduced from *The Wall Street Journal* of March 19, 2019, is an example of this sort of summary. It includes a number of indexes besides the DJIA, the S&P 500, and the Nasdaq Composite. Some of them cover firms of a particular size. For example, Standard & Poor's MidCap index covers 400 medium-size firms; its SmallCap index covers 600 small firms. And the Russell 2000 tracks the value of the smallest two-thirds of the 3,000 largest U.S. companies. Other indexes cover a particular sector or industry. Note that Dow Jones publishes indexes for transportation and utilities; others provide special indexes for biotechnology, pharmaceuticals, banks, and semiconductors. Many more indexes are published, all of them designed for specific functions. When you encounter a new index, make sure you understand both how it is constructed and what it is designed to measure.

Table 8.1 Major U.S. Stock Market Indexes
March 19, 2019

	LATEST					52-WEEK RANGE			% CHG	
	High	Low	Close	Net chg	% chg	High	Low	% chg	YTD	3-yr. ann.
Dow Jones										
Industrial Average	26109.68	25814.92	25887.38	−26.72	−0.10	26828.39	21792.20	4.7	11.0	13.7
Transportation Avg	10453.49	10253.24	10277.32	−137.04	−1.32	11570.84	8637.15	−3.9	12.1	8.4
Utility Average	777.25	765.58	768.20	−8.57	−1.10	779.36	656.93	12.5	7.8	5.3
Total Stock Market	29407.95	29116.65	29205.12	−26.20	−0.09	30390.61	24126.04	3.7	13.5	11.5
Barron's 400	702.90	692.70	694.33	−5.05	−0.72	786.73	571.68	−4.9	13.9	10.6
Nasdaq Stock Market										
Nasdaq Composite	7767.89	7699.15	7723.95	9.47	0.12	8109.69	6192.92	4.9	16.4	17.2
Nasdaq 100	7390.29	7321.93	7349.28	23.00	0.31	7660.18	5899.35	6.7	16.1	18.6
Standard & Poor's										
500 Index	2852.42	2823.27	2832.57	−0.37	−0.01	2930.75	2351.10	4.3	13.0	11.4
MidCap 400	1917.96	1895.09	1899.15	−9.86	−0.52	2050.23	1567.40	−1.0	14.2	9.9
SmallCap 600	958.89	946.04	947.56	−7.41	−0.78	1098.36	793.86	−1.2	12.1	11.8
Other Indexes										
NYSE Composite	12854.82	12728.97	12760.79	−20.63	−0.16	13236.44	10769.83	0.8	12.2	7.7
NYSE Arca Biotech	5175.12	5123.22	5138.92	3.64	0.07	5400.34	3890.37	9.3	21.8	21.9
NYSE Arca Pharma	601.56	596.95	600.62	4.57	0.77	609.15	516.32	11.0	5.6	7.0
Russell 2000	1570.89	1552.66	1554.99	−8.95	−0.57	1740.75	1266.92	−1.0	15.3	12.2
PHLX[§] Gold/Silver	76.19	75.37	75.40	0.28	0.37	85.67	61.84	−3.5	6.7	1.9
PHLX[§] Housing	288.72	283.22	283.91	−2.68	−0.93	327.81	229.82	−11.9	16.9	7.7
PHLX[§] Oil Service	99.20	96.59	96.96	−0.55	−0.56	170.81	75.70	−28.3	20.3	−15.9
PHLX[§] Semiconductor	1411.68	1398.55	1407.35	18.58	1.34	1437.94	1069.39	0.1	21.8	27.7
CBOE Volatility	13.77	12.37	13.56	0.46	3.51	36.07	10.85	−25.5	−46.7	−1.1
KBW Bank	102.13	99.82	100.00	−1.33	−1.32	112.19	80.78	−10.7	16.6	14.9
Value Line	540.31	534.79	535.89	−2.12	−0.39	593.57	446.06	−4.0	13.4	5.8

[§]Philadelphia Stock Exchange

SOURCES: SIX Financial Information; WSJ Market Data Group; historical data prior to 6/7/11: Thomson Reuters; WSJ Market Data Group

If the second firm—the one whose shares are valued at $50 apiece—has 100 million shares outstanding, its market capitalization is $5 billion. Together, the two companies are worth $6 billion.

Now look at the effect of changes in the two stocks' prices. If the first firm's per-share price rises by 15 percent, its total value goes up to $1.15 billion, and the value of the two companies together rises to $6.15 billion—an increase of 2½ percent. (Remember that in the last example, the price-weighted DJIA rose by 10 percent.) Contrast that with the effect of a 15 percent increase in the price of the second stock, which raises the total value of that firm to $5.75 billion. In this case, the value of the two firms together goes from $6 billion to $6.75 billion—an increase of 12½ percent. (In the last example, the price-weighted DJIA rose only 5 percent.)

Clearly, price-weighted and value-weighted indexes are very different. A price-weighted index gives more importance to stocks that have high prices, while a value-weighted index gives more importance to companies with a high market value. Price per se is irrelevant.

Neither price weighting nor value weighting is necessarily the best approach to constructing a stock price index. The S&P 500 is neither better nor worse than the DJIA. Rather, the two types of index simply answer different questions. Changes in a price-weighted index like the DJIA tell us the change in the value of a portfolio composed of a single share of each of the stocks in the index. This tells us the change in the price of a typical stock. Changes in a value-weighted index tell us the return to holding a portfolio of stocks weighted in proportion to the size of the firms. Thus, they accurately mirror changes in the economy's overall wealth.

Other U.S. Stock Market Indexes

Besides the S&P 500 and the DJIA, the most prominent indexes in the United States are the **Nasdaq Composite Index**, or Nasdaq for short, and the **Wilshire 5000**. The Nasdaq is a value-weighted index of more than 2,500 securities traded on the over-the-counter (OTC) market through the National Association of Securities Dealers Automatic Quotations (Nasdaq) service. The Nasdaq Composite is composed mainly of smaller, newer firms and in recent years has been dominated by technology and Internet companies. The Wilshire 5000 is the most broadly based index in use. It covers all publicly traded stocks in the United States with readily available prices, including all the stocks on national stock exchanges, which together total just over 3,500 (contrary to the index's name) as of January 2019. Like the Nasdaq and the S&P 500, the Wilshire 5000 is value-weighted. Because of its great breadth, this index is a useful measure of overall market wealth. You can find the history of this index at the Wilshire website: www.wilshire.com/indexinfo/Wilshire-5000-Total-Market-Index.html. Its latest value is available at finance.yahoo.com/quote/^W5000.

World Stock Indexes

Roughly one-third of the countries in the world have stock markets, and each of these markets has an index. Most are value-weighted indexes like the S&P 500. Listings of other countries' stock indexes are in publications such as *The Wall Street Journal,* the *Financial Times*, or *The Economist*, as well as online at websites such as www.bloomberg.com or www.finance.yahoo.com (see Table 8.2).

Table 8.2 gives some sense of the behavior of stock markets (in local currency terms) from the end of 2017 to early 2019. The index levels (in column three) don't mean much because the indexes themselves aren't comparable. No one would think

Table 8.2 World Stock Markets
January 23, 2019

		Index Level on Jan 23	One Week % Change	% Change from Dec 29, 2017
World, developed	**MSCI**	1,980.1	0.7	-5.9
Emerging markets	**MSCI**	1,011.6	0.2	-12.7
Argentina	Merval	34,819.1	2.3	15.8
Australia	All Ordinaries	5,908.7	0.3	-4.2
Brazil	Bovespa	96,558.4	2.3	26.4
Canada	S&P/TSX	15,208.3	0.6	-6.2
China	Shanghai Comp	2,581.0	0.4	-22.0
China	Shenzhen Comp	1,316.3	-0.4	-30.7
France	CAC 40	4,840.4	0.6	-8.9
Germany	DAX	11,071.5	1.3	-14.3
Hong Kong	Hang Seng	27,008.2	0.4	-9.7
Italy	FTSE/MIB	19,400.2	-0.4	-11.2
Japan	Nikkei 225	20,593.7	0.7	-9.5
Japan	TOPIX	1,547.0	0.6	-14.9
Mexico	IPC	43,697.7	-0.3	-11.5
Singapore	STI	3,171.1	-1.8	-6.8
United Kingdom	FTSE 100	6,842.9	-0.3	-11.0
United States	S&P 500	2,638.7	0.9	-1.3

SOURCE: *The Economist,* January 24, 2019.

that the Brazilian stock exchange was bigger than the New York Stock Exchange or than China's Shanghai Stock Exchange, even though the Bovespa index stood at 96,558.4, when the S&P 500 was just 2,638.7 and the Shanghai Composite index 2,581.0. Instead, we need to focus on the percentage changes in these indexes (in columns four and five). A 100-point move in the Singapore STI, with a level of 3,171.1, would be much more significant than a 100-basis-point move in the Japanese Nikkei 225, with a level of 20,593.7.

Table 8.2 also shows that, like the United States, which has the S&P 500, the Wilshire 5000 and the Nasdaq Composite, some countries also have more than one stock index. In China, the second-largest stock market by market capitalization, the leading index is that of the Shanghai exchange, but the index of the Shenzhen exchange includes some of the most rapidly growing firms. In Japan, the TOPIX index covers many more stocks than the Nikkei 225, but the key difference is that the TOPIX index (like the S&P 500) is weighted by market capitalization, while the Nikkei 225 (like the Dow Jones index) is not.

Finally, Table 8.2 shows that from the end of 2017 to late January 2019, most stock markets declined. The drop of the S&P 500 (–1.3 percent) was relatively small, while the indexes in China showed the largest declines (Shanghai Composite, –22.0 percent;

Shenzhen Composite, –30.7 percent), reflecting worries about a slowing economy and about growing trade disputes with the United States. Despite the sizable, broad-based declines in both developed (–5.9 percent) and emerging stock markets (–12.7 percent), there were a few bright spots: Brazil's Bovespa surged by 26.4 percent, while Argentina's Merval climbed by 15.8 percent.

Investors view global stock markets as a means to diversify risk away from domestic investments. While that remains correct, the benefits from such diversification have tended to decline over time. Stock markets have become increasingly linked by the choices of investors whose changing preferences are rapidly transmitted from one market to the next. The result has been an increased correlation of global markets, especially in periods of financial distress.

Valuing Stocks

People differ on how stocks should be valued. Some believe they can predict changes in a stock's price by looking at patterns in its past price movements. Because these people study charts of stock prices, they are called *chartists.* Other investors, known as *behavioralists,* estimate the value of stocks based on their perceptions of investor psychology and behavior. Still others estimate stock values based on a detailed study of companies' financial statements. In their view, the value of a firm's stock depends on both its current assets and on estimates of its future profitability—what they call the *fundamentals.* Thus, the **fundamental value** of a stock is based on the timing and uncertainty of the returns it brings.

We can use our toolbox for valuing financial instruments to compute the fundamental value of stocks. Based on the size and timing of the promised payments, we can use the present-value formula to assess how much a stock is worth in the absence of any risk. Then, realizing that the payments are uncertain in both their size and timing, we can adjust our estimate of the stock's value to accommodate those risks. Together, these two steps give us the fundamental value.

The chartists and behavioralists question the usefulness of fundamentals in understanding the level and movement of stock prices. They focus instead on estimates of the deviation of stock prices from those fundamental values. These deviations can create short-term bubbles and crashes, which we'll take up later in the chapter. First, though, let's use some familiar techniques to develop an understanding of basic stock valuation.

Fundamental Value and the Dividend-Discount Model

Like all financial instruments, a stock represents a promise to make monetary payments on future dates, under certain circumstances. With stocks, the payments are usually in the form of **dividends**, or distributions made to the owners of a company when the company makes a profit.[6] If the firm is sold, the stockholders receive a final distribution that represents their share of the purchase price.

Let's begin with an investor who plans to buy a stock today and sell it in one year. The principle of present value tells us that the price of the stock today should equal the

[6]To be precise, not all profits are distributed to shareholders. Some of these "earnings" are retained by the firm and used to increase its size. A firm may also use profits to buy back its own stock, thereby increasing the value of the remaining shares. We will ignore these complications.

present value of the payments the investor will receive from holding the stock. This is equal to the selling price of the stock in one year's time plus the dividend payments received in the interim. Thus, the current price is the present value of next year's price plus the dividend. If P_{today} is the purchase price of the stock, $P_{next\ year}$ is the sale price one year later, and $D_{next\ year}$ is the size of the dividend payment, we can write this expression as

$$P_{today} = \frac{D_{next\ year}}{(1+i)} + \frac{P_{next\ year}}{(1+i)} \qquad (1)$$

where i is the interest rate used to compute the present value (measured as a decimal).

What if the investor plans to hold the stock for two years? To figure out the answer, start by using present value to calculate that the price next year equals the value next year of the price in two years plus next year's dividend payment. Using the logic and notation from equation (1), this is

$$P_{next\ year} = \frac{D_{in\ two\ years}}{(1+i)} + \frac{P_{in\ two\ years}}{(1+i)} \qquad (2)$$

Substituting equation (2) into equation (1), we get that the current price is the present value of the price in two years plus two dividend payments, one each year, or

$$P_{today} = \frac{D_{next\ year}}{(1+i)} + \frac{D_{in\ two\ years}}{(1+i)^2} + \frac{P_{in\ two\ years}}{(1+i)^2} \qquad (3)$$

Extending this formula over an investment horizon of n years, the result is

$$P_{today} = \frac{D_{next\ year}}{(1+i)} + \frac{D_{in\ two\ years}}{(1+i)^2} + \cdots + \frac{D_{n\ years\ from\ now}}{(1+i)^n} + \frac{P_{n\ years\ from\ now}}{(1+i)^n} \qquad (4)$$

That is, the price today is the present value of the sum of the dividends plus the present value of the price at the time the stock is sold n years from now. (Notice that this equation is the same as the expression for the price of a coupon bond on page 132 of Chapter 6.)

At this point, you may be asking: What about companies that do not pay dividends? How do we figure out their stock price? The answer is that we estimate when they will start paying dividends and then use the present-value framework. From equation (4) you can see that there is no reason all of the dividends need to be positive. Some of them can be zero, and we can still do the calculation. So if we figure that the company will start paying dividends in 10 years, we just set the first 9 years' worth of dividends equal to zero, and compute the present discounted value of dividend payments starting in year 10.

Returning to our baseline case, looking at the messy equation (4) we can see that unless we know something more about the annual dividend payments, we are stuck. To proceed, we will assume that dividends grow at a constant rate of g per year. That is, the dividend next year will equal the dividend today multiplied by one plus the growth rate:

$$D_{next\ year} = D_{today}(1+g) \qquad (5)$$

As long as the growth rate remains constant, all we need to do is multiply by $(1 + g)$ to compute future dividends. Following the procedure for computing present value in n years, we can see that the dividend n years from now will be

$$D_{n\ years\ from\ now} = D_{today}(1+g)^n \qquad (6)$$

Using equation (6), we can rewrite the price equation (4) as

$$P_{today} = \frac{D_{today}(1+g)}{(1+i)} + \frac{D_{today}(1+g)^2}{(1+i)^2} + \cdots + \frac{D_{today}(1+g)^n}{(1+i)^n} + \frac{P_{n\ years\ from\ now}}{(1+i)^n} \qquad (7)$$

Even if we know the dividend today, D_{today}, and the interest rate, *i,* as well as an estimate of the dividend growth rate, *g,* we still can't compute the current price, P_{today}, unless we know the future price, $P_{n\ years\ from\ now}$. We can solve this problem by assuming the firm pays dividends forever and noting that as *n* gets big $[1/(1+i)^n]$ approaches zero until it finally disappears. This assumption turns the stock into something like a consol—the strange bond that makes fixed coupon payments forever and never repays the principal.[7] It allows us to convert equation (6) into the following simple formula:[8]

$$P_{today} = \frac{D_{today}(1+g)}{i-g} \qquad (8)$$

This relationship is the **dividend-discount model**. Using the concept of present value, together with the simplification that the firm's dividends will grow at a constant rate *g*, we have discovered that the "fundamental" price of a stock is simply the current dividend divided by the interest rate, minus the dividend growth rate. The model tells us that stock prices should be high when dividends (D_{today}) are high, when dividend growth (*g*) is rapid (that is, when *g* is large), or when the interest rate (*i*) is low. (In using the dividend-discount model, we will need to remember to write both *i* and *g* as decimals—numbers like 0.03 and 0.05.)

The dividend-discount model is simple and elegant, but we have ignored risk in deriving it. Stock prices change constantly, making investors' returns uncertain. Where does this risk come from, and how does it affect a stock's valuation? We turn now to an analysis of risk.

Why Stocks Are Risky

Recall that stockholders are the firm's owners, so they receive the firm's profits. But their profits come only after the firm has paid everyone else, including bondholders. It is as if the stockholders bought the firm by putting up some of their own wealth and borrowing the rest. This borrowing creates *leverage,* and leverage creates risk. (See the Tools of the Trade box in Chapter 5.)

A simple example will show what happens. Imagine a software business that needs only one computer. Say the computer costs \$1,000 and the purchase can be financed

[7]Because neither the consol nor the stock has a maturity date, it makes sense that they would be formally the same.

[8]To compute equation (8), begin by noticing that if we change notation slightly so that P_j and D_j are the price and dividend in year *j*, then the original pricing equation (4) can be rewritten as an infinite sum, so that $P_0 = \sum_{t=1}^{\infty} \frac{D_j}{(1+i)^t}$. Substituting in the expression for the dividend growth rate, $D_j = (1+g)^i$, this gives us $P_0 = \sum_{t=1}^{\infty} \frac{D_0(1+g)^t}{(1+i)^t}$. This expression looks exactly like the one for a consol, with the current dividend in place of the coupon payment and an interest rate equivalent to $(1+i^*) = (1+i)/(1+g)$. That is, we can write it as $P_0 = \sum_{t=1}^{\infty} \frac{D_0}{(1+i^*)^t}$. Using the techniques in the appendix to Chapter 4, we can simplify this to $\frac{D_0}{i^*}$. Rewriting $i^* = \frac{i-g}{1+g}$ and substituting, we get equation (8).

Table 8.3 Returns Distributed to Debt and Equity Holders under Different Financing Assumptions

Percent Equity (%)	Percent Debt (%)	Required Payments on 10% Bonds ($)	Payment to Equity Holders ($)	Equity Return (%)	Expected Equity Return (%)	Standard Deviation of Equity Return
100%	0	0	\$80–\$160	8–16%	12%	4%
50%	50%	\$50	\$30–\$110	6–22%	14%	8%
30%	70%	\$70	\$10–\$ 90	3⅓–30%	16⅔%	13⅓%
20%	80%	\$80	\$ 0–\$ 80	0–40%	20%	20%

Firm requires a \$1,000 capital investment that can be financed by either stock (equity) or 10% bonds (debt). Revenue is either \$80 or \$160, with equal probability.

by any combination of stock (equity) and bonds (debt). If the interest rate on bonds is 10 percent, for each \$100 borrowed the firm must pay \$10 in interest. Finally, assume that the company, which produces software, earns \$160 in good years and \$80 in bad years, with equal probability.

Table 8.3 shows what happens to the company's equity returns as its level of debt changes. The more debt, the more leverage and the greater the owners' risk (as measured by the standard deviation of the equity return). As the proportion of the firm financed by equity falls from 100 percent to 20 percent, the expected return to the equity holders rises from 12 percent to 20 percent, but the associated risk rises substantially as well.

If the firm were only 10 percent equity financed, the stockholders' limited liability could come into play. Issuing \$900 worth of bonds would mean incurring an obligation to make \$90 in interest payments. If business turned out to be bad, the firm's revenue would be only \$80—not enough to pay the interest. Without their limited liability, the common stockholders, who are the firm's legal owners, would be liable for the \$10 shortfall. Instead, the stockholders would lose only their initial \$100 investment, and no more, and the firm goes bankrupt.

Stocks are risky, then, because the shareholders are residual claimants. Because they are paid last, they never know for sure how much their return will be. Any variation in the firm's revenue flows through to them dollar for dollar, making their returns highly volatile. In contrast, bondholders receive fixed nominal payments and are paid before the stockholders in the event of a bankruptcy.

Risk and the Value of Stocks

RISK

Stockholders require compensation for the risk they face; the higher the risk, the greater the compensation. To integrate risk into stock valuation, we will return to the simple question we asked earlier: How will investors with a one-year investment horizon value a stock? Our initial answer was that the stock price equals the present value of the price of the stock in one year's time plus the dividend payments received in the interim. From this statement, we derived the dividend-discount model. But once we recognize the risk involved in buying stock, the answer to our question must change. The new answer is that an investor will buy a stock with the idea of obtaining a certain return, which includes compensation for the stock's risk.

Here is how the process works. Buying the stock for an initial price P_{today} entitles the investor to a dividend $D_{next\ year}$ plus the proceeds from the sale of the stock one year later, at price $P_{next\ year}$. The return from the purchase and subsequent sale of the stock equals the dividend plus the difference in the price, both divided by the initial price:

$$\text{Return to holding stock for one year} = \frac{D_{next\ year}}{P_{today}} + \frac{P_{next\ year} - P_{today}}{P_{today}} \quad (9)$$

Because the ultimate future sale price is unknown, the stock is risky and the investor will require compensation in the form of a risk premium. We will think of the required return as the sum of the risk-free interest rate and the risk premium (sometimes called the *equity risk premium*). We can approximate the risk-free rate as the interest rate on a U.S. Treasury security with a maturity of several months. Such an instrument has virtually no default risk, because the government isn't going to collapse, and it has almost no inflation risk, because U.S. inflation is highly persistent and so is unlikely to change sharply over a few months. In addition, there is very little price risk because interest rates normally don't move quickly and suddenly either.[9] Dividing the required stock return into its two components, we can write

$$\text{Required stock return}\,(i) = \text{Risk-free return}\,(rf) + \text{Risk premium}\,(rp) \quad (10)$$

Combining this equation with our earlier analysis is straightforward. All we need to do is recognize that the interest rate used for the present-value calculation in the dividend-discount model, equation (8), is the sum of the risk-free return and a risk premium. Using this insight, we can rewrite equation (8) as

$$P_{today} = \frac{D_{today}(1 + g)}{rf + rp - g} \quad (11)$$

Looking at equation (11), we can see that the higher the risk premium investors demand to hold a stock, the lower its price. Similarly, the higher the risk-free return, the lower the stock's price. (See Table 8.4 for a summary.)

We can use equation (11) to see if current stock prices are warranted by fundamentals. Start by finding the current level of the S&P 500 Index. At the end of 2018, it was about 2,506. Next, we need to get estimates for the various numbers in the formula. Historically, the (long-term) risk-free real interest rate has averaged around 2 percent, so $rf = 0.02$. Historical information also suggests that the risk premium is around 4 percent, so $rp = 0.04$. The dividend growth rate is about 2 percent, so $g = 0.02$. And the owner of a \$2,506 portfolio of the

Table 8.4 Implications of the Dividend-Discount Model with Risk

Stock Prices Are High When:

1. Current dividends are high (D_{today} is high).
2. Dividends are expected to grow quickly (g is high).
3. The risk-free rate is low (rf is low).
4. The risk premium on equity is low (rp is low).

[9] TIPS (Treasury Inflation-Protected Securities), mentioned in Chapter 6, are a ready source of a nearly risk-free interest rate that is adjusted for inflation. TIPS let us measure the risk-free real interest rate directly in financial markets.

China's Stock Market Boom and Bust

APPLYING THE CONCEPT

China's relatively young mainland stock market, consisting of two exchanges that began around 1990, is already the second largest in the world. In January 2019, its total capitalization of \$6.7 trillion was nearly 20 percent larger than that of Japan's market, the world's third largest. (The \$33.1 trillion combined capitalization of the New York Stock Exchange and the Nasdaq market makes the U.S. market the largest.)

The huge rise in China's stock market capitalization highlights the extraordinary spread of market-based finance in a country led for more than 70 years by its Communist Party. Vladimir Lenin once spoke of controlling an economy from the "commanding heights" at its center. In contrast, a stock market *decentralizes* economic decisions by allowing millions of investors to collectively determine the valuation of firms, thereby directing the allocation of capital. According to one report, the number of Chinese with brokerage accounts (90 million) exceeds the membership of the Chinese Communist Party (88 million).

However, the stock market boom that began in 2014 set the stage for an equally dramatic plunge in the following year. In the 12 months to the peak on June 12, 2015, the price indexes of the Shanghai Stock Exchange (SSE) and the Shenzhen exchange (SZSE) jumped by more than 150 percent. As a result, price-earnings ratios reached breathtaking levels—above 25 in Shanghai and 70 in Shenzhen!

But the 2014–2015 boom was disconnected from China's economic slowdown, and it didn't take long for the market to plunge back to earth. By the end of August 2015, the combined capitalization of the SSE and SZSE markets had fallen by one-third.

Why such a large boom and bust? The initial run-up reflected some favorable developments, including a lower risk-free rate for domestic investors and the prospect that capital controls limiting nonresident access to China's domestic equities would be relaxed. But it also reflected leveraging that was driven by millions of new retail investors buying stocks on borrowed funds (called margin loans). When the stock market turned down, the obligation to repay margin loans compelled these inexperienced investors to sell. This leverage cycle amplified both the surge in prices and the plunge that followed.

Policymakers in China intervened in various ways to halt the bust, with little success. They might have been more effective had they resisted the boom (say, by tighter limits on margin lending). If anything, their clumsy actions undermined liquidity and confidence in the market: Who would buy a stock they can't sell without risking the government's wrath? Ultimately, the integrity of China's stock market and its effectiveness in allocating resources will depend on whether policymakers accept the volatility that is inevitable in a transparent stock market.

S&P 500 stocks might expect to receive \$133.02 in dividends during 2019.[10] Putting this all into equation (11) gives us P_{today} = \$3,392.

$$P_{today} = \frac{D_{today}(1+g)}{rf + rp - g} = \frac{\$133.02(1.02)}{0.02 + 0.04 - 0.02} = \$3{,}392$$

This is 35 percent above the actual level of 2,506. There are several possible explanations for the disparity. One is that the risk premium *rp* is higher; 5.4 percent would do it. Alternatively, we can justify an S&P 500 level of 2,506 by assuming that the dividend growth rate is a bit below 0.7 percent rather than 2 percent. The conclusion is that this simple dividend-discount model is a rough approximation that is sensitive to assumptions about the risk-free interest rate, the risk premium, and the dividend growth rate.

[10]This amount is adjusted for the fact that companies commonly buy back some of their shares as a complement to paying dividends. Using an author-calculated 2018 earnings per share of \$152.71, and a 10-year payout ratio of 87 percent, the author-estimated payment for an S&P 500 portfolio share is \$133.02. The payout ratio of 87 percent is the ratio of the 10-year sum of dividends and buybacks to the 10-year sum of operating earnings. For the recent history of buybacks and dividends, see here: https://us.spindices.com/documents/index-news-and-announcements/20190325-sp-500-buybacks-2018-q4-pr.pdf.

The Theory of Efficient Markets

Stock prices change nearly continuously. Why? One explanation starts in the same place as the dividend-discount model and is based on the concept of fundamental value. When fundamentals change, prices must change with them.

This line of reasoning gives rise to what is commonly called the theory of efficient markets. The basis for the **theory of efficient markets** is the notion that the prices of all financial instruments, including stocks, reflect all available information.[11] As a result, markets adjust immediately and continuously to changes in fundamental values. If the theory of efficient markets is correct, the chartists are doomed to failure.

The theory of efficient markets implies that stock price movements are unpredictable. If they weren't—if you could accurately forecast that the price of a stock was going to rise tomorrow—you would immediately buy as many shares of the stock as possible. Your action would increase demand for the stock, driving its price up today. In other words, the fact that you think a stock's price will rise tomorrow makes it rise today.[12] When markets are efficient, the prices at which stocks currently trade reflect all available information, so future price movements are unpredictable.

If no one can predict stock price movements, then what good is investment advice? Not much! If the theory of efficient markets is correct, no one can consistently beat the market average. This means that active portfolio management—buying and selling stocks based on someone's advice—will not yield a higher return than that of a broad stock market index—the market average—year after year.

There is quite a bit of evidence to support the view that stock price changes are unpredictable and that professional money managers cannot beat an index like the S&P 500 with regularity. On average, the return on managed portfolios is about one percent *less* than average stock market returns. But we do see managers who at least claim to exceed the market average year after year.[13] How can this be? There are four possibilities: (1) They are taking advantage of insider information, which is illegal; (2) they are taking on risk, which brings added compensation but means that at times, returns will be extremely poor; (3) they are lucky; or (4) markets are not efficient.

It is intriguing to think that high (or low) investment returns could simply be the result of chance. To understand why this is so, consider the following parable, which appears in Peter Bernstein's book *Capital Ideas*.[14] Suppose that 300 million people all join in a coin-tossing contest. On the first day, each person finds a partner and they each bet a dollar on the coin toss. The winner gets $2 and the loser leaves the game. Each day the coin toss is repeated, with the losers turning their dollars over to the winners, who then stake their winnings on the next day's toss. The laws of chance tell us that, after 10 flips on 10 consecutive mornings, only 220,000 people will still be in the contest, and each will have won a little more than $1,000. Then the game heats up. Ten days later, after 20 tosses, only 286 people will still be playing, and each will have

[11]A failure by financial markets to use all information efficiently need not imply the existence of arbitrage profits, that is, of a risk-free opportunity to profit from trading securities. On the contrary, in the absence of transaction costs, two financial instruments with the same risk and expected future payments should trade at the same price. This "no arbitrage" assumption, which is weaker than the efficient markets hypothesis, is widely used in financial research today. Chapter 9 defines arbitrage and explains the pricing of futures contracts using the no-arbitrage approach.

[12]If you felt sure that a stock's price was going to fall, you could take advantage of your forecast by using a strategy called *short selling*. You would borrow shares and sell them with the idea of buying them back at a lower price in the future. This tactic increases the supply of shares for sale, driving the stock's price down.

[13]Remember that someone owns every share in the stock market, so above-average returns to one person must be matched by below-average returns to someone else.

[14]Peter Bernstein, *Capital Ideas: The Improbable Origins of Modern Wall Street* (New York: Free Press, 1993).

nearly $1,050,000. These winners had no special knowledge. No skill was involved in their accumulation of high returns, just pure chance.

You may be asking what this has to do with investment and efficient markets. The answer is that when there are lots of people placing bets—and there surely are a large number of investors trying to gain advantages in the stock market—there will be a fair number of people who do well just by pure chance. And the problem with the stock market is that the number of people who "win" is about the same as the number we would expect to be lucky.

Investing in Stocks for the Long Run

Stocks appear to be risky, yet many people hold a substantial proportion of their wealth in the form of stock. We can reconcile our perception of risk with observed behavior in two ways. Either stocks are not that risky, or people are not that averse to the risk and so do not require a large risk premium to hold stocks. Which of these explanations is more plausible?

To get a sense of the risk in holding stock, we can look at the one-year return on the S&P 500 Index since 1872. The orange line in Figure 8.2 plots the one-year real return to holding this portfolio (including dividend payments and adjusted for inflation using the consumer price index). The one-year real returns shown in Figure 8.2 averaged more than 8 percent per year. From a different perspective, the annualized real return on one dollar invested in stocks in 1871 and held until 2019 was somewhat lower, almost 6½ percent.

In looking at Figure 8.2, remember to check the axis labels. Start by noting that the scale on the vertical axis goes from −40 percent to +60 percent, a huge range. The minimum return was nearly −40 percent (in 1932), and the maximum was more than 50 percent (in 1936). Over the past 50 years the range has narrowed somewhat, to a maximum annual return of 31 percent (in 1996) and a minimum of −35 percent (in 2008). Nearly half the time, the return on holding stocks has been either less than zero (negative) or above 25 percent (substantially positive). The graph certainly gives the impression that prices fluctuate wildly and that holding stocks is extremely risky.

Figure 8.2 S&P 1-Year and 25-Year Stock Returns, 1872 to 2019
(Returns Are Real, Adjusted for Inflation Using the CPI)

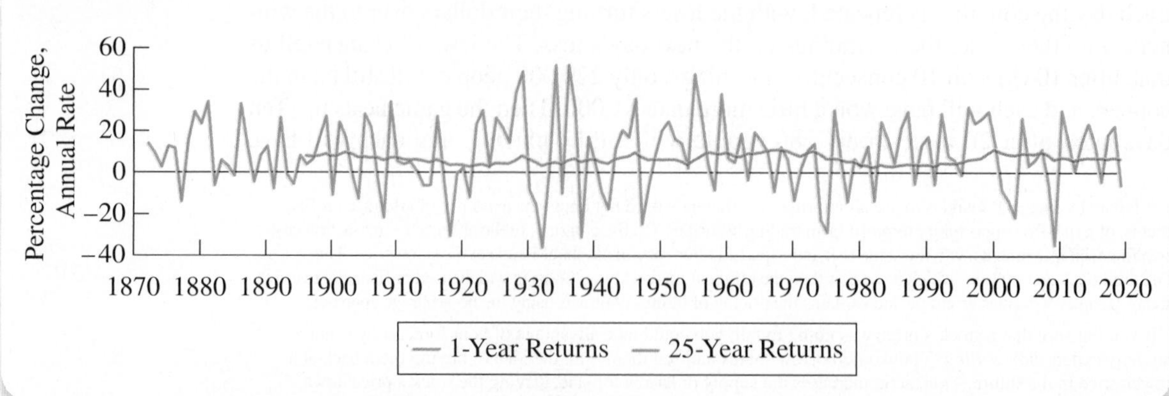

SOURCE: From *Irrational Exuberance,* 3/e, Princeton, 2015. Reprinted with permission by Robert J. Shiller. Estimated after 2004 using source data from www.econ.yale.edu/~shiller/data/ie_data.xls.

Should You Own Stocks?

YOUR FINANCIAL WORLD

Should you own stocks? The answer is yes, especially if you are young! Many people shy away from stocks and invest in bonds (or other interest-bearing assets). But remember that bonds are risky, too—even U.S. Treasury bonds carry interest rate risk and inflation risk. Though stocks may look risky, history suggests that a well-diversified portfolio of stocks held over the long term is not. The real question is *how* to buy stock.

There are five issues to think about when buying stock: affordability, liquidity, diversification, management, and cost. Prepackaged portfolios called **mutual funds** and **exchange-traded funds (ETFs)** address all these issues in one way or another. The problem is that there are literally thousands of mutual funds. So, how do we choose? Here are some points to keep in mind:

1. *Affordability.* Most mutual funds and ETFs allow a small initial investment. For a mutual fund, you can start with as little as $1,000. For an ETF, the minimum is even lower.
2. *Liquidity.* In an emergency, you may need to withdraw resources quickly. Make sure you can withdraw your investment easily if you need to.
3. *Diversification.* The vast majority of mutual funds and ETFs are much more diversified than any individual portfolio of stocks. The most popular versions hold stocks in proportion to a broad index, like the S&P 500. Even so, it is important to check before you buy.
4. *Management.* Both mutual funds and ETFs offer the advantage of professional management. You do need to be careful, as funds in which people make the decisions, so-called managed funds, tend to perform worse than passively managed index funds.
5. *Cost.* Mutual fund managers charge fees for their services. The fees for managed funds run about 0.8 percent per year, compared to 0.2 percent (or even less) for index funds. This is a significant difference. Over 20 years, an investment of $10,000 with an average annual return of 5 percent will amount to $26,533. If you pay an additional 0.6 percent fee, so that the return averages 4.4 percent, the value of the investment drops to $23,660, or $2,873 less. Expense ratios of ETFs often appear cheaper, but you need to be careful because the purchase price of an ETF is higher than the sale price–something called a *bid-ask spread.* For smaller and less frequently traded ETFs, this bid-ask spread can be large, making the investment expensive.

Taken together, these considerations persuade many people to invest in passive index funds. These funds are affordable and liquid, offer excellent diversification, and tend to be cheap. Don't take our word for it; always ask before you invest.

In 1994 though, Professor Jeremy Siegel of the University of Pennsylvania's Wharton School published a book titled *Stocks for the Long Run,*[15] in which he suggested that investing in stocks is risky only if you hold them for a short time. If you buy stocks and hold them for long enough, they really are not very risky.

To see Professor Siegel's point, we can again look at Figure 8.2, this time to see the return to holding stocks for 25 years instead of 1 year. The green line shows the average annual return from investing in the S&P 500 for a 25-year period (versus the 1-year return shown by the orange line). We can see immediately that the green line is much smoother and fluctuates over a much smaller range—and it never dips below zero. In fact, the *minimum average* annual inflation-adjusted return over 25 years was 2.5 percent, while the maximum was 11.2 percent. Siegel's point is that if you buy stocks and hold them for the long run—25 years or so—past patterns indicate that your investment is not very risky.

That was not the end of Professor Siegel's analysis. His next step was to compare the returns from holding bonds with those from holding stock. The results were startling. Siegel

[15]Jeremy J. Siegel, *Stocks for the Long Run: A Guide to Selecting Markets for Long-Term Growth,* 5th ed. (New York: McGraw-Hill, 2014).

Should I Buy or Should I Sell?

MONEY AND BANKING BLOG

If you are an investor, your goal is to buy low and sell high. Looking at the stock market, what should we do today in early 2019? Are prices too high? Are they too low? Or are they just right?

The truth is that no one can answer these questions with much confidence because the stock market makes fairly efficient use of available information. For the most part, trying to beat the market is a game for fools or for criminal insiders.

To be sure, asset prices occasionally get so far out of line with plausible fundamentals that the prudent course is to sell, put the proceeds into cash, and wait. In the late 1980s, for example, Japanese stock prices set repeated records, implying the implausible—an endlessly rapid rise of profits.

On such extreme occasions, we can be fairly sure that the prospective return on such highly priced assets will prove quite low (or even negative) in the coming years. What that statement means is that we expect the relationship of asset prices to fundamentals to revert to historical norms. Periods of extreme valuation just don't last.

To see how the U.S. equity market has been doing recently, we went to Robert Shiller's website and downloaded the data for Figure 8.3. (In 2013, Professor Shiller received the Nobel Prize in Economics, in part for the work that is behind this figure.) Each month, he computes a cyclically adjusted price-earnings (CAPE) ratio for the S&P composite index. Instead of current or forecasted earnings, the CAPE uses the average earnings of the firms in the index over the previous 10 years.

At least two big peaks highlight the mean-reverting pattern of the CAPE ratio over the entire period for which we have data; the price surge in the 1920s and in the 1990s. Neither lasted. Stock prices plummeted.

Where do we stand today? Well, that's a matter of perspective. In the 138 years since 1881, the CAPE ratio has averaged 16.93 (not shown in the figure). So its early 2019 level of 28.8 puts it 70 percent above the long-run norm.

If you think that the normal level of the CAPE is its average over its entire history, you might expect the ratio to fall. Normalization could come either from a sustained rise in earnings or from a decline in stock prices. But earnings are already quite high: In fact, in recent years, the share of corporate profits in gross domestic income has remained relatively high—above 8 percent—similar to what it was in the 1960s. So that leaves you to expect a drop in stock prices.

But there are good reasons to be less worried about prices than the overall level of the CAPE ratio would suggest. To see why, look at the 25-year lagged moving average of the CAPE ratio that we computed using Professor Shiller's data. Throughout the 20th century, this measure fluctuated between 11.80 and 17.54 (with an average of 14.71). But at the beginning of the 2000s, it broke out of this range, so that by early 2019 it stood at a record 26.9. If this represents the "new normal," then the latest CAPE reading is less than 10 percent above the new trend, rather than 70 percent above it.

So, should we look at the full history since 1881 or at just the last 25 years? Do we know which norm is the right one? Not really.

One reason stock prices are so high today is almost surely that interest rates are so low. Higher interest rates could lead to lower stock prices. But to the extent that U.S. economic growth prospects have worsened—as many people believe—then real interest rates are likely to remain lower than they were during the second half of the 20th century. So long as inflation remains tame, this means that long-term nominal interest rates also will stay lower than they used to be. To equalize risk-adjusted expected returns on stocks and bonds, the current ratio of stock prices to earnings should then be higher than in the past, as the 25-year lagged average CAPE suggests.

reported that, between 1871 and 1992, there was no 30-year period when bonds outperformed stocks. In other words, when held for the long term, *stocks are less risky than bonds!*

For many people, investing in stock is a way of saving for retirement, so their investment horizon is very long. Professor Siegel's calculations tell us that our retirement savings should be invested in stock and that we shouldn't worry about year-to-year fluctuations in their value.[16]

[16]For a more sobering view of the stock market rise of the late 1990s and the housing bubble of the subsequent decade, see Robert J. Shiller, *Irrational Exuberance,* 3rd ed. (Princeton, NJ: Princeton University Press, 2016).

Figure 8.3 Cyclically Adjusted Price-Earnings (CAPE) Ratio

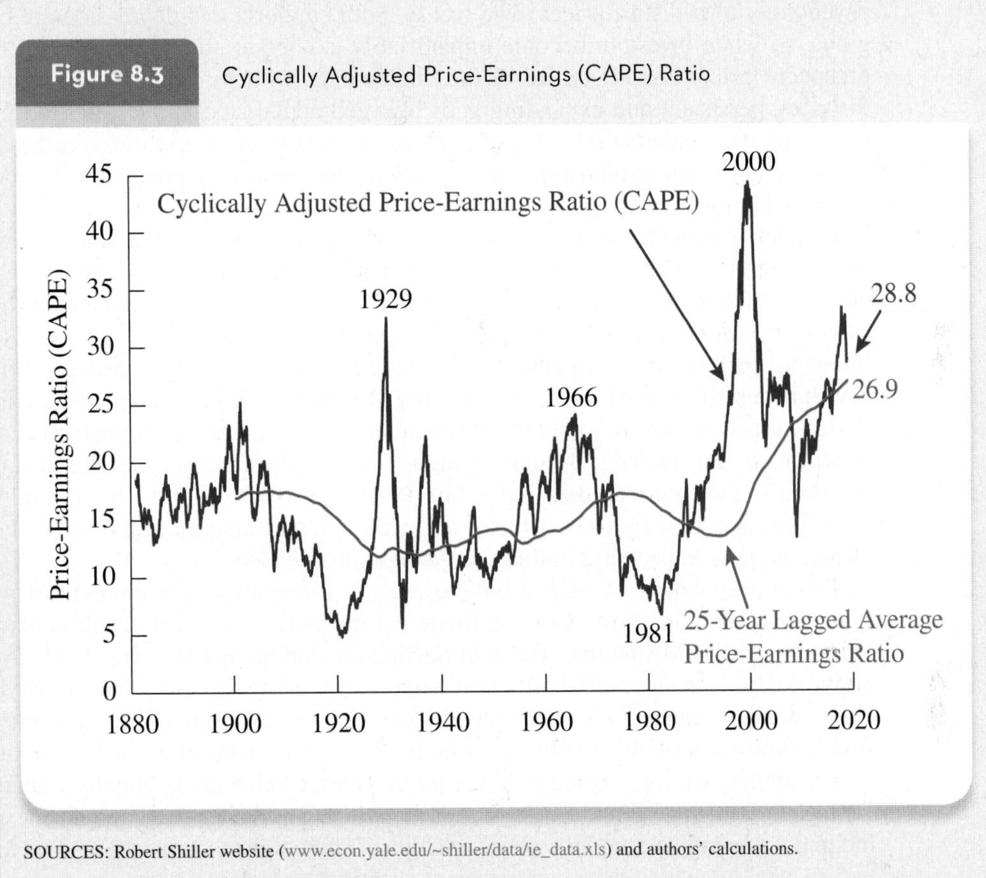

SOURCES: Robert Shiller website (www.econ.yale.edu/~shiller/data/ie_data.xls) and authors' calculations.

What should we conclude? Buy? Or sell? The honest answer is that we don't know. What we can say is that there is reason to believe that the rate of return on stocks purchased today will be lower over the longer term than it has been in the past.

The Stock Market's Role in the Economy

The stock market plays a crucial role in every modern capitalist economy. The prices determined there tell us the market value of companies, which guides the allocation of resources. Firms with a high stock market value are the ones investors prize, so they have an easier time garnering the resources they need to grow. In contrast, firms whose stock value is low have difficulty financing their operations.

So long as stock prices accurately reflect fundamental values, this resource allocation mechanism works well. The signals are accurate, and investment resources flow to their most socially beneficial uses. But at times, stock prices deviate significantly from the fundamentals and move in ways that are difficult to attribute to changes in the real interest rate, the risk premium, or the growth rate of future dividends.

While many economists believe that markets are reasonably efficient and that prices reflect fundamental values, it is worth entertaining the possibility that shifts in investor psychology may distort prices. The fact is, both euphoria and depression are contagious, so when investors become unjustifiably exuberant about the market's future prospects, prices rise regardless of the fundamentals. Such mass enthusiasm creates **bubbles**, persistent and expanding gaps between actual stock prices and those warranted by the fundamentals. These bubbles inevitably burst, creating crashes. This phenomenon is one explanation for the very jagged pattern in annual stock returns—the large gains followed by equally large losses—shown in Figure 8.2.[17]

Investors surely care about the large gains and losses they see when stock prices rise or fall serendipitously. But they are not the only ones who should be concerned. Bubbles affect all of us because they distort the economic decisions companies and consumers make. Here is what happens to companies. When their stock prices rise, financing becomes easier to obtain. They can sell shares and use the proceeds to fund new business opportunities. In the feeding frenzy of a bubble, companies can sell shares for prices that are too high, so financing new investments becomes too easy. It is not much of a challenge to identify high-technology companies that raised staggering sums in the equity markets in the late 1990s, only to crash and burn several years later. They spent the funds they raised on investments in equipment and buildings that turned out later to be worth nothing to them or anyone else.[18]

The consequences of such a bubble are not innocuous. The companies whose stock prices rise the most can raise financing the most easily. The result is that they invest too much. Meanwhile, firms in businesses that are not the objects of investor euphoria have a more difficult time raising financing, so they invest too little. The distortions can be large, and recovery can be slow, especially because companies find it almost impossible to obtain financing for new projects after the bubble bursts.

The impact of stock price bubbles on consumer behavior is equally damaging. Rising equity prices increase individual wealth. The richer we become the more income we spend and the less we save. Unjustifiably high stock prices lead us to buy luxury cars, large houses, and extravagant vacations, which fuels a boom in economic activity. People begin to think they will not need to work as long before they retire. After all, the stock market has made them wealthy, and rich people don't need to work.

The euphoria can't last. When the bubble eventually bursts, individuals are forced to reevaluate their wealth. People discover that their houses and mortgages are too large for their paychecks and their investment accounts are only a shadow of what they once were. Now they need to work harder than ever just to keep up, and their plans for an early retirement are a distant memory. That's not all. Firms that geared up to produce luxury goods for rich shoppers are in trouble. Their wealthy customers disappeared when the bubble burst, and now they are stuck with products people can't afford to buy.

If bubbles result in real investment that is both excessive and inefficiently distributed, crashes do the opposite. The shift from overoptimism to excessive pessimism

[17]The fact that large declines tend to be followed by equally large increases is what makes stocks less risky when held over a long period, as Professor Siegel noticed.

[18]Stories about the Internet boom of the late 1990s, together with data on stock prices and market values of firms, are collected in John Cassidy's *Dot.con: How America Lost Its Mind and Money in the Internet Era* (New York: HarperCollins, 2002).

Raising Equity: Public versus Private Markets
APPLYING THE CONCEPT

Since peaking at over 8,000 in 1996, the number of domestic listed U.S. firms has fallen steadily so that by 2017, it was just over 4,300. Over the same interval, the ratio of equity-market capitalization to GDP actually rose from 105 percent to 166 percent.

Compared to other countries, the dramatic decline in the number of publicly traded U.S. firms has created a "listing gap." From 1996 to 2012, as U.S. listings were *falling* by 49 percent, in a sample of 13 advanced economies, listings were *rising* by an average of 48 percent!*

A related trend is the sizable decline in the number of U.S. initial public offerings (IPOs), where companies issue publicly traded equity for the first time. IPOs also peaked in 1996 at 677, before plunging to 112 in 2017. The percentage decline was even larger among technology firms—from 274 to 30. Adjusted for the 130 percent rise of nominal GDP over the past 20 years, the absolute proceeds from these offerings also declined.

As the number of U.S. publicly traded firms has shrunk, private markets for capital have flourished. Since 2009, funds raised in the private market (that is, "exempt" from government registration requirements) for debt and equity have exceeded funds raised in the public (registered) markets by more than 20 percent. Given that only a small fraction of 1 percent of an estimated 28.8 million U.S. firms are exchange-listed, a vibrant private market plays a critical role in supporting economic activity.

Why is the private equity market displacing the public market? Regulatory changes in the early 2000s that raise the cost of going public could bear some responsibility. So could the increased willingness of wealthy investors to fund private equity and venture capital funds that provide rapidly growing firms an alternative to an IPO. But why are these investors so eager to do so?

One explanation is that small, growing firms today are worth more when they are part of a larger organization than when they remain on their own. If so, the medium-term goal of successful start-ups will be to merge into larger firms, rather than to remain independent by going public.

Instead of factories and machinery, the capital of today's start-ups tends to be *intangible*, including hard-to-value things like software, data, and other types of intellectual property. This makes market financing relatively difficult. Private equity not only fills the gap, it also allows start-ups to keep their innovations secret until they can fully exploit them in product markets. Big firms that eventually absorb them can quickly gain scale and scope economies from this intangible capital.

Fortunately, as the economy's needs change, finance evolves to allocate resources efficiently, in this case shifting away from public markets and toward private equity.

*See Craig G. Doidge, Andrew Karolyi, and René M. Stulz, "The U.S. Listing Gap," *Journal of Financial Economics* 123, no. 3 (June 2016): 464–487.

causes a collapse in investment and economic growth. Normally, the stock market works well and investment funds flow to their most beneficial uses. Occasionally the process goes awry and stock prices move far from any reasonable notion of fundamental value. When these bubbles grow large enough, especially when they lead to crashes, the stock market can destabilize the real economy.

Bubbles have arisen numerous times in stock markets, but housing bubbles appear to be more pernicious because their collapse frequently impairs other important institutions and markets that are critical for economic growth. As we saw in Chapter 3, financial intermediation and the supply of credit suffered when (shadow) banks took large losses on their mortgage-related portfolios in the financial crisis of 2007–2009. And workers whose homes were "underwater"—with market values below the outstanding balances on their mortgages—sometimes could not move to better jobs in new locations because they could neither sell nor refinance their homes. Even at the end of March 2013—nearly four years after the economic recovery began—one out of five borrowers still owed more on their mortgages than the market value of their homes.

Finally, large stock market swings alter economic prospects even when they are grounded in fundamentals. In the recent financial crisis, the disruption of liquidity and credit undermined profit prospects for many companies. As their stocks plunged, the incentive to pull back on investment intensified, helping to amplify the recession of 2007–2009.

Key Terms

bubble, 204
common stock, 185
dividend-discount model, 195
dividends, 193
Dow Jones Industrial Average (DJIA), 189
equity, 185
exchange-traded funds (EFTs), 201
fundamental value, 193
limited liability, 187
market capitalization, 189
mutual fund, 201
Nasdaq Composite Index, 191
price-weighted average, 189
residual claimant, 186
Standard & Poor's 500 Index, 189
stock market, 184
stock market indexes, 188
theory of efficient markets, 199
value-weighted index, 189
Wilshire 5000, 191

Using FRED: Codes for Data in This Chapter

Data Series	FRED Data Code
S&P 500 Stock Price Index	SP500
Dow Jones Industrial Average	DJIA
NASDAQ Composite Index	NASDAQCOM
Wilshire 5000 Price Index	WILL5000PR
Wilshire U.S. Small-Cap Total Market Index	WILLSMLCAP
Wilshire U.S. Large-Cap Total Market Index	WILLLRGCAP
CBOE Volatility Index: VIX	VIXCLS
Market value of equities of nonfarm nonfinancial corporations	NCBEILQ027S
Total net worth (market value) of nonfarm nonfinancial corporations	TNWMVBSNNCB
Total net worth (historical cost) of nonfarm nonfinancial corporations	TNWHCBSNNCB
Corporate equities held by households and nonprofits	HNOCEAQ027S
Disposable personal income	DSPI
Personal dividend income	B703RC1Q027SBEA
U.S. listed companies per million people	DDOM01USA644NWDB

To learn more about the changing financial system, visit www.moneyandbanking.com.

Chapter Lessons

1. Stockholders own the firms in which they hold shares.
   a. They are residual claimants, which means they are last in line after all other creditors.
   b. They have limited liability, so their losses cannot exceed their initial investments.
2. There are two basic types of stock market index.
   a. The Dow Jones Industrial Average is a price-weighted index.
   b. The S&P 500 is a value-weighted index.
   c. For every stock market in the world, there is a comprehensive index that is used to measure overall performance.

3. There are several ways to value stocks.
   a. Some analysts examine patterns of past performance; others follow investor psychology.
   b. The fundamental value of a stock depends on expectations for a firm's future profitability.
   c. To compensate for the fact that stocks are risky investments, investors in stock require a risk premium.
   d. The dividend-discount model is a simple way to assess fundamental value. According to this model, stock prices depend on the current level of dividends, the growth rate of dividends, the risk-free interest rate, and the equity risk premium.
   e. According to the theory of efficient markets, stock prices reflect all available information.
   f. If markets are efficient, then stock price movements are unpredictable, and investors cannot systematically outperform a comprehensive stock market index like the S&P 500.
4. Stock investments are much less risky when they are held for long periods than when they are held for short periods.
5. Stock prices are a central element in a market economy, because they ensure that investment resources flow to their most profitable uses. When occasional bubbles and crashes distort stock prices, they can destabilize the economy.

Conceptual and Analytical Problems connect

1. Explain why being a residual claimant makes stock ownership risky. *(LO1)*
2. Do individual shareholders have an effective say in corporate governance matters? *(LO1)*
3. Consider the following information on the stock market in a small economy. *(LO2)*

Company	Shares Outstanding	Price, Beginning of Year	Price, End of Year
1	100	$100	$94
2	1,000	$ 20	$25
3	10,000	$ 3	$ 6

   a. Compute a price-weighted stock price index for the beginning of the year and the end of the year. What is the percentage change?
   b. Compute a value-weighted stock price index for the beginning of the year and the end of the year. What is the percentage change?
4. To raise wealth and stimulate private spending, suppose the central bank lowers interest rates, making stock market investment relatively attractive. Which stock market index would you monitor to judge the effectiveness of the policy: the Dow Jones Industrial Average or the S&P 500? Why? *(LO2)*

5. Suppose you see evidence that the stock market is efficient. Would that make you more or less likely to invest in stocks for your 401(k) retirement plan when you get your first job? *(LO4)*

6. Professor Siegel argues that investing in stocks for retirement may be less risky than investing in bonds. Would you recommend this approach to an individual in his or her early 60s? *(LO4)*

7. How do venture capital firms, which specialize in identifying and financing promising but high-risk businesses, help the economy grow? *(LO5)*

8.* What are the advantages of holding stock in a company versus holding bonds issued by the same company? *(LO1)*

9. If Professor Siegel is correct that stocks are less risky than bonds, then the risk premium on stock should be zero. Assuming that the risk-free interest rate is 2½ percent, the growth rate of dividends is 1 percent, and the current level of dividends is $70, use the dividend-discount model to compute the level of the S&P 500 that is warranted by the fundamentals. Compare the result to the current S&P 500 level, and comment on it. *(LO4)*

10.* Why is a booming stock market not always a good thing for the economy? *(LO5)*

11. The financial press tends to become excited when the Dow Jones Industrial Average rises or falls sharply. After a particularly steep rise or fall, media outlets may publish tables ranking the day's results with other large advances or declines. What do you think of such reporting? If you were asked to construct a table of the best and worst days in stock market history, how would you do it, and why? *(LO2)*

12. You are thinking about investing in stock in a company that paid a dividend of $10 this year and whose dividends you expect will grow at 4 percent a year. The risk-free rate is 3 percent and you require a risk premium of 5 percent. If the price of the stock in the market is $200 a share, should you buy it? *(LO3)*

13.* Suppose you use the dividend-discount model to calculate the price you are willing to pay for a stock and find that this differs from the market price. What might account for the difference in the market price of the stock and the price you are willing to pay for the stock? *(LO3)*

14. You are trying to decide whether to buy stock in Company X or Company Y. Both companies need $1,000 capital investment and will earn $200 in good years (with probability 0.5) and $60 in bad years. The only difference between the companies is that Company X is planning to raise all of the $1,000 needed by issuing equity, while Company Y plans to finance $500 through equity and $500 through bonds on which 10 percent interest must be paid.

    Construct a table showing the expected value and standard deviation of the equity return for each of the companies. (You could use Table 8.3 as a guide.) Based on this table, in which company would you buy stock? Explain your choice. *(LO3)*

15. Your brother has $1,000 and a one-year investment horizon and asks your advice about whether he should invest in a particular company's stock. What information would you suggest he analyze when making his decision? Is there an alternative investment strategy to gain exposure to the stock market you might suggest he consider? *(LO4)*

*Indicates more difficult problems.

16. Given that many stock market indexes across the world fell and rose together during the financial crisis of 2007–2009, do you think investing in global stock markets is an effective way to reduce risk? Why or why not? *(LO2)*
17. Do you think a proposal to abolish limited liability for stockholders would be supported by companies issuing stock? *(LO1)*
18. You peruse the available records of some public figures in your area and notice that they persistently gain higher returns on their stock portfolios than the market average. As a believer in efficient markets, what explanation for these rates of returns seems most likely to you? *(LO5)*
19. Do you think that widespread belief in the efficient markets theory was a significant contributor to the 2007–2009 financial crisis? Why or why not? *(LO5)*
20. Based on the dividend-discount model, what do you think would happen to stock prices if there were an increase in the perceived riskiness of bonds? *(LO3)*
21.* Use the dividend-discount model to explain why an increase in stock prices is often a good indication that the economy is expected to do well. *(LO3)*
22. Memories of the 2007–2009 financial crisis have made you more risk averse, doubling the risk premium you require to purchase a stock. Suppose that your risk premium before the crisis was 4 percent and that you had been willing to pay $412 for a stock with a dividend-payment of $10 and expected dividend growth of 3 percent. Using the dividend-discount model, with unchanged risk-free rate, dividend payment, and expected dividend growth, what price (rounded to the nearest dollar) would you now be willing to pay for this stock? *(LO3)*
23. Suppose a shock to the financial system were to disproportionately hit corporate bond markets, making it much harder for companies to raise new funds via bond issuance. As a result, the proportion of equity financing rises significantly. What impact would you anticipate this would have on (i) the expected return on holding stocks and (ii) the volatility of equity returns? *(LO3)*
24.* The growth of private equity markets in the United States expands the options available to firms to raise funds, as well as the investment choices available to some investors. Why do you think private equity investing tends to be confined to institutional investors and high net worth individuals? *(LO4)*

Data Exploration Mc Graw Hill connect

For detailed instructions on using Federal Reserve Economic Data (FRED) online to answer each of the following problems, visit www.mhhe.com/moneyandbanking6e *and refer to the FRED Resources and Data Exploration Hints.*

1. How well does the stock market anticipate the behavior of the economy? Plot on a monthly basis since 1972 the percent change from a year ago of the Wilshire 5000 index (FRED code: WILL5000PR). Is the index a reliable predictor of business cycle downturns (depicted in the graph by vertical, shaded bars)? *(LO5)*
2. Why might the stocks of small firms outperform large firms over long periods of time? Will this hold over short periods of time, too? Plot since 1979 the stock indexes for small firms (FRED code: WILLSMLCAP) and large firms (FRED

*Indicates more difficult problems.

code: WILLLRGCAP) using annual data scaled to a common base year of 1979=100. *(LO3)*

3. The NASDAQ stock market index (FRED code: NASDAQCOM) is comprised of stocks that tend to be relatively small, new, and focused on technology while the Wilshire 5000 (FRED code: WILL5000PR) includes all actively traded stocks in the United States. Which do you think is more volatile? Plot on a monthly basis from 1980 the percent change from a year ago of these two indexes and discuss whether your intuition was correct. *(LO5)*
4. To see the impact of the bubble in Internet stocks on household wealth, plot on a monthly basis since 1980 the NASDAQ stock index (FRED code: NASDAQCOM) on the left axis against the market value of nonfarm nonfinancial corporations (FRED code: NCBEILQ027S) on the right axis. Comment on the impact of the bursting of the bubble on this measure of equity wealth. Aside from the NASDAQ decline, what else might have caused it to drop? *(LO5)*
5. Have stock dividends become a more important source of income to U.S. households? Plot on a quarterly basis since 1959 the share of dividend income (FRED code: B703RC1Q027SBEA) in personal disposable income (FRED code: DSPI). Can you explain the 50-year trend? *(LO5)*
6. What factors determine whether firms issue publicly traded stock to finance investment? Plot the number of publicly listed companies per million people in the United States (FRED Code: DDOM01USA644NWDB) since 1985. Describe the trend and discuss what might explain it. *(LO5)*

Chapter

9 Derivatives: Futures, Options, and Swaps

Learning Objectives

After reading this chapter, you should be able to:

LO1 Explain what derivatives are and how they transfer risk.

LO2 Distinguish between forward and futures contracts.

LO3 Define put and call options and describe how to use them.

LO4 Show how swaps can be used to manage risk or to conceal it.

Derivatives played a central role in the financial crisis of 2007–2009. One of the key events during the crisis was the fall of AIG, the world's largest insurance company. Through the use of derivatives contracts, AIG had taken enormous risks that it was able to conceal from the view both of government officials and its trading partners. Each contract was arranged over the counter (OTC)—that is, directly between AIG and a single counterparty—rather than through an organized exchange. In the crisis, these hidden risks threatened the entire financial system.

Leading up to the crisis, the tight but largely unseen links that OTC derivatives created among the largest, most important global financial institutions made the entire system vulnerable to the weakest of those institutions. Partly as a result of the *systemic vulnerabilities* posed by OTC derivatives, phrases like "too interconnected to fail" and "too big to fail" filled newspapers and the media (see Chapter 5, Lessons from the Crisis: Systemic Risk). Warren Buffett, the famed investor, called derivatives "weapons of financial mass destruction."

Even in the years before the financial crisis, stories detailing the abuse of derivatives filled the pages of the business press. Derivatives were at the bottom of the scandal that engulfed Enron immediately after it declared bankruptcy in November 2001. As we have learned since then, Enron engaged in a variety of financial transactions whose express purpose was to give the appearance of low debt, low risk, and high profitability. This sleight of hand kept the stock price high and made shareholders happy, so no one complained. In fact, no one even looked. But eventually the day of reckoning came, and the company collapsed.

Financial derivatives were also linked to the collapse of Long-Term Capital Management (LTCM), a Connecticut-based hedge fund, in fall 1998. On a single day in August 1998, LTCM lost an astounding $553 million. By late September, the fund had lost another $2 billion. That left LTCM with more than $99 billion in debt and $100 billion in assets. With loans accounting for 99 percent of total assets, repayment was nearly impossible. LTCM also had significant derivatives positions that did not show up on the balance sheet as assets or liabilities. These off-balance-sheet arrangements, which carried even more risk, were the primary cause of the fund's stunningly swift losses.

Derivatives also played a role in the euro-area crisis that began in earnest in 2010. Many banks that owned Greek government debt had hedged by purchasing derivatives that would compensate them if Greece defaulted (see Credit Default Swaps on page 232). But policymakers in the euro area sought to reduce Greece's debt burden without triggering an outright default in legal terms. In the end, Greece defaulted, and the derivatives paid off. Yet, had the policymakers succeeded, financial firms that thought they were protected would have faced large, unanticipated losses. Fears of such exposure, along with doubts about the insurance provided by derivatives, likely accelerated deleveraging and aggravated financial instability.

If derivatives are open to abuse, why do they exist? The answer is that when used properly, derivatives are extremely helpful financial instruments. They can be used to reduce risk, allowing firms and individuals to enter into agreements that they otherwise wouldn't be willing to accept. Derivatives can also be used as insurance. For example, in winter 1998, a snowmobile manufacturer named Bombardier offered a $1,000 rebate to buyers should snowfall in 44 cities total less than half what it had averaged over the preceding three years. Sales rose 38 percent. The existence of "weather derivatives" enabled Bombardier to undertake this risky marketing strategy. Paying the rebates would have bankrupted the company, but Bombardier purchased derivatives that would pay off if snowfall were low. By using this unorthodox form of insurance, Bombardier transferred the risk to someone else.

What exactly are derivatives, and why are they so important? Though they play a critical role in our financial well-being, most people barely know what they are. This chapter will provide an introduction to the uses and abuses of derivatives.

The Basics: Defining Derivatives

To understand what derivatives are, let's begin with the basics. A **derivative** is a financial instrument whose value depends on—is *derived* from—the value of some other financial instrument, called the *underlying asset.* Some common examples of underlying assets are stocks, bonds, wheat, snowfall, and orange juice.

A simple example of a derivative is a contractual agreement between two investors that obligates one to make a payment to the other, depending on the movement in interest rates over the next year. This type of derivative is called an interest rate *futures contract.* Such an arrangement is quite different from the outright purchase of a bond for two reasons. First, derivatives provide an easy way for investors to profit from price declines. The purchase of a bond, in contrast, is a bet that its price will rise.[1] Second, and more important, in a derivatives transaction, one person's loss is always another person's gain. Buyer and seller are like two people playing poker. How much each player wins or loses depends on how the game progresses, but the total amount on the table doesn't change.

[1]Investors can bet that prices will fall using a technique called *short selling*. The investor borrows an asset from its owner for a fee, sells it at the current market price, and then repurchases it later. The short seller is betting that the price of the asset will fall between the time it is sold and the time it is repurchased.

While derivatives can be used to *speculate,* or gamble on future price movements, the fact that they allow investors to manage and reduce risk makes them indispensable to a modern economy. Bombardier used a derivative to hedge the risk of having to pay rebates in the event of low snowfall (we discussed hedging in Chapter 5). As we will see, farmers use derivatives regularly, to insure themselves against fluctuations in the market prices of their crops. Risk can be bought and sold using derivatives. Thus, *the purpose of derivatives is to transfer risk from one person or firm to another.*

When people have the ability to transfer risks, they will do things that they wouldn't do otherwise. Think of a wheat farmer and a bread baker. If he or she cannot insure against a decline in the price of wheat, the farmer will plant fewer acres of wheat. And without a guarantee that the price of flour will not rise, the baker will build a smaller bakery. Those are prudent responses to the risks created by price fluctuations. Now introduce a mechanism through which the farmer and the baker can guarantee the price of wheat. As a result the farmer will plant more and the baker will build a bigger bakery. Insurance is what allows them to do it! Derivatives provide that insurance. In fact, by shifting risk to those willing and able to bear it, derivatives increase the risk-carrying capacity of the economy as a whole, improving the allocation of resources and increasing the level of output.

While derivatives allow individuals and firms to manage risk, they also allow them to conceal the true nature of certain financial transactions. In the same way that stripping a coupon bond separates the coupons from the principal payment, buying and selling derivatives can unbundle virtually any group of future payments and risks. A company that hesitates to issue a coupon bond for fear analysts will frown on the extra debt can instead issue the coupon payments and the principal payment as individual zero-coupon bonds, using derivative transactions to label them something other than borrowing. Thus, if stock market analysts penalize companies for obtaining funding in certain ways, derivatives (as we will see) allow the companies to get exactly the same resources at the same risk but under a different name.

Derivatives may be divided into three major categories: forwards and futures, options, and swaps. Let's look at each one.

Forwards and Futures

Of all derivative financial instruments, forwards and futures are the simplest to understand and the easiest to use. *A* **forward**, *or* **forward contract**, *is an agreement between a buyer and a seller to exchange a commodity or financial instrument for a specified amount of cash on a prearranged future date.* Forward contracts are private agreements between two parties. Because they are customized, forward contracts are very difficult to resell to someone else.

To see why forward contracts are difficult to resell, consider the example of a year-long apartment lease, in which the renter agrees to make a series of monthly payments to the landlord in exchange for the right to live in the apartment. Such a lease is a sequence of 12 forward contracts. Rent is paid in predetermined amounts on prearranged future dates in exchange for housing. While there is some standardization of leases, a contract between a specific renter and a specific landlord is unlike any other rental contract. Thus, there is no market for the resale or reassignment of apartment rental contracts.

In contrast, a **future**, *or* **futures contract**, *is a forward contract that has been standardized and sold through an organized exchange.* A futures contract specifies

Table 9.1 Interest Rate Futures

(1)	(2) Open	(3) High	(4) Low	(5) Last	(6) Change	(7) Open Interest
Treasury Bond Futures Settlements: $100,000 face value						
March	146'11	147'03	146'05	146'29	+'22	13,209
June	145'17	146'14	145'14	146'09	+'22	948,775

This table reports information on a contract for delivery of $100,000 face value of 10-year 6 percent coupon U.S. Treasury bonds.
Column (1). This reports the month when the contract requires delivery of the bonds from the short position/seller to the long position/buyer.
Column (2). "Open" is the price quoted when the exchange opened on the morning of March 15, 2019. This need not be the same as the preceding afternoon's close. The price in the first row, 146'11, is quoted in 32nds and represents the cost of $100 face value worth of the 10-year 6 percent coupon U.S. Treasury bonds. In this case, the open price is 146 plus 11 32nds. The price in the second row, 145'17, means 145 plus 17 32nds.
Columns (3) and (4). "High" and "Low" are the highest and lowest prices posted during the trading day.
Column (5). "Last" is the closing or settlement price at the end of the trading day on March 15, 2019. This is the price used for marking to market.
Column (6). "Change" is the change in the closing price, measured in 32nds, from the preceding day's closing price.
Column (7). "Open interest" is the number of contracts outstanding, or open. These numbers often are quite large, especially when one contract is close to expiration.

SOURCE: CME Group, March 15, 2019, www.cmegroup.com/trading/interest-rates/us-treasury/30-year-us-treasury-bond_quotes_settlements_futures.html#tradeDate=03%2F21%2F2019.

that the seller—who has the *short position*—will deliver some quantity of a commodity or financial instrument to the buyer—who has the *long position*—on a specific date, called the *settlement* or *delivery* date, for a predetermined price. No payments are made initially when the contract is agreed to. The seller/short position benefits from declines in the price of the underlying asset, while the buyer/long position benefits from increases.[2]

Take the U.S. Treasury bond futures contract that trades on the Chicago Board of Trade (CBOT, which is a part of the CME Group). The contract specifies the delivery of $100,000 face value worth of 10-year, 6 percent coupon U.S. Treasury bonds at any time during a given month, called the *delivery* month.[3] Table 9.1 shows the prices and trading activity for this contract on March 15, 2019. The fact that the contract is so specific means there is no need for negotiation. And the existence of the exchange creates a natural place for people who are interested in a particular futures contract to meet and trade. Historically, exchanges have been physical locations, but

[2]The term *short* refers to the fact that one party to the agreement is obligated to deliver something, whether or not he or she currently owns it. The term *long* signifies that the other party is obligated to buy something at a future date.

[3]A bond issued by the U.S. Treasury with an original maturity of 10 years or less is officially called a *Treasury note*, but we use the term *Treasury bond* in this chapter for simplicity. The seller of a U.S. Treasury bond futures contract need not deliver the exact bond specified in the contract. The Chicago Board of Trade, a part of the CME Group, maintains a spreadsheet of conversion factors to use in adjusting the quantity (face value) when delivery of some other bond is made. While these particular futures allow for delivery at any time during the delivery month, other futures may require delivery on a specific day. Specifications of the contract are available at: www.cmegroup.com/trading/interest-rates/us-treasury/10-year-us-treasury-note_contract_specifications.html.

with the Internet came online trading of futures. In recent years, firms have created virtual futures markets for a wide variety of products, including energy, bandwidth, and plastics.

One more thing is needed before anyone will actually buy or sell futures contracts: assurance that the buyer and seller will meet their obligations. In the case of the U.S. Treasury futures contract, the buyer must be sure that the seller will deliver the bond, and the seller must believe that the buyer will pay for it. Market participants have found an ingenious solution to this problem. Instead of making a bilateral arrangement, the two parties to a futures contract each make an agreement with a *clearing corporation.* The clearing corporation, which operates like a large insurance company, is the counterparty to both sides of a transaction, guaranteeing that they will meet their obligations. This arrangement reduces the risk buyers and sellers face. The clearing corporation has the ability to monitor traders and the incentive to limit their risk taking (see Lessons from the Crisis: Central Counterparties and Systemic Risk).

Margin Accounts and Marking to Market

To reduce the risk it faces, the clearing corporation requires both parties to a futures contract to place a deposit with the corporation itself. This practice is called posting **margin** in a *margin account.* The margin deposits guarantee that when the contract comes due, the parties will be able to meet their obligations. But the clearing corporation does more than collect the *initial margin* when a contract is signed. It also posts daily gains and losses on the contract to the margin accounts of the parties involved.[4] This process is called *marking to market,* and it is done daily.

Marking to market is analogous to what happens during a poker game. At the end of each hand, the amount wagered is transferred from the losers to the winner. In financial parlance, the account of each player is marked to market. Alternative methods of accounting are too complicated, making it difficult to identify players who should be excused from the game because they have run out of resources. For similar reasons, the clearing corporation marks futures accounts to market every day. Doing so ensures that sellers always have the resources to make delivery and that buyers always can pay. As in poker, if someone's margin account falls below the minimum, the clearing corporation will sell the contracts, ending the person's participation in the market.

An example will help you understand how marking to market works. Take the case of a futures contract for the purchase of 1,000 ounces of silver at \$20 per ounce. The contract specifies that the buyer of the contract, the long position, will pay \$20,000 in exchange for 1,000 ounces of silver. The seller of the contract, the short position, receives the \$20,000 and delivers the 1,000 ounces of silver. We can think about this contract as guaranteeing the long position the ability to buy 1,000 ounces of silver for \$20,000 and guaranteeing the short position the ability to sell 1,000 ounces of silver for \$20,000. Now consider what happens when the price of silver changes. If the price rises to \$21 per ounce, the seller needs to give the buyer \$1,000 so that the buyer pays only \$20,000 for the 1,000 ounces of silver. By contrast, if the price falls to \$19 an ounce, the

[4]On March 15, 2019, the March U.S. Treasury bond futures contract in Table 9.1 rose 22/32 per \$100 face value worth of bonds. A single contract covers 1,000 times that amount, so the value of each contract rose by (\$22/32)(1,000) = \$687.50. Marking to market means that, at the end of the day for each outstanding contract, the clearing corporation credited the long position/buyer and debited the short position/seller \$687.50.

buyer of the futures contract needs to pay $1,000 to the seller to make sure that the seller receives $20,000 for selling the 1,000 ounces of silver. Marking to market is the transfer of funds at the end of each day that ensures the buyers and sellers get what the contract promises.

Hedging and Speculating with Futures

Futures contracts allow the transfer of risk between buyer and seller. This transfer can be accomplished through hedging or speculation. Let's look at *hedging* first. Say a government securities dealer wishes to insure against declines in the value of an inventory of bonds. Recall from Chapter 5 that this type of risk can be reduced by finding another financial instrument that delivers a high payoff when bond prices fall. That is exactly what happens with the sale of a U.S. Treasury bond futures contract: the seller/short position benefits from price declines. Put differently, the seller of a futures contract—the securities dealer, in this case—can guarantee the price at which the bonds are sold. The other party to this transaction might be a pension fund manager who is planning to purchase bonds in the future and wishes to insure against possible price increases.[5] Buying a futures contract fixes the price that the fund will need to pay. In this example, *both sides use the futures contract as a hedge.* They are both *hedgers*.[6]

Producers and users of commodities employ futures markets to hedge their risks as well. Farmers, mining companies, oil drillers, and the like are sellers of futures, taking short positions. After all, they own the commodities outright, so they want to stabilize the revenue they receive when they sell. In contrast, millers, jewelers, and oil distributors want to buy futures to take long positions. They require the commodity to do business, so they buy the futures contract to reduce risk arising from fluctuations in the cost of essential inputs.

What about *speculators*? Their objective is simple: They are trying to make a profit. To do so, they bet on price movements. Sellers of futures are betting that prices will fall, while buyers are betting that prices will rise. Futures contracts are popular tools for speculation because they are cheap. An investor needs only a relatively small amount of investment—the margin—to purchase a futures contract that is worth a great deal. Margin requirements of 10 percent or less are common. In the case of a futures contract for the delivery of $100,000 face value worth of 10-year, 6 percent coupon U.S. Treasury bonds, the Chicago Board of Trade (the clearing corporation that guarantees the contract) requires maintaining margin of $1,050 per contract. That is, an investment of only $1,050 gives the investor the same returns as the purchase of $100,000 worth of bonds. It is as if the investor borrowed the remaining $98,950 without having to pay any interest.[7]

To see the impact of this kind of leverage on the return to the buyer and seller of a futures contract, recall from footnote 4 that a rise of 22/32nds in the price of the Treasury bond futures contract meant that the long position/buyer gained $687.50, while the short position/seller lost $687.50. With a minimum initial investment of $1,050 for each contract, this represents a 65.5 percent gain to the futures contract buyer and a 65.5 percent loss to the futures contract seller. In contrast, the owner of the bond itself would have

[5]Recall from Chapters 4 and 6 that bond prices and interest rates move in opposite directions. That means the bond dealer who sells the futures contract is insuring against interest rate increases.

[6]Hedgers who buy futures are called *long hedgers* and hedgers who sell futures are called *short hedgers*.

[7]It is even possible to arrange a margin account so that the balance earns interest.

Central Counterparties and Systemic Risk

LESSONS FROM THE CRISIS

We know that a loss of liquidity and transparency can threaten the financial system as a whole (see Chapter 5, Lessons from the Crisis: Systemic Risk). Lack of liquidity can make trading impossible, while lack of transparency can make traders unwilling to trust one another. Both can cause markets to seize up and trigger a cascade of failures. Transparent, liquid financial markets are less prone to such systemic disruptions.

How can we make markets more robust? One way is to shift trading from over-the-counter (OTC) markets, where products tend to be customized, to transactions with a **central counterparty (CCP)** in standardized financial instruments.*

OTC trading is bilateral, that is, directly between buyer and seller, rather than through an intermediary. By contrast, a CCP is an entity that interposes itself between the two sides of a transaction, becoming the buyer to every seller and the seller to every buyer. Trading on most stock, futures, and options exchanges goes through CCPs. As a result, when you buy or sell a stock, you neither know nor care who the ultimate seller or buyer is because you are trading with the CCP of the exchange.

When trading OTC with many partners, a firm can build up excessively large positions without other parties being aware of the risk it is acquiring. In contrast, a CCP has the *ability*, as well as the *incentive*, to monitor the riskiness of its counterparties. Because all trades occur with the CCP, it can see whether a trader is taking a large position on one side of a trade. Standardization of contracts also facilitates CCP monitoring. If it finds itself trading with a risky counterparty, a CCP can insist on a risk premium to protect itself. A CCP also can refuse to trade with a counterparty that may not be able to pay. And it can insist on frequent marking of prices to market to measure and control risks effectively.

A CCP also limits its own risk through economies of scale. Most of the trades that a CCP conducts can be offset against one another. Therefore, the volume of net payments that must occur on any given day is only a small fraction of the gross value of the trades, sharply lowering the risk of nonpayment.

The history of CCPs reveals their practical benefits. Since 1925, when all U.S. futures contracts began trading through a CCP, no contract has failed despite many subsequent financial disruptions, including the Great Depression. CCPs have helped markets function well even when traders cannot pay. For example, when one large energy futures trader (Amaranth) failed in 2006, the futures market adjusted smoothly because the CCP could use the trader's collateral to satisfy its contracts with other firms. Futures markets also absorbed the losses from the spectacular 2011 collapse of a large commodities brokerage (MF Global) that misused customer money.

In contrast, systemic threats and disruptions have arisen repeatedly with OTC contracts: in 1998, when the possible demise of the hedge fund LTCM threatened numerous counterparties of its OTC interest rate swaps; and again, during the financial crisis of 2007–2009, with a number of firms active in OTC derivatives, including Bear Stearns, Lehman Brothers, and AIG.

Over the past decade, there has been an overhaul of derivatives markets so that today more than 60 percent of the roughly $600 trillion in derivatives contracts are centrally cleared. While this reduces the dangers posed by a complex, opaque web of bilateral relationships, it concentrates risks in the CCPs themselves. To ensure that these critical components of the financial architecture are resilient and not prone to collapse, appropriate safeguards must be in place so that CCPs will always have the resources to continue operating.

*For more details on CCPs, see Stephen G. Cecchetti, Jacob Gyntelberg, and Marc Hollanders, "Central Counterparties for Over-the-Counter Derivatives," *BIS Quarterly Review*, September 2009, pp. 45–58.

gained $687.50 on an approximately $100,000 investment, which is a gain of just 0.688 percent! *Speculators, then, can use futures to obtain very large amounts of leverage at a very low cost.*

Arbitrage and the Determinants of Futures Prices

To understand how the price of a futures contract is determined, let's start at the settlement date and work backward. On the settlement or delivery date, we know that the price of the futures contract must equal the price of the underlying asset the seller is obligated to deliver. The reason is simple: If, at expiration, the futures price were to deviate from the asset's price, then it would be possible to make a risk-free profit by engaging in offsetting cash and futures transactions. If the current market price of a bond were below the futures contract price, someone could buy a bond at the low price and simultaneously sell a futures contract (take a short position and promise to deliver the bond on a future date). Immediate exercise of the futures contract and delivery of the bond would yield a profit equal to the difference between the market price and the futures price. Thinking about this example carefully, we can see that the investor who engages in these transactions has been able to make a profit without taking on any risk or making any investment.

The practice of simultaneously buying and selling financial instruments in order to benefit from temporary price differences is called **arbitrage**, and the people who engage in it are called *arbitrageurs*. Arbitrage means that two financial instruments with the same risk and promised future payments will sell for the same price. If, for example, the price of a specific bond is higher in one market than in another, an arbitrageur can buy at the low price and sell at the high price. The increase in demand in the market where the price is low drives the price up there, while the increase in supply in the market where the price is high drives the price down there, and the process continues until prices are equal in the two markets. As long as there are arbitrageurs, on the day when a futures contract is settled, the price of a bond futures contract will be the same as the market price—what is called the *spot price*—of the bond.

So we know that on the settlement date, the price of a futures contract must equal the spot price of the underlying asset. But what happens before the settlement date? The principle of arbitrage still applies. The price of the futures contract depends on the fact that someone can buy a bond and sell a futures contract simultaneously. Here's how it's done. First, the arbitrageur borrows at the current market interest rate. With the funds, the arbitrageur buys a bond and sells a bond futures contract. Now the arbitrageur has a loan on which interest must be paid, a bond that pays interest, and a promise to deliver the bond for a fixed price at the expiration of the futures contract. Because the interest owed on the loan and received from the bond will cancel out, this position costs nothing to initiate.[8] As before, if the market price of the bond is below the futures contract price, this strategy will yield a profit. *Thus, the futures price must move in lockstep with the market price of the bond.*

To see how arbitrage works, consider an example in which the spot price of a 4 percent coupon 10-year bond is $100, the current interest rate on a 3-month loan is also 4 percent (quoted at an annual rate), and the futures market price for delivery of a 4 percent, 10-year bond is $101. An investor could borrow $100, purchase the 10-year bond, and sell a bond future for $101 promising delivery of the bond in three months. The investor could use the interest payment from the bond to pay the interest on the loan and deliver the bond to the buyer of the futures contract on the delivery date. This transaction is completely riskless and nets the investor a profit of $1—without even putting up any funds. A riskless profit is extremely tempting, so the investor will continue to engage in the transactions needed to generate it. Here that means continuing to buy bonds (driving the price up) and sell futures (forcing the price down) until the prices converge and no further profits are available.[9]

Table 9.2 summarizes the positions of buyers and sellers in the futures market.

[8]Unlike you and me, the arbitrageur can borrow at an interest rate that is close to the one received from the bond. There are two reasons for this. First, the arbitrageur is likely to be a large financial intermediary with a good credit rating; second, the loan is collateralized by the bond itself.

[9]In a commodity futures contract, the futures price will equal the present value of the expected spot price on the delivery date, discounted at the risk-free interest rate.

Table 9.2 Who's Who in Futures

	Buyer of a Futures Contract	Seller of a Futures Contract
This is called the	*Long* position	*Short* position
Obligation of the party	Buy the commodity or asset on the settlement date	Deliver the commodity or asset on the settlement date
What happens to this person's margin account after a *rise* in the market price of the commodity or asset?	*Credited*	*Debited*
Who takes this position to *hedge?*	The *user* of the commodity or *buyer* of the asset who needs to insure against the price *rising*	The *producer* of the commodity or owner of the asset who needs to insure against the price *falling*
Who takes this position to *speculate?*	Someone who believes that the market price of the commodity or asset will *rise*	Someone who believes that the market price of the commodity or asset will *fall*

Options

Everyone likes to have options. Having the option to go on vacation or buy a new car is nice. The alternative to having options, having our decisions made for us, is surely worse. Because options are valuable, people are willing to pay for them when they can. Financial options are no different; because they are worth having, we can put a price on them.

Calculating the price of an option is incredibly complicated. In fact, no one knew how before Fischer Black and Myron Scholes figured it out in 1973. Traders immediately programmed their famous Black-Scholes formula into the computers available at the time, and the options markets took off. By June 2000, the market value of outstanding options was in the neighborhood of $500 billion. Today, hundreds of millions of options contracts are outstanding, and millions of them change hands every day.

Before we learn how to price options, we'll need to master the vocabulary used to describe them. Once we have the language, the next step is to move on to how to use options and how to value them.

Calls, Puts, and All That: Definitions

Like futures, options are agreements between two parties. There is a seller, called an *option writer,* and a buyer, called an *option holder.* As we will see, option writers incur obligations, while option holders obtain rights. There are two basic options, *puts* and *calls.*

A **call option** is the right to buy—"call away"—a given quantity of an underlying asset at a predetermined price, called the **strike price** (or *exercise price*), on or before a specific date. For example, a July 2019 call option on 100 shares of Apple stock at a strike price of 100 gives the option holder the right to buy 100 shares of Apple for $100 apiece prior to the third Friday of July 2019. The writer of the call option *must* sell the shares if and when the holder chooses to use the call option. The holder of the call is *not required* to buy the shares; rather, the holder has the option to buy and will do so only if buying is beneficial. When the price of Apple stock exceeds the option strike price of 100, the option holder can either call away the 100 shares from the option writer by *exercising* the option or sell the option to someone else at a profit. If the market price rose to \$105, for example, then exercising the call would allow the holder to buy the stock from the option writer for \$100 and reap a \$5 per share profit. Whenever the price of the stock is above the strike price of the call option, exercising the option is profitable for the holder, and the option is said to be *in the money* (as in "I'm in the money!"). If the price of the stock exactly equals the strike price, the option is said to be *at the money*. If the strike price exceeds the market price of the underlying asset, it is termed *out of the money*.

A **put option** gives the holder the right but not the obligation to sell the underlying asset at a predetermined price on or before a fixed date. The holder can "put" the asset in the hands of the option writer. Again, the writer of the option is obliged to buy the shares should the holder choose to exercise the option. Returning to the example of Apple stock, consider a put option with a strike price of 100. This is the right to sell 100 shares at \$100 per share, which is valuable when the market price of Apple stock falls below \$100. If the price of a share of Apple stock were \$90, then exercising the put option would yield a profit of \$10 per share.

The same terminology that is used to describe calls—in the money, at the money, and out of the money—applies to puts as well, but the circumstances in which it is used are reversed. Because the buyer of a put obtains the right to sell a stock, the put is *in the money* when the option's strike price is *above* the market price of the stock. It is *out of the money* when the strike price is *below* the market price.

While it is possible to customize options in the same way as forward contracts, many are standardized and traded on exchanges, just like futures contracts. The mechanics of trading are the same. A clearing corporation guarantees the obligations embodied in the option—those of the option writer. And the option writer is required to post margin. Because option holders incur no obligation, they are not required to post margin.

There are two types of calls and puts: American and European. **American options** can be exercised on any date from the time they are written until the day they expire. As a result, prior to the expiration date, the holder of an American option has three choices: (1) continue to hold the option, (2) sell the option to someone else, or (3) exercise the option immediately. **European options** can be exercised only on the day that they expire. Thus, the holder of a European option has two choices on a date prior to expiration: hold or sell. The vast majority of options traded in the United States are American.

Using Options

Who buys and sells options, and why? To answer this question, we need to understand how options are used. *Options transfer risk* from the buyer to the seller, so they can be used for both hedging and speculation. Let's take hedging first. Remember that a hedger is buying insurance. For someone who wants to purchase an asset such as a bond or a stock in the future, a call option ensures that the cost of buying the asset will not rise. For someone who plans to sell the asset in the future, a put option ensures that the price at which the asset can be sold will not go down.

To understand the close correspondence between options and insurance, think of the arrangement that automobile owners have with their insurance company. The owner pays an insurance premium and obtains the right to file a claim in the event

Should You Believe Corporate Financial Statements?

YOUR FINANCIAL WORLD

Corporations work hard to appear as profitable as possible. They employ squadrons of accountants and financial wizards to dress up their financial statements so that reported profits are as high and stable as possible. While financial statements must meet exacting accounting standards, that does not mean they accurately reflect a company's true financial position. The problem is that the standards are so specific they provide a road map for the creation of misleading statements. Remember that derivatives render the names attached to particular risks and payoffs arbitrary and irrelevant. But accounting regulations are all about names. That is the way the system works, and there is nothing illegal about it.

So what are investors supposed to do? First, never trust an accounting statement that doesn't meet the standards set forth by financial regulators. For example, during the Internet boom of the late 1990s, many firms published so-called pro forma financial statements based on their own definitions of revenue and costs. To look profitable, these companies had to make their own accounting rules. Such tinkering implies that a firm has something to hide.

Second, the more open a company is in its financial accounting, the more likely that it is honest. One of the lasting effects of the credit rating failures associated with the financial crisis of 2007–2009 is that investors now punish companies that publish opaque financial statements. Honesty really is the best policy; the more information a firm makes public, the more credible it will be with investors.

Finally, remember that diversification reduces risk. If you own shares in many different companies, you are better protected against the possibility that some of them will be less than honest in their disclosures.

of an accident. If the terms of the policy are met, the insurance company is obligated to pay the claim. If no accident occurs, then there is no claim and the insurance company makes no payment; the insurance premium is lost. In effect, the insurance company has sold an American call option to the car's owner where the underlying asset is a working car and the strike price is zero. This call option can be exercised if and only if the car is damaged in an accident on any day before the policy expires.

Options can be used for speculation as well. Say that you believe that interest rates are going to fall over the next few months. There are three ways to bet on this possibility. The first is to purchase a bond outright, hoping that its price will rise as interest rates fall. This is expensive, because you will need to come up with the resources to buy the bond. A second strategy is to buy a futures contract, taking the long position. If the market price of the bond rises, you will make a profit. As we saw in the last section, this is an attractive approach, because it requires only a small investment. But it is also very risky, because the investment is highly leveraged. Both the bond purchase and the futures contract carry the risk that you will take a loss, and if interest rates rise substantially, your loss will be large.

The third strategy for betting that interest rates will fall is to buy a call option on a U.S. Treasury bond. If you are right and interest rates fall, the value of the call option will rise. But if you are wrong and interest rates rise, the call will expire worthless and your losses will be limited to the price you paid for it. This bet is both highly leveraged and limited in its potential losses.

In the same way that purchasing a call option allows an investor to bet that the price of the underlying asset will rise, purchasing a put option allows the investor to bet that the price will fall. Again, if the investor is wrong, all that is lost is the price paid for the option. In the meantime, the option provides a cheap way to bet on the movement in the price of the underlying asset. The bet is highly leveraged, because a small initial investment creates the opportunity for a large gain. But unlike a futures contract, a put option has a limited potential loss.

So far we have discussed only the purchase of options. For every buyer there must be a seller. Who is it? After all, an option writer can take a large loss. Nevertheless, for a fee, some people are willing to take the risk and bet that prices will not move against them. These people are simply speculators. A second group of people who are willing to write options are insured against any losses that may arise. They are primarily dealers who engage in the regular purchase and sale of the underlying asset. These people are called *market makers* because they are always there to make the market. Because they are in the business of buying and selling, market makers both own the underlying asset so that they can deliver it and are willing to buy the underlying asset so that they have it ready to sell to someone else. If you own the underlying asset, writing a call option that obligates you to sell it at a fixed price is not that risky. These people write options to obtain the fee paid by the buyer.

Writing options can also generate clear benefits. To see how, think about the case of an electricity producer who has a plant that is worth operating only when electricity prices exceed a relatively high minimum level. Such peak-load plants are relatively common. They sit idle most of the time and are fired up only when demand is so high that prices spike. The problem is that when they are not operating—which is the normal state of affairs—the owner must pay maintenance charges. To cover these charges, the producer might choose to write a call option on electricity. Here's how the strategy works. For a fee, the plant owner sells a call option with a strike price that is higher than the price at which the plant will be brought online. The buyer of the call might be someone who uses electricity and wants insurance against a spike in prices. The option fee will cover the producer's maintenance cost while the plant is shut down. And, because the producer as option writer owns the underlying asset here—electricity—he or she is hedged against the possibility that the call option will pay off. As the price of electricity rises, the plant's revenue goes up with it.

Options are very versatile and can be bought and sold in many combinations. They allow investors to get rid of the risks they do not want and keep the ones they do want. In fact, options can be used to construct synthetic instruments that mimic the payoffs of virtually any other financial instrument. For example, the purchase of an at-the-money call and simultaneous sale of an at-the-money put gives the exact same payoff pattern as the purchase of a futures contract. If the price of the underlying asset rises, the call's value increases just as a futures contract does, while the put remains worthless. If the price falls, the put seller loses, just as a futures contract does, while the call is out of the money. Finally, options allow investors to bet that prices will be volatile. Buy a put and a call at the same strike price, and you have a bet that pays off only if the underlying asset price moves up or down significantly.

In summary, options are extremely useful. Remember the example at the beginning of the chapter, in which the snowmobile manufacturer Bombardier purchased insurance so it could offer its customers a rebate? What it bought were put options with a payoff tied to the amount of snow that fell. The puts promised payments in the event of low snowfall. This hedged the risk the company incurred when it offered rebates to the purchasers of its snowmobiles. The providers of this insurance, the sellers of the snowfall options, may have been betting that snowfall would not be low. That is, they may have been speculating—but not necessarily. After all, there are many companies whose sales and profits rise during warm weather and that are well positioned to take such a risk. Insurance companies, for instance, have lower claims during warm winters, because there are fewer accidents when there is less snow. If there is little snow, the insurance

Table 9.3 A Guide to Options

	Calls	Puts
Buyer	*Right* to *buy* the underlying asset at the strike price prior to or on the expiration date. "Hey, send it over!"	*Right* to *sell* the underlying asset at a fixed price prior to or on the expiration date. "Here it is; it's yours now!"
Seller (Writer)	*Obligation* to *sell* the underlying asset at the strike price prior to or on the expiration date.	*Obligation* to *buy* the underlying asset at the strike price prior to or on the expiration date.
Option is *in the money* when	Price of underlying asset is *above* the strike price of the call.	Price of underlying asset is *below* the strike price of the put.
Who *buys* one	Someone who: • Wants to *buy* an asset in the future and ensure the price paid will not *rise.* • Wants to bet that the price of the underlying asset will rise.	Someone who: • Wants to *sell* an asset in the future and ensure the price paid will not fall. • Wants to bet that the price of the underlying asset will fall.
Who *sells (writes)* one	• Someone who wants to bet that the market price of the underlying asset will *not* rise. • A broker who is always willing to sell the underlying asset and is paid to take the risk.	• Someone who wants to bet that the market price of the underlying asset will *not* fall. • A broker who is always willing to buy the underlying asset and is paid to take the risk.

company has the funds to make the payments, while if there is lots of snow, they can use the price they were paid to write the put to help pay the cost of the claims they face.[10]

Table 9.3 provides a summary of what options are, who buys and sells them, and why they do it.

Pricing Options: Intrinsic Value and the Time Value of the Option

An option price has two parts. The first is the value of the option if it is exercised immediately, and the second is the fee paid for the option's potential benefits. We will refer to the first of these, the value of the option if it is exercised immediately, as the *intrinsic value*. The second, the fee paid for the potential benefit from buying the option, we will call the **time value of the option** to emphasize its relationship to the time of the option's expiration. This means that

$$\text{Option price} = \text{Intrinsic value} + \text{Time value of the option}$$

As an example, before we launch into a discussion of option valuation in general, let's apply what we know about present value and risk analysis. Consider the example

[10]Bombardier purchased its snowfall insurance from Enron (prior to that company's bankruptcy). As it turned out, there was sufficient snowfall, so no payments were made either from Bombardier to the buyers of the snowmobiles or from Enron to Bombardier.

of an at-the-money European call option on the stock of XYZ Corporation that expires in one month. Recall that a European option can be exercised only at expiration and that an at-the-money option is one for which the current price equals the strike price. In this case, both equal $100. So, the intrinsic value of this call option is zero. To the extent that it has any value at all, that value resides entirely in the option's time value. Assume that, over the next month, the price of XYZ Corporation's stock will either rise or fall by $10 with equal probability. That is, there is a probability of ½ the price will go up to $110, and there is a probability of ½ it will fall to $90. What is the value of this call option?

To find the answer, we can compute the expected present value of the payoff. Let's assume that the interest rate is so low that we can ignore it. (If the payoff were postponed sufficiently far into the future or the interest rate were high enough, we could not ignore the present-value calculation but would have to divide by one plus the interest rate.) Now notice that the option is worth something only if the price goes up. In the event that XYZ's stock price falls to $90, you will allow the option to expire without exercising it. For a call option, then, we need to concern ourselves with the upside, and the expected value of that payoff is the probability, ½, times the payoff, $10, which is $5. This is the time value of the option.

Now think about what happens if, instead of rising or falling by $10, XYZ's stock will rise or fall by $20. This change increases the standard deviation of the stock price. In the terminology used in options trading, the stock price *volatility* has increased. Doing the same calculation, we see that the expected payoff is now $10. As the volatility of the stock price rises, the option's time value rises with it.

General Considerations In general, calculating the price of an option and how it might change means developing some rules for figuring out its intrinsic value and time value. We can do that using the framework from Chapter 3. Recall that the value of any financial instrument depends on four attributes: the size of the promised payment, the timing of the payment, the likelihood that the payment will be made, and the circumstances under which the payment will be made.[11] As we consider each of these, remember that the most important thing about an option is that the buyer is not obligated to exercise it. An option gives the buyer a choice! What this means is that someone holding an option will never make any additional payment to exercise it, so its value cannot be less than zero.

Because the options can either be exercised or expire worthless, we can conclude that the intrinsic value depends only on what the holder receives if the option is exercised. The intrinsic value is the difference between the price of the underlying asset and the strike price of the option. This is the *size of the payment* that the option represents, and it must be greater than or equal to zero—the intrinsic value cannot be negative. For an in-the-money call, or the option to buy, the intrinsic value to the holder (the long position) is the market price of the underlying asset minus the strike price. If the call is at the money or out of the money, it has no intrinsic value. Analogously, the intrinsic value of a put, or the option to sell, equals the strike price minus the market price of the underlying asset, or zero, whichever is greater.

TIME

At expiration, the value of an option equals its intrinsic value. But what about prior to expiration? To think about this question, consider an at-the-money option—one whose

[11]Because the pricing of European options is easier to understand, we will talk about options as if they can be exercised only at the expiration date. The principles for pricing American options are the same, however.

Should You Accept Options as Part of Your Pay?

YOUR FINANCIAL WORLD

What if someone offers you a job in return for a salary and stock options? Should you take it? Before you do, ask questions! Let's look at what you need to know. Many firms that offer options on their own stock to employees view the options as a substitute for wages. Employees receive call options that give them the right to purchase the company's stock at a fixed price. The strike price is usually set at the current market price of the stock, so that when employees receive the options, they are at the money. Normally, the expiration date is from 1 to 10 years in the future. Because the options are long-term, they will have substantial value, as measured by the option's time value. But there is a catch. Employees generally are not allowed to sell them and may need to remain with the firm to exercise them.

Nevertheless, the price of the company's stock could skyrocket, so the options may bring a substantial payoff. To take an extreme example, from January 1991 to January 2000, Microsoft's stock price rose from $2 to $116 per share. An employee with 1,000 options to purchase the stock at $2 would have made $114,000 by exercising them. Though Microsoft employees were winners, there are many losers in the options game. Employees holding options to purchase stock in General Motors or Lehman, both of which went bankrupt in 2008, got nothing.

So what should you do? If taking the options means accepting a lower salary, then you are paying for them, and you should think hard before you take the offer. Stock options are almost like lottery tickets, but with a drawing that may not occur for years. They give you a small chance to make a large profit. But investing in the same company that pays your salary is a risky business. If the company goes broke or you lose your job, the options will be worthless to you. So think hard before you trade a high-paying job for a lower-paying job with options.

intrinsic value is zero. Prior to expiration, there is always the chance that the price of the underlying asset will move so as to make the option valuable. This potential benefit is represented by the option's time value. *The longer the time to expiration,* the bigger the likely payoff when the option does expire and, thus, the more valuable it is. Remember that the option payoff is asymmetric, so what is important is the chance of making profit. In the last example, think about what will happen if the option expires in three months instead of one and the stock price has an equal probability of rising or falling $10 each month. The expected payoff rises from $5 (for the one-month call option) to $7.50 (for the three-month call option). (Over three months, the stock can either rise by $30 with probability ⅛, rise by $10 with probability ⅜, fall by $10 with probability ⅜, or fall by $30 with probability ⅛. When the price falls, the call option is not exercised, so the expected value of the three-month call is ⅛ × $30 + ⅜ × $10 = $7.50.)

The likelihood that an option will pay off depends on the volatility, or standard deviation, of the price of the underlying asset. To see this, consider an option on Apple stock that is currently at the money—one with a strike price that equals the current price of the stock. The chance of this option being in the money by the time it expires increases with the volatility of Apple's stock price. Think about an option on an asset whose price is simply fixed—that is, whose standard deviation is zero. This option will never pay off, so no one would be willing to pay for it. Add some variability to the price, however, and there is a chance that the price will rise, moving the option into the money. That is something people will pay for. Thus, the option's time value increases with the volatility of the price of the underlying asset. Taking this analysis one step further, we know that regardless of how far the price of the underlying asset falls, the holder of a call option cannot lose more. In contrast, whenever the price rises higher, the call option increases in value. Increased volatility has no cost to the option holder, only benefits.

Table 9.4 Factors Affecting the Value of Options

Option value = Intrinsic value + Time value

Increase in One Factor, Holding All Others Fixed	Call (the right to buy)	Put (the right to sell)
Increase in the strike price	Decrease (intrinsic value falls)	Increase (intrinsic value rises)
Increase in the market price of the underlying asset	Increase (intrinsic value rises)	Decrease (intrinsic value falls)
Increase in the time to expiration	Increase (time value rises)	Increase (time value rises)
Increase in the volatility of the underlying asset price	Increase (time value rises)	Increase (time value rises)

We have emphasized that options provide insurance, allowing investors to hedge particular risks. The bigger the risk being insured, the more valuable the insurance, and the higher the price investors will pay. Thus, *the circumstances under which the payment is made* have an important impact on the option's time value. Table 9.4 summarizes the factors that affect the value of options.

The Value of Options: Some Examples

To see how options are valued, we can examine a simple example. The daily news reports the prices of options that are traded on organized exchanges. Table 9.5 shows the prices of Apple's puts and calls on March 21, 2019, as reported on the website of *The Wall Street Journal.* Panel A shows the prices of options with different strike prices but the same expiration date, June 21, 2019. Panel B shows the prices of options with different expiration dates but the same strike price. From the top of the table we can see that the price of Apple's stock, the underlying asset on which these options were written, was $195.09 per share at the close of that day.

By examining the table, we can discover the following:

- At a given price of the underlying asset and time to expiration, the higher the strike price of a call option, the lower its intrinsic value and the less expensive the option. That is, as you read down the column labeled "Strike Price" in Panel A, the intrinsic value under "Calls" (Apple stock price minus the strike price) falls. For example, as the strike price goes from $190 to $195, the intrinsic value falls from $5.09 to $0.09.
- At a given price of the underlying asset and time to expiration, the higher the strike price of a put option, the higher the intrinsic value and the more expensive the option. (See the "Intrinsic Value" column for puts in Panel A.) As the strike price rises from $200 to $205, the intrinsic value of the Apple put (the strike price minus the Apple stock price) rises from $4.91 to $9.91.
- The closer the strike price is to the current price of the underlying asset, the larger the option's time value. (See the two columns in Panel A labeled "Time Value of Call" and "Time Value of Put.") For a call option with a strike price of $195 and an intrinsic value of $0.09, the time value is $9.76. As the strike price goes down to $190, the time value falls to $7.56.
- Deep in-the-money options have lower time value (see the time value of the calls in Panel A). Because a deep in-the-money call option is very likely to

Table 9.5 Prices of Apple Puts and Calls
At the close on Thursday, March 21, 2019
Apple stock price close = $195.09

A. June 21 Expiration

	Calls			Puts		
Strike Price	**Call Price**	**Intrinsic Value**	**Time Value of Call**	**Put Price**	**Intrinsic Value**	**Time Value of Put**
185.00	$15.70	$10.09	$5.61	$4.96	$0.00	$4.96
190.00	12.65	5.09	7.56	6.75	0.00	6.75
195.00	9.85	0.09	9.76	8.95	0.00	8.95
200.00	7.45	0.00	7.45	11.50	4.91	6.59
205.00	5.50	0.00	5.50	14.70	9.91	4.79
210.00	4.00	0.00	4.00	17.60	14.91	2.69

B. Strike Price of 195

	Calls			Puts		
Expiration Date	**Call Price**	**Intrinsic Value**	**Time Value of Call**	**Put Price**	**Intrinsic Value**	**Time Value of Put**
Apr 26	6.40	0.09	6.31	5.05	0.00	5.05
Jun 21	9.85	0.09	9.76	8.58	0.00	8.58
Sep 20	14.08	0.09	13.99	12.20	0.00	12.20

Intrinsic value of a call = Stock price − Strike price, or zero, whichever is larger

Intrinsic value of a put = Strike price − Stock price, or zero, whichever is larger

Time value of the option = Option price − Intrinsic value

NOTE: Prices are averages of bids and asks.

SOURCE: *The Wall Street Journal,* March 21, 2019. Used with permission of Dow Jones & Company, Inc. via Copyright Clearance Center. http://quotes.wsj.com/AAPL/options

expire in the money, buying one is much like buying the stock itself. Note that the call with a strike price of $185 and an intrinsic value of $10.09 has a time value of $5.61, much less than the $9.76 time value of a call with an intrinsic value of $0.09.

- The longer the time to expiration at a given strike price, the higher the option price. Looking at the prices of both puts and calls in Panel B of Table 9.5, you can see that as you read down those columns and the time to expiration rises, the price goes up with it. That is because the option's time value is going up. A $195 Apple call that expires in April sells for $6.40, while the price of one that expires five months later sells for $14.08. The same rule applies to puts.

Swaps

Like other derivatives, swaps are contracts that allow traders to transfer risks. Swaps come in numerous varieties. We will study two types: *Interest rate swaps* allow one swap party—for a fee—to alter the stream of payments it makes or receives. Interest rate swaps have been used widely for decades to synchronize receipts and payments. *Credit default swaps (CDS)* are more recent. CDS are a form of insurance that allow a

What Was Long-Term Capital Management Doing?
APPLYING THE CONCEPT

From mid-August to late September 1998, Long-Term Capital Management (LTCM), a *hedge fund* based in Greenwich, Connecticut, lost more than $2.5 billion, placing itself in danger of default. (For a detailed description of hedge funds, see the Tools of the Trade box in Chapter 13.) The prospect of LTCM's failure struck fear into world financial markets, prompting the Federal Reserve Bank of New York to form a group of 14 banks and investment companies to purchase the company. How did so much wealth disappear so fast, and why did so many people care? Until the crisis of 2007–2009, there was no comparable case in which the financial community was so desperate to avoid a bankruptcy.

The answer is that LTCM had engaged in a large number of complex speculative transactions, including interest rate swaps and options writing, which all failed simultaneously. One of the bets LTCM had made was based on the belief that interest rate spreads would shrink. Following the Russian government bond default on August 17, 1998, financial market participants' willingness to take on risk declined dramatically, so the risk premium exploded. (Recall the discussion of this episode in Chapter 6.) As a result, the spread between corporate bonds and U.S. Treasury bonds grew in a way that had not recently occurred. LTCM lost billions. While the interest rate spread did eventually shrink, so that the bets LTCM had made paid off in the long run, marking to market drove the fund bankrupt.

The really scary part of this episode was that many of the transactions LTCM had engaged in involved instruments that could not easily be resold. The most amazing discovery was the $1¼ trillion (yes, trillion) in interest rate swaps. Granted, this was a notional principal of all the transactions added together, but the problem is that swaps are individualized, bilateral transactions. The fact that LTCM was willing to make a swap agreement with a particular counterparty was no guarantee that some other party would. Thus, a normal bankruptcy settlement, in which assets are sold off in the marketplace and the proceeds given to the failed company's creditors, was not an option. LTCM's failure would mean it could not honor its side of the agreements, which would mean the counterparties would not be able to honor their own agreements, creating a cascade of failure. Its collapse would jeopardize the entire financial system. Large banks, insurance companies, pension funds, and mutual fund companies with whom LTCM did business were at risk of being bankrupted themselves.

In short, while one person's derivatives loss is another's gain, the system works only if the winners can collect. In this case, the Federal Reserve had no choice but to step in and ensure that the financial system remained sound. LTCM was essentially sold to its creditors—the banks from which it had borrowed—and then closed down about a year later.*

*For a detailed history of the rise and fall of Long-Term Capital Management, see Roger Lowenstein, *When Genius Failed* (New York: Random House, 2000).

buyer to own a bond or mortgage without bearing its default risk. We will see that CDS played an important role in the financial crisis of 2007–2009 and were also a factor in the euro-area crisis that began in 2010.

Interest Rate Swaps

Government debt managers—the people at the U.S. Treasury who decide when and how to issue U.S. Treasury bonds, notes, and bills—do their best to keep public borrowing costs as low as possible. That means (a) selling bonds at the lowest interest rates possible and (b) ensuring that government revenues will be available when payments must be made. Because of the structure of financial markets, keeping interest costs low usually is not a problem. Demand for long-term government bonds is high. (They are used as collateral in many financial transactions.) Thus, government debt managers can sell them at relatively high prices. Selling long-term debt also limits rollover risk if future investors come to doubt the government's willingness or ability to repay.

Managing government revenues is more of a challenge. Revenues tend to rise during economic booms and fall during recessions. Even if tax revenues fall, the government must still make its bond payments. Short-term interest rates, like tax revenues, tend to move with the business cycle, rising during booms and falling during recessions (see Chapter 21). Ensuring that future interest expenses match future tax revenues might be easier if government borrowers issued short-term bonds.

This difficulty leaves the public debt manager in a quandary. Which is more important, keeping interest costs and rollover risk down by issuing long-term debt or matching costs with tax revenues by issuing short-term debt? Fortunately, derivatives allow government debt managers to meet both these goals using a tool called an interest rate swap.

Understanding Interest Rate Swaps **Interest rate swaps** are agreements between two counterparties to exchange periodic interest rate payments over some future period, based on an agreed-upon amount of principal—what's called the **notional principal**. The term *notional* is used here because the principal of a **swap** is not borrowed, lent, or exchanged; it just serves as the basis for calculation of the periodic cash flows between the counterparties to the swap. In the simplest type of interest rate swap, one party agrees to make payments based on a fixed interest rate, and in exchange the counterparty agrees to make payments based on a floating interest rate. The effect of this agreement is to transform fixed-rate payments into floating-rate payments and vice versa. For example, as we write in 2019, the conventional five-year swap rate is the rate paid for five years by the fixed-rate payer in return for receiving floating payments of three-month LIBOR.[12]

Figure 9.1 shows a typical interest rate swap. A bank agrees to make payments to a swap dealer at a fixed interest rate, say, 7 percent, in exchange for payments based on a floating rate determined in the market. Both payments are based on the same

Figure 9.1 An Interest Rate Swap Agreement

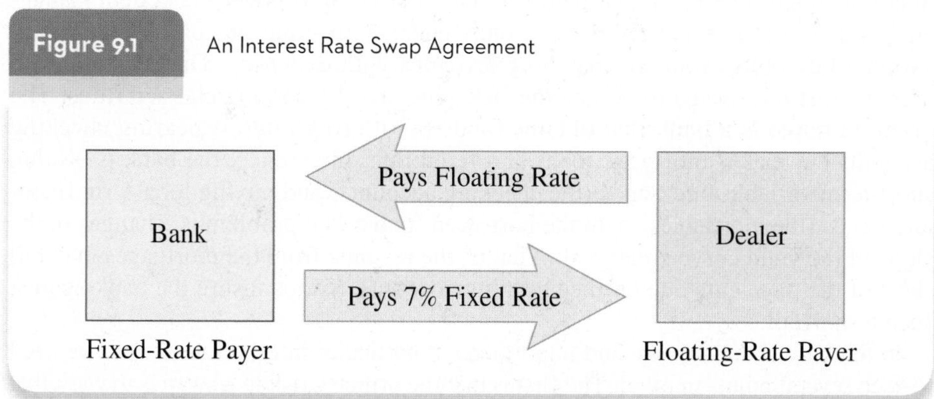

The bank agrees to pay a fixed rate to the swap dealer in exchange for payments based on a floating rate. The fixed-rate payments match the bank's loan income, while the floating-rate payments match the payments promised to the bank's deposit holders.

[12]The London Interbank Offered Rate (LIBOR), the rate at which banks in London make short-term loans to each other, often serves as the floating rate. LIBOR is expected to disappear as an interest rate benchmark after 2021. In that case, the industry will substitute a different short-term rate. (See Chapter 13 page 335.)

agreed-upon principal, say $100 million. That is, the notional principal on the swap is $100 million. The bank is the **fixed-rate payer** and the swap dealer is the **floating-rate payer**. Put slightly differently, the two parties enter into a series of forward agreements in which they agree today to exchange interest payments on a series of future dates for the life of the swap. As in a futures contract, no payment is made at the outset.

Now let's return to the government debt manager's problem. Remember that the government can issue long-term debt cheaply but its revenues tend to fluctuate with the short-term interest rate, going up when short-term interest rates rise and down when they fall. The solution is to sell long-term bonds and then enter into an interest rate swap. The government becomes the floating-rate payer for the term of the bonds.

Pricing and Using Interest Rate Swaps Pricing interest rate swaps means figuring out the fixed interest rate to be paid. To do so, financial firms begin by noting the market interest rate on a U.S. Treasury bond of the same maturity as the swap, called the *benchmark*. The rate to be paid by the fixed-rate payer, called the *swap rate*, will be the benchmark rate plus a premium. The difference between the benchmark rate and the swap rate, called the **swap spread**, is a measure of risk: For example, the spread of the 10-year swap rate over the 10-year Treasury bond yield averaged about ¼ percentage point during the 10 years through 2015. In recent years, the swap spread has attracted substantial attention as a measure of systematic risk, or overall risk in the economy (see Chapter 5). When it widens, it signals that general economic conditions are deteriorating.[13]

Interest rate swaps are just one example of the exchange of future payoffs. Investors engage in a wide variety of swaps involving foreign exchange and equities, though interest rate swaps are the most important. By one estimate, by mid-2018, the notional value of interest rate swaps worldwide was $350 trillion—more than 13 times the total of foreign currency swaps at the time.[14]

Who uses all these interest rate swaps? Two groups have a comparative advantage in issuing bonds of a particular maturity. The first group is government debt managers, who find long-term fixed-rate bonds cheaper to issue but prefer short-term variable-rate obligations for matching revenues with expenses. The second group uses interest rate swaps to reduce the risk generated by commercial activities. The prime example is a bank that obtains funds by offering interest-bearing checking accounts but makes mortgage loans at a fixed rate. In essence, the bank is issuing short-term variable-rate bonds (the checking accounts) and buying long-term fixed-rate bonds (the mortgages) with the borrowed funds. The problem is, changes in the slope of the yield curve create risk. That is, the revenue from the mortgages may fall short of the payments due on the checking accounts. Swaps insure the bank against such a shortfall.

In thinking about the size and importance of particular interest rate swaps, we need to keep several points in mind. The first is that the primary risk in a swap is the risk that one of the parties will default. Aside from a major financial crisis, that risk is not very

[13]However, the information content of swap spreads can change for a variety of reasons. For example, when they turned negative in late 2015, the likely cause was an increase in bank capital requirements that made certain types of trading more costly. For a detailed description, see Nina Boyarchenko, Pooja Gupta, Nick Steele, and Jacqueline Yen, "Negative Swap Spreads," *Economic Policy Review of the Federal Reserve Bank of New York* 25, no. 20 (October 2018).

[14]Data on interest rate swaps are collected and regularly published by the Bank for International Settlements in Basel, Switzerland. For recent information, see its website, www.bis.org.

The VIX: The Thing to Fear Is the *Lack* of Fear Itself

MONEY AND BANKING BLOG

The VIX (https://fred.stlouisfed.org/series/VIXCLS) has been called the *fear index*. It is a measure of the uncertainty and risk that investors see over the near future (specifically, the next 30 days). Constructed from options on S&P 500 Index futures, the VIX is technically a gauge of what is called implied volatility.*

The technicalities are not all that important, as the VIX and similar options-based measures of implied volatility track financial conditions pretty well. When implied volatility is low, stock market liquidity and valuations are usually high; when implied volatility is high, stock trading is more difficult and valuations suffer.

But why, then, do people worry when the VIX stays low for a long time? The concern is that unusually low volatility *breeds* risk. The logic goes like this: When implied volatility is high, investors are cautious because there is a great deal of uncertainty about the future. Conversely, when implied volatility is low, investors are confident that the likelihood of big moves in asset prices is low. Being more confident, investors are willing to take greater risk—to pay a higher price for small expected gains—because they see little downside. We call that kind of risk taking "reaching for yield."

Put differently, low volatility causes complacency. When investors underestimate market risks, the prices of risky assets rise to levels that are unwarranted by fundamentals. Lofty asset prices can plummet when events prompt investors to reassess risk. When that happens, both actual and expected volatility typically surge, causing investors to become cautious in unison.

During 2005 and 2006, before the financial crisis, the VIX fluctuated in a narrow range somewhat above 10, but it remained low—well below the 20-year average of 19.8. In October 2008, however, at the peak of the crisis, it jumped to a record above 80!

To see how the low, precrisis level of implied volatility might have made the financial system vulnerable, consider the following example: suppose that financial institutions target a certain level of risk in their portfolio of assets. Measures of portfolio risk—like the widely used "value at risk" (VaR) gauge—are *positively* related to volatility. Consequently, when intermediaries expect volatility to be unusually *low*, maintaining the targeted VaR requires that they *add* to the riskiness of their portfolios. They can do this in various ways, including by raising leverage, extending maturity transformation, and purchasing assets with a higher probability of default.

When volatility suddenly rises—as it did in the financial crisis—these intermediaries try to "de-risk" their portfolios. That means reducing leverage, reducing maturity transformation, and selling high-risk assets. Importantly, if everyone does this at the same time, as often happens when volatility jumps, their actions can trigger a "fire sale," pushing down prices and reducing capital in the financial system. This *procyclical* behavior amplifies the stock market boom–bust cycle and is very destabilizing.

Reflecting the experience of the financial crisis, both investors and policymakers now associate periods of very low volatility with a destabilizing reach for yield. For example, in her June 2014 press conference, Federal Reserve Chair Janet Yellen linked them directly: "to the extent that low levels of volatility may induce risk-taking behavior that, for example, entails [an] excessive buildup in leverage or maturity extension, things that can pose risk to financial stability later on, that is a concern."

Central banks don't claim to know when the level of volatility is "just right." Indeed, no particular level of expected volatility will always be optimal. But monetary policymakers do know that keeping interest rates low for a long time tends to stimulate the economy at least partly because it depresses expected volatility and encourages investors to take risks.

A crucial question for policymakers and investors alike is, when do policies to suppress volatility go too far? That is, when does the resulting risk of financial instability start to outweigh the potential gain from boosting output? The VIX can't answer that question, but it is a useful warning about complacency.

*Option-pricing models (like the classic Black-Scholes model) deliver a measure of future expected risk—called implied volatility because it is implied by the model—calculated from the risk-free interest rate, the price of the underlying asset, and the key attributes of the option, namely, its market price, strike price, and maturity. The model-implied volatility is the expected annualized standard deviation of the price of the underlying asset.

high because the other side can enter into another agreement to replace the one that failed. (The case of Long-Term Capital Management, described in Applying the Concept on page 228, is a notable exception when widespread default became a real possibility.) Second, unlike futures and options, swaps are not traded on organized exchanges; they are bilateral agreements between two financial intermediaries. For various reasons, a bank that enters into a swap agreement with another bank may not want to make the same kind of arrangement with a pension fund. Thus, swaps are very difficult to resell.

Credit Default Swaps

On September 16, 2008, the Federal Reserve Bank of New York, part of the U.S. central bank, made an extraordinary $85 billion loan to American International Group (AIG). AIG, the largest insurance company in the world, was on the verge of collapse because it had sold several hundred billion dollars' worth of **credit default swaps (CDS)**.

A CDS is a *credit derivative* that allows lenders to insure themselves against the risk that a borrower will default. The buyer of a CDS makes payments—like insurance premiums—to the seller, and the seller agrees to pay the buyer *if* an underlying loan or security defaults. The CDS buyer pays a fee to transfer the risk of default—the credit risk—to the CDS seller.

Using CDS, a lender can make a loan without facing the possibility of default. By combining a loan with a CDS to insure against default, a lender who is good at identifying attractive loan opportunities and collecting the loan payments can function efficiently, while letting someone else worry about the default risk. This division of labor can improve resource allocation.

A CDS agreement often lasts several years and requires that collateral be posted to protect against the inability to pay of either the seller or the buyer of the insurance. For example, the seller provides collateral to ensure that the buyer will be paid in the event that the underlying loan or security defaults and the seller is unable to pay. The collateral for a CDS varies with the credit rating of the seller and buyer.

The market for CDS expanded astronomically in the years before the financial crisis of 2007–2009 but then shrank rapidly. The volume of CDS (based on the initial value of the underlying assets), which was about $6 trillion at the end of 2004, soared to $58 trillion at the end of 2007 before plunging to $33 trillion two years later. By mid-2018, it had fallen below $8.5 trillion.

CDS contributed to the financial crisis in three important ways: (1) fostering uncertainty about who bears the credit risk on a given loan or security, (2) making the leading CDS sellers mutually vulnerable, and (3) making it easier for sellers of insurance to assume and conceal risk.

Financial institutions do not report the amount of their CDS purchases and sales, so their depositors or investors do not know how much risk they bear. This loss of transparency makes the financial system more vulnerable to a shock that threatens trust in counterparties.

Because CDS contracts are traded over the counter (OTC), even traders cannot identify others who take on concentrated positions on one side of a trade. As a result, CDS dealers—typically the largest financial institutions—are collectively exposed to a failure by any weak dealer, much like a train can go off the tracks when one flimsy car derails. When you read the phrase "too interconnected to fail" in the financial news, think of the mutual—but hidden—vulnerabilities of the large CDS vendors. So long as CDS trading lacks transparency, the lingering worry is that a failure of one institution could bring down the financial system as a whole (see Lessons from the Crisis: Central Counterparties and Systemic Risk on page 217).

As noted earlier, derivatives used properly can improve the allocation of risk and foster healthy risk taking. It follows that undermining the credibility of derivative contracts can have a damaging impact. The euro-area crisis that began in

September 2010 presents a notable example. Having observed the U.S. crisis, euro-area policymakers feared that a chaotic default on Greek sovereign debt would lead to a catastrophic financial disruption. Consequently, they hoped to restructure Greek debt without a legal "event of default" that would trigger large CDS payouts.

As an unintended consequence, however, their actions encouraged doubt about the value of CDS as insurance, making banks and others even less willing to hold the debt of other weak euro-area sovereigns (e.g., Ireland, Italy, Portugal, and Spain), not just Greece. Uncertainty encouraged banks to shrink their balance sheets, adding to downward pressure on credit supply and the economy at a delicate stage of the crisis. Eventually, Greece's default prompted a CDS payout without augmenting the crisis, but doubts about CDS and other means of hedging (such as short selling) probably had already added to the turmoil.

Key Terms

American option, 220
arbitrage, 218
call option, 219
central counterparty (CCP), 217
credit default swap (CDS), 232
derivatives, 212
European option, 220
fixed-rate payer, 230
floating-rate payer, 230
forward, 213
forward contract, 213
future, 213
futures contract, 213
interest rate swap, 229
margin, 215
notional principal, 229
put option, 220
strike price, 219
swap, 229
swap spread, 230
time value of the option, 223

Using FRED: Codes for Data in This Chapter

Data Series	FRED Data Code
5-year U.S. swap rate	ICERATES1100USD5Y
5-year U.S. Treasury yield	GS5
10-year U.S. Treasury yield	GS10
Central bank liquidity swaps held by Federal Reserve	SWPT
CBOE Volatility Index: VIX	VIXCLS
Wilshire 5000 price index	WILL5000PR
St. Louis Fed Financial Stress Index	STLFSI

Chapter Lessons

To learn more about the changing financial system, visit www.moneyandbanking.com.

1. Derivatives transfer risk from one person or firm to another. They can be used in any combination to unbundle risks and resell them.
2. Futures contracts are standardized contracts for the delivery of a specified quantity of a commodity or financial instrument on a prearranged future date, at an

agreed-upon price. They are a bet on the movement in the price of the underlying asset on which they are written, whether it is a commodity or a financial instrument.

a. Futures contracts are used both to decrease risk, which is called hedging, and to increase risk, which is called speculating.
b. The futures clearing corporation, as the counterparty to all futures contracts, guarantees the performance of both the buyer and the seller.
c. Participants in the futures market must establish a margin account with the clearing corporation and make a deposit that ensures they will meet their obligations.
d. Futures prices are marked to market daily, as if the contracts were sold and repurchased every day.
e. Because no payment is made when a futures contract is initiated, the transaction allows an investor to create a large amount of leverage at a very low cost.
f. The prices of futures contracts are determined by arbitrage within the market for immediate delivery of the underlying asset.

3. Options give the buyer (option holder) a right and the seller (option writer) an obligation to buy or sell an underlying asset at a predetermined price on or before a fixed future date.
   a. A call option gives the holder the right to buy the underlying asset.
   b. A put option gives the holder the right to sell the underlying asset.
   c. Options can be used both to reduce risk through hedging and to speculate.
   d. The option price equals the sum of its intrinsic value, which is the value if the option is exercised, plus the time value of the option.
   e. The intrinsic value depends on the strike price of the option and the price of the underlying asset on which the option is written.
   f. The time value of the option depends on the time to expiration and the volatility in the price of the underlying asset.
4. Interest rate swaps are agreements between two parties to exchange a fixed for a variable interest rate payment over a future period.
   a. The fixed rate payer in a swap typically pays the U.S. Treasury bond rate plus a risk premium.
   b. The flexible-rate payer in a swap normally pays the London Interbank Offered Rate (LIBOR).
   c. Interest rate swaps are useful when a government, firm, or investment company can borrow more cheaply at one maturity but would prefer to borrow at a different maturity.
   d. Swaps can be based on an agreed-upon exchange of any two future sequences of payments.
5. Credit default swaps (CDS) are a form of insurance in which the buyer of the insurance makes payments (like insurance premiums) to the seller, who in turn agrees to pay the buyer if an underlying loan or security defaults.
   a. A CDS agreement often lasts several years and requires that collateral be posted to protect against the inability to pay of the seller or the buyer of insurance.
   b. If financial institutions do not report CDS sales and purchases, it is not clear who bears credit risk on a given loan or security.
   c. When CDS are traded over the counter, even traders cannot identify others who take on concentrated risks on one side of a trade.
6. Derivatives allow firms to arbitrarily divide up and rename risks and future payments, rendering their actual names irrelevant.

Conceptual and Analytical Problems connect

1. An agreement to lease a car can be thought of as a set of derivative contracts. Describe them. *(LO2)*
2. How is entering into a forward contract similar to barter? Can you think of costs associated with forward contracts that are minimized or eliminated with futures contracts? *(LO2)*
3. The E-mini S&P 500 futures contract is one-fifth the size of the standard futures contract and can be traded on the 24-hour CME Globex electronic trading system. What might be some of the advantages of a futures contract with these properties? *(LO1)*
4. A hedger buys a futures contract, taking a long position in the wheat futures market. What are the hedger's obligations under this contract? Describe the risk that is hedged in this transaction, and give an example of someone who might enter into such an arrangement. *(LO1)*
5. A futures contract based on a payment of $250 times the S&P 500 Index is traded on the Chicago Mercantile Exchange. At an index level of 1,000 or more, the contract calls for a payment of over $250,000. It is settled by a cash payment between the buyer and the seller. Who are the hedgers and who are the speculators in the S&P 500 futures market? *(LO1)*
6. Explain why trading derivatives on centralized exchanges rather than in over-the-counter markets helps reduce systemic risk. Can you think of a way in which more trading on centralized exchanges might increase risk? *(LO1)*
7. What are the risks and rewards of writing and buying options? Are there any circumstances under which you would get involved? Why or why not? (*Hint:* Think of a case in which you own shares of the stock on which you are considering writing a call.) *(LO3)*
8. Suppose XYZ Corporation's stock price rises or falls with equal probability by $30 each month, starting where it ended the previous month. What is the value of a three-month at-the-money European call option on XYZ's stock if the stock is priced at $100 when the option is purchased? *(LO3)*

9.* Why might a borrower who wishes to make fixed interest rate payments and who has access to both fixed- and floating-rate loans still benefit from becoming a party to a fixed-for-floating interest rate swap? *(LO4)*

10. Concerned about possible disruptions of the supply of oil from the Middle East, the chief financial officer (CFO) of American Airlines would like to hedge the risk of an increase in the price of jet fuel. What tools could the CFO use to hedge this risk? *(LO3)*

11.* How does the existence of derivatives markets enhance an economy's ability to grow? *(LO1)*

12. Credit default swaps provide a means to insure against default risk and require the posting of collateral by buyers and sellers. Explain how these "safe-sounding" derivative products contributed to the 2007–2009 financial crisis. *(LO4)*

*Indicates more difficult problems.

13. What kind of an option should you purchase if you anticipate selling $1 million of Treasury bonds in one year's time and wish to hedge against the risk of interest rates rising? *(LO3)*

14. You sell a bond futures contract and, one day later, the clearinghouse informs you that it had credited funds to your margin account. What happened to interest rates over that day? *(LO2)*

15. You are completely convinced that the price of copper is going to rise significantly over the next year and want to take as large a position as you can in the market but have limited funds. How could you use the futures market to leverage your position? *(LO2)*

16. Suppose copper is selling at $3 a pound and the margin requirement for a futures contract for 25,000 pounds of copper is $8,000. *(LO2)*
    a. Calculate your return if you purchase one copper futures contract and copper prices rise to $3.10 a pound.
    b. How does this compare with the return you would have made if you had simply purchased $8,000 worth of copper and sold it a year later?
    c. Compare the risk involved in each of these strategies.

17. Suppose you were the manager of a bank that raised most of its funds from short-term variable-rate deposits and used these funds to make fixed-rate mortgage loans. Should you be more concerned about rises or falls in short-term interest rates? How could you use interest rate swaps to hedge against the interest rate risk you face? *(LO4)*

18.* The following table shows the interest rates on the fixed and floating borrowing choices available to three firms. Firms A and B want to be exposed to a floating interest rate while Firm C would prefer to pay a fixed interest rate. Which pair(s) of firms (if any) should borrow in the market they do not want and then enter into a fixed-for-floating interest rate swap? *(LO4)*

	Fixed Rate	Floating Rate
Firm A	7%	LIBOR + 50 bps
Firm B	12%	LIBOR + 150 bps
Firm C	10%	LIBOR + 150 bps

NOTE: LIBOR, which stands for London Interbank Offered Rate, is a floating interest rate that serves as a reference rate. It is expected to be replaced after 2021.

19. Suppose, prior to the European financial crisis, you were considering investing in Greek Government bonds but had some concerns about the creditworthiness of the Greek Government. Why, despite your concerns, might you still make such an investment? *(LO1, LO4)*

20. You and a colleague both follow the movements of the VIX, an index based on options prices that reflects investors' expectations for stock market volatility. Suppose, according to the VIX, implied volatility is expected to be low for a protracted period. Your colleague sees this as unambiguously good news. Why might you disagree? *(LO3)*

*Indicates more difficult problems.

Data Exploration connect

For detailed instructions on using Federal Reserve Economic Data (FRED) online to answer each of the following problems, visit www.mhhe.com/moneyandbanking6e *and refer to FRED Resources and Data Exploration Hints.*

1. Central banks occasionally engage in "liquidity swaps" with each other. Plot and interpret the Fed's provision of dollar liquidity swaps (FRED code: SWPT) to other central banks since 2007. To facilitate your interpretation, view the FRED "Notes" about this data series. *(LO4)*
2. Define the five-year swap rate and then plot it (FRED code: ICERATES1100USD5Y). Describe how and when parties might use the swap rate. *(LO4)*
3. Risk-averse investors care greatly about asset price volatility. Using the FRED "Notes" about the data series, briefly define the VIX Volatility Index (FRED code: VIXCLS) of the Chicago Board Options Exchange (CBOE). Plot monthly since 2004 the VIX and the percent change from a year ago of the Wilshire 5000 stock market index (FRED code: WILL5000PR). Interpret the graph. *(LO3)*
4. Is the VIX volatility index (FRED code: VIXCLS) an indicator of broader financial market volatility? Using weekly data ending on Fridays, plot from 1994 the VIX, with its scale on the left axis, and the St. Louis Federal Reserve Bank index of financial stress (FRED code: STLFSI), with its scale on the right axis. Describe the financial stress index and comment on how closely related it is to the VIX. *(LO3)*

Chapter

10 Foreign Exchange

Learning Objectives

After reading this chapter, you should be able to:

LO1 Distinguish real and nominal exchange rates.

LO2 Explain how prices and inflation affect exchange rates in the long run.

LO3 Analyze the supply of and demand for currencies to explain exchange rates in the short run.

LO4 Discuss government intervention in foreign exchange markets.

Every year, moving goods and services around the globe becomes easier. Currently, the volume of international transactions (summing exports and imports of goods and services) amounts to more than one-half of world GDP. Today, Americans buy cell phones and clothing made in China, computers assembled in Singapore, and fruit grown in Chile. But global business deals aren't limited to goods and services. Individuals, companies, and governments also invest abroad, buying and selling stocks and bonds in financial markets around the globe. The magnitude of the international flow of goods, services, and assets is impossible to ignore. To understand the nature of these transactions, we must become familiar with a key tool that makes this trade possible: *exchange rates.*

Whenever you buy something that has been made abroad, whether it is an article of clothing, a car, a stock, or a bond, someone somewhere has exchanged dollars for the currency used where the item was made. The reason is simple: You want to use dollars to pay for an imported shirt that you buy in a local store, but the Malaysian producer wants to be paid in *ringgit*. All cross-border transactions are like this; the buyer and seller both want to use their own currency. The exchange rate, at its most basic level, is the tool we use to measure the price of one currency in terms of another.

Exchange rates have broad implications both for countries and for individuals. Take the case of South Korea in the winter of 1998. As economic and financial turmoil spread through Asia starting in the summer of 1997, output and employment plunged. In Korea, large industrial companies and financial institutions approached bankruptcy. From October 1997 to January 1998, the number of South Korean *won* needed to purchase one dollar more than doubled, rising from 900 to 1,900 (see Figure 10.1). The consequences were dramatic, both inside and outside the country. When the cost of buying the won plummeted, South Korean products became much cheaper for

Figure 10.1 South Korean Won-Dollar Exchange Rate, 1997-2000

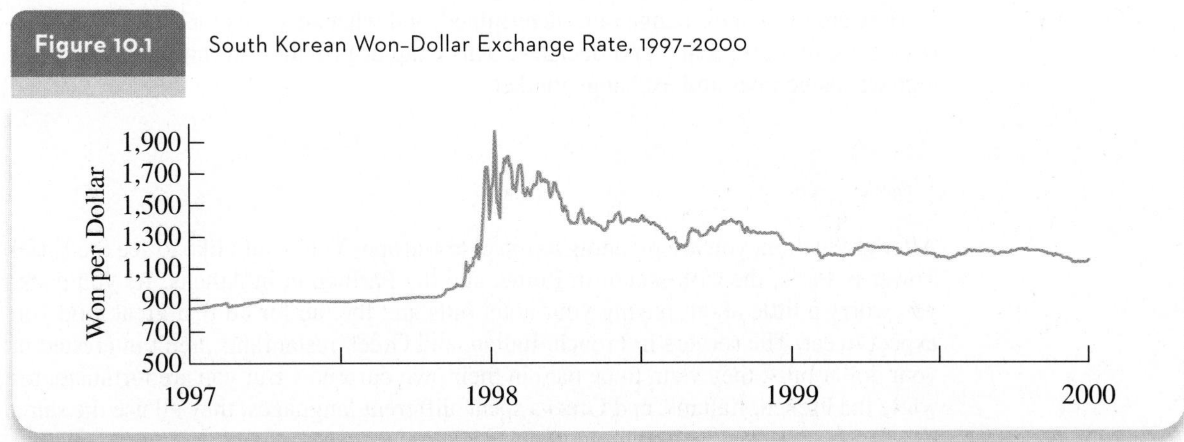

SOURCE: Federal Reserve Bank of St. Louis (FRED data code: EXKOUS).

foreigners to buy. As the value of the won dropped, the U.S. prices of Hyundai cars and Samsung televisions fell with it. At the same time, U.S.-made products became extremely expensive for South Koreans to buy. In fact, the crisis became so severe that many Korean students at U.S. colleges and universities had to go home. The price of a U.S. education, measured in won, had doubled, and many Korean students just couldn't afford to continue.

Exchange rates go through long swings as well as sudden spikes. In 1973, the currency used in the United Kingdom, the **British pound** or "pound sterling," was worth \$2.50. Over the next 46 years, its value declined by nearly 50 percent, so that by early 2019 one pound was worth \$1.28 (see Figure 10.2). Nevertheless, Americans visiting London during January 2019 did not return thinking that their vacations had been very inexpensive. At an exchange rate of \$1.28, a hotel room in London cost about the same as in New York, and dining out was no bargain either.

Figure 10.2 Dollar-Pound Exchange Rate, 1971-2019

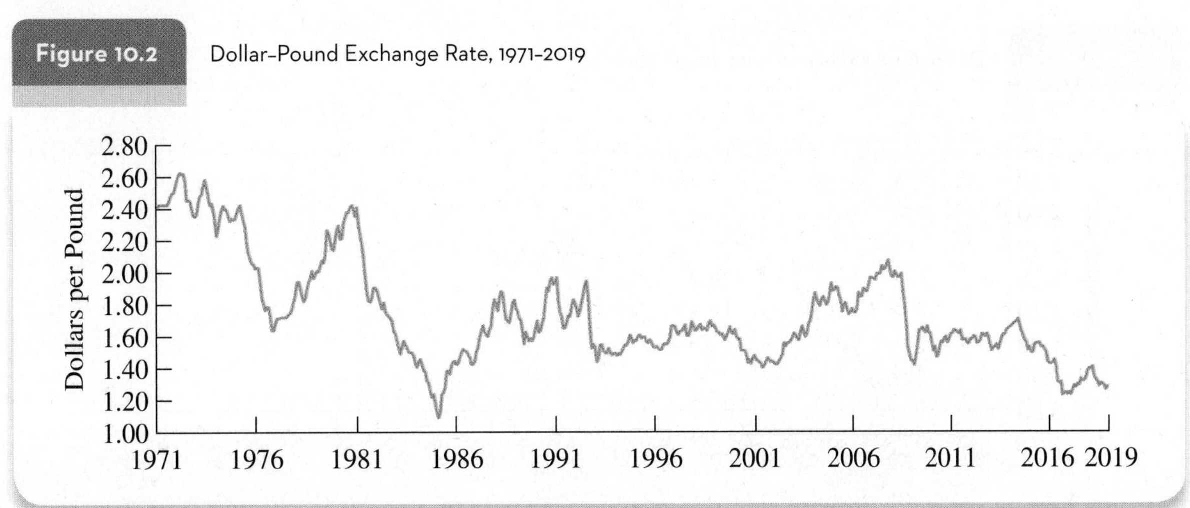

SOURCE: Federal Reserve Bank of St. Louis (FRED data code: EXUSUK).

How are foreign exchange rates determined, and what accounts for their fluctuation over days, months, years, and decades? This chapter provides an introduction to foreign exchange rates and exchange markets.

Foreign Exchange Basics

After graduation, you are planning to travel to Europe. You would like to see the Eiffel Tower in Paris, the Colosseum in Rome, and the Parthenon in Athens. As you pack, you worry a little about paying your hotel bills and the tab for all that great food you expect to eat. The servers in French, Italian, and Greek restaurants aren't interested in your dollar bills; they want to be paid in their own currency. But you are fortunate, for while the French, Italians, and Greeks speak different languages, they all use the same coins and bills. In fact, buying anything in Europe—at least in the countries that are members of the European Monetary Union—means exchanging your dollars for **euros**. So when you get to Europe, you will care about the rate of exchange between the dollar and the euro. The price of one euro in dollars is called the dollar–euro exchange rate.

The Nominal Exchange Rate

Exchanging dollars for euros is like any other economic transaction: you are using your money to buy something—in this case, money to spend in another country. The price you pay for this currency is called the nominal exchange rate, or simply the *exchange rate.* Formally defined, the **nominal exchange rate** *is the rate at which one can exchange the currency of one country for the currency of another country.* The dollar–euro exchange rate is the number of dollars you can get for each euro. In January 2019, one euro (the symbol for the euro is €) would buy roughly $1.14. So an American who went to Europe in January 2019 paid about $114 for €100.

Exchange rates change every day. Figure 10.3 shows the dollar–euro exchange rate since the inception of the euro in January 1999 to January 2019. The figure

Figure 10.3 Dollar-Euro Exchange Rate, 1999- 2019

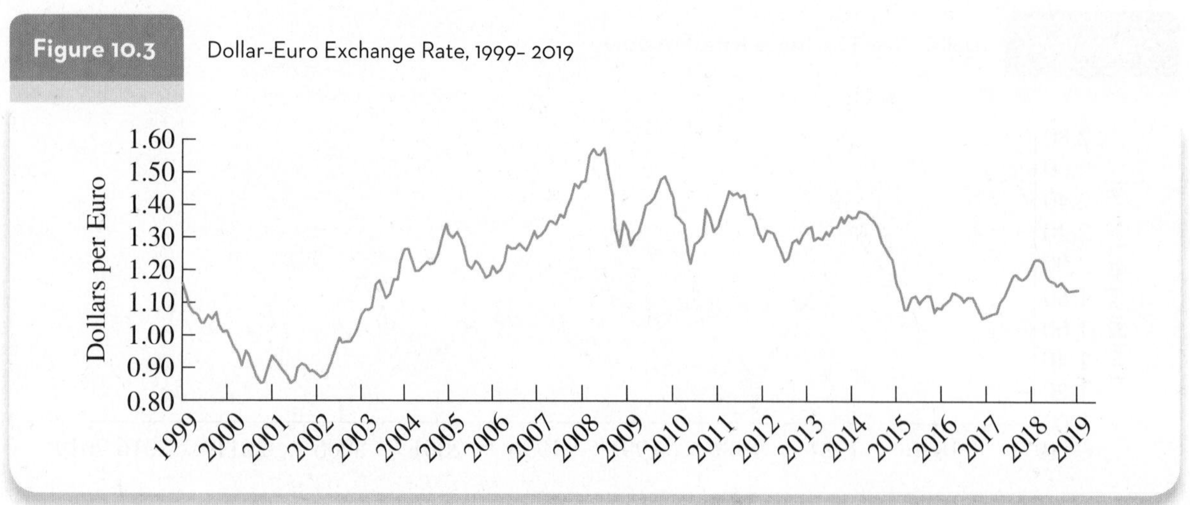

SOURCE: Federal Reserve Bank of St. Louis (FRED data code: EXUSEU).

A 20-euro note used in the countries that participate in the European Monetary Union.

Deposit Photos/Glow Images

plots the number of dollars per euro, which is the conventional way to quote the dollar–euro exchange rate. When the euro was introduced, it was worth $1.17. But by October 2000, less than two years later, it could be exchanged for only 83 cents. Such a decline in the value of one currency relative to another is called a **depreciation** of the currency that is falling in value. During the first 22 months of the euro's existence, it depreciated nearly 30 percent relative to the dollar. Later in this chapter, we will consider the reasons for large movements in exchange rates.

At the same time that the euro was falling in value, the dollar was rising. After all, if you can buy fewer dollars with one euro, you can get more euros for one dollar. The rise in the value of one currency relative to another is called an **appreciation** of the currency that is rising in value. During 1999 and 2000, the euro's depreciation was matched by the dollar's appreciation; they are really one and the same. When one currency goes up in value *relative to another,* the other currency must go down.

Note that, theoretically, exchange rates can be quoted in units of either currency—for example, as the number of dollars needed to buy one euro or as the number of euros needed to buy one dollar. The two prices are equivalent; one is simply the reciprocal of the other. In practice, however, each currency has its convention. The price of the British pound is quoted in the same way as the euro, so that people talk about the number of dollars that can be exchanged for one pound (£). The price of the Japanese **yen** (¥) is quoted as the number of yen that can be purchased with one dollar.

Unfortunately, there is no simple rule for determining which way a particular exchange rate should be quoted. Most rates tend to be quoted in the way that yields a number larger than one. The fact that €1 equaled $1.17 when the euro was created on January 1, 1999, is the likely explanation for why we talk about the number of dollars needed to purchase one euro. Ever since, people have quoted dollars per euro, even though there have been significant periods of time when the number was less than one. If you need to guess which way to quote an exchange rate, the best guess is that it is the way that yields a number larger than one. But the real solution is always to state the units explicitly, to avoid confusion.

The Real Exchange Rate

While it may be interesting to know that one euro is worth about $1.14, you are interested in more than just the rate at which one country's currency can be exchanged for another. What you really want to know when you travel to Europe is how much you can buy with that euro. When all is said and done, will you return home thinking that your trip was cheap or expensive?

Following Exchange Rates in the News
TOOLS OF THE TRADE

Exchange rates are reported in the business news. *The Wall Street Journal* carries a daily Foreign Exchange column that describes events in the markets, as well as a table reporting the most recent nominal exchange rates between the U.S. dollar and various foreign currencies. (Because the rates quoted are generally for transactions of $1 million or more, they normally are not available to tourists.) The column and the table, such as the one reprinted here, appear in both the print and online versions of the paper. Let's run through Table 10.1 to see how to read it.

Column 1: The name of the country together with the name of its currency.

Column 2: The number of dollars that could be purchased per unit of foreign currency at the close of business on Friday, December 28, 2018. Looking at the entry for "**UK** pound" we can see that on that date, one British pound purchased $1.2699.

Column 3: The numbers of units of foreign currency needed to purchase one dollar at the close of business on Friday, December 28, 2018. Looking at the entry for "**Japan** yen" we can see that on that date, you could exchange 110.27 Japanese yen for one dollar.*

Column 4: The year-to-date change in the U.S. dollar equivalent. That is, the percentage change since January 1, 2018, in the units of foreign currency that could be purchased per dollar, so positive values mean that the dollar has appreciated relative to a particular currency, while negative values imply a depreciation of the dollar. In some cases, the exchange rate hasn't moved, so the entry reads "unch" for "unchanged." To see how it works, notice that the "**Euro area** euro" in this column is 4.9 percent. This means that during 2018 the dollar appreciated against the euro, rising by 4.9 percent from roughly €0.8311 to €0.8739 per dollar.

In thinking about foreign exchange rates, be sure to keep track of whether you are quoting the number of U.S. dollars that can be exchanged for one unit of foreign currency, as in column 2 of the table, or the number of units of foreign currency that can be purchased with one dollar. They are easy to confuse. If you went to Europe and confused $1.1443 per euro with €0.8739 per dollar, you would think everything was less expensive than it really is, and you would end up buying something for more than you originally planned to pay.

*Note the reciprocal nature of the rates in columns 2 and 3. For any entry, the value in column 2 times the value in column 3 equals 1, so either value divided into 1 equals the other value.

Because nominal exchange rates do not provide an answer to this question, we now turn to the concept of a **real exchange rate**, *the rate at which one can exchange the goods and services from one country for the goods and services from another country.* It is the cost of a basket of goods in one country *relative* to the cost of the same basket of goods in another country. To grasp this concept, we will start with the real exchange rate between two cups of espresso, one American and the other Italian. The local Starbucks charges $3.42 for an espresso; in Florence, Italy, a cup of espresso costs €1.50. (Yes, the Italian version is better, but for the sake of the example, let's pretend they're the same.) Using the nominal dollar–euro exchange rate as of January 2019, $1.14 per euro, this means that to buy an espresso in Florence, you need to spend $1.71. More important, you can exchange one cup of Starbucks espresso for 2 cups of Italian espresso. This is the *real* exchange rate. You will return from your European vacation thinking that espresso was very cheap in Italy.

There is a simple relationship between the real exchange rate and the nominal exchange rate, which we can infer from our espresso calculation. To compute the real exchange rate, we took the euro price of an espresso in Italy and multiplied it by the nominal exchange rate, the number of dollars per euro. Then we divided it into the dollar price of a cup of espresso in the United States:

Table 10.1 Currencies

U.S. dollar foreign exchange rates in late New York trading, December 28, 2018

(1) Country/currency	(2) Fri in US$	(3) Fri per US$	(4) US$ vs, YTD chg (%)
Americas			
Argentina peso	.0265	37.6805	**102.5**
Brazil real	.2576	3.8814	**17.2**
Canada dollar	.7332	1.3639	**8.5**
Chile peso	.001441	694.00	**12.8**
Ecuador US dollar	1	1	**unch**
Mexico peso	.0509	19.6594	**−0.1**
Uruguay peso	.03094	32.3200	**12.2**
Venezuela b. fuerte	.00000402	248567.85	**2403414.4**
Asia-Pacific			
Australian dollar	.7040	1.4205	**10.9**
China yuan	.1454	6.8782	**5.8**
Hong Kong dollar	.1277	7.8300	**0.2**
India rupee	.01430	69.933	**9.5**
Indonesia rupiah	.0000687	14560	**8.0**
Japan yen	.009069	110.27	**−2.2**
Malaysia ringgit	.2408	4.1535	**2.3**
New Zealand dollar	.6708	1.4908	**5.7**
Pakistan rupee	.00715	139.900	**26.4**
Philippines peso	.0190	52.525	**5.1**
Singapore dollar	.7324	1.3654	**2.1**
South Korea won	.0008952	1117.05	**4.7**
Taiwan dollar	.03271	30.568	**3.0**
Thailand baht	.03072	32.550	**−0.1**
Vietnam dong	.00004311	23196	**2.1**

(1) Country/currency	(2) Fri in US$	(3) Fri per US$	(4) US$ vs, YTD chg (%)
Europe			
Czech Rep. koruna	.04445	22.498	**5.7**
Denmark krone	.1533	6.5249	**5.2**
Euro area euro	1.1443	.8739	**4.9**
Hungary forint	.003560	280.93	**8.5**
Norway krone	.1148	8.7120	**6.2**
Poland zloty	.2661	3.7587	**8.0**
Russia ruble	.01437	69.607	**20.7**
Sweden krona	.1115	8.9667	**9.5**
Switzerland franc	1.0160	.9843	**1.0**
Turkey lira	.1897	5.2725	**38.9**
Ukraine hryvnia	.0365	27.3900	**−2.7**
UK pound	1.2699	.7875	**6.4**
Middle East/Africa			
Bahrain dinar	2.6532	.3769	**−0.1**
Eqypt pound	.0559	17.8865	**0.6**
Israel shekel	.2657	3.7636	**8.2**
Saudi Arabia riyal	.2666	3.7515	**0.03**
South Africa rand	.0693	14.4305	**16.7**

	Close	NetChg	%Chg	YTD%Chg
WSJ Dollar Index	89.95	−0.24	−0.26	**4.62**

Sources: Tullett Prebon, Dow Jones Market Data

Real coffee exchange rate

$$= \frac{\text{Dollar price of espresso in the U.S. (\$3.42)}}{\text{Euro price of espresso in Italy (€1.50)} \times \text{Dollars per euro (\$1.14/€)}} \qquad (1)$$

$$= \frac{\text{Dollar price of espresso in the U.S. (\$3.42)}}{\text{Dollar price of espresso in Italy (€1.50)} \times \text{(\$1.14/€)}}$$

$$= \frac{\$3.42}{\$1.71}$$

$$= 2.00$$

At these prices and exchange rate, one cup of Starbucks espresso buys 2.0 cups of Italian espresso. Note in equation (1) that the units of measurement cancel out. In the denominator, we multiplied the price in euros times the nominal exchange rate (measured as dollars per euro) to get an amount stated in dollars. Then we divided that number into the numerator, also expressed in dollars. The real exchange rate has no units of measurement.

In summary, to figure out the real coffee exchange rate in equation (1), we divided the dollar price of coffee in the United States by the dollar price of coffee in Italy. We can use the same procedure to compute the real exchange rate more broadly by comparing the prices of a set of goods and services that are commonly purchased in any country. If we can transform a basket of goods and services produced in the United States into more than one basket produced in Europe, as in the coffee example, then we are likely to return from a trip to Paris, Rome, and Athens thinking that the cost of living there is relatively cheap. Using this idea, we can write the real exchange rate as

$$\text{Real exchange rate} = \frac{\text{Dollar price of domestic goods}}{\text{Dollar price of foreign goods}} \tag{2}$$

From this definition of the real exchange rate, we can see that whenever the ratio in equation (2) is more than one, foreign products will seem cheap.

The real exchange rate, then, is much more important than the nominal exchange rate. It is the rate that measures the relative price of goods and services across countries, telling us where things are cheap and where they are expensive. The real exchange rate is the guiding force behind international transactions. When foreign goods are less expensive than domestic goods, their prices create an incentive for people to buy imports. Competing with foreign imports becomes more difficult for local producers. Think about what would happen if you could ship cups of espresso to the United States from Italy and sell them in an import shop. Starbucks would lose business. Obviously, you can't do that with freshly brewed coffee, but you can do it with clothing, electronics, cars, airplanes, and a wide variety of other goods and services. As a result, the competitiveness of U.S. exports depends on the real exchange rate. *Appreciation* of the real exchange rate makes U.S. exports more expensive to foreigners, reducing their competitiveness, while *depreciation* of the real exchange rate makes U.S. exports seem cheaper to foreigners, improving their competitiveness.

Foreign Exchange Markets

The volume of foreign exchange transactions is enormous. On an average day in April, 2019, $6.6 trillion in foreign currency was traded in a market that operates 24 hours every business day.[1] Given 260 business days in a normal year, the annual volume of foreign exchange transactions is about $1,715 trillion. To get a sense of how huge this number is, compare it to world output and trade. The World Bank estimates that in 2018, world GDP (at market prices) was $86 trillion, and international trade transactions (measured as exports plus imports) accounted for about $50 trillion of that amount. Hence, the volume of foreign exchange transactions is about 20 times world GDP and 34 times the value of world trade.

Because of its liquidity, the U.S. dollar is one side of 88 percent of these currency transactions.[2] That means that someone who wishes to exchange Thai *baht* for Japanese

[1] This estimate, the latest available, comes from a triennial survey by the Bank for International Settlements in Basel, Switzerland. The complete survey is available at www.bis.org.

[2] The liquidity of the market for dollars creates a premium, driving up the dollar's value in the same way that liquidity increases the price of a bond.

yen is likely to make two transactions, the first to convert the baht to dollars and the second to convert the dollars to yen. Most likely these transactions will take place in London, because the United Kingdom is home to 43 percent of foreign exchange trades—more than twice the volume in New York. Other significant foreign exchange trading takes place in Hong Kong and Singapore (each more than 7 percent).

Exchange Rates in the Long Run

How are exchange rates determined? To answer this question, we will divide our discussion into two parts. This section will look at the determination of the long-run exchange rate and the forces that drive its movement over long periods, such as decades. The next section will consider what causes exchange rates to vary over the short term—a few days or months, or even years.

The Law of One Price

The starting point for understanding how long-run exchange rates are determined is *the law of one price.* The **law of one price** is based on the concept of *arbitrage*—the idea that identical products should sell for the same price. Recall from our discussion in Chapter 9 that two financial instruments with the same risk and promised future payments will sell for the same price. We might refer to this phenomenon as financial arbitrage. If we extend the concept of arbitrage from financial instruments to goods and services, we can conclude that identical goods and services should sell for the same price regardless of *where* they are sold. Identical televisions or cars should cost the same whether they are sold in St. Louis or Philadelphia. When they don't, someone can make a profit.

For instance, if a specific model television were cheaper in St. Louis than in Philadelphia, someone could buy it in St. Louis, drive to Philadelphia, and sell it at a profit. This opportunity to profit from arbitrage would increase demand for televisions in St. Louis, where the price is low, and increase the supply of televisions in Philadelphia, where the price is high. Higher demand drives prices up, while a larger supply forces them down. The process will continue until the television sells for the same price in both cities. Of course, complete price equalization occurs only in the absence of transportation costs. If it costs $10 to transport the television 900 miles from the Mississippi River to the East Coast, then arbitrage will continue until the price in St. Louis is within $10 of the price in Philadelphia.

We can extend the law of one price from cities in the same country to cities in different countries. Instead of St. Louis and Philadelphia, think of Detroit, Michigan, and Windsor, Ontario—two cities separated by the Detroit River and the Canadian border. The river can be crossed by bridge or tunnel in roughly one minute. Ignoring transportation costs, then, once we have converted a price from U.S. to Canadian dollars, the cost of a television should be the same in both cities. If a TV costs $500 in the United States, at a nominal exchange rate of 1.36 Canadian dollars per U.S. dollar (see Table 10.1), the Canadian price should be (500 × 1.36) = 680 Canadian dollars. That is, the law of one price tells us that

$$\begin{array}{c}\text{Canadian dollar price of a}\\ \text{TV in Windsor, Ontario}\end{array} = \begin{array}{l}\text{(U.S. dollar price of a TV in Detroit)}\\ \times\ \text{(Canadian dollars per U.S. dollar)}\end{array} \qquad (3)$$

This example shows once again the importance of using the correct units when working with exchange rates. In converting the U.S. dollar price to Canadian dollars, we multiply by the number of Canadian dollars needed to buy one U.S. dollar. That is, we compute (U.S. dollars) times (Canadian dollars/U.S. dollar) to equal Canadian dollars. This is the same calculation we did earlier to figure out the U.S. dollar price of an Italian cup of coffee. There, we multiplied (euros) times (U.S. dollars/euro) to get U.S. dollars.

Returning to the law of one price, we can see immediately that it fails almost all the time. The fact is that the same commodity or service sells for vastly different prices in different countries. Why? Transportation costs can be significant, especially for heavy items like marble or slate. Tariffs—the taxes countries charge at their borders—are high sometimes, especially if a country is trying to protect a domestic industry. And technical specifications can differ. A television bought in Paris will not work in St. Louis because it requires a different input signal. A car sold in Great Britain cannot be used in the United States or continental Europe because its steering wheel is on the right. Moreover, tastes differ across countries, leading to different pricing. Finally, some things simply cannot be traded. A haircut may be cheaper in New Delhi than in Philadelphia, but most Americans simply can't take advantage of that price difference.

Purchasing Power Parity

Since the law of one price fails so often, why do we bother with it? Because even with its obvious flaws, the law of one price is extremely useful in explaining the behavior of exchange rates over long periods, like 10 or 20 years. To see why, we need to extend the law from a single commodity to a basket of goods and services. The result is the theory of **purchasing power parity (PPP)**, which means that one unit of U.S. domestic currency will buy the same basket of goods and services anywhere in the world. This idea may sound absurd, but let's look at its implications.

According to the theory of purchasing power parity, the dollar price of a basket of goods and services in the United States should be the same as the dollar price of a basket of goods and services in Mexico, Japan, or the United Kingdom. In the case of the United Kingdom, this statement means that

$$\begin{matrix}\text{Dollar price of basket} \\ \text{of goods in U.S.}\end{matrix} = \begin{matrix}\text{Dollar price of basket} \\ \text{of goods in U.K.}\end{matrix} \qquad (4)$$

Rearranging this expression gives us

$$\frac{\text{Dollar price of basket of goods in U.S.}}{\text{Dollar price of basket of goods in U.K.}} = 1 \qquad (5)$$

The left-hand side of equation (5) is familiar: It is the real exchange rate [see equation (2) on page 242]. Thus, *purchasing power parity implies that the real exchange rate is always equal to one.* The implication of this conclusion is straightforward. It is that the purchasing power of a dollar is always the same, regardless of where in the world you go.

This idea must seem doubly absurd. If a dollar doesn't even buy the same number of cups of coffee in Italy and the United States, how can it have the same purchasing power all the time, everywhere in the world? On any given day, it doesn't. But over the long term, exchange rates do tend to move, so this concept helps us understand changes that happen over years or decades. To see how, remember that the dollar price of a foreign basket of goods is just the foreign currency price of the basket of goods times the number of dollars per unit of foreign currency. This means that if we quote the price of a basket of goods in the United Kingdom in pounds instead of dollars, then

$$\frac{\text{Dollar price of basket of goods in U.S.}}{(\text{Pound price of basket of goods in U.K.}) \times (\text{Dollars per pound})} = 1 \qquad (6)$$

so

$$\frac{\text{Dollar price of basket of goods in U.S.}}{\text{Pound price of basket of goods in U.K.}} = (\text{Dollars per pound}) \qquad (7)$$

That is, purchasing power parity implies that when prices change in one country but not in another, the exchange rate should change as well. When prices rise within a country, the effect is called inflation. If inflation occurs in one country but not in another, the change in prices creates an international inflation differential. So purchasing power parity tells us that changes in exchange rates are tied to differences in inflation from one country to another. Specifically, the currency of a country with high inflation will depreciate.

To see this point, think about what would happen if there were no inflation in the United Kingdom, but prices in the United States doubled. We would not expect the dollar–pound exchange rate to stay the same. Instead, we would predict that one dollar would now buy half as many British pounds as it did before (that is, twice as many dollars would be needed to purchase one pound).[3] There is strong evidence to support this conclusion, but the data must be drawn over fairly long periods, and the relationship is not perfect.

Take, for instance, the U.S. dollar–British pound exchange rate plotted in Figure 10.2 (page 239). Recall that in 1973, one pound was worth around \$2.50. By early 2019, a pound was worth \$1.28—a decline of 49 percent, or a bit more than 1.4 percent per year for 46 years. Over the same period, U.S. prices increased an average of 3.86 percent per year, while British prices increased an average of 5.08 percent per year—a difference of 1.2 percent per year. So, the relationship between the inflation and exchange rates explains most of the trend in the dollar–pound exchange rate over the 46-year period.

What is true for the United Kingdom is true for the rest of the world. To confirm it, we can look at a plot of (a) the historical difference between inflation in other countries and inflation in the United States against (b) the percentage change in the number of units of other countries' currencies required to purchase one dollar—that is, the average annual depreciation of the exchange rate.

Figure 10.4 on page 248 presents data for 62 countries. Each point represents a country. The difference between its average annual inflation and that of the U.S. is on the horizontal axis, and the average annual percentage change in the exchange rate between the country's currency and the U.S. dollar is on the vertical axis. Points further to the right represent countries with higher levels of inflation, and points higher up are countries whose dollar exchange rate experienced more depreciation over the 30-year period of the sample. The solid line is a 45-degree line that is consistent with the theoretical prediction of purchasing power parity. On the 45-degree line, exchange rate movements exactly equal differences in inflation. Granted, the points don't all lie exactly on the line, but the pattern is clearly there. The higher a country's inflation, the greater the depreciation in its exchange rate.

[3]It is possible to show this mathematically. If P represents the domestic (U.S.) currency price of a basket of goods, P^f the foreign currency price of the foreign (British) basket of goods, and e the nominal exchange rate, expressed as the domestic currency price of foreign currency (dollars per pound), then purchasing power parity tells us that $(P/eP^f) = 1$ (eq. 5), so $e = (P/P^f)$ (eq. 7). When converted from levels to rates of change, this expression implies that the percent change in the exchange rate equals the difference between domestic and foreign inflation.

Figure 10.4 Exchange Rate Movements and Inflation Differentials, 1980–2010

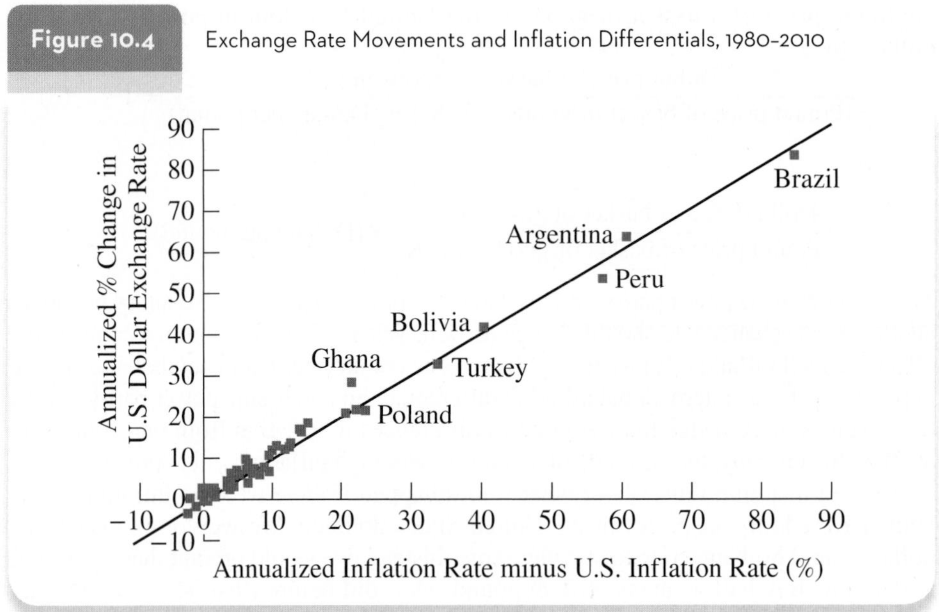

SOURCE: The International Monetary Fund.

Take the example of Bolivia. From 1980 to 2010, Bolivia's inflation minus U.S. inflation averaged 40 percent per year, and the Bolivian currency (originally the *bolivar,* now the *boliviano*) depreciated at an average annual rate of 42 percent. Putting that into perspective, the 2010 Bolivian price level was more than 465,000 times the 1980 Bolivian price level, and the exchange rate depreciated by an enormous multiple. That means purchasing one dollar in the foreign exchange market required 286,000 times as many bolivianos in 2010 as in 1980. Importantly, Figure 10.4 Shows that there are no countries with high inflation differentials and small exchange rate changes or big exchange rate changes and low inflation differentials. All of the points lie close to the 45-degree line.

The data in Figure 10.4 tell us that purchasing power parity held true over a 30-year period. Even if we look at an interval as short as a decade, the connection between movements in the exchange rate and differences in inflation across countries usually holds up to scrutiny. But the same exercise applied to periods of a few weeks, months, or even years would be a total failure. We know that from examining the plots of the Korean won–U.S. dollar exchange rate in Figure 10.1 and the dollar–euro exchange rate in Figure 10.3. Recall that the Korean won went through a sudden, steep depreciation, falling from 900 to 1,900 won to the dollar in just a few months, at the end of 1997. The pattern of Korean inflation at the time, a relatively steady 7½ percent versus 1½ percent in the United States, simply cannot explain this sudden change.

Similarly, from the euro's inception in January 1999, the dollar–euro rate fell steadily for two years, dropping more than 25 percent (see Figure 10.3). At the same time, inflation in the euro area ran a full percentage point *below* U.S. inflation. Examples like these are the norm, not the exception. Over weeks, months, and even years, nominal exchange rates can deviate substantially from the levels implied by purchasing power parity. So, while the theory can help us understand long swings in exchange rates, it provides no explanation for the short-term movements we see all the time.

The Big Mac Index

APPLYING THE CONCEPT

By the close of the 20th century, the Big Mac was available to consumers in 121 countries. Regardless of where it was sold, a Big Mac was defined as "two all-beef patties, special sauce, lettuce, cheese, pickles, onions on a sesame seed bun." Needless to say, every McDonald's restaurant requires payment in the local currency. In 1986, the staff of *The Economist* realized that this presented an opportunity. Together, the market exchange rate and the price of a Big Mac would allow them to estimate the extent to which a country's currency deviates from the level implied by purchasing power parity.

Twice a year, under headlines like "Big MacCurrencies" and "Burgernomics," *The Economist* publishes a table showing Big Mac prices in more than 40 countries. Table 10.2 is based on Big Mac prices from *The Economist* website on January 10, 2019. Using Big Mac prices as a basis for comparison, it shows the extent to which each country's currency was undervalued or overvalued relative to the U.S. dollar. As you look at the table, you will realize that all exchange rates are quoted as the number of units of local currency required to purchase one dollar.

To see how the **Big Mac index** works, take the case of Denmark. The Danish currency is called the *krone* (which means "crown") and in early 2019, a Big Mac cost DKr30 in Copenhagen. At an exchange rate of 6.52, that's equivalent to $4.60. To figure out the purchasing power parity value of one dollar in krone, we can use the relationship in equation (7), which tells us to divide the price of a Big Mac in krone by the dollar price: 30 krone per Big Mac/$5.58 per Big Mac = 5.38 krone per dollar (adjusted for rounding error). If the theory of purchasing power parity holds, then 5.38 krone should buy one dollar. But instead, the price of one dollar in the currency markets was 6.52 krone, which means that the Danish krone was undervalued by 18 percent. For the Chinese *yuan*, the same calculation implies an undervaluation of roughly – 45 percent.

The Big Mac index is a clever idea, and it works surprisingly well considering that it is based on a single commodity that is not tradeable, and whose local price surely depends on costs like wages, rent, and taxes.

Table 10.2 A Feast of Burgernomics
The Big Mac Index

Country	Big Mac prices: In local currency	Big Mac prices: In U.S. dollars*	Implied PPP† of the dollar	Actual dollar exchange rate January 1	Under(–)/over(+) valuation against the dollar, %†
United States‡	$5.58	5.58	—	—	—
Argentina	Peso 75.00	2.00	13.44	37.46	45
Australia	A$6.10	4.35	1.09	1.40	–22
Brazil	Real 16.90	4.55	3.03	3.72	–19
Britain	£3.19	4.07	0.57	0.78	–27
Canada	C$6.77	5.08	1.21	1.33	–9
Chile	Peso 2,640	3.89	473.12	678.99	–30
China**	Yuan 20.9	3.05	3.75	6.85	–45
Colombia	Peso 11,900	3.73	2,132.62	3,191.50	–33
Costa Rica	Colones 2,290	3.77	410.39	606.98	–32
Czech Republic	Koruna 85	3.81	15.23	22.31	–32
Denmark	DK 30	4.60	5.38	6.52	–18
Egypt	Pound 40	2.23	7.17	17.91	–60
Euro area‡	€4.05	4.64	0.73	0.87	–17
Hong Kong	HK$20	2.55	3.58	7.83	–54
Hungary	Forint 850	3.03	152.33	280.27	–46
India***	Rupee 178	2.55	31.90	69.69	–54
Indonesia	Rupiah 33,000	2.34	5,913.98	14,090.00	–58
Israel	Shekel 17	4.58	3.05	3.71	–18
Japan	Yen 390	3.60	69.89	108.44	–36
Malaysia	Ringgit 9.05	2.20	1.62	4.12	–61
Mexico	Peso 49	2.54	8.78	19.31	–55
New Zealand	NZ$6.20	4.19	1.11	1.48	–25
Norway	Kroner 50	5.86	8.96	8.53	5
Pakistan	Rupee 460	3.31	82.44	138.88	–41
Peru	Sol 10.50	3.14	1.88	3.35	–44
Philippines	Peso 140	2.67	25.09	52.39	–52
Poland	Zloty 10.50	2.80	1.88	3.75	–50
Russia	Rouble 110.17	1.65	19.74	66.69	–70
Saudi Arabia	Riyal 12	3.20	2.15	3.75	–43
Singapore	S$5.80	4.28	1.04	1.36	–23
South Africa	Rand 31	2.24	5.56	13.87	–60
South Korea	Won 4,500	4.02	806.45	1,118.60	–28
Sri Lanka	Rupee 580	3.18	103.94	182.25	–43
Sweden	SKr 52	5.84	9.32	8.91	5
Switzerland	SFr 6.50	6.62	1.16	0.98	19
Taiwan	NT$69	2.24	12.37	30.80	–60
Thailand	Baht 119.00	3.72	21.33	32.01	–33
Turkey	Lira 10.75	2.00	1.93	5.38	–64
UAE	Dirhams 14	3.81	2.51	3.67	–32
Ukraine	Hryvnia 54	1.94	9.68	27.80	–65
Uruguay	Peso 140	4.31	25.09	32.51	–23
Vietnam	Dong 65,000	2.80	11,648.75	23,199.00	–50

*At market exchange rate (January 1, 2019.)
†Purchasing-price parity; local price divided by price in United States.
‡Average of four cities.
**Average of five cities.
††Weighted average of prices in euro area.
***Maharaja Mac.

SOURCE: *The Economist Newspaper Limited, London* (January 10, 2019).

www.economist.com.

Fortunately, we do have some equipment in our tool kit that we can use to explain short-term movements in exchange rates.

Before continuing, we should note the meaning of two additional terms. We often hear currencies described as **undervalued** or **overvalued**. When people use these terms, they often have in mind a current market rate that deviates from what they consider to be purchasing power parity. For example, a person who thinks that one dollar should purchase one euro—that is, that one to one is somehow the "correct" long-run exchange rate—would say that if one dollar purchases only €0.90, it is *undervalued* relative to the euro, or the euro is *overvalued* relative to the dollar.

Exchange Rates in the Short Run

While purchasing power parity helps us understand movements in nominal exchange rates over decades, it cannot explain the weekly, monthly, or even yearly movements we see. What can? What sorts of phenomena are responsible for the nearly constant movement in exchange rates? To explain short-run changes in nominal exchange rates, we turn to an analysis of the supply of and demand for currencies. Because, in the short run, prices don't move much, these nominal exchange rate movements represent changes in the real exchange rate. That is, a 1 or 2 percent change in the *nominal* dollar–euro exchange rate over a day or week creates a roughly equivalent change in the *real* dollar–euro exchange rate.

The Supply of Dollars

As is always the case in discussing foreign exchange, we need to pick a home country and stick to it. The most natural choice for us is the United States, so we'll use the U.S. dollar as the domestic currency. Consistent with this, we will discuss the number of units of foreign currency that it takes to purchase one dollar. For example, we will talk about the number of euros per dollar.

Who supplies dollars to the foreign exchange markets? People who have them, of course—primarily people in the United States. There are two reasons why someone who is holding dollars would want to exchange them for euros or yen: (1) to purchase goods and services produced abroad, like a Japanese television set, dinner in Paris, or tuition at a foreign university; and (2) to invest in foreign assets, such as bonds issued by the German telecommunications company Deutsche Telekom, or shares in Honda, the Japanese manufacturer of cars and motorcycles.

Figure 10.5 The Dollar-Euro Market

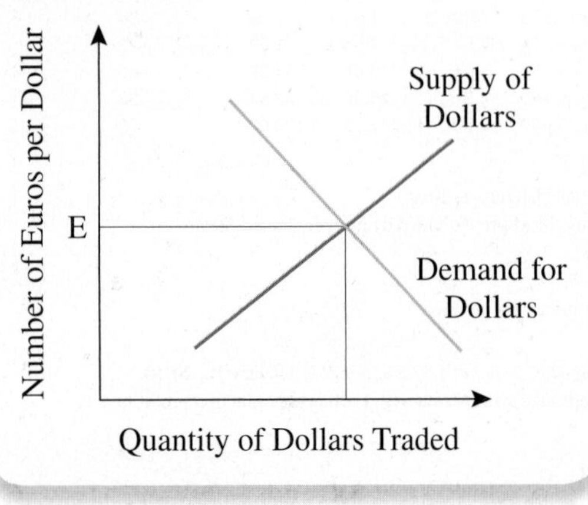

Number of Euros per Dollar
Supply of Dollars
E
Demand for Dollars
Quantity of Dollars Traded

Figure 10.5 shows the **supply of dollars** in the dollar–euro market. Just like any other supply curve, it slopes upward. The higher the price a dollar commands in the market, the more dollars are supplied. And the more valuable the dollar, the cheaper are foreign-produced goods and foreign assets *relative to domestic ones* in U.S. markets.

To see why, suppose you are planning to buy a car. You have narrowed your options to a German-made Volkswagen Jetta and an American-made Ford Focus. Price is important to you. Because the Volkswagen is

Yogi Berra and the Dollar
YOUR FINANCIAL WORLD

Former New York Yankees manager Yogi Berra once warned: "It's tough to make predictions, especially about the future." Yogi's admonition applies well to the projections that market practitioners frequently make about the value of the dollar and other currencies. Currency forecasts are rarely useful.

For decades, economists noted that exchange rates behave like a random walk—the best predictor of tomorrow's exchange rate is today's spot rate, which is the same as saying that any change in the rate from one day to the next is unpredictable. Why? Like other deep and liquid asset markets, foreign exchange markets are reasonably efficient, so spot exchange rates reflect all publicly available data.

More recently, economists have argued that a very small fraction of exchange rate variation is in fact predictable. The "carry trade" (in which investors anticipate that a high-yielding currency will depreciate less than would be necessary to equalize investment returns across currencies) is an example. But as one would suspect, this investment strategy is extremely risky. Carry trades proved particularly hazardous during the financial crisis of 2007–2009, when the sudden surge in demand for the safest assets drove low-interest rate currencies like the yen and the dollar sharply higher.

Many practitioners base their currency forecasts on projections of how economic growth and interest rates will evolve across countries. For example, someone who expects the U.S. economy to grow faster than the euro area—leading to relatively higher inflation-adjusted U.S. interest rates—might conclude that this difference will attract investment to the United States and drive up the dollar relative to the euro.

Such forecasts suffer from two big weaknesses. First, the largest impact on the currency value usually occurs as soon as the shift in relative growth rates is widely anticipated. Like other efficient markets, foreign exchange market participants don't wait for confirmation of their expectations from the publication of statistics, let alone from subsequent policymaker actions, all of which are "old news" by the time they occur.

Second, shifts in relative growth rates are only one factor among many that influence exchange rates. They can easily be overwhelmed by other developments. Recall the collapse of the carry trade during the crisis: It drove the dollar sharply higher in October 2008, just as the U.S. economy was entering the worst of the Great Recession.

The bottom line: Yogi had it right. Beware currency forecasts.

manufactured abroad, a change in the value of the dollar will affect your decision. As the dollar increases in value, the price of the Jetta falls and you become more likely to buy the Jetta. If you do, you will be supplying dollars to the foreign exchange market. What is true for your car purchase is true for everything else. The more valuable the dollar, the cheaper foreign goods, services, and assets will be and the higher the supply of dollars in the dollar–euro market. Thus, *the supply curve for dollars slopes upward,* as shown in Figure 10.5.

The Demand for Dollars

Foreigners who want to purchase American-made goods, assets, or services need dollars to do so. Suppose a European student would like to attend college in the United States. The school will accept payment only in dollars, so paying the tuition bill means exchanging euros for dollars. The lower the dollar–euro exchange rate—the fewer euros needed to buy one dollar—the cheaper the tuition bill will be from the viewpoint of a European student. At a given dollar price, the fewer euros needed to purchase one dollar, the cheaper are American-made goods and services. And the cheaper a good or service, the higher the demand for it. The same is true of investments. The cheaper the dollar—the lower the dollar–euro exchange rate—the more attractive are U.S. investments and the higher is the **demand for dollars** with which to buy them. Thus, *the demand curve for dollars slopes downward* (see Figure 10.5).

Equilibrium in the Market for Dollars

The equilibrium exchange rate, labeled *E* in Figure 10.5, equates the supply of and demand for dollars. Because the values of all the major currencies of the world (including the dollar, the euro, the yen, and the pound) float freely, they are determined by market forces. As a result, fluctuations in their value are the consequence of shifts in supply or demand.

Figure 10.6 Effect of an Increase in the Supply of Dollars in the Dollar-Euro Market

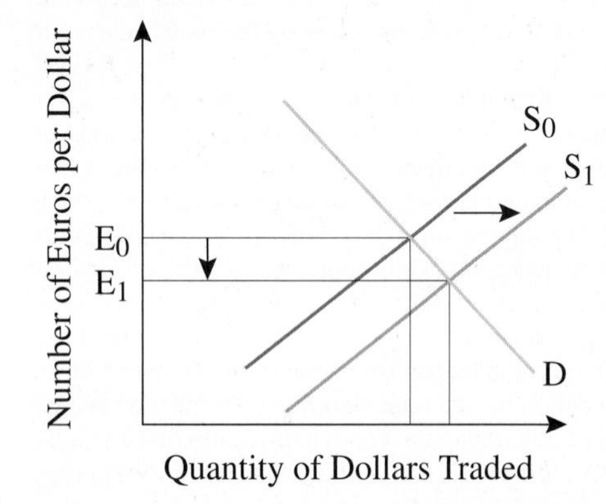

Shifts in the Supply of and Demand for Dollars

Shifts in either the supply of or the demand for dollars will change the *equilibrium exchange rate.* Let's begin with *shifts in the supply of dollars.* Remember that Americans wanting to purchase products from abroad or to buy foreign assets will supply dollars to the foreign exchange market. Anything that increases their desire to import goods and services from abroad, or their preference for foreign stocks and bonds, will increase the supply of dollars, leading to a depreciation of the dollar. Figure 10.6 shows the mechanics of this process.

What causes Americans' preferences for foreign goods, services, and assets to increase, prompting them to supply more dollars to the foreign exchange market, shifting the supply of dollars to the right? This question has many answers.

A rise in the supply of dollars Americans use to purchase foreign goods and services can be caused by:

- *An increase in Americans' preference for foreign goods.* For instance, a successful advertising campaign might convince American consumers to buy more imported olive oil. To fill the new orders, U.S. importers would exchange dollars for euros, shifting the dollar supply curve to the right.

- *An increase in the real interest rate on foreign bonds (relative to U.S. bonds).* With U.S. real interest rates holding steady, an increase in the return on foreign bonds would make them a more appealing investment. Because buying German bonds means exchanging dollars for euros, a rise in the desire to purchase foreign bonds shifts the supply curve for dollars to the right. (Remember that the real interest rate is the nominal interest rate minus expected inflation, so real interest rates increase either when the nominal interest rate rises and expected inflation holds steady or when expected inflation falls and the nominal interest rate remains the same.)
- *An increase in American wealth.* Just as an increase in income raises consumption of everything, an increase in wealth raises investment in everything. The wealthier we are, the more foreign investments we will make, and the more dollars we will exchange for euros, shifting the supply of dollars to the right.

- *A decrease in the riskiness of foreign investments relative to U.S. investments.* Lower-risk bonds are always more desirable than others, regardless of their country of origin. If the risk associated with foreign investments falls, Americans will want more of them. To get them, they will increase the supply of dollars in the foreign exchange market.

- *An expected depreciation of the dollar.* If people think the dollar is going to lose value, possibly because of inflation, they will want to exchange it for foreign currency. To see why, assume that the euro is currently worth €0.88 per dollar and that you expect it to move to €0.80 per dollar over the next year. If you exchange $100 for euros today, you will get €88. Reversing the transaction a year later, you will be left with $110: a 10 percent return. The point is simple: If investors think the dollar will decline in value—it will depreciate—they will sell dollars, increasing the supply of dollars in the foreign exchange market.

Figure 10.7 Effect of an Increase in the Demand for Dollars in the Dollar-Euro Market

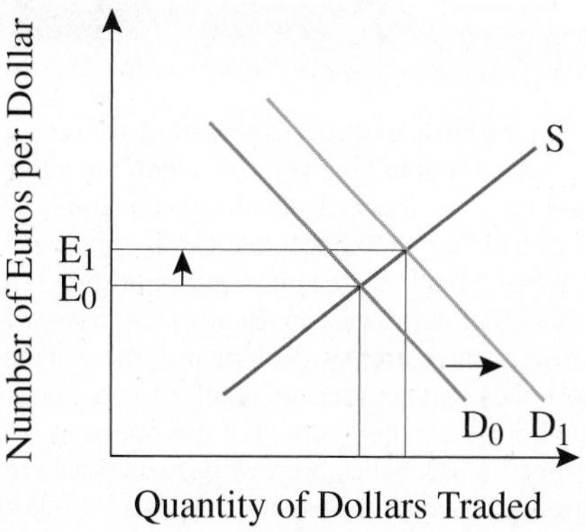

To understand *shifts in the demand for dollars,* all we need to do is review the list just presented, this time from the point of view of a foreigner. Anything that increases the desire of foreigners to buy American-made goods and services, or to invest in U.S. assets, will increase the demand for dollars and shift the demand curve to the right. Increases in demand come about when foreigners prefer more American-made goods, when the real yield on U.S. bonds rises (relative to the yield on foreign bonds), when foreign wealth increases, when the riskiness of American investments falls, and when the dollar is expected to appreciate. All these events increase demand, shifting the demand curve to the right and causing the dollar to appreciate (see Figure 10.7). Table 10.3 summarizes all the events that increase the supply of and demand for dollars in the foreign exchange market.

Explaining Exchange Rate Movements

The supply and demand model of the determination of exchange rates helps explain short-run movements in currency values. Let's return to the 30 percent appreciation of the dollar relative to the euro that occurred between January 1999 and October 2000

Table 10.3 Causes of an Increase in the Supply of and Demand for Dollars

Increased Supply Shifts Supply Curve to the Right (Leads to a fall in the value of the dollar)	***Increased Demand Shifts Demand Curve to the Right*** (Leads to a rise in the value of the dollar)
Increase in American preference for foreign goods	Increase in foreign preference for American goods
Increase in real interest rate on foreign bonds (relative to U.S. bonds)	Increase in real interest rate on U.S. bonds (relative to foreign bonds)
Increase in American wealth	Increase in foreign wealth
Reduction in riskiness of foreign investment (relative to U.S. investment)	Reduction in riskiness of U.S. investment (relative to foreign investment)
Expected depreciation of the dollar	Expected future dollar appreciation

Currency Risk and Rollover Risk
LESSONS FROM THE CRISIS

During the crisis of 2007–2009, some non-U.S. banks faced a sudden threat to their survival: When the interbank market dried up, they found it difficult to borrow the U.S. dollars needed to fund their dollar loans and securities.*

When a bank lends in a foreign currency, it typically borrows in that currency, too. Banks face *currency risk* if they borrow in one currency and lend in another. If the currency in which they lent appreciates relative to the currency in which they borrowed, they benefit. If the opposite occurs, so the currency in which they borrowed rises in value relative to the currency in which they lent, they lose. The larger the mismatch between lending and borrowing in a currency, the greater the currency risk.

But simply matching the currencies of assets and liabilities does not eliminate all the risks the bank faces. Because loans usually have a longer maturity than borrowings, banks still face a danger that funding liquidity in the foreign currency will dry up. This danger is called *rollover risk*. If a bank is unable to "roll over" its short-term foreign currency borrowing (that is, renew at maturity), it must either sell the foreign currency assets it has purchased or accept increased currency risk by borrowing in domestic currency. A crisis may eliminate even these options and thus threaten the bank's survival.

To see the relationship between currency risk and rollover risk, consider the balance sheet of a hypothetical Japanese bank (Table 10.4). The bank has borrowed short term and made long-term loans in both U.S. dollars and Japanese yen. But because of the way it did this, it has a currency mismatch of \$100 million. This is the gap between its lending and borrowing in the foreign currency. At an initial exchange rate of ¥100/US\$, in yen this gap equals ¥10 billion. What is the bank's currency risk? If the yen appreciates to ¥99/US\$—so instead of taking 100 yen to purchase 1 dollar, it now takes only 99—the bank loses ¥100 million. If the yen depreciates to ¥101/US\$, the bank gains ¥100 million. The bank also has rollover risk in dollars. If it cannot roll over its \$100 million liability, the bank must repay it by selling dollar loans or by borrowing in yen. The latter adds to its currency risk.

In the financial crisis of 2007–2009, the rollover risk facing internationally active banks became acute and posed a threat to the financial system as a whole. From a policy perspective, the goal was not just to create an adequate supply of dollars, but to deliver it to the banks that needed it. Only the central bank of the United States (the Federal Reserve) can create dollars, but the Fed is not in a position to know all about non-U.S. private banks in need of dollar funding.

So, to limit its credit exposure, the U.S. central bank arranged a series of extraordinary dollar swaps with 10 other central banks, who accepted the currency and credit risks of lending these newly created dollars to their domestic banks. Unprecedented cooperation among central banks allowed for an aggressive and successful policy response to the threat of a currency-driven meltdown.

Table 10.4 Simple Balance Sheet of a Hypothetical Japanese Bank

Assets Long Term	Liabilities Short Term
¥10 billion	¥20 billion
US\$200 million	US\$100 million

*We defined funding liquidity in Chapter 2 as the ease with which a financial institution can borrow to buy securities or make loans.

(see Figure 10.3 on page 240). Over this period, the number of euros required to purchase one dollar increased. Our model allows us to conclude that the cause was either a decrease in the dollars supplied by Americans or an increase in the dollars demanded by foreigners. The first would shift the supply curve to the left and the second would shift the demand curve to the right, increasing the equilibrium exchange rate and making dollars more valuable. To figure out which of these is right, we need to look for other evidence.

Looking at the statistics on the supply of dollars, we see that the U.S. current account deficit—exports minus imports—increased from \$200 billion at the end of 1998 to \$450 billion by the close of 2000. That is, Americans increased their net purchases of foreign goods during this period, *raising* the supply of dollars, shifting the supply curve to the right. But at the same time, investment funds were pouring into the United States from abroad. Fall 1998 was a time of financial stress, and during times of crisis, investors tend to shift into the safest place, which they view as the United States. Moreover, 1999 was the peak of the U.S. stock market bubble. Foreign capital streamed toward the dot-com companies, especially those on the Nasdaq (see the discussion at the end of Chapter 8). As a result, foreigners' demand for dollars skyrocketed, outstripping the increased supply of dollars and driving up the "price"—the exchange rate. That is, the demand for dollars shifted to the right by more than the supply for dollars did. In the long run, however, such a move was unsustainable, so the dollar eventually depreciated, returning to a level more consistent with the theory of purchasing power parity.

Government Policy and Foreign Exchange Intervention

The more a country relies on exports and imports, the more important its exchange rate. Currency appreciation drives up the price foreigners pay for a country's exports as it reduces the price residents of the country pay for imports. This shift in foreign versus domestic prices hurts domestic businesses. Companies with big export businesses suffer the most, along with businesses whose products compete with imported goods. They often respond by pressuring elected officials to reduce the value of the currency. After all, government policymakers may influence the prices of lots of goods and services. Milk, rent, and electric power are just a few possibilities. Why not exchange rates too?

Government officials can intervene in foreign exchange markets in several ways. Some countries adopt a fixed exchange rate and act to maintain it at a level of their choosing. We will discuss the implications of this approach in Chapter 19. For now, all we need to know is that exchange rates can be controlled if policymakers have the resources available and are willing to take the necessary actions.

Large industrialized countries and common currency zones like the United States, Europe, and Japan generally allow currency markets to determine their exchange rate. Even so, there are occasions when officials in these countries try to influence the currency values. Sometimes they make public statements in the hope of influencing currency traders. But talk is cheap, and such statements rarely have an impact on their own. At other times, policymakers will buy or sell currency in an attempt to affect demand or supply. This approach is called *foreign exchange intervention.*

Some countries hardly ever attempt to influence their exchange rates in this way, while others intervene in the markets frequently. Over the past two decades to 2019, the United States intervened only twice; both times it was pressured to do so by its allies. Among the major industrialized countries, the Japanese are the most frequent participants in foreign exchange markets. The spring of 2002 provides a good example of their approach.

In the latter half of the 1990s, the Japanese economy was stagnant; real GDP grew at a rate of about 1 percent. In 2001, the economic situation worsened and output fell 2 percent. After trying almost every other approach imaginable to resuscitate the economy, Japanese officials decided to see if depreciating the yen would help. The idea was to help Japanese exporters increase their foreign sales by reducing the prices foreigners paid for Japanese products. In late May 2002, Japan's Ministry of Finance sold yen in exchange for dollars, hoping to drive down the price by increasing the supply of yen. While the yen did depreciate very modestly as a result of intervention, by the end of the month its price was higher than it had been before the intervention.

To RMB or Not to RMB? Lessons from Currency History

MONEY AND BANKING BLOG

China is the world's largest economy (on a purchasing power parity basis) and the world's largest trader. It accounts for about 15 percent of global economic activity and 10 percent of global trade in goods and services.

Does this mean that China's currency, the *renminbi (RMB)*, will become the most widely used international currency as well? Will RMB-denominated assets supplant U.S. dollar assets in central banks' foreign exchange reserve holdings? Will the RMB become the leading reserve currency in the world?

This issue is not an immediate one because the RMB has not been (at least through mid-2019) freely *convertible* into other currencies. And without specific government authorization, most residents and nonresidents cannot move large quantities of RMB across the border.*

International use of the RMB remains well behind that of the U.S. dollar. But it has picked up since 2010, in part because of efforts by the Chinese government, so there are good reasons to look ahead, as these data suggest:

- At the start of 2019, according to SWIFT, the RMB ranked eighth as a cross-border payments currency, with a share of 1 percent (compared to the U.S. dollar's share of 45 percent and the euro's share of 34 percent). In 2010, the RMB ranked 35th.
- Its importance in foreign exchange markets has grown, rising from 17th place in 2010 to 8th in 2016, with a 4 percent share (the U.S. dollar share was 88 percent).
- In October 2016, the International Monetary Fund added the RMB to the small basket of currencies that make up its unit of account, called Special Drawing Rights (SDRs).

If China were to relax its still-extensive controls on cross-border finance, how far will RMB internationalization go, and how fast? No one knows for sure, but history provides some useful lessons.

Over the past 200 years, only two currencies have been widely used internationally: the British pound and the U.S. dollar. Until recently, historians viewed World War II as the turning point in their relative dominance, with the pound prevailing before the war and the dollar after. But new research concludes that the transition occurred significantly earlier. The pound's lead began to wane in 1914, after which the dollar's importance made rapid gains, and the two currencies shared the principal role during the interwar period. One study suggests that the U.S. dollar surpassed the pound in the 1920s as the currency most held by the world's central banks. As of 1929, the two currencies accounted for virtually all such foreign exchange reserves, with the dollar somewhat ahead. Similarly, by that time almost all sovereign bonds denominated in foreign currency were being issued in either pounds or dollars.

What are the general lessons of the pound–dollar history? First, beginning with the Industrial Revolution, the pound and the dollar each benefited from a stable political regime

Why did the Japanese government's policy fail? Shouldn't an increase in the supply of yen, regardless of where it comes from, lead to a depreciation? The primary reason the intervention didn't work was that, while the Japanese Ministry of Finance was selling yen, the Bank of Japan was buying them. We'll study the details of foreign exchange intervention and monetary policy when we get to Chapter 19, but here is a quick version of the story. The Bank of Japan is in charge of monetary policy in Japan, which means controlling a particular short-term interest rate. Operationally, the result was that, within a few days, the Bank of Japan reversed the Ministry's foreign exchange intervention. If it hadn't, the interest rate it wished to control would have changed. Thus, foreign exchange interventions will be ineffective unless they are accompanied by a change in the policy interest rate. That is the reason countries like the United States rarely intervene in the foreign exchange markets.

with an independent judiciary that efficiently enforced property rights.

Second, the home economy's size alone did not make its currency an international leader. By 1880, the U.S. economy was larger than the United Kingdom's, but it took more than 30 years before the dollar was widely used abroad. The dollar's ascendancy did not begin until 1914, when the United States was already the leader in world trade and its economy was more than double the size of the United Kingdom's.

Third, the rise of the dollar as a new international currency required effective financial markets and institutions and a supportive external environment. Between 1914 and 1929, two important developments stand out in that regard. The U.S. government created the Federal Reserve, the U.S. central bank, which began operating in 1914. The Fed promoted the rapid expansion of U.S. financial markets, including short-term instruments with which foreign investors could freely park their holdings of U.S. dollars and foreign borrowers could raise funds. And at virtually the same time, World War I forced the European combatants, including the United Kingdom, to leave the gold standard for the better part of a decade. In contrast, the United States was able to maintain this commitment, giving the dollar a leg up on the competition.

And fourth, although the two currencies shared a leading role for some time, history doesn't tell us whether such a regime is stable. Large economies of scale that lower transactions costs and concentrate liquidity make it more likely that one leader will emerge from the competition, as the U.S. dollar did after World War II. Recent historical research suggests that these scale economies are actually small, but the issue is far from settled.

What does all this mean for the future of the RMB? The main implication is that China's economic size per se is far from decisive. More important is that the market for a currency be especially accessible and attractive if it is to be favored for use in international finance (aside from the case of payments in international trade).

Ultimately, investors want to know they can get their funds back whenever they choose. Given the chance, they will flock to RMB markets and use the RMB in financial transactions if they see that China has credible and efficient enforcement mechanisms to secure property rights. If the RMB market is to approach the depth and breadth of markets enjoyed by other international currencies today, China will have to make vast—and politically sensitive—reforms. That could still take a long time.

*For the United States, the dollar is both the name of the currency and its unit of account. The unit of account for the renminbi is the yuan, whose symbol, ¥, is the same as that of the Japanese yen. Specific amounts of the renminbi, such as its exchange rate versus another currency, are thus called yuan.

Key Terms

appreciation (of a currency), 241
Big Mac index, 249
British pound, 239
demand for dollars, 251
depreciation (of a currency), 241
euro, 240
law of one price, 245
nominal exchange rate, 240
overvalued currency, 250
purchasing power parity (PPP), 246
real exchange rate, 242
supply of dollars, 250
undervalued currency, 250
yen, 241

Using FRED: Codes for Data in This Chapter

Data Series	FRED Data Code
U.S. dollar/euro exchange rate	EXUSEU
Japanese yen/U.S. dollar exchange rate	EXJPUS
U.S. dollar/U.K. pound exchange rate (monthly)	EXUSUK
U.S. dollar/U.K. pound exchange rate (daily)	DEXUSUK
Brazilian real/U.S. dollar exchange rate	EXBZUS
Chinese yuan/U.S. dollar exchange rate	EXCHUS
Mexican peso/U.S. dollar exchange rate	EXMXUS
South Korean won/U.S. dollar exchange rate	EXKOUS
Swiss franc/U.S. dollar exchange rate	EXSZUS
Australian dollar/U.S. dollar exchange rate	EXUSAL
Trade-weighted U.S. dollar index: broad	TWEXBMTH
Trade-weighted U.S. dollar index: major currencies	TWEXMMTH
Real trade-weighted U.S. dollar index: broad	TWEXBPA
Real trade-weighted U.S. dollar index: major currencies	TWEXMPA
U.S. consumer price index	CPIAUCSL
Euro-area index of consumer prices	CP0000EZ19M086NEST
Bank of Japan intervention: purchases of U.S. dollar against Japanese yen	JPINTDUSDJPY

To learn more about the changing financial system, visit www.moneyandbanking.com.

Chapter Lessons

1. Different areas and countries of the world use different currencies in their transactions.
   a. The nominal exchange rate is the rate at which the currency of one country can be exchanged for the currency of another.
   b. A decline in the value of one currency relative to another is called depreciation.
   c. An increase in the value of one currency relative to another is called appreciation.
   d. When the dollar appreciates relative to the euro, the euro depreciates relative to the dollar.
   e. The real exchange rate is the rate at which the goods and services of one country can be exchanged for the goods and services of another.
   f. About $5 trillion worth of currency is traded every day in markets run by brokers and foreign exchange dealers.
2. In the long run, the value of a country's currency is tied to the price of goods and services in that country.
   a. The law of one price states that two identical goods should sell for the same price, regardless of location.
   b. The law of one price fails because of transportation costs, differences in taxation and technical specifications, and the fact that some goods cannot be moved.

c. The theory of purchasing power parity applies the law of one price to international transactions; it states that the real exchange rate always equals one.
d. Purchasing power parity implies that countries with higher inflation than other countries will experience exchange rate depreciation.
e. Over decades, exchange rate changes are approximately equal to differences in inflation, implying that purchasing power parity holds.

3. In the short run, the value of a country's currency depends on the supply of and demand for the currency in foreign exchange markets.
   a. When people in the United States wish to purchase foreign goods and services or invest in foreign assets, they must supply dollars to the foreign exchange market.
   b. The more foreign currency that can be exchanged for one dollar, the greater will be the supply of dollars. That is, the supply curve for dollars slopes upward.
   c. Foreigners who wish to purchase American-made goods and services or invest in U.S. assets will demand dollars in the foreign exchange market.
   d. The fewer units of foreign currency needed to buy one dollar, the higher the demand for dollars. That is, the demand curve for dollars slopes downward.
   e. Anything that increases the desire of Americans to buy foreign-made goods and services or invest in foreign assets will increase the supply of dollars (shift the supply curve for dollars to the right), causing the dollar to depreciate.
   f. Anything that increases the desire of foreigners to buy American-made goods and services or invest in U.S. assets will increase the demand for dollars (shift the demand curve for dollars to the right), causing the dollar to appreciate.
4. Some governments buy and sell their own currency in an effort to affect the exchange rate. Such foreign exchange interventions are usually ineffective.

Conceptual and Analytical Problems Mc Graw Hill connect

1. If the U.S. dollar–British pound exchange rate is \$1.30 per pound, and the U.S. dollar–euro rate is \$1.12 per euro: *(LO1)*
   a. What is the pound-per-euro rate?
   b. How could you profit if the pound-per-euro rate were above the rate you calculated in part *a*? What if it were lower?
2. If a video game costs \$30 in the United States and £27 in the United Kingdom, what is the real "video game" exchange rate? Look up the current dollar–pound exchange rate and compare the two prices. What do you conclude? *(LO1)*
3. Suppose the euro–dollar exchange rate moves from \$0.90 per euro to \$0.92 per euro. At the same time, the prices of European-made goods and services rise 1 percent, while prices of American-made goods and services rise 3 percent. What has happened to the real exchange rate between the dollar and the euro? Assuming the same change in the nominal exchange rate, what if inflation were 3 percent in Europe and 1 percent in the United States? *(LO2)*
4. The same television set costs \$600 in the United States, €450 in France, £300 in the United Kingdom, and ¥100,000 in Japan. If the law of one price holds, what are the euro–dollar, pound–dollar, and yen–dollar exchange rates? Why might the law of one price fail? *(LO1)*

5.* What does the theory of purchasing power parity predict in the long run regarding the inflation rate of a country that fixes its exchange rate to the U.S. dollar? *(LO2)*

6.* Can purchasing power parity help predict short-term movements in exchange rates? *(LO2)*

7. You need to purchase Japanese yen and have called two brokers to get quotes. The first broker offered you a rate of 125 yen per dollar. The second broker, ignoring market convention, quoted a price of 0.0079 dollar per yen. To which broker should you give your business? Why? *(LO1)*

8. During the 1990s, the U.S. Secretary of the Treasury often stated, "A strong dollar is in the interest of the United States." *(LO4)*
   a. Is this statement true? Explain your answer.
   b. What can the Secretary of the Treasury actually do about the value of the dollar relative to other currencies?

9. The following table gives selective data on nominal exchange rates, price levels, and real exchange rates for Country A and three other countries. Country A uses the dollar (A$) as its currency. Fill in the blanks in the table. *(LO1)*

	Nominal Exchange Rate (A$ per unit of other currency)	Price Level in Country A	Price Level in Other Country	Real Exchange Rate
Country B	A$1.25 per unit of currency B	114.5	88.3	
Country C		114.5	95.6	1.23
Country D	A$0.55 per unit of currency D	114.5		0.80

10. If the price (measured in a common currency) of a particular basket of goods is 10 percent higher in the United Kingdom than it is in the United States, which country's currency is undervalued, according to the theory of purchasing power parity? *(LO2)*

11.* You hear an interview with a well-known economist who states that she expects the U.S. dollar to strengthen against the British pound over the next 5 to 10 years. This economist is known for her support of the theory of purchasing power parity. Using an equation to summarize the relationship predicted by purchasing power parity between exchange rate movements and the inflation rates in the two countries, explain whether you expect inflation in the United States to be higher or lower on average compared with that in the U.K. over the period in question. *(LO2)*

12. Using the model of demand and supply for U.S. dollars, what would you expect to happen to the U.S. dollar exchange rate if, in light of a worsening geopolitical situation, Americans viewed foreign bonds as more risky than before? (You should quote the exchange rate as number of units of foreign currency per U.S. dollar.) *(LO3)*

13. Suppose that the Chinese central bank has been intervening in the foreign exchange market, buying U.S. dollars in an effort to keep its own currency, the renminbi (measured in yuan), weak. Use the model of demand and supply for

*Indicates more difficult problems.

dollars to show what the immediate effect would be on the Chinese yuan–U.S. dollar exchange rate of a decision by China to allow its currency to float freely. *(LO3)*

14. If the Chinese renminbi appreciated against the U.S. dollar, what would you expect to happen to:
    a. U.S. exports to China?
    b. U.S. imports from China?
    c. the U.S. trade deficit with China?
    Explain your answers. *(LO4)*

15. Suppose that, driven by waves of national pride, consumers across the world (including in the United States) decide to buy home-produced products where possible. Explain how the demand for and supply of U.S. dollars would be affected. What can you say about the impact on the equilibrium dollar exchange rate? *(LO3)*

16. Suppose an Italian bank has short-term borrowings of 400 million euros and 100 million U.S. dollars and made long-term loans of 300 million euros and 250 million U.S. dollars. The euro–dollar exchange rate is initially $1.50 per euro.
    a. Ignoring other assets and liabilities, place each item on the appropriate side of the bank's balance sheet.
    b. List the risks that this bank faces.
    c. If the euro–dollar exchange rate moved to $1.60 per euro, would the bank gain or lose? Provide calculations to support your answer. *(LO3)*

17.* Suppose government officials in a small open economy decided they wanted their currency to weaken in order to boost exports. What kind of foreign exchange market intervention would they have to make to cause their currency to depreciate? What would happen to domestic interest rates in that country if its central bank doesn't take any action to offset the impact on interest rates of the foreign exchange intervention? *(LO4)*

18. Suppose the interest rate on a one-year U.S. bond is 10 percent and the interest rate on an equivalent Canadian bond is 8 percent. If the interest rate parity condition holds (see the appendix to Chapter 10), is the U.S. dollar expected to appreciate or depreciate relative to the Canadian dollar over the next year? Explain your choice. *(LO3)*

19. Most countries do not attempt to manage their exchange rates with intervention in the foreign currency markets, but some do. Under which circumstances is such an intervention likely to be ineffective? *(LO4)*

20. Suppose you see the following news headline: "Japan's Finance Ministry Sells Yen for U.S. Dollars." What is the objective of this policy? If the policy goal is achieved, what will happen to the prices of Japanese imports to the United States? What will happen to the prices of U.S. goods purchased by residents of Japan? *(LO4)*

21. Immediately following the June 2016 U.K. referendum vote to leave the European Union, the value of the British pound plummeted versus the U.S. dollar.

*Indicates more difficult problems.

Using a demand and supply framework for British pounds, identify two factors that might have contributed to this decline by shifting the demand curve for British pounds. Illustrate the shift graphically. *(LO3)*

22. Suppose events elsewhere in the world lead to an increase in demand for Japanese yen, as investors seek a "safe haven" for their funds. How would this development affect Japanese exporters and Japan's immediate economic growth prospects? What currency policy tool might Japan's Ministry of Finance utilize to counter these effects? Is it likely to be effective? *(LO4)*

Data Exploration connect

For detailed instructions on using Federal Reserve Economic Data (FRED) online to answer each of the following problems, visit www.mhhe.com/moneyandbanking6e *and refer to the FRED Resources and Data Exploration Hints.*

1. Exchange rates can exhibit sudden changes as well as long-run patterns. *(LO1)*
   a. Plot the daily U.S. dollar–British pound exchange rate (FRED code: DEXUSUK) for the first half of 2016 and identify the short-term spike. What caused this spike? Which currency is appreciating when the plotted exchange rate falls?
   b. Plot since 1971 the monthly Japanese yen–U.S. dollar exchange rate (FRED code: EXJPUS) without recession bars. Which currency is appreciating when the plotted exchange rate falls?
2. Plot since 1999, without recession bars, the real exchange rate between U.S. goods and euro-area goods according to equation (2) in the text. Use the consumer price index (divided by 2.37 to set a common base year of 2015 = 100 for the U.S. and euro-area indexes) for the price of U.S. goods (FRED code: CPIAUCSL). Use the harmonized index of consumer prices for the price of euro-area goods (FRED code: CP0000EZ19M086NEST), and use the U.S. dollar–euro exchange rate (FRED code: EXUSEU). Why might this measure of the real exchange rate be persistently below unity since 2003? *(LO1)*
3. Write in algebraic form a calculation of U.K. pounds per euro that uses U.S. dollars per U.K. pound (FRED code: EXUSUK) and U.S. dollars per euro (FRED code: EXUSEU). Then plot since 1999 (without recession bars) the exchange rate of U.K. pounds per euro using these two U.S. dollar exchange rates. What happened to the pound–euro exchange rate in 2016? *(LO1)*
4. Examine an episode of large-scale intervention by the Bank of Japan (BoJ) in the yen–dollar foreign exchange market. Plot between January 2009 and January 2013 a measure of BoJ intervention (FRED code: JPINTDUSDJPY). Do positive values of this intervention indicator reflect purchases or sales of yen by the BoJ? What was the BoJ's policy objective? To investigate whether the intervention was effective, add the Japanese yen–U.S. dollar exchange rate (FRED code: EXJPUS) to the chart, but scaled on the right axis. *(LO5)*
5. How can we assess the impact of exchange rate fluctuations on the competitiveness of U.S. exporters? Plot the real trade-weighted U.S. dollar index (FRED code: TWEXBPA), which was 100 in March 1973. When was the index more than 20 percent above its March 1973 level? How far is it today from the March 1973 level? *(LO1)*

Appendix to Chapter 10

Interest Rate Parity and Short-Run Exchange Rate Determination

There is another way to think about the determinants of exchange rates in the short run. Rather than focus on the supply of and demand for currency, we can look at exchange rates from an investor's point of view. If the bonds issued in different countries are perfect substitutes for one another, then arbitrage will equalize the returns on domestic and foreign bonds. And because investing abroad means exchanging currencies, the result is a relationship among domestic interest rates, foreign interest rates, and the exchange rate. From this intuition, we can develop an understanding of the short-run movements in exchange rates.

Let's take the example of an American investor with a one-year investment horizon and \$1,000 to invest in either a one-year U.S. Treasury bond or a one-year German government bond. Because the investor is from the United States, we will assume that at the end of the year when the bonds mature, she wants to receive dollars. The question is: Which investment is more attractive? To find the answer, we need to compute the dollar return on buying a one-year \$1,000 U.S. Treasury bond and compare it to the dollar return on converting \$1,000 to euros, buying a German government bond, and converting the proceeds back to dollars after one year. The value of the first investment is easy to find. If the one-year U.S. Treasury interest rate is i, then one year later an initial investment of \$1,000 is worth $\$1,000 \times (1 + i)$. But the currency conversion complicates the calculation of the return to the foreign investment.

Computing the return to investing \$1,000 in a one-year German bond requires a series of steps. First, the investor needs to take the \$1,000 and convert it to euros. If E is the dollar–euro exchange rate measured as the number of euros per dollar, then \$1,000 purchases $E \times 1{,}000$ euros. Next, the investor purchases the German bond. If the one-year German bond rate is i^f, a \$1,000 investment yields $E \times 1{,}000 \times (1 + i^f)$ euros in one year. Finally, at the end of the year, the investor must exchange the euros for dollars. If we call E^e the expected future exchange rate—the number of euros per dollar expected in a year's time—then the dollar return to a \$1,000 investment in foreign bonds is

$$\text{Value of \$1,000 invested in foreign bonds after one year} = \frac{\$1{,}000E(1 + i^f)}{E^e} \qquad \text{(A1)}$$

Looking at this equation, we can see that for the U.S. investor, the return to holding the German bond has two parts: (1) the interest income and (2) the expected change in the exchange rate. By doing a little algebra and using an approximation, we can rewrite equation (A1) to divide the return into these two parts. The result is

$$\text{Value of \$1,000 invested in foreign bonds after one year} = \$1{,}000(1 + i^f)\left(1 - \frac{\Delta E^e}{E}\right) \quad \text{(A2)}$$

where ΔE^e is the expected change in the exchange rate.

This expression tells us that the return on the foreign bond is the foreign interest rate minus the expected percentage change in the dollar–euro exchange rate.

To see why the return depends on the change in the exchange rate, take an example in which the dollar–euro rate is €1/$1 at the start of the year and €1.05/$1 at the end of the year. That is, at the start of the year, you exchange one dollar for one euro, but at the end of the year the dollar is worth 1.05 euros—an appreciation of 5 percent in the value of the dollar. If the German interest rate is 6 percent, then a $1,000 investment will yield $1,000 × (1.06/1.05) = $1,010. Because the dollar has appreciated by 5 percent, the return on a 6 percent German bond is only 6 percent − 5 percent = 1 percent.

Returning to our comparison of a domestic and a foreign bond, we know that if the investor is indifferent between the two, their returns must be the same. That must be the case for the two bonds to be perfect substitutes. The implication is that

$$\begin{aligned}&\text{Value of \$1,000 invested in U.S. Treasury bonds for one year}\\ &\qquad = \text{Value of \$1,000 invested in foreign bonds after one year} \quad \text{(A3)}\end{aligned}$$

This means that

$$\$1{,}000(1 + i) = \$1{,}000(1 + i^f)\left(1 - \frac{\Delta E^e}{E}\right) \quad \text{(A4)}$$

or, using an approximation,

$$i = i^f - \frac{\Delta E^e}{E}$$

This equation, called the *interest parity condition,* tells us that the U.S. interest rate equals the German interest rate minus the dollar's expected appreciation. (These calculations ignore the risk of exchange rates moving in an unexpected way.)

If the interest parity condition did not hold, people would have an incentive to shift their investments until it did. For instance, if the U.S. interest rate exceeded the German interest rate minus the expected depreciation in the dollar, then foreign and domestic investors would sell German bonds and buy U.S. Treasury bonds. Their action would drive down the price of German bonds and drive up the price of U.S. bonds, raising the foreign interest rate and lowering the domestic rate until the relationship held.

Because we know the current U.S. and German interest rates, the interest parity condition tells us what the current dollar–euro exchange rate should be for a given expected future dollar–euro exchange rate. The interest rate parity condition tells us that the current value of the dollar will be higher:

1. the higher U.S. interest rates,
2. the lower German interest rates, and
3. the higher the expected future value of the dollar.

These are the same conclusions we arrived at using supply and demand theory.

We should note that there are two types of interest rate parity conditions: *uncovered* and *covered*. These differ based on whether they include an exchange rate guarantee when the bond matures. To see what we mean, remember that we are comparing the purchase of a domestic bond with a three-step transaction: (1) exchanging domestic for foreign currency, (2) buying a foreign bond, and (3) exchanging the foreign currency proceeds of the foreign bond at maturity for domestic currency. Since the exchange rate can move during the year, the third step involves currency risk. An investor can either accept this risk or buy insurance. In the second case, at the start of the entire process, the investor enters into an agreement to exchange the two currencies when the bond matures at a rate determined when the contract is written. *Uncovered* interest rate parity, where the position included exchange rate risk, is the first case—as represented by equation (A4). *Covered* (or currency-hedged) interest rate parity is the second.

Chapter

11 The Economics of Financial Intermediation

Learning Objectives

After reading this chapter, you should be able to:

LO1 Discuss the role of financial intermediaries and how they promote efficiency.

LO2 Explain asymmetric information, the problems it causes, and solutions to these problems.

LO3 Describe how moral hazard and adverse selection are managed by intermediaries and how they influence business finance.

The financial crisis of 2007–2009 alerted everyone that general economic well-being is closely tied to the health of the financial institutions that make up the financial system. The financial system is a lot like plumbing. When it's working well, we pay little attention. But its failure almost inevitably leads to a costly economic mess. The breadth, depth, and persistence of financial disruptions in the crisis brought us closer to a second Great Depression than at any time since the first one, in the 1930s.

As described in Chapter 1, our financial system is made up of six components: money, financial instruments, financial markets, financial institutions, government regulatory agencies, and the central bank. In Parts I and II (Chapters 1–10) we covered the first three of these components. In Part III (Chapters 11–14) we focus on the fourth, financial institutions, and the fifth, government regulatory agencies. In this chapter, we examine financial institutions' purpose, which is known as *financial intermediation*. As we learned in Chapter 3, financial institutions intermediate between savers and borrowers, and so their assets and liabilities are primarily financial instruments. Various sorts of banks, brokerage firms, investment companies, insurance companies, and pension funds all fall into this category. These are the institutions that pool funds from people and firms who save and lend them to people and firms who need to borrow, transforming assets and providing access to financial markets. They funnel savers' surplus resources into home mortgages, business loans, and investments.

As we discussed briefly at the end of Chapter 3, financial intermediaries are involved in both direct finance—in which borrowers sell securities directly to lenders in the financial markets—and indirect finance, in which a third party issues claims to those who provide funds and acquires claims from those who use them. Intermediaries investigate the financial condition of the individuals and firms who want financing to figure out which have the best investment opportunities. As providers of indirect finance, banks want to make loans only to the highest-quality borrowers. When they do their job correctly, financial intermediaries increase investment and economic growth at the same time that they reduce investment risk and economic volatility.

Ensuring that the best investment opportunities and highest-quality borrowers are funded is extremely important. Any country that wants to grow must ensure that its financial system works. When a country's financial system crumbles, its economy fails with it. That is what happened in the United States in the Great Depression of the 1930s, when a series of bank closings was followed by an increase in the unemployment rate to more than 25 percent and a fall of nearly one-third in the level of economic activity (measured by GDP). The Asian crisis of 1997, in which the banking systems of Thailand and Indonesia collapsed, is a more recent example. The deep, prolonged economic plunge of 2008–2009 highlights how a financial crisis, once started, can spread devastation across the global economy, triggering a spiral of economic and financial decline that is difficult to halt. And the subsequent turmoil in the euro area depressed some economies in the region enough to rival the traumatic 1930s experience. Without a stable, smoothly functioning financial system, no country can prosper.

The strong relationship between financial development and economic development is clearly apparent from the data. Figure 11.1 plots a commonly used measure of financial activity—the ratio of credit extended to the private sector (both through financial intermediaries and markets) to gross domestic product (GDP)—against real GDP per capita. The resulting positive correlation, roughly 0.6, is no surprise. With few exceptions, rich countries display advanced levels of financial development.

Figure 11.1 Financial and Economic Development

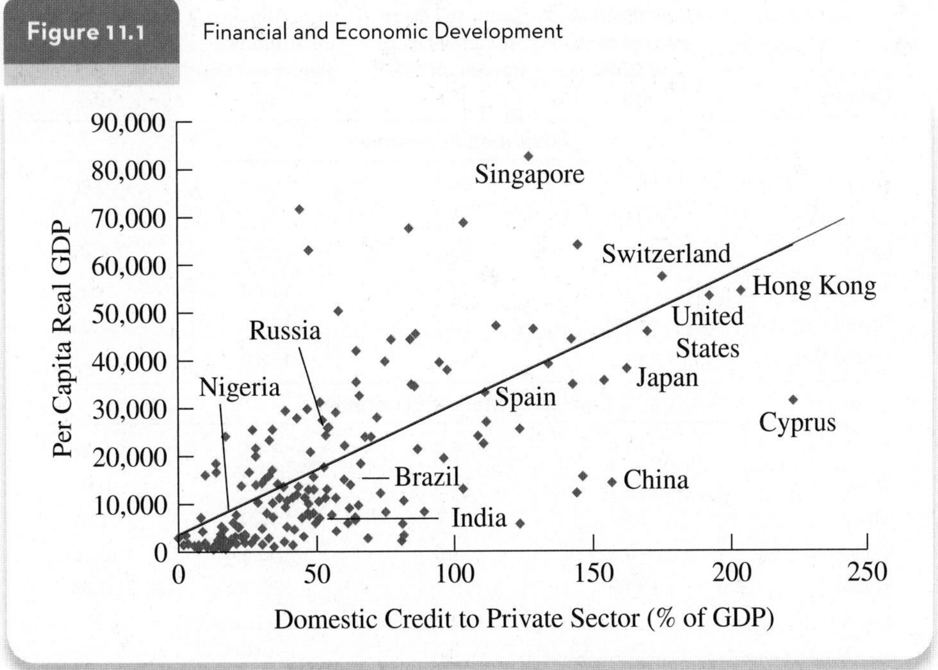

SOURCE: Financial development is measured as total financial system credit extended to the private sector. Global Financial Development Database, the World Bank. All data are for 2016. www.worldbank.org.

In theory, the market system may seem neat and simple, but the reality is that economic growth is a messy, chaotic thing. The flow of information among parties in a market system is particularly rife with problems—problems that can derail real growth unless they are addressed properly. In this chapter, we will discuss some of these information problems—including several that contributed to the financial crisis of 2007–2009—and learn how financial intermediaries attempt to solve them.

The Role of Financial Intermediaries

Markets are remarkably effective at coordinating the behavior of millions of firms and households in an economy. And financial markets are among the most important markets of all; they price economic resources and allocate them to their most productive uses. In many countries over the past 25 years, the value of stock and bond markets has come to rival or even surpass the value of outstanding loans through financial intermediaries. But as we will see, intermediaries, including banks and securities firms, continue to play a key role in both these types of finance.

Table 11.1 illustrates the importance of different channels of finance. As you look at the table, note two things. First, to make comparisons across countries of vastly

Table 11.1 The Relative Importance of Financing Channels
(Averages for 1990– 2016)

	Securities Markets		Loans	
Country	Stock Market Capitalization as a Percent of GDP (A)	Outstanding Domestic Debt Securities as a Percent of GDP (B)	Credit Extended by Banks and Other Financial Institutions as a Percent of GDP (C)	Ratio of Loans to Securities C/(A+B) (D)
Advanced Economies				
France	63.3	45.2	86.7	0.80
Germany	39.0	44.3	96.3	1.16
Italy	31.1	30.5	69.8	1.13
Japan	74.5	57.7	171.4	1.30
United Kingdom	113.5	15.1	129.5	1.01
United States	111.2	92.6	158.9	0.78
Emerging Market Economies				
Argentina	13.6	4.3	14.1	0.79
Brazil	34.5	17.8	42.3	0.81
China	35.7	18.6	103.0	1.90
India	49.2	1.5	33.5	0.66
Russia	34.9	5.1	25.7	0.64

NOTE: The items in columns A, B, and C are expressed as a percentage of GDP. But because the items are not components of GDP, there is no reason that the percentages should add to 100. Data are missing in some years for some countries. NA = not available.

(Stock Market Cap: GFDD.DM.01); (Domestic Private Debt Securities: GFDD.DM.03); (Credit by Intermediaries: GFDD.DI.12)

SOURCE: Global Financial Development Database, World Bank. https://datacatalog.worldbank.org/dataset/global-financial-development. Updates are also available through FRED.

different size, we measure everything relative to GDP. Second, there is no reason that the value of a country's stock market, bonds outstanding, or bank loans cannot be bigger than its GDP. In fact, we would expect it to be much larger, because the value of a company to its owners is often several times the level of one year's sales. This means that when you add up all the types of financing, direct and indirect, as a percentage of GDP, the numbers will generally sum to more than 100 in an advanced economy.

To see the lessons from the table, take the example of France, in the first row. The value of the French stock market (the value of the shares of all companies listed on the exchanges) is equivalent to 63.3 percent of that country's GDP (column A); the value of French debt securities is 45.2 percent of GDP (column B). Adding columns A and B tells us that, in France, securities finance equals 108.5 percent of GDP. That exceeds the amount of credit extended by French banks and other intermediaries— 86.7 percent of GDP (column C). The final column, D, reports the ratio of loans to securities. For France, the result is 0.80, which means that financing via securities markets was somewhat larger than loans. For the advanced economies in the table, the range of that ratio is between 0.78 and 1.30, so the French case is not unusual. In many emerging markets, the ratio is somewhat lower because in recent decades their stock markets have expanded notably. However, domestic private debt securities play only a small role in most emerging market economies, which underscores the costs and challenges of developing this alternative to loan and stock finance. The biggest difference among the emerging economies is in the scale of loans, which range from less than 15 percent of GDP in Argentina to more than 100 percent in China.

These data highlight the importance of intermediaries. Banks are still critical providers of financing around the world, although bank lending may not be the dominant source of financing that it once was. And intermediation is not limited to bank lending. Intermediaries determine which firms can access the stock and bond markets. Just as banks decide the size of a loan and the interest rate to be charged, securities firms set the volume and price of new stock and bond issues when they purchase them for sale to investors. And other intermediaries, like mutual funds, help individual investors sort among the thousands of stocks and bonds that are issued to develop a diversified portfolio with the desired risk characteristics.

Why are financial intermediaries so important? The answer has to do with information. To understand the importance of information in the role financial intermediaries play in the economy, consider the online company eBay. This virtual auction house may seem an unlikely place to start, but while eBay deals primarily with physical objects, it faces some of the same information problems as financial firms. As an online intermediary, eBay provides a mechanism through which almost anyone can auction off almost anything. As of late 2018, roughly 1.2 billion items were listed for sale at www.ebay.com—everything from $5 dinner plates to million-dollar antiques of all kinds. And people buy them! For just the single year 2018, eBay reported total transactions valued at nearly $95 billion, entered into by more than 175 million active users.

While millions of items are for sale on eBay, if you look carefully you'll notice an absence of financial products. You can purchase collectible coins and paper currency on eBay, but you can't borrow. There are no listings for Samantha's student loan, Chad's car loan, Chloe's credit card balance, or Mort's mortgage—at least, not yet. And though you can buy defaulted bond certificates, like the Reading Railroad bond shown in Chapter 4 (which was purchased on eBay), you can't buy or sell bonds on which the issuer is still making payments. People are selling cars and even real estate on eBay, but no one is auctioning off checking account services.

Think for a moment about why eBay doesn't auction off mortgages. First, Mort might need a $100,000 mortgage, and not many people can finance a mortgage of that size. The people who run eBay could try to establish a system in which 100 people sign up to lend Mort $1,000, but it would be extremely complex and cumbersome. Imagine collecting the payments, figuring out how to repay the lenders, and writing all the legal contracts that go with the transaction. Just as important, before offering to finance Mort's mortgage, lenders would want to know something about Mort and the house he's proposing to buy. Is Mort accurately representing his ability to repay the loan? Does he really intend to buy a house with the loan? The questions are nearly endless (see Chapter 12, Money and Banking Blog: The Cloudy Future of Peer-to-Peer Lending).

Financial intermediaries exist so that individual lenders don't have to worry about getting answers to all of these questions. Most people take for granted the ability of the financial system to shift resources from savers to investors, but when you look closely at the details, you're struck by how complicated the task is. It's amazing the enterprise works at all. Lending and borrowing involve both *transactions costs,* like the cost of writing a loan contract, and *information costs,* like the cost of figuring out whether a borrower is trustworthy. Financial institutions exist to reduce these costs.

In their role as financial intermediaries, financial institutions perform five functions (see Table 11.2): (1) pooling the resources of small savers; (2) providing safekeeping and accounting services, as well as access to the payments system; (3) supplying liquidity by converting savers' balances directly into a means of payment whenever needed; (4) providing ways to diversify risk; and (5) collecting and processing information in ways that reduce information costs. As we go through these, you'll see that the first four have to do with lowering transactions costs. That is, by specializing and providing these services to large numbers of customers, a financial firm can reduce the cost of providing them to individual customers. As in other fields, experts can do a better job than others, and more cheaply at that. The fifth function on the list, collecting and processing information, is a category all by itself, so we'll consider it in more detail.

While we will not discuss international banks in any depth, it is worth mentioning that they provide an additional set of services that complements those offered by your neighborhood bank. International banks handle transactions that cross national borders. That may mean taking deposits from savers in one country and providing them to investors in another country. It may also mean converting currencies in order to facilitate transactions for customers who do business or travel abroad.

Table 11.2 A Summary of the Role of Financial Intermediaries

1. *Pooling savings*	Accepting resources from a large number of small savers/lenders in order to provide large loans to borrowers.
2. *Safekeeping and accounting*	Keeping depositors' savings safe, giving them access to the payments system, and providing them with accounting statements that help them track their income and expenditures.
3. *Providing liquidity*	Allowing depositors to transform their financial assets into money quickly, easily, and at low cost.
4. *Diversifying risk*	Providing investors with the ability to diversify even small investments.
5. *Collecting and processing information services*	Generating large amounts of standardized financial information.

Pooling Savings

The most straightforward economic function of a financial intermediary is to pool the resources of many small savers. By accepting many small deposits, banks empower themselves to make large loans. So, for example, Mort might get his \$100,000 mortgage from a bank or finance company with access to a large group of savers, 100 of whom have \$1,000 to invest (see Figure 11.2). Similarly, a government or large company that wishes to borrow billions of dollars by issuing bonds will rely on a financial intermediary to find buyers for the bonds.

To succeed in this endeavor—pooling people's savings in order to make large loans—the intermediary must attract substantial numbers of savers. This means convincing potential depositors of the institution's soundness. Banks are adept at making sure customers feel that their funds will be safe. In the past, they did so by installing large safes in imposing bank buildings. Today, they rely on their reputations, as well as on government guarantees like deposit insurance. We'll return to this topic in Chapter 14.

Figure 11.2 Financial Intermediaries Pool Savings

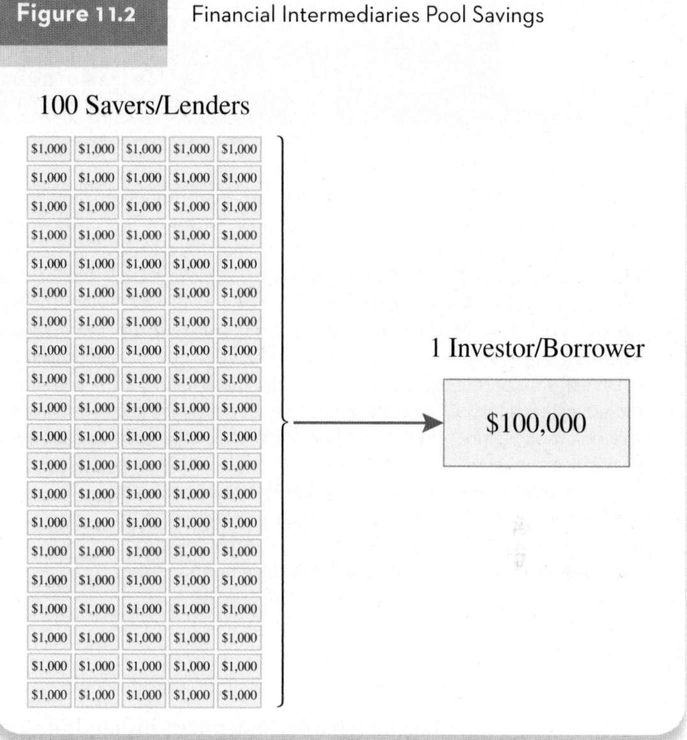

Financial intermediaries pool the funds of many small savers and lend them to one large borrower.

Safekeeping, Payments System Access, and Accounting

Goldsmiths were the original bankers. To keep their gold and jewelry safe, they had to construct vaults. Soon people began asking the goldsmiths to store gold for them in return for a receipt to prove it was there. It didn't take long for someone to realize that trading the goldsmith's receipts was easier than trading the gold itself. The next step came when the goldsmith noticed that there was quite a bit of gold left in the vault at the end of the day, so that some of it could safely be lent to others. The goldsmiths took the resources of those with gold to spare—the savers of the day—and channeled them to individuals who were short—the borrowers. Today, banks are the places where we put things for safekeeping—not just gold and jewelry, but our financial wealth as well. We deposit our paychecks and entrust our savings to a bank or other financial institution because we believe it will keep our resources safe until we need them.

When we think of banks, safekeeping is only one of several services that immediately come to mind. The others are Internet and mobile access, automated teller machines, credit and debit cards, checkbooks, and monthly bank statements. In providing depositors with these physical and electronic services, a bank gives them access to the payments system—the network that transfers funds from the account of one person or business to the account of another. The bank provides depositors a way to get cash into their wallets and to finalize payments using credit cards, debit cards, and checks. And

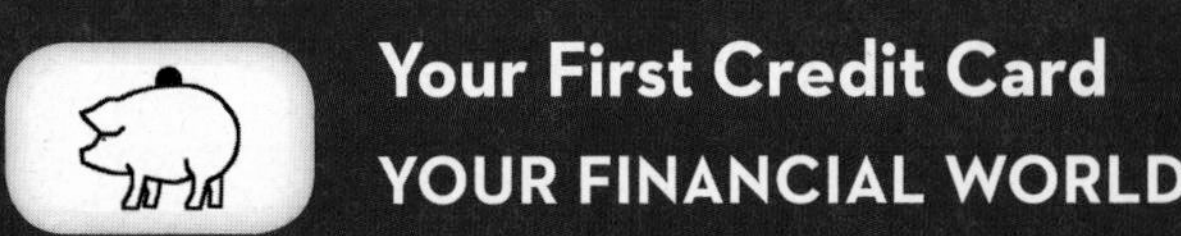

Your First Credit Card
YOUR FINANCIAL WORLD

Credit card interest rates are outrageous, running to more than 30 percent in some cases (really)! In Chapter 4, Your Financial World: What is *Your* Risk-Free Rate? explained why you should pay off your debt before building a financial portfolio. The odds are, when you get your first credit card, the interest rate will be extremely high. Why?

Unless your parent signed your credit card papers (or you worked a steady job before starting college), as a student you have no credit history, and the company that issued the card will assume the worst. So you're lumped in with people who have very poor credit, who would rather get lower-interest loans elsewhere but can't. This is adverse selection at its worst (see page 275 for a definition of adverse selection). When you get your first credit card, the assumption is that you are in a group of people who will have a high default rate. No wonder the issuers charge high interest rates. It is compensation for the risk they are taking. And just to prove the point, the industry's profitability is sensitive to the state of the economy.*

You need a credit card to build up a credit history, to establish yourself as a person who repays loans promptly. After a while, you'll be able to get a new card at a lower interest rate. But in the meantime, remember that your interest rate is extremely high, so borrowing is very expensive.

*The Federal Reserve reports annually regarding the profitability of credit card operations. The most recent report is available here: www.federalreserve.gov/publications/credit-card-profitability.htm.

because banks specialize in handling payments transactions, they can offer all these services relatively cheaply. Financial intermediaries reduce the costs of financial transactions.

This is not a trivial matter. It would be a disaster if we didn't have a convenient way to pay for things. By giving us one, financial intermediaries facilitate the exchange of goods and services, promoting specialization. Remember that in efficient economies—those that manage to get the most output from a given set of inputs—people and companies concentrate on the activities at which they are best and for which their opportunity cost is lowest. This principle of *comparative advantage* leads to specialization so that each of us ends up doing just one job and being paid in some form of money. But as specialization increases, more and more trading must take place to ensure that most of us end up with the goods and services we need and want. The more trading, the more financial transactions; and the more financial transactions, the more important it is that those transactions be cheap. If getting hold of money and using it to make payments were costly, that would put a damper on people's willingness to specialize. Financial intermediaries, by providing us with a reliable and inexpensive payments system, help our economy function more efficiently.

Beyond safekeeping and access to the payments system, financial intermediaries provide bookkeeping and accounting services. They help us manage our finances. Just think about your financial transactions over the past few months. If you work, you were paid, probably more than once. If you rent an apartment or own a home, you paid the rent or mortgage and probably the electric and gas bills. You paid your phone bill. Then there's transportation. If you have a car, you may have made a loan payment. You surely paid for gasoline and possibly for a repair. You purchased food, too, both at the grocery store and in various restaurants. And don't forget the movies and books you bought, perhaps through your mobile phone or tablet. As you get older, you may shoulder the expense of having children, along with saving for their education and your retirement. The point is, our financial lives are extraordinarily complex, and we need help keeping track of them. Financial intermediaries do the job: They provide us with bookkeeping and accounting services, noting all our transactions for us and making our lives more tolerable in the process.

Before we continue, we should note that providing safekeeping and accounting services, as well as access to the payments system, forces financial intermediaries to write legal contracts. Writing individualized contracts to ensure that each customer will maintain a checking account balance as required, or repay a loan as promised, would be extremely costly. But a financial intermediary can hire a lawyer to write one very high-quality contract that can be used over and over again, thus reducing the cost of each use. In fact, much of what financial intermediaries do takes advantage of what are known as *economies of scale*, in which the average cost of producing a good or service falls as the quantity produced increases. As we will see later, information is subject to economies of scale just as other goods and services are.

Providing Liquidity

One function that is related to access to the payments system is the provision of liquidity. Recall from Chapter 2 that *liquidity* is a measure of the ease and cost with which an asset can be turned into a means of payment. When a financial asset can be transformed into money quickly, easily, and at low cost, it is said to be very liquid. Financial intermediaries offer us the ability to transform assets into money at relatively low cost. That's what ATMs are all about—converting deposit balances into money on demand.

Financial intermediaries provide liquidity in a way that is both efficient and beneficial to all of us. To understand the process, think about your bank. Two kinds of customers visit the bank: those with funds, who want to make deposits, and those in need of funds, who want to make withdrawals or take out loans. Depositors want easy access to their funds—not just the currency they withdraw every week or so but the larger amounts they may need in an emergency. Borrowers don't want to pay the funds back for a while, and they certainly can't be expected to repay the entire amount on short notice.

In the same way that an insurance company knows that not all its policyholders will have automobile accidents on the same day, a bank knows that not all its depositors will experience an emergency and need to withdraw funds at the same time. The bank can structure its assets accordingly, keeping enough funds in short-term, liquid financial instruments to satisfy the few people who will need them and lending out the rest. And because long-term loans usually have higher interest rates than short-term money-market instruments—for instance, commercial paper and U.S. Treasury bills—the bank can offer depositors a higher interest rate than they would get otherwise.

Even the bank's short-term investments will do better than an individual depositor's could, because the bank can take advantage of economies of scale to lower its transactions costs. It isn't much more expensive to buy a $1 million U.S. Treasury bill than it is to buy one worth only $1,000. By collecting funds from a large number of small investors, the bank can reduce the cost of their combined investment, offering each individual investor both liquidity and a better rate of return. Pooling large numbers of small accounts in this way is very efficient. By doing so, an intermediary offers depositors something they can't get from the financial markets on their own.

The liquidity services financial intermediaries provide go beyond fast and easy access to account balances. Intermediaries offer both individuals and businesses lines of credit, which are similar to overdraft protection for checking accounts. A line of credit is essentially a preapproved loan that can be drawn on whenever a customer needs funds.

Home equity lines of credit, credit card cash advances, and business lines of credit are examples. Like a deposit account, the line of credit provides a customer with access to liquidity, except that in this case withdrawals may exceed deposit balances. To offer this service profitably, a financial intermediary must specialize in liquidity management. That is, it must design its balance sheet so that it can sustain sudden withdrawals.

Diversifying Risk

If you had $1,000 or $10,000 or even $100,000 to invest, would you want to keep it all in one place? Would you be willing to lend it all to a single person or firm? By now you have read Chapter 5, so you know the answer to this question: Don't put all your eggs in one basket; it's unnecessarily risky. But even without knowing much about diversifying through hedging and spreading risk, you would sense intuitively that lending $1 to each of 1,000 borrowers is less risky than lending $1,000 to just one borrower, and putting $1 in each of 1,000 different stocks is safer than putting $1,000 in one stock. Financial institutions enable us to diversify our investments and reduce risk.

Banks mitigate risk in a straightforward way: They take deposits from thousands or even millions of individuals and make thousands of loans with them. Thus, each depositor has a very small stake in each one of the loans. For example, a bank might collect $1,000 from each of one million depositors and then use the resulting $1 billion to make 10,000 loans of $100,000 each. So each depositor has a 1/1,000,000 share in each of the 10,000 loans.

RISK

To picture this, look back at Figure 11.2 (page 271) and imagine that it shows 10,000 times as many deposits and 10,000 times as many mortgages. Next, picture each of those deposits cut up into 10,000 pieces, each assigned to a different loan. That is, each deposit contributes 10 cents to each loan. That's diversification! And because the bank specializes in taking deposits and making loans, it can minimize the cost of setting up all the necessary legal contracts to do this.

All financial intermediaries provide a low-cost way for individuals to diversify their investments. Mutual fund companies offer small investors a low-cost way to purchase a diversified portfolio of stocks and eliminate the idiosyncratic risk associated with any single investment. Many of the mutual funds based on the Standard & Poor's 500 Index (described in Chapter 8) require a minimum investment of as little as a few thousand dollars. Because the average price of each stock in the index usually runs between $40 and $60, a small investor would need more than $20,000 to buy even a single share of stock in each of the 500 companies in the index (not to mention the fees the investor would need to pay to a broker to do it). Thus, the mutual fund company lets a small investor buy a fraction of a share in each of the 500 companies in the fund. And because mutual fund companies specialize in this activity, the cost remains low.

Collecting and Processing Information

One of the biggest problems individual savers face is figuring out which potential borrowers are trustworthy and which are not. Most of us do not have the time or skill to collect and process information on a wide array of potential borrowers. And we are understandably reluctant to invest in activities about which we have little reliable information. The fact that the borrower knows whether he or she is trustworthy, while the lender faces substantial costs to obtain the same information, results in an *information asymmetry*. Very simply, borrowers have information that lenders don't.

By collecting and processing standardized information, financial intermediaries reduce the problems information asymmetries create. They screen loan applicants to guarantee that they are creditworthy. They monitor loan recipients to ensure that they use the funds as they have claimed they will. To understand how this process works, and the implications it has for the financial system, we need to study information asymmetries in more detail.

Information Asymmetries and Information Costs

Information plays a central role in the structure of financial markets and financial institutions. Markets require sophisticated information to work well; when the cost of obtaining that information is too high, markets cease to function. Information costs make the financial markets, as important as they are, among the worst functioning of all markets. The fact is, the issuers of financial instruments—borrowers who want to issue bonds and firms that want to issue stock—know much more about their business prospects and their willingness to work than potential lenders or investors—those who would buy their bonds and stocks. This **asymmetric information** is a serious hindrance to the operation of financial markets. Solving this problem is one key to making our financial system work as well as it does.

To understand the nature of the problem and the possible solutions, let's go back to eBay. Why are the people who win online auctions willing to send payments totaling nearly $95 billion a year to the sellers? An amazing amount of trust is involved in these transactions. To bid at all, buyers must believe that an item has been described accurately. And winners must be sure that the seller will send the item in exchange for their payments, because the normal arrangement is for the seller to be paid first.

How can buyers be sure they won't be disappointed by their purchases when they arrive, assuming they arrive at all? The fact that sellers have much more information about the items they are selling and their own reliability creates an information asymmetry. Aware of this problem, the people who started eBay took two steps. First, they offered insurance to protect buyers who don't receive their purchases. Second, they devised a feedback forum to collect and store information about both bidders and sellers. Anyone can read the comments posted in the forum or check an overall rating that summarizes their content. Sellers who develop good reputations in the feedback forum command higher prices than others; buyers who develop bad reputations can be banned from bidding. Without this means of gathering information, eBay probably could not have been successful. Together, the buyers' insurance and the feedback forum make eBay run smoothly.[1]

The two problems eBay faced arise in financial markets, too. In fact, information problems are the key to understanding the structure of our financial system and the central role of financial intermediaries. Asymmetric information poses two important obstacles to the smooth flow of funds from savers to investors. The first, called **adverse selection**, arises before the transaction occurs. Just as buyers on eBay need to know the relative trustworthiness of sellers, lenders need to know how to distinguish good credit risks from bad. The second problem, called **moral hazard**, occurs after

[1]A low-cost, reliable payments system helps, too. The easier it is for buyers to pay sellers, the more likely both are to use the auction site. Realizing the need for a payments system, eBay acquired and integrated *PayPal,* which allows buyers and sellers to set up electronic accounts through which to make and receive payments for their eBay transactions. Because many sellers are too small to take credit cards, this innovation greatly facilitated the online exchanges. By 2015, PayPal had grown so large that it was again made independent.

Truth or Consequences: Ponzi Schemes and Other Frauds

APPLYING THE CONCEPT

In the financial world, you always have to be on the lookout for crooks. Fraud is the most extreme version of moral hazard, and it is remarkably common.

The term *Ponzi scheme* has its origins in a 1920 scam run by serial con artist Charles Ponzi. Promising a 50 percent profit within 45 days, he swindled unsuspecting investors out of something like $250 million in 2014 dollars. Ponzi never invested their money. Instead, he paid off early investors handsomely with the money he obtained from subsequent investors.

Financial laws are now far more elaborate than in Ponzi's day, and governments spend much more to enforce them, but frauds persist.

Bernie Madoff is the leading recent example. For decades, Madoff was a respected member of the investment community and able to escape detection. In the same manner as Ponzi, Madoff was redeeming requests for funds with the money he collected from more recent investors. Madoff's con, which may have begun as early as the 1970s, failed only when the financial crisis of 2007–2009 depleted his funds, making it impossible for him to pay off the final cohort of wealthy, sophisticated—yet apparently quite gullible—investors and financial firms. The Madoff scandal dwarfed Ponzi's racket: At the time the scheme blew up, the losses were estimated at $17.5 billion, and extensive efforts at recovery have put final losses in the neighborhood of $7 billion.

Unfortunately, in a complex financial system, the possibilities for fraud are widespread. Most cases are smaller and more mundane than those of Madoff or Ponzi, but their cumulative size is significant. One source devoted to tracking just Ponzi-type frauds in the United States listed 70 schemes worth an estimated $2.2 billion in 2014 alone.*

We aren't going to get rid of Ponzi schemes and other frauds (see Money and Banking Blog: Conflicts of Interest in Finance). But the mission of ferreting them out and prosecuting those responsible is essential. A well-functioning financial system is based on trust. That is, when we make a bank deposit or purchase a share of stock or a bond, we need to believe that the terms of the agreement are being accurately represented and will be carried out. Economies where property rights are weak and enforcement is unreliable also usually supply less credit to worthy endeavors. That means lower production, lower income, and lower welfare.

*See www.ponzitracker.com.

Used Cars: clean, reliable, and priced just right!

B Christopher/Alamy Stock Photo

the transaction. In the same way that buyers on eBay need reassurance that sellers will deliver their purchases after receiving payment, lenders need to find a way to tell whether borrowers will use the proceeds of a loan as they claim they will. The following sections will look at both these problems in detail to see how they affect the structure of the financial system.

Adverse Selection

Used Cars and the Market for Lemons The 2001 Nobel Prize in Economics was awarded to George A. Akerlof, A. Michael Spence, and Joseph E. Stiglitz "for their analyses of markets with asymmetric information." Professor Akerlof's contribution came first, in a paper published in 1970 titled "The Market for 'Lemons.'"[2] Akerlof's paper explained why the market for used cars—some of which may be "lemons"—doesn't function very well. Here's the logic.

[2]See "The Market for 'Lemons': Quality Uncertainty and the Market Mechanism," *Quarterly Journal of Economics*, August 1970. This paper contains very little mathematics and is quite readable. You can find it through your university library using an electronic storage system called JSTOR.

Suppose the used-car market has only two cars for sale, both 2017 model Honda Accords. One is immaculate, having been driven and maintained by a careful elderly woman who didn't travel much. The second car belonged to a young man who got it from his parents, loved to drive fast, and did not worry about the damage he might cause if he hit a pothole. The owners of these two cars know whether their own cars are in good repair, but used-car shoppers do not.

Let's say that potential buyers are willing to pay $20,000 for a well-maintained car, but only $10,000 for a "lemon"—a car with lots of mechanical problems. The elderly woman knows her car is a "peach." It's in good condition and she won't part with it for less than $20,000. The young man, knowing the poor condition of his car, will take $8,000 for it. But if buyers can't tell the difference between the two cars, without more information they will pay only the average price of $15,000. (A risk-averse buyer wouldn't even pay that much.) That is less than the owner of the good car will accept, so she won't sell her car and it disappears from the market. The problem is that if buyers are willing to pay only the average value of all the cars on the market, sellers with cars in above-average condition won't put their cars up for sale. Only the worst cars, the lemons, will be left on the market. In summary, buyers' inability to uncover the *hidden attributes* of the vehicles for sale undermines the used-car market as a whole.

Information asymmetries aside, people like to buy new cars, and when they do, they sell their old cars. People who can't afford new cars, or who would rather not pay for them, are looking to buy good used cars. Together, these potential buyers and sellers of used cars provide a substantial incentive for creative people to solve the problem of adverse selection in the used-car market. Some companies try to help buyers separate the peaches from the lemons. For instance, *Consumer Reports* has long provided information about the reliability and safety of particular makes and models. More recent is the CARFAX service, which provides potential car buyers the detailed history, including reported accidents and airbag deployments, of a specific used vehicle. Car dealers may try to maintain their reputations by refusing to pass off a clunker as a well-maintained car. For a fee, a mechanic will check out a used car for a potential buyer. Finally, many car manufacturers offer warranties on the used cars they have certified. We have found ways to overcome the information problems pointed out by Professor Akerlof, and as a result both good and bad used cars sell at prices much closer to their true value. So long as there exists a technology that lets buyers determine, at a reasonable cost, the hidden attributes of used cars for sale, the market works.

Adverse Selection in Financial Markets When it comes to information costs, financial markets are not that different from the used-car market. In the same way that the seller of a used car knows more about the car than the buyer, potential borrowers know more about the projects they wish to finance than prospective lenders. And in the same way that information asymmetries can drive good cars out of the used-car market, they can drive good stocks and bonds out of the financial market. To see why, let's start with stocks.

Think about a simple case in which there are two firms, one with good prospects and one with bad prospects. If you can't tell the difference between the two firms, you will be willing to pay a price based only on their average quality. The stock of the good company will be undervalued. Because the managers know their stock is worth more than the average price, they won't issue it in the first place. That leaves only the firm with bad prospects in the market. And because most investors aren't interested in companies with poor prospects, the market is very unlikely to get started at all.

The same thing happens in the bond market. Remember that risk requires compensation. The higher the risk, the greater the risk premium. In the bond market, this relationship between risk and return affects the cost of borrowing. The more risky the borrower, the higher the cost of borrowing. If a lender can't tell whether a borrower is a good or bad credit risk, the lender will demand a risk premium based on the average risk. Borrowers who know they are good credit risks won't want to borrow at this elevated interest rate, so they will withdraw from the market, leaving only the bad credit risks. The result is the same as for used cars and stocks: Because lenders are not eager to buy bonds issued by bad credit risks, the market will disappear.

Solving the Adverse Selection Problem

From a social perspective, the fact that managers might avoid issuing stock or bonds because they know the market will not value their company correctly is not good. It means that the company will pass up some good investments. And because some of the best investments will not be undertaken, the economy won't grow as rapidly as it could. Thus, it is extremely important to find ways for investors and lenders to distinguish well-run firms from poorly run firms. Well-run firms need to highlight their quality so they can obtain financing more cheaply. Investors need to distinguish between high- and low-risk investments so they can seek compensation corresponding to the level of risk they are taking on. The question is how to do it.

Recall how buyers and sellers in the used-car market developed ways to address the problem of distinguishing good from bad cars. The answer here is similar. First, because the problem is caused by a lack of information, we can create more information for investors. Second, we can provide guarantees in the form of financial contracts that can be written so a firm's owners suffer together with the people who invested in the company if the firm does poorly. This type of arrangement helps persuade investors that a firm's stocks and bonds are of high quality. And as we will see later, financial intermediaries can do a great deal to reduce the information costs associated with stock and bond investments.

Disclosure of Information One obvious way to solve the *hidden attributes* problem is to generate more information. This can be done in one of two ways: government-required disclosure, and the private collection and production of information (like CARFAX for used cars). In most advanced economies, *public companies*—those that issue stocks and bonds that are bought and sold in public financial markets—are required to disclose voluminous amounts of information. For example, in the United States the Securities and Exchange Commission requires firms to produce public financial statements that are prepared according to standard accounting practices. Corporations are also required to disclose, on an ongoing basis, information that could have a bearing on the value of their firms. And since August 2000, U.S. companies have been required to release to the public any information they provide to professional stock analysts.[3]

As we learned in 2001 and 2002, however, these requirements can go only so far in ensuring that investors are well informed. Despite government regulations designed to protect investors, Enron, WorldCom, Global Crossing, and numerous other companies

[3]Some people were concerned that Regulation FD, for "fair disclosure," might have the perverse effect of causing firms to make less information public. Fortunately, evidence shows that public corporations are now providing more information to both professional stock analysts and individual investors. Today, virtually all company conference calls—a mechanism frequently used to disseminate information about a firm's financial performance—are open to individual investors.

Deflation, Net Worth, and Information Costs

APPLYING THE CONCEPT

A casual reader of the business press might get the impression that **deflation**, when prices are declining on average, is a fate we would rather not contemplate. Deflation is associated with the Great Depression of the 1930s, when consumer prices and output both fell about 30 percent. It is also associated with Japan's economic underperformance since the early 1990s, when the price level peaked and began to decline.

Deflation is the opposite of the more familiar inflation. Inflation is when prices are going up, on average. Deflation is when they are going down. A primary reason deflation is so bad is that it aggravates information problems in ways that inflation does not. It does so by reducing a company's net worth. To see why, think about a typical firm's balance sheet. Its assets are buildings, machines, and product inventories. Its liabilities include various kinds of debt, much of it fixed in nominal terms. That is, companies borrow fixed numbers of dollars. Now think about the consequences of a decline in the price level. When prices fall, the dollar value of the firm's liabilities remains the same. The value of the firm's assets, however, tends to fall with the price level. Deflation drives down a firm's net worth, making it less trustworthy as a borrower. Remember, net worth solves the problems of adverse selection and moral hazard, allowing firms to obtain loans. With a low net worth, firms can no longer obtain financing because lenders cannot overcome the difficulty of asymmetric information. The same problems also afflict households, whose key assets (especially houses and stocks) usually decline in value in a deflation, reducing the capacity of households to borrow against collateral.

The connection among net worth, information, and the availability of credit to borrowers helps explain the dynamics of the business cycle. Think about what happens at the start of a recession. The value of a firm (as measured by the present value of its expected future sales) falls, compounding lenders' information problems. Lenders, suddenly more concerned about a borrower's creditworthiness, become more reluctant to make loans. The availability of investment funds falls, pushing the economy further into recession.

managed to distort the profits and debt levels published in their financial statements. With the help of some unethical accountants, company executives found a broad range of ways to manipulate the statements to disguise their firms' true financial condition. While accounting practices have changed since then and financial statements may now convey more information than they once did, everyone remains on guard. Information problems persist.

What about the private collection and sale of information? You might think that this would provide investors with what they need to solve the adverse selection problem, but unfortunately it doesn't work. While it is in everyone's interest to produce credible proof of the quality of a company's activities, such information doesn't really exist. In a limited sense there is private information collected and sold to investors. Various research services like Moody's, Value Line, and Dun and Bradstreet collect information directly from firms and produce evaluations.

These reports are not cheap. For example, Value Line charges nearly $600 a year for its weekly publication. To be credible, the companies examined can't pay directly for the research themselves, so investors have to. And while some individuals might be willing to pay, in the end they don't have to and so they won't. Private information services face what is called a free-rider problem. A **free rider** is someone who doesn't pay the cost to get the benefit of a good or service, and free riding on stock market analysis is easy to do. Even though these publications are expensive, public libraries subscribe to some of them. Reporters for *The Wall Street Journal* and other periodicals read them and write stories publicizing crucial information. And individual investors can simply follow the lead of people they know who subscribe to the publications. Of course, all these practices reduce the ability of the producers of private information to actually profit from their hard work.

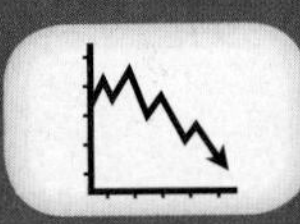

Information Asymmetry and Securitization
LESSONS FROM THE CRISIS

This chapter highlights the importance of *screening* credit risks to limit adverse selection and of *monitoring* the recipients of funds to limit moral hazard. It also warns that *free riding* can diminish screening and monitoring. A key source of the financial crisis of 2007–2009 was insufficient screening and monitoring in the securitization of mortgages (see Chapter 6, Applying the Concept: Securitization, page 148).

Mortgage securitization problems started with the initial mortgage lenders—the *originators*—who eased standards and reduced screening to increase the volume of lending and the short-term profitability of their businesses. The result was many risky mortgages: When housing prices began to fall in 2006, defaults soared.

At the next stage of securitization, the firms that assembled these mortgages into securities for sale—the *distributors*—did little to forestall the decline of lending standards by originators. Had they wished to, they could have required that the originators demonstrate a high level of net worth and invest it in the mortgages that they sold.

When lending standards decline, securitization becomes like a game of "hot potato." Players in the game try to pass risky loans—the hot potato—along to the next player as quickly as they can, while it's still possible. The game ends when defaults soar, leaving someone with the loss.

Rating agencies might have halted the game early. Instead, they awarded their top ratings to a large share of mortgage-backed securities, severely underestimating the riskiness of the loans. In retrospect, we can now see that the agencies had little incentive to expend the resources necessary to adequately screen the underlying loans or the lenders.

Finally, many investors (and government officials responsible for overseeing intermediaries) assumed they could rely on other people—they were free riders. Rather than undertake their own costly screening efforts, they assumed the assessment of the rating agencies was accurate.

Implicitly, the participants in the process acted as if the ultimate collateral—the value of houses—would always be adequate to contain the damage from adverse selection. Had housing prices risen indefinitely, as many appeared to assume they would, the collateral would have protected investors against any damage. But, when housing prices and the value of the collateral started to plunge, the effects of adverse selection threatened the financial system as a whole.

Collateral and Net Worth While government-required disclosure and private information collection are crucial, they haven't solved all the hidden attributes problems that plague investors and the firms they invest in. Fortunately, other solutions exist. One is to make sure that lenders are compensated even if borrowers default. If a loan is insured in some way, then the borrower isn't a bad credit risk.

There are two mechanisms for ensuring that a borrower is likely to repay a lender: collateral and net worth. Recall from Chapter 3 that **collateral** is something of value pledged by a borrower to the lender in the event of the borrower's default. Collateral is said to *back* or *secure* a loan. Houses serve as collateral for mortgages; cars, as collateral for car loans. If the borrower fails to keep up with the mortgage or car payments, the lender will take possession of the house or car and sell it to recover the borrowed funds. In circumstances like these, adverse selection is less of a concern; that's why collateral is so prevalent in loan agreements. When banks make loans without collateral—**unsecured loans**, like credit card debt—they typically charge very high interest rates. Adverse selection is the reason. (See Your Financial World: Your First Credit Card on page 272.)

Net worth is the owner's stake in a firm, the value of the firm's assets minus the value of its liabilities. Under many circumstances, net worth serves the same purpose as collateral. If a firm defaults on a loan, the lender can make a claim against the firm's net worth. Consider what would happen if a firm with a high net worth borrowed to undertake a project that turned out to be unsuccessful. If the firm had no net worth, the lender would be out of luck. Instead, the firm's owners can use their net worth to repay the lender.

The same is true of a home mortgage. A mortgage is much easier and cheaper to get when a homebuyer makes a substantial down payment. For the lender, the risk is that the price of the home will fall, in which case its value will not be sufficient to fully compensate the lender in the event of a default. But with a large down payment, the homeowner has a substantial stake in the house, so even if the price falls, the mortgage can likely be repaid even if the borrower defaults. From the perspective of the mortgage lender, the homeowner's equity serves exactly the same function as net worth in a business loan.

Photodisc/Getty Images

The importance of net worth in reducing adverse selection is the reason owners of new businesses have so much difficulty borrowing money. If you want to start a bakery, for example, you will need financing to buy equipment and cover the rent and payroll for the first few months. Such seed money is very hard to get. Most small business owners must put up their homes and other property as collateral for their business loans. Only after they have managed to establish a successful business and have built up some net worth in it, can they borrow without pledging their personal property.

Moral Hazard: Problem and Solutions

The phrase *moral hazard* originated when economists who were studying insurance noted that an insurance policy changes the behavior of the person who is insured. Examples are everywhere. A fire insurance policy written for more than the value of the property might induce the owner to arson; a generous automobile insurance policy might encourage reckless driving. Employment arrangements suffer from moral hazard, too. How can your boss be sure you are working as hard as you can if you'll get your paycheck at the end of the week whether you do or not? Moral hazard arises when we cannot observe people's actions and so cannot judge whether a poor outcome was intentional or just a result of bad luck.

Thus, a lender's or investor's information problems do not end with adverse selection. A second information asymmetry arises because the borrower knows more than the lender about the way borrowed funds will be used and the effort that will go into a project. Where adverse selection is about *hidden attributes,* moral hazard is about *hidden actions*. Moral hazard plagues both equity and bond financing, making it difficult for all but the biggest, best-known companies to issue either stocks or bonds successfully. Let's look at each type of financing and examine the ways people have tried to solve the problem of moral hazard.

Moral Hazard in Equity Financing If you buy a stock, how do you know the company that issued it will use the funds you have invested in the way that is best for you? The answer is that it almost surely will not. You have given your funds to managers, who will tend to run the company in the way most advantageous to them. The separation of your ownership from their control creates what is called a *principal–agent problem,* which can be more than a little costly to stockholders. Witness the luxurious offices, corporate jets, limousines, and artwork that executives surround themselves with, not to mention the millions of dollars in compensation they pay themselves. Managers gain all these personal benefits at the expense of stockholders.

A simple example will illustrate this point. Let's say that your cousin Ina, who is a whiz at writing software, has an idea for a program to speed up wireless Internet access. Together, the two of you estimate she needs $10,000 to write the program and sell it to an interested buyer. But Ina has only $1,000 in savings, so you will have to contribute $9,000. Family etiquette dictates that once you've made the investment, you won't be able to monitor Ina's progress—to tell whether she is working hard or even if she is working at all. If everything goes well, you think you can sell the program to Microsoft for $100,000, which is 10 times the initial investment. But Ina had better work quickly or someone else may make it to market first and Ina's program won't be worth nearly as much.

The difficulty in this arrangement is immediately apparent. If Ina works hard and all goes according to plan, she will get 10 percent of the $100,000 (that's $10,000) and you will get the rest, a whopping $90,000. But if Ina runs into programming problems or spends part of the time surfing instead of working, someone else may bring the product to market first, reducing the value of Ina's software to $10,000. The problem is, Ina's decision to go surfing would cost her only $9,000, but it would cost you $81,000! And because you wouldn't be able to tell why the venture failed, you're unlikely to part with your $9,000 in the first place.

Solving the Moral Hazard Problem in Equity Financing Solutions to the moral hazard problem in equity finance are hard to come by. Information on the quality of management can be useful, but only if owners have the power to fire managers—and that can be extremely difficult. Requiring managers to own a significant stake in their own firm is another possibility. If Ina comes up with the entire $10,000, then there is no separation between ownership and control and no question whether Ina will behave in the owner's interest—she is the owner. But people who have good ideas don't always have the resources to pursue them. Ina doesn't have the $10,000 she needs.

During the 1990s, a concerted attempt was made to align managers' interests with those of stockholders. Executives were given stock options that provided lucrative payoffs if a firm's stock price rose above a certain level. This approach worked until managers found ways to misrepresent their companies' profitability, driving up stock prices temporarily so they could cash in their options. Accounting methods have been reformed in an attempt to reduce such abuses, but at this writing, no one has devised a foolproof way of ensuring that managers will behave in the owners' interest instead of their own.

Moral hazard: How can you be sure that your investment isn't being used to buy one of these vacation homes in Tahiti?

Photodisc/Getty Images

Moral Hazard in Debt Finance When the managers of a company are the owners, the problem of moral hazard in equity financing disappears. This suggests that investors should prefer debt financing to equity financing. But debt financing has its problems, too. Imagine that instead of buying a 90 percent share in your cousin Ina's software venture, you lend her $9,000 at an 11 percent annual interest rate. The debt contract specifies that she will repay you $9,990 in one year's time. This arrangement dramatically changes Ina's incentives. Now, if she works hard, she gets $90,010, but if she goes surfing, she still has to repay the $9,990, leaving her nothing at the end of the year. Surely this solves your problem.

Debt does go a long way toward eliminating the moral hazard problem inherent in equity finance, but it doesn't finish the job. Because debt contracts allow owners to keep all the profits in excess of the loan payments, they encourage risk taking. Suppose Ina decides to use some or all of the $10,000 to buy lottery tickets. That's an extremely risky thing to do. The problem is, if her lottery number comes up, she gets the winnings, but if she loses, you pay the cost. That's not a very desirable outcome for you, the lender. While in the real world the danger isn't quite that extreme, the problem still exists. Lenders need to find ways to make sure borrowers don't take too many risks. Unfortunately, borrowers' limited liability has the same effect that an insurance policy has on the insured. People with risky projects are attracted to debt finance because they get the full benefit of the upside, while the downside is limited to their collateral, if any.

Solving the Moral Hazard Problem in Debt Finance To some degree, a good legal contract can solve the moral hazard problem that is inherent in debt finance. Bonds and loans often carry *restrictive covenants* that limit the amount of risk a borrower can assume. For example, a covenant may restrict the nature of the goods or services the borrower can purchase. It may require the firm to maintain a certain level of net worth, a minimum balance in a bank account, or a minimum credit rating. Home mortgages often come with restrictive covenants requiring the homeowners to purchase fire insurance or to make monthly deposits toward payment of their property taxes. (Failure to pay property taxes can lead the government to seize the borrower's house, complicating the mortgage company's attempt to recover its principal.)

Table 11.3 summarizes this section's discussion of how financial relationships are affected by information problems, together with a list of the various solutions used to address the problems information costs create.

Table 11.3 The Negative Consequences of Information Costs

1. ***Adverse selection.*** Lenders can't distinguish good from bad credit risks, which discourages transactions from taking place.

   Solutions to the hidden attributes problem include:

   - Government-required information disclosure
   - Private collection of information
   - Pledging of collateral to insure lenders against the borrower's default
   - Requiring borrowers to invest substantial resources of their own

2. ***Moral hazard.*** Lenders can't tell whether borrowers will do what they claim they will do with the borrowed resources; borrowers may take too many risks.

   Solutions to the hidden actions problem include:

   - Requiring managers to report to owners
   - Requiring managers to invest substantial resources of their own
   - Covenants that restrict what borrowers can do with borrowed funds

Conflicts of Interest in Finance
MONEY AND BANKING BLOG

Financial corruption exposed in the years since the financial crisis is breathtaking in its scale, scope, and resistance to remedy. Traders colluded to rig the foreign exchange (FX) market, where daily transactions exceed $5 trillion, and to manipulate LIBOR, the world's leading interest rate benchmark (see Chapter 13, Applying the Concept: Eclipsing LIBOR). Firms have facilitated tax evasion and money laundering. And Bernie Madoff engineered what was arguably the largest Ponzi scheme in history (see Applying the Concept: Truth or Consequences: Ponzi Schemes and Other Frauds).

In response, Congress enacted the Dodd-Frank Act, the most far-reaching financial reform since the 1930s. Authorities have leaned on financial firms to diminish risk-taking incentives in their compensation schemes. Governments and private litigants obtained ever-larger pecuniary settlements—since 2009, fines alone approached $250 billion—at the same time that prosecutors convicted both firms and individuals involved in the big trading scandals. And leading regulators have warned the largest U.S. institutions that a failure to improve their ethical culture could lead policymakers to downsize their firms.

So far, the most obvious reaction from the financial sector has been to hire thousands of compliance officers and risk managers to police the behavior of their own employees.

Yet, corruption persists.

The source of this continuing behavior is poor incentives arising from a *principal–agent* (or *agency*) *problem.* If employees and firms (the *agents*) can hide their conduct, then they can benefit greatly by acting in ways that run counter to the interests of their employers or their clients (the *principals*). Unless the principals (or the government) can prevent such concealment at a reasonable cost, it comes as no surprise that agents behave unethically, if not illegally.

Agency problems are particularly rampant in finance because both the rewards to exploitation *and* the cost of detection are so high. The incentive problems appear worst in the largest, most complex intermediaries that engage in multiple activities.

The reason is that the presence of diverse business lines both breeds conflicts of interest and makes them more difficult to contain.* To be sure, many financial activities are pursued at the same time by the same firm and rarely trigger serious conflicts of interest. For example, without harm, most banks and brokers simultaneously provide (1) safekeeping services for assets, (2) access to the payments system, and (3) accounting services to track transactions and balances. Even here, however, major frauds occasionally arise. Bernie Madoff's clients may have thought that the lack of an independent asset custodian was safe and reduced their costs. Instead, allowing

Financial Intermediaries and Information Costs

The problems of adverse selection and moral hazard make securities finance expensive and difficult to get. These drawbacks lead us immediately to loans and the role of financial institutions. Much of the information that financial intermediaries collect is used to reduce information costs and minimize the effects of adverse selection and moral hazard. To reduce the potential costs of adverse selection, intermediaries screen loan applicants. To minimize moral hazard, they monitor borrowers. And when borrowers fail to live up to their contracts with lenders, financial intermediaries penalize them by enforcing the contracts. Let's look more closely at how financial firms screen and monitor borrowers to reduce information costs. And then we will conclude with a quick look at how firms finance growth and investment.

Madoff to serve both as broker and custodian helped him conceal his fraud.

But, when pursued together, a variety of other activities are prone to widespread and costly conflicts. Perhaps the most notorious is the mix of equity underwriting, equity research, and equity sales. The incentive problem here is simple: With large underwriting fees at stake, analysts are motivated to produce optimistic company research reports to attract issuers, even if the result is that brokers sell overvalued stocks to unwitting clients. Yet, more than a decade after the legal settlement that compelled brokerage firms to erect or fortify costly "Chinese walls" between their investment banking and research staffs, reports indicate significant violations.

Overall, the most serious issues arise in the context of large, complex intermediaries, whose failure threatens the financial system as a whole. Unfortunately, the combination of increased transparency, improved market discipline, enhanced regulation, massive financial penalties, and criminal prosecution has thus far failed to halt repeated, large-scale misbehavior arising from conflicts of interest.

What to do?

The main options are to (1) break up large institutions into smaller ones with restricted scope, (2) hold individuals more accountable, and (3) do some mix of the two. Regulators may wish to consider the first option if the cost of losing economies of scope is small relative to the social costs of conflicts of interest. The case of equity research and underwriting may be a useful example.

The second remedy requires that managers face greater *personal financial liability* for their firms' excesses. Large fines that punish stockholders who have minimal corporate control may simply increase the cost of capital for big firms. In contrast, partnerships, where owners face *unlimited liability* for their own and their partners' actions, foster strong incentives to police bad behavior. Hence, compensation arrangements that create partnership-like downside risks for years into the future—even for middle-level managers with risk-taking authority—ought to be a common feature in large, systemic intermediaries. For similar reasons, more frequent criminal prosecutions (such as those for LIBOR and FX manipulation) promote individual accountability and eventually may increase deterrence.

Unfortunately, there is no panacea. Regulators and prosecutors must continue to experiment with new remedies, acknowledging that past efforts have proven remarkably ineffective. And they must remain vigilant because the financial system constantly evolves and adjusts.

*See, for example, Ingo Walter, "Conflict of Interest and Market Discipline among Financial Services Firms," NYU Working Paper No. 2451/27263, October 2003.

Screening and Certifying to Reduce Adverse Selection

To get a loan, whether from a bank, a mortgage company, or a finance company, you must fill out an application. As part of the process, you will be asked to supply your Social Security number. The lender uses the number to identify you to a company that collects and analyzes credit information, summarizing it for potential lenders in a credit score.

Your personal credit score (described in Chapter 7 in Your Financial World: Your Credit Rating) tells a lender how likely you are to repay a loan. It is analogous to eBay's feedback forum rating or to an expert appraiser's certification of the authenticity and condition of an original painting. The credit rating company *screens* you and then *certifies* your credit rating. If you are a good credit risk with a high credit score, you are more likely than others to get a loan at a relatively low interest rate. Note that the company that collects your credit information and produces your credit score charges a fee each time someone wants to see it. This overcomes the free-rider problem.

Financing Intangible Capital

APPLYING THE CONCEPT

When most people think of business investment, what comes to mind is the purchase of new equipment and structures. A restaurant might start with construction, and then fill its new building with tables, chairs, stoves, and the like. This is the world of *tangible* capital.

We still need buildings and machines (and restaurants). But, over the past few decades, the nature of business capital has changed. Much of what firms invest in today—especially the biggest and fastest-growing ones—is *intangible*. This includes software, data, market analysis, scientific research and development (R&D), employee training, organizational design, development of intellectual and entertainment products, mineral exploration, and the like.

Figure 11.3 shows the shift from tangible to intangible investment in the United States over the past 40 years. As a percent of private gross value added, tangible capital expenditure (the red line) falls, while intangible expenditure (the blue line) rises.

Figure 11.3 U.S. Tangible and Intangible Investment (Percent of Private Gross Value Added)

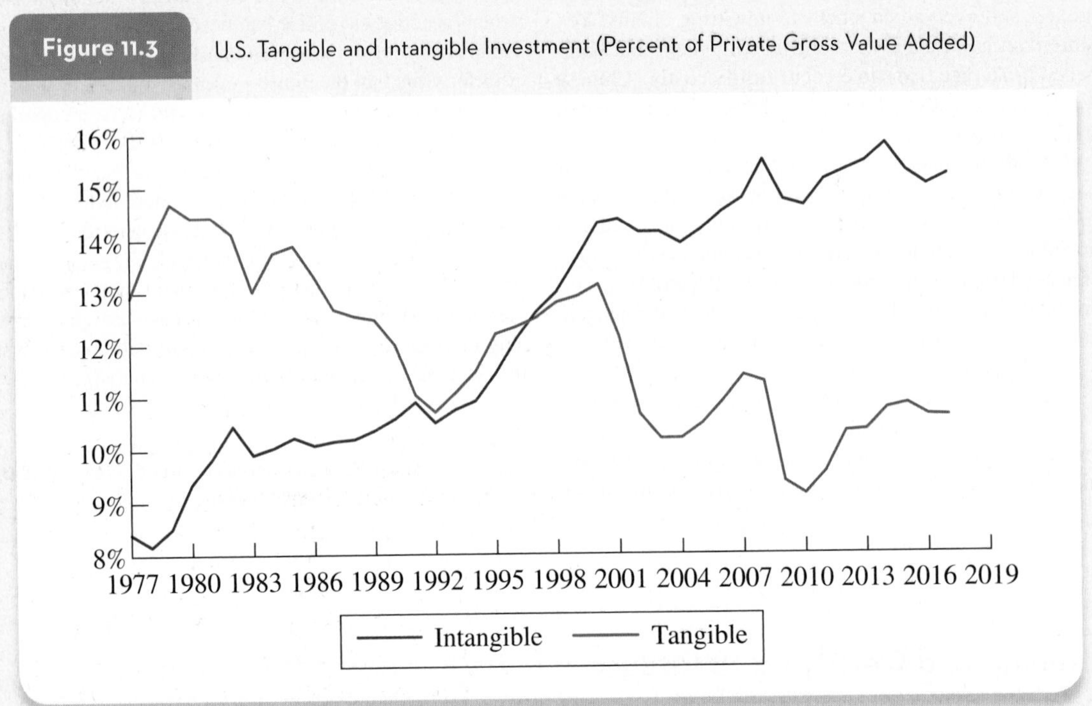

SOURCE: Lee Branstetter and Daniel Sichel, *The Case for an American Productivity Revival*, Peterson Institution for International Economics, Policy Brief 17-26, June 2017.

Banks can collect information on a borrower that goes beyond what a loan application or credit report contains. By noting the pattern of deposits and withdrawals from your account, as well as your use of your debit card if you have one, they can learn more about you than you might like. Banks monitor both their individual and their business customers in this way. Again, the information they collect is easy to protect and use. The special information banks have puts them in an almost unique position to *screen* customers and reduce the costs of adverse selection. This expertise helps explain another phenomenon, the fact that most small and medium-size businesses depend on banks for their financing.

An example from the world of information technology helps understand the pattern. Consider what has happened to prices of computer hardware and software, and the related expenditure to purchase the two. The first IBM PC, built in 1981, cost the equivalent of $8,000 today. While it came with a Microsoft operating system, most of the expenditure was for a very expensive machine—a tangible asset. Today, you could acquire hardware that runs at least 10,000 times faster for barely one-quarter of the price. But, if you want that machine to do anything useful, you will likely fork over a substantial amount for software and then spend time learning how to use it. When it comes to expenditure on computing and information technology, intangibles have gradually substituted for tangibles.

What are the implications of this shift for the structure of finance? Tangible capital can serve as collateral, providing lenders with some protection against default. As a result, firms with an abundance of physical assets can finance themselves readily by issuing debt. By contrast, a company that focuses on software development, employee training, or improvement of the efficiency of its organization will find it more difficult and costly to borrow because the resulting assets cannot easily be resold.

Indeed, the challenge for business finance is inherent in the economic characteristics of intangible capital.* Intangible assets:

- Are often *nonrival*, so one person's use does not impede someone else from using it simultaneously.
- Have *little market value*, so the cost of producing them is almost entirely sunk.
- Generate positive *spillovers* that benefit people other than the producer.
- Exhibit *synergies*, so they work more effectively when combined.

Given these properties, software firms—especially those developing Internet applications—have debt that is only about 10 percent of book equity. By contrast, the debt-to-book value of restaurants is nearly 95 percent. Scientific research and development expenditure fits this pattern as well: Software and pharmaceutical firms invest heavily in R&D, while restaurants and car dealers do almost none. All of this leads to the judgment that the traditional system based on bank lending and marketable bonds may be ill-suited to financing the increased share of economic activity requiring intangible investment.

Fortunately, finance evolves. And, once we focus on the increased importance of business activities that are nonrival, have little market value, carry spillovers, and exhibit synergies, it becomes easier to understand some important trends. In particular, we can explain the ongoing shift from public to private equity markets (see Chapter 8, Applying the Concept: Raising Equity: Public versus Private Markets).

*For a detailed discussion of the importance of intangible capital, see Jonathan Haskel and Stian Westlake, *Capitalism without Capital: The Rise of the Intangible Economy* (Princeton, NJ: Princeton University Press, 2017).

Financial intermediaries' superior ability to screen and certify borrowers extends beyond loan making to the issuance of bonds and equity. Underwriters—large financial institutions, like Goldman Sachs, JPMorgan Chase, and Morgan Stanley—screen and certify firms seeking to raise funds directly in the financial markets. Without certification by one of these firms, companies would find it difficult to raise funds. Large intermediaries go to great lengths to market their expertise as underwriters; they want people to recognize their names the world over, just as everyone recognizes Coca-Cola. A can of Coke, the best-selling soft drink in the world, is instantly recognizable, whether the fine print is in English, Chinese, Arabic, or Swedish. Financial institutions have applied this concept, which marketing people call branding, to their certification of financial products. If JPMorgan Chase, a well-known bank and securities firm, is willing to sell a bond or stock, the brand name suggests that it is a high-quality investment.

In the financial world, Goldman Sachs, JPMorgan Chase, and Morgan Stanley have as much brand recognition as Coke does in the soft-drink world.

PATRICK KOVARIK/AFP/Getty Images

Monitoring to Reduce Moral Hazard

If someone weren't watching over your shoulder, you might take the money you borrowed for a business project and fly off to Tahiti. To address the risk that sellers might take the money and run, eBay developed buyers' insurance. In the financial world, intermediaries insure against this type of moral hazard by monitoring both the firms that issue bonds and those that issue stocks.

Car dealers provide an interesting example of how this process works. Dealers have to finance all those shiny new cars that sit on the lot, waiting for buyers to show up. One way to do this is with a bank loan that is collateralized by the cars themselves. But the bank doesn't completely trust the dealer to use the loan proceeds properly. Every so often, the bank manager will send an associate to count the number of cars on the lot. The count tells the manager whether the dealer is using the borrowed funds properly. In monitoring the dealer this way, the bank is enforcing the restrictive covenants contained in the loan contract. Because banks specialize in this type of monitoring, they can do it more cheaply than individual borrowers and lenders.

Many financial intermediaries (other than banks) hold significant numbers of shares in individual firms. When they do, they find ways to monitor the companies' activities. For example, the California Public Employee Retirement System (CalPERS) manages more than $300 billion in assets, the income from which is used to pay retired employees' pensions. About 1.6 million "members" of CalPERS depend on the fund's managers to carefully monitor its investments. Before buying a company's stock, CalPERS's managers do a significant amount of research on the firm; once they have purchased the shares, they monitor the firm's activities very closely. In some cases, they place a representative on the company's board of directors to monitor and protect CalPERS's investment firsthand.

In the case of some new companies, a financial intermediary called a *venture capital firm* does the monitoring. Venture capital firms (like Kleiner Perkins or Draper Fisher) specialize in investing in risky new *ventures* in return for a stake in the ownership and a share of the profits. To guard against moral hazard and ensure that the new company has the best possible chance of success, the venture capitalist keeps a close watch on the managers' actions.

Finally, the threat of a takeover helps persuade managers to act in the interest of the stock- and bondholders. If managers don't do a good job of watching out for shareholders' interests, another company can buy the firm and replace them. In the 1980s, some firms specialized in such tactics. Today, this approach has become the business model of *private equity firms,* a few of which (like Bain Capital and Kohlberg Kravis Roberts) have become very large themselves. When the new owners put their own people in charge of the firm, they eliminate the moral hazard problem.

Key Terms

adverse selection, 275
asymmetric information, 275
collateral, 280
deflation, 279
free rider, 279
moral hazard, 275
net worth, 280
unsecured loan, 280

Using FRED: Codes for Data in This Chapter

Data Series	FRED Data Code
Total debt securities owed	ASTDSL
Total loans owed	ASTLL
Credit market liabilities of nonfinancial corporations	BCNSDODNS
Total credit market debt owed by domestic financial sector	TCMDODFS
Market value of equities (of nonfinancial corporations)	NCBEILQ027S
Population	POP
Bank loans and leases	TOTLL
Gross value added of financial corporations	A454RC1Q027SBEA
Nominal GDP	GDP
Total debt-to-equity ratio (United States)	TOTDTEUSQ163N
Total debt-to-equity ratio (Germany)	TOTDTEDEQ163N
Unemployment rate for the United States	M0892AUSM156SNBR
Harmonized unemployment rate for Greece	LRUN64TTGRQ156S
Harmonized unemployment rate for Italy	LRUN64TTITQ156S
Harmonized unemployment rate for Portugal	LRHUTTTTPTQ156S
Harmonized unemployment rate for Spain	LRUN64TTESQ156S
Consumer Price Index of All Items in Japan	JPNCPIALLQINMEI
GDP Implicit Price Deflator in Japan	JPNGDPDEFQISMEI

Chapter Lessons

To learn more about the changing financial system, visit www.moneyandbanking.com.

1. Financial intermediaries specialize in reducing costs by:
   a. Pooling the resources of small savers and lending them to large borrowers.
   b. Providing safekeeping, accounting services, and access to the payments system.
   c. Providing liquidity services.
   d. Providing the ability to diversify small investments.
   e. Providing information services.
2. For potential lenders, investigating borrowers' trustworthiness is costly. This problem, known as asymmetric information, occurs both before and after a transaction.
   a. Before a transaction, the least creditworthy borrowers are the ones most likely to apply for funds. This problem is known as adverse selection.
   b. Lenders and investors can reduce adverse selection by:
      i. Collecting and disclosing information on borrowers.
      ii. Requiring borrowers to post collateral and show sufficient net worth.
   c. After a transaction, a borrower may not use the borrowed funds as productively as possible. This problem is known as moral hazard.
      i. In equity markets, moral hazard exists when the managers' interests diverge from the owners' interests.
      ii. Finding solutions to the moral hazard problem in equity financing is difficult.
      iii. In debt markets, moral hazard exists because borrowers have limited liability. They get the benefits when a risky bet pays off, but they don't suffer a loss when it doesn't.

iv. The fact that debt financing gives managers/borrowers an incentive to take too many risks gives rise to restrictive covenants, which require borrowers to use funds in specific ways.

3. Financial intermediaries can manage the problems of adverse selection and moral hazard.
   a. They can reduce adverse selection by collecting information on borrowers and screening them to check their creditworthiness.
   b. They can reduce moral hazard by monitoring what borrowers are doing with borrowed funds.
   c. In the end, the vast majority of firms' finance comes from internal sources, suggesting that information problems are too big for even financial intermediaries to solve.

Conceptual and Analytical Problems

1. Describe the problem of asymmetric information that an employer faces in hiring a new employee. What solutions can you think of? Does the problem persist after the person has been hired? If so, how and what can be done about it? Is the problem more or less severe for employees on a fixed salary? Why or why not? *(LO2)*
2. In some cities, media outlets publish a weekly list of restaurants that have been cited for health code violations by local health inspectors. What information problem is this feature designed to solve, and how? *(LO2)*
3. In 2009, Bernard Madoff was sentenced to 150 years in prison for executing what was likely the largest Ponzi scheme in history. What problem associated with asymmetric information was central to Madoff's success in cheating so many investors for so long? *(LO2)*
4. Financial intermediation is not confined to bank lending but is also carried out by nonbank firms such as mutual fund companies. How do mutual funds help overcome information problems in financial markets? *(LO1)*
5. In some countries it is very difficult for shareholders to fire managers when they do a poor job. What type of financing would you expect to find in those countries? *(LO3)*
6. Define the term *economies of scale* and explain how a financial intermediary can take advantage of such economies. *(LO1)*
7. The Internet can have a significant influence on asymmetric information problems. *(LO2)*
   a. How can the Internet help solve information problems?
   b. Can the Internet compound some information problems?
   c. On which problem would the Internet have a greater impact, adverse selection or moral hazard?
8. The financial sector is heavily regulated. Explain how government regulations help solve information problems, increasing the effectiveness of financial markets and institutions. *(LO1)*
9. One of the solutions to the adverse selection problem associated with asymmetric information is the pledging of collateral. However, the collateral may be riskier than initially thought. As an example, explain why the collateral did not work adequately to mitigate the mortgage securitization problems associated with the financial crisis of 2007–2009. *(LO2)*

10.* Deflation causes the value of a borrower's collateral to drop. Define deflation and explain how it reduces the value of a borrower's collateral. How might a lender who anticipates deflation alter the terms of a loan? *(LO2)*

11. You are in charge of setting policies for implementing construction loans at a bank once the loan officer has approved the borrowers' applications. (Construction loans finance the development of a structure during the building process and are later converted to mortgages.) How would you protect your bank's interests? *(LO3)*

12.* Your parents give you $3,000 as a graduation gift and you decide to invest the money in the stock market. If you are risk averse, should you purchase some stock in a few different companies through a website with low transaction fees or put the entire $3,000 into a mutual fund? Explain your answer. *(LO1)*

13. Suppose a new website was launched providing up-to-date, credible information on all firms wishing to issue bonds. What would you expect to happen to the overall level of interest rates in the bond market? *(LO1)*

14. Suppose two types of firms wish to borrow in the bond market. Firms of type A are in good financial health and are relatively low risk. The appropriate premium over the risk-free rate of lending to these firms is 2 percent. Firms of type B are in poor financial health and are relatively high risk. The appropriate premium over the risk-free rate of lending to these firms is 6 percent. As an investor, you have no other information about these firms except that type A and type B firms exist in equal numbers. *(LO2)*
    a. At what interest rate would you be willing to lend if the risk-free rate were 5 percent?
    b. Would this market function well? What type of asymmetric information problem does this example illustrate?

15. Suppose you are the financial advisor to a firm that is in good financial health. What suggestions would you make to the firm's management about obtaining borrowed funds if both financially healthy and financially unhealthy firms are trying to borrow in the bond market? *(LO2)*

16. Consider a small company run by a manager who is also the owner. If this company borrows funds, why might a moral hazard problem still exist? *(LO2)*

17.* The island of Utopia has a very unusual economy. Everyone on Utopia knows everyone else and knows all about the firms they own and operate. The financial system is well developed on Utopia. Everything else being equal, how would you expect the mix on Utopia between internal finance (where companies use their own funds such as retained earnings) and external funding (where companies obtain funds through financial markets) to compare with other countries? What role would financial intermediaries play in this economy? *(LO1)*

18. You and a friend visit the headquarters of a company and are awestruck by the expensive artwork and designer furniture that grace every office. Your friend is very impressed and encourages you to consider buying stock in the company, arguing that it must be really successful to afford such elegant surroundings. Would you agree with your friend's assessment? What further information (other than the usual financial data) would you obtain before making an investment decision? *(LO2)*

*Indicates more difficult problems.

19. Under what circumstances, if any, would you be willing to participate as a lender in a peer-to-peer lending arrangement? *(LO1)*
20. Upon graduation, both you and your roommate receive your first credit cards with identical features. You use your card extensively to make purchases, always paying your credit card balance in a timely manner so that you incur no interest cost. Your roommate pays for everything in cash, reserving the credit card only for an emergency that never happened. After two years, you both look for a new credit card. Explain why you are offered a new card at a much lower interest rate than your roommate, despite both of you working in similar jobs for the same income. *(LO2)*
21. What would you expect to happen to the mix between internal and external financing for new investment projects in a country that experiences a large increase in financial market uncertainty? *(LO2)*
22. Use a core principle from Chapter 1 to explain why, everything else being equal, a software company might find it more expensive to issue debt than a furniture store? *(LO1)*

Data Exploration connect

For general information on using Federal Reserve Economic Data (FRED) online, visit www.mhhe.com/moneyandbanking6e *and refer to the FRED Resources.*

1. Financial intermediaries connect savers and borrowers. Examine growth in intermediation from the following perspectives. *(LO1)*
   a. Total credit market debt is the sum of debt securities (FRED code: ASTDSL) and loans (FRED code: ASTLL). Plot the ratio of total credit market debt owed to population (FRED code: POP). (*Hint:* Because credit market debt is expressed in millions and population in thousands, multiply credit market debt by 1,000 to correct for the difference in units.) Interpret the plot.
   b. Plot the ratio of total credit market debt to nominal GDP (FRED code: GDP). Interpret the plot.
   c. Plot the ratio to nominal GDP of the value added by financial corporate business (FRED code: A454RC1Q027SBEA). Multiply the ratio by 100 to express it in percent. Interpret the plot since 2005.
2. How has the use of credit evolved in key sectors of the economy? Plot as ratios to total credit market debt outstanding (the sum of FRED codes ASTDSL and ASTLL) the debt of (a) nonfinancial corporate businesses (FRED code: BCNSDODNS), and (b) the domestic financial sector (FRED code: TCMDODFS). What do the patterns during the financial crisis in the nonfinancial and financial sector ratios mean in terms of leverage? *(LO1)*
3. Financial crisis is often associated with rising, and then persistently high, unemployment rates. Plot the U.S. unemployment rate during the Great Depression until the end of the 1930s (FRED code: M0892AUSM156SNBR). Compare the U.S. experience then with unemployment rates in Spain (FRED code: LRUN64TTESQ156S), Greece (FRED code: LRUN64TTGRQ156S), Italy (FRED code: LRUN64TTITQ156S), and Portugal (FRED code: LRHUTTTTPTQ156S) since the beginning of the financial crisis in 2007. (Turn off the recession bars for the European data plot.) *(LO3)*

4. The rise of securities markets and the expansion of intermediation by nonbanks has come partly at the expense of commercial banks. Plot the ratio of bank credit (FRED code: TOTLL) to debt securities owed (FRED code: ASTDSL), and comment on the trend. *(LO1)*
5. Deflation raises the real burden of repaying fixed-rate debt. Japan has recently experienced a long deflation. *(LO3)*
   a. Plot the percent change from a year ago of consumer prices in Japan (FRED code: JPNCPIALLQINMEI), and discuss the long-term patterns of inflation and deflation. (Turn off the recession bars.)
   b. Plot on a new graph the percent change from a year ago of the GDP deflator in Japan (FRED code: JPNGDPDEFQISMEI). How does it compare with the post-1994 evolution of consumer prices? (Turn off the recession bars.) *(Hint:* The GDP deflator is a price index for *all* final goods and services produced domestically. It is a broader measure than the price index for goods and services consumed by households in part *a*.)
   c. Why might deflation become self-perpetuating?

Further Data Exploration: If you wish to learn more about how the channels of financing vary across countries, take a look at the World Bank's Global Financial Development Database (GFDD) (https://datacatalog.worldbank.org/dataset/global-financial-development). The GFDD can be used online or downloaded in an Excel spreadsheet. It includes annual data from 1960 for more than 200 countries. Relevant data for Chapter 11 include private credit from intermediaries (GFDD.DI.12), stock market capitalization (GFDD.DM.01), and private debt securities (GFDD.DM.03), all measured as a share of nominal GDP. These data are displayed for a few countries in Table 11.1. The GFDD includes many other indicators of financial depth, access, efficiency, and stability. All GFDD indicators are also available through FRED.

Chapter

12 Depository Institutions: Banks and Bank Management

Learning Objectives

After reading this chapter, you should be able to:

LO1 Describe a commercial bank's assets and liabilities.

LO2 Define bank capital and key measures of bank profits and returns.

LO3 Identify the types and sources of bank risk and explain how to control them.

Banks are the most visible financial intermediaries in the economy. Most of us use the word *bank* to describe what people in the financial world call **depository institutions**. These are the financial institutions that accept deposits from savers and make loans to borrowers. What distinguishes depository institutions from **nondepository institutions** is their primary source of funds—that is, the liability side of their balance sheets. Depository institutions include commercial banks, savings and loans, and credit unions—the financial intermediaries most of us encounter in the course of our day-to-day lives.

Banking is a business. Actually, it's a combination of businesses designed to deliver the services discussed in Chapter 11. One business provides the accounting and record-keeping services that track the balances in your accounts. Another grants you access to the payments system, allowing you to convert your account balances into cash or transfer them to someone else. Yet a third business pools the savings of many small depositors and uses them to make large loans to trustworthy borrowers. A fourth business offers customers diversification services, buying and selling financial instruments in the financial markets in an effort to make a profit. Banks trade in the financial markets not just as a service to their customers but in an effort to earn a profit for their owners as well.

The intent of banks, of course, is to profit from each of these lines of business. Our objective in this chapter is to see how they do it. Not all banks make a profit. While some banks are extremely large, with hundreds of billions of dollars in loans and securities on their balance sheets, their access to funds is no guarantee of profitability. The risk that banks may fail is a problem not just for their owners and managers but for the rest of us, too. In the years from 2009 to 2018, more than 500 U.S. banks failed outright, while nearly 2,000 merged, reflecting the most severe financial crisis since the 1930s.

We have emphasized repeatedly that financial and economic development go hand in hand. An economy that lacks the financial institutions to effectively channel resources from savers to investors is much less likely to thrive. This statement applies regardless of whether a country is rich or poor. The United States and Japan provide a striking example. By virtually any standard, both countries are well off. Yet during the 1990s, U.S. banks made substantial profits, while Japanese banks suffered prodigious losses. At the same time, Japan's economy grew at a rate of just over 1 percent, while the U.S. economy grew at a rate well over 3 percent. The financial problems of Japanese banks played an important role in Japan's poor economic performance. Banks are important; when they are poorly managed, we all suffer. Similarly, the damage to U.S. banks in the crisis of 2007–2009 helped make the U.S. recovery that began in 2009 the weakest since the Great Depression.

In this chapter, we will examine the business of banking. We will see where depository institutions get their funds and what they do with them. That is, we will study the sources of banks' liabilities and learn how they manage their assets. And because banking is a risky business, we will examine the sources of risk that bankers face, as well as how those risks can be managed.

The Balance Sheet of Commercial Banks

To focus our discussion of depository institutions, we will concentrate on what are called *commercial banks.* These institutions were established to provide banking services to businesses, allowing them to deposit funds safely and borrow them when necessary. Today, many commercial banks offer accounts and loans to individuals as well. To understand the business of commercial banking, we'll start by examining the commercial bank's balance sheet. Recall that a balance sheet is a list of a household's or firm's assets and liabilities: the sources of its funds (liabilities) and the uses to which those funds are put (assets). A bank's balance sheet says that

$$\text{Total bank assets} = \text{Total bank liabilities} + \text{Bank capital} \qquad (1)$$

Banks obtain their funds from individual depositors and businesses, as well as by borrowing from other financial institutions and through the financial markets. They use these funds to make loans, purchase marketable securities, and hold cash. The difference between a bank's assets and liabilities is the bank's capital, or *net worth*—the value of the bank to its owners. The bank's profits come both from service fees and from the difference between what the bank pays for its liabilities and the return it receives on its assets (a topic we'll return to later).

Table 12.1 shows a consolidated balance sheet for all the commercial banks in the United States in December 2018. It reports the sum of all the items on all the balance sheets of the more than 4,700 commercial banks that existed in the United States at the time. The government collects these statistics in the course of supervising and regulating the financial system, to ensure bank safety and soundness. The numbers in the table are also related to the measures of money discussed in Chapter 2. Recall that the monetary aggregate M2 includes deposits, which are liabilities of the banking system.

Assets: Uses of Funds

Let's start with the asset side of the balance sheet—what banks do with the funds they raise. Table 12.1 shows that assets are divided into four broad categories: cash, securities, loans, and all other assets. More than 20 percent of assets, or \$3.5 trillion, is held in the form of securities; 56 percent (\$9.6 trillion) in the form of loans; and the remaining 23 percent in the form of cash and "Other assets." The last category includes mostly

Table 12.1 Balance Sheet of U.S. Commercial Banks, December 2018

Assets in billions of dollars (numbers with % sign are percentages of total assets)				
Cash items			1,950	11.5%
Securities*			3,499	20.6%
U.S. government and agency	2,672	15.7%		
Other securities	827	4.9%		
Loans			9,578	56.3%
Commercial and industrial	2,314	13.6%		
Real estate (including mortgage)	4,413	25.9%		
Consumer	1,494	8.8%		
Interbank	15	0.1%		
Other (including loss allowance)	1,342	7.9%		
Other assets (including trade allowance)			1,994	11.7%
Total Commercial Bank Assets			**17,021**	
Liabilities in billions of dollars (numbers with % sign are percentages of total liabilities)				
Deposits			12,425	82.3%
Large time deposits	1,699	11.3%		
Borrowings			1,945	12.9%
Other liabilities			730	4.8%
Total Commercial Bank Liabilities			**15,100**	
Bank Capital = Bank Assets – Bank Liabilities			**1,921**	11.3%

*Securities include mortgage-backed securities worth $1,876 billion, equivalent to 11.0% of assets.

SOURCE: Data are for the end of 2018, seasonally adjusted, from Board of Governors of the Federal Reserve System statistical release H.8. "Assets and Liabilities of Commercial Banks in the United States," available at www.federalreserve.gov/releases/h8/current.

buildings and equipment, as well as collateral repossessed from borrowers who defaulted. In looking at consolidated figures like the ones in Table 12.1, we can get some sense of their scale by comparing them to *nominal GDP.* In the fourth quarter of 2018, U.S. nominal GDP was $20.9 trillion, so total bank assets were equivalent to more than 80 percent of one year's GDP.

Cash Items Cash assets are of three types. The first and most important is **reserves**. Banks hold reserves because regulations require it and because prudent business practice dictates it. Reserves include the cash in the bank's vault (and the currency in its ATMs), called **vault cash**, as well as the bank's deposits at the Federal Reserve System. Cash is the most liquid of the bank's assets; the bank holds it to meet customers' withdrawal requests.

Cash items also include what are called *cash items in process of collection.* When you deposit your paycheck into your checking account, several days may pass before your bank can collect the funds from your employer's bank. In the meantime, the uncollected funds are considered your bank's asset because the bank is expecting to receive them.

Figure 12.1 U.S. Commercial Bank Assets, 1979–2019

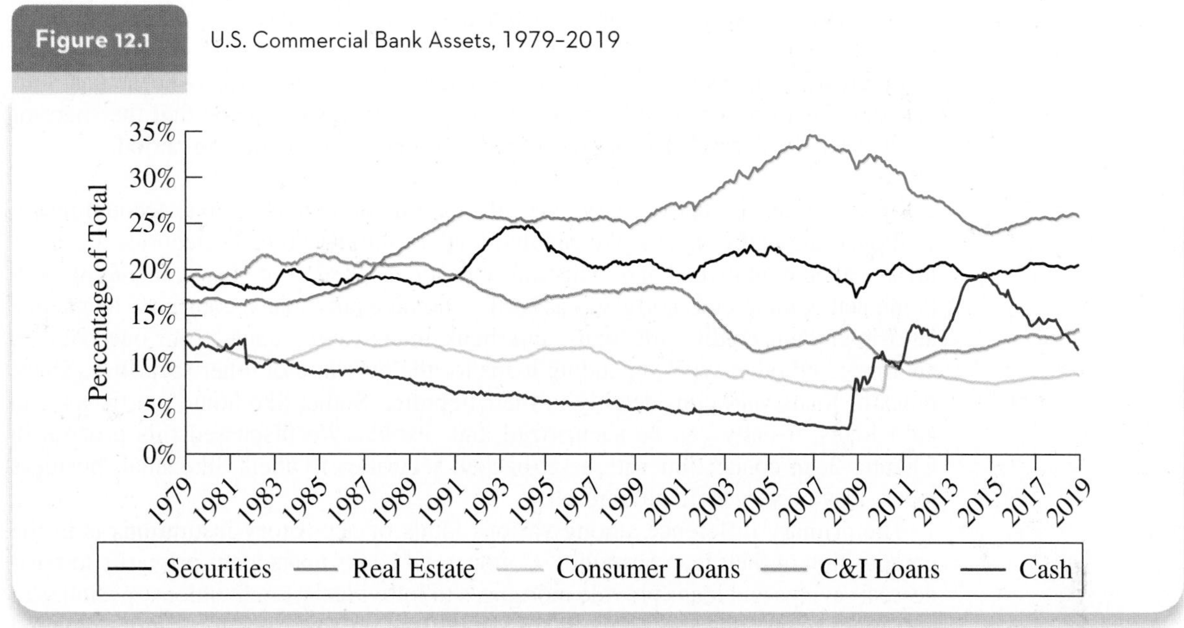

SOURCE: Monthly data, seasonally adjusted from "Assets and Liabilities of Commercial Banks in the United States," Board of Governors of the Federal Reserve System Statistical Release H.8. (FRED data codes: INVEST, REALLN, CONSUMER, BUSLOANS, CASACBM027SBOG, and TLAACBM027SBOG).

Finally, cash includes the balances of the accounts that banks hold at other banks. In the same way that individuals have checking accounts at the local bank, small banks have deposit accounts at large banks, and those accounts are classified as cash. Over the years, the practice of holding such accounts has declined, so the total quantity of these *correspondent bank* deposits has shrunk.

In December 2018, banks held more than 11 percent of their assets in cash (see Table 12.1). Up to the financial crisis of 2007–2009, that share was much smaller (in early 2007, it was about 3 percent; see Figure 12.1). Banks usually try to minimize their cash holdings because they typically earn less interest than loans or securities. However, the crisis forced them to change their strategy: A heightened possibility of bank runs, credit line takedowns, and borrower defaults prompted them to scramble for liquidity, and as market interest rates fell and the Federal Reserve began to pay interest on reserves, the opportunity cost of holding cash plummeted.

Securities The second-largest component of bank assets is marketable securities. While banks in many countries can hold stock, U.S. banks cannot, so this category of assets includes only bonds. Banks' bond holdings are split between U.S. government and agency securities, which account for 15.7 percent of their assets, and other securities (including state and local government bonds), which account for an additional 4.9 percent.[1] Note that more than half of all the securities are mortgage-backed (11.0 percent of assets). Nevertheless, a sizable proportion of the securities held by banks are very liquid. They can be sold quickly if the bank needs cash, which makes

[1]While there is nothing to prevent banks from holding corporate bonds, regulatory rules make the practice expensive. In Chapter 14, we will learn that banks are required to hold capital based on the composition of their balance sheets. The amount of capital required to extend a loan to a corporation is the same as the amount required to purchase a corporate bond. But because interest rates banks can charge on loans are generally higher than interest rates on corporate bonds, there is no price incentive to purchase a bond.

them a good backup for the bank's cash balances. For this reason securities are sometimes referred to as *secondary reserves.*

Figure 12.1 shows the trends in the composition of bank assets over the past four decades. Focusing on the line representing securities, we can see that the share of securities in bank assets has varied around 20 percent throughout the period.

Loans Loans are the primary asset of modern commercial banks, accounting for well over one-half of assets. We can divide loans into five broad categories: business loans, called commercial and industrial (C&I) loans; real estate loans, including both home and commercial mortgages as well as home equity loans; consumer loans, like auto loans and credit card loans; interbank loans (loans made from one bank to another); and other types, including loans for the purchase of other securities. These types of loans vary considerably in their liquidity. Some, like home mortgages and auto loans, usually can be securitized and resold. (We discussed this process in Chapter 3, in connection with asset-backed securities.) Others, like small business loans, may be very difficult to resell.

The primary difference among various kinds of depository institutions is in the composition of their loan portfolios. Commercial banks make loans primarily to businesses; savings and loans provide mortgages to individuals; credit unions specialize in consumer loans. See the Tools of the Trade box on page 302 for a more detailed description of the various types of depository institutions.

Figure 12.1 shows that, prior to the crisis of 2007–2009, commercial banks became more and more involved in the real estate business. Their involvement grew for a number of reasons. First, the rise of the commercial paper market made securities market debt finance more convenient for large firms, which reduced the quantity of commercial and industrial loans demanded. (Commercial paper is described in Chapter 7.) Second, the creation of mortgage-backed securities (MBS) meant that banks could sell the mortgage loans they had made. This innovation reduced the risk associated with an illiquid asset, encouraging banks to move into the business of home lending. So, on top of making more real estate loans, banks also acquired MBS, which recently accounted for more then half of securities held (see Table 12.1). Since the crisis, however, banks appear to have reduced their overall real estate exposure, underscoring the critical role that housing prices and MBS played in the 2007–2009 episode (see Lessons from the Crisis: Information Asymmetry and Securitization in Chapter 11, page 280).

Liabilities: Sources of Funds

To finance their operations, banks need funds. They get them from savers and from borrowing in the financial markets. To entice individuals and businesses to place their funds in the bank, institutions offer a range of deposit accounts that provide safekeeping and accounting services, access to the payments system, liquidity, and diversification of risk (see Chapter 11), as well as interest payments on the balance. There are two types of deposit accounts, transaction and nontransaction accounts. Transaction accounts are known as checkable deposits. As of December 2018, checkable deposits totaled $2.12 trillion, or roughly 17 percent of total deposits in the commercial banking system.

Checkable Deposits "Demand deposits," which allow a customer to withdraw funds without notice on a first-come, first-served basis, make up the largest component of checkable deposits. Banks also offer customers a variety of similar options that fall into the category of checking accounts, such as insured market rate accounts. A typical bank will offer half a dozen or more of these, each with slightly different characteristics. In addition to the names created by banks' marketing departments, economists use various other terms in speaking of checkable deposits. For example, some economists call them "sight deposits" because a depositor can show up to withdraw them when the bank is in sight.

Over the years, financial innovation has reduced the importance of checkable deposits in the day-to-day business of banking. As a share of total liabilities, checkable deposits plummeted from 40 percent in the 1970s to about 14 percent at the end of 2018. The reason for their decline is that checking accounts pay little or no interest; they are a low-cost source of funds for banks but a low-return investment for depositors. As interest rates rose through the 1970s and remained high into the 1990s, individuals and businesses realized the benefits of reducing the balances in their checking accounts and began to look for ways to earn higher interest rates. Banks obliged by offering innovative accounts whose balances could be shifted automatically when the customers' checking accounts ran low.[2] Thus, traditional checking accounts are no longer the principal source of bank funds.

Nontransaction Deposits In December 2018, nontransaction deposits, including savings and time deposits, accounted for more than half of all commercial bank liabilities. Savings deposits, commonly known as *passbook savings* accounts, were popular for many decades, though they are less so today. Time deposits are *certificates of deposit (CDs)* with a fixed maturity. When you place your savings in a CD at your local bank, it is as if you are buying a bond issued by that bank. But unlike government or corporate bonds, there isn't much of a resale market for your small CD. So if you want to withdraw your funds before the CD matures, you must get them back from the bank. To discourage early withdrawals, banks charge a significant penalty.

Certificates of deposit come in two varieties: small and large. Small CDs are issued for $100,000 or less; *large certificates of deposit* exceed $100,000 in face value. Large CDs are negotiable, which means that they can be bought and sold in the financial markets, just like bonds and commercial paper. Investors in this *wholesale money market* include corporate treasurers and others with large cash balances to manage. Because large CDs can be resold, they have become an important source of bank financing. When a bank needs funds, it can issue large CDs, in addition to commercial paper and more conventional bonds.

Borrowings Borrowing is the second most important source of bank funds. Figure 12.2 shows that borrowing grew increasingly important over the past four decades, until the financial crisis of 2007–2009 triggered greater bank caution. Today, borrowings account for about 13 percent of bank liabilities. Banks borrow in a number of ways. First, they can borrow from the Federal Reserve. We'll have much more to say about such **discount loans** in Part IV (Chapters 15–19). For now, think of this source of funds as borrowing from the government.

More often, banks borrow from other intermediaries. For example, banks with **excess reserves** can lend their surplus funds to banks that need them through an interbank market called the **federal funds market**. Loans made in the federal funds

[2]This is also related to a practice called *deposit sweeping*, in which banks take checking account balances and put them into savings deposits, thereby reducing the level of reserves they are required to hold. Over recent decades, deposit sweeping has lowered required reserves even as the monetary aggregates have risen markedly.

Figure 12.2 U.S. Commercial Bank Liabilities, 1979–2019

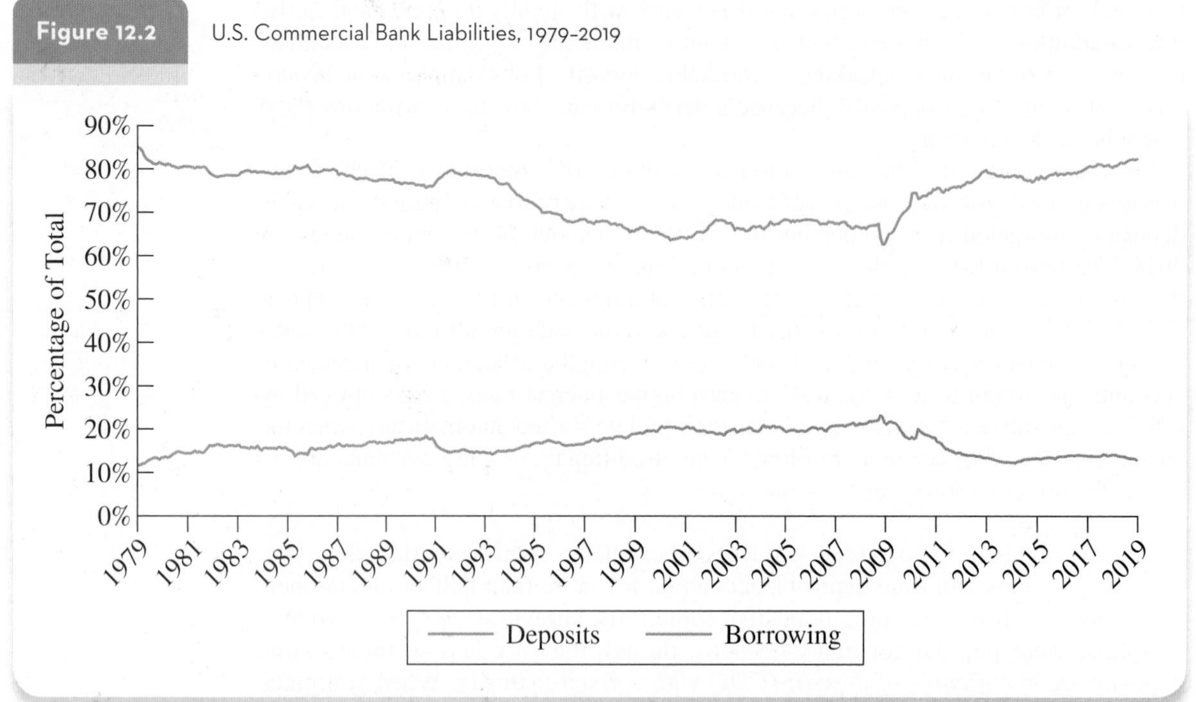

SOURCE: Monthly data, seasonally adjusted from "Assets and Liabilities of Commercial Banks in the United States," Board of Governors of the Federal Reserve System Statistical Release H.8. (FRED data codes: DPSACBM027SBOG, BOWACBM027SBOG, and TLBACBM027SBOG.)

market are unsecured—they lack collateral—so the lending bank must trust the borrowing bank. Look back at the balance sheet in Table 12.1; you will see interbank loans listed as an asset. These uncollateralized loans have become very small, while collateralized bank loans and borrowings have grown. The latter are included in Table 12.1 in "Other assets" and "Other liabilities." Some of these borrowings come from foreign banks and from U.S. government-sponsored enterprises that hold deposits at the Federal Reserve.

Finally, banks borrow using an instrument called a **repurchase agreement**, or **repo**, a short-term collateralized loan in which a security is exchanged for cash, with the agreement that the parties will reverse the transaction on a specific future date, typically the next day. For example, a bank that has a U.S. Treasury bill might need cash, while a pension fund might have cash that it doesn't need overnight. Through a repo, the bank would give the T-bill to the pension fund in exchange for cash, agreeing to buy it back—repurchase it—with interest the next day. In short, the bank gets an overnight loan and the pension fund gets some extra interest, along with the protection provided by collateral. The details are shown in Figure 12.3.

Bank Capital and Profitability

Net worth equals assets minus liabilities, whether we are talking about an individual's net worth or a bank's. In the case of banks, however, net worth is referred to as **bank capital**, or *equity capital*. (Important tip: Do not confuse bank capital and cash reserves. Capital appears on the liability side of the balance sheet, whereas reserves are an asset.) If the bank's owners sold all its assets (without taking a loss) and used

Figure 12.3 Mechanics of an Overnight Repurchase Agreement

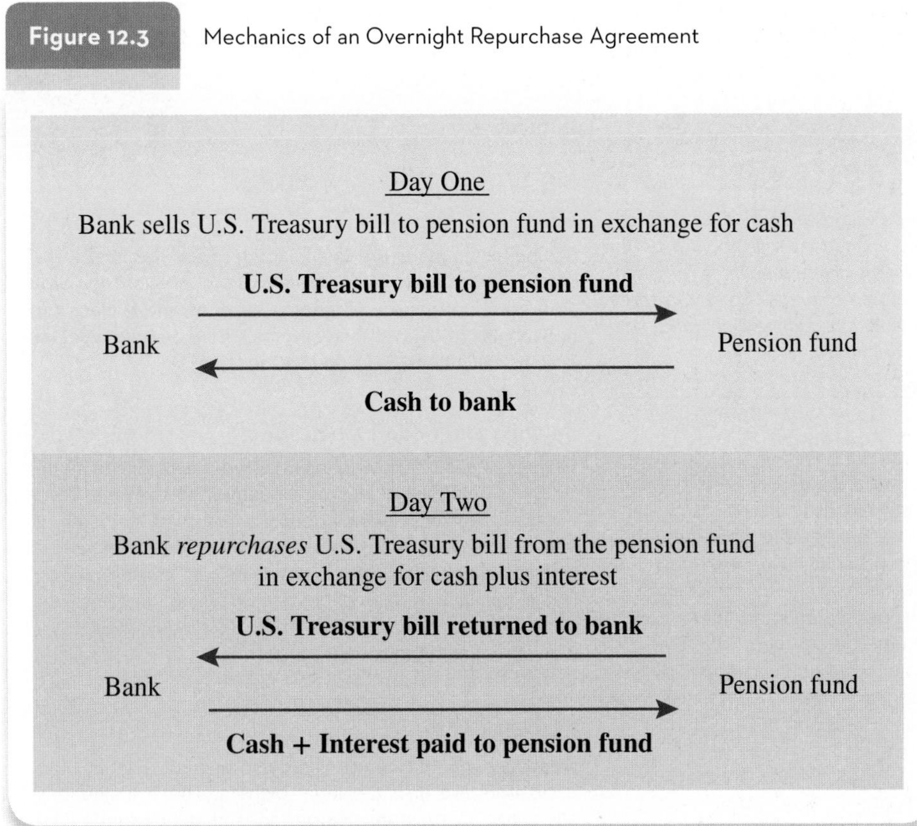

the proceeds to repay all the liabilities, capital is what would be left. We can think of capital as the owners' stake in the bank.

Capital is the cushion banks have against a sudden drop in the value of their assets or an unexpected withdrawal of liabilities. It provides some insurance against insolvency (the inability to repay debts when a firm's liabilities exceed its assets). An important component of bank capital is **loan loss reserves**, an amount the bank sets aside to cover potential losses from defaulted loans. At some point a bank gives up hope that a loan will be repaid and the loan is *written off,* or erased from the bank's balance sheet. At that point the loan loss reserve is reduced by the amount of the loan that has defaulted.

Looking once again at the balance sheet in Table 12.1 (page 296), we can see that in December of 2018, bank capital in the U.S. commercial banking system totaled $1.9 trillion. That $1.9 trillion of capital was combined with $15.1 trillion worth of liabilities to purchase $17.0 trillion in assets. So the ratio of debt to equity in the U.S. banking system was nearly 8 to 1. That's a substantial amount of leverage, but it is nearly 25 percent below the average commercial bank debt-to-equity ratio that prevailed prior to the financial crisis of 2007–2009. As we saw in Chapter 3, Lessons from the Crisis: Leverage, the crisis compelled banks to reduce their leverage sharply. (Recall that the term *leverage* refers to the portion of an asset that is purchased using borrowed funds.)

To put this ratio of 8 to 1 into perspective, we can compare it to the average debt-to-equity ratio for nonfinancial businesses in the United States, which is less than 1 to 1.

A Catalog of Depository Institutions
TOOLS OF THE TRADE

While the financial landscape is constantly shifting, it is safe to assume that depository institutions will be with us for some time. These are the financial intermediaries for whom deposits are the primary source of funds. There are three basic types of depository institution: commercial banks, savings institutions, and credit unions.

Commercial Banks

A commercial bank is an institution that accepts deposits and uses the proceeds to make consumer, commercial, and real estate loans. Originally established to meet the needs of businesses, many of these banks now serve individual customers as well. Commercial banks tend to specialize as community, regional and super-regional, or money center banks. As a result of mergers during the crisis of 2007–2009, more than one-third of U.S. commercial bank deposits are in four institutions (ranked in order of deposits): Bank of America, JPMorgan Chase, Wells Fargo, and Citigroup.

Community Banks

Community banks are small banks—those with assets of less than $1 billion—that concentrate on serving consumers and small businesses. These are the banks that take deposits from people in the local area and lend them back to local businesses and consumers. Of the roughly 5,400 commericial banks and savings institutions in the United States at the end of 2018, more than 95 percent were community banks.

Regional and Super-Regional Banks

Regional and super-regional banks are larger than community banks and much less local. Besides consumer and residential loans, these banks also make commercial and industrial loans. Regional banks obtain their funds through borrowing as well as from deposits. These banks can be very large. When the largest regional bank, Wachovia, faced a bank run in 2008, it was taken over by Wells Fargo.

Money Center Banks

A few large banks—only five or six—do not rely primarily on deposit financing. These banks rely instead on borrowing for their funding. They stand at the center of the *wholesale money market,* the market for short-term debt. Citigroup and JPMorgan Chase are two examples. (Recall from Chapter 3 that money-market instruments are bonds with a maturity of less than 12 months.)

Savings Institutions

Savings institutions are financial intermediaries that were established to serve households and individuals. They provide both mortgage and lending services and a place for households to deposit their savings. There are two types of savings institutions, S&Ls and savings banks.

Savings and Loan Institutions

Savings and loan institutions (S&Ls) were established in the 1800s to help factory workers become homeowners. They accepted workers' savings deposits and used the funds to make loans to homebuyers, most of whom were not served by traditional banks. These institutions traditionally specialized in taking short-term deposits and turning them into residential mortgages. The S&Ls that still exist today engage in a much broader range of financial activities.

Savings Banks

Most savings banks are mutually owned. That is, the depositors are also the legal owners. These institutions specialize in residential mortgages that are funded by deposits. They are permitted to exist only in certain states. When the largest savings bank, Washington Mutual, failed during the crisis of 2007–2009, JPMorgan Chase acquired its deposits.

Credit Unions

Credit unions are nonprofit depository institutions that are owned by people with a common bond—members of police associations, union members, and university students and employees. Credit unions specialize in making small consumer loans. They originated in the 19th century to meet the needs of people who could not borrow from traditional lenders. Before credit unions existed, many ordinary people had nowhere to turn when they faced unexpected home repairs or medical emergencies.

Not all these depository institutions are likely to survive the financial innovations and economic upheaval of the coming decades. Commercial banks will likely remain with us, but savings institutions have already declined in importance and are at risk of disappearing altogether due to changes in the mortgage business. Whether credit unions remain viable will depend on their continuing ability to exploit their advantage in verifying members' creditworthiness.

Household leverage is far lower, roughly 1/7 to 1.[3] Recall from Tools of the Trade in Chapter 5 that leverage increases both risk and expected return. If you contribute half the purchase price of a house and borrow the other half, both your risk and your expected return double. If you contribute one-fifth of the purchase price and borrow the other four-fifths, your risk and expected return go up by a factor of 5. So if a bank borrows $8 for each $1 in capital, its risk and expected return increase a whopping 9 times! Banking, it seems, is a very risky business. As we will see in Chapter 14, one of the explanations for the relatively high degree of leverage in banking is the existence of government guarantees like deposit insurance, which allow banks to capture the benefits of risk taking without subjecting depositors to potential losses.

There are several basic measures of bank profitability. The first is called **return on assets (ROA)**. Return on assets equals a bank's net profit after taxes divided by the bank's total assets:

$$ROA = \frac{\text{Net profit after taxes}}{\text{Total bank assets}} \tag{2}$$

ROA is an important measure of how efficiently a particular bank uses its assets. By looking at the different units' ROAs, for example, the manager of a large bank can also compare the performance of the bank's various lines of business. But for the bank's owners, return on assets is less important than the return on their own investment, which is leveraged at an average ratio of nearly 9 to 1. (The leverage ratio equals total assets divided by bank capital. It also equals the debt-to-equity ratio plus 1.) The bank's return to its owners is measured by the **return on equity (ROE)**, which equals the bank's net profit after taxes divided by the bank's capital:

$$ROE = \frac{\text{Net profit after taxes}}{\text{Bank capital}} \tag{3}$$

Not surprisingly, ROA and ROE are related to leverage. One measure of leverage is the ratio of bank assets to bank capital. Multiplying ROA by this ratio yields ROE:

$$\begin{aligned} ROA \times \frac{\text{Bank assets}}{\text{Bank capital}} &= \frac{\text{Net profit after taxes}}{\text{Total bank assets}} \times \frac{\text{Bank assets}}{\text{Bank capital}} \\ &= \frac{\text{Net profit after taxes}}{\text{Bank capital}} = ROE \end{aligned} \tag{4}$$

For a typical U.S. bank, prior to the financial crisis of 2007–2009, the return on assets was about 1.3 percent, while the return on equity was 10 to 12 times that high. For large banks, the return on equity tends to be higher than for small banks, which suggests greater leverage, a riskier mix of assets, or the existence of significant economies of scale in banking. The poor performance of many large banks in the crisis, combined with moderate returns in its aftermath, suggests that their precrisis higher returns (compared to small banks) at least partly reflected more leverage or a riskier asset mix. Nevertheless, research also points to sizable economies of scale for banks with assets exceeding $100 billion.[4]

[3]You can arrive at these figures yourself by looking at the *Financial Accounts of the United States,* which is computed by the Board of Governors of the Federal Reserve (see its website). The appropriate tables are B.101 for households and B.103 for nonfarm nonfinancial corporate business; both include assets, liabilities, and net worth for their parts of the U.S. economy.

[4]See John P. Hughes and Loretta Mester, "Who Said Large Banks Don't Experience Scale Economies? Evidence from a Risk-Return-Driven Cost Function," *Journal of Financial Intermediation* 22, no. 4 (October 2013), pp. 559–585.

Shadow Banking in China
APPLYING THE CONCEPT

By almost any measure, the residents of China save more than virtually any other population in the world. Yet, until recently, they have had few attractive avenues for investing.

Until 2015, for example, regulation capped bank deposit rates at a level far below the growth rate of the economy. This was part of a strategy whereby the government—through the large state-controlled banks—funneled an outsized proportion of national savings to favored borrowers, typically state-owned enterprises (SOEs), at low interest rates. This is an example of *financial repression*.

Enter shadow banking. In 2008, as the global economy tanked, China sought to boost domestic demand by relaxing the supply of credit. To fund the credit expansion, regulators allowed banks and others to offer new products that looked a lot like short-term deposits but with much higher interest rates—often in excess of 10 percent. Hungry household investors flocked to these products.

So, viewed in the most favorable light, the rise of shadow banking in China constituted backdoor financial liberalization. However, the rapid expansion of shadow banking occurred in a financial system plagued by poor incentives. Neither lenders (the banks and other intermediaries) nor borrowers (especially SOEs and local government financing vehicles—LGFVs) had much of an interest in controlling risk taking. This, plus the lack of clarity about who bears the risk of failure, fueled worries about financial instability in China.

As a result of rapid credit growth, the ratio of overall credit to GDP has soared since 2008 to more than 250 percent, and nonfinancial corporations in China became the most indebted among those in countries for which we have accurate data. Furthermore, a significant portion of the credit in China flowed through off-balance-sheet finance to LGFV real estate projects that had uncertain prospects for repayment. Experience teaches us that credit booms like this one are the fuel for financial crises.

Fortunately, the Chinese government has considerable wherewithal to steady the financial system even as many loans go bad. But over time, government bailouts undermine the discipline needed to make the financial system efficient. Without the force of market discipline—including the trauma of creditors bearing the losses from borrower failures—there is little incentive to limit or even monitor risk taking.

The challenge for China's authorities is to keep the benefits of shadow banking while containing the risks. The recent global crisis shows that this is difficult anywhere. For China, it may be especially so. Some of the country's most stunning successes—including its rapid infrastructure development—reflect the government's virtually unrestrained use of authority. In contrast, building a large and efficient financial system requires curbing that authority so that—consistent with Core Principle 4—markets determine prices and allocate resources. It remains to be seen whether the Chinese government can exhibit the restraint needed to reap the benefits markets have to offer.

Before continuing, it is important to introduce one more measure of bank profitability: net interest income. This measure is related to the fact that banks pay interest on their liabilities, creating interest expenses, and receive interest on their assets, creating interest income. Deposits and bank borrowing create interest expenses; securities and loans generate interest income. The difference between the two is the bank's *net interest income*.

Net interest income can also be expressed as a percentage of total assets to yield a quantity called **net interest margin**. This is the bank's **interest rate spread**, which is the (weighted) average difference between the interest rate received on assets and the interest rate paid for liabilities. A bank's net interest margin is closely related to its return on assets. Just take the bank's fee income minus its operating costs, divide by total assets, add the result to the net interest margin, and you get its ROA. Roughly equivalent to a manufacturer or retailer's gross profits and gross profit margin, net interest income and net interest margin reveal a great deal about a bank's business.

Well-run banks have high net interest income and a high net interest margin. And because we would expect most of a bank's loans to be repaid, net interest margin tells us not just current profitability but future profitability as well; it is a forward-looking measure. If a bank's net interest margin is currently improving, its profitability is likely to improve in the future.

Off-Balance-Sheet Activities

A financial firm's balance sheet provides only so much information. To generate fees, banks engage in numerous **off-balance-sheet activities**. Recall that banks exist to reduce transactions costs and information costs as well as to transfer risks. When they perform these services, bankers expect to be compensated. Yet many of these activities do not appear as either assets or liabilities on the bank's balance sheet, even though they may represent an important part of a bank's profits and may add significantly to the risks that a bank faces.

For example, banks often provide trusted customers with lines of credit, which are similar to the credit limits on credit cards. The firm pays the bank a fee in return for the ability to borrow whenever necessary. When the agreement is signed, the bank receives the payment and the firm receives a *loan commitment*. However, not until a loan has actually been made—until the firm has *drawn down* the credit line—does the transaction appear on the bank's balance sheet.

In the meantime, the bank is compensated for reducing both transactions and information costs. Without the loan commitment, the firm would find credit difficult and potentially expensive to obtain on short notice (a transactions cost). And because the bank usually knows the firms to which it grants lines of credit, the cost of establishing their creditworthiness (an information cost) is negligible.

Letters of credit are another important off-balance-sheet item for banks. These letters guarantee that a customer of the bank will be able to make a promised payment. For example, a U.S. importer of television sets may need to reassure a Chinese exporter that the firm will be able to pay for the imported goods when they arrive. This customer might request that the bank send a *commercial letter of credit* to the Chinese exporter guaranteeing payment for the goods on receipt. By issuing the letter of credit, the bank substitutes its own guarantee for the U.S. importer's credit risk, enabling the transaction to go forward. In return for taking this risk, the bank receives a fee.

A related form of the letter of credit is called a *standby letter of credit.* These letters, which are issued to firms and governments that wish to borrow in the financial markets, are a form of insurance. Commercial paper, even when it is issued by a large, well-known firm, must be backed by a standby letter of credit that promises the bank will repay the lender should the issuer default. What is true for large corporations is true for state and local governments as well: in most cases, they need a bank guarantee to issue debt. As with loan commitments, letters of credit expose the bank to risk in a way that is not readily apparent on the bank's balance sheet.

Because off-balance-sheet activities create risk for financial institutions, they have come under increasing scrutiny in recent years. Recall the case of Long-Term Capital Management (LTCM), which we discussed in Chapter 9. While LTCM's balance sheet carried assets worth over $100 billion when the firm got into trouble, the risky instruments that did *not* appear on its balance sheet—the $1.25 trillion in interest rate swaps—were what scared everyone. A similar problem arose in the financial crisis of 2007–2009, when the invisible, off-balance-sheet risks taken by some of the largest banks and other intermediaries added to doubts about their solvency (see Chapter 3, Lessons from the Crisis: Shadow Banks). By allowing for the transfer of risk, modern financial instruments enable individual institutions to concentrate risk in ways that are very difficult for outsiders to discern. When revealed, these hidden attributes can undermine financial stability.

The Cost of Payday Loans
YOUR FINANCIAL WORLD

If you drive through the streets of a U.S. city, you will eventually pass a store with a sign saying "Checks Cashed." Or, if you start looking for a loan on the Internet, you will quickly find a slew of lenders who advertise things like "Bad Credit Okay." These financial intermediaries lend to people who cannot borrow from mainstream financial institutions such as banks.

The most common type of loan these stores and websites offer is a *payday loan*. To get one, you need provide only a very limited amount of information to identify yourself. If you are doing this online, you will receive a deposit into your bank account within a day or two and must agree to let the lender directly debit your account when the loan is due, usually within two weeks. If you make the transaction in a store, you walk out with the cash.

The catch is a huge fee, typically equal to 15 percent of the loan's principal. So if you borrow $500, you will have to repay a minimum of $575. In many cases, lenders are required to disclose the implied annual interest rate on these loans. It can exceed 2,000 percent, which should give all but the most desperate borrowers pause.

But the main problem with these loans is that they trap some borrowers in a vicious cycle of new fees for repeated loan renewals. A study by the Consumer Financial Protection Bureau (CFPB) reports that more than 80 percent of payday borrowers take out another loan within two weeks.* And 15 percent of borrowers will roll over the original debt in a series of 10 loans or more. For a $500 loan, 10 renewals means the borrower will pay $825 in fees over a 22-week period and still owe the original $500!

To the extent that payday loans allow people to obtain short-term loans from legitimate financial intermediaries, they are a good thing. You will find testimonials on websites from people who were clearly helped. But when payday loans lead to a cycle of costly renewals, they can do substantial harm.

In response, governments regulate certain lending practices. At the federal level, the Military Lending Act caps lending rates and rollovers on loans to U.S. service families. States impose a variety of restrictions on the number of loans, the renewal limits and repayment requirements, as well as annual interest rates. For a listing of the legal status of payday loans by state, see https://paydayloaninfo.org/state-information.

*Consumer Financial Protection Bureau Office of Research, "CFPB Data Point: Payday Lending," March 2014.

Bank Risk: Where It Comes from and What to Do about It

Banking is risky both because depository institutions are highly leveraged and because of what they do. The bank's goal is to make a profit in each of its lines of business. Some of these are simply fee-for-service activities. For example, a financial institution might act as a broker, buying and selling stocks and bonds on a customer's behalf and charging a fee in return. Banks also transform deposit liabilities into assets such as loans and securities. In the process, they pool savings, provide liquidity services, allow for diversification of risk, and capitalize on the advantages they have in producing information. All along, the goal is to pay less for the deposits the bank receives than for the loans it makes and the securities it buys. That is, the interest rate the bank pays to attract liabilities must be lower than the return it receives on assets.

In the process of all these activities, the bank is exposed to a host of risks. They include the chance that depositors will suddenly withdraw their balances, that borrowers will not repay their loans, that interest rates will change, and that the bank's securities trading operation will do poorly. Each of these risks has a name: *liquidity risk, credit risk, interest rate risk,* and *trading risk*. To understand how these risks arise and what can be done about them, we will look at each in detail.

Liquidity Risk

All financial institutions face the risk that their liabilities holders (depositors) will seek to cash in their claims. The holder of a checking account can always take cash out at an ATM or make a transfer to someone else via mobile phone or over the Internet. This risk of a sudden demand for liquid funds is called **liquidity risk**. Banks face liquidity risk on both sides of their balance sheets. Deposit withdrawal is a liability-side risk, but there is an asset-side risk as well. Recall from our discussion of off-balance-sheet activities that banks provide households and firms with lines of credit—promises to make loans on demand. When this type of loan commitment is claimed, or *taken down,* the bank must find the liquidity to cover it.

If the bank cannot meet customers' requests for immediate funds, it runs the risk of failure. Even if a bank has a positive net worth, illiquidity can still drive it out of business. Who would put their funds in a bank that can't always provide cash on demand? For this reason, bankers must manage liquidity risk with great care. Failure to do so in the crisis of 2007–2009 led to bank runs—such as the run on Wachovia in September 2008—and to the failures of numerous bank and nonbank intermediaries.

To fully understand liquidity risk and how banks manage it, let's look at a simplified balance sheet. Figure 12.4 shows a stripped-down version of the balance sheet of a hypothetical bank. Keep in mind that the two sides of a balance sheet must always balance. Any change in the level of assets must be mirrored by an equal change in the level of liabilities.

In Figure 12.4, bank liabilities are composed primarily of deposits, along with some borrowing and $20 million of bank capital. Liabilities total $150 million. The bank's assets include $15 million in reserves. Banking regulations require that banks hold a portion of their assets either as vault cash or as deposits at the Fed. That portion is stated as a specific percentage of the bank's deposits. If we assume that **required reserves** are 10 percent of deposits, then the $100 million in deposits shown on the balance sheet means that the bank is required to hold $10 million in reserves. The fact that the bank is holding $15 million in reserves means that it has $5 million in *excess reserves.*

To assess liquidity risk, we need to ask how the bank will handle a customer's demand for funds. What happens if a corporate customer arrives at the bank and requests a withdrawal of $5 million? Because the bank has $5 million in excess reserves, it can honor the customer's request immediately, without difficulty. Similarly, if the bank were forced suddenly to honor a $5 million loan commitment, it could do so by drawing down its reserves. In the past, this was a common way to manage

Figure 12.4 Balance Sheet of a Bank Holding $5 Million in Excess Reserves

Assets		Liabilities	
Reserves	$ 15 million	Deposits	$100 million
Loans	$100 million	Borrowed funds	$ 30 million
Securities	$ 35 million	Bank capital	$ 20 million

Figure 12.5 Balance Sheet of a Bank Holding No Excess Reserves

Assets		Liabilities	
Reserves	$ 10 million	Deposits	$100 million
Loans	$100 million	Borrowed funds	$ 30 million
Securities	$ 40 million	Bank capital	$ 20 million

liquidity risk; banks would simply hold sufficient excess reserves to accommodate customers' withdrawals. This is a passive way to manage liquidity risk.

The problem is, holding excess reserves is expensive, because it means forgoing the higher rate of interest that typically can be earned on loans or securities. Banks work hard to find other ways to manage the risk of sudden withdrawals and drawdowns of loan commitments. There are two other ways to manage the risk that customers will require cash: The bank can adjust its assets or its liabilities. To see how it's done, let's look at Figure 12.5. This bank has $10 million in reserves to back its $100 million in deposits, so it has no excess reserves. If a customer makes a $5 million withdrawal, the bank can't simply deduct it from reserves. Instead, the bank will need to adjust another part of its balance sheet.[5]

This bank has two choices in responding to the shortfall created by the $5 million withdrawal: It can adjust either its assets or its liabilities. On the asset side, the bank has several options. The quickest and easiest one is to sell a portion of its securities portfolio. Because some of them are almost surely U.S. Treasury securities, they can be sold quickly and easily at relatively low cost. The result of this action is shown in the top panel of Figure 12.6. Note that assets and liabilities are both $5 million lower than they were prior to the withdrawal (compare Figure 12.5). Banks that are particularly concerned about liquidity risk can structure their securities holdings to facilitate such sales.

A second possibility is for the bank to sell some of its loans to another bank. This option is shown in the bottom panel of Figure 12.6. While not all loans can be sold, some can. Banks generally make sure that a portion of the loans they hold are marketable for just such purposes.

Yet another way to handle the bank's need for liquidity is to refuse to renew a customer loan that has come due. Corporate customers have short-term loans that are periodically renewed, so the bank always has the option of refusing to extend the loan again for another week, month, or year. But this course of action is not very appealing. Failing to renew a loan is guaranteed to alienate the customer and could well drive the customer to another bank. Recall from Chapter 11 that banks specialize in solving information problems by screening to find customers who are creditworthy and then monitoring them to ensure they repay their loans. The idea is to separate good customers from bad ones and develop long-term relationships with the good ones. The

[5]If you're thinking that the bank can finance part of the withdrawal from reserves, because the $5 million withdrawal will reduce required reserves by $500,000, you're right. But that still leaves the bank $4.5 million short.

Figure 12.6 Balance Sheet of a Bank Following a $5 Million Withdrawal and Asset Adjustment

Withdrawal Is Met by Selling Securities

Assets		Liabilities	
Reserves	$ 10 million	Deposits	$95 million
Loans	$100 million	Borrowed funds	$30 million
Securities	$ 35 million	Bank capital	$20 million

Withdrawal Is Met by Reducing Loans

Assets		Liabilities	
Reserves	$10 million	Deposits	$95 million
Loans	$95 million	Borrowed funds	$30 million
Securities	$40 million	Bank capital	$20 million

last thing a bank wants to do is to refuse a loan to a creditworthy customer it has gone to some trouble and expense to find.

Moreover, bankers do not like to meet their deposit outflows by contracting the asset side of the balance sheet because doing so shrinks the size of the bank. And because banks make a profit by turning liabilities into assets, the smaller their balance sheets, the lower their profits. For this reason alone, today's bankers prefer to use liability management to address liquidity risk. That is, instead of selling assets in response to a deposit withdrawal, they find other sources of funds.

There are two ways for banks to obtain additional funds. First, they can borrow to meet the shortfall, either from the Federal Reserve or from another bank. The result of such an action is shown in the top panel of Figure 12.7. As you can see, while deposits have fallen by $5 million, borrowing has made up the difference.

A second way to adjust liabilities in response to a deposit outflow is to attract additional deposits. The most common way to do so is to issue large-denomination CDs (with a value over $100,000), effectively borrowing in the wholesale money market.[6] In the bottom panel of Figure 12.7, these nontransaction deposits are combined with checking accounts. As we saw earlier, large certificates of deposit have become an increasingly important source of funds for banks. Now we know why: It is because they allow banks to manage their liquidity risk without changing the asset side of their balance sheets.

In the crisis of 2007–2009, many of the usual mechanisms for managing liquidity risk failed. Banks could neither sell their illiquid assets nor obtain at a reasonable cost the funding needed to hold those assets. The sudden and unanticipated loss of both market and funding liquidity threatened the financial system as a whole.

[6]Unlike transactions deposits such as checking accounts, CDs are not subject to a reserve requirement. Thus, a change in the composition of a bank's deposits affects the level of reserves it is required to hold and hence its balance sheet.

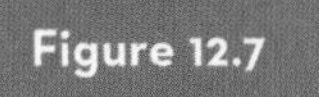

Figure 12.7 Balance Sheet of a Bank Following a $5 Million Withdrawal and Liability Adjustment

Withdrawal Is Met by Borrowing

Assets		Liabilities	
Reserves	$ 10 million	Deposits	$95 million
Loans	$100 million	Borrowed funds	$35 million
Securities	$ 40 million	Bank capital	$20 million

Withdrawal Is Met by Attracting Deposits

Assets		Liabilities	
Reserves	$ 10 million	Deposits	$100 million
Loans	$100 million	Borrowed funds	$ 30 million
Securities	$ 40 million	Bank capital	$ 20 million

Credit Risk

Banks profit from the difference between the interest rate they pay to depositors and the interest rate they receive from borrowers. That is, the return on their assets exceeds the cost of their liabilities. At least, that's the idea. But to ensure that this profit-making process works, for the bank to make a profit, borrowers must repay their loans. There is always some risk that they won't. The risk that a bank's loans will not be repaid is called **credit risk**. To manage their credit risk, banks use a variety of tools. The most basic are diversification, in which the bank makes a variety of different loans to spread the risk, and credit risk analysis, in which the bank examines the borrower's credit history to determine the appropriate interest rate to charge.

INFORMATION

Diversification means spreading risk, which can be difficult for banks, especially those that focus on certain kinds of lending. Because banks specialize in information gathering, it is tempting to try to gain a competitive advantage in a narrow line of business. The problem is, if a bank lends in only one geographic area or only one industry, it exposes itself to economic downturns that are local or industry-specific. It is important that banks find a way to hedge such risks.

Credit risk analysis produces information that is very similar to the bond rating systems discussed in Chapter 7. There we saw that rating agencies like Moody's and Standard & Poor's produce letter ratings for large corporations wishing to issue bonds. Banks do the same for small firms wishing to borrow, and specialized firms gather information about the credit history of individual borrowers (see Your Financial World: Your Credit Rating in Chapter 7, page 166). Credit risk analysis uses a combination of statistical models and information that is specific to the loan applicant. The result is an assessment of the likelihood that a particular borrower will default. When the bank's loan officers decide to make a loan, they use the customer's credit rating to determine how high an interest rate to charge. To the interest rate they must pay on their liabilities, they add a markup that will allow them to make a profit. The poorer a borrower's credit rating, the higher the interest rate they will charge.[7]

In the crisis of 2007–2009, many banks seriously underestimated the risks associated with mortgage and other household credit. They had not anticipated the first decline of nationwide housing prices since the Great Depression or the surge of unemployment to double-digit rates. As a consequence, they overestimated the value of the collateral. Rising defaults prompted large losses and impaired their capital, although not as much as crisis-driven trading losses on mortgage-backed and related securities (see pages 314–315).

Interest Rate Risk

Because banks are in the business of turning deposit liabilities into loan assets, the two sides of their balance sheet do not match up. One important difference is that a bank's liabilities tend to be short term, while its assets tend to be long term. This mismatch between the maturities of the two sides of the balance sheet creates **interest rate risk**.

To understand the problem, think of both the bank's assets and its liabilities as bonds. That is, the bank's deposit liabilities are just like bonds, as are its loan assets. (The bank must have some capital as well.) We know that a change in interest rates will affect the value of a bond; when interest rates rise, the price of a bond falls. More important, the longer the term of the bond is, the greater the change in the bond's price at any given change in the interest rate. (Refer back to Chapter 4 to refresh your memory.) Thus, when interest rates rise, banks face the risk that the value of their assets will fall more than the value of their liabilities (reducing the bank's capital). Put another way, if a bank makes long-term loans, it receives payments from borrowers that do not vary with the interest rate. But its short-term liabilities—those with variable interest rates—require the bank to make larger payments when interest rates rise. So rising interest rates reduce revenues relative to expenses, directly lowering the bank's profits.

The best way to see this point is to focus on a bank's revenue and expenses. Let's start by dividing the bank's assets and liabilities into two categories, those that are interest rate sensitive and those that are not. The term *interest rate sensitive* means that a change in interest rates will change the revenue produced by an asset. Because newly purchased short-term bonds always reflect a change in interest rates, short-term bonds that are constantly maturing and being replaced with new ones produce interest rate sensitive revenue. In contrast, when the bank purchases long-term bonds, it receives a fixed stream of revenue. Purchasing a 5 percent, 10-year bond means getting $5 per $100 of face value for 10 years, regardless of what happens to interest rates in the meantime. So the revenue stream from a long-term bond is not interest rate sensitive.

Suppose that 20 percent of a bank's assets fall into the first category, those that are sensitive to changes in the interest rate. Another 80 percent fall into the second category, those that are not sensitive to changes in the interest rate. If the interest rate has been stable at 5 percent for some time, then for each $100 in assets, the bank receives $5 in interest.

The bank's liabilities tend to have a different structure. Let's assume that half the bank's deposits are interest rate sensitive and half are not. In other words, half the

[7]Banks can also manage their credit risk by purchasing *credit default swaps* (*CDS*), a type of derivative that allows lenders to insure themselves against the chance that a borrower will default. For a discussion of CDS, see pages 232–233 of Chapter 9.

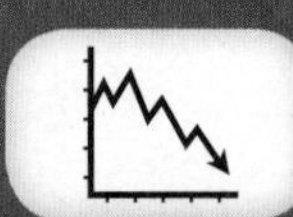

Insufficient Bank Capital
LESSONS FROM THE CRISIS

The financial crisis of 2007–2009 and the recession that it triggered led to projected losses on U.S. bank assets of nearly $1 trillion.* For comparison, the total capital of U.S. depositories before the crisis began was about $1.3 trillion. Had the U.S. government not provided massive support to the banking system, many banks probably would have become *insolvent*—unable to repay their debts because their liabilities would have exceeded their assets.

What is bank capital? Why do banks hold it? Through what mechanism did the crisis erode capital?

A bank's capital is its net worth—the difference between the value of its assets and the value of its liabilities. The capital a bank holds cushions it against many risks, including declines in the market value of assets—so-called *market risk*. The larger a bank's capital cushion, the less likely that it will be made insolvent by an adverse surprise.

In the financial crisis, U.S. bank capital was insufficient to cushion against the market risks that surfaced. Put another way, banks were too leveraged: They had too many assets for each unit of capital, making them vulnerable to market risk.

How did declines in the market value of assets arise in the crisis? The process began in 2007 when surging mortgage defaults depressed the value of many mortgage-backed securities. U.S. banks were sensitive to such declines because they held more than $4 trillion in mortgages.

Even when borrowers make timely interest payments, mortgages and the securities backed by them can pose market risk. *Mark-to-market* accounting rules require banks to adjust the recorded value of the assets on their balance sheets when the market value of those assets changes. When the market price rises, the value of the assets is "written up." When the price falls, the value is "written down." Because bank capital is the difference between assets and liabilities, *writedowns* reduce a bank's capital.

Why didn't banks hold a larger capital cushion against market and other risks? The answer is that capital is costly. Financial institutions must pay for capital, compensating the investors that provide it with dividends and the like.

To boost profits, intermediaries try to reduce costs, including the amount of capital they require. They also may take more risk by increasing leverage. The more leverage, the greater the possible reward for each unit of costly capital—and the greater the risk. Highly leveraged firms are vulnerable even to modest declines in market prices. When a financial institution is leveraged 30 times—as some were before the crisis—a drop in asset prices of as little as 3 percent can wipe out the capital cushion and lead to bankruptcy. Yet, even some top-rated mortgage securities plunged in price by one-third, threatening widespread insolvency among the institutions that held them.

*See the projection in the IMF *Global Financial Stability Report*, April 2009, Table 1.15.

bank's liabilities are deposits that earn variable interest rates, so the costs associated with them move with the market rate. Interest-bearing checking accounts fall into this category. The remainder of the bank's liabilities are time deposits such as certificates of deposit, which have fixed interest rates. The payment a bank makes to the holder of an existing CD does not change with the interest rate.

For the bank to make a profit, the interest rate on its liabilities must be lower than the interest rate on its assets. The difference between the two rates is the bank's net interest margin. Assuming that the interest rate on its liabilities has been 3 percent, the bank has been paying out $3 per $100 in liabilities. Because the bank is receiving 5 percent interest on its assets, its net interest margin is 2 percent (5 minus 3). This margin is the bank's profit.

Now look at what happens if interest rates rise 1 percent for interest-sensitive assets and liabilities. For each $100 in assets, the bank's revenue goes up from (0.05 × $100) = $5 to [(0.05 × $80) + (0.06 × $20)] = $5.20. But the cost of its liabilities goes up too, from (0.03 × $100) = $3 to [(0.03 × $50) + (0.04 × $50)] = $3.50. So a one-percentage point rise in the interest rate reduces the bank's profit from ($5 − $3) = $2 per $100 in assets to ($5.20 − $3.50) = $1.70, a decline of $0.30, or

15 percent. This example illustrates a general principle: When a bank's liabilities are more interest rate sensitive than its assets are, an increase in interest rates will cut into the bank's profits.

The first step in managing interest rate risk is to determine how sensitive the bank's balance sheet is to a change in interest rates. Managers must compute an estimate of the change in the bank's profit for each one-percentage point change in the interest rate. This procedure is called *gap analysis,* because it highlights the gap, or difference, between the yield on interest rate sensitive assets and the yield on interest rate sensitive liabilities. In our example, the asset-liability gap is (20 percent − 50 percent) = −30. Multiplying this gap times the projected change in the interest rate yields the change in the bank's profit. A gap of −30 tells us that a one-percentage point increase in the interest rate will reduce the bank's profit by 30 cents per $100 in assets, which is the same answer we got in the last paragraph. Gap analysis can be refined to take account of differences in the maturity of assets and liabilities, but the analysis quickly becomes complicated.[8] Table 12.2 summarizes all of these calculations.

Table 12.2 An Example of Interest Rate Risk

The impact of an interest rate increase on bank profits (per $100 of assets)

	Assets	**Liabilities**
Interest rate sensitive	$20	$50
Not interest rate sensitive	$80	$50
Initial interest rate	5%	3%
New interest rate on interest rate sensitive assets and liabilities	6%	4%
	Revenue from Assets	**Cost of Liabilities**
At initial interest rate	(0.05 × $20) + (0.05 × $80) = $5.00	(0.03 × $50) + (0.03 × $50) = $3.00
After interest rate change	(0.06 × $20) + (0.05 × $80) = $5.20	(0.04 × $50) + (0.03 × $50) = $3.50
Profits at initial interest rate: ($5.00) – ($3.00) = $2.00 per $100 in assets		
Profits after interest rate change: ($5.20) – ($3.50) = $1.70 per $100 in assets		

Gap Analysis

Gap between interest rate sensitive assets and interest rate sensitive liabilities:

(Interest rate sensitive assets of $20) – (Interest rate sensitive liabilities of $50) = (Gap of –$30)

[8]A more sophisticated examination of interest rate risk, called *duration analysis,* includes a measure of the interest rate sensitivity of bond prices. A bond's duration is related to its maturity. The percentage change in the market value = −(Duration of the bond) × (Percentage-point change in the interest rate). Bankers compute the weighted-average duration of their liabilities and subtract it from the weighted-average duration of their assets to get a duration gap, which can be used to guide the bank's risk management strategy. For a complete treatment, see Chapter 9 in Anthony Saunders and Marcia Millon Cornett, *Financial Institutions Management: A Modern Perspective,* 9th ed. (New York: McGraw-Hill, 2018).

Bank managers can use a number of tools to manage interest rate risk. The simplest approach is to match the interest rate sensitivity of assets with the interest rate sensitivity of liabilities. For instance, if the bank accepts a variable-rate deposit, it then uses the funds to purchase short-term securities. A similar strategy is to make long-term loans at a floating interest rate—as in adjustable-rate mortgages (ARMs)—instead of at the fixed interest rate characteristic of a conventional mortgage. But while this approach reduces interest rate risk, it increases credit risk. Rising interest rates put additional strain on floating-rate borrowers, increasing the likelihood that they will default on their payments.

While restructuring assets to better match liabilities can reduce risk, the fact that it also reduces potential profitability has led bankers to look for other ways to control interest rate risk. Alternatives include the use of derivatives, specifically interest rate swaps, to manage interest rate risk. Recall from Chapter 9 that an interest rate swap is an agreement in which one party promises to make fixed-interest rate payments in exchange for floating-interest-rate payments. For a bank that is holding long-term assets and short-term liabilities, an interest rate swap is exactly the sort of financial instrument that will transfer the risk of rising interest rates to another party.

Trading Risk

There was a time when banks merely took deposits and made loans, holding them until they were completely paid off. Today, banks not only engage in sophisticated asset and liability management but they hire traders to actively buy and sell securities, loans, and derivatives using a portion of the bank's capital, in the hope of making additional profits for the bank's owners. But trading financial instruments is risky. If the price at which an instrument is purchased differs from the price at which it is sold, the risk is that the instrument may go down in value rather than up. This type of risk is called **trading risk**, or sometimes *market risk*.[9]

Managing trading risk is a major concern for today's banks. Some of the largest banks in the world have sustained billions of dollars in losses as a result of unsupervised risk taking by employees in their trading operations. The problem is that traders normally share in the profits from good investments, but the bank pays for the losses. Heads, the trader wins; tails, the bank loses. This arrangement creates moral hazard: Traders have an incentive to take more risk than bank managers would like.

The solution to the moral hazard problem in trading is to compute the risk the portfolios traders generate using measures like standard deviation and value at risk (see Chapter 5). The bank's risk manager then limits the amount of risk any individual trader is allowed to assume and monitors each trader's holdings closely, at least once a day. Yet, large banks find it difficult to monitor their traders (and the managers who are supposed to be the monitors). As a result, multi-billion-dollar losses due to trading risk are surprisingly frequent at large banks—even those that are well managed. The higher the risk inherent in the bank's portfolio, the more capital the bank will need to hold to make sure the institution remains solvent.

[9]Because regulators in the United States won't allow banks to hold stock (equity), the traders employed by the bank can't, either. But because the traders buy and sell derivatives that are based on bonds, commodities, and foreign exchange, the rule against stock ownership doesn't restrict their ability to take risks.

The Cloudy Future of Peer-to-Peer Lending
MONEY AND BANKING BLOG

Peer-to-peer (P2P) lending started in the mid-2000s with the founding of firms like Lending Club and Prosper. The notion was that the lenders and borrowers could cut out the intermediary—usually a bank—"disrupting" traditional finance.

Browsing through the loan listings on www.prosper.com—the second-largest P2P lender in the United States—you will see that Prosper rates potential borrowers, with those rated "A" having the greatest likelihood of repaying their loans (and who therefore receive the lowest interest rates). You will also find that, while some people are looking to finance home improvements or borrow to go on vacation, many are trying to consolidate their debts to reduce their interest payments.

Lending Club, the largest U.S. P2P lender, originated more than $6 billion in loans in 2018, about three times the amount just five years earlier. Some borrowers may be getting loans they would have difficulty getting from a bank. And after adjusting for losses, investors appear to be reaping very favorable returns.

Improving the lot of borrowers will be great if this new lending channel works over time. But the key question for its longevity is whether lenders will continue to get an attractive risk-adjusted return on their investment over the long run. To do so, P2P lending systems will have to match or beat the borrower-assessment technologies that traditional banks use. Whether they can meet this challenge remains in doubt. Here's why.

Perhaps the most critical function of financial intermediaries is to address the information asymmetries in lending—figuring out whether a borrower is willing and able to repay. Determining that in advance is costly; and once a loan is made, it is difficult to confirm that the borrower is using the funds as intended. To overcome these *adverse selection and moral hazard* problems, banks screen potential borrowers and monitor them after a loan has been made.

The difficulty of monitoring is the reason that banks tend to employ a very fine screen when evaluating potential borrowers for direct loans. They favor borrowers with whom they have established relationships, and, when possible, obtain collateral—the car for an auto loan, the house for a mortgage—to limit their exposure and contain moral hazard.

Against this background, it seems natural that borrowers who already have credit card debt are relatively common on P2P sites. Credit card lending resembles P2P lending in several ways. The lender faces important information asymmetries, and the loan is uncollateralized. Card issuers can screen using credit histories and FICO scores, set interest rates high enough to encourage healthy borrowers to pay quickly, and set spending limits to control use—all very much like the process for a P2P loan.

Consequently, the real question is whether P2P technology for screening is as good as that of banks. Put differently, are the relatively high returns over the past decade indicative of long-term prospects? There are reasons to believe experience so far may *not* be a good guide for things to come. Instead, the next time the unemployment rate starts to go up, default rates likely will rise, too. And when that happens, P2P lending returns will likely plummet.

Indeed, this cyclical pattern is what we see with credit card loans, the type of debt that is closest to P2P lending and for which we have a long history. For each one-percentage-point rise in the unemployment rate, credit card default rates climb by nearly a full percentage point.

Overall, our guess is that if you have a good credit rating and are looking to reduce the burden of your existing debt payments, a P2P loan could be very attractive. But if you are looking to be a P2P lender, be especially cautious. Financial intermediaries have been around for a long time, and there is tremendous competition in the consumer lending business. If websites are to have a big impact on lowering credit card financing costs, perhaps they could better do so by directing borrowers to the lowest-cost card providers—much like some mortgage lending sites do today.

It would be nice if replacing the most competitive card providers with a website would result in consistently higher returns to investors and lower costs to borrowers, but the burden of proof will stay on the P2P lenders at least through the next recession.

In the crisis of 2007–2009, some banks, especially large ones, sharply underestimated the risks associated with mortgage-backed securities and related derivatives. As market prices on these financial instruments plunged, losses on their large holdings of these instruments seriously depleted their bank capital and threatened insolvency (see Lessons from the Crisis: Insufficient Bank Capital on page 312).

Cyber Risk and Other Operational Risks

Natural and human-made disasters highlight another set of risks that banks face. Severe weather, such as Hurricane Sandy that flooded Manhattan in 2012 or Hurricane Irma that paralyzed the Gulf Coast of Florida in 2017, raises questions about the resilience of infrastructure. When terrorists attacked the World Trade Center on September 11, 2001, they destroyed critical financial systems threatening to shut down banks, ATMs, and credit card operations across the country.[10] More recently, the extraordinary data breach at Equifax, affecting 143 million people, highlights the damage that hackers can wreck.

These episodes emphasize the importance of **operational risk**, defined as the risk of loss resulting from inadequate or failed internal processes, people and systems. Addressing natural disasters is part of virtually every large firm's business continuity plans. To limit disruptions, some firms create backup sites with duplicate infrastructure that is physically distant from the primary site.

Operational risk also includes **cyber risk**—the losses that arise when information technology systems fail or are compromised. This encompasses a variety of risks, some of which—like equipment failure—are increasingly addressed using "cloud computing" and other redundant systems. At the top of the list today, however, are the personal data breaches that are increasingly common, and especially likely to occur in financial services. From 2005 to 2018, the Privacy Rights Clearinghouse reports nearly 800 financial data breaches exposing 650 million records!

It's not difficult to imagine why the financial sector is both vulnerable and a target. Financial institutions, markets, and third-party vendors are especially reliant on information and communication technology to supply instantaneous on-demand services in large volumes at low cost. They have enormous client databases. They form an extensive network—domestically and globally—through the payments mechanism, exchanges, clearing and settlement systems, and the like. Cyberattackers can and do seek out the weakest links in these chains in order to achieve their goals—whether to steal property or, as may be the case with some hostile state actors, to destroy it and undermine confidence. And, it is no mystery why they target data related to finance. As bank robber Willie Sutton supposedly said, that's where the money is.

The burden of protecting electronic records and networks falls on individual firms. This creates a problem because of the potential for spillovers when data breaches occur: If key personal identifiers can be used fraudulently, the entire financial system may be at risk. Because firms cannot reap the full benefits of their data security investments, they lack the incentive to ensure the socially optimal level of cybersecurity or cyber resilience (see Chapter 7 of the 2018 *Economic Report of the President*). Left on its own, the private market will underinvest. This means that there is a role for government—in cooperation with the private sector—in promoting cybersecurity.

What should the government do? One key role is to encourage disclosure and information sharing. Firms have strong incentives—for legal and reputational reasons—to conceal cyberattacks that successfully exploit their vulnerabilities. As a result, it is widely believed that most events go unreported. The lack of reporting makes the financial system even more vulnerable. First, firms find it difficult to manage rapidly

[10]For a discussion of the problems that occurred in the U.S. financial system following the destruction of the World Trade Center towers, see the Federal Reserve Bank of New York's *Economic Policy Review*, November 2002, special issue on the economic effects of September 11. Of particular note are Michael J. Fleming and Kenneth D. Garbade, "When the Back Office Moved to the Front Burner: Settlement Fails in the Treasury Market after September 11," and James J. McAndrews and Simon Potter, "Liquidity Effects of the Event of September 11, 2001."

changing threats if they do not know the different types of attack that may occur, let alone their probability. Second, concealment contributes to long lags in recognizing ongoing attacks, allowing them to spread across vulnerable firms. As a result, it is difficult or impossible to prevent contagion and reduce widespread damage. Third, the lack of a sufficient data history means that it is impossible to build actuarial models for pricing insurance against losses from cyberattack. Consequently, financial institutions likely are underinsured against cyber risk.

The good news is that widespread public attention to these threats—along with frequent, sizable losses—has prompted both firms and governments to promote cybersafety. While spending is still relatively low—by one estimate financial institutions spent \$16 billion on cybersecurity in 2017—amounts are growing. In the United States, firms also have formed associations (like Financial Services Information Sharing and Analysis Center [FS-ISAC]) to share insights and data, and to establish reliable safety procedures in the event of infrastructure failures. And, together with the private sector, financial regulators have developed a range of "tabletop exercises" in which authorities and bank managers come together to simulate an emergency, thereby identifying vulnerabilities before hackers do so.

The challenge will be to keep up with the malicious actors. Financial firms are in an arms race. To stay competitive, firms and regulators will need to anticipate and focus on *prospective* risks, rather than merely ensure compliance with rules that address past incidents. Most important, they will need to avoid the kind of "failure of imagination" that the 9/11 Commission cited as one of the key sources of U.S. vulnerability to that attack. The rapid changes in both technology and the financial system bring not only new opportunities, but the possibility for previously unimagined catastrophes as well. If anything, the odds of disaster rise with the increased complexity and interconnectedness of finance.

Other Risks

Beyond liquidity, credit, interest rate, trading, cyber, and operational risk, banks face an assortment of other risks. A bank that operates internationally will face foreign exchange risk and sovereign risk. *Foreign exchange risk* comes from holding assets denominated in one currency and liabilities denominated in another. For example, a U.S. bank that holds dollar-denominated liabilities might purchase bonds issued by Sony Corporation or make a loan to a Japanese business. Both those assets would be denominated in yen. Thus, when the dollar–yen exchange rate moves, the dollar value of the bank's assets will change. Banks manage their foreign exchange risk in two ways. They work to attract deposits that are denominated in the same currency as their loans, thereby matching their assets with their liabilities, and they use foreign exchange futures and swaps to hedge the risk. But both approaches can introduce other risks that need to be managed (see Chapter 10, Lessons from the Crisis: Currency Risk and Rollover Risk).

Sovereign risk arises from the fact that some foreign borrowers may not repay their loans, not because they are unwilling to, but because their government prohibits them from doing so. When a foreign country is experiencing a financial crisis, the government may decide to restrict dollar-denominated payments, in which case a U.S. bank would have difficulty collecting payments on its loans in the country. Such circumstances have arisen on numerous occasions. Examples include Asia in 1997, Russia in 1998, and Argentina in 2002. In all these cases governments and corporations alike had difficulty raising enough dollars to repay their dollar-denominated debts. In such crises, a bank has very little recourse in the courts and little hope of recovering the loans. In

The Tri-Party Repo Market*
APPLYING THE CONCEPT

Repurchase agreements (repos) are a key form of short-term finance for many intermediaries. For lenders, like the treasurers of corporations or municipalities, repo is a close substitute for cash, making it a virtual component of the payments system. On the borrowing side, securities dealers use the repo market to fund their inventories of stocks and bonds, giving it a critical role in the capital markets.

Economists at the Bank for International Settlements (BIS) estimate that the volume of outstanding repos approached $5 trillion at the end of 2007, or nearly half the overall liabilities of the commercial banking system.† But in 2008, anxious repo lenders sought to avoid receiving illiquid or questionable collateral (such as mortgage-backed securities) as protection if repo borrowers failed to repay, so the repo lenders stopped lending and the repo market shriveled, aggravating the financial crisis.

Since the crisis, policymakers have focused on lingering sources of fragility in the repo market. The peculiar mechanism for clearing repo trades remains a key concern. A large share of repo transactions occurs in the "tri-party" market, in which a borrower and a lender each contract with a third party (a bank) to transfer the collateral first from the borrower to the lender and then back to the borrower when the repo unwinds.

In the United States, two banks—BNY Mellon and JPMorgan Chase—provide these repo safekeeping and transfer (also called clearing) services using a process that creates operational and liquidity risks for the financial system as a whole. In the interval between the usual late-afternoon implementation of a new repo agreement and the early-morning expiration of a previous one, these two banks become large creditors to the repo borrowers. This intraday exposure to individual borrowers makes them vulnerable to counterparty and collateral risks. In a crisis, such concentrated exposures can lead to fire sales and the paradox of leverage, in which collateral sales depress asset prices and aggravate the loss of capital in the financial system (see Chapter 3, Lessons from the Crisis: Leverage).

Policymakers concerned about systemic fragilities have promoted reforms in the tri-party repo market to synchronize the creation of new repo loans and the settlement of expiring loans. Making these transactions simultaneous would reduce the intraday lending exposure of the two clearing banks and the overall fragility of the market. However, the reform process remained ongoing in 2013, partly because of the technical challenges of allocating various types of collateral across multiple repo contracts and counterparties in a speedy, cost-effective manner. By 2015, the Federal Reserve Bank of New York estimated that intraday credit needs for tri-party repo had plunged to 3 to 5 percent of volume, down from 100 percent as recently as 2012. However, there remained a risk of disorderly fire sales of collateral from a defaulted dealer. Partly as a result, the repo market remains an important source of vulnerability in the U.S. financial system.

*This article is based largely on Copeland et al., "Key Mechanics of the Tri-Party Repo Market," *FRBNY Economic Policy Review* 18, no. 3 (November 2012).

†Peter Hördahl and Michael King, "Developments in Repo Markets during the Financial Turmoil," *BIS Quarterly Review*, December 2008.

2011–2012, Europe's sovereign debt crisis prompted sufficient fear that some countries would give up the euro (and re-create their own currencies) that many banks moved assets out of countries on the geographic periphery of the euro area to avoid so-called *redenomination risk*. The result was a capital flight that threatened the euro itself.

Managing sovereign risk is difficult. Banks have three options. The first is diversification, which means distributing the bank's loans and securities holdings throughout the world, carefully avoiding too much exposure in any country where a crisis might arise. Second, the bank can simply refuse to do business in a particular country or set of countries. And third, the bank can use derivatives to hedge sovereign risk.

It should go without saying that bank managers need accurate and timely information to control all these "other risks," in addition to the risks related to liquidity, credit, interest rates, trading, and operations. Yet, one of the lessons of the 2007–2009 financial crisis is that many banks lacked real-time information that would allow them to assess their various risk exposures at the bankwide level. Most important, some large banks with many business lines and legal entities operating across national borders lacked facilities to quickly aggregate and report the information that management

Table 12.3 Risks Banks Face and How They Manage Them

Type of Risk	Source of Risk	Recommended Responses
Liquidity risk	Sudden withdrawals by depositors or takedowns of credit lines	1. Hold sufficient cash reserves to meet customer demand. 2. Manage assets—sell securities or loans (contracts the size of the balance sheet). 3. Manage liabilities—attract more deposits (maintains the size of the balance sheet).
Credit risk	Default by borrowers on their loans	1. Diversify to spread risk. 2. Use statistical models to screen for creditworthy borrowers. 3. Monitor to reduce moral hazard.
Interest rate risk	Mismatch in maturity of assets and liabilities coupled with a change in interest rates	1. Closely match the maturity of both sides of the balance sheet. 2. Use derivatives such as interest rate swaps.
Trading (Market) risk	Trading losses in the bank's own account	Closely monitor traders using risk management tools, including value at risk.
Operational risk	Losses from inadequate or failed internal processes, people, and systems	1. Firms invest in redundant systems to limit vulnerability. 2. Government plays a role in helping to expose and limit malicious threats.

needed for effective risk control. The resulting uncertainties deepened anxieties about counterparty risks among intermediaries and contributed to the crisis. Unsurprisingly, governments now keep closer tabs on large banks' risk management efforts, including the quality of their analysis and reporting systems.

Table 12.3 summarizes the five major risks banks face and the recommended risk management strategies.

Key Terms

bank capital, 300
credit risk, 310
cyber risk, 316
depository institution, 294
discount loans, 299
excess reserves, 299
federal funds market, 299
interest rate risk, 311
interest rate spread, 304
liquidity risk, 307
loan loss reserves, 301
net interest margin, 304
nondepository institution, 294
off-balance-sheet activities, 305
operational risk, 316
repurchase agreement (repo), 300
required reserves, 307
reserves, 296
return on assets (ROA), 303
return on equity (ROE), 303
trading risk, 314
vault cash, 296

Using FRED: Codes for Data in This Chapter

Data Series	FRED Data Code
Number of commercial banks	USNUM
Bank failures	BKFTTLA641N
Net interest margin	USNIM
Return on equity	USROE
Net loan losses/Average total loans	USLSTL
Loan loss reserve/Total loans	USLLRTL
Commercial bank assets	TLAACBM027SBOG
Cash assets	CASACBM027SBOG
Securities	INVEST
Loans	LOANS
Real estate loans, all commercial banks	REALLN
Commercial bank liabilities	TLBACBM027SBOG
Deposits	DPSACBM027SBOG
Deposits, domestically chartered banks	DPSDCBM027SBOG
Deposits, large domestically chartered banks	DPSLCBM027SBOG
Large time deposits, all commercial banks	LTDACBM027SBOG
Bank capital or net worth (assets less liabilities)	RALACBM027SBOG
Return on average equity for U.S. banks with average assets under $1B	US1ROE
Return on average equity for U.S. banks with average assets greater than $15B	USG15ROE
Five-bank asset concentration in U.S.	DDOI06USA156NWDB

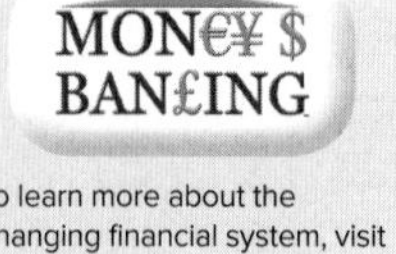

To learn more about the changing financial system, visit www.moneyandbanking.com.

Chapter Lessons

1. Bank assets equal bank liabilities plus bank capital.
   a. Bank assets are the uses for bank funds.
      i. They include reserves, securities, and loans.
      ii. Over the years, commercial and industrial loans have become less important and mortgages more important as a use for bank funds.
   b. Bank liabilities are the sources of bank funds.
      i. They include transaction and nontransaction deposits as well as borrowings.
      ii. Over the years, transaction deposits have become less important as a source of bank funds.
   c. Bank capital is the contribution of the bank's owners; it acts as a cushion against a fall in the value of the bank's assets or a withdrawal of its liabilities.
   d. Banks make a profit for their owners. Measures of a bank's profitability include return on assets (ROA), return on equity (ROE), net interest income, and net interest margin.

   e. Banks' off-balance-sheet activities have become increasingly important in recent years. They include:
      i. Loan commitments, which are lines of credit firms and households can use whenever necessary.
      ii. Letters of credit, which are guarantees that a customer will make a promised payment.

2. Banks face several types of risk in day-to-day business. They include:
   a. Liquidity risk—the risk that customers will demand cash immediately.
      i. Liability-side liquidity risk arises from deposit withdrawals.
      ii. Asset-side liquidity risk arises from the use of loan commitments to borrow.
      iii. Banks can manage liquidity risk by adjusting either their assets or their liabilities.
   b. Credit risk—the risk that customers will not repay their loans. Banks can manage credit risk by:
      i. Diversifying their loan portfolios.
      ii. Using statistical models to analyze borrowers' creditworthiness.
      iii. Monitoring borrowers to ensure that they use borrowed funds properly.
      iv. Purchasing credit default swaps (CDS) to insure against borrower default.
   c. Interest rate risk—the risk that a movement in interest rates will change the value of the bank's assets more than the value of its liabilities.
      i. When a bank lends long and borrows short, increases in interest rates will drive down the bank's profits.
      ii. Banks use a variety of tools, such as gap analysis, to assess the sensitivity of their balance sheets to a change in interest rates.
      iii. Banks manage interest rate risk by matching the maturity of their assets and liabilities and using derivatives like interest rate swaps.
   d. Trading risk—the risk that traders who work for the bank will create losses on the bank's own account. Banks can manage this risk using complex statistical models and closely monitoring traders.
   e. Cyber risk and other operational risks—the risk of loss resulting from inadequate or failed internal processes, people, or systems. This includes losses arising when information technology systems fail or are compromised.
      i. These risks can be very difficult to manage, as it is difficult to keep up with malicious actors.
      ii. While the burden of protecting individual systems falls on individuals, the presence of spillovers means there is a role for government to ensure a sufficient level of resilience.
   f. Other risks banks face include foreign exchange risk and sovereign risk.

Conceptual and Analytical Problems Mc Graw Hill connect

1. Explain how a bank manager uses Core Principles 1, 2, and 3 (time has value, risk requires compensation, and information is the basis for decisions) to select assets and issue liabilities consistent with shareholder preferences. *(LO1)*

2. Consider a bank with the following balance sheet, as shown on the next page. You read online that the bank's return on assets (ROA) was 1 percent. What were the bank's after-tax profits? *(LO2)*

Bank Balance Sheet (in millions)

Assets		Liabilities	
Reserves	$200	Deposits	$2,000
Loans	$950	Borrowing	$ 0
Securities	$950	Bank capital	$ 100

3. Based on the following information about Banks A and B, compute for each bank its return on assets (ROA), return on equity (ROE), and leverage ratio. *(LO2)*
   a. Bank A has net profit after taxes of $1.8 million and the following balance sheet:

Bank A (in millions)

Assets		Liabilities	
Reserves	$ 5	Deposits	$75
Loans	$45	Borrowing	$10
Securities	$45	Bank capital	$10

   b. Bank B has net profit after taxes of $1 million and the following balance sheet:

Bank B (in millions)

Assets		Liabilities	
Reserves	$ 8	Deposits	$80
Loans	$50	Borrowing	$ 2
Securities	$22	Bank capital	$ 8

4. Banks hold more liquid assets than do most businesses. Explain why. *(LO1)*
5. Explain why banks' holdings of cash have increased significantly as a portion of their balance sheets in recent times. *(LO1)*
6. Why are checking accounts no longer the primary source of funds for commercial banks in the United States? *(LO2)*

7. The volume of commercial and industrial loans made by banks has declined over the past few decades, while the volume of real estate loans has risen. Explain why this trend occurred and how it contributed to banks' difficulties during the financial crisis of 2007–2009. *(LO2)*

8.* Why do you think that U.S. banks are prohibited from holding equity as part of their own portfolios? *(LO3)*

9. Explain how a bank uses liability management to respond to a deposit outflow. Why do banks prefer liability management to asset management in this circumstance? *(LO1)*

10. A bank with a two-year investment horizon has issued a one-year certificate of deposit for $50 million at an interest rate of 3 percent. With the proceeds, the bank has purchased a two-year Treasury note that pays 5 percent interest. What risk does the bank face in entering into these transactions? What would happen if all interest rates were to rise by 1 percent? *(LO3)*

11.* In response to changes in banking legislation, recent decades have seen a significant increase in interstate branching by banks in the United States. How do you think a development of this type would affect the level of risk in the banking business? *(LO3)*

12. Consider the balance sheets of Bank A and Bank B. Suppose that reserve requirements are 10 percent of transaction deposits and both banks have equal access to the interbank market and funds from the Federal Reserve.
    a. Which bank appears to face a greater liquidity risk?
    b. Which bank appears to face a greater risk of insolvency? What other information might you use to assess the risk of insolvency of these banks?

    Explain your answers. *(LO3)*

Bank A (in millions)

Assets		Liabilities	
Reserves	$ 50	Transaction deposits	$200
Loans	$920	Nontransaction deposits	$600
Securities	$250	Borrowings	$100

Bank B (in millions)

Assets		Liabilities	
Reserves	$ 30	Transaction deposits	$200
Loans	$920	Nontransaction deposits	$600
Securities	$ 50	Borrowings	$100

13. Bank Y and Bank Z both have assets of $1 billion. The return on assets for both banks is the same. Bank Y has liabilities of $800 million while Bank Z's liabilities are $900 million. In which bank would you prefer to hold an equity stake? Explain your choice. *(LO2)*

14.* You are a bank manager and have been approached by a swap dealer about participating in fixed-for-floating interest rate swaps. If your bank has the typical maturity structure, which side of the swap might you be interested in paying and which side would you want to receive? *(LO3)*

*Indicates more difficult problems.

15. If lines of credit and other off-balance-sheet activities do not, by definition, appear on the bank's balance sheet, how can they influence the level of liquidity risk to which the bank is exposed? *(LO3)*

16. Suppose a bank faces a gap of −20 between its interest-sensitive assets and its interest-sensitive liabilities. What would happen to bank profits if interest rates were to fall by one percentage point? You should report your answer in terms of the change in profit per $100 in assets. *(LO2)*

17.* Duration analysis is an alternative to gap analysis for measuring interest rate risk. (See footnote 8 on page 313.) The duration of an asset or liability measures how sensitive its market value is to a change in the interest rate: the more sensitive, the longer the duration. In Chapter 6, you saw that the longer the term of a bond, the larger the price change for a given change in the interest rate.

    Using this information and the knowledge that interest rate increases tend to hurt banks, would you say that the average duration of a bank's assets is longer or shorter than that of its liabilities? *(LO1)*

18. Suppose you were the manager of a bank with the following balance sheet:

Bank Balance Sheet
(in millions)

Assets		Liabilities	
Reserves	$ 30	Checkable deposits	$200
Securities	$150	Time deposits	$600
Loans	$820	Borrowings	$100

    You are required to hold 10 percent of checkable deposits as reserves. If you were faced with unexpected withdrawals of $30 million from time deposits, would you rather:

    a. Draw down $10 million of excess reserves and borrow $20 million from other banks?
    b. Draw down $10 million of excess reserves and sell securities of $20 million?

    Explain your choice. *(LO1)*

19. Suppose you are advising a bank on the management of its balance sheet. In light of the financial crisis of 2007–2009, what arguments might you make to convince the bank to hold additional capital? *(LO2)*

20. The financial crisis compelled banks to reduce their leverage sharply. Consider the following two views (on the next page) of the balance sheet of a bank before and after the financial crisis. Which balance sheet view is more likely to be that of the bank after the financial crisis? Support your choice with calculations. *(LO2)*

*Indicates more difficult problems.

Bank Balance Sheet: View 1 (in millions)

Assets		Liabilities	
Reserves	$ 30	Deposits	$800
Securities	$150	Other borrowed funds	$ 90
Loans	$820	Bank capital	$110

Bank Balance Sheet: View 2 (in millions)

Assets		Liabilities	
Reserves	$ 30	Deposits	$800
Securities	$150	Other borrowed funds	$110
Loans	$820	Bank capital	$ 90

21. Suppose you operate a bank in a country where the central bank is expected to embark on a series of interest rate increases. Based on gap analysis, would this scenario be more likely to hurt or help your bank's profitability, assuming the bank's liabilities are more interest sensitive than its assets? What steps might your bank take to prepare for this scenario? *(LO3)*
22. Cyber risk has been recognized as a growing source of operational risk for financial institutions. Why might managing this risk at an individual firm level not be adequate? *(LO3)*

Data Exploration

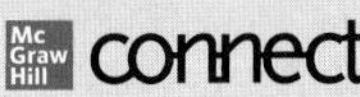

For general information on using Federal Reserve Economic Data (FRED) online, visit www.mhhe.com/moneyandbanking6e *and refer to the FRED Resources.*

1. Are U.S. banks increasing in size? Plot since 1984 on a quarterly basis the number of U.S. commercial banks (FRED code: USNUM) and, on the right scale, the volume of their deposits (FRED code: DPSACBM027SBOG). Download the data and compute the average deposit size of banks in the first quarters of 1984 and 2019. Do these sizes accurately portray a *typical* commercial bank? *(LO1)*
2. Commercial banks have become increasingly involved in the real estate market. Plot the percent change from a year ago of real estate loans made by commercial banks (FRED code: REALLN), and discuss the relationship between the booms and busts in real estate lending and the expansions and recessions of the U.S. economy. *(LO3)*
3. Plot since 1990 the return on equity of small banks (banks with assets of less than $1 billion; FRED code: US1ROE) and of large banks (banks with assets greater than $15 billion; FRED code: USG15ROE). How do you explain the long-run pattern? *(LO2)*
4. Banks sometimes manage liquidity risk by issuing large, marketable certificates of deposit when other deposits decline. How important is this practice? Plot the share of large time deposits (FRED code: LTDACBM027SBOG) in total deposits (FRED code: DPSACBM027SBOG). Explain how this share evolved over the long run and after 2004. *(LO3)*
5. What share of U.S. banks fail? Plot since 2000 the fraction (in percent) of bank failures (FRED code: BKFTTLA641N) relative to the number of banks (FRED code: USNUM). Comment on the timing and the proportion of failures. Were most of the failing banks large or small? *(LO3)*

Chapter

13 Financial Industry Structure

Learning Objectives

After reading this chapter, you should be able to:

LO1 Explain the structure, current trends, and future prospects of the banking industry.

LO2 Discuss the functions and characteristics of nondepository institutions.

Canada, a nation of 37 million people, has 35 domestic banks. If the United States had the same ratio of banks to population, it would have something like 312 banks. In fact, at the beginning of 2019, more than 4,700 commercial banks existed within U.S. borders, all vying to serve some 330 million Americans. The U.S. banking system is the outlier: Most countries' systems more closely resemble the Canadian structure. In Japan, for example, 125 million people depend on 119 banks, while in the United Kingdom, 67 million people are served by 154 domestically incorporated banks.

Amazingly, the United States once had even more banks than it does today. As Figure 13.1 shows, the number of commercial banks peaked at nearly 15,000 in 1984 and has been falling ever since. The figure also shows an odd pattern in the structure of banks. For decades, most U.S. banks were **unit banks**, or banks without branches. Throughout the 1950s and 1960s, more than two-thirds of banks were unit banks. Over the last quarter of the 20th century, however, the pattern changed. Today, less than one-fourth of banks in the United States are unit banks. What explains this change in structure?

The decline in the total number of banks and the increase in the number of banks with branches are not the only changes the U.S. banking industry has seen in recent years. In April 1998, the Traveler's Insurance Company, together with its investment banking and brokerage subsidiary Salomon Smith Barney, merged with Citibank, then the second-largest commercial bank in the country, to become Citigroup. At the time of its creation, Citigroup had $700 billion in assets and more than 100 million customers in 100 countries. It was also illegal. But by the end of 1999, the law that forbade such combinations had been repealed, and Citigroup began buying up even more financial firms. Today, Citigroup and a few other megabanks provide a broad assortment of products offered by almost all other financial institutions. These may

Figure 13.1 Number of Insured Commercial Banks in the United States, 1935-2017

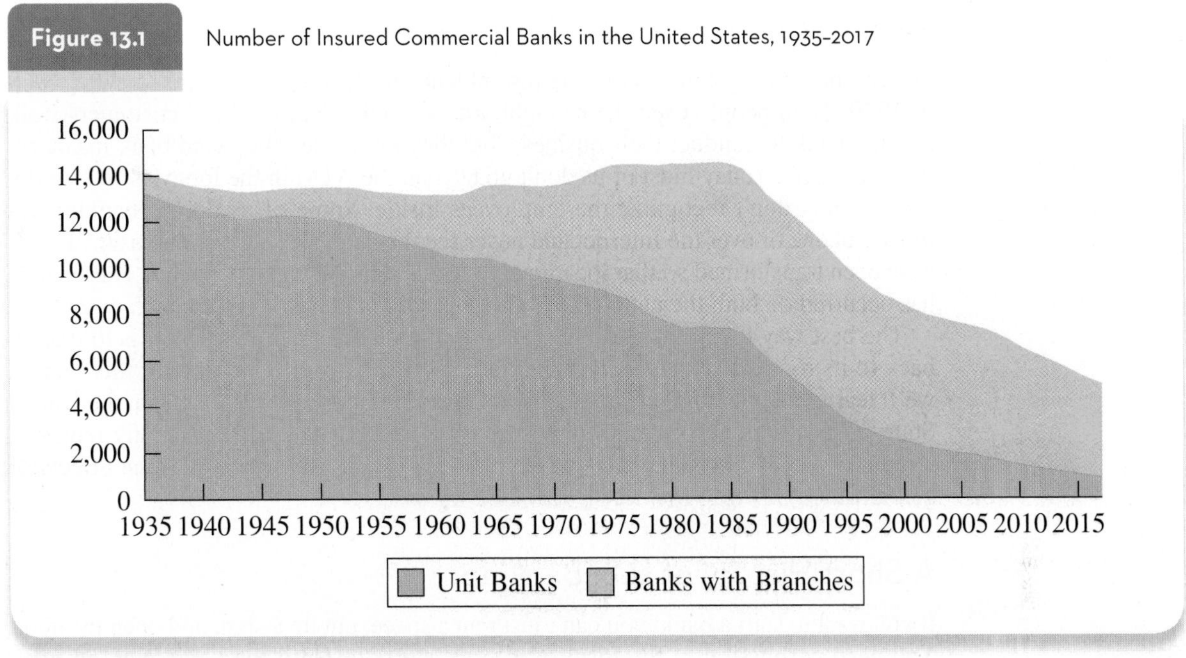

SOURCE: FDIC Historical Statistics on Banking, www.fdic.gov/open/datatools.html (FRED data code for total number of banks: USNUM.)

include the functions of an insurance company, a pension fund, a securities broker, a collection of mutual funds, a finance company and—of course—a commercial bank, all rolled into one.

The crisis of 2007–2009 has transformed the U.S. financial industry. The failure or forced merger of several large banks and other depository institutions accelerated concentration, boosting the domestic deposit share of the top four commercial banks by about seven percentage points, to around 40 percent of the total. In July 2008, the U.S. government placed the two massive government-sponsored enterprises (GSEs, see page 67) for housing finance in conservatorship (wiping out their private shareholders, but allowing them to operate while insolvent). In September 2008, the investment banking era that had prevailed since the 1930s came to an abrupt end as the four largest independent investment banks failed, merged, or became bank holding companies. The ensuing run on money-market mutual funds (MMMFs) was stopped only by a government guarantee of MMMF liabilities. And the federal government invested several hundred billion dollars to restore the capital of the largest U.S. financial institutions, bailing out their creditors to stabilize the financial system.

To understand the changing structure of the financial industry, we will discuss the services offered by both depository and nondepository financial institutions. Together, they provide a broad menu of services: buying and selling securities; offering loans, insurance, and pensions; and providing checking accounts, credit cards, and debit cards. Most financial institutions perform at least a few of these functions. Visit the website of any large bank, for instance, and you will discover that you can get not only checking and savings accounts, loans, and credit cards, but insurance and stockbrokerage services. The first half of this chapter will consider current trends in the banking industry, including the tendency toward consolidation with nondepository institutions. The second half of the chapter will study the functions and characteristics of nondepository institutions.

Banking Industry Structure

Today's banking system bears little resemblance to the one Americans knew in 1960 or 1970. Then people used their neighborhood banks. Not only did customers walk into the bank to conduct their business, but they knew the tellers and bank managers they saw there. Today most of us don't go beyond the ATM in the lobby, and if we do, we probably don't recognize the employees inside. Some of us do our banking via mobile phone or over the Internet and never see the bank's "bricks and mortar." Banks have been transformed so that location doesn't matter the way it once did. This change has occurred on both the national and the international level.

The best way to understand the structure of today's banking industry is to trace it back to its roots. That means looking at the legal history of banking. In this section we'll learn that banking legislation is the reason we have so many banks in the United States. We'll look at the trend toward consolidation that has been steadily reducing the number of banks since the mid-1980s. And we'll briefly consider the effects of globalization.

A Short History of U.S. Banking

If you want to start a bank, you can't just rent a space, put up a sign, and open the door. You need permission in the form of a **bank charter**. Until the Civil War, all bank charters were issued by state banking authorities. Because the authors of the U.S. Constitution feared a strong central government, in the early years of the Republic the federal government was weak and sometimes ineffectual. State governments were often more powerful. Until 1863, in fact, there was no national currency. Instead, state banks issued banknotes that circulated in much the way dollar bills do today. But while the state-chartered banks usually promised to redeem their banknotes in gold, they did so only if the bearer presented them at the bank. As the bearer traveled farther and farther from the bank, the value of the notes fell. So a note issued by a New York bank was worth less in Philadelphia than it was in New York.

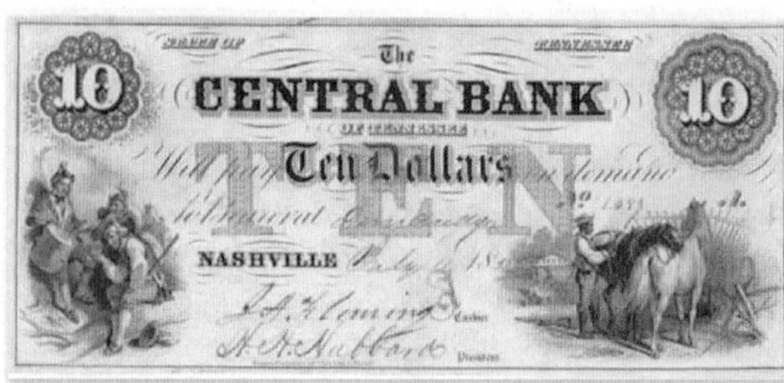

A $10 banknote issued by the Central Bank of Tennessee in 1853.

Courtesy of Stephen Cecchetti.

Besides currency that did not hold its value from one place to another, the early American financial system was plagued by insufficient capital and fraud. Banks regularly failed, and when they did, their banknotes became worthless. As we saw in Chapter 2, given the license to print money, most people will print too much. With so many different banknotes circulating, telling the sound money from the unsound became inordinately confusing and inefficient. The whole point of printing money is to reduce information costs and facilitate trade. Still, reasonable people hesitated to accept banknotes issued by banks they weren't familiar with, so money was not widely accepted. In the end, the system just didn't work.

Radical change came during the Civil War, when Congress passed the National Banking Act of 1863, initiating a gradual shift in power away from the states. Although the new law didn't eliminate state-chartered banks, it did impose a 10 percent tax on their issue of banknotes. At the same time, the act created a system of federally chartered banks, or *national banks,* which would be supervised by the Office of the Comptroller of the Currency, inside the U.S. Department of the Treasury. These new national banks could issue banknotes tax-free. Congress's intent was to put the state banks out of business by taking away their source of funds.

While the act did get rid of state-issued banknotes, state banks devised another way to raise funds, by creating demand deposits. This explains the origin of the **dual banking system** we have today, in which banks can choose whether to get their charters from the Comptroller of the Currency at the U.S. Treasury or from state officials. Roughly three-quarters of U.S. banks now have a state charter and the rest have a federal charter. The decision is related to a bank's profitability. State banking authorities have been more permissive than federal authorities in the types of operations they allow. Because greater flexibility in a bank's operations means a better chance of making a profit, state charters have been the overwhelming choice.

Furthermore, if the Comptroller of the Currency won't allow a bank to engage in a particular practice, the bank can always change its charter. This ability to switch back and forth between state and federal charters created what amounts to regulatory competition, which has hastened innovation in the financial industry. In the 1990s, changes in banking law required federal and state agencies to coordinate their oversight of financial intermediaries. But the globalization of the financial system, together with banks' ability to move funds easily across international boundaries, means that today regulatory competition exists not so much between state and federal government regulators but between regulators of different countries.

The first national banknote issued in 1863.

Courtesy of Stephen Cecchetti.

Following the Banking Act of 1863, the next major event in U.S. banking history occurred in 1933, in the midst of the Great Depression. From 1929 to 1933, more than a third of all U.S. banks failed; individual depositors lost $1.5 billion, or about 3 percent of total bank deposits. Millions of small savers lost their life savings.

To protect depositors and make banks safer, Congress enacted the Glass-Steagall Act of 1933, which created the Federal Deposit Insurance Corporation (FDIC) and severely limited the activities of commercial banks. The FDIC provided insurance to individual depositors, so they would not lose their savings in the event that a bank failed. The act also restricted bank assets to certain approved forms of debt and forbade banks from dealing in securities, providing insurance, or engaging in any of the other activities undertaken by nondepository institutions.

By separating commercial banks from investment banking, the law limited the ability of financial institutions to take advantage of economies of scale and scope that might exist in various lines of business. Nevertheless, this restriction on banks' activities remained in place until 1999, when the Gramm-Leach-Bliley Financial Services Modernization Act repealed the Glass-Steagall Act. We will return to this topic shortly. The repeal of the Glass-Steagall Act in 1999 eliminated the restrictions on banks' activities, but it renewed concerns about potential mismanagement of large financial holding companies.

The financial crisis of 2007–2009 underscored these concerns and led to the biggest financial reform since the Great Depression, the Dodd-Frank Wall Street Reform and Consumer Protection Act of 2010. Dodd-Frank aims to prevent financial crises and new government bailouts of financial intermediaries. In more than 800 pages of complex legislation, it sets out new rules for financial institutions and markets; requires closer government oversight over key establishments, called **systemically important financial institutions (SIFIs)**, regardless of their legal form; and sharply alters the authorities of the government agencies that govern the financial system. Like Glass-Steagall, the Volcker rule—a part of Dodd-Frank named after the former Federal Reserve chair who advocated it—also forbids insured depositories from proprietary trading, segmenting this and other business activities so that deposit insurance cannot subsidize bank risk taking.

We will explore the Dodd-Frank Act and its implications, along with more recent regulatory developments, in some depth in Chapter 14. But it is already clear that Dodd-Frank—and the hundreds of rules and procedures that the government is still developing to implement it—will continue to change the financial landscape significantly in coming years, much like the reforms of the 1930s did in their time. What remains unclear is how successful it will be in preventing another financial crisis.

Competition and Consolidation

None of the historical events we have discussed explains why there were more than 4,700 commercial banks in the United States at the beginning of 2019 or why that number had been shrinking since the mid-1980s. To unravel the mystery, let's return to Figure 13.1. Notice the division between banks with branches and banks that don't have branches. As we mentioned in the introduction, banks that do not have branches are called *unit banks*. The alternative, which is familiar to most of us today, is a bank with many branches spread out over a wide geographic area. Large banks like the Big Four—Bank of America, Citibank, JPMorgan Chase, and Wells Fargo—maintain branches in many cities across many states and foreign countries. We'll return to these banks in a moment. For now, notice from the figure that in 1935, the vast majority of banks had no branches; today, more than 80 percent of them do. In fact, if we look at the numbers, we see that in 1935 there were 14,125 commercial banks in the United States, with a total of 17,237 offices; by 2019, there were roughly 4,700 commercial banks, but they operated more than 80,000 offices. Today's banks not only have branches; they have lots of them.

The number of banks and bank branches in the United States tells only part of the story; we also need to look at bank size. Table 13.1 shows that the U.S. banking system is composed of a large number of very small banks and a small number of very large ones. Fewer than 3 percent of the banks hold more than 85 percent of commercial bank assets. Ranked by asset size, the top nine banks alone hold more than one-half of commercial bank assets.

Table 13.1 Number and Assets of Commercial Banks in the United States

Size of Institution (Assets)	Number	Percent of Total Assets
Less than $100 million	1,333	0.4%
$100 million to $1 billion	2,941	5.7%
$1 billion to $10 billion	518	8.3%
$10 billion or more	123	85.6%
Total	4,715	100% ($17.9 trillion)

SOURCE: Table III-A, FDIC Quarterly Banking Profile, Fourth Quarter 2018.

The primary reason for this structure is the McFadden Act of 1927, which required that nationally chartered banks meet the branching restrictions of the states in which they were located.[1] Because some states had laws that forbade branch banking, the result was a large number of very small banks.[2] Advocates of legal limits on branching argued that they prevented concentration and monopoly in banking in the same way that antitrust laws prevented concentration in manufacturing.

The McFadden Act produced a fragmented banking system nearly devoid of large institutions. The result was a network of small, geographically dispersed banks that faced virtually no competition. In many states, more efficient and modern banks were legally precluded from opening branches to compete with the small, inefficient ones that were already there. In these states, the result was a network of small community banks that faced no competitive pressures to innovate.

Not only that, but the system was prone to failure. Because the only loan applications these local banks received were from residents of their own communities, their loan portfolios were insufficiently diversified. In a farming town, the bank's fortunes depended on the weather, because its loan portfolio was composed almost entirely of agricultural loans. Aware of the problem, the bank manager would eventually stop making loans because the risk was simply too great. When credit ceased to flow into the community, farmers curtailed their operations. In the end, the bank's owners made a healthy profit because the bank was protected from competition—but everyone else in town suffered.

Some banks reacted to branching restrictions by creating **bank holding companies**. A holding company is a corporation that owns a group of other firms. In some contexts, it may be thought of as the *parent firm* for a group of subsidiaries. Bank holding companies have been around since the early 1900s. Initially, they were created not just as a way to evade branching restrictions but as a way to provide nonbank financial services in more than one state. In 1956, the U.S. Congress passed the Bank Holding Company Act, which broadened the scope of what bank holding companies could do, allowing them to provide various nonbank financial services. Over the years, changes in laws and regulations have added asset management, investment advice, insurance, leasing, collections, and real estate services to the list of allowable activities.

Beginning in the early 1970s, technology enabled banks to borrow and lend at a distance. The combination of the U.S. mail, telephone service, and finally the Internet dramatically reduced the importance of physical location in banking. Without the need to personally visit the bank to conduct their business, people ceased to care whether a bank was chartered in the state where they lived. Today, ATMs, laptop computers, smartphones, and debit and credit cards allow depositors access to means of payment even when they are far from home. Credit companies can evaluate any individual or firm's creditworthiness, so a bank can make a loan regardless of the borrower's location.

In changing the way people use the financial system, technology eroded the value of the local banking monopoly. In the 1970s and 1980s, states responded by loosening their

[1]The 1956 Douglas Amendment applied the same restrictions to bank holding companies, requiring that any out-of-state expansion be expressly approved by the host state.

[2]In the nation's early years, the states were starved for revenue; they could neither issue their own currency nor tax interstate trade. The fees the states earned for granting bank charters and the taxes they levied on bank profits became important sources of revenue for state government. The fees gave the state governments an incentive to create many small banks, while the taxes gave them an interest in protecting banks and ensuring they would be profitable. The result was a fragmented banking system with little competition. See R. Kroszner and P. Strahan, "What Drives Deregulation? Economics and Politics of the Relaxation of Bank Branching Restrictions," *Quarterly Journal of Economics* 114 (November 1999), pp. 1437–1467.

branching restrictions.[3] Then in 1994, Congress passed the Riegle-Neal Interstate Banking and Branching Efficiency Act. This legislation reversed the restrictions put in place almost 70 years earlier by the McFadden Act. Since 1997, banks have been able to acquire an unlimited number of branches nationwide. While some banks couldn't handle the new competition and went out of business, the vast majority that ceased independent operations disappeared through mergers with other banks. The number of commercial banks has thus fallen by about one-half over the past two decades, and the number of savings institutions—savings and loans plus savings banks—has fallen even more.

The Riegle-Neal Act allowed banks to diversify geographically. Today a bank that wants to establish operations in a new state can purchase a bank already located in that state. In doing so, it acquires the bank's customers, as well as its employees and their knowledge of the state's business and legal environment. The results have been dramatic. Banks became more profitable: their operating costs and loan losses fell; the interest rates paid to depositors rose while the interest rates charged to borrowers fell. The only people who suffered were the employees of inefficient banks, who had to work harder and were paid less as a result of the new competition. So, the deregulation of banks provided sizable benefits for the economy.[4]

Table 13.2 summarizes the key events in the evolution of the U.S. banking industry over the last century.

The financial crisis of 2007–2009 focused attention on the costs of deregulation. Did the poor management of some megabanks reveal the limits to expanding institutional scale and scope? Have the biggest banks already outrun those economies? Has

Table 13.2 Key Legislation Affecting the U.S. Banking Industry

1927 McFadden Act	Outlawed interstate branching and required national banks to abide by the laws of the states in which they operated.
1933 Glass-Steagall Act	Established federal deposit insurance and prohibited commercial banks from engaging in the insurance and securities businesses.
1994 Riegle-Neal Act	Repealed the McFadden Act's prohibition of interstate branching.
1999 Gramm-Leach-Bliley Act	Repealed the Glass-Steagall Act's prohibition of mergers between commercial banks and insurance companies or securities firms.
2010 Dodd-Frank Act	Aimed to prevent financial crises and government bailouts of intermediaries, partly through government oversight of systemically important financial institutions (SIFIs).
2018 Economic Growth, Regulatory Relief, and Consumer Protection Act	Reduced the regulatory burden on small and medium-sized banks, but also relaxed requirements on some larger banks.

[3]A number of other changes took place as well. For example, until 1980, federal law restricted the interest rate banks could pay on deposits. Under Regulation Q, they were prohibited from paying interest on checking accounts, and were limited to a maximum rate of just over 5 percent on savings deposits. As inflation and interest rates rose in the late 1970s, these restrictions became prohibitive. Many depositors withdrew their funds from banks and placed them in money-market mutual funds, whose interest rates were not restricted by law.

[4]One way to tell that deregulation improved growth is to look at what happened in different states. Separating the impact of deregulation from that of a variety of other effects on growth can be tricky. The fact that states deregulated at different times allows economists to disentangle the effects. See J. Jayaranthe and P. Strahan, "The Finance-Growth Nexus: Evidence from Bank Branch Deregulation," *Quarterly Journal of Economics* 111 (1996), pp. 639–670.

deregulation encouraged banks to take on too much risk? Has deregulation motivated some banks to become *too big to fail (TBTF)* in order to secure a government bailout in the event of distress?

More recently, the regulatory costs associated with Dodd-Frank posed the question whether the U.S. government is using the most effective means to make the financial system more resilient, and whether it has achieved the proper balance between safety and efficiency. The Economic Growth, Regulatory Reform and Consumer Protection Act (EGRRCPA) of 2018 scaled back some of the regulatory burden imposed after 2010 on small- and medium-sized banks, but also eased some of the requirements set by Dodd-Frank for larger institutions. After the 2016 election, the U.S. Treasury also sought ways to ease the regulatory burden in the absence of new legislation.

Addressing these complex questions is mostly an issue for government supervision, which is the subject of Chapter 14.

The Globalization of Banking

Toward the end of the 20th century, U.S. banking underwent not just a national but an international transformation. An explosion in international trade had increased the need for international financial services. Very simply, every time a Japanese company purchased software produced in the United States or an American bought a television set manufactured in China, payments had to be made across national boundaries. Today, the international banking system has adjusted to the needs of an interdependent, globalized world. Large U.S. banks like JPMorgan Chase and Citibank have stationed ATMs on the streets of Frankfurt, Buenos Aires, and other major capitals. In New York, keen observers can spot the foreign offices of Barclays, Deutsche Bank, and Tokyo-Mitsubishi. In 2018, U.S. banks had foreign exposure in excess of $2.5 trillion. And, nearly 200 foreign banking organizations with assets totaling over $2.5 trillion had a presence in the United States.

There are a number of ways banks can operate in foreign countries, depending on such factors as the legal environment. The most straightforward approach is to open a foreign branch that offers the same services as those in the home country. Certain legal structures also allow U.S. banks to engage in operations outside of the country, opening what looks to the casual observer like a branch (but may have a different legal status). For example, a bank can create an international banking facility (IBF), which allows it to accept deposits from and make loans to foreigners outside the country. Or the bank can create a subsidiary called an Edge Act corporation, which is established specifically to engage in international banking transactions. Alternatively, a bank holding company can purchase a controlling interest in a foreign bank. From our point of view, the classification of the particular enterprise is less important than the fact that U.S. banks take advantage of various methods to operate outside the country.

Foreign banks, of course, can take advantage of similar options. They can purchase an interest in a U.S. bank, open branches on U.S. soil, create a U.S. subsidiary, or open what is called an *agency office*. These alternatives differ in the spectrum of financial services they can provide.

The growth of international banking has had an economic impact similar to that of deregulation in the United States. Today, a borrower in France, Brazil, or Singapore can shop for a loan virtually anywhere in the world, and a depositor seeking the highest return can do the same. All this competition has made banking a tougher business. Profits are harder for bankers to come by today than they were in 1970, when depositors and borrowers were captive to small local banks. But while bankers' lives may be more difficult, on balance the improved efficiency of the financial system has enhanced growth everywhere.

One of the most important aspects of international banking is the eurodollar market. **Eurodollars** are dollar-denominated deposits in foreign banks. For reasons we will explain shortly, a bank in London, Zurich, or the Cayman Islands might offer its best customers the ability to make their deposits in dollars. In response, Ford Motor Corporation might convert a $1 million deposit in its New York bank to a eurodollar deposit in the bank's Cayman Islands subsidiary. After the $1 million has been deposited in Ford's Cayman Islands account, it is lent back to the New York bank. So, the account continues to provide Ford with all the same functions of the deposit at the same time that the New York bank now has a loan liability from its offshore subsidiary.

Both Ford and the New York bank have an incentive to do this. For the bank, the Cayman Islands deposit is cheaper. It is not subject to U.S. reserve requirements, nor is the bank required to pay a deposit insurance premium on the balance. Moreover, regulatory supervision is more lax in the middle of the Gulf of Mexico than it is in the United States, which reduces the cost of compliance. Finally, profits from the offshore bank may be subject to a lower corporate income tax rate than profits originating inside the United States. These advantages allow the bank to pay Ford a higher interest rate on the deposit, and they increase the bank's net interest margin.

A number of forces conspired to create the eurodollar market. Originally, it was a response to restrictions on the movement of international capital that were instituted at the end of World War II with the creation of the Bretton Woods system of exchange rate management. (We will learn more about the international monetary system and capital controls in Chapter 19.) To ensure that the pound would retain its value, the British government imposed restrictions on the ability of British banks to finance international transactions. In an attempt to evade these restrictions, London banks began to offer dollar deposits and dollar-denominated loans to foreigners. The result was what we know today as the eurodollar market. The Cold War accelerated the market's development when the Soviet government, fearful that the U.S. government might freeze or confiscate them, shifted its dollar deposits from New York to London. In the United States, a combination of factors propelled the eurodollar market forward. In the 1960s, U.S. authorities tried to prevent dollars from leaving the country and made it costly for foreigners to borrow dollars in the United States for use elsewhere in the world. Then in the early 1970s, a combination of domestic interest rate controls and high inflation rates made domestic deposits much less attractive than eurodollar deposits, which paid comparatively high interest rates.

Today, the eurodollar market in London is one of the biggest and most important financial markets in the world. And the interest rate at which banks lend each other eurodollars, called the **London Interbank Offered Rate (LIBOR)**, serves as the benchmark for many trillions of dollars (notional principal) of interest rate derivatives, making it the leading global interest rate indicator. It also is the standard against which many private loan rates are measured. For example, some adjustable-rate home mortgages in the United States carry an interest rate that is pegged to LIBOR. LIBOR figured prominently in the financial crisis of 2007–2009 when the interbank lending market dried up: the gap between LIBOR and the expected Federal Reserve policy interest rate provided a key measure of the intensity and persistence of the liquidity crisis. However, revelations in 2012 that LIBOR had been widely manipulated by global banks raised serious doubts about its future as an interest rate benchmark and led to government intervention to reform the way LIBOR is determined. As a result, LIBOR is now expected to disappear after 2021, to be replaced by one or more new short-term interest rate benchmarks that are currently in development (see Applying the Concept: Eclipsing LIBOR, on the next page).

Eclipsing LIBOR
APPLYING THE CONCEPT

The manipulation of the London Interbank Offered Rate (LIBOR) began in the mid-2000s. Employees of leading global firms submitted false reports to the British Banking Association (BBA), first to influence the value of LIBOR-linked derivatives, and later (during the financial crisis) to conceal the deterioration of their employers' creditworthiness. In response, U.S. and European regulators imposed $9 billion in fines on a dozen financial firms, forced out management, and jailed some individuals.

Despite this costly scandal, and the resulting challenges in maintaining it, as of 2019 LIBOR remains the world's leading benchmark for short-term interest rates. The current administrator (ICE Benchmark Administration), which replaced the BBA in 2014, estimates that it is the reference rate for contracts with cumulative value in excess of $300 *trillion*.

The basic rationale for financial benchmarks, ranging from the S&P 500 to the Brent oil price, is threefold. First, they lower transaction costs by providing an agreed basis for settling trades. Second, by focusing trades on a particular instrument, benchmarks foster competition and improve market depth. Third, benchmark-linked assets provide a mechanism for hedging common risks, increasing the overall risk-bearing capacity of the financial system.

So, what's the problem with LIBOR? Unlike the S&P 500 index or the Brent oil standard, LIBOR is *not* based on transactions. In its pre-2014 incarnation, the BBA calculated LIBOR from a *survey* of a panel of large London banks every business day to estimate their cost of *uncollateralized* borrowing in a specific currency at a specific maturity. Overall, the BBA reported 150 LIBOR benchmarks, covering 10 currencies at 15 maturities ranging from overnight to 12 months.

To reduce the risk of manipulation, the new administrator implemented a number of useful reforms. These include promoting the use of data based on transactions, reducing the number of benchmarks constructed, and establishing a code of conduct to emphasize integrity. Despite these worthy improvements, the paucity of transactions at some currency-maturity pairs makes it impossible for participating banks to escape the need for *expert judgment* in making their daily submissions. Wherever submissions rely on expert judgment, rather than transactions, there is the potential for manipulation.

To give some sense of the scale of the problem, note that daily transactions at the key three-month maturity in LIBOR-based U.S. dollar derivatives markets are about *1,000 times larger* than the roughly $1 billion in daily cash market transactions for unsecured bank funding. Furthermore, the stock of derivatives affected by price movements is about *100,000 times larger*, creating the possibility for enormous derivatives market gains or losses in response to tiny changes in LIBOR. Under such conditions, the temptation for manipulation can be overwhelming, even in the face of strong compliance oversight.*

Yet, as of 2019, LIBOR is on life support. Authorities, cajoling hesitant banks to participate, have committed to keeping it alive only through 2021.† Meanwhile, groups of government and industry experts are looking for a replacement. This effort has produced several measures of *secured* financing costs, including one called the *Secured Overnight Financing Rate* (SOFR). SOFR has a number of things going for it, starting with the fact that it is based on a deep, liquid market, with average daily transactions exceeding one trillion dollars, making it difficult to manipulate. It also is as close to default-risk-free as we are likely to get. In 2018, Fannie Mae issued the first SOFR-linked bond, while the CME established a platform for trading one- and three-month SOFR futures. That sounds great, but it is still missing features that have been integral to LIBOR: (1) a range of maturities, and (2) the funding risk premium of banks.

There also is another problem with replacing LIBOR—the legacy contracts that reference it as a benchmark. In some markets it would probably take less than 5 years for these contracts to mature and disappear. However, some LIBOR-based debt instruments—like the 30-year floating-rate mortgages included in mortgage-backed securities—have especially long lives, so they could be with us for decades. The private sector is working—with the support of regulators—on adding to new LIBOR contracts "fallback" clauses that allow for a smooth transition to another benchmark if LIBOR disappears. However, in the case of legacy contracts that lack such fallbacks, financial firms and the authorities will need to address the legal uncertainties and disputes that LIBOR's disappearance would trigger.

The good news is that the international regulators and leading market participants—including the largest banks that dominate the derivatives markets—are keenly aware of the risks arising from the need to replace LIBOR soon. While there is no way to guarantee a disruption-free transition, the partial eclipse of LIBOR already is well underway. It is only a matter of time until we reach totality.

*See Darrell Duffie and Jeremy C. Stein, "Reforming LIBOR and Other Financial Market Benchmarks," *Journal of Economic Perspectives* 29, no. 2 (Spring 2015), pp. 191–212.

†Andrew Bailey, "The Future of LIBOR," Financial Conduct Authority, July 27, 2017, www.fca.org.uk/news/speeches/the-future-of-libor.

The Future of Banks

Today's banks are bigger, fewer in number, and more international in reach than the banks of yesteryear; they also have more to offer in the way of services. A typical large commercial bank now offers investment and insurance products as well as the more conventional deposit accounts and loans. This trend began in 1998 with Citigroup's creation (see the chapter introduction).

In November 1999, the Gramm-Leach-Bliley Financial Services Modernization Act effectively repealed the Glass-Steagall Act of 1933, allowing a commercial bank, investment bank, and insurance company to merge and form a **financial holding company**. Citigroup, which already included all three, became legal. Since then, investment firms like J.P. Morgan, which once dealt only in securities, were acquired by commercial banks (in this case, Chase Manhattan), while commercial banks like Bank of America have purchased large securities dealers and retail brokers (Merrill Lynch). To serve all their customers' financial needs, bank holding companies are converting to financial holding companies.

Financial holding companies are a limited form of **universal bank**, a type of firm that engages in a wide range of financial (and possibly nonfinancial) activities. Depending on the country, such an arrangement provides more or less separation among the banking, insurance, and securities industries. The most extreme example is Germany, where universal banks do everything under one roof, including direct investment in the shares of nonfinancial firms. In the United States, different financial activities must be undertaken in separate subsidiaries, and financial holding companies are still prohibited from making equity investments in nonfinancial companies.

The owners and managers of these large financial firms cite three reasons to create them. First, their range of activities, properly managed, permits them to be well diversified, so their profitability does not rely on one particular line of business. This reduced risk should increase the value of the firm.[5] Second, these firms are large enough to take advantage of **economies of scale**. A financial holding company needs only one CEO and one board of directors regardless of its size. Only one accounting system is required to run the company. Third, these companies hope to benefit from **economies of scope**. In the same way that a supermarket offers all sorts of food and nonfood items under one roof, financial holding companies offer customers a wide variety of services, all under the same brand name. This, too, should reduce costs—or maybe the people who run these firms are just trying to build empires.

While Citigroup was creating the first of these full-service financial firms in the United States, the rest of the financial world was not standing still. Individual firms were working to provide customers with the same services they could obtain from more traditional financial intermediaries. Money-market mutual funds competed with banks in providing liquidity services to customers. Mortgage brokers gave consumers a choice in how to borrow for the purchase of a home and then sold the mortgages in the financial marketplace. Today, people who need an auto loan or any kind of insurance can get dozens of price quotes in a few hours just by logging onto the Internet. The screening of loan applicants, which was once the job of the neighborhood banker, has been standardized and now can be done by virtually anyone. Then there are discount brokerage firms like Charles Schwab and E-Trade, which provide low-cost access to the financial markets. Unlike the banks of

[5]Financial economists disagree on whether the reduced risk would actually increase the firm's value. Some people argue that firms should not diversify themselves but leave the choice to their stockholders. An investor can always purchase shares in two companies that would otherwise merge, in proportion to whatever risk exposure the investor desires. There also is concern that a firm with many different lines of business may not be as well managed as specialized firms.

the past, these alternative financial intermediaries don't have balance sheets of their own. Instead, for a fee they provide their customers with access to financial markets.

In fact, thanks to recent technological advances, almost every service traditionally provided by financial intermediaries can now be produced independently, without the help of a large organization. Loan brokers can give large borrowers access to the pooled funds of many small savers. A variety of financial firms, including brokerage firms and mutual fund companies, provide connections to the payments system, as well as the ability to transform assets into money quickly and at low cost. One of these days, even the electric company may get into the act. Or, as we have seen in Kenya's M-Pesa system, perhaps the cell phone provider will do so (see Chapter 2). And many intermediaries, including mutual fund companies and pension funds, help customers spread, share, and transfer risk. Finally, the production of information to mitigate the problems of adverse selection and moral hazard has become a business in and of itself.

As we survey the financial industry, then, we see two trends running in opposite directions. On the one hand, large firms are working hard to provide one-stop shopping for financial services. On the other hand, as we will see in Chapter 14, pressures are growing on governments to restrain or even break up the largest, most complex intermediaries that might need government support in a crisis. In addition, the industry is splintering into a host of small firms, each of which serves a very specific purpose. Will the future be one of generalists, specialists, or both? We will have to wait and see. In the meantime, let's look more closely at the role of nondepository financial institutions. And as we do, let's think about whether their products can be provided more easily and cheaply alone or together with other financial services.

Nondepository Institutions

A survey of the financial industry reveals a broad array of intermediaries. Besides depository institutions, there are five major categories of nondepository institution: insurance companies; pension funds; securities firms, including brokers, mutual fund companies, and investment banks; finance companies; and government-sponsored enterprises. This classification is neither exhaustive nor meant to imply that an institution's activities are restricted to a particular category. Nondepository institutions also include an assortment of alternative intermediaries, such as payday loan centers (see Chapter 12, Your Financial World: The Cost of Payday Loans, page 306), rent-to-own centers, peer-to-peer lending firms (see Chapter 12, Money and Banking Blog: The Cloudy Future of Peer-to-Peer Lending, page 315), pawnshops, and even loan sharks.

Table 13.3 shows that depository institutions accounted for less than one-quarter of the nearly $78 trillion in assets held by financial intermediaries in 2018. In the decades after 1970, the share of intermediation handled by banks fell steadily until the crisis of 2007–2009 temporarily depressed the assets of many nonbanks, but the relative decline of depositories subsequently resumed. Insurance companies suffered a more modest decline as their share of intermediation fell from 17.1 percent in 1970 to 13 percent in 2018. Meanwhile, mutual funds have been the big winners, growing from a 3.6 percent share in 1970 to more than 25 percent by 2018.

Our goal in this section is to understand the role of each of these types of nondepository institution in our financial system. We will do so by focusing on the functions of each. Recall from Chapter 11 that the functions of financial institutions can be divided into five categories: (1) pooling the resources of small savers; (2) providing safekeeping and accounting services, which allow people to make payments and track their

Table 13.3 Relative Size of U.S. Financial Intermediaries, 1970–2018

	Assets ($ billions)	Percent of All Intermediary Assets		
	2018	1970	1990	2018
Depository Institutions				
U.S.-chartered institutions	$15,407	51.0%	35.3%	19.8%
Foreign-banking offices	2,059	0.6%	3.1%	2.6%
Credit unions	1,408	1.0%	1.7%	1.8%
Insurance Companies				
Life insurance	7,709	13.7%	11.5%	9.9%
Property and casualty	2,436	3.4%	4.6%	3.1%
Pension Funds				
Private pension funds	10,003	12.6%	15.3%	12.8%
Government pension funds	7,145	6.0%	9.3%	9.2%
Mutual Funds				
Money-market funds	2,867	0.0%	4.3%	3.7%
Stock and bond funds	20,531	3.6%	5.6%	26.4%
Finance Companies	1,466	4.9%	5.3%	1.9%
Government-Sponsored Enterprises	6,887	3.2%	4.1%	8.8%
Total Assets of These Financial Institutions in 2018 = $77,917 billion				

NOTE: As of 2018, mutual funds include closed-end and exchange-traded funds, and government pension funds exclude unfunded claims on fund sponsors.

SOURCE: Board of Governors of the Federal Reserve, Financial Accounts of the United States, December 6, 2018, Tables L.111 to L.128.

assets; (3) supplying liquidity by converting resources into means of payment whenever needed; (4) providing diversification services; and (5) collecting and processing information in order to reduce information costs. We will use the same system to classify nondepository institutions.

Insurance Companies

Insurance companies began with long sea voyages. Centuries ago, distant trade and exploration were fraught with risk, and that risk generated a demand for insurance. Modern forms of insurance can be traced back to around 1400, when wool merchants insured their overland shipments from London to Italy for 12 to 15 percent of their value. (Overseas shipments were even more expensive to insure.) The first insurance codes were developed in Florence in 1523. They specified the standard provisions for a general insurance policy, such as the beginning and end of the coverage period and the time frame for receipt of payment following a loss. They also stipulated procedures for handling fraudulent claims in an attempt to reduce the moral hazard problem.

In 1688, Lloyd's of London was established. Today, Lloyd's is famous for insuring singers' voices, dancers' legs, even food critics' taste buds, as well as more traditional assets like airplanes and ships. The best-known insurance company in the world, Lloyd's

Why You Are Obliged to Buy Health Insurance

YOUR FINANCIAL WORLD

In its landmark 2015 decision upholding the Affordable Care Act (ACA, also known as Obamacare), the U.S. Supreme Court explained why health insurance that is always available to everyone at a common price requires a mandatory element: "Why buy insurance when you are healthy, if you can buy the same coverage at the same price when you are ill?"

The justices went on to describe how such *adverse selection* can trigger a "death spiral" for health insurance programs. To see what they meant, suppose that an insurer initially bases the policy premium on the nation's average cost of health care per person. If participation is voluntary, healthier people—typically young adults—will be less willing to enroll than those who anticipate greater-than-usual health care costs. Consequently, insurance outlays will exceed the norm, leading to losses for the insurance firm. If the insurer then raises the premium, the relatively healthy will drop their insurance. The higher the premium, the smaller the enrollment, and the worse the health of those still insured. Eventually, the program becomes unviable.

The adverse selection problem can be addressed in one of two ways: (1) allow price discrimination based on health status, or (2) make insurance mandatory. Under the first option, allowing insurers to set premiums according to the health of the applicant—the way they do for life insurance—makes the system workable: the more healthy the person, the lower the premium. The low premium reduces the incentive to drop out.

But concerns about fairness often lead governments to forbid this kind of price discrimination. Poor health is usually a result of poor fortune, and it is precisely bad luck against which people need insurance. Consequently, in most advanced economies, the solution to the adverse selection problem is the second option—compel participation.

How was adverse selection managed in the United States before passage of the ACA? For the most part, employers who provided health insurance promised insurers broad participation, limiting the risk that healthy workers would drop out. However, the health insurance system had major shortcomings. For example, an estimated 47 million U.S. residents—about 18 percent of the population—went uninsured before the ACA was introduced. In addition, persons with "preexisting conditions" could not obtain new coverage, so many stayed in their jobs (even when that was inefficient) just to keep their health insurance.

The science of genomics is adding to the problem of adverse selection: Advances in DNA testing are making it more feasible to anticipate an individual's future illnesses, another reason why health insurance will be broadly available at a common price only if it is mandatory.

began in a small London coffeehouse whose proprietor, Edward Lloyd, catered to retired sea captains who had prospered in the East Indies spice trade. Having sailed many of the trade routes themselves, these captains possessed special knowledge of the hazards of sea voyages. They used their knowledge to assess the risks associated with particular routes and to dabble in marine insurance. The risks were not inconsequential. In the 17th century, a typical voyage to the Spice Islands (part of Indonesia) and back lasted three years. Only one in three ships returned with its cargo, and as few as one in eight sailors lived to tell of the adventure. The rewards of a successful voyage were coveted spices like nutmeg, a single sack of which could make a sea captain wealthy for the rest of his life.

To obtain insurance, a ship's owner would write the details of the proposed voyage on a piece of paper, together with the amount he was willing to pay for the service, and then circulate the paper among the patrons at Edward Lloyd's coffeehouse. Interested individuals would decide how much of the risk to accept and then sign their names under the description of the voyage. This customary way of doing business became the source of the term *underwriter.* Underwriting was open to anyone who wished to assume the risk associated with sea voyages. Because Lloyd's predated by several centuries the concept of limited liability, in which investors' losses were confined to the amount of their investment, underwriting implied unlimited liability. The saying was that an underwriter was liable down to his last cufflink.

Today Lloyd's provides insurance through the more conventional structure of a limited liability company. The losses of individual investors in a syndicate are limited to the amount of their initial investment, and no person is exposed to the possibility of financial ruin.

Two Types of Insurance At their most basic level, all insurance companies operate like Lloyd's of London. They accept premiums from policyholders in exchange for the promise of compensation if certain events occur. A homeowner pays a premium in return for the promise that if the house burns down, the insurance company will pay to rebuild it. For the individual policyholder, then, insurance is a way to transfer risk. In terms of the financial system as a whole, insurance companies specialize in three of the five functions performed by intermediaries: They pool small premiums and make large investments with them; they diversify risks across a large population; and they screen and monitor policyholders to mitigate the problem of asymmetric information.

Insurance companies offer two types of insurance: life insurance and **property and casualty insurance**. Life insurers—companies like Prudential of America, Metropolitan Life, and John Hancock Mutual Life—sell policies that protect the insured against the loss of earnings from disability, retirement, or death. Property and casualty companies sell policies that protect households and businesses from losses arising from accident, fire, and natural disaster. Both types of intermediary allow individuals to transfer their risk to a group. While a single company may provide both kinds of insurance, the two businesses operate very differently.

Life insurance comes in two basic forms, called term and whole life insurance, as well as a variety of hybrids. **Term life insurance** provides a payment to the policyholder's beneficiaries in the event of the insured's death at any time during the policy's term. The premium depends on the very predictable proportion of people (of a given age) who will die. Term policies are generally renewable every year so long as the policyholder is less than 65 years old. Many people obtain term life insurance through their employers, an arrangement called group life insurance.

Whole life insurance is a combination of term life insurance and a savings account. The policyholder pays a fixed premium over his or her lifetime in return for a fixed benefit when the policyholder dies. Should the policyholder decide to discontinue the policy, its cash value will be refunded. As time passes and the policyholder ages, the emphasis of the whole life policy shifts from insurance to savings. Someone who lives to a ripe old age will have accumulated substantial savings in a whole life policy, which can be cashed in if the policyholder chooses. Whole life insurance tends to be an expensive way to save, though, so its use as a savings vehicle has declined markedly as people have discovered cheaper alternatives.

Most adults have experience with property and casualty insurance because driving a car without it is illegal. Auto insurance is a combination of property insurance on the car itself and casualty insurance on the driver, who is protected against liability for harm or injury to other people or their property. Holders of property and casualty insurance pay premiums in exchange for protection during the term of the policy.

On the balance sheets of insurance companies, these promises to policyholders show up as liabilities. While some claims may already be in process, most of them are future claims. On the asset side, insurance companies hold a combination of stocks, bonds, and other assets. Property and casualty companies profit from the fees they charge for administering the policies they write; the claims are covered by the premiums. Because the assets are essentially reserves against sudden claims, they have to be

How Much Life Insurance Do You Need?
YOUR FINANCIAL WORLD

We discussed disability insurance in Chapter 3 and automobile insurance in Chapter 5. What about life insurance? How much should you buy? The first question is whether you should buy any at all. The purpose of life insurance is to take care of the people you are supporting should something unpleasant happen to you. Think of it as replacement income that will be there when you're not. People with young children are the ones who need life insurance the most. If a parent dies, someone will have to raise those children and put them through school, and a life insurance policy will pay the bills. Life insurance is not for a single college student with no obligations, so don't let anyone sell it to you if you don't need it.

If you think you need life insurance, the next step is to decide what kind. The best approach is to buy term life insurance, which will pay off only if you die. Because other kinds of life insurance include investment components, they are more costly. And because the people who need life insurance most are young families with limited incomes and big expenses, the more affordable the policy, the better. Making your insurance and investment decisions separately is also easier than trying to achieve all your goals with a single vehicle.*

Finally, how much life insurance should you buy? If you are married with two small children, most advisors recommend that you buy a term policy worth six to eight times your annual income. While that might cover your family's living expenses until the children are grown, consider carefully whether it will be enough to send them to college. If you and your spouse each earn $45,000 a year, each of you might need $500,000 worth of life insurance. For someone who is between 30 and 40 years old, a $500,000 policy might cost about $500 a year, so out of your joint annual income of $90,000, you and your spouse would be spending $1,000 on term life insurance. That's expensive, so don't buy more than you need.

*Your parents and grandparents may have purchased whole life insurance policies for two reasons. First, in the past, individuals did not have access to all the investment choices that are available today. Second, tax laws were different; for some people, saving through a whole life insurance policy had tax advantages. But with the creation of tax-deferred savings vehicles like individual retirement accounts (IRAs), those benefits disappeared. Today, you would likely pay a life insurance company much more than the value of any tax benefits to you to administer a whole life insurance policy.

liquid. A look at the balance sheet of a property and casualty insurer will show a preponderance of government and other liquid securities and money-market instruments.

Life insurance companies hold assets of longer maturity than property and casualty insurers. Because most life insurance payments will be made well into the future, this better matches the maturity of the companies' assets and liabilities. Furthermore, while stocks may carry a relatively low degree of risk when held for periods of 25 years or more (recall the discussion in Chapter 8), insurance companies cannot risk the possibility that they may be forced to sell stocks when prices are low in order to pay policyholders' claims. As a result, life insurance companies hold mostly bonds.

The Role of Insurance Companies Like life insurers, property and casualty insurers pool risks to generate predictable payouts. That is, they reduce risk by spreading it across many policies. Recall from Chapter 5 that a group of investments with uncorrelated returns is less risky than any individual investment. The same is true of insurance contracts. While there is no way to know exactly which policies will require payment—who will have an automobile accident, lose a house to fire, or die—the insurance company can accurately estimate the percentage of policyholders who will file claims. Doing so allows managers to compute, with little uncertainty, how much the firm will need to pay out in any given year. From the point of view of policyholders, property and casualty insurance allows them to spread the risk of accident and damage across a large group of individuals.

In Chapter 11, we discussed the problem of asymmetric information in stock and bond finance. Recall that when a lender or investor cannot tell a good borrower or investment from a bad one, the tendency is for only the worst opportunities to present themselves. This phenomenon is called adverse selection. Furthermore, once borrowers or entrepreneurs have received financing, they have less incentive to avoid risk than the lender or investor. That problem is called moral hazard.

While adverse selection and moral hazard create significant problems in the stock and bond markets, they create worse problems in the insurance market. A person who has terminal cancer surely has an incentive to buy life insurance for the largest amount possible—that's adverse selection. And without fire insurance, people would have more fire extinguishers in their houses. Fire insurance creates moral hazard, encouraging homeowners to be less careful in protecting their homes than they would otherwise. Insurance companies work hard to reduce both these problems. By screening applicants, they can reduce adverse selection. A person who wants to buy a life insurance policy often must undergo a physical evaluation: weight, blood pressure, blood tests, and health history. Only those who pass the exam are allowed to purchase policies. And people who want automobile insurance must provide their driving records, including traffic citations and accident histories. While bad drivers may be allowed to buy car insurance, they will need to pay more for it. By screening drivers and adjusting their premiums accordingly, then, insurance companies can reduce their losses due to adverse selection.

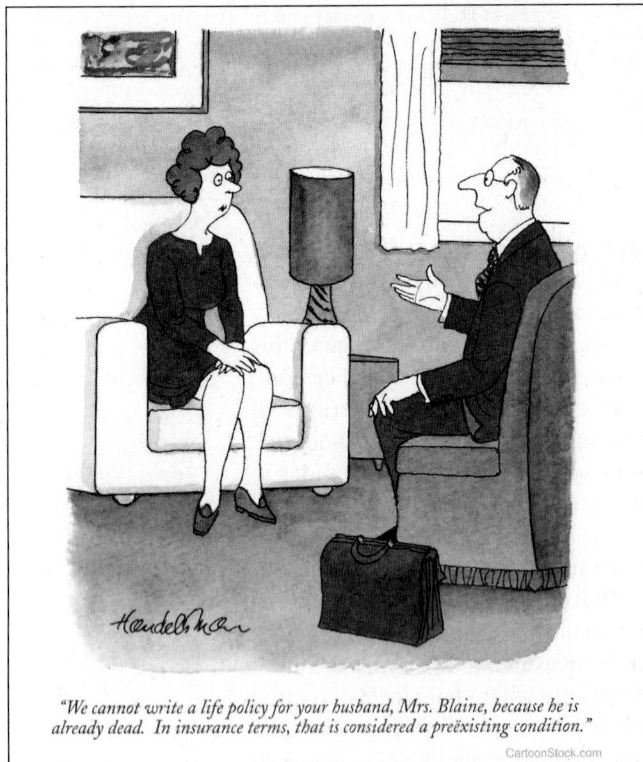

"We cannot write a life policy for your husband, Mrs. Blaine, because he is already dead. In insurance terms, that is considered a preëxisting condition."

www.CartoonStock.com.

Insurance companies have ways to reduce moral hazard as well. Policies usually include restrictive covenants that require the insured to engage or not to engage in certain activities. To qualify for fire insurance, a restaurant owner might be required to have the sprinkler system examined periodically; to obtain insurance against physical injury, a baseball or basketball player might be precluded from riding a motorcycle. Beyond such covenants, insurance policies often include *deductibles,* which require the insured to pay the initial cost of repairing accidental damage, up to some maximum amount. Or they may require *coinsurance,* in which the insurance company shoulders a percentage of the claim, perhaps 80 or 90 percent, and the insured assumes the rest of the cost.

It is interesting to speculate about the future of insurance in an age in which firms can collect more and more information at lower and lower cost. Remember that insurance is meant to shift risk from individuals to groups, not to shift the responsibility for events that are certain to happen. For example, no one expects an insurance company to sell life insurance to a person with a terminal disease.

Herein lies a potential problem. If, with the decoding of the human genome, tests become available whereby individuals can determine their probability of developing a

Reinsurance and "Cat Bonds"

APPLYING THE CONCEPT

To get a mortgage on a home, you'll need insurance. Regardless of where you live, your lender will require you to have fire insurance, and in some places you may also need insurance against natural disasters like floods, earthquakes, or hurricanes. Without such insurance you won't get a mortgage, and without a mortgage you won't buy a house. Clearly, it's in everyone's interest for insurance companies to provide such insurance and spread the risk. But sometimes this kind of insurance isn't easy to obtain.

Imagine that an insurer is thinking of offering earthquake insurance in California. Unlike automobile accidents, when an earthquake hits, a large number of policyholders will all file claims at the same time. The result for the insurance company is a large, undiversified risk. To offer earthquake insurance and stay in business, a property and casualty insurance company must find some way to insure itself against catastrophic risks—large natural disasters that generate a significant number of payouts simultaneously.

Reinsurance companies offer a solution to this problem by providing insurance to insurance companies. Say the California insurer estimates that an earthquake would generate payments of $15 billion (the approximate loss in the 1994 earthquake in Northridge, Los Angeles). The company may have the resources to cover only the first $1 billion of policyholders' claims. To write the full $15 billion worth of insurance, the company will need to buy $14 billion of reinsurance.

Reinsurance companies are enormous; they operate all over the world. Their geographic spread allows them to diversify their risk, because earthquakes don't happen at the same time in both California and Japan. The fact that reinsurance companies can spread their risk globally gives them the ability to withstand individual losses, even if they are catastrophic. For this to work, reinsurers have to be big. So big, in fact, that they have become near monopolies, driving up the price of reinsurance in the process.

The rising cost of reinsurance has spurred the creation of a second solution to the problem of insuring catastrophic risk. Financial experts have designed catastrophic bonds, or *cat bonds,* which allow individual investors to share a very small portion of the reinsurance risk. It works like this: through an investment bank, an insurance company will sell a quantity of cat bonds, immediately investing proceeds in low-risk financial instruments like U.S. Treasury bonds. If a catastrophe occurs, the U.S. Treasury bonds are sold and the resulting funds used to pay the claims the insurance company faces. But if no earthquake, fire, or hurricane hits during the policy period, the cat bond owners receive a substantial return that can be as high as 10 percentage points above the yield on U.S. Treasury bonds of equal maturity.* This high level of compensation, coupled with a very low correlation with the return on most other investments, means that cat bonds can both improve the expected return and lower the risk of a typical investor's portfolio. Nevertheless, the demand for cat bonds remains limited, with issuance of less than $15 billion in 2018.

The existence of reinsurance and cat bonds has clear benefits. These mechanisms for transferring and spreading the risk of catastrophic disaster improve the risk–return tradeoff for individual investors, enable insurance companies to offer more insurance than they could otherwise, and allow prospective homeowners to get the insurance they need—and the mortgage financing they want—to purchase a home.

*One of the first cat bonds to be issued was a $400 million offering in 1997 by the United Services Automobile Association (USAA), an insurer of current and past military personnel and their families. The bond agreement provided that if USAA's losses from a hurricane rated category 3, 4, or 5 exceeded $1 billion over the next year, bondholders would pay 80 percent of the next $500 million in claims.

terminal disease, then they may be able to use this information to get a fairly good idea of their life expectancy and relative cost of health care. If applicants for health insurance were to withhold this information from insurance companies, the adverse selection problem could become severe enough to cause the industry to collapse. By contrast, if applicants chose to reveal this information, they might not be able to obtain insurance. Someone who has a high probability of getting heart disease at a young age will still be able to get automobile insurance, but getting life or health insurance will be very difficult. Providing affordable insurance for such "preexisting conditions" was one of the leading motivations for the U.S. health care reforms that were enacted by Congress in 2010.

Pension Funds

Like an insurance company, a pension fund offers people the ability to make premium payments today in exchange for promised payments under certain future circumstances. Also like an insurance company, pension funds do not accept deposits. They do help people develop the discipline of saving regularly, getting them started early and helping them stick with it. As we saw in Chapter 4, the earlier a person begins saving and the more disciplined he or she is, the better off that person will be later in life. Saving from an early age means enjoying a higher income at retirement. Pension plans not only provide an easy way to make sure that a worker saves and has sufficient resources in retirement; they help savers diversify their risk. By pooling the savings of many small investors, pension funds spread the risk, ensuring that funds will be available to investors in their old age.

People can use a variety of methods to save for retirement, including employer-sponsored plans and individual savings plans, both of which allow workers to defer income tax on their savings until they retire. Nearly everyone who works for a large corporation in the United States has an employer-administered pension plan. There are two basic types: defined-benefit (DB) pension plans and defined-contribution (DC) pension plans. Regardless of the type, many employer-sponsored plans require a person to work for a certain number of years before qualifying for benefits. This qualifying process is called **vesting**. Think of vesting as the point at which the contributions your employer has made to the pension plan on your behalf belong to you. Changing jobs before your pension contributions have been vested can be very costly.

Let's take a look at how the two types of pension plan work. **Defined-benefit plans** were once more common than they are today. Participants in DB plans receive a lifetime retirement income based on the number of years they worked at the company and their final salary. For example, someone who worked for the same company for 30 years and retired at a salary of \$100,000 might receive 2 percent of that salary for each year of service, or \$60,000 per year. That may seem good, but to reap such benefits, most people would need to work a very long time for the same firm.

Defined-contribution plans are replacing defined-benefit plans, and they are very different. These plans are sometimes referred to by names like "401(k)" after their designations in the Internal Revenue Service code. In a defined-contribution plan, the employee and employer both make contributions into an investment account that belongs to the employee. Unlike a defined-benefit plan, in a DC plan the employer takes no responsibility for the size of the employee's retirement income. Instead, at retirement the employee receives the accumulated funds in the account and must decide what to do with them. The options include accepting a lump sum, removing small amounts at a time, or converting the balance to a fixed monthly payment for life by purchasing an annuity.

You can think of a pension plan as the opposite of life insurance. One pays off if you live, the other if you don't. The two vehicles are similar enough that the same institution often offers both. And not surprisingly, the balance sheets of pension funds look a lot like those of life insurance companies; both hold long-term assets like corporate bonds and stocks. The only difference is that life insurance companies hold only half the equities that pension funds do.[6]

[6]The heavier emphasis on equities makes pension funds more risky. This is a risk that is potentially borne by the plans' participants. But, as mentioned later in this section, defined-benefit pension plans are insured by the U.S. government, so in reality this is a risk borne broadly by everyone.

Public Pensions and the Social Security System

APPLYING THE CONCEPT

Providing for older adults is a tremendous challenge for any society. Traditionally, children cared for their parents as they aged. But with the advent of modern industrial societies and an associated increase in geographic mobility, many elderly parents no longer live with their children. Today the expectation is that people will save enough while they are working to pay their own way when they retire. If they don't, the general view is that in a civilized society, government should care for the poor.

grzegorz knec/Alamy Stock Photo

During the 20th century, the governments of many countries created pension systems that provided a guaranteed income to elderly people. These programs were financed by tax revenues paid by younger workers. As long as workers' incomes were growing quickly enough and the population itself was growing, the arrangement worked well. Around 1970, however, both economic growth and population growth began to slow in industrialized countries. At the same time, medical care was improving, raising the prospect of a longer life for everyone. Gradually the ratio of workers to retirees began to fall, so fewer and fewer working people were supporting more and more retirees.

Today, to remain financially viable, these systems must change. One solution—to raise the age at which full retirement benefits are received to 70 instead of 67—has so far been politically unpalatable. Failure to deal with the problem has set the stage for a crisis. In the United States, the Social Security system will eventually be unable to meet the obligations currently on its books.

Social Security is not a pension system in the traditional sense of the term. All U.S. workers pay Social Security tax (see the line labeled "FICA" on your pay stub); in return, the government promises to make payments to them when they retire. But with the Social Security taxes it collects from workers, the government can do only one of two things: it can give it to current retirees or spend it on general programs. As such, Social Security is a "pay-as-you-go" system that transfers revenues directly from current workers to current retirees.

This is a very different arrangement from a private pension fund, in which contributions accumulate and are invested for the long term and only after many years are paid out to retirees. Not only is the source of funds different but the allocation of risk differs too. In the current Social Security system, the responsibility to pay retirees belongs to younger generations. They foot the bill; they face the risk. If the economy does poorly, for example, wages of younger workers will fall, making it more burdensome to pay the taxes required to honor promises to retirees. In contrast, in a private pension system, individuals' own savings provide their retirement incomes and they themselves face the risk that the return on their investments may be low.

The Social Security system's finances are in bad shape. According to the government's 2018 estimates, by 2034 tax income will be sufficient to finance only 79 percent of promised benefits. There are only a few ways the problem can be repaired. The government can reduce the benefits promised to future retirees, raise the tax rate that future workers pay, apply the Social Security contribution to incomes above the current cap, or convert the system into one that mirrors a private pension plan, with individual accounts. Most proposals to fix the system involve some combination of all three of these approaches. For example, suggestions to *privatize* the system involve reducing benefits to those who are currently working, raising their Social Security taxes, and placing new revenues into individual accounts similar to defined-contribution pension funds. In such a system, the government would continue to guarantee that the poor do not starve, but those who are well off enough to take care of themselves would have to do so.

At this point, all anyone knows is that the Social Security system will have to change and the faster the better. In evaluating the proposals to fix it, keep in mind two key questions: Who will pay the bills and who will shoulder the risks?

Finally, it is worth noting that the U.S. government does provide insurance for private, defined-benefit pension systems. If a company goes bankrupt, the Pension Benefit Guaranty Corporation (PBGC) will take over the fund's liabilities. The PBGC currently guarantees more than 24,000 pension funds covering nearly 40 million workers. While the PBGC's insurance is capped, so that highly paid employees like airline pilots are not fully protected, it still increases the incentive for a firm's managers to engage in risky behavior. To guard against this possibility, regulators monitor pension funds closely. Even so, as of fiscal 2017, the PBGC reported a deficit exceeding $50 billion.

Securities Firms: Brokers, Mutual Funds, and Investment Banks

The broad class of securities firms includes brokerages, investment banks, and mutual fund companies. In one way or another, these are all financial intermediaries. The primary services of brokerage firms are accounting (to keep track of customers' investment balances), custody services (to make sure valuable records such as stock certificates are safe), and access to secondary markets (in which customers can buy and sell financial instruments). Brokers also provide loans to customers who wish to purchase stock on margin. And they provide liquidity, both by offering check-writing privileges with their investment accounts and by allowing investors to sell assets quickly. Mutual fund companies like Vanguard, Fidelity, and Dreyfus offer liquidity services as well; their money-market mutual funds are a key example. But the primary function of mutual funds is to pool the small savings of individuals in diversified portfolios that are composed of a wide variety of financial instruments.

All securities firms are very much in the business of producing information. But while brokers and mutual funds provide some investment advice to their retail customers, information is at the heart of the investment banking business. Investment banks like Goldman Sachs, Morgan Stanley, and JPMorgan Chase—all now divisions of bank holding companies—are the conduits through which firms raise funds in the capital markets. Through their **underwriting** services, these investment banks issue new stocks and a variety of other debt instruments. Most commonly, the underwriter guarantees the price of a new issue and then sells it to investors at a higher price, a practice called *placing the issue*. The underwriter profits from the difference between the price guaranteed to the firm that issues the security and the price at which the bond or stock is sold to investors. But because the price at which the investment bank sells the bonds or stocks in financial markets can turn out to be lower than the price guaranteed to the issuing company, there is some risk to underwriting. For most large issues, a group of investment banks will band together and spread the risk among themselves rather than one of them taking the risk alone.

INFORMATION

Information and reputation are central to the underwriting business. Underwriters collect information to determine the price of the new securities and then put their reputations on the line when they go out to sell the issues. A large, well-established investment bank will not underwrite issues indiscriminately. To do so would reduce the value of the bank's brand, along with the fees the bank can charge.

In addition to underwriting, investment banks provide advice to firms that want to merge with or acquire other firms. Investment bankers do the research to identify potential *mergers and acquisitions* and estimate the value of the new, combined company. The information they collect and the advice they give must be valuable because they are paid handsomely for them. In facilitating these combinations, investment banks perform a service to the economy. Mergers and acquisitions help ensure that the people who manage firms do the best job possible. Managers who don't get the most out of the resources entrusted to them risk having their company purchased by executives who can do a better job. This threat of a takeover—sometimes described as the *market for corporate control*—provides discipline in the management of individual companies and improves the allocation of resources across the economy.

Hedge Funds
TOOLS OF THE TRADE

Hedge funds are strictly for millionaires. These investment partnerships (sometimes referred to as *nontraditional investment funds*) bring together small groups of people who meet certain wealth requirements. To avoid various legal regulations, hedge funds come in two basic sizes: (1) they can have a maximum of either 99 investors, each of whom has at least $1 million in net worth, or (2) 499 investors, each of whom has at least $5 million in net worth. The larger hedge funds can also accept funds from institutional investors like pension funds, mutual funds, and insurance companies so long as their net worth is at least $25 million. The minimum investment in a hedge fund is usually $100,000. These really are millionaires' investment clubs.

Hedge funds are run by a general partner, or manager, who is in charge of day-to-day decisions. Managers are very well paid, receiving an annual fee of at least 2 percent of assets plus 20 percent of profits. In a year in which the fund's return on investment is 10 percent, the manager of an average-size fund of $500 million will receive $20 million in fees.

Because these funds are unregulated, finding out what their portfolios contain can be a challenge even for the fund's investors: the manager need not tell anyone. This secrecy creates the very real possibility of moral hazard. If a fund starts to incur losses, determining the reason for the fall in value is often impossible. To ensure that the manager's incentives match those of the investors, the manager is required to keep a large fraction of his or her own wealth in the fund. By and large, this requirement solves the problem of moral hazard; fraudulent behavior is extremely rare.

The name *hedge fund* may suggest that these funds employ the diversification techniques discussed in Chapter 5, but they do not. Hedging reduces risk by grouping together individual investments whose returns tend to move in opposite directions, but hedge funds are not low-risk enterprises. Because they are organized as private partnerships, hedge funds are not constrained in their investment strategies; they can trade in derivatives and borrow to create leverage.

A. W. Jones founded the first hedge fund in 1949. His fund combined leverage with short selling (the practice of borrowing a stock or bond whose price you believe will fall, selling it, and then buying it back at a lower price before repaying the lender). Jones divided the fund's equities into two groups: companies whose stock prices he thought would fall and companies whose stock prices he thought would rise. He sold the first group short and used the proceeds to buy shares in the second group. The term *hedge* in the name *hedge fund* comes from the fact that when the market in general went up or down, moving all stocks in the same direction, the fund would take losses on one group of stock but turn a profit on the second. It was hedged against movements in the market as a whole. Jones turned a profit when the stocks he sold short went down relative to the stocks he purchased. And those profits were substantial.

Today we would refer to Jones's fund as a "long-short hedge fund" because he was long on some stocks and short on others. As of 2018, according to Hedge Fund Research, more than 8,000 hedge funds managed roughly $3.25 trillion. The long-short approach is only one of the strategies their managers follow. *Macro fund* managers take unhedged positions in the hope of benefiting from shifts in interest rates or national market conditions. *Global fund* managers engage in international stock picking. And the managers of *relative value funds* try to exploit small, transitory differences in the prices of related securities, such as U.S. Treasury bills and bonds. Long-Term Capital Management, the hedge fund that collapsed in September 1998 (see Chapter 9), was following this last strategy, trying to take advantage of price differences between U.S. Treasury bonds of slightly different maturities. Playing games with interest rates is what led the firm to amass $1.25 trillion in interest rate swaps.*

Regardless of the strategies they use, hedge fund managers typically strive to create returns that roughly equal those of the stock market (as measured by a comprehensive index like the S&P 500) but are uncorrelated with it. So while individual hedge funds are very risky—something like 10 percent of them close down every year—a portfolio that invests in a large number of these funds can expect returns equal to the stock market average with less risk. That is why people like hedge funds and why successful hedge fund managers are so well paid.

*For an insightful history and analysis of hedge funds, see Sebastian Mallaby, *More Money Than God: Hedge Funds and the Making of a New Elite* (New York: Penguin Press, 2011).

Finance Companies

Finance companies are in the lending business. They raise funds directly in the financial markets by issuing commercial paper and securities and then use them to make loans to individuals and corporations. Because these companies specialize in making loans, they are concerned largely with reducing the transactions and information costs that are associated with intermediated finance. And because of their narrow focus, finance companies are particularly good at screening potential borrowers' creditworthiness, monitoring their performance during the term of the loan, and seizing collateral in the event of a default.

Most finance companies specialize in one of three loan types: consumer loans, business loans, and what are called sales loans. Some also provide commercial and home mortgages. *Consumer finance* firms provide small installment loans to individual consumers. If you visit an appliance store to purchase a new refrigerator, you may be offered a deal that includes "no money down and no payments for six months." If you accept this loan offer, you'll be asked to fill out an application and to wait a few minutes while someone checks your credit. The credit is usually supplied not by the store but by a finance company like Wells Fargo. This kind of consumer credit allows people without sufficient savings to purchase appliances such as television sets, washing machines, and microwave ovens.

Business finance companies provide loans to businesses. If you want to start your own airline, for example, you will need to acquire some airplanes. That isn't as difficult as it may sound, because you don't need to shell out the entire $100 million price of a new plane. Airplanes, like automobiles, can be leased. That is, a business finance company buys the plane and then leases it back to you, an approach that significantly reduces the cost of starting your new enterprise. While this example is extreme, finance companies will purchase many types of equipment and lease them back to firms.

In addition to equipment leasing, business finance companies provide both inventory loans and accounts receivable loans. Inventory loans enable firms to keep their shelves stocked so that when a customer asks for a product, the firm can fill the order. Accounts receivable loans provide firms with immediate resources in anticipation of receipt of customers' payments. The purpose of both these loan types is to provide short-term liquidity to firms.

Sales finance companies specialize in larger loans for major purchases, such as automobiles. Car dealers customarily offer financing to people who are shopping for a new car. When you purchase a car, at a certain point in the negotiations the salesperson will ask how you intend to pay for it. Unless you have sizable savings or are buying a very cheap car, you will need to borrow. The car business is organized so that you don't need to leave the dealership to get your loan; someone there will take care of it for you. The financing is arranged through a finance company, possibly a finance division of the manufacturer, that specializes in making car loans.

Government-Sponsored Enterprises

You will not be surprised to learn that the U.S. government is directly involved in the financial intermediation system and that the risk taking of government-related intermediaries contributed importantly to the financial crisis of 2007–2009. You might be surprised that intermediation by a variety of government agencies grew markedly after the crisis and accounted for most new home mortgages.

In some cases, the government provides loan guarantees; in others, it charters financial institutions to provide specific types of financing, such as home, farm, and student loans. In 1968, when Congress wanted to expand its support for mortgage lending to low- and moderate-income families, it privatized the Depression-era Federal National Mortgage Association (**Fannie Mae**) and, in 1970, issued a similar charter for a competing entity, the Federal Home Loan Mortgage Corporation (*Freddie Mac*). Each was thus chartered by the government

MON€¥ $ BAN£ING

Still Riding the GSE Train

MONEY AND BANKING BLOG

The U.S. federal government is trapped. Its role in mortgage finance has become so large that a rapid exit is simply not an option. At least not anytime soon.

How did we get into this mess?

In September 2008, as the financial crisis intensified, investors shunned the debt of Fannie Mae and Freddie Mac, so the U.S. Treasury put these government-sponsored enterprises (GSEs) into federal conservatorship—in effect, wiping out shareholders and taking ownership. Not long after, the CBO estimated the fair value of the GSEs losses at $291 billion (or more than 5 percent of their end-2009 mortgage portfolios).

At the time, it was widely agreed that the GSEs needed to change. There was even a building consensus to eliminate them completely, and in 2011 the Treasury proposed reforms to do just that—restore private involvement (and risk management) in the mortgage market, and protect taxpayers from future GSE losses. But the plan went nowhere. In fact, in 2014, the agency that regulates the GSEs proposed to *reduce* the down payment needed to obtain a guarantee to as little as 3 percent of the purchase price. Doing so would merely increase the indebtedness of homeowners and raise the burden on U.S. taxpayers if the mortgages could not be repaid.

We have known for a long time about the systemic risks lurking in the current mortgage finance system. In 2001, well before the financial crisis, Federal Reserve officials warned about the GSEs, whose assets then already equaled 40 times their equity. More recently, academics showed how these mortgage giants' leveraged balance sheets made them "guaranteed to fail." And other research highlights the role of household leverage in prompting the deepest economic slump in U.S. postwar history. Yet the GSEs have continued to grow. As of end -2015, the fraction of outstanding residential mortgages attributable to the two GSEs reached a record 61.5 percent.

And the federal government's overall role in the housing market has also continued to grow. Collectively, federal agencies—including the GSEs, the Federal Housing Administration (FHA), and the Department of Veterans Affairs (VA)—backed nearly 70 percent of mortgages issued in 2017, up from 35 percent in 2006.

So, why do we remain stuck with a mortgage finance system completely dominated by the federal government? For now, the GSEs are profitable again, reducing the pressure on Congress to act. More fundamentally, many people benefit from the system: the GSEs' own employees and managers; real estate brokers; mortgage originators and servicers; builders and construction workers; and last, but hardly least, homeowners who can borrow up to $625,500 (the current limit for conforming loans in high-cost areas) at a below-market interest rate. The CBO estimates that GSE backing of new mortgages over the period 2017–2023 will result in a total subsidy averaging around $1.3 billion per year. The recipients of these benefits are so numerous that it is hard to imagine how to even start reforming the system.

The massive federal intervention in the mortgage market has failed to raise the rate of U.S. home ownership. On the contrary, it has been dropping—in 2018, it was 64.4 percent, below the average of the previous three decades. Moreover, despite the relatively high U.S. ratio of mortgage debt to GDP and the extensive government role in mortgage finance, the U.S. home ownership rate is unexceptional among advanced economies. Italy and Spain stand out, with homeownership rates at 73 percent and 78 percent, respectively.

If boosting home ownership were truly the policy goal, focusing the federal subsidy on first-time buyers (or at least on houses below the 2018 median sales price of $257,000 for existing homes) would probably be more effective. And to make the subsidy less risky for the financial system as a whole, policymakers could transform it from a debt subsidy to an equity subsidy of roughly the same size.

Imagine, for example, that the federal government fully matched each dollar saved by a low-income family, up to 10 percent of the value of a $200,000 starter home (call it a 21st-century land grant). The combined amount would be enough for the family to put 20 percent down on the purchase. Keeping the annual cost at $1.3 billion (the CBO estimate of the GSE subsidy) would allow the government to support the purchase of 65,000 such homes *every year*. With a bigger equity cushion, the resulting mortgages would be less risky (and easier to securitize, thus making them even more attractive to potential lenders).

The dangers of the GSE system and the possibility of a better way to boost home ownership are unlikely to translate into serious reform anytime soon. Congress has made little progress on financial reform since the 2010 Dodd-Frank Act, which failed to tackle the problem of the GSEs. And any effort to wind down the debt subsidy is likely to widen the yield spread of mortgages over Treasury bonds, which would raise conventional mortgage rates and drive down house prices. What politician wants that?

Table 13.4 Summary of Financial Industry Structure

Financial Intermediary	Primary Sources of Funds (Liabilities)	Primary Uses of Funds (Assets)	Services Provided
Depository Institution (Bank)	Checkable deposits Savings and time deposits Borrowing from other banks	Cash Loans Securities	• Pooling of small savings to provide large loans • Diversified, liquid deposit accounts • Access to payments system • Screening and monitoring of borrowers
Insurance Company	Expected claims	Corporate bonds Government bonds Stocks Mortgages	• Pooling of risk • Screening and monitoring of policyholders
Securities Firm	Short-term loans	Commercial paper Bonds Stocks	• Management of asset pools • Clearing and settling trades
Investment Bank			• Immediate sale of assets • Access to spectrum of assets, allowing diversification • Evaluation of firms wishing to issue securities • Research and advice for investors
Mutual Fund Company (including exchange-traded funds, ETFs)	Shares sold to customers	Commercial paper Bonds Mortgages Stocks Real estate	• Pooling of small savings to provide access to large, diversified portfolios, which can be liquid
Finance Company	Bonds Bank loans Commercial paper	Mortgages Consumer loans Business loans	• Screening and monitoring of borrowers
Pension Fund	Policy benefits to be paid out to future retirees	Stocks Government bonds Corporate bonds Commercial paper	• Pooling of employees' and employers' contributions • Diversification of long-term investments to ensure future income for retirees
Government-Sponsored Enterprise	Bonds Loan guarantees	Mortgages Farm loans Guarantee payments	• Largest share of housing finance • Access to financing for borrowers who cannot obtain it elsewhere

as a corporation with a public purpose, a hybrid corporate form known as a government-sponsored enterprise (GSE). While the debt issued by Fannie and Freddie was not guaranteed by the government, market participants generally assumed that it would be in a crisis.

In 1968, Congress also established the Government National Mortgage Corporation (*Ginnie Mae*) as a GSE that is wholly owned by the federal government. The U.S. government explicitly guarantees Ginnie Mae debt. (To provide student loans, Congress in 1974 chartered the Student Loan Marketing Association—Sallie Mae—as a GSE but by 2004 had terminated the charter, making Sallie Mae a wholly private-sector firm).

At their founding, the GSEs had similar financial characteristics. They issued short-term bonds and used the proceeds to provide loans or guarantees of one form or another. Because of their explicit or implicit relationship to the government, they paid less than private borrowers for their liabilities and passed on some of these benefits in the form of subsidized mortgages and loans.

As the crisis of 2007–2009 highlighted, housing intermediation is by far the largest of these government-sponsored activities. And, even though many people see them as a continuing risk to the financial system, Fannie and Freddie (along with a few federal agencies) dominate housing finance in the United States (see Money and Banking Blog: Still Riding the GSE Train).

Table 13.4 summarizes the characteristics and roles of financial intermediaries.

Key Terms

bank charter, 328
bank holding company, 331
defined-benefit pension plan, 344
defined-contribution pension plan, 344
dual banking system, 329
economies of scale, 336
economies of scope, 336
eurodollars, 334
Fannie Mae, 348
financial holding company, 336
hedge fund, 347
London Interbank Offered Rate (LIBOR), 334
property and casualty insurance, 340
systemically important financial institutions (SIFIs), 330
term life insurance, 340
underwriting, 346
unit bank, 326
universal bank, 336
vesting, 344
whole life insurance, 340

Using FRED: Codes for Data in This Chapter

Data Series	FRED Data Code
Commercial banks	USNUM
Banks with total assets over $20 billion	FREQ5
Bank failures	BKFTTLA641N
Return on equity	USROE
Equity-to-assets ratio	EQTA
3-month U.S. dollar LIBOR	USD3MTD156N
1-week U.S. dollar LIBOR	USD1WKD156N
Effective federal funds rate (weekly)	FF
Institutional money market mutual funds	WIMFSL
Retail money market mutual funds	WRMFSL
Savings deposits at savings institutions	SVGTI
Time deposits at savings institutions	STDTI
Household holdings of mutual funds	HNOMFAQ027S
Commercial bank assets	TLAACBM027SBOG
Foreign bank assets	TLAFRIM027SBOG
U.S. nominal gross domestic product	GDP

To learn more about the changing financial system, visit www.moneyandbanking.com.

Chapter Lessons

1. The United States has a comparatively large but declining number of banks.
   a. The large number of banks in the United States is explained by restrictions on branching, both within and across state lines, that were imposed by the federal government in 1927.
   b. The large number of banks in the United States is a sign of an anticompetitive legal environment.
   c. Since 1997, banks have been permitted to operate in more than one state. This change has increased competition and driven many small, inefficient banks out of business.
   d. Between 1933 and 1999, banks were prohibited from engaging in the securities and insurance businesses.
   e. Banking has been expanding not just across state boundaries but across international boundaries.
      i. Many U.S. banks operate abroad, and a large number of foreign banks do business in the United States.
      ii. Eurodollars—dollar deposits in foreign banks—play an important part in the international financial system.
   f. The financial industry is constantly evolving. With changes in regulations, financial services can now be provided in two ways:
      i. Through a large universal bank, which provides all the services anyone could possibly need.
      ii. Through small specialized firms, which supply a limited number of services at a low price.

2. Nondepository institutions are playing an increasingly important role in the financial system. Five types of financial intermediary may be classified as nondepository institutions.
   a. Insurance companies.
      i. Life insurance companies insure policyholders against death through term life insurance and provide a vehicle for saving through whole life insurance.
      ii. Property and casualty companies insure individuals and businesses against losses arising from specific events, like accidents and fires.
      iii. The two primary functions of insurance companies are to
         - allow policyholders to transfer risk.
         - screen and monitor policyholders to reduce adverse selection and moral hazard.
   b. Pension funds perform two basic services.
      i. They allow employees and employers to make payments today so that employees will receive an income after retirement.
      ii. They spread risk by ensuring that those employees who live longer than others will continue to receive an income. For this reason, pension funds may be thought of as the opposite of life insurance.
   c. Securities firms include three basic types of financial intermediary: brokers, mutual fund companies, and investment banks.
      i. Brokers give customers access to the financial markets, allowing them to buy and sell securities.
      ii. Mutual fund companies provide savers with small-denomination shares in large, diversified investment pools.
      iii. Investment banks screen and monitor firms before issuing their securities.
   d. Finance companies specialize in making loans to consumers and businesses for the purchase or lease of specific products, such as cars and business equipment.
   e. Government-sponsored enterprises supply direct financing and provide loan guarantees for low-interest mortgages, student loans, and agricultural loans.

Conceptual and Analytical Problems Mc Graw Hill connect

1. For many years you have used your local, small-town bank. One day you hear that the bank is about to be purchased by Bank of America. From your vantage point as a retail bank customer, what are the costs and benefits of such a merger? *(LO1)*
2. Why have technological advances hindered the enforcement of legal restrictions on bank branching? *(LO1)*
3. How did the financial crisis of 2007–2009 affect the degree of concentration in the U.S. banking industry? *(LO1)*
4. Depository institutions have been losing their advantage over other financial intermediaries in attracting customers' funds. Why? *(LO2)*
5. An industry with a large number of small firms is usually thought to be highly competitive. Is that supposition true of the banking industry? What are the costs and benefits to consumers of the current structure of the U.S. banking industry? *(LO1)*

6.* What was the main rationale behind the separation of commercial and investment banking activities in the Glass-Steagall Act of 1933? Why was the act repealed? *(LO1)*

7. Explain what the phrase *too big to fail* means in reference to financial institutions. How did the policy responses to the financial crisis of 2007–2009 affect the too-big-to-fail problem? *(LO1)*

8. Discuss the problems life insurance companies will face as genetic information becomes more widely available. *(LO2)*

9. When the values of stocks and bonds fluctuate, they have an impact on the balance sheets of insurance companies. Why is that impact more likely to be a problem for life insurance companies than for property and casualty companies? *(LO2)*

10.* Compare and contrast the structures of bank holding companies, financial holding companies, and universal banks. *(LO1)*

11. What are the benefits of collaboration between a large appliance retailer and a finance company? *(LO2)*

12. Why did government-sponsored enterprises (GSEs) such as Freddie Mac and Fannie Mae have substantially higher leverage ratios than the average U.S. bank in the years preceding the financial crisis of 2007–2009? Explain how this made the enterprises more vulnerable to the house price declines that precipitated the crisis. *(LO2)*

13. Consider two countries with the following characteristics. Country A has no restrictions on bank branching and banks in Country A are permitted to offer investment and insurance products along with traditional banking services. In Country B, there are strict limits on branch banking and on the geographic spread of a bank's business. In addition, banks in Country B are not permitted to offer investment or insurance services. Explain each of your choices for the following. *(LO1)*
    a. In which country do you think the banking system is more concentrated?
    b. In which country do you think the banking system is more competitive?
    c. In which country do you think, everything else being equal, banking products are cheaper?

14. You examine the balance sheet of an insurance company and note that its assets are made up mainly of U.S. Treasury bills and commercial paper. Is this more likely to be the balance sheet of a property and casualty insurance company or a life insurance company? Explain your answer. *(LO2)*

15.* Statistically, teenage drivers are more likely to have an automobile accident than adult drivers. As a result, insurance companies charge higher insurance premiums for teenage drivers. Suppose one insurance company decided to charge teenagers and adults the same premium based on the average risk of an accident for all drivers. Using your knowledge of the problems associated with asymmetric information, explain whether you think this insurance company will be profitable. *(LO2)*

16. Use your knowledge of the problems associated with asymmetric information to explain why insurance companies often include deductibles as part of their policies. *(LO2)*

*Indicates more difficult problems.

17. Suppose you have a defined-contribution pension plan. As you go through your working life, in what order would you choose to have the following portfolio allocations: (a) 100 percent bonds and money-market instruments, (b) 100 percent stocks, (c) 50 percent bonds and 50 percent stocks? *(LO2)*
18. As an employee, would you prefer to participate in a defined-benefit pension plan or a defined-contribution pension plan? Explain your answer. *(LO2)*
19. In the aftermath of the financial crisis of 2007–2009, there were calls to reinstate the separation of commercial and investment banking activities that was removed with the repeal of the Glass-Steagall Act, but this did not happen. What might be some of the benefits and shortcomings of segmenting financial activities for reducing systemic risk? *(LO1)*
20. Suppose a well-known financial holding company agreed to be the underwriter for a new stock issue. After guaranteeing the price to the issuing company but before selling the stocks, a scandal surrounding the business practices of the holding company is revealed. How would you expect this scandal to affect (a) the financial holding company and (b) the issuing company? *(LO1)*
21. Consider three possible health insurance programs with the following characteristics:

    Program A: Participation in the program is voluntary and the policy premium charged varies with an individual's health status, with those in relatively better health paying less.

    Program B: Participation in the program is voluntary and the policy premium is the same for everyone, based on the nation's average cost of health care per person.

    Program C: Participation in the program is mandatory and the policy premium is the same for everyone, based on the nation's average cost of health care per person.

    Which of the three programs is least likely to be viable? Explain your answer. *(LO2)*
22. Suppose a U.S. bank is considering providing its services abroad. List one possible advantage and one possible disadvantage of expanding via the acquisition of a controlling interest in a foreign bank versus the establishment of an international banking facility (IBF)? *(LO1)*
23. The globalization of banking has led to the need for global benchmarks for interest rates. In light of the LIBOR scandal, what characteristic do you think is most central to any new interest rate benchmark that might replace LIBOR? *(LO2)*

Data Exploration

For general information on using Federal Reserve Economic Data (FRED) online, visit www.mhhe.com/moneyandbanking6e *and refer to the FRED Resources.*

1. One aspect of the 2007–2009 financial crisis was a run on some money-market mutual funds (MMMFs). Plot weekly data (without the recession bars) for 2008 on institutional MMMF deposits (FRED code: WIMFSL) and identify the timing of the run visually. Next, download the data, and report the size of the deposit outflow in the week that the run peaked. Why did this run end? *(LO1)*
2. When did the financial crisis of 2007–2009 peak and why? Plot weekly data for 2006–2010 for 1-week U.S. dollar LIBOR (FRED code: USD1WKD156N) and the

effective federal funds rate (FRED code: FF). (For consistency, plot both series on the same basis by specifying "Weekly, ending Wednesday" in the "Modify Frequency" dropdown box.) Explain the pattern. *(LO1)*

3. How did competition from money-market mutual funds affect traditional savings institutions that provided mortgages at fixed interest rates? Beginning with 1981, plot the ratio of retail money-market mutual funds (FRED code: WRMFSL) to the sum of savings and small time deposits at savings institutions (FRED codes: SVGTI and STDTI). What favored money funds in the 1980s and 1990s? Why did the ratio shrink in the first half of the 2000s? *(LO1)*
4. Mutual funds allow small savers to pool their resources and purchase diversified portfolios of assets with low transactions costs. To see whether savers have taken advantage of these (and other) benefits, plot since 1980 mutual fund holdings (FRED code: HNOMFAQ027S) as a percentage of GDP (FRED code: GDP). Explain the pattern. *(LO2)*
5. Both U.S. and foreign banks are active in the United States. To compare them, plot the share (in percent) of foreign banks' assets (FRED code: TLAFRIM027SBOG) in the assets of all commercial banks (FRED code: TLAACBM027SBOG). Describe the trend since the 1970s and explain how the trend might have arisen. *(LO1)*

Further Data Exploration: The FDIC's website (www.fdic.gov/bank/statistical) provides several databases that allow for further exploration of the U.S. banking system. For example, the "Historical Statistics on Banking" section (www.fdic.gov/open/datatools.html) provides data on the evolution of the insured banking system since the FDIC's origin in 1934.

Chapter

14 Regulating the Financial System

Learning Objectives

After reading this chapter, you should be able to:

LO1 Identify the sources and discuss the consequences of bank runs, bank panics, and financial crises.

LO2 Explain why and how the government intervenes in the financial system, and the problems the government safety net creates.

LO3 Analyze how a government regulates and supervises the financial system to contain risk.

The painful effects of the global crisis of 2007–2009 brought home the importance of the financial system in our lives. Millions of people lost their jobs, their homes, and their wealth. Healthy firms needing to borrow temporarily to pay their employees or suppliers faced ruin. As the crisis peaked in the fall of 2008, the global economy suffered its deepest and broadest downturn since the Great Depression, and policymakers took unprecedented action to keep the crisis from precipitating a second Great Depression. In 2010, after financial conditions stabilized, the U.S. government enacted the most ambitious financial reforms since the 1930s. The Dodd-Frank Wall Street Reform and Consumer Protection Act aims to prevent another crisis and to limit the moral hazard from the government's interventions during the global crisis.

Although no financial crisis since the 1930s has matched the severity of the 2007–2009 episode, disruptions to the financial system are surprisingly frequent and widespread. After 2010, millions of people in the euro area faced devastating losses from the combination of a plunge in their sovereigns' creditworthiness, the weakening of banks holding risky debt, and rising doubts about the viability of the euro. More broadly, since 1970, some 120 countries experienced 151 banking crises. Including other types of financial disruptions, a crisis has occurred in an average of eight countries each year since 1970.[1]

And virtually no part of the world has been spared from banking crises; large, advanced economies have suffered along with smaller, less developed ones. Indeed, banking disruptions appear to cause greater damage and persist longer in advanced

[1]Adding in currency and sovereign debt crises, the total number of serious financial disturbances between 1970 and 2017 approached 500. See Luc Laeven and Fabian Valencia, "Systemic Banking Crises Revisited," IMF Working Paper WP/18/206, September 2018.

economies, perhaps because the financial systems are deeper and more critical for sustaining economic efficiency. Partly as a result, governments in advanced economies also are likely to undertake a wider range of actions to support their banks, including liquidity support, guarantees of bank liabilities, and recapitalizations of weakened banks.

When financial crises occur, governments step in and put financial intermediaries back on track. They often do so by assuming responsibility for the banking system's liabilities so that depositors won't lose their savings. But the cleanup can also require the injection of capital into failed institutions. Not only are these crises expensive to clean up, but they also can have a dramatic impact on growth in the countries where they occur.

Table 14.1 shows information on the economic impact and fiscal cost of selected banking crises between 1970 and 2017. The data show what one would expect: Bigger

Table 14.1 Banking Crises: Output Losses, Fiscal Costs, and Public Debt Increases (Percent of GDP), 1970–2017

Country	Crisis Dates	Output Loss	Fiscal Cost	Public Debt Increase
ADVANCED ECONOMIES				
Ireland	2008–2012	107.7	37.6	76.5
Finland	1991–1995	69.6	12.8	43.6
Greece	2008–2012	64.9	28.7	43.9
Spain	1977–1981	58.5	7.7	3.8
Japan	1997–2001	45.0	8.6	41.7
Portugal	2008–2012	35.0	11.1	38.5
Sweden	1991–1995	32.9	3.6	36.2
Italy	2008–2009	32.2	0.7	8.6
United States	2007–2011	30.0	4.5	21.9
United Kingdom	2007–2011	25.3	8.8	27.0
EMERGING ECONOMIES				
Thailand	1997–2000	109.3	43.8	42.1
Latvia	2008–2012	93.9	8.1	27.6
Ukraine	2014–	93.2	13.9	53.4
Philippines	1983–1986	91.7	3.0	44.8
Panama	1988–1989	85.0	12.9	−2.6
Argentina	2001–2003	71.0	9.6	81.9
Indonesia	1997–2001	69.0	56.8	67.6
Brazil	1990–1994	62.3	0.0	−22.6
Korea	1997–1998	57.6	31.2	9.9
Cote d'Ivoire	1988–1992	45.0	25.0	13.6
Median (full sample)		23.3	8.7	12.7

NOTE: Output loss is the gap between actual and precrisis trend growth. Both output loss and the increase of the public debt ratio cover three years from the crisis start. Fiscal cost covers direct outlays to the financial sector. The specific country episodes are the top 10 (ranked by output loss) for which all three measures are available. The medians are calculated from the full sample of 151 banking crises.

SOURCE: Laeven, Luc, and Fabián Valencia. "Systemic Banking Crises Revisited." IMF Working Paper WP/18/206, September 2018.

crises are worse for output. And crises in advanced economies lead to a larger increase in public debt as a percent of GDP.

Some degree of default is normal at every bank, including well-run ones. But in 1998, when 35 percent of all loans made by Korean banks defaulted, it was more than just bad luck. Clearly, the Korean financial system was failing to perform one of its primary functions, the efficient channeling of resources from savers to borrowers so that credit goes to firms based on the merit of their proposed investments. Instead, borrowers who shouldn't have received loans got them, and projects that shouldn't have been funded went ahead. Because resources were wasted, Korea's growth and income were lower than they could have been. To put the output loss shown in Table 14.1 into perspective, Korea has invested an average of 31 percent of GDP annually since 1970, so the country lost nearly two years' worth of business investment.

Banking crises are not a recent phenomenon; the history of commercial banking over the last two centuries is replete with periods of turmoil and failure. By their very nature, financial systems are fragile and vulnerable to crisis. Unfortunately, when a country's financial system collapses, its economy goes with it, and with economic crisis comes the risk of violence and revolution. Keeping banks open and operating, then, is as essential to maintaining our way of life as a ready military defense. Because a healthy financial system benefits everyone, governments are deeply involved in the way banks and other intermediaries function. As a result, the financial sector is subject to voluminous rules and regulations, and financial institutions must withstand constant scrutiny by official examiners. The importance of this government oversight in ensuring financial stability is hard to exaggerate. When government oversight fails, as it did in many countries in the years before the crisis of 2007–2009 and in the run-up to the euro-area crisis that erupted in 2010, the costs can be enormous.

The purpose of this chapter is fourfold. First, we will look at the sources and consequences of financial fragility. By and large, financial crises are banking crises, so we will focus on that sector. Included in this group are **shadow banks** that, like banks, have liabilities that can be withdrawn at face value virtually without notice but are usually subject to less oversight than banks.[2] Next, we will look at the institutional safeguards—for instance, deposit insurance—the government has built into the system in an attempt to avert financial crises. Third, we'll study the regulatory and supervisory environment of the banking industry. Finally, we'll examine emerging approaches to regulation that focus on the safety of the financial system rather than on individual institutions.

The Sources and Consequences of Runs, Panics, and Crises

In a market-based economy, the opportunity to succeed is also an opportunity to fail. New restaurants open and others go out of business. Only 1 in 10 restaurants survives as long as three years. In principle, banks should be no different from restaurants: new ones should open and unpopular ones close. But few of us would want to live in a world where banks fail at the same rate as restaurants. Banks serve some essential functions in

[2]Some types of intermediaries routinely depend on short-term funding that closely substitutes for deposits, completely fulfilling this definition of a shadow bank. These intermediaries typically include money-market mutual funds and securities brokers. Other classes of intermediaries—such as hedge funds—include a range of firms that vary more in the extent to which they depend on short-term funding (like the repo and asset-backed commercial paper markets) and leverage.

our economy: They provide access to the payments system, and they screen and monitor borrowers to reduce information problems. If your favorite restaurant closes suddenly, you can still eat, but if your bank closes, you lose your ability to make purchases and pay your rent. So while no one suggests that the government appoint officials to minimize restaurant closings, everyone expects the government to safeguard banks.

Banks' fragility arises from the fact that they provide liquidity to depositors. That is, they allow depositors to withdraw their balances on demand. If you want the entire amount in your checking account converted into cash, all you need to do is go to your bank and ask for it; the teller is obligated to give it to you. If a bank cannot meet this promise of withdrawal on demand because of insufficient liquid assets, it will fail.

Banks not only guarantee their depositors immediate cash on demand; they promise to satisfy depositors' withdrawal requests on a first-come, first-served basis. This commitment has some important implications. Suppose depositors begin to lose confidence in a bank's ability to meet their withdrawal requests. They have heard a rumor that one of the bank's largest loans has defaulted, so that the bank's assets may no longer cover its liabilities. True or not, reports that a bank has become **insolvent** can spread fear that it will run out of cash and close its doors. Mindful of the bank's first-come, first-served policy, frenzied depositors may rush to the bank to convert their balances to cash before other customers arrive. In effect, they hope that getting to the bank early will let them withdraw their "investment" (deposit) at a price above its true value (the value of the banks' assets). Such a **bank run** can cause a bank to fail.

In short, a bank run can be the result of either real or imagined problems. No bank is immune to the loss of depositors' confidence just because it is profitable and sound. In practice, runs often start with shakier banks and then spread to healthier ones as confidence erodes.

The financial crisis of 2007–2009 is replete with examples of runs on banks and on the much less regulated shadow banks, which also provide liquidity to the financial system. The United Kingdom faced its first run on a large bank in more than a century when, in September 2007, depositors rushed to withdraw funds from Northern Rock, a major housing lender (see neighboring photos). Meanwhile, the largest savings bank in the United States, Washington Mutual, failed when depositors fled in September 2008. That same month, withdrawals from Wachovia Bank—at the time the fourth-largest U.S. commercial bank—led to its emergency sale.

Quiet, invisible runs on shadow banks were even more dramatic, as they punctuated the peaks of the financial crisis. In March 2008, short-term lenders and other creditors stopped lending to Bear Stearns, the fifth-largest U.S. investment bank. The run halted only when the Federal Reserve Bank of New York stepped in to help the then-second-largest U.S. commercial bank, JPMorgan Chase, acquire Bear. A similar sudden stop in private lending led the U.S. government to take over Fannie Mae and Freddie Mac (the huge government-sponsored housing finance enterprises described in Chapter 13) in September 2008. The financial crisis peaked later that month when a run on Lehman Brothers—the fourth-largest U.S. investment bank—precipitated its bankruptcy. Shortly thereafter, losses

Crowds trying to get into the Northern Rock bank in Kingston upon Thames, United Kingdom, on September 17, 2007.

Peter Macdiarmid/Getty Images (both images)

on Lehman debt compelled a money-market mutual fund (MMMF) to "break the buck"—that is, to lower its share value below $1; that fixed value is traditionally promised by all MMMFs so that their customers can treat their shares as if they were bank deposits. Fearful that other MMMFs would break the buck, investors in those funds rushed to withdraw their investments at the promised $1 per share, a value they thought might exceed the true market value of the fund's assets. The resulting runs undermined a key component of the U.S. intermediation mechanism.

What matters during a bank run is not whether a bank is solvent, but whether it is liquid. Solvency means that the value of the bank's assets exceeds the value of its liabilities—that is, the bank has a positive net worth. Liquidity means that the bank has sufficient reserves and immediately marketable assets to meet depositors' demand for withdrawals. False rumors that a bank is *insolvent* can lead to a run that renders a bank **illiquid**. If people believe that a bank is in trouble, that belief alone can make it so.

When a bank fails, depositors may lose some or all of their deposits, and information about borrowers' creditworthiness may disappear. For these reasons alone, government officials work to ensure that all banks are operated in a way that minimizes their chance of failure. But that is not their main worry. The primary concern is that a single bank's failure might cause a small-scale bank run that could turn into a systemwide **bank panic**. This phenomenon of spreading panic on the part of depositors in banks (or of creditors to shadow banks like MMMFs) is called **contagion**. Contagion was powerful at the peak of the 2007–2009 financial crisis, as depositors and creditors grew anxious about the well-being of financial intermediaries around the world.

Information asymmetries are the reason that a run on a single bank can turn into a bank panic that threatens the entire financial system. Recall from Chapter 11 that if there is no way to tell a good used car from a bad one, the only used cars on the market will be lemons. What is true for cars is even truer for banks. Most of us are not in a position to assess the quality of a bank's balance sheet. In fact, because banks often make loans based on sophisticated statistical models, only an expert with knowledge of market conditions and access to all details about a bank's assets can estimate their worth. Depositors, then, are in the same position as uninformed buyers in the used-car market: They can't tell the difference between a good bank and a bad bank. And if the cost of withdrawal is tiny, who wants to keep a deposit in a bank if there is even a small chance that it could be insolvent? So when rumors spread that a certain bank is in trouble, depositors and other creditors begin to worry about their own banks' financial condition. Concern about even one bank can create a panic that causes profitable banks throughout the nation to fail, leading to a complete collapse of the banking system.

While banking panics and financial crises can easily result from false rumors, they can also occur for more concrete reasons. Because a bank's assets are a combination of loans and securities, anything that affects borrowers' ability to make their loan payments or drives down the market value of securities has the potential to imperil the bank's finances. The decline of U.S. housing prices and the resulting wave of mortgage defaults that began in 2006 set the stage for the crisis of 2007–2009 by lowering the value of assets on the balance sheets of intermediaries around the world. Recessions—widespread downturns in business activity—have a clear negative impact on a bank's balance sheet. When business slows, firms have a harder time paying their debts. People lose their jobs and suddenly can't make their loan payments. As default rates rise, bank assets lose value, and bank capital drops. With less capital, banks are forced to contract their balance sheets, making fewer loans. This decline in loans, in turn, means less business investment, which amplifies the downturn. Large asset price declines and deep recessions can lead to widespread failure of banks and shadow banks.

The Three Phases of the Financial Crisis of 2007–2009

LESSONS FROM THE CRISIS

The Financial Crisis (FC) of 2007–2009 had three distinct phases: a liquidity crisis, a solvency crisis, and a recapitalization of the system. It is worth going through each of these. Before we get to that, we provide a definition: a financial crisis is the sudden, unanticipated shift from a reasonably healthy equilibrium—characterized by highly liquid financial markets, high valuations, narrow risk spreads, easily available credit, and low asset price volatility—to a very unhealthy one with precisely the opposite features. The term *equilibrium* reflects a *persistent state* of financial conditions and note that—as was the case for Humpty Dumpty—it is easy to shift from a good financial state to a bad one, but very difficult to shift back again. The bad state is usually associated with increased *co-movement* and volatility of asset prices; *contagion* across firms, markets, and geographic jurisdictions; and an *adverse feedback* between the financial system and the real economy, so that as one deteriorates it makes the other even worse.

The first phase of the FC began on August 9, 2007, when the large French bank BNP Paribas suspended redemptions from three mutual funds invested in U.S. subprime mortgage debt. The result was an immediate scramble for liquidity, *combined* with doubts about the capital adequacy of a widening circle of intermediaries. Market and funding liquidity dried up for financial institutions, as investors shunned all but the safest instruments and slashed lending to intermediaries that might be stuck with toxic, low-quality assets like subprime debt. Having failed to screen the ultimate mortgage borrowers adequately in advance, post-Paribas *adverse selection* undermined financing mechanisms that relied on the collateral value of structured credit based on these mortgages. The aggregate supply of credit to financial firms shriveled precisely when their need for funds surged.

The March 14, 2008, collapse of Bear Stearns kicked off the second phase of the crisis. In the period between Paribas and Bear, both liquidity and counterparty risk rose, increasing stress in the financial system. During this period, the Federal Reserve acted on an ad hoc basis to create and implement a broad array of lending tools, acting as a lender of last resort (LOLR) to key parts of the financial system. One of the most important LOLR innovations prior to Bear was the December 2007 authorization of dollar swap lines with foreign central banks. Providing other central banks with dollars (collateralized by foreign currency) that they could lend to private intermediaries in their jurisdictions diminished the pressure for global fire sales of U.S. dollar assets.

With the run on Bear, everything changed. For the first time since the Great Depression of the 1930s, the Fed provided support to a supposedly solvent, but illiquid, *nonbank*. Doing so required that the Federal Reserve Board invoke its virtually forgotten emergency authority that (until the 2010 Dodd-Frank eliminated it) allowed collateralized lending "in unusual and exigent circumstances" to "any individual, partnership or corporation."

The failure of Lehman Brothers on September 15, 2008, ushered in the most intense period of the deepest financial crisis in the United States and Europe since the Great Depression. The credit freeze spread broadly; not just uncollateralized lending, but short-term lending backed by *investment-grade* collateral also dried up. In mid-September, measures of financial stress spiked far above levels seen before or since. And, the spillover to the real economy was rapid and dramatic, with the U.S. economy plunging that autumn at the fastest pace since quarterly reporting began in 1947.

Three, interrelated policy responses proved critical in arresting the crisis and promoting recovery. First, the Fed undertook aggressive monetary stimulus, including the introduction of unconventional policy tools, such as quantitative easing, targeted asset purchases, and forward guidance, at the effective lower bound for interest rates (see Chapter 18). After Lehman, within its mandate, the Fed did "whatever it took" to end the crisis, utilizing its authority to the limit. Second, officials used taxpayer funds—authorized by Congress within days of the Lehman shock—to recapitalize the U.S. financial system. And third, there was the exceptional disclosure mechanism—the first round of macro-prudential stress tests—introduced by the Federal Reserve in early 2009 to overcome the challenge of adverse selection. Released in May 2009, the test results assuaged the worst fears about U.S. banks (see the section in this chapter on pages 377–380).

While scholars will surely continue to debate the causes of the weak postcrisis recovery for years to come, one thing is certain: it could have been much worse. Without the aggressive economic stabilization policy, speedy government-led recapitalization of the financial system, and innovative bank supervision, the United States and Europe probably would have had a second Great Depression. Given the inevitability of financial crises, it is important not to forget these policy lessons: Crisis management requires government and private financial leaders who have the knowledge, authority, resources, and willingness to act quickly and decisively. It is essential that everyone be ready to do whatever it takes.

The history of banking in the United States shows clear evidence that downturns in the business cycle put pressure on banks, substantially increasing the risk of panics. To see this, we can look at the period from 1871 to 1914, prior to the creation of the Federal Reserve System. Over those four-plus decades, there were 11 business cycles—booms followed by recessions. Bank panics occurred during seven of them, five of which were very severe. They often started near the business cycle peak, when investors began to anticipate a downturn. The next series of severe bank panics occurred during the Great Depression of the 1930s, when output fell by roughly one-third. Bank panics usually start with real economic events or their prospect, not just rumors.[3]

Financial disruptions can also occur whenever borrowers' net worth falls, as it does during a deflation (see Applying the Concept: Deflation, Net Worth, and Information Costs in Chapter 11). Companies borrow a fixed number of dollars to invest in real assets like buildings and machines, whose values fall with deflation. The same applies to households acquiring houses. So a drop in prices reduces companies' and households' net worth (but not their loan payments). This decline in net worth aggravates the adverse selection and moral hazard problems caused by information asymmetries, making loans more difficult to obtain. If borrowers cannot get new financing, business and residential investment will fall, reducing overall economic activity and raising the number of defaults on loans. As more and more borrowers default, banks' balance sheets deteriorate, compounding information problems and creating a full-blown crisis. This **adverse feedback** between financial and economic activity is a key characteristic of deep crises.

The Government Safety Net

There are three reasons for the government to get involved in the financial system:

1. To protect investors.
2. To protect bank customers from monopolistic exploitation.
3. To safeguard the stability of the financial system.

First, the government is obligated to protect small investors, many of whom are unable to judge the soundness of their financial institutions. While competition is supposed to discipline all the institutions in the industry, in practice only the force of law can ensure a bank's integrity. As small investors, we rely on the government to protect us from mismanagement and malfeasance.

Second, the tendency for small firms to merge into large ones reduces competition, ultimately ending in monopolies. In general, monopolies exploit their customers, raising prices to earn unwarranted profits. Because monopolies are inefficient, the government intervenes to prevent the firms in an industry from becoming too large. In the financial system, that means ensuring that even large banks face competition.

Third, the combustible mix of liquidity risk and information asymmetries means that the financial system is inherently unstable. A financial firm can collapse much more quickly than an industrial company. For a steel corporation, an electronics manufacturer, or an automobile maker, failure occurs slowly as customers disappear one by one. But a

[3]To better understand the role of business cycles in the U.S. bank runs of the 19th and 20th centuries up through the Great Depression, see Gary B. Gorton, *Misunderstanding Financial Crises: Why We Don't See Them Coming* (New York: Oxford University Press, 2012).

financial institution can create and destroy the value of its assets in an astonishingly short period, and a single firm's failure can bring down the entire system.[4]

Government officials employ a combination of strategies to protect investors and ensure the stability of the financial system. First, they provide the safety net to insure small depositors. Authorities both operate as the *lender of last resort,* making loans to banks that face sudden deposit outflows, and provide *deposit insurance,* guaranteeing that depositors receive the full value of their accounts should an institution fail. But this safety net causes bank managers to take on too much risk, leading to the regulation and supervision that we will discuss later in the chapter.

This section will examine the unique role of depository institutions in our financial system. The point is that we need banks. While they are essential, they are also fragile. This leads to a discussion of the components of the safety net and the problems it creates. The next section will look at the government's responses to these problems.

The Unique Role of Banks and Shadow Banks

As the key providers of liquidity, banks ensure a sufficient supply of the means of payment for the economy to operate smoothly and efficiently. This critical role and the problems associated with it make banks a key focus of attention for government regulators. Shadow banks are also major providers of liquidity, and following their role in the financial crisis of 2007–2009, they also have attracted intense attention from regulators around the world.

We all rely heavily on these intermediaries for access to the payments system. If banks, MMMFs, and securities brokers were to disappear, we would no longer be able to transfer funds—at least not until someone stepped forward to take their place. Other financial institutions—insurance companies, pension funds, and the like—do not have this essential day-to-day function of facilitating payments.

Furthermore, because of their role in liquidity provision, banks and shadow banks are prone to runs. These intermediaries hold illiquid assets to back their liquid liabilities. In the case of banks, their promise of full and constant value to depositors is based on assets of uncertain value. The fixed-value shares of MMMFs are like bank deposits in all but name. The liabilities of other shadow banks are less similar but have important deposit-like characteristics. For example, repurchase agreements are usually overnight contracts, so a repo lender can refuse to roll over the loan to a securities broker at virtually any time, an action similar to a deposit withdrawal. In contrast, pension funds and insurance companies (and even some hedge funds) may hold illiquid assets, but their liability holders cannot withdraw funds whenever they want.

Moreover, banks and shadow banks are linked to one another both on their balance sheets and in their customers' minds. Take a quick look back at Table 12.1 (page 296) and you will see that in January 2019 interbank loans made up just 0.1 percent of U.S.

[4]One culprit in creating this high degree of risk is derivatives. Like dynamite, when used properly derivatives are extremely beneficial, allowing the transfer of risk to those who can best bear it. But in the wrong hands, derivatives can bring down even the largest, most respected institutions. The failure of Barings Bank in 1995 is an example. One of the oldest and best-known banks in England, Barings collapsed in just two months after a single trader wiped out the bank's capital with losses of more than $1 billion on futures positions worth more than $17 billion. Large, opaque bets like that can be made only using derivatives. And, because they can be made in ways that are extremely difficult for government regulators to detect, these high-risk actions have the potential to put the entire financial system at risk. In the crisis of 2007–2009, the most dramatic example of a system-threatening derivatives exposure was that of American International Group (AIG), the largest U.S. insurer. In September 2008, AIG became unable to meet the obligations arising from hundreds of billions of dollars of credit default swaps (see page 232).

commercial banking system assets—which was less than 1 percent of all bank capital. Prior to the crisis, interbank lending had been substantially greater and represented roughly one-third of all bank capital. If a bank begins to fail, it will default on its loan payments to other banks and thereby transmit its financial distress to them. Similarly, MMMFs hold large volumes of commercial paper, most of which was issued by banks. And (shadow) banks are among the key repo lenders to securities brokers and hedge funds. Banks and shadow banks are so interdependent that they are capable of initiating contagion throughout the financial system.

Other financial institutions also may pose such risks, but these intermediaries typically are very large and few in number (see footnote 4 regarding the derivatives exposure of AIG, the largest U.S. insurer when the crisis of 2007–2009 hit). While the ramifications of a financial crisis outside the system of banks and shadow banks may be more limited, they are still damaging. As a result, the government also protects individuals who do business with finance companies, pension funds, and insurance companies.

For example, government regulations require insurance companies to provide proper information to policyholders and restrict the ways the companies manage their assets. The same is true for securities firms and pension funds, whose assets must be structured to ensure that they will be able to meet their obligations many years into the future.[5]

The Government as Lender of Last Resort

The best way to stop a bank failure from turning into a bank panic is to make sure solvent institutions can meet their depositors' withdrawal demands. In 1873 the British economist Walter Bagehot suggested the need for a **lender of last resort** to perform this function. Such an institution could make loans to prevent the failure of solvent banks and could provide liquidity in sufficient quantity to prevent or end a financial panic. Specifically, Bagehot proposed that Britain's central bank should lend freely on good collateral at a high rate of interest. By lending freely he meant providing liquidity on demand to any intermediary that asked for it. Good collateral would provide assurance of the borrowing institution's solvency, and the high interest rate would penalize the borrower for failing to hold enough reserves or easily salable assets to meet deposit outflows and would promote rapid repayment when funding conditions normalized.

The existence of a lender of last resort significantly reduces, but does not eliminate, contagion. The series of three bank panics that occurred during the Great Depression of the 1930s is one example of the failure of a lender of last resort. While the Federal Reserve had the capacity and the mandate to operate as a lender of last resort in the 1930s, it chose not to do so. In effect, policymakers acted as if the "fire" would burn itself out. Instead, the conflagration spread and intensified. The result was the worst financial disaster in the 100-plus-year history of the Federal Reserve.

There is another flaw in the concept of a lender of last resort. For the system to work, central bank officials who approve the loan applications must be able to distinguish an illiquid from an insolvent institution. But during a crisis, computing the market value of a bank's assets is almost impossible, because there are no market prices. (If a bank could sell its marketable assets in the financial markets, it wouldn't need a loan from the

[5]All nondepository institutions are subject to some form of regulation. State regulators oversee insurance companies; the Pension Benefits Guaranty Corporation regulates private pension funds. Securities firms are overseen by a combination of the Securities and Exchange Commission, a government agency, and a self-regulatory organization, the Financial Industry Regulatory Authority. The Commodity Futures Trading Commission oversees commodity brokers and derivatives exchanges. Finance companies are regulated by state agencies, as well as by the Federal Reserve if they are subsidiaries of bank holding companies.

The Securities Investor Protection Corporation
YOUR FINANCIAL WORLD

Brokerage firms will advertise that they are members of the SIPC—that's the Securities Investor Protection Corporation. The SIPC provides insurance in the event that a brokerage firm fails, owing its customers cash and securities. It is insurance against fraud.

It is important to understand what SIPC insurance is and what it is not. If a bank accepts your deposits and uses the funds to make bad loans, your savings are protected by the FDIC against the bank's failure. By contrast, SIPC insurance replaces missing securities or cash that was supposed to be there—up to a limit of $500,000. It does not compensate individuals for investments that lost value because market prices fell, nor will it cover individuals who were sold worthless securities. The SIPC protects against theft by a broker. One sizable SIPC payout in recent years was to the victims of Bernard Madoff's Ponzi scheme (see Chapter 11, Applying the Concept: Truth or Consequences: Ponzi Schemes and Other Frauds, page 276).

For more information on the SIPC, go to www.sipc.org. For comprehensive information on investor rights, look at the website of the Financial Industry Regulatory Authority (FINRA)—the industry's self-regulatory body—at www.finra.org/investors/ProtectYourself.

central bank.) Because a bank will go to the central bank for a direct loan only after having exhausted all opportunities to sell its assets and borrow from other banks without collateral, its illiquidity and its need to seek a loan from the government raise the question of its solvency. Officials, anxious to keep the crisis from deepening, are likely to be generous in evaluating the bank's assets and to grant a loan even if they suspect the bank may be insolvent. Knowing this, bank managers will tend to take too many risks.

In other words, the central bank's difficulty in distinguishing a bank's insolvency from its illiquidity creates moral hazard for bank managers. It is important for a lender of last resort to operate in a manner that minimizes the tendency for bankers to take too much risk in their operations.

Finally, as we learned in the crisis of 2007–2009, the U.S. lender-of-last-resort mechanism has not kept pace with the evolution of the financial system. Like many government practices in the financial arena, the conventional rules for Fed discount lending were (and remain) based on the legal *form* of the borrower rather than on its economic *function.* Some intermediaries facing sudden flight by their very short-term creditors were not banks—to whom the Fed usually lends—but shadow banks, which do not normally have access to Fed loans. Only by using its emergency lending authority—something last done in the Great Depression of the 1930s—was the Fed able to lend to such nonbank intermediaries to stem the crisis.[6]

During the turmoil, the Fed utilized this emergency authority repeatedly when it needed to lend to securities brokers, MMMFs, insurers, other nonbank intermediaries, and even to nonfinancial firms. Based on this emergency authority, it developed a variety of new policy tools—including the Primary Dealer Credit Facility through which the authorities lent directly to nonbank securities dealers—to deliver liquidity where and when it was needed. While this ad hoc, reactive approach helped both stem runs and counter their impact, it had limited value in preventing them in the first place.

[6]The Fed's authority to lend to nonbanks during the 2007–2009 crisis was based on Section 13(3) of the Federal Reserve Act. At the time, this rule allowed the Board of Governors "in unusual and exigent circumstances" to lend against collateral to any "individual, partnership, or corporation"—that is, to nonbanks. However, as you will see later in this chapter, the Dodd-Frank Act curtailed this emergency authority. You can view the current Federal Reserve Act at www.federalreserve.gov/aboutthefed/fract.htm.

The Day the Bank of New York Borrowed $23 Billion
APPLYING THE CONCEPT

While the existence of a lender of last resort may encourage bank managers to take too many risks, very few people would argue for abolishing the safeguard outright. There have been days when the system worked exactly as it should. November 20, 1985, was one of them. On that day the Bank of New York's computer system went haywire. BONY, as it was known, plays a central role in the U.S. Treasury securities market. The bank (now Bank of New York Mellon) acts as a clearinghouse, buying bonds from sellers and then reselling them to buyers.

On November 20, a software error prevented BONY from keeping track of its Treasury bond trades.* For 90 minutes transactions poured in, and the bank accumulated and paid for U.S. Treasury bonds, notes, and bills. Importantly, BONY promised to make payments without actually having the funds. But when the time came to deliver the securities and collect from the buyers, BONY employees could not tell who the buyers and sellers were or what quantities and prices they had agreed to. The information had been erased. By the end of the day, the Bank of New York had bought and failed to deliver so many securities that it was committed to paying out $23 billion that it did not have, at least until it could correct for the computer error.

Without a way to come up with $23 billion quickly, BONY wasn't able to make payments to sellers who had delivered their securities. These sellers had made additional transactions in the expectation that they would be paid. Unless BONY found a way to make the promised payments, the problem would spread to other institutions. The Federal Reserve, as lender of last resort, stepped in and made a collateralized loan of $23 billion, preventing a computer problem at one very important bank from becoming a full-blown financial crisis.

*BONY's computers could store only 32,000 transactions at a time. When more transactions arrived than the computer could handle, the software's counter restarted at zero. Because the counter number was the key to where the trading information was stored, the information was effectively erased. (Had all the original transactions been processed before the counter restarted, there would have been no problem.)

Lending to nonbank intermediaries also added massively to the moral hazard usually associated with the lender of last resort. These intermediaries generally are not subject to regulation or supervision by the Federal Reserve, and the level of oversight they received from other agencies was typically less intense and intrusive than that applied to banks. Accordingly, in the absence of new oversight, the access to central bank loans granted by the Fed in the crisis will encourage these borrowers to take greater risks in the future.

Government Deposit Insurance

Congress's response to the Federal Reserve's failure to stem the bank panics of the 1930s was to create nationwide **deposit insurance**. The Federal Deposit Insurance Corporation guarantees that a depositor will receive the full account balance up to some maximum amount even if a bank fails. Bank failures, in effect, become the problem of the insurer; bank customers need not concern themselves with their bank's risk taking. So long as a bank has deposit insurance, customers' deposits are safe, even in the event of a run or bank failure.

Here's how the system works. When a bank fails, the FDIC resolves the insolvency either by closing the institution or by finding a buyer. The first approach, closing the bank, is called the *payoff method*. The FDIC pays off all the bank's depositors and then sells all the bank's assets in an attempt to recover the amount paid out. Under the payoff method, depositors whose balances exceed the insurance limit, currently $250,000, suffer some losses.

The second approach, called the *purchase-and-assumption method*, is more commonly applied than the payoff method. In a "P&A" transaction, the FDIC finds a firm that is willing to take over the failed bank. Because the failed institution is insolvent—on the balance sheet, its liabilities exceed its assets—no purchaser will do so for free. In fact, the FDIC has to pay banks to purchase failed institutions. That is, the FDIC sells the failed bank at a negative price. Depositors prefer the P&A method to the payoff method because the transition is typically seamless, with the bank closing as usual at the end of the week and reopening on Monday morning under new ownership. In a purchase and assumption, no depositors, even those whose account balances exceed the deposit insurance limit, suffer a loss.

No private or small public-sector insurance fund would be able to withstand a run on all the banks it insures—but the FDIC can. Because the U.S. Treasury backs the FDIC, it can withstand any crisis that does not undermine the nation's sovereign credit standing.

Since its inception, deposit insurance clearly helped prevent runs on commercial banks. Even so, it did not prevent the crisis of 2007–2009 and the runs associated with it. The prime reason is that deposit insurance covers only depository institutions. But as the financial system developed, shadow banks—money market funds, securities brokers, and the like—gained importance. Those entities are sufficiently like banks that they, too, face the risk of runs by their short-term creditors. However, these nonbanks lack the benefits of deposit insurance, and, until the latter part of the crisis, they had no access to a lender of last resort. Although some traditional banks suffered runs during the crisis—mostly by large depositors with balances in excess of the insurance limit—most of the runs were against shadow banks that bid for funds in the competitive ("wholesale") money markets.

Problems Created by the Government Safety Net

We know that insurance changes people's behavior. Protected depositors have no incentive to monitor their bankers. Knowing this, bankers take on more risk than they would normally, because they get the benefits while the government assumes the costs. In protecting depositors, then, the government creates moral hazard. This is not just a theory. We can find evidence for this assertion by comparing bank balance sheets before and after the implementation of deposit insurance. Recall from Chapter 12 that commercial banks in the United States have significant leverage; their assets are nearly 9 times the size of their capital. In the 1920s, before the deposit insurance system was created, banks' ratio of assets to capital was about 4 to 1. Most economic and financial historians believe that government insurance led directly to the rise in risk.

And that is not the only problem. Government officials are especially worried about the largest institutions because they can pose a threat to the entire financial system. Although the failure of a community bank is unfortunate, the prospect of a large financial conglomerate going under is a regulator's worst nightmare. The financial havoc that could be caused by the collapse of an institution holding more than a trillion dollars in assets is too much for most people even to contemplate.

What this means is that some intermediaries are treated as *too big to fail* or *too interconnected to fail*. Putting such an institution through the usual mechanism for resolving a business failure—bankruptcy court—may force the bankruptcy of many households, firms, and other intermediaries that have contracted with the failed institution. Thus, too big to fail really means too big or too complex to shut down or sell in an orderly fashion without large and painful spillovers. Regulators call such an institution *too big to resolve*, and the Dodd-Frank law gave rise to a special legal designation for such a firm: systemically important financial institution (SIFI).

Experience has led the managers of these too-big-to-fail intermediaries to expect that if their institutions begin to founder, the government will find a way to bail them out. Regulators allowed Lehman Brothers to fail in September 2008, but the painful financial and economic disruptions that ensued served only to reinforce the widespread expectation that government will bail out the largest and most interconnected financial institutions.

A bailout of a failed bank can take many forms. In most cases, the deposit insurer quickly finds a buyer; otherwise, the government, as lender of last resort, usually makes a loan to buy time to fashion a solution. Depositors whose balances do not exceed the insurance limit will be made whole. But in the crisis of 2007–2009, most of the creditors to banks were protected, not just the insured depositors. Following the Lehman failure, governments in Europe and the United States guaranteed all of the liabilities of their largest banks. In particular, they promised that the holders of new bonds issued by the banks would not incur losses. Without these guarantees, the evaporation of funding liquidity probably would have led to a rapid cascade of failures because banks would be unable to fund themselves. In a number of cases, unlike in a normal bankruptcy, the managers of failing banks also kept their jobs.

During the crisis, governments also *recapitalized* some intermediaries—that is, gave them public money in return for partial ownership rights—to prevent a run by their creditors. In effect, governments declared recapitalized intermediaries to be too big to fail while they allowed many smaller institutions to go under. In the United States, for example, the FDIC shut down 297 banks in 2009 and 2010, the largest number in a two-year period since 1991–1992. In these ways, the government, not the market, chose the winners and the losers.

Because it undermines the market discipline that depositors and creditors impose on banks and shadow banks, this **too-big-to-fail policy** is ripe for reform. Given the $250,000 insurance limit, a corporation with millions of dollars to deposit would normally be concerned about the quality and riskiness of the assets a bank holds. If the bank or MMMF were to fail, the corporation would face significant losses. Thus, the threat of withdrawal of these large balances restrains the bank or MMMF from taking on too much risk.[7] But for very large banks, the too-big-to-fail policy renders the deposit insurance ceiling meaningless. In the aftermath of the crisis of 2007–2009, everyone knew which banks were too big to fail and that the authorities would support them. With little threat that depositors will flee, bank managers are inclined to take greater risk than they otherwise would. The too-big-to-fail policy compounds the problem of moral hazard, encouraging managers of large banks to engage in extremely risky behavior (and putting small banks at a competitive disadvantage).

During the financial crisis, many shadow banks also received government bailouts and guarantees that foster moral hazard. Like their bank brethren, some of the largest shadow banks obtained government support because their failure was perceived as too costly in a crisis. And the problem is not limited to the too-big-to-fail class. The U.S. government guaranteed the liabilities of all MMMFs—most of which are small—in order to halt a run. Whenever the government provides such a safety net without charging an appropriate fee for it in advance of the protection, the government creates an incentive for financial institutions to take risks that can threaten the system as a whole.

[7]Intermediaries can suffer what is known as a *silent run* when repo lenders refuse to roll over their loans to a securities broker or when investors electronically sell their shares in a MMMF rumored to be in trouble. Today, even traditional banks can suffer a silent run. If depositors with balances that exceed the insurance limit fear that their bank is in trouble, they needn't line up at the teller window to get their money. They can simply go online to initiate an electronic withdrawal.

Why do government authorities provide this free safety net in a crisis? After all, they know that some quick-fix policies create bad incentives and impose large burdens on taxpayers. In the midst of a crisis, however, they must balance the often-conflicting goals of *crisis mitigation* and *crisis prevention*. Frequently, there are no good choices. Like an emergency room doctor trying to save a dying patient, a government official will occasionally act to rescue the financial system from urgent threats that, if left to play out on their own, would lead to an economic catastrophe. Of course, the taxpayer foots the bill.

Naturally, in the aftermath of a crisis, limiting the unintended consequences of the government safety net is the leading problem facing regulators. Some argue that too-big-to-fail institutions are simply too big to exist and that they need to be broken up, removing certain business activities from them in ways that limit incentives for risk taking. However, that approach does not eliminate the bad incentives arising from deposit insurance and from the government guarantees provided to smaller institutions during the crisis. Later in this chapter, we'll analyze how the Dodd-Frank law addresses these challenges, and we will assess its shortcomings. We'll also discuss how, through a variety of fees and charges, governments could discourage certain kinds of risk taking, thereby limiting systemic threats.

The conflict between crisis prevention and crisis mitigation exemplifies the problem of *time consistency* (see page 27). In good times, governments and central banks typically promise not to bail out financial behemoths and other intermediaries, hoping to limit their risk taking and thus prevent a crisis. But these intermediaries know that, in bad times, policymakers will have an overwhelming incentive to bail them out to limit a crisis. If these policymakers also have the tools to implement a bailout, their good-times promises will lack credibility. When it is not feasible to make a credible commitment, policy cannot be time consistent.

One approach to this problem is to remove the policy tools entirely—to substitute legal rules for discretionary bailouts. Following the crisis of 2007–2009, bankruptcy lawyers proposed to modify the bankruptcy code to make it safely applicable to the resolution of large financial intermediaries.[8] In 2017, the House passed the Financial Institution Bankruptcy Act that incorporated these ideas. However, the Senate did not, so it remains to be seen whether such reform will become law. Another approach—which characterizes the postcrisis regulatory reform in the United States—is to make bailouts more difficult, but not impossible, for policymakers to implement. The more difficult a bailout, the less likely a crisis, but the more dangerous an actual crisis will be. There is no costless way to overcome the time-consistency challenge. As you think about the Dodd-Frank legislation, consider the extent to which it reduces this time-consistency problem, and the cost at which it does so.

Regulation and Supervision of the Financial System

Government officials employ three strategies to ensure that the risks created by the safety net are contained. Government *regulation* establishes a set of specific rules for intermediaries to follow. Government *supervision* provides general oversight of

[8]See, for example, Kenneth E. Scott, Thomas H. Jackson, and John B. Taylor (eds.), *Making Failure Feasible: How Bankruptcy Reform Can End "Too Big to Fail"* (Stanford, CA: Hoover Institution Press, 2015).

Better Capitalized Banks Lend *More* and Lend *Better*

APPLYING THE CONCEPT

Many people seem to think that when authorities increase capital requirements, banks lend less. The advocates of this view go on to argue that, since credit is essential for economic growth, we should not impose overly tough constraints on banks. Put another way, there is a common belief that Basel III and the Dodd-Frank Act have gone too far in making the financial system safe and the cost is lower growth and employment.

There are three reasons to be doubtful. First, there is little evidence that higher bank capital is associated with lower lending. In fact, quite the opposite. Second, given that the 2007–2009 financial crisis was the result of *too much* borrowing—and that overborrowing is a leading indicator of financial crises—it follows that not all reductions in lending are bad. Third, for most banks, which are very small and pose little threat to the financial system, regulators can ease the burden by shifting toward *simpler* capital requirements—so long as they are high enough. For the few very large, systemic intermediaries, strict oversight still should accompany higher capital requirements.

Focusing on the first of these, higher capital does *not* hamper the aggregate supply of credit. The evidence is compelling: strong banks lend to healthy borrowers, weak banks don't. Those countries with better-capitalized banking systems in 2006, prior to the start of the crisis, experienced stronger lending growth during and after the crisis. In addition, better-capitalized banks experience lower funding costs, higher growth of debt funding, and higher growth of lending volumes.

Further evidence comes from looking at Japan and Europe. In the 1990s, regulatory forbearance delayed a thorough recapitalization of Japan's banks for more than a decade. As a consequence, insolvent banks made loans to keep insolvent borrowers afloat. More recently, there is evidence that the impact of extremely low interest rates was that undercapitalized euro-area banks were able to continue making loans to low-quality firms.

Finally, there is the fact that decreases in lending are not necessarily bad: again, quite the opposite. As the studies from Japan and Europe highlight, loans made by weak banks to insolvent, zombie firms result in an inefficient allocation of savings and lead to slower economic growth. And, who would wish to return to the overindebtedness of U.S. households that contributed to the vulnerability of the financial system in 2007? Given the experience of the financial crisis, lenders need to ensure that borrowers are able to pay, both to protect the financial system and to protect taxpayers.

financial institutions. And formal *examination* of an institution's books by specialists provides detailed information on the firm's operation.

As we look at each of these, keep in mind that the goal of government regulation is not to remove all the risk that investors face. Financial intermediaries themselves facilitate the transfer and allocation of risk, improving economic efficiency in the process. Regulating risk out of existence would eliminate one of the purposes of financial institutions. Consider also that efforts to tighten regulations on banks may push risk taking somewhere outside the view of the authorities. The result may not be a safer financial system.

Wary of asking taxpayers to pick up the bill for bank insolvencies, officials created regulatory requirements that are designed to minimize the cost of such failures to the public. The first screen, put in place to make sure the people who own and run banks are not criminals, is for a new bank to obtain a charter. Once a bank has been chartered and has opened for business, a complex web of detailed **regulations** restricts competition, specifies what assets the bank can and cannot hold, requires the bank to hold a minimum level of capital, and makes public information about the bank's balance sheet.

As we all know, rules are one thing; enforcement is another. Posting a speed limit on an interstate highway is just the first step in preventing people from driving too fast. Unless the police patrol the highways and penalize speeding drivers, such laws are worthless. The same is true of banking regulations. The best-designed regulatory

Table 14.2 Regulators of Depository Institutions

Type of Intermediary	Regulators
Commercial banks	1. Federal Deposit Insurance Corporation 2. Office of the Comptroller of the Currency (nationally chartered banks) 3. Federal Reserve System (state-chartered banks that are Federal Reserve members) 4. State authorities (all state-chartered banks)
Savings banks Savings and loans	1. Office of the Comptroller of the Currency (since 2011) 2. Federal Deposit Insurance Corporation 3. State authorities
Credit unions	1. National Credit Union Administration 2. State authorities

structure in the world won't be worth the paper it's written on unless someone monitors banks' compliance. Government supervisors are the highway patrol of the banking world. They monitor, inspect, and examine banks and other intermediaries to make sure their business practices conform to regulatory requirements.

Banks are regulated and supervised by a combination of the U.S. Treasury, the Federal Reserve, the FDIC, and state banking authorities (see Table 14.2). The overlapping nature of this regulatory structure means that more than one agency works to safeguard the soundness of each bank. A bank can effectively choose its regulators by choosing whether to be a state or national bank and whether or not to belong to the Federal Reserve System. Banks can also change their *legal form*—say, to become a securities broker-dealer—leading to yet a different regulator (the Securities and Exchange Commission) and regulatory framework. If one regulator allows an activity that another prohibits, a bank's managers can threaten to switch, or argue that a competitor who answers to a more permissive regulator has an unfair advantage.

The consequences of such **regulatory competition** are twofold. First, regulators force each other to innovate, improving the quality of the regulations they write. But regulatory competition has a less desirable outcome: It allows bank managers to shop for the most lenient regulator—the one whose rules and enforcement are the least stringent. Especially since the repeal of the ban on interstate branching, regulatory agencies have tried to prevent this outcome. Today state authorities usually defer to the Federal Reserve, whose supervisors impose uniform regulations on all state-chartered banks. The Comptroller of the Currency cooperates with the Fed to ensure that national banks receive similar treatment.

However, the financial crisis of 2007–2009 highlighted cases of "regulator shopping" that resulted in ineffective oversight. One example was the supervision of AIG—then the largest U.S. insurer—by the small U.S. Office of Thrift Supervision (OTS) that also had supervised failed savings banks like Countrywide, IndyMac, and Washington Mutual. OTS naturally had less experience than other supervisors with the insurance business—especially with the complex derivatives that AIG sold and with its business of lending securities. In effect, AIG had chosen its supervisor by purchasing a small

Are Your Deposits Insured?

YOUR FINANCIAL WORLD

The sign says "Each depositor insured to $250,000." But what does it really mean? Are your deposits fully insured? The answer to this question can be complicated. Here are a few things to keep in mind.

First, deposit insurance covers individuals, not accounts. It insures depositors. This means that if you hold your accounts jointly with a spouse, parent, sibling, friend, or business partner, the FDIC will insure each of you up to $250,000, assuming that each person has an equal share in the account. For instance, if you hold a savings account jointly with your spouse or partner, deposit insurance will cover a total balance of $500,000, or $250,000 for each of you.

Second, because deposit insurance covers individuals rather than accounts, if you have more than one account at the same bank, all in your own name, they will be insured together up to the insurance limit. For example, if you have a checking account, a savings account, and a personal business account (an account for what is known legally as a sole proprietorship), they will be added together and insured up to the $250,000 maximum.

Finally, if you have accounts at more than one bank, they will be insured separately, up to a total of $250,000 at each bank. But if the two banks merge, your accounts will be covered as if they had been opened at the same bank.

Most people are unlikely to accumulate $250,000 in even a combination of their checking and savings accounts, so the $250,000 insurance limit is not something to be too concerned about. But the FDIC also insures "self-directed retirement accounts" as well. These retirement savings that you control are in individual retirement accounts (IRAs) and the like. Many people will hit the limit well before they retire. If the interest rate is 4 percent, and you deposit $400 per month in one of these accounts, you will hit the $250,000 insurance limit in less than 30 years. But $250,000 in retirement savings is not all that much. So insuring your retirement savings is something you will need to worry about.

Finally, like all government regulations, the rules for government deposit insurance can change. If you really need to know whether you are insured or just want the peace of mind of knowing that your information is current, you can check the FDIC's website, www.fdic.gov.

savings bank years earlier. In 2010, the Dodd-Frank Act closed the OTS—the only regulatory agency that was shut down following the crisis—and merged it with the Office of the Comptroller of the Currency.

The arbitrary and complex structure of U.S. financial regulators does not stop with the banks. Some shadow banks—such as securities brokers—are subject to regulation by both the Securities and Exchange Commission (SEC) and the Commodity Futures Trading Commission (CFTC). The SEC also regulates MMMFs. Even after the Dodd-Frank Act, hedge funds remain lightly regulated: Aside from registering with the SEC, and fulfilling reporting requirements, they need only act with care (i.e., as a fiduciary).

Restrictions on Competition

One long-standing goal of financial regulators has been to prevent banks from growing too big and powerful, both because their failure might threaten the financial system and because banks that have no real competition exploit their customers. As we saw in Chapter 13, throughout most of the 20th century banks faced numerous restrictions that kept them small. And until 1999, banks could not own securities firms or insurance companies.

While recent legislation has changed the banking industry, restrictions on bank size remain. Bank mergers still require government approval. Before granting it, officials must be convinced on two points. First, the new bank must not constitute a monopoly in any geographic region. Second, if a small community bank is to be taken over by a large regional bank, the small bank's customers must be well served by the merger.

But government officials also worry that the greater the competition among banks, the more difficulty banks will have making a profit. Competition reduces the prices customers must pay and forces companies to innovate in order to survive. These effects are as true of the market for deposits and loans as they are of the markets for cars and computers. Competition raises the interest rate bankers pay on deposits and lowers the interest rate they receive on loans; it spurs them to improve the quality of the services they provide. Normally we think of these effects of competition as being positive, but there is a negative side as well. Lower interest margins and reduced fee income cause bankers to look for other ways to turn a profit. Some may be tempted to assume more risk—that is, to make loans and purchase securities that are riskier than advisable, to increase leverage, or to rely excessively on short-term funding.

There are two ways to avoid this type of moral hazard. First, government officials can explicitly restrict competition. That is the solution regulators have chosen in a number of countries; it was also one of the purposes of branching restrictions.[9] (Branching restrictions create networks of small, geographically separated independent banks that face very little competition in their regions.) A second way to combat bankers' tendency to take on too much risk is to prohibit them from making certain types of loans and from purchasing particular securities.

The financial crisis of 2007–2009 accelerated the ongoing concentration in the U.S. financial system. When banks and shadow banks weakened or failed during the crisis, regulators encouraged other institutions to buy them. JPMorgan Chase, already the second-largest U.S. bank, acquired both Bear Stearns, the fifth-largest broker, and Washington Mutual, the largest savings bank. Bank of America, the number one bank in the country, purchased both Merrill Lynch, the largest broker, and Countrywide, the biggest housing lender. And Wells Fargo, the fifth-largest commercial bank, took over Wachovia, the fourth-largest. As of 2018, 36 percent of deposits at U.S. commercial banks were held in only four banks—Bank of America, Citi, JPMorgan Chase, and Wells Fargo.

Thus, in the process of trying to keep the crisis from deepening by merging failing banks with the largest ones, authorities made the too-big-to-fail problem even bigger—in a future crisis, it will be even costlier to allow these swollen intermediaries to fail. Unless their risk taking is restrained, the protected status of these megabanks will encourage their managers to take greater risks, increasing the likelihood of another crisis. Later in this chapter, we'll see how a combination of capital requirements, limits on leverage, regulatory scrutiny, and restrictions on their activities can help limit such systemic risks.

Asset Holding Restrictions and Minimum Capital Requirements

One way to prevent bankers from exploiting their safety net is to restrict banks' balance sheets. Such regulations take two forms: restrictions on the types of asset banks can hold and requirements that they maintain minimum levels of capital. While banks are allowed to build big office buildings and buy corporate jets for top executives, their financial assets are heavily restricted. U.S. banks cannot hold common stock.[10] Regulations also restrict both the grade and quantity of bonds a bank can hold. For example, banks are generally prohibited from purchasing bonds that are below investment grade, and their holdings from any single private issuer cannot exceed 25 percent of their capital. The size of the loans they can make to particular borrowers is also limited. For

[9]In addition, until the early 1970s, regulation restricted the interest rates U.S. banks could pay on deposits. Regulation Q prohibited interest payments on demand deposits and placed a ceiling on interest payments on time and savings deposits. Its purpose was to restrict competition in order to improve banks' profitability.

[10]Common stock holdings were one of the sources of the problems Japanese banks faced in the 1990s. As the Japanese stock market collapsed, the value of Japanese bank assets declined precipitously, to the point where many banks became insolvent.

example, the Federal Reserve requires that one bank's exposure to another not exceed 25 percent of the bank's capital. While these restrictions on asset holdings are quite detailed, they are really just a matter of common sense and sound risk management. In effect, regulators are telling bankers to do what they should be doing already: holding a well-diversified portfolio of liquid, high-grade bonds and loans.

Minimum capital requirements complement these limitations on bank assets. Recall that bank capital represents the net worth of the bank to its owners. Capital serves as both a cushion against declines in the value of the bank's assets, lowering the likelihood of the bank's failure, and a way to reduce the problem of moral hazard. Capital requirements take two basic forms. The first requires most banks to keep their ratio of capital to assets above some minimum level, regardless of the structure of their balance sheets. This approach is equivalent to capping leverage, which (as we saw in Chapter 3, Lessons from the Crisis: Leverage) is a key means of taking risk.

The second requires banks to finance their activities with capital in proportion to the riskiness of their operations. The computation is extremely complicated and the rules change frequently, but basically a bank must first compute the risk-adjusted level of its assets given the likelihood of a loan or bond default. Then a capital charge is assessed against that level. Of course, banks face a multitude of other risks, including trading risk, operational risk, and the risk associated with their off-balance sheet operations. Regulators require banks to finance their activities with capital based on assessments of those risks as well. (See Tools of the Trade for a description of recent changes in capital requirements.)

Unfortunately, over time, banks can learn to evade or "game" any fixed set of rules. For example, in the half-dozen years leading up to the 2007–2009 crisis, banks in the United States and Europe purchased large volumes of U.S. mortgage-backed securities precisely because these assets carried (misleadingly) high ratings, which reduced the capital they needed to hold under their national capital rules. Lower capital meant more leverage, which increased both risk and expected return. (See Chapter 5, Tools of the Trade.) Prior to the financial crisis, overall assets of the largest banks in Europe and the United States rose much faster than their risk-weighted assets. To change bank incentives, regulators of many countries have agreed to impose a cap on leverage and to reform the risk-weighted capital requirements that proved too easy to game (see Tools of the Trade in this chapter).

Disclosure Requirements

Many intermediaries are required to provide information, both to their customers about the cost of their products and to the financial markets about their balance sheets. Regulations regarding disclosures to customers are responsible for the small print on loan applications and deposit account agreements; their purpose is to protect consumers. A bank must tell you the interest rate charged on a loan and must do so in a standardized way that allows you to compare interest rates at competing banks. (This regulation is similar to the one that requires grocery stores to show the price of cheese, peanut butter, or popcorn per ounce, allowing customers to tell which brand or size is cheapest.) The bank must also tell you the fees it charges to maintain a checking account—the cost of check clearing, the monthly service charge, the fee for overdrafts, and the interest rate paid on the balance, if any.

Disclosure of accounting information to the financial markets protects depositors in a different way. It allows both regulators and the financial markets to assess the quality of a bank's balance sheet. Because the information is published in a standardized format according to clearly specified accounting rules, government officials can tell whether a bank is obeying the regulations, and financial analysts can compare one bank to another. With this information, both regulators and the financial markets can penalize banks that are taking too much risk.[11]

One example of where disclosure is important is the measurement of a bank's capital and its leverage (the ratio of assets to capital). As we learned in Chapter 12, a bank's capital—its net worth or equity—equals its assets minus its liabilities. In practice, capital turns out to be quite difficult to compute primarily because assets are challenging to measure.

Measurement problems arise both with a simple unweighted measure of assets and with the regulatory quantity known as *risk-weighted assets.* The computation of the first is complicated by the presence of derivatives on the balance sheet of the bank. How should you treat the fact that large banks engage in both the buying and selling of interest rate swaps, among other things? (For an explanation of interest rate swaps, see Chapter 9, pages 228–232.) And, because it requires the computation of the relative riskiness of portfolios of assets that differ across banks, calculating the level of risk-weighted assets is quite difficult as well.

To see what difference this can make, Figure 14.1 plots three measures of the capital ratio of U.S. banks with assets in excess of $1 trillion. The three metrics are based

Figure 14.1 Risk-Weighted and Unweighted Capital Ratios for Largest U.S. Banks (ranked by asset size), December 2017

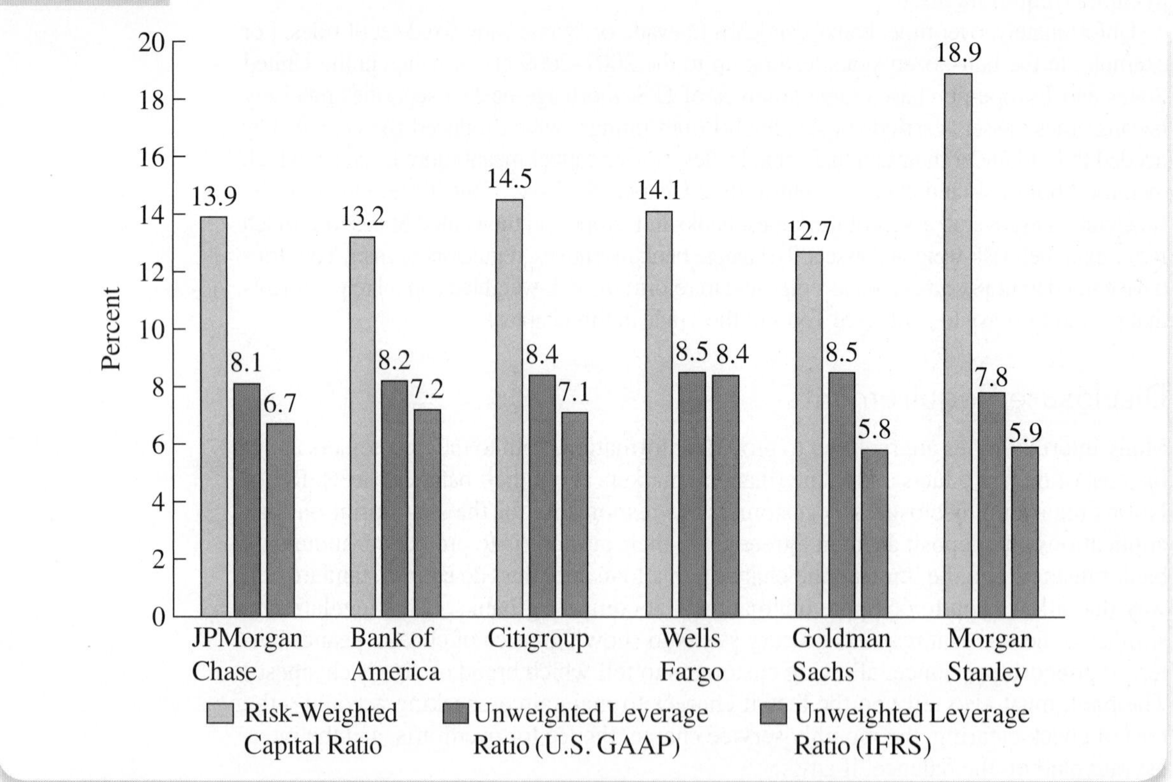

SOURCE: FDIC, Global Capital Index, December 2017.

[11]Writing disclosure rules turns out to be extremely difficult, especially for off-balance sheet activities. For example, regulators need to know whether a bank that buys or sells interest rate swaps is hedging risk on its balance sheet or taking on more risk. Because positions can change very quickly, sometimes minute by minute, regulators are challenged to figure out exactly what should be reported and when.

on (1) risk-weighted assets; (2) overall assets measured according to U.S. Generally Accepted Accounting Principles (GAAP) that use *net* derivatives positions; and (3) overall assets measured according to International Financial Reporting Standards (IFRS) that use *gross* derivatives positions. What we see is that reported capital varies substantially according to the measure that is used: between 12.7 and 18.9 percent of risk-weighted assets, between 6.3 and 8.5 percent of total assets measured using U.S. GAAP, and between 5.8 and 8.4 percent of assets under IFRS.

Supervision and Examination

The government enforces banking rules and regulations through an elaborate oversight process called **supervision**, which relies on a combination of monitoring and inspection. Supervision is done both remotely, using the detailed reports banks are required to file, and through on-site **examination**. All chartered banks must file quarterly reports known as *call reports*. (Their official name is the *Consolidated Reports of Condition and Income*.) These reports detail the level and sources of banks' earnings, asset holdings, and liabilities. Supervisors process the reports using a statistical model that allows them to identify institutions whose solvency is deteriorating and to spot industry trends.

Examiners also visit banks in person. Every depository institution that is insured by the FDIC is examined at least once a year. Examiners arrive at a bank unannounced and look into virtually every aspect of its operation. They once counted the cash in each teller's drawer. While they no longer do that, they do call borrowers randomly to confirm that they actually have a loan and that the balance on the bank's books is correct. Examiners also verify that the loan collateral really exists, even visiting farms to make sure the grain that backs a farm loan is actually in the silo. At the largest institutions, examiners are on-site all the time. They follow a process known as *continuous examination,* which is a bit like bridge painting—once they get to the end of the process, they go back to the beginning and start over.

The most important part of a bank examination is the evaluation of past-due loans. Bank managers are understandably reluctant to write off a loan, wanting to keep it on the books as long as possible after the borrower has begun to miss payments. Loan officers exercise substantial discretion in deciding when to declare a loan in default. For example, they can choose to increase the size of the loan by the missed interest payments. The examiner's job is to make sure that when borrowers stop making payments, loans are written off and the bank's balance sheet properly reflects the losses.

Supervisors use what are called the **CAMELS** criteria to evaluate the health of the banks they monitor. This acronym stands for **C**apital adequacy, **A**sset quality, **M**anagement, **E**arnings, **L**iquidity, and **S**ensitivity to risk. Examiners give the bank a rating from one to five in each of these categories, one being the best, and then combine the scores to determine the overall rating. The CAMELS ratings are *not* made public. Instead, they are used to make decisions about whether to take formal action against a bank or even to close it. Current practice is for supervisors to act as consultants, advising banks how to get the highest return possible while keeping risk at an acceptable level that ensures they will stay in business.

Stress Tests

In late 2008, the solvency of the largest U.S. intermediaries was in doubt. That uncertainty made their own managers cautious about taking risk and it made potential lenders wary of doing business with them. The doubts and hesitancy contributed to the extreme fragility in many financial markets, leading to a virtual collapse of interbank lending.

The Basel Accords: I, II, III, and Counting . . .

TOOLS OF THE TRADE

Global financing took off in the 1980s as bankers realized they could expand their operations across national boundaries and turn a profit internationally. While this was a welcome development for most bank customers, not everyone appreciated the competition from abroad. In some countries, bankers complained that the foreign banks that were invading their turf held an unfair competitive advantage.

Because no one likes competition, we should always be suspicious of this sort of complaint. But in this case, the bankers did have a point. Competing with a foreign bank whose home country allows it to hold a lower level of capital is impossible. Holding extra capital is costly. Banks that hold less capital than others, and therefore take on more leverage, have lower costs and can offer borrowers lower interest rates.

This legitimate complaint led to a movement to create international regulations that would promote financial stability within countries and ensure a competitive balance with banks that operate globally. The result was the 1988 **Basel Accord**, named after the Swiss town where the world's bank regulators meet. The accord established a requirement that internationally active banks must finance their activities with capital equal to or greater than 8 percent of their risk-adjusted assets. Assets would be placed in one of four different categories based on their risk of default. The associated risk weights would range from zero to 100 percent (see Table 14.3).

Table 14.3 1988 Basel Accord Risk Weights

Borrower	Risk Weight
Sovereign debt issued by industrialized countries*	Zero
Claims on industrialized countries' banks	20%
Residential mortgages	50%
Consumer and corporate loans	100%

*Industrialized countries are defined as members of the Organization for Economic Cooperation and Development (OECD). Currently, 36 countries belong to the OECD, including Mexico, Turkey, and Korea as well as the United States, Germany, Japan, and Great Britain.

The Basel Accord is not a law but a set of recommendations for banking regulation and supervision. The committee that writes and amends the accord has no direct authority over the banks in any country. Instead, its members work to develop a code of best practice that will help government officials around the world ensure the safety and soundness of their banking systems.

The Basel Accord had several positive effects. First, by linking minimum capital requirements to the risk a bank takes on, it forced regulators to change the way they thought about bank capital. Second, it created a uniform international system. Finally, the accord provided a framework that less developed countries could use to improve the regulation of their banks.

While the original Basel Accord was constructive, it had—and still has—limitations. In adjusting for asset risk, the accord failed to differentiate between bonds issued by the U.S. government and those issued by emerging market countries like Turkey: both received a weight of zero. And a corporate bond received a weight of 100 percent regardless of whether it was AAA-rated or junk. Not only that, but a bank got no credit for reducing risk through diversification. Making one

Part of the remedy was a special disclosure procedure in which the U.S. Treasury conducted an extraordinary set of "stress tests" on banks and, in May 2009, published the results. The tests evaluated, on a common basis, the prospective capital needs of the 19 largest U.S. banks in light of the deep recession that waswell under way. While observers questioned whether the tests were stringent enough—the "stress" scenario quickly turned into the central economic forecast—the results were sufficient to reassure the government, market participants, and the banks themselves that most of the institutions were in fact solvent. Conditions in financial markets quickly improved. And, armed with the stress-test evidence of their well-being, most large banks were able to attract new private capital for the first time since the Lehman failure the previous September.

Partly as a consequence of this favorable experience, stress tests have become a permanent part of the regulatory landscape. In the United States, the Dodd-Frank Act loan of $100 million received the same risk weight as making 1,000 loans of $100,000 each. These shortcomings encouraged banks to shift their holdings toward riskier assets in ways that did not increase their required bank capital.

By the mid-1990s, bank regulators and supervisors had concluded that the Basel Accord needed revision. Starting in 1998, the Basel Committee on Banking Supervision, which wrote the original accord, negotiated a revised framework for determining whether banks have sufficient capital. The new Basel Accord is based on three pillars: a revised set of minimum capital requirements; supervisory review of bank balance sheets; and increased reliance on market discipline to encourage sound risk management practices.

The first measure refines the estimation of risk-adjusted assets to reflect more accurately the risk banks actually take. For example, bonds issued by highly rated corporations receive a 20 percent weight; junk bonds, a 150 percent weight. However, the low risk weights on mortgage-backed securities helped encourage risky leverage in the run-up to the crisis of 2007—2009 (see page 375). The second measure requires supervisors to attest to the soundness of bank managers' risk estimation and control methods. Supervisors now review the way banks assess their risk and determine the level of capital financing needed. The third measure requires banks to make public their risk exposure and level of capital. Banks that can show they are behaving responsibly will be rewarded in the market with better credit ratings and higher stock prices.*

In the aftermath of the financial crisis of 2007–2009, regulators refined and extended the Basel Accord, and in 2010 they agreed on Basel III, which was implemented in stages through 2018. The new agreement combines micro- and macro-prudential reforms that address both institution-level and system-level risks (see the section on macro-prudential regulation starting on page 382). While the details are quite complex, the basics are not. By expanding the coverage of assets for which banks are required to finance their activities with capital, by raising the risk weights, and by tightening the definition of capital itself, Basel III more than doubled the capital cushion a typical bank is required to hold.

Basel III goes beyond the refinements of Basel II by making three important additions. First, it set restrictions on leverage—the ratio of total assets to equity—that supplement capital requirements based on risk-weighting of assets. Because risk-weighting is difficult, subjective, and subject to evasion by banks, a leverage ratio forms a second line of defense in case some assets turn out to be much riskier than anyone thought.

Second, the newest agreement introduces a set of three buffers over and above the minimum capital requirement itself. Should a bank's capital position deteriorate, Basel III's new *capital conservation buffer* restricts the payment of dividends and bonuses. The purpose is to preserve the bank as a going concern. Next, the *countercyclical capital buffer* rises in good times and declines in bad times, helping reduce the procyclicality of credit supply. Finally, the *systemic capital surcharge* raises the minimum capital requirement on SIFIs.

Third, Basel III adds a *liquidity requirement* that compels banks to hold an amount of high-quality liquid assets (like U.S. Treasury securities) to meet deposit outflows and the exercise of contingent (preexisting) loan commitments that might occur during a crisis. The goal is to ensure that banks can meet their obligations without relying on fire sales of their assets—something that has a negative impact on everyone else—or on borrowing from the lender of last resort, the central bank.

*The Basel Committee on Banking Supervision constantly revises its recommendations to bank regulators. For information about the committee's activities and the Basel Accords in general, see its website at www.bis.org/bcbs/aboutbcbs.htm.

now requires the Fed to conduct annual tests for SIFIs. In Europe, the European Banking Authority has developed a similar testing regime for banks in the European Union.

The idea behind stress testing is simple: following an episode of falling asset values, rising default rates, and funding strains (including deposit withdrawals and inability to roll over maturing liabilities), banks and other financial intermediaries should nevertheless have sufficient capital and liquidity to meet regulatory requirements. Put differently, the goal is for banks that experience a large loss of capital and of liquidity to remain able and willing to provide credit to healthy borrowers.

A prominent example of a stress test is the Federal Reserve's Comprehensive Capital Analysis and Review (CCAR), which examines the resilience of the largest bank holding companies in the United States. In 2018, the CCAR's most severe stress

Narrow Banks Won't Stop Bank Runs

MONEY AND BANKING BLOG

Every financial crisis generates calls to restrict the activities of banks. One frequent proposal is to create "narrow banks," that is, change the legal and regulatory framework in a way that severely limits the assets that traditional deposit-taking banks can hold. One approach to creating narrow banks would require that all demand deposits be invested at the central bank as the equivalent of cash. This is the "100 percent reserves" model of narrow banking.

In the aftermath of the financial crisis of 2007–2009, numerous commentators and experts took up a version of the narrow bank idea by proposing to split banks into two parts, neither of which, supposedly, would be "runnable" (subject to runs).* The first part of each institution would be a narrow bank, providing deposits that are as safe as cash. The second part would operate like a mutual fund or investment company with 100 percent equity finance; thus, unlike with fixed-dollar deposits, the value of its assets would fluctuate, and that "net asset value" would flow directly to the investor.

Proposals vary in how the narrow-banking system would ensure the supply of liquidity demanded by the public and in how it would thwart the entry of runnable shadow banks. Accomplishing the latter would require another government intervention, such as John Cochrane's proposal for a tax on runnable short-term debt.†

Naturally, we share the objective of preventing runs. But how? And at what cost?

Banks as we know them—deposit-financed lending institutions with fractional rather than 100 percent reserves—first made an appearance in early Renaissance Italy and have been operating in that form for nearly a thousand years. No country today requires 100 percent reserves, nor are we aware of any major jurisdiction that ever has. The reason is pretty clear: traditional banks are extremely useful. Given the chance, people will create them.

Banks serve clients in two ways that are costly to replicate. First, they are experts in providing liquidity to creditors in the form of deposits, and to borrowers in the form of prearranged lines of credit (such as home equity loans that can be used when the borrower needs funds). Second, banks have expertise both in screening potential borrowers and then in monitoring those to whom they make loans. That is, they specialize in mitigating the information problems that plague all financial transactions.

Narrow-banking proponents correctly insist that these screening and monitoring functions can be carried out by mutual funds without having the risk reside on the balance sheets of the narrow banks. However, the need to tax potential shadow banks, making it costly for them to engage in traditional banking activities, suggests that the service to the economy of lending out demand deposits—a service that would be lost under narrow banking—is at least privately valuable even if it creates externalities.

scenario assumed, among other things, that the unemployment rate would rise to 10 percent, real GDP would shrink by 9 percent, the stock market would fall by 30 percent, and residential housing values would drop by one-fourth. Together with bank employees, supervisors then computed the impact on the level of each bank's capital. Those institutions that were unable to withstand the stress were then forced to raise additional capital. Specifically, banks deemed to have failed the test would be required to postpone payouts to shareholders, reduce bonuses to managers, or issue additional equity into financial markets.

Stress tests are arguably the most powerful prudential tool we currently have for safeguarding the resilience of the financial system. Importantly, authorities can alter the stress scenarios as conditions change in the economy and in financial markets. If, for example, real estate markets boom, the new stress test might require that banks be able to withstand larger real estate price declines. Or, if commodity prices rise sharply, the scenario may include a more precipitous fall. By changing the stress scenarios, regulatory authorities are implicitly changing the level of capital that banks are required to hold. Passing tests with higher stresses requires more capital.

This brings us to the main point: would narrow banking really eliminate runs? Would it solve the fragility problem its proponents suggest is a consequence of fractional reserve banking? We doubt it.

While the narrow banks themselves would not be runnable, the mutual funds that provide the loans to households and businesses probably would be. This seems paradoxical: many people believe that mutual funds with floating asset values are run-proof. However, recent research shows that—in the presence of small investors—relatively illiquid mutual funds are more likely to face redemptions in the event of bad performance. The reason is the presence of "first mover" advantage: The first investors to redeem their mutual fund holdings may prompt the fund to sell its relatively liquid assets. Those who redeem late suffer because they receive the diminished value of the fund's remaining, relatively illiquid assets that it is forced to sell. Thus, in a world of mutual funds with many investors, illiquidity plays a role that is analogous to its role in the world of traditional banks.

Without deposit insurance, mutual fund runs could be devastating. Even modest declines in confidence, for reasons that are either real or imaginary, could turn into panics. Since the mutual funds would be holding illiquid loans—remember, they are taking over that business from banks—collective attempts at liquidation to meet withdrawal requests would force the mutual funds to conduct ruinous fire sales. After this happens even once, people would simply flock to the narrow banks, and there would be no source of lending. That is, a financial panic in a system with narrow banks would undermine the provision of credit.

Such a credit crisis would probably trigger a massive government intervention to support the not-so-narrow intermediaries. As a result, any government precommitment to let the mutual fund values collapse in a crisis would not be credible, adding to the funds' incentive to take on credit and liquidity risk and—contrary to the goals of narrow banking—raising the probability and cost of a future crisis. In short, we suspect that narrow banking lacks time consistency.

Requirements for transparency, high levels of capital and liquidity, and deposit insurance, combined with a central bank lender of last resort, make a financial system more resilient. We doubt that narrow banking would.

*One of many examples is Christophe Chamley, Laurence J. Kotlikoff, and Herakles Polemarchakis, "Limited-Purpose Banking— Moving from 'Trust Me' to 'Show Me' Banking," *American Economic Review: Papers & Proceedings* 102, no. 3 (May 2012), pp. 1–10.

†See http://faculty.chicagobooth.edu/john.cochrane/research/papers/run_free.pdf.

Evolving Challenges for Regulators and Supervisors

Thus far, our discussion has focused on the regulation and supervision of depository institutions. But globalization and technological innovation, combined with changes in the law, have challenged the traditional structure of regulation and supervision. Today, we bank in a bazaar where a wide range of intermediaries offers a broad array of financial services. We no longer know or care whether the product or service we buy is supplied by someone in town or on the other side of the country. In fact, when you call the bank, the person who answers the phone may live in India, for all you know. Telecommunication has made the location of financial service providers irrelevant.

Besides the globalization of financial services, other changes have challenged regulators and supervisors. First, today's marketplace offers financial instruments that allow individuals and institutions to price and trade almost any risk imaginable. Moreover, because derivatives allow the transfer of risk without a shift in the ownership of assets, a financial institution's balance sheet need not say much about its health. To understand the meaning of this change, consider the traditional rules for computing the minimum required level of bank capital. Historically, the minimum capital level was based on measures such as the default risk of a bank's assets. But in a world where banks can buy and sell derivatives that promise payment in the event of default—like the *credit default swaps* discussed in Chapter 9—such measures become almost meaningless. Regulators and supervisors need to adapt. (See Tools of the Trade on pages 378–379 for a discussion of recent attempts at modernizing financial regulations.)

Added to the challenge of globalization and financial innovation is the fact that during the 1990s, Congress removed the functional and geographic barriers that once separated commercial banking from other forms of intermediation and outlawed interstate banking. Institutions like Bank of America and JPMorgan Chase now are not just commercial banks but investment banks, insurance companies, and securities firms all rolled into one. Each part of these large organizations is regulated and supervised by different agencies, both functionally and geographically. Surely it would serve the public interest more to minimize the likelihood that such an institution as a whole might fail rather than examine each business line separately.

Realizing this truth, regulators and supervisors have begun to think about their jobs in a different way. In the future they will have no choice but to combine forces along both geographic and functional lines. State and federal agencies must either cooperate or merge, as must regulators of banks, insurance companies, and securities firms. A compelling case can be made for a super-regulator that would make the entire process more uniform and coherent, avoiding rules and practices that merely shift risk taking from an intermediary of one legal form to another. Finally, as the international financial system becomes more and more integrated, the need for cooperation across national borders continues to increase. The day may come when the world needs an international agency to formulate the rules for the global financial system.

Micro-Prudential versus Macro-Prudential Regulation

Just as important, regulators must recognize that the goal of financial stability does not mean the stability of individual financial institutions. Too often supervisors have viewed their role as ensuring that no firm fails. The government official's job is not to stabilize the profits of an individual bank or insurance company. To do so would be to defeat the purpose of competition, rendering the entire system less efficient than it could be. Rather, the regulator's goal should be to prevent large-scale catastrophes.

The financial crisis of 2007–2009 has made avoidance of systemic threats a top priority for government (see Chapter 5, Lessons from the Crisis: Systemic Risk). As a result, regulators are broadening their focus beyond **micro-prudential** oversight to encompass **macro-prudential** regulation. Traditional regulation is micro-prudential—it aims at limiting the risks *within* intermediaries in order to reduce (but not eliminate) the possibility of an individual institution's failure. Before the crisis, micro-prudential had been the sole focus of regulators, but it is insufficient to prevent systemic risks. That is the goal of macro-prudential regulation.[12]

How does macro-prudential regulation aim to limit systemic risks?[13] It treats systemic risk taking by an intermediary as a kind of *pollution* that spills over to other financial institutions and markets. To limit such costly spillovers, or **externalities**, regulators can use an evolving set of macro-prudential tools that work like the taxes and fees that governments use to limit pollution.

[12]Indeed, most failures of intermediaries do not threaten the financial system, so efforts to secure the solvency of individual institutions may do little to make the financial system more secure.

[13]The following section draws significantly on the discussion of systemic risk in the BIS *Annual Report*, June 2009, pp. 128–135.

There are two types of externalities that pose systemic risks requiring regulatory intervention. These are known as (1) **common exposure** and (2) **pro-cyclicality**, which refers to the links between the financial sector and the economy that amplify boom and bust cycles.

Common Exposure When many institutions have an exposure to the same specific risk factor, it can make the system vulnerable to a shock to that factor. The shock may be small, but the institutions with an exposure to it can all be brought down at once. In biology, for example, the animals in an ecosystem may be sensitive to changes in climate or chemistry or to the introduction of a new life form. Imagine the risks posed to the indigenous elk when wolves were returned to Yellowstone National Park. More dramatically, think of the mass extinctions that punctuate the history of life on Earth. Mass extinctions occur only infrequently, but they represent occasions in which many forms of life were similarly vulnerable to a change in their environment.

In finance, common exposures arise directly and indirectly. Intermediaries may be directly exposed to a frail institution through financial contracts. Or they may be exposed unknowingly through their counterparties, which are themselves directly exposed to the frail institution. Institutions might be damaged if a vulnerable intermediary is driven into a *fire sale* of its assets at depressed prices that further undermines market liquidity. Finally, all institutions may be vulnerable to the same underlying risks, such as a wave of mortgage defaults or the inability to roll over short-term debt.

In the crisis of 2007–2009, risky mortgages were embedded in many financial instruments, infecting financial markets such as those for asset-backed commercial paper (see Chapter 7, Lessons from the Crisis: Asset-Backed Commercial Paper) and for repo loans, which are the lifeblood of securities brokers (Chapter 12). The infection damaged financial institutions through their portfolios and through their access to credit. When the contagion spread to the repo market, a biologist might say that the crisis became an "extinction-level event" for the species known as large U.S. investment banks: In the week after the fall of the Lehman Brothers investment bank in September 2008, the three largest of the remaining investment banks merged with a bank or became bank holding companies themselves to qualify for support from the U.S. government.

The problem of common exposure may be related to the size of the institution, but it does not have to be. Large intermediaries usually are more interconnected, so they are typically a greater source of systemic risk. However, even a set of small institutions (like MMMFs) that have identical balance sheets face common risks and in doing so can represent a systemic hazard. Once again, a biological analogy is instructive. To survive, living creatures need water in its liquid form: Their size does not matter. Liquidity is a matter of survival in finance, too.

Pro-Cyclicality How do the cyclical patterns in finance and other economic activity pose systemic risks? As the crisis of 2007–2009 illustrates, financial activity is prone to virtuous and vicious cycles. The interaction between financial and economic activity can be mutually reinforcing—recall the concept of adverse feedback mentioned on page 363—leading to unsustainable booms and busts.

In a boom, investor complacency lowers market risk premiums (i.e., investors' optimism causes them to accept compensation that is too low for the risks they are taking). The lower risk premiums boost asset prices, spending, and profits and thus reinforce the prevailing optimism. Rising asset prices raise wealth and the value of collateral, making it easier for lenders to overcome the information asymmetries that lead to adverse selection and moral hazard. Both the value of intermediary capital and the willingness to leverage that capital rise, increasing credit supply and spurring new economic activity that encourages further euphoria—even among regulators. Rising asset prices also lower the cost of making markets, adding to liquidity and complacency.

As we saw in the crisis that began in 2007, busts reverse this process. Falling asset prices depress wealth, collateral, bank capital, credit supply, and liquidity. Leveraged intermediaries scramble to deleverage (to reduce risk taking), but the financial system cannot deleverage all at once in a safe fashion. The liquidity and deleveraging spirals highlighted in the Lessons from the Crisis in Chapters 2 and 3 reinforce the vicious cycle both in finance and in economic activity. The depletion of capital makes the financial system vulnerable even to a modest shock. And regulators typically become more cautious, urging banks to limit risky lending (even though the riskiest loans were made during the boom). Only an entity outside the financial system—usually the government—can supply the liquidity to counter a systemic crisis and, if necessary, restore the capital of the damaged intermediaries.

Macro-Prudential Policy To limit the kind of risk taking that can lead to a systemic crisis, macro-prudential regulation aims to make intermediaries bear—or *internalize*—the costs that their behavior imposes on others. In the same way, pollution taxes are designed to make the polluter bear the cost of the pollution.

Macro-prudential policy applies some familiar regulatory tools in unfamiliar ways. For example, regulatory capital requirements might vary with an institution's contribution to systemic risk. That contribution depends on an intermediary's interconnectedness and the riskiness of its balance sheet and is often correlated with its size. To be effective in limiting systemic threats, a *systemic capital surcharge*—think of a tax on pollution—would be disproportionately larger for firms that contribute the most to systemic risk.[14] In this way, intermediaries would have an incentive to limit the systemic risks that they create, just as a pollution tax encourages polluters to clean up their act. Consistent with this approach, the Federal Reserve began in 2016 to phase in higher capital requirements corresponding to each firm's overall systemic risk for the largest, most interconnected, U.S.-based global intermediaries. In line with international regulatory efforts, to reduce the probability of contagion, the Fed also has required that the largest, most systemic intermediaries issue a large volume of long-term debt that can be safely written down when necessary to replenish equity capital eroded by asset losses.

To counter the systemic risks from boom–bust finance, macro-prudential regulators also could make capital requirements vary with the business cycle. In good times, capital requirements would rise above the long-run average to create a capital buffer against adverse shocks and to discourage euphoria. When leaner times arrive, regulators would allow intermediaries to use their ample capital buffer to meet the credit needs of healthy borrowers. Overall, the effect would be to dampen the cyclical swings of credit supply that can be an important source of economic instability.

Other macro-prudential tools may be new and different.[15] For example, regulators could require banks to buy catastrophe insurance: In the event of a systemic crisis, the payout from the insurance contract would replenish bank capital precisely when the financial system needs it. Another approach would be to have banks issue so-called

[14]See Nikola Tarashev, Claudio Borio, and Kostas Tsatsaronis, "The Systemic Importance of Financial Institutions," *BIS Quarterly Review*, September 2009, pp. 75–87. For one measure of U.S. financial institutions' contributions to systemic risk, see the website of the NYU Stern Volatility Lab: http://vlab.stern.nyu.edu/analysis/RISK.USFIN-MR.MES.

[15]See, for example, Samuel Hanson, Anil Kashyap, and Jeremy Stein, "A Macroprudential Approach to Financial Regulation," *Journal of Economic Perspectives* 25, no. 1 (Winter 2011), available at http://pubs.aeaweb.org/doi/pdfplus/10.1257/jep.25.1.3.

contingent convertible (CoCo) bonds that convert to equity in the event of a capital shortfall. In these ways, intermediaries would pay in advance for the potential cost of restoring the system's capital in a crisis rather than relying on a future government capital infusion that burdens taxpayers. The price of the insurance (or the cost of issuing the CoCo bond) would also function as a brake on risk taking if it rises with the intermediary's contribution to systemic risk.

Ultimately, addressing systemic risk will require a broad framework of macroprudential supervision that includes (1) rules and mechanisms that promote better risk management on the part of intermediaries and (2) reforms that reduce the vulnerability of the financial system to the liquidation of any single financial firm. In the final section of this chapter, we will see how the Dodd-Frank reform addresses these needs.

Regulatory Reform: The Dodd-Frank Act of 2010

The Dodd-Frank Wall Street Reform and Consumer Protection Act imposes the most far-reaching changes in U.S. financial regulation since the 1930s, when the Glass-Steagall Act separated the commercial side from the investment side of banking and when many of today's federal financial agencies (including the FDIC and the SEC) were born. Like the 1930s reforms, Dodd-Frank will significantly alter the structure of finance—its institutions, markets, and practices—perhaps for decades.

The act has led to a significant and unavoidable increase in the complexity of financial regulation. Government officials have had to design and implement hundreds of new rules for a wide range of financial activities, including banking, derivatives, and insurance. Some of these, like the Volcker rule (Section 619 of the act that restricts the ability of insured depository institutions to trade for their own account, invest in private equity funds, and own hedge funds), took years to elaborate and have resulted in hundreds of pages of new regulations.

The Act's Goals and Means

Dodd-Frank has four primary goals: (1) to make the financial system robust; (2) to anticipate and prevent financial crises by limiting systemic risk; (3) to end too big to fail; and (4) to reduce the moral hazard resulting from policy actions such as those taken in the 2007–2009 crisis, including the risks to U.S. taxpayers from government bailouts. The act addresses each of these goals in multiple ways.

Strengthening the Financial System Dodd-Frank encourages transparency and simplification throughout the financial system and improves its resilience. Reminiscent of limits imposed on banks before 1999, Dodd-Frank forbids depositories from engaging in a variety of risky activities (as in the Volcker rule described above). It increases the liability of credit rating agencies for ratings errors while compelling greater disclosure to limit the agencies' conflicts of interest (see Chapter 7, page 163, Money and Banking Blog: In Search of Better Credit Assessments). It requires intermediaries that originate and distribute asset-backed securities to have "skin in the game" through partial ownership of the instruments. And, consistent with the new Basel III international standards (see Tools of the Trade earlier in this chapter), it also encourages regulators to increase the capital banks hold.

Preventing Crises through Systemic Risk Management Led by the Treasury Secretary, Dodd-Frank's super-committee of top U.S. regulators, the Financial System Oversight Council (FSOC), aims to identify and forestall threats to the system. The Office of Financial Research (OFR), which expands the regulators' data-gathering and analysis capacity, supports the FSOC's effort to locate and quantify systemic risks. The FSOC has the authority to designate nonbanks and banks as systemically important financial institutions (SIFIs), making them subject to enhanced oversight by the Federal Reserve, including heightened capital requirements consistent with systemic risk.[16] At the height of its activities, the FSOC had designated four *nonbank* intermediaries—American International Group (AIG), General Electric Capital Corporation (GECC), MetLife (MET), and Prudential (PRU)—as SIFIs. Should a SIFI's weakness "gravely threaten" the financial system, the FSOC, together with the Federal Reserve Board and the FDIC, can require it to close down under Dodd-Frank's new resolution procedure (using the FDIC's "Orderly Liquidation Authority"), which aims to avoid a disruptive bankruptcy like the Lehman Brothers fiasco of September 2008. However, as of 2019, there were no nonbanks designated as SIFIs, renewing doubts about the government's effort to limit too big to fail.[17]

Ending Too Big to Fail and Reducing Moral Hazard One leading motivation for Dodd-Frank was the desire to eliminate government bailouts of institutions whose failure would be deemed too risky for the financial system. Not only are bailouts unpopular, but even the possibility of them lowers the borrowing costs of the largest banks and gives those banks an incentive to take too much risk. Simply put, bailouts create moral hazard. Among other things, the act makes it much more difficult for the Federal Reserve to make loans to nonbank intermediaries. (We will discuss central bank lending in more detail in Chapter 18.) Dodd-Frank also constrains the FDIC's guarantee powers, which were used extensively in the crisis to sustain banks' funding capacity. Finally, the act requires all SIFIs to have resolution plans ("living wills") and gives the FDIC new powers to take over SIFIs, even if they are not banks.

Where Dodd-Frank Falls Short

Despite its length and complexity, the Dodd-Frank Act fails to address several glaring problems that contributed to the crisis of 2007–2009. It also has created a broad new difficulty.[18]

Here are some of the biggest shortcomings:

1. The act fails to streamline the U.S. regulatory apparatus, which remains complex and unwieldy, with a multiplicity of regulators that have overlapping responsibilities.
2. Many government guarantees still largely come for free. The failure to charge a fee commensurate with the risk sustains moral hazard.
3. As of mid-2019, Fannie Mae and Freddie Mac remain under direct federal control, and still dominate U.S. housing finance (see Chapter 13, page 349, Money and Banking Blog: Still Riding the GSE Train).
4. The act largely ignores key shadow banks like money-market mutual funds (MMMFs), which received a blanket federal guarantee during the crisis. MMMFs generally are too small to be SIFIs, but collectively they create systemic risk through common exposures—namely, their vulnerable short-term funding and their herdlike asset management. Dodd-Frank also does not address potentially

[16]The act also requires that SIFIs undergo annual stress tests, such as those carried out under the Fed's annual Comprehensive Capital Analysis and Review (see www.federalreserve.gov/bankinforeg/ccar.htm).

[17] In an effort to end their SIFI status after having been designated by the FSOC, two of the four—GE Capital and MetLife—took steps to alter their structure and reduce their systemic importance, and were subsequently de-designated. In April 2016, MetLife's designation as a SIFI was rescinded by a federal judge. The FSOC de-designated Prudential, the remaining nonbank SIFI, in 2018.

[18]Many of the ideas in this section are based on Viral Acharya, Thomas F. Cooley, Matthew P. Richardson, and Ingo Walter, *Regulating Wall Street: The Dodd-Frank Act and the New Architecture of Global Finance* (Hoboken, NJ: Wiley, 2010).

systemic financial markets—like the market for repurchase agreements (repos)—that may themselves be vulnerable to a run and a fire sale.

5. Dodd-Frank continues to regulate according to institutional *form* rather than *function*. Supervisors who compel banks and nonbank SIFIs to reduce their risk taking may find, over time, that as a result of financial innovation and efforts of intermediaries to circumvent regulation, systemic risk has migrated to shadow banks with different legal forms.
6. Perhaps most important, many observers still doubt that Dodd-Frank will end big bailouts. A major reason is the perception that designation as a SIFI implies a government guarantee for some creditors (e.g., uninsured depositors). So long as private market participants expect bailouts of SIFIs, these institutions will enjoy lower funding costs than other intermediaries when capital in the financial system as a whole is diminished. This funding advantage tilts the playing field further in favor of SIFIs and promotes financial concentration. Over time, the greater the concentration, the more that SIFIs will be seen as public utilities that cannot be allowed to fail in a crisis. Breaking this vicious cycle is possible only if intermediaries can fail without systemic repercussions.

And here is the new difficulty: While Dodd-Frank may reduce the chances of a crisis, past experience and the powerful dynamics of financial innovation make it likely that one will eventually occur. And when it does, regulators will find that Dodd-Frank limits policy flexibility (such as the new constraints on action by the Federal Reserve and the FDIC) in ways that could make the crisis more difficult to contain.

U.S. Regulatory Backlash The Dodd-Frank Act aimed to reduce systemic risk, but it prompted sustained resistance from the financial industry and from some members of Congress. From their perspective, Dodd-Frank imposes excessive costs on the industry.

Some of these higher costs—such as the increase in capital requirements—seem unavoidable. Indeed, to the extent that higher capital requirements reduce distortions arising from the government safety net and from too big to fail, the *social* cost of greater regulation may be negligible, even if the *private* cost is substantial. And the benefits—the reduced frequency and severity of a crisis—appear *very* large.

However, Dodd-Frank also included policies—including renewed restrictions on the scope of bank activity—that add significantly to the regulatory burden without necessarily trimming systemic risk. Because there are simpler, less costly mechanisms (such as higher capital and liquidity requirements) to make the financial system more resilient, the law is "relatively" inefficient. Consequently, with years of experience since the 2010 passage of Dodd-Frank, it is natural for policymakers and practitioners to review what is working, what isn't, and what was overlooked.

Following the 2016 elections that altered party control in the U.S. legislative and executive branches, the resistance to Dodd-Frank became partly enshrined in both law and regulatory changes. For example, in 2018 Congress passed the Economic Growth, Regulatory Relief, and Consumer Protection Act (EGRRCPA, also known as S.2155), scaling back the regulatory burden on small- and medium-sized banks as well as raising the minimum asset threshold for designating a large bank as a SIFI. Similarly, the Treasury encouraged U.S. regulators to ease requirements that, in their view, made U.S. financial intermediaries less competitive internationally, while FSOC de-designated the remaining nonbank SIFI. At the same time, the Federal Reserve and the FDIC began to review Dodd-Frank restrictions on the scope of bank activities that probably did little to make the financial system more resilient.

Nevertheless, it is difficult to argue that the United States has found a sustainable balance between the safety and the efficiency of the financial system. Most of the shortcomings of Dodd-Frank remain in place—the U.S. regulatory apparatus remains uniquely complex; the charges for federal guarantees often are too low; the GSEs are still under federal control; the tendency to regulate by legal form remains strong; and the concerns about "too big to fail" persist. Finally, the wave of "deregulation" could reduce the resilience of the U.S. financial system. As one keen observer put it, "The history of bank regulation in the United States is of progressive dilutions of core regulatory requirements over a number of years, leaving the banking system as a whole vulnerable to crisis."[19]

[19]Paul Tucker, Chair, The Systemic Risk Council, "Letter to Senate Banking Committee Leaders," February 21, 2018.

Key Terms

Using FRED: Codes for Data in This Chapter

Data Series	FRED Data Code
Failures of depositories	BKFTTLA641N
FDIC failure and assistance transactions	BKIFDCA641N
Purchase and assumption transactions	BKTTPIA641N
Payout transactions	BKTTPOA641N
Commercial bank equity/assets ratio	EQTA
Commercial bank equity/assets ratio for banks with assets less than $300 million	EQTA1
Commercial bank equity/assets ratio for banks with assets over $20 billion	EQTA5
Retail MMMFs	RMFSL
Institutional MMMFs	IMFSL
Discount window borrowings	DISCBORR
Assets of the Federal Reserve System	WRESCRT
Asset-backed commercial paper outstanding	ABCOMP
Deposits in suspended banks	M09039USM144NNBR

Chapter Lessons

To learn more about the changing financial system, visit www.moneyandbanking.com.

1. The collapse of banks and the banking system disrupts both the payments system and the screening and monitoring of borrowers.
   a. Intermediaries are insolvent when their liabilities exceed their assets.
   b. Because banks guarantee their depositors cash on demand on a first-come, first-served basis, they are subject to runs. Shadow banks like MMMFs and securities brokers also face runs because some of their liabilities can be withdrawn at face value without notice.
   c. A bank run can occur simply because depositors have become worried about a bank's soundness. Shadow banks also may face runs due to a loss of confidence.
   d. The inability of depositors to tell a sound from an unsound bank can turn a single bank's failure into a bank panic, causing even sound banks to fail through a process called contagion. Shadow banks face similar risks.
   e. A financial crisis in which the entire system of banks and shadow banks ceases to function can be caused by:
      i. False rumors.
      ii. The actual deterioration of balance sheets for economic reasons.
2. The government is involved in every part of the financial system.
   a. Government officials may intervene in the financial system in order to:
      i. Protect small depositors.
      ii. Protect bank customers from exploitation.
      iii. Safeguard the stability of the financial system.
   b. Most financial regulations apply to depository institutions, while shadow banks usually face less regulation.
   c. Intermediaries that are less prone to runs, such as pension funds and most insurers, face less intrusive government oversight than the banking industry.
   d. The U.S. government has established a two-part safety net to protect the nation's financial system.
      i. The Federal Reserve acts as the lender of last resort, providing liquidity to solvent institutions in order to prevent the failure of a single intermediary from becoming a systemwide panic.
      ii. The Federal Deposit Insurance Corporation (FDIC) insures individual depositors, helping prevent bank runs by reducing depositors' incentive to flee at the first whiff of trouble.
   e. The government's safety net encourages bank managers to take more risk than they would otherwise, increasing the problem of moral hazard.
3. Through regulation and supervision, government officials reduce the amount of risk banks can take, lowering their chances of failure. Regulators and supervisors:
   a. Restrict competition.
   b. Restrict the types of assets banks can hold.
   c. Require banks to hold minimum levels of capital.
   d. Require banks to disclose their fees to customers and their financial indicators to investors.
   e. Monitor banks' compliance with government regulations.
4. Regulators use macro-prudential tools to limit systemic threats to the financial system. Such risks usually arise from externalities—costly spillovers from the behavior of intermediaries. These externalities have two sources: (1) *common exposure* of

intermediaries to frail institutions or to underlying risks and (2) *pro-cyclicality* of the links between financial and economic activity, which amplifies boom and bust cycles.

Conceptual and Analytical Problems connect

1. Explain how a bank run can turn into a bank panic. *(LO1)*
2. Current technology allows large bank depositors to withdraw their funds electronically at a moment's notice. They can do so all at the same time, without anyone's knowledge, in what is called a silent run. When might a silent run happen, and why? *(LO1)*
3. Explain why financial institutions such as pension funds and insurance companies are not as vulnerable to runs as money-market mutual funds and securities dealers. *(LO1)*
4. Explain the link between falling house prices and bank failures during the financial crisis of 2007–2009. *(LO1)*
5. Discuss the regulations that are designed to reduce the moral hazard created by deposit insurance. *(LO3)*
6. During the financial crisis of 2007–2009, the Federal Reserve used its emergency authority to lend to nonbank intermediaries. Explain how this extension of the lender-of-last-resort function added to moral hazard. *(LO2)*

7.* Why is the banking system much more heavily regulated than other areas of the economy? *(LO3)*

8.* Explain why, in seeking to avoid financial crises, the government's role as regulator of the financial system does not imply it should protect individual institutions from failure. *(LO2)*

9. Explain how macro-prudential regulations work to limit systemic risk in the financial system. *(LO3)*
10. Why were runs during the financial crisis of 2007–2009 not limited to institutions with large exposures to subprime mortgage lending? *(LO1)*
11. Suppose you have two deposits totaling $280,000 with a bank that has just been declared insolvent. Would you prefer that the FDIC resolve the insolvency under the payoff method or the purchase-and-assumption method? Explain your choice. *(LO2)*

12.* In the absence of limits on the behavior of large intermediaries, how might the perception of institutions being "too-big-to-fail" lead to increased concentration in the banking industry? *(LO2)*

13. One goal of the regulatory reforms that followed the 2007-2009 financial crisis was to address the "too-big-to-fail" problem associated with large institutions. How did the reforms try to address this problem? Why might they not be sufficient? *(LO3)*
14. A government can overcome the challenge of time consistency only if it is both *able* and *willing* to make credible commitments. With this in mind, how might the U.S. laws and procedures for bankruptcy affect the too-big-to-fail problem? *(LO2)*

*Indicates more difficult problems.

15. If banks' fragility arises from the fact that they provide liquidity to depositors, as a bank manager, how might you reduce the fragility of your institution? *(LO1)*
16.* Why do you think bank managers are not always willing to pursue strategies to reduce the fragility of their institutions? *(LO1)*
17. Regulators have traditionally required banks to maintain capital-asset ratios of a certain level to ensure adequate net worth based on the size and composition of the bank's assets on its balance sheet. Why might such capital adequacy requirements not be effective? *(LO3)*
18. You are the lender of last resort and an institution approaches you for a loan. You assess that the institution has $800 million in assets, mostly in long-term loans, and $600 million in liabilities. The institution is experiencing unusually high withdrawal rates on its demand deposits and is requesting a loan to tide it over. Would you grant the loan? *(LO2)*
19. You are a bank examiner and have concerns that the bank you are examining may have a solvency problem. On examining the bank's assets, you notice that the loan sizes of a significant portion of the bank's loans are increasing in relatively small increments each month. What do you think might be going on and what should you do about it? *(LO3)*
20. Deflation is the rate of decline in the aggregate price level. Why might unexpected deflation be of particular concern to someone managing a bank? *(LO1)*
21. Explain how regulations that require banks to finance a greater portion of their activities with equity capital might hinder economic growth. How might such regulations help economic growth? *(LO3)*

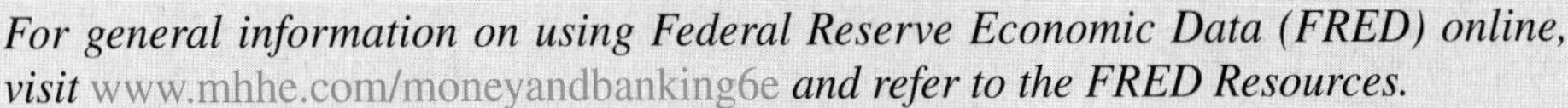

Data Exploration

For general information on using Federal Reserve Economic Data (FRED) online, visit www.mhhe.com/moneyandbanking6e *and refer to the FRED Resources.*

1. When banks failed in the 1929–1933 period, the lack of deposit insurance meant that depositors experienced sizable losses. How big were these losses? For September 1929 through February 1933, plot the deposits in suspended banks (FRED code: M09039USM144NNBR). Download the data and sum the deposits lost to bank failures in 1931. Using this total, compute its ratio to 1931 gross domestic product of $77.4 billion. Using that ratio, how large would the losses be compared to first-quarter 2016 nominal GDP of $18.3 trillion. *(LO1)*
2. How frequently are the payoff and the purchase-and-assumption methods used by the FDIC? Plot the total number of institutions receiving such assistance (FRED codes: BKTTPIA641N for purchase-and-assumption; BKTTPOA641N for the payoff method). On the same graph, plot as a second line the purchase-and-assumption data separately (so that your graph will show one line with the total and a second line with the purchase-and-assumption data only). Describe the evolution over the long run. From what you know about the total number of depository institutions, does the total number of resolutions seem high or low? *(LO2)*

*Indicates more difficult problems.

3. Examine the capital ratios of large banks (FRED code: EQTA5) and small banks (FRED code: EQTA1). What can you say about the risk-taking propensity of these banks over the long run? How did the financial crisis of 2007–2009 influence the risk-taking behavior of large banks? *(LO3)*
4. How important was the lender-of-last-resort function of the Federal Reserve in the financial crisis of 2007–2009? Beginning in 2000, plot the ratio (in percent) of borrowing from the Fed (FRED code: DISCBORR) to its asset holdings (FRED code: WRESCRT). What happened to the borrowing ratio during the 2007–2009 financial crisis? *(LO2)*
5. Shadow banks typically fund their assets by issuing liabilities of shorter maturity that are close substitutes for bank deposits. The maturity mismatch between their assets and liabilities creates *rollover risk* that can trigger *fire sales* and systemic disruption. Plot the outstanding level of one such liability—asset-backed commercial paper (FRED code: ABCOMP)—from the start of 2002 to the end of 2007. Based on the plot, discuss how the use of asset-backed commercial paper influenced the financial crisis of 2007–2009. *(LO1)*

Chapter

15 Central Banks in the World Today

Learning Objectives

After reading this chapter, you should be able to:

LO1 Explain the origin and functions of central banks.

LO2 Analyze the objectives of central banks.

LO3 Describe the features of an effective central bank.

LO4 Discuss the relationship between monetary and fiscal policy.

Beginning in the summer of 2007, the most severe and persistent financial crisis since the Great Depression shook intermediaries, markets, and economies around the globe. Some of the largest financial institutions failed, and the market disruptions triggered the worst global recession since World War II. The panic peaked after the September 2008 run on Lehman Brothers—the fourth-largest U.S. investment bank—as investors around the globe sought to hold only the safest, most liquid assets they could find. Investors stopped lending to intermediaries, which stopped lending to each other. As the storm spread, the global financial system bordered on complete collapse for the first time in 75 years.

Central banks neither foresaw nor prevented the crisis of 2007–2009. Even long after the tempest began, they did not see how menacing it would become. Yet, as the expanding storm continuously poked new holes in the financial boat, policymakers developed new tools to plug the holes. When the financial hurricane finally reached its late-2008 crescendo, the world's leading central banks played a key role in bringing the financial system and the economy back to safe harbor. They acted in unprecedented fashion—on their own as well as with other central banks and with government finance ministries—to prevent the financial system from capsizing and, over time, to restore financial and economic stability.

The **central bank** of the United States is the Federal Reserve (widely known as the Fed for short). The people who work there are responsible for making sure that our financial system functions smoothly so that the average citizen can carry on without worrying about it. During the financial crisis, the Fed fell short of this goal. Nevertheless, it managed in 2008 to prevent the looming collapse of the financial system and to foster a vast improvement of financial conditions in 2009 that helped end the long, deep economic slump.

The euro area consists of 19 countries (as of January 2020) that have adopted the euro as their common currency (the euro area is a subset of the European Union). The central bank of the euro area is the European Central Bank (ECB). After working to safeguard the euro during the global crisis of 2007–2009, the ECB in 2010 began to face a banking and sovereign debt crisis in several euro-area countries. A flight of capital and deposits out of those countries threatened an end to the euro itself, but extraordinary liquidity provision by the ECB purchased time for governments to begin addressing the euro area's vulnerabilities. Strengthened euro-area institutions helped limit renewed contagion when, in 2015, Greece teetered on the edge of leaving the euro area.

Earlier caution under similar circumstances on the part of Japan's central bank, the Bank of Japan, had provided a negative lesson to the Fed and the ECB: Beginning in the 1990s, the Bank of Japan allowed the country to sink into deflation following the collapse of huge bubbles in the stock market and real estate market. Over the next two decades, Japan's price deflator for gross domestic product sank by nearly 20 percent from its peak, adding to the real burden of debt. It wasn't until 2014, following a new round of aggressive monetary expansion by the Bank of Japan, that this generation-long deflation was interrupted.

These watershed events will leave a lasting imprint on global economies, the financial system, and policymaking. Many changes resulting from recent crises are likely to prove permanent rather than temporary. As we saw in Chapters 12 and 13, the crisis of 2007–2009 has already transformed the structure of the financial industry in the United States, with further change on the horizon. Chapter 14 highlighted the new regulatory environment, especially Basel III, Dodd-Frank, and new approaches to managing systemic risk.

In Part IV (Chapters 15–19), we will study the evolving role of central banks. Central banks do not act only during times of crisis. Their work is vital to the day-to-day operation of any modern economy. Today there are about 180 central banks in the world: Virtually every country has one.[1] Yet, despite the vast powers of these institutions and the constant news reports on their activities, most people have only a vague idea of what they are and what they do.

This chapter begins to explain the role of central banks in our economic and financial system. It describes the origins of modern central banking and examines the complexities policymakers now face in meeting their responsibilities. It also highlights a central question that has become politically controversial following the crisis actions of the Fed, the ECB, and other central banks; namely, what is the proper relationship between a central bank and the government?

The Basics: How Central Banks Originated and Their Role Today

The central bank started out as the government's bank and over the years added various other functions. A modern central bank not only manages the government's finances but provides an array of services to commercial banks. It is the bankers' bank. Let's see how this arrangement came about.

The Government's Bank

Governments have financial needs of their own. Some rulers, like King William of Orange, created the central bank to finance wars. Others, like Napoléon Bonaparte, did it in an effort to stabilize their country's economic and financial system.[2]

[1]For a list of the world's central banks and their websites, see the website of the Bank for International Settlements: www.bis.org/cbanks.htm.

[2]The Bank of England was chartered in 1694 for the express purpose of raising taxes and borrowing to finance a war between Austria, England, and the Netherlands on one side and Louis XIV's France on the other. The Banque de France was created in 1800 in the aftermath of the deep recession and hyperinflation of the French Revolutionary period. For a more detailed discussion, see Glyn Davies's *A History of Money: From Ancient Times to the Present Day* (Cardiff: University of Wales Press, 2002).

While central banks have been around since the late 1600s, these early examples are really the exceptions, as central banking is largely a 20th-century phenomenon. In 1900, only 18 countries had central banks. Even the U.S. Federal Reserve did not begin operating until 1914.[3] As the importance of the government and the financial system grew, the need for a central bank grew along with it. Today it is hard to imagine not having one.

As the government's bank, the central bank occupies a privileged position: It has a monopoly on the issuance of currency. *The central bank creates money.* Historically, central bank money has been seen as more trustworthy than that issued by kings, queens, or emperors. Rulers have had a tendency to default on their debts, rendering their currencies worthless. By contrast, early central banks kept sufficient reserves to redeem their notes in gold. People must have faith in money if they are to use it, and experience tells us that this type of institutional arrangement creates that faith. Today the Federal Reserve has the sole legal authority to issue U.S. dollar bills.[4]

The ability to print currency means that the central bank can control the availability of money and credit in a country's economy. As we'll see in later chapters, most central banks go about this by adjusting short-term interest rates. This activity is what we usually refer to as **monetary policy**. In today's world, central banks use monetary policy to stabilize economic growth and inflation. An expansionary or accommodative policy, through lower interest rates, raises both growth and inflation over the short run, while tighter or restrictive policy reduces them. We will discuss the mechanics of monetary policy in more detail in later chapters.

Understanding why a country would want to have its own monetary policy is important. At its most basic level, printing paper money is a very profitable business. A $100 bill costs less than 15 cents to print, but it can be exchanged for $100 worth of goods and services. It is logical that governments would want to maintain a monopoly on printing paper money and to use the revenue it generates to benefit the general public. (Although, when we list the objectives of the central bank later in this chapter, profit maximization will not be one of them.)

Government officials also know that losing control of the printing presses means losing control of inflation. A high rate of money growth creates a high inflation rate. Giving the currency-printing monopoly to someone else can be disastrous, resulting in high inflation and damage to the economy's ability to function smoothly. (In fact, attempts to destabilize the value of a country's currency through counterfeiting have been used as a weapon in wars. See Applying the Concept: Why Is Stable Money Such a Big Deal?) Nevertheless, some countries have done it. The leading example is the euro area, whose member-states ceded the conduct of monetary policy to the ECB as part of a broader move toward economic integration. To limit inflation risks, they enshrined rules for the ECB in a treaty, helping to secure the ECB's credibility even amid crisis. We will see, however, that securing price stability and the viability of the euro over the long run also requires sound management of the euro area's government budgets, debt, and banking systems.

[3]For two short periods in the 19th century, the United States did have a national bank that served many of the functions of a central bank. Early American dislike for the centralization of power doomed these institutions, the First Bank of the United States (1791–1811) and the Second Bank of the United States (1816–1836). In the next chapter, we will see how economic and financial development after the Civil War convinced people that they could not live without a central bank. See Michael F. Bryan and Bruce Champ's "Fear and Loathing of Central Banks in America," *Economic Commentary* of the Federal Reserve Bank of Cleveland, June 2002, for a brief description of this history. To learn about the origins of the Federal Reserve, see Roger Lowenstein, *America's Bank: The Epic Struggle to Create the Federal Reserve* (New York: Penguin Press, 2015).

[4]While once upon a time you could redeem dollar bills for gold, today all the Federal Reserve promises is that it will give you a crisp new dollar bill for a worn old one—and that is enough for the average person, given the public's faith in the Federal Reserve.

Why Is Stable Money Such a Big Deal?

APPLYING THE CONCEPT

by David E. Altig*

On Wednesday, July 10, 1940, Adolf Hitler's Luftwaffe attacked British air bases along the coasts of Scotland and eastern and southeastern England. Four months later, the Battle of Britain was over, bringing an end to German hopes of direct military conquest of the British Isles.

But the end of the air raids would not end the attack on the United Kingdom. Shortly after their defeat in the Battle of Britain, the Germans began to produce a new weapon that, while less obviously violent than Luftwaffe bombs, was recognized as no less virulent. That weapon was counterfeit British pounds.

Operation Bernhard, as the counterfeiting enterprise would be known, was named for Bernhard Kruger, the SS officer who oversaw the production of the bogus notes by slave labor in the Sachsenhausen concentration camp near Berlin. By contemporary accounts, the plan resulted in the manufacture of about £150,000,000 in counterfeit notes of various denominations—in the neighborhood of $7 billion by today's standards. Kruger's operation enlisted the support of known counterfeiters as well as professionals and skilled tradesmen among the camp's population. It incorporated production techniques that ran the gamut from detailed material analyses to the manual labor of prisoners who "seasoned" the bogus bills by passing them from one another, folding and soiling them to give them a realistic worn appearance.

The objective was simple, devious, and pernicious: To undermine public confidence in the pound and, by so doing, irreparably damage the British economy. In the end, the plot did not succeed in destroying confidence in Britain's currency, and eventually, the counterfeiting program shifted toward financing various clandestine Nazi activities outside the United Kingdom. Ironically, this shift in the operation's focus was made possible precisely because the initial goal of undermining the pound's value was not realized.

Operation Bernhard is a particularly interesting example of the use of counterfeiting as warfare, but it is by no means unique or unprecedented. One of the earliest known instances of counterfeiting as a weapon occurred during the city-state conflicts of Renaissance Italy (the historical period that would inspire Machiavelli's *The Prince*). The instigator in this case was one Galeazzo Sforza, a Milanese duke, who in 1470 (when Machiavelli was an infant) attempted to undermine the economic well-being of his enemies in the rival city-state of Venice by adding counterfeiting Venetian currency to the corpus of general treachery that he regularly practiced. (History records the duke as a particularly odious character, whose cruelty led to a successful assassination plot by Milanese elites in 1476.)

There are many, many more examples, including American counterfeiting of North Vietnamese dong during the Vietnam War and modern terrorist aggressions. The ubiquitous impulse to undermine the value of, and confidence in, the currency of one's enemies is testament to the indispensable role of a stable and reliable monetary standard in modern economies. In fact, so broad and deep is the potential damage of a successful counterfeiting campaign, some reports indicate that professional German military officers initially opposed Operation Bernhard partly on the grounds that it constituted an unacceptable attack on civilian populations. What do attempts to counterfeit an enemy's currency during wartime have in common with decisions to adopt another country's currency during peacetime? Both are inspired by the power of a stable monetary standard and, conversely, the consequences of losing it. Both illustrate why preserving the value of the nation's currency is one of a central bank's most important responsibilities.

*Excerpt from David E. Altig's *Why Is Stable Money Such a Big Deal?* Economic Commentary of the Federal Reserve Bank of Cleveland, May 1, 2002.

The Bankers' Bank

The political backing of the government, together with their sizable gold reserves, made early central banks the biggest and most reliable banks around. The notes issued by the central bank were viewed as safer than those of smaller banks, making it easier for holders to convert their deposits into cash. This safety and convenience quickly persuaded most other banks to hold deposits at the central bank as well.

As the bankers' bank, the central bank took on key roles it plays today. The important day-to-day jobs of the central bank are to (1) provide loans during times of financial stress, (2) manage the payments system, and (3) oversee commercial banks and the financial system. The central bank's ability to create money means that it can make loans even when no one else can, including during a crisis. We discussed this "lender of last resort" function in Chapter 14 and will provide more detail in Chapter 18. For now, all we need to say is that by ensuring that sound banks and financial institutions can continue to operate, the central bank makes the whole financial system more stable. Many people believe this is the most important function of any modern central bank.

Second, every country needs a secure and efficient payments system. People require ways to pay each other, and financial institutions need a cheap and reliable way to transfer funds to one another.[5] The fact that all banks have accounts there makes the central bank the natural place for these *interbank* payments to be settled. In today's world, interbank payments are extremely important. Look at the daily volume on the Federal Reserve's *Fedwire* system. In 2018, an average of more than \$2.8 trillion per day was transferred over the Fedwire—nearly one-seventh of the annual U.S. gross domestic product.

Finally, as we saw in our discussion of banking regulation, someone has to watch over commercial banks and nonbank financial institutions so that savers and investors can be confident they are sound. Those who monitor the financial system must have sensitive information. For example, they need to know the exact methods institutions use to make lending and credit decisions. Needless to say, such knowledge would be very useful to the institutions' competitors. Government examiners and supervisors are the only ones who can handle such information without conflict of interest. In some countries they are housed in the central bank, while in others they work in separate agencies. In the United States, as we saw in Chapter 14, the examiners work in various places, including the Federal Reserve.

As the government's bank and the bankers' bank, central banks are the biggest, most powerful players in a country's financial and economic system. Central bankers are supposed to use this power to stabilize the economy, making us all better off. And for the most part, that is what they do. But any institution with the power to ensure that the economic and financial systems run smoothly also has the power to create problems. By limiting its lending early in the financial crisis of 2007–2009, the Bank of England may have contributed to the first depositor run on a major British bank in more than a century. And following the breakup of the Soviet Union, the failure of the Bank of Russia to exert any control over the expansion of money and credit led to a very high inflation rate, while Russian economic activity in the 1990s was virtually halved.

Before we go on to examine the goals and objectives of central bankers in detail, it is essential that we understand what a modern central bank is *not*. First, a central bank does not control securities markets, though it may monitor and participate in bond and stock markets. Second, the central bank does not control the government's budget. In the United States, the budget is determined by Congress and the president through **fiscal policy**. The U.S. Treasury then administers the government, managing the collection of funds through the tax system and writing checks to pay for the government's expenditures. The Fed acts only as the Treasury's bank, providing a place for money paid to the government to be deposited, making good on the government's checks, and

[5]Prior to the creation of the Federal Reserve's payment system, banks were not always willing to honor the obligations of other banks at par. Thus, a \$100 bank note from a particular Philadelphia bank might be worth only \$95 in New York. And the discount would vary depending on the perceived creditworthiness of the Philadelphia bank. This system was very cumbersome and expensive. One of the jobs of the Federal Reserve is to act as an intermediary, ensuring that all banks' commitments are valued at par so that the rest of us don't have to worry. In the same way, the ECB acts today to facilitate payments in euros at par from, say, a bank in Rome to one in Berlin.

Table 15.1 The Functions of a Modern Central Bank

1. *The Government's Bank*
   a. Executes financial transactions for the government.
   b. Through interest rates, controls the availability of money and credit.
2. *The Bankers' Bank*
   a. Guarantees that sound intermediaries can do business by *lending* to them, even during crises.
   b. Operates a *payments system* for interbank payments.
   c. *Oversees* financial institutions to ensure confidence in their soundness.

helping to borrow funds when they are needed. Not just in the United States but throughout the world, the common arrangement today is for the central bank to serve the government in the same way that a commercial bank serves a business or an individual. The treasury or finance ministry manages fiscal policy, and the central bank offers a set of services that make such management possible.

Table 15.1 lists the functions of a modern central bank.

Stability: The Primary Objective of All Central Banks

The central bank is essentially part of the government.[6] Whenever we see an agency of the government involving itself in the economy, we need to ask why. What makes individuals incapable of doing what we have entrusted to the government? In the case of national defense and pollution regulation, the reasons are obvious. Most people will not voluntarily contribute their resources to the army. Nor will they spontaneously clean up their own air. To put it slightly differently, government involvement is justified by the presence of externalities (the uncompensated impact on one entity from the actions of another; see page 382) or **public goods** (those that the public cannot be excluded from using and whose use does not limit use by others).

The rationale for the existence of a central bank is equally clear. While economic and financial systems may be fairly stable most of the time, when left on their own they are prone to episodes of extreme volatility. Prior to the advent of the Fed, the U.S. financial system was extremely unstable. It was plagued by frequent panics. Even with a central bank, these systems don't necessarily work well.

The historical record is filled with examples of failure, like the Great Depression of the 1930s, when the banking system collapsed, economic activity plunged by one-third, and, at its worst, one-quarter of Americans were unemployed for nearly a decade. Economic historians blame the Federal Reserve for the severity of that episode. The claim is that monetary policymakers failed to provide adequate money and credit, with the result that 10,000 of the country's 25,000 banks, accounting for 13 percent of all

[6]Technically, the legal organization of central banks can be quite complex. Some are inside their country's government, some are private banks, and others are a combination. As we will see in Chapter 16, the Federal Reserve is in that last category, part government and part private bank. As a practical matter, because they all have a set of tasks that only they are allowed to perform, we will treat central banks as if they are a part of the government.

Time Consistency
APPLYING THE CONCEPT

The problem of time consistency is one of the most profound in social science. With applications in areas ranging from economic policy to counterterrorism, it arises whenever the effectiveness of a policy today depends on the credibility of the commitment to implement that policy in the future.

A time-consistent policy is one where a future policymaker lacks the opportunity or the incentive to renege. Conversely, a policy lacks time consistency when a future policymaker has both the means and the motivation to break the commitment.

Finn Kydland and Edward Prescott introduced the notion in 1977, opening up a rich field of research that eventually earned them the 2004 Nobel Prize. They describe how policymakers operating with complete discretion at each moment in time might *not* obtain the best possible long-term outcome. Rather, in important circumstances, it is possible to improve outcomes by limiting discretion.

This startling conclusion is a result of the fact that, rather than playing a "game against nature," economic and social policy influences the behavior of thoughtful people. Importantly, what people do today depends on their expectations about the future—including their expectations of future policy. This means that economic behavior depends on the ability of a policymaker to commit credibly to a future course of action; and, as a result, there are important circumstances where long-run economic outcomes are worse if policymakers have the option to make period-by-period choices without constraint.

This line of reasoning means that an effective policy must be a *strategy* for the future, including a *commitment* that influences expectations and behavior today. A strategy has to be more than a mere "promise," which will lack credibility unless there is some mechanism to ensure policymakers make good on their word. To make a commitment *credible*, we need institutions and practices—a policy framework—that make it costly for future policymakers to renege. The more effective the framework, the more likely that policy will prove effective.

The irony of this logic is that limiting the discretion of policymakers can lead to better outcomes. As a simple example, consider the case of kidnapping. In any particular instance, paying a large ransom may result in the release of hostages. However, bigger payments can lead to more frequent abductions. Over the long run, it may be useful to limit the discretion of hostage negotiators (as well as to impose harsh penalties on the crime).

The time-consistency problem surfaces nearly everywhere in economic policy. A prominent example is the problem of regulating too-big-to fail (TBTF) financial intermediaries (see Chapter 14). It is tempting for policymakers merely to pass legislation banning bailouts. The problem is that such commitments are not credible. If, in a future crisis, the perceived alternative is the collapse of the financial system and a depression, policymakers will renege on any "no bailout" promise they could possibly make. Only a regulatory regime that forces financial behemoths to internalize the spillovers of their behavior on to the financial system as a whole will credibly contain the TBTF problem.

deposits, were closed. The Fed also bears considerable responsibility for the crisis of 2007–2009. It was largely passive as intermediaries took on increasing risk amid an unprecedented housing bubble, and it allowed the financial hurricane to intensify for more than a year after the storms began. Unlike the Great Depression, however, the Fed used all its emergency authority in historically unprecedented ways to steady the financial system when the crisis peaked in 2008. The Fed's tenacity and flexibility helped promote a huge recovery of financial conditions in 2009 and avoid a second Great Depression. Similarly, increasingly aggressive liquidity provision by the ECB beginning in 2010 (and continuing as of 2016) was essential to sustaining euro-area banks in the face of runs on several countries' banking systems.

Central bankers work to reduce the volatility of the economic and financial systems by pursuing five specific objectives:

1. Low and stable inflation.
2. High and stable real growth, together with high employment.
3. Stable financial markets and institutions.
4. Stable interest rates.
5. A stable exchange rate.

The job of the central bank is to improve general economic welfare by managing and reducing systematic risk. As we learned in Chapter 5, through diversification, people can manage idiosyncratic risk—the risk associated with individual persons or organizations—but not systematic risk, which affects everyone (and is distinct from *systemic* risk, which we generally use to refer to the financial sector of the economy). Instability in any of these five objectives poses a systematic or economywide risk. Keep in mind that it is probably impossible to achieve all five of the central bank's objectives simultaneously. Tradeoffs must be made. As we will see, stabilizing inflation may result in less stable growth, and stable interest rates may be inconsistent with all the other objectives.

Low, Stable Inflation

Several years ago, Federal Reserve Board chair Janet L. Yellen summarized virtually every economist's view when she said "inflation that is high, excessively low, or unstable imposes significant costs on households and businesses."[7] That is why many central banks take as their primary job the maintenance of **price stability**. As a practical matter, that means keeping inflation low and stable. The consensus is that when inflation rises too high or falls too low, and remains there for an extended period, the central bank is at fault.

The rationale for seeking price stability is straightforward. Standards, everyone agrees, should be standard. A pound should always weigh a pound, a cup should always hold a cup, and a yard should always measure a yard. Similarly, a dollar should always be worth a dollar. What is true for physical weights and measures should be true for the unit of account as well. The purchasing power of one dollar, one yen, or one euro should remain stable over long periods. Maintaining price stability enhances money's usefulness both as a unit of account and as a store of value.

Prices are central to everything that happens in a market-based economy. They provide the information individuals and firms need to ensure that resources are allocated to their most productive uses. When a seller can raise the price of a product, for example, that is supposed to signal that demand has increased, so producing more is worthwhile. But volatile inflation degrades the information content of prices. When all prices are rising together, understanding the reasons becomes difficult. Did consumers decide they liked an item, shifting demand? Did the cost of producing the item rise, shifting supply? Or was inflation responsible for the jump in price? If the economy is to run efficiently, we need to be able to tell the difference.

If the inflation rate were predictable—say, 10 percent year in and year out—we might be able to adjust, eventually. But unfortunately, as inflation rises, it becomes less stable. If our best guess is that the rate of inflation will be 2 percent over the coming year, we can be fairly certain that the result will be a price level increase of between 1 and 3 percent. But experience tells us that when we expect the inflation rate to be around 10 percent, we shouldn't be surprised if it ends up anywhere between 8 and 12 percent. The higher inflation is, the less predictable it is, and the more systematic risk it creates.[8]

Moreover, high inflation is bad for growth. This fact is obvious in extreme cases, such as the one in Zimbabwe, where prices doubled every day in November 2008,

[7] Janet Yellen, "Inflation Dynamics and Monetary Policy," Speech at University of Massachusetts, Amherst, September 24, 2015.

[8] Inflation is costly for other reasons as well. They include the cost of going to the bank more often, the cost of changing prices more often, and distortions created by the way the tax rules are written.

resulting in the second-largest inflation on record.[9] In such cases of **hyperinflation**, prices contain virtually no information, and people use all their energy just coping with the crisis, so growth plummets. The Zimbabwe economy shrank by nearly 20 percent the year inflation peaked. Only when Zimbabweans gave up using the local currency in favor of the U.S. dollar (a process called *dollarization*) did the economy begin to grow again.

Because low inflation is the basis for general economic prosperity, most people agree that it should be the primary objective of monetary policy. But how low should inflation be? Zero is probably too low. There are several reasons for this. First, if the central bank tries to keep the inflation rate at zero, there is a risk of deflation—a drop in prices. Deflation makes debts more difficult to repay, which increases the default rate on loans, affecting the health of banks. Recall from Chapter 11 (Applying the Concept: Deflation, Net Worth, and Information Costs) that deflation lowers the value of collateral and may prevent some borrowers from obtaining loans. Second, if the inflation rate were zero, an employer wishing to cut labor costs would need to cut nominal wages, which is difficult to do. With a small amount of inflation, the employer can simply leave wages as they are, and workers' real wages will fall. So a small amount of inflation makes labor markets work better, at least from the employer's point of view (see Applying the Concept: Zero Matters in Chapter 21).

High, Stable Real Growth

When Ben S. Bernanke was sworn in as the 14th chair of the Board of Governors of the Federal Reserve System, he said, "Our mission, as set forth by the Congress, is a critical one: to preserve price stability, to foster maximum sustainable growth in output and employment, and to promote a stable and efficient financial system that serves all Americans well and fairly."[10] We just discussed the first of these; preserving price stability requires keeping inflation low and stable. And we will look at financial stability in a moment. For now, let's examine the second item on Bernanke's list: to foster maximum sustainable growth in output and employment. When central bankers talk like this, what they mean is that they are working to dampen the fluctuations of the business cycle. Booms are popular, but recessions are not. In recessions, people get laid off and businesses fail. Without a steady income, individuals struggle to make their auto, credit card, and mortgage payments. Consumers pull back, hurting businesses that rely on them to buy products. Reduced sales lead to more layoffs, and so on. The longer the downturn goes on, the worse it gets.

By adjusting interest rates, central bankers work to moderate these cycles and stabilize growth and employment. The idea is that there is some long-run *normal* level of production called **potential output** that depends on things like technology, the size of the capital stock, the number of people who can work, and their usual working hours. Growth in these *inputs* leads to growth in *potential output*—**sustainable growth**. In

[9]For a table of hyperinflations ranked by their scale, see Steve Hanke and Nicholas Krus, "World Hyperinflations," Cato Institute Working Paper No. 8, August 2012 (www.cato.org/publications/working-paper/world-hyperinflations). The largest hyperinflation on record occurred in Austria, where, in July 1946, prices doubled on average every 15 hours. As of mid-2019, Venezuela had been suffering inflation of more than 50 percent per month for more than two years—making it one of the longest hyperinflations on record—but the pace of inflation has not placed it in history's top 10.

[10]Remarks by former chair Ben S. Bernanke at the ceremonial swearing-in by President George W. Bush, Board of Governors of the Federal Reserve System, Washington, D.C., February 6, 2006.

the United States, growth averages 2 to 3 percent per year. Over the short run, output may deviate from its potential level, and growth may deviate from its long-run sustainable rate. In recessions, the economy stalls, incomes stagnate, and unemployment rises. By lowering interest rates, monetary policymakers can moderate such declines.[11]

Similarly, there are times when growth rises above sustainable rates, and the economy overheats. These periods may seem to bring increased prosperity, but because they don't last forever, they are followed by reduced spending, lower business investment, and layoffs. A period of above-average growth has to be followed by a period of below-average growth. The job of the central bank during such periods is to raise interest rates and keep the economy from operating at unsustainable levels.

Importantly, in the long run, stability leads to higher growth. The reason is that unstable growth creates risk for which investors need to be compensated in the form of higher interest rates. With higher interest rates, businesses and households borrow less, which means that they have fewer resources to spend. To understand how this works, think about getting a loan to buy a car. The more certain you are that you will have a good, steady job over the next few years, the larger the loan you will feel comfortable taking on. If you are nervous that you might lose your job, you will be cautious. What is true for you and your car loan is true for every person and every company. The greater the uncertainty about future business conditions, the more cautious people will be in spending. Stability leads to higher growth.[12]

The importance of keeping sustainable growth as high as possible is hard to overstate. The difference between an economy that grows at 4 percent per year and one that grows at 2 percent per year is the difference between an economy that doubles in size over 18 years and one that grows by less than 50 percent in the same period. (This calculation uses the rule of 72 described in Your Financial World: How Long Does Your Investment Take to Double? in Chapter 4.) Keeping employment high is equally important. In the same way that you can never get back the study time you lost when you went to the movies before an exam, it is impossible for the economy to recover what unemployed people would have produced had they been working during a downturn. You can't get the lost time back. Our hope is that policymakers can manage the country's affairs so that we will stay on a high and sustainable growth path.

The levels of growth and employment aren't the only things of importance, though. Stability matters too. Together with financial crises, fluctuations in general business conditions are the primary source of systematic risk. As we have said a number of times, uncertainty about the future makes planning more difficult, so getting rid of uncertainty makes everyone better off.

Financial System Stability

The Federal Reserve was founded to stop the financial panics that plagued the United States during the late 19th and early 20th centuries. It took awhile to work out the kinks in the system. As we have seen, the U.S. financial system collapsed again in the early 1930s, as policymakers at the Federal Reserve watched. Between then and

[11]Financial crises typically depress economic growth below their prior sustainable path for many years. In the most extreme U.S. example, the Great Depression, the U.S. economy did not regain its pre-1929 trend until 1942, when wartime production was in full swing. As of 2016, the U.S. economy is more than 10 percent below the trend that prevailed before the financial crisis of 2007–2009.

[12]For a discussion on the relationship between the level and volatility of growth, both the evidence and the theory, see Philippe Aghion and Abhijit Banerjee, *Volatility and Growth* (Cambridge, UK: Oxford University Press, 2005).

2007, the Fed's track record in preventing or mitigating crises improved substantially. However, recent experience demonstrates that financial and economic catastrophes are not limited to history books. Accordingly, **financial system stability** is an integral part of every modern central banker's job. It is essential for policymakers to ensure that the markets for stocks, bonds, and the like continue to operate smoothly and efficiently.

If people lose faith in financial institutions and markets, they will rush to low-risk alternatives, and intermediation will stop. Savers will not lend and borrowers will not be able to borrow. Getting a car loan or a home mortgage becomes impossible, as does selling a bond to maintain or expand a business. When the financial system collapses, economic activity does, too.

The possibility of a severe disruption in the financial markets is a type of systematic risk. Nothing that a single individual does can eliminate it. Central banks must control this risk, making sure that the financial system remains in good working order. The *value at risk,* not the standard deviation, is the important measure here. Recall from Chapter 5 that value at risk measures the risk of the maximum potential loss of a specific intermediary. Newer measures of risk seek to quantify the impact that losses at an individual intermediary could have on the stability of the *financial system as a whole.*[13] When thinking about financial stability, central bankers want to minimize the risk of a disaster and keep the chance of this maximum loss as small as possible. Their struggles in the crisis of 2007–2009 revealed just how difficult it can be to achieve these goals.

Interest Rate and Exchange Rate Stability

If you ask them, most central bankers will tell you that they do their best to keep interest rates and exchange rates from fluctuating too much. They want to eliminate abrupt changes. But if you press them further, they will tell you that these goals are secondary to those of low inflation, stable growth, and financial stability. The reason for this hierarchy is that *interest rate stability* and *exchange rate stability* are means for achieving the ultimate goal of stabilizing the economy; they are not ends unto themselves.

It is easy to see why interest rate volatility is a problem. First, most people respond to low interest rates by borrowing and spending more. Individuals take out loans to purchase cars, new appliances, and the like, while corporations issue more bonds and use the proceeds to enlarge their operations. Conversely, when interest rates rise, people borrow and spend less. So, by raising expenditure when interest rates are low and reducing expenditure when interest rates are high, interest rate volatility makes output unstable. Second, interest rate volatility means higher risk—and a higher risk premium—on long-term bonds. (Remember from Chapter 7 that the long-term interest rate is the average of expected future short term interest rates plus a risk premium that compensates for the volatility of short term interest rates.) Risk makes financial decisions more difficult, lowering productivity and making the economy less efficient. Because central bankers control short-term interest rates, they are in a position to control this risk and stabilize the economy.

Stabilizing exchange rates is the last item on the list of central bank objectives. The value of a country's currency affects the cost of imports to domestic consumers and

[13]To view estimated contributions of specific U.S. intermediaries to systemic risk, see http://vlab.stern.nyu.edu/analysis/RISK.USFIN-MR.MES.

Table 15.2 The Objectives of a Modern Central Bank

1. *Low, stable inflation*	Inflation creates confusion and makes planning difficult. When inflation is high, growth is low.
2. *High, stable growth*	Stable, predictable growth is higher than unstable, unpredictable growth.
3. *Financial system stability*	Stable financial markets and institutions are a necessity for an economy to operate efficiently.
4. *Stable interest rates*	Interest rate volatility creates risk for both lenders and borrowers.
5. *Stable exchange rates*	Variable exchange rates make the revenues from foreign sales and the cost of purchasing imported goods hard to predict.

the cost of exports to foreign buyers. When the exchange rate is stable, the dollar price of a car produced in Germany is predictable, making life easier for the foreign automobile manufacturer, the domestic retailer, and the American car buyer. Planning ahead is easier for everyone.

Different countries have different priorities. While the Federal Reserve and the European Central Bank may not care much about exchange rate stability, the heads of central banks in more trade-oriented countries do. In countries where exports and imports are central to the structure of the economy, officials might reasonably argue that good overall macroeconomic performance follows from a stable exchange rate.

Table 15.2 summarizes the five objectives of a modern central bank.

Meeting the Challenge: Creating a Successful Central Bank

The decades prior to the global crisis of 2007–2009 were amazing in many ways. The Internet and cell phones came into widespread use. Overall economic conditions improved nearly everywhere, and especially in rapidly growing emerging economies, such as those of Brazil, China, and India. Virtually across the globe, inflation was lower and more stable than in the 1980s. In the United States, the inflation rate fell from an average of 5.6 percent in the 1980s to 2.6 percent in the first decade of the 21st century and continued to edge lower.

Outside the United States, improvements were even more dramatic. In 1980, nearly two-thirds of the countries in the world were experiencing an inflation rate in excess of 10 percent per year and nearly one in three was experiencing negative growth. Thirty years later, only one country in nine had a two-digit inflation rate, while something like 150 countries were growing at rates in excess of 2 percent per year. And not only was inflation lower and growth higher for many countries, but both were more stable, until the global financial crisis struck.

What explains this long period of stability? A prime candidate is that technology sparked a boom just as central banks became better at their jobs. First, monetary policymakers realized that sustainable growth had gone up, so they could keep interest rates low without worrying about inflation. Second, central banks were

The Threat to Fed Independence
APPLYING THE CONCEPT

Beginning in July 2018, and with increasing frequency and intensity, President Donald Trump openly criticized the Federal Reserve and Chairman Jay Powell (whom he appointed earlier that year) for raising interest rates. The president's growing attacks interrupted several decades of presidential restraint regarding the Federal Reserve's monetary policy decisions. By late 2018, the situation reached the point where the U.S. Treasury Secretary and the head of the Council of Economic Advisers felt compelled to deny that the President would fire the chair, an event that has never occurred over more than a century of Federal Reserve history.

Legal experts can debate whether the President has the authority to dismiss the Fed chair (the Federal Reserve Act requires that firing a governor be "for cause"—that is, for wrongdoing, rather than for policy reasons—but does not directly address removing a chair). However, there is little doubt that doing so would severely undermine the independence of the Federal Reserve and pose substantial risks for the U.S. economy. Unsurprisingly, media reports about the President's possible actions triggered large gyrations in U.S. stock prices.

The Fed's operational independence is fragile. As a body led by unelected officials, it has a weak hand to play in a public battle with any President. The disastrous experience with President Lyndon Johnson—when the Fed last faced a commander in chief who wanted to keep interest rates low despite a large pro-cyclical fiscal stimulus—is a case in point. The Fed's imprudent reaction in the mid-1960s helped set the stage for the greatest peacetime inflation in U.S. history.

Current Federal Reserve officials are unlikely to repeat this error. Since the mid-1980s, the Federal Reserve has been largely successful in keeping inflation low and stable, a sharp contrast to the Great Inflation of the 1970s. The result is that long-term inflation expectations have settled close to the Fed's inflation target of 2 percent. At the same time, both the volatility of inflation and of economic growth have declined, helping to diminish uncertainty regarding the prospective returns on other assets, like stocks and real estate.

Precisely because of this success, blatantly undermining Fed independence likely would add a risk premium, driving down prices of U.S. assets ranging from Treasury and corporate bonds to stocks and real estate. As of mid-2019, investors appear to doubt that President Trump would try to fire Chairman Powell. But President Trump's penchant for challenging other key institutions makes the Fed's independence more precarious than at any time in the past 50 years.

redesigned. It wasn't just that new central banks were established, like the ECB. The structure of existing central banks changed significantly. The Bank of England is more than three centuries old (its building in London has stood for more than 200 years) but its operating charter was completely rewritten in 1998. The same year brought major changes in the organizational structure of the Bank of Japan. Federal Reserve operations have changed, too, fostering transparency and accountability. The first public announcement of a move in the federal funds rate was made on February 4, 1994. By 2012, the Federal Reserve had announced an official inflation goal and had begun quarterly disclosures of economic growth and inflation forecasts along with policy rate projections.

Many people believe that improvements in economic performance after the 1980s were related at least in part to the policy followed by these restructured central banks. Improving monetary policy is not just a matter of finding the right person for the job. There is an ample supply of highly qualified people. In fact, in many countries there is a long history of central bankers who have tried but failed because they weren't free to pursue effective policies. Successful policymaking is as much a consequence of the institutional structure and context as of the people who work in the institutions. Nowhere is that more true than in central banking.

Today, in the aftermath of the financial crisis, economists are exploring how to improve financial regulation, and reconsidering the role that central banks should play in financial supervision. However, there remains a strong consensus among economists about the best way to design a central bank for making effective monetary policy. To be successful, a central bank must (1) be independent of political pressure, (2) be accountable to the public and transparent in communicating its policy actions, (3) operate within an explicit framework that clearly states its goals and makes clear the tradeoffs among them, and (4) make decisions by committee.

The Need for Independence

The idea of **central bank independence**—that central banks should be independent of political pressure—is a new one. After all, the central bank originated as the government's bank. It did the bidding first of the king or emperor and then of the democratically elected congress or parliament. Politicians rarely give up control over anything, much less something as important as monetary policy. But in the 1990s, nearly every advanced-economy government that hadn't already done so made the central bank independent of the finance ministry. The Banque de France became independent in 1993. Political control of the Bank of England and the Bank of Japan ended in 1998. And the new European Central Bank was independent from the day it opened on July 1, 1998.

Independence has two operational components. First, monetary policymakers must be free to control their own budgets. If politicians can starve the central bank of funding, then they can control the bank's decisions. Second, the bank's policies must not be reversible by people outside the central bank. Prior to 1998, policymakers at the Bank of England merely recommended interest rate changes to the Chancellor of the Exchequer, a political official. That is, interest rate policy was ultimately decided by the British equivalent of the U.S. Secretary of the Treasury. Since 1998, the Bank of England's Monetary Policy Committee has made those decisions autonomously. The same is true in the United States, where the Federal Open Market Committee's decisions on when to raise or lower interest rates cannot be overridden by the president, Congress, or the Supreme Court.

Successful monetary policy requires a long time horizon. The impact of today's decisions won't be felt for a while—several years, in many instances. Democratically elected politicians are not a particularly patient bunch; their time horizon extends usually to the next election. The political system encourages members of Parliament and members of Congress to do everything they can for their constituents before the next election—including manipulating interest rates to bring short-term prosperity at the expense of long-term stability. The temptation to forsake long-term goals for short-term gains is difficult for most politicians to resist. In many instances, for example, politicians would be inclined to select monetary policies that are overly accommodative. They will keep interest rates too low, raising output and employment quickly (before the election), but causing inflation to go up later (after the election). Low interest rates are very popular because there are more borrowers than lenders. Politicians with a short horizon also may be reluctant to use specific central bank tools that are highly unpopular, even if doing so is the surest way to prevent deflation or a financial crisis.

You can think of central bank independence as a means to overcome a classic version of the time-consistency problem: If monetary policy were always made by decision makers with a short horizon, people would doubt the long-run commitment to price stability. (See the Applying the Concept: Time Consistency on page 405.) For example, they might expect politicians to run inflationary policies at some time in the future when it would be expedient to temporarily boost economic growth. As a result, inflation expectations would tend to be high today. This implies that independent central banks will deliver lower inflation—a conclusion for which there is substantial evidence.[14]

In the same way, societies may be able to stabilize inflation and inflation expectations efficiently if they delegate monetary policy to an independent central bank that *strongly* prefers price stability.[15] The reason is that the central bank's commitment to keep inflation low and steady in the future would be made credible by its prudent inflation preferences, making policy time consistent. Like many problems involving time consistency, this example illustrates how a constraint on policy discretion (when legislators tie their hands and entrust monetary policy decisions to the stability-oriented central bank) can lead to a more favorable policy outcome (in this case, lower inflation).

In light of these considerations, governments have moved responsibility for monetary policy into a separate, largely apolitical, institution. To insulate policymakers from the daily pressures faced by politicians, governments must give central bankers control of their budgets and authority to make irreversible decisions and must appoint them to long terms of office. A similar need for independence applies to the central bank's role as lender of last resort, which may require unpopular decisions (say, regarding the provision of credit to large banks or foreign banks) to secure financial stability.

The Fed's extraordinary actions during the crisis of 2007–2009, however successful in stemming a second Great Depression, led to a political backlash in the United States against central bank independence. The consensus among economists is strongly in favor of central bank independence.[16] Yet, the Fed's emergency actions in the crisis—including large bailouts and extraordinary credit provisions—may invite legislative interference in the day-to-day conduct of conventional monetary policy, making it less effective in keeping inflation low and stable. A far more acute threat arose during 2018, as President Donald Trump openly attacked the Federal Reserve and his appointed chair, Jay Powell, for raising interest rates (see Applying the Concept: The Threat to Fed Independence on page 405). In 2019, the President also proposed to nominate to the Board of Governors several candidates who were widely seen as malleable, making the threat to Fed independence seems greater than at any time in recent decades.

The Need for Accountability and Transparency

There is a big problem with central bank independence: It is inconsistent with representative democracy. The idea of putting appointed technocrats in charge of one

[14]The original work showing the negative relationship between central bank independence and inflation is Alberto Alesina and Lawrence H. Summers, "Central Bank Independence and Macroeconomic Performance: Some Comparative Evidence," *Journal of Money, Credit, and Banking* 25 (May 1993), pp. 151–162. For a more recent update and extension, see N. Nergiz Dinçer and Barry Eichengreen, "Central Bank Transparency and Independence: Updates and New Measures," *International Journal of Central Banking* 10, no. 1 (March 2014), pp. 189–259.

[15]For readers with advanced math skills, see Kenneth Rogoff, "The Optimal Degree of Commitment to an Intermediate Monetary Target," *The Quarterly Journal of Economics* 100, no. 4 (November 1985), pp. 1169–1189.

[16]Naturally, there is some dissent. For the case against central bank independence, see Nobel Prize winner Joseph Stiglitz, "A Revolution in Monetary Policy: Lessons in the Wake of the Global Financial Crisis." C.D. Deshmukh Memorial Lecture, Reserve Bank of India, January 2013, available at http://rbidocs.rbi.org.in/rdocs/Speeches/PDFs/PSS030113FL.pdf.

of the most important government functions is inherently undemocratic.[17] Politicians answer to the voters; by design, independent central bankers don't. How can we have faith in our financial system if there are no checks on what the central bankers are doing? The economy will not operate efficiently unless we trust our policymakers.

Proponents of central bank independence realized they would need to solve this problem if their proposals were going to be adopted. Their solution was twofold. First, politicians would establish a set of goals; second, the policymakers would publicly report their progress in pursuing those goals. Explicit goals foster **accountability** and disclosure requirements create **transparency**. While central bankers are powerful, our elected representatives tell them what to do and then monitor their progress. Technically speaking, legislatures usually grant central banks **instrument independence**—the authority to use their tools as they see fit to achieve mandated objectives—not **goal independence**. That means requiring plausible explanations for their decisions, along with supporting data.

That is precisely the approach endorsed by current Federal Reserve chair Jay Powell at his 2018 ceremonial swearing-in: "Congress has wisely entrusted us with an important degree of independence so that we can pursue our monetary policy goals without concern for short-term political pressures. As a public institution, we must be transparent about our actions, so that the public, through its elected representatives, can hold us accountable."

The institutional means for ensuring accountability and transparency differ from one country to the next. In some cases, the government establishes an explicit numerical target for inflation, while in others the central bank defines the target. In the United Kingdom, the government sets a specific target each year; in the European Union, the central bank is asked only to pursue "price stability" as its primary objective; in the United States, the Federal Reserve is asked to deliver price stability as one of a number of objectives. Similar differences exist in the timing and content of information made public by central banks. Today every central bank announces its policy actions almost immediately, but the extent of the statements that accompany the announcement and the willingness to answer questions vary. The Federal Reserve's statements tend to be only a few paragraphs long, while the statements of the ECB president and vice president may be several pages. The Fed holds a long press conference quarterly when forecasts are updated; the ECB every month.

INFORMATION

Over time, these differences in communications strategy have narrowed substantially, and central bank statements are far more informative today than they were in the early 1990s. Until 1994, for example, the Federal Reserve didn't announce its policy decisions publicly. Secrecy, once the hallmark of central banking, is now understood to damage both the policymakers and the economies they are trying to manage. For monetary policy to be a stabilizing force, central bankers need to explain their actions in periodic public statements, like the ones that follow every Federal Open Market Committee (FOMC) meeting. In essence, the economy and financial markets should respond to information that everyone receives, not to speculation about what policymakers are doing. Thus, policymakers need to be as clear as possible about what they are trying to achieve and how they intend to achieve it. There really shouldn't be any surprises.

[17]High courts, such as the U.S. Supreme Court, provide the leading example in democracies of an independent body of unelected experts making key policy decisions. In Germany, where the Bundesbank was unusually powerful, the central bank was widely known as the "fourth branch of government."

The crisis of 2007–2009 heightened the importance of transparency, both to make policy effective and to secure popular support for unprecedented actions. As we will see in Chapter 18, some unconventional monetary policies can be implemented *only* by communicating them. And transparency can help counter the uncertainties and anxieties that feed liquidity and deleveraging spirals (see Chapter 3, Lessons from the Crisis: Leverage).

The Policy Framework, Policy Tradeoffs, and Credibility

We've seen that a modern central bank has a long list of objectives—low, stable inflation; high, stable growth; a stable financial system; and stable interest and exchange rates. To meet these objectives, central bankers must be independent, accountable, and good communicators. Together these qualities make up what we will call the **monetary policy framework**. The framework exists to resolve ambiguities that arise in the course of the central bank's work.

Looking at the bank's objectives, we can see the problem. Setting a goal of low inflation is easy, but there are many ways to measure inflation. The central bank needs to decide which measure to use and then stick with it. Thus, the FOMC stated in each year since 2012 that an annual inflation of 2 percent in the price index of personal consumption expenditures is consistent over the long run with its mandate as given in the Federal Reserve Act. In the euro area, the ECB seeks a rise of less than, but close to, 2 percent, in the harmonized index of consumer prices, or HICP. More important than the details, though, is the fact that officials have told us what they are trying to do. Their statement helps people plan at the same time that it holds officials accountable to the public.

The monetary policy framework also clarifies the likely responses when goals conflict with one another. There is simply no way that policymakers can meet all their objectives at the same time. Often, they have only one instrument—the interest rate—with which to work, and it is impossible to use a single instrument to achieve a long list of objectives. To take one example, by mid-2004, the U.S. economy had recovered completely from the recession of 2001, and the inflation rate had started to rise. When this happens, the appropriate response is to tighten policy, raising interest rates. So, starting on June 30, 2004, the FOMC did just that. Seventeen times over the next two years policymakers raised the target interest rate—each time by 25 basis points. Obviously, if interest rates are changing every few months, they are not stable. More important, raising the interest rate means reducing the availability of money and credit at the risk of slowing growth. The goal of keeping inflation low and stable, then, can be inconsistent with the goal of avoiding a recession. By the end of 2006, inflation remained low while growth had slowed slightly. The financial crisis that erupted in August 2007 began more than a year after the Fed had stopped raising rates.

Central bankers face the tradeoff between inflation and growth on a daily basis. In March 2008, with inflation soon to rise above 5 percent for the first time since 1991, the Federal Open Market Committee nevertheless cut its policy rate by an outsized 75 basis points to 2.25 percent and highlighted in its statement that "downside risks to growth remain." Although the committee members expressed concern about indications of rising inflation expectations, they judged that it was more important to cut the policy rate in an effort to halt the financial contagion that had resulted from the run on Bear Stearns, the fifth-largest U.S. investment bank. As is often the case, policymakers were forced to choose among competing objectives amid great uncertainty. Indeed, two FOMC members dissented, preferring a less aggressive rate cut. As it turned out, when the financial crisis intensified later that year, inflation worries gave way to deflation fears and the prospect of the deepest recession since World War II.

Because policy goals often conflict, central bankers must make their priorities clear. The public needs to know whether policymakers are focusing primarily on price stability or whether they are willing to allow a modest rise in inflation to avoid a slowdown in economic activity. The public also needs to know the roles that interest rate and exchange rate stability play in policy deliberations. This important part of the policy framework limits the discretionary authority of the central bankers, ensuring that they will do the job they have been entrusted with. Thus, it is an essential part of the bank's communication responsibilities.

Finally, a well-designed policy framework helps policymakers establish **credibility**. For central bankers to achieve their objectives, everyone must trust them to do what they say they are going to do. This is particularly important when it comes to keeping inflation low and stable. The reason is that most economic decisions are based on expectations about future inflation. We saw this relationship when we studied the determination of interest rates: The nominal interest rate equals the real interest rate plus expected inflation. The same is true for wage and price decisions. Firms set prices based partly on what they believe inflation will be in the future. They make wage agreements with workers based on expected future inflation. The higher their expectations for future inflation, the higher prices, wages, and interest rates will be. Expected inflation creates inflation. Stable inflation expectations help prevent both high inflation and deflation.

Successful monetary policy, then, requires that inflation expectations be kept under control. The most straightforward way for the central bank to do so is to announce its objectives, show resolve in meeting them, and explain its actions clearly along the way. By making their preferences clear and their commitments reliable, policymakers can overcome the time-consistency challenge. If, instead, they are seen as likely to renege on a promise—such as the promise to keep inflation low and stable—their policy's impact will be diminished.

Table 15.3 summarizes the principles of central bank design and can serve as a checklist for evaluating the operation of any central bank we come across.

Table 15.3 The Principles of Central Bank Design

1. *Independence*	To keep inflation low, monetary decisions must be made free of political influence.
2. *Accountability and transparency*	Policymakers must be held accountable to the public they serve and clearly communicate their objectives, decisions, and methods.
3. *Policy framework*	Policymakers must clearly state their policy goals and the tradeoffs among them.
4. *Decision making by committee*	Pooling the knowledge of a number of people yields better decisions than decision making by an individual. But effective crisis response requires a clear chain of command.

Decision Making by Committee

Should important decisions be made by an individual or by a committee? Military planners know they can't have groups making decisions in the heat of a battle; someone has to be in charge. But monetary policy isn't war. Monetary policy decisions are made deliberately, after significant amounts of information are collected and examined. Occasionally a crisis does occur, and in those times someone does need to be in charge. But in the course of normal operations, it is better to rely on a committee than an individual. Though extraordinary individuals can be trusted to make policy as well as a committee, building an institution on the assumption that someone of exemplary ability will always be available to run it is unwise. And given the difficulty of removing a central bank governor—a feature that is built into the central bank system—the cost of putting the wrong person in charge can be very high (the same reason is often cited for preferring legislatures over monarchs).

The solution, then, is to make policy by committee. Pooling the knowledge, experience, and opinions of a group of people reduces the risk that policy will be dictated by an individual's quirks. Besides, in a democracy, vesting so much power in one individual poses a legitimacy problem. For these reasons, monetary policy decisions are made by committee in all major central banks in the world: The Federal Reserve has its Federal Open Market Committee the European Central Bank its Governing Council, and the Bank of Japan its Policy Board. The number of members varies from 9 in the United Kingdom and Japan to (currently) 25 at the ECB—but, crucially, it is always bigger than one.

Fitting Everything Together: Central Banks and Fiscal Policy

Before a European country can join the common currency area and adopt the euro, it is supposed to meet a number of conditions. Two of the most important are that the country's annual budget deficit—the excess of government spending over revenues each year—cannot exceed 3 percent of GDP and the government's total debt—its accumulated level of outstanding bonds and other borrowings—cannot exceed 60 percent of GDP.[18] Once a country gains membership in the monetary union, failure to maintain these standards is supposed to lead to pressure from other member countries and (in theory) even to substantial penalties.[19]

Remember that the central bank does not control the government's budget. Fiscal policy, the decisions about taxes and spending, are the responsibility of elected officials. But by specifying a range of "acceptable" levels of borrowing, Europeans sought to restrict the fiscal policies that member countries enact. For the European Central Bank to do its job effectively, all the member countries' governments must behave responsibly.

While fiscal and monetary policymakers share the same ultimate goal—to improve the well-being of the population—conflicts can arise between them. Fiscal

[18]In practice, these limits were open to political interpretation, so countries that failed to meet them were allowed to join anyway. For example, in fall of 1998, Belgium's debt was 122 percent of its GDP—more than double the stated limit. But because the debt was forecast to decline in the future, the requirement was waived.

[19]The Stability and Growth Pact of 1997 (SGP) dictated that "medium-term budgets" must be "close to balance or in surplus." That mechanism first came under significant strain in 2003. The previously agreed-upon penalties that would be triggered by budget deficits in excess of 3 percent of GDP were not levied on the offending countries. In the aftermath of the 2007–2009 financial crisis, many countries far surpassed the deficit limit. In 2011, additional rules (called the "sixpack") enhanced mutual surveillance of fiscal policies. By 2014, the new Fiscal Stability Treaty—a stronger and broader version of the earlier SGP—had come into force in all euro-area countries and most other members of the European Union as well.

Fiscal Sustainability
MONEY AND BANKING BLOG

Since the financial crisis of 2007–2009, public debt in a number of advanced economies has surged and now exceeds 100 percent of GDP. In the United States, the Congressional Budget Office (CBO) projects that—in the absence of policy changes—federal debt held by the public will approach this level in the coming decade.

Importantly, there is a *real* (inflation-adjusted) limit to how much public debt a government can issue. Beyond that ceiling, the consequences are outright default or, if the debt is in domestic currency bonds that the central bank acquires, inflation that erodes its real value leading to a partial default. Importantly, when debt gets very large, the government can compel the central bank to use expansionary monetary policy to erode the real value of the debt through inflation—a situation called *fiscal dominance*.

Sovereign defaults are significant events. Countries typically lose access to financial markets, compelling them to restore fiscal balance immediately. The consequences are nearly always disastrous, including plunging incomes and surging unemployment.

Furthermore, there is a clear link between persistent increases in public debt and slower long-run growth. One reason is that rising public debt *crowds out* private borrowing by raising the equilibrium real interest rate. Another is that persistent debt increases create concern about *debt sustainability—the willingness and ability of a government to pay its debt*—leading to a rising risk premium on the debt to compensate investors for default risk.

Debt sustainability requires that a country's ratio of public debt to GDP stabilize. Otherwise, debt eventually will rise above the real limit. The steady-state condition necessary for this fiscal stabilization is straightforward: A government's *primary surplus*—the excess of government revenues over *noninterest* spending (as a ratio to GDP)—must be at least as large as the stock of outstanding sovereign debt as a ratio to GDP (b) times the difference between the nominal interest rate (i) the government has to pay and the rate of growth of nominal GDP (g). We can write this as the following simple equation:

$$\text{Ratio of primary budget surplus to GDP} \geq b \times [i - g]$$

A useful way to interpret this expression is that the right-hand-side coefficient shown in square brackets (the difference between the nominal interest rate and the nominal GDP growth rate) is a *risk premium* on the outstanding debt. Sustainability requires that the budget surplus be sufficient to cover this risk premium times the level of debt. So, the larger the risk premium, the greater the primary surplus must be for a given stock of debt. And, the larger the debt, the larger the necessary primary surplus.

Table 15.4 highlights the impact of the debt ratio (columns) and the risk premium (rows) on sustainable fiscal policy. The number in each cell is the minimum steady-state primary surplus as a percent of GDP that a country needs to meet the sustainability condition. For example, a country with a government debt ratio of 120 percent of GDP would require a primary surplus of at least 2.4 percent of GDP if the market risk premium were 2 percent. Should the risk

policymakers are responsible for providing national defense, educating children, building and maintaining transportation systems, and aiding the sick and poor. They need resources to pay for these services. Thus, funding needs create a natural conflict between monetary and fiscal policymakers. Central bankers, in their effort to stabilize prices and provide the foundation for high sustainable growth, take a long-term view, imposing limits on how fast the quantity of money and credit can grow. In contrast, fiscal policymakers tend to ignore the long-term inflationary effects of their actions and look for ways to spend resources today at the expense of prosperity tomorrow. For better or worse, their time horizon often extends only until the next election. Some fiscal policymakers resort to actions intended to get around restrictions imposed by the central bank, eroding what is otherwise an effective and responsible monetary policy.

In the earliest days of central banks, a government that needed money would simply order the bank to print some. Of course, the result was inflation and occasionally hyperinflation. That is what led to the evolution of the independent central banks. Today the premium to jump to 7 percent, the primary surplus needed to prevent a debt explosion would climb to 8.4 percent of GDP.

A five-percentage-point jump in the market risk premium is large, but not without precedent. This is what happened in Italy several years ago. As doubts about the viability of the euro grew in the period from 2010 to 2012, the interest rate on Italian sovereign debt rose by about 1½ percentage points to 5½ percent, while the growth rate of nominal GDP plunged from roughly 2 percent to −1½ percent. (So [$i-g$] rose by five percentage points.) Any short-run attempt to tighten fiscal policy sufficiently to offset such a rise in the risk premium would mean a staggering six-percentage-point rise in the primary surplus ratio. Even attempting this would almost surely create a far deeper economic downturn, making the needed adjustment even larger.

Table 15.4 Primary Surplus as a Percent of GDP Required for Debt Sustainability

Risk Premium	Ratio of Debt to GDP (b)			
[i-g]	60%	90%	120%	150%
1%	0.6%	0.9%	1.2%	1.5%
2%	1.2%	1.8%	2.4%	3.0%
3%	1.8%	2.7%	3.6%	4.5%
4%	2.4%	3.6%	4.8%	6.0%
5%	3.0%	4.5%	6.0%	7.5%
6%	3.6%	5.4%	7.2%	9.0%
7%	4.2%	6.3%	8.4%	10.5%

NOTE: The number in each cell corresponds to the minimum primary surplus-to-GDP ratio sufficient to stabilize the debt-to-GDP ratio at each combination of the debt-to-GDP ratio (column) and market risk premium (row).

central bank's autonomy leaves fiscal policymakers with two options for financing government spending. They can take a share of income and wealth from the country's citizens through taxes, or they can borrow by issuing bonds in the financial markets.

Because no one likes taxes, and officials fear angering the electorate, politicians often turn to borrowing in order to finance some portion of their spending. But a country can issue only so much debt. Beyond some limit, future tax revenues will not cover the payments that are due to lenders. At that point, the only solution is to turn to the central bank for the means to finance spending. As a technical matter, the government will "sell" new bonds directly to the central bank—bonds that no one else wants to buy. This process, often referred to as "monetizing the debt," eventually leads to inflation. In fact, if officials can't raise taxes and are having trouble borrowing, inflation is the only way out.

While central bankers hate it, inflation is a real temptation to shortsighted fiscal policymakers. It is a way to get resources in their hands. The mechanism is straightforward.

The government forces the central bank to buy its bonds and then uses the proceeds to finance spending. But doing so increases the quantity of money in circulation, sparking inflation. The rise in inflation may ultimately do great damage to the country's well-being, but it also benefits fiscal policymakers: It reduces the value of the bonds the government has already sold, making them easier to repay. Inflation is a way for governments to default on a portion of the debt they owe.

U.S. fiscal and monetary policies to combat the crisis of 2007–2009 led many observers to worry both about future inflation risks and about renewed financial instability. On the fiscal side, in 2009, the federal government's deficit neared 10 percent of GDP for the first time since World War II. On the monetary policy side, the Federal Reserve lowered the policy interest rate close to zero and accumulated assets at an unprecedented pace as it sought to prevent a meltdown of the financial system.

U.S. policymakers understood that both these policies eventually must be reversed to prevent a large future inflation. A failure to reverse them eventually would undermine investor confidence in U.S. Treasuries. By 2016, the federal deficit was running below 3 percent of GDP, the Fed had begun to normalize its policy interest rate, and it planned to shrink its balance sheet once that normalization was well advanced. Partly as a result, long-term Treasury yields set record lows amid low inflation expectations.

While many politicians do act in their countries' long-term interests, there are plenty of examples of poor fiscal policymaking. In early 2002, Argentina's economy collapsed when banks refused to honor their depositors' withdrawal requests. Unemployment skyrocketed, output plummeted, and the president was forced to resign. The full story is complicated, but we can understand one aspect of it without much trouble. During 2001, Argentina's provincial governments (the equivalent of the state governments in the United States) began to experience significant budget problems. Their response was to start paying their employees with government bonds. But unlike the bonds we normally see, these were in small denominations—1, 2, 5, 10, 20 pesos, and so on. Not surprisingly, these small-denomination bonds were immediately used as means of payment, becoming money in effect. By mid-2002, this new form of money accounted for roughly 40 percent of the currency circulating in Argentina and the Central Bank of Argentina lost control over the amount of money circulating in the economy.

So, we see that the actions of fiscal policymakers can subvert the best efforts of central bankers. If the government can shut down the banking system and issue its own money, then the central bank's independence is irrelevant. The Federal Reserve, the European Central Bank, the Bank of Japan, and the other central banks around the world are independent only for as long as their governments let them be. When faced with a fiscal crisis, politicians often look for the easiest way out. If that way is inflating the value of the currency today, they will worry about the consequences tomorrow.

This brings us back to the criteria for inclusion in the European Monetary Union. The founders of the system wanted to ensure that participating governments kept their fiscal houses in order so that none of them would be tempted to pressure the European Central Bank to create inflation and bail them out. Monetary policy can meet its objective of price stability only if the government lives within its budget and never forces the central bank to finance a fiscal deficit. In 2010, large fiscal deficits propelled government bond yields sharply higher in several euro-area countries and triggered a financing crisis in Greece, helping to weaken the euro. And, over the next two years, the crisis spread to Ireland, Portugal, Spain, and then Italy. In response, euro-area governments created a facility for lending to member states that face difficulty borrowing in markets. As a condition of borrowing, a government is required to restore fiscal discipline. As of this writing, the credibility and independence of the European Central Bank have kept euro-area inflation expectations low despite the region's fiscal problems.

Stepping back and looking at the problem more broadly, we can say that governments face the challenge of time consistency in setting fiscal policy, just as they do in making monetary and regulatory policy. The value of any debt depends on investors' belief that they will be paid back (see Chapter 6). For a government, the problem is that future fiscal authorities may have an incentive to renege on the promises their predecessors made. If lenders believe that future developments will compel default, the value of the debt will plunge today, regardless of how cautious the current government may be. If, as a result, today's government can no longer borrow, it may turn to the central bank for direct monetary finance.

Laws and other rules that constrain future governments—such as the constitutional commitments of many U.S. states to run balanced budgets or the mutual fiscal surveillance of the member countries of the euro area—address the time-consistency challenge by making today's fiscal promises more credible.

In the absence of fiscal credibility, rapid government debt accumulation can lead to higher inflation expectations even in the face of cautious monetary policy. Indeed, in a famous analysis, 2011 Nobel Prize winner Thomas Sargent and coauthor Neil Wallace show that an otherwise credible, anti-inflationary central bank cannot prevent high inflation if a government issues debt without end.[20] Put differently, to keep inflation low over the long run, (1) institutions must ensure the time consistency of both monetary *and* fiscal policy, and (2) fiscal policy must not dominate monetary policy.

In summary, responsible fiscal policy is essential to the success of monetary policy. Our discussions earlier in the chapter allowed us to conclude that there is no way for a poorly designed central bank to stabilize prices, output, the financial system, and interest and exchange rates, regardless of the government's behavior. To be successful, a central bank must be independent, accountable, and clear about its goals. It must also have a well-articulated communications strategy and a sound decision-making mechanism. We turn in Chapter 16 to a detailed discussion of the structure of major central banks to see what makes them successful.

[20]Thomas Sargent and Neil Wallace, "Some Unpleasant Monetarist Arithmetic," Federal Reserve Bank of Minneapolis *Quarterly Review,* Fall 1981.

Key Terms

accountability, 408
central bank, 393
central bank independence, 406
credibility, 410
financial system stability, 403
fiscal policy, 397
goal independence, 408
hyperinflation, 401
instrument independence, 408
monetary policy, 395
monetary policy framework, 409
potential output, 401
price stability, 400
public goods, 398
sustainable growth, 401
time consistency, 399
transparency, 408

Using FRED: Codes for Data in This Chapter

Data Series	FRED Data Code
U.S. potential GDP	GDPPOT
U.S. real GDP	GDPC1
U.S. 10-year Treasury constant maturity rate	GS10
U.S. 10-year Treasury inflation-indexed yield	FII10
U.S. consumer price index	CPIAUCSL
U.S. consumer price index (less food and energy)	CPILFESL
Personal consumption expenditures price index	PCEPI
Personal consumption expenditures price index (less food and energy)	PCEPILFE
Euro area harmonized index of consumer prices	CP0000EZ19M086NEST
Euro area harmonized index of consumer prices (less unprocessed food and energy)	00XFUNEZ19M086NEST
Consumer price index less food and energy for New Zealand	CPGRLE01NZQ659N
Central bank assets for the euro area	ECBASSETS
Euro area nominal GDP	EUNNGDP
Effective federal funds rate	FEDFUNDS
Gross federal debt	FYGFD
Federal debt held by Federal Reserve Banks	FDHBFRBN

To learn more about the changing financial system, visit www.moneyandbanking.com.

Chapter Lessons

1. The functions of a modern central bank are to:
   a. Adjust interest rates and other tools to control the quantity of money and credit in the economy.
   b. Operate a payments system.
   c. Lend to sound banks during times of stress.
   d. Oversee the financial system.
2. The objective of a central bank is to reduce systematic risk in the economic and financial system. Specific objectives include:
   a. Low and stable inflation.
   b. High and stable growth and employment.
   c. Stable financial markets and institutions.
   d. Stable interest rates.
   e. Stable exchange rates.

   Because these objectives often conflict, policymakers must have clear priorities.
3. The best central banks:
   a. Are independent of political pressure.
   b. Are accountable to elected representatives and the public.
   c. Communicate their objectives, actions, and policy deliberations clearly to the public.

d. Articulate clearly how they will act when their goals conflict.
e. Are credible in their efforts to meet their objectives.
f. Make decisions by committee rather than by an individual.

4. Fiscal policy can make the central bank's job impossible because:
   a. Politicians tend to take a short-term view, encouraging doubt about the commitment to price stability or financial stability.
   b. In some cases, politicians are predisposed toward financing techniques that will create inflation.
   c. Inflation provides immediate revenue and reduces the value of the government's outstanding debt.
   d. Responsible fiscal policy is a precondition for successful monetary policy.
   e. Central banks remain independent at the pleasure of politicians.

Conceptual and Analytical Problems

1. In 1900, there were 18 central banks in the world; today, there are about 180. Why does nearly every country in the world now have a central bank? *(LO1)*
2. The power of a central bank is based on its monopoly over the issuance of currency. Economics teaches us that monopolies are bad and competition is good. Would competition among several central banks be better? Provide arguments both for and against. *(LO1)*
3. Explain the costs of each of the following conditions and explain who bears them. *(LO2)*
   a. Interest rate instability
   b. Exchange rate instability
   c. Inflation
   d. Unstable growth
4. Provide arguments for and against the proposition that a central bank should be allowed to set its own objectives. *(LO2, LO3)*
5. A euro-area country that runs very large public deficits or shows a persistently high and rising debt-to-GDP ratio violates the provisions of a 2012 treaty aimed at promoting fiscal stability. Explain how such fiscal violations pose a challenge for the ECB in the form of moral hazard. *(LO4)*
6. How does the time consistency problem apply to the conduct of monetary policy? How might long terms of office for central bankers help overcome it? *(LO4)*
7. What problems does a central bank face in a country with inefficient methods of tax collection? *(LO4)*
8. The Maastricht Treaty, which established the European Central Bank, states that the governments of the countries in the euro area must not seek to influence the members of the central bank's decision-making bodies. Why is freedom from political influence crucial to the ECB's ability to maintain price stability? *(LO3)*
9. Transparency is a key element of the monetary policy framework. *(LO3)*
   a. Explain how transparency helps eliminate the problems that are created by central bank independence.
   b. In what ways did the financial crisis of 2007–2009 emphasize the importance of central bank transparency?

c. Since 1993, the Bank of England has published a quarterly *Inflation Report.* Find a copy of the report on the bank's website, www.bankofengland.co.uk. Describe its contents and explain why the bank might publish such a document.

10.* While central bank transparency is widely accepted as desirable, too much openness may have disadvantages. Discuss what some of these drawbacks might be. *(LO3)*

11. Which do you think would be more harmful to the economy—an inflation rate that averages 5 percent a year and has a high standard deviation or an inflation rate of 7 percent that has a standard deviation close to zero? *(LO2)*

12. Suppose the central bank in your country has price stability as its primary goal. Faced with a choice of having monetary policy decisions made by a well-qualified individual with an extremely strong dislike of inflation or a committee of equally well-qualified people with a wide range of views, which choice would you recommend? *(LO3)*

13. Suppose the president of a newly independent country asks you for advice in designing the country's new central bank. For each of the following design features, choose which one you would recommend and briefly explain your choice. *(LO3)*
    a. Central bank policy decisions that are irreversible or central bank policy decisions that can be overturned by the democratically elected government.
    b. The central bank has to submit a proposal for funding to the government each year or the central bank finances itself from the earnings on its assets and turns the balance over to the government.
    c. The central bank policymakers are appointed for periods of four years to coincide with the electoral cycle for the government or the central bank policymakers are appointed for 14-year terms.

14. "A central bank should remain vague about the relative importance it places on its various objectives. That way, it has the freedom to choose which objective to follow at any point in time." Assess this statement in light of what you know about good central bank design. *(LO3)*

15.* The long list of central bank goals includes the stability of interest rates and exchange rates. You look on the central bank website and note that the bank has increased interest rates at every one of its meetings over the last year. You read the financial press and see references to how the exchange rate has moved in response to these interest rate changes. How could you reconcile this behavior with the central bank pursuing its objectives? *(LO2)*

16. While there is strong consensus among economists in favor of central bank independence, political support seems to be waning. What factors may have contributed to the rise in the political threat to the Federal Reserve's independence? What economic consequences might ensue? *(LO3)*

17. Suppose in an election year the economy started to slow down. At the same time, clear signs of inflationary pressures were apparent. How might the central bank with a primary goal of price stability react? How might members of the incumbent political party who are up for reelection react? *(LO2)*

18. Assuming that they could, which of the following governments do you think would be more likely to pursue policies that would seriously

*Indicates more difficult problems.

hinder the central bank's pursuit of low and stable inflation? Explain your choice. *(LO4)*

a. A government that is considered highly creditworthy both at home and abroad in a politically stable country with a well-developed tax system, or
b. A government of a politically unstable country that is heavily indebted and considered an undesirable borrower in international markets.

19.* Suppose the government is heavily in debt. Why might it be tempting for the fiscal policymakers to sell additional bonds to the central bank in a move that it knows would be inflationary? *(LO4)*

20. In 2012, the Federal Reserve joined many other central banks by making explicit a numerical target for inflation. Explain how stating that an annual inflation rate of 2 percent over the long run is most consistent with its mandate can help the Federal Reserve fulfill that mandate? *(LO2, LO3)*

21. Consider the following data for Country A and Country B:

	Country A	Country B
Primary Budget Surplus/GDP	2.8%	1.5%
Sovereign Debt/GDP	90%	60%
Nominal GDP Growth Rate	2%	4%
Nominal Interest Rate on Debt	5%	7%

Use these data to show that the ratio of public debt to GDP is expected to stabilize in Country A but not in Country B. How might this impact monetary policy in Country B? *(LO4)*

Data Exploration Mc Graw Hill connect

For general information on using Federal Reserve Economic Data (FRED) online, visit www.mhhe.com/moneyandbanking6e *and refer to the FRED Resources.*

1. New Zealand in the 1970s and 1980s combined high inflation with relatively little central bank independence. In 1989, New Zealand became the first country to adopt an inflation target. How did this policy regime shift affect inflation? Plot the inflation rate based on New Zealand's "core" consumer price index (FRED code: CPGRLE01NZQ659N) beginning in 1970. Was inflation after 1990 lower and more stable than before? Download the data and compute the average and the standard deviation of inflation for (a) the period through 1989 and (b) the period from 1990 to the present. *(LO1)*

2. Financial stability is a goal of most central banks. To see this, plot the European Central Bank's assets (FRED code: ECBASSETS) as a percent of nominal GDP (FRED code: EUNNGDP). (Note: to match units, divide the ratio by 4.) Based on this chart, how important was the goal of financial stability for the ECB (a) before 2007, (b) during the crisis period of 2007–2009, (c) when the euro-area crisis intensified in 2011–2012, and (d) in the period following 2013 as the euro-area crisis subsided? *(LO2)*

*Indicates more difficult problems.

3. Interest rate stability is a common goal of central banks. When has the Federal Reserve been relatively successful at keeping interest rates stable? Compare quarterly *changes* since 1965 of the federal funds rate (FRED code: FEDFUNDS) with the *level* of inflation based on the percentage change from year-ago levels of the consumer price index (FRED code: CPIAUCSL). Are stable interest rates associated with high or low inflation? Why? *(LO2)*
4. To what extent has the Federal Reserve "monetized" government debt? Plot since 1970 the change from a year ago (measured in billions of dollars) in gross federal debt (FRED code: FYGFD) and the change from a year ago (measured in billions of dollars) in the federal debt held by the Federal Reserve System (FRED code: FDHBFRBN). *(LO4)*

Chapter

16 The Structure of Central Banks: The Federal Reserve and the European Central Bank

Learning Objectives

After reading this chapter, you should be able to:

LO1 Explain the structure of the Federal Reserve System.

LO2 Assess the effectiveness of the Federal Reserve System.

LO3 Describe the European Central Bank and analyze the euro-area crisis.

The instability and chaos that accompany financial panics damage more than just the banks that are directly involved. Fear of losing one's savings is a great disincentive to making deposits in banks, and making fewer deposits means smaller banks and fewer loans. Everyone is slow to regain confidence in the financial system after a panic, making it hard for anyone to get financing. New businesses can't get the resources they need to get started; established companies can't find the financing they need to expand. The more frequent the panics, the worse the situation gets, and the slower the economy grows.

That description sounds like the world after the financial crisis of 2007–2009. But it describes even more aptly the financial flaws of the United States during the late 19th and early 20th centuries. Between 1870 and 1907, the nation experienced 21 financial panics of varying severity. In the mostly agrarian economy of the time, a typical crisis began with either a crop failure that left farmers with nothing to sell or a bumper crop that drove prices down below costs. Either way, farmers defaulted on their loans. The losses damaged the balance sheets of rural banks, leading them to withdraw funds from larger banks in New York or Chicago, where they held deposits. If the rural banks' withdrawals were large enough, the urban banks would be forced to call in their own loans or to refuse renewal of loans that were coming due. As word of the financial difficulties spread, other banks would become concerned and begin to call in their loans as well. Finally, when average people (small depositors) heard of the problem, they would flock to their local banks, demanding to receive their balances in the form of currency or gold.[1]

Unless confidence in the system was restored quickly, such runs left bankers with no choice but to close their doors. During the Panic of 1907, an astonishing two-thirds of banks found themselves temporarily unable to redeem deposits in cash. The situation

[1]The process could also go the other way, from the big banks to the small ones. A large loan default in New York, for example, would force the large city bank to try to acquire reserves from the small country banks. The small banks would then be forced to start calling in loans, and the process would go on from there.

led one prominent German banker to observe that the U.S. banking system was at the same point in the early 1900s that Europe's had been in the 1400s. In the intervening centuries, Europeans had developed a system of central banks; Americans hadn't.

The prevailing philosophy of many 19th-century Americans was that centralized government of any form should be kept to a minimum. But the punishing effects of frequent financial panics led people to reconsider the merits of a powerful central bank. In 1913, Congress passed the Federal Reserve Act, which created the U.S. Federal Reserve System. As the central bank's knowledge of how policy mechanisms worked grew, its governance improved. By the 1990s, the Fed was widely recognized as a key promoter of low inflation and maximum sustainable growth.

While central banking had stabilized European financial systems before 1900, the 20th century was another story. In that century, Europe experienced high inflation rates, low growth, high and volatile interest rates, and unstable exchange rates. After two world wars, governments' free spending led to unrelenting fiscal deficits. When European economies stagnated in the 1970s and 1980s, a consensus built that inflation was a key problem and poor monetary policy was to blame. Leaders came to believe that the only way to ensure both political and economic stability was to forge closer ties among the continent's countries. They decided the best solution was a common currency and a single central bank. The result was the *European Economic and Monetary Union (EMU)* with its common currency, the euro, and its central bank, the *European Central Bank (ECB)*.

Jerome H. Powell, 16th chair of the Board of Governors of the Federal Reserve System, congratulated by Janet Yellen, 15th chair.

SOURCE: Board of Governors of the Federal Reserve System.

Europe's monetary union—born in 1999—was the natural outgrowth of a decades-long process that established the free movement of goods, services, and capital throughout the continent of more than 500 million people. Like the Fed, the ECB is based on principles that support the goal of price stability (principles we learned about in Chapter 15). We turn now to an examination of these two central banks to see how their structure helps them meet their objectives.

The Structure of the Federal Reserve System

The Federal Reserve Act, passed in 1913 and amended numerous times since then, established what is now known as the **Federal Reserve System**. It is composed of three branches with overlapping responsibilities.[2] There are 12 regional *Federal Reserve Banks,* distributed throughout the country; a central governmental agency, called the *Board of Governors of the Federal Reserve System,* located in Washington, D.C.; and the *Federal Open Market Committee (FOMC)*. In addition, a series of advisory committees make recommendations to the board and the Federal Reserve Banks. Finally, there are the private banks that are members of the system. This complex structure diffuses power in a way that is typical of the U.S. government, creating a system of checks and balances that reduces the tendency for power to concentrate at the center.

[2]The Dodd-Frank Act of 2010, discussed in Chapter 14, was the most recent source of extensive changes in the Federal Reserve Act. It curtailed the Fed's authority as a lender of last resort but made it the supervisor of systemically important financial institutions (SIFIs).

All national banks (those chartered by the federal government) are required to belong to the Federal Reserve System. State banks that receive their charters from individual state banking authorities have the option of joining, but most do not. The original reason was cost. Prior to a change in the law in 1980, member banks were required to hold noninterest-bearing reserve deposits at the Fed, while nonmember banks could hold reserves in interest-bearing securities, such as U.S. Treasury bills. Today, members and nonmembers alike must hold reserve deposits at the Fed on which the Fed pays interest, so there is no real distinction between them.

The Federal Reserve Banks

In the heart of Wall Street, two blocks from the Freedom Tower that replaced the twin World Trade Center towers, sits a large, fortresslike building that is the home of the Federal Reserve Bank of New York. Deep in the fourth subbasement is the largest gold vault in the world, stocked with many more bars than are in Fort Knox. All of this gold belongs to foreign countries and international organizations like the International Monetary Fund. It is stored there for free. You can take a tour to see the gold vault if you call ahead, but you won't get into the rest of the building without an invitation. When the bank was built, one of the vaults held cash, but today that vault is filled with excess furniture. Cash is stored across the Hudson River in New Jersey, in a three-story vault the size of a football field. People rarely enter the vault, and there are no tours—just thick walls, fences, security cameras, and armed guards. (The cash is stored on pallets of about 160 shrink-wrapped blocks of 4,000 notes each. It is moved around entirely by small robotic forklifts.)

The gold vault at the Federal Reserve Bank of New York contains about one-fifth of official gold reserves in the world: more than 180 million troy ounces worth over $200 billion at early-2019 prices. A single gold bar weighs 400 ounces and is worth more than $500,000.

Stockbyte Silver/Alamy Stock Photo

The Federal Reserve Bank of New York is the largest of the 12 **Federal Reserve Banks**, accounting for about one-fifth of all Reserve Bank employment. The Reserve Banks, together with their branches, constitute the operational arm of the Federal Reserve System; and with more than 22,000 employees as of 2018, they account for the bulk of Reserve System employment. (All 12 have cash vaults, but only New York has gold.) Figure 16.1 shows the location of the banks and the region or "district" each one serves. From a modern vantage point, this map looks very odd. Why is nearly one-third of the continental United States served by a single bank in San Francisco while the Philadelphia district is so small? And why are two of the 12 banks in Missouri?

One explanation is that the lines were drawn in 1914, so they represent the population density at the time. Then there was politics. Senator Carter Glass, one of the authors of the Federal Reserve Act, was from Richmond, Virginia, the headquarters of the fifth district; Speaker of the House Champ Clark came from Missouri, the state with two Reserve Banks. But more important, politicians decided that no district should coincide with a single state. The Federal Reserve Bank of New York, for example, serves all of New York State as well as northern New Jersey (where the cash vault is), a small slice of southwestern Connecticut, Puerto Rico, and the Virgin Islands. The purpose of this arrangement is twofold: to ensure that every district contains as broad a mixture of economic interests as possible and that no person or group can obtain preferential treatment from the Reserve Bank.

Reserve Banks are strange creations, part public and part private. They are federally chartered banks and private, nonprofit organizations, owned by the commercial banks in their districts. As such, they are overseen by both their own boards of directors and the Board of Governors, an arm of the federal government. The method for choosing

Figure 16.1 The Federal Reserve System

The 12 Federal Reserve Banks and Their Districts

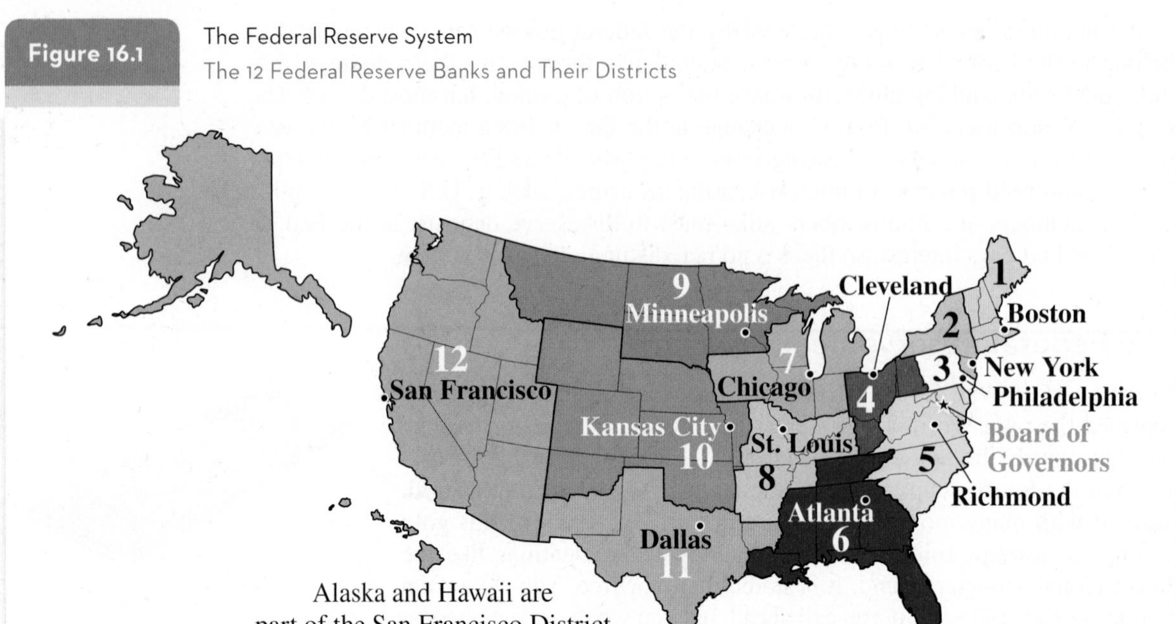

the nine members of each Reserve Bank's board of directors ensures the inclusion of not only bankers but other business leaders and people who represent the public interest. Six directors are elected by the commercial bank members of the Reserve Bank (three directors representing commercial banks and three representing the public), and the remaining three directors (also representing the public) are appointed by the Board of Governors. Though the range of views represented is wide, everyone has an interest in ensuring economic and financial stability.

Each Reserve Bank has a president, one of whose key responsibilities, as we will discuss later, is to sit periodically as a voting member of the Federal Open Market Committee. Subject to the approval of the Board of Governors, the president is selected for a five-year term by the six members of the bank's board of directors who represent the public.[3] (All 12 presidents' terms run concurrently, starting and ending at exactly the same time.) Reserve Bank presidents tend to come from one of three groups. Some have worked their way up inside the Federal Reserve System and are experts on the business of the district banks. Others are academic economists who have studied the financial system. Then there are former bankers, people who were once customers of the Federal Reserve. Because the presidents work together, the fact that they come from diverse backgrounds means that collectively they have the experience to manage the wide-ranging responsibilities of the Federal Reserve Banks.

The Reserve Banks conduct the day-to-day business of the central bank, serving as both the government's bank and the bankers' bank. Here is a brief list of the functions they perform:

1. As the bank for the U.S. government, they
   a. Issue new currency (Federal Reserve notes) and destroy old, worn currency.

[3]All nine directors used to appoint the Reserve Bank president, but the bailouts during the crisis of 2007–2009 fed the perception that the Federal Reserve System was too sympathetic to the financial institutions they regulate. In reaction, the Dodd-Frank Act of 2010 excluded the three commercial bank representatives on the Reserve Bank board from the process of selecting the president.

   b. Maintain the U.S. Treasury's bank account and process electronic payments.
   c. Manage the U.S. Treasury's borrowings. That means issuing, transferring, and redeeming U.S. Treasury bonds, notes, and bills. But like you and your bank, the Treasury decides what it wants, and the Federal Reserve Banks just do it.
2. As the bankers' bank, they
   a. Hold deposits for the banks in their districts.
   b. Operate and ensure the integrity of a payments network for transferring funds.
   c. Make funds available to commercial banks within the district through *discount loans* on which they charge interest at the *discount rate.*
   d. Supervise and regulate financial institutions in the district to ensure their safety and soundness, as well as evaluate proposed bank mergers and new operations.
   e. Collect and make available data on business conditions.

In addition to these duties, the Federal Reserve Bank of New York provides services to foreign central banks and to certain international organizations that hold accounts there. The Federal Reserve Bank of New York is also the system's point of contact with financial markets. It is where Treasury securities are auctioned, foreign currency is bought and sold, and the Federal Reserve's own portfolio is managed through what are called *open market operations.* In the financial crisis of 2007–2009, the Federal Reserve Bank of New York also operated a variety of special new *liquidity and credit facilities* that supplied funds to intermediaries and allowed the Fed to acquire a portfolio of non-Treasury assets, ranging from commercial paper to mortgage-backed securities (see Chapter 18 Tools of the Trade).

Finally, the Reserve Banks play an important part in formulating monetary policy. They do it primarily through their representation on the Federal Open Market Committee (FOMC), which makes interest rate decisions and determines the size and composition of the Fed's balance sheet, and less importantly through their participation in setting the **discount rate**, the interest rate charged on loans to commercial banks. The Federal Reserve Act specifies that the discount rate is to be set by each of the Reserve Bank's board of directors, with the approval of the Board of Governors, and strictly speaking, it is. But the directors have virtually no say over the discount rate, because it is set in practice at a premium above the interest rate on excess reserves (IOER rate, see Chapter 18) that the FOMC controls. Once the FOMC makes its decision, there is nothing left for anyone else to do.[4] That's why in Figure 16.2 detailing the complex structure of the Federal Reserve System a solid line labeled "Controls" runs from the FOMC to the discount rate. (We will learn more about this topic in Chapter 18.)

The Board of Governors

The headquarters of the Federal Reserve System sits at the corner of 20th Street and Constitution Avenue in northwest Washington, D.C., a short walk from the White House in one direction and the State Department in the other. The seven members of the Board, who are called governors, are appointed by the president and confirmed by the U.S. Senate for 14-year terms. The long terms are intended to protect the Board from political pressure. The fact that the terms are staggered—one beginning every two years—limits any individual president's influence over the membership. The

[4]The only exception so far was during the financial crisis of 2007–2009, when the governors reduced the spread of the discount rate above the federal funds rate to encourage borrowing.

Figure 16.2 The Structure and Policy Organization of the Federal Reserve System

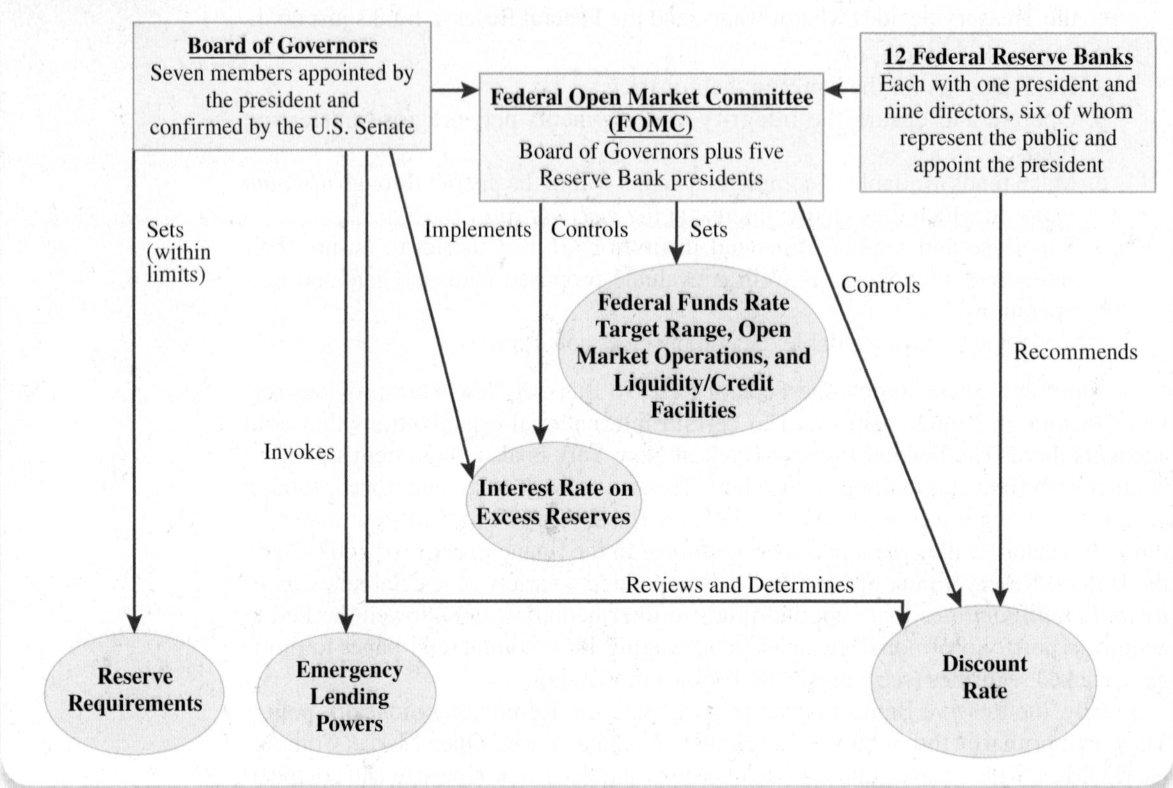

Board has a chairperson and two vice chairs, appointed by the president from among the seven governors for four-year renewable terms.[5] The Board's membership usually includes academic economists, bank regulators, and bankers. To ensure adequate regional representation on the Board, no two governors can come from the same Federal Reserve district. The Federal Reserve Act explicitly requires "a fair representation of the financial, agricultural, industrial, and commercial interests."

Together with a staff of more than 2,800, the **Board of Governors of the Federal Reserve System** performs the following duties:

- Sets the reserve requirement, which determines the level of reserves banks are required to hold.
- Approves or disapproves discount rate recommendations made by the Federal Reserve Banks.
- Approves changes in the interest rate paid on excess reserves (IOER rate, see Chapter 18) consistent with changes in the range for the target federal funds rate set by the Federal Open Market Committee (FOMC).
- Acts as rule-writing agency for consumer credit protection laws (with enforcement by the Consumer Financial Protection Bureau).

[5]To elevate the Board's mandate for financial stability, the Dodd-Frank Act of 2010 created the new role of vice chair for supervision.

Central Bank Digital Currency
APPLYING THE CONCEPT

How will financial innovation alter the role of central banks? Over the past several decades, with the development of inflation targeting, central banks have delivered price stability. And, improved prudential policies are making the financial system more resilient. Will advances in *fintech*—ranging from the use of electronic platforms to algorithm-driven bots that disrupt the traditional provision and implementation of financial services—change any of this?

Some people suggest that central banks should help speed innovation by issuing *digital currency*.* A simple way to do this, one that satisfies the varied goals of advocates, would be for the central bank to offer universal, unlimited access to deposit accounts. Call it *universal central bank digital currency* (UCBDC).

Does it make sense for central banks to compete with commercial banks in providing deposit accounts? Probably not. At virtually every central bank today, only commercial banks have interest-bearing deposits. This is not an accident. Changing it would risk destabilizing the financial system.

To see why, recall the wide range of functions that commercial banks perform (see Chapter 11). A central bank that takes deposits from anyone who wants one may not provide all these services, but it will have to offer accounting, payments system access, liquidity, and the tracking of information. Consequently, the central bank will need to have compliance and risk management functions—including procedures that prevent money laundering, tax evasion, and other illegal activities potentially aided by finance. Private-sector experience suggests this will be expensive, costing 2 to 3 percent of the size of the assets annually.

Ironically, the key risks of UCBDC arise from the likely popularity of central bank accounts. Because they are inherently safer than those offered by their private competitors, we expect that direct deposits at the central bank will attract strong demand. How big might the reallocation out of private banks be if the Federal Reserve today were to offer demandable deposits without limit? While there is no sure way to know, the shift could be very large, and probably would accelerate in response to slight disturbances in the financial system. In other words, UCBDC will likely increase the risk of commercial bank runs.

It also would lead to profound political economy challenges. Competition from UCBDC will make it more difficult for private banks to fund the relatively illiquid loans that they make to households and firms. With a shortage of private loans, the central bank would face pressure to become a massive *state bank*. Even laws could change to allow the state bank to become the economy's primary supplier of credit. Indeed, it is not difficult to imagine pressure on the central bank to supply credit directly to a failing General Motors, Japan Airlines, Sears, or what have you. The result would be a government bank that not only controls money and interest rates, but directs credit as well.

The bottom line is that the introduction of UCBDC would profoundly alter the balance between the private and public provision of financial services. It probably would add to, rather than diminish, the risk of bank runs; and it would turn the central bank into the premier lender to broad swaths of the economy. Until there are ways to address these concerns, we remain skeptical about the universal and unlimited provision of central bank deposit accounts.

*See John Barrdear and Michael Kumhof, "The Macroeconomics of Central Bank Issued Digital Currencies," Bank of England Working Paper No. 605, July 2016.

- Approves bank merger applications.
- Supervises and regulates the Reserve Banks, including their budgets and their presidents' salaries.
- Along with the Reserve Banks, regulates and supervises the banking system, examining individual banks, nonbank systemically important financial institutions (SIFIs), and financial market utilities (FMUs) for safety and soundness and for compliance with the law.
- Invokes **emergency powers** to lend to nonbanks when circumstances are deemed "unusual and exigent." These powers provided the authority for much of the Fed's emergency lending in the crisis of 2007–2009 but were curtailed by the Dodd-Frank Act of 2010 (see Chapter 14, page 387).
- Analyzes financial and economic conditions, both domestic and international.
- Collects and publishes detailed statistics about the system's activities and the economy at large. As you have seen throughout this book, the Federal Reserve

Economic Database (FRED) provides a wide variety of information about the United States and other economies, including data collected directly by the Fed about the amount of money in the economy (M1 and M2), interest rates, exchange rates, the banking system's assets and liabilities, the level of production in U.S. industry, and the level of household wealth.

The seven governors do not have their own support staff. Instead, they request help and information from the directors of various departments, who assign individuals to specific tasks. The directors answer to the chair of the Board of Governors.

The Federal Open Market Committee

When most people think about the Federal Reserve, what comes to mind is not the payments system or bank supervision but interest rate setting. And when the business press discusses the Fed, its attention is really on the **Federal Open Market Committee (FOMC)**. This is the group that sets the key interest rates and adjusts the Fed's balance sheet to control the availability of money and credit to the economy. The FOMC has been around since 1936 and has 12 voting members. These are the seven governors, the president of the Federal Reserve Bank of New York, and a rotating selection of 4 of the remaining 11 Reserve Bank presidents. The chair of the Board of Governors chairs the FOMC as well, and the committee's vice chair is the president of the Federal Reserve Bank of New York. While only five of the 12 Reserve Bank presidents vote at any one time, all of them participate in the meeting.

The FOMC could control any interest rate, but the rate it chooses to control is the **federal funds rate**, the rate banks charge each other for unsecured overnight loans on their excess deposits at the Fed. We will discuss the details of this arrangement in the next two chapters. For now, keep in mind that the rate the FOMC controls is a nominal interest rate. However, because inflation expectations don't change quickly when a credible central bank aims at price stability, the FOMC in effect controls the *real* interest rate. (Recall that the real interest rate equals the nominal interest rate minus expected inflation.) The real interest rate plays a central role in economic decisions. The higher the real interest rate, the more expensive borrowing is, and the less likely a company is to build a new factory or an individual is to purchase a new car. Furthermore, the lower the level of purchases by firms and households, the lower the level of growth will be. So by controlling the federal funds rate, the FOMC influences real growth.

The Board Room at the Federal Reserve in Washington, D.C., with its oblong table. This is the meeting place of the Federal Open Market Committee and Board of Governors of the Federal Reserve System.

Dennis Brack/Black Star

The FOMC currently meets eight times a year, or roughly once every six weeks, in the Board Room at the Federal Reserve in Washington, D.C. During times of crisis, the committee can confer and change policy over the telephone. Because these "inter-meeting" policy shifts signal the financial markets that the FOMC believes conditions are dire, they are reserved for extraordinary times, like the aftermath of the terrorist attacks on the World Trade Center of September 2001. One measure of the financial crisis of 2007–2009 is that it prompted 12 unscheduled FOMC meetings, surpassing the cumulative total of recent decades!

FOMC meetings take place over a two-day period, starting one afternoon, and finishing the next day. In addition to the seven governors and 12 Reserve Bank presidents, numerous Board staff members attend, along with at least one senior staff member from each Reserve Bank. In all, between 50 and 60 people are there. The primary purpose of the meeting is to decide on the target range for the federal funds rate and, in response to the crisis of 2007–2009, on the scale and mix of assets to acquire. No less important, the FOMC agrees on how to communicate its policies to the public, including any **forward guidance** about likely future policy. The FOMC itself does not engage in the financial market transactions that are required to keep the market federal funds rate near this target or to manage the Fed's portfolio. That job falls to the system open market account (SOMA) manager, who, together with his or her staff, works for the Federal Reserve Bank of New York. The policy directive simply instructs the New York Fed's staff to buy and sell securities, or to adjust the IOER rate, so as to maintain the market federal funds rate in the target range or to assemble the desired asset mix.

To figure out who really controls these key policy decisions, we need to look closely at how the FOMC works, focusing on the information that is distributed in advance and the mechanics of the meeting. Two important documents are distributed to all attendees prior to each meeting: the *Beige Book* and the *Tealbook*. The Beige Book is a compilation of anecdotal information about current business activity, collected by the staffs of the Reserve Banks and published about two weeks before the meeting. This is the only FOMC document that is released to the public before the meeting. The Tealbook contains two parts: the Board staff's economic forecast for the next few years (until 2010, this part was called the *Greenbook*) and a discussion of financial markets and current policy options (formerly called the *Bluebook*). The Tealbook is distributed electronically during the week preceding the meeting. It is a confidential document and is not released to the public until five years after the meeting. On a quarterly basis, the governors and the Reserve Bank presidents also submit in advance of the meeting their own projections for economic growth, unemployment, inflation, and (since 2012) the timing and pace of future changes to the target range for the federal funds rate. The final versions of their projections are submitted on the second day of the FOMC meeting.

An FOMC meeting is a formal proceeding that includes staff reports and discussion comments by all of the meeting's participants (consisting of the 12 voting members and the remaining seven Reserve Bank presidents). The staff may respond to questions following their presentations, and there is some give-and-take among the meeting participants. One advantage of two-day meetings is that members also can engage each other informally—for example, over dinner on the first night. At 2 p.m. on the second day, shortly after the meeting adjourns, the committee releases a policy statement containing its decisions and a brief explanation of them. Around 2:30 p.m., the chair then holds a press conference to discuss the FOMC's assessment and policy plans. At a quarterly frequency, an update to the economic and target federal funds rate projections of the 19 FOMC participants is provided to the committee before its meeting; after those meetings, a summary of these projections is released simultaneously with the policy statement. Finally, three weeks after each meeting, the FOMC releases detailed minutes summarizing the deliberations on the Federal Reserve Board's public website, and providing information regarding the uncertainty and risks around the FOMC participants' projections.

To see where the committee's power lies and who controls interest rate and asset-mix decisions, notice a few things (see Table 16.1). First, and foremost, the chair is the voice of the Federal Reserve System. He or she speaks to Congress and the public on behalf of the FOMC. Second, note that the governors make up a majority of the

Table 16.1 A User's Guide to the Fed

The Federal Reserve System is complicated, so here is a list of the key players:

Chair of the Board of Governors	Most powerful person in the Federal Reserve System. Effectively controls FOMC meetings and monetary policy. Appointed by the U.S. president to a four-year term, subject to U.S. Senate confirmation; must be one of the governors. Also elected by the FOMC as its chair.
Other members of the Board of Governors	Supervise and regulate an important portion of the financial industry. All are voting members of the FOMC. Appointed by the president to 14-year terms, subject to U.S. Senate confirmation. The two vice chairs (of which one is designated for supervision) must be members of the Board of Governors.
President of the Federal Reserve Bank of New York	Runs the biggest and most important of the Reserve Banks, where monetary policy operations are carried out and much of the Fed's work for the Treasury is done. Also provides services to commercial banks in the district. As with the presidents of the other Reserve Banks, appointed by the nonbanking members of the bank's board of directors, with the approval of the Board of Governors, for a five-year term. Also vice chair of the FOMC.
Presidents of the 11 other Federal Reserve Banks	Provide services to commercial banks in their districts. All participate in every FOMC meeting and four serve one-year terms as voting members of the FOMC on a rotating basis.

The Board of Governors and each of the Reserve Banks maintain websites that publish data, economic research, speeches, and information about customer services. In addition, the FOMC maintains a list of its meeting times on the Board of Governors website, along with links to the committee's statements, minutes, transcripts, and economic projections, as well as the chair's press conferences. The place to start is www.federalreserve.gov.

committee, and they work together daily at the headquarters of the Federal Reserve in Washington, D.C. Third, aside from the quarterly projections of FOMC members, the most important information distributed to all committee members before a meeting is the Tealbook forecast and policy options. The Tealbook is prepared by the Federal Reserve Board staff, which is controlled by the chair. Fourth, the chair sets the agenda for the FOMC meeting, determines the order in which people speak, and proposes the FOMC policy statement (see Tools of the Trade on the next page). Finally, though the votes are made public immediately after the meeting, committee members observe a blackout period from a week preceding an FOMC meeting to a week following the meeting, during which they do not speak publicly about the economic outlook or current monetary policy. Dissenters, who are identified immediately in the press release that comes the afternoon of the meeting, usually wait a week to explain their views in public. And remember, the Board of Governors controls the Reserve Banks' budgets, as well as the salaries of their presidents.

Press reports, then, do give a good sense of where the FOMC's power lies. The chair of the Fed is the FOMC's most important member. So, if you want to know whether interest rates are likely to go up or down, or whether the Fed will alter the size and composition of its portfolio, that is the person you should listen to most closely. To have an impact on policy, governors or Reserve Bank presidents must build support for their positions through their statements at the meeting and in public speeches. While the chair is very powerful, the committee structure provides an important check on his or her power. Indeed, even two dissents on an FOMC vote are unusual, while three dissents—an outcome that has occurred only once since the 1980s—could raise doubts about the chair's leadership.

Decoding the FOMC Statement

TOOLS OF THE TRADE

As the financial crisis deepened in 2008, the range of FOMC policy actions broadened, and financial stability rose to the top of the Fed's agenda. Accordingly, the form of the **FOMC statement** released at the end of the FOMC's regularly scheduled meetings changed markedly. Nevertheless, some of the statement's familiar components remained:

- A clear statement of the committee's decision at the meeting regarding its target or target range for the federal funds rate (the interest rate that the FOMC controls).
- A summary of the committee's view of economic conditions, especially the inflation outlook.
- A description of how the outlook is expected to influence *future* policy.
- A description of the policy tools, in addition to the federal funds rate, that the Fed will use to achieve its objectives (to understand these, you have to follow current events very closely).
- A report of the voting.

Consider, for example, the following FOMC statement of December 18, 2018, announcing the eighth interest rate increase since December 2015:

> *Information received since the Federal Open Market Committee met in November indicates that the labor market has continued to strengthen and that economic activity has been rising at a strong rate. Job gains have been strong, on average, in recent months, and the unemployment rate has remained low. Household spending has continued to grow strongly, while growth of business fixed investment has moderated from its rapid pace earlier in the year. On a 12-month basis, both overall inflation and inflation for items other than food and energy remain near 2 percent. Indicators of longer-term inflation expectations are little changed, on balance.*
>
> *Consistent with its statutory mandate, the Committee seeks to foster maximum employment and price stability. The Committee judges that some further gradual increases in the target range for the federal funds rate will be consistent with sustained expansion of economic activity, strong labor market conditions, and inflation near the Committee's symmetric 2 percent objective over the medium term. The Committee judges that risks to the economic outlook are roughly balanced, but will continue to monitor global economic and financial developments and assess their implications for the economic outlook.*
>
> *In view of realized and expected labor market conditions and inflation, the Committee decided to raise the target range for the federal funds rate to 2¼ to 2½ percent.*
>
> *In determining the timing and size of future adjustments to the target range for the federal funds rate, the Committee will assess realized and expected economic conditions relative to its maximum employment objective and its symmetric 2 percent inflation objective. This assessment will take into account a wide range of information, including measures of labor market conditions, indicators of inflation pressures and inflation expectations, and readings on financial and international developments.*
>
> *Voting for the FOMC monetary policy action were: Jerome H. Powell, Chairman; John C. Williams, Vice Chairman; Thomas I. Barkin; Raphael W. Bostic; Michelle W. Bowman; Lael Brainard; Richard H. Clarida; Mary C. Daly; Loretta J. Mester; and Randal K. Quarles.*
>
> NOTE: At the time of this meeting, two positions were vacant, so there were only five governors. That left only 10 voters, who voted unanimously.

Interpreting these statements takes some practice. A summary of this one might go like this: "With inflation near the Fed's medium-term objective against a background of solid economic growth and a tight labor market, interest rates are likely to rise again during the course of the next year. But, uncertainty about a number of things means that the timing and scale of future policy moves will depend on a range of economic data as well as on the evolution of financial conditions." As it turned out, the next Fed interest rate policy change—in July 2019—was a rate cut that reversed the December 2018 hike!

By going to the FOMC's website at www.federalreserve.gov/fomc, you can look at recent statements and see how they have been changing. What do you think the Fed will do next?

Assessing the Federal Reserve System's Structure

In the previous chapter, we developed a checklist for assessing a central bank's structure. We said that an effective central bank is one in which policymakers are largely independent of political influence, make decisions by committee, are accountable and transparent, and state their objectives clearly. Let's evaluate the Federal Reserve System using these criteria.

Independence from Political Influence

We set out three criteria for judging a central bank's independence: budgetary independence, irreversible decisions, and long terms in office. The Fed meets each of these. It controls its own budget. The Fed's substantial revenue is a combination of interest on the government securities it holds and fees charged to banks for payments system services, including check clearing, electronic funds transfers, and the like. In fact, the Fed's income is so large that, in a typical year, 95 percent of it is returned to the U.S. Treasury.[6] Interest rate changes are implemented immediately and can be changed only by the FOMC—no one else can reverse or change them. The terms of the governors are 14 years; the chair's term runs for four years; and the Reserve Bank presidents serve for five years (and they aren't even appointed by politicians).

Even though the structural elements required to maintain an independent monetary policy are in place, the Fed occasionally comes under political attack. As we have said, raising interest rates is never popular. In 2009, public outrage over the financial crisis and the bailouts of large intermediaries made the Fed a political target, posing the biggest threat to its independence in many years. Ultimately, the Dodd-Frank Act of 2010 curtailed the Fed's emergency lending powers and required new disclosures of Fed transactions, but it also widened Fed supervisory responsibility (see Chapter 14). The greatest threat to Federal Reserve independence in recent decades surfaced in 2018, when President Donald Trump began to criticize aggressively Fed rate hikes and his appointed chair of the Federal Reserve Board, Jerome Powell (see Chapter 15, Applying the Concept: The Threat to Fed Independence).

Decision Making by Committee

The Fed clearly makes decisions by committee, because the FOMC *is* a committee. While the chair of the Board of Governors may dominate policy decisions, the fact that there are 12 voting members provides an important safeguard against arbitrary action by a single individual. In the Federal Reserve, no one person can become a dictator.

Accountability and Transparency

INFORMATION

The FOMC releases huge amounts of information to the public. Prior to each meeting, the committee publishes the Beige Book and makes it publicly available. Within a couple of hours of the meeting's adjournment, the committee releases and posts on its website a brief policy statement giving its decisions and its reasoning, while the chair holds a press conference to explain the FOMC's assessment and actions (At quarterly intervals, committee members' economic and target federal funds rate projections are released at the same time as the policy statement.) Then, three weeks later, the committee publishes a detailed summary of the meeting—the minutes—that also states how each member voted and gives the reasons for any dissenting votes. And after a five-year waiting period, the FOMC publishes the word-for-word transcript of the meeting along with the Tealbook and other staff presentations.

[6]In 2017, the Federal Reserve transferred $80.2 billion to the Treasury. This is the difference between the $113.6 billion in interest income on a roughly $4 trillion securities portfolio and the sum of $29.3 billion in interest expense and $4.1 billion in operating expense.

The Evolution of Federal Reserve Independence
APPLYING THE CONCEPT

Like most large bureaucracies, the Federal Reserve moves very slowly and deliberately. Nevertheless, there have been some defining moments when the Fed's structure changed suddenly and significantly. The first one came in 1935, after the economywide financial failures that led to the Great Depression of the 1930s. To remove monetary policy from the political arena, the Secretary of the Treasury and the Comptroller of the Currency, two political appointees who served at the pleasure of the president, were kicked off the Federal Reserve Board, and the FOMC was created.

But independence in name is not independence in fact. During World War II, the Federal Reserve became part of the war effort, which meant ensuring a cheap source of funds for the Treasury. The Fed worked to keep interest rates low by making sure that bond prices remained high. Importantly, when the Treasury went to issue securities, to keep prices high the Fed would buy what the public refused to purchase. Early in 1951, the Secretary of the Treasury, who was under pressure to finance the new Korean War, tried to force the Fed to purchase significant quantities of bonds directly from the Treasury. Faced with rising inflation, the FOMC had announced its desire to curtail credit growth by reducing the rate at which it purchased government debt. President Truman was forced to step in and resolve the standoff. On March 4, 1951, the president, the secretary of the Treasury, and the Federal Reserve chair reached an "accord" and issued a joint announcement establishing the FOMC's independence in setting interest rates and controlling the rate of monetary expansion.*

These two events provided the foundation for the Federal Reserve's independence in forming monetary policy. Of course, the FOMC's ability to do its job still depends on the willingness of politicians to refrain from interference. The President and the Secretary of the Treasury can make comments criticizing the FOMC's monetary policy decisions, and Congress does have the ability to revoke the Fed's independence. Following the financial crisis of 2007–2009, congressional criticism of the Fed became unusually intense, while proposals to limit Fed independence flourished. In contrast, the U.S. government proposed to expand the Fed's supervisory powers to help prevent another financial crisis.

*For a brief summary of this history, see Carl E. Walsh, "Federal Reserve Independence and the Accord of 1951," *Federal Reserve Bank of San Francisco Weekly Letter,* No. 93-21, May 28, 1993.

Added to these documents is the Federal Reserve Board's twice-yearly "Monetary Policy Report to the Congress," which provides great detail about the outlook and the considerations behind policy setting. This report is accompanied by the chair's appearance before Congress to discuss the state of the nation's economy. Similarly, the Board vice chair for supervision testifies twice annually regarding the state of the financial system. Members of the FOMC also give frequent public speeches, and occasionally they testify before Congress. In an average year, the chair gives 15 to 20 speeches, and other governors and Reserve Bank presidents speak 5 to 10 times each. All of these communications—the Beige Book, the statement, the press conference, the minutes, the transcripts, the biannual report, the testimony, and the speeches—can be found on various Fed websites.

This avalanche of information seems enough to give everyone a sense of what the FOMC is doing and why. But some things are still missing from the Fed's communications. For example, unlike some central banks, the FOMC does not agree on or publish a *consensus* economic or interest rate projection (the individual members' projections are summarized anonymously in a table). In addition, key inputs into the decision-making process—documents like the staff forecast and the policy options in the Tealbook—and the meeting transcript are not made public until five years after the fact. The Fed also delays the dissemination of information about the recipients of its loans because it does not want to trigger a run on a fragile—or even on a healthy—intermediary. On the other hand, as we will discuss in a moment, the Fed's 2012 shift to an inflation-targeting strategy helps focus Fed communications, making both the message and the policy more effective (see also Tools of the Trade).

Policy Framework

The U.S. Congress has set the Federal Reserve's objectives: "The Board of Governors of the Federal Reserve System and the Federal Open Market Committee shall maintain long run growth of the monetary and credit aggregates commensurate with the economy's long run potential to increase production, so as to promote effectively the goals of maximum employment, stable prices, and moderate long-term interest rates."

What should we make of this vague statement? Some people see ambiguity as advantageous. Because laws are difficult to change, they argue, we wouldn't want the Fed's objectives to be extremely specific; the imprecision of the language means the Fed has considerable leeway in setting its own goals. For most of its existence, the FOMC was unable or unwilling to tell us exactly how it interprets this broad mandate.

STABILITY

Today, however, the FOMC's approach is largely transparent, and (although Fed officials resist being labeled inflation-targeters) the strategy is consistent with the **inflation-targeting** framework that is now utilized by most leading central banks around the world. The strategic shift was enshrined in the FOMC's January 2012 special Statement on Longer-Run Goals and Monetary Policy Strategy, which the committee expects to reaffirm each year.[7] This FOMC consensus on longer-run strategy is likely to prove a key legacy of former Board chair Bernanke's leadership.

Most important, the FOMC statement quantifies the inflation goal over the longer term—namely, an annual rise of 2 percent in the price index for personal consumption expenditures. With each monthly release of that price index (which is somewhat different from the consumer price index reported monthly in the news media), observers can judge whether inflation is headed toward that objective. "In setting monetary policy," the statement said, "the Committee seeks to mitigate deviations of inflation from its longer-run goal and deviations of employment from the Committee's assessments of its maximum level."

Importantly, the FOMC does *not* set a specific standing goal for longer-run "normal" economic growth, for maximum employment, or for the "normal" level of unemployment because—unlike the longer-run inflation rate—the Fed does not control these outcomes. The FOMC's quarterly "Summary of Economic Projections" does, however, give the latest anonymous estimates of each of the 19 FOMC participants for longer-run unemployment, inflation, and output growth. Finally, the strategy specifies a "balanced approach" whenever the FOMC faces a tradeoff between its goals of minimizing deviations of inflation from the 2 percent target and deviations of employment from the FOMC's assessment of its maximum sustainable level. Put differently, the speeds at which the FOMC seeks to realize each of these two goals can differ when the goals conflict with each other.

The European Central Bank

As recently as 1998, Romans shopped with *lire,* Berliners with *deutsche marks,* and Parisians with *francs.* The Banca d'Italia, Italy's central bank, controlled the number of lire that circulated, while the Bundesbank managed the quantity of deutsche marks, and the Banque de France the volume of francs. But on January 1, 1999, the majority of

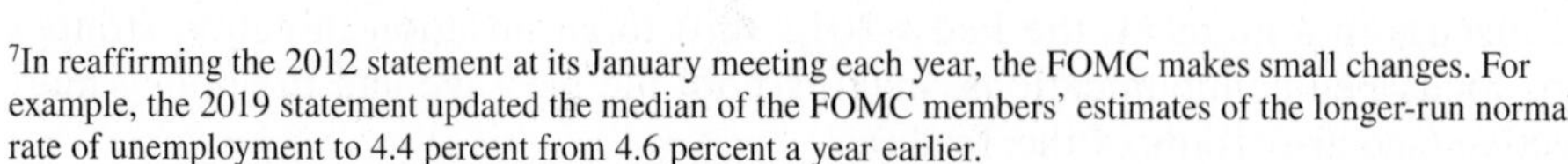
[7]In reaffirming the 2012 statement at its January meeting each year, the FOMC makes small changes. For example, the 2019 statement updated the median of the FOMC members' estimates of the longer-run normal rate of unemployment to 4.4 percent from 4.6 percent a year earlier.

Figure 16.3 The European System of Central Banks

Western European countries adopted a common currency. Today, residents of Rome, Berlin, and Paris all make their purchases in euros, and monetary policy is the job of the **European Central Bank (ECB)**. In the same way that a dollar bill is worth a dollar everywhere in the United States, a euro note is worth a euro everywhere in the **euro area**. By 2020, the euro had become the currency of 19 countries (see the map in Figure 16.3).[8]

The agreement to form a European monetary union was formalized in the Treaty of Maastricht, named for the Dutch city in which it was signed in 1992. The treaty initiated

[8] Despite the 2016 referendum to leave the European Union, the future status of the United Kingdom remained uncertain even as of August 2019.

a lengthy process that led ultimately to the creation of the **European System of Central Banks (ESCB)**, which is composed of the European Central Bank (ECB) in Frankfurt, Germany, and the national central banks (NCBs) in every country in the European Union. The ECB and the NCBs of the 19 countries that participate in the monetary union make up what is known as the **Eurosystem**, which shares a common currency and common monetary policy. As of August 2019, Denmark, Sweden, and the United Kingdom, as well as 6 of the 13 countries that joined the European Union since May 1, 2004, remained outside the Eurosystem and retained control over their monetary policy.

A myriad of names and abbreviations are associated with central banking in Europe. To avoid confusion, we will refer to the institution that is responsible for monetary policy in the euro area as the European Central Bank. Our goal is to understand its basic organizational structure.[9] As we examine the ECB, keep in mind that, in economic terms, Europe is larger, and the euro area is only a bit smaller, than the United States.

Organizational Structure

The Eurosystem mirrors the structure of the Federal Reserve System in several ways. There is the six-member **Executive Board of the ECB**, which is similar to the Board of Governors; the **national central banks NCBs)**, which play many of the same roles as the Federal Reserve Banks; and the **Governing Council**, which formulates monetary policy, just as the FOMC does.[10] The Executive Board has a President (Christine Lagarde of France) and a Vice President (Luis de Guindos of Spain) who play the same role as the leaders of the Federal Reserve's Board of Governors. ECB Executive Board members are appointed by a committee composed of the heads of state of the countries that participate in the monetary union (see Table 16.2).

The ECB and the NCBs together perform the traditional operational functions of a central bank, which we learned about in the last chapter. In addition to using interest rates to control the availability of money and credit in the economy, they are responsible for the smooth operation of the payments system and the issuance of currency. Together, they also serve as the lender of last resort. In 2014, under the newly implemented Single Supervisory Mechanism, the ECB became the euro area's leading bank supervisor. Like the Fed, it directly supervises the large systemic banks. While the details differ from country to country, the national central banks continue to serve as bankers to the banks and governments in their countries, just as the Federal Reserve Banks serve the banks in their districts and the U.S. government.

There are several important differences between the Fed and the ECB, however. Some exist by design and others as a result of the way the system came into being (see Table 16.3). First, the implementation of monetary policy—the ECB's day-to-day interaction with the financial markets—is accomplished at all the national central banks, rather than being centralized as it is in the United States. Second, the

[9] Three publications are helpful in understanding European monetary policy. The first chief economist of the ECB, Otmar Issing, who also served on the ECB Executive Board in its first eight years, explains the evolution of ECB policies in *The Birth of the Euro* (Cambridge, UK: Cambridge University Press, 2008). *The Monetary Policy of the ECB,* published by the ECB in 2011, provides a technical description of how things work. More recently, Philipp Hartmann and Frank Smets of the ECB reviewed "The First 20 Years of the European Central Bank: Monetary Policy," *Brookings Papers on Economic Activity*, September 2018.

[10] While the ECB may appear to be modeled after the Federal Reserve System, its structure is actually based on that of the Deutsche Bundesbank, the German central bank. Europeans uniformly viewed the Bundesbank as being successful in stabilizing the post–World War II German economy, so it was a natural model, but the real reason for the new structure was politics. The designers of the ECB had to find a way to create a common central bank that incorporated all of the existing national central banks. This meant adding a new central administration while retaining the NCBs, which already existed.

Table 16.2 Key Aspects of the European Central Bank

European Central Bank (ECB)	The central authority in Frankfurt, Germany, that oversees monetary policy in the common currency area. (Established July 1, 1998.)
National central banks (NCBs)	The central banks of the countries that belong to the European Union.
European System of Central Banks (ESCB)	The ECB plus the NCBs of all the countries in the European Union, including those that do not participate in the monetary union.
Eurosystem	The ECB plus the NCBs of euro-area countries; together, they carry out the tasks of central banking in the euro area.
ECB Executive Board	The six-member body in Frankfurt that oversees the operation of the ECB and the Eurosystem.
Governing Council	The (currently) 25-member committee that makes monetary policy in the common currency area.
Euro	The currency used in the countries of the European Monetary Union.
Euro area	The countries that use the euro as their currency.

ECB's budget is controlled by the national central banks, not the other way around. This arrangement means that the NCBs control the finances of the Executive Board and its headquarters in Frankfurt. Third, the ECB still supplies a large volume of reserves through collateralized lending to the banks, in addition to sales and purchases of securities.

Aside from its regulatory role, the focus of the ECB's activity is on the control of money and credit in the Eurosystem—that is, on monetary policy. The Governing Council, the equivalent of the Fed's FOMC, is composed of the six Executive Board members and the governors of the 19 central banks in the euro area. Meetings to consider monetary policy actions are held eight times a year. While decisions are made by formal votes of the Governing Council, the votes are not published. The rationale for not disclosing the votes is to ensure that Governing Council members focus on setting policy for the euro area as a whole, regardless of economic conditions in the individual countries they come from. For the governor of the Banque de France to vote to raise interest rates at a time when the French economy is on its way into a recession would be difficult, even if it is the right thing to do for the euro area as a whole. Occasionally, however, Governing Council members air their dissent in public.[11]

A number of important safeguards were included in the Treaty of Maastricht to ensure the central bank's independence. First, there are the terms of office: Executive Board members serve eight-year terms (without the possibility of reappointment), and member nations must appoint their central bank governors for a minimum of five years. Second, the ECB's financial interests must remain separate from any political organization. Third, the treaty states explicitly that the Governing Council cannot take instructions from any government, so its policy decisions are irreversible. The fact that the ECB is the product of a treaty agreed to by all of the countries of the European Union makes it extraordinarily difficult to change any of the terms under which it

[11]An important difference between the ECB's Governing Council and the FOMC is that the governors of the Federal Reserve Board generally hold the majority of the seats on the FOMC (7 out of 12) while the Executive Board members are always a minority on the Governing Council (6 versus 15 NCB governors voting at each meeting). In the Eurosystem, power is less centralized than it is at the Fed.

Table 16.3 Comparing the FOMC with the ECB's Governing Council

	FOMC	Governing Council
Independence		
Budgetary control	Controlled by the Board of Governors	Controlled by the NCBs
Decisions irreversible	Yes	Yes
Terms of appointment	Governors 14 years, Reserve Bank presidents 5 years	Executive Board members 8 years; heads of NCBs minimum of 5 years
Threat of legislative change	Requires an act of Congress	Requires agreement of all signatories to Treaty of Maastricht
Decision making		
	Committee of 19 members; governors and New York Reserve Bank president always vote; 11 other Reserve Bank presidents rotate 4 voting slots	Committee of 25 members, with 6 Executive Board members and 15 of 19 NCB governors voting at each meeting
Accountability and transparency		
Policy deliberations	Immediate release of target interest rate with a brief statement including the votes of the committee members, followed by a press conference by the chair; quarterly forecasts of economy and interest rates	Immediate release of target interest rate with an explanatory statement; the president and vice president answer questions
	Minutes of the meeting released after three weeks	Account of the meeting released after about one month
	Transcripts released after 5 years	No transcripts
Other information	Twice-yearly reports to Congress	Quarterly report to the European Parliament
	Public speeches of members	Public speeches of members
	Data collection and dissemination	Data collection and dissemination
	Publication of research reports, along with FOMC participants' quarterly forecasts of inflation and growth	Publication of research reports, along with twice-yearly staff forecasts of inflation and growth
Policy framework		
	Dual mandate of price stability and maximum sustainable employment; "balanced approach" to tradeoffs between goals; price stability defined numerically	Price stability is paramount and defined numerically. All other goals are secondary
Cooperation with fiscal policymakers		
	No explicit mechanism	Stated requirements for member countries' deficits and debt levels that are frequently violated
	Not authorized to purchase most state and municipal debt	Selectively purchases sovereign debt of member-states

operates. People who study central banks generally agree that these provisions make the ECB's legal mandate the strongest in the world.

In order to continue operating efficiently as the monetary union enlarged to include new members, in 2015 the Governing Council of the ECB implemented a complex system of rotation that bears a passing resemblance to the system used by the FOMC. Executive Board members have permanent votes on the Governing Council, just as the Board of Governors of the Federal Reserve System does, while the leaders of the NCBs rotate each month, with 15 of 19 current leaders voting at each meeting. In contrast to the FOMC's annual voting rotation, the Governing Council's monthly rotation ensures that each member country (including the smallest) has effective representation in every year.

Accountability and Transparency

Like the Federal Reserve, the ECB distributes large volumes of information on its website, in all of the ECB's official languages. Included are a weekly balance sheet, a monthly statistical bulletin, an analysis of current economic conditions, biannual forecasts of inflation and growth, research reports relevant to current policy, and an annual report. In addition, the president of the ECB appears before the European Parliament every quarter to report on monetary policy and answer questions, and Governing Council members speak regularly in public. But the most important aspect of the ECB's communication strategy concerns statements about the Governing Council's policy deliberations. (Like the FOMC, the Governing Council of the ECB targets a short-term interest rate on interbank loans, provides forward guidance, and has developed several liquidity-supplying facilities that alter its asset scale and mix in order to counter widespread financial disruptions.)

Following each of the Governing Council's monthly meetings on monetary policy, the president and vice president of the ECB hold a news conference in Frankfurt. The proceedings begin with the president reading a several-page statement announcing the council's interest rate decision, together with a brief report on current economic and financial conditions in the euro area. The president and vice president then answer questions. A transcript of all their remarks is posted on the ECB's website (www.ecb.int) soon afterward. This procedure was the model for the Fed chair's press conference that began in 2011. And, in 2015, the ECB began to issue a written "account" of Governing Council meetings that is comparable to the minutes published by the FOMC. However, the ECB's accounts do not detail votes of the Governing Council; nor does the ECB keep verbatim transcripts.

In assessing whether the ECB's communications strategy is sufficient, we need to ask two questions. First, does the information that is released minimize the extent to which people will be surprised by future policy actions? Second, does it hold policymakers accountable for their decisions? On the first issue, uncertainties arise when conflicting opinions are expressed, but this information helps the public understand the range and complexity of policy debate in the Governing Council. On the second issue, most indications are that the system is working and that there is accountability. The ECB is forced to justify its actions to the euro-area public, explaining its policies and responding to criticisms in more than a dozen languages.

The Price Stability Objective and Monetary Policy Strategy

The Treaty of Maastricht states, "The primary objective of the European System of Central Banks [ESCB] shall be to maintain price stability. Without prejudice to the objective of price stability, the ESCB shall support the general economic policies in

The Euro-Area Crisis and the ECB
LESSONS FROM THE CRISIS

The Maastricht Treaty provided the European Central Bank (ECB) with a legal foundation that makes it highly independent. But even a strong central bank depends on the support of other authorities: it cannot secure price stability over the long term if fiscal policymakers do not control the rise of public debt, and it cannot ensure economic stability if prudential regulators allow a systemwide capital shortfall that fosters bank runs. Yet the treaty failed to create the euro-area institutions that would provide the support needed by the monetary union's central bank.

Put another way, the treaty mastered the time-consistency problems of monetary policy but not of fiscal and prudential policy. When the euro-area crisis began in earnest in 2010, policymakers had to scramble to prevent a breakup of the monetary union. Here's what happened.

The global financial crisis of 2007–2009 severely damaged euro-area banks and plunged euro-area economies into a deep recession. Where fiscal deficits were already large, as in Greece, they widened much further. Where fiscal deficits were contained but the entire banking sector had overextended itself with risky lending, as in Spain, the national government was forced to borrow heavily to bail out the banks. These two problems—weakened banks and overstretched sovereigns—fed on each other. Insolvent countries could no longer support insolvent banks. Banks and other investors—often from other countries—ran from the hard-hit sovereigns, refusing to lend more, and depositors ran from hard-hit banks. Everyone sought safety in countries where they felt they could trust the government.

The runs hit Greece, Ireland, and Portugal first (and worst) and then moved on to Italy and Spain. In Figure 16.4, we can see the consequences for bonds issued by these countries on the geographic periphery of the euro area. The yield spreads for these sovereigns had been driven unrealistically low, in part by what turned out to be unwise purchases of their debt by banks and other investors in the core euro area. In 2011, these spreads exploded. As the crisis deepened, depositors and bondholders feared both sovereign default and "redenomination" risk—the reintroduction of a domestic currency that would depreciate versus the euro.

As this story makes clear, the weaknesses of fiscal policy and prudential regulation in some countries had spillover effects on other countries. Much like bank runs, bad news in one country led to contagion elsewhere.

Addressing the euro-area crisis fell initially to the ECB. On July 26, 2012, then-ECB President Mario Draghi famously said that "the ECB is ready to do whatever it takes to preserve the euro. And believe me, it will be enough." To back up that pledge, the ECB instituted a mechanism to purchase government bonds to lower the market interest rates faced by countries subject to speculation that they might leave the euro. It also offered unlimited reserves to euro-area banks. Figure 16.4 shows that these policies indeed helped narrow interest rate spreads.

But the euro area must still face the more fundamental and persistent challenge avoided by the Maastricht Treaty: building the institutions necessary to prevent or manage spillovers and thus support the efficacy of the euro-area central bank. On the financial stability side, this means having common banking supervision, resolution arrangements, and deposit insurance that cover the entire euro area so that depositors don't care if their deposits are in a bank in Athens, Frankfurt, or Madrid.

Euro-area policymakers have made headway on the first two of these three goals. They established common banking supervision through the Single Supervisory Mechanism, a new arm of the ECB. And they have come somewhat closer to a common resolution framework through the European Stability Mechanism, which offers funding for governments, especially when used to support their banks; and through the Single Resolution Mechanism for funding and restructuring insolvent banks. A tax on banks is being used to provide the resources for the resolution fund, which is expected to reach its target size by 2023.

These policy developments help explain why the 2015 resurgence of crisis in Greece involved only minimal

the [European] Community," including the objective of sustainable and noninflationary growth. Like the Fed's legislatively dictated objectives, this statement is quite vague. However, the treaty is widely understood to place priority on price stability as the top objective for the ECB, while the Fed's mandate does not. The Governing Council's response has been to explain its interpretation of the statement and describe the factors that guide its policy decisions. Before assuming operational responsibility on January 1, 1999, the council prepared a press release titled "A Stability-Oriented Monetary Policy Strategy." The strategy has two parts. First, there is a numerical definition of price stability. Second, the Governing Council announces its intention to

Figure 16.4 10-Year Yield Spreads of Selected Euro-Area Government Bonds over German Government Bonds (Basis Points), 1990–2019

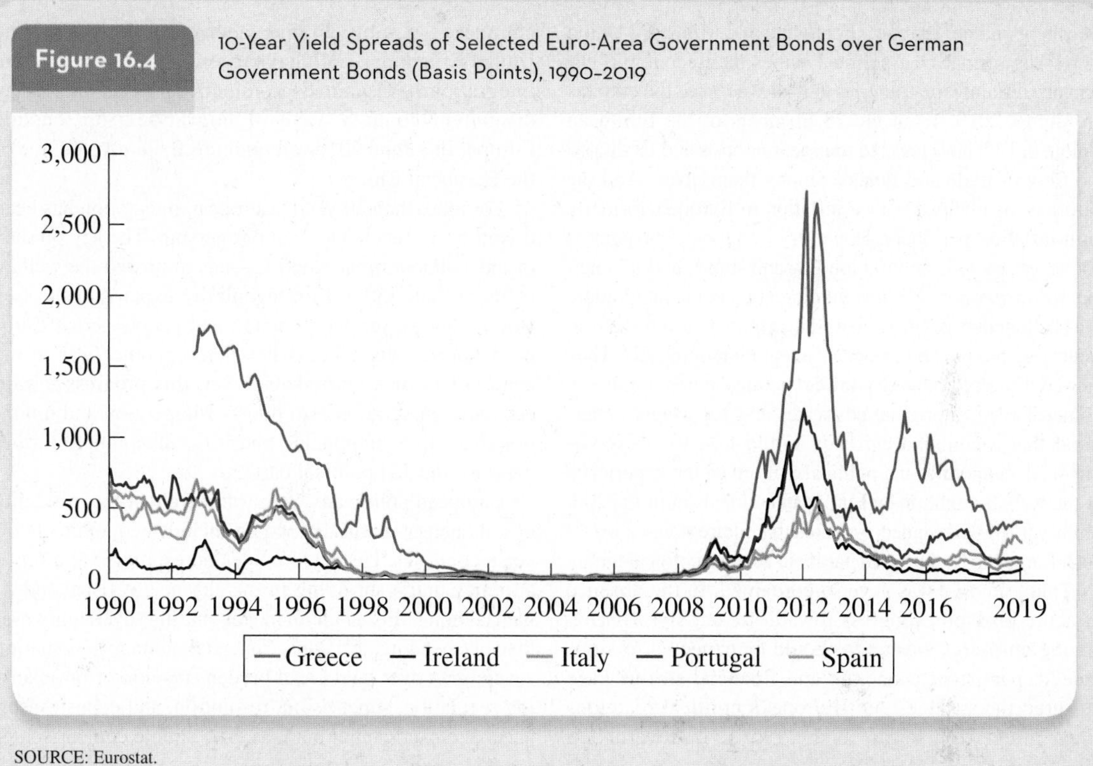

SOURCE: Eurostat.

spillovers (have a look again at the pattern of interest rates in Figure 16.4). In short, the steps taken by policymakers to fill the void left by the Maastricht Treaty were sufficient to prevent contagion in 2015.

Nevertheless, the construction of the banking union is far from complete, especially regarding resolution and deposit insurance. Once all aspects of the financial system become a joint responsibility of all euro-area countries, then—and only then—will euro-area depositors be secure regardless of where their banks are located. At least until then, it will remain premature to confirm that the euro-area crisis is over.

focus on a broad-based assessment of the outlook for future prices, with money playing a prominent role.[12]

The ECB's Governing Council defines price stability as an inflation rate of close to, but less than, 2 percent, based on a euro-area-wide measure of consumer prices. The index, called the harmonized index of consumer prices (HICP), is similar to the U.S.

[12]The ECB refers to this statement as its "two-pillar" strategy. Observers have been critical of the way money is included in the policy framework. If the goal is to stabilize prices, why isn't money growth just one of a wide range of indicators that are factored into policy decisions? Following a 2004 policy review, ECB practice downgraded the importance of the monetary pillar, blunting this type of criticism.

The Importance of Being Europe

MONEY AND BANKING BLOG

Despite its name, Europe's Economic and Monetary Union (EMU) is primarily a political rather than economic endeavor. Certainly the countries that have adopted the euro (as of August 2019, 19 of the 28 members of the European Union, or EU) have lowered transactions costs and facilitated the flow of trade and finance among themselves. And the euro has also helped reduce inflation in Europe's formerly high-inflation periphery. However, a common currency is not necessary to keep inflation low and stable, and it is neither *necessary* nor *sufficient* for closer economic integration.

The founders of EMU viewed it as more than a process to achieve economic and monetary integration of the EU. They viewed it as a profound step toward political union in Europe. Some of EMU's original advocates and supporters understood that a common currency would lead to stresses—financial, economic, and political. But given the experience of the wars brought on by European nationalism in the 20th century, EMU's designers expected that future stresses would push European leaders even harder to achieve political union.

That outcome was never preordained. In the absence of acute pressure, progress toward greater risk sharing among euro-area sovereigns could be expected to slow. Indeed, persistent economic and financial strains have nurtured the strongest anti-European political reactions since integration began in the 1950s. In several EU countries—notably France, Germany, Italy, and the United Kingdom—political parties opposed to European integration have gained prominence, fueled in part by discontent about a wave of migration from outside Europe. In a June 2016 referendum, Britain voted to exit the European Union.

For more than 60 years, European integration has been driven by a French–German partnership. The key product of this collaboration—the EU—has improved the welfare of more than 450 million people by expanding the free flow of goods, services, capital, and people across European borders. Its success has made another war in the center of Europe unthinkable. Yet, this progress toward economic integration also boosts competition and migration that can be unpopular, and it is vulnerable to further gains by anti-EU political parties.

European politicians were warned about the instability of a monetary union that would include economically diverse countries. History provides no examples of a broad currency union surviving in the absence of fiscal and financial union. Fiscal union means sharing sovereignty over tax and spending decisions. Financial union means sharing sovereignty over (and fiscal burdens resulting from) banking regulation, supervision, resolution, and deposit insurance, and over capital markets. The simple comparison of

consumer price index (CPI). The HICP is an average of retail price inflation in all the countries of the monetary union, weighted by the size of their gross domestic products. So inflation in Germany, where nearly 30 percent of the total economic activity in the euro area occurs, is much more important to policy decisions than inflation in Portugal, whose economy is about one-sixteenth the size of Germany's. This arrangement has important implications for monetary policy operations, because there are times when the proper policy for Portugal is to lower interest rates but the proper policy for Germany is to raise them. Given Portugal's relative size, a change in inflation or growth there has little impact on the euro area as a whole. The same is true for other small countries in the union.

The fact that the economically large countries matter much more than the small ones can affect the dynamics of the Governing Council's interest rate decisions—remember the Council includes the heads of all the euro-area national central banks, as well as the members of the Executive Board. While the Governing Council's job is to stabilize prices in the euro area as a whole, one wonders whether the smaller countries might have undue influence on its policy decisions. To understand this concern, imagine what would happen if all the Governing Council's members pressed for actions appropriate to their own countries. The result would be a policy

EMU with the U.S. monetary union—which has enjoyed fiscal union since 1789 and financial union since the Great Depression—makes these differences clear.

To make EMU work, euro-area institutions still need to adapt in big ways. In 2014, the euro area transferred the regulation and supervision of its largest banks to the Single Supervisory Mechanism, housed inside the European Central Bank (ECB). And the European Stability Mechanism was created in 2012 as a precursor to a joint bank resolution fund. Even so, as of 2019, euro-area banks and their sovereigns remain at risk of a "doom loop." That is, on the one hand, individual countries within the euro area still bear the financial burden for resolutions of impaired domestic banks, which weighs on the quality of their debt securities; and on the other, these banks hold large amounts of their government's liabilities. Finally, there is no consensus on a euro-area-wide deposit insurance mechanism.

Against this background, the burden of maintaining financial stability in EMU has fallen on the ECB—easily the euro area's strongest institution. Considering the context, the ECB has been extraordinarily effective. Without the ECB's 2012 commitment to do "whatever it takes" to save the euro, it is doubtful that the euro area today would have 19 members.

To preserve price stability—its primary mandate—the ECB has gone further than most people thought possible. Beginning in 2015, the central bank expanded its balance sheet massively through the purchase of government and private debt. Yet these aggressive actions remain a point of conflict among euro-area countries.

Ultimately, even if the ECB achieves its inflation objective—close to, but below, 2 percent—it is merely buying time. Ironically, the ECB's success in containing euro-area financial strains diminishes the incentives of countries and policymakers to address the structural weaknesses of EMU. Yet, these prolonged and repeated strains expose EMU's underlying instability; preserving it will entail *greater* sharing of risk and sovereignty among its member states.

The architects of the Maastricht Treaty, which laid the basis for EMU, likely envisioned a strong political union, not just a monetary union. But Europe's citizenry has never exhibited strong support for a strong, federal regime, so Europeans are faced with a stark choice. They can either embrace a closer union along with its financial, fiscal, and political consequences; or they can walk away from the broad-based euro, with at least some countries reintroducing the national currencies that disappeared nearly two decades ago. While the first option remains much more likely, the political challenges are daunting.

appropriate to the median country. And because there are only four large countries in the ECB—Germany, France, Italy, and Spain—the median country is likely to be small: Ranked by nominal GDP, Portugal is the median country, accounting for less than 2 percent of 2018 euro-area GDP. The custom of drawing half the Executive Board members from the large countries and half from the small ones is not a foolproof counterweight to this tendency.

These potential shortcomings notwithstanding, evidence strongly suggests that the ECB is doing the job it is supposed to do. Despite an extraordinary crisis since 2010, the long-run inflation projections of professional forecasters remain modestly shy of 2 percent as of early 2019, highlighting the ECB's credibility. Put differently, the Governing Council's policy has been largely appropriate to the euro area as a whole; it has not been skewed toward smaller countries' concerns. The specificity of the price stability objective set forth in the Treaty of Maastricht holds policymakers accountable, limiting discretion in their decision making.[13]

[13] Strong evidence for the effectiveness and credibility of the ECB can be found in Stephen Cecchetti and Kermit Schoenholtz, "How Central Bankers See It: The First Decade of ECB Policy and Beyond," NBER Working Paper 14489, November 2008.

Key Terms

Using FRED: Codes for Data in This Chapter

Data Series	FRED Data Code
Federal funds rate	FEDFUNDS
Discount rate (primary credit)	DPCREDIT
Personal consumption expenditures price index	PCEPI
Personal consumption expenditures index (less food and energy)	PCEPILFE
Euro-area harmonized index of consumer prices	CP0000EZ19M086NEST
France gross sovereign debt (percent of GDP)	GGGDTAFRA188N
Germany gross sovereign debt (percent of GDP)	GGGDTADEA188N
Italy gross sovereign debt (percent of GDP)	GGGDTAITA188N
Japan gross sovereign debt (percent of GDP)	GGGDTAJPA188N
Spain gross sovereign debt (percent of GDP)	GGGDTAESA188N
U.S. gross sovereign debt (percent of GDP)	GGGDTAUSA188N
Projection of Germany gross sovereign debt (percent of GDP)	GGGDTPDEA188N
Projection of Italy gross sovereign debt (percent of GDP)	GGGDTPITA188N
U.S. unemployment rate	UNRATE
FOMC long-run projection for unemployment rate	UNRATECTMLR
Discount window borrowings from Federal Reserve	DISCBORR
Federal funds target rate	DFEDTAR

To learn more about the changing financial system, visit www.moneyandbanking.com.

Chapter Lessons

1. The Federal Reserve System is the central bank of the United States. Its decentralized structure comprises three primary elements:
   a. Twelve Federal Reserve Banks, each with its own board of directors, that
      i. Serve as the government's bank, issuing currency, maintaining the U.S. Treasury's bank account, and handling the Treasury's securities.
      ii. Serve as the bankers' bank, holding deposits, operating a payments system, making loans, and evaluating the safety and soundness of financial institutions in their districts.

   b. The seven-member Board of Governors in Washington, D.C., including the chair:
      i. Regulates and supervises the financial system.
      ii. Oversees the Federal Reserve Banks.
      iii. Publishes economic data.
   c. The Federal Open Market Committee:
      i. Makes monetary policy by setting interest rates or altering the balance sheet.
      ii. Has 12 voting members, including the seven governors and five of the 12 Reserve Bank presidents.
      iii. Meets eight times a year.
      iv. Is controlled largely by the chair.
2. The FOMC's success in meeting its objectives is enhanced by:
   a. Its independence, which comes from its members' long terms, budgetary autonomy, and the irreversibility of its policy decisions.
   b. Clear communication of its policy decisions through an explanatory statement that is distributed immediately, through a quarterly press conference, and through minutes that are published three weeks after each scheduled meeting.
   c. Regular public appearances of the committee's members.
3. The European Central Bank (ECB) is the central bank for the countries that participate in the European Monetary Union—the euro area.
   a. The Eurosystem is composed of three distinct parts:
      i. The national central banks (NCBs) provide services to the banks and governments in their countries.
      ii. The European Central Bank (ECB) in Frankfurt, with its six-member Executive Board, oversees the monetary system.
      iii. The Governing Council makes monetary policy decisions.
   b. The ECB's primary objective is to stabilize prices in the common currency area.
   c. The ECB's success in meeting its monetary policy objectives is aided by the timely announcement of policy decisions, press conferences in which top ECB officials respond to questions, published accounts of meetings, and the release of twice-yearly forecasts.
   d. The ECB also is the leading supervisor of euro-area banks, directly supervising the region's largest banks.

Conceptual and Analytical Problems Mc Graw Hill connect

1. What are the Federal Reserve's goals, and who established them? How are Fed officials held accountable for meeting them? Explain why the chair is the most influential Fed official. *(LO1)*
2. Go to the Federal Reserve Board's website and locate the FOMC's most recent statement. What did the committee members say at their last meeting regarding the target range for the Federal funds rate and the two goals of price stability and sustainable economic growth? *(LO2)*
3. Some people have argued that the high inflation of the late 1970s was a consequence of the fact that Federal Reserve Board Chair Arthur Burns did what President Richard Nixon wanted him to do. What policy do you think President Nixon might have wanted? *(LO2)*
4. How might the ECB's pursuit of price stability as its primary objective have restricted its response to the sovereign debt crisis in the euro area? *(LO3)*
5. Evaluate the following statement: "The Maastricht Treaty helped solve the time-consistency problem in monetary policy but not fiscal policy." *(LO3)*

6. How did the response to the financial crisis of 2007–2009 alter the appointment process of presidents of the Federal Reserve Banks? *(LO1)*
7. What are the goals of the ECB? How are its officials held accountable for meeting them? *(LO3)*
8. Why did the sovereign debt problem of Greece—a country that accounts for less than 2 percent of euro-area GDP—threaten the banking system throughout the euro area? *(LO3)*
9. Go to the ECB's website and locate the most recent introductory statement made by the president of the ECB at the press conference following a Governing Council meeting. What was the Governing Council's policy decision? How was it justified? *(LO3)*
10. Do you think the FOMC has an easier or a harder time agreeing on monetary policy than the Governing Council of the ECB? Why? *(LO3)*
11. Why did the "no-bailout" clause of the Maastricht Treaty come under stress during and after the financial crisis of 2007–2009? *(LO3)*
12. Do you think the current procedures for appointing members to the Board of Governors are consistent with the principles of good central bank design? Explain your answer. *(LO1)*
13.* Currently, all the national central banks in the Eurosystem are involved with the implementation of monetary policy. What do you think the advantage would be of centralizing the conduct of these day-to-day interactions with financial markets at the ECB in Frankfurt? Are there any disadvantages you can think of? *(LO3)*
14. If you were charged with redrawing the boundaries of the Federal Reserve districts, what criteria would you use to complete the task? *(LO1)*
15. Why do you think the statement released after each Federal Open Market Committee meeting retains the same basic structure? *(LO2)*
16. Do you think, in the interest of transparency, the chair of the Federal Reserve Board should explain in detail the subtleties surrounding policy decisions? Why or why not? *(LO2)*
17. Suppose a fellow student in your money and banking class made the following statement: "Since the Federal Reserve introduced a specific numerical target for inflation in 2012 but does not have one for maximum employment, it has, in effect, a hierarchical mandate like the ECB, placing primacy on the price stability part of its mandate." On what basis could you disagree with this student? *(LO1, LO3)*
18. Compare the communication strategies of the Federal Reserve and the ECB. In what ways are they similar? Identify two key elements of the Fed's strategy that are *not* part of the ECB's strategy and discuss whether you think the ECB is justified in omitting each of them. *(LO1, LO3)*
19. During the euro-area crisis, interest rate spreads between the sovereign debt of peripheral countries and Germany widened most sharply when it was feared that one or more countries might leave the euro area. These spreads narrowed when ECB actions restored confidence in the monetary union. What accounts for this pattern? *(LO3)*
20. Like most central banks around the world, the Federal Reserve currently does not provide deposit accounts for individuals. Suppose the Fed decided to issue digital currency by offering unlimited access to interest-paying deposit accounts for individuals. What problems might this change cause for the financial system? *(LO2)*

*Indicates more difficult problems.

Data Exploration

For general information on using Federal Reserve Economic Data (FRED) online, visit www.mhhe.com/moneyandbanking6e *and refer to the FRED Resources.*

1. How large are the public debt burdens of key euro-area economies? Are they rising or falling? Plot without recession bars the debt-to-GDP ratios of Germany (FRED code: GGGDTADEA188N), and Italy (FRED code: GGGDTAITA188N). Extend each line (matching its color) using the projections of the International Monetary Fund (FRED codes: GGGDTPDEA188N, and GGGDTPITA188N, respectively). Are these ratios consistent with the Maastricht Treaty's public debt-to-GDP guideline of 60 percent? *(LO3)*
2. The European Central Bank (ECB) has translated its primary objective of price stability into an explicit, quantitative goal of keeping euro-area annual inflation close to, but below, 2 percent over the medium term. Plot the percent change from a year ago of the euro-area price level, called the *harmonized index of consumer prices* (FRED code: CP0000EZ19M086NEST). Evaluate the performance of the ECB on average since 2000 and over shorter intervals. Download the data and compute the average inflation rate for the full period and for the periods 2008–2009, 2010–2011, and 2012–present. *(LO3)*
3. In 2012, the Federal Reserve announced an inflation objective of 2 percent "over the longer run" for the price index of personal consumption expenditures (FRED code: PCEPI). However, many analysts focus on the "core" price index (FRED code: PCEPILFE), which omits the volatile food and energy components. For the Fed's horizon, does this difference matter? Plot the percent change from a year ago of both price measures since 2000. Download the data and compute the averages and standard deviations over that period. What do you conclude? *(LO2)*
4. In its statement of March 20, 2019, the FOMC indicated that it would pursue policies to meet its objectives of "maximum employment and price stability." Plot since 2009 the evolution of the FOMC's longer run projection for the unemployment rate (FRED Code: UNRATECTMLR), the actual unemployment rate (FRED Code: UNRATE), and the percent change from a year ago of the core personal consumption expenditures price index (FRED Code: PCEPILFE). Summarize the description provided by FRED (beneath the plot) of the FOMC longer-run unemployment projection. Then use the plot to explain why the March 2019 statement indicated that the FOMC "will be patient as it determines what future adjustments to the target range for the federal funds rate may be appropriate." *(LO2)*
5. In August 2007 and in March 2008, the Federal Reserve Board reduced the discount rate to ease liquidity conditions for banks. Plot discount window borrowing (FRED code: DISCBORR) between January 2007 and December 2008. As a second line, plot on the right axis the difference between the discount rate (FRED code: DPCREDIT) and the federal funds rate target (FRED code: DFEDTAR). Did narrowing the spread between the discount rate and the federal funds target rate trigger the borrowing surge in September–October 2008? *(LO2)*

Chapter

17 The Central Bank Balance Sheet and the Money Supply Process

Learning Objectives

After reading this chapter, you should be able to:

LO1 Describe the central bank's balance sheet and the monetary base.

LO2 Explain how the central bank's balance sheet changes.

LO3 Calculate the deposit expansion multiplier.

LO4 Analyze the link between the monetary base and the money supply.

On the morning of September 11, 2001, four hijacked planes crashed: two into the World Trade Center towers in New York City, one into the Pentagon in Washington, D.C., and one in a field in western Pennsylvania. Thousands of people died, and the world changed. The disruptions were enormous. All nonmilitary aircraft in the United States were immediately grounded and U.S. airspace was closed. In the Wall Street area, power and communications networks were shut down, closing the financial markets. Yet New Yorkers found they could still go to an ATM anywhere outside the immediate neighborhood of the attacks and withdraw cash. Despite the massive disruptions in the Wall Street area, the electronic network that processed the withdrawals continued to work.

Conditions were anything but normal inside the financial community, where the risk of a systemwide collapse was very real. But because of the immediate action of Federal Reserve officials, the financial system held together, and most of us never realized how close we came to catastrophe. At 11:45 a.m., three hours after the attacks began, the Federal Reserve Board issued a terse statement: "The Federal Reserve is open and operating. The discount window is available to meet liquidity needs." Over the next week, people throughout the Federal Reserve System made sure there was enough money circulating to keep the economy going. They bought nearly $100 billion worth of U.S. Treasury securities, extended tens of billions of dollars in loans to U.S. banks, and provided foreign central banks with the billions of dollars they needed to ensure that commercial banks in their countries could meet their obligations. They did it all from backup sites because the Federal Reserve's primary operating site, two blocks from the World Trade Center, was inaccessible.

This was one of the great successes of modern central banking. In extraordinary circumstances, quick action by the Fed kept the financial markets afloat. While some institutions and individuals will never recover from the terrorist attacks, the financial system—one of the terrorists' primary targets—returned to near normal within weeks.

Many observers assign part of the blame for the financial crisis of 2007–2009 to the policies of the Federal Reserve. However, most would agree that the Fed's extraordinary actions in 2008–2009 were critical in preventing a complete meltdown of the U.S. (and global) financial system. As one former Fed chair put it, the Fed under Chairman Ben Bernanke went to the limits of its powers to secure financial stability in the depths of crisis.

Many of the Fed's actions in the crisis of 2007–2009 were unprecedented or had not been seen since the 1930s. For the first time since the Great Depression, the Fed lent to nonbanks and even to nonfinancial companies. The central bank created new mechanisms to increase the overall supply of liquidity and to deliver it where and when it was needed. Following the failure of Lehman Brothers in September 2008, the Fed became the "intermediary of last resort," allowing its assets to double in a matter of weeks—an unparalleled expansion. To substitute for markets that had stopped functioning normally, the Fed acquired more than $1 trillion of loans and securities that had previously been traded in the market. More than a decade later, these extraordinary actions still affect the Fed's balance sheet, in contrast to the brief and much smaller policy actions after September 11, 2001.

The stories of the financial crises of September 11, 2001, and of 2007–2009 stand in stark contrast to what happened in the 1930s, when policy failures led to the collapse of the U.S. banking system and precipitated the Great Depression. At the time, Federal Reserve officials didn't fully understand how their actions affected the supply of credit in the economy. They failed to recognize the link between changes in the Fed's balance sheet and the growth rate of money. They thought that so long as they supplied more and more cash to the economy, and so long as commercial bank account balances at the Federal Reserve banks were growing, money and credit were easily available. They were wrong. The financial system collapsed because the Fed officials had failed to provide the liquidity that sound banks needed to stay in business. As a result, virtually no one could borrow; both the amount of credit and the quantity of money in the economy plummeted.

The Fed's policymakers did their best in the 1930s, and their best wasn't very good. But at least they did it in public, which is not always the case. When the economy is suffering, or when central bankers are taking actions they aren't supposed to, they have a tendency to hide what they are doing. At times, central bankers have delayed publication of statistics or distorted the information they did provide. That's what the central bank of Thailand did in 1997. The Bank of Thailand was committed to stabilizing the value of its currency, the Thai baht, at an exchange rate of about 26 to one U.S. dollar. To do so, officials had to convince foreign exchange traders that they had enough dollars to buy baht if market participants started to sell. To be convinced, currency traders had to see the numbers. But in summer 1997, officials at the Bank of Thailand refused to tell anyone, even their own Minister of Finance, how many dollars the bank held.[1] When the truth got out, and everyone learned that the cupboard was bare, the baht collapsed, ending 1997 at 50 to one dollar.

[1]The Bank of Thailand hadn't actually sold its dollar reserves on the open market. Officials had engaged in forward transactions that committed them to sell the dollars in the future. Thus, they could claim to have dollars that in reality were committed to others. For a detailed description of this episode, see Paul Blustein, *The Chastening: Inside the Crisis That Rocked the Global Financial System and Humbled the IMF* (New York: PublicAffairs, 2001).

To appreciate what went right in the Fed's response to September 2001 and to the crisis of 2007–2009—and what went wrong both in the United States in the 1930s and in Thailand in 1997—we need to understand how the central bank interacts with the financial system. What is it that central banks buy and sell? What are the assets and liabilities on their balance sheets? How do they control those assets and liabilities, and why might they want to hide them from the public? More to the point, how is the central bank's balance sheet connected to the money and credit that flow through the economy? Where *do* the trillions of dollars in our bank accounts actually come from? In answering these questions, we will combine our knowledge of how central banks work with our understanding of commercial bank operations. Let's see how the system works.

The Central Bank's Balance Sheet

As the government's banker and the bankers' banker, the central bank engages in numerous financial transactions. It supplies currency, provides deposit accounts to the government and commercial banks, makes loans, and buys and sells securities and foreign currency. All these activities cause changes in the **central bank's balance sheet**. Because the balance sheet is the foundation of any financial institution, understanding the day-to-day operation of a central bank must start with an understanding of its assets and liabilities and how they change. The structure of the balance sheet gives us a window through which we can study how the institution operates.

Central banks publish their balance sheets regularly. The Federal Reserve and the European Central Bank both do so weekly; you can find the information on their websites. (To get a sense of the changing scale and composition of the Fed's balance sheet, see Applying the Concept on page 452.) Publication is a critical part of the transparency that makes monetary policy effective. The actual published data are complicated and include items we don't need to worry about here. Instead, we'll focus on a stripped-down version of the balance sheet, one that has been reduced to the most important components. Figure 17.1 shows the major assets and liabilities that appear in every central bank's balance sheet in one form or another. Note that the entries are divided not only into columns, with assets on the left and liabilities on the right, but into categories as well. The top row shows the assets and liabilities the central bank holds in its role as the government's bank, and the bottom row shows the assets and liabilities it holds as the bankers' bank. Let's examine each entry, starting with the assets.

Figure 17.1 The Central Bank's Balance Sheet

	Assets	Liabilities
Government's bank	Securities Foreign exchange reserves	Currency Government's account
Bankers' bank	Loans	Accounts of the commercial banks (reserves)

Assets

The central bank's balance sheet shows three basic assets: securities, foreign exchange reserves, and loans. The first two are needed so that the central bank can perform its role as the government's bank; the loans are a service to commercial banks. Let's look at each one in detail.

1. *Securities* are the primary assets of most central banks. Traditionally, the Fed exclusively held Treasury securities, mostly short maturity. However, during the 2007–2009 financial crisis, the central bank chose to acquire a variety of riskier assets, including more than $1 trillion of mortgage-backed securities (MBS, page 52), making MBS temporarily the largest component of Federal Reserve assets. Later, the central bank sharply boosted purchases of medium- and long-term Treasury instruments, restoring U.S. government debt to the top rank. The quantity of securities that the Fed holds is controlled through purchases and sales known as *open market operations.* It is important to emphasize that independent central banks, not fiscal authorities, determine the quantity and mix of securities they purchase.
2. **Foreign exchange reserves** are the central bank's and government's balances of foreign currency. These are held in the form of bonds issued by foreign governments. For example, the Fed holds euro-denominated bonds issued by the German government as well as yen-denominated bonds issued by the Japanese government. These reserves are used in **foreign exchange interventions**, when officials attempt to change the market values of various currencies.
3. *Loans* are usually extended to commercial banks. But, in 2008 and 2009, as part of its extraordinary response to the financial crisis, the Fed made substantial loans to nonbanks as well. There are several kinds of loans, and their importance varies depending on how the central bank operates. **Discount loans** are the loans the Fed makes when commercial banks need short-term cash. Discount loans usually are in the millions of dollars, but the volume temporarily surged in 2008 to beyond $400 billion as the Fed battled the liquidity crisis (see Chapter 2, Lessons from the Crisis: Market Liquidity, Funding Liquidity, and Making Markets).

Prior to the financial crisis of 2007–2009, the Fed controlled the federal funds rate and the availability of money and credit by adjusting its holdings of liquid securities, primarily short-term Treasury bills (see Chapter 18). Foreign exchange reserves play only a small role in Fed policy, and (aside from crises) loans are almost always modest. At other central banks, this ranking of assets often differs. For example, the ECB's primary assets prior to the euro-area crisis were collateralized loans (repos) to the banks, rather than securities, but that ranking has reversed in recent years as the ECB expanded its securities holdings rapidly.[2] In many trade-dependent economies, the primary focus is often on the level of foreign exchange reserves.

Liabilities

Turning to the liabilities side of the central bank's balance sheet, we see three major entries: currency, the government's deposit account, and the deposit accounts of the commercial banks. Again, these can be divided into two groups based on their purpose. The first two items allow the central bank to perform its role as the government's bank,

[2]Where the government debt market is neither deep nor liquid—as in many euro-area countries—adjustments in bank lending can be more effective than purchases and sales of securities as a means of central bank control.

The Fed's Balance Sheet: Impact of the Crisis
APPLYING THE CONCEPT

The Federal Reserve's response to the crisis of 2007–2009 transformed the size and composition of its assets and liabilities in unprecedented fashion. Table 17.1 contrasts the balance sheet at an early stage of the crisis (December 2007) with that after the worst of the crisis had passed (December 2009).

The massive expansion of the balance sheet stands out. At the end of the two-year period, the amount of assets was 2.5 times larger—$2.2 trillion versus $900 billion. Most of this increase occurred in September and October 2008, following the collapse of Lehman Brothers. Under normal circumstances, such an increase would be expected to drive up prices and nominal GDP. But this time, nominal GDP barely moved. Instead, the Fed's actions helped prevent a repeat of the plunge of the money supply and nominal GDP that occurred in the Great Depression (see In the Blog: Monetary Policy: A Lesson Learned on page 473).

As for the composition of the assets, we can see that the increase was concentrated in securities, which surged by more than $1 trillion to reach 2.3 times the amount held at the beginning of the period. Purchases of mortgage-backed and U.S. agency securities more than accounted for this gain. The Fed also boosted its lending sharply, accepting a wide variety of collateral. Some of the most illiquid assets acquired in its emergency operations (including those related to the failure of Bear Stearns in March 2008 and the collapse of AIG in September 2008) remain on the Fed's books as of 2016. In the discussion of unconventional monetary policy in Chapter 18, we will take a closer look at the changing scale and mix of the Fed's assets during the crisis.

The liability side of the balance sheet also was transformed during the crisis: commercial bank deposits rose nearly 100 times! This surge was triggered by the post-Lehman panic, when the Fed sought to calm banks desperately seeking a liquidity cushion by purchasing more securities and boosting discount lending. Yet, even after the liquidity crisis subsided in 2009, banks showed a clear desire to hold massive excess reserves. Lending their reserves at low interest rates to risky borrowers was unattractive for banks that faced a much higher cost of capital than before the crisis. Beginning in October 2008, banks also received interest on their reserves held at the Fed (the policy tool of paying interest on reserves is discussed in Chapter 18), further diminishing the opportunity cost of holding reserves.

Table 17.1 Balance Sheet of the Federal Reserve: December 2009 and December 2007 (Billions of dollars, month-end)

	2009	**2007**
Assets		
Securities	$ 1,835	$ 797
Of which:		
Mortgage-backed	901	0
Federal agency debt	158	0
Foreign exchange reserves	25	47
Loans	276	25
Gold	11	11
Other assets	91	14
Total	**2,239**	**894**
Liabilities		
Currency	$ 883	$ 792
Governments' accounts	149	5
Commercial bank deposits	1,073	11
Other liabilities	81	49
Total	**2,187**	**857**
Capital (Assets minus Liabilities)	$ 52	$ 37
Notes (period mean):		
Nominal GDP	$14,454	$14,338
M1	1,696	1,376
M2	8,544	7,501

NOTE: "Securities" includes all forms of repurchase agreements. "Foreign exchange reserves" does not include the U.S. Treasury Exchange Stabilization fund.

SOURCE: *Federal Reserve release H.4.1* and *U.S. Treasury and Federal Reserve Foreign Exchange Operations, Quarterly Report,* Table 1.

while the third allows it to fulfill its role as the bankers' bank. Let's look at each in turn, again using the example of the United States to illustrate some important details.

1. *Currency.* Nearly all central banks have a monopoly on the issuance of the currency used in everyday transactions. Take a look at the top of any dollar bill and

you will see the words "Federal Reserve Note." Currency—that is, currency circulating in the hands of the *nonbank* public—is the principal liability of most central banks.

2. *Government's account.* Governments need a bank account just like the rest of us. They must have a place to deposit their income and a way to pay for the things they buy. The central bank provides the government with an account into which the government deposits funds (primarily tax revenues) and from which the government writes checks and makes electronic payments. By shifting funds between its accounts at commercial banks and the Fed, the Treasury usually keeps its account balance at the Fed fairly constant. However, to improve the Fed's ability to purchase assets during the financial crisis, the Treasury temporarily increased its central bank deposits, which peaked at more than $500 billion in November 2008.
3. *Commercial bank accounts* (**reserves**). Commercial bank reserves are the sum of two parts: deposits at the central bank *plus* the cash in the bank's own vault. The first of these functions like the commercial bank's checking account. In the same way that you can take cash out of a commercial bank, the bank can withdraw its deposits at the central bank. And just as you can instruct your bank to transfer some part of your account balance to someone else, a commercial bank can transfer a portion of its deposit account balance to another bank. **Vault cash** is part of reserves; it is not part of item 1, which includes only cash held by the nonbank public. Because a bank's vault cash is available to meet depositors' withdrawal demands, it serves the insurance function for which reserves are designed. Reserves are assets of the commercial banking system and liabilities of the central bank. Reflecting policy actions taken during and after financial crises, reserves constitute the largest liability of both the Fed and the ECB as of 2019.

Of all central bank liabilities, bank reserves are the most important in determining the quantity of money and credit in the economy, and for this reason, they play a central role in monetary policy operations. Increases normally lead to a rise in deposits and to growth in the availability of money and credit; decreases do the opposite. As we saw in Chapter 12, there are two types of reserves: those that banks are required to hold, called **required reserves**, and those they hold voluntarily, called **excess reserves**. Originally, the government required banks to hold a certain level of reserves to ensure banks' safety and soundness. However, as a result of financial innovations that reduce the demand for checkable deposits, required reserves declined well below the level of overall reserves that banks wish to hold. Indeed, today's bankers hold excess reserves both as insurance against unexpected outflows and for use in conducting their day-to-day business.

The Importance of Disclosure

Buried in the mountain of paper that every central bank publishes is a statement of the bank's own financial condition. This balance sheet contains what is probably the most important information that any central bank makes public. Every responsible central bank in the world discloses its financial position regularly, most of them every week. In the same way that shareholders require a periodic accounting of the activities of the companies they own, we are all entitled to the information on our central bank's balance sheet. Without public disclosure of the level and change in the size of foreign exchange reserves and currency holdings, it is impossible for us to tell whether the policymakers are doing their job properly. Publication of the balance sheet is an essential aspect of central bank transparency. Delays, like those during the Mexican debt crisis of 1994–1995, are a clear sign of impending disaster.

Another sign of trouble is misrepresentation of the central bank's financial position. A particularly egregious case of lying by a central bank occurred in the Philippines in 1986, when then-President Ferdinand Marcos was desperate to remain in power. We know now that Marcos ordered the central bank to print enormous amounts of currency so that he could try to buy enough individual votes to win the election. And the central bank kept quiet about the elaborate scheme to conceal the monetary expansion.[3]

The Monetary Base

Together, currency in the hands of the public and reserves in the banking system—the privately held liabilities of the central bank—make up the **monetary base**, also called **high-powered money**. As we will see in the next section, the central bank can control the size of the monetary base, the base on which all other forms of money stand. (The term *high-powered* comes from the fact that the quantity of money and credit in the economy is a multiple of currency plus banking system reserves.) As we will see later in this chapter, when the monetary base increases by a dollar, the quantity of money typically rises by several dollars.

To get some sense of the relationship between the monetary base and the quantity of money, we can look at a few numbers. In January 2019, the U.S. monetary base was $3.34 trillion. At the same time, M1 was $3.74 trillion and M2 was $14.47 trillion. So M1 was was barely 12 percent larger than the monetary base, while M2 was more than four times greater than the monetary base. Later in the chapter we'll return to these relationships and learn how the financial crisis of 2007–2009 altered them. But first, let's see how the central bank adjusts its balance sheet and changes the size of the monetary base.

Changing the Size and Composition of the Balance Sheet

Unlike you and me, the central bank controls the size of its balance sheet. That is, policymakers can enlarge or reduce their assets and liabilities at will, without asking anyone. We can't do that. To see the point, think about a simple transaction you engage in regularly, like buying $50 worth of groceries. When you arrive at the checkout counter, you have to pay for your purchases. Let's say you do it with a check. When the supermarket deposits your check in the bank, your $50 moves through the payments system. It is credited to the supermarket's account and, eventually, debited from yours. As long as you started with at least $50 in your checking account, the process works smoothly. The grocery store's bank account is $50 larger and yours is $50 smaller.

Now think about a standard transaction in which the central bank buys a $1 million government security. What's the difference between this purchase and yours at the grocery store? First, there is its size. The central bank's transaction is 20,000 times as big as yours. But that's not all. To see another important difference, let's look at the mechanics of the security purchase. To pay for the bond, the central bank writes a

[3]Newspaper stories at the time documented what happened in the Philippines. See, for example, Chris Sherwell, "Banknotes in Triplicate Add to Filipino's Confusion," *Financial Times*, February 22, 1986.

$1 million check payable to the bond dealer who sells the bond. (In real life, the transaction is done electronically.) After the check is deposited, the dealer's commercial bank account is credited $1 million. The commercial bank then sends the check back to the central bank. When it gets there, something unusual happens. Remember, at the end of your check's journey, your bank debited your checking account $50. But when the central bank's $1 million check is returned, the central bank credits the reserve account of the bank presenting it $1 million. And that's it. The central bank can simply buy things (the $1 million bond, for instance) and then create liabilities to pay for them (the $1 million increase in reserves in the banking system). It can increase the size of its balance sheet as much as it wants.

Turning to the specifics of this process, we'll look at four types of transactions: (1) an *open market operation,* in which the central bank buys or sells a security; (2) a *foreign exchange intervention,* in which the central bank buys or sells foreign currency reserves; (3) the extension of a *discount loan* to a commercial bank by the central bank; and (4) the decision by an individual to *withdraw cash* from the bank. Each of these has an impact on both the central bank's balance sheet and the banking system's balance sheet. Open market operations, foreign exchange interventions, and discount loans all affect the *size* of the central bank's balance sheet and change the size of the monetary base. Cash withdrawals by the public are different. They shift components of the monetary base, changing the composition of the central bank's balance sheet but leaving its size unaffected.

To figure out the impact of each of these four transactions on the central bank's balance sheet, we need to remember one simple rule: When the value of an asset on the balance sheet increases, either the value of another asset decreases so that the net change is zero or the value of a liability rises by the same amount. What's true for assets is also true for liabilities. An increase in a liability is balanced either by a decrease in another liability or by an increase in an asset. The principle is the same regardless of whose balance sheet we are looking at.

In the following sections, we will discuss these transactions in the context of the Federal Reserve's institutional structure. As we go through the examples, remember that the securities and foreign exchange transactions are managed by the Federal Reserve Bank of New York, while discount loans are extended by all 12 Reserve Banks.

Open Market Operations

When the Federal Reserve buys or sells securities in financial markets, it engages in **open market operations**. These open market purchases and sales have a straightforward impact on the Fed's balance sheet. To see how the process works, take the common case in which the Federal Reserve Bank of New York purchases $1 billion in U.S. Treasury bonds from a commercial bank.[4] To pay for the bonds, the Fed transfers $1 billion into the reserve account of the seller. The exchange is done electronically. Panel A of Figure 17.2 shows the change in the Federal Reserve's balance sheet. This is called a **T-account**. The left side shows the change in assets and the right side gives the change in liabilities. Panel A of Figure 17.2 shows the impact of this **open market purchase** on the Fed's balance sheet: its assets and liabilities both go up $1 billion, increasing the monetary base by the same amount.

[4]The Fed purchases securities from a list of *primary government securities dealers,* which includes a combination of banks and securities dealers. While we could examine the mechanics of the Fed's purchase assuming the other side is a dealer, it would complicate the analysis without providing additional insight.

Figure 17.2 Balance Sheet Changes after the Federal Reserve Purchases a U.S. Treasury Bond

A. Federal Reserve's Balance Sheet

Assets		Liabilities	
Securities (U.S. Treasury bond)	+$1 billion	Reserves	+$1 billion

B. Banking System's Balance Sheet

Assets		Liabilities
Reserves	+$1 billion	
Securities (U.S. Treasury bond)	−$1 billion	

What is the impact of the Fed's open market purchase on the banking system's balance sheet? The Fed exchanged $1 billion in securities for $1 billion in reserves, both of which are banking system assets. Panel B of Figure 17.2 shows the balance sheet effect of the exchange.

Note that there are no changes on the liabilities side of the banking system's balance sheet, and the changes on the asset side sum to zero.

Looking at Figure 17.2, you'll notice that reserves are an asset to the banking system but a liability to the Federal Reserve. This may seem confusing, but it shouldn't. It's like your own bank account. The balance in that account is your asset, but it is your bank's liability.

Before we move on, we should note that if the Fed *sells* a U.S. Treasury bond through what is known as an **open market sale**, the impact on everyone's balance sheet is reversed. All the credits in the two figures become debits and vice versa. The Fed's balance sheet shrinks, as does the monetary base; the banking system's reserves decline, while its securities holdings increase.[5]

Foreign Exchange Intervention

What happens if the U.S. Treasury instructs the Federal Reserve to buy $1 billion worth of euros? The answer is that the Federal Reserve Bank of New York buys German government bonds, denominated in euros, from the foreign exchange departments of large commercial banks and pays for them with dollars.[6] Like an open market bond purchase, this transaction is done electronically and the $1 billion payment is credited directly to the reserve account of the bank from which the bonds were bought. The impact on the Fed's balance sheet is almost identical to that of the open market operation, as Panel A of Figure 17.3 shows. The Fed's assets and liabilities both rise by $1 billion, and the monetary base expands with them.

Because the Federal Reserve bought the euros from a commercial bank, the impact on the banking system's balance sheet is straightforward. The result, shown in Panel B of Figure 17.3, is nearly identical to the impact when the Fed bought bonds through an

[5]Prior to the financial crisis of 2007–2009, the Fed virtually never sold securities. It always bought; the only question was how much. The Fed had always intentionally left itself in a position in which it needed to buy securities on a temporary basis through repurchase agreements. In the early stages of the crisis, however, the Fed sold securities to limit the expansion of its balance sheet. From 2017 to 2019, the Fed gradually reduced its balance sheet by limiting the replacement of maturing securities.

[6]As a technical matter, the Fed first purchases euro currency with dollars and then uses the proceeds to buy the German government bonds. But because it owns the euro currency for a very short time, only a few hours, we are ignoring that intermediate transaction.

What Should the Fed Own?
APPLYING THE CONCEPT

There is always a great deal of discussion about the *size* of the Fed's balance sheet. The total quantity of securities owned rose from less than $800 *billion* in 2007 to more than $4.5 *trillion* in 2015. Meanwhile, the *composition* of the balance changed dramatically. Prior to the crisis, the Fed owned exclusively U.S. Treasury securities. From 2008 to 2010, it purchased substantial quantities of mortgage-backed securities (MBS), driving the fraction of Treasurys down to as low as 37 percent. As of August 2019, the Fed held a total of $3.8 trillion in securities, 42 percent ($1.5 trillion) of which were MBS.

All of this brings up an important question: What *should* the Fed own? More specifically, what is the appropriate *mix* (rather than the *scale*) of the Fed's asset holdings?

A simple and compelling answer is that in normal times, when the economy is expanding and absent any financial strains, the Fed should aim for a balance sheet that has *minimal liquidity, maturity, and credit risk*. In practical terms, this means a securities portfolio composed largely of Treasury bills and short-term notes, with an average maturity that is very short.

Such a minimalist portfolio satisfies two objectives. First, the holdings are as riskless as possible. And second, the actions of the Fed distort financial markets as little as possible. Because the federal government issues or guarantees the domestic securities held by the Fed, credit risk already is minimal. To reduce liquidity and maturity risk, holdings should be short maturity.

A minimum-risk portfolio has three distinct advantages. First, holding entirely short-term Treasury debt counters the frequent criticism from Congress and others that by purchasing MBS to support the housing market, the Fed strays into fiscal policy ("picking winners" among the users of funds) and oversteps its mandate. Second, a low-risk portfolio removes the Fed from interference in the market determination of liquidity and maturity risk premia, in line with its approach to credit risk. Third, by sharply dialing back the riskiness of its portfolio in normal times, the Fed maximizes the firepower available to counter threats to financial and economic stability when they inevitably arise.

Importantly, however, saying that the Fed should own exclusively short-term Treasury notes and bills says nothing about the appropriate quantity it should hold. Should the balance sheet be equivalent to its level in 2007, when authorities held enough Treasury securities to accommodate the demand for currency and very little more? Or, should the balance sheet be much larger, providing abundant reserves to the banking system? In early 2019, the FOMC decided that it will maintain a relatively abundant supply of reserves over the medium term and will continue to exercise policy control primarily through interest rate tools (see Chapter 18 for details). In any case, to the extent that banks are indifferent between holding reserves at the Fed and Treasury bills, a low-risk portfolio in normal times makes the magnitude of the Fed's balance sheet less salient.

open market purchase (see Figure 17.2). In both cases, the banking system's securities portfolio falls by $1 billion and reserve balances rise by an equal amount. The only difference is the exact assets that decline. In a standard open market operation, the reduction is in bank holdings of U.S. government bonds; here it is in their holdings of euro-denominated assets.

Figure 17.3 Balance Sheet Changes after the Federal Reserve Purchases a German Government Bond

A. Federal Reserve's Balance Sheet

Assets		Liabilities	
Foreign exchange reserves (German government bonds in euros)	+$1 billion	Reserves	+$1 billion

B. Banking System's Balance Sheet

Assets		Liabilities
Reserves	+$1 billion	
Securities (German government bonds)	−$1 billion	

Figure 17.4 Balance Sheet Changes after the Federal Reserve Makes a Discount Loan

A. Federal Reserve's Balance Sheet

Assets		Liabilities	
Discount loans	+$100 million	Reserves	+$100 million

B. Banking System's Balance Sheet

Assets		Liabilities	
Reserves	+$100 million	Discount loans	+$100 million

Discount Loans

The Federal Reserve does not force commercial banks to borrow money; the banks ask for loans. To get one, a borrowing bank must provide collateral.[7] While this usually takes the form of U.S. Treasury bonds, the Fed has always been willing to accept a broad range of securities and loans as the collateral for lending to banks. During the crisis, when discount loans surged, this willingness facilitated lending. Not surprisingly, when the Fed makes such a loan, it changes the balance sheet of both institutions. For the borrowing bank, the loan is a liability that is matched by an offsetting increase in the level of its reserve account. For the Fed, the loan is an asset that is created in exchange for a credit to the borrower's reserve account. The impact on the Federal Reserve's balance sheet is shown in Panel A of Figure 17.4.

Note that the increase in loans is an asset to the Fed, while the change in reserves increases its liabilities. Once again, the impact on the Fed's balance sheet is the same as that of an open market purchase or an increase in foreign exchange reserves. The extension of credit to the banking system raises the level of reserves and expands the monetary base.

The impact on the banking system's balance sheet mirrors the impact on the Fed, with reserves and loans both increasing. In this case, however, commercial banks have increased the size of their balance sheet by borrowing from the Fed (see Panel B of Figure 17.4).

In summary, open market purchases, an increase in foreign exchange reserves, and the extension of discount loans all increase the reserves available to the banking system, expanding the monetary base. We turn now to a different type of transaction, one that affects only the composition—not the size—of the monetary base.

Cash Withdrawal

The Federal Reserve can always shift its holdings of various assets, selling U.S. Treasury bonds and using the proceeds to buy Japanese yen, or engaging in an offsetting sale of a U.S. Treasury security after a bank takes out a discount loan. But the same is not true of its liabilities. Because the Fed stands ready to exchange reserves for

[7]Remember, *collateral* is the term used to describe specific assets pledged by a borrower that a lender can seize in the event of nonpayment. To obtain a discount loan, a bank must identify specific assets (usually bonds) that the Fed can take if the bank doesn't repay the loan. The ECB, which relies primarily on collateralized lending to implement policy, publishes each day a list of eligible collateral. As of January 2019, that list contained more than 28,000 financial instruments.

Figure 17.5 Balance Sheet Changes after a Private Person Withdraws Cash from His or Her Bank Account

A. Nonbank Public's Balance Sheet

Assets		Liabilities
Currency	+$100	
Checkable deposits	−$100	

B. Federal Reserve's Balance Sheet

Assets	Liabilities	
	Currency	+$100
	Reserves	−$100

C. Banking System's Balance Sheet

Assets		Liabilities	
Reserves	−$100	Checkable deposits	−$100

currency on demand, it does not control the mix between the two. The nonbank public—the people who hold the cash—controls that.

You may be surprised to learn that when you take cash from an ATM, you are changing the Federal Reserve's balance sheet. The reason is that vault cash is part of reserves, while the currency holdings of the nonbank public—your cash and ours—are not. By moving your own assets out of your bank and into currency, you force a shift from reserves to currency on the Fed's balance sheet. The transaction is complicated, involving the nonbank public (you and me), the banking system, and the central bank, so understanding it means looking at three balance sheets.

Consider an example in which you withdraw $100 from your checking account. This transaction changes the composition of the asset side of your balance sheet, as shown in Panel A of Figure 17.5. (Because there is no change in your liabilities, the changes in the asset side of your balance sheet must sum to zero.)

But that isn't all. By taking $100 out of the cash machine, you had an impact on your bank's balance sheet as well. Remember, cash inside the bank—vault cash—counts as reserves, so by withdrawing cash from your bank, you decreased the banking system's reserves. The change in the banking system's T-account is shown in Panel C of Figure 17.5.

It should come as no surprise to you that when you take your money out of the bank, the bank's balance sheet shrinks. Here we see that your cash withdrawal forced the banking system to contract its balance sheet. Note that the change in bank assets equals the change in bank liabilities.

Finally, there is the Federal Reserve. Remember, the Fed controls the size of its own balance sheet, so your transactions can't affect that. But what you can do is change the composition of the Fed's liabilities. By withdrawing cash, you changed the amount of currency outstanding—a change that shows up on the Fed's balance sheet as a shift from reserves to currency. Both are liabilities. Panel B of Figure 17.5 shows what the Fed's balance sheet looks like. Note that the monetary base hasn't changed. Remember that the monetary base equals currency plus reserves, and one went up while the other went down. But the *relative size* of each component of the monetary base has changed.

Table 17.2 Changes in the Size and Composition of the Federal Reserve's Balance Sheet and the Monetary Base

Transaction	Initiated by	Typical Action	Impact
Open market operation	Central bank	Purchase of Treasury bond	Increases reserves, the size of the Fed's balance sheet, and the monetary base
Foreign exchange intervention	Central bank	Purchase of German government bond	Increases reserves, the size of the Fed's balance sheet, and the monetary base
Discount loan	Commercial bank	Extension of loan to commercial bank	Increases reserves, the size of the Fed's balance sheet, and the monetary base
Cash withdrawal	Nonbank public	Withdrawal of cash from ATM	Decreases reserves and increases currency, leaving the size of the Fed's balance sheet and the monetary base unchanged

Table 17.2 summarizes the impact of each of the four transactions we have just studied on the size and composition of the Federal Reserve's balance sheet. Open market operations and foreign exchange interventions are both done at the discretion of the central bank, while the level of discount borrowing is decided by the commercial banks. The nonbank public decides how much currency to hold.

It is worth noting that there are countries where the process works differently. As we will see in Chapter 19, when a central bank wishes to control its country's exchange rate rather than the domestic interest rate, one way to do so is to stand ready to buy and sell foreign currency. In such cases, foreign exchange intervention is not truly under the central bank's control. Instead, the private sector decides when the purchases and sales are made and how large they are. That is essentially what the Bank of Thailand was doing in 1997, and when it started to run out of foreign currency reserves, the system collapsed.

The Deposit Expansion Multiplier

Central bank liabilities form the base on which the supplies of money and credit are built; that is why they are called the *monetary base*. The central bank controls the monetary base, causing it to expand and contract. But most of us don't focus much attention on the monetary base. Our primary interest is in the broader measures of money, M1 and M2, which are mostly liabilities of private banks. Recall from Chapter 2 that M1 is currency plus demand deposits and M2 adds time deposits to M1. This is the *money* we think of as available for transactions. What is the relationship between the central bank's liabilities and these broader measures of money? How do reserves become bank deposits? The answer is that the banking system makes them, in a process called **multiple deposit creation**.

Deposit Creation in a Single Bank

To see how deposits are created, let's start with an open market purchase in which the Federal Reserve buys $100,000 worth of securities from a bank called *First Bank*.

Figure 17.6 Changes in First Bank's Balance Sheet after the Fed's Purchase of a U.S. Treasury Bond

A. Immediate Impact

Assets		Liabilities
Reserves	+$100,000	
Securities	–$100,000	

B. After the Extension of a Loan

Assets		Liabilities	
Reserves	+$100,000	Checkable deposits	+$100,000
Securities	–$100,000		
Loans	+$100,000		

C. After Withdrawal by the Borrower

Assets		Liabilities	
Reserves	$0	Checkable deposits	$0
Securities	–$100,000		
Loans	+$100,000		

While First Bank may have its own reasons for selling the securities, we are assuming that the Fed initiated the transaction. So if First Bank doesn't sell the securities, some other bank will.

The Fed's purchase leaves the bank's total assets unchanged, but it shifts $100,000 out of securities and into reserves, increasing reserves by the amount of the open market purchase. The impact on First Bank's balance sheet is shown in Panel A of Figure 17.6. (It is similar to Panel B of Figure 17.2.)

TIME

What does First Bank do in response to this change in the composition of its assets? The bank's management must do something. After all, it just sold a U.S. Treasury bond to the Fed and received reserves that typically bear a lower interest rate in exchange. If it does nothing, the bank's revenue will fall, and so will its profits. With liabilities unchanged, the increase in First Bank's reserves doesn't affect the quantity of reserves the bank is required to hold, so it counts as an increase in *excess reserves*. Remember that banks hold reserves for two reasons: because regulators require them and because banks need them to conduct their daily business. But when reserves rise in response to the sale of a security, something profitable has to be done with the proceeds.

The most natural thing for a bank to do is to lend out the excess—and no more. To keep the example simple, assume that First Bank has just received a loan application from Office Builders Incorporated (OBI). OBI is seeking $100,000 to finance the continued construction of an office building. First Bank approves the loan and credits OBI's checking account with an additional $100,000. Figure 17.6 Panel B shows First Bank's balance sheet immediately after the loan is made.

OBI did not take out its $100,000 loan to leave it in First Bank's checking account. The company borrowed to pay suppliers and employees. So OBI's financial officer proceeds to write checks totaling $100,000. As First Bank makes good on OBI's checks, OBI's checking account balance falls, but so does First Bank's reserve account balance. When the entire $100,000 loan has been spent, First Bank's balance sheet looks like Panel C of Figure 17.6.

In summary, following a $100,000 open market purchase of securities by the Fed, First Bank makes a loan equal to the amount of newly created excess reserves. That loan replaces the securities as an asset on First Bank's balance sheet.

Deposit Expansion in a System of Banks

First Bank's loan and OBI's expenditures can't be the end of the story because the suppliers and employees paid by OBI took their checks to the bank and deposited them. As the checks made their way through the payments system, First Bank's reserves were transferred to the reserve accounts of the suppliers' and employees' banks. *Only the Fed (the central bank) can create and destroy the monetary base.* The nonbank public determines how much of it ends up as reserves in the banking system and how much is in currency; all the banks can do is move the reserves they have around among themselves. So, assuming cash holdings don't change following an open market purchase, the reserves created by the Fed must end up somewhere. Let's follow them to see where they go.

We'll start by making four assumptions that allow us to focus on the essential parts of the story: (1) banks hold no excess reserves; (2) the reserve requirement is 10 percent of checking account deposits; (3) when the level of checking account deposits and loans changes, the quantity of currency held by the nonbank public does not; and (4) when a borrower writes a check, none of the recipients of the funds deposit them back in the bank that initially made the loan. Now, let's say that OBI uses the $100,000 loan to pay for steel girders from American Steel Co. American Steel deposits the $100,000 in its bank, Second Bank, which credits American's checking account. When OBI's check clears, Second Bank's reserve account at the Federal Reserve Bank is credited with $100,000. That's the transfer of reserves from First Bank. The result is shown in Panel A of Figure 17.7.

The additional $100,000 in American Steel's checking account is costly for Second Bank to service. American Steel will want to receive interest on its idle balance as well as access to it for payments. And the reserves Second Bank just received usually pay less

Figure 17.7 Changes in Balance Sheets

A. Second Bank after American Steel's Deposit

Assets		Liabilities	
Reserves	+$100,000	American Steel's checking account	+$100,000

B. Second Bank after Extension of a Loan

Assets		Liabilities	
Reserves	+$10,000	American Steel's checking account	+$100,000
Loan	+$90,000		

C. Third Bank after Deposit and Extension of a Loan

Assets		Liabilities	
Reserves	+$ 9,000	Checking account	+$90,000
Loan	+$81,000		

Assuming a 10 percent reserve requirement, banks hold no excess reserves, and there are no changes in currency holdings.

interest than a loan. In the same way that First Bank lent out its new reserves following the Fed's open market purchase, Second Bank will make a loan after American Steel has made its deposit. How large will the loan be? Because the reserve requirement is 10 percent, Second Bank must hold an additional $10,000 in reserves against the new $100,000 deposit. Individual banks can't make loans that exceed their excess reserves, so the largest loan Second Bank can make is $90,000—and that's what it does. (Remember, we're assuming banks hold no excess reserves.) If the borrower immediately uses the $90,000 loan, Second Bank's balance sheet will look like Figure 17.7 Panel B.

This new loan, and the reserves that go with it, must go somewhere, too. Let's say that it is deposited in yet another bank, Third Bank, which makes a loan equal to 90 percent of the new deposit. The change in Third Bank's balance sheet is shown in Panel C of Figure 17.7. (Recall, we're assuming that the owner of the checking account at Third Bank doesn't withdraw any cash.)

At this point, a $100,000 open market purchase has created $100,000 + $90,000 = $190,000 in new checking account deposits at Second Bank and Third Bank and $100,000 + $90,000 + $81,000 = $271,000 in new combined loans at First Bank, Second Bank, and Third Bank. But the process doesn't stop there. The $81,000 loan from Third Bank is deposited into Fourth Bank, where it creates an additional $81,000 in checking account deposits. Fourth Bank then makes a loan that is 90 percent of $81,000, or $72,900, and the $72,900 is deposited. And so on, as shown in Figure 17.8.

Table 17.3 shows the consequences of a $100,000 open market purchase for the banking system as a whole. As the $100,000 in new reserves spreads through the banking system, it generates $1,000,000 in deposits and $1,000,000 in loans. With a 10 percent reserve requirement, each added dollar in reserves expands to $10 in deposits, increasing the quantity of money by a factor of 10.

With a bit of algebra, we can derive a formula for the **deposit expansion multiplier**—the increase in commercial bank deposits following a one-dollar open market purchase, (assuming there are no excess reserves in the banking system and no changes in the amount of currency held by the nonbank public).

Figure 17.8 Multiple Deposit Creation

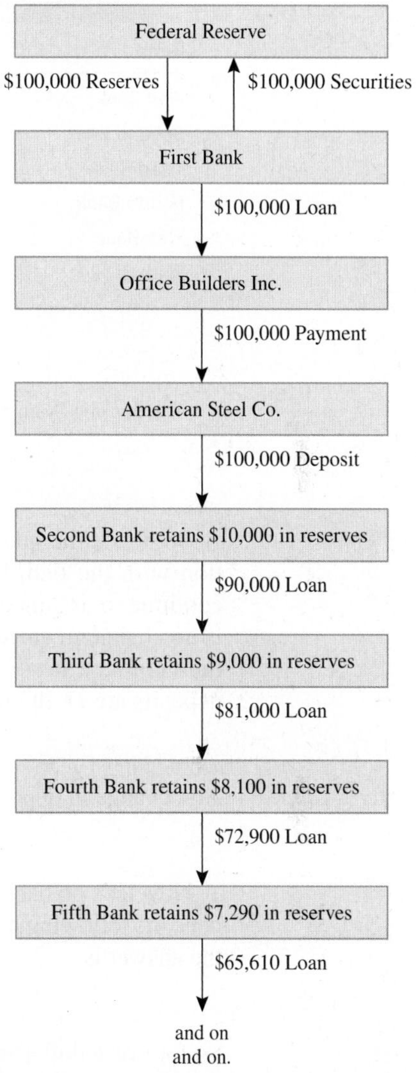

Federal Reserve
$100,000 Reserves ↓ ↑ $100,000 Securities
First Bank
↓ $100,000 Loan
Office Builders Inc.
↓ $100,000 Payment
American Steel Co.
↓ $100,000 Deposit
Second Bank retains $10,000 in reserves
↓ $90,000 Loan
Third Bank retains $9,000 in reserves
↓ $81,000 Loan
Fourth Bank retains $8,100 in reserves
↓ $72,900 Loan
Fifth Bank retains $7,290 in reserves
↓ $65,610 Loan
and on and on.

Assuming a 10 percent reserve requirement, banks hold no excess reserves, and there are no changes in currency holdings.

There's an easy way and a hard way to figure out the size of the deposit expansion multiplier. Let's start with the easy way. Imagine that the entire banking system is composed of a single bank—call it the Monopoly Bank. When the country's banking system is made up of just one bank, everyone has to use it. That means that any payment made from one person to another is just a transfer between two accounts in the Monopoly Bank. Because the managers of the Monopoly Bank know this, they don't need to worry about losing reserves when they make a loan.

Table 17.3 Multiple Deposit Expansion following a $100,000 Open Market Purchase Assuming a 10% Reserve Requirement

Bank	Increase in Deposits	Increase in Loans	Increase in Reserves
First Bank	$ 0	$ 100,000	$ 0
Second Bank	$ 100,000	$ 90,000	$ 10,000
Third Bank	$ 90,000	$ 81,000	$ 9,000
Fourth Bank	$ 81,000	$ 72,900	$ 8,100
Fifth Bank	$ 72,900	$ 65,610	$ 7,290
Sixth Bank	$ 65,610	$ 59,049	$ 6,561
.	.	.	.
.	.	.	.
.	.	.	.
The Banking System	$1,000,000	$1,000,000	$100,000

So here's the question. For each dollar change in reserves arising from a transaction with the Fed, how much can the Monopoly Bank change its deposits? If we continue to assume that the Monopoly Bank holds no excess reserves and that there is no change in currency held by the nonbank public, then its level of reserves is just the **required reserve ratio** r_D times its deposits. If required reserves are RR and deposits are D, the level of reserves can be expressed as

$$RR = r_D D \tag{1}$$

Any change in deposits creates a corresponding change in reserves, expressed as

$$\Delta RR = r_D \Delta D \tag{2}$$

Now let's go back to the question we started with: What is the change in the level of deposits following a one-dollar change in reserves? From equation (2), we can see that the answer is

$$\Delta D = \frac{1}{r_D} \Delta RR \tag{3}$$

So for every dollar increase in reserves, deposits increase by $(1/r_D)$. This is the simple deposit expansion multiplier. If the reserve requirement is 10 percent, as it was in our example, then the simple deposit expansion multiplier equals (1/0.1) = 10, and a \$100,000 open market purchase generates a \$1,000,000 = 10 × \$100,000 increase in the quantity of money. To see why this makes sense, note that if deposits rose by more than \$1,000,000 following the addition of \$100,000 in reserves, the banking system would violate the reserve requirement. And if deposits rose by less than 10 times the change in reserves, some banks would be holding excess reserves, which violates one of the assumptions we made at the outset.

The hard way to compute the simple deposit expansion multiplier is to look at Table 17.3 and add up the entries. Notice that starting with Third Bank, each entry in the column "Increase in Deposits" equals $(1 - r_D)$ times the entry above it, where r_D is the reserve requirement (measured as a decimal). With a reserve requirement of 10 percent, $r_D = 0.10$, $(1 - r_D) = 0.90$, so each entry is 0.90 times the one above it.

For example, \$90,000 equals 0.90 times \$100,000; \$81,000 equals 0.90 times \$90,000. Thus, a one-dollar increase in reserves creates an increase in deposits equal to the sum of this series: $[1 + (1 - r_D) + (1 - r_D)^2 + (1 - r_D)^3 + \cdots]$. Using a formula from the appendix to Chapter 4, we can determine that this expression equals $(1/r_D)$.

Before we continue, it is important to emphasize that there is nothing magical about *increases* in reserves and deposit *expansion*. A *decrease* in reserves will generate a deposit *contraction* in exactly the same way. That is, a \$100,000 open market sale, in which the Fed sells a security in exchange for reserves, will reduce the level of deposits. From equation (3), we see that with a 10 percent reserve requirement, the contraction in deposits is $10 \times \$100,000 = \$1,000,000$.

The Monetary Base and the Money Supply

We have made considerable headway in understanding the link between the central bank's balance sheet and the quantity of money in the economy. A change in reserves precipitates a significant change in the level of loans and checkable deposits in the banking system. But the simple deposit expansion multiplier is too simple. In deriving it, we ignored a few important details.

First, we assumed that banks lent out the entirety of the reserves that were not required, leaving no excess reserves in the banking system. In fact, banks do hold some excess reserves, in part to protect against unexpected deposit outflows, but also for other reasons. Demand for excess reserves can change dramatically and unpredictably. For example, during the financial crisis of 2007–2009, excess reserves surged as banks built a safety cushion to insure themselves against the loss of funding liquidity (see Chapter 2, Lessons from the Crisis: Market Liquidity, Funding Liquidity, and Making Markets) and unanticipated drawdowns of credit lines.

Second, we ignored the fact that the nonbank public holds cash. As people's account balances rise, they have a tendency to hold more cash. From our discussion of the central bank's balance sheet, we know that when individuals change their cash holdings, they change the level of reserves in the banking system. Both these considerations affect the relationship among reserves, the monetary base, and the quantity of money in the economy. Let's look at the relationship in more detail.

Deposit Expansion with Excess Reserves and Cash Withdrawals

To see how important excess reserves and cash holdings are, we can go back through the deposit expansion story, this time taking them into account. Assume that banks want to hold excess reserves equal to 5 percent of checking account deposits and that the holder of a checking account withdraws 5 percent of a deposit in cash. Recall that the reserve requirement is 10 percent.

To understand the implication of these changes, let's go back to the example in the last section, in which the Fed purchased \$100,000 worth of securities from First Bank (Panel A of Figure 17.6), which proceeded to make a \$100,000 loan to Office Builders Incorporated (Panel B of Figure 17.6). OBI then used the \$100,000 to purchase steel from American Steel, which withdrew the funds from First Bank and deposited them in a checking account in Second Bank. This brings us to the T-account in Panel A of Figure 17.7. If American Steel takes some of the \$100,000 in cash and Second Bank wishes to hold excess reserves, then the next loan cannot be \$90,000.

Has Paper Money Outlived Its Purpose?
YOUR FINANCIAL WORLD

Serious people have suggested that we eliminate paper currency.* Paper money facilitates criminality and establishes the effective lower bound for nominal interest rates. So why not just get rid of it? We could replace it with electronic money that could be monitored for illicit transactions and would carry an interest rate as low as policymakers wish—even a sizably negative rate (see Applying the Concept: Negative Nominal Interest Rates: Blast from the Past?, page 469).

There is an enormous amount of currency out there. For dollars, the value in circulation worldwide is in the range of $5,300 per U.S. resident and about €3,600 per euro-area resident. In Japan, the number is more than 40 percent greater. than in the United States And most of the notes in circulation are in large denominations: 80 percent of U.S. currency is in $100 bills, 48 percent of euros is in bills of €100 or more, and ¥10,000 notes account for 93 percent of Japanese paper currency. Out of concern that high-value notes facilitate criminality, in 2016 the ECB decided to eliminate further issuance of the €500 note.

Law-abiding taxpayers simply do not keep this amount of cash around. The natural conclusion is that the extraordinary volume of currency—especially the large-denomination component—results from illegal activity ranging from tax evasion to organized crime.

In the absence of paper money, central banks could reduce the nominal interest rate as far as they want by setting a negative interest rate on banks' reserve deposits; and banks would presumably turn around and charge their customers for holding deposit balances. Very negative interest rates could help battle deep economic slumps like the Great Recession of 2007–2009.

Not so fast, you say. If the United States eliminated its paper currency, criminals would shift to euros, yen, sterling, and the like—so then, wouldn't *all* major currencies have to be made electronic in order to combat criminality? The answer is surely yes. If one major currency goes electronic, any other country that issues a trusted currency would have to get rid of at least its large-denomination notes. In addition, countries would have to tax or forbid private currencies that could substitute for the public varieties.

However, paper currency carries significant economic benefits. Governments receive *seignorage* (the ability to acquire real goods and services in exchange for fiat currency) for issuing notes and coin. That income probably exceeds by a significant margin the revenue gained from reducing tax evasion.

Another, very different, and more powerful argument for keeping cash around is this: the anonymity of paper currency is a source of freedom. Yes, people sometimes misuse that freedom for criminal gain. But in a society with only electronic currency, the government could use the resulting detailed knowledge of payments to exert tyrannical control. There is a very real sense in which we are what we buy, so protecting our privacy requires having the option of anonymity in payments. Cash provides that option.

Paper currency is at the heart of how we choose to organize our society. There are means other than eliminating cash—less effective but also less threatening to personal liberties—to expose the shadow economy. And as the recent financial crisis has shown, central banks still have policy alternatives when the short-term interest rate hits zero.

*See Kenneth S. Rogoff, *The Curse of Cash* (Princeton, NJ: Princeton University Press, 2016).

Assuming that American Steel removes 5 percent of its new funds in cash, that leaves $95,000 in the checking account and $95,000 in Second Bank's reserve account. (Look back at Panel C of Figure 17.5 to see the impact of a cash withdrawal on the banking system's balance sheet.) Because Second Bank wishes to hold excess reserves equal to 5 percent of deposits, it will want to keep reserves of 15 percent of $95,000, or $14,250. That means making a loan of only $80,750. Instead of Panel B of Figure 17.7, Second Bank's balance sheet looks like Figure 17.9.

We can continue as before, following the proceeds of Second Bank's loan as it is deposited in Third Bank. Assuming that the depositor of the loan's proceeds wishes to hold 5 percent of the deposit in cash and that Third Bank wants to hold excess reserves equal to 5 percent of deposits, the increase in deposits will be $80,750 minus $4,037.50 equals $76,712.50, and Third Bank will make a loan of $65,205.63, keeping reserves of $11,506.87. Compare these numbers with the ones in Table 17.3 and you will see

Figure 17.9 Change in Second Bank's Balance Sheet following a Deposit and Extension of a Loan

Assets		Liabilities	
Required reserves	+$ 9,500	American Steel's checking account	+$95,000
Excess reserves	+$ 4,750		
Loan	+$80,750		

Assuming excess reserves and cash holdings. Note: American Steel also has $5,000 in cash.

how much smaller the deposit expansion becomes if we take into account excess reserves and cash withdrawals.

In the last section, we derived the result that a one-dollar change in reserves created a change in deposits equal to one over the reserve requirement, or $(1/r_D)$. So, for an r_D of 10 percent, a $1 change in reserves generated a $10 change in deposits. But now the analysis is more complicated and the deposit expansion is smaller. The desire of banks to hold excess reserves and the desire of account holders to withdraw cash both reduce the impact of a given change in reserves on the total deposits in the system. The more excess reserves banks desire to hold, and the more cash the public withdraws, the smaller the impact. In fact, these two factors operate in the same way as an increase in the reserve requirement.

The Arithmetic of the Money Multiplier

To better understand the relationship between deposits and reserves, we can derive the *money multiplier,* which shows how the quantity of money (checking account deposits plus currency) is related to the monetary base (reserves in the banking system plus currency held by the nonbank public). Keep in mind that the monetary base is the quantity that the central bank can control.

If we label the quantity of money M and the monetary base MB, the money multiplier m is defined by the relationship

$$M = m \times MB \tag{4}$$

To derive the money multiplier, we start with a few simple relationships: money equals currency (C) plus checkable deposits (D); the monetary base (MB) equals currency plus reserves in the banking system (R); and reserves equal required reserves (RR) plus excess reserves (ER). Writing these relationships as simple equations, we have

$$M = C + D \quad \text{Money} = \text{Currency} + \text{Checkable deposits} \tag{5}$$

$$MB = C + R \quad \text{Monetary base} = \text{Currency} + \text{Reserves} \tag{6}$$

$$R = RR + ER \quad \text{Reserves} = \text{Required reserves} + \text{Excess reserves} \tag{7}$$

These are just accounting definitions; the next step is to incorporate the behavior of banks and individuals. Starting with banks, we know that their holdings of required reserves depend on the required reserve ratio r_D. But what about excess reserves? In our earlier discussion, we assumed that banks hold excess reserves as a proportion of their deposits, and that *the amount of excess reserves a bank holds depends on the costs and benefits of holding them.* The cost of excess reserves is the interest on the loans that could be made with them, less the interest received on reserve balances, while the benefits have to do with safety should deposits be withdrawn suddenly. The higher the interest rate on loans, the lower banks' excess reserves will be; the greater banks' concern over the possibility of deposit withdrawals, the higher their excess reserves will be.

Labeling the **excess reserve-to-deposit ratio** $\{ER/D\}$, we can rewrite the reserve equation (7) as

$$\begin{aligned} R &= RR + ER \quad \text{Reserves} = \text{Required reserves} + \text{Excess reserves} \\ &= r_D D + \{ER/D\}D \\ &= (r_D + \{ER/D\})D \end{aligned} \tag{8}$$

That is, banks hold reserves as a proportion of their deposits.

Turning to the nonbank public, we need to take account of their currency holdings. Again, as in the preceding example, we assume that people hold currency as a fraction of their deposits. That is,

$$C = \{C/D\}D \tag{9}$$

where $\{C/D\}$ is the **currency-to-deposit ratio**. The *decision of how much currency to hold depends on costs and benefits* in the same way as the decision to hold excess reserves. The cost of currency is the interest it would earn on deposit, while the benefit is its lower risk and greater liquidity. As interest rates rise, cash becomes less desirable. But if the riskiness of alternative holdings rises or liquidity falls, then cash becomes more desirable, and $\{C/D\}$ will rise.

Bringing all these elements together, we can rewrite the expression for the monetary base using the reserve and currency expressions. That gives us

$$\begin{aligned} MB &= C + R \quad \text{Monetary base} = \text{Currency} + \text{Reserves} \\ &= \{C/D\}D + (r_D + \{ER/D\})D \\ &= (\{C/D\} + r_D + \{ER/D\})D \end{aligned} \tag{10}$$

We see now that the monetary base has three uses: required reserves, excess reserves, and cash in the hands of the nonbank public. But our interest is in the relationship between the quantity of money and the monetary base. To find this, we can solve equation (10) for the level of deposits.

$$D = \frac{1}{\{C/D\} + r_D + \{ER/D\}} \times MB \tag{11}$$

This expression tells us how much deposits change with a change in the monetary base. Notice that if we ignore excess reserves and cash withdrawals, so that $\{ER/D\}$ and $\{C/D\}$ both equal zero, we get the same result as in equation (3), that a change in deposits equals $(\frac{1}{r_D})$ times the change in the monetary base. For a reserve requirement of 10 percent, that meant that a one-dollar change in the monetary base increased deposits by \$10. Adding the excess reserve-to-deposit and currency-to-deposit ratios that we used in the example after Figure 17.9, 5 percent each, this equation tells us that a one-dollar increase in the monetary base will increase deposits by $[1/(0.10 + 0.05 + 0.05)] = 5$.

Returning to the derivation of the money multiplier, we can take the expression for money and rewrite it as

$$\begin{aligned} M &= C + D \quad \text{Money} = \text{Currency} + \text{Checkable deposits} \\ &= \{C/D\}D + D \\ &= (\{C/D\} + 1)D \end{aligned} \tag{12}$$

Negative Nominal Interest Rates: Blast from the Past?
APPLYING THE CONCEPT

Goldsmiths were the forerunners of modern bankers. Originally, they issued receipts to those who paid them a fee to place gold in their vaults. These receipts eventually gave rise to *fractional reserve banking*, as goldsmiths used a portion of the gold to make loans.

Today, we might be on our way back to the original form of goldsmith safekeeping, but instead of guarding our gold, banks will be storing our physical cash—our dollar, Swiss franc, yen, or euro notes!

This story is tied to an important puzzle regarding negative nominal interest rates: how far below zero can they go? Answer: somewhat, but beyond that still-unknown level, a point exists at which our handling of cash will revert to the early days of the goldsmiths.

Starting in late 2014, several central banks indeed pushed their deposit rates below zero. The ECB's was set at –0.20 percent, while the Swiss National Bank set its at –0.75 percent, meaning commercial banks had to pay to make deposits at the central bank. If the rates had gone sharply lower, the commercial banks might have started to charge *their* depositors—the general public—to hold their funds.

This seems upside down. Lenders paying borrowers to borrow? Isn't there a zero lower bound for nominal interest rates? Could those central banks have pushed their rates even further below zero?

We don't know what the "effective lower bound" (ELB) is. But, if central banks try to lower rates below the ELB, commercial bank depositors would shift their funds into cash and banks would shrink their balance sheets. So long as there is abundant cash that earns a zero interest rate, there exists an ELB on nominal interest rates: namely, zero less the costs of storing, transferring, and insuring cash.

Why? Recall that bankers run what is called a "spread" business, charging borrowers a higher rate for loans than they pay customers for their deposits. As a matter of arithmetic, that would mean that if the bank's interest rate spread is three percentage points (a fairly representative level) and assets yielded –1 percent, the bank would offer depositors –4 percent.

But who would want to pay 4 percent of their deposit balance each year to the bank when they can hold cash instead? Of course, people willingly pay for services that come with a deposit account, like safekeeping, check writing, automated payments, and web access to their accounts. If these services are worth about 1 percent of the balance, then that leaves 3 percent more that depositors would have to pay the bank. However, since withdrawing all your money from the bank and holding it as cash would be highly inconvenient, banks can still help businesses and households in this case. How? Like the goldsmiths of yore, banks can rent out vault space.

Suppose, for example, that banks were to offer to convert customers' deposit accounts into "cash reserve accounts" (CRAs), which hold only currency and so do not represent reserve balances at the central bank. Bankers can organize CRAs so that a customer's funds are available during the business day, and at night they are held as piles of currency in the bank's vault. At night, the currency belongs to customers; during the day it is the asset balancing the CRA liability on the bank's own account.

Crucially, the CRA cash in the bank's vault is not available to be lent out. That is, the deposit expansion multiplier does not operate when depositors hold currency.

What would happen if policymakers try to stimulate the economy by reducing interest rates below the ELB threshold that prompts bank customers to favor CRAs over deposits? Banks would store customers' cash for a small fee and let them use it to make payments. Thus, instead of providing further economic stimulus, such a rate cut would reduce the supply of bank credit and tighten monetary conditions!

Substituting D from equation (11) gives us the final answer:

$$\boxed{M = \frac{\{C/D\} + 1}{\{C/D\} + r_D + \{ER/D\}} \times MB} \qquad (13)$$

Money = Money multiplier × Monetary base

This result is somewhat complicated, but it is worth studying. Equation (13), highlighted by the red rectangle, tells us that the quantity of money in the economy depends on four variables:

1. The monetary base, which is controlled by the central bank.
2. The reserve requirement imposed by regulators on banks that accept deposits.
3. The desire on the part of banks to hold excess reserves.
4. The demand for currency by the nonbank public.

To see how the quantity of money in the economy changes, we can look at the impact of each of these four elements. The first is the easiest. We know that if the monetary base increases, holding bank and public behavior constant, the quantity of money increases. Looking at the second and third elements—those factors affecting reserves—we see that an increase in either the reserve requirement or banks' excess reserve holdings decreases the money multiplier. So for a fixed level of the monetary base, an increase in either r_D or $\{ER/D\}$ reduces M.

Finally, there is the currency-to-deposit ratio. What happens when individuals increase their currency holdings at a fixed level of the monetary base? Because $\{C/D\}$ appears in both the numerator and the denominator of the money multiplier in equation (13), we can't immediately tell whether the change creates an expansion or a contraction. Fortunately, logic gives us the answer that is correct whenever, as has usually been the case, deposits exceed total reserves. (Reserves have surpassed checkable deposits since 2008 but remain well below total deposits.) When an individual withdraws cash from the bank, he or she increases currency in the hands of the public and decreases reserves, so the monetary base is unaffected. But the decline in reserves creates a multiple deposit contraction. (Remember, every dollar in reserves creates more than a dollar's worth of deposits, raising the quantity of money more than a dollar.) Because each extra dollar held in currency raises M by only a dollar, when reserves are converted to currency, the money supply contracts. Table 17.4 summarizes the effect of changes in the four components of the money supply.

A short numerical example illustrates the computation of the money multiplier.[8] At the end of 2018, banks held required reserves of \$123.7 billion and excess reserves of \$1,567.7 billion. Currency in the hands of the public was \$1,709.3 billion, while deposit accounts (demand deposits plus other checkable deposits) amounted to \$2,158.5 billion. These amounts imply that the required reserve ratio (r_D) was (123.7/2,158.5) = 0.06; the excess reserve-to-deposit ratio $\{ER/D\}$ was (1,567.7/2,158.5) = 0.73; and the currency-to-deposit ratio $\{C/D\}$ was (1,709.3/2,158.5) = 0.79. Substituting these amounts into equation (13), we get the M1 money multiplier:

$$m = \frac{0.79 + 1}{0.79 + 0.06 + 0.73} = \frac{1.79}{1.58} = 1.13 \qquad (14)$$

That year-end 2018 value for the M1 multiplier is nearly 30 percent less than the value preceding the financial crisis of 2007–2009. The plunge reflected a surge in excess reserves, which boosted the excess reserve-to-deposit ratio $\{ER/D\}$ from only 0.03 at the end of 2006 to 0.73 at the end of 2018. Replacing 0.73 with 0.03 in equation (14) raises the multiplier to 1.87. The enormous level of excess reserves at the end of 2018 reflected both the low opportunity cost of holding reserve balances and the lingering caution among banks in the aftermath of the financial crisis.

[8]The example in the following paragraph is based on the Federal Reserve Board's H.3 and H.6 releases that are neither seasonally adjusted nor adjusted for changes in reserve requirements. In addition, the excess reserve number used is not the official one, but includes "surplus vault cash," which serves the same economic purpose as conventionally calculated excess reserves. While the H.3 release no longer reports excess reserves, these can be estimated by subtracting reserve balances required (FRED code: RESBALREQ) from total reserve balances maintained (FRED code: RESBALNS). Note that these new measures of reserves exclude vault cash.

The Impact on Money Supply
LESSONS FROM THE CRISIS

The central bank supplies the *monetary base*—the sum of bank reserves and currency in circulation—but it is banks and the banking system that supply money. This chapter explains this useful adage: Bank behavior determines the *deposit expansion multiplier*—the increase in the quantity of money that comes from an extra dollar of reserves.

The financial crisis of 2007–2009 highlighted the role of bank behavior in the money supply process. When the crisis peaked in September 2008, the deposit expansion multiplier plummeted to a fraction of its normal value. Why?

The standard process of deposit expansion assumes that banks wish to lend out most of an additional dollar of reserves supplied by the Fed. Multiple deposit expansion occurs as the banking system repeatedly lends the extra asset until the Fed's addition to reserves is used up.

However, following the collapse of Lehman Brothers in September 2008, banks panicked. In seeking to hold more excess reserves, they short-circuited the deposit expansion process, and the deposit expansion multiplier collapsed.

What caused the panic? The liquidity crisis threatened the banks' survival (see Chapter 2, Lessons from the Crisis: Market Liquidity, Funding Liquidity, and Making Markets). Excess reserves that banks hold at the Fed are the most liquid assets in the U.S. financial system. They can be used to make a payment or be converted into cash immediately. Amid the crisis, the extra profits that banks might be able to make by lending out their excess reserves were far too small to be worth the risk they faced—failure if they couldn't make a payment or honor a withdrawal request when necessary.

The Fed met the surge in liquidity demand in unprecedented fashion. During the five months following August 2008, officials added more than $800 billion to reserves—an increase of nearly 20 times. And because banks had virtually no interest in lending out these reserves, almost all of the increase flowed into excess reserves.*

The behavior of the monetary aggregates M1 and M2 highlights the impact of bank caution. Over those five months, the absolute increase of M2—$538 billion—was *smaller* than the Fed's addition to reserves! Instead of the normal multiple deposit expansion, the crisis led to only a fractional expansion. Banks were so wary that they accumulated reserves in excess of demand deposits. As a result, the M2 money multiplier plunged by about half, while the M1 multiplier dropped below 1 (see Figure 17.10).

What would have happened if the Federal Reserve had not met the radical increase in the demand for excess reserves? The experience of the Great Depression suggests that banks, desperate for liquid assets, would have cut back loans to healthy borrowers much more aggressively, and the money supply would have collapsed (see In the Blog: Monetary Policy: A Lesson Learned on page 473).

The Fed learned a key lesson from its 1930s failure: A panic by banks can undermine the money supply even if bank reserves and currency in circulation are growing. Supporting the money supply may require an explosion of the monetary base until the panic-driven demand for reserves recedes. The lesson paid off: the aggressive liquidity supply by the Federal Reserve in the financial crisis of 2007–2009 was a critical difference between this episode and the Great Depression.

*In October 2008, the Federal Reserve began paying interest on reserves (see the Chapter 18 discussion of this policy tool). This shift helps explain why reserve demand stayed high even as the crisis receded.

Table 17.4 Factors Affecting the Quantity of Money

Factor	Who Controls It	Change	Impact on *M*
Monetary base	Central bank	Increase	Increase
Required reserve-to-deposit ratio	Central bank	Increase	Decrease
Excess reserve-to-deposit ratio	Commercial banks	Increase	Decrease
Currency-to-deposit ratio	Nonbank public	Increase	Decrease

The Limits of the Central Bank's Ability to Control the Quantity of Money

At this point, we might discuss why the various factors affecting the quantity of money change over time. For example, market interest rates affect the cost of holding both excess reserves and currency. So as interest rates increase, we would expect to see both $\{ER/D\}$ and $\{C/D\}$ fall, increasing the money multiplier and the quantity of money. If these changes in the money multiplier were predictable, a tight link would exist between the monetary base and the quantity of money—a link the central bank might choose to exploit in its policymaking. While such a link made sense in a discussion of the U.S. economy in the 1930s, and might still be important in some emerging economies, for countries with sophisticated financial systems it no longer is. In places like the United States, Europe, and Japan, the link between the central bank's balance sheet and the quantity of money circulating in the economy has become too weak and unpredictable to be exploited for policy purposes.[9]

The problem is that the money multiplier is just too variable; you can see it in the data. Figure 17.10 plots the ratio of M1 and M2 to the monetary base from 1980 to 2019. The results are striking. Both money multipliers were reasonably stable during the 1980s, but then began to fall steadily over the next decade or so, and then plunged after the failure of Lehman Brothers in 2008 (see Lessons from the Crisis: The Impact on Money Supply on page 471). From 1994 to 2019, the M1 multiplier fell from almost 3 to a bit more than 1.

Figure 17.10 The M1 and M2 Money Multipliers, 1980-2019

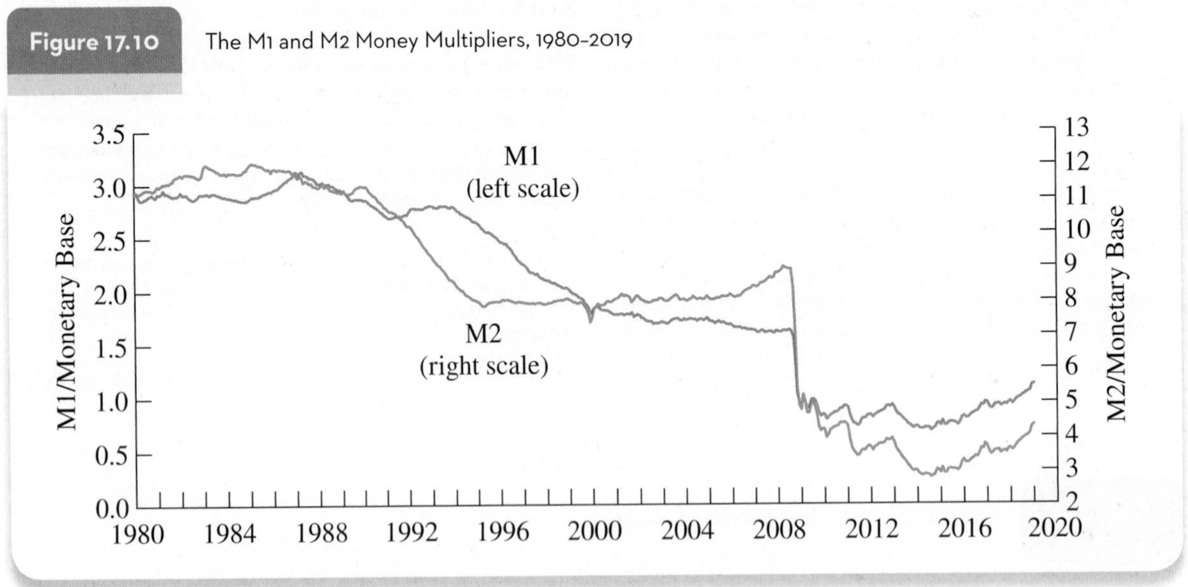

SOURCE: Board of Governors of the Federal Reserve System (FRED data codes: M1SL, M2SL, and AMBSL).

[9]For 20 years, the Federal Reserve was required to publish target ranges for the growth rate of the monetary aggregates. Twice a year, in the *Monetary Policy Report to Congress,* we could count on getting a look at the FOMC's targets for money growth. That is, until the July 2000 issue. Buried in a footnote of that report was the following announcement: "At its June meeting, the FOMC did not establish ranges for growth of money and debt in 2000 and 2001. The legal requirement to establish and to announce such ranges had expired, and . . . for many years [they] have not provided useful benchmarks for the conduct of monetary policy." See footnote 2 in Section 1 of the report, available on the Federal Reserve Board's website.

Monetary Policy: A Lesson Learned
MONEY AND BANKING BLOG

In October 2014, the Federal Reserve completed the final round of asset purchases in the extraordinary cycle of monetary easing that the Federal Open Market Committee (FOMC) began in 2007. These massive balance sheet expansions were designed to counter the impact of the Great Financial Crisis. It is worth examining what they achieved.

Back in November 2002, then-Governor Ben Bernanke gave a speech titled "Deflation: Making Sure 'It' Doesn't Happen Here." His message: The 1930s taught us that avoiding deflation after a financial crisis required aggressive monetary accommodation. Having learned this lesson, Chairman Bernanke and his FOMC colleagues in 2007 and thereafter took actions that their 1930s predecessors had not.* The result was the Great Recession, not another Great Depression.

The depth and duration of these two "Great" downturns differed markedly. During the Great Depression, consumer prices and output each plunged by nearly 30 percent from their 1929 peak to their 1933 trough. And, it took until 1936 for real GDP to regain its pre-Depression level. By contrast, in the Great Recession, the consumer price index fell by 3.2 percent during the second half of 2008 but then regained its previous level in less than a year. Likewise, output fell by 4.2 percent from end-2007 to mid-2009 but regained its precrisis peak by late 2010.

Although other government policies (including fiscal stimulus, deposit insurance, and bank recapitalizations) played important roles, we credit the Federal Reserve with having prevented another depression. To see why, let's compare the evolution of reserves in the U.S. banking system over the two periods. Reserves are the deposits of commercial banks at the Federal Reserve. The Fed controls the overall volume of reserves through its purchase and sale of securities.

During the Great Depression, the Fed failed to respond to the worst financial crisis in U.S. history. It held aggregate reserves roughly constant from 1928 to 1933 while nearly 40 percent of U.S. banks failed. As a result, the quantity of broad money—M2—plunged by 36 percent from its peak in 1929 to its trough in 1932, while the M2 money multiplier fell by nearly half. The predictable result was a historic plunge in prices, output, and employment.

The contrast with the recent episode could not be more striking. The M2 money multiplier fell by two-thirds after 2008 (see Figure 17.10 in the text). That is, the ability and willingness of the banking system to convert reserves into loans and deposits fell even more sharply than it did in the 1930s—yet, there was far less damage. The reason is that, immediately following the collapse of Lehman Brothers in September 2008, the Fed boosted the supply of reserves from \$45 billion to more than \$800 billion in a matter of weeks. Over the next four years, the monetary policymakers continued this massive expansion of reserves through its policy known as *quantitative easing* (see Chapter 18 for a detailed description of QE).

The Federal Reserve's dramatic QE operations, along with the efforts of prudential and fiscal policymakers to stabilize the banks, prevented another collapse of the broad money supply. Instead, from early 2008 to early 2019, M2 grew at a 5.9 percent annual rate, while annual CPI inflation averaged 1.7 percent.

The success of the Fed's actions and the responses of the banks reveal a key insight about the relationship of money, banking, and inflation. Quite a few observers argued that the massive increase in reserves would lead to an uncontrolled inflation. Had the money multiplier been stable, they would have been right. However, when a financial crisis impairs the banking system, increases in reserves typically do *not* translate into broad money creation, so they are *not* inflationary. In fact, the experience of the 1930s taught us that, without aggressive action by the Federal Reserve, a financial crisis leads to deflation and depression.

Returning to where we started, then-governor Bernanke had preceded his November 2002 speech about deflation with one earlier in the month on the occasion of Milton Friedman's 90th birthday. He described how Friedman and Anna Schwartz, in their *A Monetary History of the United States*, connected money and monetary policy to growth and employment. Bernanke concluded with the following promise:

> *Let me end my talk by abusing slightly my status as an official representative of the Federal Reserve. I would like to say to Milton and Anna: Regarding the Great Depression. You're right, we did it. We're very sorry. But thanks to you, we won't do it again.*
>
> And they didn't!

* For a firsthand account of U.S. monetary policy during and after the crisis, see Ben S. Bernanke, *The Courage to Act: A Memoir of a Crisis and Its Aftermath (New York: Norton, 2015).*

If the problem were confined to M1, policymakers could turn to controlling M2. But as the data show, the M2 multiplier has followed roughly the same pattern as the M1 multiplier, falling from 12 in the mid-1980s to 8 by the end of the 1990s, and plunging to 4 as of 2019.

The conclusion is clear: The relationship between the monetary base and the quantity of money is not something that a central bank can exploit for short-run policy purposes. Instead, interest rates have become the monetary policy tool of choice, while, in a financial crisis, other balance sheet tools help address liquidity needs and market disruptions more directly. That is the subject of the next chapter.

Key Terms

Using FRED: Codes for Data in This Chapter

Data Series	FRED Data Code
Nominal GDP	GDP
M1	M1SL
M2	M2SL
Monetary base	AMBSL
Monetary base (NSA)	BOGMBASE
Currency in circulation (weekly)	CURRENCY
Currency in circulation (monthly)	CURRSL
Checkable deposits (weekly)	TCD
Checkable deposits (monthly)	TCDSL
Total reserve balances maintained (NSA)	RESBALNS
Reserve balance requirements (NSA)	RESBALREQ
Discount window borrowings	DISCBORR
Treasury securities held by Fed (NSA)	TREAST
Federal Reserve assets (NSA)	WALCL
MBS held by Fed (NSA)	WSHOMCB

NSA, not seasonally adjusted.

Chapter Lessons

To learn more about the changing financial system, visit www.moneyandbanking.com.

1. The central bank uses its balance sheet to control the quantity of money and credit in the economy.
   a. The central bank holds assets and liabilities to meet its responsibilities as the government's bank and the bankers' bank.
   b. Central bank assets include securities, foreign exchange reserves, and loans.
   c. Central bank liabilities include currency, the government's account, and reserves.
   d. Reserves equal commercial bank account balances at the central bank plus vault cash.
   e. The monetary base, also called high-powered money, is the sum of currency and reserves, the two primary liabilities of the central bank.
2. The central bank can manage the size of its balance sheet.
   a. The central bank can increase the size of its balance sheet, raising reserve liabilities and expanding the monetary base, through:
      i. Open market purchases of domestic securities.
      ii. The purchase of foreign exchange reserves (in the form of bonds issued by a foreign government).
      iii. The extension of a loan to a commercial bank.
   b. The central bank can decrease the size of its balance sheet, lowering reserve liabilities and reducing the monetary base, through the sale of domestic or foreign securities.
   c. The public's cash withdrawals from banks shift the central bank's liabilities from reserves to currency and shrink the size of the banking system balance sheet.
3. Bank reserves are transformed into checkable deposits through multiple deposit creation. In the simplest case, this process is limited by the reserve requirement.
   a. When a bank's reserves increase, the bank makes a loan that becomes a deposit at a second bank.
   b. The second bank then makes another loan, but the amount of the loan is limited by the reserve requirement.
   c. This process continues until deposits have increased by a multiple that is equal to one over the reserve requirement.
4. The money multiplier links the monetary base to the quantity of money in the economy.
   a. The size of the money multiplier depends on:
      i. The reserve requirement.
      ii. Banks' desire to hold excess reserves.
      iii. The public's desire to hold currency.
   b. While the central bank controls the level of the monetary base, it cannot control the money multiplier. Financial crises can trigger dramatic changes in the multiplier.
   c. Changing payments technology has weakened the connection between the central bank's balance sheet and the quantity of money.

Conceptual and Analytical Problems Mc Graw Hill connect

1. Follow the impact of a $100 cash withdrawal through the entire banking system, assuming that the reserve requirement is 10 percent and that banks have no desire to hold excess reserves. *(LO3)*

2. Suppose a major bank needs to borrow $20 billion overnight that it cannot obtain from private creditors. The Fed is willing to make a discount loan of $20 billion provided that it will not alter interbank lending rates. How can it do so? *(LO1)*
3. Compute the impact on the money multiplier of a fall in the currency-to-deposit ratio from 10 percent to 8 percent when the reserve requirement is 10 percent of deposits, and banks' desired excess reserves are 3 percent of deposits. *(LO3)*
4. Does the Federal Reserve frequently purchase or sell gold or foreign exchange as part of its efforts to change the money supply? *(LO1)*
5. Consider an open market purchase by the Fed of $5 billion of Treasury bonds. What is the impact of the purchase on the bank from which the Fed bought the securities. Compute the impact on M1 assuming that (1) the required reserve ratio is 10 percent, (2) the bank does not wish to hold extra reserves, and (3) the public does not wish to hold currency. *(LO3)*
6. When you withdraw cash from your bank's ATM, what happens to the size of the Fed's balance sheet? Is there any reason for the Fed to react to your action? *(LO1)*
7.* Why is currency circulating in the hands of the nonbank public considered a liability of the central bank? *(LO1)*
8. How did the financial crisis of 2007–2009 affect the size and composition of the balance sheet of the Federal Reserve? *(LO1)*
9. Suppose the currency-to-deposit ratio is 0.25, the excess reserve-to-deposit ratio is 0.05, and the required reserve ratio is 0.10. Which will have a larger impact on the money multiplier: a rise of 0.05 in the currency ratio or in the excess reserves ratio? *(LO4)*
10. Is the money multiplier model still useful for policymakers in the United States? If not, why not? *(LO4)*
11. Based on Figure 17.10, explain why the multipliers fell sharply with the onset of the financial crisis of 2007–2009. Why did they remain at this lower level after the crisis ended? *(LO3)*
12. The U.S. Treasury maintains accounts at commercial banks. What would be the consequences for the money supply if the Treasury shifted funds from one of those banks to the Fed? *(LO2)*
13.* Explain how an incomplete understanding at the Federal Reserve of the relationship between the central bank's balance sheet and the money supply contributed to the Great Depression. How did the Fed's behavior during the financial crisis of 2007–2009 illustrate that it had learned a valuable lesson from the Great Depression? *(LO4)*
14. Suppose you examine the central bank's balance sheet and observe that since the previous day, reserves had fallen by $100 million. In addition, on the asset side of the central bank's balance sheet, securities had fallen by $100 million. What activity did the central bank carry out earlier in the day to lead to these changes in the balance sheet? Do you think the central bank was aiming to increase, decrease, or maintain the size of the money supply? *(LO3, LO4)*
15. Suppose you observe a fall in reserves of $100 million on the central bank's balance sheet as well as a fall of $100 million in securities held by the central bank.

*Indicates more difficult problems.

Do you think the size of the banking system's balance sheet would be affected immediately by these changes to the central bank's balance sheet? Explain your answer. *(LO2)*

16. Do you think the Federal Reserve successfully carried out its role as lender of last resort in the wake of the terrorist attacks on September 11, 2001? Why or why not? *(LO2)*

17.* In carrying out open market operations, the Federal Reserve usually buys and sells U.S. Treasury securities. Suppose the U.S. government paid off all its debt. Could the Federal Reserve continue to carry out open market operations? *(LO2)*

18. In which of the following cases will the size of the central bank's balance sheet change? *(LO2)*
    a. The Federal Reserve conducts an open market purchase of $100 million U.S. Treasury securities.
    b. A commercial bank borrows $100 million from the Federal Reserve.
    c. The amount of cash in the vaults of commercial banks falls by $100 million due to withdrawals by the public.

19.* You read a story reporting a major scandal about the Federal Deposit Insurance Corporation that is likely to undermine the public's confidence in the banking system. What impact, if any, do you think this scandal might have on the relationship between the monetary base and the money supply? *(LO4)*

20. Use your knowledge of the money multiplier to explain why the massive increase in bank reserves that began in the 2007–2009 financial crisis has not resulted in uncontrolled inflation. *(LO3)*

21. Explain the distinction between the "zero lower bound" and the "effective lower bound" on nominal interest rates. If interest rates were pushed below the effective lower bound, what would be the likely impact on the money multiplier and the supply of bank credit? *(LO3, LO4)*

22. Assuming normal financial and economic conditions, what are the main advantages of a central bank maintaining low-risk, short-term assets on its balance sheet? *(LO2)*

Data Exploration Mc Graw Hill connect

FRED ECONOMIC DATA | ST. LOUIS FED

For general information on using Federal Reserve Economic Data (FRED) online, visit www.mhhe.com/moneyandbanking6e *and refer to the FRED Resources.*

1. Plot on a weekly basis the ratio of currency (FRED code: CURRENCY) to checkable deposits (FRED code: TCD) from the start of 2000 through 2002 and then remove the recession bar. Download the data and identify the week of the downward spike in the graph. Do you think the spike reflects the currency term in the numerator or the deposits term in the denominator? Explain your reasoning. *(LO2)*

2.* Figure 17.10 shows a sharp decline of the M1 money multiplier in 2008. What caused the drop? Using the monthly indicators for currency (FRED code: CURRSL), total reserve balances maintained (FRED code: RESBALNS), reserve balances required (FRED code: RESBALREQ), and checkable deposits

*Indicates more difficult problems.

(FRED code: TCDSL), plot since 2000 the currency-to-deposit ratio and the excess reserve-to-deposit ratio. Which one caused the M1 money multiplier to plunge? (*Hint:* To estimate excess reserves, see footnote 8. Divide RESBALREQ by 1,000 to convert the units to billions of dollars.) *(LO3)*

3. In the Great Depression, the Fed allowed the money supply to decline. To confirm that the Federal Reserve learned from this lesson, plot since 2000 the M2 multiplier—the ratio of M2 (FRED code: M2SL) to the monetary base (FRED code: AMBSL)—and, on the right axis, the level of M2. Explain how the Fed was conducting policy in order to sustain the expansion of M2. *(LO4)*

4. Prior to the financial crisis of 2007–2009, the Fed seldom reduced its holdings of Treasury securities. Plot for the 2007–2009 period the Fed's Treasury holdings (FRED code: TREAST) and its total assets (FRED code: WALCL) on a weekly basis. Did the Fed's practices change during the crisis? If so, how? (*Hint:* Examine Table 17.1 to help with your response.) *(LO2)*

5. Thousands of the data series on FRED are provided directly by the Board of Governors of the Federal Reserve System, including hundreds of indicators from the Fed's weekly balance sheet report (H.4.1 Factors Affecting Reserve Balances). How does this balance sheet transparency affect the conduct of monetary policy? *(LO1)*

Chapter

18 Monetary Policy: Stabilizing the Domestic Economy

Learning Objectives

After reading this chapter, you should be able to:

LO1 Explain the conventional policy tools used by major central banks.

LO2 Discuss the links between monetary policy tools and objectives.

LO3 Use a simple guide to analyze monetary policy.

LO4 Describe unconventional monetary policy tools and how they work.

Central bankers have a long list of goals and a short list of tools they can use to achieve them. They are supposed to stabilize prices, output, the financial system, exchange rates, and interest rates, yet the only real power they have comes from their control over their own balance sheet and their monopoly on the supply of currency and reserves. To achieve their goals, policymakers can change the size of the monetary base by buying and selling assets—primarily government securities in the case of the Fed—and by making loans to banks. They can also alter the mix of assets they hold.

Traditionally, central banks choose a target for the market interest rate on overnight interbank loans and adjust the scale of the monetary base to hit that target. In the United States, the rate at which banks make overnight loans to each other is known as the federal funds rate. Today, the Fed influences the market federal funds rate by adjusting the interest rate it pays on excess reserves that banks hold at the central bank (the IOER rate). The target range for the federal funds rate and the IOER rate are the primary tools of monetary policy when interest rates are above zero and reserves are abundant, as they are now.[1] However, when key markets do not function properly, as in a financial crisis, or when policymakers judge conventional interest rate policy to be inadequate, central banks may also adjust the size and composition of their balance sheet to achieve key policy goals. In addition, they can use communications with the public to influence expectations about *future* interest rate policy.

Interest rates play a central role in all of our lives. They are the cost of borrowing for those of us who need resources and the reward for lending for those of us with savings. Higher interest rates tend to restrict the growth of credit, making it harder for businesses

[1]As we will see, the Fed has other conventional tools, including reserve requirements and the discount rate, but these have taken a backseat to the other two in macroeconomic management.

and households to get financing and for individuals to find or keep jobs. Little wonder that everyone is preoccupied with interest rates and that the business press is constantly speculating about whether the Federal Open Market Committee will change its target.

Between September 2007 and December 2008, the FOMC lowered its target for the federal funds rate 10 times, including once between normally scheduled meetings, taking it from 5.25 percent to a range of 0 to 0.25 percent. This marked the first time since the 1930s that the nominal federal funds rate hit zero.

The term **zero lower bound (ZLB)** for nominal interest rates has been in common use for some time because of the widespread belief that commercial banks could always hold cash in lieu of reserves, and so central banks could not reduce policy rates below zero. Recent experience shows that, due to the transactions costs of holding cash—which include storage, transportation, and insurance—it is possible to lower rates below zero, but there is still an **effective lower bound (ELB)** at which intermediaries and their customers will switch to holding cash.[2] (See Chapter 17, Applying the Concept: Negative Nominal Interest Rates: Blast from the Past?, page 469)

The Fed's extraordinary reduction of the federal funds rate was a direct consequence of policymakers' belief that real economic activity was plunging amid the worst global financial crisis since the Great Depression. From the start of 2008, real GDP fell in five of the succeeding six quarters. When it hit bottom in the spring of 2009, GDP was about 4 percent lower than a year earlier, the largest drop in more than 60 years. The unemployment rate climbed nearly 6 percentage points—a post–World War II record—from its trough of 4.4 percent to a peak of 10 percent. For a few months in mid-2008 during an oil-related inflation spike, the Fed's rate cutting briefly paused, but as the deep recession lowered inflation, policy rates resumed their march to zero.

Remarkably, even setting the federal funds rate target at essentially zero wasn't enough to stabilize the economy! The crisis had undermined the willingness and ability of major financial intermediaries to lend. It had disrupted the function of key financial markets, including those for interbank loans, commercial paper, home mortgages, and even municipal bonds. Healthy nonfinancial firms that had always been able to borrow short term in order to pay their employees, purchase materials for production, and the like suddenly couldn't find access to funds and faced ruin. At the same time, fears of deflation (akin to Japan's experience in the 1990s) threatened to keep the real interest rate (the nominal interest rate minus the expected inflation rate) from falling as the Fed eased. As we will see in Chapter 21, it is the real interest rate that drives economic activity.

In this environment, the Federal Reserve moved to substitute itself for dysfunctional intermediaries and markets. To do that, policymakers undertook the most dramatic alteration of the Fed's balance sheet in history (see Figure 18.1). Beginning with the Bear Stearns rescue in March 2008, the Fed lent massively to fragile financial institutions. Then, after the September 2008 failure of Lehman Brothers, the Fed's balance sheet exploded in unprecedented fashion (see Chapter 17, Table 17.1, and Figure 18.1). Authorities created a variety of new programs aimed at supplying funds to key financial markets by directly or indirectly purchasing a wide variety of financial instruments. At various points during 2008 and 2009, the Fed lent more than $100 billion through the discount window, offered nearly $500 billion of credit at auction, acquired more than $300 billion of long-term Treasury securities and $1 trillion of mortgage-backed

[2]In theory, altering the unit of account (e-dollars) would make it feasible to pay deeply negative interest rates. One way to make this work would be to give universal access to a central bank digital currency. See Michael Bordo and Andrew Levin, "Central Bank Digital Currency and the Future of Monetary Policy," September 22, 2017, https://voxeu.org/article/benefits-central-bank-digital-currency.

Figure 18.1 U.S. Federal Reserve Assets (billions of U.S. dollars), July 2007–February 2019

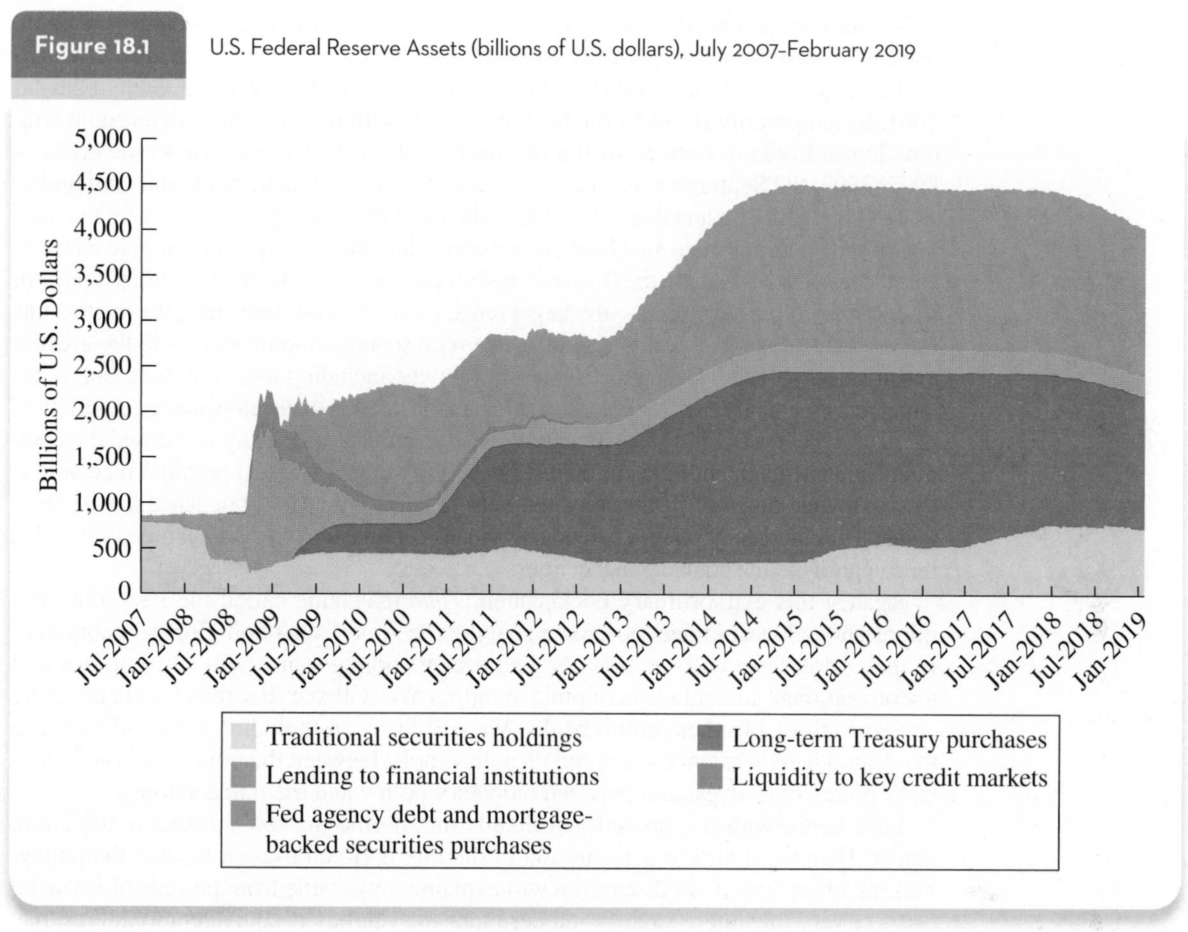

SOURCE: Board of Governors of the Federal Reserve System and authors' calculations.

securities, and had net holdings of commercial paper (CP) in excess of $300 billion. Over time, as financial conditions normalized and the economy bottomed, the Fed's discount lending and its interventions in the CP market wound down.

Yet, the Fed's balance sheet continued to expand in unprecedented fashion, peaking above $4.5 trillion in early 2015, about five times the precrisis level. Despite this rapid expansion of the monetary base and a near-zero federal funds rate, the economic recovery from the Great Contraction of 2007–2009 proceeded at the slowest pace in postwar experience—after five years of anemic growth, the unemployment rate dropped back only to the peak of the previous business cycle.

Other major central banks, including the Bank of England, the Bank of Japan, and the ECB, pursued similar policies. In each case, policy interest rates fell to record lows (even below zero in Europe and Japan), while the size of the central bank balance sheets expanded in extraordinary fashion.

The Federal Reserve has been widely accused of failing to anticipate the financial crisis and even of contributing to it. And its aggressive actions to restore financial and economic stability following the crisis have proven controversial, attracting radically different reactions, including praise for effective monetary policy stabilization, criticism for massive market intervention, and warnings about severe inflation risks.

We have emphasized on several occasions that the economy relies on the central bank to ensure the stability of the financial system when it is under stress. In Chapter 17, we saw that the Federal Reserve reacted to the terrorist attacks of September 11, 2001, by temporarily flooding the banking system with reserves through discount window loans. Looking back from the perspective of the Fed's response to the crisis of 2007–2009, the September 11 episode seems remarkably small, brief, and contained.

To sum up, the financial crisis of 2007–2009 and the ensuing recession were the most severe and enduring since the Great Depression, while the subsequent economic recovery was the weakest. To steady the financial system and the economy, the Fed utilized three of its **conventional policy tools**—the target range for the federal funds rate, the interest rate on excess reserves (IOER rate), and the rate on discount window loans—to the greatest extent since the 1930s to support economic activity, including lowering its federal funds target rate essentially to zero. Policymakers then proceeded to develop and use a variety of **unconventional policy tools**—including massive purchases of risky assets and the communication of its intent to keep interest rates low over an extended period. To be able to lend to a wide range of institutions, the Fed—again for the first time since the 1930s—invoked its emergency powers to lend to nonbanks. These unconventional measures added meaningfully to the conventional actions.

Against this extraordinary background, *Time* magazine called the Fed "the most important and least understood force shaping the American—and global—economy." In this chapter, we will see how the Fed uses its policy tools, both conventional and unconventional, to achieve economic stability. We will see that those tools are quite similar to those of other central banks. We will focus on three links: the link between the central bank's balance sheet and its policy tools; between the policy tools and monetary policy objectives; and between monetary policy and the real economy.

Let's begin with the operational details that define the tools available to central banks. Then we'll turn to a discussion of the link between those tools and the policymakers' objectives. That discussion will explain why—aside from periods of financial crisis or very low interest rates—modern monetary policy is equivalent to interest rate policy. We'll examine how policymakers arrive at a target for the federal funds rate. Finally, we'll turn to a discussion of a number of unconventional policy tools that were used in the crisis of 2007–2009 and in the postcrisis recovery and explain how they augment conventional policy. We'll also look briefly at the Fed's exit from unconventional policy that began in 2015.

To keep the discussion manageable, we'll focus on monetary policy in large economies like that of the United States (where trade is a relatively small part of GDP) and of the euro area (a more "open" economy—i.e., where trade is a somewhat larger part of GDP). Chapter 19 will discuss exchange rates and other issues that are important to central banks in more trade-dependent (more open) economies.

The Federal Reserve's Conventional Policy Toolbox

Like all central banks, the Federal Reserve can alter the quantity of reserves that depository institutions hold. Reserves are injected into the banking system through an increase in the size of the Fed's balance sheet, either because of a decision by the Fed to buy securities or because of a bank's decision to borrow from the Fed. Besides controlling the quantity of reserves, the central bank can control either the size of the monetary base or the price of its components. (We will revisit these control options when discussing the role of interest paid on excess reserves.) Like most modern central banks, the Fed usually sets policy by focusing its attention on prices, rather than quantities. The prices it concentrates on are the interest rate at which banks borrow and lend reserves overnight and the interest rate that the Fed pays on reserves that banks hold at the central bank.[3]

Understanding day-to-day monetary policy requires a familiarity with the institutional structure of the central bank and financial markets. What is true in one country may or may not be true elsewhere. Because cataloging the structure and tools of monetary policy around the world is too big a task, we will begin with the Federal Reserve and financial markets in the United States. In the next section, we will look at the ECB's operating procedures to see how they differ.

The Federal Reserve has four leading conventional policy tools, also known as policy instruments (see Table 18.1).

1. The **target federal funds rate range**, the interest rate at which banks borrow overnight from each other or from other intermediaries.
2. The **interest rate on excess reserves (IOER rate)**—the interest rate paid by the Fed on reserves that banks hold in their accounts at the central bank in excess of reserve requirements.
3. The **discount rate**—the interest rate charged by the Fed on its loans to banks. These loans provide liquidity to banks and are used to stabilize the financial system rather than as a tool to alter day-to-day monetary policy.
4. The **reserve requirement**, the level of balances a bank is required to hold either as vault cash or as a deposit at a Federal Reserve Bank.

Table 18.1 The Conventional Tools of the Federal Reserve

	What Is It?	How Is It Controlled?	What Is Its Impact?
Target Federal Funds Rate Range	Range for the interest rate charged by financial intermediaries on overnight, uncollateralized loans to banks	Announced by the FOMC as the target range for the market federal funds rate	Influences interest rates throughout the economy
Interest Rate on Excess Reserves (IOER Rate)	Interest rate paid by the Federal Reserve on excess reserves held by banks	Announced by the FOMC as a rate to be paid on all excess reserves	Changes interest rates at which banks will lend and borrow
Discount Rate	Interest rate charged by the Federal Reserve on its loans to banks	Set by Reserve Banks, subject to approval by the Federal Reserve Board, at a premium over the interest rate on excess reserves (IOER rate)	Provides liquidity to banks in times of crisis; not used to alter monetary policy
Reserve Requirement	Fraction of deposits that banks must keep either on deposit at the Federal Reserve or as cash in their vaults	Set by the Federal Reserve Board within a legally imposed range	Influences the demand for reserves; not used to alter monetary policy

[3]In October 2008, at the peak of the financial crisis, Congress authorized the Fed to pay interest on reserves, and it began to do so immediately. This authority brought the Fed's set of conventional policy tools in line with that of other major central banks, like the ECB. In the course of this chapter, we will see how important this tool has become.

Before we examine these four tools in detail, it is worth noting that the target for the Fed could change in the next few years. In recent years *collateralized* lending, such as repurchase agreements, has virtually replaced *uncollateralized* lending, which forms the basis for the federal funds rate. Private organizations have developed various secured short-term reference rates as alternatives to the federal funds rate. The Fed is exploring whether to shift its day-to-day interest rate instrument to one of these new benchmarks. While such a shift is unlikely to have broad macroeconomic implications, it will alter the details of Fed operations.[4]

The Target Federal Funds Rate and the Interest on Excess Reserves

Prior to the financial crisis, the target federal funds rate was the Federal Open Market Committee's primary policy instrument. Financial market participants constantly speculated about movements in this rate. FOMC meetings always ended with a decision on the target level, and the statement released after the meeting began with an announcement of that decision. To a large extent, that decision constituted U.S. monetary policy. But because the federal funds rate was, and remains, the rate at which banks borrow from other financial intermediaries overnight, it is determined in the market, not controlled by the Fed. With this qualification in mind, we distinguish between the target federal funds rate set by the FOMC and the **market federal funds rate**, at which transactions between banks and their overnight lenders take place.[5]

The name *federal funds* refers to the fact that the funds are the reserve balances held by banks at the Federal Reserve Banks. For many years before the September 2008 failure of Lehman Brothers, aggregate reserves were scarce—on the order of $10 billion—and excess reserves were less than $2 billion. As a result, banks economized on their reserve holdings. Day-to-day discrepancies between actual and desired reserves gave rise to a market for reserves, with some banks lending out their excess and others borrowing to cover a shortfall in their required balance. Without this market, banks would have needed to hold substantial quantities of excess reserves as insurance against shortfalls. Because the loans are unsecured—there is no collateral to fall back on in the event of nonpayment—the borrowing bank must be creditworthy in the eyes of the lending bank, or the loan will not be made.

As one would expect, demand for reserves (banks' deposits at the Fed) has always been negatively related to the cost of holding them. And since one of the closest alternatives to holding reserves has been an overnight loan to another bank at the market federal funds rate, this interest rate remains a good proxy for the opportunity cost of holding reserves. Consistent with the downward-sloping line in Figure 18.2, banks demand fewer reserves as the market federal funds rate rises.

The Fed continues to be the monopoly supplier of aggregate bank reserves. On any particular day, the Fed can choose the amount of reserves to supply, so that the supply curve is vertical at that level (as in Figure 18.2). Until September 2008, the Fed faced the kind of downward-sloping demand for its product that typically confronts a monopolist.

[4]The Fed also has a supplementary tool: the overnight reverse repo (ON RRP) rate. The ON RRP rate is the interest rate paid by the Federal Reserve on funds from nonbank intermediaries supplied via overnight reverse repurchase agreements. It is currently used to set a floor on the market federal funds rate.

[5]The market federal funds rate is often referred to as the "effective" federal funds rate. Published daily by the Fed, it is the average of the interest rates on market transactions in federal funds weighted by the size of the transactions.

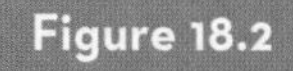

Figure 18.2 The Market for Bank Reserves prior to September 2008

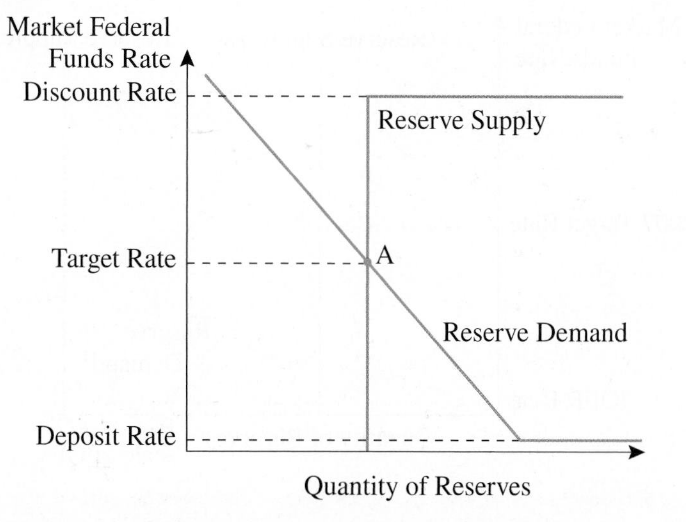

Reserve demand generally slopes down because the higher the market federal funds rate, the more costly it is to hold reserves, which paid a zero rate of interest (labeled "Deposit Rate" in the chart) prior to October 2008. Reserve demand turns flat at the deposit rate because banks have no better alternative to holding reserves at that rate. For levels of the market federal funds rate below the discount rate, reserve supply is vertical at the point that the Open Market Trading Desk estimates reserve demand will equal the target funds rate. At the discount rate, reserve supply becomes horizontal because the Fed stands willing to lend to banks at this rate.

By buying or selling securities in the market through an open market operation (OMO), the Fed could increase or decrease the supply of reserves (shifting the supply curve to the right or the left) in order to lower or raise the market federal funds rate.

The use of OMOs in small volume—no more than a few billion dollars on any given day—allowed the Fed to hit its federal funds target with reasonable accuracy. And if the demand for reserves was unexpectedly high on a particular day, the Fed could lend elastically at the discount rate (set at a spread above the federal funds target rate) to prevent the market federal funds rate from rising too far. In Figure 18.2, this elastic lending is depicted by the horizontal portion of the supply curve at the discount rate.

That was the state of affairs up to the failure of Lehman Brothers in September 2008. But as the financial crisis intensified in the fall of 2008, the Fed first lowered its policy target close to zero and then, over the next five years or so, engaged in several rounds of large-scale asset purchases (LSAPs) that boosted the supply of reserves far beyond the level needed to keep the federal funds rate near zero. Figure 18.3 depicts the scale of this **quantitative easing (QE)** as the gap between the point where reserve demand becomes flat (point *B*) and the point at which the reserve supply curve on the right intersects the near-zero IOER rate (point *C*). By mid-2014, reserves had ballooned dramatically: Total reserves peaked at $2.8 trillion, more than 300 times their 2007 average; and excess reserves were $2.7 trillion, over 1,400 times larger!

Awash in excess reserves, banks are now largely indifferent to holding a few hundred billion dollars more or less. Graphically, this indifference is reflected by the horizontal portion of the demand curve in Figure 18.3, which is shown at the level of the IOER rate.

Figure 18.3 The Market for Reserves with Quantitative Easing (QE) after September 2008

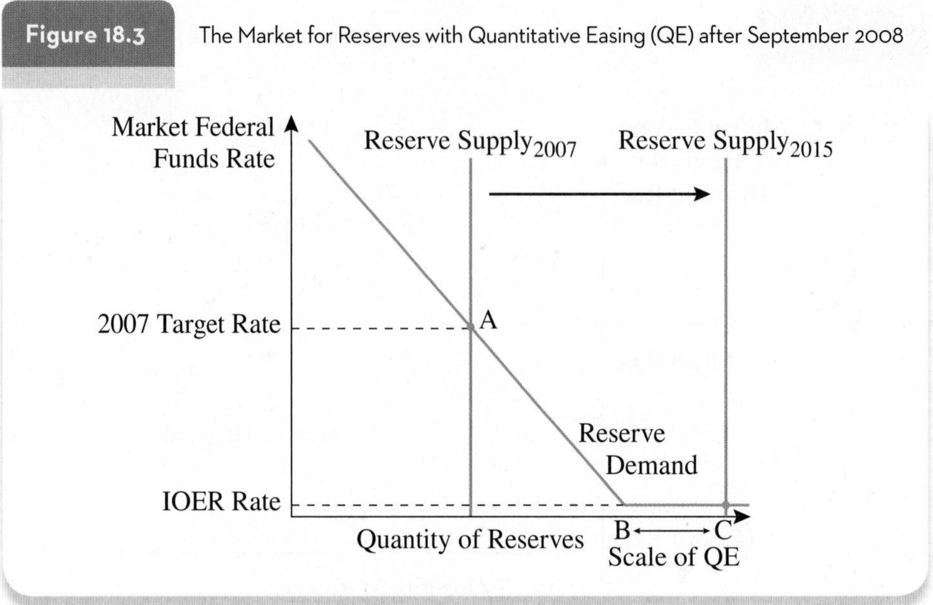

From 2008 to 2014, through quantitative easing described later in this chapter, the Fed increased the supply of reserves by nearly $3 trillion, shifting the supply curve far to the right along the horizontal portion of the reserve demand curve and moving the equilibrium from point *A* to point C. (The figure is not drawn to scale.) Reserve demand is depicted as flat at the IOER rate because banks have no better alternative to holding reserves at that rate. Put differently, they will not make loans at a rate below the IOER rate.

An additional change occurred at the height of the financial crisis: Beginning in December 2008, policymakers began specifying a target *range*, instead of a target *level*, for the federal funds rate. The range was initially set as 0.00 to 0.25 percent. It was not until December 2015, when the Federal Open Market Committee began to normalize monetary policy, that they raised this range, by 25 basis points (making it 0.25 to 0.50 percent). Initially, the IOER rate corresponded with the upper limit of the target range, but as of mid-2019, it is set within the target range. (The appendix to this chapter discusses the mechanics of holding the market federal funds rate within the target range and describes how the market federal funds rate itself is determined in the current environment.).

STABILITY

This is the backdrop of monetary policy today (2020) and probably in coming years. Reserves remain so abundant that, unless the Fed is willing to sell hundreds of billions of dollars worth of securities, it cannot get back to the point where small OMOs would have any impact on the federal funds rate. Any attempt to operate within the precrisis framework faces two insurmountable obstacles. First, given the introduction of interest on reserves in October 2008, no one knows much about the demand for reserves, including the location of the kink shown in Figure 18.3 and the steepness of the line to the left of the kink. Second, sales of securities on such a massive scale would lead to unpredictable and potentially serious disruptions in financial markets.

So instead, the Fed has begun to employ a relatively new set of tools to tighten monetary policy and drive up interest rates in financial markets. The principal device is the IOER rate, at which banks would prefer to deposit at the Federal Reserve rather than provide loans to other institutions. When the FOMC announces an increase in its target range, the Fed implements the change by raising the IOER rate; it thereby raises the minimum rate at which banks are willing to lend. No less important, a higher IOER rate encourages

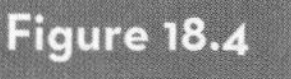

Figure 18.4 Tightening Monetary Policy by Increasing the IOER Rate

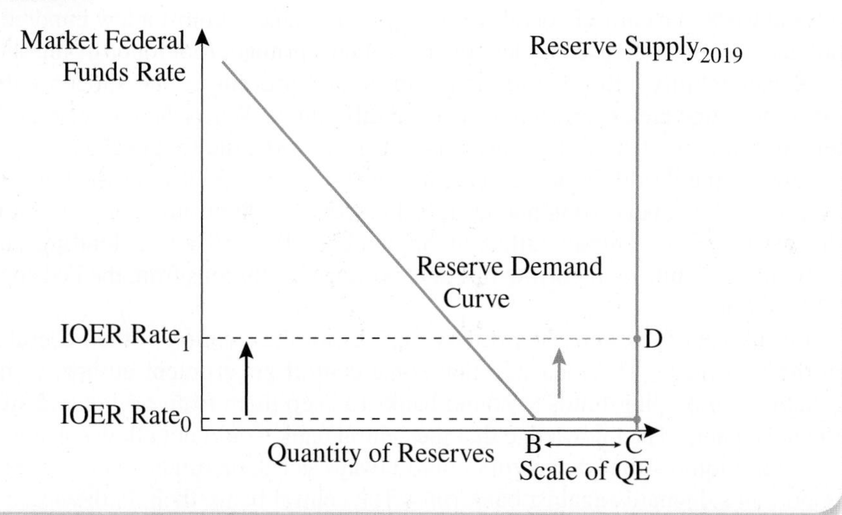

Beginning in December 2015, the FOMC started to raise interest rates in order to tighten monetary policy. Since excess reserve levels were so large, it did this by raising the interest paid on excess reserves, the IOER rate. This is shown as an increase from IOER Rate_0 to IOER Rate_1. The impact was to shift the equilibrium in the market for reserves from point C to point *D*, leaving the quantity of reserves unchanged.

banks to bid aggressively for funds from other money-market participants in order to deposit them in their reserve accounts at the Fed's riskless IOER rate. So, when the Fed hikes the IOER rate, other short-term rates are dragged upward by the banks' actions.

Graphically, raising the IOER rate raises the flat portion of the reserve demand curve shown in Figure 18.4. This moves the equilibrium in the market for bank reserves from point *C* to point *D*.

So, the Fed sets monetary policy primarily by using the IOER rate. Importantly, this interest rate tool allows the FOMC to raise interest rates in the economy, thereby tightening financial conditions, without altering the supply of reserves. In effect, the Fed has developed a clever way to independently set both the price (the interest rate) and the quantity of the product (aggregate reserves) that it supplies. Most monopolists have to choose one or the other.

From 2017 until August 2019, the Fed shrank its balance sheet. Going forward, however, policymakers aim to ensure an abundant supply of reserves in order to remain on the flat portion of the reserve demand curve. Consequently, in the future, the balance sheet will expand to accommodate the demand for reserves, as well as increases in the demand for non-reserve liabilities, such as currency and the deposits of the federal government at the Fed.

Discount Lending, the Lender of Last Resort, and Crisis Management

When a central bank extends credit to commercial banks, its balance sheet changes. So by controlling the quantity of loans it makes, a central bank can control the size of reserves, the size of the monetary base, and ultimately interest rates. While the Fed

could take this approach (and did for the first decade of its existence in the early 20th century), today it does not. Lending by Federal Reserve Banks to commercial banks, called **discount lending**, is usually small aside from crisis periods. During a normal week, the entire Federal Reserve System makes at most a few hundred million dollars in loans. Yet, discount lending is the Fed's primary tool for ensuring short-term financial stability, eliminating bank panics, and preventing the sudden collapse of institutions that are experiencing financial difficulties. When there is a crisis, discount lending explodes. On Wednesday, September 12, 2001, the first business day after the collapse of the World Trade Center, banks borrowed $45.5 billion from the Fed! In the preceding week, borrowing had averaged just over $100 million per day. Similarly, in the weeks after Lehman failed in September 2008, discount lending surged to $110 billion, while total borrowings of depository institutions from the Fed approached $700 billion!

Recall that crises were the primary impetus for the creation of the Federal Reserve in the first place. The idea was that some central government authority should be capable of providing funds to sound banks to keep them from failing and sparking a financial panic. The knowledge that the central bank would not allow solvent banks to become illiquid—that depositors could always get their funds—became one of the important safeguards against bank runs. The central bank, then, is the **lender of last resort**, making loans to banks when no one else will or can. But a bank is supposed to show that it is sound to get a loan in a crisis. This means having assets that the central bank is willing to take as collateral, because the central bank does not make uncollateralized loans. A bank that does not have assets it can use as collateral for a discount loan is a bank that should probably fail. Indeed, this is the principal reason that Fed officials gave when they explained why they could not prevent Lehman's failure in September 2008.

For most of its history, the Federal Reserve loaned reserves to banks at a rate *below* the target federal funds rate. Borrowing from the Fed was cheaper than borrowing from another bank. Even so, no one borrowed, because the Fed required banks to exhaust all other sources of funding before they applied for a loan. Moreover, banks that used discount loans regularly faced the possibility of being denied loans in the future. Needless to say, these practices created quite a disincentive to borrow from the Fed. Almost everyone was willing to pay high rates in the marketplace rather than ask the Fed for a loan; only banks with nowhere else to go went to the Fed. But by severely discouraging banks from borrowing, the Fed created volatility in the market for reserves. Eventually, officials decided to make the process more rational. In 2002, they instituted the discount lending procedures that are in place today.

To see how this all works, we need to look at the details of how lending functions. The Federal Reserve makes three types of loans, called *primary credit, secondary credit,* and *seasonal credit.* The Fed controls the interest rate on these loans, not the quantity of credit extended. The banks decide how much to borrow, and the rules are not very complicated. Let's look at each one in turn.

Primary Credit **Primary credit** is extended on a very short-term basis, usually overnight, to institutions that the Fed's bank supervisors deem to be sound (as measured by the standardized ratings they produce).[6] Banks seeking to borrow must post

[6]Banks with CAMELS ratings of 1 or 2 qualify for primary credit. The ratings are described in Chapter 14.

acceptable collateral to back the loan.[7] The interest rate on primary credit is set at a spread *above* the IOER rate. This is called the **primary discount rate**.[8] The term *discount rate* usually refers to this primary discount rate.

As long as a bank qualifies and is willing to pay the penalty interest rate, it can get the loan. The rules allow a borrowing bank to lend the funds again if it wishes. Primary credit adds to the Fed's supply of reserves to the banks. When reserves were scarce—as they were prior to September 2008—providing a facility through which banks could borrow at a penalty rate above the target kept the market federal funds rate from rising above the discount rate. That's because, if it rose above, banks that would normally borrow in the federal funds market could instead go to the discount window and borrow reserves from the Fed.

Secondary Credit Secondary credit is available to institutions that are not sufficiently sound to qualify for primary credit. Because secondary credit is provided to banks that are in trouble, the **secondary discount rate** is set above the primary discount rate. There are two reasons a bank might seek secondary credit. The first is the standard one: a temporary shortfall in reserves. But short-run secondary borrowing is very unusual. Banks that request secondary credit from the Fed are banks that can't borrow from anyone else. By offering to pay a rate above the primary discount rate, a bank signals other banks that it doesn't qualify for primary credit. By paying the Fed the secondary discount rate for funds, the bank advertises that it is in trouble. It is hard to see any but the most desperate banker doing this. Indeed, even during the crisis of 2007–2009, secondary credit did not exceed $1 billion.

So who is secondary credit for, anyway? It is for banks that are experiencing longer-term problems that they need some time to work out. There are times when banks have serious financial difficulties that they can resolve without failing. A bank that takes a large loss from poor lending decisions will become undercapitalized, but it may be able to raise funds to continue operating if it is given enough time. Such a bank has nothing to lose by requesting secondary credit. Without it, it will fail anyway. But before the Fed makes the loan, it has to believe there is a good chance the bank will be able to survive. You can see why secondary credit is rare.

Seasonal Credit Seasonal credit is used primarily by small agricultural banks in the Midwest to help in managing the cyclical nature of farmers' loans and deposits.[9] Historically, these banks had poor access to national money markets, so the Fed stepped in to provide credit, charging them a market-based interest rate.[10] In recent years, however, there has been a move to eliminate seasonal credit. While the Fed still extends more than $250 million of seasonal credit during the summer months, there seems little justification for the practice any longer. Banks that used seasonal credit in the past now have easy access to longer-term loans from large commercial banks.

[7]The list of acceptable collateral is fairly broad, including not only government securities and investment-grade corporate bonds but also consumer loans, commercial and agricultural loans, and some mortgage obligations.

[8]In the case of a financial emergency resulting from an act of war, military or terrorist attack, natural disaster, or other catastrophic event, the primary discount rate can be reduced to the IOER rate.

[9]During spring and summer, as farmers plant and cultivate their crops, the demand for loans rises and deposits decline, driving down bank reserves. Harvests and crop sales bring repayment of loans and increases in deposits, raising bank reserves.

[10]The interest rate charged on seasonal credit is the average of the market (effective) federal funds rate and the market rate on 90-day negotiable certificates of deposit, both averaged over the previous two weeks.

Reserve Requirements

Reserve requirements are an additional tool in the monetary policymaker's toolbox. Since 1935, the Federal Reserve Board has had the authority to set the reserve requirements, the minimum level of reserves banks must hold either as vault cash or on deposit at the Fed.[11] Required reserves equal the required reserve ratio times the level of deposits to which the requirement is applied.[12] (In Chapter 17, we wrote this relationship as $RR = r_D D$.) As we saw in the last chapter, changes in the reserve requirement affect the money multiplier and the quantity of money and credit circulating in the economy. Increasing it reduces the deposit expansion potential of the banking system, lowering the level of money supported by a given monetary base. So, by adjusting the reserve requirement, the central bank can influence economic activity. For example, the People's Bank of China often adjusts the reserve requirement rate up or down in order to tighten or loosen bank credit supply.

In the United States, however, the reserve requirement turns out not to be very useful. One reason is that small changes in the reserve requirement may have little impact when the banking system is awash with reserves—keep in mind that required reserves have been considerably less than 10 percent of total reserves since 2009. At the same time, we cannot predict accurately how large changes in the requirement would affect the level of deposits.

The case against using the reserve requirement as a direct policy tool also is based on U.S. historical experience. Following the banking crises of the Great Depression, U.S. banks began accumulating excess reserves. By the beginning of 1936, less than half of the $5.6 billion of reserves held in the banking system were required; the rest were excess reserves. The Federal Reserve Board was puzzled and became concerned that the high level of excess reserves could be used to support a rapid expansion of deposits and loans, which would lead to inflation. To head off the possibility, beginning in August 1936 the Fed used its newly acquired powers and in three steps doubled the reserve requirement. Suddenly, $3 billion in excess reserves was reduced to $1 billion. But the Fed had underestimated banks' desire to hold excess reserves to protect against the possibility of renewed bank runs. So, bank executives spent the next year rebuilding their reserve balances until excess reserves were back to the level where they had been before the reserve requirement was raised. The consequences for the economy were grim. While the monetary base remained relatively stable, the money multiplier plummeted, driving M1 and M2 down. As monetary aggregates fell, the economy went along with them. From its peak in spring 1937 to its trough less than a year later, real GDP fell more than 10 percent.

Operational Policy at the European Central Bank

Like the Federal Reserve's, the ECB's monetary policy toolbox contains an overnight interbank rate (equivalent to the federal funds rate), a rate at which the central bank lends to commercial banks (equivalent to the discount rate), a reserve deposit rate,

[11] Originally, the requirements were specified in the Federal Reserve Act and could not be changed. For a concise history of reserve requirements, see Joshua N. Feinman, "Reserve Requirements: History, Current Practice, and Potential Reform," *Federal Reserve Bulletin* 79, no. 6 (June 1993), pp. 569–589.

[12] To limit the costs small banks face, a limited volume of deposits is exempt from reserves. The level at which the higher reserve requirement kicks in changes every year, based on the amount of transaction deposits in the banking system. In 2019, the reserve requirement was zero for the first $16.3 million in deposits, 3 percent for deposits up to $124.2 million, and 10 percent above that. For updates, see www.federalreserve.gov/monetarypolicy/reservereq.htm.

(equivalent to the IOER rate), and a reserve requirement. While the conventional toolkit is the same, the details are different, so let's have a look at them.

The ECB's Target Interest Rate and Open Market Operations

Like the Federal Reserve, the ECB now frequently uses outright purchases of securities to inject reserves into the banking systems of countries that use the euro. But prior to 2012, it provided reserves primarily through collateralized loans in what it calls refinancing operations. Originally, the *main* refinancing operation was a weekly auction of **repurchase agreements (repos)** in which the ECB—through the 19 (as of 2020) national central banks (NCBs) of Eurosystem countries—provided reserves to banks in exchange for securities, and then reversed the transaction up to three weeks later. When reserves were scarce, the ECB's usual policy instrument was the **minimum bid rate**, set by the ECB's Governing Council as the minimum interest rate accepted at these refinancing auctions. The minimum bid rate is the ECB equivalent of the Fed's target federal funds rate, so we will refer to it as the *target refinancing rate*. Now that reserves are plentiful, we will see that the effective refinancing rate is determined by the ECB's analog to the IOER rate, namely, the rate offered by the *ECB's deposit facility*.

Beginning in 2007, in an effort to steady financial markets, the ECB increased the supply of reserves through longer-term refinancing operations (LTROs) at maturities ranging from one month to one year. And to stabilize bank funding in late 2011 and early 2012—a period of intense financial turmoil in the euro area—the ECB extended LTRO maturities to three years, a move that supplied more than €1 trillion to banks. The financial turmoil also led the ECB to boost open market purchases of securities, including the debt of euro-area sovereigns that had difficulties borrowing in private markets. By early 2019, the ECB's holdings of securities denominated in euros accounted for over 60 percent of its €4.7 trillion in assets, while bank refinancing operations (mostly LTROs) represented only 17 percent.

With these changes, the ECB's operations have become more similar to the Fed's. But there are still notable differences. The most important difference is that ECB operations are conducted simultaneously at all the NCBs. The Fed's open market operations are executed from only one location, the Federal Reserve Bank of New York. And while the Fed solicits prices from a short list of primary dealers (24 as of 2019) in the course of its normal operations, hundreds of European banks participate in the ECB's weekly auctions. Finally, because of the differences in financial structure across euro-area countries, the collateral that is accepted in refinancing operations differs from country to country. Under normal circumstances, the Fed takes only U.S. government and agency securities (although the range of accepted collateral widened during the crisis of 2007–2009). In contrast, the ECB and the NCBs accept tens of thousands of different marketable assets as collateral, including privately issued bonds and bank loans as well as government bonds. Even when the government of Greece was on the verge of default in 2012 and again in 2015, the ECB continued to accept its debt as collateral.

The Marginal Lending Facility

The **ECB's marginal lending facility** is the analog to the Federal Reserve's primary credit facility. Through this facility, the ECB provides overnight loans to banks at a rate that is normally well *above* the target refinancing rate. The spread between the marginal lending rate and the target refinancing rate is set by the Governing Council and was 25 basis points at the start of 2019. As in the case of discount borrowing from the Fed, commercial banks initiate these borrowing transactions when they face a reserve deficiency that they cannot satisfy more cheaply in the marketplace. Banks do borrow regularly, and on occasion the amounts they borrow are large. The similarity between this procedure and the Federal Reserve's primary credit facility is no accident, because the ECB's system (which is itself based on the German Bundesbank's) was the model for the 2002 redesign of the Fed's discount window.

The Deposit Facility

Banks with excess reserves at the end of the day can deposit them overnight in the **ECB's deposit facility** at an interest rate *below* the target refinancing rate. The rate paid by the deposit facility is set by the ECB Governing Council; as of early 2019, it was 40 basis points below the target refinancing rate. Because a bank can always deposit its excess reserves in the riskless deposit facility, it will never make a loan at a lower rate. Therefore the deposit facility places a floor under the market interest rate charged on loans made by banks. Once again, the ECB served as a model for the Fed, which based the design of its IOER rate (introduced in October 2008) on the ECB's deposit facility.

Prior to the crisis, the deposit facility contained nearly all of the excess reserves in the Eurosystem's banks. Amounts were small, averaging €350 million or so. In recent years, two developments have altered this pattern. First, the deposit facility rate fell, hitting zero in mid-2012 before becoming negative two years later. As a result, banks became indifferent between keeping their deposits in a "current account" and shifting them into the deposit facility itself, as both paid the same interest rate.[13] Second, in 2014, the ECB began buying large quantities of sovereign bonds as part of its quantitative easing policy. As a result, banks' excess reserve levels rose dramatically so that at the start of 2019 they stood at €1.9 trillion.

It is interesting to note that, even though the ECB charges a fee for accepting excess reserves—at the beginning of 2019 the rate was –0.40 percent—banks did not switch from holding reserves to holding cash in their vaults. Were they to make that switch, the policy impact of the negative deposit rate would become contractionary rather than expansionary (see Applying the Concept: Negative Nominal Interest Rates: Blast from the Past?, page 469).

Reserve Requirements

The ECB requires that banks hold minimum reserves based on the level of their liabilities. The reserve requirement of 1 percent is applied to deposits and debt securities with a maturity of up to two years. The level of these liabilities is averaged over a month, and reserve levels must be held over the following month.

The European system is designed to give the ECB tight control over the short-term money market in the euro area. And it usually works well. Figure 18.5 shows the target refinancing rate, which is the minimum bid rate in the weekly auctions, as the red line running through the center of the graph, with the marginal lending rate above and the deposit rate below (both in blue). The **overnight cash rate** is the European analog to

[13]Deposits in banks' current accounts receive an interest rate equal to zero, or the deposit facility rate, whichever is lower. So, when the deposit rate facility pays a positive rate, banks prefer using that facility to their current account.

Figure 18.5 Euro-Area Overnight Cash Rate and ECB Interest Rates, 1999–2019

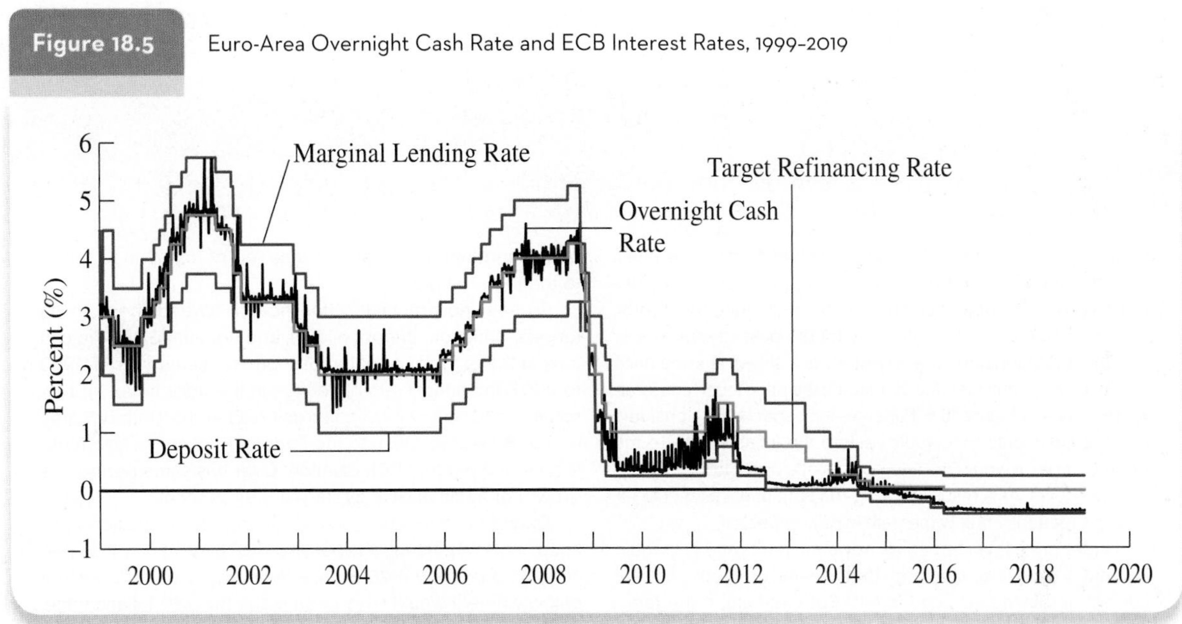

SOURCE: European Central Bank.

the market federal funds rate, the rate banks charge each other for overnight loans. As you can see, this rate fluctuates quite a bit. After the Lehman failure in 2008, it stayed below the target refinancing rate for most of the period, as the ECB flooded the system with liquidity. Yet, even in this period, the overnight cash rate remained within the band formed by the marginal lending rate and the deposit rate. Indeed, until the Fed began to pay interest on reserves in 2008, the ECB was notably more successful in keeping the short-term interest rate close to target.

Linking Tools to Objectives: Making Choices

Monetary policymakers use the various tools they have to meet the objectives society gives them. Their goals—low and stable inflation, high and stable growth, a stable financial system, stable interest and exchange rates—are (or should be) given to them by their elected officials. But day-to-day policy is left to the technicians, who must then decide which tools are the best for the job.

Over the years, a consensus has developed among monetary policy experts, both inside and outside most central banks, that (1) the reserve requirement is not useful as an operational instrument, (2) central bank lending is necessary to ensure financial stability, and (3) short-term interest rates are the conventional tool to use to stabilize short-term fluctuations in prices and output. Later in this chapter, we will see how exceptional conditions—such as dysfunctional financial markets or nominal short-term interest rates near the effective lower bound—can lead to the use of unconventional policy tools, but even those tools aim to influence some market interest rate. The logic of this conclusion is straightforward. To follow it, let's start by listing the features that distinguish good policy instruments from bad ones.

Alternative Monetary Policy Targets: Inflation, Price Level, and Nominal GDP

APPLYING THE CONCEPT

Should central banks aim to control inflation, the price level, or nominal GDP? The question of the appropriate policy target has been a subject of analysis at least since the 1980s, and it has been debated intensely for the past several years.

Under inflation targeting, a central bank strives to keep price increases at a particular rate. If, instead, the price level temporarily declines—as Figure 18.6, Panel A—the central bank considers policy adjustments that would restore the inflation rate to the desired target. It would *not* attempt to make up for lost ground in the price level. As a result, the long-run path of prices would remain permanently below the path initially expected.

Under price level targeting, however, policymakers would commit to closing any gap that opens up between the current and targeted price levels. For example, if the long-run objective is for prices to rise 2 percent per year but in the preceding period the price level unexpectedly fell, the central bank would be obliged to engineer an inflation rate *faster* than 2 percent to raise prices to their originally intended level (see Panel B of Figure 18.6). Consequently, there would be no gap between the long-run path of prices and the path initially expected. Nominal GDP targeting is much like price level targeting, with policymakers aiming to keep the level of nominal GDP on a particular trajectory.

Proponents of price level or nominal GDP targeting argue that—by credibly committing to make up for shortfalls—policymakers gain the ability to raise *expected* inflation by more than under inflation targeting. Following an undershoot of the target, this would drive the real interest rate further down and stimulate economic expansion. Advocates view this approach as more effective than quantitative easing (QE) at the effective lower bound. Skeptics point to the uncertainty about the inflation rate under price level and nominal GDP targeting as a downside of those policy regimes. They also worry that—in the event of a temporary but large price level or nominal GDP *overshoot*—the central bank might need to engineer a period of deflation to return to the long-run path.

To see the practical differences between these three targets—inflation, the price level, and nominal GDP—we can look at the experience of the past quarter century. From 1990 to 2007, the annual rate of change in the price index for personal consumption expenditures (PCE) in the United States was 2.18 percent, close to the Federal Reserve's current objective of 2 percent PCE inflation. Over this same period, the growth of nominal GDP averaged 5.34 percent.

During the following 11 years, through 2018, inflation averaged only 1.54 percent, and nominal GDP grew at only 3.23 percent. As a result, the 2018 price level was about 5½ percent below where it would have been at the precrisis inflation rate, while nominal GDP was a whopping 26 percent lower.

In practical terms, trying to go back to the 1990–2007 price path in the three years that began in 2019 would require an annual inflation rate of nearly 4 percent, before returning to the long-run inflation objective of 2 percent during 2022.

However, under nominal GDP targeting, restoring the target to the level implied by its precrisis path is a monumental task. To do it in three years beginning in 2019 would require annual growth in nominal GDP of more than 13 percent—a pace that we haven't seen in the United States since the late 1970s and early 1980s, when inflation was running in double digits.

This is unlikely to be what we would want to do. The reason is that, under nominal GDP targeting, inflation uncertainty rises when (as in recent years) the economy's trend rate of real economic growth unexpectedly changes. From 1990 to 2007, that trend rate averaged 3 percent, so a nominal GDP target of 5 percent would have yielded inflation of 2 percent. That seems sensible. But more recently, the trend real growth rate looks to have fallen closer to 2 percent. If that persists, then the same 5 percent nominal GDP target will yield 3 percent inflation. And the more uncertain we are

Desirable Features of a Policy Instrument

A good monetary policy instrument has three features.

1. It is easily *observable* by everyone.
2. It is *controllable* and quickly changed.
3. It is tightly *linked* to the policymakers' objectives.

These features seem obvious. After all, a policy tool wouldn't be very useful if you couldn't observe it, control it, or predict its impact on your objectives. But beyond the obvious, it is important that a policy instrument be easily observable to ensure

Figure 18.6 Inflation Targeting versus Price Level or Nominal GDP Targeting

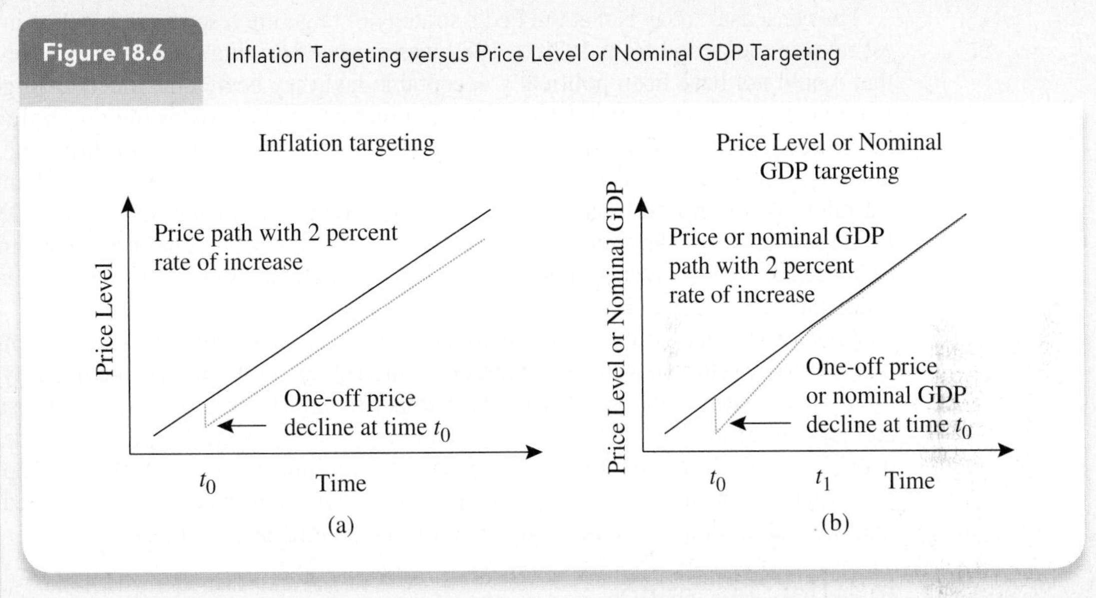

about real growth, the less certain we are going to be about inflation.

So, the price level and nominal GDP policy frameworks might help borrowers who rely on future nominal income repay their debt. But they would complicate decisions for consumers and businesspeople who must distinguish relative price changes from inflation surprises in order to make efficient choices.

Over the past quarter century, dozens of central banks have adopted formal, or at least de facto, inflation-targeting frameworks, so that roughly two-thirds of global GDP (measured by PPP) now is produced under an inflation-targeting regime. The result has been lower, more stable inflation around the world. Is it worth risking this hard-won credibility to change the policy regime? Or, to put it another way, are the benefits of price level and nominal GDP targeting small enough that central banks should continue targeting inflation and let bygones be bygones when it comes to price and output shortfalls? As of 2019, the debate persists, but inflation targeting remains the dominant framework.

transparency in policymaking, which enhances accountability. Controllability is important in both the short term and the long term. An instrument that can be adjusted quickly in the face of a sudden change in economic conditions is clearly more useful than one that takes time to adjust. And the more predictable the impact of an instrument, the easier it will be for policymakers to meet their objectives.

Requiring that a monetary policy instrument be observable and controllable and have predictable impact leaves us with only a few options to choose from. The reserve requirement won't work, as we have seen, because the effect of changes in the requirement is difficult to anticipate. Then there are the components of the central bank's balance sheet—commercial bank reserves, the monetary base, loans, and foreign exchange reserves—as well as their prices—various interest rates and the exchange rate. (Exchange-rate policy is discussed in the next chapter.) But how do we choose between controlling quantities and controlling prices? Over the years, central banks have switched from one to the other. For example, from 1979 to 1982, the Fed did try targeting bank reserves, with an eye toward reducing the inflation rate from double-digit levels. Inflation fell quickly, so in a sense the policy was a success. But one side effect of choosing to control reserves was that interest rates became highly variable, rising from 14 percent to over 20 percent and then falling to less than 9 percent, all in a period of less than six months.

The consensus today is that the Fed's strategy of targeting reserves rather than interest rates in the period from 1979 to 1982 was a way of driving interest rates to levels that would not have been politically acceptable had they been announced as targets. Even in an environment of double-digit inflation rates, the FOMC could not explicitly raise the target federal funds rate to 20 percent. By saying they were targeting the quantity of reserves, the committee members escaped responsibility for the high interest rates. When inflation had fallen and interest rates came back down, the FOMC reverted to targeting the overnight interest rate. And that is what it has done ever since. (Although the Fed's balance sheet expansion after 2008 did not aim to alter the federal funds rate target, it did aim to reduce longer-term interest rates.)

Appearances and politics aside, there is a very good reason that the leading central banks in the world today choose to target an interest rate rather than some quantity on their balance sheet. Interest rates are the primary linkage between the financial system and the real economy, so stabilizing growth means keeping interest rates from being overly volatile. In the context of choosing an operating target, that means keeping unpredictable changes in reserve demand from influencing interest rates and feeding into the real economy. The best way to do this is to target interest rates.[14]

Inflation Targeting

When you focus central bankers' attention on a well-articulated objective, you get better policy. During the 1990s, a number of countries adopted a policy framework called **inflation targeting** in an effort to improve monetary policy performance. Today, central banks in countries that produce nearly two-thirds of global GDP operate a de jure or a de facto inflation-targeting regime. Countries that embraced inflation targeting achieved both lower inflation and (at least until the financial crisis of 2007–2009) more stable real economic growth.

Inflation targeting focuses directly on the objective of low and stable inflation. It is a monetary policy strategy that involves public announcement of a numerical inflation target and underscores the central bank's commitment to price stability. When the target is credible—because the central bank routinely acts to achieve it—everyone believes that inflation will be low. Long-term expectations of low inflation act to anchor low long-term interest rates and promote economic growth. So inflation targeting is designed to convince people that monetary policy will deliver low inflation, and if central bankers are resolute, it usually works. (To compare inflation targeting with other policy regimes, see Applying the Concept: Alternative Monetary Policy Targets: Inflation, Price Level, and Nominal GDP on pages 494–495.)

[14]More than 50 years ago, William Poole observed that the decision to target either interest rates, or an aggregate like reserves or the monetary base, depends on what is less predictable. Is it the money multiplier that links the monetary base to monetary aggregates? Or is it the linkage between money and the real economy? (This is the velocity of money, which we will discuss in Chapter 20.) Poole showed that if the money multiplier is less predictable, policymakers should target interest rates; otherwise, it is better to target the monetary base. See William Poole, "Optimal Choice of Monetary Policy Instruments in a Simple Stochastic Macro Model," *Quarterly Journal of Economics* 84, no. 2 (1970), pp. 197–216.

Often, central banks that employ inflation targeting operate under what has been described as a *hierarchical mandate*, in which price stability comes first and everything else comes second. Australia, Chile, South Africa, and the United Kingdom are among the roughly two dozen countries that target inflation in this way. Most observers put the ECB in this group as well. The hierarchical approach contrasts with the Fed's *dual mandate*, in which the goal of price stability (together with low long-term interest rates) and the goal of maximum employment are on equal footing. Nevertheless, consistent with inflation targeting, the Fed announced a quantitative inflation objective in January 2012 but set no employment target.

To understand how inflation targeting works, let's look at the British example. The Bank of England Act of 1998 granted the Bank of England independence but also dictated its objective: to deliver price stability, as defined by the government's inflation target. A nine-member Monetary Policy Committee (MPC) meets monthly to determine short-term interest rates in an effort to meet this objective, which has been defined as annual consumer price inflation of 2 percent. Because transparency is a crucial part of inflation targeting, the Bank of England releases the interest rate decisions of the MPC along with the minutes of its meetings the day after they conclude and publishes quarterly forecasts of inflation in its *Inflation Report*.

By focusing on a clearly defined and easily observable numerical inflation statistic and by requiring frequent public communication, inflation targeting increases policymakers' accountability and helps establish their credibility. Not only do central bankers know what they are supposed to do, but everyone else does, too. By reducing any incentive that future policymakers might have to renege on the commitment to low inflation, this framework of communication and accountability helps overcome the time-consistency problem.

The result is not just lower and more stable inflation but—usually—higher and more stable economic growth. Nevertheless, as we saw in the global crisis of 2007–2009, inflation targeting is not sufficient to prevent financial disruptions that undermine economic stability.

A Guide to Central Bank Interest Rates: The Taylor Rule

Interest rate setting is about numbers. Policymakers both pick a specific target and choose when to implement it. How do they do it? The answer is that they have a large staff who distill huge amounts of information into manageable sets of policy recommendations. Committee members digest all the information, meet, and reach a decision. We could try to list all the factors they consider and explain how each influences the committee's decision, but that would take another book.

What we can do is study a simple formula that approximates what the FOMC does. Called the **Taylor rule** after the economist who created it, Professor John Taylor of Stanford University, it tracks the actual behavior of the target federal funds rate and relates it to the real interest rate, inflation, and output.[15] The formula is

$$\text{Target fed funds rate} = \text{Natural rate of interest} + \text{Current inflation} + \tfrac{1}{2}(\text{Inflation gap}) + \tfrac{1}{2}(\text{Output gap}) \quad (1)$$

[15]The Taylor rule first appeared in "Discretion versus Policy Rules in Practice," *Carnegie-Rochester Conference Series on Public Policy* 39 (1993), pp. 195–214. For a retrospective on the rule's influence, see Evan F. Koenig, Robert Leeson, and George A. Kahn, eds., *The Taylor Rule and the Transformation of Monetary Policy* (Stanford, CA: Hoover Institution Press, 2012).

The **natural rate of interest** is the real short-term interest rate that prevails when the economy is using resources normally. Taylor originally used 2 percent, which had been close to the average real short-term rate. The inflation gap is current inflation minus an inflation target, both measured as percentages; the output gap is the percentage deviation of current output (real GDP) from potential output. (As Chapter 21 discusses in detail, potential output is what the economy is capable of producing when its resources are being used at normal rates.) When inflation exceeds the target level, the inflation gap is positive; when current output is above potential output, the output gap is positive.

The Taylor rule says that the target federal funds rate should be set equal to the natural rate of interest plus the current level of inflation, plus a factor related to the deviations of inflation and output from their target or normal levels. For example, if the natural rate of interest is 2 percent, inflation is currently 2 percent, the inflation target is 2 percent, and real GDP equals its potential level so there is no output gap, then the target federal funds rate should be set at $2 + 2 + 0 + 0 = 4$ percent.

This rule functions like a thermostat, tuning the policy interest rate target if the economy (measured as inflation and output) is too hot or cold. It makes intuitive sense: When inflation rises above its target level, the response is to raise interest rates; when output falls below the target level, the response is to lower interest rates. If inflation is currently on target and there is no output gap (current real GDP equals potential GDP), then the target federal funds rate should be set at the natural rate of interest plus target inflation.

The Taylor rule has some interesting properties. Consider what happens if inflation rises by 1 percentage point, from 2 percent to 3 percent, and the inflation target is 2 percent (assume that everything else remains the same). What happens to the target federal funds rate? The increase in inflation affects two terms in the Taylor rule, current inflation and the inflation gap. Because the inflation target doesn't change, both these terms rise 1 percentage point. The increase in current inflation feeds one for one into the target federal funds rate, but the increase in the inflation gap is halved. *A 1-percentage-point increase in the inflation rate raises the target federal funds rate 1½ percentage points.*

Significantly, the Taylor rule tells us that for each percentage-point increase in inflation, the real interest rate, which is equal to the nominal interest rate minus expected inflation, goes up half a percentage point (assuming that expected inflation matches actual inflation). Because economic decisions depend on the real interest rate, this means that higher inflation leads policymakers to raise the inflation-adjusted cost of borrowing, thereby slowing the economy and ultimately reducing inflation. If central banks failed to do this, if they allowed the real interest rate to fall following an increase in inflation, the result would be further increases in production and further increases in inflation.

The Taylor rule also states that for each percentage point output is above potential—that is, for each percentage point in the output gap—interest rates will go up half a percentage point.

The fractions that precede the terms for the inflation and output gaps—the halves in equation (1)—depend both on how sensitive the economy is to interest rate changes and on the preferences of central bankers. The more central bankers care about inflation, the bigger the multiplier for the inflation gap and the lower the multiplier for the output gap. When a shock occurs, these differences influence the speed with which the inflation target is restored, or the output gap eliminated.

Returning to the United States, we see that implementing the Taylor rule requires four inputs: (1) the natural rate of interest; (2) a measure of inflation; (3) a measure of the inflation gap; and (4) a measure of the output gap. The natural rate of interest can and does change. Although 2 percent remains a common estimate, as a result of the weak postcrisis recovery many observers have lowered their estimate of the natural rate.

Next we need to add measures of current inflation and the inflation gap. What index should we use? While the CPI is widely known, economists believe that the price index of personal consumption expenditure (PCE) is a more accurate measure of inflation and, in 2012, the Fed set its inflation goal in terms of the annual rise of this measure. The index comes from the national income accounts and is based on the "C" in "Y = C + I + G + X − M." Using the Fed's inflation goal of 2 percent, and assuming the natural rate of interest is 2 percent, the neutral target federal funds rate is 4 percent (2 plus 2).

For the output gap, the usual choice is the percentage by which GDP deviates from a measure of its trend, or potential.[16] Figure 18.7 plots the FOMC's actual target federal funds rate, together with the rate predicted by the Taylor rule (assuming 2 percent for both the natural rate of interest and the inflation target). The result is striking: The two

Figure 18.7 The Taylor Rule, 1990–2018

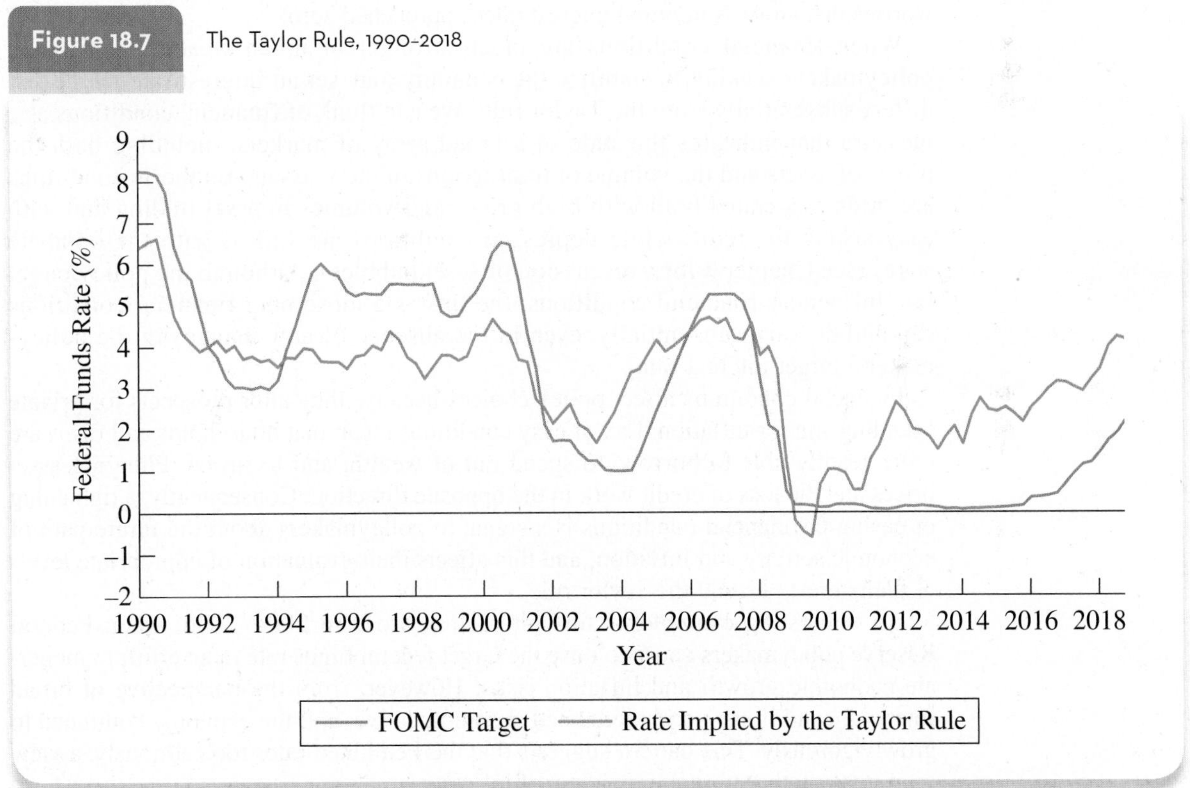

SOURCE: Board of Governors of the Federal Reserve System and authors' calculations as of February 2019 (FRED data codes: GDPPOT, GDPC1, JCFXE, and FEDFUNDS).

[16]In the "Money and Banking Blog: Is 2 Percent Still the Right Inflation Target?" on page 509, we use a modified form of the Taylor rule that substitutes the "unemployment rate gap" for the output gap. The unemployment rate gap is the difference between the actual unemployment rate and the frictional or equilibrium unemployment rate that is also called "the natural rate of unemployment." The unemployment gap rises when the output gap declines. In U.S. experience, it is usually about one-half of the output gap (a regularity that is called Okun's law, after economist Arthur Okun). Consequently, the coefficient on the unemployment rate gap in the modified Taylor rule becomes −1 rather than +½.

lines are reasonably close to each other. The FOMC usually changed the target federal funds rate when the Taylor rule predicted it should. While the rule didn't match policy exactly, it did predict what policymakers would do in a general way. And what is really remarkable is that Professor Taylor created his rule around 1992, at the beginning of the period shown in the graph. (To understand the Taylor rule, you can try different assumptions online at www.frbatlanta.org/cqer/research/taylor-rule.aspx?panel=1.)

Before we get carried away and replace the FOMC with an equation, or begin betting in the financial markets based on the Taylor rule's predictions, we should recognize some caveats. First, at times the target rate does deviate from the Taylor rule, and with good reason. The Taylor rule is too simple to take account of sudden threats to financial stability, such as the terrorist attacks of September 11, 2001.

Indeed, we can learn from the periods in which the policy rate deviates from the Taylor rule. For example, why did the FOMC set the federal funds rate target below the Taylor rule in 1992–1993, 2002–2005, and 2008–2013 (see Figure 18.7)? The answer is that these periods were characterized by at least one of two factors: (1) unusually stringent conditions across an array of financial markets or (2) deflationary worries that arose as nominal interest rates approached zero.

When financial conditions are much stronger or much weaker than usual, policymakers seeking to stabilize the economy may set an interest rate target that differs substantially from the Taylor rule. We can think of financial conditions as a measure that indicates the state of a broad array of markets, including both the prices of assets and the volume of transactions in these assets. Euphoric conditions are often associated both with high prices and volumes in asset trading and with easy access to credit, while depressed conditions are linked with the opposite states (see Chapter 8 for a discussion of asset bubbles). Although the policy target rate influences financial conditions, the link is a loose one: financial conditions can and do vary substantially, even in the absence of any changes in the policymakers' target interest rate.

Financial conditions affect policy choices because they alter prospects for private spending and for inflation. Lax or easy conditions mean that households and firms are more readily able to borrow, to spend out of wealth, and to invest. Plunging asset prices and the loss of credit work in the opposite direction. Consequently, a tightening or easing in financial conditions is a signal to policymakers about the future path of economic activity and inflation, and this affects their evaluation of appropriate levels of the interest rate and the Taylor rule.

An interesting example of this interaction arose in 2004–2006, when Federal Reserve policymakers chose to raise the target federal funds rate in an effort to moderate economic growth and inflation risks. However, from the perspective of broad financial conditions, policy remained accommodative, and the economy continued to grow vigorously. This pattern suggests that the Fed hiked rates too cautiously, a view reinforced by the subsequent pickup of inflation.

In 2008, even though the Fed cut rates below the Taylor rule, the collapse of financial conditions and the economy suggests that it was too cautious. Just like Japan in the 1990s, the Fed did not act early enough to prevent the interest rate implied by the Taylor rule from sinking below zero. Indeed, for the first time in at least 50 years, in 2009 the Taylor rule suggested that the appropriate policy rate was negative for the United States as well as for several other major economies. In this environment, even a zero-rate target probably was too high to counter weakness in the global economy. Yet, as we have seen, a central bank is unable to set its policy rate below the effective lower bound (ELB) on nominal rates, which (so long as cash offers a zero rate of return) is not far below zero.

Because of this ELB, central banks naturally wish to avoid circumstances that would require a very negative policy rate. Thus, if the economy is weak and inflation is both low and falling below the central bank's objective, policymakers might set their target rate temporarily below the one implied by the Taylor rule. This approach accepts as a cost the possibility that inflation will rise temporarily above the objective in the future. The benefit is a lower risk of hitting the ELB. Such a *risk management* approach to policy was a key element of the FOMC's thinking when during 2002–2005 it set the target federal funds rate below the level implied by the Taylor rule. Yet, some economists—including the creator of the Taylor rule—now argue that the Fed's low rate target during this period amplified the housing bubble and contributed to the crisis that followed.[17]

Finally, two other problems cast doubt on the practicality of the Taylor rule as a guide for monetary policy decisions. The first is uncertainty about the natural rate of interest. As of early 2019, one estimate by Fed researchers put the natural rate at around $\frac{1}{2}$ percent rather than the historical level of 2 percent.[18] That's a big difference for policymakers.

The second problem is the lack of reliable real-time data. Figure 18.7 was drawn from data available in early 2019—data that were revised many times after their first release (see Applying the Concept: GDP: One Size No Longer Fits All). So, while researchers might be able to make good monetary policy for, say, 2015 using the Taylor rule and the data available to us today, that ability really isn't of much practical use. Policymakers are not "Monday-morning quarterbacks": they have no choice but to base their decisions on the available information, which is generally less than completely accurate. Their good judgment is the key to successful monetary policy.

Unconventional Policy Tools

We have seen that most central banks set a target for the overnight interbank lending rate in an effort to stabilize the economy and keep inflation low. However, there are two circumstances when additional policy tools can play a useful stabilization role: (1) when lowering the target interest rate to zero (or to the ELB) is not sufficient to stimulate the economy and (2) when an impaired financial system prevents conventional interest rate policy from supporting economic growth.[19] In both cases, unconventional monetary policy can add to the stimulus already coming from conventional policy. When these circumstances arose during the financial crisis of 2007–2009, in the euro-area crisis that followed, and in the course of Japan's long battle against deflation, central banks used a variety of unconventional policy tools to supplement conventional interest rate policy. With continued use by many central banks, these tools have become less and less "unconventional," but we continue to categorize them in this way to simplify matters. In this section, we'll examine some of those tools.

First, however, let's dismiss a common belief: that monetary policy becomes ineffective when the target rate is at the ELB and the financial system is impaired. In these circumstances, skeptics often speak of a "liquidity trap," in which monetary expansion has no impact. Central banks are said to be "pushing on a string." In fact, central banks have powerful tools at their disposal, even in such extreme circumstances. But the

[17]See, for example, John Taylor, "The Financial Crisis and the Policy Responses: An Empirical Analysis of What Went Wrong," November 2008 (www.stanford.edu/~johntayl/FCPR.pdf).

[18]Kathryn Holston, Thomas Laubach, and John C. Williams, "Measuring the Natural Rate of Interest: International Trends and Determinants," *Journal of International Economics* 108, supplement 1 (May 2017), pp. S39–S75.

[19]In that circumstance we say that the *transmission* of monetary policy to the economy is impaired. In Chapter 23 we will look at how the usual transmission mechanism can be undermined.

GDP: One Size No Longer Fits All
APPLYING THE CONCEPT

Even the most casual reader of financial and economic news knows that the speed of economic growth matters. Businesses need to know so that they can decide how much to invest and produce, as well as how many people to employ. Fiscal policymakers need to do their budgeting. And monetary policymakers need to adjust their policies in an effort to meet their inflation and growth objectives.

But, does it make sense for all of these people to focus on fresh estimates of GDP? How much attention should we pay when the U.S. Bureau of Economic Analysis (BEA) announces that its initial estimate of growth for the quarter just ended is 2 percent or 3 percent or 4 percent? While GDP was once a key cyclical indicator, its usefulness has declined substantially for at least three reasons: timeliness, seasonal adjustment, and revisions. Not surprisingly, in the era of big data, those who need information on growth are turning to more up-to-date, customized indicators.

Starting with timeliness, because of the delay in obtaining a broad swathe of information, national accounts data are lagging. By the time we get the first estimate of GDP for a given three-month period–nearly a full month after the end of the quarter–we already have a myriad of indicators for the same period. We know employment, retail sales, industrial production, housing starts, motor vehicle sales, and the list goes on. As a result, GDP announcements may carry little added information.

Turning to seasonality, Figure 18.8 plots GDP growth–quarterly at an annual rate–using the seasonally unadjusted (green line) and seasonally adjusted (orange line) data. This is a striking figure. First, note the vertical scale goes from –20 to +20 percent! Second, the unadjusted data exhibit an enormous annual drop and rebound. Most people would be surprised to learn that the United States experiences a depression that averages about 20 percent of GDP every winter, followed by a boom every spring.

Finally, there is the problem of revisions. The BEA is receiving additional data–tax information, new census and survey results, and the like–as well as improving its methodology. This means that revisions occur constantly and continue for decades! Take as an example the data for GDP in the second quarter of a given year. BEA publishes the initial estimate at the end of July. Then for three succeeding months–in August, September, and October–there are revisions. Every July for the next five years brings another set of revisions. And, every five years there is a comprehensive update that goes back further. This means that over the past 30 years statisticians have revised the 1990 GDP data a dozen times.

These updates can be large. The changes from the initial estimate to the latest reading average 1.3 percentage points. Importantly, the changes tend to be especially large around business cycle turning points—that is, when a recession is starting or ending—precisely when we really need high-frequency cyclical information. The third quarter of 2008—at the height of the financial crisis—is a stark example. Estimates of the economic collapse following the Lehman bankruptcy in 2008 were initially much too optimistic, showing a roughly 4 percent contraction. This was revised almost immediately to less than –5 percent. But it took three years, until mid-2011, for the estimate to go below –8 percent, where it has stayed. By that time, the recovery was well under way—far too late to revise monetary or fiscal policy to stabilize activity.

We draw two conclusions from this. First, quarterly changes in GDP are extremely noisy. And, initial estimates are even noisier. So, it makes little sense to pay close attention. Second, other guides to economic performance may be more useful. A firm producing cars needs a different set of information from one selling pizzas. And governments in different locales need data that are specific to their region. So, now that we have timely access to enormous amounts of raw data about consumption, investment, production, and the like, people are looking to a range of alternatives to GDP.

An analogy to the pharmaceutical industry seems apt: Medical researchers are in the process of harnessing modern genetic technology to develop individually tailored drug therapies. Over time, we probably will do something similar for economic indicators: employ the combination of analytic tools, cheap computing power, and large datasets to develop custom economic indicators designed to address narrow questions.

When it comes to measuring economic activity, one size no longer fits all.

problem for central bankers is that the impact of these unconventional tools is less predictable than that of day-to-day interest rate policy. And being responsible public officials, policymakers are loath to treat the economy as a laboratory, risking sudden increases in inflation and the like. This means that using unconventional policies is much more complicated than simply changing an interest rate target. In addition, the exit from unconventional policies poses risks. For these reasons, central bankers use unconventional tools only in situations when interest rate policy is clearly insufficient for economic stabilization.

Figure 18.8 Seasonally Adjusted and Unadjusted Quarter-to-Quarter Annualized GDP Growth (Percent), 2002–1Q 2019

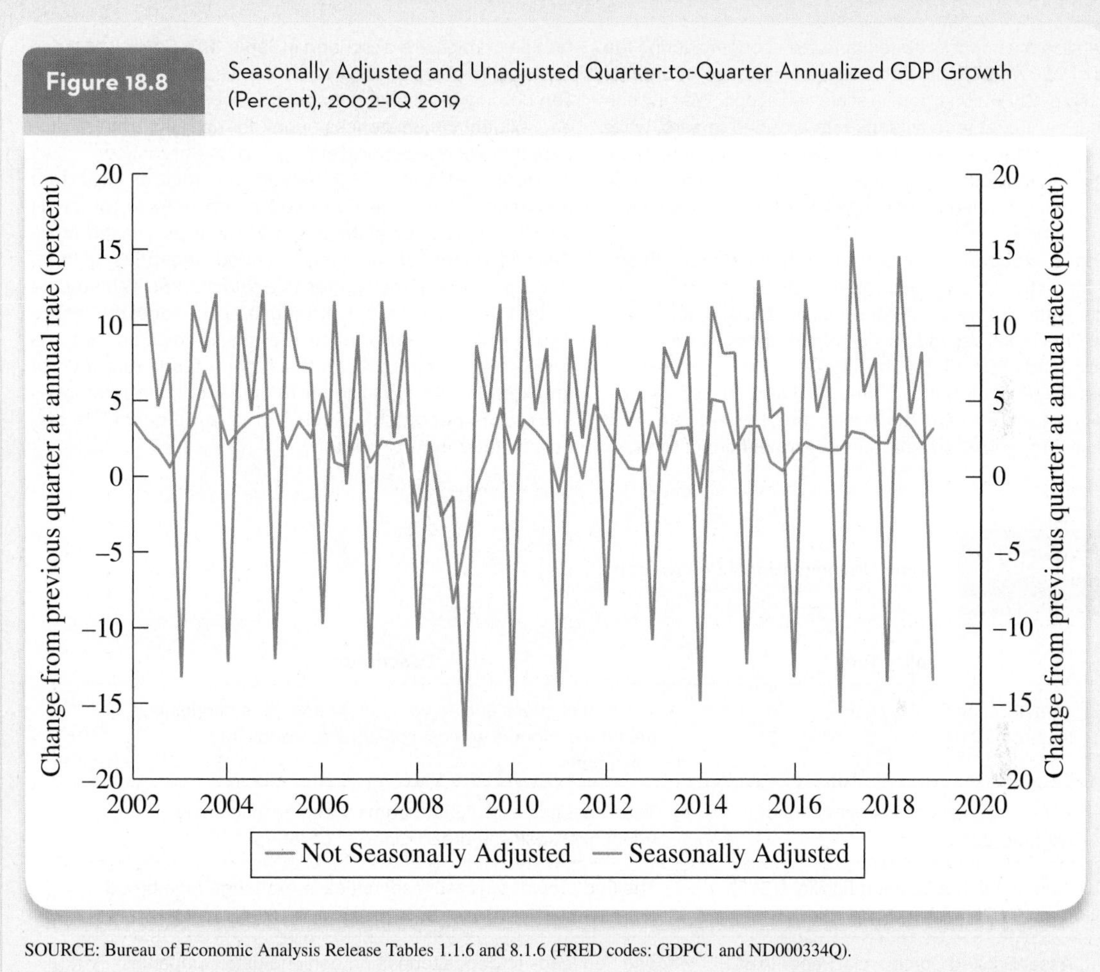

SOURCE: Bureau of Economic Analysis Release Tables 1.1.6 and 8.1.6 (FRED codes: GDPC1 and ND000334Q).

What are the key unconventional policy approaches? While various central banks may label them differently, there are three broad categories: (1) **forward guidance**, in which the central bank communicates its intentions regarding the future path of monetary policy; (2) *quantitative easing (QE)*, in which the central bank supplies aggregate reserves beyond the quantity needed to lower the policy rate (such as the federal funds rate in the United States) to its target (usually zero or lower); and (3) **targeted asset purchases (TAP)**, in which the central bank alters the mix of assets it holds on its balance sheet in order to change their relative prices (interest rates) in a way that

Some Unconventional Policy Tools
TOOLS OF THE TRADE

To stabilize the financial system and the economy during the crisis of 2007–2009, the Fed undertook a range of unprecedented policy actions, both in scale and scope. We saw earlier that the target federal funds rate dropped to zero, while the Fed's balance sheet ballooned. We also saw that the authorities purchased a large volume of assets with credit risk, while cutting traditional holdings of short-term Treasuries (Figure 18.1).

These extraordinary (and frequently controversial) policy interventions were made possible by the introduction of a wide variety of new, temporary policy tools. In this chapter, we have discussed four *conventional* tools: the target federal funds rate range, the interest rate on excess reserves (IOER rate), the discount rate, and the reserve requirement. In addition to these, the Federal Reserve officially recognizes several other unconventional tools, or facilities, which are described in Table 18.2. Several of these facilities involved lending to nonbanks, something the Fed can do only by invoking its emergency powers in "unusual and exigent circumstances." Look for updates of the Fed's toolkit at www.federalreserve.gov/monetarypolicy.

Note that Table 18.2 leaves out several important mechanisms that the Fed used extensively in the crisis and thereafter. For example, in 2009, it purchased more than $1 trillion of mortgage-backed securities to help lower the cost of mortgages in a thin market. The volume of that "targeted asset purchase" exceeded the entire Fed balance sheet prior to the crisis! The Fed also expressed its intent to keep the federal funds rate low for an extended period in order to influence long-term interest rate expectations. Such "forward guidance" is discussed later in this chapter.

Table 18.2 Some Unconventional Policy Tools

Policy Tool	Description
Term Auction Facility (TAF) (expired 2010)	The Fed auctions a fixed volume of funds at maturities less than three months against collateral to depository institutions.
Primary Dealer Credit Facility (PDCF) (expired 2010)	The Fed lends overnight to primary dealers (including nonbanks) against a broad range of collateral.
Term Securities Lending Facility (TSLF) (expired 2010)	The Fed provides Treasury securities in exchange for a broad range of collateral in order to promote market liquidity.
Asset-Backed Commercial Paper (ABCP) Money-Market Mutual Fund (MMMF) Liquidity Facility (expired 2009)	The Fed lends to depositories and bank holding companies to finance purchases of ABCP from MMMFs.
Commercial Paper Funding Facility (CPFF) (expired 2010)	The Federal Reserve Bank (FRB) of New York finances the purchase of commercial paper from eligible issuers via primary dealers.
Money-Market Investor Funding Facility (MMIFF) (expired 2009)	The FRB New York funds investment vehicles that purchase assets from MMMFs.
Term Asset-Backed Securities Loan Facility (TALF) (expired 2010)	The FRB New York lends to holders of high-rated newly issued asset-backed securities (ABS), using the ABS as collateral.

stimulates economic activity. When the Fed refers to its unconventional policy of *large-scale asset purchases,* the term covers both targeted asset purchases and, if the purchases are unsterilized, quantitative easing. That is, Fed large-scale asset purchases are QE, TAP, or both.

In the next section we describe how these three unconventional mechanisms work. Finally, we'll look at how one of the four conventional policy tools—paying interest on reserves—helps a central bank exit smoothly from unconventional policies (like QE and TAP) that expand the central bank's balance sheet or result in the acquisition of illiquid assets.

Forward Guidance

The simplest unconventional approach a central bank can take is to provide "forward guidance"—guidance today about policy target rates in the *future*. For example, if policymakers believe that inflation will stay well below their objective, they might express the intention to keep the policy target rate low for an extended period (see the section Inflation Targeting on pages 496–497). This forward guidance could have a specific termination date, or its duration could be made contingent on a future change in economic conditions (say, an upturn in business activity or a rise of employment).

How does forward guidance influence the economy and inflation? To stimulate activity, central bank forward guidance aims at lowering the long-term interest rates that affect private spending. As Chapter 7 highlights, long-term bond yields depend in part on expectations about future short-term rates, which the central bank has the power to alter. Consequently, what central bankers say about their future plans can be very important. However, to be effective, forward guidance needs to be credible. Otherwise, long-term market interest rates may not respond as the central bank hopes.

In the past, policymakers used several mechanisms to make their commitments about future policy credible. For example, from the late 1930s until 1951, the Fed purchased long-term Treasury bonds with the objective of capping their interest rates at an artificially low level.[20] However, exiting from such intervention can be disruptive because investors face the prospect of immediate capital losses when yields rise. Consequently, if bondholders fear that the central bank will stop intervening, they may sell immediately. In such circumstances, the only way to sustain the cap on long-term interest rates would be for the central bank to buy *all* the bonds.

As discussed in this chapter, many central banks engage in inflation targeting; this policy framework affects the credibility of forward guidance and can be reinforced by it. For example, forward guidance aimed at keeping interest rates low will be most credible for an inflation-targeting central bank precisely when inflation is expected to stay below target for some time. The reason is that the guidance is time consistent: Future policymakers will not wish to renege. For the same reason, forward guidance can be used to counter the risk of deflation when the target interest rate is at the ELB.

How has the Federal Reserve used forward guidance? The answer is, with increasing frequency and refinement. In 2002–2004, the FOMC believed that inflation would sink undesirably low and worried about the possibility of deflation. Accordingly, the FOMC stated that its target federal funds rate would stay low for the "foreseeable future" or for a "considerable period." When the Fed began to tighten in 2004, it assured markets that the withdrawal of accommodation would occur at a "measured pace" to avoid fears of sharp rate hikes.

[20]The 10-year Treasury bond yield remained close to 2 percent in this period.

In late 2008, having lowered the policy target to zero during the crisis, policymakers announced that "weak economic conditions are likely to warrant exceptionally low levels of the federal funds rate for some time."[21] In December 2012, the FOMC went further, stating its expectation that "highly accommodative monetary policy will remain appropriate for a considerable time after . . . the economic recovery strengthens."[22] It also introduced specific thresholds (projected inflation above 2½ percent or an unemployment rate of less than 6½ percent) for raising the target rate.

Although forward guidance can be effective, the Fed's experience suggests that it is difficult to anticipate and reach consensus on the desirable policy path and to communicate these policy intentions in a simple yet precise way. Another concern is the potential for disturbing side effects, including asset price bubbles. Consequently, forward guidance is provided most often in extraordinary circumstances—when a general understanding of how the Fed usually responds to economic and financial conditions is insufficient to manage expectations.

Quantitative Easing

Quantitative easing (QE) is perhaps the most well-known mechanism to relax the monetary stance when policymakers no longer wish to lower the target rate. As we saw earlier in this chapter, QE occurs when the central bank expands the supply of aggregate reserves to the banking system *beyond* the level that would be needed to maintain its policy rate target. The central bank uses the proceeds from this reserve expansion to buy assets, thereby expanding its overall balance sheet. In the example in Table 18.3, the central bank adds $1 billion to commercial bank reserves held in their accounts at the Fed and acquires $1 billion in Treasury bonds.

The impact of QE on supply and demand in the federal funds market was shown in Figure 18.3 on page 486. At a market federal funds rate equal to the interest on excess reserves, an addition to aggregate reserves no longer reduces the funds rate. As a result, the Fed can add limitlessly to reserves—and to the assets on its balance sheet—without depressing the market federal funds rate. The amount of QE is the volume of reserves in excess of the level needed to keep the policy rate at its target, in this case the IOER rate. In Figure 18.3, it is the gap between points *B* and *C*.

A simple thought experiment shows that QE *can* shape the path of economic growth and inflation, even if the financial system is impaired. Imagine that the central bank expands reserves to the point where it (or the fiscal authority that it finances with new reserve issuance) purchases *all* of the assets in the economy. For QE to be ineffective, it would imply that the central bank could do so without influencing the level of prices! This nonsensical outcome means that QE, applied with sufficient vigor, and with the cooperation of the government, can alter economic growth and inflation prospects.

Nonetheless, it is difficult to predict the effects of QE. Fed policymakers argue that their balance sheet expansion helped lower long-term interest rates, but there is disagreement among experts about the

Table 18.3 How Quantitative Easing Affects the Central Bank Balance Sheet

Assets		Liabilities	
Treasury bonds	(+$1 billion)	Reserves	(+$1 billion)

[21]Statement of the Federal Open Market Committee, December 16, 2008. See www.federalreserve.gov/newsevents/press/monetary/20081216b.htm.

[22]Statement of the Federal Open Market Committee, December 12, 2012. See www.federalreserve.gov/newsevents/press/monetary/20121212a.htm.

impact—especially in deep, liquid markets.[23] Moreover, the mechanism by which QE affects economic prospects is not clear. When interest rates are at the rate paid on excess reserves, banks are indifferent between reserve deposits at the central bank and short-term government debt. These assets are riskless, so an increase in the supply of reserves (QE) may simply lead banks to hold more of them rather than provide additional loans to households and firms. This is one version of a "liquidity trap."

Such claims of QE's ineffectiveness were common when the Bank of Japan undertook the practice in the late 1990s. Japanese banks accumulated massive excess reserves, but lending continued to decline. We can see why this happened. After sustaining devastating losses, banks sought to rebuild their financial positions by *deleveraging*—that is, their objective was to lower the ratio of their assets to bank capital (recall Chapter 3, Lessons from the Crisis: Leverage).

How, then, might QE succeed in practice? One mechanism is that it can add credibility to a policymaker's expressed intention to keep interest rates low. Suppose that investors believe that a central bank will keep its policy rate at zero until after it will have exited from QE. Then, announcements of asset purchases that will expand aggregate reserves (QE) could lower bond yields by extending the time horizon over which bondholders expect a zero policy rate. This helps explain why the Fed announces its asset purchase plans well in advance: In doing so, it reinforces the impact of its forward guidance.

A key problem with QE is that central banks do not know how much is needed to be effective. They can only calibrate the appropriate level of reserves by experimentation. As the central bank boosts aggregate reserves (and expands its balance sheet), it can observe the impact on financial conditions and the economy. Naturally, this lack of predictability makes policymakers uncomfortable. Nevertheless, when conventional policy tools have been exhausted, QE can be an important tool for central bankers to prevent a sustained deflation.

How has the Federal Reserve used QE? Its first and largest application since the Great Depression occurred immediately after the Lehman failure in September 2008, and was subsequently labeled "QE1" (see how the Fed's balance sheet jumped in Figure 18.1 on page 481). In 2010, and again in 2012, the FOMC judged that inflation was likely to remain below its goal and unemployment would stay far above long-term norms. Consequently, in each of those years, the committee introduced a new round of balance sheet expansion, but perhaps with diminishing marginal impact. Overall, the combination of QE1, QE2, and QE3 boosted the Fed's assets to $4.5 trillion as of the end of 2014, up from the pre-QE1 level of less than $900 billion in August 2008. Over the same period, excess reserves in the banking system jumped from less than $2 *billion* to $2.6 *trillion.* Ultimately, the Fed's experience highlights policymakers' uncertainty about the appropriate dosage of QE.

Other major central banks—including the Bank of England, the ECB, and the Bank of Japan—also applied sizable doses of QE beginning in 2008. In each of these instances, central bank balance sheets expanded as policy interest rates sank to record lows. Were the policies effective? These economies showed less resilience than the United States, but their performance might have been even worse without QE.

The biggest QE experiment began in April 2013, when the Bank of Japan announced a round of asset purchases that doubled its monetary base in two years. Using QE, the bank aims to end Japan's deflation that began in the 1990s and to achieve a 2 percent inflation target. While progress has been slow, with inflation averaging roughly

[23]For differing opinions on the impact of QE, see the favorable view of Ben Bernanke ("Opening Remarks," pp. 6–9, www.federalreserve.gov/newsevents/speech/bernanke20120831a.htm) and the skeptical view of Michael Woodford ("Accommodation at the Zero Lower Bound," pp. 240–243, www.kc.frb.org/publicat/sympos/2012/Woodford_final.pdf) that were presented at the Federal Reserve Bank of Kansas City's August 2012 Economic Policy Symposium.

1 percent per year over the succeeding five years, the Bank of Japan is committed to using unconventional policy tools aggressively to reach the goal. Japan's experience with QE is bound to influence how policymakers in many countries judge the effectiveness of this policy tool.

Targeted Asset Purchases

In contrast to quantitative easing, which increases the *size* of the central bank's balance sheet, targeted asset purchases (TAP) shift the *composition* of the balance sheet toward selected assets in order to boost their relative price and stimulate economic activity.[24]

A simple example of TAP would be for the central bank to sell short-term U.S. Treasury bills and buy mortgage-backed securities (MBS, see page 52) of similar maturity. As seen in Table 18.4, this shift leaves the size of the balance sheet unchanged. Only the mix of assets is altered.

How does TAP alter the outlook for the economy and inflation? The central bank's actions can influence both the *cost* and *availability* of credit. When the central bank acquires an asset, such as MBS, it increases the overall demand for the asset. Increased demand tends to boost its price while driving its yield down. In the absence of private demand for the targeted asset, the central bank's purchase makes credit available where none existed.

The impact of TAP is likely to be greater in thin, illiquid markets. Under such conditions, even small interventions can have a magnified effect on market prices. The impact of TAP is also likely to be larger the bigger the difference between the yield on the asset that the central bank buys and the yield on the asset that the central bank sells. Assets with similar yields and risk characteristics are usually *close substitutes*. Assets with different risk characteristics and yields are less substitutable. By altering the relative supply of such assets to private investors, TAP narrows their interest rate differences.

The Federal Reserve's use of TAP in the financial crisis was unprecedented. In Figure 18.1, assets with default risk ("Lending to financial institutions" and "Liquidity to key credit markets") temporarily became the largest component of the Fed's balance sheet. Over time, the largest examples of TAP were the Fed's acquisitions of nearly $1.8 trillion of MBS and more than $2 trillion of long-term Treasury debt. The goal was to lower yields on mortgages and other long-term bonds and support interest-sensitive outlays, especially for housing.

Like the Fed, the ECB used TAP (and other targeted actions) aggressively in seeking to calm the euro-area crisis. To limit the widening yield spreads on the sovereign debt of countries on the periphery of the euro area (namely, Greece, Ireland, Italy, Portugal, and Spain), the ECB acquired more than €200 billion of this debt in its "securities market program." It also offered to purchase without limit the secondary-market debt (up to three years in maturity) of any country that accepted the stringent fiscal conditions for such "outright monetary transactions." Finally, the

Table 18.4 How Targeted Asset Purchases Affect the Central Bank's Balance Sheet

Assets		Liabilities
3-month Treasury bills	(−$1 billion)	
Mortgage-backed securities	(+$1 billion)	

[24]For the theory of targeted asset purchases, see pp. 243–252 in Michael Woodford, "Accommodation at the Zero Lower Bound," Federal Reserve Bank of Kansas City Economic Policy Symposium, August 2012, www.kc.frb.org/publicat/sympos/2012/Woodford_final.pdf.

ECB widened the range of acceptable collateral in order to boost the relative prices of troubled assets and to make funds available to periphery banks lacking better collateral.

Like QE, TAP is significantly more unwieldy for central bankers than conventional interest rate policy. A central bank cannot reliably anticipate the impact of TAP on the cost of credit. And TAP poses concerns that need not arise with QE. For example, like fiscal policy, TAP favors some users of credit over others. The special access that the Fed provided to issuers of commercial paper during the crisis is one example. In normal times, using conventional policy techniques, a central bank typically avoids such direct allocation of credit, promoting market competition rather than picking winners. TAP purposely deviates from such *asset neutrality* in order to influence relative prices.

Exiting from TAP probably also is more difficult than unwinding QE. TAP assets are generally harder to sell—that is, they are less liquid—than short-term Treasuries, so the central bank may not be able to get rid of them exactly when it wants without a significant price discount. In addition, political influences can become important if powerful users of credit and their government representatives seek to hinder the central bank from selling specific assets for fear of raising the costs of a particular class of borrowers.

Making an Effective Exit

When central banks pursue conventional interest rate targets, officials think about the policy choices they face every six to eight weeks. Deliberations are continuous, forming a *strategy* that influences expectations about the future path of their instrument and their objective. Decisions are not a series of one-time, separate choices. We can think of central bankers setting interest rates as participating in a complicated game—like chess—that requires them to make moves today while keeping in mind moves they may need to make far in the future.

The introduction of and exit from unconventional policies—such as forward guidance, quantitative easing, and targeted asset purchases—also require looking into the future. Without a consistent and credible approach, policymakers may be unable to keep inflation expectations close to their inflation objective. And, if they fail, unstable inflation expectations could lead to broader economic instability.

Compared with conventional policy, exiting from QE and TAP poses additional obstacles that appear technical but have important implications. The key question is whether a central bank that wishes to raise interest rates in order to tighten policy conditions will be able to do so as quickly as desired. With conventional policy, the answer is yes. In the case of QE and TAP, the answer depends on the size and composition of the central bank's balance sheet and on the toolset available to the policymakers.

When reserves are scarce, a central bank that wishes to hike the policy rate can do so by modestly trimming the aggregate reserves that it supplies to the banking system. A central bank may hold enough short-term risk-free assets (such as Treasury bills) to reduce the supply of reserves merely by allowing some of these assets to mature. If necessary, the authorities also could sell a portion of these assets, which are among the most liquid.

What happens when QE and TAP have vastly expanded the amount of reserves and assets on the central bank's balance sheet? The answer—as we saw earlier in this chapter—is that the central bank may need to sell a large volume of assets to reduce reserve supply sufficiently to raise the policy rate target. But TAP assets are typically more difficult to sell (less liquid) than Treasury bills. Moreover, the value of any TAP assets that default will plunge. In these circumstances, a central bank may be unable to sell assets and withdraw reserves from the banking system rapidly enough to hike the policy interest rate when it desires. So what can authorities do?

Is 2 Percent Still the Right Inflation Target?

MONEY AND BANKING BLOG

Policymakers in Europe, Japan, and the United States have struggled over the past decade to stimulate their weak economies and stabilize prices with near-zero nominal interest rates and a range of unconventional monetary policies. Along the way, observers have increasingly wondered whether central banks should raise their inflation target in order to reduce the need to use unconventional policies.

The concept of inflation targeting became widely accepted after the 1970s and early 1980s, when a number of advanced economies experienced inflation as high as 20 percent. A broad consensus developed that, if central banks adopted an inflation target, people would have more confidence that inflation would stay low and stable. Today, most advanced economies have chosen 2 percent as their desired level of inflation, even though the inflation-targeting concept says nothing about what, exactly, the target should be.*

So, why 2 percent? First, a target of zero percent would require policy to continually flirt with deflation, which conventional policy tools are ill-suited to address (see Chapter 21, Applying the Concept: Zero Matters, page 606). Second, research has convinced many policymakers that inflation is commonly overstated by about 1 percentage point.[†] At a measured inflation rate of about 2 percent, actual inflation would be about 1 percent, providing some buffer against the risk of deflation in a recession. Once a small group of central banks began to pick 2 percent as their objective, others soon followed.

Then why are some policy experts now questioning the 2 percent inflation target? Despite ultra-low policy interest rates, the weak postcrisis recovery kept advanced-economy inflation below 2 percent for an extended period. Central bankers are no longer confident that lowering the policy rate to zero will be sufficient to recover from a severe recession with an inflation target of 2 percent.

To illustrate the connection between the inflation target, economic activity, and the policy interest rate, consider a modified version of the Taylor rule based on the unemployment rate (instead of real GDP). Under this rule, the proper level of the policy interest rate is the sum of (1) the neutral real interest rate (also called the natural or equilibrium rate of interest), (2) the inflation target, (3) one-half of the difference between current inflation and the inflation target, and (4) −1 times the **unemployment gap**, which is the difference between the current unemployment rate and what is called the frictional, equilibrium, or **natural rate of unemployment**.

In the long run, item 3 in the Taylor rule will be zero because current inflation will be at the target rate, and item 4 will be zero because the current jobless rate will equal the natural rate. If the neutral *real* interest rate (the neutral *nominal* rate minus the expected inflation rate) is 2 percent, and the target inflation rate is 2 percent, then the equation tells us that the policy interest rate in the long run should be set to 4 percent. Starting from this long-run position and with the inflation rate at the target of 2 percent, a rise in the unemployment rate to four percentage points above the natural rate yields a nominal policy rate of zero. (To see why nominal interest rates cannot decline far below zero, see Applying the Concept: Negative Nominal Interest Rates: Blast from the Past?, page 469).

Put another way, a policy interest rate of zero when the actual and expected inflation rate is 2 percent should restore full employment to an economy in which unemployment is four percentage points above the minimum rate. But what if unemployment is more than four points above the natural rate? Since 1960, that has happened twice, in the recession of 1982–1983 and during the Great Recession, 2009–2010—roughly once every 25 years (see Figure 18.9). In these episodes, a central bank with a 2 percent inflation target could use unconventional policy tools after cutting the policy rate to zero.

Other things equal, raising the inflation target by even one percentage point, to 3 percent, would accommodate an unemployment gap of five percentage points—and even in the Great Recession, the U.S. unemployment gap did not reach five percentage points.

But other things may not be equal. Two important factors would favor an even higher inflation target. First, recent estimates put the neutral real rate below 1 percent—more than a full percentage point lower than in a conventional Taylor rule. Second, when the

Following the financial crisis of 2007–2009, many people worried that the swollen balance sheets of the Fed and other central banks would lead to runaway inflation. Everybody knows that a timely exit from QE and TAP is necessary to keep inflation low. But is it possible?

Figure 18.9 U.S. Unemployment Gap, 1960–2018 (percentage points)

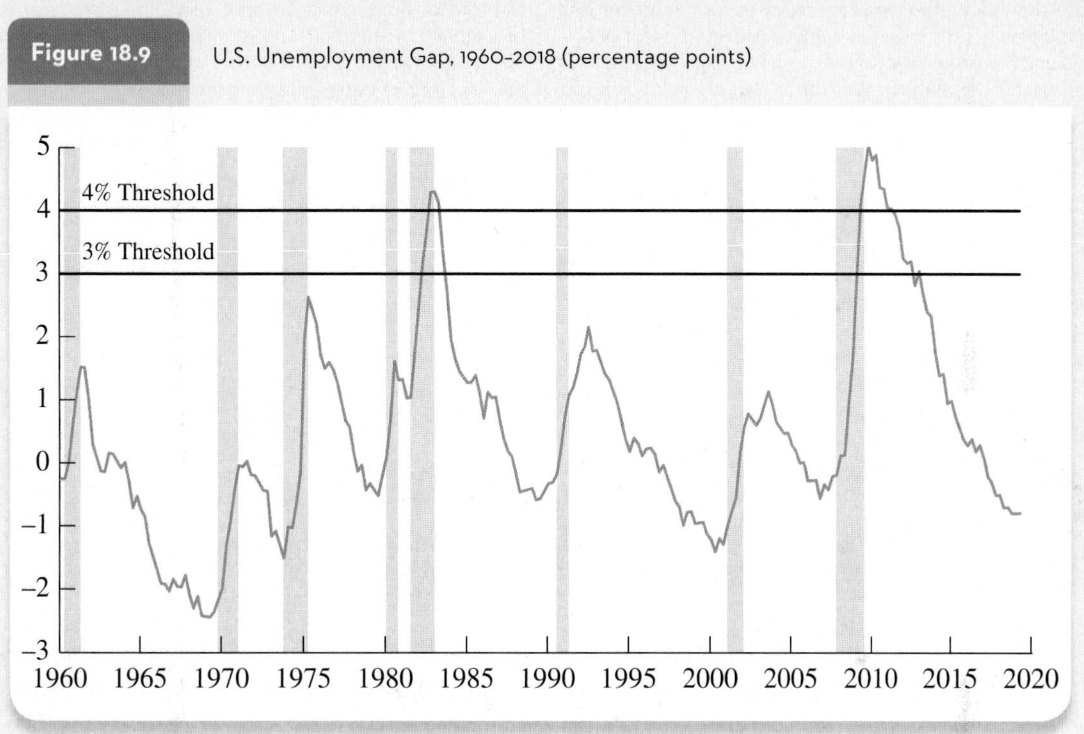

NOTE: Shaded areas denote recessions. The gap is the civilian unemployment rate (FRED code: UNRATE) less the natural rate of unemployment (FRED code: NROU).

SOURCE: Federal Reserve Bank of St. Louis and author's calculations.

unemployment rate begins to rise in some future downturn, inflation could be below the 2 percent target, reducing the unemployment gap that could be cured by a zero policy rate. Putting all of this together, even a 3 percent inflation target may not be high enough to avoid the occasional need for negative interest rates or unconventional monetary policies.

For these reasons, policymakers might wish they had initially chosen a higher target rate of inflation. But having educated their publics that the right inflation target is 2 percent, and having settled on that level internationally as a useful form of monetary policy coordination, making such a fundamental change in the policy framework could pose a risk to their credibility.

*Emerging market economies have picked higher targets—in 2014, for example, India chose 4 percent. The difference is sensible. As emerging economies catch up with advanced economies, they are likely to face a transitional period of higher inflation for nontraded goods and services.

†For a discussion of why measured inflation overstates the true level, see Stephen G. Cecchetti and Kermit L. Schoenholtz, "Inflation and Price Measurement: A Primer," October 8, 2018, www.moneyandbanking.com.

You already know that the answer is yes. Central banks holding large quantities of illiquid assets can tighten while avoiding a fire sale if they can raise the rate that they pay on reserves. Today, leading central banks like the Fed and the ECB have this authority and use it. In the case of the Fed, the IOER rate establishes a floor below

The Financial Stability-Monetary Policy Nexus

LESSONS FROM THE CRISIS

All central bankers worry about financial stability. They know that when they ease monetary policy to bolster growth and employment, they boost risk taking, drive up asset prices, and encourage borrowing. They also know that these effects can go too far, turning asset price and credit booms into busts. The result is credit defaults by households, firms, and intermediaries. On all of this everyone agrees.

The question is what to do about it. The broad consensus is that prudential tools, both micro and macro (including stress tests), should remain the first line of defense against financial instability.

But what about the risks that remain even after policymakers have used their prudential tools? Should central bankers alter interest rate policy to promote financial stability? On this, there is much less agreement. The difficulty is that conventional monetary policy is a highly practical endeavor. For example, central bankers must continually decide whether they should change their target interest rate, and if so, by exactly how much and on what date.

So, in asking monetary policymakers to use interest rate policy to secure financial stability, proponents need to be precise about what should they do and when should they do it.

No one disagrees that monetary policies aimed at economic stabilization today can create financial stability risks tomorrow. But how big are these risks? And what is the interest rate policy that should be used to combat them without undue sacrifice to the objectives of stable prices and maximum employment?

To answer these questions, we need a measure of financial-sector vulnerability and some idea of the extent to which it is influenced by monetary policy. Yet, as of 2019, empirical investigations of these connections remain at an early stage. We don't even have a commonly accepted definition of systemic risk: One recent paper explores 17 definitions for the United States and 10 for Europe and the United Kingdom. As for the impact of monetary policy on systemic risk, by some measures it is quite limited.

While monetary policy can in theory create financial stability risks, changing the path of policy in specific cases to reduce these risks is still difficult to justify. So, for the time being, micro- and macro-prudential regulation remain the principal tools to contain systemic risk. And central banks will be reluctant to alter monetary policy for this purpose unless policy's influence on future financial stability can be reliably quantified.

which banks are unwilling to lend. Hence, the Fed—and other central banks, like the ECB, with a similar policy tool—can raise interest rates throughout the economy without reducing the level of reserve supply or changing the composition of its balance sheet. The example for the Fed in Figure 18.4 on page 487 shows that, to tighten policy, the Fed raises the IOER rate from IOER Rate_0 to IOER Rate_1. As a result, the flat portion of the reserve demand curve rises, and the equilibrium between reserve demand and reserve supply moves from point *C* to point *D*.

Paying interest on reserves thus allows a central bank, unlike a typical monopolist, to control both price and quantity, two powerful monetary policy tools, independently of one another: (1) For price, it can adjust the target short-term interest rate (or range) and the IOER rate without changing the size or composition of its balance sheet; and (2) for quantity, it can adjust *the size and composition of its balance sheet* without changing the target short-term rate or the IOER rate. This flexibility means that the central bank can change its balance sheet in a fashion consistent with financial stability while keeping inflation under control.

As the first of the major central banks to exit from unconventional policy, the Fed used this ability to make separate decisions regarding its interest rate target and its balance sheet. The first shift came when it stopped expanding its assets in 2015. By the end of that year, wanting to tighten, the Fed began to raise the IOER rate, while leaving the size of its balance sheet largely unchanged. Only in late 2017, after multiple hikes of the IOER rate, did it begin to allow some of the assets on its balance sheet to mature without replacement (see Figure 18.1 on page 481). In the third quarter of 2019, the Fed halted the shrinkage of its balance sheet, even as it lowered the IOER rate.

Concluding Remarks

In truth, central bankers have a nearly impossible job. They are supposed to stabilize the economy and financial system at the same time that they provide services to commercial banks and the government. To perform this task, we give them control over their own balance sheet, allowing them to buy and sell securities in the financial markets and make loans to banks. In normal times, they choose to control the price of reserves, which is an interest rate. Because movements in interest rates affect the entire economic system, control over interest rates usually gives monetary policymakers the leverage they need to stabilize inflation rates, growth rates, and the financial system. As we will see in detail in Part V, Chapters 20–23, higher interest rates slow inflation and growth by reducing the availability of credit; lower interest rates stimulate economic activity by making credit cheaper and easier to get. But monetary policy requires unconventional tools when interest rates sink to the effective lower bound, or when financial institutions or markets become dysfunctional.

Over the years, central bankers have learned from their mistakes. They understand the importance of keeping the financial system running smoothly and have refined their ability to lend quickly in times of crisis. And because everyone understands the importance of keeping inflation low, we have designed our central banks to deliver price stability. The outcome is that the inflation rate is lower now in many countries than it was from 1970 to 1995.

Today we have a set of principles that tells us how central banks should be designed and how they should use interest rates to stabilize their economy. But central bankers cannot do the job alone. Sound monetary policy must be combined with responsible fiscal policy to build a healthy economic and financial system. Moreover, with the fading economic importance of national borders, the time has passed when even large central banks could avoid taking international conditions into account. To fill this hole in our analysis, we turn in Chapter 19 to a study of exchange rate management and the international financial system.

Key Terms

conventional policy tools, 482
discount lending, 488
discount rate, 483
ECB's deposit facility, 492
ECB's marginal lending facility, 491
effective lower bound (ELB), 480
forward guidance, 503
inflation targeting, 496
interest rate on excess reserves (IOER rate) 483
lender of last resort, 488
market federal funds rate, 484
minimum bid rate, 491
natural rate of interest, 498
natural rate of unemployment, 510
overnight cash rate, 492
overnight reverse repo (ON RRP) rate, 519
primary credit, 488
primary discount rate, 489
quantitative easing (QE), 485
repurchase agreement (repo), 491
reserve requirement, 483
secondary discount rate, 489
target federal funds rate range, 483
targeted asset purchases (TAP), 503
Taylor rule, 497
unconventional policy tools, 482
unemployment gap, 510
zero lower bound (ZLB), 480

Using FRED: Codes for Data in This Chapter

Data Series	FRED Data Code
Federal Reserve assets	WALCL
MBS	WSHOMCB
Treasuries	WSHOTSL
Agencies	WSHOFADSL
Repos	WORAL
Loans	WLCFLL
Federal funds rate (monthly)	FEDFUNDS
Federal funds rate (weekly)	FF
Discount rate (through 2002)	MDISCRT
Discount rate (beginning 2003)	WPCREDIT
Interest paid on excess reserves	IOER
Required reserves	REQRESNS
Total reserves	TOTRESNS
Primary credit	WPC
Potential GDP	GDPPOT
Real GDP	GDPC1
Real GDP (not seasonally adjusted)	ND000334Q
Personal consumption expenditures price index	PCEPI
Personal consumption expenditures price index (less food and energy)	JCXFE
30-year fixed mortgage rate	MORTGAGE30US
Discount window borrowing	DISCBORR
Japan Treasury bill rates	INTGSTJPM193N
Japan consumer price index	JPNCPIALLMINMEI

To learn more about the changing financial system, visit www.moneyandbanking.com.

Chapter Lessons

1. The Federal Reserve has four tools of conventional monetary policy.
   a. The target range for the federal funds rate:
      i. Set by the FOMC, it is the intended range for the interest rate charged by financial intermediaries on overnight, uncollateralized loans to banks.
      ii. The target level of the federal funds rate was the primary tool of policy before 2008.
   b. The interest rate on excess reserves (IOER rate):
      i. Set by the FOMC, it is the interest rate paid by the Federal Reserve on excess reserves held by banks.
      ii. It determines the short-term market rate (the federal funds rate) because banks prefer to deposit at the Fed rather than lend to others at or below the IOER rate.
      iii. It is currently the primary tool for influencing financial conditions in the economy.

   c. The discount rate:
      i. Set by the Reserve Banks, subject to approval by the Federal Reserve Board, it is the interest rate on discount lending, used by the Fed as the lender of last resort to supply funds to banks in need to maintain financial stability.
      ii. The "primary rate" for discount lending is set at a spread above the interest rate on excess reserves (IOER rate).
   d. Reserve requirements:
      i. Set by the Federal Reserve Board, the requirements determine how much banks are required to hold in reserve against certain deposits.
      ii. Banks hold required reserves in the form of interest-bearing reserve deposits at Federal Reserve Banks or as vault cash.
      iii. Required reserves have a limited policy role today because they are much smaller than excess reserves, and the impact of changes in reserve requirements is difficult to predict.

2. The European Central Bank's primary objective is price stability.
   a. The ECB provides liquidity to the banking system both through open market purchases of securities and through auctions called refinancing operations.
   b. When reserves are scarce, the minimum bid rate on the main refinancing operations, also known as the target refinancing rate, is the target interest rate controlled by the ECB Governing Council.
   c. The ECB allows banks to borrow from its marginal lending facility at an interest rate that is set above the target refinancing rate.
   d. Banks with excess reserves can deposit them at national central banks and receive interest at a spread below the target refinancing rate. Banks will not lend to others below this riskless deposit rate, which is equivalent to the Fed's IOER rate.

3. Monetary policymakers use several tools to meet their objectives.
   a. The best tools are observable, controllable, and tightly linked to objectives.
   b. Short-term interest rates are the primary tools for monetary policymaking.
   c. Most modern central banks employ inflation targeting, a policy strategy that involves the public announcement of a numerical inflation target, underscoring the central bank's commitment to price stability.

4. The Taylor rule is a simple equation that describes movements in the target federal funds rate. It suggests that:
   a. When inflation rises, the FOMC raises the target rate by 1½ times the increase in inflation.
   b. When output rises above potential by 1 percent, the FOMC raises the target rate by ½ percentage point.

5. Unconventional monetary policy can supplement conventional policy when policymakers are no longer willing or able to lower the target rate or when an impaired financial system prevents conventional interest rate policy from working.

6. Central banks have three principal tools of unconventional monetary policy:
   a. *Forward guidance:* communication regarding expected future policy target rates.
   b. *Quantitative easing:* supplying aggregate reserves beyond the quantity needed to lower the policy rate to the target.
   c. *Targeted asset purchases:* changing the mix of assets at the central bank to alter their relative market prices.

7. Unconventional monetary policy is less predictable than conventional policy and potentially disruptive, so it is used only when the conventional toolkit is insufficient to stabilize the economy. One conventional policy tool—the payment of interest on reserves—can help a central bank exit smoothly from unconventional monetary policy.

Conceptual and Analytical Problems

1. Explain how the Federal Reserve would implement a rise in the target range for the federal funds rate? How does its action influence the market federal funds rate? *(LO1)*
2. Using a graph of the market for bank reserves, show how, in the post-2008 environment, the Federal Reserve can control independently both the price and quantity of aggregate bank reserves. *(LO1)*
3. Why might the market federal funds rate deviate from the interest rate on excess reserves? *(LO1)*
4. Federal Reserve buying of mortgage-backed securities is an example of a targeted asset purchase. Explain how the Fed's actions are intended to work. *(LO4)*
5. The strategy of inflation targeting, which seeks to keep inflation close to a numerical goal over a reasonable horizon, has been referred to as a policy framework of "constrained discretion." What features of the inflation targeting framework make this an appropriate description? *(LO2)*
6. The charge given by Congress to the Federal Reserve is to "promote effectively the goals of maximum employment, stable prices, and moderate long-term interest rates." Discuss whether the Taylor rule conforms to this mandate. *(LO3)*
7. Use the following Taylor rule to calculate what would happen to the real interest rate if inflation increased by three percentage points. *(LO3)*

   $$\text{Target federal funds rate} = \text{Natural rate of interest} + \text{Current inflation} + \tfrac{1}{2}(\text{Inflation gap}) + \tfrac{1}{2}(\text{Output gap})$$

8.* The conventional Taylor rule places weights of one-half on the inflation gap and output gap, corresponding to the "dual mandate" of the U.S. central bank. Taking into account what you know about the policy goals of the ECB, how might you amend the Taylor rule to better approximate policymaking behavior by the ECB? *(LO3)*

9.* Use your knowledge of the problems associated with asymmetric information to explain why, prior to the change in the Federal Reserve's discount lending facility in 2002, banks were extremely unlikely to borrow from the facility despite funds being available at a rate below the target federal funds rate. *(LO1)*

10. Based on the liquidity premium theory of the term structure of interest rates, explain how forward guidance about monetary policy can lower long-term interest rates today. Be sure to account both for future short-term rates and for the risk

*Indicates more difficult problems.

premium. How does the effectiveness of forward guidance depend on its time consistency? *(LO4)*

11. With the policy interest rate at the effective lower bound, how might a central bank counter unwanted deflation? *(LO4)*

12.* Outline and compare the ways in which the Federal Reserve and the ECB added to or adjusted their monetary policy tools in response to the financial crisis of 2007–2009 and the subsequent financial crisis in the euro area. *(LO4)*

13. The central bank of a country facing economic and financial market difficulties asks for your advice. The bank cut its policy interest rate to the effective lower bound, but it was not low enough to stabilize the economy. Drawing on the actions taken by the Federal Reserve during the financial crisis of 2007–2009, what might you advise this central bank to do? *(LO4)*

14.* Suppose ECB officials ask your opinion about their operational framework for monetary policy. You respond by commenting on their success at keeping short-term interest rates close to target but also express concern about the complexity of their process for managing the supply of reserves. What specific changes would you suggest the ECB make to its system in the future? *(LO3)*

15. The interest rate paid by the European Central Bank (ECB) on excess reserves declined below zero in 2014 (and remained there as of 2019). What was the rationale behind this move to a negative deposit rate, and why would banks be willing to pay to keep deposits with the ECB? *(LO1)*

16. Suppose, immediately after the European Central Bank (ECB) began charging banks a fee for holding their excess reserves, the banks switched to holding cash in their vaults (rather than holding excess reserves), and also began charging customers for holding their deposits. Do you think the ECB would have kept the deposit rate in negative territory? Explain your answer. *(LO2)*

17. Inflation, rather than the price level or nominal GDP, is the policy target of choice for many of the world's central banks. Provide a reason why you think this is the case. *(LO2)*

18. You have been asked about the appropriate use of data in policy decisions by officials from a new central bank in a country that is economically similar to the United States. These officials currently use non-seasonally adjusted GDP to gauge the state of economic activity in real time. What advice would you offer these policymakers? *(LO2)*

19 Suppose you were given the following information about two inflation–targeting economies.
   - Economy A has been volatile historically with the unemployment rate fluctuating widely around the natural rate, with the neutral real interest rate estimated to be around 1.5 percent. Despite the economic volatility, the well-designed central bank has enjoyed many decades of credibility.
   - Economy B has seen unemployment rates stay relatively close to the natural rate, with the neutral real interest rate estimated to be around 3 percent. Despite the stable unemployment rate, the credibility of the central bank is somewhat fragile.

   Based on this information, assuming everything else equal, which Economy should adopt a higher inflation target? Explain your answer. *(LO3)*

*Indicates more difficult problems.

Data Exploration connect

For general information on using Federal Reserve Economic Data (FRED) online, visit www.mhhe.com/moneyandbanking6e *and refer to the FRED Resources.*

1. Plot the Taylor rule since 1990 on a quarterly basis (similar to Figure 18.7). For the output gap, use the percent deviations of real GDP (FRED code: GDPC1) from potential output (FRED code: GDPPOT). For inflation, use the percent change from a year ago of the price index for personal consumption expenditures (FRED code: PCEPI). Assume that the long-run risk-free rate averages 2 percent and the target inflation rate is 2 percent. When complete, compare the Taylor rule rate against the actual federal funds rate (FRED code: FEDFUNDS) after 2007. *(LO3)*

2. On December 15, 2015, the FOMC began to raise the target range for the federal funds rate in a series of small steps over several years. To see the impact, plot (on a "Weekly, ending Wednesday" basis beginning July 15, 2015) the interest rate on excess reserves (FRED code: IOER) and the effective federal funds rate (FRED code: FF). Explain the plot, noting the impact of the FOMC decisions on these two interest rates *(LO4)*

3. Assess the impact of targeted asset purchases by plotting since 2003 on a monthly basis the Federal Reserve's holdings of mortgage-backed securities (FRED code: WSHOMCB) and (on the right scale) the average yield on 30-year fixed-rate mortgages (FRED code: MORTGAGE30US). Discuss how these purchases might support both the housing market and the banking system. *(LO4)*

4. In 2002, the Federal Reserve began to set the discount rate *above* the federal funds rate, reversing its previous practice of keeping the discount rate below the funds rate. To assess the impact, plot on a monthly basis from 1990 to 2007 the difference between the federal funds rate and the discount rate *before* (FRED codes: FEDFUNDS and MDISCRT) and after the policy shift (FRED codes: FEDFUNDS and WPCREDIT), using the same line color. On the right scale, plot the level of discount window borrowing (FRED code: DISCBORR). Did the new penalty rate for discount loans significantly diminish borrowing? What might account for the behavior of discount window borrowing? *(LO1)*

5. Examine the real interest rate in Japan, plotting since 2000 the nominal interest rate on Japanese Treasury bills (FRED code: INTGSTJPM193N), the inflation rate based on the percent change from a year ago of Japan's consumer price index (FRED code: JPNCPIALLMINMEI), and an estimate of the real interest rate based on the difference between these two indicators. Comment on the lengthy period of positive real rates since 2000 and the role of deflation in determining the real rate. Discuss the risks that deflation poses in an economy with the nominal interest rate at the effective lower bound. *(LO1)*

Appendix to Chapter 18

Monetary Policy Operations and the Reverse Repo Rate

Prior to 2007, day-to-day monetary policy was straightforward. The FOMC would announce a target for the level of the federal funds rate, and then the Open Market Operations Desk of the Federal Reserve Bank of New York would do its best to supply the quantity of reserves that matched the target federal funds rate on the reserve demand curve. (Take a look back at Figure 18.2, page 485.) But with reserves in the banking system now so abundant, this mechanism for controlling the federal funds rate no longer works. The FOMC sets a target for the range of the federal funds rate, but the Fed has shifted to the IOER rate as its primary tool for hitting that target. In this appendix, we describe the current procedures.[25]

To understand how the system works, start by noting that the market federal funds rate generally fluctuates in a range *near* the IOER rate. From 2008 to 2018, the IOER rate marked the top of the 25-basis-point target range for the federal funds rate, but as of 2019 it is set *within* this target range. How does the IOER rate influence the market federal funds rate? One way is by affecting bank lending: No bank will provide credit to a risky counterparty below the Fed's IOER rate, when it can earn a higher return free of default risk and liquidity risk by holding reserves.

Today, the most common lenders in the federal funds rate market are not banks, but government-sponsored enterprises (GSEs)—like Fannie Mae, Freddie Mac, and the Federal Home Loan Banks (FHLBs). In practice, with the banking system awash in excess reserves, the rate at which these nonbanks are willing to lend to banks determines the market federal funds rate.

So, the IOER rate is the principal device the Fed now uses to tighten or loosen monetary policy and influence interest rates in financial markets. How does the Fed control the bottom end of its target range for the federal funds rate? This is where the **overnight reverse repo (ON RRP) rate** comes in as a supplementary tool.

Since 2008, the Fed has set the ON RRP rate at the bottom of the target range. As of August 2019, that rate is 10 basis points below the IOER rate, while more than 120 intermediaries—including the GSEs and money-market mutual funds (MMMFs)—are eligible to participate in Fed ON RRP operations. ON RRPs constitute a default-free loan to the Fed. So, provided that the Fed offers them in sufficient volume, ON RRPs set a floor below the rate at which this broad array of short-term market participants is willing to lend to a bank.

[25]For a look at how the Fed's tools affect a range of short-term interest rates, see the video produced by economists at the Federal Reserve Bank of Chicago at http://youtu.be/IkGH5qRy-zE.

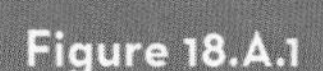

Figure 18.A.1 The Market for Reserves with the IOER and the ON RRP Rate

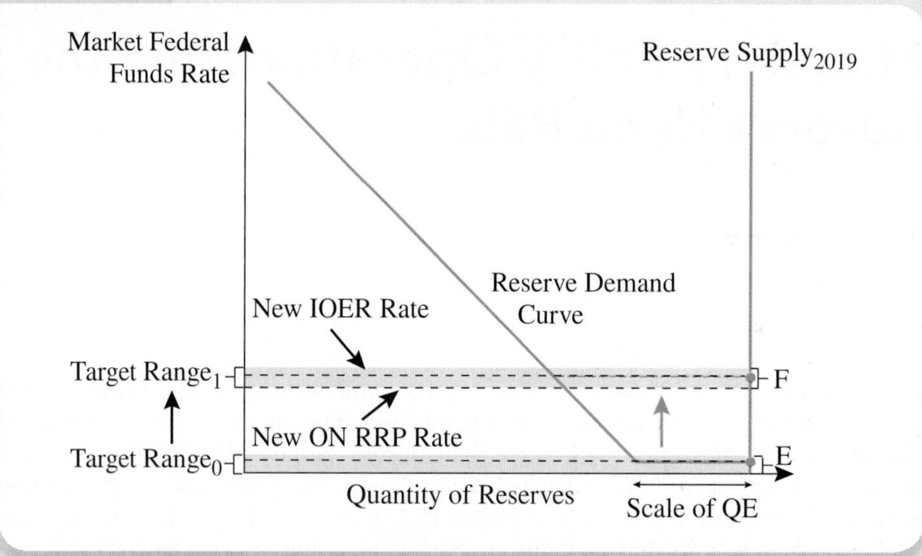

The FOMC announces a target range for the federal funds rate, shown as the shaded area. The IOER and ON RRP rate are set so that the federal funds rate will remain inside this range. Reserve demand slopes down but then becomes horizontal. Reserve supply is vertical and far to the right of the kink in the demand curve. Because some large lenders to banks are not banks themselves and thus not entitled to earn interest on deposits at the Fed, the IOER virtually determines the level of the horizontal portion of reserve demand. Policy tightening is achieved by raising the federal funds rate target range, which means raising the IOER rate and the ON RRP rate. This shifts the equilibrium in the market for reserves from point *E* to point *F*.

As a result, the Fed can adjust the IOER and ON RRP rates to maintain or alter its target range for federal funds rate. Prior to the financial crisis, many central banks allowed the overnight interbank lending rate to fluctuate in a wide channel between the central bank deposit rate (much like the IOER rate) and the central bank lending rate (a ceiling equivalent to the Fed's discount rate). Today, the effective channel is far narrower—only 25 basis points. In this new framework, the Fed's discount rate no longer has relevance for monetary policy, but (as you have seen in this chapter) it still plays a central role when the Fed acts as lender of last resort.

Figure 18.A.1 shows all of this graphically. Note first that reserve demand slopes down, but because banks seek to minimize their borrowing cost, which is virtually determined by the IOER rate, the flat portion is below the top of the target range. Second, we have labeled the bottom of the target range as the ON RRP rate. Because nonbank intermediaries can engage in overnight reverse repos with the Fed, they will not be willing to lend to banks at a rate below this level, provided that the Fed accepts a sufficient volume of funds at this rate. Alternatively, should the Fed limit the funds accepted via ON RRP, the market federal funds rate could drop below the target range depicted in the figure.

Third, the figure shows that tightening policy is straightforward. All the FOMC has to do is to raise the target range for the federal funds rate. It does so by raising both the IOER rate and the ON RRP rate. As long as reserves remain plentiful, the equilibrium in the market for reserves will be on the flat part of the reserve demand curve, which (like the IOER rate) is inside the target range for the federal funds rate.

Chapter

19 Exchange Rate Policy and the Central Bank

Learning Objectives

After reading this chapter, you should be able to:

LO1 Explain the links between exchange rates and monetary policy.

LO2 Describe the mechanics of exchange rate management.

LO3 Assess the costs, benefits, and risks of fixed exchange rates.

LO4 Analyze how fixed exchange rate regimes work.

On the morning of September 22, 2000, the Federal Reserve Bank of New York's foreign exchange desk began buying euros for the first time since the currency came into existence 21 months earlier. Meanwhile, central bank officials in Frankfurt, London, Tokyo, and Ottawa (Canada) did the same. Among them, they bought between €4 and €6 billion. The Fed alone bought €1.5 billion for \$1.34 billion. At this writing, the Fed has conducted only one **foreign exchange intervention** since the September 2000 operation.[1]

The whole operation took about two hours; when it was over, the central banks announced what they had done. As the ECB wrote in its press release, they did it because of "shared concern about the potential implications of recent movements in the euro exchange rate for the world economy." Since its inception on January 1, 1999, the euro had fallen steadily from \$1.18 to \$0.85, a decline of more than 25 percent. Though its low value had made exports cheap, bolstering the foreign sales of European-made products, it had also forced up the prices of imports. ECB officials, charged with maintaining price stability, found the high price of imports particularly troubling because they really did not want to raise interest rates just to bolster the value of their currency (which is what they would have had to do). Experts debated whether the euro should be worth \$1.10 or \$1.00, but most agreed that \$0.85 was too low.

The coordinated intervention in the foreign exchange market made headlines around the world. The euro appreciated briefly, rising to \$0.89 on the day of the intervention,

[1]On March 18, 2011, the Fed sold \$1 billion of Japanese yen in a coordinated intervention involving the ECB and the central banks of Canada, Japan, and the United Kingdom. The central banks acted jointly to counter the sudden rise in the value of the yen that followed Japan's March 11 earthquake and tsunami. After those natural disasters, currency speculators purchased yen, believing that Japanese holders of foreign assets would sell their investments abroad and repatriate the funds to finance domestic reconstruction. The intervention weakened the yen for a few weeks, but it began to appreciate again and surpassed the March peak by July.

but by mid-October, it had returned to $0.85. The action may have been dramatic, but it wasn't effective. To understand why the intervention didn't work, and why the Fed almost never engages in such foreign currency transactions, we need to examine the mechanics of how a central bank manages its country's exchange rate.

The United States economy is huge and largely self-contained. Exports and imports together account for less than 30 percent of GDP. For the most part, the U.S. economy produces what it consumes and invests, so, on most days, policymakers at the Fed are justified in concentrating on the domestic economy and letting the exchange rate take care of itself. In other large economies, trade plays a somewhat larger role, approaching 40 percent of GDP in China and exceeding 50 percent in the euro area. In contrast, highly *open* economies are far more exposed to trade developments in the rest of the world, so changes in their exchange rates can have a dramatic impact on them. For example, in small economies, imports and exports together frequently exceed 100 percent of GDP, so their central banks do not have the luxury of ignoring the exchange rate.

Argentina provides an interesting example of how external and domestic factors interact in the making of monetary policy. Over the years, Argentina has suffered from severe inflation. During the 1970s, inflation averaged about 100 percent, meaning that prices doubled every year, while the economy grew about 3 percent a year. By 1989, inflation had climbed to more than 2,000 percent per year and the price level was *60 billion* times what it had been 20 years before. Needless to say, growth fell. In 1990, real GDP was below its 1973 level and Argentina's economy was at a standstill.

The cause of such high inflation is often a combination of failed fiscal policy and failed monetary policy. Politicians want to spend too much, so they lean on central bankers to print more money. To discipline policymakers, in 1991 Argentineans implemented a mechanism called a *currency board,* which had two important attributes. First, Argentina's central bank, the Banco Central de la Republica Argentina, guaranteed that it would exchange Argentinean pesos for U.S. dollars on a one-for-one basis; it fixed its exchange rate. Second, the central bank was required to hold dollar assets equal to its domestic currency liabilities, again at a one-to-one exchange rate. For every peso note that was issued and every peso in commercial bank reserves that it created, the Central Bank of Argentina had to hold one U.S. dollar.

The results were almost miraculous. Inflation fell immediately; after a few years, it had completely disappeared. But as we will see later, the victory didn't last. By early January 2002, the currency board had collapsed, GDP had fallen by a quarter, and inflation had risen to more than 30 percent.

The examples of the euro purchases in 2000 and the Argentine exchange rate actions suggest a connection between domestic monetary policy and exchange rate policy. To avoid raising domestic interest rates, the ECB organized a coordinated intervention to shore up the value of the euro. To control the inflationary impulses of fiscal and monetary authorities, Argentina fixed its exchange rate to the dollar. If exchange rate policy is inseparable from interest rate policy, we have left something essential out of our analysis by ignoring cross-border transactions. To rectify the omission, we turn now to a discussion of exchange rate regimes. Why is a country's exchange rate linked to its domestic monetary policy? Are there circumstances when exchange rate stabilization becomes the overriding objective of central bankers? If so, should they try to fix the rate at which their currency can be exchanged for some other currency? Should a country even consider giving up its currency entirely?

Linking Exchange Rate Policy with Domestic Monetary Policy

Exchange rate policy is integral to any monetary policy regime. The city of Chicago, for instance, has a fixed exchange rate with the rest of the United States—both use the dollar—so it has no independent monetary policy. Because Chicago's monetary policy is made by the FOMC, interest rates in Chicago are the same as interest rates everywhere else in the United States. Any discrepancy between the price of a bond in Chicago and the price of the same bond in San Francisco is wiped out instantly by arbitrage, as investors buy the bond where it is cheap and sell it where it is expensive (all this is done electronically). What is true for Chicago is true for any country: *When capital flows freely across a country's borders, a fixed exchange rate means giving up domestic monetary policy.*

There are two ways to see the connection between exchange rates and monetary policy. The first comes from thinking about the market for goods and *purchasing power parity;* the second builds on the Chicago/San Francisco bond market arbitrage example. Purchasing power parity tells us about the long-run tendencies of exchange rates, while capital market arbitrage shows us how short-run movements in exchange rates are tied to the supply and demand in the currency markets. Let's look at each of these approaches in more detail.

Inflation and the Long-Run Implications of Purchasing Power Parity

In Chapter 10, we studied the long-run determinants of exchange rates starting with the *law of one price.* Ignoring transportation costs, the law of one price says that identical goods should sell for the same price regardless of where they are sold. That is, the same television set should sell for the same price in Philadelphia and St. Louis. The concept of purchasing power parity extends the logic of the law of one price to a basket of goods and services. As long as goods can move freely across international boundaries, one unit of domestic currency should buy the same basket of goods anywhere in the world.

This apparently simple idea has important implications. It means that when prices change in one country but not in another, the exchange rate will adjust to reflect the change. If Mexican inflation is higher than U.S. inflation, for instance, the Mexican peso should depreciate relative to the dollar. If everything in Mexico costs more pesos, dollars should cost more pesos, too. Figure 10.4 confirmed that this principle works well over periods of several decades. *In the long run, changes in the exchange rate are tied to differences in inflation.*

To understand how this works, recall that purchasing power parity means that

$$\text{Pesos per dollar} = \frac{\text{Peso price of basket of goods in Mexico}}{\text{Dollar price of basket of goods in U.S.}} \qquad (1)$$

Taking the percent change of both sides of this expression, we get[2]

$$\begin{bmatrix}\text{Percent change in} \\ \text{number of pesos} \\ \text{per dollar}\end{bmatrix} = \begin{bmatrix}\text{Percent change in} \\ \text{peso price of basket} \\ \text{of goods in Mexico}\end{bmatrix} - \begin{bmatrix}\text{Percent change in} \\ \text{dollar price of basket} \\ \text{of goods in U.S.}\end{bmatrix} \qquad (2)$$

[2]In going from equation (1) to equation (2), we are using the approximation that the percent change in (*X/Y*) equals the percent change in *X minus* the percent change in *Y*. This approximation works best for small percent changes.

Because the percent change in the price of the basket of goods is the same as inflation, we can rewrite this expression as

$$\begin{bmatrix}\text{Percent change in} \\ \text{number of pesos} \\ \text{per dollar}\end{bmatrix} = [\text{Mexican inflation rate}] - [\text{U.S. inflation rate}] \qquad (3)$$

Thus, when the Mexican inflation rate is higher than the U.S. inflation rate, the number of pesos needed to buy a dollar rises. When the U.S. inflation rate is higher than the Mexican inflation rate, the reverse is true. An example can help us see how this works. Say we need 10 pesos to purchase a dollar (so a peso is worth 10 cents) at the beginning of the year. During the year, the Mexican inflation rate is 5 percent, and the U.S. inflation rate is 2 percent. At the end of the year, we would expect the exchange rate to change so we need 3 percent more pesos to purchase a dollar, or 10.3 pesos per dollar.

Purchasing power parity has immediate implications for monetary policy. If the Banco de México, Mexico's central bank, wants to fix its exchange rate, then Mexican monetary policy must be conducted so that Mexican inflation matches U.S. inflation. Alternatively, if Mexico wants its inflation rate to diverge from the U.S. inflation rate, the peso–dollar exchange rate must be allowed to vary. *The central bank must choose between a fixed exchange rate and an independent inflation policy; it cannot have both.*

We could stop here, except for the fact that purchasing power parity works only over long periods, like decades. That is, even though the exchange rate *eventually* adjusts to differences between prices at home and abroad, deviations from purchasing power parity can last for years. While this time lag in exchange rate movements might appear to ease restrictions on monetary policy, in fact it does not. To understand why, we need to examine what happens in the capital markets when investors can move their funds freely across international boundaries.

Interest Rates and the Short-Run Implications of Capital Market Arbitrage

In the short run, a country's exchange rate is determined by supply and demand. The exchange value of the dollar depends on factors such as the preferences of Americans for foreign assets and the preferences of foreign investors for U.S. assets. In the short run, investors play a crucial role, because they are the ones who can move large quantities of dollars, euros, pounds, or pesos across international borders. Assuming that governments allow funds to flow into and out of their countries, these movements can occur very quickly.

To understand the implications of international capital mobility, we need to look at how investors decide whether to purchase a foreign or a domestic bond. Given two bonds of equal risk, investors will always buy the one with the higher expected return. And when two otherwise identical bonds differ in yield, investors will bid up the price of the high-return bond and bid down the price of the low-return bond until the two converge. Thus, arbitrage in the capital market ensures that two equally risky bonds have the same expected return.

Like purchasing power parity, capital market arbitrage has immediate implications for monetary policy. Think about two bonds that are identical except that one is issued in Chicago and the other in San Francisco. The two bonds are equally risky, with the same time to maturity and the same coupon rate. Arbitrage ensures that they will sell

Is International Diversification Dead?

YOUR FINANCIAL WORLD

Diversification has long been viewed as the key to an efficient portfolio—one that minimizes risk for a given expected rate of return. When James Tobin received his Nobel Prize in 1981, he summarized this view in the classic fashion: "Don't put all your eggs in one basket."

Over the years, experts extended this fundamental principle from the domestic to the global asset universe, highlighting the benefits of *international* diversification.

More recently, however, investors have lamented diminishing benefits from owning foreign assets. Because swings in key securities markets across countries have become more synchronized, owning foreign assets does less to reduce portfolio risk than it once did. It turns out, however, that—at least in the case of equity portfolios—it is principally the *short-run* benefits that have eroded. For long-horizon investors, international diversification still has advantages.

To see why, let's start by recalling the basic case for diversification. In building an efficient portfolio of assets, investors face a tradeoff between the portfolio's risk and its expected return. Provided that two asset classes are not perfectly correlated (that is, their statistical correlation is less than 1), holding a mix of assets in the portfolio can reduce risk for a given rate of return.

So even though the variance of returns in a broad collection of foreign stocks may be higher than that on a diversified group of U.S. stocks, adding a portion of foreign stocks to the U.S. portfolio can lower the overall portfolio variance because these assets are not perfectly correlated.

The problem for investors is that the correlations across country stock markets (measured in their own currencies) have risen notably since the start of this century. Even worse, in recent years, international equity markets have become more synchronized when movements have been the largest—as in the Great Financial Crisis of 2007–2009. Thus, at the precise moment that a reduction of risk is most valuable—when one market makes a big move up or down—international diversification may not provide it.

Why might cross-market correlations have risen? One reason is the trend toward the global integration of economic and financial markets. This trend makes equity markets everywhere more sensitive to changes in the global discount rate applied to long-term assets (recall the dividend-discount model of Chapter 8).

Fortunately, there is still good news for devotees of international stock diversification. First, holding assets that are priced in different currencies whose exchange rates move unpredictably continues to provide a diversification benefit. And most important, while correlations have increased for returns over the short term—say, one year—research by market professionals shows that country stock markets are less likely to move in unison over long periods.

So if you are an investor who follows a buy-and-hold strategy—as economists typically advise (see, for example, Burton Malkiel's classic book, *A Random Walk Down Wall Street*)—the traditional benefits of international equity diversification persist: you can still lower risk for a given rate of return.

for the same price and so have the same interest rate. Does it matter that both these bonds make payments in dollars?

To answer this question, we can substitute bonds issued in different countries that promise payments in their currencies. What happens if we compare a Chicago bond to an otherwise identical bond issued in London and denominated in pounds? At what interest rates will investors be indifferent between the Chicago bond and the London bond?

Consider a hypothetical case in which the Bank of England decides to fix the exchange rate at \$1.50 per pound. If the pound–dollar exchange rate is fixed, and everyone expects that it will remain fixed, we can ignore the fact that the two investments are denominated in different currencies. Say a U.S. investor is considering what to do with \$1,500 over the next year. The options are to buy a one-year Chicago bond with an interest rate we will call simply i or a one-year London bond with an interest rate i^f (the superscript f stands for *foreign*). Investing in London requires converting dollars to pounds and buying the bond at the beginning of the year and then taking the proceeds and reconverting them to dollars at the end of the year.

At a fixed exchange rate of \$1.50 per pound, \$1,500 becomes £1,000 ("£" is the symbol used for the pound). After a year, this amount becomes £1,000 $(1 + i^f)$.

Reconverting to dollars, again at the fixed exchange rate of \$1.50 per pound, the U.S. investor has \$1,500 $(1 + i^f)$. In deciding which bond to buy, then, the investor should compare \$1,500 $(1 + i^f)$ to the return from the Chicago bond, which is \$1,500 $(1 + i)$. Because arbitrage in the capital market equates these two returns, under a fixed exchange rate

$$\$1{,}500(1 + i^f) = \$1{,}500(1 + i) \tag{4}$$

and so

$$i^f = i \tag{5}$$

Thus, investors will be indifferent between investing in a dollar-denominated bond in Chicago or a pound-denominated bond in London only when the interest rates in the two cities are the same. If interest rates differ in Chicago and London, and the dollar–pound exchange rate is fixed, investors will move funds back and forth, wiping out the difference. This example is analogous to the comparison between bonds sold in Chicago and in San Francisco. Because the dollar exchange rate between the two cities is fixed and capital is free to move between them, their interest rates must be the same.[3]

Capital Controls and the Policymakers' Choice

At first glance, it may seem as if policymakers can choose between stabilizing the domestic interest rate and stabilizing the exchange rate. But our discussion of interest rates and arbitrage in the last section depended critically on the ability of investors to move capital across international boundaries. If capital cannot flow freely between London and Chicago, there is no mechanism to equate interest rates in the two countries, and our logic falls apart. Thus, we need to revise our conclusion: so long as capital can flow freely between countries, monetary policymakers must choose between fixing their exchange rate and fixing their interest rate. A country *cannot:*

- be open to international capital flows,
- control its domestic interest rate, *and*
- fix its exchange rate.

Policymakers must choose two of these three options. (This is called the "impossible trinity" or the "trilemma" of open-economy macroeconomics.)

Looking around the world, we see that different countries have made different choices. The United States, for example, has an open capital market, a controlled domestic interest rate, and a freely floating dollar. During the 1990s, Argentina maintained an open capital market but fixed its exchange rate with the dollar, giving up control of domestic interest rates. But these are not the only alternatives; there is another possibility that is worth exploring. If a country is willing to forgo participation in international capital markets, it can impose **capital controls**, fix its exchange rate, and still use monetary policy to pursue its domestic objectives.

Capital controls go very much against the grain of modern economic thinking. Among economists, there is strong support for the view that open capital markets are beneficial. In the same way that international trade allows countries to exploit their comparative advantage, internationally integrated capital markets help allocate capital

[3]Taking the analysis one step further, when the exchange rate is free to move, capital market arbitrage ensures that the expected return on bonds of similar maturity and risk will be the same when expressed in the same currency. This is the logic that leads to the covered interest rate parity condition discussed in the appendix to Chapter 10.

to its most efficient uses. The free flow of capital across borders enhances competition, improves opportunities for diversification, and tends to equalize rates of return (adjusted for risk). As this view took hold in the late 20th century, countries removed the restrictions on the flow of capital that had been initiated earlier in the century.[4]

When we look at large industrialized countries, the benefits of open capital markets are easy to see. U.S. workers benefit from the jobs at Honda's U.S. operations, which have produced more than 25 million vehicles. U.S. investors also benefit from their access to Brazilian and Indian stocks. On the downside, disturbances in one country's financial market—such as the U.S. mortgage securities market in 2007—can be quickly transmitted to markets and institutions in other countries through their various interconnections. The global financial crisis of 2007–2009 and the euro-area crisis that followed are prime examples.

For emerging market countries, greater openness of capital markets poses other risks, too. The problem is that capital that flows into a country can also flow out, and it can do so quickly. That means that countries with open capital markets are vulnerable to sudden changes in investor sentiment. Investors may decide to sell a country's bonds, driving their prices down and their interest rates up. They convert the proceeds of the sale into foreign currency, driving the value of the domestic currency down. If everyone loses confidence in a country at the same time, the result—known as a *sudden stop*—is similar to a bank run: All foreign investors leave at once, precipitating a financial collapse (see Money and Banking Blog: Sudden Stops: Understanding Balance-of-Payments Crises on page 541). Thailand in 1997 (discussed in Chapter 17), Korea in 1998 (described in Chapter 10), and the euro-area economies overwhelmed by sovereign debt and banking crises in 2012 are just three examples. (We will examine the mechanics of these crises in the next section of this chapter.)

It is tempting for government officials to try to avert such crises by restricting people's ability to move capital into and out of a country—by imposing controls on the flow of capital. There are two basic types of capital control. *Inflow controls* restrict the ability of foreigners to invest in a country; *outflow controls* place obstacles in the way of selling investments and taking funds out. China has long operated with extensive capital controls in both directions that have been only partly relaxed (see Applying the Concept: China's Changing Exchange Rate Regime, pages 539–540). During much of the 1990s, foreigners wishing to invest in Chile were required to make a one-year, zero-interest deposit of 20 percent of the investment at the central bank. This inflow control penalized short-term investments, encouraging investors to invest for a longer period. In 2009, rapid capital inflows and a rising currency led Brazil to impose a tax on foreign purchases of domestic securities.

Outflow controls include restrictions on the ability of domestic residents to purchase foreign assets, and often include prohibitions on removing currency from the country. In the fall of 1998, Malaysian citizens were prohibited from taking more than 1,000 ringgit in cash (worth a bit more than $250 at the time) out of the country, while the most foreigners could take out of the country was the amount they had brought

[4]Like central banks, controls on international capital flows are a 20th-century innovation. One of the hallmarks of the period between the world wars (the 1920s and 1930s) was the strong movement toward national autonomy. As the world economy collapsed during the Great Depression, countries tried to isolate themselves by instituting restrictions on both the trade in goods and services and the transfer of capital. Restrictions on the ability of foreigners to own domestic assets, and on everyone's ability to transfer currency or gold out of a country, became common. Many of these became part of the international financial system after World War II and were maintained by industrialized countries into the 1970s and beyond. Until 1979, the British government maintained controls on investments made abroad by U.K. residents. Until 1974, the United States imposed a special tax on interest received by Americans on foreign bonds.

with them when they entered the country. Any nonresident who sold a Malaysian security was required to hold the proceeds in the country for at least 12 months before taking them out. These controls temporarily cut Malaysia off from the world capital market.

Mechanics of Exchange Rate Management

Because both the Federal Reserve and the European Central Bank adjust their balance sheets to maintain their overnight interbank interest rates at their target level or range (or to influence longer-term interest rates), they must have given up control of their exchange rates. No wonder their intervention on September 22, 2000, had almost no effect on the value of the euro. Even so, Fed and ECB policies *do* have an impact on the value of the dollar and the euro. And if either central bank chose to, it could give up controlling interest rates and target the exchange rate instead.

How would they do it? What are the mechanics of exchange rate management and exchange rate intervention? We have seen that virtually everything the central bank does has something to do with its balance sheet. Foreign exchange intervention is no exception. So to look at the mechanics of exchange rate management, we'll start with the central bank's balance sheet. Once we understand the balance sheet effects of foreign currency intervention, we can look more closely at what large central banks like the Fed and the ECB actually do.

The Central Bank's Balance Sheet

If all policymakers want to do is to fix the exchange rate, there is a simple way to do it: They can offer to buy and sell their country's currency at a fixed rate. For example, if officials at the Federal Reserve decided to fix the dollar–euro exchange rate at one to one, they would simply stand ready to exchange dollars for euros whenever anyone asked. Buying euros wouldn't be much of a problem, because the Federal Reserve can print all the dollars it needs. But selling euros in exchange for dollars might pose some difficulty unless the Fed had a substantial euro reserve. We will ignore this complication for now and return to it in the next section, when we discuss the problem of speculative attacks.

In this example, as the Fed works to maintain a fixed dollar–euro exchange rate, its balance sheet shifts. When it buys euros, it increases its dollar liabilities; when it sells euros, it reduces its dollar liabilities (refer back to the section of Chapter 17 titled "Foreign Exchange Intervention"). When reserves are scarce, as they were in the United States prior to the Lehman failure in 2008, buying euros and selling dollars increases the supply of reserves to the banking system in a way that puts downward pressure on interest rates.

To see how this process works in practice, let's go back to September 2000, when the largest central banks in the world intervened to bolster the value of the euro. We'll focus on the Federal Reserve's decision to purchase €1.5 billion in exchange for $1.34 billion, ignoring the actions of the other central banks on that day as well as the open market operations that followed. When Fed employees bought euros, they did it the same way they buy anything else: They created liabilities to the commercial banks. Then, as soon as they received the €1.5 billion from foreign exchange dealers, they spent it on bonds issued by euro-area governments. We will refer to these bonds as German government bonds, because that is primarily how the Fed holds its euro-denominated reserves.

The balance sheet implications of this exchange are straightforward. Figure 19.1 shows the results of the intervention. Looking at the asset side, and following the

Figure 19.1 Change in the Federal Reserve's Balance Sheet Immediately following a Purchase of Euros

Assets		Liabilities	
Euro reserves (German government bonds)	+ $1.34 billion	Commercial bank reserves	+ $1.34 billion

standard convention of reporting the value of the central bank's foreign exchange reserves in domestic currency units, we see that the Fed has increased its euro-denominated foreign exchange reserve assets by $1.34 billion. On the liabilities side of the balance sheet, we see that commercial bank reserves have increased by the same amount.

This T-account should look familiar. If we focus on the liabilities side of the balance sheet, we see that the purchase of German government bonds is identical to a purchase of U.S. Treasury bonds. That is, the purchase of a security has added reserves to the banking system. The only difference is the issuer of the bond. Like any other change in reserves, this one has a direct impact on the quantity of money in the economy. In other words, it is expansionary, so it reduces domestic interest rates. *A foreign exchange intervention has the same impact on reserves as a domestic open market operation.*

As we already have seen in Chapter 18, the impact of balance-sheet changes on the policy interest rate depends on whether reserves are scarce or abundant. The balance-sheet impact on foreign exchange exhibits the same pattern.

If reserves are scarce, the policy interest rate falls when the Fed expands its balance sheet through an open market purchase, regardless of whether the assets it buys are foreign or domestic. Figure 19.2 shows what happens to the value of the dollar when the U.S. interest rate declines, while European interest rates remain the same. Remember that whenever investing in the United States becomes less attractive relative to investing somewhere else, the result is a decrease in the demand for dollars that will be used by foreigners to purchase U.S. assets and an increase in the supply of dollars that will be used by Americans to purchase foreign assets. The demand and supply shifts shown in Figure 19.2 together drive the value of the dollar down and the value of the euro up. The dollar depreciates and the euro appreciates, reducing the number of euros offered per dollar in the foreign exchange market.

Put differently, it is the relative shift in interest rates that alters the value of the dollar when—in a world of scarce reserves—the Fed alters the size of its balance sheet. You may think there is something strange about this discussion. We started with a foreign exchange intervention in which the Fed purchased euros and noted its impact on the dollar–euro exchange rate. But the reason the exchange rate moved was that the domestic interest rate changed, shifting the demand for dollars in the foreign exchange market. By making domestic U.S. investment less attractive, the intervention prompted people to purchase fewer dollars, driving the price of dollars down. Our conclusion is that *a foreign exchange intervention affects the value of a country's currency by changing domestic interest rates.*

This conclusion has an important implication. It means that *any central bank policy that influences the domestic interest rate will affect the exchange rate.* The fact that we started with an exchange rate intervention is irrelevant. Whenever reserves

Figure 19.2 Effect of a Decrease in U.S. Interest Rates Relative to Interest Rates in the Euro Area

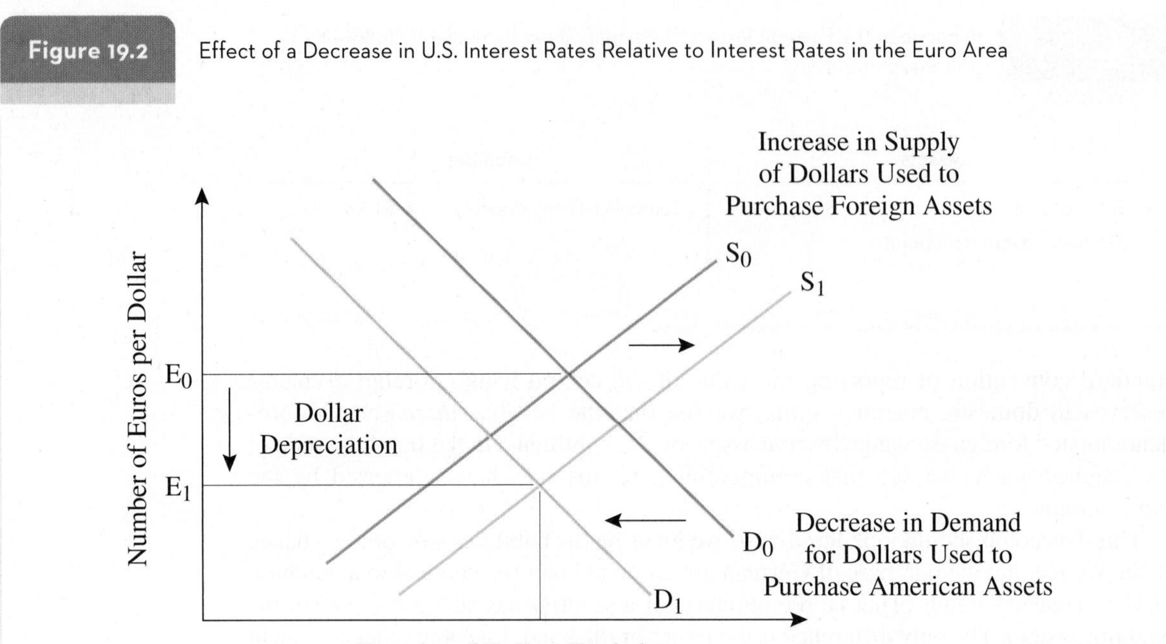

are scarce, an open market purchase or sale works exactly the same way. If the Federal Reserve bought U.S. Treasury bonds instead of euro-denominated bonds, the action would drive down U.S. interest rates, decreasing the demand for dollars in the foreign exchange market and causing a decline in the value of the dollar. There is nothing special about a foreign exchange intervention.

What, then, is the impact on the exchange rate of a balance sheet change when there is an abundance of reserves, as there has been in the United States since late 2008? Recall from Chapter 18 that in this case interest rates are unaffected by the size of the central bank's balance sheet. Instead, they are determined by the interest rate on excess reserves (IOER). So, when the Federal Reserve purchases euro-denominated bonds, as in the example in Figure 19.2, nothing happens to the interest rate. Consequently, the interest rate mechanism that affects the exchange rate when reserves are scarce no longer operates.

In theory, there is another mechanism to consider. When the central bank purchases foreign assets—as in Figure 19.1—the supply of dollars does increase. Consequently, so long as the central bank can continue to purchase foreign securities *without limit*, it can keep its currency from appreciating. Conversely, with sufficient foreign exchange resources, by selling foreign assets and reducing the supply of their domestic currency continuously, the central bank can fight off a depreciation.

In practice, however, each of these policies—buying or selling foreign assets when reserves are abundant—has limits. Central banks have finite holdings of foreign assets, so they will eventually run out if they keep selling them (see the discussion of speculative attacks on page 534). And, while there is no technical limit to the quantity of foreign assets that a central bank can buy, major currency markets are very deep and liquid, so the central bank may have to expand its balance sheet massively in order to limit currency appreciation. That is precisely what the Swiss central bank began to do in 2011 in order to cap the rise of the Swiss franc versus the euro. Yet, the political reaction to the central bank's surging balance sheet eventually led Swiss authorities to give up the effort, triggering a jump in the value of the Swiss franc (see Lessons from the Crisis: Oasis of Stability? on page 538).

Sterilized Intervention

On September 22, 2000, when the ECB, the Federal Reserve, the Bank of Japan, the Bank of England, and the Bank of Canada all intervened to buy euros, none of them changed their domestic interest rate targets. No wonder the value of the euro didn't change! But that means their transactions must have been different from the one we just studied. We assumed that when the Fed bought euros, it increased commercial bank reserves, which would reduce interest rates in the absence of any other action. Such a move is an example of an **unsterilized foreign exchange intervention**, one that changes central bank liabilities. But in large countries, central banks don't operate that way. Instead, they engage in **sterilized foreign exchange interventions**, in which a change in foreign exchange reserves alters the asset side of the central bank's balance sheet but the domestic monetary base remains unaffected.

A sterilized intervention is actually a combination of two transactions. First there is the purchase or sale of foreign currency reserves, which by itself changes the central bank's liabilities. But this is immediately followed by an open market operation of exactly the same size, designed to offset the impact of the first transaction on the monetary base. For example, the Fed's purchase of a German government bond, which would increase reserves, is offset by the sale of a U.S. Treasury bond. Together, these two actions leave the level of reserves unchanged. Such an intervention is sterilized with respect to its effect on the monetary base, or the size of the central bank's balance sheet. *An intervention is unsterilized if it changes the monetary base and sterilized if it does not change the monetary base.*

To see what happens in practice, let's go back to September 22, 2000, one last time. Between 7:11 a.m. and 9:20 a.m., the Federal Reserve Bank of New York sold $1.34 billion in exchange for €1.5 billion. We have already seen that the initial impact on the Fed's balance sheet was to increase the level of reserves in the banking system. But the FOMC had not changed the target federal funds rate, so the job of the Open Market Trading Desk was the same as it had been every day since May 17, when the prevailing 6½ percent target rate had been put in place.

To do their job, the Federal Reserve Bank of New York staff entered the intervention numbers into their spreadsheet before estimating the size of the day's temporary operation. In figuring out what to do to keep the federal funds rate on target, they took account of the quantity of reserves their colleagues had already added. By 10:00 a.m., when the open market operations were completed, the impact of the foreign exchange intervention on the Fed's liabilities had disappeared. The foreign exchange desk had purchased bonds issued by a euro-area government, paying for them with reserves, and the Open Market Desk had sold U.S. Treasury bonds to reverse the potential impact.

Figure 19.3 shows the result on the Fed's balance sheet. Notice two things. First, commercial bank reserves remain unchanged following a sterilized intervention, so domestic monetary policy does not change. Second, the intervention changes the *composition* of the asset side of the central bank's balance sheet. The Fed has swapped U.S. Treasury bonds for bonds issued by the German government.

Could this change in the mix of assets on the central bank's balance sheet alter the exchange rate in a sustained fashion? In normal times, the answer is no: as we observed,

Figure 19.3 Change in the Federal Reserve's Balance Sheet following a *Sterilized* Purchase of Euro-Denominated Bonds

Assets		Liabilities
Euro reserves (German government bonds)	+$1.34 billion	Commercial bank reserves unchanged
Securities (U.S. Treasury bonds)	−$1.34 billion	

the sterilized intervention in support of the euro in 2000 had no sustained effect. In deep, well-functioning markets, small shifts in central bank assets are dwarfed by the actions of private traders. Recall from Chapter 10 that the daily volume of foreign exchange transactions averaged $6.6 trillion in 2019! A change of a few billion dollars in central bank assets is a mere drop in this ocean.

However, as we saw in the discussion of targeted asset purchases (TAP) in Chapter 18, changes in the composition of a central bank balance sheet can alter the relative prices of assets if (1) markets are thin or functioning poorly and (2) the policy shift is large compared to the level of market transactions. The Fed's 2009 purchase of more than $1 trillion of mortgage-backed securities in crisis-weakened markets is a prime example. Most observers believe that these Fed actions did what they were intended to do: lower mortgage yields at a time when loans were very difficult to get.

Just like the yield on mortgage securities, an exchange rate is an asset price. And during the 2007–2009 crisis, virtually all financial markets, including foreign exchange markets, were thinner and less effective than usual. In that setting, sterilized currency intervention might have had a bigger impact than in normal times, but there was no intervention that would allow us to judge.

The Costs, Benefits, and Risks of Fixed Exchange Rates

STABILITY

Many countries allow their exchange rates to float freely, so that the value of their currencies is determined in the financial markets. But others—especially small, emerging market countries—fix their exchange rates. That is, officials of the central bank and the finance ministry agree that the best policy is to maintain a predictable value for their currency, so they target the exchange rate. Why do some countries make that decision? Surely fixing the exchange rate has costs as well as benefits. We now turn to a brief discussion of the tradeoffs.

Assessing the Costs and Benefits

The owners of the Blue Jays, Toronto's major league baseball team, probably wouldn't mind if the Bank of Canada decided to fix the exchange rate for U.S. and Canadian dollars. They face a common problem for companies engaged in international trade: they pay most of their expenses in one currency and receive the bulk of their revenues in another. Suppose that the team receives about 80 percent of its annual revenue in Canadian dollars (equivalent to roughly U.S. $280 million), but pays 80 percent of its expenses—including a $118 million annual payroll (in 2019) and the bills for chartered planes and fancy hotel rooms—in U.S. dollars. So if the Canadian dollar depreciates, as it did during 2018, the team incurs a financial loss. Unless it hedges this exchange rate risk, for each 10 percent drop in the value of the Canadian dollar it will lose something like $22 million. The more volatile exchange rates become, the worse the problem gets. If the exchange rates were fixed, the Blue Jays's risk would disappear.[5]

Goods and services aren't the only things that cross international borders; capital does, too. Fixed exchange rates not only simplify operations for businesses that trade internationally; they also reduce the risk that investors face when they hold foreign stocks and bonds. Think of what happens if you buy a Korean government bond. Unlike a U.S. Treasury bond, on which the interest rate tells you the return, a Korean bond involves the possibility that the dollar–Korean *won* exchange rate may change. An increase in the number of won needed to purchase one dollar—so that the dollar becomes more valuable—would reduce the return on the Korean bond by the amount of the dollar's appreciation.[6]

So fixed exchange rates seem to be a good idea for both businesses and investors. They also have another potential benefit. A fixed exchange rate ties policymakers' hands. Remember that in the long run, the exchange rate is determined by inflation differentials. In countries that are prone to bouts of high inflation, a fixed exchange rate may be the only way to establish a credible low-inflation policy. It enforces low-inflation discipline on both central bankers and politicians, and an exchange rate target enhances transparency and accountability.

There is one serious drawback to a fixed exchange rate, however. It *imports* monetary policy. Fixing your currency's value to that of another country means adopting the other country's interest rate policy. When Argentina fixed the exchange rate of the peso to the U.S. dollar, policymakers gave up control of Argentinean interest rates and effectively handed it over to the FOMC. Needless to say, when the FOMC set the target federal funds rate, committee members didn't worry much about what was going on in Argentina. What this means is that a fixed exchange rate makes the most sense when the two countries involved have similar macroeconomic fluctuations. Ideally, their cyclical ups and downs are perfectly synchronized. Otherwise, the country with the flexible exchange rate that is in control of monetary policy (e.g., the United States) might be raising interest rates to combat domestic inflation at the same time that the other country (e.g., Argentina) is going into recession.

In deciding whether to fix their country's exchange rate, policymakers should consider several additional matters. First, when a country fixes its exchange rate, the

[5]The Toronto Blue Jays team may hedge its foreign exchange risk in the derivatives market. In effect, it can pay someone for insurance against moves in the exchange rate. Doing so makes the team's expenses and profits more predictable, but it isn't costless.

[6]A numerical example helps clarify this point. Assume that a U.S. investor converts $1,000 into Korean won at a rate of 1,000 won per dollar and then buys a one-year, 5 percent Korean government bond. At the end of the year, the bond pays 1,050,000 won. If the exchange rate has not changed, this amount can be exchanged for $1,050. But if the dollar appreciates 5 percent during the year, so that the exchange rate rises to 1,050 won per dollar, then the American investor is left with only $1,000. The total return to holding the Korean bond equals the Korean interest rate minus the dollar's appreciation. The appendix to Chapter 10 describes this phenomenon in more detail.

central bank is offering to buy and sell its own currency at a fixed rate. To honor this commitment to purchase currency, monetary policymakers will need ample currency reserves. For instance, a country that fixes its exchange rate to the dollar needs to hold dollars in reserve. Living up to this promise in a world of free-flowing capital requires a high level of foreign exchange reserves. For many countries, the billions of dollars required are both difficult to obtain and expensive to keep.

Second, because floating exchange rates act as automatic macroeconomic stabilizers, fixing the exchange rate means reducing the domestic economy's natural ability to respond to macroeconomic shocks. Imagine a country on the verge of recession. If monetary policymakers can, they will react by lowering interest rates in an attempt to keep the economy from slowing. Beyond the direct effect on investment and consumption, lower interest rates make domestic bonds less attractive to foreigners, reducing the demand for the domestic currency and driving down its value. The resulting currency depreciation drives down the price foreigners must pay for domestic exports, increasing the demand for them and amplifying the impact of the initial interest rate reduction. With a fixed exchange rate, this stabilization mechanism is completely shut down.

Third, if the nominal exchange rate is fixed, a country may need its prices and wages to decline to offset any loss of ability to compete in world markets. If, instead, prices and wages are inflexible, a country that loses *competitiveness* may experience persistently high levels of unemployment, income losses, and government deficits (like the economies on the geographic periphery of the euro area amid that region's crisis).

Fourth, policymakers need to consider the robustness of the banking system. To fix an exchange rate, a central bank may need to accommodate large swings in reserve demand that bring about booms and busts in money, credit, the economy, and the well-being of banks. Yet, the ability of the central bank to serve as lender of last resort may be limited if it must sell assets to defend the exchange rate.

The Danger of Speculative Attacks

While fixed exchange rates may have benefits for a country's economy, they are fragile and prone to a type of crisis called a **speculative attack**. To understand the nature of a speculative attack, imagine that a country is trying to maintain a fixed exchange rate. Now suppose that for some reason, financial market participants come to believe that the government will need to devalue its currency in the near future. The problem is usually one of time consistency: If investors expect policymakers to renege on their promise to defend the exchange rate, they will attack the currency now and force an immediate devaluation.

The mechanics of the attack are straightforward. Take the example of the attack on the Thai baht in 1997. Through the mid-1990s, the Bank of Thailand was committed to maintaining a fixed exchange rate of approximately 26 baht to the U.S. dollar. To do so, officials had to make sure foreign currency traders believed that the Bank of Thailand had enough dollars on hand to buy however many baht the traders wanted to sell. In summer 1997, financial market participants began to question whether the reserves at the central bank really were big enough, and they swung into action. Speculators borrowed baht at domestic Thai interest rates, took them to the central bank to convert them to dollars at the rate of 26 to 1, and then invested the dollars in short-term, interest-bearing securities in the United States. The immediate impact of these transactions was to drain the Bank of Thailand's dollar reserves. The lower the dollar reserves, the less likely that the Thais would be able to meet further requests to convert baht into

The Gold Standard: An Exchange Rate Regime Whose Time Has Passed

APPLYING THE CONCEPT

If you take a dollar bill to the Federal Reserve, officials will give you a new one. Should they offer to give you gold instead? That would be returning to the time when the dollar was "as good as gold." Today, advocates of a return to the **gold standard** claim that it would eliminate inflation. As evidence, they point to the time before World War I, when the United States was on the gold standard and inflation averaged less than 1 percent per year. What these advocates don't advertise is that, while inflation was low on *average*, it was highly variable, fluctuating between +3¼ percent and −3¼ percent. In fact, for much of the late 19th century, prices fell steadily. Only early in the 20th century did they rise back to a level not far above where they started in 1880.

The focus on past inflation obscures the long list of reasons few economists today advocate a return to the gold standard. To begin with, the gold standard obligates the central bank to fix the price of something we don't really care about. Instead of stabilizing the prices of the goods and services we buy and consume, the central bank fixes the dollar price of gold. In place of fluctuations in the market price of gold, there are fluctuations in the dollar price of goods.

Then there is the fact that, under the gold standard, the amount of money in the economy would depend on the amount of gold available. More gold equals more money. Because, in the long run, inflation is tied to money growth, this means that inflation depends on the rate at which gold is mined. Why should monetary policy be determined by the rate at which South Africa and Russia dig gold from the ground? Moreover, any political disruption in those parts of the world could have dramatic monetary policy effects.

The case for gold grows even less persuasive when we realize that the gold standard is an exchange rate policy, too. The promise to convert dollars into gold means that international transactions must be settled in gold. So when the value of imports does not exactly match the value of exports, gold is transferred from one country to another. Thus, a country with a current account deficit—whose imports exceed its exports—has to pay the difference by transferring gold to countries with current account surpluses. (See the appendix to this chapter for a description of balance-of-payments accounting.) With less gold, the country's central bank must contract its balance sheet, raising interest rates, reducing the quantity of money and credit in the economy, and driving domestic prices down. Under a gold standard, countries running current account deficits will be forced into deflation. Meanwhile, countries with current account surpluses can allow their gold inflows to generate inflation, but they need not. Under the gold standard, a central bank can have too little gold, but it can never have too much.

Economic historians believe that gold flows played a central role in spreading the Great Depression of the 1930s throughout the world. After World War I, all the major countries in the world worked to reconstruct the gold standard. By the late 1920s, they had succeeded. At the time, both the United States and France were running current account surpluses, absorbing the world's gold into their vaults. But instead of allowing the gold inflows to expand the quantity of money in their financial systems, authorities in both countries tightened monetary policy in an attempt to cool off their overheated, inflation-prone economies. The result was catastrophic, because it forced countries with current account deficits and gold outflows to tighten their monetary policies even more. The resulting deflation increased the likelihood that people would default on loans, destroying the economic and financial system in the United States and elsewhere.* Economic historians place the blame squarely on the gold standard. What makes their argument truly convincing is the fact that the sooner a country left the gold standard and regained control of its monetary policy, the faster its economy recovered.

From our vantage point in the 21st century, the gold standard is a historical artifact that caused great trouble. Most economic experts do not wish to see it restored.† Doing so would not even be time consistent: In bad times, investors would expect governments to exit the gold standard—as they eventually did in the 1930s—encouraging self-fulfilling speculative attacks.

*In Applying the Concept: Deflation, Net Worth, and Information Costs in Chapter 11, we discussed how deflation increases the adverse selection problems caused by information asymmetries. This is one of the mechanisms people today believe made the Great Depression of the 1930s so deep.

†For a survey of academic economists, see www.igmchicago.org/igm-economic-experts-panel/poll-results?SurveyID=SV_cw1nNUYOXSAKwrq.

dollars. And the more baht speculators borrowed to convert into dollars, the further the reserves fell.

The details are instructive. Imagine that, anticipating a severe depreciation, you borrow 2.6 million baht. You take them to the Bank of Thailand and convert them into $100,000 at the fixed rate of 26 to 1. With the proceeds, you buy U.S. Treasury bills. One week later, your expectations are realized and the baht depreciates by 10 percent. Now you need only $90,909 to obtain the 2.6 million baht with which to repay the loan. You've made an almost instant profit of over $9,000.[7] Because international currency speculators have very deep pockets, they can quickly drain billions of dollars from a central bank this way—and make a huge profit in the process.[8]

What causes a speculative attack? There are three possibilities. The first brings us back to fiscal policy: remember that politicians can make the central banker's job impossible. Ensuring that a currency retains its value means keeping domestic inflation at the same level as that of the country to which your exchange rate is pegged. If investors begin to think that at current levels, government spending must ultimately increase inflation, they will stop believing that officials can maintain the exchange rate at its fixed level. This seems to have been an important part of what happened during the Asian crisis of 1997.

A second possibility arises from financial instability. If a country's banking system is insufficiently capitalized or otherwise unsound, a central bank may face pressure to relax monetary policy to avoid or contain a financial crisis. If investors doubt that the central bank will keep interest rates high enough for a sufficient time to defend the currency peg, an attack may follow. This may be one reason territories with successful fixed exchange rate arrangements, like Hong Kong, favor high bank capital ratios.

Finally, speculative attacks can occur even when policymakers are behaving responsibly and financial institutions are healthy. They can arise spontaneously out of nowhere. If by chance enough currency speculators simply decide that a central bank cannot maintain its exchange rate, they will attack it, mobilizing tens of billions of dollars virtually overnight. To make matters even worse, spontaneous speculative attacks are a bit like bank runs; they can be contagious.

Many observers suspect that in today's world, no central bank has the resources to withstand such an attack in the absence of capital controls. It would take substantial foreign exchange reserves to even think about trying.

Summarizing the Case for a Fixed Exchange Rate

The easiest way to summarize this discussion is to make a list of the conditions under which adopting a fixed exchange rate makes sense for a country. A country will be better off fixing its exchange rate if it has all five of these:

- A poor reputation for controlling inflation on its own.
- An economy that is well integrated with the one to whose currency the rate is fixed, trading significantly with it and sharing similar macroeconomic characteristics, especially a synchronized business cycle.

[7]This simple example ignores both the interest you would need to pay to borrow the baht and the interest you would receive on the Treasury bills. An exact calculation would take the difference between the two interest rates into account and would likely reduce the profit. But because such transactions are usually done over days or weeks at most, this adjustment would have only a modest impact on the return. The point is that this is a very profitable transaction.

[8]In September 1992, the Bank of England belonged to the European Exchange Rate Mechanism, which linked the exchange rates of many countries. It effectively pegged the pound to the then-independent German currency, the deutsche mark. In an attempt to contain domestic inflation, the Germans raised interest rates dramatically, a policy the British did not want to follow. When speculators realized that the situation was untenable—that the Bank of England could not fix its exchange rate and have a lower interest rate than the Germans—they attacked. Investor George Soros is reputed to have made more than $1 billion betting that the pound would be devalued.

- A high level of foreign exchange reserves.
- A high degree of price and wage flexibility.
- A robust banking system.

Regardless of how closely a country meets these criteria, fixed exchange rates are still risky to adopt and difficult to maintain.

Fixed Exchange Rate Regimes

Our final task in this chapter is to study some examples of fixed exchange rate regimes, to see how they work. We will look at managed exchange rate pegs, in which policymakers try to restrict the exchange rate to a certain range; at currency boards, in which the central bank holds foreign currency assets as backing for the domestic monetary base; and at dollarization (or euroization), in which a country eliminates its own currency and begins using one issued by another country.

Exchange Rate Pegs and the Bretton Woods System

Despite the calamity of the 1930s, the world remained enamored of fixed exchange rates and the gold standard. So in 1944, a group of 44 countries agreed to form the *Bretton Woods system.* Named for the New Hampshire resort where the agreement was signed, it was a system of fixed exchange rates that offered more policy flexibility over the short term than had been possible under the gold standard.

The Bretton Woods system lasted from 1945 to 1971. Though the details of the system were complex, the basic idea is not. Each country maintained an agreed-upon exchange rate with the U.S. dollar—that is, it *pegged* its exchange rate to the dollar. To make the system work, every country had to hold dollar reserves and stand ready to exchange its own currency for dollars at the fixed rate. The dollar was what is known as a *reserve currency,* and it was convertible into gold at a rate of $35 per ounce. The choice of the dollar as the reserve currency was based on several factors. First, the United States was the biggest of the Allies (the victors in World War II), both economically and militarily. Second, dollars were relatively abundant.

Because other countries did not want to adopt U.S. monetary policy, their fixed exchange rates required complex capital controls. Even so, countries had to intervene regularly, buying or selling dollars to maintain their exchange rates at the peg. Adjustments were made to the *exchange rate pegs,* but only in response to perceived long-term imbalances. What gave the system some flexibility was the *International Monetary Fund (IMF).* The IMF was created to manage the Bretton Woods system by making loans to countries in need of short-term financing to pay for an excess of imports over exports. For a number of years, the system worked reasonably well, but as capital markets started to open up, it came under increasing strain.

With a fixed exchange rate and the free movements of capital across international borders, countries could not have their own discretionary monetary policies. Recall the example of Mexico cited earlier in this chapter. The long-run implications of purchasing power parity meant that, if Mexican inflation deviated from U.S. inflation, the dollar–peso exchange rate had to change. In the late 1960s, the countries in the Bretton Woods system were in the same position as Mexico. Because their exchange rate was

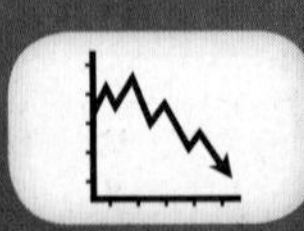

Oasis of Stability?

LESSONS FROM THE CRISIS

How does a central bank preserve stability in a crisis? There is no easy answer. One requirement is that monetary policy be *time consistent*: it must be feasible for policymakers to commit to future policy actions that ensure stability; and for that commitment to be credible today, policymakers typically must face a costly penalty for reneging.

Switzerland's experience during the euro-area crisis highlights the time-consistency challenge.

In 2010 and 2011, investors who worried about a potential breakup of the euro area fled that currency in favor of the Swiss franc. In the 20 months from January 2010 to August 2011, the value of the euro in terms of the Swiss franc plummeted from about CHF 1.50 to a bottom of CHF 1.04. Switzerland has a small, open economy with a cross-border trade that accounts for more than 90 percent of its GDP. The overvalued franc rendered many Swiss firms uncompetitive and pushed Switzerland into an unanticipated deflation.

Yet, Switzerland's central bank—the Swiss National Bank (SNB)—had already lowered interest rates close to zero. So, on September 6, 2011, the SNB committed itself to weaken the currency by preventing the Swiss franc from falling below CHF 1.20 per euro. To do so, the SNB stated that it was "prepared to buy foreign currency in unlimited quantities."

The key word is "unlimited." To stop the runaway franc, the central bank offered to supply investors with as many Swiss francs as they wished at a fixed price of CHF 1.20 per euro. In the midst of a crisis, anything less than a commitment to unlimited sales of the franc (and unlimited purchases of the euro) might have stimulated demand for francs, aggravating the crisis. In principle, a central bank has the capacity to carry out this pledge because it can create any amount of its currency indefinitely.

To fulfill its commitment, the SNB stopped using discretionary monetary tools (like interest rates) to set policy; instead, it let its balance sheet be determined by the demand for Swiss francs at its stated price. Between September 2011 the end of 2014, foreign exchange reserves at the SNB ballooned from $190 billion to more than $500 billion, making it the world's sixth-largest holder of foreign reserves.

The SNB's policy prevented sustained deflation and supported economic growth, but it was nevertheless highly controversial. Critics worried about the potential losses to taxpayers from SNB holdings of euros. The political controversy indicated to speculators that a further large expansion of the SNB balance sheet would increase doubts about the central bank's exchange rate commitment. This encouraged investors to buy more francs, betting that the SNB would eventually relent.

In January 2015, with the Greek crisis intensifying and the ECB expected to begin quantitative easing, the SNB indeed gave up and let the franc float. The result was an immediate depreciation of the euro against the franc, causing the franc to drop more than 10 percent below its previous floor, to CHF 1.05/€. To counter the deflationary impulse that was created, the SNB slashed the interest rate it pays on reserves to *minus* 0.75 percent, the lowest of any central bank. Even so, Swiss consumer prices in 2015 fell by 1 percent.

Fixed exchange rate commitments typically fail when a central bank is trying to prevent the domestic currency from depreciating. Doing so means either selling foreign exchange, which is always in limited supply, or raising interest rates, which risks harming what may already be a weak economy. In the absence of capital controls, neither of these actions can be maintained for long, and everyone knows it. That is, the policy fails for lack of time consistency.

What makes the Swiss case so interesting is that it exposes the difficulty that a central bank faces even when it wishes to *weaken* its currency. As we noted, this should in theory be sustainable indefinitely. But, as the Swiss discovered, the commitment can be sufficiently controversial that it, too, lacks credibility.

No matter how you look at it, time consistency remains one of the biggest policy challenges for central banks.

fixed to the dollar, participating countries were forced to adopt policies that resulted in the same amount of inflation as in the United States. When U.S. inflation began to rise in the late 1960s (yet another disastrous side effect of the Vietnam War), many countries balked; they didn't want to match the rise in inflation.

By 1971, the system had completely fallen apart. The response of American officials has been to allow the dollar to float freely ever since. Europeans took a different tack; for much of the time from the collapse of the Bretton Woods system to the adoption of the euro in 1999, they maintained various fixed exchange rate mechanisms. Because capital flowed freely among these countries, that meant giving up their ability to set interest rates.

Hard Pegs: Currency Boards and Dollarization

The international monetary system took a big hit in 1971 when the Bretton Woods system collapsed. Since then, a consensus has developed that countries whose economies are open to international capital flows must choose between completely flexible, market-determined exchange rates and what have come to be known as **hard pegs**. In a hard-peg system, the central bank implements an institutional mechanism that ensures its ability to convert a domestic currency into the foreign currency to which it is pegged. The danger of a speculative attack means anything less is unworkable. As one leading monetary policymaker and scholar put it, "Pegs are not sustainable unless they are very hard indeed."[9]

Only two exchange rate regimes can be considered hard pegs: currency boards and dollarization. With a **currency board**, the central bank commits to holding enough foreign currency assets to back all domestic currency liabilities at a fixed rate. With **dollarization** or euroization, one country formally adopts the currency of another country for use in all its financial transactions. Let's look at examples of both systems.

Currency Boards and the Argentinean Experience

Somewhere between 10 and 20 currency boards operate in the world today. The best known is the one in Hong Kong. The Hong Kong Monetary Authority (HKMA) operates a system whose sole objective is to maintain a fixed exchange rate of 7.8 Hong Kong dollars to one U.S. dollar. Because (as of December 2018) the HKMA holds roughly $483 billion in foreign currency (dollar) assets, it can issue nearly 3.4 trillion Hong Kong dollars in liabilities. The rules of the currency board provide that the HKMA can increase the size of Hong Kong's monetary base only if it can accumulate additional dollar reserves.

As this example suggests, with a currency board, the central bank's only job is to maintain the exchange rate. While that means that policymakers cannot adjust monetary policy in response to domestic economic shocks, the system does have its advantages. Prime among them is the control of inflation. As we noted in the introduction to this chapter, Argentina decided to adopt a currency board in April 1991 to end triple-digit inflation, and the approach worked. After three years, the inflation rate had dropped to 4 percent; by 1998, it was nearly zero. Forgoing the ability to stabilize domestic growth seems like a small price to pay for this sort of inflation performance, especially in an inflation-prone economy.

But currency boards do have their problems. First, by giving up the ability to control the size of its balance sheet, the central bank loses its role as the lender of last resort to the domestic banking system. The Banco Central de la Republica Argentina solved this problem by establishing standby letters of credit (described in Chapter 12) from large U.S. banks. When the time came to make emergency loans to local banks, officials borrowed dollars from U.S. banks and then made loans in pesos. But their lending was limited to the amount of dollar credit that foreign banks were willing to extend.

In 2001, the Argentinean currency board collapsed and authorities were forced to allow the peso to float. Within a few months, dollars that had once cost one peso apiece cost three. What caused the collapse? Entire books have been written to answer

[9]See Stanley Fischer, "Exchange Rate Regimes: Is the Bipolar View Correct?" *Journal of Economic Perspectives* 15, no. 2 (Spring 2001), pp. 3–24.

China's Changing Exchange Rate Regime

APPLYING THE CONCEPT

In June 2014, China's massive stockpile of foreign exchange reserves peaked at $4 trillion. That amount accounted for more than one-fourth of all the currency reserves in the world and represented a 25-fold increase since 2000! Subsequently, however, the stockpile declined rapidly, sinking to $3 trillion as of January 2017, before stabilizing (see Figure 19.4).

What prompted China to embark on an accumulation of reserves that far outstripped any before seen in history? And what triggered the sharp reversal beginning in 2014?

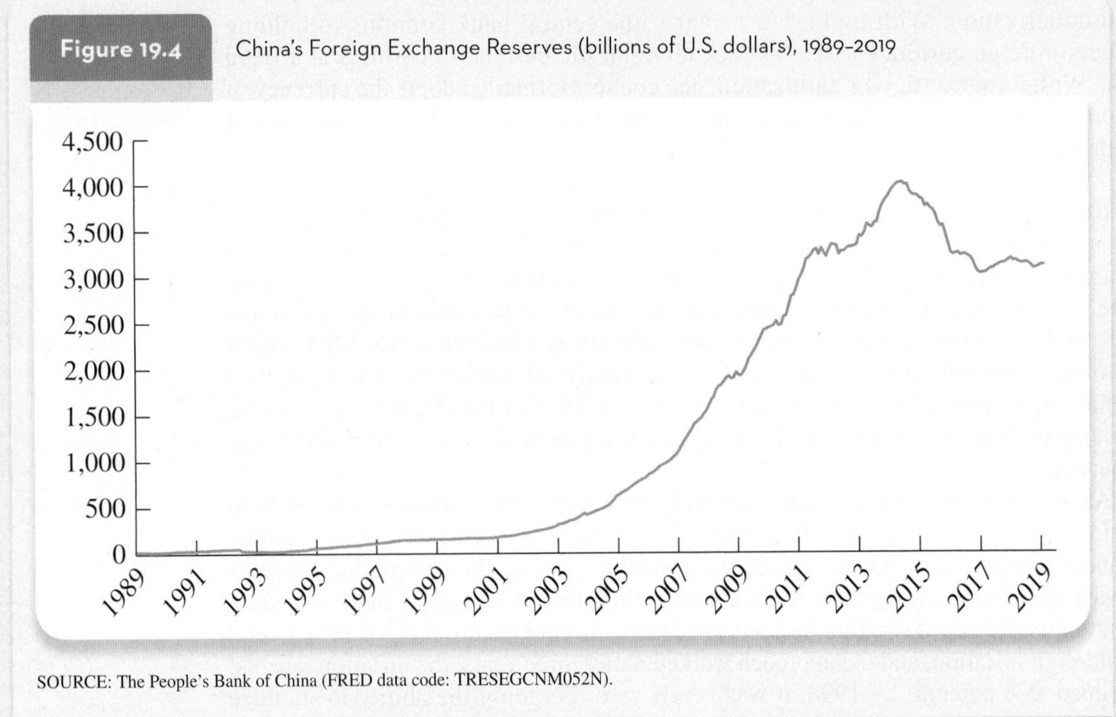

Figure 19.4 China's Foreign Exchange Reserves (billions of U.S. dollars), 1989–2019

SOURCE: The People's Bank of China (FRED data code: TRESEGCNM052N).

this question, but several points will take us a long way toward understanding what happened. First, the peso was pegged to the U.S. dollar, despite the fact that Argentina's economy doesn't have much to do with the U.S. economy. When the dollar appreciated in the 1990s, it made the peso more valuable as well. The overvalued peso priced Argentinean exporters out of their markets, which were not in the United States. Over a period of years, the fact that their exports were too expensive ended up severely damaging Argentina's economy.

A 5-peso note issued by the government of the Province of Buenos Aires in 2001.

Courtesy of Stephen Cecchetti

But the overvalued exchange rate was only part of the story; fiscal policy was the other part. While the Argentinean economy grew at a healthy rate of nearly 4½ percent per year through much of the 1990s, government spending rose even faster—so fast that the

The massive growth in China's reserves up to mid-2014 reflected a combination of its fixed exchange rate regime and its sustained current account surpluses—the excess of exports over imports. Exporters were typically paid in dollars, which they then exchanged for Chinese currency at a fixed exchange rate. The result was that dollars flowed into the central bank.

China's fixed exchange rate provided strong support for its export growth. The country's leaders promoted export-led expansion by pegging their currency, the **renminbi (RMB)**, to the U.S. dollar (the unit of account of the renminbi is the **yuan**, and its exchange rate is reported as the number of yuan per unit of foreign currency). Helped by the stability of the nominal exchange rate relative to the dollar, China became the world's largest exporter. And, in 2008, its current account surplus peaked at a whopping 10 percent of GDP.

Starting in mid-2005, however, Chinese policymakers began adjusting the dollar peg, allowing the RMB to appreciate over the next decade by more than 25 percent versus the dollar. On a real trade-weighted basis, over the same period, China's currency rose in value by 60 percent! Although China has remained the world's premier goods manufacturer, this large real appreciation offset the country's rapid gains in international competitiveness. That is, it became more difficult for Chinese producers to sell traded products at prices lower than anyone else.

What has China been doing with its immense stock of foreign exchange reserves? When a country runs a current account surplus, it also runs a financial account deficit (see the appendix to this chapter). This means that it is either making loans to foreigners or buying assets from them. China has been mostly a lender, purchasing U.S. government bonds. As of May 2019, according to the U.S. Treasury, China owned about $1.32 trillion of Treasury and agency debt, making it the second-leading financier of the U.S. government. Besides these bond holdings, investors based in China held nearly $200 billion of U.S. corporate bonds and equities, while Chinese firms also have increased their direct investment abroad.

Since mid-2014, China's capital flow and exchange rate developments have reflected a number of cross-currents. From July 2014 until January 2017, unprecedented capital outflows triggered the $1 trillion plunge in China's reserves shown in Figure 19.4. A gradual easing of capital controls—aimed partly at encouraging greater international use of the RMB—initially facilitated this shift. However, following a modest devaluation of the RMB in mid-2015, capital outflows accelerated as investors began to expect a further weakening of the currency.

In 2017, a partial restoration of capital controls, combined with the perception that policymakers were aiming to limit devaluation, helped steady both the value of the currency and the level of reserves. While worries about intensifying trade conflict with the United States weighed on China's currency in 2018, capital controls limited outflows. In 2019, when the China-U.S. trade conflict intensified, the Chinese authorities allowed a renewed devaluation.

From a monetary policy perspective, the benefits of capital controls became especially clear in 2018: Despite the fixed exchange rate regime, China's central bank was able to lower interest rates to stimulate a slowing economy, even as the Fed raised interest rates to limit inflation risks and encourage a sustainable rate of growth. In the absence of capital controls, the differences in cyclical conditions would have invited a speculative attack on the RMB.

government needed to borrow an average of nearly 4 percent of GDP per year just to pay its bills. The more the government borrowed, the more wary lenders became of continuing to lend. Undeterred, politicians spent until they simply ran out of money.

The problem was worst at the provincial government level (analogous to the state governments in the United States), where borrowing became impossible even to meet the payroll. So provincial government officials began printing a sort of bond and using it to pay their employees. The bonds issued by the provincial government of Buenos Aires, called *patacones,* paid 7 percent annual interest and matured in one to five years (see the photo). What made them special was that they were the same physical size as currency and were issued in small denominations of 1 to 100 pesos in order to pay employees and retirees. Observers estimated that Argentina's provincial governments eventually issued 40 percent of the currency in circulation. When politicians began printing their own money, the claim that Argentinean inflation would roughly mirror U.S. inflation—a requirement for the long-run viability of the fixed

Sudden Stops: Understanding Balance-of-Payments Crises

MONEY AND BANKING BLOG

*"It is not speed that kills, it is the sudden stop."**

Balance-of-payments (BoP) crises—*sudden stops* or capital flow reversals—compel countries to restore their external balance between exports and imports or shift to export surpluses rapidly. To understand the process, start by noting that the BoP is an accounting identity stating that net cross-border flows of goods and services—the *current account*—must be matched by net flows of financial claims (including those arising from portfolio shifts and from direct investment)—the *financial account*. Simply put, if one country is importing more than it is exporting from another country, it must find a way to finance that difference. (See the appendix to this chapter.)

Importantly, the current account is the consequence of domestic consumption, investment, and saving behavior. To see this, consider the relationship between national income and domestic spending (the sum of consumption, investment, and government outlays). When income falls short of spending, the result is a current account deficit. Similarly, when the current account is in surplus (deficit), savings must exceed (fall short of) investment.

Consequently, current account balances are a *macroeconomic* phenomenon determined both by long-run factors including demographics that influence aggregate savings and by cyclical factors that shift investment. If a country has a current account deficit that it wishes to bring closer to balance, then it must raise saving, lower investment, or both. Equivalently, when imports exceed exports, reducing the gap requires lowering domestic spending relative to national income.

Yet another way to think about the drivers of the current account is in terms of the financial account, which is the other side of the balance of payments. Consider a simple example where a country's domestic saving is insufficient to meet its investment demand. Unable to find resources at home, the natural response is to seek funds abroad. This creates a capital inflow. Since the balance of payments is an identity, the only way for this to balance is with a current account deficit.

When a country can no longer finance a current account deficit, it must adjust very quickly. This usually means cuts in government spending (raising public savings) along with a recession that depresses both consumption and investment. These large, rapid shifts typically are associated with bouts of high unemployment, excess capacity, reduced productivity, lost income, and business failures.

Such BoP crises occur precisely when the inward flow of capital needed to finance a current account deficit (or to offset gross capital outflows) abruptly halts. Such a *sudden stop* typically reflects foreign creditors' doubts about the likelihood of full and timely repayment. When these concerns are mild, the result can be a simple rise in risk premia. But, if concerns become acute, risk premia can skyrocket, eventually halting financing altogether.

Even more disruptive than a sudden stop is a *capital flow reversal*—when sentiment turns so negative that inward capital flows transform into capital flight. Such reversals compel a shift to a current account surplus, resulting in an even deeper recession.

Sudden stops are a frequent occurrence. Figure 19.5 shows the pattern over the period from 1993 to 2015. Note that the episodes tend to occur in waves, at least partly reflecting global conditions (such as the Asian financial crisis of 1997–1998 and the financial crisis of 2007–2009). Not only are sudden stops common, but when they strike, they persist on average for about a year and are associated with a shift from capital inflows to outflows averaging about 3 percent of GDP. The real economic consequences of this are severe, with GDP falling on average by about 4 percent in the first year as investment plunges.

Today, governments and international financial authorities understand a great deal more about sudden stops and capital flow reversals than they did a few decades ago. They know that fixed exchange rates are generally incompatible with the free flow of capital across borders, so most countries have shifted to flexible or managed-exchange-rate regimes. Furthermore, to defend against the need for large, sudden adjustments and improve financial resilience, many countries also have built up foreign exchange reserves. And, the IMF now acknowledges the potential usefulness of some types of capital controls, especially where financial systems remain vulnerable and undeveloped.

*Cited by Rudiger Dornbusch, Ilan Goldfajn, and Rodrigo O. Valdés, "Currency Crises and Collapses," *Brookings Papers on Economic Activity* 26, no. 2 (1995), pp. 219–294.

Figure 19.5 Number of Countries Experiencing a Sudden Stop (quarterly), 1993–2015

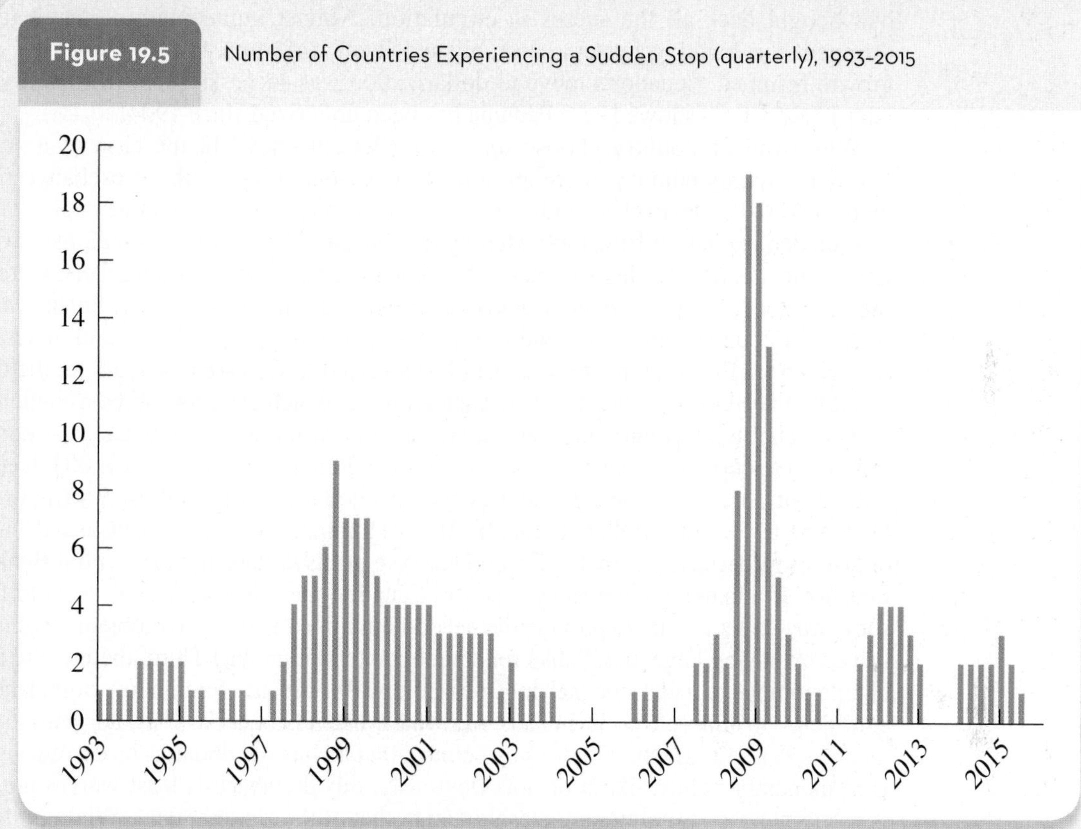

SOURCE: Based on Appendix A in Barry Eichengreen & Poonam Gupta, "Managing Sudden Stops," Central Banking, Analysis, and Economic Policies Book Series, in Enrique G. Mendoza, Ernesto Pastén, and Diego Saravia, editors, *Monetary Policy and Global Spillovers: Mechanisms, Effects and Policy Measures*, Central Bank of Chile, 2018, p. 9-47.

exchange rate—was no longer credible and the currency board collapsed. Always remember, irresponsible politicians can undermine any monetary policy regime.

Dollarization in Ecuador Some countries just give up and adopt the currency of another country for all their transactions, completely eliminating their own monetary policy. This practice need not be based on the dollar. Monaco, the small country for the rich and famous on the southern coast of France, adopted the French franc in 1865 and uses the euro today.[10]

[10]Other small countries that have euroized include Andorra, Kosovo, Montenegro, San Marino, and Vatican City.

Monaco is very small, covering less than 50 square miles (about twice the size of Manhattan), with a population of fewer than 40,000. Ecuador, with a population of 15 million spread over 100,000 square miles, is another story. In 1999, Ecuador experienced a severe financial crisis. Real GDP fell more than 7 percent, the inflation rate rose to 50 percent, the banking system nearly collapsed, and the currency, the *sucre,* went into freefall, losing two-thirds of its value relative to the dollar in a year. In January 2000, Ecuador officially gave up its currency. Within six months, the central bank had bought back all the sucres in circulation. Almost immediately, interest rates dropped, the banking system reestablished itself, inflation fell dramatically, and growth resumed. Ecuador's move to dollarization was successful enough that a year later El Salvador followed suit. Panama has been dollarized since 1904.

Why would a country choose to give up its currency? In the case of a small emerging market country, there are a host of reasons. First, with no exchange rate, there is no risk of an exchange rate crisis—no possibility of either a large depreciation or a sudden capital outflow motivated by the fear of depreciation. Second, using dollars or euros or yen can help a country become integrated into world markets, increasing its trade and investment. Finally, by rejecting the possibility of inflationary finance, a country can reduce the risk premium it must pay on loans and generally strengthen its financial institutions. But it does need to find some way to get the dollars it will need to keep the monetary base growing, which can prove to be a challenge.

The benefits of dollarization are balanced against the loss of revenue that comes from issuing currency—what is called *seignorage.* Remember, printing a $100 bill costs only about 13 cents. When Ecuador decided to dollarize, it gave those profits to the United States. Second, dollarization effectively eliminates the central bank as the lender of last resort because, again, the Federal Reserve prints dollars, not the Central Bank of Ecuador. If a banking emergency arises in Ecuador, the government will need to find some way to get dollars to provide the needed liquidity. (This is the problem Argentina solved by paying large U.S. banks for standby letters of credit.) Third, there is the loss of autonomous monetary or exchange rate policy. But because foreign investors' lack of confidence in domestic policymakers was what created Ecuador's crisis, it is hard to see that loss as a serious one. Finally, any country that adopts the dollar as its currency gets U.S. monetary policy, like it or not. Obviously, this drawback is least worrisome for countries whose economies are closely tied to that of the United States. While it might make sense for countries like Mexico or Canada, for Ecuador the decision isn't so clear.

Note that dollarization is not the same as a monetary union. The decision by European countries to adopt a common currency, the euro, was fundamentally different from a country's decision to adopt the dollar. When the FOMC makes its decisions, the affairs of Ecuador and El Salvador carry no weight. And as we have already noted, dollarized countries forgo the revenue from issuing currency and are forced to make special arrangements to provide emergency loans to domestic banks. In contrast, all European countries participating in the monetary union take part in monetary policy decisions, and all share in the revenue that comes from printing euros. Europe's national banks still operate as lenders of last resort in making euro loans. In sum, a monetary union is shared governance; euroization is not.[11] Moreover, with its shared institutions, a monetary union generally is even harder than a hard peg (see page 540). Yet, because a member country of a monetary union cannot control the money supply by itself, some important characteristics

[11]The willingness of the ECB to continue lending to Greece's national central bank in 2015—despite concerns that the country would default and exit the euro area—exemplifies how shared governance in the European Economic and Monetary Union favors many forms of risk sharing.

of monetary unions are analogous to those of dollarized or euroized countries. And, because a country may be able to withdraw from a monetary union (and reintroduce its own currency), investors may still require a currency-related risk premium to hold that country's liabilities.

Key Terms

capital controls, 526
currency board, 539
dollarization, 539
foreign exchange intervention, 521
gold standard, 535
hard peg, 539
renminbi (RMB), 541
speculative attack, 534
sterilized foreign exchange intervention, 531
unsterilized foreign exchange intervention, 531
yuan, 541

Using FRED: Codes for Data in This Chapter

Data Series	FRED Data Code
U.S. dollar/euro exchange rate	EXUSEU
Deutsche mark/U.S. dollar exchange rate	EXGEUS
Germany discount rate	INTDSRDEM193N
U.K. discount rate	INTDSRGBM193N
U.S. interventions in market for euros	USINTDMRKTDM
U.S. index of general price level	M0401USM324NNBR
Japanese yen/U.S. dollar exchange rate	EXJPUS
Mexican peso/U.S. dollar exchange rate	EXMXUS
Ecuador consumer price index	DDOE02ECA086NWDB
El Salvador consumer price index	DDOE01SVA086NWDB
Japan consumer price index	JPNCPIALLMINMEI
Mexico consumer price index	MEXCPIALLMINMEI
Panama consumer price index	DDOE02PAA086NWDB
U.S. consumer price index	CPIAUCSL
U.S. dollar/U.K. pound exchange rate	EXUSUK
12-month U.S. dollar LIBOR	USD12MD156N
12-month U.K. pound LIBOR	GBP12MD156N
Thai baht/U.S. dollar exchange rate	EXTHUS
Korean won/U.S. dollar exchange rate	EXKOUS
Chinese yuan/U.S. dollar exchange rate	EXCHUS
Malaysian ringgit/U.S. dollar exchange rate	EXMAUS
Canadian dollar/U.S. dollar exchange rate	EXCAUS
Swiss franc/U.S. dollar exchange rate	EXSZUS
Price of gold (U.S. dollars)	GOLDAMGBD228NLBM
China foreign exchange reserves (excluding gold)	TRESEGCNM052N

To learn more about the changing financial system, visit www.moneyandbanking.com.

Chapter Lessons

1. When capital flows freely across a country's borders, fixing the exchange rate means giving up discretionary monetary policy.
   a. Purchasing power parity implies that in the long run exchange rates are tied to inflation differentials across countries.
   b. Capital market arbitrage means that in the short run the exchange rate is tied to differences in interest rates.
   c. Monetary policymakers can have only two of the following three options: open capital markets, control of domestic interest rates, and a fixed exchange rate.
   d. Countries that impose controls on capital flowing in and/or out can fix the exchange rate without giving up discretionary monetary policy.
2. Central banks can intervene in foreign exchange markets.
   a. When they do, it affects their balance sheet in the same way as an open market operation.
   b. When reserves in the domestic banking system are scarce, foreign exchange intervention affects the exchange rate by changing domestic interest rates. This is called unsterilized intervention.
   c. When reserves in the domestic banking system are abundant, foreign exchange intervention can influence the exchange rate by shifting the supply of domestic currency, but there are limits. Policymakers wishing to drive the value of their currency up (an appreciation) can run out of foreign assets to sell, while those desiring to drive the value of their currency down (a depreciation) may need to do so on a very large scale, risking a political reaction as their balance sheet grows.
   d. A sterilized intervention is a purchase or sale of foreign exchange reserves that leaves the central bank's total liabilities unchanged. It has no lasting impact on the exchange rate in a deep, well-functioning currency market.
3. The decision to fix the exchange rate has costs, benefits, and risks.
   a. Both corporations and investors benefit from predictable exchange rates.
   b. Fixed exchange rates can reduce domestic inflation by importing the monetary policy of a country with low inflation.
   c. Fixed exchange rate regimes are fragile and leave countries open to speculative attacks.
   d. The right conditions for choosing to fix the exchange rate include:
      i. A poor reputation for inflation control.
      ii. An economy that is well integrated and cyclically synchronized with the one to whose currency the rate is fixed.
      iii. A high level of foreign exchange reserves.
      iv. A high degree of price and wage flexibility.
      v. A robust banking system.
4. There are a number of examples of exchange rate systems.
   a. The Bretton Woods system, set up after World War II, pegged exchange rates to the U.S. dollar. It collapsed in 1971 after U.S. inflation began to rise.
   b. Most fixed exchange rate regimes are no longer thought to be viable in the absence of capital controls.
   c. Two that may work are currency boards and dollarization (or euroization).
   d. With a currency board, the central bank holds enough foreign currency reserves to exchange the entire monetary base at the promised exchange rate.

e. Argentina's currency board collapsed when the regional governments began printing their own money.
f. Dollarization is the total conversion of an economy from its own currency to the currency of another country.
g. Several Latin American countries have adopted the dollar recently, with good results over the short run. Several small European countries have adopted the euro.

Conceptual and Analytical Problems Mc Graw Hill connect

1. Explain the mechanics of a speculative attack on the currency of a country with a fixed exchange rate regime. *(LO4)*
2. Country A frequently experiences large business cycle swings. Under what conditions might it be appropriate for Country A to dollarize? *(LO1)*
3. In the first half of 1997, the Bank of Thailand maintained a fixed exchange rate of 26 Thai baht to the U.S. dollar, but Thai interest rates were substantially higher than those in the United States and Japan. Thai bankers were borrowing money in Japan and lending it in Thailand. *(LO3)*
   a. Why was this transaction profitable?
   b. What risks were associated with this method of financing?
   c. Describe the impact of a depreciation of the baht on the balance sheets of Thai banks involved in these transactions.
4. During the time of the currency board, Argentinean banks offered accounts in both dollars and pesos, but loans were made largely in pesos. Describe the impact on banks of the collapse of the currency board. *(LO4)*
5. Consider a scenario where investors become nervous just before a key government election. As a result, the risk premium on sovereign debt in that country increases dramatically and its currency depreciates significantly. *(LO1)*
   a. How could concern over an election drive up the risk premium?
   b. How is the risk premium connected to the value of the currency?
6. Explain why a well-capitalized domestic banking system might be important for the successful maintenance of a fixed exchange rate regime. *(LO4)*
7.* Explain why, in the absence of the time consistency problem, you might expect a central bank to be effective at holding the value of its domestic currency at an artificially low level for a sustained period but not at an artificially high level. *(LO3)*
8. Describe how the time consistency challenge for monetary policy can make it difficult for a central bank to cap the value of its domestic currency. *(LO3)*
9. Why might a sterilized foreign exchange market intervention have a greater impact on the exchange rate in times of financial stress than in times of normal market conditions? *(LO2)*
10. When asked about the value of the dollar, the chair of the Federal Reserve Board answers, "The foreign exchange policy of the United States is the responsibility of the secretary of the Treasury; I have no comment." Discuss this answer. *(LO1)*
11.* Explain why a consensus has developed that countries should either allow their exchange rates to float freely or adopt a hard peg as an exchange rate regime? *(LO3)*

*Indicates more difficult problems.

12. Dollarizing and joining a monetary union both involve giving up a country's own currency, but there are key differences between these two options. Identify one factor that might lead a country to choose to dollarize (rather than join a monetary union) and one factor that could lead to the opposite choice. *(LO4)*
13. You observe that two countries with a fixed exchange rate have current inflation rates that differ from each other. You check the recent historical data and find that inflation differentials have been present for several months and that they have not remained constant. How would you explain these observations in light of the theory of purchasing power parity? *(LO2)*
14. Assuming the country is open to international capital flows, which of the following combinations of monetary and exchange rate policies are viable? Explain your reasoning. *(LO1)*
    a. A domestic interest rate as a policy instrument and a floating exchange rate.
    b. A domestic interest rate as a policy instrument and a fixed exchange rate.
    c. The monetary base as a policy instrument and a floating exchange rate.
15. Show the impact on the Federal Reserve's balance sheet of a foreign exchange market intervention where the Fed purchases $5,000 worth of foreign exchange reserves. Explain what impact, if any, the intervention will have on the domestic money supply. Under what circumstances, if any, will this unsterilized intervention impact the dollar exchange rate? *(LO2)*
16. Suppose that a central bank that is operating on the downward-sloping portion of the reserve demand curve decides to purchase $1,000 worth of foreign exchange reserves and then sterilize this foreign exchange market intervention. Show the impact on the central bank's balance sheet. What would the overall impact be on the monetary base? What would be the impact, if any, on the exchange rate? Assume that the intervention took place in a deep, well-functioning foreign exchange market. *(LO2)*
17.* Consider a small open economy with a wide array of trading partners all operating in different currencies. The economy's business cycles are not well synchronized with any of the world's largest economies, and the policymakers in this country have a well-earned reputation for being fiscally prudent and honest. In your view, should this small open economy adopt a fixed exchange rate regime? *(LO3)*
18. A small eastern European economy asks your opinion about whether it should pursue the path to joining the European Economic and Monetary Union (EMU) or simply "euroize" (i.e., dollarize by using the euro for all domestic transactions). What advice would you give? *(LO3)*
19. In the face of increased short-run synchronization of global stock markets, what strategies could you employ to continue to benefit from international diversification? *(LO3)*
20. In an increasingly integrated financial world, under what circumstances might you support the imposition of capital controls? *(LO1)*

*Indicates more difficult problems.

Data Exploration connect

FRED
ECONOMIC DATA | ST. LOUIS FED

For general information on using Federal Reserve Economic Data (FRED) online, visit www.mhhe.com/moneyandbanking6e.com *and refer to the FRED resources.*

1. Panama, Ecuador, and El Salvador began using the U.S. dollar as their domestic currency in 1904, 2000, and 2001, respectively. How do you expect their inflation rates to compare with U.S. inflation? Plot since 1960 the percent change from a year ago of consumer prices in Panama (FRED code: DDOE02PAA086NWDB), Ecuador (FRED code: DDOE02ECA086NWDB), El Salvador (FRED code: DDOE01SVA086NWDB), and the United States (FRED code: PCEPI). Download these data and (starting with the country's date of dollarization) compare the average inflation rate in each country with U.S. inflation. *(LO4)*

2. Did the September 2000 currency intervention by the United States and other countries influence the dollar–euro exchange rate? Plot for the September–October 2000 period the daily dollar–euro exchange rate (FRED code: DEXUSEU) and, on the right scale, the Fed's sales of dollars for euros (FRED code: USINTDMRKTDM). Was the intervention successful? If not, why not? *(LO2)*

3. Some claim that adoption of a gold standard would contribute to price stability. Was price stability a feature of the U.S. gold standard that prevailed prior to World War I (see Applying the Concept on page 535)? Based on a plot of the general price level (FRED code: M04051USM324NNBR), discuss U.S. price developments from 1880 to 1914. *(LO4)*

4. Does purchasing power parity (PPP) hold in the long run? Does it hold in the short run? Following equation (3) on page 524, plot for Japan and the United States beginning in 1972 the percent change from a year ago of the Japanese yen/U.S. dollar exchange rate (FRED code: EXJPUS) *minus* the annual inflation rate in Japan (FRED code: JPNCPIALLMINMEI) plus the annual inflation rate in the United States (FRED code: CPIAUCSL). If PPP holds in the long run, what should this expression equal on average? Download the data and compute the average for the full period. Is the result consistent with long-run PPP? Observing the plot, does PPP seem to hold in the short run? *(LO1)*

5. In September 1992, a speculative attack compelled the United Kingdom to devalue the British pound versus the German currency (the deutsche mark). How did monetary policies in both countries influence this outcome? Plot from 1990 to 1992 the discount rates in the United Kingdom (FRED code: INTDSRGBM193N) and Germany (FRED code: INTDSRDEM193N), and (on the right scale) the exchange rate of German marks per British pound [obtained by multiplying the number of U.S. dollars per pound (FRED code: EXUSUK) by the number of deutsche marks per U.S. dollar (FRED code: EXGEUS)]. What do you conclude? *(LO3)*

Appendix to Chapter 19

What You Really Need to Know about the Balance of Payments

The international financial system exists to sustain the flow of capital and goods among countries. To understand how it works, we need to define three important terms connected with the international balance of payments. They are the current account balance, the financial account balance, and the official settlements balance.

The *current account* tracks the flow of payments across national boundaries. When an American purchases a television set made in Korea, or a Japanese consumer buys a copy of Microsoft Windows, the transaction shows up as part of the U.S. current account. The *current account balance* is simply the difference between a country's exports and imports of goods and services. A full accounting would include unilateral transfers, such as the money foreign workers send home to relatives, as well as investment income, such as the interest payments Americans receive on Mexican bonds. But we will ignore these and stick to the simple version: when a country's exports exceed its imports, its current account balance will be positive—that is, it will have a *current account surplus*.

To grasp the importance of the current account, you need to realize that countries have budgets, just like individuals. If you spend more than your income, you have two options: sell something you own or get a loan. What is true for an individual is also true for a country. Think of the revenue earned from selling exports to foreigners as the country's income, and the cost of imports bought from overseas as its spending. When spending exceeds income, the result is a current account deficit. To pay for its overspending, the country must either sell something it owns or borrow.

Take an example in which there is only one international transaction, your purchase of a new television set made in South Korea. When you buy your new TV, you want to pay in dollars, but the Samsung dealer wants to be paid in Korean won. Because you have sold nothing to anyone in South Korea, you have no won to pay. There are two ways to get the won you need. You can appeal to a South Korean to purchase some asset you own, like a share of IBM stock, or you can try to get a South Korean to give you a loan—in essence, to buy a bond that you issue. Only after you have sold an asset to someone who has Korean won will you be able to pay for and import the television set.

The *financial account* tracks the purchase and sale of assets—stocks, bonds, real estate, and the like—between countries. When a German buys shares in IBM or an American purchases a Brazilian government bond, the transaction appears in the financial account. The *financial account balance* is the difference between a country's capital inflows and capital outflows. When a country's financial account is in surplus, it has a net capital inflow. Its residents are either selling assets to foreigners or borrowing money from abroad.

Finally, the *official settlements balance* is the change in a country's official reserve holdings. During the time of the gold standard, these reserves took the form of gold bars. It shows the change in the central bank's foreign exchange reserves (or gold reserves).

The international balance of payments is an accounting framework that relates these three pieces. Their relationship is simple: They must sum to zero.

$$\text{Current account balance } (CA) + \text{Financial account balance } (FA) + \text{Official settlements balance } (OB) = 0$$

This accounting identity has important implications. If, as is normally the case in developed economies today, official reserve positions are unchanged so the official settlements balance is zero, then the current account balance plus the financial account balance sum to zero. That is

$$\text{Current account balance } (CA) = -\text{ Financial account balance } (FA)$$

That is, when a country's current account is in deficit—imports exceed exports ($CA < 0$)—the financial account is in surplus ($FA > 0$): capital inflows exceed outflows. Put differently, foreigners accrue financial claims on a net-importing country in compensation for their net sales of goods and services. As a result, a persistent flow of current account surpluses (deficits) leads over time to a rising stock of net foreign assets (liabilities).

When we add the official settlements balance, the analysis changes slightly. Now we see that if a country is running a current account deficit, there are two ways to pay for it. A country can run a financial account surplus or it can draw down its foreign exchange reserves. If foreigners want to sell their investments and take the proceeds home, they will force a country either to run a current account surplus—something it cannot do quickly without a severe economic contraction—or to drain foreign exchange from the central bank's reserves.

The balance of payments is an identity: it says nothing about causality. While changes in the current account can trigger changes in the financial account, the reverse is not only possible, but quite common. For example, a country that liberalizes cross-border capital flows may attract large net capital inflows ($FA > 0$) that then lead it to become a net importer of goods and services ($CA < 0$). Similarly, a net-importing country that loses the confidence of foreign investors may face an abrupt halt to capital inflows (or even a reversal). Such a *sudden stop* of net financing from abroad would compel an immediate restoration of current account balance (see In the Blog: Sudden Stops: Understanding Balance-of-Payment Crises).

To help understand the factors driving the current account, we can explore its relationship with national savings and investment. The national accounting identity states that national income or gross national product (Y) is the sum of consumption (C), investment (I), government spending (G), and net exports (NX):

$$Y = C + I + G + NX$$

Net exports equal the current account (CA) in the balance of payments. Thus, when imports exceed exports ($NX < 0$) the current account is in deficit. This also means that domestic spending ($C + I + G$) exceeds national income (Y).

To further draw out the implications, define national savings (S) as the gap between national income (Y) and noninvestment domestic spending, which is the sum of consumption (C) and government spending (G):

$$S = Y - C - G$$

Combining these, we see that the gap between savings and investment is equal to the current account balance:

$$S - I = NX = CA$$

This relationship has profound implications. First, a nation has a current account deficit (surplus) if and only if investment exceeds (falls short of) national savings. This means that macroeconomic factors—like demographic influences on saving or cyclical swings in investment—determine the current account balance. Moreover, to improve its current account balance, a country must raise savings, lower investment, or both. Equivalently, it must lower domestic spending relative to national income.

Absent a change in the official settlements balance that would come from the sale of foreign exchange reserves, when a sudden stop occurs and the financial account shifts toward outflows, the current account balance must improve. In theory, this current account shift can occur through an increase of savings or a decline of investment. In practice, much of the short-run adjustment usually occurs through a cyclical downturn (a recession) associated with a plunge of investment. In such a recession, national income falls, but the current account improves so long as domestic spending falls by more. Such a painful economic adjustment is a routine feature of balance-of-payments crises.

Chapter

20 Money Growth, Money Demand, and Modern Monetary Policy

Learning Objectives

After reading this chapter, you should be able to:

LO1 Discuss the role of the monetary aggregates.

LO2 Define the velocity of money and its role in the quantity theory of money.

LO3 Describe the transactions demand and the portfolio demand for money.

LO4 Explain why key central banks have shifted away from targeting money growth.

Anyone who listens carefully to what central bankers say, or reads what they write, will form the clear impression that 21st-century monetary policy has very little to do with money, despite its focus on inflation. That impression is reinforced by the technical papers that monetary economists write. Everyone talks about interest rates and exchange rates; no one talks about money.

But digging deeper, you will find that central bankers and monetary economists *do* care about money. After decades of studying the economy, the Nobel Prize–winning economist Milton Friedman wrote, "Inflation is always and everywhere a monetary phenomenon." Most economists would agree. We see concern for money, too, in statements made by officials of the European Central Bank (ECB). In Chapter 16, we discussed the stability-oriented strategy that the ECB's Governing Council adopted in the fall of 1998 to achieve the objective of price stability. The council's strategy assigned money a prominent role that was, in its members' words, "signaled by the announcement of a quantitative reference value for the growth rate of a broad monetary aggregate." The idea was that deviations of money growth from the reference value signaled a risk to European price stability. Since then, the ECB's monthly announcements of its target interest rate have regularly mentioned money growth.

Obviously, money plays a significant role in the formulation of European monetary policy. The contrast with the United States could not be more striking. In July 2000, after roughly a quarter century of publishing twice-yearly target ranges for the monetary aggregates, the Federal Open Market Committee (FOMC) stopped doing so, explaining that "these ranges [no longer] provide useful benchmarks for monetary policy."[1] While the Federal Reserve still collects and publishes data on the monetary aggregates, FOMC members now mention them only in passing. They rarely make any

[1]This announcement appeared as a footnote in the biannual *Monetary Policy Report to Congress.*

reference to money in public announcements of the federal funds target rate. In 2001, Federal Reserve Board Governor Laurence H. Meyer even went so far as to say that money "plays virtually no role in the conduct of monetary policy."[2]

What accounts for the distinctly different treatment of money growth in the two largest central banks in the world? Why does the ECB make regular public references to money growth, while the Fed never does? If money growth is tied to inflation, why don't central bankers in the United States pay more attention to it? The goal of this chapter is twofold. First, it examines the link between money growth and inflation in order to clarify the role of money in monetary policy. Second, it explains the logic underlying central bankers' focus on interest rates.

Why We Care about Monetary Aggregates

We start with the single most important fact in monetary economics: the relationship between money growth and inflation rates. Panel A of Figure 20.1 shows the average annual inflation and money growth in 160 countries over the three decades that began in 1980. This graph is striking for two reasons. The first is its scale: Some countries suffered inflation that averaged more than 200 percent *a year* over three decades. Second, every country with high inflation had high money growth. History provides no

Figure 20.1 Inflation Rates and Money Growth

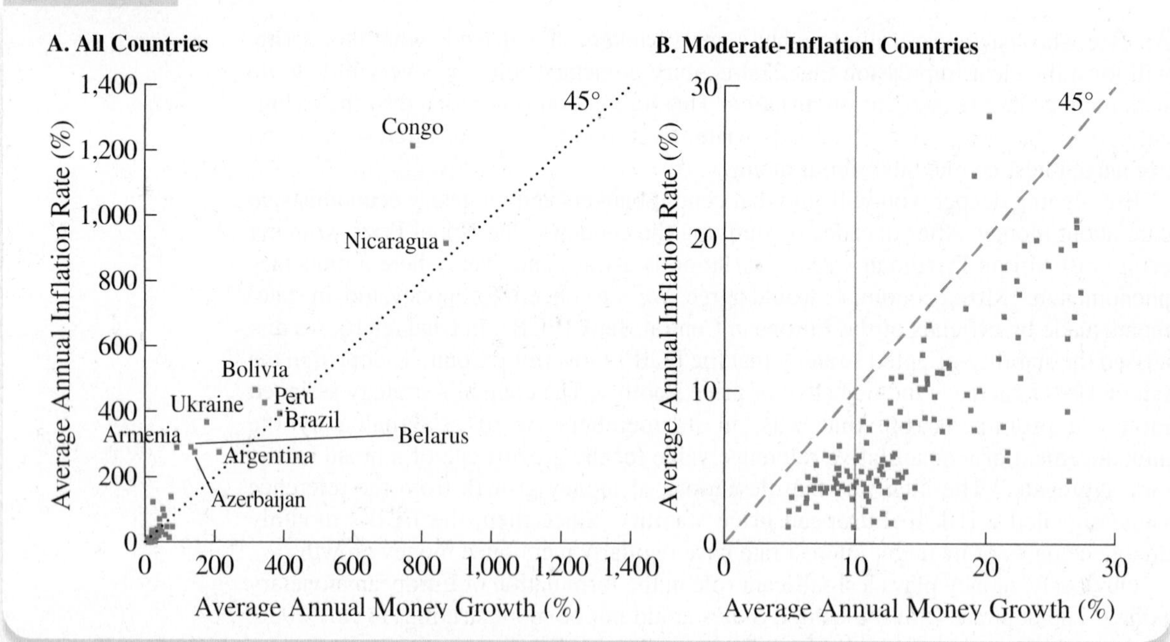

Inflation was computed from each country's analog to the consumer price index; money is the rough equivalent of M2. Data are for the 30 years beginning in 1980.

SOURCE: These figures are based on data from the International Monetary Fund's International Financial Statistics.

[2]Laurence H. Meyer, "Does Money Matter?" The 2001 Homer Jones Memorial Lecture, Washington University, St. Louis, Missouri, March 28, 2001.

examples of countries with high inflation and low money growth or with low inflation and high money growth.

One thing the figure does not show because of its scale is the huge number of points that fall very close to the origin, representing countries with both low inflation and low money growth. Panel B of Figure 20.1 displays the data for the 130 countries that experienced moderate money growth (averaging less than 30 percent) over the three decades from 1980 to 2009. While the relationship between money growth and inflation is less striking it is still clearly there. The higher the rate of money growth is, the higher the inflation rate is likely to be. The two variables move together. This evidence alone tells us that *to avoid sustained episodes of high inflation, a central bank must be concerned with money growth. Avoiding high inflation means avoiding persistent rapid money growth.*

Both panels of Figures 20.1 include a 45-degree line. Note that the points representing countries with very high inflation tend to lie above the line, while the points representing countries with moderate to low inflation tend to fall below it. As the simplified graph in Figure 20.2 shows, points lying above the 45-degree line represent countries where average inflation exceeds average money growth; points lying below the 45-degree line represent countries where money growth exceeds inflation. To understand this relationship, think about what would happen if the inflation rate rose to 900 percent a year, as was the case in Nicaragua (see Panel A of Figure 20.1). That means prices would be rising about 4½ percent a week. When the currency that people are holding loses value that rapidly, they will work to spend what they have as quickly as possible.[3] As we will see shortly, spending money more quickly has the same effect on inflation as an increase in money growth.

Figure 20.2 Money Growth and Inflation

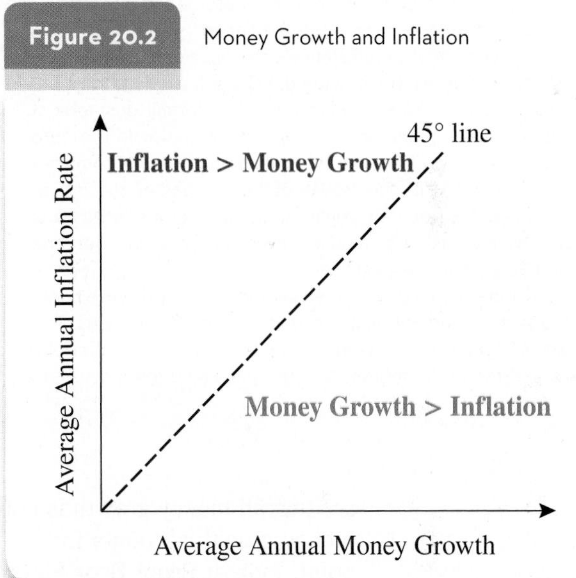

Connecting this relationship to central bank policy is straightforward. Recall from Chapter 17 that the central bank controls the size of its own balance sheet. Policymakers can purchase as many assets as they want, issuing currency and commercial bank reserve liabilities to do so. Those liabilities, in turn, form the monetary base. Through the process of deposit expansion, the banking system turns the monetary base into the monetary aggregates. Thus, the monetary aggregates cannot grow rapidly without at least the tacit consent of the central bank. By limiting the rate at which they purchase securities, policymakers can control the rate at which aggregates like M2 grow. In other words, *it is impossible to have high, sustained inflation without monetary accommodation.*

Not surprisingly, evidence of the link between inflation and money growth is the foundation on which modern monetary policy is built. That is why the ECB pays close attention to growth in the monetary aggregates. But to use the link as a policy guide, central bankers must understand how it works. Looking back at Figure 20.1, we can

[3]In some countries suffering from hyperinflation, workers may be paid more than once a day because cash loses value so quickly.

Central Bank Money Without Inflation?

APPLYING THE CONCEPT

From July 2007 to December 2018, the assets of the European Central Bank, the Bank of Japan, and the Federal Reserve surged by 385 percent, 512 percent, and 469 percent, respectively. Yet, over the same period, prices in these regions rose *cumulatively* by about 18 percent, 5 percent, and 22 percent, respectively!

Having learned that inflation is a monetary phenomenon, people are confused. Shouldn't this massive injection of central bank money have resulted in inflation?

Under normal circumstances, the answer would be yes. But since August 2007, when the Great Financial Crisis began, conditions have been anything but normal. Just look at roughly comparable *broad* measures of money in the euro area (M3), Japan (M2), and the United States (M2). From mid-2007 to mid-2018, the growth of these broad monetary aggregates has been far smaller than the rise of central bank money, increasing by a cumulative 37 percent, 40 percent, and 96 percent, respectively.

Normally the central bank provides reserves to the banking system, and the banks respond by increasing loans. The loans expand deposits in the banking system as a whole, raising the broad monetary aggregates (see the discussion of the deposit expansion multiplier in Chapter 17). Over time, higher growth of broad money leads to higher inflation.

In recent years, however, banks have *not* been lending much. Instead, as the quantity of central bank money surged, banks' holdings of reserves skyrocketed without a sizable impact on broad money. For example, from mid-2007 to the end of 2018, total reserves in the United States rose from less than $50 billion to nearly $1.8 trillion, but the ratio of M2 to the monetary base—the M2 money multiplier—plunged from 8.6 to 4.2 (see Figure 17.10 on page 472).

The big question has been, why are banks not lending more? Are their credit standards too high? Or is the demand for loans too low? During the crisis and shortly thereafter, banks were likely wary of supplying credit. In the euro area and Japan, this may still be the case. But banks in the United States were willing and able to lend at a healthy pace after 2013.

Regardless of why so little central bank money has turned into broad money, inflation has remained low. But, in the United States, where the credit and broader economic expansions picked up first, inflation edged up gradually. Not surprisingly, the Federal Reserve also was the first of the Big Three central banks to begin raising interest rates.

see that all money growth is not created equal. Something beyond just differences in money growth accounts for the differences in inflation across countries. To see the point, look at Panel B of Figure 20.1 and note the vertical line drawn at the point where annual money growth averages 10 percent. Points lying on or near the line represent countries that experienced average annual inflation rates of between 1 percent and 8 percent. What accounted for the differences in inflation among those countries?

Still other questions arise. For instance, Figure 20.1 shows average inflation and money growth over a 30-year period. The results suggest that money growth is a useful guide to understanding long-term movements in inflation. But what happens over shorter periods of a few months or years? Answering this question requires moving beyond the simple statistical relationship shown in Figure 20.1. We need to develop a deeper understanding of the link between money growth and inflation, one that is based on economic decisions.

The Quantity Theory and the Velocity of Money

What accounts for the fact that high money growth is accompanied by high inflation? Recall that during times of inflation, the value of money is falling. If we think about the value or purchasing power of money in terms of the goods needed to get money, the impact of inflation becomes clear. Normally, we think of how many dollars we need to buy a cup of coffee or a sandwich; that's the money price of the sandwich. But we can turn the question around and ask how many cups of coffee or sandwiches a person needs to buy one dollar. A fall in the number of cups of coffee it takes to buy one dollar represents a decline in the price, or value, of money.

If someone asked you how the price of a cup of coffee is determined, having learned your microeconomics, you would answer that it depends on the supply of and demand for coffee. When the supply of coffee rises but demand does not, the price falls. Not surprisingly, the same is true of the price of money: it is determined by supply and demand. Given steady demand, an increase in the supply of money drives the price of money down. That's inflation. If the central bank continuously floods the economy with large amounts of money, inflation will reach very high levels.

Velocity and the Equation of Exchange

To understand the relationship between inflation and money growth, we need to focus on money as a means of payment. Imagine a simple economy that is composed of four college students: one has \$100 in currency; the second has two tickets to the weekend football game, worth \$50 each; the third has a \$100 calculator; and the fourth has a set of 25 high-quality drawing pencils that sell for \$4 apiece. Each of these students wants something else. The one with the \$100 in currency needs a calculator, so she buys it. The student who sold the calculator to her wants to see the football game, so he uses the cash she paid him to buy the two tickets. Finally, the student who sold the football tickets needs some pencils for a drawing class, so the cash changes hands again.

Let's analyze the effect of these transactions. Their total value is \$100 × (1 calculator) + \$50 × (2 football tickets) + \$4 × (25 drawing pencils) = \$300. In this four-person economy, the \$100 was used three times, resulting in \$300 worth of transactions. In general terms, we can write this as

$$\text{(Number of dollars)} \times \text{(Number of times each dollar is used)} = \text{Dollar value of transactions} \quad (1)$$

To interpret this expression, note that the number of dollars is the quantity of money in the economy. The number of times each dollar is used (per unit of time) is called the **velocity of money**. The more frequently each dollar is used, the higher the velocity of money.

Applying this same logic to the economy as a whole is straightforward because virtually every transaction uses money at some stage. For our purposes here, we will restrict the analysis to sales and purchases of final goods and services produced in a country during a given period and measured at market prices. That is, we will focus on

Courtesy of Stephen Cecchetti

This note, issued by the Central Bank of Hungary in 1946, is the highest-denomination currency note ever issued. Its face value is 100 million trillion *pengö* (that's a 1 followed by 20 zeros). The note was produced for use during one of the most extreme hyperinflations in history, which took place in Hungary following World War II. Starting in 1944, the amount of currency in circulation grew from 12 billion pengö (a number with 11 digits) to a 27-digit total in 1946. In two short years, the quantity of money had increased by a factor of about 10,000 trillion, reducing the value of this note to the equivalent of 20 cents.

nominal gross domestic product. Every one of the purchases counted in nominal GDP requires the use of money. So,

$$\text{(Quantity of money)} \times \text{(Velocity of money)} = \text{Nominal GDP} \qquad (2)$$

Because we have data on both the quantity of money and nominal GDP, we can use equation (2) to compute the velocity of money. Each definition of money—each monetary aggregate—has its own velocity. In the final quarter of 2018, GDP equaled \$20.89 trillion and M1 equaled \$3.76 trillion, so M1 had a velocity of 5.56. In the same period, M2 equaled \$14.48 trillion, so the velocity of M2 was 1.44. We will come back to this topic shortly.

To manipulate the expression for velocity in equation (2), we can rewrite it using algebraic symbols. We'll use the letter M to represent money and V to represent velocity. Nominal GDP can be divided into two parts, the price level and the quantity of real output (or real GDP). Calling these two factors P and Y, we can state that nominal GDP = P times Y. Using this notation, we can rewrite equation (2) as

$$MV = PY \qquad (3)$$

This expression, called the **equation of exchange**, tells us that *the quantity of money multiplied by its velocity equals the level of nominal GDP,* written as the price level times the quantity of real output.

With money on the left-hand side and prices on the right, the equation of exchange provides the link between money and prices that we are looking for. But our real concern is with inflation, not the price level, and money growth, not the quantity of money. We need to manipulate equation (3) to allow for the percentage change in each factor. Noting that the percentage change of a product like MV or PY is the sum of the percentage changes in each factor,[4] we can write

$$\begin{array}{ccccccc} \%\Delta M & + & \%\Delta V & = & \%\Delta P & + & \%\Delta Y \\ \text{Money growth} & + & \text{Velocity growth} & = & \text{Inflation} & + & \text{Real growth} \end{array} \qquad (4)$$

where the symbol "%Δ" stands for percentage change. We know that the percentage change in the quantity of money is money growth; the percentage change in the price level is inflation; and the percentage change in real GDP is real growth. So equation (4) tells us that *money growth plus velocity growth equals inflation plus real growth.*

The Quantity Theory of Money

In the early 20th century, the economist Irving Fisher wrote down the equation of exchange and derived the implication in equation (4). Next, he assumed that no important changes occur in payment methods or the cost of holding money. If the

[4]This statement is based on the approximation that the change in the natural log of a variable x is approximately equal to its percentage change. To see how it works, first take the natural log of the product M_tV_t: $ln(M_tV_t) = ln(M_t) + ln(V_t)$. Now subtract $ln(M_{t-1}V_{t-1})$ from the left-hand side and $ln(M_{t-1}) + ln(V_{t-1})$ from the right-hand side to get $ln(M_tV_t) - ln(M_{t-1}V_{t-1}) = [ln(M_t) - ln(M_{t-1})] + [ln(V_t) - ln(V_{t-1})]$. This means that the change in the natural log of MV equals the change in the natural log of M plus the change in the natural log of V. Next, use the fact that the difference in the log is the log of the ratio, $[ln(M_t) - ln(M_{t-1})] = ln(M_t/M_{t-1})$. We can rewrite this as $ln[1 + (M_t - M_{t-1})/M_{t-1}]$, and use the fact that the natural log of one plus a small number is approximately equal to the small number, so $ln(M_t/M_{t-1}) \approx (M_t - M_{t-1})/M_{t-1}$, which is the percentage change. Putting all of this together gives us the fact that the percentage change of a product is the sum of the percentage change of the elements: $\%\Delta(MV) = \%\Delta M + \%\Delta V$.

interest rate is fixed and there is no financial innovation, then velocity will be constant. Fisher also assumed that real output is determined solely by economic resources and production technology, so it too is fixed in the short run. In other words, Fisher assumed that $\%\Delta V = 0$ and $\%\Delta Y = 0$. He concluded that money growth translates directly into inflation, an assertion that is termed the **quantity theory of money**. According to Fisher's theory, changes in the aggregate price level are caused solely by changes in the quantity of money. So if the central bank pours more money into the economy, it drives up the prices of existing goods and services. Raising the quantity of money by 10 percent raises prices by 10 percent; doubling the quantity of money doubles the price level. As Milton Friedman said, *inflation is a monetary phenomenon.*

The fact that individuals require money to complete transactions means that we can reinterpret the quantity theory of money to describe the equilibrium between money demand and money supply. Note that in the classroom economy described earlier, the number of dollars needed equaled the total dollar value of the transactions divided by the number of times each dollar was used. That is, money demanded (M^d) equals the total value of transactions divided by the velocity of money. For the economy as a whole, the demand for money equals nominal GDP divided by velocity:

$$M^d = \frac{1}{V}PY \qquad (5)$$

Next, recall that the supply of money (M^S) is determined by the central bank and the behavior of the banking system. Equilibrium in the money market means that supply equals demand ($M^d = M^S$), which equals the quantity of money in the economy (M). Rearranging equation (5) gives us $MV = PY$. Assuming that velocity and real output are both constant, as Irving Fisher did, we can once again conclude that money growth equals inflation.

The quantity theory of money accounts for some important characteristics of the patterns shown in Figure 20.1. First, it tells us why high inflation and high money growth go together. Second, it explains the tendency for moderate- and low-inflation countries to fall below the 45-degree line in Panel B of Figure 20.1. That is, money growth tends to be higher than inflation in those countries because they are experiencing real growth. Looking at equation (4), we can see that if velocity is constant, then money growth equals the sum of inflation and real growth. At a given level of money growth, the higher the level of real growth is, the lower the level of inflation will be. So in countries that are growing, inflation will be lower than money growth, causing their economies to fall below the 45-degree line in Panel B of Figure 20.1.

The Facts about Velocity

If Irving Fisher was correct in assuming that the velocity of money is constant, his assumption would have important implications for monetary policy. Because the trend in real growth is determined by the structure of the economy and the rate of technological progress, countries could control inflation directly by limiting money growth. This logic led Milton Friedman to conclude that central banks should simply set money growth at a constant rate.[5] That is, policymakers should strive to ensure that the

[5]The original statement of what has come to be known as Friedman's *k-percent rule* is in Milton Friedman, *A Program for Monetary Stability* (New York: Fordham University Press, 1960).

monetary aggregates like M1 and M2 grow at a rate equal to the rate of real growth plus the desired level of inflation. Friedman was aware that the central bank does not control the monetary aggregates precisely and that the link between the monetary base and M1 and M2 fluctuates over time. Policymakers cannot control the money multiplier because it depends both on how much currency individuals decide to hold and how much excess reserves banks decide to maintain. To make the rule viable, he suggested changes in regulations that would limit banks' discretion in creating money and tighten the relationship between the monetary aggregates and the monetary base, reducing fluctuations in the money multiplier. For example, an increase in the reserve requirement or restrictions on the number and types of loans banks could make would have such an effect.

But even if the relationship between the monetary base and the monetary aggregates were constant, Friedman's recommendation that the central bank should keep money growth constant would stabilize inflation only if velocity were constant. In countries with inflation rates above 10 or 20 percent per year, changes in velocity can probably be safely ignored. In those economies, lowering inflation really does require lowering money growth. But in countries where the inflation rate is below 10 percent per year, changes in the velocity of money could have a significant impact on the relationship between money growth and inflation.

How much does the velocity of money fluctuate? To find out, we can look at some data. Panel A of Figure 20.3 shows the velocity of M2 from 1959 to 2018. There appear to be two distinct periods. Until 1998, the trend rises; thereafter, it falls. However, over the full 59 years, the net effect is only a moderate decline of velocity at an annual rate of 0.3 percent. Taken as a whole, these historical data seem reasonably consistent with Fisher's conclusion that *in the long run, the velocity of money is stable, so that controlling inflation means controlling the growth of the monetary aggregates.*

But central bankers are concerned with inflation rates over quarters or years, not half a century. The monetary aggregates, even broad ones, can be useful guides to short-term policy only to the extent that they signal changes in inflation during the periods monetary policymakers care about. And the long-run view in the top panel of Figure 20.3 masks some important short-run movements. To see them, we can look at the four-quarter (short-run) percentage change in M2 velocity, shown in Panel B of Figure 20.3. The shaded bars in the figure represent recessions. Looking at the figure, we can see that in the short run, velocity fluctuates quite a bit, sometimes by very large amounts. The scale of the figure runs from −12 to +8 percent!

The first step in understanding short-run movements in velocity is to examine what happened in the past. Returning to Figure 20.3, notice the increase in velocity in the late 1970s and early 1980s. This was a period when nominal interest rates peaked at more than 20 percent, triggering significant financial innovations, including the introduction of stock and bond mutual funds that allow investors checking privileges. The first of these developments made holding money very costly; the second allowed individuals to economize on the amount of money they held. Neither currency nor the checking accounts of the time paid interest, so with a 10 percent rate of inflation, the real rate of interest on money was −10 percent. Meanwhile, innovations like mutual funds outside of M2 (which allow for small-denomination withdrawals and provide transactions services similar to those of checking accounts) mean that individuals no longer needed to hold as much money. Together these reduced the amount of money individuals held for a given level of transactions, raising the velocity of money. In contrast, since the late 1990s, falling

Figure 20.3 The Velocity of M2, 1959–2018

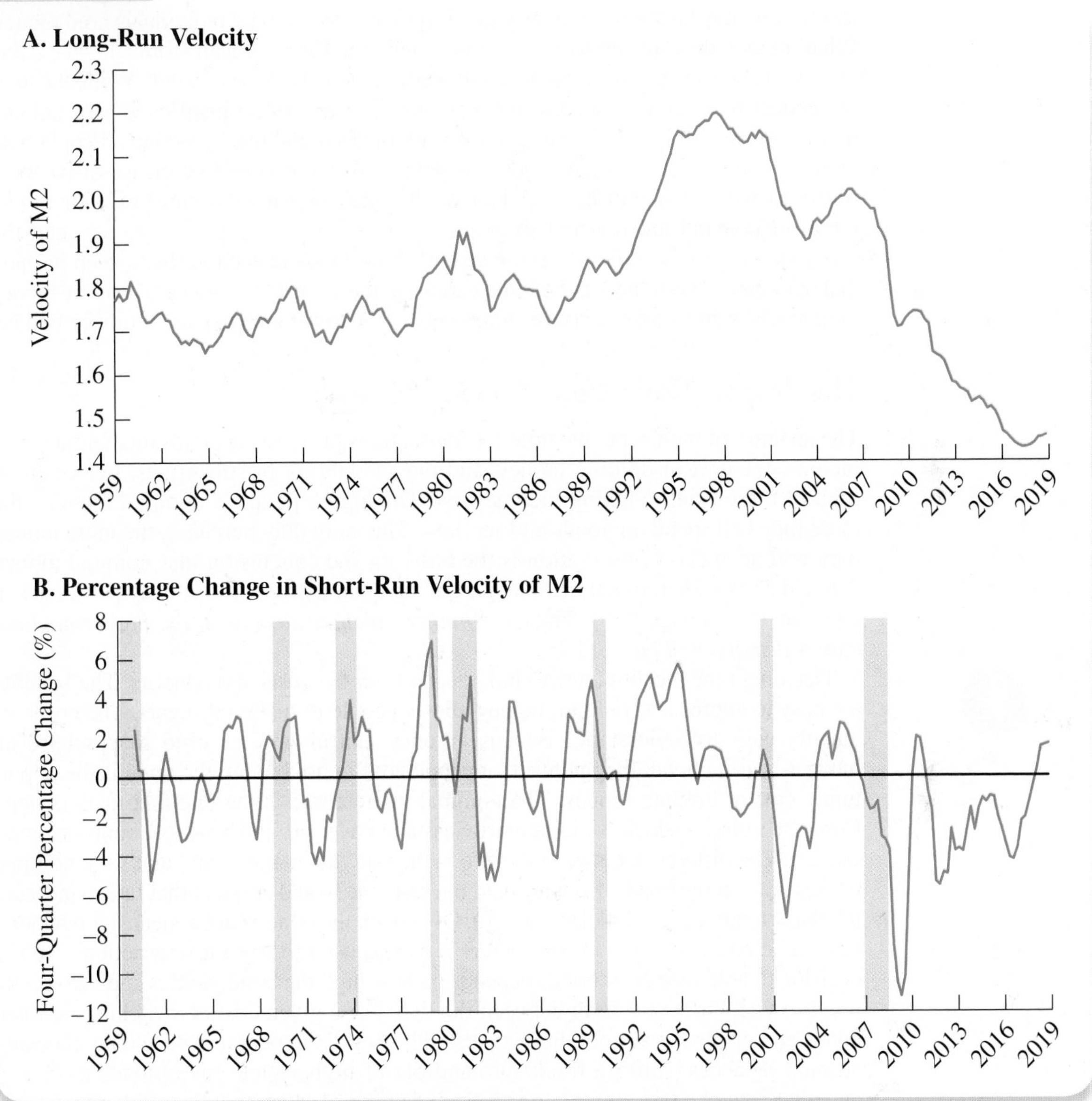

SOURCE: Panel A is seasonally adjusted quarterly U.S. nominal GDP from the Bureau of Economic Analysis, divided by quarterly averages of monthly seasonally adjusted M2 from the Board of Governors of the Federal Reserve System. Panel B is four-quarter percentage changes in the velocity of M2, plotted in Panel A. Shaded areas depict recessions (FRED data code: M2V).

interest rates, combined with innovations that slashed the cost of holding money, lowered M2 velocity.

These data clearly suggest that fluctuations in the velocity of money are tied to changes in people's desire to hold money. To understand and predict changes in the velocity of money, then, policymakers must understand the demand for money. We turn to that topic next.

The Demand for Money

The best way to understand money demand, the determinants of the velocity of money, and the relationship between money and inflation is to ask why individuals hold money. What do they do with the money that is supplied to them? Recall from Chapter 2 that money can be a means of payment, a unit of account, and a store of value. While the unit-of-account function is crucial to the economy, it provides no justification for holding money, so we will ignore it here and focus on the first and third functions. People hold money in order to pay for the goods and services they consume (the means-of-payment function) and as a way of holding their wealth (the store-of-value function). These two forms of demand are referred to as the **transactions demand for money** and the **portfolio demand for money**, respectively.[6] As we look at each of them, keep in mind that our objective is to understand fluctuations in the velocity of money. The more money individuals want to hold (all other things equal), the lower the velocity of money will be.

The Transactions Demand for Money

The quantity of money people hold for transactions purposes depends on their nominal income, the cost of holding money, and the availability of substitutes. Let's look at each of these briefly, taking income first. The higher people's nominal income, the more they will spend on goods and services. The more they purchase, the more money they will need. This observation is the basis for the conclusion that nominal money demand rises with nominal income, part of the quantity theory of money [look back at equation (5) on page 559]. Thus, *the higher nominal income is, the higher nominal money demand will be.*

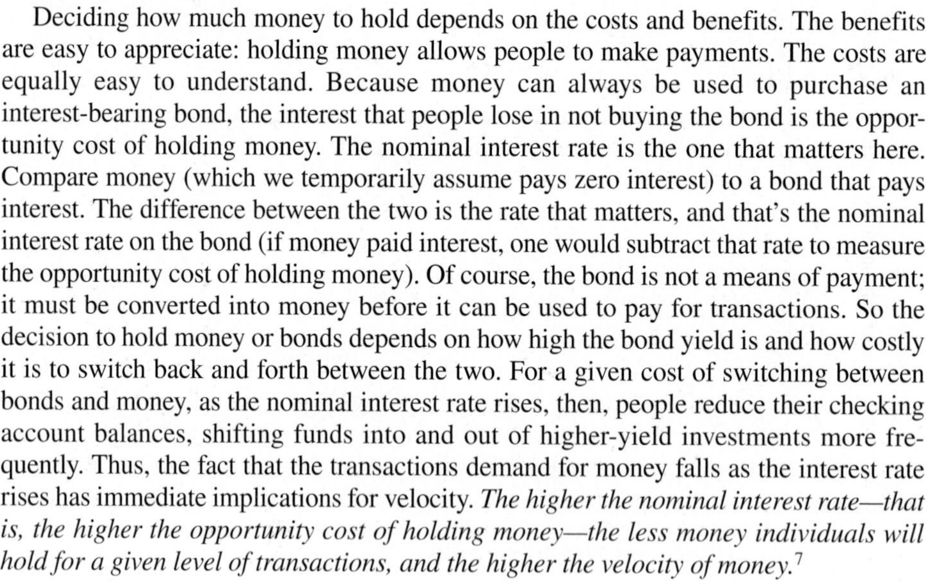

Deciding how much money to hold depends on the costs and benefits. The benefits are easy to appreciate: holding money allows people to make payments. The costs are equally easy to understand. Because money can always be used to purchase an interest-bearing bond, the interest that people lose in not buying the bond is the opportunity cost of holding money. The nominal interest rate is the one that matters here. Compare money (which we temporarily assume pays zero interest) to a bond that pays interest. The difference between the two is the rate that matters, and that's the nominal interest rate on the bond (if money paid interest, one would subtract that rate to measure the opportunity cost of holding money). Of course, the bond is not a means of payment; it must be converted into money before it can be used to pay for transactions. So the decision to hold money or bonds depends on how high the bond yield is and how costly it is to switch back and forth between the two. For a given cost of switching between bonds and money, as the nominal interest rate rises, then, people reduce their checking account balances, shifting funds into and out of higher-yield investments more frequently. Thus, the fact that the transactions demand for money falls as the interest rate rises has immediate implications for velocity. *The higher the nominal interest rate—that is, the higher the opportunity cost of holding money—the less money individuals will hold for a given level of transactions, and the higher the velocity of money.*[7]

[6]This framework for discussing the demand for money was originally developed by John Maynard Keynes and is known as Keynes's liquidity preference theory.

[7]The fact that higher interest rates raise velocity means that they put upward pressure on inflation. And yet, as we will see in the following chapters, monetary policymakers combat high inflation by raising interest rates. The apparent contradiction is resolved by the fact that, while interest rate increases might drive velocity higher, they reduce real growth by even more—enough to make the overall effect the one that we have come to expect.

The ECB's Reference Value for Money Growth
APPLYING THE CONCEPT

At the start of the European Monetary Union in 1999, the monetary policy strategy of the European Central Bank assigned a prominent role to money. Many of the ECB's practices are modeled on those of its predecessor, the German Bundesbank, widely viewed as one of the most successful central banks in the world. In the 1970s, as inflation rose into the double digits in the United States and throughout most of Europe, the Bundesbank kept inflation in Germany at levels that would be acceptable even today. Policymakers there did so by setting annual targets for the monetary aggregates. Several decades later, in the hope that the Bundesbank's reputation for controlling inflation would rub off on them, ECB policymakers decided to set a "quantitative reference value for the growth rate of a broad monetary aggregate."

For the first four years of its existence, the ECB announced what amounted to a target growth rate of 4½ percent for euro-area M3 (the region's equivalent of M2). Officials computed the rate using the percentage-change version of the equation of exchange [equation (4)]. That meant they had to make assumptions about real growth, velocity growth, and the desired level of inflation. They assumed the euro-area economy was growing at a rate of 2 to 2½ percent per year, velocity was declining by ½ to 1 percent per year, and inflation should be 1 to 2 percent annually. Substituting the midpoints of those ranges into equation (4), we get

$$\text{Money growth} - \tfrac{3}{4} = 1\tfrac{1}{2} + 2\tfrac{1}{4},$$

$$\text{so Money growth} = 4\tfrac{1}{2}\text{ percent}$$

The ECB was heavily criticized for its use of money growth targets. Observers claimed that the relationship between money growth and inflation was too unpredictable to be useful in the short run. They argued that the velocity of money in the newly created euro area would be difficult to forecast (see Figure 20.5 on page 571). For a new central bank with no proven record of controlling inflation, they charged, this was a potentially dangerous move that could damage policymakers' credibility. Possibly in response to their critics, in May 2003 ECB policymakers decided to downgrade the role of money growth in their strategy. From then on, money growth would be used as "a crosscheck," not a major part of their strategy. And the Governing Council would no longer review the reference value every year, emphasizing its usefulness only as a long-run benchmark.

This relationship explains why inflation tends to exceed money growth in the high-inflation countries shown in Panel A of Figure 20.1; that is why the points representing high-inflation countries tend to lie above the 45-degree line. At high levels of inflation, when prices are rising at a rate of 1,000 or 1,500 percent a year, money is losing value very quickly. At those levels, the opportunity cost of holding money is equivalent to the cost of inflation, a real return of −1,000 or −1,500 percent a year. People respond to the high cost of holding money by keeping as little of it as possible, getting rid of it as quickly as they can. They purchase durable goods that have a zero real return, which is quite a bit better than the real return of −1,000 percent they would get from holding money. Their frantic spending drives up the velocity of money. The quantity theory of money tells us that with national income held constant, inflation equals money growth plus growth in velocity. Because high inflation brings an increase in velocity, inflation must be higher than money growth in these countries, placing them above the 45-degree line in Panel A of Figure 20.1.

Besides interest rates, *the transactions demand for money is affected by technology*. Financial innovation allows people to limit the amount of money they hold. The best way to think about this is to imagine that innovation reduces the cost of shifting funds from an interest-bearing bond to a checking account. The lower the transactions cost, the more frequently people will shift money from their bond funds to their checking accounts, and the less money people will choose to hold.

This has direct implications for the impact of financial innovation on the transactions demand for money. To see what they are, think about a case in which your bank offers a new kind of product that features free automatic transfers between an account with interest at the level of a bond and your traditional checking account. You sign up for the account, but continue using your old checks and debit card. This new account has the feature that each time you make a purchase, your bank automatically shifts the amount of the purchase from the bonds you are holding to your checking account, where it remains for one day before being paid to your creditor. As a result your checking account will never have more than one day's worth of purchases in it, so you will hold much less money. Financial innovations that lower the cost of shifting money between bonds (or other investments) and a checking account will lower money holdings at a given level of income. The immediate implication is that financial innovations that economize on money holding increase the velocity of your money.

Thus, an increase in the liquidity of stocks, bonds, or any other asset reduces the transactions demand for money. The advent of automatic teller machines and financial products that allow customers to make payments directly from their stock or bond mutual funds, often at no extra cost, means that today people don't need to hold as much cash in their wallets and their checking accounts as their parents and grandparents once did.

Finally, *we all hold money to ensure ourselves against unexpected expenses*. We will include this form of demand, sometimes called the **precautionary demand for money**, as a part of transactions demand. The idea is that emergencies may arise that require immediate payments, for which we hold some amount of money in reserve. The rainy-day fund that an individual keeps to cope with unexpected expenses that can't be postponed is analogous to a bank's excess reserves. The level of precautionary balances we hold in such funds is usually related to our income and our level of expenditures. The higher our normal expenses, the larger our rainy-day funds will be. The precautionary demand for money also rises with risk. While this effect is probably small, the higher the level of uncertainty about the future, the higher the demand for money and the lower the velocity of money will be.

The Portfolio Demand for Money

Money is just one of many financial instruments that we can hold in our investment portfolios. As a store of value, money provides diversification when held along with a wide variety of other assets, including stocks and bonds. To understand the portfolio demand for money, note that a checking account balance or a money-market account is really just a "bond" with zero time to maturity. That means we can use the framework presented in Chapter 6, where we discussed the demand for bonds, to understand the portfolio demand for money.

Recall that the demand for bonds depends on several factors, including wealth, the return relative to alternative investments, expected future interest rates on bonds, risk relative to alternative investments, and liquidity relative to alternative investments. Each of these affects the portfolio demand for money. As wealth increases, individuals increase their holdings of all assets. A prudent person holds a diversified portfolio that includes stocks, bonds, real estate, and money. As wealth rises, the quantity of all these investments, including money, rises with it. So money demand varies directly with wealth. Note that this rule applies even at a fixed level of expenditures: A rich person who has the same expenses as a poor person will still hold more money.

In studying the demand for bonds, we noted that an investor's desire to hold any specific financial instrument depends on how well it compares with alternative investments. The higher the expected return relative to the alternatives, the higher the demand for an asset will be. The same is true for money: The higher its return relative to the alternatives, the higher the demand. Put slightly differently, a decline in bond yields will increase the portfolio demand for money.

Because expectations that interest rates will change in the future are related to the expected return on a bond, they will affect the demand for money as well. To understand why, remember that the price of a bond varies inversely with the interest rate. When interest rates rise, bond prices drop and bondholders suffer a capital loss. So if you think interest rates are likely to rise, bonds will become less attractive than money to you. (Recall that the prices of short-term bonds fluctuate less than the prices of long-term bonds. Money is the ultimate short-term bond because it has zero time to maturity.) As a result, you will sell the bonds in your portfolio and increase your money holdings—at least until interest rates stop rising. When interest rates are expected to rise, then, money demand goes up.

Next there is risk. In our discussion of bonds, we noted that a decline in risk relative to that of alternative investments increases the demand for bonds. While the riskiness of money can decrease, what usually happens is that the riskiness of other assets increases, driving up the demand for money.[8] Looking back at Panel B of Figure 20.3, we can see that during and after the financial crisis of 2007–2009, the velocity of M2 plunged. One cause was an increase in uncertainty (risk), which drove investors to shift their funds into money.

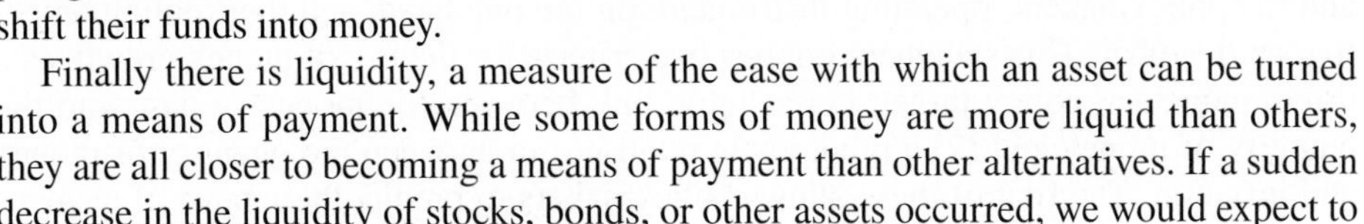

Finally there is liquidity, a measure of the ease with which an asset can be turned into a means of payment. While some forms of money are more liquid than others, they are all closer to becoming a means of payment than other alternatives. If a sudden decrease in the liquidity of stocks, bonds, or other assets occurred, we would expect to see an increase in the demand for money.

Table 20.1 summarizes all of the factors that influence the demand for money.

Table 20.1 Determinants of Money Demand: Factors That Cause Individuals to Hold More Money

	Transactions Demand for Money
Nominal income	The higher nominal income, the higher the demand for money.
Interest rates	The lower interest rates, the higher the demand for money.
Availability of alternative means of payment	The less available alternative means of payment, the higher the demand for money.
	Portfolio Demand for Money
Wealth	As wealth rises, the demand for money goes up.
Return relative to alternatives	As the return on alternatives falls, the demand for money goes up.
Expected future interest rates	As expected future interest rates rise, the demand for money goes up.
Risk relative to alternatives	As the riskiness of alternatives rises, the demand for money goes up.
Liquidity relative to alternatives	As the liquidity of alternatives falls, the demand for money goes up.

[8]To grasp why money can be risky, think of an example in which the nominal interest rate on money is zero (that is literally true for cash and nearly true for many bank deposits). When money pays no interest, its return is minus inflation. That is, money loses value at the rate of inflation. The less certain inflation is, the more uncertain the return on money, and the more risky it is. So inflation uncertainty increases the riskiness of holding money.

Targeting Money Growth in a Low-Inflation Environment

So here is where we stand. In the long run, inflation is tied to money growth. In a high-inflation environment, where money growth and inflation are both running higher than 100 percent, moderate variations in the growth of velocity are a mere annoyance. What is important is the resolve of central bank officials (and politicians) to bring inflation down. There is no magic to it; the only solution is to reduce money growth.

In a low-inflation environment, controlling inflation is not so simple. The quantity theory of money tells us that our ability to use money growth as a policy guide depends on the stability of the velocity of money. In the United States, the velocity of the broad monetary aggregate M2 appears sufficiently stable for M2 to serve as a benchmark for controlling inflation over the long run—over periods of several decades. In the short run, the velocity of money varies substantially. Yet the mere fact that velocity fluctuates is not reason enough to dismiss money growth as a policy target.

In theory, an intermediate target can be useful when stable links exist between it and the policymakers' operating instrument, on the one hand, and their policy objective on the other. This statement implies two criteria for the use of money growth as a direct monetary policy target: (1) a stable link between the monetary base and the quantity of money and (2) a predictable relationship between the quantity of money and inflation. The first of these allows policymakers to predict the impact of changes in the central bank's balance sheet on the quantity of money. The second allows them to translate changes in money growth into changes in inflation. These criteria cannot be solely qualitative in nature; central bankers need numerical estimates of these relationships. Policymakers must be able to say that a 1 percent change in the monetary base will generate an x percent change in a monetary aggregate like M2, which will then translate into a y percent change in inflation, and over what time period. The relationship between money demand and its determinants listed in Table 20.1 must be stable and predictable—a problem for U.S. policymakers.

The Instability of U.S. Money Demand

To study the demand for money quantitatively, we will focus on the impact of the two factors that affect the transactions demand for money, nominal income and interest rates. Recalling the logic of the equation of exchange [equation (3) on page 558], we can conclude that the first factor, nominal income, is roughly proportional to money demand. Doubling people's nominal income means doubling the dollar value of the transactions they engage in, which requires double the original amount of money. That means we can focus on nominal income divided by the quantity of money, which equals velocity. This brings us to the second factor, interest rates (or more precisely, the opportunity cost of holding money). Is there a stable relationship between the velocity of money and the opportunity cost of holding it?

The data displayed in Figure 20.4 bear directly on this question. The figure shows the velocity of M2 on the vertical axis and the opportunity cost of holding M2 on the horizontal axis. The opportunity cost of M2 is defined as the yield on a three-month U.S. Treasury bill (an alternative asset) minus the return on holding M2, as computed by the Federal Reserve Bank of St. Louis. Note that this opportunity cost is a measure of the real return that individuals give up when they decide to

Figure 20.4 M2 Velocity and Opportunity Cost, 1979–2018

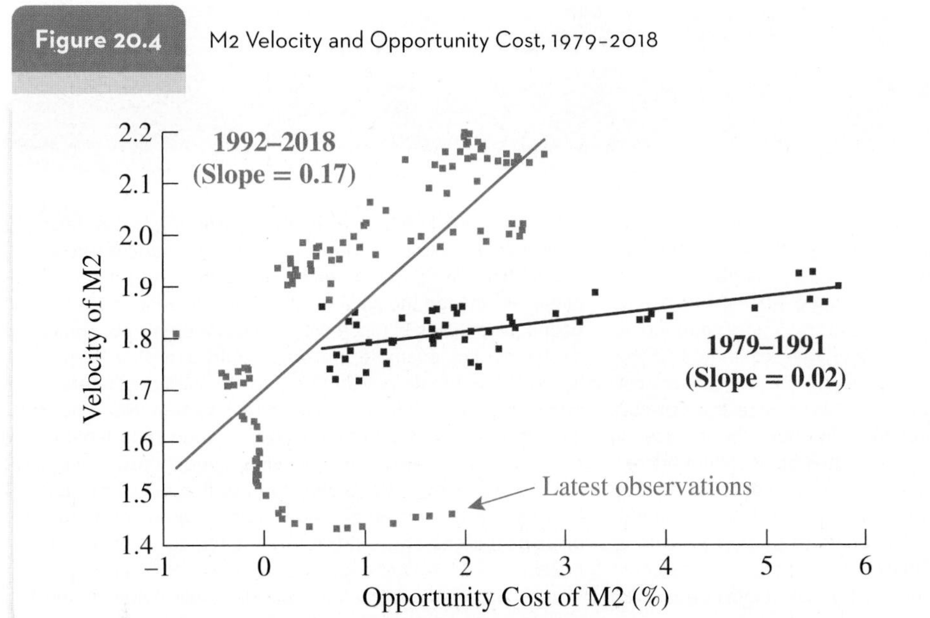

Data are quarterly. Velocity was computed as the ratio of nominal GDP to M2. The opportunity cost of M2 was computed as the three-month Treasury bill rate less the rate of return on M2. The two solid lines are regression lines fitted to the separate samples.

SOURCE: Federal Reserve Bank of St. Louis (FRED data codes: M2V, TB3MS, and M2OWN).

hold M2 rather than a three-month Treasury bill. Each point on the figure represents a particular quarter. They fall into at least two distinct groups. The first group, shown as dark blue squares, covers the decade of the 1980s. The second group, shown as red squares, covers the 1990s through 2018. What we want to know is whether an increase in the opportunity cost of holding money can be used to forecast an increase in velocity. (Recall that higher interest rates raise the opportunity cost of holding money, reducing the demand for money at a given level of income and increasing its velocity.)

The answer to our question is yes, there is a relationship between the velocity of money and the opportunity cost of holding money, but that relationship shifted quite a bit between the two periods. To see how much it shifted, consider an increase from 1 to 2 percent in the opportunity cost of holding M2. In the 1980s, the implication of a 1 percent increase in opportunity cost was an increase of almost 1¼ percent in the velocity of M2, from roughly 1.79 to 1.82. Since the early 1990s, the same change in opportunity cost drove velocity up 9 percent, from 1.88 to 2.05. That is, the sensitivity of money demand to a change in the interest rate rose by a factor greater than seven. The relationship between money demand and interest rates that held in the 1980s broke down in the 1990s. Using the relationship from the 1980s as a basis for policymaking in the 1990s and thereafter would not have produced the desired result. (Since 2015, the slope of the money demand curve has again flattened—see the "latest observations" in Figure 20.4—but it is unclear how long this new pattern will persist.)

There are several possible explanations for the instability of U.S. money demand over these three decades. The primary one has to do with the introduction of

Using Statistical Models in Policy Evaluation
TOOLS OF THE TRADE

For policymakers to do their jobs, they need to know how changes in policy will affect their objectives. An essential question in any monetary policy decision is how much to adjust interest rates in order to keep prices stable and economic growth high. Unlike theory, policymaking is about numbers; it requires quantitative estimates of the relative impact of alternative policies. These estimates are based on statistical models that summarize the correlations among economic variables. To obtain the necessary information, economists at the central bank collect historical information and analyze it in an attempt to determine how past changes in policy have affected the economy. Their estimates allow policymakers to answer questions such as "If we raise the federal funds rate by one percentage point, how much lower will the rate of inflation be two years from now?"

Such an exercise may seem straightforward, but it has pitfalls. For an economic prediction to be valid, it must be based on data drawn from a historical period in which the same set of policies—sometimes called the policy *framework* or the policy *regime*—was in place. If it isn't, the results can be seriously misleading. A sports analogy will help make the point. In the United States, a football team has four downs to make 10 yards, but in Canada, a football team gets only three downs before being forced to give up the ball. As a result, Canadian football teams regularly kick the ball away on the third down. Needless to say, no one would think of using data from Canadian football games to predict third-down behavior in a U.S. game.

In the mid-1970s, Nobel Prize–winning economist Robert Lucas observed that what is true in sports is true in economics.* In the same way that altering the rules of a game will change the players' strategies, altering the set of economic policies in place will change people's economic decisions. For example, no one would use data from a fixed exchange rate period to model the impact of interest rate policy in a floating exchange rate system. Nor would anyone use information from a period when central bankers targeted money growth, allowing interest rates to vary, to predict the impact of a shift to targeting interest rates. Economic and financial decisions, Lucas noted, are based on expectations about the future, including what policymakers will do. Any change in policymakers' behavior will change people's expectations, altering their behavior and the observed relationships among economic variables.

This observation, known as the **Lucas critique**, has had a profound influence on the way policymakers formulate their recommendations. It implies that in predicting the effects of a change in policy, policymakers must take into account how people's economic behavior will change with it. To understand the impact of policies never before implemented, Lucas emphasized, policymakers must rely heavily on economic theory, modeling people's reactions to changes in their environment.

*The original Lucas critique is described in Robert E. Lucas Jr., "Econometric Policy Evaluation: A Critique," *Carnegie-Rochester Conference Series on Public Policy* 1 (1976), pp. 19–46.

financial instruments that paid higher returns than money but could still be used as means of payment. While officials have tried to account for the new instruments by changing the composition of the monetary aggregates, money demand continues to appear unstable.

A second explanation for the shift in the relationship between the velocity of M2 and its opportunity cost has to do with changes in mortgage refinancing rates. As long-term interest rates fell throughout the 1990s and into the 21st century, they spurred periods of intense activity in the mortgage market. Because every U.S. mortgage comes with the right to repay early, the holder of a conventional 30-year, fixed-rate mortgage can terminate the loan contract at any time by simply repaying the balance. When mortgage interest rates fall dramatically, large numbers of people pay off their old, high-interest mortgages and replace them with new, low-interest mortgages. The incentive to refinance a mortgage can be significant, even for what might seem a small decline in interest rates.

When a mortgage is refinanced, it creates demand for money in several ways. Many people who are refinancing take the opportunity to remove some of their equity in their home. The proceeds go into liquid deposit accounts, which are part of M2, until they are spent on home renovations or other major purchases. In addition, funds for the new mortgage must be collected from investors and transferred to holders of the old mortgage. Along the way, they flow through an account that is part of M2. So when mortgage interest rates fall, M2 tends to grow rapidly. Once interest rates stabilize and the wave of refinancing subsides, M2 settles down and even shrinks. But in the meantime, velocity fluctuates.

The breakdown in the relationship between money demand and interest rates that occurred in the United States during the early 1990s drove researchers back to their computers to build better, more robust statistical models. It also continues to serve as a cautionary note for policymakers.

Targeting Money Growth: The Fed and the ECB

Though today virtually no central bank targets money growth, the practice was common in the 1970s. In the United States, the FOMC first adopted explicit objectives for money growth on January 15, 1970. Five years later, Congress passed a law directing the chair of the Federal Reserve Board to make quarterly appearances to testify to the Fed's money growth targets for the coming year. In addition, the Full Employment and Balanced Growth Act, passed in 1978, required the Fed to publish ranges for money growth in its twice-yearly *Monetary Policy Report to Congress.*

But announcing an objective is one thing; achieving it is something else. The FOMC rarely hit its money growth targets. Finally in July 2000, after the requirements of the 1978 legislation had expired, the committee stopped publishing them. A number of observers, including some inside the Federal Reserve, have argued that policymakers could have hit their money growth targets using procedures that were then in place. But to do so would have meant adjusting the federal funds rate target frequently, and by large amounts—something policymakers were unwilling to do. By the summer of 2003, even Milton Friedman had given up. "The use of the quantity of money as a target has not been a success," he conceded. "I'm not sure I would as of today push it as hard as I once did."[9]

European monetary policymakers view matters differently. As we saw at the beginning of the chapter and in Applying the Concept: The ECB's Reference Value for Money Growth on page 563, the ECB's Governing Council periodically announces a money growth rate that is intended to serve as a long-run reference value. Large deviations from this reference value require an explanation. The difference of opinion between the Fed and the ECB on this matter can be traced to their divergent views on the stability of money demand. Researchers who study the demand for money in the euro area have concluded that it is stable, which implies that changes in velocity are predictable. This assumption is the justification for the ECB's emphasis on money in its monetary policy framework.

The ECB's strategy is based on data like those shown in Figure 20.5 on page 571. From 1995 to 2018, the velocity of euro-area M3 (the equivalent of U.S. M2) declined from 0.38 to less than 0.24. While short-run fluctuations in velocity were significant, European policymakers point to the tendency of velocity to return to its long-run downward trend over periods of a few years. (Recall that in computing the ECB's reference value for money growth, described in Applying the Concept on page 563,

[9]Simon London, "Lunch with the FT: Milton Friedman," *Financial Times,* June 6, 2003.

We Are Still Overstating Inflation

MONEY AND BANKING BLOG

More than twenty years ago, a government-appointed group of experts—the "Boskin Commission"—concluded that the U.S. consumer price index (CPI) systematically overstated inflation by 0.8 to 1.6 percentage points each year. Taking these findings to heart, the Bureau of Labor Statistics (BLS) got to work reducing this bias so that, by the mid-2000s, experts felt it had fallen by as much as half a percentage point.

More recently, the concern about overestimation of inflation has resurfaced because of the way we (mis) measure changes in the quality of information technology (IT), digital content, and health care.

Price measurement is central to our understanding of the economy. To measure economic growth, we use prices to distinguish nominal from real quantities. We also use prices to deflate nominal incomes to measure the evolution of living standards. And, considering price stability to be the foundation of sustainable and balanced growth, central bankers obsess over whether inflation is too high or too low.

The CPI tends to overstate inflation for two main reasons: (1) Consumers are continually shifting their "consumption basket," usually toward goods that have become relatively less expensive, while the composition of the measured basket changes less frequently. And (2) new welfare-enhancing goods are included in the CPI only with a significant lag (if at all), while the improvements they provide are difficult to estimate and often understated.

Persistently overstating inflation has important consequences. So long as the upward bias is constant, central bankers can set their inflation targets accordingly. But price indexes are used to adjust entitlement benefits without correcting for any bias. And wage measurement exemplifies how the sustained upward bias of the CPI can affect public discourse, as it means the median *real* wage may have risen substantially over past decades, in contrast to reported stagnation.

There is good reason to think that the price mismeasurement problem has gotten worse in recent years. Failure to fully reflect quality advances has probably increased the overstatement of prices in IT (computer hardware and software) and health care. In the case of IT hardware, for example, the graphics card in a 2018-model iPhone could make nearly 3,500 times the number of floating point operations per second (FLOPS) as a 1975 Cray-1 supercomputer, which (adjusting for inflation) cost something like 100,000 times as much as the phone. If we imagine FLOPS as a consumer product, that represents an almost incomprehensible price decline.[*] In the case of software, vast improvements and new programs (like Google Maps) are often available free of charge; and this free digital content has recently expanded far beyond what broadcast radio and TV long provided.

But, perhaps surprisingly, the bias in IT probably is *not* a big source of overall consumer price mismeasurement. Households spend less than 3.4 percent of their budget on all IT goods and services. As a result, even a 10-percentage-point overstatement of IT inflation would result in less than a 0.4 percent overstatement of overall inflation.

Health care is potentially more important: its weight in the consumer price index is 8.6 percent.[†] Quality changes in both the health care process and the effectiveness of treatment have, as in IT, been enormous. In terms of process, hospitals and clinics now offer online medical histories, including nearly instantaneous test results, allowing

statisticians assumed that velocity would decline between ½ and 1 percent a year. In fact, the annual rate of decline has averaged more than 2 percent.)

Even given this difference in their emphasis on money growth, the ECB and the Fed have both chosen interest rates as their conventional operating target. The reason is that interest rates are the link between the financial system and the real economy. Changes in interest rates are one of the primary tools central bankers have for influencing the economy. By keeping interest rates stable, policymakers can insulate the real economy from disturbances that arise in the financial system. For example, the payments system can change quickly. The introduction of more liquid financial instruments or newly configured electronic systems can have a direct impact on the doctors to proceed rapidly with life- and limb-saving steps. These reduce hospital stays and patient recovery time, increasing the quality of care dramatically.

As rough indicators of the improved effectiveness of medical treatment, consider just two of many successes: the death rate from heart disease in the United States plunged by one-third in the decade to 2013. And today we speak of "bad cancers" because medicine has advanced to the point where we can cure many of them. Not long ago, *all* cancers were bad.

These quality improvements have contributed to the *reported* decline in health care cost inflation—from an average of more than 6 percent per year from 1975 to 2010 to closer to 2¾ percent since then. The high share of health care in the consumption basket means that from 2010 to 2018, the drop in health care inflation reduced overall CPI inflation by 0.3 percentage point per year. Might the *true* reduction have been even greater? Probably, but it is difficult to prove.

The bottom line is that the CPI has long overstated inflation, so the rise of living standards has been understated for decades. In recent years, IT price mismeasurement has probably made the bias worsen slightly. However, because U.S. consumers spend much more on health care than on IT, the CPI impact of understating quality improvements has been, and will likely remain, much greater in health care than in IT. So as we work to improve the quality of inflation data, the health sector is where we should be putting our effort.

*Recent reported readings could be understating actual hardware deflation by as much as 7 percentage points. See David M. Byrne, Stephen D. Oliner, and Daniel E. Sichel, "How Fast Are Semiconductor Prices Falling?" NBER Working Paper No. 21074, April 2015.

†Health care outlays constitute a whopping 17 percent of personal consumption expenditures, which include payments by insurers, but the CPI excludes spending that is not out of pocket.

Figure 20.5 Velocity of Euro-Area M3, 1995–2018

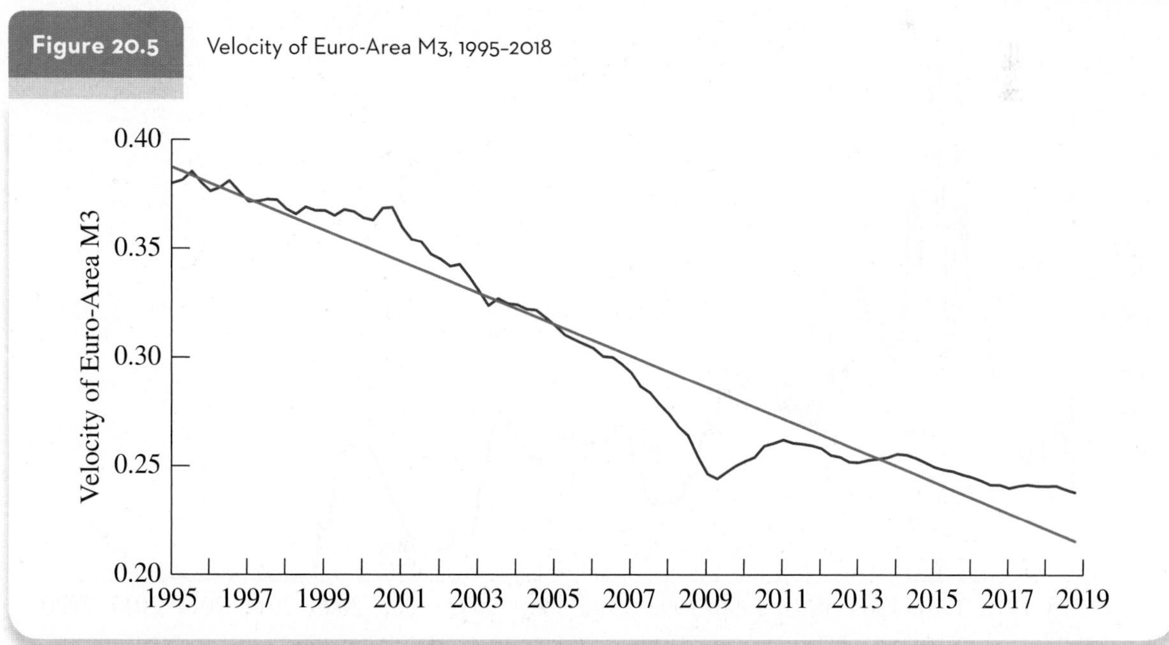

Velocity is measured as nominal GDP divided by M3 for the 19 countries of the euro area as of 2019. The red line is a simple time trend.
SOURCE: Eurostat and International Monetary Fund (FRED data codes: EUNNGDP and MABMM301EZQ189S).

way money is used and therefore on velocity. If policymakers wanted to, they could keep money growth constant in the face of such innovations. But doing so would create volatility in interest rates, which could destabilize the real economy. This point was made in Chapter 18, which discussed the rationale for choosing the interest rate rather than the quantity of reserves as an operating instrument. There we noted that the best way to keep changes in reserves from influencing interest rates and affecting the real economy is to target interest rates. While inflation is tied to money growth in the long run, interest rates are the tool policymakers use to stabilize inflation in the short run.

The idea that targeting money growth destabilizes interest rates is not just a theoretical possibility. For roughly three years from October 1979 to October 1982, as part of the effort to reduce inflation from more than 10 percent the FOMC used reserves to target money growth, allowing the federal funds rate to fluctuate. Figure 20.6 shows the results. The shaded area represents the period when the FOMC targeted the quantity of money. Notice how volatile the interest rate was during that three-year period. In fact, over intervals as short as three to four months, the federal funds rate fluctuated as much as 10 percentage points, rising from 11½ percent in September 1979 to 20 percent in March 1980, then falling to 10 percent in July 1980 before climbing back to 20 percent in December 1980. This sort of volatility, caused by policymakers' inability to forecast shifts in the velocity of money, would surely damage the real economy. Realizing the problem, policymakers have turned to the only viable alternative: targeting and smoothing fluctuations in interest rates. In the next chapter, we will study how they use interest rates to stabilize inflation and growth.

Figure 20.6 The Federal Funds Rate, 1975–2019

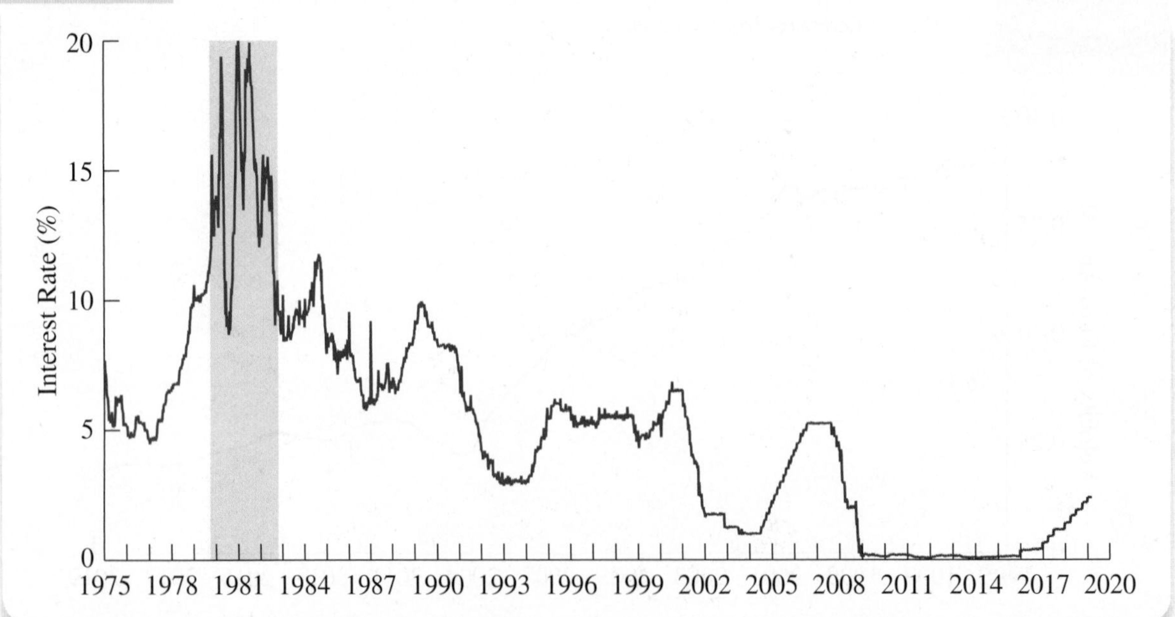

The shaded bar represents the period from October 1979 to October 1982, when the Federal Reserve targeted the quantity of money.
SOURCE: Data are the effective federal funds rate, weekly, from the Board of Governors of the Federal Reserve System (FRED data code: FF).

Key Terms

equation of exchange, 558
Lucas critique, 568
nominal gross domestic product, 558
portfolio demand for money, 562
precautionary demand for money, 564
quantity theory of money, 559
transactions demand for money, 562
velocity of money, 557

Using FRED: Codes for Data in This Chapter

Data Series	FRED Data Code
M1	M1SL
M2	M2SL
U.S. consumer price index	CPIAUCSL
Brazil consumer price index	BRACPIALLMINMEI
Mexico consumer price index	MEXCPIALLQINMEI
Mexico M1	MYAGM1MXM189N
Nominal GDP	GDP
M2 velocity	M2V
M1 velocity	M1V
U.S. historical velocity (annual)	A14187USA163NNBR
U.S. chained consumer price index	SUUR0000SA0
GDP deflator	GDPDEF
M2 own rate of return	M2OWN
U.S. 3-month Treasury bill rate	TB3MS
Federal funds rate	FEDFUNDS

Chapter Lessons

1. There is a strong positive correlation between money growth and inflation.
   a. Every country that has had high rates of sustained money growth has experienced high rates of inflation.
   b. At very high levels of inflation, inflation exceeds money growth.
   c. At moderate to low inflation, money growth exceeds inflation.
   d. Ultimately, the central bank controls the rate of money growth.
2. The quantity theory of money explains the link between inflation and money growth.
   a. The equation of exchange tells us that:
      i. The quantity of money times the velocity of money equals nominal GDP.
      ii. Money growth plus velocity growth equals inflation plus real growth.
   b. If velocity and real growth were constant, the central bank could control inflation by keeping money growth constant.
   c. In the long run, velocity is stable, so controlling inflation means controlling money growth.
   d. In the short run, the velocity of money is volatile.

To learn more about the changing financial system, visit www.moneyandbanking.com.

3. Shifts in velocity are caused by changes in the demand for money.
   a. The transactions demand for money depends on income, interest rates, and the availability of alternative means of payment.
   b. The portfolio demand for money depends on the same factors that determine the demand for bonds: wealth, expected future interest rates, and the return, risk, and liquidity associated with money relative to alternative investments.
4. The quantity theory of money and theories of money demand have a number of implications for monetary policy.
   a. Countries with high inflation can reduce inflation by controlling money growth.
   b. Countries with low inflation can control inflation by targeting money growth only if the demand for money is stable in the short run.
   c. In the United States, the relationship between the velocity of M2 and its opportunity cost (the yield on an alternative investment) has proven unstable over time.
   d. The instability of money demand in the United States has caused Federal Reserve policymakers to pay less attention to money growth than to interest rates.
   e. In the euro area, ECB officials view money demand as relatively stable, so they pay more attention to money growth than the Fed does.
   f. Regardless of the stability of money demand, central banks target interest rates to insulate the real economy from disturbances in the financial sector.

Conceptual and Analytical Problems

1. Why is inflation higher than money growth in high-inflation countries and lower than money growth in low-inflation countries? *(LO1)*

2.* Explain why giving an independent central bank control over the quantity of money in the economy should reduce the occurrences of periods of extremely high inflation, especially in developing economies. *(LO1)*

3. If velocity were constant at 1.5 while M2 rose from $11 trillion to $12 trillion in a single year, what would happen to nominal GDP? If real GDP rose 2.09 percent, what would be the level of inflation? *(LO2)*

4. According to Irving Fisher, when velocity and output are fixed, the quantity theory of money implies that inflation equals money growth. What does the quantity theory imply for inflation in the long run in an economy with growing output and stable velocity? *(LO2)*

5. If velocity were predictable but not constant, would a monetary policy that fixed the growth rate of money work? *(LO2)*

6. Describe the impact of financial innovations on the demand for money and velocity. *(LO3)*

7. Suppose that expected inflation rises by 2 percent at the same time that the yields on money and on nonmoney assets both rise by 2 percent. What will happen to the demand for money? What if expected inflation rose by only 3 percent? What if the yield on nonmoney assets rose by 4 percent? *(LO3)*

8.* Explain how money growth reduces the purchasing power of money. *(LO2)*

*Indicates more difficult problems.

9. Provide arguments both for and against the Federal Reserve's adoption of a target growth rate for M2. What assumptions would be necessary to compute such a target rate? *(LO1)*
10. Explain why we observed a fall in the velocity of M2 during the financial crisis of 2007–2009. *(LO3)*
11. Comment on the role given to money in the monetary policy strategy of the ECB. *(LO1)*
12. Countries A and B both have the same money growth rate and in both countries, real output is constant. In Country A velocity is constant while in Country B velocity has fallen. In which country will inflation be higher? Explain why. *(LO2)*
13. Consider a country where the level of excess reserves fluctuates widely and unpredictably. Would such a country be a good candidate for a money growth rule to guide monetary policy? Explain your answer. *(LO4)*
14. Draw a graph of money demand and money supply with the nominal interest rate on the vertical axis and money balances on the horizontal axis. Assume the central bank is following a money growth rule where it sets the growth rate of money supply to zero. Use the graph to illustrate how fluctuations in velocity imply that targeting money growth results in greater volatility of interest rates. *(LO4)*
15. In a chart of money demand and money supply with the nominal interest rate on the vertical axis, show how a central bank could use its control over the quantity of money to target a particular level of interest rate in the face of changes in velocity. *(LO4)*
16. Why might targeting the money supply lead to lower output growth than targeting the rate of interest? *(LO4)*
17. Which of the following factors would increase the transactions demand for money? Explain your choices. *(LO3)*
    a. Lower nominal interest rates.
    b. Rumors that a computer virus had invaded the ATM network.
    c. A fall in nominal income.
18. Which of the following factors would increase the portfolio demand for money? Explain your choices. *(LO3)*
    a. A new website allows you to liquidate your stock holdings quickly and cheaply.
    b. You expect future interest rates to rise.
    c. A financial crisis is looming.
19.* Suppose a central bank is trying to decide whether to target money growth. Proponents of the move are confident that the new policy would be successful as, under the existing policy regime, they observed a stable statistical relationship between money growth and inflation. What warning might you issue to the central bank when it asks your advice? *(LO1)*
20. If "inflation is always and everywhere a monetary phenomenon," why did the huge expansions of central bank money by the Federal Reserve, the ECB, and the Bank of Japan between 2007 and 2015 not result in high inflation in those economies? *(LO1)*
21. Why might the ECB place somewhat greater emphasis than the Federal Reserve on money growth rates in discussing monetary policy? *(LO4)*

*Indicates more difficult problems.

Data Exploration connect

For general information on using Federal Reserve Economic Data (FRED) online, visit www.mhhe.com/moneyandbanking6e.com *and refer to the FRED resources.*

1. A scatterplot may reveal a relationship between two indicators. Construct a scatterplot of annual data beginning in 1959 for inflation and money growth. Measure these as the percent change from a year ago of consumer prices (FRED code: CPIAUCSL) and M2 (FRED code: M2SL), respectively. Then, display a second scatterplot of annual data beginning in 1959 for inflation (measured as before) and the federal funds rate (FRED code: FEDFUNDS). Which indicator is more closely linked to inflation: money growth or the interest rate? Does that tell us which policy instrument is better? *(LO2)*
2. Plot the percent change from a year ago of the velocity of money (FRED code: A14187USA163NNBR) between 1922 and 1939. Compare the typical scales of the velocity declines during the recessions of this interwar period and the velocity declines during the recessions shown in Panel B of Figure 20.3. Were the 1929–1933 and 2007–2009 periods special? What role might wealth have played in these two episodes? *(LO3)*
3. Plot annually since 1950 the reciprocal of the consumer price index (FRED code: CPIAUCSL) to see how inflation erodes the purchasing power of money. To start with an initial value of 1.0, in the Units dropdown box in FRED, select the option "Index (Scale to value to 100 for the chosen date)" and then apply the formula "(1/a) × 100." If a dollar bought one unit of goods and serves in 1950, as of which year did the dollar buy only one-half unit? As of 2019, how many units of goods and services did a dollar buy? *(LO1)*
4. In Figure 20.1, which compares money growth and inflation over an extended time period, would Mexico be above or below the 45-degree line? Plot since 1987 on a quarterly basis the percent change from a year ago of the consumer price index (FRED code: MEXCPIALLQINMEI) and M1 (FRED code: MYAGM1MXM189N) in Mexico. Then download the data and calculate the averages of these inflation and money growth measures. Where would Mexico appear on Figure 20.1? Were there episodes since 1987 when Mexico was on the other side of the 45-degree line? If so, why? *(LO2)*
5. In theory, the velocity of money should rise with the cost of holding it. To assess the theory, plot the opportunity cost of holding M2—defined as the difference between the three-month Treasury bill rate (FRED code: TB3MS) and the interest rate on M2 components (FRED code: M2OWN)—and (on the right scale) the percent change from a year ago of M2 velocity (FRED code: M2V). What do you conclude? *(LO4)*

Chapter

21 Output, Inflation, and Monetary Policy

Learning Objectives

After reading this chapter, you should be able to:

LO1 Describe the determinants of output and inflation in the long run.

LO2 Show the role of monetary policy in the dynamic aggregate demand curve.

LO3 Characterize aggregate supply in the short run and the long run.

LO4 Explain short-run and long-run equilibrium using the dynamic aggregate demand and aggregate supply curves.

Governments publish economic data constantly. Almost every day we receive new information on some aspect of the economy with news stories quoting experts on what it all means. Is inflation on the way up? Is the economy on the verge of recession? An important part of such analyses is speculation about the impact of the new data on monetary policy. In our discussion of central banking, we noted that conjecture about policymakers' likely reaction fills the financial news. And no wonder, for members of the committees that set interest rates—the FOMC in the United States and the Governing Council in the euro area—always tie their policy actions to current and expected future economic conditions.

Needless to say, everyone is preoccupied with monetary policy. While traders in the financial markets are trying to outguess each other, to make a profit by betting on the next move in interest rates, the rest of us are just hoping the central bank will succeed in keeping inflation low and real growth high. How do policymakers do it? What is the mechanism through which changes in the interest rate influence inflation and output? And what are the limits of policymakers' power to control the economy?

As we just learned in Chapter 20, in the long run, inflation is tied to money growth. Over periods of several decades, high money growth leads to high inflation. Furthermore, long-run growth depends on technology, the size of the capital stock, the number of people who can work, and the skills of the workers. But over shorter periods of months or years, changes in the rate of money growth tell us little about future movements in the inflation rate. That is especially true when inflation is low, as it has been throughout much of the industrialized world over the past two decades.

The objective of this chapter is to understand fluctuations in inflation and real output and how central banks use conventional interest rate policy to stabilize them. To do it, we will develop a macroeconomic model of fluctuations in the business cycle in which monetary policy plays a central role. From this, we will see that short-run movements in inflation and output can arise from two sources: shifts in the quantity of aggregate output demanded (i.e., changes in consumption, investment, government spending, or net exports) and shifts in the quantity of aggregate output supplied (that is, changes in normal production and in the use of that capacity). Modern monetary policymakers work to reduce the volatility that each of these creates by adjusting the target interest rate.

We will develop our macroeconomic model in three steps, beginning with a description of long-run equilibrium. We then move on to derive the *dynamic aggregate demand curve,* which shows the quantity of real output demanded by those people who use it at each level of inflation, that is, how real output is related to changes in the prices, not just their level. Here we will see the critical role of monetary policy. Then, we introduce aggregate supply, which is the level of real output supplied by firms at each level of inflation. There is both a short-run and a long-run version of the aggregate supply curve. In the short run, equating dynamic aggregate demand with short-run aggregate supply gives us the equilibrium levels of output and inflation. Business cycles are movements in this short-run equilibrium. And because we have built monetary policy into the model, we will see how modern central banks can use their policy tools to stabilize short-run fluctuations in output and inflation. (The appendix to this chapter contains an algebraic version of the model.)

As we proceed through the chapter, keep in mind that our ultimate objective is to understand how modern central bankers determine the level or range of the target interest rate. When policymakers change the target rate, what are they reacting to, and what is the impact on the economy?

Output and Inflation in the Long Run

A useful way to understand fluctuations in the business cycle is as deviations from some benchmark or long-run equilibrium level. The booms and recessions that make up business cycles are temporary movements away from this long-run equilibrium level. So we begin with the following question: What would the levels of inflation and output be if nothing unexpected happened for a long time? The answer to this question is that in the long run, current output equals **potential output**—the level of output given existing technology and normal use of resources—and the inflation rate equals the level implied by the rate of money growth.

Potential Output

Potential output is what the economy is capable of producing when its resources are used at normal rates. Imagine you are running a company that produces baseball bats for the Milwaukee market. You have estimated the demand for bats based on the information available to you, purchased machines, and hired workers to operate them. If everything goes according to plan, you'll make a nice profit. But suddenly the Milwaukee Brewers, a team that has never won a World Series, wins the championship and the number of kids who play baseball in your area increases dramatically. Your bat sales skyrocket. To meet the increased demand, you begin running your factory around the clock.

What happened? The fact that the Brewers have won the World Series has driven your output above the normal level—that is, above your potential output. Now, what if the local professional basketball team, the Milwaukee Bucks, were suddenly successful? This would create a boom in the sale of basketballs at the expense of baseball equipment, forcing you to cut back on production below normal levels. The reduction

Distinguishing Inflation, Deflation, and Disinflation
YOUR FINANCIAL WORLD

What do people mean when they refer to *inflation* and *deflation*?

In normal conversation, people often use the word *inflation* when they are referring to price increases. If the price of gasoline or the cost of a basket of groceries rises, that's inflation. When *The Wall Street Journal* reports that the inflation rate was one-tenth of 1 percent over the past month, it means that the average price level went up. But these common uses of the term *inflation* do not distinguish such one-time changes in the price level from an ongoing rise in prices.

Economists use the term in the latter sense. To them, inflation means a continuously rising price level—that is, a sustained rise that continues for a substantial period. In discussing changes in inflation, economists emphasize the distinction between temporary and permanent changes. A temporary change is a one-time adjustment in the price level that does not change the trend of inflation, while a permanent change is a rise or fall in the trend.

To see the difference, consider an example in which the inflation rate is zero. Then, gasoline prices suddenly rise, driving up that month's consumer price index (CPI) by 1 percent. The next month, however, prices don't change, so the CPI is unchanged as well. At the end of this episode, the month-to-month inflation rate is where it started, at zero, but the price level as measured by the CPI is 1 percent higher.

In recent years, as price increases have slowed and even turned negative, *deflation* and *disinflation* also have been added to the common vocabulary, but these two words mean very different things. Deflation is simply the opposite of inflation: inflation is a sustained rise in the price level, whereas deflation is a sustained decline. And just as a one-time rise in prices has no impact on the trend of inflation, a one-time drop in prices has no impact on the trend of deflation.

In contrast, disinflation means a slowdown in the pace of inflation, not a decline in prices. But it could lead there. Consider the recent history of global price developments. Over the past two decades, disinflation has reduced inflation to such a low level in a few advanced economies that they face the risk of outright deflation.

in the rate at which you use your resources would drive your output level below the potential level at which you could produce.

Over time, conditions at your baseball bat factory are likely to change. First, if you come to believe that an increase or decrease in the demand for your product is permanent, you will change the scale of your factory, redesigning it to enlarge or reduce its size. And second, technological improvements allow you to increase the factory's production at given levels of capital and labor. In other words, your factory's normal level of output evolves over time—usually going up, but occasionally going down. So, in the short run production can deviate from normal, while in the long run the normal level itself changes.

What is true for the Milwaukee bat manufacturer is true for the economy as a whole. There is a normal level of production that defines potential output. But potential output is not a fixed level. Because the amount of labor and capital in an economy can grow, and improved technology can increase the efficiency of the production process, potential output tends to rise over time. Furthermore, unexpected events can push current output away from potential output, creating what is called an **output gap**. When current output climbs above potential it creates an **expansionary output gap**; when current output falls below potential, it creates a **recessionary output gap**. These output gaps eventually cancel each other out, so that *in the long run, current output equals potential output.*

Long-Run Inflation

The other key to long-run equilibrium is inflation. In the last chapter, we saw that the equation of exchange, $MV = PY$, implies that money growth plus the change in the velocity of money equals inflation plus real growth:

$$\%\Delta M + \%\Delta V = \%\Delta P + \%\Delta Y$$

where M is the quantity of money, V is the velocity of money, P is the price level, Y is real output, and "%Δ" stands for percentage change. We can restate this equation in terms of potential output, which we will call Y^P. In the long run, because current output equals potential output, real growth must equal growth in potential output ($\%\Delta Y = \%\Delta Y^P$) and changes in velocity are unimportant ($\%\Delta V = 0$). From this we can conclude that, *in the long run, inflation equals money growth minus growth in potential output* ($\%\Delta P = \%\Delta M - \%\Delta Y^P$).

While central bankers focus primarily on controlling short-term nominal interest rates, they keep an eye on money growth. They know that when they adjust the target nominal interest rate, their action affects the rate at which money grows. That is what ultimately determines inflation. But in the short run, over periods even as long as a few years, fluctuations in velocity weaken this link substantially.

We turn now to a discussion of the role of monetary policy in the determination of fluctuations in current output and inflation. To understand that role, we need to develop a simple macroeconomic model—a shorthand description of the economy that helps us organize our thinking.

Monetary Policy and the Dynamic Aggregate Demand Curve

Policymakers know that money growth is an important benchmark for tracking long-run inflation trends. In fact, when faced with very high inflation, central bankers will focus almost exclusively on controlling money growth. Reducing the growth of the money supply is the only way to bring down inflation of 50 or 100 percent per year.

But with 1 or 2 or even 5 percent inflation, restraining money growth is not a central short-run policy objective. Under such circumstances, modern central bankers concentrate on manipulating interest rates in order to keep inflation low and close the gap between current and potential output. Thus, the Federal Reserve Open Market Committee's policy statements announce and explain interest rate decisions or planned changes in the scale and composition of Fed assets, but make virtually no mention of money growth. If we want to understand the role of central bankers in stabilizing the economy—and particularly how policymakers themselves think about their role—we need to examine the connection between short-term interest rates and policymakers' inflation and output objectives.

Because our task is somewhat complex, it is useful to have an overview of where we are going. The goal is to understand the relationship between inflation and the quantity of aggregate output demanded by those people that use it. To get there, we will proceed in three steps. First, we examine the relationship between aggregate expenditure and the real interest rate. Next, we study how monetary policymakers adjust their interest rate instrument in response to changes in inflation. And finally, we put these two together to construct the dynamic aggregate demand curve that relates output and inflation. A short summary, also shown in Figure 21.1, is as follows:

1. ***Aggregate expenditure and the real interest rate.*** We begin with a description of how *aggregate expenditure*—primarily investment and consumption—depends on the real interest rate. As the real interest rate rises, investment and consumption fall, reducing the level of aggregate expenditure. There is a

Figure 21.1 Inflation, Monetary Policy, and Aggregate Demand

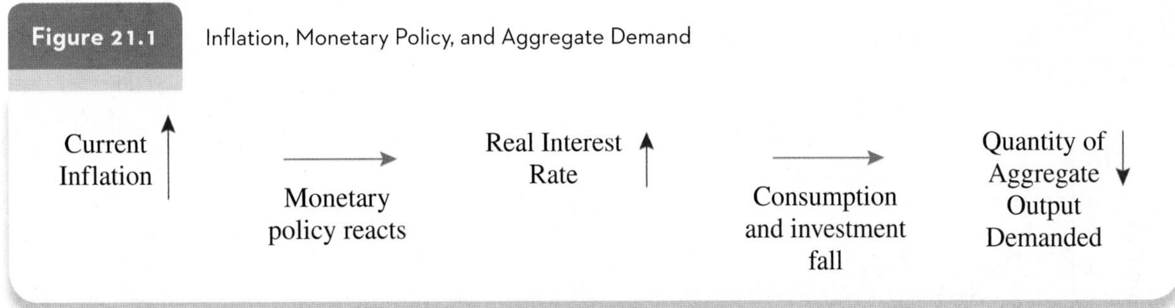

When inflation rises, policymakers react by raising the real interest rate. Higher real interest rates reduce consumption and investment, lowering the quantity of aggregate output demanded.

downward-sloping relationship between the quantity of aggregate expenditure and the real interest rate.

2. ***Inflation, the real interest rate, and the monetary policy reaction curve***. Next, we will see that monetary policymakers respond to increases in inflation by raising their policy-controlled interest rate. And, importantly, they raise their nominal policy rate by more than the change in inflation (see, for example, the Taylor rule on pages 497–503). So, because of the way policymakers react, when inflation rises, the real interest rate goes up. There is an *upward-sloping* relationship between inflation and the real interest rate that we will call the *monetary policy reaction curve*.
3. ***The dynamic aggregate demand curve***. Putting 1 and 2 together—the fact that monetary policymakers react to higher inflation by raising the real interest rate and that a higher real interest rate reduces the level of aggregate expenditure—gives us a relationship between inflation and the quantity of aggregate output demanded that we will call the *dynamic aggregate demand curve*. And like conventional demand curves, this one slopes down, so that's how we will draw it. The dynamic aggregate demand curve is a downward-sloping relationship between inflation and aggregate output.

Before continuing, it is important to keep in mind that economic decisions of households to consume and of firms to invest depend on the *real* interest rate, not the nominal rate. So, to alter the course of the economy, central banks must influence the real interest rate. As it turns out, in the short run, when monetary policymakers operating in a credible policy framework change the nominal interest rate, they change the real interest rate. To see why, remember that the nominal interest rate (i) equals the real interest rate (r) plus expected inflation (π^e): $i = r + \pi^e$. Solving this for r tells us that $r = i - \pi^e$, or the real interest rate equals the nominal interest rate minus expected inflation. Importantly, inflation expectations reflect the credibility of the central bank—its record of matching word and deed (see the discussion of credibility on pages 409–410). For a central bank that is effective at stabilizing inflation and output, inflation expectations adjust slowly in response to changes in economic conditions. This means that when policymakers alter i, π^e doesn't change, so changes in the nominal interest rate alter the real interest rate.

Data for the past several decades make it clear that movements in the short-term nominal interest rate are also movements in the short-term real interest rate. To see this, look at Figure 21.2, which plots the nominal and real three-month Treasury bill rates.

Figure 21.2 The Nominal and Real Three-Month Treasury Bill Rates

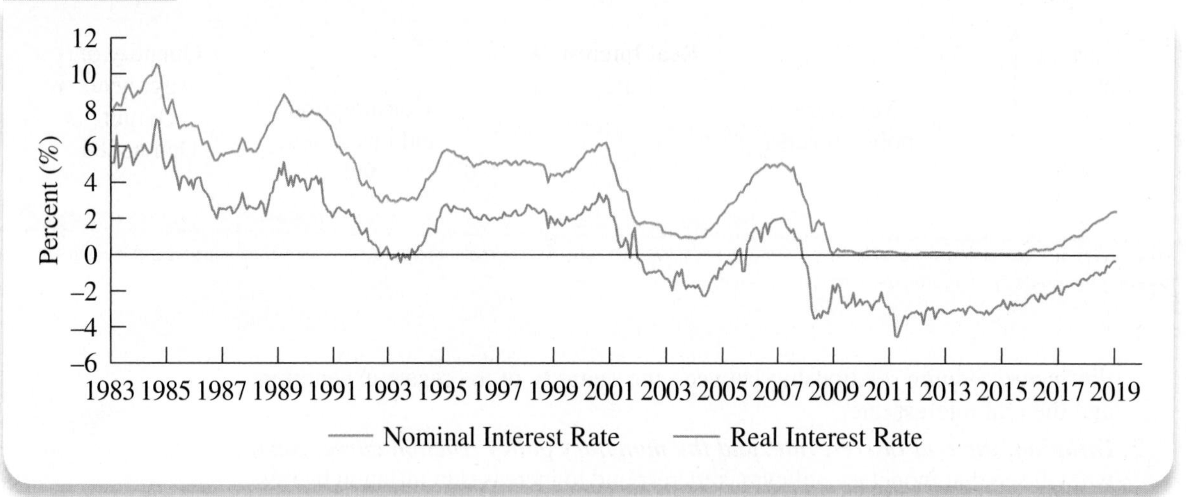

The real Treasury bill rate is computed as the monthly nominal three-month Treasury bill rate minus expected inflation for the next year from the University of Michigan's Survey of Consumers. The FRED data codes are TB3MS and MICH, respectively.

SOURCE: Federal funds rate data are from the Federal Reserve; inflation expectations data are drawn from the median expected change in prices during the next 12 months, Table 32 of the Michigan Survey, available at www.sca.isr.umich.edu.

The figure shows that these two short-term interest rates rise and fall together (with a correlation of 0.98). So, when one changes, so does the other. We also know that the interest rate on three-month Treasury bills moves closely with the overnight interest rate that the FOMC controls. This means that when the Federal Reserve raises its nominal interest rate target, it raises the real interest rate with it.

The real interest rate, then, is the lever through which monetary policymakers influence the real economy. In changing real interest rates, they influence consumption, investment, and other components of aggregate expenditure. Let's see how this all works.

Aggregate Expenditure and the Real Interest Rate

The Components of Aggregate Expenditure and the Real Interest Rate

To understand the impact of monetary policy on the economy we need to link the real interest rate to the level of output. This task requires a detailed description of aggregate expenditure and its relationship to the real interest rate. The best way is to start with the national income accounting identity from principles of economics that analyzes the uses of the economy's output. Doing so allows us to divide aggregate expenditure into four parts:

$$\begin{array}{ccccccccccc} \textit{Aggregate expenditure} & = & \textit{Consumption} & + & \textit{Investment} & + & \textit{Government purchases} & + & (\textit{Exports} & - & \textit{Imports}) \\ Y & = & C & + & I & + & G & + & (X & - & M) \end{array}$$

The terms in this expression are defined as follows:

1. **Consumption** (C) is spending by individuals for items like food, clothing, housing, transportation, entertainment, and education, accounting for around 68 percent of GDP.

2. **Investment** (I) is spending by firms for additions to the physical capital they use to produce goods and services.[1] Examples would include new buildings and equipment. The cost of newly constructed residential homes, as well as the change in the level of business inventories, is also included. All together, these expenditures averaged 17 percent of U.S. GDP since 2000.
3. **Government purchases** (G) is spending on goods and services by federal, state, and local governments. New military equipment and schools fall into this category, as well as the salaries of public school teachers, police officers, and firefighters; but transfers, like unemployment insurance payments and Social Security, are not included. Total federal, state, and local government purchases in the United States averaged around 19 percent of GDP since 2000.
4. **Net exports** equals *exports* minus *imports* ($X - M$). Remember that exports are goods and services produced in one country and sold to residents of another country; imports are purchases of foreign-made goods and services. The difference between the two represents the net expenditure for domestically produced goods.[2] Since 2000, U.S. net exports have been negative, averaging −4 percent of GDP.

TIME

For our purposes, it is helpful to think of aggregate expenditure as having two parts, one that is sensitive to changes in the real interest rate and one that is not. Three of the four components of aggregate expenditure—consumption, investment, and net exports—are *sensitive* to changes in the real interest rate. Among these, investment is the most important. Deciding whether to replace an existing machine or purchase a new one is a complicated matter, dependent on a comparison of the revenue generated by the investment with the cost of financing it. This decision boils down to a comparison of the return on the investment and the cost of borrowing to finance it.[3] An investment can be profitable only if its internal rate of return exceeds the cost of borrowing. From this, we can conclude that the higher the cost of borrowing, the less likely that an investment will be profitable. Because borrowers and lenders both care about the real return, we see immediately that the higher the real interest rate, the lower the level of investment. Higher interest rates also reduce residential investment—the construction of new homes—as larger mortgage payments make houses less affordable.

While investment may be the most important component of aggregate expenditure that is sensitive to real interest rates, it isn't the only one. Consumption and net exports respond to the real interest rate as well. What is true for a business considering an investment, for example, is true for a family thinking of buying a new car. Higher real interest rates mean higher inflation-adjusted car-loan payments, which make new cars more costly. Furthermore, as the real interest rate rises, the reward to saving goes up. More saving means lower consumption.

The case of net exports is more complicated. Briefly, when the real interest rate in the United States rises, U.S. financial assets become more attractive to foreigners.[4]

[1]Remember that economists use the term *investment* differently from the way it is used in the business press. In the business press, an investment is a financial instrument like a stock or bond that people use as a means of holding their wealth. Importantly, though, people who make such a "financial investment" or who purchase a house from its current owner aren't creating anything new; they are buying something that already exists. To an economist, investment is the creation of new physical capital.

[2]Net exports are often referred to as the *current account surplus:* see the appendix to Chapter 19, What You Really Need to Know about the Balance of Payments.

[3]See the discussion of internal rate of return in Chapter 4.

[4]There is a more detailed discussion in Chapter 10.

This rise in the desirability of U.S. assets to foreigners increases the foreign demand for dollars, causing the dollar to appreciate (see Chapter 10, pages 251–253, for the impact of the policy interest rate on the exchange rate). The higher the value of the dollar, the more expensive U.S. exports will be, and the cheaper U.S. imports will be. Together, lower exports and higher imports mean lower net exports. Again, the higher real interest rate has reduced a component of aggregate expenditure.

Finally, there is government expenditure. While changes in the real interest rate may have an impact on the government's budget by raising the cost of borrowing, the effect is likely to be small, so we will ignore it.

For three of the four components of aggregate expenditure, then, our conclusion is the same: When the real interest rate *rises:*

- Consumption (C) *falls* because the reward to saving and the cost of financing purchases are now higher.
- Investment (I) *falls* because the cost of financing has gone up.
- Net exports ($X - M$) *fall* because the domestic currency has appreciated, making imports cheaper and exports more expensive.

Thus, as shown in Figure 21.3, *a rise in the real interest rate reduces the level of aggregate expenditure.*[5]

Bear in mind, though, that the components of aggregate expenditure can change for reasons unrelated to the real interest rate. Consumption or investment can rise when individuals or businesses become more confident about their future income or sales, or when their net worth increases. Government purchases can increase because of a change in fiscal policy, and net exports can climb because of movement in the exchange rate. Any of these would shift the aggregate expenditure curve in Figure 21.3, increasing the level of aggregate expenditure at every level of the real interest rate.

Figure 21.3 Aggregate Expenditure and the Real Interest Rate

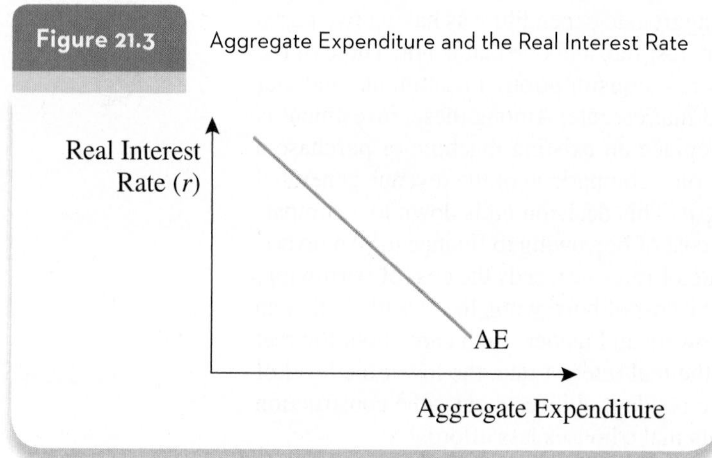

A fall in the real interest rate leads to an increase in aggregate expenditure.

Table 21.1 provides a summary of the relationship between aggregate expenditure and the real interest rate.

We can see immediately how the relationship between the real interest rate and the level of aggregate expenditure helps central bankers achieve one of their objectives: stabilizing current output at a level close to potential output. When economic activity speeds up or slows down and current output moves above or below potential output, policymakers can adjust the real interest rate in an effort to close the expansionary or recessionary gap. But as we have emphasized repeatedly throughout our study of monetary policy, central bankers spend much of their time worrying instead about keeping inflation low.

The Long-Run Real Interest Rate Before diving into a description of the relationship between monetary policy and inflation, there is one more thing we must do. We need to figure out what happens to the real interest rate over the long run. Earlier

[5]If you have studied intermediate macroeconomics, you will recognize this relationship as the "IS" curve.

Table 21.1 The Relationship between Aggregate Expenditure and the Real Interest Rate

What is it?	The downward-sloping relationship between the quantity of aggregate expenditure ($C + I + G + NX$) and the real interest rate (r).
Why does it slope down?	When the real interest rate rises, the components of aggregate expenditure, especially consumption and investment, fall.
When does it shift?	When aggregate expenditure goes up for reasons unrelated to changes in the real interest rate, the relationship shifts to the right. Examples include: 1. Increases in optimism that drive up consumption or investment. 2. Rising net worth that increases spending. 3. Changes in fiscal policy that raise government expenditure or reduce taxes. 4. Increases in net exports that are unrelated to changes in the real interest rate.

we discussed the concept of potential output and noted the economy's tendency to move toward that normal level over time. In this section we have examined how various components of aggregate expenditure respond to the real interest rate. We have seen that higher real interest rates, holding constant things like business and consumer confidence as well as government expenditure, are associated with lower levels of aggregate expenditure. Putting these two discussions together, we can conclude that there must be some level of the real interest rate at which aggregate expenditure equals potential output. That is, there is some level of aggregate expenditure that is consistent with the normal level of output toward which the economy moves over the long run. This concept is important enough that we will give it a name, the **long-run real interest rate**. *The long-run real interest rate, which we will call call r^* ("r-star"), equates the level of aggregate expenditure to the quantity of potential output.* (Note that r^* is the same as the neutral or "natural" rate of interest that we described in Chapter 18.)

To figure out the level of r^*, take the aggregate expenditure curve drawn in Figure 21.3 and find the interest rate that is consistent with the quantity of potential output (Y^P).[6] You can see how to do it in Figure 21.4. This figure helps us understand the two possible reasons that the long-run real interest rate can change: (1) shifts in the aggregate expenditure curve, and (2) changes in the level of potential output.

First, take the case in which the level of potential output remains fixed, but there is a rise in some of the components of aggregate expenditure that do not respond to the real interest rate. One example of this is a rise in government purchases (all other things held equal). When G goes up, it increases the level of aggregate expenditure at every real interest rate, shifting the aggregate expenditure curve to the right. The result

[6]Computing a numerical estimate for the long-run real interest rate is unfortunately complicated because it is related to the return on capital investment (adjusted for risk) in the economy as a whole, a quantity that is very difficult to calculate. Furthermore, it can change over time. For example, in the early 2000s, one estimate of the "natural rate" of interest in the United States put it in the range of 2½ to 3 percent. More recently it has fallen, and appears to be in the range between ½ and 1 percent. See Kathryn Holston, Thomas Laubach, and John C. Williams, "Measuring the Natural Rate of Interest: International Trends and Determinants," *Journal of International Economics* 108, supplement 1 (May 2017), pp. S39–S75. For recent data, see www.newyorkfed.org/research/policy/rstar.

Figure 21.4 The Long-Run Real Interest Rate

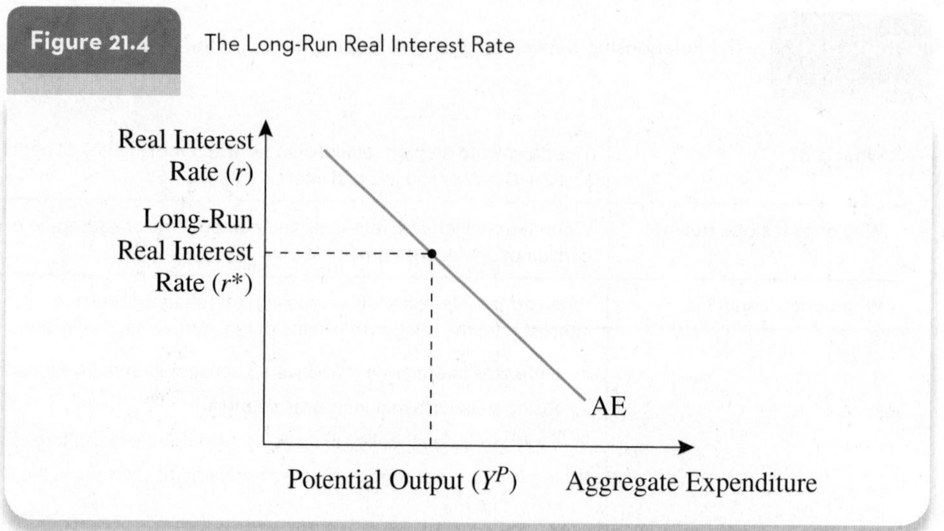

The long-run real interest rate (r^*) equates aggregate expenditure with potential output (Y^P).

is shown in Panel A of Figure 21.5. For the level of aggregate expenditure to remain equal to the (unchanged) quantity of potential output, the interest-sensitive components of aggregate expenditure must fall. For that to happen, r^* must rise.[7] Besides government purchases, there are portions of consumption, investment, and net exports that are not sensitive to the real interest rate. If any of those components rises, driving aggregate expenditure up at every level of the real interest rate, r^* must go up.

What about the second case in which a change in potential output causes a change in r^*? This has an inverse effect on the real interest rate. When the quantity of potential output rises, the level of aggregate expenditure must rise with it. As we have seen, an increase in the level of aggregate expenditure requires a decline in the real interest rate. (Take a look at Panel B of Figure 21.5.) In addition, when potential output goes up, r^* falls.

In summary, the long-run real interest rate (r^*) is that level at which aggregate expenditure ($C + I + G + NX$) equals potential output (Y^P). When components of aggregate expenditure that are not sensitive to the real interest rate rise, r^* rises with them. But when potential output rises, r^* falls. Importantly, the level of r^* is a consequence of the structure of the economy; it is *not* something policymakers can choose.

Inflation, the Real Interest Rate, and the Monetary Policy Reaction Curve

We now move to the *second of the three steps* in our derivation of the relationship between inflation and the level of aggregate output demanded: In response to changes in inflation, policymakers adjust their policy-controlled interest rate.

[7]This effect is related to what is sometimes called "crowding out." The idea is that government spending can take the place of investment. The more common type of crowding out occurs when the government borrows funds to increase spending, thereby increasing the supply of bonds. An increase in the supply of bonds drives the price of bonds down, increasing the interest rate, and reducing investment. When the economy is operating at its potential and the government borrows, firms can't, so investment is crowded out.

Figure 21.5 Change in the Long-Run Real Interest Rate

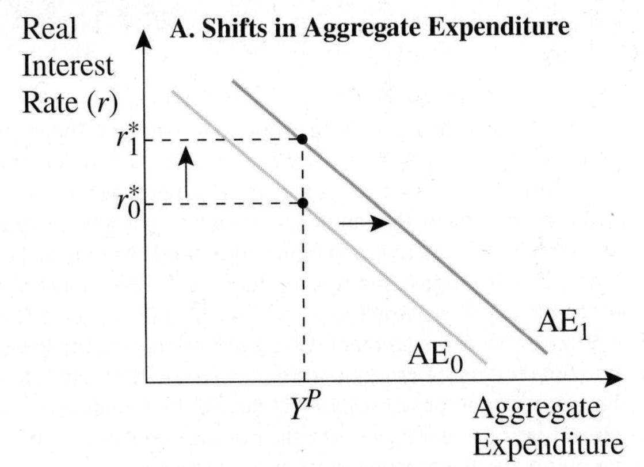

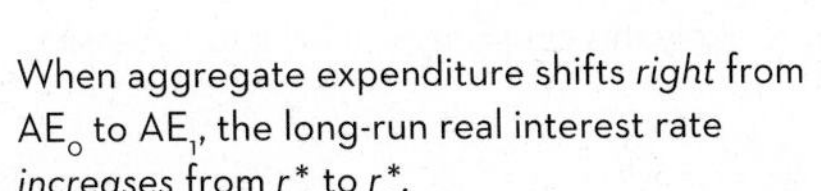
When aggregate expenditure shifts *right* from AE$_0$ to AE$_1$, the long-run real interest rate *increases* from r_0^* to r_1^*.

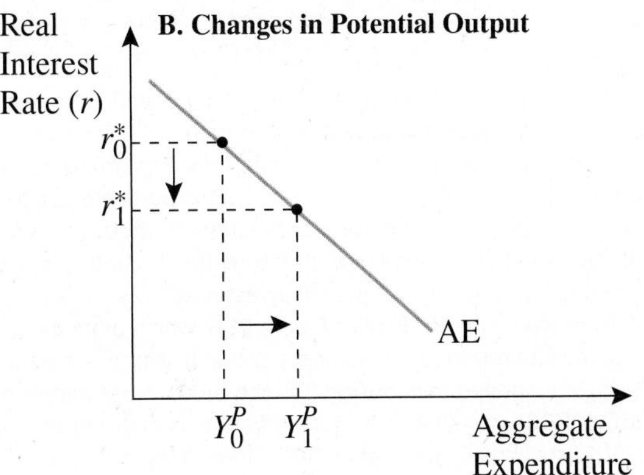

When potential output *increases* from Y_0^P to Y_1^P, the long-run real interest rate *falls* from r_0^* to r_1^*.

In early 2019, consumer price inflation in the United States was rising at a rate of around 2 percent per year, while current output was roughly equal to the Congressional Budget Office's estimate of potential output. In this context, at the conclusion of its meeting on December 18, 2018, the Federal Open Market Committee released a statement that read, in part: "The Committee judges that some further gradual increases in the target range for the federal funds rate will be consistent with sustained expansion of economic activity, strong labor market conditions, and inflation near the Committee's symmetric 2 percent objective over the medium term."

That is, FOMC members had concluded that economic conditions justified raising the real interest rate in an effort to ensure that output would grow consistently with its potential and that inflation would remain near its target. Furthermore, they made clear the likelihood that, provided the economy expanded in line with their projections, there would be additional interest rate increases in the coming year.

Statements made by the European Central Bank's Governing Council following its meeting the previous week revealed a somewhat different perspective. On December 13, 2018, the ECB left the interest rate on its deposit facility at a then-record low (of −0.4 percent). There, circumstances were quite different. With inflation at 1.6 percent and slowly rising toward the target, the statement following the meeting read, "Based on our regular economic and monetary analyses, we decided to keep . . . interest rates unchanged. We continue to expect them to remain at their present levels at least through the summer of 2019, and in any case for as long as necessary to ensure the continued sustained convergence of inflation to levels that are below, but close to, 2% over the medium term." While the Governing Council made clear that interest rates were not going to rise for at least another nine months, it did announce the end of its asset purchase program, which had begun in early 2015 (see Chapter 18 on unconventional monetary policy tools beginning on page 503).

Investment and the Business Cycle
APPLYING THE CONCEPT

Fluctuations in investment are one of the most important sources of changes in aggregate expenditure. Over short periods of a quarter or a year, consumption and government purchases tend to be fairly stable; and net exports are just too small to account for much of the variation in aggregate output. So understanding fluctuations in the business cycle means understanding changes in investment.

To grasp this point, look at Figure 21.6, which plots the ratio of investment to gross domestic product over the past 58 years. The shaded bars designate recessions. Note that from 1960 to 2018, investment fluctuated from less than 13 percent of GDP to nearly 21 percent of GDP. More to the point, during every recession, investment itself falls by between 2 and 5 percent of GDP, which is roughly the same size as the fall in GDP itself. In other words, when we talk about a recession, what we are really talking about is a drop in investment.

What causes the level of investment to change? The tools we have developed suggest two possibilities: changes in the real interest rate and changes in expectations about future business conditions. Remember, an investment will be profitable when its real internal rate of return exceeds its real cost of financing. Once again, the real interest rate is what matters in economic decisions. The higher the real cost of financing, the less likely that an investment will be profitable. And the lower the expected future revenue from an investment is, the lower the real internal rate of return will be. So the higher the real interest rate and the less optimistic businesspeople are about the future, the fewer investments firms will undertake and the more likely the economy will fall into recession.

Figure 21.6 Investment and the Business Cycle: The Ratio of Investment to GDP

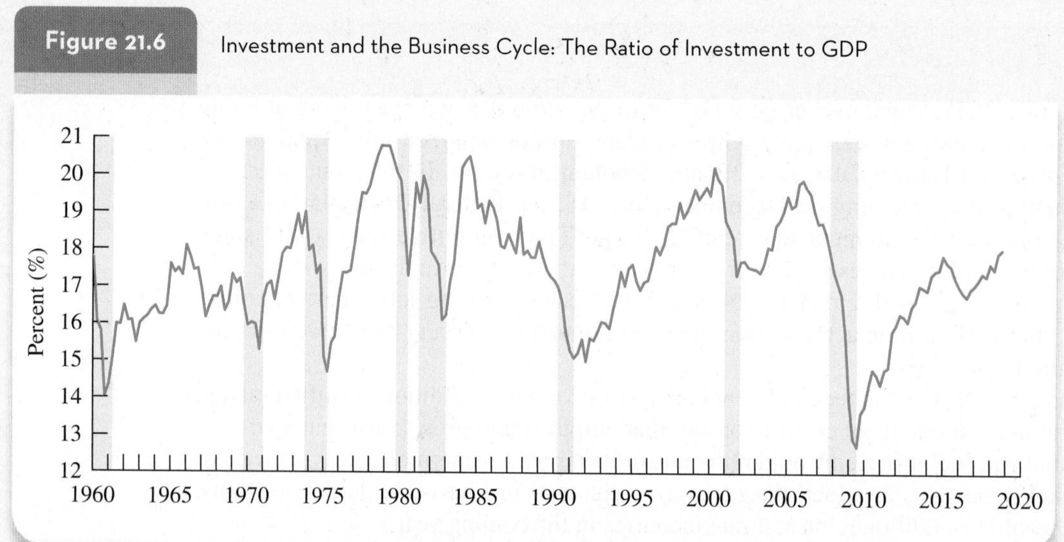

SOURCE: Ratio of nominal gross domestic investment (FRED code: GPDI) to nominal gross domestic product (FRED code: GDP), seasonally adjusted at annual rates, from the Department of Commerce, Bureau of Economic Analysis. Shaded bars denote recessions, dated by the National Bureau of Economic Research.

While the specifics differ, both statements clearly indicate that policymakers set their short-run nominal interest rate targets in response to economic conditions in general, and inflation in particular.[8] Low inflation leads central banks to ease monetary conditions by lowering interest rates.

[8]The fact that policy does not have an immediate impact on either inflation or output complicates matters substantially. In fact, interest rate changes must anticipate changes in inflation and output, so they must be based on forecasts as much as on current levels. That is why, in their public comments, central bankers nearly always refer to inflation expectations and to likely future developments.

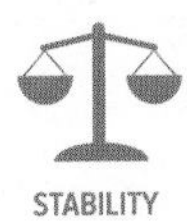

These two examples are representative of the sorts of things central bankers commonly say. Looking at the details, we can conclude that when current inflation is high or current output is running above potential output, central bankers will set a relatively high policy interest rate; when current inflation is low or current output is well below potential, they will set a low policy interest rate. Importantly, central bankers envision themselves as reacting to changes in the economic environment. And while they state their policies in terms of nominal interest rates, they do so knowing that changes in the nominal interest rate will translate into changes in the real interest rate. As we have discussed, these changes in the real interest rate influence the economic decisions of firms and households. We can summarize all of this in the form of a **monetary policy reaction curve (MPRC)** that approximates the behavior of central bankers.

Deriving the Monetary Policy Reaction Curve We introduced a version of the monetary policy reaction curve in Chapter 18 when we looked at a rule of thumb (the Taylor rule) for understanding how the FOMC sets its federal funds rate target. There we saw that in order to ensure that deviations of inflation from the target rate are only temporary, policymakers respond to changes in inflation by changing the real interest rate in the same direction. That is, *higher current inflation requires a policy response that raises the real interest rate,* and *lower current inflation requires a policy response that lowers the real interest rate.* This means that the monetary policy reaction curve slopes upward as shown in Figure 21.7.

Where do we draw the reaction curve? What determines its location? The location depends on where policymakers would like the economy to end up in the long run, which is the equilibrium toward which the economy tends over time. For the real interest rate, the economy moves toward the long-run real interest rate that equates aggregate expenditure with potential output. That interest rate is shown as r^* in Figure 21.7. For inflation, the answer is the central bank's target level (π^T). *The monetary policy*

Figure 21.7 The Monetary Policy Reaction Curve

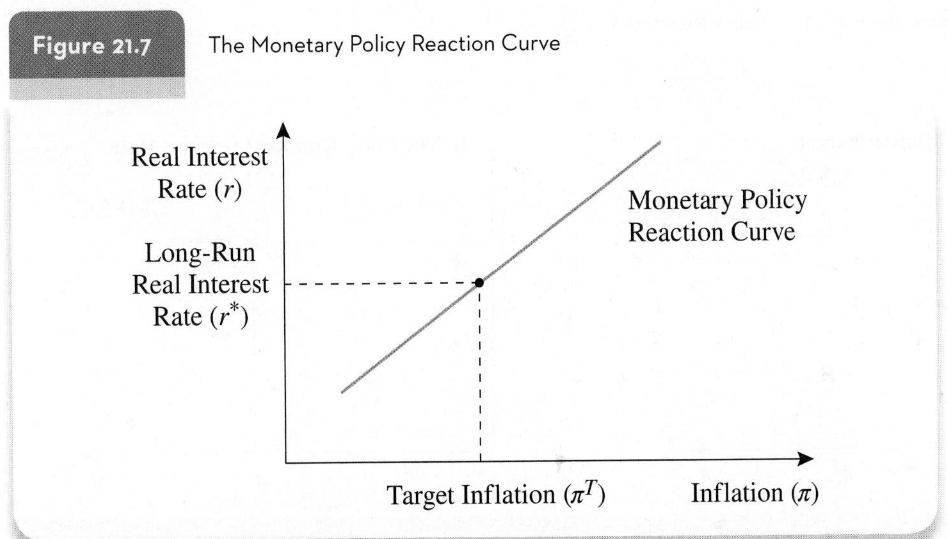

Monetary policymakers react to increases in current inflation by raising the real interest rate, while decreases lead them to lower it. The monetary policy reaction curve is located so that the central bank's target inflation is consistent with the long-run real interest rate, which equates aggregate expenditure with potential output.

reaction curve is set so that when current inflation equals target inflation, the real interest rate equals the long-run real interest rate. That is, $r = r^*$ when $\pi = \pi^T$.

While the long-run real interest rate and the inflation target tell us the location of the monetary policy reaction curve, what governs its slope? Is the curve steep or flat? The answer is that the slope depends on policymakers' objectives. When central bankers decide how aggressively to pursue their inflation target, and how willing they are to tolerate temporary changes in inflation, they are determining the slope of the monetary policy reaction curve. They are deciding whether to respond to deviations of current inflation from target inflation with small or large changes in the real interest rate. Policymakers who are aggressive in keeping current inflation near target will have a steep monetary policy reaction curve; while those who are less concerned will have a reaction curve that is relatively flat. We look at the implications of this difference at the end of the next chapter.

Shifting the Monetary Policy Reaction Curve When policymakers adjust the real interest rate, they are either moving along a fixed monetary policy reaction curve or shifting the curve. A movement along the curve is a reaction to a change in current inflation. A shift in the curve represents a change in the level of the real interest rate at every level of inflation. To see what can shift the monetary policy reaction curve, we need to examine the variables we held constant when we drew the curve in Figure 21.7. In that analysis, we held both target inflation π^T and the long-run real interest rate r^* fixed. If either of these variables changes, the entire curve shifts. Looking at Figure 21.8, we can see that a *decrease* in π^T shifts the curve to the left (Panel A), as does an *increase* in r^* (Panel B). Analogously, a decline in the long-run real interest rate r^*, or an increase in the inflation target π^T, shifts the monetary policy reaction curve to the right.

From our earlier discussion, we know that the long-run real interest rate r^* is determined by the structure of the economy. Central bank policymakers cannot choose it. What if r^* were to rise as a consequence of an increase in government purchases, or

Figure 21.8 Shifting the Monetary Policy Reaction Curve

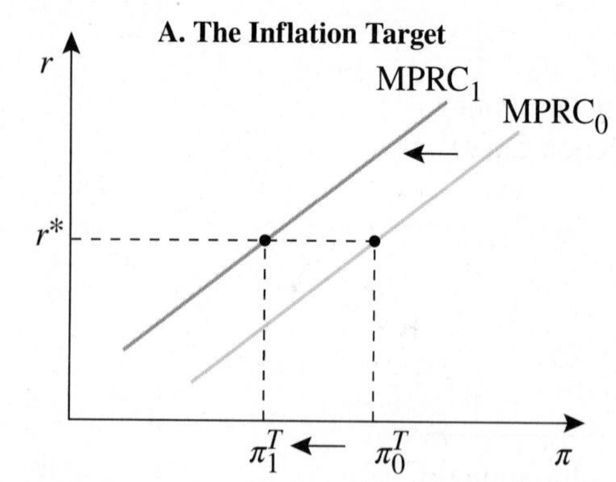

A decline in the inflation target from π_0^T to π_1^T shifts the monetary policy reaction curve to the left from MPRC$_0$ to MPRC$_1$.

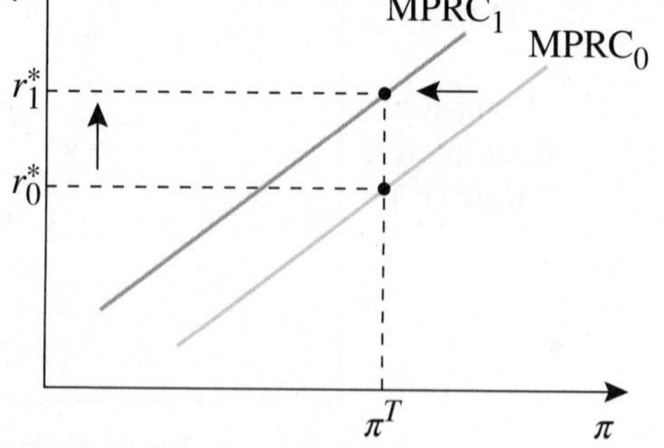

An increase in the long-run real interest rate from r_0^* to r_1^* shifts the monetary policy reaction curve to the left from MPRC$_0$ to MPRC$_1$.

Table 21.2 The Monetary Policy Reaction Curve

What is it?	The upward-sloping relationship between inflation (π) and the real interest rate (r) set by monetary policymakers.
Why does it slope upward?	When inflation rises, monetary policymakers raise the real interest rate.
What determines its location?	Drawn so that, when current inflation equals target inflation ($\pi = \pi^T$), policymakers set the real interest rate equal to the long-run real interest rate ($r = r^*$).
When does it shift?	1. When the central bank's inflation target (π^T) changes. A decline shifts the curve to the left. 2. When the long-run real interest rate (r^*) changes. An increase shifts the curve to the left.

some other component of aggregate expenditure that is not sensitive to the real interest rate? The result of such an increase is a shift to the left in the monetary policy reaction curve as shown in Panel B of Figure 21.8. Remember that the curve is drawn so that the real interest rate equals its long-run level at the point where inflation meets the central bank's target. An increase in r^* means that policymakers have to set a higher real interest rate at every level of current inflation. Assuming that policymakers have not changed their inflation target, this shift means that the long-run nominal interest rate rises as well.

Table 21.2 summarizes the properties of the monetary policy reaction curve (MPRC).

The Dynamic Aggregate Demand Curve

Deriving the Dynamic Aggregate Demand Curve We are now ready to move to the *third* and *final step* outlined at the beginning of this section: The construction of the **dynamic aggregate demand (AD) curve** that relates inflation and the level of output, accounting for the fact that monetary policymakers respond to changes in current inflation by changing the interest rate. Doing it means answering the following question: What happens to the quantity of aggregate output demanded when current inflation changes? From our earlier discussion, we know that central bankers respond to an increase in current inflation by raising the real interest rate. That is, they move along their monetary policy reaction curve (shown in Figure 21.7). We also know that a higher real interest rate lowers the level of aggregate expenditure by reducing investment, consumption, and net exports. (That's in Figure 21.3.) Putting these two together, we see that when inflation rises, the quantity of aggregate output demanded falls. Inflation and the quantity of aggregate output demanded move in opposite directions, so the *dynamic aggregate demand curve* shown in Figure 21.9 slopes downward.[9]

[9]Figuring out the location of the dynamic aggregate demand curve is somewhat complicated. To do it, recall that along the monetary policy reaction curve the real interest rate equals the long-run real interest rate r^* at the point where inflation equals the central bank's target level. And r^* is the level at which aggregate expenditure equals potential output. This all means that the dynamic aggregate demand curve must go through the point where output equals potential output at the same time that inflation equals target inflation. We will come back to this in the next chapter.

Figure 21.9 The Dynamic Aggregate Curve

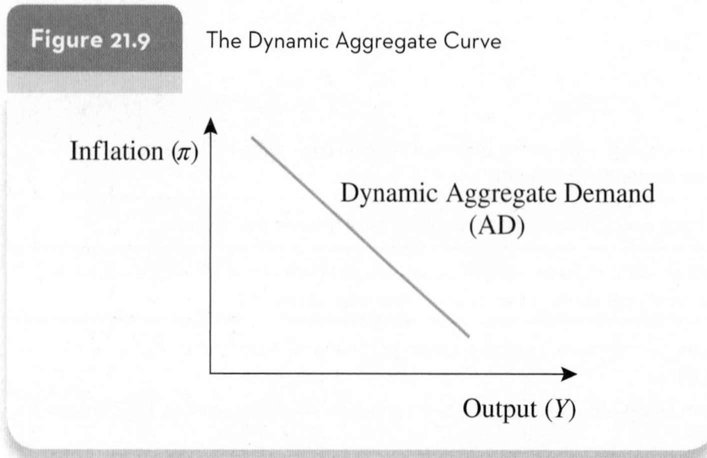

As inflation rises, monetary policymakers increase the real interest rate, lowering interest rate-sensitive components of aggregate expenditure.

To understand the dynamic aggregate demand curve, think about what happens when current inflation rises. In response, monetary policymakers raise the real interest rate, moving the economy upward along the monetary policy reaction curve. The higher real interest rate reduces the interest-sensitive components of aggregate expenditure (consumption, investment, and net exports), causing a fall in the quantity of aggregate output demanded by the people in the economy who use it. Higher current inflation means less aggregate output demanded. In contrast, in response to lower current inflation, policymakers reduce the real interest rate, moving downward along the monetary policy reaction curve. Their action raises consumption, investment, and net exports, causing the quantity of aggregate output demanded to rise. Thus, *changes in current inflation move the economy along a downward-sloping dynamic aggregate demand curve.* (Take a look back at Figure 21.1 and the summary that goes along with it.)

Why the Dynamic Aggregate Demand Curve Slopes Down To recap, the dynamic aggregate demand curve slopes down because higher current inflation induces policymakers to raise the real interest rate, depressing various components of aggregate expenditure. But this is only one reason that increases in inflation are associated with falling levels of aggregate output demanded by the people who use it. Economists have suggested a number of others. One is that the higher the rate of inflation for a given rate of money growth, the lower the level of real money balances in the economy. That is, when P grows faster than M, (M/P) falls. And with a lower level of real money balances, people purchase fewer goods. This is the implication of the equation of exchange ($MV = PY$). So, even if the monetary policymakers do not change the real interest rate when inflation goes up—the monetary policy reaction curve is flat—the effect of inflation on real money balances causes the dynamic aggregate demand curve to slope down.

In addition, higher inflation reduces wealth, which lowers consumption. It does this in two ways. First, inflation means that the money everyone holds is gradually declining in value. Second, inflation is bad for the stock market, because as it rises, uncertainty about inflation rises with it, rendering equities a relatively more risky and hence less attractive investment. A drop in the value of stocks reduces wealth.

Yet another reason for the downward slope of the dynamic aggregate demand curve is that inflation can have a greater impact on the poor than it does on the wealthy, redistributing income to those who are better off. For example, minimum-wage workers tend to have incomes that are fixed in dollar terms, so inflation erodes their purchasing power. And because the rich consume a smaller portion of their income than others, saving a greater portion than the poor (who can't afford to save at all), this redistribution lowers consumption in the economy as a whole, reducing the quantity of aggregate output demanded.

Then there is the fact that inflation creates risk; the higher the inflation rate, the greater the risk. Most people want to insure themselves against risk, and that means increased saving, just in case. More saving means a lower level of consumption and lower quantity of aggregate output demanded. Finally, there is the fact that rising inflation makes foreign goods cheaper in relation to domestic goods, driving imports up and net exports down. In every case, *higher inflation means a lower level of aggregate output demanded,* causing the dynamic aggregate demand curve to slope downward.

Shifting the Dynamic Aggregate Demand Curve In deriving the dynamic aggregate demand curve, we saw that increases in inflation bring a monetary policy response that raises the real interest rate. Those movements in the real interest rate, in turn, cause changes in the quantity of aggregate output demanded by those who use it, moving the economy *along* the dynamic aggregate demand curve. In our derivation we held constant the location of both the aggregate expenditure curve and the monetary policy reaction curve. In the first case, we assumed that factors influencing demand other than the real interest rate were fixed; and in the second, that the inflation target and the long-run real interest rate were fixed. Shifts in any of these will *shift* the dynamic aggregate demand curve.

Let's start by looking at shifts in the aggregate expenditure curve. In the absence of any change in monetary policy, changes in components of aggregate expenditure not caused by movements in the real interest rate shift the dynamic aggregate demand curve. That is, changes in consumption, investment, government purchases, or net exports that are unrelated to changes in the real interest rate shift the dynamic aggregate demand curve, with declines leading to contractions and increases leading to expansions.

To understand these sources of shifts in the dynamic aggregate demand curve, take the case of an increase in consumer confidence. When people become more optimistic about the future, believing that the risk of being laid off has eased, they are more likely to purchase a new car or go on an expensive vacation. Increases in consumer confidence tend to raise consumption at every level of the real interest rate, increasing the level of aggregate expenditure. Assuming unchanged monetary policy, this shifts the dynamic aggregate demand curve to the right (as shown in the top panel of Figure 21.10 on page 594).

What is true for consumer confidence is true for all of the components of aggregate expenditure. Increased optimism about future business prospects raises investment at every level of the real interest rate, shifting the dynamic aggregate demand curve to the right. Increases in government spending (or decreases in taxes) increase aggregate expenditure and have the same effect. And increases in net exports that are unrelated to the real interest rate do the same thing—they are expansionary, shifting the dynamic aggregate demand curve to the right.

Turning to the monetary policy reaction curve, whenever it shifts, the dynamic aggregate demand curve shifts, too. To see why, consider an increase in the central bank's inflation target, what some people might characterize as a permanent easing of monetary policy. The result is the opposite of the decline shown in Panel A of Figure 21.8. The rise in the inflation target shifts the monetary policy reaction curve to the right, lowering the real interest rate that policymakers set at every level of

Figure 21.10 Shifting the Dynamic Aggregate Demand Curve

Changes in Components of Aggregate Expenditure

$C\uparrow, I\uparrow, G\uparrow, NX\uparrow$

Increases in consumption, investment, government expenditure, or net exports (all unrelated to the real interest rate) shift the dynamic aggregate demand curve to the *right*.

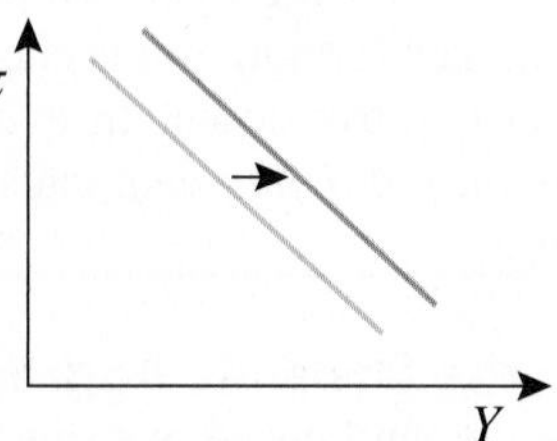

Shifts in the Monetary Policy Reaction Curve

$\pi^T\uparrow$

Increases in the central bank's inflation target shift the dynamic aggregate demand curve to the *right*.

Decreases in the long-run real interest rate shift the dynamic aggregate demand curve to the *right*.

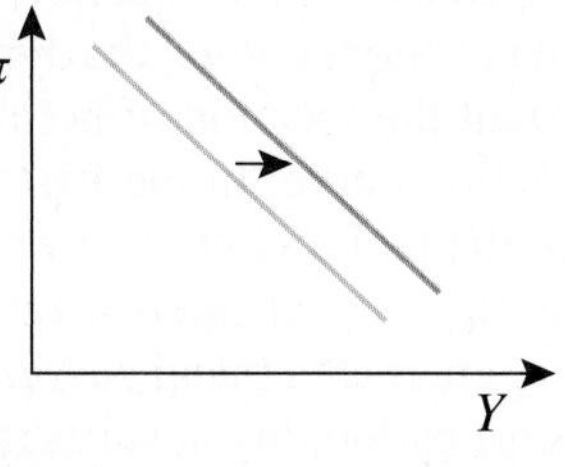

inflation. At the new, higher inflation target, the lower real interest rate increases the quantity of aggregate output demanded at every level of inflation, shifting the dynamic aggregate demand curve to the right.

Changes in the long-run real interest rate r^* shift the dynamic aggregate demand curve as well. To see why, consider a case in which the level of potential output increases. Because r^* equates aggregate expenditure with potential output, when potential output rises, r^* must fall, driving up the interest-rate-sensitive components of aggregate expenditure. This has the same effect on the monetary policy reaction curve as an increase in policymakers' inflation target. A fall in the long-run real interest rate r^* shifts the curve to the right, reducing the real interest rate policymakers set at every level of inflation and shifting the dynamic aggregate demand curve to the right.[10]

Looking at these two changes, we see that any shift in the monetary policy reaction curve shifts the dynamic aggregate demand curve in the same direction. Expansionary monetary policy that lowers the interest rate associated with each level of inflation increases the quantity of aggregate output demanded at each level of inflation and shifts the dynamic aggregate demand curve to the right (as shown in the bottom panel of Figure 21.10). And contractionary monetary policy that raises the interest rate associated with each level of inflation decreases the quantity of aggregate output demanded at each level of inflation, shifting the dynamic aggregate demand curve to the left.

[10]In the next chapter, we will examine what happens if the central bank observes the change in potential output only with a lag, temporarily delaying the shift of the MPRC curve shown in Panel B of Figure 21.8.

Table 21.3 The Dynamic Aggregate Demand Curve

What is it?	The downward-sloping relationship between inflation and the quantity of aggregate output demanded by the people who use it.
Why does it slope down?	1. A rise in inflation leads monetary policymakers to raise the real interest rate (along the monetary policy reaction curve). 2. A higher real interest rate drives down the interest-sensitive components of aggregate expenditure (especially consumption and investment).
When does it shift?	When aggregate demand goes up for reasons unrelated to changes in the real interest rate, the relationship shifts to the right. Examples include: 1. Changes in components of aggregate expenditure not sensitive to the real interest rate (monetary policy unchanged). 2. Shifts in the monetary policy reaction curve.

Table 21.3 summarizes the properties of the dynamic aggregate demand curve.

Aggregate Supply

The dynamic aggregate demand curve is downward-sloping. It tells us that higher current inflation is associated with a lower quantity of aggregate output demanded. But this alone doesn't explain how inflation and the quantity of output are determined by those people who use it. To do that, we need to introduce an aggregate supply curve. The aggregate supply curve tells us where along the dynamic aggregate demand curve the economy ends up. So, to complete the analysis, we now move to an examination of aggregate supply and the behavior of the firms that produce the economy's output. Critically, there are short-run and long-run versions of the aggregate supply curve. When combined with the dynamic aggregate demand curve, the short-run aggregate supply curve tells us where the economy settles at any particular time; while the long-run curve, together with dynamic aggregate demand, tells us the levels of inflation and the quantity of output that the economy is moving toward in the long term.

Short-Run Aggregate Supply

The **short-run aggregate supply (SRAS) curve** *is the upward-sloping relationship between current inflation and the quantity of output.*[11] It tells us that as inflation rises, producers increase the quantity of output supplied. The reason is that prices of factors used as inputs in production, especially wages paid to workers, are costly

[11]The short-run aggregate supply curve is a close relative of the *Phillips curve* that you may have already seen. The Phillips curve is the downward-sloping relationship between inflation and unemployment. Because unemployment is related to the level of output—higher output means lower unemployment—there is a clear correspondence.

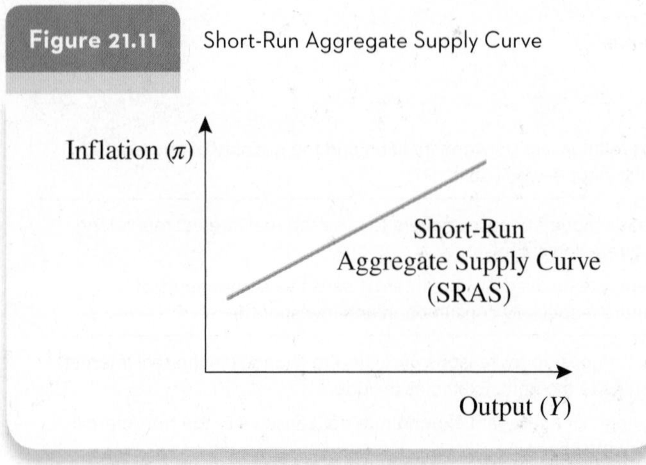

Inflation persistence means the short-run aggregate supply curve slopes up.

to adjust, so they change infrequently. In the short run, they are sticky. For producers, this means that costs of production—wages paid to workers, rents paid for buildings, prices paid for raw material inputs—are fixed in the short run, so increases in prices of the things that firms sell mean higher profits and more supply. Put another way, in the short term, production costs don't change much, so when product (or retail) prices rise firms increase supply in order to take advantage. From this we can conclude that in the short run, higher inflation elicits more aggregate output supplied by the firms that produce it (see Figure 21.11).

Shifts in the Short-Run Aggregate Supply Curve

Changes in product-price inflation create movements *along* a short-run aggregate supply curve. In coming to this conclusion, we assumed that production costs didn't change. What if they do? When production costs change, the short-run aggregate supply curve *shifts.* A shift of the SRAS curve can happen for one of two reasons:

1. Changes in expectations of future inflation.
2. Factors that drive production costs up or down.

Let's look at each one of these in some detail.

To understand the importance of inflation expectations in determining the location of the short-run aggregate supply curve, note that workers and firms care about real wages and real product prices—the level of compensation and profits measured in goods and services that they can purchase. As we mentioned earlier, it is costly to adjust wages and prices, so they change infrequently. More importantly, during months or even years for which they are fixed, inflation erodes the real wages paid to workers and real prices charged by firms. This makes everyone concerned about future inflation, and the higher expected inflation is, the faster nominal wages and nominal prices will rise. As a result, changes in inflation expectations are analogous to changes in production costs. An increase in expected inflation increases production costs, lowering production at every level of current inflation and shifting the short-run aggregate supply curve to the left as shown in the top panel of Figure 21.12.

Given the key role of inflation expectations in determining the location of the short-run aggregate supply curve, it is important to understand how these expectations are determined. To keep things simple, we assume that people form their expectations based on their recent experience. That is, inflation expectations this year are roughly equal to actual inflation last year. This assumption has the important implication that when actual inflation rises above what is currently expected, inflation expectations will go up. And, analogously, if actual inflation turns out to be lower than expected inflation, expectations will go down.

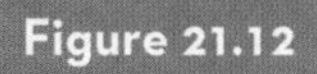
Figure 21.12 Shifting the Short-Run Aggregate Supply Curve

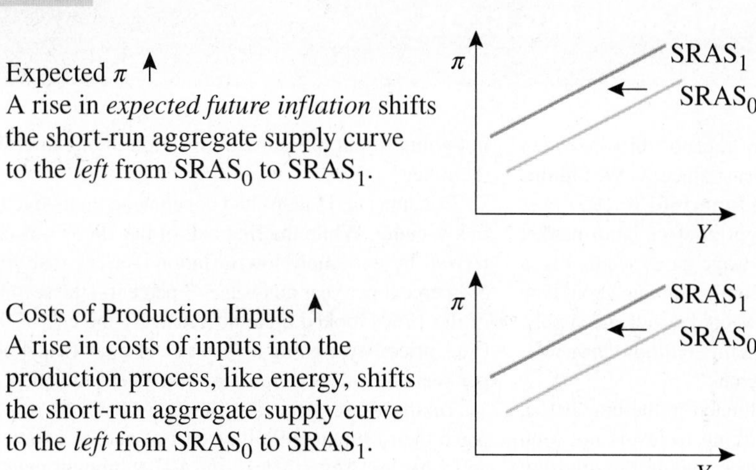

Expected π ↑
A rise in *expected future inflation* shifts the short-run aggregate supply curve to the *left* from $SRAS_0$ to $SRAS_1$.
π
$SRAS_1$
$SRAS_0$
Y
Costs of Production Inputs ↑
A rise in costs of inputs into the production process, like energy, shifts the short-run aggregate supply curve to the *left* from $SRAS_0$ to $SRAS_1$.
π
$SRAS_1$
$SRAS_0$
Y

Changes in the prices of raw material inputs, as well as other external factors that change production costs, shift the short-run aggregate supply curve as well. The most common example of an input price change is a movement in the price of energy. When oil prices rise, increasing the cost of production, firms are forced to raise the prices of their products. The sharp increases in oil prices in the 1970s, from \$3.50 a barrel in 1973 to \$10 a barrel in 1976 and \$39 a barrel in 1980, contributed to inflation during that decade.[12] Conversely, when oil prices fall, as they did in 1986 and again in 1999, inflation tends to fall. The same thing happens when labor costs rise, as they do when payroll taxes increase or the cost of employer-provided health insurance rises. *An increase in production costs causes the short-run aggregate supply curve to shift to the left*, as shown in the lower panel of Figure 21.12.

The Long-Run Aggregate Supply Curve

The final step in completing our discussion of output and inflation fluctuations is to examine the long run. What happens after prices and wages have had time to make the adjustments that in the long run bring output and inflation back to normal? The answer (from the first part of this chapter) is that the economy moves to the point where current output equals potential output, and inflation equals expected inflation, while the level of inflation itself is determined by money growth. The implications of this answer are that in the long run, current output must equal potential output, and inflation must be determined by monetary policy. That is, in the long run, output and inflation are unrelated, and *the* **long-run aggregate supply (LRAS) curve** *is vertical at the point where current output equals potential output.*

[12]Compared with this episode, the surge of oil prices in 2007–2008 had far less impact on inflation because long-term inflation expectations were well anchored.

The Phillips Curve
MONEY AND BANKING BLOG

Economists have debated the relationship between inflation and unemployment at least since A. W. Phillips published his study of U.K. data from 1861 to 1957 over 60 years ago.* The idea that a tight or slack labor market should result in faster or slower wage gains seems like a natural corollary to standard economic thinking about how prices respond to imbalances between demand and supply. But, over the years, disputes about this *Phillips curve* relationship have been and remain fierce.

As the U.S. labor market tightened in the late 2010s, with the unemployment rate sinking to levels not seen since the 1960s, policymakers were facing the question whether inflation would make a comeback. How useful is the Phillips curve as a guide for Federal Reserve policymakers who wish to achieve a 2 percent inflation target over the long run?

Despite evidence of a negative relationship between wage inflation and unemployment, there are reasons to believe that central banks ought not to rely on a stable Phillips curve for setting monetary policy. To understand why, we can look at some data. Figure 21.13 plots the civilian unemployment rate (horizontal axis) and wage inflation two years later (vertical axis). It divides the observations into three distinct periods: the 1960s (red squares); the 1970s, 1980s, and 1990s (blue triangles); and 2000 to 2016 (black circles). Amid the scatter plots, the chart also shows simple regression estimates for each period. While there appears to be a relationship in the early and later periods (the lines fit well), the three intervening decades are another story altogether.

Looking at these data, it is unsurprising that, based on experience through the early 1960s, many U.S. observers concluded that there was a stable, negative relationship between the *level* of unemployment and the *level* of inflation. As a result, policymakers thought they could choose where along this tradeoff they wanted the economy to operate.

But, to the extent that there was a consensus, it was short-lived. In the late 1960s, Milton Friedman and Edmund Phelps noted that Phillips had failed to distinguish real wages from nominal wages, and it is deviations of unemployment from some normal (or *natural*) rate that should matter for wage changes. The first point means that it is essential to take account of *expected* inflation, while the second implies that changes in economic structure can lead to movements in unemployment that are not going to put pressure on inflation in one direction or the other.†

Friedman and Phelps had not come to their conclusions in a vacuum. While the first half of the 1960s was characterized by extremely low inflation—prices rose roughly 1¼ percent per year and wages 3 percent—the second half of the 1960s looked quite different. By the end of the decade, prices were going up at a rate of more than 4 percent per year and wages were rising at a 6 percent annual rate.

Taking these lessons to heart, researchers sought to patch their estimated Phillips curves, adding various bells and whistles. Nevertheless, the 1970s brought major new challenges for Phillips-curve adherents. First, there was the combination of high inflation and high unemployment, known as *stagflation* (the blue triangles in the upper part of the Figure 21.13). Second, building on the Friedman and Phelps logic, Robert Lucas emphasized the importance of focusing on deviations of inflation from what is expected.‡ In this formulation, the inflation–unemployment relationship becomes a mere artifact that is inherently unstable, not something policymakers can exploit.

The policy lessons following from these developments are profound. For example, if *forward-looking* expectations dominate inflation dynamics, then it should be possible to lower inflation without inducing high levels of unemployment. Instead, a credible policy commitment, which convinces people that a resolute central bank will set policy to lower inflation, can itself be sufficient to lower inflation. Put differently, if people believe policymakers will act to lower inflation, the authorities can achieve this goal without inducing a recession.

Today, economists agree that commitment is key to promoting price stability. Many people believe that an aggressive, speedy effort to lower inflation (buttressed by a policy commitment) is less costly in terms of unemployment than a gradual one. In practice, however, commitment has its limits. The Volcker disinflation of the early 1980s that was accompanied by a large rise in the unemployment rate is a case in point.

Macroeconomic models like the one that we study in this chapter clearly link inflation to economic slack. That is, they incorporate a Phillips curve. However, unlike their antecedents, these formulations do not lead to an exploitable tradeoff between inflation and unemployment. Instead, they imply that there is a tradeoff between the *volatility* of inflation and the *volatility* of the

Figure 21.13 Wage Inflation and the Unemployment Rate (quarterly), 1960-2016

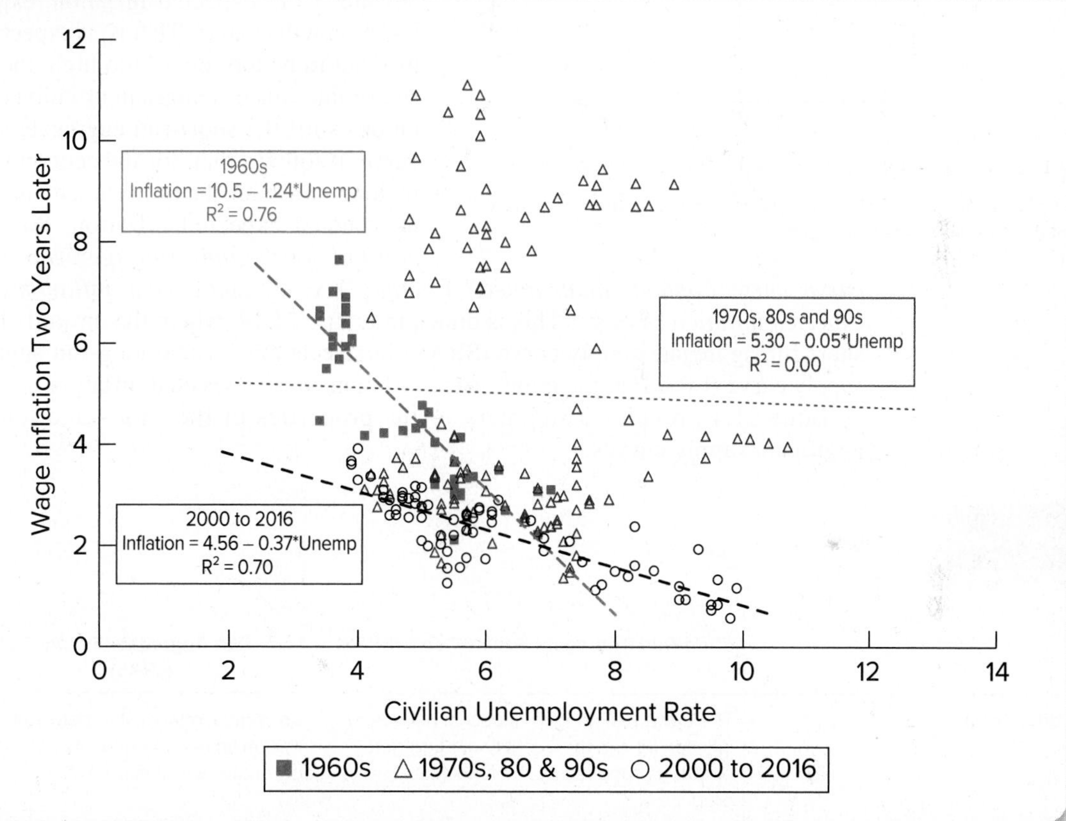

SOURCE: FRED.

output gap (see Chapter 22, page 638). Put differently, the models that frequently guide central bank thinking today allow policymakers to choose only the relative speed at which they wish to return inflation to its target or the unemployment rate to its norm. As a guide for policy, the simple relationship between inflation and the unemployment rate is no more reliable today than it was 50 years ago.

*A. W. Phillips, "The Relation between Unemployment and the Rate of Change of Money Wage Rates in the United Kingdom, 1861–1957," *Economica* 25, no. 100 (November 1958), pp. 283–299.

†Milton Friedman, "The Role of Monetary Policy." Presidential address delivered at the 80th Annual Meeting of the American Economic Association; published in *American Economic Review* 58, no. 1 (March 1968), pp. 1–17; Edmund S. Phelps, "Phillips Curves, Expectations of Inflation and Optimal Unemployment over Time," *Economica* 34, no. 135 (August 1967), pp. 254–281.

‡Robert Lucas Jr., "Expectations and the Neutrality of Money," *Journal of Economic Theory* 4, no. 2 (April 1972), pp. 103–124.

Figure 21.14 Short- and Long-Run Aggregate Supply Curves

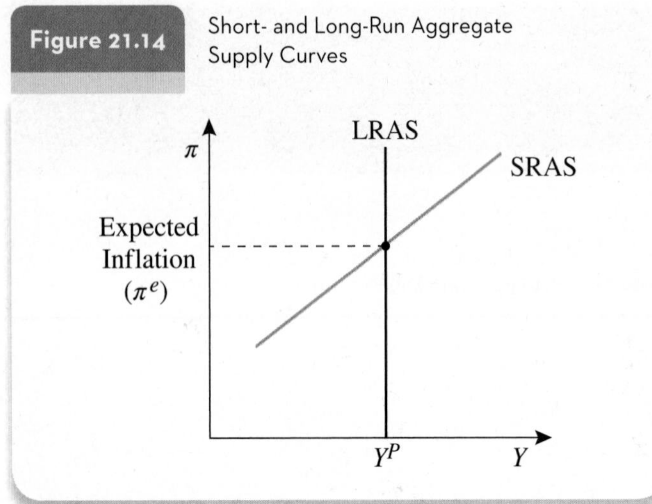

The long-run aggregate supply curve (LRAS) is vertical at the point where current output equals potential output.

This conclusion makes sense. In deriving the short-run aggregate supply curve, we noted that inflation depends on inflation expectations. That is, when workers and firms make the wage and price decisions that determine today's inflation, they do it with an eye toward future inflation. And an increase in expected inflation shifts the short-run aggregate supply curve to the left (as in Figure 21.12).

We also noted that when current inflation deviates from expected inflation, expected inflation will change. That is, if expectations turn out to be too low or too high, they will rise or fall. Since changes in inflation expectations shift the short-run aggregate supply curve, it follows that, for the economy to be in long-run equilibrium, current inflation must equal expected inflation. So *at any point along the long-run aggregate supply curve, current output equals potential output ($Y = Y^P$) and current inflation equals expected inflation ($\pi = \pi^e$).* This is drawn in Figure 21.14, where the upward-sloping short-run aggregate supply curve (SRAS) intersects the vertical long-run aggregate supply curve (LRAS) at the point where inflation equals expected inflation.

Table 21.4 provides a summary of the properties of the short- and long-run aggregate supply curves.

Table 21.4 Aggregate Supply

	Short-Run Aggregate Supply Curve (SRAS)	**Long-Run Aggregate Supply Curve (LRAS)**
What is it?	The upward-sloping relationship between inflation (π) and the quantity of aggregate output (Y) supplied by the firms that produce it.	The vertical relationship between inflation (π) and the quantity of aggregate output supplied.
What is its slope?	Because production costs adjust slowly, increases in product prices make it profitable to increase quantity supplied, so the SRAS is upward sloping.	In the long run, all prices and wages adjust and the economy moves to the point where current output equals potential output, so the LRAS is vertical at $Y = Y^P$.
What determines its location?	It intersects the long-run aggregate supply curve (LRAS) where inflation equals expected inflation ($\pi = \pi^e$).	The LRAS is vertical at potential output.
When does it shift?	1. When expected inflation increases, the SRAS shifts to the left. 2. When production costs rise, the SRAS shifts to the left.	When potential output (Y^P) changes, the LRAS shifts. An increase in Y^P shifts the LRAS to the right; a decrease shifts it to the left.

Equilibrium and the Determination of Output and Inflation

Short-Run Equilibrium

We now have the tools we need to understand both the movements in output and inflation in the short run and their determination in the long run. Short-run equilibrium is determined by the intersection of the dynamic aggregate demand curve (AD) with the short-run aggregate supply curve (SRAS). Combining the AD curve from Figure 21.9 and the SRAS curve from Figure 21.11, we get Figure 21.15. Current output and inflation are determined by the intersection at point *E* in the figure. And, like all supply and demand diagrams, changes in inflation and output arise from shifts in either supply, demand, or both. We'll have a detailed look at the sources and consequences of these shifts in Chapter 22.[13]

Adjustment to Long-Run Equilibrium

What happens when current inflation deviates from expected inflation? Earlier we saw that changes in expected inflation *shift* the short-run aggregate supply curve. This means that unless current inflation equals expected inflation, the economy cannot be in long-run equilibrium. To see how adjustment to long-run equilibrium works, let's look at two cases: one in which current inflation is above expected inflation ($\pi > \pi^e$) and one in which it is below expected inflation ($\pi < \pi^e$). These two cases correspond to situations in which current output is above ($Y > Y^P$) or

Figure 21.15 Short-Run Determination of Output and Inflation

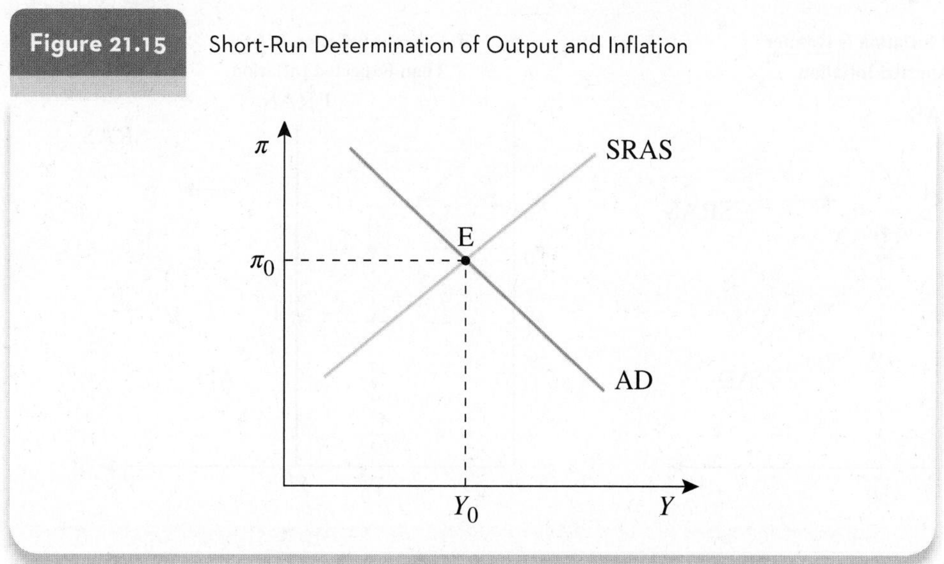

In the short run, inflation and output are determined by the intersection of the short-run aggregate supply curve (SRAS) and the dynamic aggregate demand curve (AD), at point *E* above.

[13]The appendix to this chapter derives the short-run equilibrium in an algebraic model.

below potential output ($Y < Y^P$). That is, these reflect movements along short-run aggregate supply curves in which expansionary output gaps push current inflation above expected inflation and recessionary output gaps depress current inflation below expected inflation.

Turning to the details, in the first case current inflation exceeds expected inflation ($\pi_0 > \pi_0^e$) and current output exceeds potential output ($Y_0 > Y^P$). Because inflation expectations follow current inflation, they will rise, exerting upward pressure on wages and production costs, shifting the short-run aggregate supply curve to the left. This process continues until inflation expectations are equal to the current level of inflation, which will occur at the point where output equals potential output ($Y = Y^P$), as shown in Panel A of Figure 21.16. At first, the quantity of aggregate output demanded equals the quantity supplied in the short run at point 0, but current inflation (π_0) is greater than expected inflation (π_0^e). As a result, inflation expectations rise, shifting the short-run aggregate supply curve to the left until it reaches point 1, where current inflation equals expected inflation. Only at this point do inflation and output stop changing.

Now consider the second case, in which current inflation is below expected inflation ($\pi_0 < \pi_0^e$) and current output is lower than potential output ($Y_0 < Y^P$). Because people form their expectations based on recent experience, inflation expectations begin to fall, shifting the short-run aggregate supply curve to the right. Again, the process continues until current inflation equals expected inflation, at which point current output will be equal to potential output. This is shown in Panel B of Figure 21.16.

Figure 21.16 Adjustment to Long-Run Equilibrium

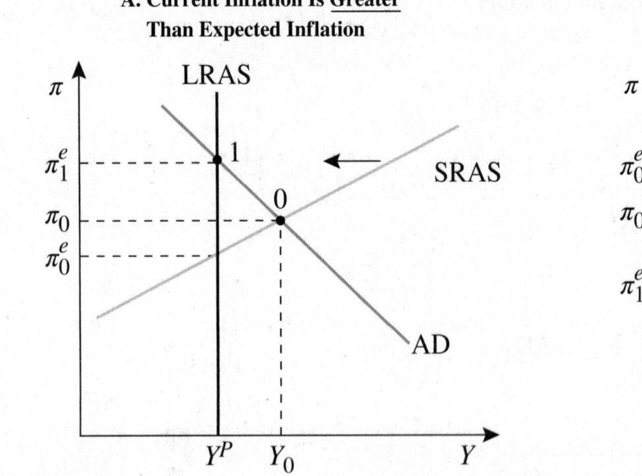

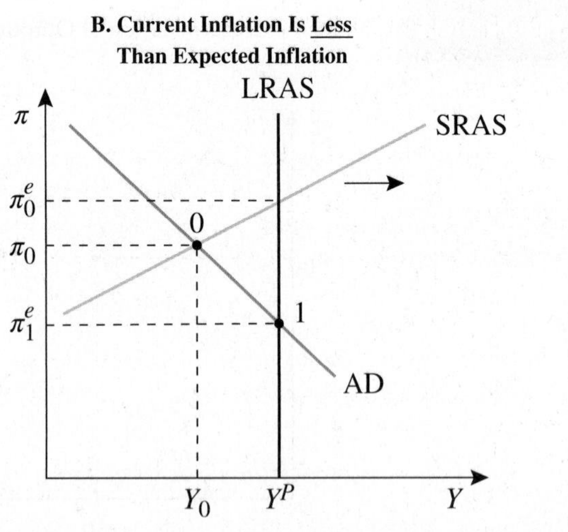

Panel A: At the initial short-run equilibrium point 0, current inflation is greater than expected inflation ($\pi > \pi_0^e$), so expected inflation rises. This shifts the short-run aggregate supply curve (SRAS) to the left. This process continues until the economy reaches point 1, where current inflation and expected inflation are equal ($\pi = \pi_1^e$).

Panel B: At the initial short-run equilibrium point 0, current inflation is less than expected inflation ($\pi < \pi_0^e$), so expected inflation falls. This shifts the short-run aggregate supply curve (SRAS) to the right. This process continues until the economy reaches point 1, where current inflation and expected inflation are equal ($\pi = \pi_1^e$).

This example has several important implications. First, it shows that the economy has a self-correcting mechanism. When actual inflation moves away from expected inflation, output moves away from its long-run equilibrium level. Furthermore, at this point inflation also moves away from the central bank's target and policymakers respond by changing the real interest rate. This moves the economy along the dynamic aggregate demand curve until it returns to its long-run equilibrium. Second, the fact that inflation changes whenever there is an output gap reinforces our conclusion that in the long run output returns to potential output. This is why we drew the long-run aggregate supply curves as a vertical line in the figures.

Long-run equilibrium is the point at which the economy comes to rest. Because we will be using it as a benchmark for understanding fluctuations, it is important to list its properties. As we noted earlier, in the long run, current inflation must equal expected inflation. Furthermore, when current output equals potential output, the real interest rate equals the long-run real interest rate. And going back to the monetary policy reaction curve, we know that policymakers set the real interest rate equal to this long-run level when current inflation equals their inflation target. So there are three conditions for long-run equilibrium:

1. Current inflation equals expected inflation ($\pi = \pi^e$),
2. Current output equals potential output ($Y = Y^P$), and
3. Current inflation is steady and equal to target inflation ($\pi = \pi^T$).

The Sources of Fluctuations in Output and Inflation

The next chapter uses the framework we have just developed to help us understand a series of problems that are of direct interest to policymakers. But before getting to that, let's finish up with a brief discussion of the possible sources of fluctuations in U.S. inflation and real growth and then a quick examination of the data. What might have caused these fluctuations over the past half century?

Looking at the macroeconomic model, we can see that output and inflation movements can arise from either demand or supply shifts. To figure how we might tell them apart, notice that while shifts in either the dynamic aggregate demand curve or the short-run aggregate supply curve can have the same effect on inflation, they have opposite effects on output. So, if the dynamic aggregate demand curve shifts to the right, increasing inflation, it will result in higher output as well. By contrast, when the short-run aggregate supply curve shifts to the left, inflation rises and output falls. That is, the possible sources of fluctuations are: (1) shifts in the dynamic aggregate demand curve that cause output and inflation to rise and fall together, moving in the *same* direction; and (2) shifts in the short-run aggregate supply curve that move output and inflation in *opposite* directions, one rises when the other one falls.

So, what are the likely sources of economic fluctuations? Let's start with inflation. Recall that in long-run equilibrium, inflation equals the central bank's target, which is equal to inflation expectations. So, if we see inflation rise or fall permanently, it must be that policymakers changed their inflation target, consciously or not. By contrast, short-run inflation fluctuations have more than one possible source. Inflation goes up in the short run either when the dynamic aggregate demand curve shifts to the right, or when the short-run aggregate supply curve shifts to the left. The first of these comes from either increases in the components of aggregate expenditure that are not sensitive to the real interest rate (higher government expenditure, business optimism, or consumer confidence) or a permanent easing of monetary policy (when the monetary policy reaction curve shifts to lower the real interest rate at every level of inflation). Each of these shifts dynamic aggregate demand to the right, increasing inflation. The second comes from higher inflation expectations or increases in the costs of production, like a rise in oil prices—each of which shifts the short-run aggregate supply curve to the left, driving inflation up.[14]

Turning to output, there are again two possible sources of fluctuations. Output drops when either the dynamic aggregate demand curve or the short-run aggregate supply curve shift to the left. For demand, either a decline in aggregate expenditure or a shift to the left in the monetary policy reaction curve drives current output below potential output. This brings up the interesting possibility that policymakers could be the sources of recessions. On the supply side, increases in either production costs or inflation expectations drive output down (at the same time that they drive inflation up). Which is it? Let's see if we can figure it out.

What Causes Recessions?

For years, economists have argued over the cause of recessions. Is it (1) shifts in the dynamic aggregate demand curve brought about by changes in consumer confidence, business optimism, or monetary policy; or (2) shifts in the short-run aggregate supply curve caused by increases in oil prices and other production costs? We can make some progress toward figuring out the answer by recalling that with a shift in the dynamic aggregate demand curve output and inflation move in the same direction, while a shift in short-run aggregate supply moves output and inflation in opposite directions. So if demand shifts were the cause of recessions, we should see inflation decline when output falls. And if production cost increases were the source, then we should see inflation rise as the economy weakens.

Table 21.5 lists the dates of recessions since the mid-1950s. The peak (column 1) is the beginning of the recession, when economic activity was at its highest before beginning to slide, and the trough (column 2) is the lowest point of the recession, when economic activity began to rise. The third column of the table shows the change in inflation from the beginning to the end of the recession. Note that inflation fell in seven of the past nine recessions. The recession of 1973–1975 (in bold) is the only case in which inflation rose. Oil prices tripled in 1973, driving up production costs and shifting the short-run aggregate supply curve to the left. The result was a protracted recession and a dramatic increase in inflation.

It appears that three-quarters of the recessions in the past half century can be traced to shifts in the dynamic aggregate demand curve. Let's go further and figure out what caused these AD shifts. Was it falling aggregate expenditure brought about by changes in people's attitudes, or was it the actions of monetary policymakers? To see, we can look at one more piece of evidence: the behavior of interest rates. Figure 21.17 shows that shortly before each recession starts, just to the left of each of the shaded bars, the interest rate tends to rise. This suggests that Federal Reserve policy is at least partly to blame for the business cycle downturns over the past half century. But why would policymakers have chosen to cause these recessions? The answer is to bring down inflation. Especially in the late 1970s, when the

[14]As we will discuss in the next chapter, when oil prices rise, the long-run aggregate supply curve may shift as well.

Table 21.5 Inflation during Recessions

Peak	Trough	Inflation Change
August 1957	April 1958	3.6 to 3.5 ↓
April 1960	February 1961	1.7 to 1.4 ↓
December 1969	November 1970	5.7 to 5.4 ↓
November 1973	**March 1975**	**7.9 to 10.0 ↑**
January 1980	July 1980	13.0 to 12.4 ↓
July 1981	November 1982	10.3 to 4.4 ↓
July 1990	March 1991	4.7 to 4.7 =
March 2001	November 2001	2.9 to 1.8 ↓
December 2007	June 2009	4.2 to −1.2 ↓

SOURCE: Inflation is the 12-month percent change in the all-items CPI-U from the Bureau of Labor Statistics (CPIAUCSL). Business cycle peaks and troughs are from the NBER (USREC). FRED data codes are in parentheses.

inflation rate was over 10 percent per year, something had to be done. The only thing the Fed could do under such circumstances was to raise interest rates, reducing the interest-sensitive components of aggregate expenditure in the process and triggering a recession. The low inflation we enjoy today is the result of the Fed's tough policy decisions.

Figure 21.17 Interest Rates and the Business Cycle

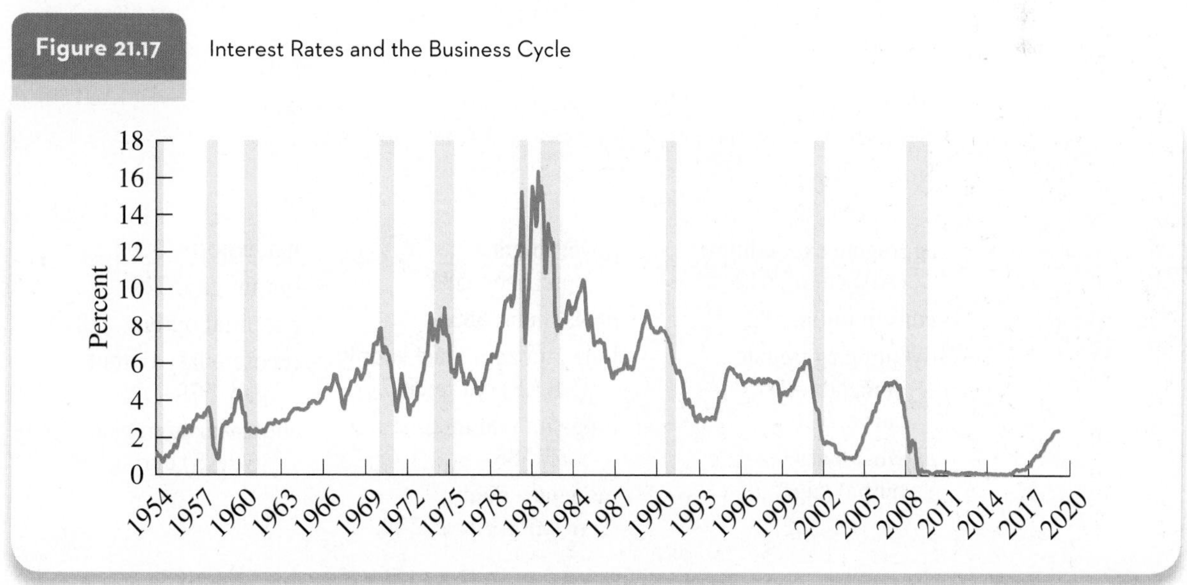

SOURCE: The solid line represents the three-month Treasury bill rate (TB3MS); the shaded bars denote recessions, as dated by the National Bureau of Economic Research. The FRED data code is in parentheses.

Zero Matters
APPLYING THE CONCEPT

The invention of the number zero transformed mathematics and laid the foundations for modern science.

Zero matters in economics, too. Arithmetically, it separates economic growth from contraction. It also divides inflation from deflation. But, in two important economic senses, inflation and deflation are not symmetrical: first, central banks cannot lower interest rates much below zero; and second, employers find it more difficult to cut wages than to raise them.

In setting their interest rate policies, central banks face an effective lower bound (see Chapter 18). This makes inflation of 2 percent and deflation of 2 percent very different. When inflation is 2 percent and the central bank lowers the nominal interest rate to zero to battle a recession, it thus lowers the expected real interest rate (the nominal interest rate minus the expected rate of inflation) to −2 percent (that's minus 2 percent). In contrast, with deflation of 2 percent, the real rate is +2 percent. Since the real, rather than the nominal, interest rate is what influences employment and growth, monetary policymakers are better able to stabilize economic activity using conventional interest rate policy in a world of modest inflation than in a world of modest deflation.

Added to this constraint on nominal interest rates is downward nominal wage rigidity. You might think wages are just another price that can go down as easily as it can go up. Experience indicates otherwise. When average wage inflation is low, there are fewer wage cuts and more instances of zero wage change than you would expect if wages were completely flexible. What that means is that deflation pushes real labor costs up in a destabilizing way.

Downward wage rigidity makes mild deflations more troublesome than mild inflations. The experience of some periphery euro-area countries over the past few years illustrates the problem. Despite the record levels of unemployment in those countries, institutional factors hindered firms' ability to cut workers' wages, which depressed the demand for labor. Spain's experience is especially instructive: its unemployment rate rose by 15 percentage points at the same time that hourly wages rose by nearly 14 percent!

Fears of deflation can easily be overdone: the economic impact of an annual price change of −0.1 percent is virtually indistinguishable from that of +0.1 percent. Yet, because they are limited by the effective lower bound for nominal interest rates, conventional monetary policy tools are ill-suited to restoring price stability in the face of a persistent annual deflation rate of 1 or 2 percent. And the presence of downward wage rigidities makes things even worse.

The bottom line: zero matters.

Key Terms

aggregate expenditure (AE) curve, 612
consumption, 582
dynamic aggregate demand (AD) curve, 591
expansionary output gap, 579
government purchases, 583
investment, 583
long-run aggregate supply (LRAS) curve, 597
long-run real interest rate, 585
monetary policy reaction curve, 589
net exports, 583
output gap, 579
potential output, 578
recessionary output gap, 579
short-run aggregate supply (SRAS) curve, 595

Using FRED: Codes for Data in This Chapter

Data Series	FRED Data Code
Real GDP	GDPC1
Potential real GDP	GDPPOT
Consumer price index less food and energy	CPILFESL
Federal funds rate	FEDFUNDS
U.S. 10-year Treasury constant maturity rate	GS10
U.S. 5-year Treasury constant maturity rate	GS5
U.S. 5-year Treasury inflation-indexed yield	FII5
Moody's Baa yield	BAA
U.S. 3-month Treasury bill rate	TB3MS
1-year inflation expectations (Michigan survey)	MICH
Real personal consumption expenditures	PCECC96
Real gross private domestic investment	GPDIC1
Real net exports of goods and services	NETEXC
Real government outlays	GCEC1
NBER recession dates (0 = expansion, 1 = recession)	USREC
CBOE volatility index: VIX	VIXCLS
Index of consumer sentiment (Michigan survey)	UMCSENT
Price of oil	WTISPLC

Chapter Lessons

1. In the long run:
   a. Current output equals potential output, which is the level of output the economy produces when its resources are used at normal rates.
   b. Inflation equals money growth minus growth in potential output.
2. The dynamic aggregate demand curve is a downward-sloping relationship between inflation and the quantity of output demanded by those who use it:
   a. Aggregate expenditure = Consumption + Investment + Government purchases + Net exports.
      i. Aggregate expenditure falls when the real interest rate rises.
      ii. The long-run real interest rate r^* equates aggregate expenditure with potential output.
   b. Monetary policy is described by an upward-sloping monetary policy reaction curve.
      i. When policymakers change the nominal interest rate, they change the real interest rate as well, because expected inflation usually doesn't change quickly.
      ii. Policymakers react to increases in inflation by increasing the real interest rate (as the Taylor rule indicates).

To learn more about the changing financial system, visit www.moneyandbanking.com.

iii. The monetary policy reaction curve is set so that the real interest rate equals the long-run real interest rate r^* when inflation equals the central bank's target.
iv. The monetary policy reaction curve shifts when either the inflation target changes or r^* changes.

c. Movements along the dynamic aggregate demand curve occur when monetary policymakers react to changes in inflation by adjusting the real interest rate.
d. The dynamic aggregate demand curve shifts when:
   i. An increase in consumer confidence, business optimism, government purchases, or net exports shifts the dynamic aggregate demand curve to the right.
   ii. The monetary policy reaction curve shifts to the right, shifting the dynamic aggregate demand curve to the right.

3. The aggregate supply curve tells us the amount of output producers are willing to supply at given levels of inflation.
   a. The short-run aggregate supply curve slopes up because, in the short run, costs of production adjust more slowly than output prices.
   b. Production cost changes shift the short-run aggregate supply curve. These occur when:
      i. Expectations about future inflation change.
      ii. Raw material prices, such as the cost of energy, change.
   c. The long-run aggregate supply curve is vertical at potential output.
      i. Along the long-run aggregate supply curve, expected inflation equals current inflation.
      ii. The long-run aggregate supply curve shifts when either the amounts of capital and labor used in the economy change or productivity changes.
      iii. The short-run aggregate supply curve intersects the long-run aggregate supply curve at the point where inflation equals expected inflation.
4. Equilibrium output and inflation are determined by the intersection of the dynamic aggregate demand curve and either the short-run or long-run aggregate supply curve.
   a. The short-run equilibrium point is located where the dynamic aggregate demand curve intersects the short-run aggregate supply curve.
   b. The long-run equilibrium point is located where the dynamic aggregate demand curve intersects the long-run aggregate supply curve. At that point, inflation equals expected inflation, which equals the inflation target, and current output equals potential output.
   c. Fluctuations in output and inflation come from either:
      i. Demand shifts, which cause them to rise and fall together.
      ii. Supply shifts, which cause one to rise as the other falls.

Conceptual and Analytical Problems Mc Graw Hill connect

1. Explain the determinants of potential output growth. *(LO1)*
2.* Explain how a recessionary output gap would emerge in an economy where the long-run aggregate supply curve is persistently shifting to the right. *(LO1)*
3. Describe the determinants of the long-run real interest rate, r^*, and speculate on the sort of events that would make it fluctuate. *(LO1)*

*Indicates more difficult problems.

4. Explain how and why the components of aggregate expenditure depend on the real interest rate. Be sure to distinguish between real and nominal interest rates, and explain why the distinction matters. *(LO2)*

5.* Suppose that the aggregate expenditure curve for an economy can be expressed algebraically as

$$AE = 3{,}000 - 2{,}500r$$

where AE is aggregate expenditures and r is the real interest rate expressed as a decimal. If the level of potential output in this economy is 2,975, what is the long-run real interest rate, r^*? *(LO2)*

6. Suppose the U.S. economy is in equilibrium at the long-run real interest rate (r^*) that prevails when aggregate expenditure equals potential output. Draw a diagram of aggregate expenditure showing this initial equilibrium. Then suppose that foreign demand for U.S. exports falls due to a recession abroad. Show how r^* will change and explain your results. *(LO1)*

7. The European Central Bank's primary objective is price stability. Policymakers interpret this objective to mean keeping inflation below, but close to, 2 percent, as measured by a euro-area consumer price index. In contrast, the Fed has a dual objective of price stability and maximum sustainable employment. How might you expect the monetary policy reaction curves of the two central banks to differ? Why? *(LO2)*

8.* Explain why the short-run aggregate supply curve is upward sloping. Under what circumstances might it be vertical? *(LO3)*

9.* Assume the short-run aggregate supply curve can be expressed algebraically as

$$Y_s = 4{,}200 + 4{,}000\pi$$

where Y_s is aggregate supply, and the dynamic aggregate demand curve can be written as

$$Y_d = 4{,}300 - 1{,}000\pi$$

where Y_d is aggregate demand. Find the numerical values for equilibrium output, Y, and the equilibrium inflation rate, π, in the short run. *(LO4)*

10. Consider Panel B of Figure 21.16 where, at the initial short-run equilibrium point 0, current inflation is below expected inflation and output is below potential output. Suppose that the initial inflation target was at the level corresponding to point 1, but the central bank chooses to stimulate demand to speed the adjustment to long-run equilibrium. What action must the central bank take and what are the costs and benefits of such a policy? *(LO4)*

11. Suppose the real interest rate unexpectedly falls in the absence of other economic changes. What would you expect to happen to (a) consumption, (b) investment, and (c) net exports in the economy? *(LO3)*

12.* Economy A and Economy B are similar in every way except that in Economy A, 50 percent of aggregate expenditure is sensitive to changes in the real interest rate and in Economy B, 70 percent of aggregate expenditure is sensitive to changes in the real interest rate. *(LO2)*
   a. Which economy will have a steeper aggregate expenditure curve?
   b. How would the dynamic aggregate demand curves differ given that the monetary policy reaction curve is the same in both countries?

   Explain your answers.

*Indicates more difficult problems.

13. Given the expected relationship between the real interest rate and investment, how would you explain a scenario where investment continued to fall despite low or even negative real interest rates? *(LO3)*
14. State whether each of the following will result in a movement along or a shift in the monetary policy reaction curve and in which direction the effect will be. *(LO2)*
    a. Policymakers increase the real interest rate in response to a rise in current inflation.
    b. Policymakers increase their inflation target.
    c. The long-run real interest rate falls.
15. Suppose a natural disaster wipes out a significant portion of the economy's capital stock, reducing the potential level of output. What would you expect to happen to the long-run real interest rate, r^*? What impact would this have on the monetary policy reaction curve and the dynamic aggregate demand curve? *(LO2)*
16. Suppose there were a wave of investor optimism in the economy. What would the impact be on the dynamic aggregate demand curve? *(LO2)*
17. Explain how each of the following affects the short-run aggregate supply curve. *(LO3)*
    a. Firms and workers reduce their expectations of future inflation.
    b. There is a fall in current inflation.
    c. There is a fall in oil prices.
18. Suppose the economy is in short-run equilibrium at a level of output that exceeds potential output. How would the economy self-adjust to return to long-run equilibrium? *(LO4)*
19. Why do you think the surge in oil prices in 2007–2008 had a much smaller impact on inflation expectations compared with the oil price shocks of the 1970s? *(LO4)*
20.* You read a news story blaming the central bank for pushing the economy into recession. The article goes on to mention that not only has output fallen below its potential level but that inflation had also risen. If you were to respond defending the central bank, what argument would you make? *(LO4)*
21. For each of the following economies, select the term—inflation, deflation, or disinflation—that best describes what the economy is experiencing. *(LO1)*

	March	April	May
Annual percent change in the consumer price index			
Economy A	−1.5%	−1.5%	−1.5%
Economy B	3.2%	2.3%	0.8%
Economy C	1.5%	1.5%	1.5%

22. As a monetary policymaker, would you be more concerned if the aggregate price level were persistently rising by 2 percent or persistently falling by 1 percent? Explain your answer. *(LO3)*

*Indicates more difficult problems.

23. A Phillips Curve postulates a negative relationship between inflation and economic slack. However, the relationship between wage inflation and lagged unemployment appeared more negative in the 1960s than in the period since 2000. In the macroeconomic model presented in this chapter, which curve would be altered by this "flattening" of the Phillips Curve? *(LO3)*

Data Exploration Mc Graw Hill connect

For general information on using Federal Reserve Economic Data (FRED) online, visit www.mhhe.com/moneyandbanking6e.com *and refer to the FRED resources.*

1. Are long-term inflation expectations "well anchored"? Using monthly data since 2003, plot a measure of long-term inflation expectations based on the difference between the yields on a five-year Treasury bond (FRED code: GS5) and a five-year Treasury Inflation-Protected Securities (TIPS) bond (FRED code: FII5). What do you conclude? How did the financial crisis of 2007–2009 affect the measure? *(LO1)*
2. Is investment sensitive to the real interest rate? Plot since 1990 a measure of the real interest rate—based on the difference between Moody's Baa corporate bond yield (FRED code: BAA) and a survey of expected inflation (FRED code: MICH)—and (on the right scale) the share of investment (FRED code: GPDIC96) in real GDP (FRED code: GDPC1). Explain the cyclical pattern. *(LO2)*
3. How sensitive is private investment to risk? Plot since 2004 the share of real gross private domestic investment (FRED code: GPDIC96) in real GDP (FRED code: GDPC1) and (on the right scale) a measure of anticipated stock market volatility (FRED code: VIXCLS). Explain the pattern. *(LO2)*
4. A recession may reflect declines in aggregate demand, aggregate supply, or both. Are swings in consumer sentiment characteristic of recessions? Plot a measure of sentiment (FRED code: UMCSENT), and discuss its evolution during the recessions since 1980. Explain why consumer sentiment is an important example of an aggregate demand shock. *(LO2, LO3)*
5. How often are negative supply shocks associated with recessions? Plot on a quarterly basis since 1971 the real price of oil—measured as the ratio of the nominal spot price of West Texas intermediate oil (FRED code: WTISPLC) to the U.S. consumer price index (CPIAUCSL). Identify recessions that may have been triggered in part by an oil price shock. *(LO4)*

Appendix to Chapter 21

The Dynamic Aggregate Demand–Aggregate Supply Model

An algebraic version of the macroeconomic model presented in Chapter 21 begins with the **aggregate expenditure (AE) curve** shown in Figure 21.4.[15] Because consumption and investment are sensitive to the real interest rate, we can write this as

$$Y_t = \overline{Y} - \alpha r_t + d_t \qquad \text{(A1)}$$

where Y_t is current real output; r_t is the current level of the real interest rate; d_t is a transitory change in demand; and $\overline{Y}$ is the level of autonomous components of aggregate demand that are not sensitive to the interest rate, including government spending and the portions of consumption and investment driven by consumer and business confidence. The positive parameter α represents the sensitivity of aggregate expenditure to changes in the real interest rate. The larger α is, the steeper the slope of the AE curve in Figure 21.4. (You may be familiar with a version of equation (A1) from introductory macroeconomics, where it is labeled as an "IS" curve.)

In the chapter, we noted that the long-run real interest rate (r^*) equates the level of aggregate expenditure (Y_t) to potential output (Y^P). Equation (A1) allows us to derive that as

$$r^* = \frac{\overline{Y} - Y^P}{\alpha} \qquad \text{(A2)}$$

Note that r^* also is the same as the natural rate of interest that we defined in Chapter 18. Equation (A2) has the immediate implication that increases in $\overline{Y}$ drive r^* up. For example, as government expenditure rises or improved business confidence boosts investment, the long-run real interest rate will rise.

Next, we turn to the monetary policy reaction curve (MPRC). To simplify the exposition, we use a version of the Taylor rule from Chapter 18 that focuses only on deviations of current inflation from the central bank's target and excludes the output gap. Following the discussion in this chapter associated with Figure 21.7, we can write this as

$$r_t = r^* + \gamma(\pi_t - \pi^T) \qquad \text{(A3)}$$

[15] This algebraic model also is a simplified version of the model presented in Chapter 15 of the ninth edition of N. Gregory Mankiw's *Macroeconomics* (New York: Worth, 2016).

where π_t is current inflation, π^T denotes the central bank's inflation target, r^* is the natural rate of interest, and the positive parameter γ represents how aggressively policymakers react to inflation deviations from their target.[16]

Substituting equation (A3) into equation (A1), and using the solution for the long-run real interest rate in equation (A2) gives us the dynamic aggregate demand (AD) curve shown in Figure 21.7:

$$\pi_t = \pi^T - \left(\frac{1}{\alpha\gamma}\right)(Y_t - Y^P) + \left(\frac{1}{\alpha\gamma}\right)d_t \tag{A4}$$

Looking at this, we see first that when current output equals potential output, and in the absence of any transitory shocks, then current inflation equals the central bank's target level ($\pi_t = \pi^T$). Second, consistent with the negative slope of the AD curve in Figure 21.7, as output rises, inflation falls. Third, the larger the sensitivities of expenditure to the real interest rate (α) and of monetary policy to the inflation gap (γ), the flatter the AD curve.

Next, we turn to the short-run aggregate supply (SRAS) curve drawn in Figure 21.11. We can write this as

$$\pi_t = \pi_t^e + \beta(Y_t - Y^P) + s_t \tag{A5}$$

where π_t^e is expected inflation, β is a positive parameter equal to the reciprocal of the responsiveness of output to a pickup in current output price inflation relative to expected inflation, and s_t represents things that drive up production costs, like increases in the price of oil. You may recognize this as a version of the Phillips curve.

To complete the model, we need to characterize how inflation expectations are formed. There are a number of ways to do this. For our purposes, the simplest is to assume that people simply set their current inflation expectations at the same level of actual inflation they have recently experienced. Often referred to as "adaptive expectations," we can write this as

$$\pi_t^e = \pi_{t-1} \tag{A6}$$

Substituting equation (A5) into equation (A4), we get

$$\pi_t = \pi_{t-1} + \beta(Y_t - Y^P) + s_t \tag{A7}$$

The short-run equilibrium of the economy is characterized by the point where the AD curve (A3) crosses the SRAS curve (A6). The solution for inflation is as follows:

$$(\pi_t - \pi^T) = \left(\frac{1}{1 + \alpha\beta\gamma}\right)(\pi_{t-1} - \pi^T) + \left(\frac{\beta}{1 + \alpha\beta\gamma}\right)d_t + \left(\frac{1}{1 + \alpha\beta\gamma}\right)s_t \tag{A8}$$

And for output, we get something similar:

$$(Y_t - Y^P) = \left(\frac{1}{1 + \alpha\beta\gamma}\right)(Y_{t-1} - Y^P) + \left(\frac{1}{1 + \alpha\beta\gamma}\right)(d_t - d_{t-1}) - \left(\frac{\alpha\gamma}{1 + \alpha\beta\gamma}\right)s_t \tag{A9}$$

The algebraic model of inflation and output reflected in equations (A8) and (A9) incorporates key features of the geometric version presented in the chapter. These include the following (some of which will be explored further in Chapter 22):

[16] This formulation assumes that the nominal interest rate implied by the sum of the real interest rate (r_t) and the expected inflation rate (π_t^e) remains above the effective lower bound. For simplicity of exposition, equation (A3) also implicitly incorporates the Fisher equation described in Chapter 4—namely, the nominal interest rate equals the real interest rate plus expected inflation—by assuming that the central bank alters the real interest rate when it changes the nominal interest rate.

- A demand shock, d_t, shifts the AD curve along the SRAS curve, moving output and inflation in the *same* direction.
- A supply shock, s_t, shifts the SRAS curve along the AD curve, moving output and inflation in *opposite* directions.
- An aggressive central bank that is highly responsive to inflation deviations (so that γ is high) has a steep MPRC, resulting in a flat AD curve.
- In the face of a demand shock, d_t, an aggressive central bank that is highly responsive to inflation (so that γ is high) can keep inflation close to target in the short run, while also minimizing the impact of the shock on the output gap.
- In the face of a supply shock, s_t, an aggressive central bank that is highly responsive to inflation deviations (so that γ is high) can keep inflation close to target in the short run, but doing so will amplify the impact of the supply shock on the output gap.
- Shocks die out slowly. Here's the logic: The terms α, β, and γ are all positive, so their product, $(\alpha\beta\gamma)$, is positive as well. This means that the term in the denominator on the right-hand side of equations (A8) and (A9), namely $(1 + \alpha\beta\gamma)$, is *greater* than one. Consequently, the coefficients on lagged inflation in (A8) and on lagged output in (A9) are *less* than one. This means that the shock fades gradually with time.

Chapter

22 Understanding Business Cycle Fluctuations*

Learning Objectives

After reading this chapter, you should be able to:

LO1 Discuss the sources of fluctuations in output and inflation.

LO2 Use AS/AD tools to analyze changes in output and inflation.

LO3 Explain the challenges and tradeoffs that monetary policymakers face in stabilizing the economy.

In the last chapter we constructed a framework for understanding fluctuations in output and inflation. We discussed the fact that central bankers respond to rising inflation by increasing the real interest rate, causing interest-sensitive components of aggregate expenditure—especially investment—to fall, driving down the quantity of aggregate output demanded by the people who use it. So, higher inflation means a lower level of demand in the economy as a whole. The *dynamic aggregate demand curve slopes down.*

On the supply side, we saw that the sluggish response of production costs means that higher inflation elicits more production from firms, and is associated with a greater level of output supplied in the short run. The *short-run aggregate supply curve slopes up.* Finally, we learned that in the long run, the economy moves to the point where output equals potential output, so the *long-run aggregate supply curve is vertical.* While the economy can and does move away from this long-run equilibrium, it has a natural self-correcting mechanism that returns it to the point where resources are being used at their normal rates and gaps between current and potential output disappear.

We will now use this framework to improve our understanding of business cycle fluctuations. Why is it that output and inflation vary from quarter to quarter and year to year, and what determines the extent of fluctuations? Figure 22.1 illustrates the long-run trends in the U.S. inflation rate over more than 60 years. In 1965, prices in the United States were rising at an average rate of just 1½ percent per year. Fifteen years later, consumer price inflation had climbed to nearly 14 percent. For the next decade the inflation rate fell, at first sharply and then gradually. By 1991, prices were increasing at a rate of less than 4 percent per year. Finally, amid the financial crisis of 2007–2009, prices began to fall for the first time in more than 50 years.

*The starred sections in the second half of this chapter are more difficult than the nonstarred sections preceding them.

Figure 22.1 Inflation and the Business Cycle, 1955–2019

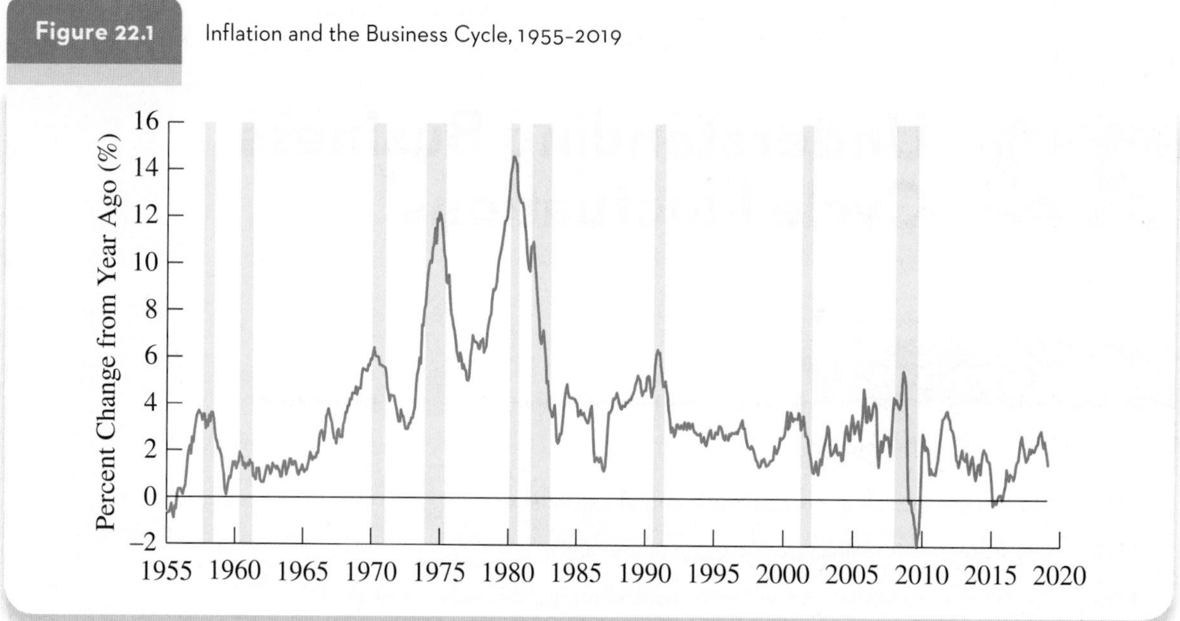

This figure shows the 12-month change in consumer prices, calculated by the Bureau of Labor Statistics (FRED code: CPIAUCSL). The bars represent recessions, as dated by the National Bureau of Economic Research.

SOURCE: FRED.

In addition to data on the rate of inflation, Figure 22.1 displays a series of shaded bars representing recessions—periods when the U.S. real GDP was falling. While there is no apparent relationship between the *level* of inflation and these recessions, it does appear that the inflation rate falls when the economy is contracting and rises when it is expanding. At least, that's what happens most of the time. The recession of 1974–1975 is an exception. During that episode, the inflation rate rose dramatically even as the economy was slumping. And during much of the boom of the 1990s, the inflation rate remained below its level at the end of the last recession. But in general, there appears to be a connection between growth and changes in inflation: The lower the growth, the more likely inflation is to fall.

One final point about Figure 22.1 is worth noting. In recent decades, the frequency of recessions has fallen. In the 30 years from 1955 to 1984, there were six recessions; in the 35 years since then, there have been three, including the deep one that ended in 2009. Recessions used to occur once every five years, but more recently, they have occurred on average about every 8 to 10 years. Until the record plunge of 2008–2009, the recessions after 1982 were milder than before as well. This reduction in the volatility of real growth has been called the "Great Moderation." We examine its possible sources later in the chapter and identify factors that could prevent its resumption in coming years.

To help understand the patterns in Figure 22.1, we will start by cataloging the various reasons that the dynamic aggregate demand curve and the aggregate supply curve shift. These are the potential sources of fluctuations in both output and inflation described at the end of the last chapter. We trace the initial impact of shifts in aggregate demand such as an increase in government spending or shifts in short-run aggregate supply such as a movement in oil prices. Next, we examine what happens during the transition as the economy moves to long-run equilibrium. Our goal is to take the macroeconomic model and use it to understand practical real-world examples.

Then, in the second part of the chapter, we will use the model to understand how central bankers work to achieve their stabilization objectives, together with a series of examples that highlight the pitfalls and limitations that monetary policymakers face. The section is organized around a series of questions of increasing complexity. We will examine how, in practice, policymakers work to achieve their stabilization goals; the appropriate actions to take when potential output changes; and the difficulty central bankers have figuring out why output has fallen, among other things.

Sources of Fluctuations in Output and Inflation

In the earlier discussion we learned that the economy naturally moves toward its long-run equilibrium where output equals potential output ($Y = Y^P$) and inflation equals the central bank's target ($\pi = \pi^T$), which equals the level of inflation firms and individuals expect ($\pi = \pi^e$). This tells us that the long-run aggregate supply curve is vertical at potential output. But because costs of production adjust slowly, higher inflation temporarily means higher profits and more supply; that is, the short-run aggregate supply curve slopes upward. Short-run equilibrium is the point where the dynamic aggregate demand curve intersects this short-run aggregate supply curve. So, immediately after either the short-run aggregate supply curve or the dynamic aggregate demand curve shift, the economy will move away from its long-run equilibrium. This means that understanding short-run fluctuations in output and inflation requires that we study shifts in dynamic aggregate demand and short-run aggregate supply.

Before moving to an analysis of various demand and supply curve shifts, let's take a brief detour to define one of the few new terms in this chapter: *shock*. Economists use the word *shock* to mean something unexpected. For example, when oil prices rise or when consumers become less confident about the future, these are almost always unpredictable *shocks*. In our framework, a shock shifts the dynamic aggregate demand or short-run aggregate supply curve. Because it affects costs of production, the oil price increase is a **supply shock**, while the shift in consumer confidence, which affects consumption expenditure, is a **demand shock**. So, a shock is something that creates a shift in the demand or supply curve.

Shifts in the Dynamic Aggregate Demand Curve

Recall that a shift in the dynamic aggregate demand curve can be caused by either a shift in the monetary policy reaction curve or a change in components that are not sensitive to the real interest rate (like government purchases) that shifts aggregate expenditure. Let's look at the impact of each of these. We will first look at a decline in the central bank's inflation target that shifts the monetary policy reaction curve, and then at a fiscal policy easing that increases government purchases and shifts the aggregate expenditure curve.

A Decline in the Central Bank's Inflation Target Over the past several decades, numerous countries have succeeded in reducing their inflation rates from fairly high levels to the modest ones we see today. For example, Chile was able to reduce its inflation rate from over 20 percent in the early 1990s to roughly 2 percent today. In the mid-1980s, Israel's inflation rate peaked at nearly 400 percent before it was brought down in a series of steps, first to 20 percent and eventually to 2 percent.

Figure 22.2 A Decline in the Central Bank's Inflation Target

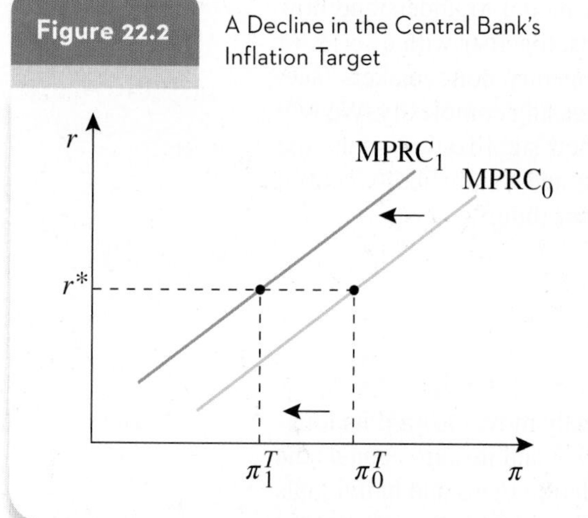

A decline in the inflation target from π_0^T to π_1^T shifts the monetary policy reaction curve to the left from $MPRC_0$ to $MPRC_1$.

And Sweden entered the 1990s with an inflation rate that was over 10 percent. The Riksbank, the Swedish central bank, spent a number of years driving the country's inflation rate down below 3 percent, where it has generally stayed. All of these cases involved permanent declines in inflation that must have been a result of a decrease in the central bank's inflation target.

To analyze the impact of a reduction in the policymaker's inflation target, let's begin with the monetary policy reaction curve. A fall in π^T shifts the monetary policy reaction curve to the left, as shown in Figure 22.2 (which reproduces Panel A of Figure 21.8 on page 590). The decrease in the inflation target raises the real interest rate policymakers set at each level of inflation.

We know from our earlier analysis that shifts in the monetary policy reaction curve shift the dynamic aggregate demand curve in the same direction. A decrease in the central bank's inflation target means a higher real interest rate at every level of inflation, shifting the monetary policy reaction curve to the left. This reduces aggregate expenditure at every level of inflation, shifting the dynamic aggregate demand curve to the left as well, as shown in Panel A of Figure 22.3. You can see that as the dynamic aggregate demand curve shifts to the left, from AD_0 to AD_1, the economy moves from the original short-run equilibrium

Figure 22.3 A Decline in the Central Bank's Inflation Target

A. Short-Run Equilibrium

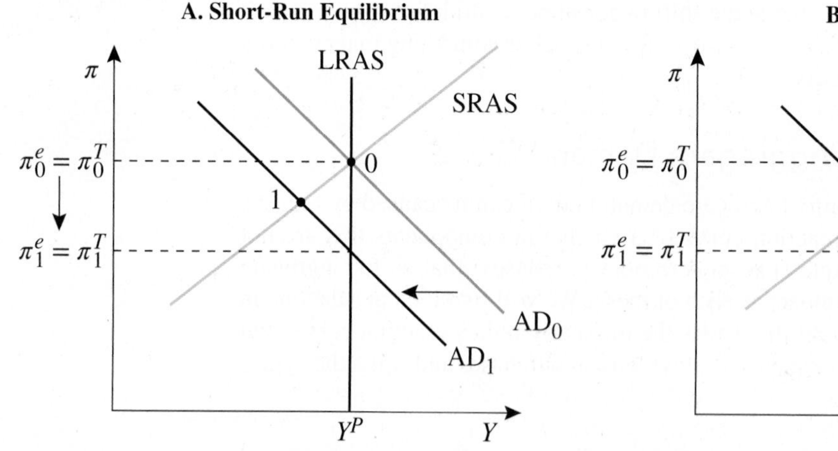

A decrease in the central bank's inflation target shifts the dynamic aggregate demand curve to the left from AD_0 to AD_1, moving the economy from point 0 to point 1.

B. Adjustment

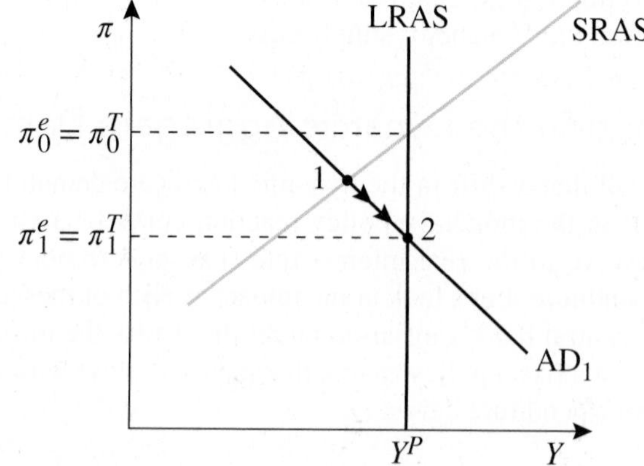

When the economy is at point 1, current inflation is less than the initial level of expected inflation (π_0^e). As a result, expected inflation falls, shifting the short-run aggregate supply curve to the right. The process continues until the economy reaches point 2, where expected inflation equals the new inflation target ($\pi_1^e = \pi_1^T$).

point, 0, to the new short-run equilibrium point, 1. At point 1, inflation and current output are both lower than they were prior to the monetary policy tightening. The immediate consequence of the reduction in the central bank's inflation target is to shift the dynamic aggregate demand curve to the left, moving the economy along the short-run aggregate supply curve (SRAS), driving both current output and inflation down.

Following the policy change, current inflation is less than expected inflation. As a result, expected inflation falls, shifting the short-run aggregate supply curve to the right. Eventually, the economy moves along the new dynamic aggregate demand curve AD_1 from point 1 to the new long-run equilibrium at point 2 in Panel B of Figure 22.3. There, inflation equals the central bank's (new) target and output equals potential output.[1]

An Increase in Government Purchases In response to the deep recession that began in December 2007, President George W. Bush signed legislation in February 2008 to cut income taxes temporarily. One year later, President Barack Obama approved a much larger package of temporary tax cuts and increases in government spending to counter the economic slump. Driven by the recession and these fiscal policy actions, the U.S. federal budget deficit surged from 1.2 percent of GDP in fiscal year 2007 (which ended September 2007) to 9.8 percent in 2009—the largest proportion since 1945. What are the macroeconomic implications of such a large expansionary move in fiscal policy?

In the last chapter we learned that increases in government purchases and cuts in taxes both represent an increase in components of aggregate expenditure that are not sensitive to the interest rate. For example, an increase in *G* shifts the dynamic aggregate demand curve to the right. Panel A of Figure 22.4 on page 620 shows how such a change in fiscal policy shifts the dynamic aggregate demand curve from its original position AD_0 to its new position AD_1. As a result, the economy moves from the original short-run equilibrium point 0 to the new short-run equilibrium point 1. Not surprisingly, the immediate impact of this increase in government purchases is to raise both current output and inflation. But, because current inflation exceeds expected inflation, this can't be the long-run effect. Instead, expected inflation rises, shifting the short-run aggregate supply curve to the left. Eventually, as the economy travels along AD_1, current inflation rises and current output falls until the economy reaches the point at which the dynamic aggregate demand curve crosses the long-run aggregate supply curve. At that point, current inflation equals expected inflation and target inflation, while current output equals potential output.

Unless something else happens, the economy settles at point 2 in Panel B of Figure 22.4, where AD_1 crosses the long-run aggregate supply curve (LRAS) and current output once again equals potential output. It is extremely important to realize that at point 2, inflation is above where it started at point 0, and that this is above the policymakers' original inflation target π^T. Unless monetary policy adjusts, when the dynamic aggregate demand curve shifts to the right, inflation will rise. Thus, Panel B shows the central bank acquiescing to a rise of its inflation target to point 2.

While central bankers could allow an increase in government purchases to drive up their inflation target, permanently increasing inflation and the monetary growth rate, it seems unlikely. So long as monetary policymakers remain committed to their original inflation target, they need to do something to get the economy back to the point where it began—point 0 in Panel A of Figure 22.4, at the intersection of the original dynamic

[1]With a lower inflation target (π^T), we also know that at the new long-run equilibrium, expected inflation (π^e) must be lower as well.

Figure 22.4 An Increase in Government Expenditure

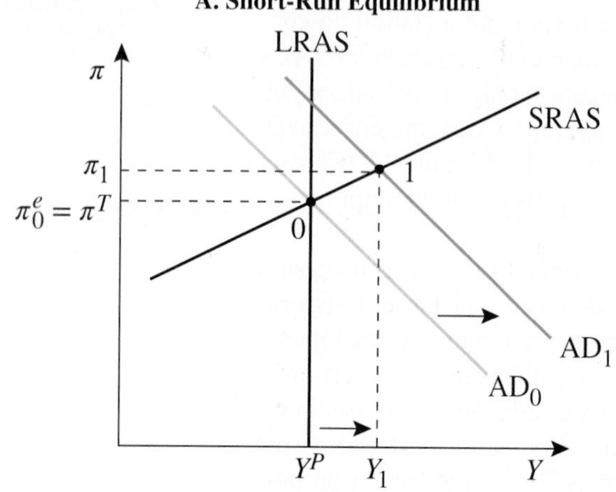

An increase in government expenditure shifts the AD curve to the right from AD_0 to AD_1. This moves the economy from point 0 to point 1. In the short run, output rises to Y_1 while inflation increases to π_1.

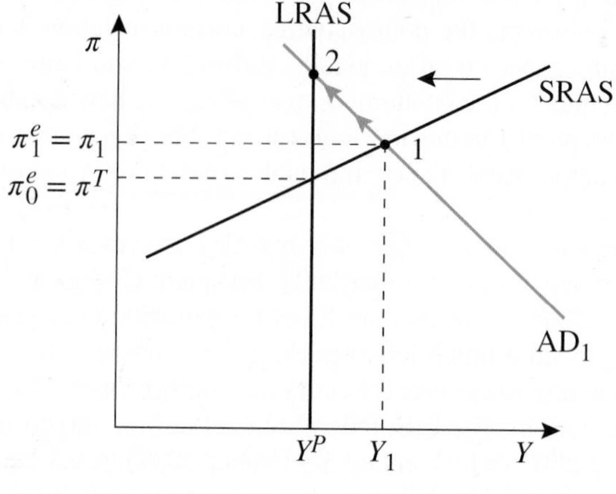

When the economy is at point 1, current inflation is initially above expected inflation ($\pi_1 > \pi_0^e$) As expected inflation rises in response, the short-run aggregate supply curve shifts to the left, moving the economy along AD_1 toward point 2.

aggregate demand curve with the long-run aggregate supply curve. This is the point where current output equals potential output, and current inflation equals the policymaker's original inflation target.

In Chapter 21, we noted that an increase in government purchases raises the long-term real interest rate. The higher the level of government purchases, the higher the level of the real interest rate needed to equate aggregate expenditure with potential output. (You can look back and see this in Figure 21.5 on page 587.) Realizing this, monetary policymakers react by shifting their monetary policy reaction curve to the left, increasing the real interest rate at every level of inflation. Remember, the central bank controls the real interest rate in the short run. When the monetary policy reaction curve shifts, the dynamic aggregate demand curve shifts with it. In this case, tighter monetary policy shifts the dynamic aggregate demand curve to the left, bringing the economy back to long-run equilibrium where output equals potential output and inflation equals the central bank's target.

We can summarize the path the economy takes after an increase in government purchases as follows: Current inflation rises above expected inflation and current output rises above potential output. Policymakers then react, shifting their monetary policy reaction curve, pushing the economy back to its long-run equilibrium level. From this we can conclude that, without a change in target inflation, *an increase in government purchases causes a temporary increase in both output and inflation.*

The same is true for any factor that shifts the dynamic aggregate demand curve to the right. Immediately following such a shift and in the absence of any monetary policy response, output and inflation both rise (see Table 22.1). If the central bank maintains its inflation target, the monetary policy reaction curve (MPRC) will shift to the left, returning inflation and output to their original long-run levels. In the absence of any monetary policy response, because current inflation exceeds expected inflation,

Table 22.1 Impact of an Increase in Dynamic Aggregate Demand on Output and Inflation

Source	Shift in the monetary policy reaction curve • Increase in inflation target • Decrease in long-run real interest rate Increase in aggregate expenditure • Consumer confidence up • Business optimism up • Government purchases up • Net exports up
Result	Dynamic aggregate demand shifts right
Short-run impact	Y increases π increases

expected inflation rises, shifting the short-run aggregate supply curve to the left, moving the economy along the new dynamic aggregate demand curve. This movement drives inflation up further as current output falls, returning to the level of potential output, but at a higher inflation rate. In effect, the central bank will have raised its inflation target.

A decline in aggregate expenditure, perhaps caused by a fall in consumer or business confidence, has the opposite impact from an increase in government expenditure. The dynamic aggregate demand curve shifts to the left, driving inflation and output down. With time, and in the absence of any monetary policy response, as lower current inflation drives inflation expectations down, the short-run aggregate supply curve shifts to the right, moving the economy along the new dynamic aggregate demand curve. This movement drives inflation down further, and current output begins to rise toward potential output. In effect, the central bank has set a new, lower inflation target. If, instead, policymakers do react, inflation and output will return to their original long-run levels.

Over the years, policymakers have reacted to shifts in aggregate expenditure in different ways, with differing results. In response to increases in government spending during the escalation of the Vietnam War in the late 1960s, when defense expenditure rose from 7.4 percent to 9.4 percent of GDP over a three-year period (twice what it was at the peak of the Iraq war in 2005), the Fed simply allowed inflation to rise. Look back at Figure 22.1 and you can see that inflation rose from less than 2 percent in 1965 to more than 5 percent in 1970. What could have been a temporary increase in inflation became a permanent one, in effect increasing the Fed's inflation target to the point where the new dynamic aggregate demand curve intersected the long-run aggregate supply curve.

Large tax cuts in 2001, and the subsequent rise of defense spending associated with the war in Iraq, did not have the same inflationary impact as the similar policy in the 1960s. There are two reasons for this. First, the fiscal stimulus came at a time when the economy was weakening for other reasons. That is to say, the timing was very fortunate. Second, by 2001 the Federal Reserve had learned the important lesson that it may need to raise interest rates to counter the risk of inflation from expansionary fiscal policy. So, a combination of good luck and better understanding meant that inflation stayed low.[2]

This discussion implies that whenever we see a *permanent* increase in inflation, it must be the result of monetary policy. That is, if inflation goes up or down and remains at its new level, the only explanation is that central bankers must be allowing it to happen. They have changed their inflation target, whether or not they acknowledge the change explicitly.

Shifts in the Short-Run Aggregate Supply Curve

Changes in production costs *shift the short-run aggregate supply curve.* Using the aggregate demand–aggregate supply diagram, we can trace the effects of such an increase in the costs of production—a *negative supply shock.* The immediate effect of something like an oil price rise that increases production costs is to move the short-run aggregate supply curve to the left, reducing the amount supplied at every level of inflation. (These bad consequences—higher inflation and lower growth—are why we label such a shock as "negative.") Figure 22.5 shows the result. Short-run equilibrium—the point where the short-run aggregate supply and dynamic aggregate demand curves intersect—moves to point 1 in the figure, where output is lower and inflation is higher. This creates a condition that is sometimes referred to as *stagflation*—economic stagnation coupled with increased inflation (see Table 22.2).

Figure 22.5 A Negative Supply Shock

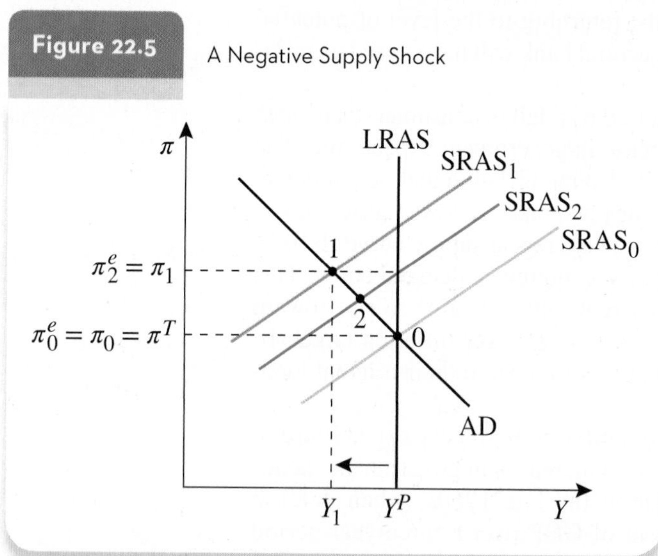

A negative supply shock shifts the SRAS curve to the left, moving the short-run equilibrium from point 0 to point 1, raising inflation to $\pi_1 > \pi^T$. At point 1, current inflation is *below* the intersection of $SRAS_1$ and LRAS that marks expected inflation in the long run, so the SRAS curve shifts back right to $SRAS_2$, which intersects the LRAS at the point where expected inflation (π_2^e) equals π_1. The SRAS curve continues to shift right until inflation and expected inflation again equal target inflation at point 0.

What happens next? Initially, expected inflation equals the inflation target. So, when inflation rises, and the economy moves from point 0 to point 1 in Figure 22.5, expected inflation rises as well. Recall that the short-run aggregate supply curve intersects the long-run aggregate supply curve at the point where current inflation equals expected inflation in the long run. Because current inflation (π_1) is below this level, the SRAS curve next shifts back to the right. This is shown in Figure 22.5 as a move from $SRAS_1$ to $SRAS_2$. The result is that the economy goes from point 1 to point 2. However, current inflation at point 2 remains below the expected inflation in the long run where $SRAS_2$ intersects the LRAS. Consequently, inflation continues to fall and output continues to rise until current inflation and expected inflation return to the central bank's inflation target, and output equals potential output. Put another way, inflation is at its highest and output at its lowest immediately following a negative shock to short-run aggregate supply. Over

[2]President George W. Bush initially proposed the personal income tax cuts to fulfill a pledge from the presidential campaign of 2000. Because the pledge occurred before anyone suspected that the economy would weaken the following year, it would seem that a substantial amount of luck was involved.

Table 22.2 Impact of a Decline in Short-Run Aggregate Supply on Output and Inflation

Source	Negative supply shock • Increase in production costs • Increase in expected inflation
Result	Short-run aggregate supply curve shifts left
Short-run impact	Y falls π increases

time, self-correcting forces in the economy unwind the shock, restoring long-run equilibrium.

As was the case with the increase in government purchases (when combined with an appropriate monetary policy response), a supply shock has no effect on the economy's long-run equilibrium point. Only a change in either potential output or the central bank's inflation target can accomplish that. Instead, a negative supply shock moves output and inflation temporarily away from potential output and the inflation target. Over time, as expected inflation first rises and then falls, the short-run aggregate supply curve shifts back to the right. As it does, the economy moves along the dynamic aggregate demand curve until output and inflation finally return to the initial equilibrium point 0 in Figure 22.5. Thus, a supply shock causes inflation to rise temporarily and then fall, at the same time that current output falls temporarily and then rises. But, as always, in the long run the economy returns to the point where output equals potential output and inflation equals the central bank's target.

Using the Aggregate Demand–Aggregate Supply Framework

We are now ready to use the macroeconomic framework to address a series of interesting questions. We examine the following (in increasing order of complexity):

1. How do policymakers achieve their stabilization objectives?
2. What accounts for what has been called the "Great Moderation," the time period from the mid-1980s until 2007 (and possibly beyond) when U.S. growth and inflation were less volatile than they were historically?
3. What happens when potential output changes?
4. What are the implications of globalization for monetary policy?
5. Can policymakers stabilize output and inflation simultaneously?

How Do Policymakers Achieve Their Stabilization Objectives?

The aggregate demand–aggregate supply framework is useful in understanding how monetary and fiscal policymakers seek to stabilize output and inflation using what is called *stabilization policy*.

Defining a Recession: The NBER Reference Cycle
TOOLS OF THE TRADE

From reading the business press, you might conclude that a recession is any episode in which real gross domestic product (GDP) declines for two consecutive quarters. While that casual definition may work in most instances, it has some drawbacks. One is that because GDP is computed and published quarterly, a definition that is based on GDP cannot indicate the specific months in which a recession started and ended. To determine that information, we need a definition that is based on measures like production, employment, sales, and income—all of which are available monthly and provide valuable information about the health of the economy.

Ultimately, the arbiter for declaring "official" recessions in the United States is the National Bureau of Economic Research (NBER). The NBER, founded in 1920, is a research organization devoted to studying how the economy works. Early work at the NBER led to the construction of much of the economic data we use today. Two of the NBER's pioneering researchers, Wesley Mitchell and Arthur Burns, dated the beginning and end of all the recessions in the United States from the Civil War through World War II.* In their book *Measuring Business Cycles* (1946), they called this dating a "reference cycle."

The NBER's definition of a recession is as follows:

> *A recession is a significant decline in activity spread across the economy, lasting more than a few months, normally visible in real GDP, real income, employment, industrial production, and wholesale–retail sales. A recession begins just after the economy reaches a peak of activity and ends as the economy reaches its trough. Between trough and peak, the economy is in an expansion.*

This definition has three important implications. First, a recession is a decline in activity, not just a dip in the growth rate. Second, the exact length of the economic contraction is ambiguous. A severe decline in economic activity that lasted less than two quarters could still be considered a recession according to this definition. And third, because key economic indicators often change direction at different times, there is an element of judgment in dating the peaks and

Table 22.3 NBER Business Cycle Reference Dates, 1946–2019

Peak	Trough	Length of Recession in Months Peak to Trough	Length of Expansion in Months Previous Trough to Peak
November 1948	October 1949	11	37
July 1953	May 1954	10	45
August 1957	April 1958	8	39
April 1960	February 1961	10	24
December 1969	November 1970	11	106
November 1973	March 1975	16	36
January 1980	July 1980	6	58
July 1981	November 1982	16	12
July 1990	March 1991	8	92
March 2001	November 2001	8	120
December 2007	June 2009	19	73

SOURCE: National Bureau of Economic Research. The FRED code is USREC (which represents a recession month as a 1 and an expansion month as a 0).

troughs of business cycles. As a result, the NBER's Business Cycle Dating Committee takes its time in declaring the beginning and end of a recession. Delays of six months to a year are common.

The term *business cycle* is somewhat misleading when used to refer to fluctuations in economic activity. The word *cycle* calls up images of recurring waves that rise and fall in a periodic pattern. Economic fluctuations aren't like that. Both the length of recessions and the time between them are irregular. As Burns and Mitchell wrote in their book, "A cycle consists of expansions . . . followed by contractions and revivals which merge into the expansion phase of the next cycle; this sequence of changes is recurrent but not periodic."

Table 22.3 displays the results of the NBER's analyses of the business cycle since the end of World War II. Figure 22.6 plots the bureau's business cycle reference dates against the growth in real GDP over the period. The figure clearly shows the tendency for real growth to be low—usually below zero—during recessions. Recessions differ along several dimensions, including the so-called 3 D's: depth, duration, and diffusion across business sectors, geographic regions, or markets. The table illustrates the remarkable fact that recessions are much shorter than expansions in the U.S. economy. Most people credit this fact to a combination of successful policy and the economy's capacity for self-correction.

For more information on the procedures used to date business cycles, go to the NBER's website at www.nber.org.

*Burns later became chair of the Federal Reserve Board, serving from 1970 to 1978.

Figure 22.6 Growth in Real GDP over the Business Cycle

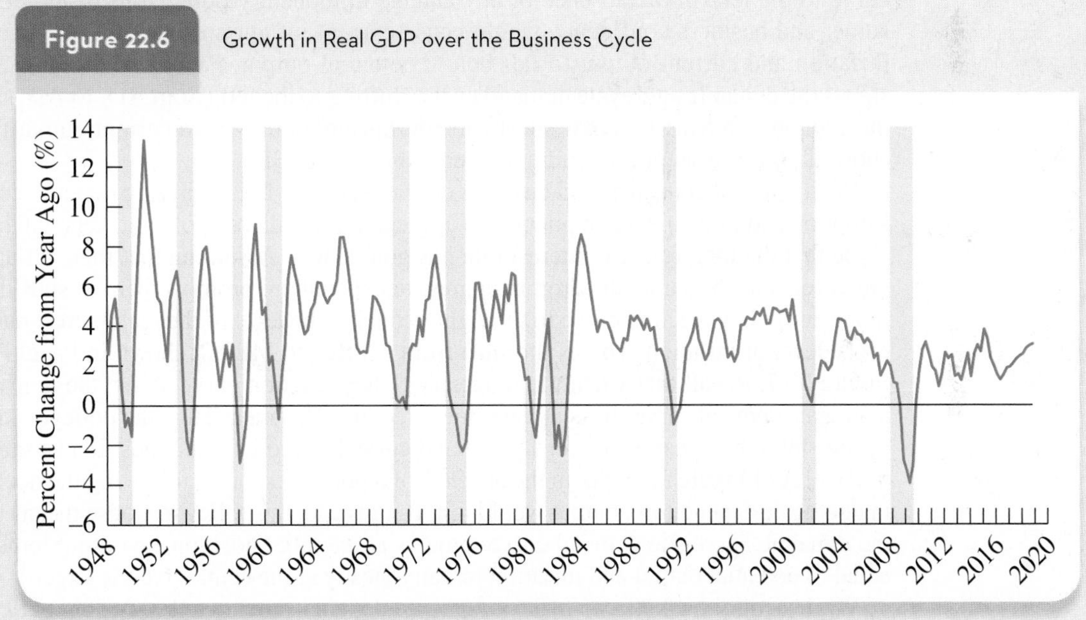

The figure shows the four-quarter percentage change in real GDP from the Bureau of Economic Analysis, and the shaded bars represent recessions as determined by the NBER. (FRED codes: GDPC1 for GDP and USREC for recession dates.)

In thinking about the way monetary policy can be used to reduce economic fluctuations, recall that movements in output and inflation can be caused both by shifts in the dynamic aggregate demand curve and in the short-run aggregate supply curve. But when shifting their reaction curve, central bankers shift the dynamic aggregate demand curve. They cannot shift the short-run aggregate supply curve. What this means is that monetary policymakers can neutralize demand shocks, but they cannot offset supply shocks. That is to say, they can counter aggregate expenditure changes that shift the dynamic aggregate demand curve, but they cannot eliminate the effects of changes in

production costs that shift the short-run aggregate supply curve. Nevertheless, as we will see, positive supply shocks that raise output and lower inflation provide policymakers with an opportunity. If they wish, following a positive supply shock, central bankers can guide the economy to a new, lower inflation target without inducing a recessionary output gap.

As for fiscal policy, our macroeconomic framework allows us to study the impact of changes in government taxes and expenditures as well. As we have seen in the previous section, these shift the dynamic aggregate demand curve. This means that fiscal policy can work to stabilize the economy. While this is true in principle, as we will discuss, the active use of fiscal policy faces great challenges. The conclusion is that stabilization policy is usually best left to central bankers.

Monetary Policy To see how monetary policy can stabilize the economy following a shift in the dynamic aggregate demand curve, consider what happens when consumers and businesses suddenly become more pessimistic about the future. Such a change reduces consumption and investment, shifting the dynamic aggregate demand curve to the left. In the absence of any change in monetary policy, this drop in consumer and business confidence would cause current inflation to fall below expected inflation and current output to fall below potential output. Panel A of Figure 22.7 shows the dynamic aggregate demand curve shifting to the left (from AD_0 to AD_1) and the economy moving to a new short-run equilibrium point where current output falls short of potential output (at point 1, where AD_1 crosses SRAS).

Realizing that consumer and business confidence have fallen, driving down the consumption and investment components of aggregate expenditure, policymakers will conclude that the long-run real interest rate has gone down. Assuming that their inflation target remains the same, the drop in aggregate expenditure prompts them to shift their monetary policy reaction curve to the right, reducing the level of the real interest rate at every level of inflation. This is the shift from $MPRC_0$ to $MPRC_1$ shown in Panel B of Figure 22.7. Recall that when the monetary policy reaction curve shifts, the dynamic aggregate demand curve shifts in the same direction. This means that the policymakers' action shifts the dynamic aggregate demand curve back to its initial position as shown in Panel A of Figure 22.7. So, in the absence of a policy response, following the decline in aggregate expenditure, output would fall. But instead, the policy response means that the dynamic aggregate demand curve remains at its initial position, so output remains equal to potential output and inflation remains steady at the central bank's target.[3]

While central bankers can offset aggregate demand shocks in theory, in practice it is extremely difficult to keep inflation and output from fluctuating when aggregate expenditure changes. There are two reasons for this. First, it takes time to recognize what has happened. Fluctuations in the quantity of aggregate output demanded arising from things like changes in consumer or business confidence can be very difficult to recognize as they are occurring. Second, changes in interest rates—the tool monetary policymakers use to offset aggregate demand shocks—do not have an immediate impact on the economy. Instead, when interest rates rise or fall, it takes time for output and inflation to respond. A good rule of thumb is that interest rate changes start to influence output in 6 to 9 months and inflation after 18 months, but our knowledge is not all that precise. In short, while in theory we can neutralize aggregate demand shocks, in reality they create short-run fluctuations in output and inflation.

[3]Stabilizing aggregate demand shocks in this way also ensures that expected inflation remains equal to the central bank's inflation target.

Figure 22.7 Stabilizing a Shift in Dynamic Aggregate Demand

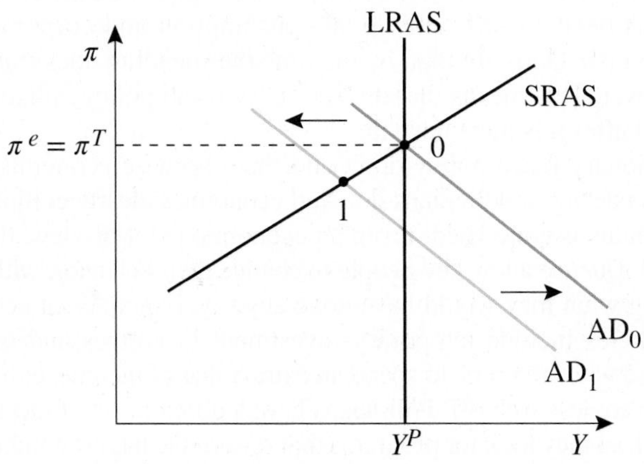

B. Monetary Policy Response

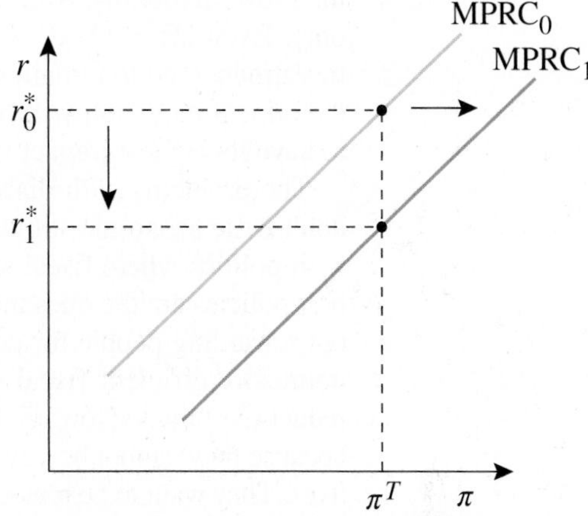

Following a drop in consumer or business confidence the dynamic aggregate demand shifts to the left from AD_0 to AD_1, moving the economy from point 0 to point 1. Realizing this, monetary policymakers shift their MPRC to the right, shifting the dynamic aggregate demand curve back to where it started and returning the economy to point 0.

Following a drop in consumer confidence, the long-run real interest rate falls from r_0^* to r_1^*. Policymakers respond by shifting their reaction curve from $MPRC_0$ to $MPRC_1$, shifting the AD curve back to its original position, AD_0.

Discretionary Fiscal Policy There are two very different types of fiscal policy. One is automatic, operating without any further actions on the part of government officials, and the other is discretionary, relying on fiscal policymakers' decisions. Automatic stabilizers, including unemployment insurance and the proportional nature of the tax system, are in the first group. These adjust mechanically to stimulate an economy that is slowing down and put the brakes on an economy that is speeding up. They operate countercyclically to eliminate fluctuations in aggregate expenditure and keep the economy stable. But there are times when automatic stabilizers are not enough; and that's when politicians face the temptation to enact temporary expenditure increases and tax reductions—what is called *discretionary* fiscal policy. Discretionary fiscal policy changes aggregate expenditure, shifting the dynamic aggregate demand curve.

As noted earlier in the chapter, a rise in government purchases or a decrease in taxes drives up aggregate expenditure, shifting the dynamic aggregate demand curve to the right. Thus, fiscal policy can act just like monetary policy to offset shifts in the dynamic aggregate demand curve and stabilize inflation and output. In fact, it has been used exactly this way on a number of occasions. As we discussed earlier, for example, the 2008–2009 federal tax cuts and spending increases boosted aggregate expenditure, helping moderate the recession.

At least in principle, then, discretionary fiscal policy offers a clear alternative to monetary policy. On closer examination, however, it has at least two shortcomings. First, discretionary fiscal policy works slowly, and second, it is very difficult to implement effectively. Most recessions are short, lasting a year or less. Until the financial crisis of 2007–2009, the longest post–World War II recession in the United States spanned 16 months (see Table 22.3 on page 624). Furthermore, because economic data only become available several months after they are collected, the economy is often halfway through a recession before there is a consensus that a downturn has actually started. Under most circumstances, Congress can't pass new legislation in less than several months. And fiscal policies do not have an immediate impact on the economy. Even after a tax cut has been passed, individual consumption and corporate investment tend to remain sluggish. Odds are that, by the time the spending does start, the typical recession will be over. This means that discretionary fiscal policy is likely to have its biggest impact well after it is most needed.

The problems with discretionary fiscal policy don't end there because economists don't write economic stimulus packages; politicians do. And economics clearly collides with politics where fiscal stimulus is concerned. From an economic point of view, the best policies are the ones that influence a few key people to change their behavior, without rewarding people for doing what they would have done anyway. Examples of economically efficient fiscal policies include temporary investment incentives and tax reductions targeted toward those who are prone to spend an extra dollar of income, either because they cannot borrow or are less well off. Politicians have a different set of incentives. They want to be reelected, so they look for programs that reward the largest number of people possible, to ensure their reelection. This means that discretionary fiscal policy is likely to be based more on political calculation than on economic logic. Though we can't hold public officials' opportunism against them, we need to recognize its existence. Because politicians want to remain popular with their constituencies, economic slowdowns—when some voters are suffering and the rest are worried—play to their worst instincts. In short, discretionary fiscal policy is a poor stabilization tool. While an economically sensible stimulus package can be designed, such legislation does not often become law.

Under most circumstances, then, stabilization policy is probably best left to the central bankers. They have both the ability to act quickly and the independence to put the economy before politics. Fiscal policy's automatic stabilizers are clearly important parts of the economic landscape, but discretionary government expenditure and tax changes only have a role after monetary policy has run its course—that is, when conditions are so bad that using every available tool makes sense.

From this perspective, the deep recession of 2007–2009 provided the strongest case in many decades for discretionary fiscal stimulus in the United States and other countries. The downturn was the longest since the 1930s, providing fiscal policymakers time to respond. It also was the deepest and most widespread, while the subsequent recovery was the weakest, posing an unusual risk of deflation in several economies. As we saw in Chapter 11 (Applying the Concept: Deflation, Net Worth, and Information Costs), deflation can be highly destabilizing. Finally, and perhaps most importantly, central banks had lowered their policy interest rates close to zero, limiting their scope for further conventional policy stimulus. Consequently, it should come as no surprise that many industrial countries undertook large-scale discretionary fiscal stimulus in this episode. The 2008 and 2009 U.S. tax cuts and spending increases and the massive 2009 budget deficit that we previously discussed fit in this category.

Positive Supply Shocks and the Opportunity They Create Next, let's consider what happens when production costs fall, creating a positive supply shock. This shifts the short-run aggregate supply curve to the right, from $SRAS_0$ to $SRAS_1$, as shown in Figure 22.8. The immediate impact of this is to drive inflation down and output up. We know that at this new short-run equilibrium (point 1 in Figure 22.8), current inflation (π_1) is below expected inflation (π_0^e). In the absence of any other change, inflation expectations initially fall. But at the next stage, inflation is above expected inflation (where the $SRAS_1$ curve intersects the LRAS), and expectations start to rise. This shifts the short-run aggregate supply curve to the left until the economy returns to the original long-run equilibrium at point 0, where output equals potential output and inflation equals the central bank's target.

Figure 22.8 A Positive Supply Shock

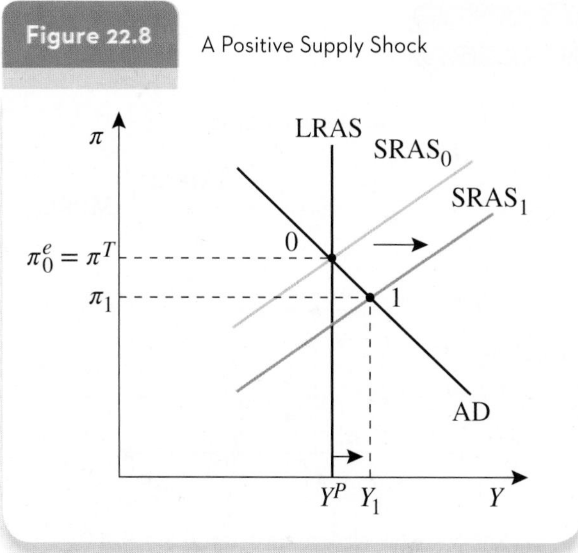

A positive supply shock shifts the short-run aggregate supply curve to the right, moving the short-run equilibrium from point 0 to point 1. Inflation falls and output rises.

While policymakers could simply allow the economy to take its natural course, with inflation falling to π_1 (at point 1) and then rising back to π^T (at point 0), there is an alternative. A positive supply shock creates an opportunity for policymakers to guide the economy to a new, lower inflation target without inducing a recession. The standard mechanism for permanently reducing inflation is to raise the real interest rate at every level of inflation. Central bankers do this by shifting the monetary policy reaction curve to the left, which then shifts the dynamic aggregate demand curve to the left as well. This drives inflation down, and inflation expectations will follow. (Look back at Figures 22.2 and 22.3 on page 618.) As a result, inflation falls to the new, lower target level. This is the mechanism that links monetary policy to economic downturns and inflation declines as shown in Figure 22.1 on page 616.

Here's how central bankers can exploit the opportunity created by a positive supply shock. Because potential output is unchanged following the fall in production costs, the long-run real interest rate r^* hasn't changed either. This means that a lower inflation target requires a higher real interest rate at every level of current inflation (that's a leftward shift in the monetary policy reaction curve as shown in Panel A of Figure 22.9 on page 630). So, policymakers wishing to lower their inflation target in response to a positive supply shock will raise interest rates, shifting the dynamic aggregate demand curve to the left until it reaches the point where the new short-run aggregate supply curve ($SRAS_1$) intersects the long-run aggregate supply curve (LRAS). If policymakers choose this course, as shown in Panel B of Figure 22.9, output will not rise above potential.[4]

What Accounts for the Great Moderation?

By any measure, the 1990s were remarkable. Information technology came of age, bringing the benefits of computerization into our lives through everything from cars to dishwashers. Because of the Internet, incredible libraries are now available to us in our homes and offices. That includes FRED, the Federal Reserve Bank of St. Louis's online database that is the source for many figures and end-of-chapter problems in this book.

What may be even more extraordinary is that the 1990s brought unprecedented economic stability—the "Great Moderation" in the volatility of real growth. In the

[4]Again, recall that at the long-run equilibrium, inflation must equal expected inflation. So, if following a positive supply shock, policymakers choose to reduce their inflation target, inflation expectations must fall as well.

Figure 22.9 Lowering the Inflation Target

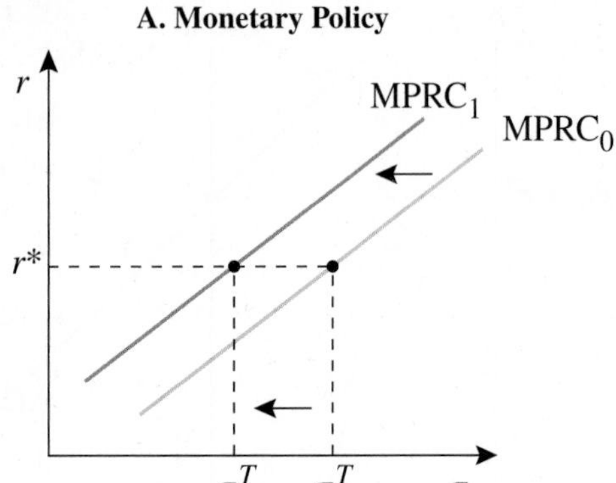

A decline in the inflation target from π_0^T to π_1^T shifts the monetary policy reaction curve to the left from $MPRC_0$ to $MPRC_1$.

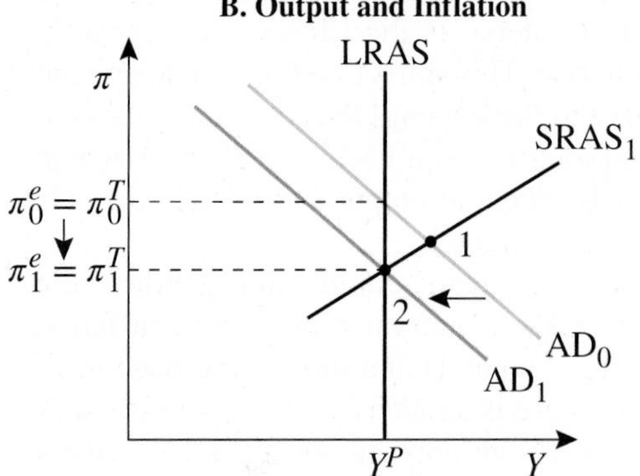

Following a positive supply shock, policymakers can reduce their inflation target by shifting the dynamic aggregate demand curve from AD_0 to AD_1. This lowers expected inflation from π_0^e to π_1^e. Instead of going to point 1, the economy moves to point 2.

"Please stand by for a series of tones. The first indicates the official end of the recession, the second indicates prosperity, and the third the return of the recession."

CartoonStock.com

SOURCE: 1991 © Robert Mankoff/ The New Yorker Collection, www.CartoonStock.com.

decade from 1991 to 2001, the U.S. economy did not suffer a single decline in output. During these 10 years of solid growth, inflation fell steadily, from more than 5 percent in 1991 to less than 2 percent by the end of the decade. Comparing the 1980s with the 1990s, researchers find that the volatility of inflation and growth dropped by more than half.[5] And if you look back at Figures 22.1 and 22.6 you can see that both inflation and growth were substantially less variable between 1982 and 2007 than in the prior period.

This prosperity and stability was shared across the industrialized world. Looking at a broad cross-section of the 63 countries for which we have reliable data, we can see that inflation dropped dramatically between the 1980s and the 1990s. Median inflation fell from an annual rate of 7 percent in the period 1985–1994 to 3 percent in the period 1995–1999. The decline in average inflation was even sharper, from 83 percent to just 8½ percent. Inflation rose in only 10 of the 63 countries.

There are three possible explanations for this phenomenal worldwide economic performance. One is that everyone was extremely lucky, and the 1990s were simply an

[5]This decline in volatility, along with the rebound of volatility during the financial crisis of 2007–2009, is documented by Todd Clark in "Is the Great Moderation Over? An Empirical Analysis," Federal Reserve Bank of Kansas City *Economic Review,* 4th Quarter, 2009.

GDP-Linked Bonds
APPLYING THE CONCEPT

As of 2019, gross government debt in advanced economies exceeded 100 percent of GDP, up by more than 30 percentage points since 2007, prior to the financial crisis. Very large debts in some countries—including Greece (177 percent), Italy (129 percent), and Portugal (117 percent)—pose a risk not only to these countries, but to others as well. As a result, policymakers and economists have been looking for ways to make it easier to manage these heavier debt burdens.

One prominent suggestion is that countries should issue *GDP-linked bonds* that tie the size of debt payments to their economy's cyclical performance. Proponents point to two major advantages of these bonds. First, these bonds reduce the likelihood of explosive paths for sovereign debt, lowering default risk. This would increase the maximum level of sustainable debt, and provide greater capacity for countercyclical fiscal policies. Second, GDP-linked bonds offer investors a low-cost way to diversify both domestically and internationally. Within a country, bonds with payoffs tied to GDP provide exposure to changes in returns to labor as well as capital. The two are only weakly associated, with the correlation between annual growth in U.S. labor income and capital income over the last half century at less than 0.2. Internationally, a portfolio of GDP-linked bonds allows diversification of idiosyncratic, country-specific risks.

However, there are a number of practical obstacles. First, might a government game this GDP-linked debt structure? It seems highly doubtful that a country's policymakers would intentionally depress its economy just to reduce its debt service. However, investors would need to trust the reporting of the national accounts that determine the returns on GDP-linked instruments. Even a temporary loss of investor confidence would raise the risk premium on GDP-linked debt.

A related concern is the issue of GDP data revisions, which are both frequent and sizable. Over the past 50 years, fully half of the time U.S. revisions exceeded one percentage point (at an annual rate) either up or down (see Applying the Concept, GDP: One Size No Longer Fits All, page 501). It is hard to see a timely solution to this problem.

Finally, there is the market price of the bonds. Government debt managers might find the risk premium that investors demand to be too high. For advanced economies, most estimates of the likely premium are in the range of 150 to 300 basis points. Unsurprisingly, for emerging market economies the numbers are much larger, and can easily exceed 500 basis points.

The bottom line: While issuing GDP-linked bonds has clear benefits, building and sustaining investor confidence in these instruments will require both an irreversible commitment to independent statistical analysis by issuing governments and a clever approach to the obstacles posed by data revisions.

exceptionally calm period. The second is that economies became more flexible in absorbing external economic disturbances. And the third is that monetary policymakers figured out how to do their job more effectively. Which one of these is most likely?

It's difficult to argue that the stability of the 1990s was mere good fortune. Surely, the decade was not a calm one for the financial markets. Major economic crises occurred in Latin America and Asia, and Long-Term Capital Management, the large hedge fund, nearly collapsed, paralyzing the bond markets. Raw materials prices fluctuated wildly. The price of oil spiked above $35 a barrel late in 1990 and then plunged below $12 a barrel at the end of 1998 before beginning a steady rise to $30 a barrel by the beginning of 2000.

If the size and frequency of external disturbances did not diminish, something must be cushioning the blows. Advances in information technology have increased manufacturers' flexibility in responding to changes in demand. The result has been a dramatic decline in inventories at every stage of the production process. In durable manufacturing, the new supply method called "just-in-time" cut the ratio of inventories to sales in half in the period from the early 1990s, to the beginning of 2002. Today, an automobile assembly plant keeps only a few hours worth of parts on hand; the rest are in transit to the factory, timed to arrive at just the right moment. Similarly, a supermarket or superstore like Walmart or Target holds only one to two days' supply of most products. The result is a great deal of flexibility in responding to changes in demand and sales.

While improvements in inventory management are part of the explanation for the long period of prosperity in the 1990s, they aren't the whole story. Every description of the recession that began in March 2001 points to the impact of an inventory adjustment. The most persistent problems emerged in the high-technology sector—semiconductors, computers, and communications equipment. Inventories also plunged sharply in the recession that began in 2007. So while the U.S. economy has become more flexible, it hasn't changed enough to prevent fluctuations caused by unexpected events.

Financial innovation probably played some role in reducing economic volatility after the early 1980s—that is, until the financial crisis of 2007–2009. Innovations in mortgages and other forms of personal credit made it easier for households and businesses to borrow. As a result, they were better able to smooth their spending during periods of temporary income fluctuations.[6] As we now know, however, rising levels of risky debt eventually led to record defaults on mortgages and other forms of personal credit during the financial crisis. And the loss of credit availability during the crisis helps explain the depth and duration of the recession that began in December 2007.

That leaves monetary policy as the only remaining explanation for the improved economic performance. Economists now have a much better understanding of how to implement monetary policy than they did as recently as 25 years ago. To succeed in keeping inflation low and stable while at the same time keeping real growth high and stable, central bankers must focus on raising real interest rates when inflation goes up and lowering them when inflation goes down. One example is the Taylor rule (see Chapter 18) that raises the policy interest rate by 1.5 percentage points for every 1 percent rise of inflation. By focusing on long-run inflation, policymakers have succeeded in bringing the inflation rate down and keeping it low.

Yet, while keeping inflation low and stable is *necessary* for reducing economic volatility, the deep recession that began in December 2007 shows that it is not *sufficient*. Low inflation did not prevent the financial crisis of 2007–2009, and history shows that such crises often are associated with deep recessions (the Great Depression being the most extreme example). It remains to be seen whether the crisis marks the end of the Great Moderation or whether it was simply a huge exception in an otherwise stable period. If households and businesses are no longer able or willing to use credit to smooth their spending over time, it may not be possible for Fed policymakers to sustain the low economic volatility of the 1985–2007 period, even if they remain effective in keeping inflation low.

What Happens When Potential Output Changes?*

In order to concentrate on the impact of shifts in dynamic aggregate demand and short-run supply, we have neglected movements in potential output. But potential output does change, and the consequences are important both for short-run movements in output and inflation and for long-run equilibrium.

[6]See, for example, Karen E. Dynan, Douglas W. Elmendorf, and Daniel Sichel, "Can Financial Innovation Help Explain the Reduced Volatility of Economic Activity?" Federal Reserve Board, FEDs Working Paper No. 2005-54, August 2006.

Figure 22.10 An Increase in Potential Output

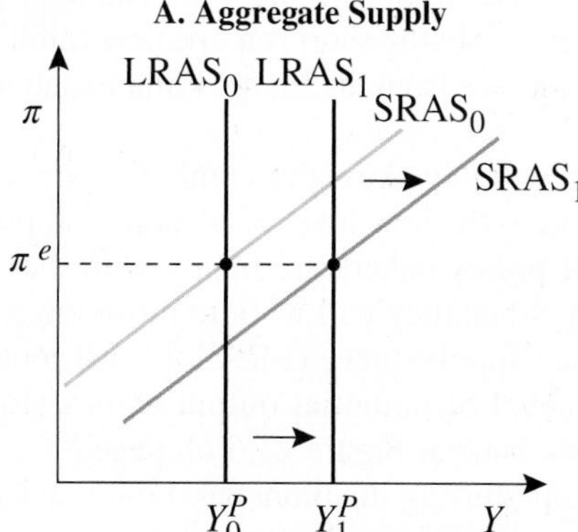

An increase in potential output shifts both the short- and long-run aggregate supply curves to the right. Before and after the shift, the short-run aggregate supply curve crosses the long-run aggregate supply curve at the point where $\pi = \pi^e$.

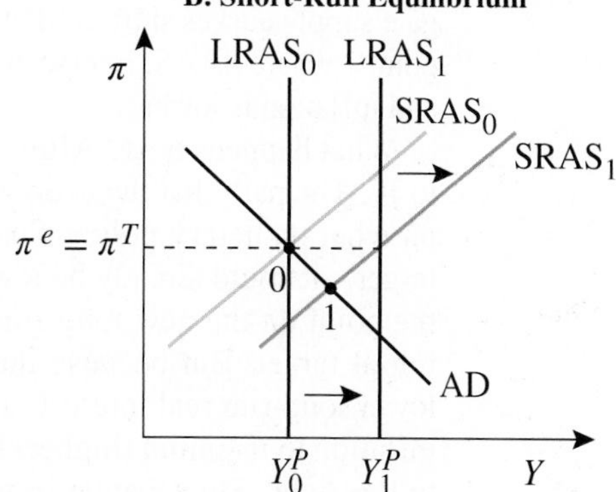

In the short run, the economy moves from point 0 to point 1.

To understand what happens when potential output changes, let's trace out the consequences of a rise in Y^P brought on by an increase in productivity. First, recall that the long-run aggregate supply curve (LRAS) is vertical at the point where current output equals potential output, so when potential output rises this curve shifts to the right. But that's not all. An increase in productivity reduces costs of production, so it is a positive supply shock as well. This shifts the short-run aggregate supply curve (SRAS) to the right. But how far does SRAS shift? To see, recall from Chapter 21 that the short-run aggregate supply curve intersects the long-run aggregate supply curve at the point where current inflation equals expected inflation (π^e)—that's where production costs are not changing. Immediately following the increase in potential output, expected inflation does not change, so the SRAS shifts the same horizontal distance as the LRAS does. From this we can conclude that an *increase in potential output shifts both the long- and short-run aggregate supply curves to the right* as shown in Panel A of Figure 22.10.

The short-run impact of an increase in potential output is straightforward. Assuming the central bank recognizes the change in potential output only with a lag, we can trace out the short-term impact of a change. First, because policymakers are slow to recognize the increase in Y^P, MPRC does not shift immediately: It still passes through the old level of potential output (Y_0^P). As a result, the AD curve also is unchanged until the MPRC shifts.[7] In the short run, output and inflation are determined by the intersection of the short-run aggregate supply (SRAS) curve and the dynamic aggregate demand (AD) curve. Panel B of Figure 22.10 shows what happens. The economy starts at point 0 where

[7]This "lagged recognition" assumption allows us to trace out graphically the impact over time of the policy response to the change in potential output. It does not alter the direction of the eventual shifts in MPRC and AD, but it makes them easier to explain. In the remainder of the chapter, we use this simplifying assumption to help illustrate the impact of changes in potential output.

the original short-run aggregate supply curve ($SRAS_0$) intersects the dynamic aggregate demand curve (AD). At this original equilibrium point, output equals the initial level of potential (Y_0^P) and inflation equals the central bank's target (π^T), which equals expected inflation (π^e). When potential output increases to Y_1^P, the short-run and long-run aggregate supply curves shift to $SRAS_1$ and $LRAS_1$. In the short run, the new equilibrium is at point 1 where $SRAS_1$ intersects AD. We can see from the figure, initially output is higher and inflation is lower.

What happens next? After a lag, the central bank realizes potential output has risen to Y_1^P. The path that the economy follows to the new level of potential output depends on what monetary policymakers do. If policymakers are happy with their inflation target—it could already be low enough—then they will work to move the economy to the point on the new long-run aggregate supply curve ($LRAS_1$) consistent with that initial target. But because the higher level of potential output comes along with a lower long-run real interest rate r^* (look back at Figure 21.5 on page 587), returning inflation to its initial (higher) level means shifting the monetary policy reaction curve to the right. This change in monetary policy shifts the dynamic aggregate demand curve to the right. The policy adjustment will drive output and inflation up until they reach their new long-run equilibrium levels where output equals Y_1^P and inflation equals its original target π^T (which equals expected inflation). This case is shown in Panel A of Figure 22.11, which continues the sequential numbering scheme from Panel B of Figure 22.10.

But as we saw earlier, a positive supply shock creates an opportunity for policymakers to reduce their inflation target. Without a conscious shift in monetary policy, at point 1 in Panel B of Figure 22.11 expected inflation exceeds current inflation, so it starts to fall, shifting the short-run aggregate supply curve to the right, driving

Figure 22.11 Policy Options following an Increase in Potential Output

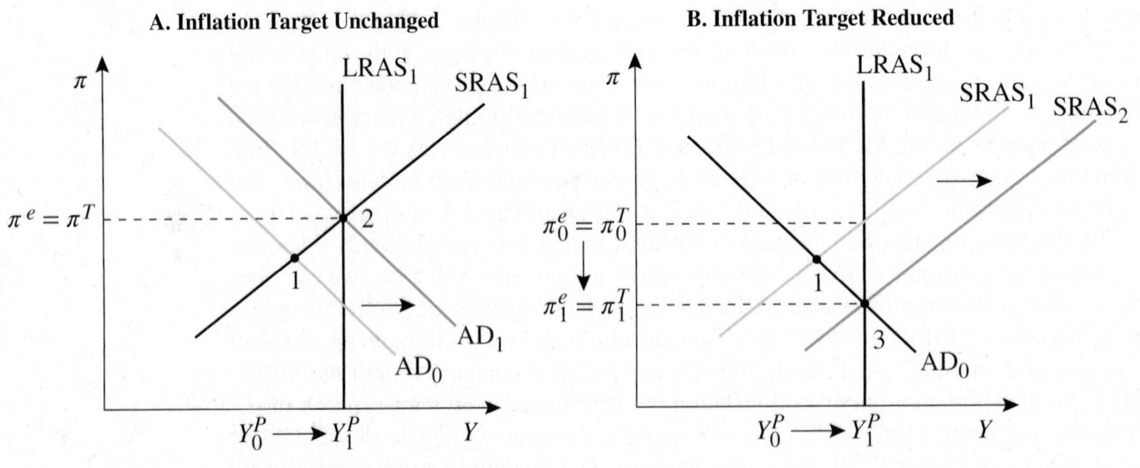

If, following an increase in potential output, policymakers' inflation target is unchanged, they must shift the dynamic aggregate demand curve to the right, bringing output and inflation to point 2.

If, following an increase in potential output, policymakers wish to lower their inflation target, they will allow the economy to move to point 3.

inflation down even further. We know that the SRAS continues to shift until expected inflation equals current inflation and current output equals potential output. Looking at Panel B of Figure 22.11, which continues sequentially from Panel B of Figure 22.10, we see that this process naturally brings us to point 3, where output equals the new higher level of potential output Y_1^P and inflation is below the original target level π_0^T. With inflation now lower, monetary policymakers have the opportunity to lower their inflation target to the level labeled π_1^T. They can do this by ensuring that the AD curve doesn't shift, which means leaving their monetary policy reaction curve where it started.[8]

Federal Reserve policymakers took advantage of an increase in potential output to drive the U.S. inflation rate down during the 1990s. Looking back at Figure 22.1, we see that inflation fell gradually from 5 percent at the end of the 1990–1991 recession to 1½ percent in 1998. This drop in inflation occurred during an economic boom. Over the last half of the 1990s, economic growth averaged 1½ percentage points above the rate for the preceding 20 years. That is, U.S. productivity (and potential output) grew more rapidly from 1996 to 1999 than it did from 1975 to 1995. In effect, the economy's long-run aggregate supply curve shifted to the right, and when it did the Federal Reserve took the opportunity to reduce its implicit inflation target from near 5 percent to 2 percent. At the time, this was referred to as *opportunistic disinflation.* **Disinflation** is the term used to describe declines in inflation; the word *opportunistic* indicates an opportunity to reduce the target inflation level.[9] During the 1990s, Fed policymakers exploited the opportunity afforded them by positive supply shocks to permanently lower inflation.

Throughout our discussion of business cycle fluctuations, we have assigned a major role to shifts in the quantity of aggregate output demanded. This has led us to focus on how shifts in the dynamic aggregate demand curve change its point of intersection with an upward-sloping short-run aggregate supply curve and lead to movements in output and inflation.

An alternative explanation for business cycle fluctuations focuses on shifts in potential output. This view, known as **real-business-cycle theory**, starts with the assumption that prices and wages are flexible, so that inflation adjusts rapidly. That is to say, the short-run aggregate supply curve shifts rapidly in response to deviations of current inflation from expected inflation. This assumption renders the short-run aggregate supply curve irrelevant. Equilibrium output and inflation are determined by the point of intersection of the dynamic aggregate demand curve and the long-run aggregate supply curve, where current inflation equals expected inflation and current output equals potential output. Thus, any shift in the dynamic aggregate demand curve, regardless of its source, influences inflation but not output. Neither changes in aggregate expenditure nor changes in monetary policy have any impact on the level of output. Because inflation ultimately depends on the level of money growth, it is determined by monetary policy.

To explain recessions and booms, real-business-cycle theorists look to fluctuations in potential output. They focus on changes in productivity and their impact on GDP.

[8]Recall that a decline in the central bank's inflation target shifts the monetary policy reaction curve to the left. But in this case, that will exactly offset the rightward shift resulting from the decline in the long-run real interest rate r^* caused by the rise in potential output, leaving the position of the monetary policy reaction curve unchanged.

[9]*Disinflation* is very different from *deflation,* which is the opposite of inflation. *Deflation* means that aggregate prices are consistently *falling; disinflation* means falling inflation. (See Chapter 21, Your Financial World: Distinguishing Inflation, Deflation, and Disinflation, page 579.)

Productivity is a measure of output at a fixed level of inputs. An increase in productivity means an increase in GDP for a given quantity of capital and number of workers. Shifts in productivity can be either temporary or permanent. Examples of such shifts would include changes in the availability of raw materials, changes in government regulation of labor and product markets, and inventions or management innovations that improve the economy's productive capacity. Any of these events will shift potential output. According to real-business-cycle theory, they are the only sources of fluctuations in output.[10]

What Are the Implications of Globalization for Monetary Policy?*

If you look at the label of the shirt or blouse you are wearing, chances are it was imported from India, the Philippines, Vietnam, or somewhere else in Asia. The reason is that it is less costly to manufacture clothing in places where labor is inexpensive. The result is that clothes are cheaper in the United States: trade lowers prices. But does it also lower inflation?

The simplest way to understand the macroeconomic impact of international trade is to think about it as a source of productivity-enhancing technological progress. Shifting production of clothes from domestic factories to foreign ones is the same as U.S. producers finding a new, cheaper technology for producing the same things at home. And improvements in technology increase potential output. That is something we understand.

Recall from the previous section that an increase in potential output shifts both the long-run and short-run aggregate supply curves to the right. This has the immediate impact of shifting the economy along its dynamic aggregate demand curve to a point where output is higher and inflation is lower. All of this is shown in Figure 22.10 on page 633. In the long run, we know that output goes to the new, higher level of potential output. But, as we discussed in the previous section, the long-run level of inflation depends on how monetary policymakers respond. Our conclusion is that globalization and trade do reduce inflation in the short run and just like any positive supply shock they provide an opportunity to reduce inflation permanently.

Is globalization likely to have a sizeable impact on inflation even in the short run? Economists estimate that nearly 14 percent of personal consumption expenditures reflect the direct cost of imported final goods (excluding the contribution from U.S. services) combined with the imported content of U.S.-made goods and services.[11] If import prices are stable and then start dropping at 5 percent per year, which is what happened in 2001, this would reduce the rate of inflation by about 0.7 percentage point per year. With inflation averaging 2 percent per year, that is a moderate but temporary impact. In the long run, $MV = PY$, so (assuming velocity is constant) the inflation rate equals the money growth rate less the growth rate of potential output ($\pi = \%\Delta M - \%\Delta Y^P$). We just can't get away from the fact that domestic inflation is tied to domestic monetary policy.

Can Policymakers Stabilize Output and Inflation Simultaneously?*

Our analysis of business cycles has been based on the idea that short-run fluctuations in output and inflation are caused by either demand shifts or supply shifts. And, as we

[10]For a more detailed discussion of real-business-cycle theory, see Charles Plosser, "Understanding Real Business Cycles," *Journal of Economic Perspectives* 3, no. 3 (Summer 1989), pp. 51–77.

[11]See Galina Hale and Bart Hobijn, "The U.S. Content of 'Made in China,'" FRBSF *Economic Letter,* August 8, 2011.

The Problem with Measuring Nominal GDP
YOUR FINANCIAL WORLD

In order to set their policy-controlled interest rate as accurately as possible, central bankers need to know the size of the output gap. This requires measuring the level (and growth rate) of both current and potential real gross domestic product (GDP) accurately. Unfortunately, this is made difficult by the fact that estimates of GDP for a specific quarter are revised for many years after the fact; and the revisions tend to be large (see Applying the Concept: GDP: One Size No Longer Fits All in Chapter 18 on pages 501–502). One of the reasons for these revisions is that government statisticians have to reconcile two methods of measuring *nominal* GDP that are supposed to give the same answer. Here's the problem.

Looking at the economy as a whole, we know that expenditures must equal income. Eventually, every dollar that is earned as income must be spent on something. This means that one way to calculate nominal GDP is to divide it into the various categories for which the product is used—consumption, investment, government purchases, and net exports—and then measure expenditure on each of these.

But because one person's expenditure is another's income, total expenditure equals total income. This means that we can also measure nominal GDP by dividing income into categories and computing what economists call gross domestic income (GDI). Income categories would include wages, rental income, interest income, and dividend income. And because everyone is supposed to pay taxes on their income, measuring it should be straightforward.

The fact that income and expenditure are supposed to be equal doesn't mean that they are, however. Looking at tables constructed by the Department of Commerce's Bureau of Economic Analysis, we find a line labeled "Statistical discrepancy." The amount on this line, which represents GDP calculated from expenditures data minus GDI computed from the income data, is quite large. From 1990 to 2018, the statistical discrepancy between the two measures was between −1.7 and +2.3 percent of nominal GDP. Table 22.4 shows some examples for recent years. Because nominal GDP usually grows from 3 to 6½ percent a year—that figure includes inflation plus real growth—changes in the statistical discrepancy can have a big impact on official estimates of overall economic performance.

Although it directly affects nominal GDP, the practical implication of the statistical discrepancy is that it makes us unsure about the current level of real output. Uncertainty about something so crucial adds to the difficulty of making monetary policy.

Table 22.4 Nominal Gross Domestic Product and Income (US$ billions except as noted)

	1993	1997	2014	2018
Nominal gross domestic product	6,858.6	8,608.5	17,521.7	20,500.6
Nominal gross domestic income	6,702.6	8,596.2	17,820.8	20,556.5
Statistical discrepancy	156.0	12.3	−299.1	−55.9
Statistical discrepancy (percent of GDP)	2.3%	0.1%	−1.7%	−0.3%
Nominal GDP growth from previous year	5.2%	6.3%	4.4%	5.2%

SOURCE: Bureau of Economic Analysis, Department of Commerce, National Income and Product Accounts Tables 1.1.5 and 1.10.

have seen repeatedly, dynamic aggregate demand curve shifts move inflation and output in the same direction; while short-run aggregate supply shifts move inflation and output in opposite directions. Early in this chapter, we discussed how, by shifting their monetary policy reaction curve, policymakers offset demand shocks. (This is shown in Figure 22.7 on page 627.)

Unfortunately, supply shocks are a different story. There is no way to neutralize them. For instance, take the case of a negative supply shock like an oil price increase that raises production costs. This has the immediate effect of driving output down and inflation up (see Figure 22.5 on page 622). Now consider the tools that are available to policymakers. By shifting the monetary policy reaction curve, central bankers can shift the dynamic aggregate demand curve. Is there any way to use this tool to bring the economy back to its original long-run equilibrium point quickly and painlessly? The answer is no. Monetary policymakers can shift the dynamic aggregate demand curve, but they are powerless to move the short-run aggregate supply curve. And there is no shift in the dynamic aggregate demand curve that can quickly move the economy back to its long-run equilibrium point, where current output equals potential output and current inflation equals the central bank's target.

But that's not the end of the story. Central bankers can choose how aggressively they react to deviations of inflation from their target caused by supply shocks. They can do this by picking the slope of their monetary policy reaction curve, which then determines the slope of the dynamic aggregate demand curve. The more aggressive policymakers are in keeping current inflation close to target, the steeper their monetary policy reaction curve and the flatter the dynamic aggregate demand curve. And by controlling the slope of the dynamic aggregate demand curve policymakers choose the extent to which supply shocks translate into changes in output or changes in inflation. This means that the slope of the monetary policy reaction curve—how aggressively to react to deviations of inflation from their target—is really a choice about the relative volatility of inflation and output. The more central bankers stabilize inflation, the more volatile output will be, and vice versa. There is a tradeoff.

To see why policymakers face a tradeoff between inflation and output volatility, we can compare two policymakers, one with a relatively steep monetary policy reaction curve (as in Panel A of Figure 22.12), and one with a relatively flat monetary policy reaction curve (as in Panel B of Figure 22.12). The first policymaker cares more about keeping inflation close to its target level than the second one does.

Turning to the dynamic aggregate demand curve, Panel A of Figure 22.13 shows the relatively flat AD curve implied by the steep monetary policy reaction curve in which small deviations in inflation from the target level elicit large changes in the real interest rate. A flat dynamic aggregate demand curve, corresponding to the steep monetary policy reaction curve in Panel A of Figure 22.12, means that a negative supply shock prompts a large decline in current output and only a small increase in current inflation. By reacting aggressively, policymakers ensure that inflation (and inflation expectations) remain close to their target. The cost of following this path, however, is that stable inflation means volatile output. This is depicted in Panel A of Figure 22.13.

Panel B of Figure 22.13 shows what happens when policymakers are less concerned about keeping inflation close to target in the short run, and more concerned about keeping current output near potential output. When policymakers worry more about short-run fluctuations in output than about temporary movements in inflation, they will choose a relatively flat monetary policy reaction curve in which movements in the real interest rate are small, even when inflation strays far from its target level. The result is a steep dynamic aggregate demand curve like the one drawn in the right panel of the figure. Notice what happens in this case following

Figure 22.12 The Slope of the Monetary Policy Reaction Curve

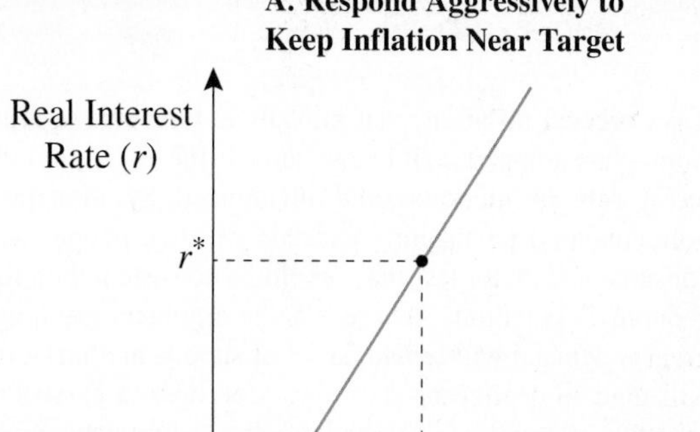

Central bankers who are intent on keeping inflation close to the target will move interest rates aggressively when inflation rises.

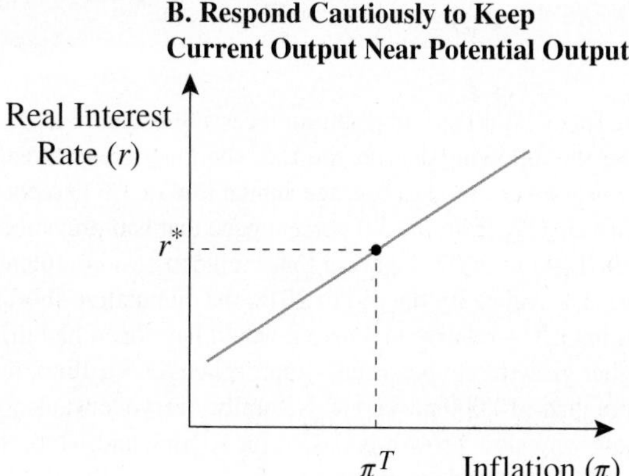

Central bankers more concerned about keeping output close to potential will move interest rates by less in reaction to an inflation increase.

Figure 22.13 The Policymaker's Choice

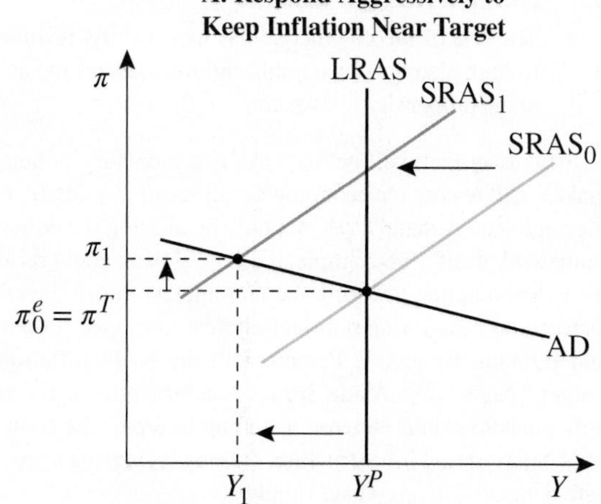

Central bankers intent on keeping inflation close to the target will move interest rates aggressively when inflation rises and create bigger fluctuations in output.

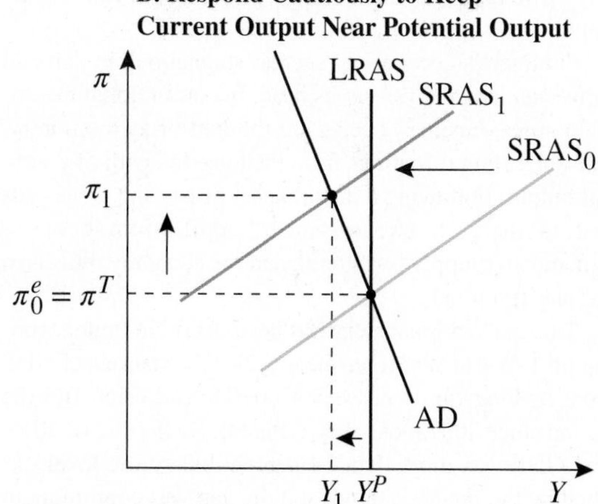

Policymakers more concerned about keeping output close to potential will move interest rates by less in reaction to an inflation change, resulting in bigger fluctuations in inflation.

A Guide to "Secular Stagnation"

MONEY AND BANKING BLOG

The financial crisis and resulting recession began in 2007. Over the following decade, the U.S. economy grew in real terms at a very modest average annual rate of 1.6 percent, down sharply from the 3.0 percent pace that had prevailed from 1990 to 2007, a period that included two complete business cycles. By the end of 2018, the cumulative shortfall in GDP—relative to where it would have been had the higher growth rate persisted—approached $3.5 trillion, or more than $10,000 per capita. Naturally, everyone wants to know why slow growth persisted for so long and what, if anything, can be done about it.

The conventional explanation for the postcrisis downshift is that the trend growth rate of potential output slowed sharply. Potential output is a supply concept: In the long run, when all prices (including wages and interest rates) have adjusted, aggregate supply is determined by the available capital and labor and by the technology used to combine them to produce output. From this perspective, a long-term decline in the growth rate of real GDP means a slowing in the contribution to growth from one or more of those three sources.

An alternative hypothesis—proposed by former Treasury Secretary Lawrence Summers—is that the feeble growth performance of the past decade reflects an unusually prolonged shortfall of aggregate demand rather than diminished supply.*

Summers's account of "secular stagnation" in demand turns standard analysis on its head. In conventional macroeconomics, business cycles are thought of as temporary, self-correcting deviations from the long-run path of potential output. Following a disturbance, prices and wages adjust to the new circumstances, equilibrium between demand and supply is restored, and the economy returns to its long-run trend.

This conventional story has been useful in understanding post–World War II business cycles. Deviations of GDP from its long-run trend were moderate and brief. But the period since 2007 looks very different. By the end of 2018, real GDP was more than 14 percent below the level implied by the precrisis trend, and the gap was continuing to widen. Not surprisingly, analysts have lowered estimates of U.S. potential GDP.

The secular stagnation story shifts the focus from supply to demand. Proponents argue that the *natural rate of interest*—the real interest rate r^* (the nominal interest rate less expected inflation) that prevails in long-run equilibrium—has dropped well below zero. If the actual real interest rate in markets (and influenced by monetary policymakers) persistently exceeds r^*, then people will consume and invest less than would be consistent with the economy's potential. As a result, the argument goes, aggregate demand will remain short of supply, and inflation will tend to decline or stay low. Moreover, a persistent shortfall of aggregate demand can itself diminish supply through the atrophying effect of unemployment on worker skills, through the depreciation of the capital stock, and through damage to intermediaries that allocate savings to the most productive uses.

Why might the natural rate of interest r^* be unusually low? Proponents of secular stagnation offer a number of possibilities:

- High saving, which drives asset prices up and expected returns down.
- The declining cost of investment goods (think "software" versus "hardware"), which reduces investment outlays relative to savings.
- Increased risk (or awareness of risk) following the financial crisis, which fosters greater caution among providers and users of funds.
- The rise of income inequality, which shifts income to high-savings households and thus lowers the average propensity to consume.

If r^* is in fact well below zero, can monetary policymakers still restore the economy's equilibrium by stimulating aggregate demand? Yes, but only by altering the policy framework itself. For example, the central bank could raise its inflation target, lowering the real interest rate at the *effective lower bound* on nominal interest rates (see Money and Banking Blog: Is 2 Percent Still the Right Inflation Target? page 509). Aside from monetary policy, fiscal policymakers could increase spending to repair the country's deteriorating infrastructure, thereby increasing aggregate demand *and* aggregate supply.†

So, can we distinguish between these competing accounts of the ongoing growth slowdown? Is it primarily a supply story of slowing productivity or a demand story of insufficiently low real interest rates? Table 22.5 highlights some of the differences in these two perspectives. But

Table 22.5 Possible Contributors to the Growth Slowdown: Supply versus Demand

Supply	Demand
Demographics: slow labor force growth	High private debt: reduced propensity to consume
Limited innovation: slow productivity growth	High public debt: reduced public investment
Education: reduced gains in labor quality	Falling price of investment goods: lower outlays
Skill atrophy: reduced gains in labor quality	Preference for safe assets: reduced investment
Regulation: slower firm creation	Increased inequality: reduced propensity to consume
Regulation: trend decline in rate of job-finding	

accurately measuring the contributions of these factors isn't easy. After 2014, the acceleration of wages suggests that supply factors were limiting economic growth but—consistent with the claims of stagnationists—the process of eliminating labor slack took far longer than in previous recoveries, while the pickup of wages was unusually modest.

*See Lawrence H. Summers, "U.S. Economic Prospects: Secular Stagnation, Hysteresis, and the Zero Lower Bound," *Business Economics* 49, no. 2 (April 2014), pp. 65–73.

†Structural reforms—such as improvements in competition and in hiring and firing flexibility—can stimulate growth by expanding aggregate supply and raising r^* in the process. See Coen Teulings and Richard Baldwin, eds., *Secular Stagnation: Facts, Causes and Cures* (London: CEPR Press and VoxEU.org, 2014).

a negative supply shock. Once more, inflation rises and output falls. But the output gap is small, while the deviation of inflation from expected inflation is large. The consequence is that expected inflation rises significantly, and adjusts only slowly back to the target. Stable output means volatile inflation.

When choosing how aggressively to respond to supply shocks, central bankers are deciding how to conduct stabilization policy. Do they want to ensure that inflation remains near target, or that output remains close to potential? When faced with a supply shock, policymakers cannot stabilize both output and inflation. And by stabilizing one, the other becomes more volatile. Monetary policymakers face an inflation-output volatility tradeoff.

Key Terms

demand shock, 617
disinflation, 635
real-business-cycle theory, 635
supply shock, 617

Using FRED: Codes for Data in This Chapter

Data Series	FRED Data Code
U.S. consumer price index	CPIAUCSL
Real GDP	GDPC1
NBER recession dates (0 = expansion, 1 = recession)	USREC
Recession periods, Germany	DEURECM
Recession periods, Italy	ITARECM
Recession periods, Spain	ESPRECM
Estimated probability of U.S. recession	RECPROUSM156N
Ratio of manufacturers' inventories to shipments	AMTMIS
Total credit market debt owed by households	CMDEBT
Nominal GDP	GDP
Real potential GDP	GDPPOT
Gross domestic income	GDI
Chile consumer price index	CHLCPIALLMINMEI
Israel consumer price index	ISRCPIALLMINMEI
U.S. federal deficit (percent of GDP)	FYFSGDA188S

To learn more about the changing financial system, visit www.moneyandbanking.com.

Chapter Lessons

1. Short-run fluctuations in output and inflation arise from shifts in either the dynamic aggregate demand curve or the short-run aggregate supply curve.
   a. A decrease in the central bank's inflation target shifts the dynamic aggregate demand curve to the left.
      i. In the short run, this decreases both output and inflation.
      ii. It drives current inflation below expected inflation.
      iii. In the long run, inflation and expected inflation fall to the new target as output returns to potential output.
   b. A government expenditure increase shifts the dynamic aggregate demand curve to the right.
      i. In the short run, this increases both output and inflation.
      ii. It drives current inflation above expected inflation.
      iii. To keep inflation from rising, monetary policymakers shift their reaction curve to the left, raising the real interest rate at every level of inflation.
      iv. Unless the central bank's target inflation changes, the economy eventually returns to its original long-run equilibrium point.
   c. A negative supply shock shifts the short-run aggregate supply curve to the left.
      i. In the short run, this decreases output and increases inflation.
      ii. The rise of inflation initially drives expected inflation up, but both inflation and expected inflation then begin to decline.
      iii. Unless the central bank's target inflation changes, the economy returns to its original long-run equilibrium point.

2. Applying the dynamic aggregate demand–aggregate supply framework we see that:
   a. Stabilization policy is the use of monetary and fiscal policy tools to stabilize output and inflation.
      i. Monetary policy can be used to shift the dynamic aggregate demand curve to offset changes in the quantity of aggregate output demanded. In practice, lack of information and lags in the impact of policy changes make this very difficult.
      ii. Fiscal policy can shift the dynamic aggregate demand curve as well, but it is difficult to do in a timely and effective way.
      iii. A positive supply shock that lowers production costs and shifts the short-run aggregate supply curve to the right creates an opportunity for policymakers to permanently lower inflation.
   b. Better monetary policy is the most likely explanation for the increased stability of the U.S. economy from the mid-1980s until 2007.
   c. An increase in potential output shifts both the short- and long-run aggregate supply curves to the right, driving output up and inflation down, resulting in expected inflation being above current inflation.
   d. Globalization has the same impact as an increase in potential output. In the long run it raises output but inflation only changes if the central bank adjusts its target.
   e. When confronted with a shift in the short-run aggregate supply curve, central bankers face a tradeoff between output and inflation volatility.

Conceptual and Analytical Problems McGraw Hill connect

1. Define the term *stabilization policy* and describe how it can be used to reduce the volatility of economic growth and inflation. Do stabilization policies improve welfare? *(LO2)*
2. Explain why stabilization policies are usually pursued using monetary rather than fiscal policy. *(LO3)*
3. Explain why fiscal policy played a greater role than usual in the response to the 2007–2009 recession. *(LO3)*
4. Explain why monetary policymakers cannot restore the original long-run equilibrium of the economy if, in the short run, the economy has moved to a point where inflation is above target inflation and output is below potential output. *(LO2)*
5. Explain why the rise in oil prices in 2008 created a particularly difficult situation for Federal Reserve policymakers. *(LO2)*
6. Will changes in technology affect the rate at which the short-run aggregate supply curve shifts in response to an output gap? Why or why not? Provide some specific examples of how technology will change the rate of adjustment. *(LO1)*
7. After examining Figure 22.6, explain the potential link between innovations in financial markets and output volatility since the 1980s. You should consider both the "Great Moderation" and the recession of 2007–2009 in your answer. *(LO1)*

8.* According to real-business-cycle theory, can monetary policy affect equilibrium output in either the short run or the long run? *(LO1)*

*Indicates more difficult problems.

9. The economy has been sluggish, so in an effort to increase output in the short run, government officials have decided to cut taxes. They are considering two possible temporary tax cuts of equal size in terms of lost revenue. The first would reduce the taxes on people with incomes *above* the median for one year. The second would cut taxes on people with incomes *below* the median for one year. Which change would shift the aggregate demand curve further to the right? Why? *(LO2)*
10. Suppose that conflict over international trade leads to a fall in consumer confidence. Starting with the economy in long-run equilibrium, use the aggregate demand–aggregate supply framework to illustrate what would happen to inflation and output in the short run. Assuming the central bank takes no action to offset this fall in confidence, what would happen to inflation and output in the long run? By taking no action, how has the central bank implicitly altered its policy goal? *(LO2)*
11. If there is a fall in consumer confidence, what would happen to inflation and output in the long run if the central bank remained committed to its original inflation target and responded with an immediate policy change? Use the aggregate demand-aggregate supply framework to illustrate your answer, starting with the economy in long-run equilibrium. Compare the outcome to what the outcome would be if the central bank did not respond explicitly to the change in consumer confidence. *(LO2)*
12. How would a shock that reduces production costs in the economy (a positive supply shock) affect equilibrium output and inflation in both the short run and the long run? Illustrate your answer using the aggregate demand–aggregate supply framework. You should assume that the shock does not affect the potential output of the economy. *(LO2)*
13. Suppose the central bank took advantage of a temporary positive supply shock to lower its inflation target. Illustrate the impact of this change in the inflation target using an aggregate demand–aggregate supply diagram. Compare this with a chart of a situation where the central bank lowers its inflation target in the absence of a positive supply shock. *(LO3)*
14.* Suppose a natural disaster reduces the productive capacity of the economy. How would the equilibrium long-run real interest rate r^* be affected? Assuming the central bank maintains its existing inflation target, illustrate the impact on the monetary policy reaction function and on equilibrium inflation and output both in the short run and in the long run. *(LO1)*
15.* Monetary policymakers observe an increase in output in the economy and believe it is a result of an increase in potential output. If they were correct, what would the appropriate policy response be to maintain the existing inflation target? If they were incorrect and the increase in output resulted simply from a positive supply shock, what would the long-run impact be of their policy response? *(LO3)*
16.* Consider a previously closed economy that opens up to international trade. Use the aggregate demand–aggregate supply framework to illustrate a situation where this would lead to lower inflation in this economy in the long run. *(LO2)*

*Indicates more difficult problems.

17.* How could you use the aggregate demand–aggregate supply framework to explain the impact of the financial crisis of 2007–2009 on inflation and output in the economy? *(LO1)*

18.* Changes in oil prices shift the short-run aggregate supply curve (SRAS). Consider how *volatility* in oil prices may influence the economy's short-run equilibrium, which occurs at the intersection of the dynamic aggregate demand (AD) curve and the SRAS curve. *(LO3)*
   a. Suppose the monetary policy reaction curve is relatively steep. What does this imply about the slope of the AD curve? What does it imply about the variability of output and inflation when the SRAS curve shifts? Explain.
   b. Suppose the monetary policy reaction curve is relatively flat. What does this imply about the slope of the AD curve? What does it imply about the variability of output and inflation when the SRAS curve shifts? Explain.

19.* Suppose that a government imposes trade barriers that raise the domestic cost of production and lower potential output. What would you expect to happen to inflation and output in the short run and the long run, assuming monetary policymakers only recognize the fall in potential output with a lag and keep their inflation target unchanged? *(LO1)*

20. High debt ratios led many countries in recent years to reduce government spending. Suppose the cut in spending started from a point with the economy at long-run equilibrium. How might monetary policymakers react, assuming their inflation target remained unchanged? *(LO1)*

21. Suppose that the anemic growth of the U.S. economy following the financial crisis of 2007–2009 was a result of "secular stagnation." Use the Fisher equation to explain why raising the central bank's inflation target could help boost economic growth in circumstances where nominal interest rates are close to the effective lower bound. *(LO2)*

22.* Do you think GDP-linked bonds would be more useful in a relatively stable economy or in an economy that is frequently buffeted in the short run by demand and supply shocks, assuming these economies have similar sovereign debt burdens? Explain your choice. *(LO2)*

Data Exploration

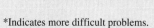

For general information on using Federal Reserve Economic Data (FRED) online, visit www.mhhe.com/moneyandbanking6e.com *and refer to the FRED resources.*

1. Display as a bar chart the periods since 1854 that are designated as U.S. recessions by the National Bureau of Economic Research (FRED code: USREC). Why has the frequency of recessions declined over time? Could improvements in monetary policy have played a role? Improvements in fiscal policy? Can you think of any other causes? *(LO1)*
2. In the past, policymakers occasionally became aware of a recession only well after it began. Can they do better? Plot the probability of a recession from a statistical model (FRED code: RECPROUSM156N). To what extent could this model help improve monetary or fiscal policy or both? *(LO3)*

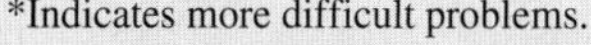

3. Compare the frequency and timing of recessions in key European economies since 1960. Make separate bar charts for Germany (FRED code: DEURECM), Italy (FRED code: ITARECM), and Spain (FRED code: ESPRECM). Do their business cycles appear sufficiently well aligned to make them operate easily in a single currency area with a common monetary policy? *(LO3)*
4. To keep inflation low and steady, central banks would like to keep output reasonably close to its potential level, but can they anticipate changes in potential GDP? Plot since 1960 the percent change from a year ago of the Congressional Budget Office's estimate of potential GDP (FRED code: GDPPOT). Suppose that the FOMC assumed that the growth rate of potential GDP remained permanently at its 1960s average. What would you expect to happen to inflation? Why? *(LO1)*
5. The Taylor rule includes a resource gap that can be measured either as the percent difference between actual and potential real GDP (FRED codes: GDPC1 and GDPPOT) or, alternatively, as the gap between the actual and natural unemployment rates (FRED codes: UNRATE and NROU). Plot these two measures of the resource gap since 1960. Show the unemployment gap as the difference between the actual and natural unemployment rates. Show the output gap as 100 times the difference between actual and potential real GDP, all divided by potential GDP. Compare the cyclical characteristics of these two measures. *(LO3)*

Chapter

23 Modern Monetary Policy and the Challenges Facing Central Bankers

Learning Objectives

After reading this chapter, you should be able to:

LO1 Analyze the monetary policy transmission mechanism.

LO2 Discuss key challenges facing monetary policymakers.

As we saw earlier, the financial crisis of 2007–2009 and the recession it triggered were by far the most widespread and costly since the Great Depression. And, although the financial disruptions began in the United States, they spread to almost all corners of the global economy. Indeed, the peak-to-trough decline of GDP was greater in many countries than in the United States (see Panel A of Figure 23.1). The subsequent crisis in the euro area triggered even larger economic losses in Greece, Ireland, Italy, Portugal, and Spain.

The response of monetary policymakers was likewise unprecedented. Interbank lending rates—the target of central bank policy—plunged in the United States, Japan, and much of Europe (see Panel B of Figure 23.1). And many central banks deployed unconventional monetary policy tools—including forward guidance, quantitative easing, and targeted asset purchases—to compensate for the collapse of intermediation and the fragility of financial markets. Although monetary policies failed to prevent the global crisis, they nevertheless helped contain it. Around mid-2009, the worldwide plunge in GDP bottomed out, and most economies began growing again. Some, like China's, had regained strength even earlier, partly because of an extraordinary fiscal expansion. Similarly, the threat of an imminent breakup of the euro area receded in the latter half of 2012 following the ECB's extraordinary interventions (see Chapter 16).

Yet, many observers worried that the aftermath of these financial crises would dim the economic outlook for years to come. Some of the concerns stemmed from the deterioration of fiscal conditions—a number of countries racked up record fiscal deficits and surges in government debt in reaction to the crisis. But the damage to the global financial system posed at least as big and pervasive a problem.

Deep, long recessions are frequently followed by unusually sharp and long-lived economic rebounds. But the experience of previous financial crises—especially the Great Depression and the 1990s breakdown in Japan—led policymakers to worry that the rebound from the crisis of 2007–2009 would be weaker than the norm. They

Figure 23.1 Economic Activity and Policy Rates during the Financial Crisis of 2007–2009 and Thereafter

A. Peak-to-Trough Percent Change of Real GDP during the Financial Crisis of 2007–2009

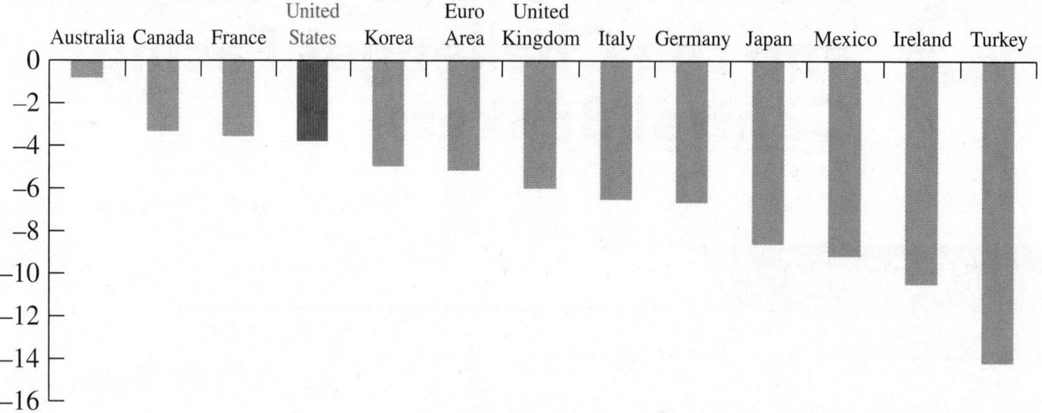

NOTE: The U.S. peak and trough occurred in fourth quarter 2007 and second quarter 2009, respectively. In the other countries, the dates differed somewhat, but the troughs occurred by third quarter 2009.

SOURCES: Organization for Economic Co-operation and Development and authors' calculations.

B. Overnight Interbank Lending Rates, 2006–2019

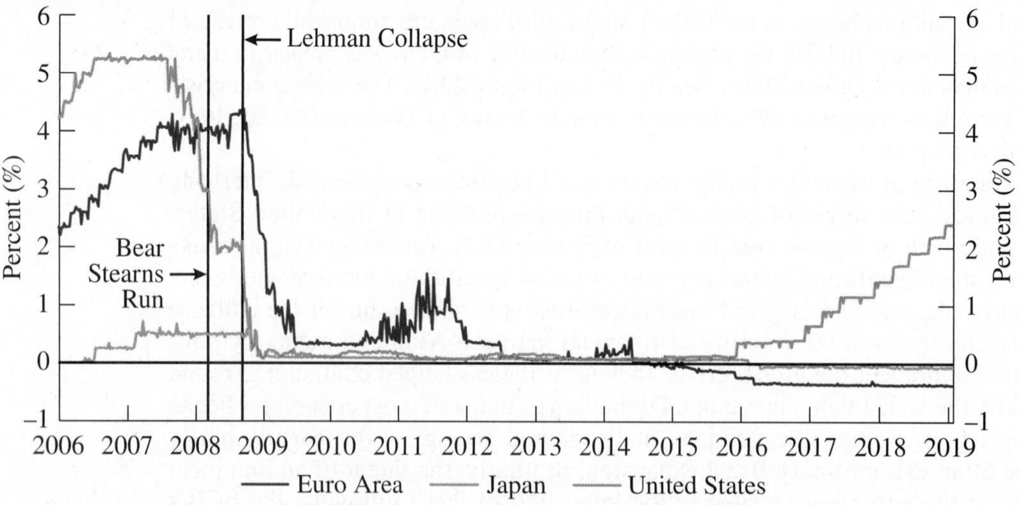

SOURCES: Bank of Japan, European Central Bank, and Federal Reserve Board.

expected that anxious banks would make credit expensive and difficult to obtain, that investors would be cautious about buying securitized assets, and that U.S. households would prefer to save more and borrow less. Policymakers also made clear that a period of increased regulation and prolonged fiscal repair lay ahead, which added to the hesitancy among intermediaries.

The aggregate demand and supply framework described in Chapter 21 helps us understand many sources of inflation and fluctuations in the business cycle as well as how stabilization policy works. But it does not explain why policymakers in many countries doubted that conventional monetary policy would be sufficient to counter the crisis of 2007–2009. And it does not explain the weakness of the recoveries following financial crises. To understand these concerns, we must return to the question of *how* monetary policy affects the economy.

Chapter 17 described how central banks influence the economy by controlling their balance sheet. Chapter 18 described how, in normal times, monetary policymakers use their balance sheet to control the interest rate banks charge each other for overnight loans. We learned that the real interest rate is the nominal interest rate minus the rate of expected inflation. Because the expected rate of inflation generally changes only slowly in low- and moderate-inflation economies, changing the target for the policy interest rate also changes the short-run real interest rate. In Chapter 21, we saw that the components of aggregate expenditure are sensitive to the real interest rate, so by changing the real interest rate, policymakers can influence real economic activity. Yet, the 2007–2009 experience (as well as that of Japan in the 1990s) suggests that conventional interest rate policy does not always work. Even lowering their policy rates *below* zero—as the Bank of Japan, the ECB, and several smaller central banks did—has not prompted a strong expansion in these economies. To see why not, we need to look at all the ways that monetary policy actions affect real economic activity—that is, all the channels through which monetary policy is transmitted.

Examining the transmission mechanism of monetary policy is the first of this chapter's two main topics. The second topic is the question of why, in the aftermath of financial crises like the 2007–2009 episode, monetary policy and the challenges facing central bankers are especially difficult.

The Monetary Policy Transmission Mechanism

Anytime the central bank alters the size of its balance sheet, the effects ripple through the economy, changing nearly everyone's behavior. Households adjust their spending on houses and cars. Companies rethink their decisions about how much and how fast to grow. Exchange rates change, bond and stock prices move, and banks adjust their balance sheets. In fact, we would be challenged to find a financial or economic decision that is unaffected. To fully appreciate how conventional monetary policy works, then, we need to examine the various ways in which changes in the policy-controlled interest influence the quantity of aggregate output demanded in the economy as a whole. These are referred to collectively as the channels of the **monetary policy transmission mechanism**. We will begin with the traditional **interest rate** and **exchange rate channels**. Next we will study the role of banks and finally the importance of asset price movements, including the prices of stocks and houses.

The Traditional Channels: Interest Rates and Exchange Rates

Central banks, such as the Federal Reserve, the European Central Bank, and the Bank of Japan, target a very short-term (usually overnight) interest rate. In the Fed's case, for example, a change of conventional policy is a change in the target range for the federal funds rate. And as we saw in Chapter 21, a change in a central bank's policy interest rate represents a change in the real interest rate, which has a direct effect on total spending. The lower the real interest rate, the higher investment, consumption, and net exports will be.

Let's review this process. As the real interest rate falls, financing becomes less expensive, so firms become more likely to undertake investment projects and families more likely to purchase new cars. Changes in the real interest rate also affect the exchange rate. When the real interest rate falls, investor demand for U.S. assets falls with it, lowering the demand for and increasing the supply of dollars, reducing the dollar's value (see Chapter 19, Figure 19.2). That is, an easing of monetary policy—by which we mean a decrease in the target nominal interest rate, which lowers the real interest rate—leads to a depreciation of the dollar. A less valuable dollar, in turn, drives up the cost of imported goods and services, reducing imports from abroad. At the same time, however, the lower value of the dollar makes U.S. goods and services cheaper to foreigners, so they will buy more of them. Together, lower imports and higher exports mean higher net exports, or an increase in total spending.

INFORMATION

While these traditional channels of monetary policy transmission make sense theoretically, they present a practical problem. Though changes in monetary policy do influence firms' decisions to purchase new equipment and build new buildings, the interest rate channel is not very powerful. That is, data suggest that the investment component of total spending isn't very sensitive to interest rates, which should not be a surprise to us. At the end of our discussion of financial intermediation in Chapter 11, we saw that information problems often make external financing too difficult and costly for firms to obtain, either directly in the financial markets or indirectly through institutions. As a result, the vast majority of investments are financed by businesses themselves, through their own funds. While a small change in the interest rate does change the cost of external financing, it doesn't have much of an effect on investment decisions.

The impact of short-term interest rates on household decisions is also rather modest. The problem is that people's decisions to purchase cars or houses depend on longer-term interest rates rather than the policymakers' short-run target rate. So household consumption decisions will change only to the extent that changing the target interest rate affects long-term interest rates. And the overall effect isn't that large.

As for the effect of monetary policy on the exchange rate, once again, theory and practice differ. In the real world, the policy-controlled interest rate is just one of many factors that shift the demand and supply for the dollar on foreign exchange markets. The rather long list, described in Chapter 10, includes a change in the riskiness of domestic investment relative to foreign investment; a change in the preference of U.S. consumers for foreign-produced goods and services; and a change in foreigners' income and wealth. The influence of these other factors may overwhelm the impact of monetary policy on the exchange rate and net exports.

Thus, after careful analysis, we must conclude that the traditional channels of monetary policy transmission aren't very powerful. Yet evidence shows that monetary policy *is* effective. When policy-controlled interest rates go up, the quantity of aggregate output demanded does go down. The dynamic aggregate demand curve slopes down. Something else must be amplifying the impact of monetary policy changes on real economic activity. Otherwise, no one would care about the central bank's periodic policy statements. To figure out what that link might be, we turn now to a discussion of two alternative transmission channels: the behavior of banks, and the impact of stock and real estate markets.

Bank-Lending and Balance-Sheet Channels

Four times a year the Federal Reserve conducts an opinion survey on bank-lending practices. Addressed to the senior loan officers who oversee lending policies at the 60

Correlation Does Not Imply Causality

TOOLS OF THE TRADE

Suppose we notice that the higher the crime rate in a neighborhood, the more often police are present. Should we infer that the police are causing crime? Surely not. Nor should we conclude from the fact that hospitals are filled with doctors that doctors make people ill. A fundamental principle of sound logical reasoning is that correlation does not imply causality. The fact that two events happened together does not indicate a causal link.

In the physical sciences, where researchers can conduct controlled experiments, establishing a causal link is not a serious challenge. We know from scientific trials that antibiotic drugs really do eliminate infections. It's not just chance that the people who take them feel better. But in economics, establishing a causal relationship is much more difficult. How can we be sure that monetary policy affects real economic activity? Our theories tell us that when policymakers raise the nominal interest rate, the real interest rate goes up, depressing aggregate expenditure and lowering real economic activity. But do we have any hard-and-fast evidence of this relationship?

The answer is that we do have some evidence that higher interest rates are associated with lower levels of real growth. Look back at Figure 21.17 (page 605), and you'll see the pattern: when interest rates rise, growth falls. But does that mean that increases in the interest rate cause recessions? What if, simultaneously, an increase in oil prices depresses real growth, causing policymakers to raise the interest rate in order to head off rising inflation? That is, what if some third factor drives up the interest rate, forcing growth down at the same time? In that case, the interest rate becomes another implication of the fundamental cause of recession, an increase in oil prices.

How can we eliminate this problem and determine the extent to which monetary policy actually causes economic fluctuations? The answer is that we need to look for clear evidence that particular monetary policy actions are unrelated to this sort of third factor. Some years ago, Christina Romer and David Romer of the University of California at Berkeley read through the records of the Federal Reserve's interest rate decisions since 1946. They identified a series of dates on which FOMC members stated unambiguously that they were raising interest rates to combat inflation. Each of these episodes was followed by a recession. Romer and Romer argued that, because the intention in each of these instances was to fight inflation, the FOMC's actions were not the result of the level of GDP at the time. Instead, it was monetary policy actions that were the fundamental cause.* With hard work and ingenuity, economists are ultimately able to distinguish causality from correlation.

*See Christina D. Romer and David H. Romer, "Does Monetary Policy Matter? A New Test in the Spirit of Friedman and Schwartz," in O. J. Blanchard and S. Fischer, eds., *NBER Macroeconomic Annual* (Cambridge, MA: MIT Press, 1989), pp. 121–170.

or so largest banks in the country, the survey contains questions about both the demand for and the supply of loans. On the demand side, the questions have to do with the quantity and quality of loan applications. On the supply side, they have to do with the relative difficulty of getting a loan, as well as the rates borrowers must pay. This survey provides important information to monetary policymakers. Without it, they would not be able to tell whether a change in the quantity of new loans granted resulted from a shift in supply or a shift in demand. Was a drop in the quantity of new loans the result of fewer applications or a tightening of credit standards? Did interest rate spreads climb because the quality of borrowers declined or because banks became more risk averse? Policymakers at the Fed care about the answers to these questions because if banks stop making loans, some businesses can't borrow to finance their investment projects, and economic growth slows.

The fact is that banks are essential to the operation of a modern economy. They direct resources from savers to investors and solve problems caused by information asymmetries. Financial intermediaries specialize in screening borrowers to ensure they are creditworthy and in monitoring loan recipients to guarantee that they use borrowed funds as they said they would. But banks are not only the hub of the financial system; they are also the conduit through which monetary policy is transmitted to

the economy. When policymakers change the size of the central bank's balance sheet, their action has an immediate impact on commercial bank balance sheets because it affects the level of reserves they hold. To understand monetary policy changes completely, then, we need to look carefully at how they affect the banking system. That means we need to examine the impact of policy changes on banks and bank lending.

Banks and Bank Lending For the vast majority of individuals and firms, the cost of issuing either stocks or bonds is prohibitive. These borrowers do not have access to capital market financing; instead, they must go to banks, which step in to reduce the information costs small borrowers face. A small business that is denied a bank loan has nowhere else to turn, so the project it wishes to undertake goes unfunded. When banks stop lending, then, a large class of borrowers simply can't obtain financing. Thus, bank lending is an important channel through which monetary policy affects the economy.[1] By altering the supply of funds to the banking system, policymakers can affect banks' ability and willingness to lend. This policy mechanism is referred to as the **bank-lending channel** of monetary policy transmission.

To see how the bank-lending channel works, think about the immediate consequences of an open market purchase (see Figure 17.2 on page 456). Recall that an open market operation involves an exchange of securities for reserves between the banking system and the central bank. When the central bank purchases securities from commercial banks, it pays for them with reserves. So after an open market purchase, banks have fewer securities and more reserves that usually bear lower interest. Unless bank managers do something, their revenues will fall. The natural reaction of the banks is to lend the new funds. These new loans work their way through the banking system through the process of multiple deposit creation, increasing the supply of loans throughout the economy. (Take a look back at the section on the deposit expansion multiplier in Chapter 17, pages 460 to 465.) In short, an open market purchase has a direct impact on the supply of loans, increasing their availability to those who depend on banks for financing.

Monetary policymakers are not the only people who can influence bank-lending practices. Financial regulators can, too. Changes in financial regulations, such as an increase or decrease in the amount of capital banks are required to hold when they make certain types of loans, will have an impact on the amount of bank lending as well. In 1980, for example, President Jimmy Carter authorized the Federal Reserve to impose a series of credit controls in an attempt to reduce bank lending and, with it, the level of output and inflation. A mild recession followed. In the early 1990s, the economy failed to make a strong recovery from the recession after the first Gulf War. Careful examination of the historical record suggests that the disappointing economic performance was a direct consequence of a slowdown in bank lending. At the time, bank balance sheets were very weak, having been eroded by large loan losses during the banking crises of the 1980s. Subsequent experience in Japan and the euro area confirms that undercapitalized banks are less able to lend to healthy borrowers.

Figure 23.2 plots two surveys of how credit conditions for large and small nonfarm businesses vary over time. One line shows the net share of banks tightening standards for loans to large firms (at least $50 million in annual sales); the other shows the share of small firms that view credit as harder to obtain (than three months earlier) minus the

[1]Studies of how and why monetary policy is transmitted through bank lending and balance sheets include Ben Bernanke and Mark Gertler, "Inside the Black Box: The Credit Channel of Monetary Policy Transmission," *Journal of Economic Perspectives* 9 (Fall 1995), pp. 27–45. The role of the bank-lending channel during the global financial crisis is the focus of Leonardo Gambacorta and David Marqués-Ibañez, "The Bank Lending Channel: Lessons from the Crisis," *Economic Policy* 26 (April 2011), pp. 135–182.

Figure 23.2 Survey Measures of Changing Credit Conditions by Firm Size

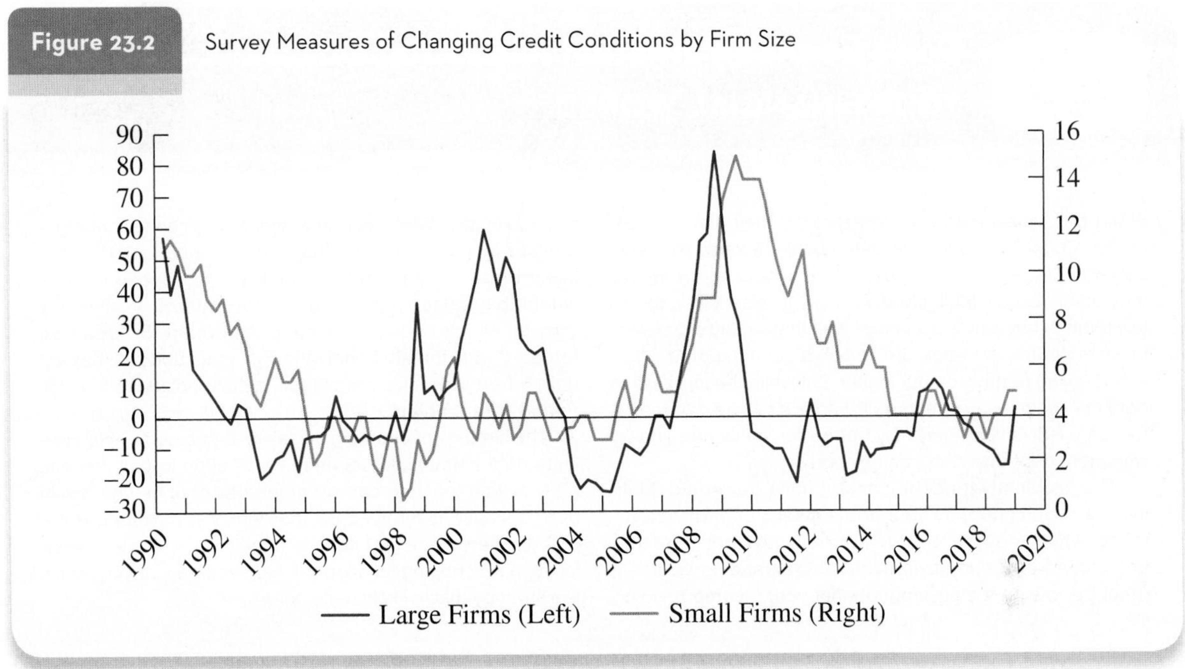

NOTE: For large firms, credit conditions are tightening when the figure is above zero and easing when it is below zero. For small firms, a higher figure indicates that the net share of firms concerned about credit availability is greater than before.

SOURCES: For large businesses, Federal Reserve Board's survey of senior loan officers at selected banks; for small businesses, survey of firms by the National Federation of Independent Business. (FRED code: DRTSCILM.)

share that view credit as easier to obtain. In both cases, credit conditions typically tighten in recessions and ease in booms. Note, however, that small firms—which depend more on bank loans than large firms—sometimes face tight credit conditions even in economic recoveries.[2] The figure shows that happening in 1992 and again in the aftermath of the financial crisis of 2007–2009. A cutback in lending to creditworthy small firms that want to expand or to qualified households that wish to buy a home creates "financial headwinds" that limit the pace of national economic growth during recovery. This is a key reason policymakers worry that the recovery from a recession caused by a financial crisis may be weaker than the recovery from a recession caused by other factors.

Firms' Balance Sheets and Household Net Worth Besides its influence on the willingness of banks to lend, monetary policy has an important effect on the creditworthiness of borrowers—or at least on their perceived creditworthiness. This **balance sheet channel** of monetary policy transmission works because monetary policy has a direct influence on the net worth of potential borrowers. Specifically, an easing of monetary policy improves firms' and households' balance sheets, increasing their net worth. In turn, these increases in net worth reduce the problems of moral hazard and adverse selection, lowering the information costs of lending and allowing borrowers to obtain financing more easily. Recall that the higher the net worth of a borrower, the more likely that the lender will be repaid. The result is a smaller credit risk premium.

[2]Small firms are critical to private, nonfarm U.S. economic activity and employment: they account for about half of output and generate up to 80 percent of net new jobs each year (see Traci L. Mach and John D. Wolken, "Financial Services Used by Small Businesses: Evidence from the 2003 Survey of Small Business Finances," *Federal Reserve Bulletin*, October 2006, pp. A167–A195).

Don't Count on Inflation to Bail You Out

YOUR FINANCIAL WORLD

When policymakers lower interest rates, their aim is to encourage people to borrow. Central bankers know that low-interest mortgages make it possible for people to buy homes they otherwise couldn't afford. And low-interest car loans allow them to buy a new car earlier than they would otherwise. In lowering interest rates, the FOMC is counting on a surge in borrowing to drive output higher. But while the increase in debt may help the economy as a whole, it can be dangerous for some individuals. They may borrow too much and end up with more debt than they can manage.

The problem with debt is that it must be repaid. Making sure you can repay your debts means carefully calculating what you can afford—not just now but over the entire term of the loan. To avoid overextending yourself, don't borrow on the assumption that your income is going to rise rapidly. While you will typically receive annual increases in your real wage (adjusted for inflation), they are likely to be fairly modest. In fact, for the economy as a whole, pay raises tend to match the rate of productivity growth, which is usually around 2 percent. So don't be tempted into thinking that, though your budget may be tight when you take out a loan, future salary raises will remedy the problem.

The strategy of counting on salary increases to help eliminate debt amounts to counting on inflation to bail you out. It's true that inflation can be helpful to people who are in debt because it reduces the burden of repayment. But if policymakers at the Fed are doing their job, which is to keep inflation low, hoping inflation will help you pay off your loans is a strategy that is likely to backfire.

There are two ways in which a monetary policy expansion can improve borrowers' net worth. First, as we have already discussed, an expansionary policy drives up asset prices, increasing the value of firms and the wealth of households. Higher equity and property prices mean higher net worth, which implies lower information costs and greater ease in obtaining financing. The increase in home equity loans that follows a real estate boom is an example of this process. With an increase in household wealth, banks are willing to step up their lending.

The second way that a monetary policy expansion can improve borrowers' net worth has to do with the drop in interest rates. Most borrowers already have loans that they are in the process of repaying; lower interest rates reduce the burden of repayment. For a firm, the drop in the cost of financing increases the difference between revenues and expenses, raising profits and increasing the firm's value. Something similar happens for individuals. When interest rates fall, people who hold variable-rate loans enjoy lower interest payments.

For both businesses and households, the resulting improvement in net worth reduces the information problems that plague the lending relationship. Why? To evaluate a borrower's creditworthiness, banks look at the percentage of revenue or income that is devoted to loan payments. At lower interest rates, that percentage will be lower, making it easier to qualify for larger loans. The conclusion is that *as interest rates fall, the supply of loans increases.*

It is worth pausing to emphasize that information is the driving force in the bank-lending and balance sheet channels of monetary policy transmission. Information services are central to banks' role in the financial system because they help address the problems of adverse selection and moral hazard. The primacy of information in banking has some important implications for our understanding of the link between the financial system and the real economy. It means that financial instability, which is characterized by large and unpredictable moves in asset prices, accompanied by widespread bankruptcy, will reduce lenders' willingness to supply financing. It also means that accounting scandals, such as the ones that plagued U.S. companies in 2001 and 2002, will have an effect on the economy as a whole. When bankers are worried about the accuracy of accounting information, they will be less willing to make loans to anyone. Inferior information leads to an increase in adverse selection, reducing bank lending, lowering investment, and ultimately depressing the quantity of aggregate output demanded.

The channels of monetary policy transmission depend on the structure of the financial system. To the extent that banks are unimportant sources of funds for firms and individuals, the bank-lending channel is minor. As we will see at the end of this chapter, the rise of loan brokers and asset-backed securities diminished the importance of the bank-lending channel until the financial crisis of 2007–2009. But, following that crisis, information problems and the resulting balance sheet effects persisted for some time. While technology has made the processing of increasing amounts of information easier and cheaper, it seems unlikely to solve the problems of adverse selection and moral hazard, which make net worth such an important determinant of a borrower's creditworthiness.

Asset-Price Channels: Wealth and Investment

When the interest rate moves, so do asset prices. Specifically, a fall in the interest rate tends to push stock and real estate prices up. This relationship between the interest rate and the stock and real estate markets is referred to as the **asset-price channel** of monetary policy transmission. To understand it, we must first figure out why a change in the interest rate might cause a movement in asset prices. Then we must explain how a change in asset prices can influence the quantity of aggregate output demanded.

To see how the interest rate influences stock prices, recall that the fundamental value of a stock is the present value of the stream of its future dividends. The lower the interest rate is, the higher the present value is and, therefore, the higher the stock price will be. Added to this relationship is the fact that an easing of monetary policy might well improve consumer and business confidence in the prospects for future growth. More growth means more revenue and higher profits and that, too, will drive up stock prices. In fact, because current stock prices are based largely on expectations of future growth and future interest rates, they tend to move in anticipation of a cut in interest rates.

Monetary policy affects real estate markets in the same way that it influences stock markets. The mechanism is straightforward. When policymakers reduce their interest rate target, it drives the mortgage rate down. Lower mortgage rates mean higher demand for residential housing, driving up the prices of existing homes.

In short, when the central bank reduces its target interest rate, the stock and real estate markets are likely to boom. Then what? Stock and property prices affect both individual consumption and business investment. For individuals, a rise in stock and real estate prices means an increase in wealth. The richer people become, the more they will consume. If stock values go high enough, shareholders can actually buy the luxury cars they have been wanting, or take the fancy vacations they've been dreaming of, or maybe both. The conclusion is that higher asset prices mean increased wealth and consumption.

Just as consumption is affected by stock price movements, so is investment. As stock prices rise, firms find it easier to raise funds by issuing new shares. That is, they gain access to financing in the primary capital market. To see why, think of a simple example in which the price of a company's stock suddenly increases. In the meantime, nothing has happened to the cost of a new investment and hence to its internal rate of return. But at the higher stock price, financing is now cheaper. This story

Table 23.1 The Monetary Policy Transmission Mechanism

Channel	Mechanism
Interest rates (traditional channel)	Lower interest rates reduce the cost of investment, making more projects profitable.
Exchange rates (traditional channel)	Lower interest rates reduce the attractiveness of domestic investment, depressing the value of the currency and increasing net exports.
Bank lending	An easing of monetary policy raises the level of bank reserves and bank deposits, increasing the supply of funds.
Firms' balance sheets	Lower interest rates raise firms' profits, increasing their net worth and reducing the problems of adverse selection and moral hazard.
Household net worth	Lower interest rates raise individuals' net worth, improving their creditworthiness and allowing them to increase their borrowing.
Asset prices	Higher stock prices and real estate values fuel an increase in both business investment and household consumption.

should sound familiar. Recall the way in which the traditional *interest rate channel* influences investment: a lower real interest rate means a lower cost of financing, which raises the profitability of investment projects. As a result, borderline investment projects suddenly become profitable when real interest rates fall. The same thing happens when stock prices rise. As financing becomes less expensive, more investments become profitable. In short, when asset markets boom, so does business investment in new equipment and buildings.[3]

Overall, changes in monetary policy influence aggregate expenditure in the economy through a variety of channels that are summarized in Table 23.1. Each of the transmission mechanisms works slightly differently, but they all lead us to the same conclusion: When interest rates rise, the quantity of aggregate output demanded falls so the dynamic aggregate demand curve slopes down.

Financial Crises and the Transmission of Monetary Policy

We have seen that monetary policy is transmitted to the economy through financial intermediaries and through asset prices. Yet, financial conditions deteriorated through much of the crisis of 2007–2009, even as central bankers were cutting interest rates aggressively. What prevented policy easing from being transmitted as usual to the real economy?

The answer is that the crisis intensified the fundamental problems of asymmetric information—adverse selection and moral hazard—that affect the provision of credit in a modern economy. In general, a reduction in the quality of information about

[3]This line of reasoning, known as *Tobin's q-theory*, was originally developed by the Nobel Prize–winning economist James Tobin. Tobin pointed out that the question of whether or not a firm invests should depend on the ratio of the market value of its shares to the replacement cost of its plant and equipment, which he called q. When q is greater than one—that is, when a firm's stock-market value exceeds its cost of rebuilding—investment in new plant and equipment is cheap relative to the value placed on it in the financial markets. When q is less than one, embarking on new investments isn't worthwhile.

potential borrowers makes it more difficult for them to borrow. In the financial crisis, the widespread losses at intermediaries in general and the heightened uncertainty about the damage suffered by specific intermediaries reduced confidence in their ability to repay loans and thus virtually shut off the availability of credit to many of them. The hesitancy to lend in this episode was not unlike the common reluctance of buyers to acquire a used car when it might be a lemon (see pages 276–278). In short, funding liquidity dried up. As for households and nonfinancial firms, their net worth fell substantially, which greatly reduced their ability to borrow, so they responded by cutting spending. The result of this was a destabilizing feedback loop between worsening economic prospects and the deterioration of financial conditions that influence spending.

The process started in 2006 with the downturn in U.S. housing prices that led to widespread mortgage defaults. Major lenders—particularly in the United States and Europe—faced enormous and growing losses. Insufficient screening and monitoring had resulted in too many risky mortgages (see Chapter 11, Lessons from the Crisis: Information Asymmetry and Securitization, page 280). Losses from U.S. mortgage-backed securities and related financial instruments sharply depressed the capital in the financial system (see Chapter 12, Lessons from the Crisis: Insufficient Bank Capital, page 312). As a result, intermediaries were compelled to deleverage (see Chapter 3, Lessons from the Crisis: Leverage, page 49). They even stopped lending to each other—especially in the aftermath of the Lehman failure in September 2008—because they doubted the solvency of their counterparties or were simply uncertain about who would bear the losses (recall the Chapter 9 discussion of credit default swaps).

The result was an intense scramble for funding that led to a near collapse of the financial system. Only the aggressive supply of reserves from central banks and of new capital from governments made it possible to restore the basic function of financial intermediaries and markets. With the usual policy transmission mechanism obstructed during the crisis, the Federal Reserve and other central banks also used unconventional policy tools to directly influence key financial conditions that affect spending in the economy. The Fed's acquisitions of mortgage-backed securities and commercial paper stand out in this regard. Over time, expressions of central bank intent to keep interest rates low over an extended period (forward guidance) also influenced the willingness of investors to purchase other important assets, like equities and private-sector debt.

The bottom line: when the policy transmission mechanism is obstructed, central banks cannot assume that a cut in their target policy rate will ease the financial conditions that influence the economy. Indeed, through most of the crisis of 2007–2009, rate cuts did not even halt the deterioration of financial conditions, let alone improve them. Even after policy rates had fallen close to zero, financial conditions remained weak for some time.

The impairment of monetary policy transmission was at least as severe in the crisis of the euro area. In general, firms and households cannot borrow at a cost less than their governments, so rising default premiums on sovereign debt in 2011 and 2012 also worsened financial conditions for private borrowers in several of the countries on the geographic periphery of the euro area—Greece, Ireland, Italy, Portugal, and Spain. The ECB found it extremely difficult to offset this differential in funding access and cost. The central bank lowered its target interest rate and became the lender of last resort to these countries' banks. Yet, the supply of credit by the banks to firms and households diminished sharply. Only in the summer of 2012, when the ECB offered to become a lender of last resort to the crisis-stricken periphery governments, did the resulting

Debt, the Great Recession, and the Awful Recovery
APPLYING THE CONCEPT

Was a high level of household debt a major cause of the Great Recession, which began in 2007, and the weak recovery, which started in 2009? If so, would reforming debt contracts make the economy less prone to severe disruptions?

Cycles make it difficult to distinguish cause and effect. Did rising debt boost house prices, or was it the other way around? And what was the relationship between the fall in house prices and the decline in household spending and employment?

House of Debt, an important recent book, shows that (1) a dramatic easing of credit standards for low-quality borrowers fed the U.S. mortgage boom in the years leading up to the Great Recession, (2) the mortgage boom was a major force driving up U.S. housing prices, and (3) the burden of high mortgage debt among those with lower incomes drove down consumption as house prices sank, contributing to the loss of jobs.*

The book shows that housing prices rose more sharply in zip codes where less-qualified borrowers (with lower incomes and wealth) were relatively numerous and gained access to mortgage credit. Beginning as early as 2005, residents in these same zip codes then cut their consumption on cars and other durable goods by the most as house price increases began to slow and then reverse. Having risen the most, house prices in those places also fell the furthest when the nationwide bubble burst. And workers who provided services nearby were the most likely to lose their jobs.

In other words, an extraordinary credit expansion stoked the housing boom, especially among families with lower incomes. And the cooling of the boom drove down consumption more sharply than in a normal recession, exacerbating the bust that was the Great Recession.

These facts do not diminish the critical role of intermediation in the 2007–2009 crisis, which turned vicious only after the September 2008 failure of Lehman Brothers.

But high levels of household debt, which led to foreclosure and bankruptcy, made things worse than they otherwise would have been. And securitization of many of the mortgages made it nearly impossible for lenders and borrowers to agree on what might have been mutually beneficial write-downs.

This has led some economists to propose new "mortgages" that shift part of the risk of house price declines to lenders and away from borrowers. Instead of merely being lenders, the suppliers of funds would become part owners of the collateral. In exchange, they would receive a portion of the increased value of the house when it is sold.

We now know that a boom in conventional mortgages can lead to a housing bust and debt burdens that generate and prolong a deep recession. But we still need to know much more about the relationship between debt and the business cycle; that would help us understand whether changing the form of debt contracts can further stabilize the economy.

*See Atif Mian and Amir Sufi, *House of Debt* (Princeton, NJ: Princeton University Press, 2014).

decline of sovereign risk premiums begin to relieve private-sector financial stress. Even in 2016, the ECB continued to introduce new policy tools designed to promote bank lending and to narrow the differential lending rates across member countries.

Financial conditions matter in economic upturns, too. When central banks hike rates to slow an economy, their success will depend on whether financial conditions respond. If an asset price bubble is under way, as it was in the United States in 2004–2006, the economic impact of central bank policy tightening probably will be smaller than usual. As a result, central banks must always take into account the workings of the monetary policy transmission mechanism in order to achieve their goals of economic and price stability.

The Challenges Modern Monetary Policymakers Face

The financial crisis of 2007–2009 was a "game changer" for the practitioners and theorists of monetary policy. Surely no one assumes now that monetary policy is a hard-and-fast science—that a few equations coupled with some statistical analysis and the help of a big computer will suffice. To do their job well, central bankers need a detailed understanding of how both the financial system and the real economy will react to their policy changes.

That job would be tough enough in a world that is standing still, but the dynamism that is such a pervasive and desirable feature of today's economy makes the job all the more difficult. In fact, modern monetary policymakers face a series of daunting challenges. In this section, we will look at three that grew more prominent thanks to the financial crisis of 2007–2009. First, stock prices and property values have a tendency to go through boom and bust cycles. Second, policymakers' options are limited, as we have seen by the fact that the nominal interest rate cannot fall below the effective lower bound (somewhat below zero). Third, the structures of the economy and the financial system are constantly evolving, and the latter may be affected greatly by changing regulation in the years ahead.

Booms and Busts in Property and Equity Prices

Nearly everyone agrees that we would all be better off without skyrocketing increases in property and stock prices followed by sudden collapses. The unprecedented surge and collapse in U.S. housing prices was the ultimate source of the financial crisis of 2007–2009. Since the Great Depression of the 1930s, housing prices had declined nationwide in only three years, and then only slightly. Real house prices had been reasonably stable, because inflation offset the trend rise of nominal house prices. The spike in house prices in the years preceding the crisis was spectacularly unprecedented (see Figure 23.3). At the time, some argued that it was a bubble and therefore must burst and cause severe economic damage. Others said that housing fundamentals—growing household income, lower mortgage rates, and the like—had boosted affordability, which both justified the price surge and made it sustainable.[4] The ensuing

Figure 23.3 U.S. Real Housing Price Index, 1890-2019 (1890 = 100)

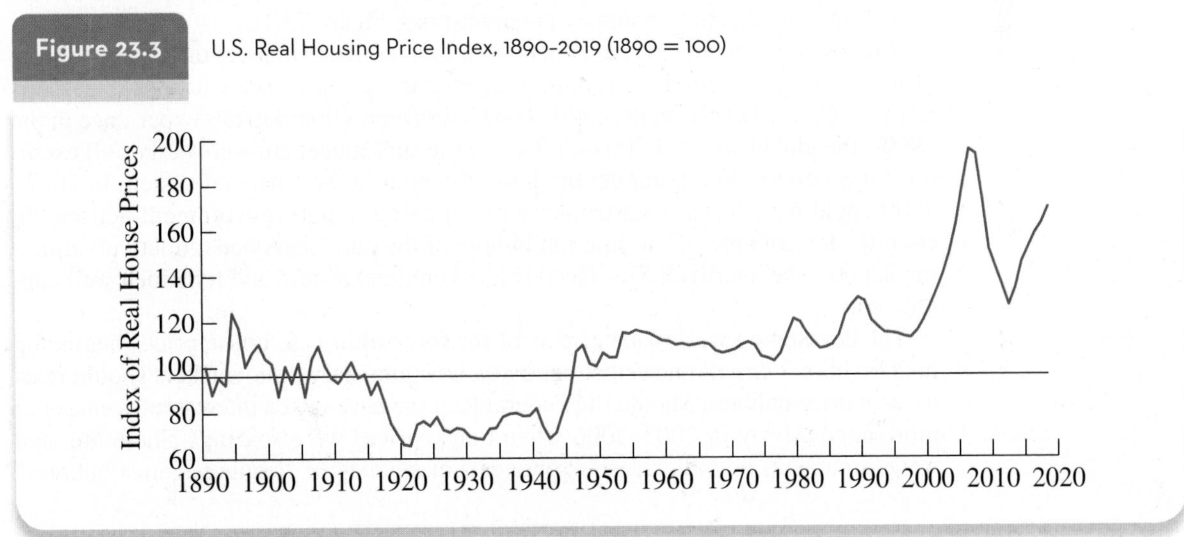

SOURCE: From *Irrational Exuberance*, 3rd ed. (Princeton, NJ: 2015). Updates from www.econ.yale.edu/~shiller/ data/Fig3-1.xls.

[4]For an assessment of the role of monetary policy in the housing bubble, see Jane Dokko et al., "Monetary Policy and the Global Housing Bubble," *Economic Policy* 26, no. 66 (2011), pp. 233–283.

Figure 23.4 The Nasdaq Composite Index, 1985–2019

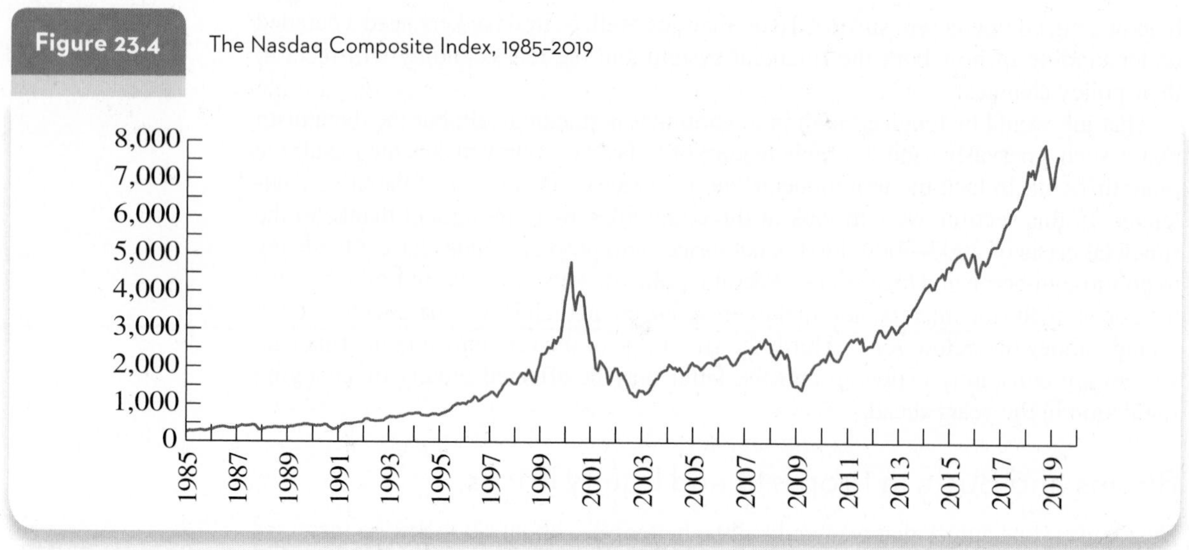

SOURCE: NASDAQ OMX Group (FRED code: NASDAQCOM).

collapse in home prices settled the debate, bringing on a financial and economic contraction more severe and widespread than even most pessimists expected.

Abrupt changes in asset prices, like the U.S. house price bubble, affect virtually every aspect of economic activity. Looking back at the first part of this chapter, we can see that changes in asset prices have a direct impact on both consumption and investment. Bubbles—which are identified after the fact by a sharp rise and then a sharp decline in prices—are damaging in part because the wealth effects they create cause consumption to surge and then contract just as rapidly. Equity bubbles—like the boom in the Internet sector in the late 1990s—allow firms to finance new projects more easily, causing investment to boom and then bust (see Figure 23.4).

Bubbles are particularly damaging when their collapse impairs the balance sheets of leveraged intermediaries, risking a deleveraging spiral (see Chapter 3, Lessons from the Crisis: Leverage, page 49). The Great Depression, Japan's experience in the 1990s, the global crisis of 2007–2009, and the subsequent euro-area crisis all exemplify this pattern. For example, the loss of capital in the financial system in 2007–2009 could have led to catastrophe without extraordinary government actions. In contrast, the collapse of the Internet bubble of the late 1990s had a relatively minor impact because intermediaries faced limited credit exposure and remained well capitalized.

The devastating worldwide effects of the reversal in U.S. house prices beginning in 2006 have focused renewed attention on how monetary policymakers should react to asset price bubbles. Should the Federal Reserve have raised interest rates earlier or more aggressively in 2003–2006 when house prices were soaring? There are, and were, arguments on both sides.[5] Proponents of a policy of "leaning against bubbles"

[5]An early example of the case for intervention may be found in Stephen G. Cecchetti, Hans Genberg, and Sushil Wadhwani, "Asset Prices in a Flexible Inflation Targeting Framework," in William C. Hunter, George G. Kaufman, and Michael Pomerleano, eds., *Asset Price Bubbles: Implications for Monetary, Regulatory and International Policies* (Cambridge, MA: MIT Press, 2002), pp. 427–444. For an early version of the case against, see Ben Bernanke and Mark Gertler, "Should Central Banks Respond to Movements in Asset Prices?" *American Economic Review*, May 2001, pp. 253–257.

say that stabilizing inflation and real growth means raising interest rates to discourage bubbles from developing in the first place. If successful, this policy would reduce the credit booms that accompany bubbles, along with the busts that inevitably follow.

Opponents of this interventionist view argue that bubbles are too difficult to identify when they are developing. They point to the debate about U.S. housing prices in 2004 and 2005 as evidence that views were not unanimous. However, the fact that an economic phenomenon is difficult to measure is no excuse for ignoring it. Indeed, we have no choice: As we saw in the discussion of monetary policy transmission, macroeconomic forecasts rest on estimates of future wealth and stock prices. Without them, there is no way to forecast either consumption or investment.

Opponents of leaning against bubbles used to argue that central banks should simply wait until the bubble bursts and only then react aggressively to limit the fallout on the economy by cleaning up the mess. They pointed to the Great Depression and the 1990s in Japan as examples of what can happen if the central bank attempts to prick a bubble with interest rate policy. Critics of an activist response also pointed to the mild U.S. recession in 2001—despite the collapse of the bubble for Internet stocks—as a successful instance of how policy can stabilize inflation and the economy in the face of a burst asset price bubble.

The crisis of 2007–2009 undermined the rosy view that policymakers can sit back and clean up after a bubble bursts. Having seen financial conditions collapse even with the policy rate set at zero, and having experienced the deepest global downturn since World War II, few central bankers remain sanguine about using conventional interest rate policy to limit the fallout from asset price bubbles after they burst. However, central bankers still worry that interest rates are only a blunt tool and that pricking an asset price bubble could require rate hikes so severe that they would bludgeon the economy and reduce the likelihood of hitting a central bank's objective for inflation. If the rate hikes were applied more cautiously to halt, say, a housing price bubble, it would be, as one economist put it, "like adding a grain of sand a day to a scale that is weighing a car."

Today, there is a more nuanced case against using interest rates to prick asset price bubbles: namely, that the proper policy toolkit for addressing bubbles is not interest rates but the macro-prudential regulatory tools that we discussed in Chapter 14. According to this view, bubbles are a major threat when they are associated with an expansion of credit that exposes the financial system to the eventual collapse of asset prices. As a result, the best response may be to adjust regulatory rules, including temporarily raising capital requirements, in an effort to inhibit intermediaries from extending such risky credits in economic booms.

The macro-prudential regulatory approach would help avoid the more destructive option of having to tighten interest rates across the whole economy to address a bubble in a specific asset. Yet, this approach still depends on the foresight and judgment of regulators to limit the buildup of a menacing asset price bubble. Moreover, policymakers acknowledge the difficulty of limiting systemic risks through the use of macroprudential policies alone. The ability of intermediaries to evade regulations and to conceal risk taking reduces the effectiveness of regulation and supervision, while raising interest rates allows policy "to get into all of the cracks" in the financial system, including shadow banks and systemically important financial markets.[6]

[6]Federal Reserve Board Governor Jeremy Stein articulated the potential benefits of using interest rate policy to limit systemic risk in a speech at the Federal Reserve Bank of St. Louis: "Overheating in Credit Markets: Origins, Measurement, and Policy Responses," February 7, 2013.

While the crisis of 2007–2009 has not settled this debate, it has advanced the discussion substantially.[7] Many policymakers remain reluctant to raise interest rates to address asset bubbles, but they no longer rule it out. Using interest rates to combat asset price bubbles now is more likely to be viewed as a backup approach for extreme circumstances, if the first-best methods of macro-prudential regulation fail to limit a systemic threat.

Deflation and the Effective Lower Interest Rate Bound

In Chapter 18, we noted that nominal interest rates cannot be deeply negative—that there is an *effective lower bound (ELB)*. In contrast to the concept of a *zero lower bound (ZLB)*, the ELB is below zero due to the transactions costs of storing, transporting, and insuring cash. The reason is that investors can always hold cash, so bonds must have yields above the ELB to attract bondholders. While this point may strike you as something only investors should worry about, it is not. The fact that nominal interest rates can't fall below the ELB restricts what monetary policymakers can do. Look back at Panel B of Figure 23.1 on page 648 and you will see that the policy target rate in 2009 was virtually zero in Japan and the United States, and only modestly higher in the euro area. Even though the global economy was sinking, policymakers believed that they had little scope to lower rates further. (As of 2016, policy rates in the euro area and Japan declined somewhat below zero, as central bankers experimented with getting closer to the ELB, the level of which is not precisely known.) The risk of becoming caught in precisely such a predicament has concerned central bankers around the world at least since Japan's experience with near-zero interest rates in the 1990s.

The problem posed by the ELB is a serious one. To understand why, we can do an exercise based on the macroeconomic model presented in Chapters 21 and 22. Think about the consequences of a shock that depresses aggregate expenditure. The shock could be caused by a decline in investment due to a fall in business prospects; by an appreciation of the dollar due to a deteriorating investment climate abroad, which has increased foreign demand for dollars; or by a decline in individuals' confidence in the future. Regardless of the source, the slowdown drives spending down at every level of inflation and the real interest rate, shifting the dynamic aggregate demand curve to the left. The immediate consequence of this drop in the quantity of aggregate output demanded is that real output falls below potential output, creating a recessionary output gap that puts downward pressure on inflation. Under normal circumstances, monetary policymakers would react to the decline in inflation by cutting the nominal interest rate enough to lower the real interest rate. Their action would increase spending, raise real output, and eliminate the output gap.

Now let's make a small adjustment to this story and assume that, when the shock occurs, inflation is zero and the policy interest rate that central bankers control is at the ELB. Under these conditions, the decline in aggregate demand still drives real output below potential output, placing downward pressure on inflation. But when inflation falls, it drops below zero so that, on average, prices are falling. The result is *deflation.*

Deflation isn't necessarily a problem, unless the shock that moves the economy away from its long-run equilibrium is big enough to drive output down to such a low level that policymakers can't bring it up, even by setting their nominal interest rate target at the ELB. At that point, we have arrived at one of the central banker's worst nightmares: a

[7]For one view of how the financial crisis should alter monetary policy practices more generally, see Olivier Blanchard, Giovanni Dell'Ariccia, and Paulo Mauro, "Rethinking Macroeconomic Policy," IMF Staff Position Note, February 12, 2010, SPN/10/03.

nominal interest rate that cannot be reduced, accompanied by deflation and real output that is below potential. Recall that when current output is below potential output, so that there is a recessionary output gap, current inflation is below expected inflation and expected inflation falls. In this case, that drives deflation down further. Because the nominal interest rate is at the ELB, policymakers cannot counter the worsening deflation by lowering it. Instead, the real interest rate *rises*, reducing spending, shifting the dynamic aggregate demand curve to the left, and expanding the recessionary output gap even more. The result is a *deflationary spiral* in which deflation grows worse and worse.

Deflation also aggravates information problems in ways that inflation does not. Deflation makes it more difficult for businesses to obtain financing for new projects. Without financing there is no investment; without investment there is no growth. The primary reason this happens is that debt is measured in fixed dollars, and deflation makes those dollars more valuable. Thus, deflation increases the real value of a firm's liabilities without affecting the real value of its assets. At a lower net worth, companies are suddenly less creditworthy.

In short, the combination of deflation and the effective lower bound can have a devastating impact on growth by short-circuiting the process that normally stabilizes the economy so that it is no longer self-correcting. Concern about the instabilities of a deflationary spiral helped animate the central bank response to the crisis of 2007–2009, even though the crisis began with inflation above desirable levels. Policymakers were concerned that the deep recession itself could lower inflation expectations too far and raise real interest rates in a destabilizing manner.

Can policymakers do anything to avoid this pitfall? The answer is yes; there are ways to minimize the chances of this sort of catastrophe. Policymakers can choose from three strategies. First, they can set their inflation objective with the perils of deflation in mind; second, they can act boldly when there is even a hint of deflation; and third, they can utilize the unconventional policy tools that we discussed in Chapter 18.

The difficulties posed by the effective lower bound arise only when central bankers have achieved their objective of low, stable inflation. When inflation is high, so is the nominal interest rate; chances are therefore remote that the interest rate will hit the ELB. This observation suggests that central bankers should set their inflation objective high enough to minimize the possibility of a deflationary spiral. Indeed, some economists have proposed raising the inflation level that many central banks target (see Chapter 18, Money and Banking Blog: Is 2 Percent Still the Right Inflation Target? pages 509–510).

Reducing the interest rate significantly and rapidly when faced with the possibility of hitting the ELB is another approach to avoiding deflation. Central bankers call this strategy "acting preemptively," which means working hard to avoid ever reaching the point where interest rates hit their hard bottom. Acting preemptively was one reason why the FOMC reduced the target federal funds rate by 5.25 percentage points toward zero in a series of 10 cuts between September 2007 and December 2008. Dramatic actions of that sort are meant to ensure that the economy will recover before deflation can take hold.

Finally, as we saw in Chapter 18, central bankers have at their disposal a range of unconventional policy tools that they can employ when the traditional interest rate target, an overnight rate, hits the lower bound.[8] These include forward guidance,

[8]For an early discussion of unconventional monetary policy options, see the speech by then-Federal Reserve Board governor, later chair, Ben S. Bernanke, "Deflation: Making Sure 'It' Doesn't Happen Here," remarks before the National Economists Club, Washington, D.C., November 21, 2001. The speech is available on the Federal Reserve Board's website at www.federalreserve.gov.

MONEY $ BANKING

GDP at Risk

MONEY AND BANKING BLOG

A policy framework for financial stability has three essential elements: a measurable objective, a set of tools, and a dynamic model that links the two. Researchers and policymakers remain at an early stage in developing such a framework. Here, we describe a useful step in constructing a quantifiable objective: the concept and measurement of *GDP at risk*.

Whether considering the risks of the economy as a whole or those of a single financial intermediary, risk management requires controlling the probability of catastrophe. So, to understand GDP at risk, start with *Value at Risk* (VaR, see Chapter 5, page 109). Financial intermediaries use VaR to quantify, at a given probability, the worst possible loss over a specific time horizon. Thus, a commercial bank risk manager might limit the daily worst-case loss of a trader who controls $100 million in assets to $10 million at a 0.1 percent probability. That means that, given the historical experience, the trader cannot take a position that has more than one chance in a thousand of losing 10 percent in a single day.

Like VaR, GDP at risk aims to measure the worst outcomes that could occur. These are the low-probability, high-cost events that are commonly known as *tail risks*. Simple measures of dispersion, like the standard deviation, often fail to account for the size of the bad (left) tail of the distribution. There are circumstances when the lower tail gets fatter—the probability of very bad events rises—without materially raising the standard deviation.

Consider, for example, what happened in the fall of 1998, when Russia defaulted on its domestic debt and Long Term Capital Management, the large hedge fund, collapsed. At the time, point forecasts for the aggregate price level and the GDP gap, as well as the standard deviation of these projections, stayed roughly the same. But the probability in the left tail of the distribution—the chance of a very bad outcome—rose. When such tail risks rise, acting as risk managers, policymakers reasonably respond to their perception that *GDP at risk* has gone up.

How can we measure GDP at risk? Using a complex statistical technique, researchers at the IMF computed the probability distribution of the one-year-ahead forecast for global growth.* Figure 23.5 displays their results. The solid red line is the median of their forecast distribution: this is the central forecast for global growth. The upper and lower dashed lines are the 5th and 95th percentiles of the distribution, respectively. So, for example, in the fourth quarter of 2016, the median forecast for growth in 2017 was 3.67 percent—that's the final point on the red line. The dashed lines tell us there is a 5 percent chance that growth will be above 5.58 percent and a 5 percent chance that it will be below 2.86 percent. The lower dashed line—the one that spikes down in late 2008—is a gauge of GDP at risk.

Figure 23.5 also reveals some fundamental properties of the IMF's estimates. The level of the top dashed line hardly changes. In fact, over the entire 25-year period, the 95th percentile of the GDP growth distribution moves between a high of 5.99 percent and a low of 4.57 percent. This is in sharp contrast with the gauge of GDP at risk (the lower dashed line), which ranges from +3.59 percent to −14.53 percent. Importantly, these large downward movements are temporary: For most of the period since 1991, GDP at risk is not far below the median.

Why does the lower tail of the growth distribution have such a wider range than the upper tail? At the top, there are short-run capacity constraints that make producing more very costly. By contrast, on the downside, the only limit is that firms shut down. That's a decline of 100 percent.

The GDP-at-risk gauge represents a notable step forward for policymakers. It has three useful characteristics. First, the concept is based on agreed social objectives: high real economic growth and low unemployment. Second, because GDP itself is widely known, focusing on GDP at risk simplifies communication. Finally, quantifying GDP at risk can help discipline discussions of policy tradeoffs. At short horizons, central bankers *aim* to encourage risk taking when they lower interest rates: Faced with an economic slowdown, they wish to stimulate lending. Over longer horizons, however, increased private leverage can create fragilities. So, policymakers want to know the extent to which lower interest rates reduce GDP at risk in the near term, and raise it in the longer term.

For several decades prior to the 2007–2009 crisis, many central banks with a price stability objective had achieved low and stable inflation. Today, with financial stability taking on such importance, we also expect central bank policies that will lower the probability and the severity of a crisis. But delivering on this means having appropriate risk measures, the tools for maintaining stability, and models that show how to use the tools to achieve the stability objective. GDP at risk is an important step forward in meeting this challenge.

*The IMF's October 2017 *Global Financial Stability Report* describes how to use quantile regression techniques to estimate the distribution of growth outcomes.

Figure 23.5 One-Year-Ahead Density Forecast for Global Growth, 1991–2016

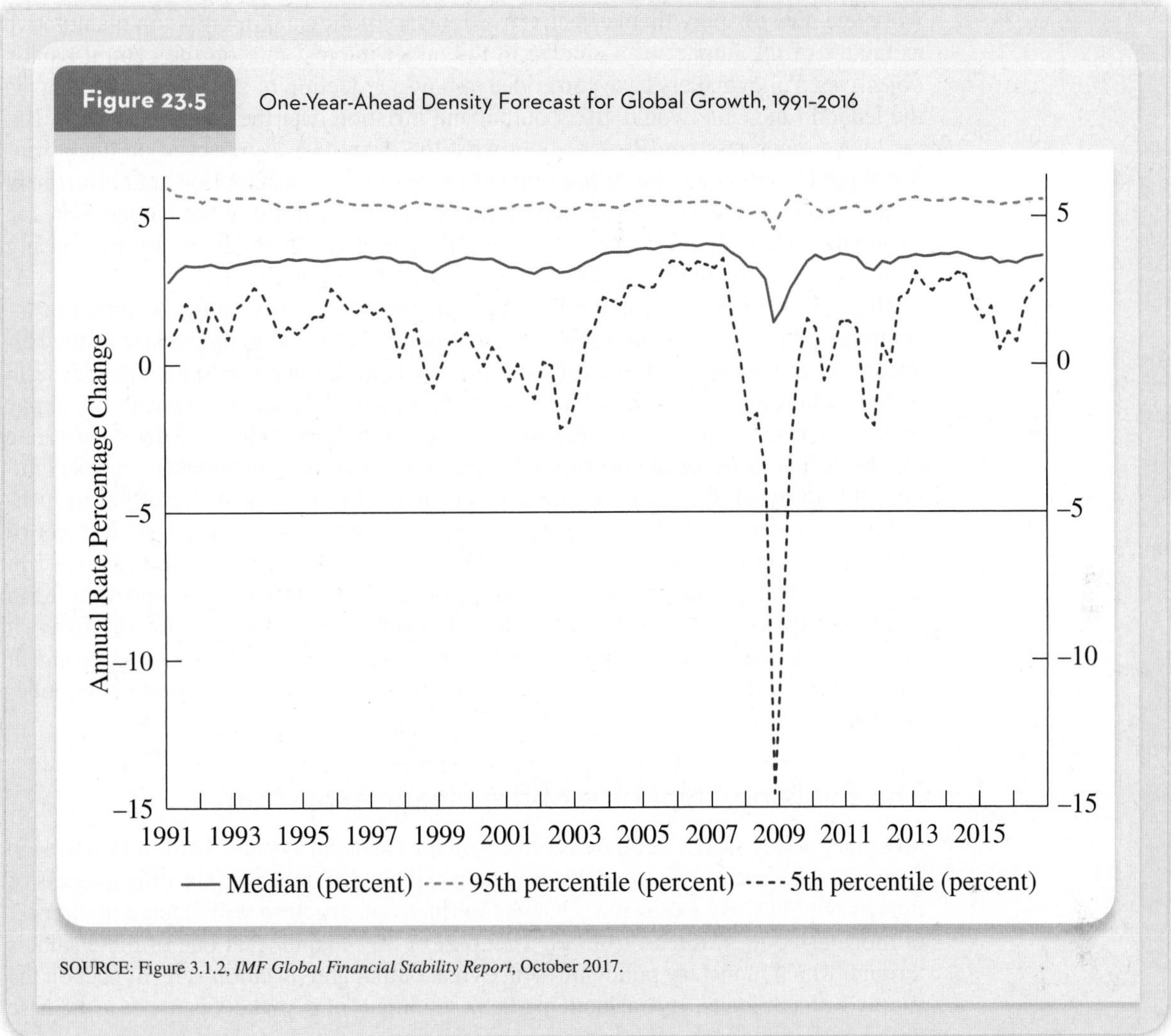

SOURCE: Figure 3.1.2, *IMF Global Financial Stability Report*, October 2017.

quantitative easing, and targeted asset purchases—all of which were actively employed by central bankers in the financial crisis of 2007–2009, by the ECB in the euro-area crisis and by the Bank of Japan in its battle against deflation. The mechanics are straightforward. Central bankers use forward guidance to influence long-term bond yields, which depend in part on expectations about future policy rates. They use quantitative easing and targeted asset purchases to control the size of their balance sheet and the mix of assets that they hold. During normal times, policymakers control the supply of their reserve liabilities in order to meet a target interest rate. But even if the short-run target rate drops to the lower bound, monetary policymakers retain their ability to expand their balance sheet. They can continue to purchase securities or make loans to banks to increase the size of the monetary base.

Everyone agrees that unconventional policy options are feasible. And we have seen their frequent use over the past decade in Europe, Japan, and the United States. Nevertheless, central bankers are reluctant to use such tools and, when used, are eager to exit as soon as improvements in the economy make it safe for them to do so. One reason for this aversion to unconventional tools is continued uncertainty about how and why they work and how to apply them effectively. Monetary policymaking rests on quantitative estimates of the impact of a change in the target interest rate on the central bank's objectives. Policymakers have some idea of how a reduction of 25 or 50 basis points in the federal funds rate would affect output and inflation over the next year or two. But they have much less confidence about what the quantitative impact of an unconventional policy option will be. What is the effect on prices, consumption, and investment if the supply of reserves increases by a factor of 100 (as it did in the United States in September–October 2008) or if the central bank doubles its assets by purchasing $1 trillion of mortgage-backed securities (as the Fed did in 2009)?

Beyond the uncertainty about their impact, another key reason for keeping unconventional policy tools unconventional is that policy exit—reducing the size of the balance sheet and restoring the mix of securities to a conventional portfolio of shorter-term government instruments—may be difficult. As we saw in Chapter 18, the ability to pay interest on reserves allows a central bank to tighten policy—by hiking the deposit rate that forms the floor for the overnight lending rate—even if policymakers choose temporarily not to sell the unconventional assets on the balance sheet. Nevertheless, central banks prefer assets that are liquid and that do not tilt the playing field in favor of specific private borrowers. And although they may wish to sell assets acquired in unconventional policy moves—including bonds with default risk and long-term bonds—in doing so they may suffer a loss. If a central bank faced sufficient losses, it might wish to ask the government to replenish its capital. Such reliance on government could add to inflation expectations if it were viewed as a threat to central bank independence.

The Evolving Structure of the Financial System

Monetary policy works through its effects on the financial system. Thus, differences in financial structure across countries may help explain differences in the effectiveness of monetary policy. By extension, changes in financial structure will change the impact of monetary policy. Recall from the first part of this chapter that one of the channels through which monetary policy influences real output and inflation is its impact on the supply of bank loans. By influencing bank lending, policymakers can affect the ease with which individuals and firms obtain financing.

Banks are crucial to this mechanism. As the nature of banking changes, we would expect the importance of this channel of monetary policy transmission to change along with it, and that has been the case. In the United States, for example, banks are no longer as important a source of financing as they once were. Thirty years ago, they accounted for virtually all the credit in the U.S. economy. At the time the crisis of 2007–2009 hit, direct bank loans had fallen to less than 60 percent of total credit extended.

The shift away from bank financing and toward securities financing in the capital markets means that the bank-lending channel of monetary policy became less important in the decades before the financial crisis that began in 2007. The decline of banks as a source of finance was accompanied by a corresponding rise in the importance of securities markets and of shadow banks—including securities brokers, money-market mutual funds, and government-sponsored enterprises (GSEs). Recall the asset-backed securities discussed in Chapter 3. Mortgage-backed and other asset-backed securities surged in volume over the past 30 years. In 1980, mortgage-backed securities accounted for only $0.1 trillion of the $1.5 trillion in U.S. mortgages outstanding. By 2009, they surpassed half of the nearly $15 trillion in mortgages outstanding.

To create mortgage-backed securities, a broker bundles together a large number of home mortgages and then sells shares in the pool. Investors in mortgage-backed securities purchase shares in the revenue from the underlying financial instruments—in this case, the mortgage payments made by homebuyers. Although their home purchase began with a bank loan, homebuyers in this way ultimately obtain a form of financing that is almost equivalent to capital market financing. Over the years, securitization—the process of pooling streams of revenue from loans and other receivables into marketable securities—has expanded in scope and size; it now includes car loans, credit card debt, student loans, equipment leases, and even movie box-office receipts.

Yet, the financial crisis that ended in 2009 is having a greater impact on the shape of the financial system than any event since the Great Depression. Importantly, it has interrupted the trend toward capital market finance: securitization has declined or slowed since 2006. For example, the volume of asset-backed commercial paper in the United States, which surpassed $1.2 trillion in the summer of 2007, stood at just 21 percent of that level at the end of 2018.

In the aftermath of the financial crisis, U.S. government agencies became the dominant source of new housing finance, either through direct loans or through guarantees. More than a decade after the crisis began, the GSEs and federal agencies still backed nearly two-thirds of U.S. mortgage originations, up from less than 40 percent in the 2004–2006 period.[9] Yet, the future of the housing-related GSEs remains highly uncertain, with many observers calling for them to be dismantled. After the GSEs were placed under the direct control of the federal government in 2008, the government injected more than $150 billion to restore their positive net worth. In 2011, the U.S. Treasury proposed to wind them down gradually by raising their guarantee fees, reducing the size of loans eligible for a guarantee, and shrinking their portfolios of mortgages.[10] In 2012, the GSEs doubled their guarantee fees. And, by 2018, their mortgage portfolios had plunged by about three-fourths from the peaks prior to 2010. Yet, as of early 2019, they remained under federal control, and the prospects for reform remained uncertain.

And, at this writing, the impact of the most far-reaching U.S. regulatory reform since the 1930s—the Dodd-Frank Act of 2010—remains far from clear. First, many key elements of the new financial regulatory measures remain untried, including the Dodd-Frank apparatus for resolving a systemic intermediary. Second, the election of 2016 brought to power a new U.S. legislature and administration that sought to reduce the regulatory burdens of Dodd-Frank, both by changing the law and through regulatory discretion. In addition to reducing the costs imposed on small banks, the 2018 Economic Growth, Regulatory Relief, and Consumer Protection Act also eased the capital requirements on medium-sized institutions. Separately, in a series of reports assessing the regulatory landscape, the Treasury proposed a number of changes that would ease supervision of the largest institutions. Finally, the Financial Stability Oversight Council reversed its own prior decisions, removing the last two large nonbanks from the category of "systemically important financial intermediaries" that are subject to the strict supervision of the Federal Reserve.

Amid all this change, it is too soon to say how the postcrisis financial system will evolve. Will the trend toward securities finance resume? In part, that will depend on

[9]See Urban Institute Housing Finance Policy Center, "Housing Finance at a Glance: Monthly Chartbook," page 8, December 2018, www.urban.org/sites/default/files/publication/99554/december_chartbook_2018_0.pdf.

[10]See U.S. Treasury, "Reforming America's Housing Finance Market: A Report to Congress," February 2011, www.treasury.gov/initiatives/documents/reforming%20america%27s%20housing%20finance%20market.pdf.

how regulators behave. A macro-prudential regulator—of the kind that we discussed in Chapter 14—will try to limit intermediaries' incentives for taking systemic risk.

Will macro-prudential regulation prevent the restoration of securitization? Probably not: regulators are aware that effective securitization can lead to a better diversification of risk. But unlike the incomplete securitization that prevailed earlier, effective securitization must avoid leaving concentrations of securitized assets on the balance sheets of intermediaries that make them vulnerable to collapsing asset price bubbles. Consequently, macro-prudential regulation will tend to restrain the future pace of securitization, at least compared to the boom years preceding the financial crisis.

However the financial system evolves, the pattern will be a critical one for central bankers, who need to know the quantitative impact their policies are likely to have. As the structure of the financial system changes, the effect of a 25- or 50-basis-point move in the federal funds rate will doubtless change with it. The changing effectiveness of conventional monetary policy likely will require central bankers to update their unconventional policy tools, too. Central bankers will always have to assess how the financial system is altering the monetary transmission mechanism.

The changing nature of the financial system is important for individuals as well as policymakers. As the characteristics of money, banks, and loans evolve, we will all adjust how we pay for our purchases, how we hold our wealth, and how we obtain credit. Our use of currency will likely continue to decline. U.S. banks that now receive interest on their reserves may continue to hold far more of them than before the financial crisis. In Europe and Japan, investors may turn to cash if central banks try to lower the policy rate even closer to the effective lower bound. Perhaps some country will eliminate cash altogether, allowing for deeply negative interest rates.

No one can predict exactly when or to what extent these changes will occur, but now that you have reached the end of this book, you know how to think about them. And your skills in finding and analyzing economic and financial data will help you stay up to date as the financial system evolves. You understand the economic role of financial institutions as well as what a central bank is and how it operates. Together with the aggregate demand–aggregate supply model, this knowledge gives you a framework with which to comprehend the evolution of the financial system, its effects on monetary policy, and its effects on you personally.

Key Terms

asset price channel, 655
balance sheet channel, 653
bank-lending channel, 652
exchange rate channel, 649
interest rate channel, 649
monetary policy transmission mechanism, 649

Using FRED: Codes for Data in This Chapter

Data Series	FRED Data Code
Real GDP	GDPC1
U.S. 3-month Treasury bill rate	TB3MS
U.S. 10-year Treasury constant maturity rate	GS10
German government bond yield	INTGSBDEM193N
Italian government bond yield	INTGSBITM193N
Spanish government bond yield	INTGSBESM193N
1-year inflation expectations (Michigan survey)	MICH
Real trade-weighted U.S. dollar index: Broad	TWEXBPA
Trade-weighted U.S. dollar index: Broad	TWEXBMTH
Household net worth	TNWBSHNO
Disposable personal income	DPI
Personal saving rate	PSAVERT
S&P Case-Shiller 20-city home price index	SPCS20RSA
S&P Case-Shiller U.S. National Home Price Index	CSUSHPISA
Consumer price index	CPIAUCSL
Net percentage of domestic banks tightening standards on credit cards	DRTSCLCC
Gross federal debt held by the public as percent of gross domestic product	FYPUGDA188S

Chapter Lessons

To learn more about the changing financial system, visit www.moneyandbanking.com.

1. Monetary policy influences the economy through several channels.
   a. The traditional channels of monetary policy transmission are interest rates and exchange rates.
      i. Interest rates influence consumption and investment.
      ii. Exchange rates affect net exports.
   b. Monetary policy affects the supply of bank loans, changing the availability of bank financing to firms and individuals.
   c. Monetary policy can change firms' and households' net worth, affecting their creditworthiness as borrowers.
   d. The asset-price channel of monetary policy transmission works through stock and real estate prices.
      i. Stock and property prices influence household wealth and consumption.
      ii. Stock prices also affect businesses' ability and incentive to raise funds and make investments.
2. Monetary policymakers face significant challenges. To be successful, they require
   a. Accurate estimates of potential GDP, even when its growth trend is shifting.
   b. An understanding of how to cope with the problems created by the effective lower bound on nominal interest rates and the possibility of deflation.

c. A knowledge of how and when to react to the possibility of a stock or real estate boom (and bust).

d. An awareness of the changing structure of the financial system and a knowledge of how to react to it.

Conceptual and Analytical Problems connect

1. Explain how an open market purchase of securities by a central bank affects the banking system's balance sheet, and discuss the potential impact on the supply of bank loans. (You may wish to refer to Chapter 17 in answering this question.) *(LO1)*

2. Explain why you might expect the recovery from the 2007–2009 recession to be weaker than normal. *(LO1)*

3.* Explain why the traditional interest rate channel of monetary policy transmission from monetary policy actions to changes in investment and consumption decisions may be relatively weak. *(LO1)*

4. Explain why monetary policymakers' actions in cutting the target range for the federal funds rate to 0 to ¼ percent were not sufficient to boost economic activity during the recession of 2007–2009. *(LO2)*

5. When monetary policymakers hit the effective lower bound with their policy rate, they have the option to turn to unconventional tools of monetary policy. How do these unconventional tools work, and why might policymakers be reluctant to use them except in very difficult circumstances? *(LO2)*

6. The government decides to place limits on the interest rates banks can pay their depositors. Seeing that alternative investments pay higher interest rates, depositors withdraw their funds from banks and place them in bonds. Will their action have an impact on the economy? If so, how? *(LO1)*

7. New developments in information technology have simplified the assessment of individual borrowers' creditworthiness. What are the likely consequences for the structure of the financial system? For monetary policy? *(LO2)*

8.* Describe the theory of the exchange rate channel of the monetary transmission mechanism. How, through the exchange rate, does an interest rate increase influence output? Why is this link difficult to find in practice? *(LO1)*

9. Why might the effective lower bound on nominal interest rates lead policymakers to raise their inflation objective? *(LO2)*

10. Considering the role of the U.S. house price bubble in the financial crisis of 2007–2009, how do you think monetary policymakers should respond to bubbles in asset markets? *(LO2)*

11. For each of the following, explain whether the response is theoretically consistent with a tightening of monetary policy and identify which of the traditional channels of monetary policy is at work: *(LO1)*
    a. Firms become more likely to undertake investment projects.
    b. Households become less likely to purchase refrigerators and washing machines.
    c. Net exports fall.

*Indicates more difficult problems.

12. In Country A suppose that changes in short-term interest rates translate quickly into changes in long-term interest rates, while in Country B long-term interest rates do not respond much to changes in short-term rates. In which country would you expect the interest rate channel of monetary policy to be stronger? Explain your answer. *(LO1)*

13. Consider a situation where central bank officials repeatedly express concern that output exceeds potential output, implying that the economy is overheating. Although they haven't implemented any policy moves as yet, the data show that consumption of luxury goods has begun to slow. Explain how this behavior could reflect the asset-price channel of monetary policy at work. *(LO1)*

14. Do you think the balance sheet channel of monetary policy would be stronger or weaker if: *(LO1)*
    a. Firms' balance sheets in general are very healthy?
    b. Firms have a lot of existing variable-rate debt?

15. In the wake of the financial crisis of 2007–2009, would you expect the bank-lending channel to have become more or less important in the United States? Explain your answer. *(LO2)*

16.* Suppose there is an unexpected slowdown in the rate of productivity growth in the economy so that forecasters consistently overestimate the growth rate of GDP. If the central bank bases its policy decisions on the consensus forecast, what would be the likely consequences for inflation assuming it maintains its existing inflation target? *(LO2)*

17. Suppose the policy interest rate controlled by the central bank and the inflation rate were both zero. Explain in terms of the aggregate demand–aggregate supply framework how the economy could fall into a deflationary spiral if it were hit by a negative aggregate demand shock. *(LO2)*

18.* Use the aggregate demand–aggregate supply framework to show how a boom in equity prices might affect inflation and output in the short run. Describe the long-run impact on inflation and output (a) if the central bank implicitly allows its inflation target to rise and (b) if it retains its original inflation target. *(LO2)*

19. Compare the impact of a given change in monetary policy in two economies that are similar in every way except that in Economy A the financial system has a large shadow banking system providing many alternatives to bank financing, while in Economy B bank loans account for almost all of the financing in the economy. *(LO1)*

20. If the anemic growth experienced in the U.S. economy since the financial crisis primarily reflects slower growth of the labor force and slowing technological innovation, can monetary policy be used to address the problem? *(LO2)*

21. In which of the following economies do you think the bank lending channel would play a more important role, everything else being equal: an economy dominated by large, financially sophisticated firms, or an economy consisting of a large number of small firms. Explain your choice. *(LO1)*

22. How might the concept of *GDP at Risk* help central banks pursue a financial stability objective? *(LO2)*

*Indicates more difficult problems.

23. Recent financial regulatory reforms have eased capital requirements for banks. Under what circumstances might lowering capital requirements affect economic growth? *(LO1)*

Data Exploration connect

For general information on using Federal Reserve Economic Data (FRED) online, visit www.mhhe.com/moneyandbanking6e.com *and refer to the FRED resources.*

1. In conducting monetary policy, the European Central Bank (ECB) must balance the needs of euro-area countries with differing economic conditions. Plot since 1990 the yield spread between government bonds in Italy (FRED code: INTGSBITM193N) and Germany (FRED code: INTGSBDEM193N), along with the yield spread between government bonds in Spain (FRED code: INTGSBESM193N) and Germany. Discuss the yield spreads after 2008, and explain how they reflect policy challenges for the ECB. *(LO2)*
2. How important is the balance sheet channel of monetary policy? Plot since 1996 the net tightening of credit standards for consumer and credit card loans (FRED code: DRTSCLCC) and (on the right scale) household net worth (FRED code: TNWBSHNO). Do banks adjust lending conditions when household balance sheets improve or deteriorate? *(LO1)*
3. Among the challenges facing central banks around the world is the elevated level of public debt. Plot U.S. federal debt held by the public as a percent of gross domestic product (FRED code: FYPUGDA188S), and discuss the problems that government debt could pose for the Federal Reserve in the future. *(LO2)*
4.* Some critics argue that the Federal Reserve stoked the housing price bubble after 2000 by keeping monetary policy too stimulative. To investigate, first plot from 2000 to 2007 on a quarterly basis the Taylor rule gap—the difference between the Taylor rule (as described in Chapter 18 Data Exploration Problem 1) and the federal funds rate. Add to this plot on the right scale an index of U.S. housing prices (FRED code: SPCS20RSA). Does the evidence support the critics' claim? What other evidence might be sought? *(LO1)*
5. Prior to the crisis, neither policymakers nor investors anticipated the impact of falling housing prices on the U.S. financial system. To see whether similar risks exist today, plot since 1990 U.S. real housing prices: namely, the Case-Shiller U.S. National Home Price index divided by the level of consumer prices (FRED code: CSUSHPISA and CPIAUCSL). Discuss the result and explain why housing matters so much for the financial system. *(LO2)*

*Indicates more difficult problems.

Glossary

NOTE: The number in parentheses at the end of each entry is the number of the chapter in which the term is introduced. On occasion, we list a second chapter in which the term appears prominently.

A

accommodative monetary policy A policy that is aimed at increasing output and raising inflation, usually a lowering of the central bank's interest rate target. (15)

accountability The idea that central bankers should be held responsible for their policies. (15)

adverse feedback Mutually aggravating interactions between the financial sector and the economy in a systemic crisis. (14)

adverse selection The problem of distinguishing a good risk from a bad one before making a loan or providing insurance; it is caused by asymmetric information. (11)

aggregate expenditure The total demand for the economy's production; the sum of consumption, investment, government purchases, and net exports. (21)

aggregate expenditure (AE) curve The graph of the negative relationship between aggregate expenditure and the real interest rate. (21)

American option An option that can be exercised anytime up to the expiration date, in contrast to a *European option.* (9)

appreciation of a currency The increase in the value of a country's currency relative to the value of another country's currency. (10)

arbitrage The practice of simultaneously buying and selling financial instruments to benefit from temporary price differences; eliminates a riskless profit opportunity. (9)

asset Something of value that can be owned; a financial claim or property that serves as a store of value. (3)

asset-backed securities (ABS) Shares in the returns or payments arising from a specific asset or pool of assets, such as home mortgages or student loans. (3)

asset-price channel The channel of the monetary policy transmission mechanism where changes in policy affect aggregate expenditure through their impact on stock prices and the value of real estate. (23)

asymmetric information The fact that the two parties to a transaction have unequal knowledge about each other. A borrower, for example, has more information about his or her abilities and prospects than a lender. (11)

at-the-money option An option whose strike price equals the current market price for the underlying instrument. (9)

automated clearinghouse (ACH) transaction The most common form of electronic funds transfers. (2)

average See *expected value.* (5)

B

balance of payments An accounting system for tracking both the flow of goods and services and the flow of assets across international boundaries. (19)

balance sheet The list of assets and liabilities that shows an individual's or firm's financial position. (3)

balance sheet channel The channel of the monetary policy transmission mechanism where changes in policy affect aggregate expenditure through their impact on household and firm balance sheets. (23)

bank See *depository institution.* (12)

bank capital Bank assets minus bank liabilities. The net worth of the bank. The value of the bank to its owners. (12)

bank charter The license authorizing the operation of a bank. (13)

bank holding company A company that owns one or more banks and possibly other nonbank subsidiaries. (13)

bank-lending channel The channel of the monetary policy transmission mechanism in which changes in policy affect aggregate expenditure through their impact on banks' willingness to make loans. (23)

bank panic The simultaneous failure of many banks during a financial crisis. (14)

bank run An event when depositors lose confidence in a bank and make withdrawals, exhausting the bank's reserves. (14)

bank supervision Government oversight of commercial banks; see also *supervision (financial).* (14)

Basel Accord An agreement requiring internationally active banks to hold capital equal to or greater than a specified share (8 percent or as agreed by regulators) of their risk-adjusted assets. (14)

Basel III The 2011 version of the Basel Accord on the regulation of internationally active banks. (1)

basis point One one hundredth of a percentage point. (4)

benchmark The performance of a group of experienced investment advisors or money managers. (5)

benchmark bond A low-risk bond, usually a U.S. Treasury bond, to which the yield on a risky bond is compared to assess its risk. (7)

Big Mac index The index used to estimate whether currencies are under- or overvalued that is based on the price of the Big Mac in various countries. (10)

Board of Governors of the Federal Reserve System The seven-member board that oversees the Federal Reserve System, including participation in both monetary policy and financial regulatory decisions. (16)

bond A financial instrument that promises a series of future payments on specific dates. Also known as a *fixed-income security*. (4)

bond market A financial market in which debt instruments with a maturity of more than one year are traded. (3)

bond principal value The final payment made to the holder of a bond; also known as the *par value* and the *face value*. (4)

Bretton Woods system The international monetary system in place from 1945 to 1971, in which exchange rates were fixed to the U.S. dollar, and the dollar was convertible into gold at $35 per ounce. (19)

British pound The name of the currency used in the United Kingdom. (10)

broker Financial intermediary that provides accounting and custody services, access to secondary markets, liquidity, loans, and advice; see also *dealer.* (3, 13)

brokerage firm See *broker.* (3, 13)

bubble A persistent and expanding gap between actual asset prices and those warranted by the fundamentals; usually created by mass enthusiasm. (8)

business cycles The periodic fluctuations in aggregate economic output. (1)

C

call option A contract that confers the right, but not the obligation, to purchase a financial instrument at a predetermined price on or prior to an agreed-upon date. (9)

call reports The detailed financial reports banks are required to file every three months. Officially known as the *Consolidated Reports of Conditions and Income.* (14)

CAMELS The system used by U.S. bank examiners to summarize their evaluation of a bank's health. The acronym stands for Capital adequacy, Asset quality, Management, Earnings, Liquidity, and Sensitivity to risk. (14)

capital account The part of the balance of payments accounts that measures the flow of assets among countries; also called the *financial account.* (19)

capital account deficit/surplus A country's capital inflows minus its capital outflows. (19)

capital controls Government-imposed barriers to investment across international boundaries; restrictions on the ability of foreigners to buy and sell domestic assets; see also *capital inflow controls* and *capital outflow controls*. (19)

capital gain The difference between the price that has been paid for an asset and the higher price at which it is sold; contrasts with a *capital loss,* where the price paid exceeds the price at which the asset is sold. (6)

capital inflow controls Government restrictions that restrict the flow of funds into a country to purchase domestic assets. (19)

capital loss The difference between the price that has been paid for an asset and the lower price at which it is sold; contrasts with *capital gain.* (6)

capital market See *bond market* and *equity market.* (8)

capital outflow controls Government restrictions on the flow of funds out of a country to purchase foreign assets. (19)

cash items in process of collection Checks and transfers due to a bank that have not yet been collected; a bank asset. (12)

central bank The financial institution that manages the government's finances, controls the availability of money and credit in the economy, and serves as the bank to commercial banks. (1, 15)

central bank independence The central bank's freedom from political pressure. (15)

central bank's balance sheet The statement of the assets and liabilities of the central bank. (17)

central counterparty (CCP) An entity that interposes itself between the two sides of a transaction, becoming the buyer to every seller and the seller to every buyer. (9)

centralized exchange A financial market in which financial instruments are traded in a single physical location. (3)

check An instruction to the bank to take funds from one account and transfer them to another. (2)

clearing corporation The institution that acts as the counterparty to both sides of all futures market transactions, guaranteeing that the parties to the contract will meet their obligations. (9)

collateral Assets pledged to pay for a loan in the event that the borrower doesn't make the required payments. (3, 11)

commercial banks Financial intermediaries that provide banking services to businesses and households, allowing them to deposit funds safely and borrow them when necessary. (2)

commercial paper Short-term, privately issued zero-coupon debt that is low risk and very liquid and usually has a maturity of less than 270 days. (7)

commodity money Precious metals or other items with intrinsic value that are used as money. (2)

common exposure Exposure of many financial institutions to the same risk factor. (14)

common stock Ownership shares in a firm; also called just *stock* and *equity.* (8)

compound interest The interest you get on interest as it accumulates over time. (4)

consol or perpetuity A coupon bond in which the issuer makes regular interest payments forever, never repaying the principal; a coupon bond with infinite time to maturity. (6)

consumption Spending by individuals for items like food, clothing, housing, transportation, entertainment, and education. (21)

contagion When the failure of one bank causes a run on other banks. (14)

conventional (monetary) policy tools The federal funds rate target, the rate for discount window lending, and the deposit rate. (18)

counterparty The person or institution that is on the other side of a financial contract. (3)

coupon bond A bond offering annual coupon payments at regular intervals until the maturity date, at which time the principal is repaid. (4)

coupon payment Yearly payment made to the holder of a coupon bond. (4)

coupon rate Annual interest rate equal to the yearly coupon payment divided by the face value of a coupon bond. (4)

credibility The idea that everyone trusts central bankers to do what they say they are going to do. (15)

credit card A promise by a bank to lend the cardholder money in order to make purchases. (2)

credit default swap (CDS) A credit derivative that makes a payment if a borrower defaults; allows lenders to insure themselves against the risk that a borrower will default. (9)

credit risk The probability that a borrower will not repay a loan; see also *default risk.* (12)

credit union A nonprofit depository institution that is owned by people with a common bond, such as members of police associations, union members, university students, and employees. (12)

currency Paper money; for example, dollar bills or euro notes. (2)

currency board A fixed exchange rate system in which the central bank commits to holding enough foreign currency assets (often dollars) to back domestic currency liabilities at a fixed rate. (19)

currency in the hands of the public The quantity of dollar bills held by the nonbank public; part of M1. (2, 17)

currency-to-deposit ratio The ratio of publicly held currency to demand deposits held at commercial banks. (17)

current account The part of the balance-of-payments account that measures the flow of currently produced goods and services among countries. (10, 19)

current account deficit/surplus A country's goods and services exports minus its goods and services imports. (10, 19)

current yield A bond's yearly coupon payment divided by its current market price. (6)

cyber risk The losses that arise when information technology systems fail or are compromised (12).

D

dealer Financial intermediary that acts as a counterparty in a securities transaction; see also *broker.* (3)

debit card A card that provides instructions to the bank to transfer funds from the cardholder's account directly to a merchant's account. (2)

debt A loan obligating the borrower to make payments to the lender. (2)

debt market A financial market where bonds, loans, and mortgages are traded. (3)

default Failure to meet an obligation; in the case of a debt, the failure of the borrower to make required payments to the lender. (1)

default risk The probability that a borrower will not repay a loan; see also *credit risk.* (6)

defined-benefit pension plan A pension plan in which beneficiaries receive a lifetime retirement income based on the number of years they worked at the company and their final salary. (13)

defined-contribution pension plan A pension plan in which beneficiaries make payments into an account and then receive the accumulation, plus the investment income, on retirement, at which time they must decide what to do with the funds. The options include accepting a lump sum, removing small amounts at a time, or converting the balance to a fixed monthly payment for life by purchasing an annuity. (13)

deflation A sustained fall in the general price level; the opposite of *inflation.* (11, 23)

demand deposits Standard checking accounts that pay no interest; part of M1. (2)

demand for dollars Dollars demanded in the foreign exchange market as a function of the nominal exchange rate. (10)

demand shock An unexpected change in aggregate expenditure, such as a rise or fall in consumer confidence, that shifts the dynamic aggregate demand curve. (22)

deposit expansion multiplier The formula for the increase in commercial bank deposits following a one-dollar increase in reserves. (17)

deposit insurance The government guarantee that depositors will receive the full value of their accounts (up to a legal limit) should a bank fail. (14)

depository institution A financial institution that accepts deposits and makes loans. (12)

deposit rate The interest rate paid by the Federal Reserve to depository institutions on the balances they hold in their reserve accounts that exceed the amount required by the central bank. (18)

depreciation The decrease in the value of a country's currency relative to the value of another country's currency. (10)

derivative See *derivative instrument.* (9)

derivative instrument A financial instrument, such as a futures contract or an option, whose value and payoff are "derived from" the behavior of underlying instruments. (3)

direct finance Financing in which borrowers sell securities directly to lenders in the financial markets. (3)

discount lending Lending by the Federal Reserve, usually to commercial banks. (18)

discount loan A loan from the Federal Reserve, usually to a commercial bank. (12, 17)

discount rate The interest rate at which the Federal Reserve makes discount loans to commercial banks. (16, 18)

disinflation The term used to describe declines in inflation. (22)

diversification Splitting wealth among a variety of assets to reduce risk. (5)

dividend-discount model The theory that the fundamental value of a stock equals the present value of expected future dividend payments. (8)

dividends The payments made to a company's stockholders when the company makes a profit. (8)

Dodd-Frank Act Major financial reform signed into law in July 2010 as the Dodd-Frank Wall Street Reform and Consumer Protection Act. (1)

dollarization One country's formal adoption of the currency of another country for use in all its financial transactions. (19)

Dow Jones Industrial Average (DJIA) The best-known index of stock market performance, it measures the average price of a single share in 30 very large and well-known American companies. (8)

dual banking system The system in the United States in which banks supervised by federal government and state government authorities coexist. (13)

dynamic aggregate demand (AD) curve The graph of the relationship between inflation and the quantity of spending on domestically produced goods and services. (21)

E

ECB's deposit facility Where euro-area banks with excess reserves can deposit them overnight and earn interest. (18)

ECB's main refinancing operations The weekly auction of two-week repurchase agreements in which the ECB, through the National Central Banks, provides reserves to banks in exchange for securities. (18)

ECB's marginal lending facility The facility through which the ECB provides overnight loans to banks; the analog to the Federal Reserve's primary credit facility. (18)

ECB's target refinancing rate The minimum bid rate on the main refinancing operations of the ECB; the interest rate set by the Governing Council. (18)

economies of scale When the average cost of producing a good or service falls as the quantity produced increases. (13)

economies of scope When the average cost of producing a good or service falls as the number of different types of goods produced increases. (13)

effective lower bound (ELB) The nominal interest rate level below which people will switch from bank deposits to cash. (18)

electronic communication networks (ECNs) Financial markets organized as an electronic network, such as Arca or Instinet. (3)

electronic funds transfer (EFT) Movements of funds directly from one account to another over an electronic network. (2)

emergency powers The Federal Reserve's extraordinary authority to lend to nonbanks when circumstances are deemed "unusual and exigent." (16)

equation of exchange The equation stating that nominal income equals the quantity of money times the velocity of money; $MV = PY$. (20)

equity Ownership shares in a firm; also called *stock* and *common stock.* (8)

equity market A financial market where stocks are bought and sold. (3)

euro The name of the currency used in the countries of the European Monetary Union. (10)

euro area The countries in Europe that use the euro as their common currency. (16)

eurodollars Dollar-denominated deposits outside the U.S. (13)

European Central Bank (ECB) The central authority, located in Frankfurt, Germany, which oversees monetary policy in the common currency area. (1, 16)

European option An option that can be exercised only on the expiration date, not before, in contrast with an *American option.* (9)

European System of Central Banks (ESCB) The European Central Bank plus the National Central Banks of all the countries in the European Union, including those that do not participate in the monetary union. (16)

Eurosystem The European Central Bank plus the National Central Banks of participating countries; together, they carry out the tasks of central banking in the euro area. (16)

examination (of banks) The formal process by which government specialists evaluate a bank's financial condition. (14)

excess reserves Reserves in excess of required reserves. (12, 17)

excess reserve-to-deposit ratio The ratio of banks' excess reserves to their demand deposit liabilities. (17)

exchange rate See *nominal exchange rate.* (10)

exchange rate channel The channel of the monetary policy transmission mechanism where changes in policy affect aggregate expenditure through their impact on exchange rates. (23)

exchange rate stability One of the objectives of the central bank is to reduce exchange rate fluctuations making it stable. (15)

exchange traded fund (ETF) A marketable security that tracks a basket of assets like an index fund. (3, 8)

Executive Board of the ECB The six-member body in Frankfurt that oversees the operation of the European Central Bank and the Eurosystem. (16)

exercise price The predetermined price at which a call or put option specifies that the underlying asset can be bought (call) or sold (put); also called the *strike price.* (9)

expansionary output gap When current output exceeds potential output; the gap puts upward pressure on inflation. (21)

expectations hypothesis of the term structure The proposition that long-term interest rates are the average of expected future short-term interest rates. (7)

expected return The probability-weighted sum of possible returns to an investment. (5)

expected value The probability-weighted sum of possible values of an investment; also known as the *mean* or *average*. (5)

externality Spillover impact from an activity of one party on to other parties who are not compensated (such as may occur when a firm creates pollution or systemic risk). (14)

F

face value See *bond principal value.* (4)

fallen angel A low-grade bond that was initially a high-grade bond but whose issuer fell on hard times. (7)

Fannie Mae The Federal National Mortgage Association; a government-sponsored entity that aids in the financing of home mortgages. (13)

federal funds market The market where banks lend their excess reserves to other banks; the loans are unsecured. (12)

federal funds rate The interest rate banks charge each other for overnight loans on their excess deposits at the Fed; the interest rate targeted by the FOMC. (16)

Federal Open Market Committee (FOMC) The 12-member committee that makes monetary policy decisions in the United States. Members include the seven members of the Board of Governors, the president of the Federal Reserve Bank of New York, and the presidents of four Federal Reserve Banks. (16)

Federal Reserve Banks The 12 regional banks in the Federal Reserve System. (16)

Federal Reserve System The central bank responsible for monetary policy in the United States. (1, 16)

fiat money Currency with no intrinsic value, it has value as a consequence of government decree. (2)

finance company A nondepository financial institution that raises funds directly in financial markets to provide loans to businesses and households. (13)

financial holding company A company that owns a variety of financial intermediaries. (13)

financial institutions Firms, such as banks and insurance companies, that provide access to the financial markets, both to savers who wish to purchase financial instruments directly and to borrowers who want to issue them; also known as *financial intermediaries*. (1, 3)

financial instrument The written legal obligation of one party to transfer something of value (usually money) to another party at some future date, under certain conditions. (1, 3)

financial intermediaries See *financial institutions.* (1, 3)

financial market The part of the financial system that allows people to buy and sell financial instruments quickly and cheaply. (1, 3)

financial system The system that allows people to engage in economic transactions. It is composed of six parts: money, financial instruments, financial markets, financial institutions, regulatory agencies, and central banks. (1)

financial system stability One objective of the central bank is to eliminate financial system volatility, ensuring that it remains stable. (15)

fiscal policy The government's tax and expenditure policies, usually formulated by elected officials. (15)

fixed payment loan A type of loan that requires a fixed number of equal payments at regular intervals; home mortgages and car loans are examples. (4)

fixed rate payer The party to an interest rate swap that is making fixed payments. (9)

flexible rate payer The party to an interest rate swap that is making variable payments. Also called *floating rate payer*. (9)

flight to quality An increase in the demand for low-risk government bonds, coupled with a decrease in the demand for virtually every risky investment. (7)

floating rate payer See *flexible rate payer*. (9)

FOMC statement The press release that immediately follows every FOMC meeting; usually contains an announcement of the federal funds rate target, an evaluation of the current economic environment, and a statement of the risks to the economy. (16)

forbearance Willingness of regulators to allow banks with insufficient capital to continue to operate. (23)

foreign exchange intervention The purchase or sale of foreign exchange by government officials with the intention of moving the nominal exchange rate. (17, 19)

foreign exchange reserves Assets of the central bank denominated in foreign currency. (17)

foreign exchange risk The risk arising from holding assets denominated in one currency and liabilities denominated in another. (12)

forward See *forward contract*. (9)

forward contract An agreement to exchange an asset for money in the future at a currently agreed-upon price. (9)

forward guidance Communication by the central bank about future policy prospects. (16, 18)

free rider Someone who doesn't pay the cost but still gets the benefit of a good or service. (11)

fundamental value The present value of the expected future returns to owning an asset, which equals the asset's price in an efficient market. (8)

funding liquidity The ability to borrow money. (2)

future See *futures contract*. (9)

future value The value on some future date of an investment made today. (4)

futures contract A standardized agreement specifying the delivery of an underlying asset (commodity or financial instrument) at a given future date for a currently agreed-upon price. (9)

G

goal independence In the case of a central bank, the authority to determine autonomously the objectives of monetary policy (such as price stability); see also *instrument independence.* (15)

gold standard A fixed exchange rate regime in which the currencies of participating countries are directly convertible into gold. (19)

Governing Council of the ECB The (currently) 25-member committee that makes monetary policy in the euro area. (16)

government purchases Spending on goods and services by federal, state, and local governments. (21)

government-sponsored enterprises (GSEs) Federal credit agencies that provide loans directly for farm and home mortgages as well as guaranteeing programs that insure the loans made by private lenders. (3)

gross domestic product (GDP) The market value of final goods and services produced in the economy during a year. (2)

H

hard peg An exchange rate system in which the central bank implements an institutional mechanism that ensures its ability to convert a domestic currency into the foreign currency to which it is pegged. (19)

hedge funds Private, largely unregulated, investment partnerships that bring together small groups of people who meet certain (high) wealth requirements. (13)

hedger Someone who uses financial instruments, like derivatives, to reduce risk. (9)

hedging Reducing overall risk by investing in two assets with opposing payoffs. (5)

high-frequency trader (HFT) A trader who engages in the computerized trading of thousands of shares of stock in a few seconds. (3)

high-powered money See *monetary base.* (17)

holding period return The return from purchasing and selling a bond (applies to bonds sold before or at maturity). (6)

hyperinflation Very high inflation; when prices double every two to three months. (15)

I

idiosyncratic risk Risk affecting a small number of people (a specific firm or industry). (5)

illiquid The inability to meet immediate payment obligations. For a bank, reserves are insufficient to honor current withdrawal requests. (14)

indirect finance An institution like a bank stands between the lender and the borrower, borrowing from the lender and providing the funds to the borrower. (3)

inflation A sustained rise in the general price level; the opposite of *deflation.* (2)

inflation-indexed bond A bond whose yield equals a fixed real interest rate plus realized (as opposed to expected) inflation. (6)

inflation persistence A term used to describe the phenomenon that when inflation is low one year, it tends to be low the next, and when it is high, it tends to stay high. (21)

inflation rate The measurement of inflation. (2)

inflation risk The risk that the real value of the payments from owning a bond will be different from what was expected; that the real interest rate on a bond will differ from what was expected. (6)

inflation targeting A monetary policy strategy that involves the public announcement of a numerical inflation target, together with a commitment to make price stability a leading objective. (16, 18)

information A collection of facts. The basis for the third core principle of money and banking: Information is the basis for decisions. (1)

information costs The costs lenders must pay to screen potential borrowers to determine their creditworthiness and monitor how they use the loans. (3)

insolvent When the value of a firm's or bank's assets is less than the value of its liabilities; negative net worth. (14)

instrument independence In the case of a central bank, the authority to adjust as it sees fit the tools of monetary policy (such as interest rates) in order to achieve its policy objectives (which may be mandated by the government); see also *goal independence.* (15)

insurance company A financial intermediary that accepts premiums, which it invests in securities and real estate (its assets) in return for promising compensation to policyholders should certain events occur (its liabilities). (3)

interest rate The cost of borrowing and the reward to lending. See also *yield.* (4)

interest rate channel The traditional channel of the monetary policy transmission mechanism where changes in policy affect aggregate expenditure through their impact on interest rates. (23)

interest rate on excess reserves (IOER rate) The interest rate paid by the Federal Reserve on reserves that the banks hold in their accounts at the central bank in excess of reserve requirements. (18)

interest rate risk 1. The risk that the interest rate will change, causing the price of a bond to change with it. (6) 2. The risk that changes in interest rates will affect a financial intermediary's net worth. It arises from a mismatch in the maturity of assets and liabilities. (12)

interest rate spread 1. The difference between the interest rate a bank receives on its assets and the interest rate it pays to obtain liabilities. (12) 2. Can also be used as a synonym for *risk spread.* (7, 12)

interest rate stability One of the objectives of the central bank is to reduce interest rate fluctuations keeping it stable. (15)

interest rate swap A contract between two counterparties specifying the exchange of interest payments on a series of future dates. (9)

intermediary See *financial institutions.* (1, 3)

intermediate targets Variables that are not directly under the central bank's control but lie somewhere between the tools policymakers do control and their objectives; the quantity of money is an example. (18)

internal rate of return The interest rate that equates the present value of an investment with its cost. (4)

International Monetary Fund (IMF) The international organization created to administer the Bretton Woods system of fixed exchange rates, provide technical assistance helping countries design their financial and economic systems, and make loans to countries in crisis. (19)

in-the-money option An option that would yield a profit if exercised immediately. A call option is in the money when the strike price is less than the current market price for the underlying instrument. (9)

inverted yield curve When the term structure of interest rates slopes down. (7)

investment Spending by firms for additions to the physical capital they use to produce goods and services; also includes construction of new houses. (21)

investment bank A financial intermediary that issues (underwrites) stocks and bonds for corporate customers and advises customers. (3)

investment-grade bond Bond with low default risk; Moody's rating of Baa or higher; and Standard & Poor's rating of BBB or higher. (7)

investment horizon The length of time an investor plans on holding an asset. (6)

J

junk bond A bond with a high risk of default. Also called a *high-yield bond.* (7)

L

lagged-reserve accounting The procedure where a bank's reserve requirement is computed based on the level of deposits several weeks earlier. (18)

large certificates of deposit Certificates of deposit that exceed $100,000 in face value. They can be bought and sold in financial markets. (12)

law of one price The principle that two identical goods should sell for the same price regardless of location. (10)

lender of last resort The ultimate source of credit to banks during a panic. A role for the central bank. (14, 18)

letter of credit A financial guarantee provided for a fee, usually by a bank, that insures a payment by one of its customers. (12)

leverage Borrowing to finance part of an investment; increases expected return and risk. (5)

liability Something you owe. (3)

life insurance Insurance that makes payment on the death of the policyholder; see also *term life insurance* and *whole life insurance.* (13)

limited liability The provision that even if a company fails completely, the maximum amount that shareholders can lose is their initial investment. (8)

liquidity A measure of the ease with which an asset can be turned into a means of payment. (2)

liquidity premium theory of the term structure The proposition that long-term interest rates equal the average of expected short-term interest rates plus a risk premium that rises with the time to maturity. (7)

liquidity risk The risk that a financial institution's liability holders will suddenly seek to cash in their claims; for a bank this is the risk that depositors will unexpectedly withdraw deposit balances. (12)

loan commitment A line of credit, similar to an individual's credit card limit, provided by a bank or other lender that gives a firm the ability to borrow whenever necessary. (12)

loan loss reserves A portion of a bank's capital that is set aside to cover potential losses from defaulted loans. (12)

London Interbank Offered Rate (LIBOR) The interest rate at which banks lend eurodollars to other banks. (13)

long futures position The position held by a buyer of a futures contract. (9)

long-run aggregate supply (LRAS) curve The quantity of output supplied in the long run at any level of inflation; the LRAS curve is vertical at potential output. (21)

long-run real interest rate The real interest rate that equates aggregate demand with potential output. (21)

Lucas critique Economist Robert Lucas's observation that changes in policymakers' behavior will change people's expectations, altering their behavior and the observed relationships among economic variables. (20)

M

M1 The narrowest monetary aggregate, which measures the most liquid means of payment available: currency, traveler's checks, demand deposits, and other checkable deposits. (2)

M2 The monetary aggregate most commonly used in the United States, it includes M1 plus somewhat less liquid financial instruments: small-denomination time deposits, savings deposits, money-market deposit accounts, and retail money-market mutual fund shares. (2)

macro-prudential (regulation) Aimed at limiting systemic risks in the financial system. (14)

margin 1. A minimum down payment legally required to purchase a stock. 2. A deposit placed by the buyer and seller of a futures contract with the clearing corporation. (9)

marked to market Accounting rule in which a financial instrument is repriced and funds transferred from the loser to the winner at the end of every day. (9)

market capitalization The total market value of a company; the price of a share of stock times the total number of shares outstanding. (8)

market federal funds rate The overnight interest rate at which lending between banks takes place in the market; differs from the federal funds rate target set by the FOMC. (18)

market liquidity The ability to sell assets. (2)

markets A virtual or physical place where goods, services, and financial instruments are purchased and sold. The basis for the fourth core principle of money and banking: Markets determine prices and allocate resources. (1)

matched-sale purchase (reverse repo) A short-term arrangement in which the Federal Reserve's open market trading desk sells a security and agrees to repurchase it in the near future. (18)

maturity date The time to the expiration of a debt instrument; the time until a bond's last promised payment is made. (4)

mean See *expected value.* (5)

means of payment Something that can be used to purchase goods and services; one of the functions of money. (2)

micro-prudential (regulation) Aimed at limiting the risks within intermediaries in order to reduce the probability of an individual institution's failure. (14)

minimum bid rate The minimum interest rate that banks can bid for reserves in the ECB's weekly refinancing operation; the European equivalent of the Fed's target federal funds rate; also known as the *target refinancing rate*. (18)

monetary aggregates Measures of the quantity of money; M1 and M2. (2)

monetary base The currency in the hands of the public plus reserves in the banking system; the central bank's liabilities. (17)

monetary policy The central bank's management of money, credit, and interest rates. (15)

monetary policy framework A structure in which central bankers clearly state their goals and the tradeoffs among them. (15)

monetary policy reaction curve The relationship between the real interest rate set by the central bank and the level of inflation. (21)

monetary policy transmission mechanism The channels through which changes in the central bank balance sheet influence real economic activity. (23)

money An asset that is generally accepted as payment for goods and services or repayment of debt, acts as a unit of account, and serves as a store of value. (1, 2)

money market A market in which debt instruments with a maturity of less than one year are traded. (3)

money-market deposit accounts Accounts that pay interest and offer limited check-writing privileges; part of M2. (2)

money-market mutual fund shares Shares in funds that collect relatively small sums from individuals, pool them together, and invest them in short-term marketable debt issued by large corporations; retail shares are part of M2. (2)

money multiplier The ratio between the quantity of money and the monetary base; the quantity of money (M) equals the money multiplier (m) times the monetary base (MB). $M = m \times MB$. (17)

moral hazard The risk that a borrower or someone who is insured will behave in a way that is not in the interest of the lender or insurer; it is caused by asymmetric information. (11)

mortgage-backed security (MBS) A financial instrument that provides its owner with a share of the mortgage payments from a large pool of mortgages. (3)

multiple deposit creation Part of the money supply process whereby a $1 increase in the quantity of reserves works its way through the banking system, increasing the quantity of money by more than $1. (17)

municipal bonds Bonds issued by state and local governments to finance public projects; the coupon payments are exempt from federal and state income taxes. Also called *tax-exempt bonds*. (7)

mutual fund A fund that pools the resources of a large number of small investors and invests them in portfolios of bonds, stocks, and real estate; managed by professional managers. (8)

mutual fund company Financial intermediary that pools the resources of a large number of small investors and invests them in portfolios of bonds, stocks, and real estate. (3)

N

Nasdaq Composite Index The value-weighted index of more than 3,000 companies traded on the over-the-counter (OTC) market through the National Association of Securities Dealers Automatic Quotations service; the index is composed mainly of smaller, newer firms and in recent years has been dominated by technology and Internet companies. (8)

national central banks (NCBs) The central banks of the countries that belong to the European Union. (16)

natural rate of interest The real short-term interest rate that prevails when the economy is using resources normally. (18)

natural rate of unemployment The rate of unemployment that persists in an economy when labor and other resources are used normally. (18)

net exports Exports minus imports; it represents an addition to the demand for domestically produced goods. (21)

net interest income A bank's interest income minus its interest expenses. (12)

net interest margin A bank's interest income minus its interest expenses divided by total bank assets; net interest income as a percentage of total bank assets. (12)

net worth The difference between a firm's or household's assets and liabilities. (11)

nominal exchange rate The value of one unit of a country's currency in terms of another country's currency. (10)

nominal gross domestic product The market value of final goods and services produced in the economy during a year measured at current (dollar) prices. (20)

nominal interest rate An interest rate expressed in dollar terms; the real interest rate plus expected inflation. (4)

nondepository institution A financial intermediary that does not issue deposit liabilities. (12)

notional principal The amount upon which the interest payments in an interest rate swap are based. (9)

O

off-balance-sheet activities Bank activities, such as trading in derivatives and issuing loan commitments, that are neither assets nor liabilities on the bank's balance sheet. (12)

open market operations When the central bank buys or sells a security in the open market; also includes central bank *repurchase agreements.* (17)

open market purchase The purchase of a security by the central bank. (17)

open market sale The sale of a security by the central bank. (17)

open market trading desk The group of people at the Federal Reserve Bank of New York who purchase and sell securities for the Fed's System Open Market Account. (18)

operating instruments The policy instruments that the central bank controls directly; the federal funds rate is an example. (18)

operational risk The risk a financial institution faces from computer hardware or software failure, natural disaster, terrorist attacks, and the like. (12)

organized exchange See *centralized exchange.* (3)

out-of-the-money option An option that would not yield a profit if exercised immediately. A call option is out of the money when the strike price is more than the current market price for the underlying instrument. (9)

output gap The difference between current output and potential output. (21)

overnight cash rate The overnight interest rate on interbank loans in Europe; the European analog to the market federal funds rate. (18)

overnight reverse repo (ON RRP) rate The interest paid by the Federal Reserve on funds from intermediaries supplied via overnight reverse purchase (repo) agreements. (18)

over-the-counter (OTC) market A financial market in which trades occur through networks of dealers connected together electronically. (3)

overvalued currency A country's currency when it is worth more than purchasing power parity implies. (10)

P

par value See *bond principal value.* (4)

payments system The web of arrangements that allow for the exchange of goods and services, as well as assets, among different people. (2)

payoff The amount an investor receives in return for an investment. (5)

payoff method Where the Federal Deposit Insurance Corporation sells or pays off a failed bank's depositors and then sells the failed bank's assets in an attempt to recover the amount paid out. (14)

pension fund company Financial intermediary that invests individual and company contributions into stocks, bonds, and real estate (its assets) in order to provide payments to retired workers (its liabilities). (3)

perpetuity See *consol or perpetuity.* (6)

policy directive The instructions from the FOMC to the System Open Market Account manager specifying the federal funds rate target. (16)

portfolio A collection or group of investments held by a person or company. (3)

portfolio demand for money The theory of the demand for money based on the use of money as a store of value; the theory that treats money as an asset analogous to a bond. (20)

potential output What the economy is capable of producing when its resources are used at normal rates; also called *sustainable output.* (15, 21)

precautionary demand for money The theory of the demand for money based on the idea that people hold money to ensure they have resources when faced with unexpected events. (20)

present discounted value See *present value.* (4)

present value The value today (in the present) of a payment that is promised to be made in the future. (4)

price stability One objective of the central bank is to keep inflation low so that prices are stable on average. (15)

price-weighted average An index based on the average price of a collection of individual stocks. Price-weighted averages give greater weight to shares with higher prices. (8)

primary credit The term used to describe short-term, usually overnight, discount loans made by the Federal Reserve to commercial banks. (18)

primary discount rate The interest rate charged by the Federal Reserve on primary credit; also known as the *discount rate*, it is set at a spread above the target federal funds rate. (18)

primary financial market A financial market in which a borrower obtains funds from a lender by selling newly issued securities. (3)

prime-grade commercial paper Commercial paper with a low risk of default. (7)

principal See *bond principal value.* (4)

probability A measure of the likelihood that an event will occur. (5)

pro-cyclicality Refers to the mutually reinforcing interaction between financial and economic activity that amplifies economic booms and busts Note: The more general term *pro-cyclical* means moving in tandem with the swings of the business cycle. (14)

property and casualty insurance Insurance against damage from events like automobile accidents, fire, and theft. (13)

public goods Goods that others cannot be excluded from using and whose consumption does not reduce availability. (15)

purchase-and-assumption method Where Federal Deposit Insurance Corporation finds a firm that is willing to take over a failed bank. (14)

purchasing power parity (PPP) The principle that a unit of currency will purchase the same basket of goods anywhere in the world. (10)

pure discount bond See *zero-coupon bond.* (6)

put option A contract that confers the right, but not the obligation, to sell a financial instrument at a predetermined price on or prior to an agreed-upon date. (9)

Q

quantitative easing (QE) Unconventional monetary policy action by the central bank to supply aggregate reserves beyond the quantity needed to lower the policy rate to zero. (18)

quantity theory of money The theory that changes in nominal income are determined by changes in the quantity of money. (20)

R

rating A measure of the default risk associated with a company's debt; normally a series of letters going from AAA for bonds with the lowest risk of default to D for bonds that have defaulted. (7)

rating downgrade When a bond-rating agency lowers the rating of a company, signaling that its bonds have an increased risk of default. (7)

rating upgrade When a bond-rating agency raises the rating of a company, signaling that its bonds have a reduced risk of default. (7)

real-business-cycle theory The theory that prices and wages are flexible, so inflation adjusts rapidly, current output always equals potential output, and all business cycle fluctuations arise from changes in potential output. (22)

real exchange rate The exchange rate at which one can exchange the goods and services from one country for goods and services from another country. (10)

real interest rate The interest rate measured in terms of constant (real) dollars; the nominal interest rate minus expected inflation. (4)

recession A decline in overall economic activity, as defined by the National Bureau of Economic Research. (21, 22)

recessionary output gap When current output is below potential output; the gap puts downward pressure on inflation. (21)

regulation (financial) A set of specific rules imposed by the government that the managers of financial institutions and participants in financial markets must follow. (1, 14)

regulatory agencies Entities responsible for making sure that the elements of the financial system operate in a safe and reliable manner. (1)

regulatory competition A situation where more than one regulatory agency works to safeguard the soundness of a bank. (14)

reinsurance company A very large company that provides insurance to insurance companies. (13)

renminbi (RMB) The name of the currency used in China; the unit of account is the *yuan.* (19)

repurchase agreement (repo) A short-term collateralized loan in which a security is exchanged for cash, with the agreement that the parties will reverse the transaction on a specific future date, as soon as the next day. (12, 18)

required reserve ratio The ratio of required reserves to demand deposit liabilities. (17)

required reserves Reserves that a bank must hold to meet the requirements set by regulators. In the United States, the requirements are established by the Federal Reserve. (12, 17)

reserve requirement Regulation obligating depository institutions to hold a certain fraction of their demand deposits as either vault cash or deposits at the central bank. (18)

reserves A bank's vault cash plus the balance in its account at the Federal Reserve. (12, 17)

residual claimant The final person to be paid. Stockholders are residual claimants; if the company runs into financial trouble, only after all other creditors have been paid will they receive what is left, if anything. (8)

return on assets (ROA) Bank net profits after taxes divided by total bank assets; a measure of bank profitability. (12)

return on equity (ROE) Bank net profits after taxes divided by bank capital; a measure of the return to the bank's owners. (12)

risk A measure of uncertainty about the future payoff to an investment, measured over some time horizon and relative to a benchmark. The basis for the second core principle of money and banking: Risk requires compensation. (1, 5)

risk-averse investor Someone who prefers an investment with a certain return to one with the same expected return but any amount of uncertainty. (5)

risk-free asset An investment whose future value is known with certainty. (5)

risk-free rate of return The rate of return on a risk-free asset. (5)

risk-neutral investor Someone who is indifferent between investments with different risks but the same expected return. (5)

risk premium The expected return minus the risk-free rate of return; the payment to the buyer of an asset for taking on risk. (5)

risk sharing The ability of individuals to combine and share the financial risks that they face; one of the services provided by a financial intermediary. (11)

risk spread The yield over and above that on a low-risk bond such as a U.S. Treasury with the same time to maturity, it is a measure of the compensation investors require for the risk they are bearing. Also called a *default risk premium*. (7)

risk structure of interest rates The relationship among the yields of bonds with the same time to maturity but different levels of risk. (7)

rule of 72 The rule that allows you to find out how many years it will take for the value of an investment to double; divide 72 by the annual interest rate. (4)

S

savings deposits The general term used to describe interest-bearing deposits that may have limited withdrawal privileges, but have no expiration date. (2)

seasonal credit Discount lending made in response to local, seasonal liquidity needs; used primarily by small agricultural banks in the Midwest to help manage the cyclical nature of farmers' loans and deposits. (18)

secondary credit Discount lending to banks that are not sufficiently sound to qualify for primary credit. (18)

secondary discount rate The interest rate charged on secondary credit; it is usually 50 basis points above the primary discount rate. (18)

secondary financial market A financial market in which previously issued securities are bought and sold. (3)

secondary reserves Short-term U.S. Treasury securities held as bank assets. (12)

securities Financial instruments representing ownership or debt; stocks, bonds, and derivatives. (3)

shadow bank Institution with liabilities that, like bank deposits, can be withdrawn at face value with little or no notice but that are usually subject to less oversight than banks. (14)

short futures position The position held by the seller of a futures contract. (9)

short-run aggregate supply (SRAS) curve The quantity of output supplied in the short run at any level of inflation; the SRAS curve is upward sloping with inflation. (21)

SIFI See *systemically important financial institution*. (13, 14)

sovereign risk The risk that a foreign borrower will not repay a loan because its government prohibits it from doing so. (12)

speculative attack A crisis in which financial market participants believe the government will become unable to maintain its exchange rate at the current fixed level, so they sell the currency, forcing an immediate devaluation. (19)

speculator Someone who takes risks for the purpose of making a profit. (9)

spot price The market price paid for immediate delivery of a commodity or financial instrument. (9)

spread over Treasuries The difference between the yield on a bond and that on a U.S. Treasury with the same time to maturity; a measure of the riskiness of the bond. (7)

spreading risk Reducing overall risk by investing in assets whose payoffs are unrelated. (5)

stability Steady and lacking in variation. The basis for the fifth core principle of money and banking: Stability improves welfare. (1)

stabilization policy Monetary and fiscal policies designed to stabilize output and inflation. (22)

Standard & Poor's 500 Index A stock market index that is based on the value of 500 of the largest firms in the U.S. economy. (8)

standard deviation Square root of the variance measure of risk; measures the dispersion of possible outcomes. (5)

sterilized foreign exchange intervention A foreign exchange intervention that alters the composition of the central bank's assets but leaves the size of its liabilities unchanged. (19)

stock Ownership shares in a firm; also called *common stock* and *equity*. (3)

stock market The market where the prices of common stock are determined. (8)

stock market indexes Index numbers that provide a sense of whether the value of the stock market is going up or down. (8)

store of value Allows movement of purchasing power into the future; one of the functions of money. (2)

strike price See *exercise price*. (9)

supervision (financial) General government oversight of financial institutions. (1, 14)

supply of dollars The number of dollars supplied in the foreign exchange market as a function of the nominal exchange rate. (10)

supply shock An unexpected change in the costs of production, such as a rise or fall in oil prices, that shifts the short-run aggregate supply curve. (22)

sustainable growth When the economy is growing at the rate dictated by potential output. (15)

swap A financial contract obligating one party to exchange one set of payments for a second set of payments made by a counterparty. (9)

swap spread The difference between the benchmark interest rate and the swap rate, it is a measure of risk. (9)

System Open Market Account (SOMA) The official name for the securities holdings of the Federal Reserve System. (18)

systematic risk Economywide risk that affects everyone and cannot be diversified. (5)

systemically important financial institution (SIFI) An intermediary whose failure could undermine the entire financial system. (13, 14)

T

T-account A simplified balance sheet in the form of a *T* that shows the changes in assets on one side and the changes in liabilities on the other. (17)

target federal funds rate range The Federal Open Market Committee's target range for the interest rate that banks pay on overnight loans from other intermediaries; the FOMC's primary policy instrument. (18)

targeted asset purchase (TAP) An unconventional monetary policy in which the central bank alters the mix of assets on its balance sheet in order to change their relative prices (and hence interest rates) in a way that stimulates economic activity. (18)

taxable bond A bond whose coupon payments are not exempt from income tax. (7)

tax-exempt bonds See *municipal bonds.* (7)

Taylor rule A rule of thumb for explaining movements in the federal funds rate; the monetary policy rule developed by economist John Taylor. (18)

term life insurance Insurance that provides a payment to the policyholder's beneficiaries in the event of the insured's death at any time during the policy's term. (13)

term spread The gap between yields to maturity on a long- and a short-term bond (usually free of default risk); see also *yield curve.* (7)

term structure of interest rates The relationship among bonds with the same risk characteristics but different maturities. (7)

term to maturity The length of time until a bond's final payment. (4)

theory of efficient markets The notion that the prices of all financial instruments, including stocks, reflect all available information. (8)

time A measurable period during which something can happen. The basis for the first core principle of money and banking: Time has value. (1)

time consistency The condition in which there is no future incentive to renege on a promise or policy commitment made today. (2)

time deposits Deposits that cannot be withdrawn before a specified date. Small-denomination time deposits are part of M2. (2)

time value (of the option) The price the buyer of an option pays to the seller that is in excess of the value of the option if it were immediately exercised. (9)

too-big-to-fail policy The idea that some financial institutions are so large that government officials cannot allow them to fail because their failure will put the entire financial system at risk. (14)

trading algorithm A rule-based computer program for automatically executing thousands of trades. (3)

trading or market risk The risk that traders who work for a bank will create losses on the bank's own account. (12)

transactions costs The costs, including time, associated with buying and selling financial instruments, as well as goods and services. (3)

transactions demand for money The demand for money based on the use of money as a means of payment, for transactions purposes. (20)

transmission mechanism of monetary policy The way changes in central bank policy influence the real economy. (23)

transparency The central bank's communication of its policy decisions and how they are made clearly to the financial markets and the public. (15)

Treasury Direct The system that allows individuals to purchase U.S. Treasury securities directly from the government without the use of a broker. (16)

U

unconventional (monetary) policy tools Policy mechanisms (including policy duration commitments, quantitative easing, and credit easing) that are usually reserved for extraordinary episodes when conventional interest rate policy is insufficient for economic stabilization. (18)

unemployment gap The difference between the current unemployment rate and the *natural rate of unemployment.* (18)

underlying instrument A financial instrument used by saver-lenders to transfer resources directly to investor-borrowers; also known as a *primitive security.* (3)

undervalued currency A country's currency when it is worth less than purchasing power parity implies. (10)

underwriter A financial intermediary that sells a firm's stocks or bonds to the public, guaranteeing the price the issuer will receive. (11)

underwriting The process through which an investment bank guarantees the price of a new security to a corporation and then sells it to the public. (13)

unit bank A bank without branches. (13)

unit of account The units (like dollars) used to quote prices and other financial quantities; one of the functions of money. (2)

universal bank An institution that engages in all aspects of financial intermediation, including banking, insurance, real estate, brokerage services, and investment banking. (13)

unsecured loan A loan that is not guaranteed by collateral. (11)

unsterilized foreign exchange intervention A foreign exchange intervention that both alters the composition and changes the size of the central bank's balance sheet. (19)

U.S. Treasury bill (T-bill) A zero-coupon bond in which the U.S. government agrees to pay the bondholder a fixed dollar amount on a specific future date; has a maturity of less than one year. (6)

U.S. Treasury bond A coupon bond issued by the U.S. Treasury to finance government activities. (6)

V

value at risk (VaR) The worst possible loss over a specific time horizon at a given probability; a measure of risk. (5)

value-weighted index An index that is based on the value of the firms, like the S&P 500. Value-weighted indexes give greater weight to larger firms. (8)

variance The probability-weighted sum of the squared deviations of the possible outcomes from their expected value. (5)

vault cash Currency that is physically held inside a bank's vaults and automated teller machines (ATMs). (12, 17)

velocity of money The average number of times each unit of money is used per unit of time. (20)

venture capital firm A financial intermediary that specializes in investing in risky new "ventures" in return for a stake in the ownership and a share of the profits. (11)

vesting When the contributions your employer has made to the pension plan on your behalf belong to you. (13)

W

wealth The total value of all assets; the net worth of an individual. (2)

whole life insurance A combination of term life insurance and a savings account in which a policyholder pays a fixed premium over his or her lifetime in return for a fixed benefit when the policyholder dies. (13)

Wilshire 5000 The most broadly based value-weighted stock index in use. It covers the roughly 6,500 publicly traded stocks in the United States. (8)

Y

yen The currency used in Japan. (10)

yield The interest rate that equates the price of a bond with the present value of its payments. (4)

yield curve A plot showing the yields to maturity of different bonds of the same riskiness against the time to maturity. (7)

yield to maturity The yield bondholders receive if they hold the bond to its maturity when the final principal payment is made. (6)

yuan The unit of account of the Chinese currency; the name of the currency is the *renminbi.* (19)

Z

zero lower bound (ZLB) The idea that a nominal interest rate cannot fall below zero. (18, 23)

zero-coupon bond A promise to pay the face value of the bond on a specific future date, with no coupon payments. (6)

zero nominal-interest rate bound See *zero lower bound.* (18, 23)

Notation Index

Commonly Occurring Symbols

Symbol	Definition	Introduced in:
M1	M1 monetary aggregate	Chapter 2
M2	M2 monetary aggregate	Chapter 2
FV	Future value	Chapter 4
i	Nominal interest rate (usually at an annual rate)	Chapter 4
PV	Present value	Chapter 4
FV_n	Future value in n years	Chapter 4
F	Final payment of a bond (principal, face value, par value)	Chapter 4
P_{BP}	Present value of bond principal payment	Chapter 4
P_{CP}	Present value of bond coupon payment	Chapter 4
C	Coupon payment	Chapter 4
P_{CB}	Price of a coupon bond	Chapter 4
r	Real interest rate	Chapter 4
π^e	Expected inflation	Chapter 4
St. Dev.	Standard deviation	Chapter 5
VaR	Value at risk	Chapter 5
i^e	Expected interest rate	Chapter 7
i_{nt}	Interest rate on a bond with n years to maturity at time t	Chapter 7
rp_n	Risk premium on an n-year bond	Chapter 7
D	Stock dividend payment	Chapter 8
P	Price of a stock	Chapter 8
g	Dividend growth rate	Chapter 8
rf	Risk-free return	Chapter 8
i^f	Foreign interest rate	Chapter 9
ROA	Return on assets	Chapter 12
ROE	Return on equity	Chapter 12
Δ	Change in a variable	Chapter 17
D	Checkable deposits	Chapter 17
r_D	Required deposit reserve ratio	Chapter 17
RR	Required reserves	Chapter 17
M	Quantity of money	Chapter 17

m	Money multiplier	Chapter 17
MB	Monetary base	Chapter 17
$\{C/D\}$	Currency-to-deposit ratio	Chapter 17
$\{ER/D\}$	Excess-reserves-to-deposit ratio	Chapter 17
C	Currency in the hands of the public	Chapter 17
ER	Excess reserves	Chapter 17
R	Total quantity of reserves	Chapter 17
M3	M3 monetary aggregate	Chapter 20
$\%\Delta$	Percentage change in a variable	Chapter 20
P	Aggregate price level	Chapter 20
V	Velocity of money	Chapter 20
Y	Real GDP	Chapter 20
M^d	Quantity of money demanded	Chapter 20
M^S	Quantity of money supplied	Chapter 20
Y^{ad}	Aggregate demand	Chapter 21
C	Consumption	Chapter 21
G	Government purchases	Chapter 21
I	Investment	Chapter 21
NX	Net exports	Chapter 21
r^*	Long-run real interest rate	Chapter 21
π^T	Central bank's inflation target	Chapter 21
Y^P	Potential output	Chapter 21

Rarely Occurring Symbols

Symbol	**Definition**	**Introduced in:**
N	Time	Chapter 4
i^m	Nominal interest rate at a monthly rate	Chapter 4
$E(x) = \bar{x}$	Expected value, or mean, of x	Appendix to Chapter 5
$Var(x) = \sigma_x^2$	Variance of x	Appendix to Chapter 5
$Cov(x,y)$	Covariance between x and y	Appendix to Chapter 5
E	Nominal exchange rate	Appendix to Chapter 10
E^e	Expected future nominal exchange rate	Appendix to Chapter 10

Index

Page numbers followed by n indicate notes.

C

D

F

G

H

I

J

K

L

M

N

O

P

Q

R

S

T

U